Johnny Weissmuller swam at the **BILTMORE HOTEL'S POOL (left)**. So did Esther Williams. But you don't need to be a swim champ to take a dip in Miami's largest pool, where, at times, it can feel like you're all alone on a deserted island. Peace and quiet abound at this pool, where size, indeed, does matter.

It may not be healthy to smoke, but watching someone hand roll cigars may tempt you to puff on one, if only for the experience. Most **LITTLE HAVANA CIGAR ROLLERS (above)** are authentic, having honed their skills in Cuba, but leaving when things got bad. In Miami, things are good, and there are plenty of reasons to celebrate with a hand-rolled stogie.

South Florida will never leave you bored at night. Hit the techno-beaten path of celeb-saturated **DANCE CLUBS ON SOUTH BEACH (left)**. Imbibe some of Fort Lauderdale's old Florida kitsch—like the **HAWAIIAN-THEMED MAI KAI (below)**, where happy hour should be renamed Elation Hour and where drinks are larger than the size of most coconuts. Kick back in flip-flops and a t-shirt at **KEY WEST'S LEGENDARY SLOPPY JOE'S BAR (above right)**. Or chug a beer with one of the many **HEMINGWAY DOPPELGANGERS (below right)** down in Margaritaville. While South Beach nightlife is a bit more stringent in terms of dress code and price (those mojito-minty-fresh-Cristal-champagne-infused 'tinis don't come cheap), Fort Lauderdale and the Florida Keys are much more laid back and old school (just order the drink straight up).

When you wish upon a star . . . dreams come true for kids of all ages in Mickeyland, where spinning in tea cups is just the beginning of the fun at **WALT DISNEY WORLD (left)**. But WDW isn't all there is to do in Orlando. World-class hotels (some themed to keep the fantasy going, if you choose), outlet shopping, and, yes, other theme parks, are there in case you want them, too.

Thrill rides, theme rides, animated characters, animals, shows, and so much more are sure to entertain you and yours during your stay in Orlando. Don't miss out on the area's roller coasters—some of the best in the world, including the **INCREDIBLE HULK COASTER (above)**, at Universal Orlando's Islands of Adventure.

At Cape Canaveral and the **JOHN F. KENNEDY SPACE CENTER (left)**, you can have lunch with an astronaut, feel a rock from the moon, learn how to get lost in space, eat astronaut ice cream, or, if you're lucky, watch an exhilarating shuttle launch or landing. Just keep your eyes on the sky.

Start your engines and plug your ears, because Daytona's racing culture is loud, not to mention exciting. NASCAR is a way of life in Daytona, as well it should be, but you needn't be a NASCAR fan to appreciate the thrill of speed at the **DAYTONA INTERNATIONAL SPEEDWAY (below)**. Hear it, feel it, taste it. Just don't attempt it yourself—unless, of course, you're on one of Daytona's many tracks made just for those of us who don't speed for a living.

A long way from czarist Russia, **SOLOMON'S CASTLE (above)** epitomizes the American dream as seen by three generations of a family that escaped Russia in the early 1900s and landed in Ona, Florida. Sculptor and castle-maker Howard Solomon built and resides in this wacky attraction he created mostly from other people's "trash"—the outside of the castle is entirely made of printing plates. Solomon also sculpts, makes other art (a chair made of beer cans, anyone?), creates stained glass, and gives tours of the place. Don't miss this off-the-beaten-track attraction.

Japan is alive and well in South Florida, where the **MORIKAMI MUSEUM AND JAPANESE GARDENS (right)** brings Japanese culture to the state with gardens, a tea house, educational programs, and stunning flora and fauna indigenous to the Yamato Colony, a Japanese farming community that existed in South Florida over 100 years ago.

© Michiko Kurisu/Morikami Museum and Japanese Gardens

Don't linger over the state's unnatural wonders of silicone, botox, and saline, because Florida's got way too much natural beauty to be overlooked. First and foremost is the **EVERGLADES,** Florida's River of Grass, which is undeniably beautiful despite its beastly reputation. Take an **AIRBOAT RIDE (left)** to get a good feel for the area.

Although some people think the **MANATEE (below)** looks like a piece of gefilte fish, these endangered gentle giants are cute in their own peaceful way.

Look, but don't even think of touching the **ALLIGATORS (above right)** and crocs you may see across the state.

Under Florida's waters, you'll find a technicolor wonderland that even Mickey can't match. Try **SCUBA DIVING (below right)** and gawk at the coral reefs, neon-colored fish, and other things you'd only expect to see in a Pixar movie. Florida has spectacular scuba spots, both natural and manmade, including Jupiter Beach, where the remains of a Spanish galleon dating back to the 1600s lies in wreck, waiting for you to visit.

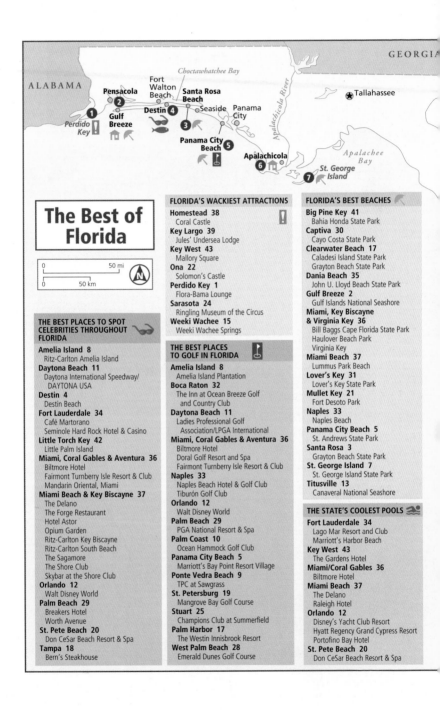

ALABAMA

GEORGIA

Choctawhatchee Bay

Pensacola ②
Gulf Breeze
Perdido Key ①

Fort Walton Beach
Destin ④
Santa Rosa Beach
Seaside ③
Panama City
Tallahassee

Apalachicola River

Panama City Beach ⑤
Apalachicola ⑥

Apalachee Bay

St. George Island ⑦

The Best of Florida

0   50 mi
0   50 km
Ⓝ

THE BEST PLACES TO SPOT CELEBRITIES THROUGHOUT FLORIDA

Amelia Island 8
  Ritz-Carlton Amelia Island
Daytona Beach 11
  Daytona International Speedway/
    DAYTONA USA
Destin 4
  Destin Beach
Fort Lauderdale 34
  Café Martorano
  Seminole Hard Rock Hotel & Casino
Little Torch Key 42
  Little Palm Island
Miami, Coral Gables & Aventura 36
  Biltmore Hotel
  Fairmont Turnberry Isle Resort & Club
  Mandarin Oriental, Miami
Miami Beach & Key Biscayne 37
  The Delano
  The Forge Restaurant
  Hotel Astor
  Opium Garden
  Ritz-Carlton Key Biscayne
  Ritz-Carlton South Beach
  The Sagamore
  The Shore Club
  Skybar at the Shore Club
Orlando 12
  Walt Disney World
Palm Beach 29
  Breakers Hotel
  Worth Avenue
St. Pete Beach 20
  Don CeSar Beach Resort & Spa
Tampa 18
  Bern's Steakhouse

FLORIDA'S WACKIEST ATTRACTIONS

Homestead 38
  Coral Castle
Key Largo 39
  Jules' Undersea Lodge
Key West 43
  Mallory Square
Ona 22
  Solomon's Castle
Perdido Key 1
  Flora-Bama Lounge
Sarasota 24
  Ringling Museum of the Circus
Weeki Wachee 15
  Weeki Wachee Springs

THE BEST PLACES TO GOLF IN FLORIDA

Amelia Island 8
  Amelia Island Plantation
Boca Raton 32
  The Inn at Ocean Breeze Golf
    and Country Club
Daytona Beach 11
  Ladies Professional Golf
    Association/LPGA International
Miami, Coral Gables & Aventura 36
  Biltmore Hotel
  Doral Golf Resort and Spa
  Fairmont Turnberry Isle Resort & Club
Naples 33
  Naples Beach Hotel & Golf Club
  Tiburón Golf Club
Orlando 12
  Walt Disney World
Palm Beach 29
  PGA National Resort & Spa
Palm Coast 10
  Ocean Hammock Golf Club
Panama City Beach 5
  Marriott's Bay Point Resort Village
Ponte Vedra Beach 9
  TPC at Sawgrass
St. Petersburg 19
  Mangrove Bay Golf Course
Stuart 25
  Champions Club at Summerfield
Palm Harbor 17
  The Westin Innisbrook Resort
West Palm Beach 28
  Emerald Dunes Golf Course

FLORIDA'S BEST BEACHES

Big Pine Key 41
  Bahia Honda State Park
Captiva 30
  Cayo Costa State Park
Clearwater Beach 17
  Caladesi Island State Park
  Grayton Beach State Park
Dania Beach 35
  John U. Lloyd Beach State Park
Gulf Breeze 2
  Gulf Islands National Seashore
**Miami, Key Biscayne
& Virginia Key 36**
  Bill Baggs Cape Florida State Park
  Haulover Beach Park
  Virginia Key
Miami Beach 37
  Lummus Park Beach
Lover's Key 31
  Lover's Key State Park
Mullet Key 21
  Fort Desoto Park
Naples 33
  Naples Beach
Panama City Beach 5
  St. Andrews State Park
Santa Rosa 3
  Grayton Beach State Park
St. George Island 7
  St. George Island State Park
Titusville 13
  Canaveral National Seashore

THE STATE'S COOLEST POOLS

Fort Lauderdale 34
  Lago Mar Resort and Club
  Marriott's Harbor Beach
Key West 43
  The Gardens Hotel
Miami/Coral Gables 36
  Biltmore Hotel
Miami Beach 37
  The Delano
  Raleigh Hotel
Orlando 12
  Disney's Yacht Club Resort
  Hyatt Regency Grand Cypress Resort
  Portofino Bay Hotel
St. Pete Beach 20
  Don CeSar Beach Resort & Spa

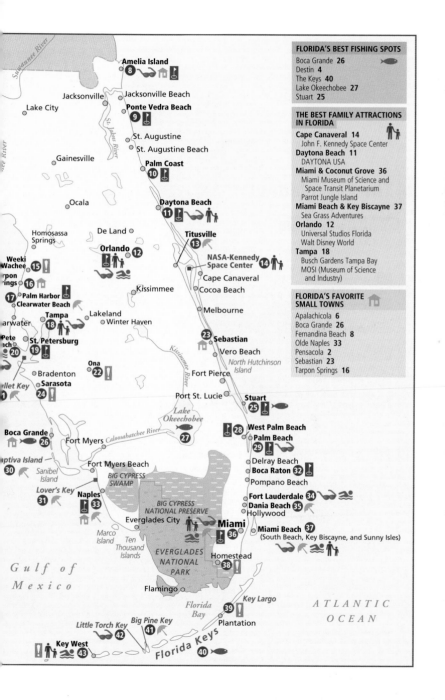

FLORIDA'S BEST FISHING SPOTS

Boca Grande **26**
Destin **4**
The Keys **40**
Lake Okeechobee **27**
Stuart **25**

THE BEST FAMILY ATTRACTIONS IN FLORIDA

Cape Canaveral 14
John F. Kennedy Space Center
Daytona Beach 11
DAYTONA USA
Miami & Coconut Grove 36
Miami Museum of Science and
Space Transit Planetarium
Parrot Jungle Island
Miami Beach & Key Biscayne 37
Sea Grass Adventures
Orlando 12
Universal Studios Florida
Walt Disney World
Tampa 18
Busch Gardens Tampa Bay
MOSI (Museum of Science
and Industry)

FLORIDA'S FAVORITE SMALL TOWNS

Apalachicola **6**
Boca Grande **26**
Fernandina Beach **8**
Olde Naples **33**
Pensacola **2**
Sebastian **23**
Tarpon Springs **16**

Suwannee River

Amelia Island **8**

Jacksonville
Jacksonville Beach
Ponte Vedra Beach 9

Lake City

St. Johns River

St. Augustine
St. Augustine Beach

Gainesville

Palm Coast 10

Ocala

Daytona Beach **11**

Homosassa Springs
De Land

Titusville 13

Weeki Wachee **15**
Orlando **12**

NASA-Kennedy Space Center **14**

Tarpon Springs **16**
Palm Harbor **17**
Clearwater Beach
Tampa 18
Lakeland
Winter Haven
Kissimmee
Cape Canaveral
Cocoa Beach

Melbourne

Pete ach
St. Petersburg **19**

Ona **22**

Sebastian 23
Vero Beach
North Hutchinson Island
Fort Pierce

Kissimmee River

llet Key **20**
Bradenton
Sarasota 24

Port St. Lucie

Lake Okeechobee

Stuart 25

West Palm Beach 28
Palm Beach 29

Boca Grande 26
Fort Myers
Caloosahatchee River

27

ptiva Island
Sanibel Island **30**

Fort Myers Beach
BIG CYPRESS SWAMP

Delray Beach
Boca Raton 32
Pompano Beach

Lover's Key **31**
Naples 33

BIG CYPRESS NATIONAL PRESERVE

Fort Lauderdale 34
Dania Beach 35
Hollywood

Marco Island
Ten Thousand Islands

Everglades City
Miami
36

Miami Beach 37
(South Beach, Key Biscayne, and Sunny Isles)

EVERGLADES NATIONAL PARK
Homestead
38

Gulf of Mexico

Flamingo

Florida Bay

Key Largo

39

A T L A N T I C
O C E A N

Little Torch Key **42**
Big Pine Key **41**
Plantation

Key West **43**

Florida Keys

40

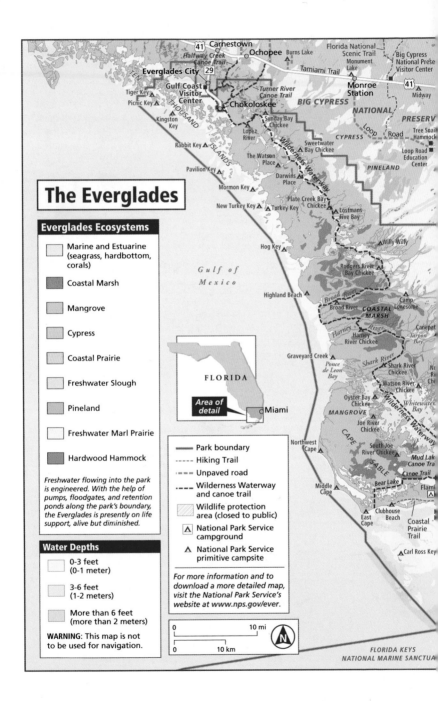

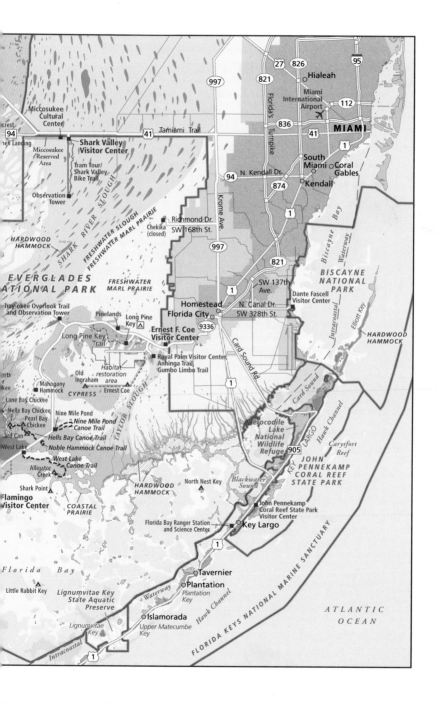

Notorious South Beach

ONLY ON SOUTH BEACH

crobar 7
This is where Microsoftie Bill Gates was rejected at the velvet ropes for being too 'geeky:' The door goon had no clue who he was!

Hotel Victor 12
P. Diddy hosted this hotel's grand opening and got in trouble by PETA (People for the Ethical Treatment of Animals) for using penguins as props. Also at the Hotel Victor, Shaquille O' Neal's wife Shaunie threw #32 a surprise 33rd birthday party. She got a cake that was a life-sized replica of Shaq— nearly six feet tall and costing $10,000!

Mansion 9
Here, Shannen Doherty fought with Tara Reid over spilled drinks and J-Lo and Mark Anthony staged a photo op to prove they were married.

Raleigh Hotel 2
Madonna, Guy Ritchie, Demi Moore, and boytoy Ashton Kutcher played in the sand here with Madonna's kids while they were all in town for a Kabbalah meeting.

Rumi 5
Singer Seal told a chatty audience at Rumi: "No wonder they say American audiences are rude. I'll never play here again."

Skybar at the Shore Club 1
At Skybar, Jay Z asked a cocktail waitress if she could get him chicken wings (something that establishment would normally never dream of serving). Nevertheless, the cocktail waitress ran to KFC to accommodate his order.

Versace Mansion 12
The unfortunate spot where fashion designer Gianni Versace was gunned down by an obsessed fan.

FILMED ON SOUTH BEACH

Big Pink 21
In *There's Something About Mary*, Big Pink is where Cameron Diaz and her friends whined and dined.

Current site of Johnny Rocket's 18
Remember the brutal chain saw scene in *Scarface*? The site where that was filmed is now a Johnny Rocket's… Mmm. Pass the ketchup!

Miami Beach Community Church 4
This church was used to simulate California as Cher and Greg Kinnear drank margaritas in *Stuck on You*.

National Hotel 3
This hotel's famous pool was wrongly identified as being the pool from The Delano in the 1999 Sydney Pollack, Harrison Ford film *Random Hearts*.

Nikki Beach Club 22
Justin Guarini and Kelly Clarkson filmed *From Justin to Kelly* here.

South Pointe Park 23
Justin Guarini arrived on the beach at South Pointe via hovercraft in *From Justin to Kelly*.

You might think that more or better films have been made on South Beach, but the pickings are actually quite slim. Perhaps that's because all the stars, crew, and so forth are so busy partying in South Beach's clubs 24/7 during shooting that nothing ever actually gets done.

SOUTH BEACH'S BEST ART DECO BUILDINGS

Breakwater Hotel **16**
Cardozo Hotel **10**
Carlyle Hotel **11**
Colony Hotel **18**
Crobar/Old Cameo Theatre **7**
Essex House **13**
Hotel Astor **14**
Hotel Chelsea **14**
Imperial **19**
Leslie **11**
Miami Beach Post Office **8**
Park Central Hotel **19**
Waldorf Towers **17**

THE HIPPEST PLACES ON SOUTH BEACH

China Grill **20**
The Delano **3**
Mansion **9**
Metro Kitchen + Bar **14**
Nikki Beach Club **22**
Opium Garden **21**
Prime 112 **22**
The Sagamore **3**
Skybar at the Shore Club **1**
The Room **21**

THE BEST PLACES TO SPOT CELEBRITIES ON SOUTH BEACH

The Delano **3**
Hotel Astor **14**
Opium Garden **21**
Ritz-Carlton South Beach **6**
The Sagamore **3**
The Shore Club **1**
Skybar at the Shore Club **1**

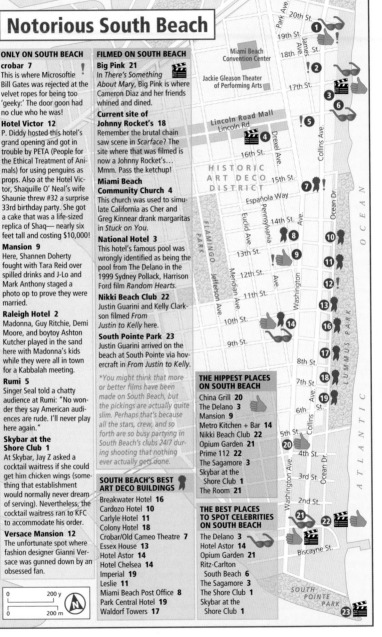

Miami Beach Convention Center

Jackie Gleason Theater of Performing Arts

Lincoln Road Mall
Lincoln Rd.

HISTORIC ART DECO DISTRICT

Española Way

FLAMINGO PARK

LUMMUS PARK

ATLANTIC OCEAN

SOUTH POINTE PARK

0   200 y
0   200 m

Frommer's®

Florida

2007

by Lesley Abravanel

with Laura Lea Miller

Here's what the critics say about Frommer's:

"Amazingly easy to use. Very portable, very complete."

—*Booklist*

"Detailed, accurate, and easy-to-read information for all price ranges."
—*Glamour Magazine*

"Hotel information is close to encyclopedic."

—*Des Moines Sunday Register*

"Frommer's Guides have a way of giving you a real feel for a place."
—*Knight Ridder Newspapers*

Wiley Publishing, Inc.

Published by:

Wiley Publishing, Inc.

111 River St.
Hoboken, NJ 07030-5774

ISBN-13: 978-0-470-03721-8
ISBN-10: 0-470-03721-0

Editor: Elizabeth Heath
Production Editor: Eric T. Schroeder
Cartographer: Guy Ruggiero
Photo Editor: Richard Fox
Production by Wiley Indianapolis Composition Services

Front cover photo: Fort Walton Beach: young man doing flip on ocean shore
Back cover photo: Great Blue Heron, close-up of head and neck

For information on our other products and services or to obtain technical support, please contact our Customer Care Department within the U.S. at 800/762-2974, outside the U.S. at 317/572-3993 or fax 317/572-4002.

Wiley also publishes its books in a variety of electronic formats. Some content that appears in print may not be available in electronic formats.

Manufactured in the United States of America

5   4   3   2   1

Contents

List of Maps

About the Authors

Lesley Abravanel is a freelance journalist and a graduate of the University of Miami School of Communication. When she isn't combing South Florida for the latest hotels, restaurants and attractions, she is on the lookout for vacationing celebrities, about whom she writes in the weekly nightlife and gossip column, "Velvet Underground," for the *Miami Herald*. She is a contributor to *Condé Nast Traveler, Time out,* and all three illustrous supermarket tabloids, and is author of *Frommer's South Florida, Florida For Dummies,* and *Frommer's Portable Miami.*

Laura Lea Miller is a freelance writer based in Orchard Park, New York, though she's spent countless hours scouring Central Florida's theme parks, hotels, and restaurants over the years—with and without the help of her five children. A family travel-expert who religiously makes more than just a few trips to the Land the Mouse built, she is also writing a guide and creating a website to Florida just for families.

Acknowledgments

To my mother and father, without whose influence, encouragement, and support I would never have ended up in Miami doing what I'm doing.

To all the publicists and proprietors for putting up with the endless e-mails, inquiries, and spur-of-the-moment visits, I thank you for your cooperation and eagerness to answer pressing questions about hair dryers, irons, hours, and credit cards.

Thanks to all my friends and colleagues who know that I'm more than a party girl and accept my quirkiness, compulsive behavior, and genuine penchant for all things bizarre.

And, last but not at all least, thanks to my husband, the Swede, for putting up with me and my inanity and insanity. Mwah!

—Lesley Abravanel

An Invitation to the Reader

In researching this book, we discovered many wonderful places—hotels, restaurants, shops, and more. We're sure you'll find others. Please tell us about them, so we can share the information with your fellow travelers in upcoming editions. If you were disappointed with a recommendation, we'd love to know that, too. Please write to:

Frommer's Florida 2007
Wiley Publishing, Inc. • 111 River St. • Hoboken, NJ 07030-5774

An Additional Note

Please be advised that travel information is subject to change at any time—and this is especially true of prices. We therefore suggest that you write or call ahead for confirmation when making your travel plans. The authors, editors, and publisher cannot be held responsible for the experiences of readers while traveling. Your safety is important to us, however, so we encourage you to stay alert and be aware of your surroundings. Keep a close eye on cameras, purses, and wallets, all favorite targets of thieves and pickpockets.

Other Great Guides for Your Trip:

Frommer's South Florida

Frommer's Walt Disney World® & Orlando

Frommer's Caribbean Cruises & Ports of Call

Frommer's Florida's Best-Loved Driving Tour

Frommer's Irreverent Guide to Walt Disney World®

The Unofficial Guide to Florida with Kids

The Unofficial Guide to Walt Disney World®

The Unofficial Guide to Walt Disney World® with Kids

The Unofficial Guide to Walt Disney World® for Grown-Ups

The Unofficial Guide to the Best RV & Tent Campgrounds in Florida & the Southeast

Frommer's Portable Miami

Frommer's Portable Tampa & St. Petersburg

Frommer's Star Ratings, Icons & Abbreviations

Every hotel, restaurant, and attraction listing in this guide has been ranked for quality, value, service, amenities, and special features using a **star-rating system.** In country, state, and regional guides, we also rate towns and regions to help you narrow down your choices and budget your time accordingly. Hotels and restaurants are rated on a scale of zero (recommended) to three stars (exceptional). Attractions, shopping, nightlife, towns, and regions are rated according to the following scale: zero stars (recommended), one star (highly recommended), two stars (very highly recommended), and three stars (must-see).

In addition to the star-rating system, we also use **eight feature icons** that point you to the great deals, in-the-know advice, and unique experiences that separate travelers from tourists. Throughout the book, look for:

Then&Now	A look back at the early days of Frommer's, highlighting timeless bits of travel wisdom as well as hotels and restaurants that have stood the test of time
Finds	Special finds—those places only insiders know about
Fun Fact	Fun facts—details that make travelers more informed and their trips more fun
Kids	Best bets for kids and advice for the whole family
Moments	Special moments—those experiences that memories are made of
Overrated	Places or experiences not worth your time or money
Tips	Insider tips—great ways to save time and money
Value	Great values—where to get the best deals

The following **abbreviations** are used for credit cards:

AE	American Express	DISC	Discover	V	Visa
DC	Diners Club	MC	MasterCard		

Frommers.com

Now that you have the guidebook to a great trip, visit our website at **www.frommers.com** for travel information on more than 3,000 destinations. With features updated regularly, we give you instant access to the most current trip-planning information available. At Frommers.com, you'll also find the best prices on airfares, accommodations, and car rentals—and you can even book travel online through our travel booking partners. At Frommers.com, you'll also find the following:

- Online updates to our most popular guidebooks
- Vacation sweepstakes and contest giveaways
- Newsletter highlighting the hottest travel trends
- Online travel message boards with featured travel discussions

What's New in Florida

MIAMI Miami's a city on the verge—of everything. Whereas supermodels were once the city's cottage industry, today it's more like condo models are all the rage. Look at the skyline and you'll see what we mean. Still beautiful, especially at night and during sunset, the photogenic Miami skyline is peppered with cranes working hard trying to raise swank, zillion-dollar condos and hotels—or, for the really trendy, condo-hotels in which buyers plunk down millions to live like Eloise in a bona fide hotel. A cash crop of hyperluxe hotels and restaurants have proven that, yes, people will spend thousands of dollars a night on a hotel room and $30 a drink. And soon there will be more culture than that which is dubiously found inside the city's nightclubs. The nearly $500 million Miami Performing Arts Center is almost done and ready for its own close-up.

Where to Stay Miami's first Rosewood Resort, **Aqualina,** 17780 Collins Ave. (✆ **305/918-8000**is slated to open in early 2006, featuring a 51-story Renaissance-inspired tower with 97 ultraluxury suites that include everything from Wi-Fi to iPods.

Regent Bal Harbour (✆ **800/545-4000**) is set to open in late 2007, with 17 stories, panoramic views of the Atlantic, and 1,650-square-foot guest rooms. Same goes for the **Regent South Beach,** 1458 Ocean Dr. (✆ **305/674-4554**), an 80-suite swank stay with rooftop garden and haute eatery.

Not too far away is Le Meridien's first Miami property, **Le Meridien Sunny Isles Beach,** 18683 Collins Ave. (✆ **800/543-4300**), a 25-story resort. It features a second Miami location of the swank Italian restaurant **Bice,** which should bring fine dining to the chain restaurant–dotted area.

NYC's hot meatpacking district **Hotel Gansevoort** has taken over the old Roney Palace Hotel at 23rd Street and Collins Avenue on South Beach, and plans to reopen in early 2007 as a 332-room boutique hotel featuring a rooftop pool, an upgraded oceanfront pool deck, a spa, a beach club, and a block of upscale shops and restaurants.

Nearby, at 2201 Collins Ave., the **W** hotel chain plans to take over an old Holiday Inn and turn it into a 25-story hotel/condo with 511 units, trademark Bliss spa, two pools, and a Rande Gerber–owned hip hotel bar. Completion is slated for mid-2007.

Where to Dine Two more star chefs will soon call Miami home. David Bouley is taking the helm at the **Ritz-Carlton South Beach,** 1 Lincoln Rd. (✆ **786/276-4000**), opening his first signature restaurant outside of Manhattan. Although this has been the buzz for several years now, it seems as if it may finally happen in early 2007.

And over at the soon-to-open **Regent South Beach**, 1458 Ocean Dr. (✆ **800/545-4000**) L.A.'s golden child, Govind Armstrong, debuts in 2006 his Miami branch of the hauter-than-thou **Table 8** eatery. Another star chef, Michelle Bernstein, will soon (mid-2006, at press time) open **Michy's,** 6927 Biscayne Blvd., a 100-seat bistro and raw bar in the Biscayne Corridor.

After Dark   Over the causeway, a burgeoning nocturnal buzz is emanating from the once-desolate area of downtown Miami off Biscayne Boulevard.

For aspiring DJs, a branch of the renowned **Scratch DJ Academy,** 642 6th St. (© **305/535-2599**), opened; for $300 a session, you, too, can become a master of the turntables.

Rumor had it at the time of this writing that **Cirque du Soleil** is about to make the Jackie Gleason Theatre of the Performing Arts its new permanent home, now that the **Miami Performing Arts Center** is about to open and become the focal point of what was once the Gleason's forte.

THE KEYS   Big families and groups who want to explore the Florida Keys can now hire a **TransFloridianStarCraft Vehicle** (© **954/523-0859**), a 26-foot luxury car that holds up to 14 people and features reclining leather seats with footrests and adjustable headrests. There's also 24 inches of legroom per person, wireless Internet service, in-seat power ports for electronic devices, personal headphone jacks, multichannel audio entertainment, overhead DVD monitors, and service by on-board attendants. Transportation from Miami, Fort Lauderdale, or Orlando to and from the Florida Keys ranges from $500 to $850.

If you want to see the Keys from an aerial point of view, commercial pilot **Dan Baker** (© **305/731-0000**) offers 18- to 20-minute aerial coral reef and island tours of the Middle Keys and Marathon areas aboard an Aerospatiale Alouette II turbine helicopter. Tours depart from Florida Keys Marathon Airport, MM 52.2 bayside. Up to four passengers can be

accommodated on each tour, depending on weight. Cost is $75 per person for four, $100 per person for three, and $150 per person for two.

A new boat tour combines Florida Keys sunsets with delectable Keys cuisine. **Sunset Culinaire Tours** (© **305/296-0982**) is a cruise aboard the vessel RB's Lady and includes a tour of Key West Harbor as the sun sinks below the horizon, and a gourmet dinner prepared by Chef Brian Kirkpatrick. The vessel departs from Sunset Marina, off U.S. 1 at 5555 College Road, at 5:30 p.m. nightly. Boarding time is 5 p.m. and cost is $65 per person.

The Florida Keys Eco-Discovery Center overlooking the waterfront at the Truman Annex (© **301/608-3040**), featuring 6,000 square feet of interactive exhibits depicting Florida Keys underwater and upland habitats—with emphasis on the ecosystem of North America's only living contiguous barrier coral reef, which parallels the Keys—is set to open in summer 2006.

THE GOLD COAST   While the Gold Coast's beaches remain less congested than those in Miami, the area isn't impervious to development—especially when it comes to resorts, restaurants, and nightlife.

Where to Stay   Still under construction is Florida's first **St. Regis Resort** (© **954/568-4623**), a $135-million, 23-story luxe property in Fort Lauderdale with nearly 200 rooms, a gourmet restaurant, an air-conditioned walkway to the beach, a massive spa, and more. It's scheduled to open in mid-2006.

In the winter of 2007, the **W Hotel** (© **954/525-8133**) will open on Fort Lauderdale Beach. The $220-million boutique-hotel-condominium features the usual W Hotel bells and whistles, including the signature bar and restaurant.

Donald Trump is converting a private condo on Fort Lauderdale Beach into the

Trump International Beach Club. True to Trump's character, some of the 14-story building's suites will be available for purchase. Opening mid-2006.

SOUTHWEST FLORIDA In Fort Myers, Southwest Florida International Airport's (RSW) new midfield terminal opened, bringing vastly increased gate capacity and enhanced air service to the area's main international airport. Southwest Airlines now services the airport with nine daily nonstop flights to Baltimore (BWI), Chicago–Midway (MDW), New York–Islip (ISP), Orlando (MCO), and Philadelphia (PHL).

Waterside Shops at Pelican Bay, 5415 Tamiami Trail (© 239/598-1605), is undergoing an extreme makeover, bringing in a selection of high-end stores, including Tiffany & Co., Hermes, Louis Vuitton, Coach, Gucci, Nordstrom, and more. Completion is expected in 2006.

The Children's Museum of Naples, www.cmon.org, will open in spring 2007 with a unique array of quality, interactive educational experiences for children. The museum will be located in North Naples Regional Park, a new Collier County public park that will also feature a water park attraction, nature trails, and extensive team sports facilities.

The **Naples Beach Hotel & Golf Club,** 851 Gulf Shore Blvd. (© 239/261-2222), has a much-needed, brand-new, $5-million lobby. **The Registry Resort & Club,** a Naples landmark for 20 years, is now known as **Naples Grande Resort & Club,** 475 Seagate Dr. (© 888/422-6177), and features a newly redone lobby with contemporary design, a new restaurant, and additional ballroom space. **The Inn on Fifth,** 699 5th Ave. (© 888/403-8778), opened a new spa facility, The Spa on Fifth. The Spa on Fifth is shaped by feng shui elements and mixes Asian influences with tropical accents, providing an extensive array of antiaging and rejuvenating treatments.

Hilton Marco Island Beach Resort, 560 S. Collier Blvd. (© 239/394-5000), has completed an expansive upgrade and renovation project to its lobby and restaurant areas, a new scenic ambiance, and a revamped menu at the Paradise Café. A new spa is planned for 2007.

THE TAMPA BAY AREA The beloved **Clearwater Beach Hotel** has been taken over by a luxe hotel group and will redebut in early 2007 as the swanky **Sandpearl Resort,** 470 Mandalay Ave. (© 800/572-1882), a 253-room resort with views of the Gulf and situated on 5½ acres of Clearwater Beach front.

A 20-story, 360-unit **Embassy Suites Hotel** (© 800/445-8667) is expected to open in mid-2006 opposite the Tampa Convention Center.

WALT DISNEY WORLD & ORLANDO The Orlando Convention & Visitors Bureau now not only offers the official Orlando website (www.orlando info.com) and the official tourist center (8723 International Dr.), but now offers the services of travel counselors (© 800/551-0181 or 407/363-5872) to help plan your Orlando vacation.

Where to Stay The **Four Seasons,** world renowned for the highest of standards in hospitality, is scheduled to open its newest resort (and fourth in Florida) in the picture-perfect town of Celebration in 2007. Lavish accommodations and indulgent amenities are a signature of this resort.

And other properties in town aren't resting on their laurels. **The Polynesian** (© 407/939-6244) has completely redecorated its rooms (and renovated the great ceremonial house) as well. They now feature more space-conscious furnishings, though the island feel still remains. The **Renaissance Orlando Resort at SeaWorld** (© 800/327-6677 or 407/351-5555) recently gave its pool and outdoor recreational area a major face-lift and outfitted rooms with luxurious bedding. Now it's undergoing a $20-million makeover that includes the addition of an 8,000-square-foot full-service spa. The **Hotel Royal Plaza** (© **407/828-2828**) recently underwent extensive renovations and upgrades, adding new carpeting, furnishings, and in-room media packages. Universal's **Portofino** (© **407/503-1000**) has also redecorated. Rooms now feature a more sophisticated decor and added amenities.

Where to Dine   Making a return is the **Chef's Table** at the Hyatt Grand Cypress (© **407/239-3853**). Offered Thursday through Sunday evenings, it's an experience like no other in town. Guests dine in the very upscale setting of the chef's kitchen, transformed into an intimate private dining room. Chef Orlando, accompanied by additional staff, personally brings your five magnificent and artfully presented courses to the table, thoroughly explaining what is being served and exactly how it was prepared. Even at $85 per person (or $135 with wine pairing), it's well worth splurging for.

Raglan Road, located at Downtown Disney's Pleasure Island (© **407/938-0300**), is an impressive addition to Disney's collection of unique eateries. The lively atmosphere, where singing, dancing, and clapping are all encouraged, is enhanced by the nightly entertainment. And the food's pretty good, too, thanks to the culinary creations of Kevin Dundon, one of Ireland's most celebrated chef's.

The **Bubba Gump Shrimp Co.** (www. bubbagump.com or www.universal orlando.com) is the latest addition to Universal's CityWalk restaurant lineup. It takes the place of Decades Café near the CityWalk entrance (across from the Cineplex). This family-friendly eatery, based on the blockbuster hit *Forrest Gump*, offers a diverse menu to please almost every palate, So don't let the name fool you—it's not just for seafood lovers.

Exploring Walt Disney World   The big news at Disney is the addition of **Expedition Everest** at Disney's Animal Kingdom (www.disneyworld. com). It's the most impressive addition since Mission: Space at Epcot just a few years back. Set in the Himalayan Mountains, guests find themselves touring by steam train through some of the most impressive scenery and surroundings that Disney has ever created. Suddenly, there's an unexpected turn of events, (okay, it's not entirely unexpected, given the numerous warnings posted along the way), and riders find themselves face to face with the mythical Yeti. The train is sent speeding off almost uncontrollably, twisting, turning, and spiraling both forward and backward through the darkness of the mountain, before finally plummeting an incredible 80 feet to escape the formidable beast.

At **MGM Studios,** guests can walk through a gigantic wardrobe and onto a wintry set similar to that seen in *The Chronicles of Narnia: The Lion, The Witch, and the Wardrobe.* Props, costumes, and creatures straight from the movie fill the gallery at the end of the attraction.

Exploring Universal Orlando & SeaWorld   In keeping with the "what you can do, I can do better" culture that ensures Orlando offers an ever-changing array of attractions to keep visitors coming back for more, SeaWorld has announced the addition of an innovative ecothemed water park. Scheduled to open in 2007, the as-yet-unnamed park will feature an array of interactive experiences that combine the ecological themes of SeaWorld, the naturalistic setting of Discovery Cove, and the fun and excitement of a water park. Back at **SeaWorld** two new shows have been added to the lineup. *Believe*, an all-new killer whale show, has spectacular choreography and an exciting musical score guaranteed to impress guests. *Blue Horizons* combines elements of the sea and sky with a storyline that follows the dream of a young girl in the almost Broadway-like dolphin spectacular. Three new rides have sprung up at **Shamu's Happy Harbor** and include the **Shamu Express**, a kid-friendly coaster, a jelly fish–themed samba tower, and a beach bucket–, tea cup–style ride. At **Discovery Cove,** guests now enjoy breakfast, lunch, and unlimited snacks and beverages as part of their regular admission.

Other big news includes an impressive online ticket offer geared at enticing families to experience Universal's various offerings. One child, under age 9, will be admitted to the parks at no charge for every full-price adult 2-day, two-park ticket purchased *online.*

Elsewhere in Orlando   The highly anticipated **Ron Jon Surf Park** (www. ronjon.com) is scheduled to open in late 2006 at the Festival Bay shopping center. It's one of those one-of-a-kind experiences that Orlando is so well known for—and given that Orlando's about 70 miles inland, one that most wouldn't otherwise be able to try.

NORTHEAST FLORIDA   Already a popular biker destination, Daytona Beach will soon have **Bruce Rossmeyer's Destination Daytona**, 1637 N. Hwy. US1 (© **866/NICEHOG**), a motorcycle complex complete with visitor information center, Harley-Davidson dealership, and restaurants.

Jacksonville Zoo and Gardens, 8605 Zoo Pkwy. (© **904/757-4462**), has broken ground on the $6.7-million, 2½-acre Kids' Zone, featuring a splash zone area that will incorporate life-size models of Florida's coastal animals, including whales, dolphins, and manta rays.

Over in St. Augustine, the 72-room **Hilton St. Augustine Historic Bayfront**, 32 Avenida Menendez (© **904/ 829-2777**), opened in late 2005. The buildings' designs were inspired by the architecture of the city's Second Spanish Period (1784–1821), with wooden balconies, cedar-shake and tile roofs, and historically accurate exterior colors. The 60-room luxury **Castillo Real,** 531 A1A Beach Blvd. (© **904/471-3505**), opened as part of the Clarion Hotel chain's luxury collection.

NORTHWEST FLORIDA: THE PANHANDLE   At press time, **Portofino** (© **850/916-5000**), a $250-million residence and resort community on Pensacola Beach, was about to complete its fourth and fifth towers. The development features five 21-story towers, a 20,000-square-foot, $4.5-million European Spa, gourmet bistro, heated Olympic pool, lounge, tennis courts, and many other amenities.

Pensacola Beach recently completed a beach renourishment that has expanded the shoreline by pumping new sand through a submerged pipeline into our coastline, replacing 2.3 million cubic yards of sand washed away during Hurricane Ivan in September 2004. This new sand brought seashells of all sorts to shore, creating a collector's delight.

1

The Best of Florida

Although it's the state nickname, describing Florida as the Sunshine State is like calling Katie Couric "perky." Sure, it's true, but not all the time—and it doesn't nearly begin to describe the state's other marketable assets. There's a lot more to Florida than just sunshine—and, yes, we get those pesky hurricanes. Weather aside, choosing the best of Florida is by no means simple. While millions of visitors flock here to escape the bleakness of winter and landlocked locations, they don't all come down for sun, fun, and Mickey Mouse. Granted, the promise of (mostly) clear skies and 800 miles of sparkling, sandy beaches is alluring, as are the animatronics and roller coasters in Orlando and Tampa, but there's much more to the state than that. In fact, in many ways, Florida is like a beautiful, blond beauty queen whom everyone thinks is all fluff until they find out she happens to be a Rhodes scholar.

Here you can choose from a colorful, often kitschy assortment of accommodations, from deluxe resorts to mom-and-pop motels. You can visit remote little towns like Apalachicola or a multicultural megalopolis like Miami. You can devour fresh seafood, from amberjack to oysters—and then work off those calories in such outdoor pursuits as bicycling, golfing, or kayaking. Despite overdevelopment in many parts of the state, Floridians have maintained thousands of acres of wilderness areas, from the little respite of Clam Pass County Park in downtown Naples to the magnificent Everglades National Park, which stretches across the state's southern tip.

Choosing the "best" of all of this is a daunting task, and the selections in this chapter are only highlights. You'll find numerous other outstanding resorts, hotels, destinations, activities, and attractions described in this book. And with an open mind and a sense of adventure, you'll come up with bests of your own.

1 The Best Beaches

- **Virginia Key** (Key Biscayne): The producers of *Survivor* or *Lost* could feasibly shoot their show on this ultra-secluded, picturesque, and deserted key, where people go purposely not to be found. See p. 138.
- **Bill Baggs Cape Florida State Park** (Key Biscayne): The pot of gold at the end of the rainbow, Bill Baggs ⸱⸱⸱es serenity with 1¼ miles of ⸱⸱⸱ nature trails, and even a ⸱⸱⸱ that recalls an era ⸱⸱⸱ like this one

gave way to avaricious developers and pollutants. See p. 147.
- **Lummus Park Beach** (South Beach): This beach is world renowned, not necessarily for its pristine sands, but for its more common name of **South Beach,** on which seeing, being seen, and, at times, the obscene, go hand in hand with the sunscreen and beach towels. The 12th Street section is the beach of choice for gay residents and travelers. Often this beach is the venue for some of the liveliest parties

South Beach has ever seen. See p. 81.

- **Haulover Beach** (Miami Beach): Nestled between the Intracoastal Waterway and the ocean, especially at the north end, is the place to be for that all-over tan: Haulover is the city's only clothing-optional (aka nude) beach. See p. 155.

- **Bahia Honda State Park** (Bahia Honda Key): This is one of the nicest and most peaceful beaches in Florida. It's located amid 635 acres of nature trails and a portion of Henry Flagler's railroad. See p. 204.

- **John U. Lloyd Beach State Park** (Dania Beach): Unfettered by high-rise condominiums, T-shirt shops, and hotels, this wonderful beach boasts an untouched shoreline surrounded by a canopy of Australian pine to ensure complete seclusion. See p. 260.

- **Lover's Key State Park** (Fort Myers Beach): You'll have to walk or take a tram through a bird-filled forest of mangroves to this gorgeous, unspoiled beach just a few miles south of busy Fort Myers Beach. Although Sanibel Island gets the accolades, the shelling here is just as good, if not better. See p. 344.

- **Cayo Costa State Park** (off Captiva Island): These days, deserted tropical islands with great beaches are scarce in Florida, but this 2,132-acre barrier strip of sand, pine forest, mangrove swamp, oak hammock, and grassland provides a genuine get-away-from-it-all experience. Access is only by boat from nearby Gasparilla, Pine, and Captiva islands. See p. 369.

- **Naples Beach** (Naples): Many Florida cities and towns have beaches, but few are as lovely as the gorgeous strip that fronts Naples's famous Millionaires' Row. You don't have to be rich to wander its length,

peer at the mansions, or stroll on historic Naples Pier to catch a sunset over the Gulf. See p. 376.

- **Caladesi Island State Park** (Clearwater Beach): Even though 3½-mile-long Caladesi Island is in the heavily developed Tampa Bay area, it has a lovely, relatively secluded beach with soft sand edged in sea grass and palmettos. In the park itself, there's a nature trail where you might see one of the rattlesnakes, black racers, raccoons, armadillos, or rabbits that live here. The park is accessible only by ferry from Honeymoon Island State Recreation Area, off Dunedin. See p. 431.

- **Fort DeSoto Park** (St. Petersburg): Where else can you get a good tan *and* a history lesson? At Fort DeSoto Park, you have not only 1,136 acres of five interconnected islands and 3 miles of unfettered beaches, but also a fort that's listed on the National Register of Historic Places. There are also nature trails, fishing piers, a 2.25-mile canoe trail, and spectacular views of Tampa Bay and the Gulf. See p. 431.

- **Canaveral National Seashore** (Cape Canaveral): Midway between the crowded attractions at Daytona Beach and Kennedy Space Center is a protected stretch of coastline 24 miles long, backed by cabbage palms, sea grapes, and palmettos. See p. 528.

- **Gulf Islands National Seashore** (Pensacola): All of Northwest Florida's Gulf shore is one of America's great beaches—an almost uninterrupted stretch of pure white sand that runs the entire length of the Panhandle, from Perdido Key to St. George Island. The Gulf Islands National Seashore preserves much of this natural wonder in its undeveloped state. Countless terns, snowy plovers, black skimmers, and other birds nest along the dunes topped

Florida

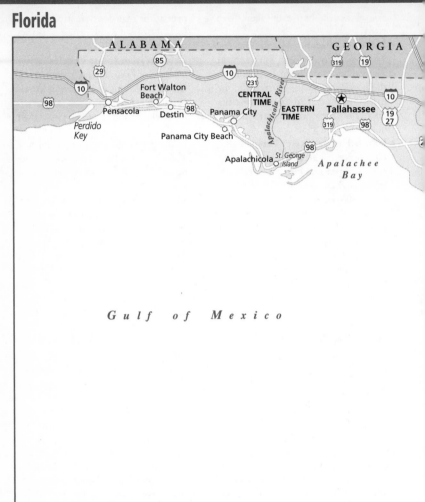

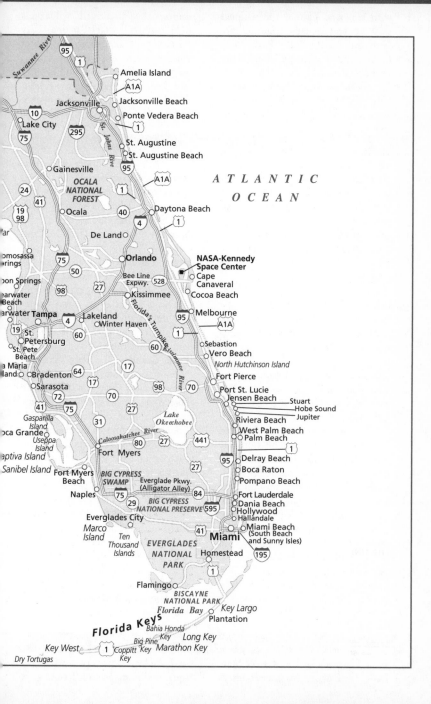

with sea oats. East of the national seashore and equally beautiful are **Grayton Beach State Park,** near Destin; and **St. George Island State Park,** off Apalachicola. See p. 590.

• **St. Andrews State Park** (Panama City Beach): With more than 1,000 acres of dazzling white sand and dunes, this preserved wilderness demonstrates what Panama City Beach looked like before motels and condominiums lined its shore. Lacy, golden sea oats sway in Gulf breezes, and fragrant rosemary grows wild. The area is home to foxes, coyotes, and a herd of deer. See p. 619.

2 The Best Fishing

• **The Keys:** The Keys boast world-class deep-sea fishing; the prize is such big-game fish as marlin, sailfish, and tuna. There's reef fishing as well, for "eating fish" like snapper and grouper; and backcountry fishing for bonefish, tarpon, and other "stalking" fish. Dozens of charter-fishing boats operate from Key West marinas and from other, less popular keys. Islamorada, in the Upper Keys, is the sport-fishing capital of the world. Seven-mile Bridge, linking the Middle and Lower keys, is known as "the longest fishing bridge in the world"; it's also a favorite spot for local fishers who wait for barracuda, yellowtail, and dolphin to bite. See p. 189.

• **Lake Okeechobee:** Many visitors to the Treasure Coast come to fish, and they certainly get their fill from the miles of Atlantic shore and from inland rivers. If you want to fish freshwater and nothing else, head for Lake Okeechobee, the state's largest lake, which is chock-full of good eating fish. It covers more than 467,000 acres—that's more than 730 square miles. At one time, the lake supported an enormous commercial fishing industry. Due to a commercial fishing-net ban, however, much of that industry has died off, leaving the sport fishers all the rich bounty of the lake. *Note:* 2005's Hurricane Wilma stirred up the polluted sediments at the bottom of the lake. As of press time, cleanup was ongoing. See p. 329.

• **Stuart:** Known as the "Sailfish Capital of the World," Stuart is an angler's haven. The fish bite year-round, but peak months are December through March and June through July. Sailfishing is an art of its own—beginners must learn that exact moment to let the reel drag so that the fish run with the lure. See p. 316.

• **Boca Grande:** The deep, shadowy holes of Boca Grande Pass, between Gasparilla and Cayo Costa islands off Fort Myers, harbor the mighty tarpon, the "silver king of the seas." Teddy Roosevelt and his rich buddies used to bag tarpon in these waters, and anglers from around the globe still compete every July in the World's Richest Tarpon Tournament. See p. 368.

• **Destin:** Florida's largest charter-boat fleet, with more than 140 vessels, is based in this Panhandle town, which calls itself the "World's Luckiest Fishing Village." Anglers here have landed championship catches of grouper, amberjack, snapper, mackerel, cobia, sailfish, wahoo, tuna, and blue marlin. See p. 605.

3 The Best Snorkeling & Diving

• **John Pennekamp Coral Reef State Park** (Key Largo): This is the country's first undersea preserve, with 188 square miles of protected coral reefs.

The water throughout much of the park is shallow, so it's an especially great place for snorkelers to see an incredibly vibrant array of coral, including tree-size elkhorn coral and giant brain coral. See p. 191.

- **Looe Key National Marine Sanctuary** (Bahia Honda State Park): With 5⅓ square miles of gorgeous coral reef, rock ledges up to 35 feet tall, and a colorful and motley marine community, you may never want to come up for air. See p. 206.

- **Hutchinson Island:** Three popular artificial reefs off this island provide excellent scenery for divers of any level. The **USS *Rankin,*** sunk in 120 feet of water in 1988, lies 7 miles east-northeast of the St. Lucie Inlet. **Donaldson Reef** consists of a cluster of plumbing fixtures sunk in 58 feet of water. **Ernst Reef,** made from old tires, is a 60-foot dive located 4½ miles east-southeast of the St. Lucie inlet. See p. 316.

4 The Best Golf Courses

- **Biltmore Hotel** (Miami): The beautiful, rolling, 18-hole golf course designed by Donald Ross and located at the majestic Biltmore Hotel in Coral Gables is open to the public and is a favorite of Bill Clinton. See p. 104.

- **Doral Golf Resort and Spa** (Miami): Four championship courses make the Doral one of Miami's best golf destinations. One course, the legendary Blue Monster is the site of the annual Doral-Ryder Open. See p. 100.

- **Fairmont Turnberry Isle Resort & Club** (Aventura, North Miami Beach): These two 18-hole courses by Robert Trent Jones, Sr., are open only to guests but are among the city's best. See p. 102.

- **PGA National Resort & Spa** (Palm Beach): This rambling resort, the national headquarters of the PGA, is a premier golf destination with five 18-hole courses on more than 2,300 acres. See p. 309.

- **Emerald Dunes Golf Course** (West Palm Beach): This gorgeous Tom Fazio–designed course (featuring 60 acres of water and stunning views of the ocean) is pricey, but one of only a few in the area open to the public. See p. 293.

- **Tiburón Golf Club** (Naples): Greg Norman designed this course's 36 championship holes to play like a British Open—but without the thick thatch rough. The course is now home to the luxurious Ritz-Carlton Golf Resort, Naples. See p. 375.

- **Naples Beach Hotel & Golf Club** (Naples): One of the state's oldest, this resort course is relatively flat, but small greens and masterful bunkers will test your skills. In addition, one of Florida's most charming resort hotels is across the street. See p. 379.

- **Mangrove Bay Golf Course** (St. Petersburg): One of the nation's top 50 municipal courses, the Mangrove Bay course hugs the inlets of Old Tampa Bay and offers 18-hole, par-72 play. Facilities include a driving range; lessons and golf-club rental are also available. See p. 420.

- **The Westin Innisbrook Resort** (Tarpon Springs): *Golfweek* has called Innisbrook's Copperhead Course, former home of the annual JCPenney Classic, number one in Florida. Each year, 1,000 students go through Innisbrook's Golf Institute. Golfers from around the world come to play the 600 acres of courses. See p. 438.

- **Walt Disney World** (Orlando): The resorts surrounding the theme parks have 99 regulation holes that let you walk in the footsteps (and share the frustrations) of the game's greatest players. Those with a shorter stroke can play the master miniature courses: Fantasia Gardens and Winter Summerland. See p. 509.

- **Grand Cypress Resort** (Orlando): No Bermuda shorts allowed on the four Jack Nicklaus–designed courses, including three 9-hole courses that are played in three 18-hole combinations, and an 18-hole course called the New Courses. See p. 477.

- **Ladies Professional Golf Association/LPGA International** (Daytona Beach): This "women-friendly" course has multiple tee settings, unrestricted tee times, a great pro shop, and state-of-the-art facilities. Designed by Rees-Jones, the older of the two courses here was chosen as one of the "Top Ten You Can Play" by *Golf* magazine. See p. 537.

- **TPC at Sawgrass** (Ponte Vedra Beach, near Jacksonville): With 99 holes, Pete Dye's Tournament Players Club (TPC) at Sawgrass makes top-10 lists everywhere. The 17th hole, on a tricky island, is one of the most photographed holes in the world. See p. 567.

- **Ocean Hammock Golf Club** (Palm Coast, between Daytona Beach and St. Augustine): With six of its holes actually skirting the Atlantic Ocean, this Jack Nicklaus–designed course is the first authentic seaside links built in Florida since the 1920s. See p. 555.

- **Amelia Island Plantation** (Amelia Island): This exclusive resort has three of the state's best courses. Long Point Club, designed by Tom Fazio, is the most beautiful and challenging. Pete Dye's Amelia Links comprises two courses, Oak Marsh and Ocean Links. All are open only to resort guests. See p. 580.

- **Marriott's Bay Point Resort Village** (Panama City Beach): Thirty-six holes of championship golf at this Marriott include the Lagoon Legends course, one of the country's most difficult. Nearby is the Hombre, an 18-holer where O. J. Simpson played a round right after his acquittal. See p. 621.

5 The Best Luxury Resorts

- **The Setai** (South Beach; ✆ **305/520-6100**): Simply put, there is no hotel like this anywhere in Florida. With a *discounted* rate of $1,000 per night, this hotel breaks the bank and takes luxury to a new level with its imported, not imitated, Asian decor and staff; outstanding pan-Asian cuisine; and celebrity clientele. Who else can afford these prices? See p. 86.

- **Ritz-Carlton Key Biscayne** (Key Biscayne; ✆ **800/241-3333** or 305/365-4500): In addition to consistently superior services and amenities, this British colonial–style version of the Ritz rises above its casual Key Biscayne surroundings with a stellar view of the Atlantic Ocean, not to mention an equally impressive 20,000-square-foot spa. See p. 96.

- **Mandarin Oriental, Miami** (Brickell Key, Miami; ✆ **305/913-8383**): The swank and stunning Mandarin Oriental features a waterfront location, residential-style rooms, superb service, a spa frequented by J-Lo, and several upscale dining and bar facilities. See p. 99.

- **Ritz-Carlton South Beach** (South Beach; ✆ **800/241-3333** or 786/276-4000): Taking the concept of swanky South Beach to a very literal level, the Ritz-Carlton South Beach may be a landmark building restored to its original 1950s Art Moderne style, but in terms of the hotel's standout service (a tanning butler!), amenities, and ocean frontage, everything else is very much in the immediate present. See p. 84.

- **The Atlantic** (Fort Lauderdale; ✆ **800/325-3589** or 954/567-8020): Set on a golden sand beach, the Mediterranean-style Atlantic brings a fresh sense of modern luxury to Fort Lauderdale, not to mention a fabulous chef hailing from NYC's acclaimed Tribeca Grill. See p. 267.

- **The Breakers** (Palm Beach; ✆ **800/833-3141** or 561/655-6611): This stately, historic hotel epitomizes *la dolce vita,* Palm Beach style, featuring an elegant lobby, impeccable service, expansive manicured lawns, and a very scenic golf course that is the state's oldest. See p. 297.

- **Four Seasons Resort Palm Beach** (Palm Beach; ✆ **800/432-2335** or 561/582-2800): "Exquisite" is the adjective most often used to describe this posher-than-posh hotel. Luxurious but hardly stuffy, the Four Seasons was the stay of choice for quintessential aging rockers Aerosmith, who took great advantage of post-concert pampering. See p. 298.

- **LaPlaya Beach & Golf Resort** (Naples; ✆ **800/237-6883** or 239/597-3123): More intimate than the Ritz, the equally luxe LaPlaya Beach & Golf Resort offers spacious rooms, each with a completely private balcony overlooking the pristine waters of the Gulf or Vanderbilt Bay. The resort features four unique pools, two lagoons, an outdoor whirlpool, the Tiki Bar, the 4,500-square-foot Spa-Terre, the 2,700-square-foot fitness center, the Gulf-view Baleen restaurant, and a 6,907-yard championship 18-hole golf course designed by Bob Cupp. See p. 380.

- **Ritz-Carlton Golf Resort, Naples** (Naples; ✆ **888/856-4372** or 239/593-2000): This luxurious Mediterranean-style resort takes full advantage of the Greg Norman–designed Tiburón Golf Club. Guests here can use the beach and spa at the Ritz-Carlton, Naples, nearby. See p. 381.

- **Ritz-Carlton, Naples** (Naples; ✆ **888/856-4372** or 239/598-3300): This opulent 14-story Mediterranean-style hotel at Vanderbilt Beach is a favorite of affluent types who like standard Ritz amenities such as imported marble floors, antique art, Oriental rugs, Waterford chandeliers, and afternoon British-style high tea. Guests relax in high-backed rockers on the verandas or unwind by the heated pool set in a landscaped terrace. See p. 381.

- **Don CeSar Beach Resort & Spa** (St. Pete Beach; ✆ **866/728-2206** or 727/360-1881): Dating back to 1928 and listed on the National Register of Historic Places, this "Pink Palace" tropical getaway is so romantic, you may bump into six or seven honeymooning couples in one weekend. The lobby has classic high windows and archways, crystal chandeliers, marble floors, and original artwork. Most rooms have high ceilings and offer views of the Gulf or Boca Ciega Bay. See p. 434.

- **Disney's Grand Floridian Resort & Spa** (Lake Buena Vista; ✆ **407/934-7639**): This magnificent Victorian inn has a grand five-story lobby topped by an opulent Tiffany–style glass dome. The glass-enclosed brass cage elevator and Chinese Chippendale aviary are examples of the very refined style that runs throughout the entire resort. An orchestra plays big-band music every evening near Victoria & Albert's, the resort's five-star restaurant, and afternoon tea is a daily event. See p. 470.

- **Hyatt Regency Grand Cypress Resort** (Orlando; ✆ **800/233-1234** or 407/239-1234): The impressive facilities at this luxury resort include a half-acre pool with a dozen waterfalls, caves, and gottos; three spas; 12 tennis courts; four Jack Nicklaus–designed golf courses; a 45-acre nature walk; a private lake with its own stretch of white sand beach; and some of Orlando's best restaurants. See p. 477.

- **Amelia Island Plantation** (Amelia Island; ✆ **888/261-6161** or 904/ 261-6161): Set amid magnolias, oak trees, and the Atlantic Ocean, this gracious resort is straight out of the Deep South. It's more rustic than the nearby Ritz, but it has excellent hiking and biking paths, tennis, swimming, horseback riding, and boating. Golfers can enjoy exclusive use of two of Florida's top courses. See p. 580.

6 The Best Romantic Hideaways

- **Hotel Place St. Michel** (Coral Gables; ✆ **800/848-HOTEL** or 305/444-1666): This European-style hotel in the heart of Coral Gables is one of the city's most romantic options. The accommodations and hospitality are very old-world European, complete with dark-wood paneled walls, cozy beds, beautiful antiques, and a quiet elegance that seems startlingly out of place in trendy Miami. See p. 104.

- **Hotel Impala** (South Beach; ✆ **800/ 646-7252** or 305/673-2021): During the heyday of 1990s excess, Miami Beach was known for the fabulous parties thrown by the eclectic designer Gianni Versace. The late Versace desired an intimate European-style guesthouse that would please well-seasoned travelers, and the Impala is the result. His personal touch on this renovated Mediterranean inn is still evident, from the Greco-Roman frescoes and friezes to an intimate garden perfumed by strategically planted hanging lilies and gardenias. See p. 88.

- **Jules' Undersea Lodge** (Key Largo; ✆ **305/451-2353**): Submerge yourself in this single-room Atlantis-like hotel that offers a surprisingly comfortable suite 30 feet underwater. Don't worry; there's plenty of breathing room. See p. 197.

- **Little Palm Island** (Little Torch Key; ✆ **800/343-8567** or 305/872-2524): Accessible only by boat, this private 5-acre island is not only remote, it's romantic—there are no TVs, telephones, or faxes in the luxurious thatched cottages. See p. 206.

- **Marquesa Hotel** (Key West; ✆ **800/ 869-4631** or 305/292-1919): Don't be fooled by the Marquesa's location on heavily populated Key West: This charming B&B is in a wonderful world of its own, far enough from the tumult, yet close enough if you want it. See p. 225.

- **The Gardens Hotel** (Key West; ✆ **800/526-2664** or 305/294-2661): A well-kept secret (until now), The Gardens Hotel is an exotic, lush, serene, and sultry escape from the frat-boy madness that ensues on nearby Duval Street. See p. 223.

- **Sundy House** (Delray Beach; ✆ **877/439-9601** or 561/272-5678): With just 11 suites surrounded by over 5,000 species of exotic plants and flowers, gazebos, and flowing streams, Sundy House is a gorgeous getaway close enough to access the beach, but safely hidden from the mood-ruining madness and conventionality of your typical tourist-class beach hotel. See p. 285.

- **Island's End Resort** (St. Pete Beach; ✆ **727/360-5023**): Sitting right on

Pass-a-Grille, where the Gulf of Mexico meets Tampa Bay, this little all-cottage retreat is a great hideaway from the crowds of St. Pete Beach. You won't have an on-site restaurant, bar, and other such amenities, but you can step from your cottage right onto the beach. And if you get the unit with two living rooms, you'll have a whirlpool tub and your own Gulf-side pool. See p. 436.

- **Turtle Beach Resort** (Siesta Key, off Sarasota; © **941/349-4554**): Sitting beside the bay, this intimate little charmer began life years ago as a traditional Old Florida fishing camp, but today it's one of the state's most romantic retreats. It's a tightly packed little place, but high wooden fences surround each unit's private outdoor hot tub, and one-way mirror walls let you lounge in bed while passersby see only reflections of themselves. See p. 454.
- **Disney's Wilderness Lodge & Villas** (Lake Buena Vista; © **407/934-7639**): This impressive resort is reminiscent of the grand lodge at Yellowstone National Park. The spewing geyser out back, the mammoth stone hearth in the lobby, the Artist's Point 360-degree view of Bay Lake, and the towering forest sheltering the resort from the rest of the world are just a few of the reasons to stay here. Some guest rooms have patios or balconies overlooking the lake, woodlands, or meadow. See p. 473.
- **The Villas of Grand Cypress** (Orlando; © **800/835-7377** or 407/

239-4700): This luxury condominium resort offers lush grounds dotted with bougainvillea and hibiscus, lakes fat with largemouth bass and bream, and grounds speckled with trumpeter swans, wood ducks, and the occasional fox or bobcat. It shares a golf academy, racquet club, and equestrian center with the Hyatt Regency Grand Cypress. Best of all, the woodsy grounds make you feel as if you're far, far from Disney, which is right next door. See p. 477.

- **The Lodge & Club at Ponte Vedra Beach** (Ponte Vedra Beach, near Jacksonville; © **800/243-4304** or 904/273-9500): Every unit at this intimate hotel in upscale Ponte Vedra Beach has a romantic seat built into its oceanview window, plus a big bathroom with a two-person tub and separate shower. Gas fireplaces in most units add even more charm. One of the three pools and whirlpools here is reserved exclusively for couples. You can even get married in the semicircular meeting room overlooking the Atlantic. See p. 570.
- **Seaside** (near Destin; © **800/277-8696** or 850/231-1320): If residents of Northwest Florida don't stay at Henderson Park Inn for their getaways, they head for the romantic Gulf-front cottages at Seaside. Built in the 1980s but evoking the 1880s, the Victorian-style village of Seaside (a short drive east of Destin) has several cozy cottages designed especially for honeymooners. See p. 602.

7 The Best Moderately Priced Accommodations

- **Lily Leon Hotel** (South Beach; © **305/673-3767**): A true value, this charismatic and hip sliver of property has won the loyalty of fashion industrialists and romantics alike. Built in 1929 and restored in 1996, the hotel

retains many original details such as facades, woodwork, and fireplaces. See p. 90.

- **Catalina Hotel & Beach Club** (South Beach; © **877/SOBEGRP** or 305/674-1160): Affordable and hip, the Catalina is a retro fab stay with stylish rooms, Swedish Tempur-Pedic mattresses, a hot bar, and VIP hookups at all the clubs in South Beach. See p. 90.

- **Pelican Hotel** (South Beach; © **800/ 7-PELICAN** or 305/673-3373): Owned by the creative owners of the Diesel jeans company, the Pelican is South Beach's only self-professed "toy-hotel," and each of its 30 rooms and suites is decorated as outrageously as some of the area's more colorful drag queens. See p. 91.

- **Whitelaw Hotel** (South Beach; © **305/398-7000**): With a slogan that reads, "Clean sheets, hot water, and stiff drinks," the Whitelaw stands apart from the other boutique hotels with its fierce sense of humor and happening happy hours. See p. 91.

- **Conch Key Cottages** (Marathon; © **800/330-1577** or 305/289-1377): This oceanfront hideaway offers rustic but immaculate and well-outfitted cottages that are especially popular with families. Each has a hammock, barbecue grill, and kitchen. See p. 198.

- **Banyan Marina Resort** (Fort Lauderdale; © **954/524-4430**): These fabulous waterfront apartments located on a beautifully landscaped residential island may hear you vow never to stay in a hotel again. See p. 270.

- **Hotel Biba** (West Palm Beach; © **561/832-0094**): The mod squad has adopted—and adapted—this '40s-style motel into a Jetsonian, jet-set hangout that provides swank and sleek shelter from the upper-crusty hotels that surround it. See p. 301.

- **Island's End Resort** (St. Pete Beach; © **727/360-5023**): A wonderful respite from the madding crowd, and a great bargain, to boot, this little all-cottage hideaway sits on the southern tip of St. Pete Beach, smack-dab on Pass-a-Grille, where the Gulf of Mexico meets Tampa Bay. You can step from the six contemporary cottages right onto the beach. One unit even has a private pool. See p. 436.

- **Disney's Port Orleans Resort** (Lake Buena Vista; © **407/934-7639** or 407/934-5000): This resort's Southern charm appeals to all tastes, thanks to the varied landscapes of its Riverside and French Quarter sections; stately or casual, you'll find it here. The French Quarter's pool sports a water slide that curves from the mouth of a colorful sea serpent, while Riverside's Ol' Man Island has a water hole and playground with a very Tom Sawyer–ish feel. See p. 473.

- **Staybridge Suites** (Lake Buena Vista; © **800/866-4549** or 407/238-0777): Close to the action of Downtown Disney and the theme parks, this resort's one- and two-bedroom suites have full kitchens and are larger and more comfortable than most of the competition's. And to help you relax, the resort will do your grocery shopping for you so you don't have to deal with the hassle. See p. 479.

- **Casa Monica Hotel** (St. Augustine; © **800/648-1888** or 904/827-1888): Built in 1888 as a luxury hotel, this Spanish-style building was gutted and restored to its previous elegance in 1998. Most interesting of the guest quarters are suites installed in two tile-topped towers and a fortresslike central turret. One suite in the turret has a half-round living room with gunport windows overlooking St. Augustine's historic district. See p. 556.

- **Gibson Inn** (Apalachicola; © **850/ 653-2191**): Built in 1907 as a seamen's hotel and gorgeously restored in 1985, this cupola-topped inn is such a brilliant example of Victorian architecture that it's listed on the National Register of Historic Inns.

No two guest rooms are alike (some still have the original sinks in the sleeping area), but all are richly furnished with period reproductions.

Grab a drink from the bar and relax in one of the high-backed rockers on the old-fashioned veranda. See p. 631.

8 The Best Family Attractions

- **Parrot Jungle Island** (Miami): We adults think it's overrated and touristy, but kids love it. You'll need to watch your head, however, since flying above are hundreds of parrots, macaws, peacocks, cockatoos, and flamingos. Continuous suitable but cheesy shows star roller-skating cockatoos, card-playing macaws, and numerous stunt-happy parrots. There are also tortoises, iguanas, and a rare albino alligator on exhibit. See p. 164.

- **Miami Children's Museum** (Miami): In addition to hundreds of bilingual, interactive exhibits; and programs and classes and learning materials related to arts, culture, community, and communication, the museum has a re-creation of the NBC 6 television studio and a working music studio in which aspiring rock stars can lay down tracks and play instruments.

- **Sea Grass Adventures** (Miami): This is not your typical nature tour. With Sea Grass Adventures, you will be able to wade in the water on Key Biscayne with your guide and catch an assortment of sea life in the provided nets. At the end of the program, participants gather on the beach while the guide explains what everyone's just caught, passing the creatures around in miniature viewing tanks. See p. 164.

- **Miami Museum of Science and Space Transit Planetarium** (Miami): The Museum of Science features more than 140 hands-on exhibits that explore the mysteries of the universe. Live demonstrations and collections of rare natural-history specimens make a visit here fun and informative. Many of the demos involve audience participation, which can be lots of fun for willing and able kids and adults alike. See p. 144.

- **Busch Gardens Tampa Bay** (Tampa): Although the thrill rides, live entertainment, shops, restaurants, and games get most of the ink at this 335-acre family theme park, Busch Gardens also ranks among the top zoos in the country, with several thousand animals living in naturalistic environments. If you can get them off the roller coasters, kids can find out what all those wild beasts they've seen on the Discovery Channel look like in person. See p. 395.

- **MOSI (Museum of Science and Industry)** (Tampa): One of the largest educational science centers in the Southeast, MOSI has more than 450 interactive exhibits in which the kids can experience hurricane-force winds, defy the laws of gravity, cruise the mysterious world of microbes, explore the human body, and more. They can also watch stunning movies in MOSIMAX, Florida's first IMAX dome theater. See p. 403.

- **Universal Studios Florida** (Orlando): Universal Orlando's original Florida park has many rides based on Hollywood blockbusters or cartoon heroes, such as Shrek, Spiderman, Jaws, and Jimmy Neutron's Nicktoon Blast. Kids can get slimed at Nickelodeon Studios or get thrilled by the pint-size roller coaster and other fun in Woody Woodpecker's KidZone. See p. 509.

- **Walt Disney World's Magic Kingdom** (Orlando): Introduce your wee ones to many of the Disney characters at Mickey's Toontown Fair in the Magic Kingdom, Disney's premier park. There's also a ton of fun on rides themed after Winnie the Pooh, Peter Pan, Dumbo, Cinderella, Aladdin, and Buzz Lightyear. Rides like Splash Mountain make sure older guests have fun, too. See p. 496.

- **Kennedy Space Center** (Cape Canaveral): Especially since the recent multimillion-dollar renovation and expansion, this family destination is a must-see. There is plenty to keep kids and parents busy for at least a full day, including interactive computer games,

IMAX films, and dozens of informative displays on the space program. Try to schedule a trip during a real launch; there are more than a dozen each year. See p. 526.

- **DAYTONA USA** (Daytona Beach): Opened in late 1996 on Daytona International Speedway grounds, this huge state-of-the-art interactive attraction is an exciting and fast-paced stop even for nonrace fans. Kids can see real stock cars, go-karts, and motorcycles, and even participate in a pit stop on a NASCAR Winston Cup race car. See p. 534.

9 The Best Offbeat Travel Experiences

- **Jimbo's** (Miami): Located at the very end of Virginia Key, in Key Biscayne, on the lagoon where they shot *Flipper,* Jimbo's has become the quintessential, albeit hard-to-find, South Florida watering hole, snack bar, and hangout for a wacky assortment of colorful characters, from shrimpers and yachters to politicos. Dollar beers and excellent smoked fish are sold from a cooler, vacant shacks serve as backdrops for films, and visitors are able to test their skills in a game of bocce ball. See p. 130.

- **Alabama Jack's** (Key Largo): En route to the Keys, veer off onto Card Sound Road, once the only way to get down there, and follow the Harley-Davidsons to Alabama Jack's. A waterfront biker bar, restaurant, and live music joint built on two barges, Alabama Jack's on Sunday is the place to be for country line dancers, many of whom are in full Hee Haw regalia; lazy folks whiling away the day over beer, conch fritters, and the best Key Lime and peanut butter pie ever; and just good ol', interesting folks passin' through. See p. 186.

- **Columbus Day Regatta** (Miami): This unique observation of Columbus

Day revolves around a so-called regatta in Biscayne Bay but always ends with participants stripping down to their bare, ahem, necessities and partying at the sandbar in the middle of the bay. There is a boat race at some point of the day, but most people are too preoccupied to notice. See p. 35.

- **People-Watching on South Beach and Worth Avenue** (Miami and Palm Beach): As cliché as the notion of people-watching may seem, it's never the same old scenario on Miami's neon-hued Riviera, where equally colorful locals and luminaries proudly prance as if every day was the Easter parade. In Palm Beach, titled nobility, bejeweled socialites, and an assortment of upper crusties put on the ritz on the city's version of Rodeo Drive. See p. 138.

- **Swimming with the Dolphins at the Dolphin Research Center** (Marathon): Of the four such centers in the continental United States, the Dolphin Research Center is the most impressive. With advance reservations, you can splash around with dolphins in their natural lagoon homes. It's an amazing experience. See p. 190.

- **Underwater Stay at Jules' Undersea Lodge** (Key Largo): We give this a vote as one of Florida's most romantic retreats, but this underwater hotel is also, hands down, its most unusual. Where else can you have a pizza delivered via scuba diver?. See p. 197.
- **Fantasy Fest** (Key West): Mardi Gras takes a Floridian vacation as the streets of Key West are overtaken by wildly costumed revelers who have no shame and no parental guidance. This weeklong, hedonistic, X-rated Halloween party is *not* for children under 18. See p. 36.
- **Babcock Wilderness Adventures** (Fort Myers): Experienced naturalists lead "swamp buggy" tours through the Babcock Ranch, including the mysterious Telegraph Swamp, where alligators lounge in the sun. Although the Babcock Ranch is the largest cattle operation east of the Mississippi (with bison and quarter horses, too), it is also a major wildlife preserve inhabited by countless birds and other creatures. See p. 339.
- **Swimming with the Manatees** (Crystal River, north of Clearwater):

Some 360 manatees spend the winter in the Crystal River, and you can swim, snorkel, or scuba with them in the warm-water natural spring of Kings Bay, about 7 miles north of Homosassa Springs. It's not uncommon to be surrounded in the 72°F (21°C) water by 30 to 40 "sea cows," which nudge and caress you as you swim with them. See p. 422.
- **Wrangling an Alligator** (Orlando): Play trainer for a day and meet some of the toothy stars up close and *real* personal at Gatorland. You might even get to hop on "Pop," the 12-foot, 750-pound big daddy—or momma, rather—of the breeding march. See p. 517.
- **Learning to Surf the Big Curls at Cocoa Beach Surfing School** (Cocoa Beach): Even if you don't know how to hang ten, this school will get you riding the waves with the best of them. It offers equipment and lessons for all skill levels—beginner to pro—at the best surf beaches in Florida. See p. 530.

10 The Best Spas

- **Agua at The Delano Hotel** (Miami; ✆ 800/555-5001 or 305/672-2000): One trip to this sublime, celebrity-saturated rooftop spa in a haute hotel overlooking the Atlantic, and you'll feel like you're in heaven. Try the milk-and-honey massage and you'll understand. See p. 81.
- **The Spa at Mandarin Oriental Miami** (Miami; ✆ 866/526-6567 or 305/913-8383): If it's good enough for J-Lo, then it must be good enough for the rest of us. But seriously, this star-studded spa isn't the best because of its clientele, but because of its Chinese, Balinese, Indian, and European treatments

applied by professionals well versed in the inimitable Mandarin Oriental brand of pampering. See p. 99.
- **The Spa at The Setai** (South Beach; ✆ 305/520-6100): Nirvana is alive and well at the Spa at The Setai, where the philosophy of relaxation is derived from an ancient Sanskrit legend, natural elixirs, eternal youth, and Asian treatments and ingredients such as green tea. See p. 86.
- **The Spa at The Standard Hotel** (South Beach; ✆ 305/673-1717) What used to be an old-school, Borscht Belt–style Miami Beach health spa is now one of the hottest, trendiest places to take a Turkish bath

in a bona fide Hamam, let out steam in a cedar sauna, or get spritzed in the hotel's sublime Wall of Sound Shower.

- **The Ritz-Carlton Spa, Key Biscayne** (Key Biscayne; © 305/365-4158: This spa is a sublime, 20,000-square-foot West Indies colonial-style Eden in which you can treat yourself to over 60 treatments, including the Key Lime Coconut Body Scrub and the Everglades Grass Body Wrap in one of 21 treatment rooms. For a real splurge, the Fountain of Youth Balance treatment is a 6-hour indulgence featuring a facial, massage, manicure, pedicure, shampoo, styling, and lunch served on the oceanfront terrace. See p. 96.

- **Marriott's Harbor Beach** (Fort Lauderdale; © 800/222-6543 and 954/525-4000): This $8-million, 24,000-square-foot European spa is the first full-service seaside facility of its kind in Fort Lauderdale. See p. 268.

- **PGA National Resort & Spa** (Palm Beach Gardens; © 800/633-9150 or 561/627-2000): This lauded golf resort provides the perfect pampering for sore golfers and bored nongolfers, with its Mediterranean Spa featuring just about every treatment imaginable, including special ones for pregnant women. See p. 309.

- **Sanibel Harbour Resort & Spa** (Fort Myers; © 800/767-7777 or 239/466-4000): Many call this high-rise resort overlooking Sanibel Island the best spa value in the country. Regardless of the price, the spa obliges your every whim. Try the amazing Betar Bed, a suspended "bed of music" that floats you to a level where stresses disappear. There are

also mud, algae, seaweed, and mineral wraps; Swiss showers; paraffin facials; and more. Day packages, makeovers, and men's sports packages are popular. The fitness center is also state-of-the-art. See p. 341.

- **Naples Beach Hotel & Golf Club** (Naples; © 800/237-7600 or 239/261-2222): This modern spa adds complete relaxation to a stay at this venerable hotel, already one of Florida's most relaxing resorts. A deep-body massage followed by a milk-and-honey wrap will leave you on cloud nine, and a special wedding package will have you primed for the big day. See p. 379.

- **The Ritz-Carlton, Naples** (Naples; © 888/856-4372 or 239/598-3300): An impressive, hard-to-leave, full-service spa will leave you thoroughly relaxed before or after your stroll through the mangrove forest to the white-sand beach at one of Florida's finest luxury resorts. See p. 381.

- **Safety Harbor Resort and Spa** (Tampa Bay Area; © 888/237-8772 or 727/726-1161): Tucked away off the beaten track amid moss-draped oaks and cobblestone streets, Safety Harbor is the oldest continually running spa in the United States, and Florida's only spa built around natural healing springs—the feeling is very European. The Phil Green tennis school is also on the grounds, and many tennis programs are available. See p. 425.

- **Amelia Island Plantation** (Amelia Island; © 888/261-6161 or 904/261-6161): Besides a spectacular resort and a stunning spa facility, the Amelia Island Plantation has a dedicated Watsu Massage facility on its own small island right near the spa.

11 The Best Seafood Restaurants

- **Joe's Stone Crab Restaurant** (South Beach; ✆ 305/673-0365): Open only during stone-crab season (Oct–May), this always-packed Miami institution knows how to reel in the crowds with the freshest, meatiest stone crabs and the essential accouterments that go with them, from creamed spinach to excellent sweet-potato french fries. See p. 109.
- **The Fish Joint** (North Miami Beach; ✆ 305/936-8333): Although the name does this fantastic seafood restaurant no justice, the food makes up for it tenfold. See p. 124.
- **Grillfish** (South Beach; ✆ 305/538-9908): The Liza Minelli of South Beach, Grillfish has weathered the trendy storm of South Beach and still manages to pay the exorbitant South Beach rent by having a loyal following of locals who come for fresh, simple seafood in a relaxed but upscale atmosphere. See p. 116.
- **Seven Fish** (Key West; ✆ 305/296-2777): It may be a little tough to find and it doesn't have a water view, but the tiny, hip Seven Fish isn't about the frills. A mostly locals' seafood spot, the motto here is "simple.good.food." We disagree. The food isn't simple; it's simply the best seafood in town, with fresh catches of the day, phenomenal crab cakes, friendly servers, and a cool, in-the-know crowd. See p. 231.
- **Atlantic's Edge** (Islamorada; ✆ 305/664-4651): Of the many seafood restaurants in the Keys, this one is tops, with an innovative menu that includes some of the freshest and tastiest fish around. It's also the most elegant offering in the Keys. See p. 201.
- **Marker 88** (Islamorada; ✆ 305/852-9315): Bahamian conch, stone crabs from the Florida Bay, and shrimp from the West Coast are just some of the fresh items, innovatively prepared, at this Upper Keys institution. See p. 202.
- **Hobo's Fish Joint** (Coral Springs; ✆ 954/346-5484): Huge portions of extremely fresh fish are prepared in well over a dozen ways at this steak-house-style restaurant with wood floors and white tablecloths. Despite the fact that it's located away from the ocean in the utterly suburban enclave of Coral Springs, this joint is definitely worth a jaunt. See p. 274.
- **Sunfish Grill** (Pompano Beach; ✆ 954/788-2434): Some argue that this is the best seafood restaurant on the entire Gold Coast, and we won't argue against them, thanks to the chef/owner who buys seafood fresh from local fishermen and prepares it with stunning results. See p. 274.
- **Conchy Joe's Seafood** (Jensen Beach; ✆ 561/334-1130): Known for fresh seafood and Old Florida hospitality, Conchy Joe's enjoys an excellent reputation that's far bigger than the restaurant itself. Dining is either indoors or on a covered patio overlooking the St. Lucie River. See p. 320.
- **Channel Mark** (Fort Myers Beach; ✆ 239/463-9127): Every table looks out on a maze of channel markers on Hurricane Bay, and a dock with palms growing through it makes the Channel Mark a relaxing place for a waterside lunch. The atmosphere changes dramatically at night, when the relaxed tropical ambience is ideal for kindling romance. Congenial owners Mike McGuigan and Andy Welsh put a creative spin on their seafood dishes, and their delicately seasoned crab cakes are tops. See p. 349.
- **Lobster Pot** (Redington Shores, near St. Pete Beach; ✆ 727/391-8592): Come here for some of the finest seafood dishes on the St. Pete and

Clearwater beaches. Among the amazing variety of lobster dishes is one flambéed in brandy with garlic, and the bouillabaisse is as authentic as any you'll find in the South of France. See p. 439.

- **Fulton's Crab House** (Lake Buena Vista; ⓒ 407/934-2628): Located in a riverboat replica, Fulton's has a nostalgic mood and an array of good seafood, though meals can get a bit pricey if you opt for stone or king crab. There's also an excellent wine list. See p. 490.

- **Ted Peters' Famous Smoked Fish** (near St. Pete Beach; ⓒ 727/381-7931): The Peters clan has been watering mouths since 1948, when they started smoking fish and icing draft beer at the end of the causeway that leads from St. Pete Beach to the St. Petersburg mainland. Options include mullet, mackerel, and salmon, or you can bring your own

fish to be smoked over the red oak coals, at $1.50 per pound. See p. 439.

- **Back Porch** (Destin; ⓒ 850/837-2022): The food isn't gourmet at this cedar-shingled shack, whose long porch offers glorious beach and Gulf views, but this is where charcoal-grilled amberjack originated. Today you'll see it on menus throughout Florida. Other fish and seafood, as well as chicken and juicy hamburgers, also come from the coals. See p. 613.

- **Chef Eddie's Magnolia Grill** (Apalachicola; ⓒ 850/653-8000): Chef Eddie Cass's pleasant restaurant occupies a small bungalow built in the 1880s that is still in possession of the original black cypress paneling in its central hallway. Nightly specials emphasize fresh local seafood and New Orleans–style sauces. Chef Eddie received more than 2,000 orders for his spicy seafood gumbo at a recent Florida Seafood Festival. See p. 632.

12 The Best Local Dining Experiences

- **Azul** (downtown Miami; ⓒ 305/913-8254): Topping nearly every food critic's "best of" list is this culinary tour de force overlooking Biscayne Bay and located in the posh Mandarin Oriental. Star chef Michelle Bernstein's global fusion fare is a marvel that has elevated Miami to a new level of epicurean idolatry. See p. 124.

- **The Setai** (South Beach; ⓒ 305/520-6100): A Bombay native and a Singapore native—both Miamians now—celebrated when they tasted the uber-authentic (and uber-pricey) Asian cuisine here. It may be expensive, but it's a lot cheaper than a ticket to Asia! See p. 86

- **Big Fish** (downtown Miami; ⓒ 305/373-1770): Located on the Miami River across from the spectacular

Miami skyline, Big Fish is indeed just that, in a little pond—or river—whose scenic value is priceless. See p. 125.

- **Versailles** (Little Havana; ⓒ 305/444-0240): This iconoclastic Cuban diner isn't as swanky as its palatial French namesake, but it is full of mirrors, through which you can view the colorful—and audible—Cuban clientele that congregates here for down-home cuisine and hearty conversation. See p. 129.

- **Islamorada Fish Company** (Islamorada; ⓒ 800/258-2559 or 305/664-9271): We're not sure which is better, the view or the seafood—but whichever it is, it's a winning combination. See p. 203.

- **Blue Heaven** (Key West; ⓒ 305/296-8666): What was once a well-kept secret in Key West's Bahama Village is now a popular eatery known for fresh food (it's some of the best in town) and a motley, bohemian crowd. See p. 231.

- **Mai Kai** (Fort Lauderdale; ✆ **954/563-3272**): At this fabulous vestige of Polynesian kitsch, you're expected to forget that you're in the middle of a tacky stretch of Fort Lauderdale and pretend you're somewhere in Hawaii or Tahiti as hula dancers and fire-eaters entertain, and potent and sickly sweet cocktails are served in coconuts. See p. 278.

- **Taverna Opa** (South Beach, Hollywood and Ft. Lauderdale; ✆ **954/929-4010** or 954/567-1630): Don't get nervous if you hear plates breaking when you enter this raucous, authentic Greek taverna situated directly on the Intracoastal Waterway—it's just the restaurant's lively waitstaff making sure your experience here is 100% Greek. See p. 171.

- **Cap's Place Island Restaurant** (Lighthouse Point; ✆ **954/941-0418**): The only way to get to this rustic seafood restaurant, the former bootlegging and gambling hangout of Al Capone, is by boat, but don't be dismayed—it's not the least bit Disneyfied. Churchill, Roosevelt, Marilyn Monroe, and Sly Stallone have all indulged in this delicious taste of Old Florida. See p. 274.

- **Farmers Market Restaurant** (Fort Myers; ✆ **239/334-1687**): The retail Farmers Market next door may be tiny, but the best of the cabbage, okra, green beans, and tomatoes ends up here at this simple eatery, frequented by everyone from business executives to truck drivers. The specialties of the house are Southern favorites like smoked ham hocks with a bowl of black-eyed peas. See p. 342.

- **Fourth Street Shrimp Store** (St. Petersburg; ✆ **727/822-0325**): The outside of this place looks like it's covered with graffiti, but it's actually a gigantic drawing of people eating. Inside, murals on two walls seem to look out on an early-19th-century seaport (one painted sailor permanently peers in to see what you're eating). This is the best and certainly the most interesting bargain in St. Petersburg. See p. 427.

- **Moore's Stone Crab** (Longboat Key, off Sarasota; ✆ **941/383-1748**): Located in Longbeach, the old fishing village on the north end of Longboat Key, this popular bay-front restaurant still looks a little like a packing house (it's an offshoot of a family seafood business), but the view of the bay (dotted with mangrove islands) makes a fine complement to stone crabs fresh from the family's own traps. See p. 459.

- **Singleton's Seafood Shack** (Mayport/Jacksonville; ✆ **904/246-4442**): This rustic Old Florida fish camp has kept up with the times by offering fresh fish in more ways than just battered and fried. Yet it has still managed to retain the charming casualness of a riverside fish camp. Even if you don't want seafood, this spot is worth stopping at, if only for a feel of Old Florida. See p. 574.

- **The Boss Oyster** (Apalachicola; ✆ **850/653-9364**): This rustic, dockside eatery is a good place to see if what they say about the aphrodisiac properties of Apalachicola oysters is true. The bivalves are served raw, steamed, or under a dozen toppings ranging from capers to crab meat. They'll even steam three dozen of them and let you do the shucking. Dine inside or at picnic tables on a screened dockside porch. See p. 632.

13 The Best Bars & Nightspots

- **The Room** (South Beach; ☎ 305/531-6061): This NYC import exudes that hip Meatpacking District vibe with its simple yet chic concept of an impressive international collection of beer and wine only, comfy seats, candelight only, and a contingency of locals who know about this place and refuse to share it with the other poor souls who don't. See p. 170.

- **Pawn Shop Lounge** (Miami; ☎ 305/373-3511): Where else can you party with Paris, do shots with Colin Farrell, and jam with Jamie Foxx—all in an Airstream Trailer? Pawn Shop Lounge is Miami's most innovative club, with a full-blown Airstream, a school, bus and even the interior of a jetliner as its hubs of hipster action. See p. 175.

- **Opium/Prive and Mansion** (South Beach; ☎ 305/531-5535): This trendy troika of night spots is among the hottest in Miami for dancing, drinking, and slews of celebrity sightings. Friday and Saturday are the hottest nights at any of them, and you're almost guaranteed to spot a celeb at any given moment. See p. 174.

- **Tobacco Road** (Downtown Miami; ☎ 305/374-1198): Al Capone used to hang out here when it was a speakeasy. Now locals flock to this road-well-traveled place to hear live, local bands perform, as well as national acts such as George Clinton and the P-Funk All-Stars, Koko Taylor, and the Radiators. It's small, it's gritty, and it's meant to be that way here at the proud owner of Miami's very first liquor license. See p. 176.

- **Upstairs at the Van Dyke Cafe** (South Beach; ☎ 305/534-3600): Even though this jazz bar isn't located in a basement, but rather on the second floor of the Van Dyke Café, it resembles a classy speakeasy in which local jazz performers play to an intimate, enthusiastic crowd of mostly adults and sophisticated young things who huddle at the small tables often until the wee hours. See p. 176.

- **La Covacha** (West Miami; ☎ 305/594-3717): This hut, located virtually in the middle of nowhere, is the hottest Latin joint in the entire city. Do not wear silk here, as you *will* sweat. Friday is *the* night, so much so that the owners had to place a red velvet rope out front to maintain some semblance of order. See p. 177.

- **crobar** (South Beach; ☎ 305/531-8225): With its intense, dance-heavy sound system, an industrially chic ambience, and huge crowds, this Chicago import has raised the bar on South Beach nightlife with crazy theme nights (the monthly Sex Night is particularly, uh, stimulating), top-name deejays, and the occasional celebrity appearance. See p. 174.

- **Nikki Beach Club** (South Beach; ☎ 305/538-1111): What the Playboy Mansion is to Hollywood, the Nikki Beach Club is to South Beach. It's here where *Survivor* meets *The Brady Bunch in Hawaii,* with a bit of St.-Tropez thrown in for taste. See p. 174.

- **Automatic Slim's** (South Beach; ☎ 305/695-0795): Proudly billing itself as a place where "the beautiful people come to get ugly," Automatic Slim's is a good-time bar in which anything goes and pretenses are left at the door. See p. 168.

- **Twist** (South Beach; ☎ 305/538-9478): South Beach's most popular and long-lasting gay bar, Twist is where the who's who of the gay community convene for cocktails, consorting, and, at times, contorting. See p. 177.

- **Le Tub** (Hollywood; © **954/931-9425**): This former 1959 Sunoco gas station was transformed into a kitschy waterfront oasis whose resplendent scenery is almost secondary to the decor: old toilet bowls, bathtubs, and sinks—seriously. Not the least bit as gross as it sounds, Le Tub also has the best hamburgers, chili, a 4am close time and a strict "no children" policy. See p. 277.
- **Duval Street** (Key West): South Florida's own version of Bourbon Street, Duval Street is party central, with bars galore. See p. 209.
- **Clematis Street** (West Palm Beach): Until recently, nightlife in Palm Beach County was either an oxymoron or reserved for haughty private clubs on the island of Palm Beach. Thanks to a downtown revitalization, downtown West Palm now boasts a strip of its own, with trendy restaurants, clubs, and bars. See p. 304.
- **Las Olas Boulevard/Riverwalk** (Fort Lauderdale): Moving off the beachfront strip and onto the more quaint (but no less calm) riverside, Fort Lauderdale now boasts its very own downtown nightlife scene with restaurants, bars, and clubs. See p. 266.
- **Biba Bar** (West Palm Beach; © **561/832-0094**): The harder to find, the hipper it is, so they say, which is why this dimly lit, loungey hotel bar is tucked away in the middle of this mod motor inn—a hangout for in-the-know locals and visitors. See p. 301.
- **The Dock at Crayton Cove** (Naples; © **239/263-9940**): Right on the City Dock, this lively pub is a perfect place for an open-air meal or libation while watching the action on Naples Bay. See p. 384.
- **CityWalk** (Orlando; © **407/363-8000**): This 12-acre entertainment complex is a collection of eateries and nighttime entertainment spots. It's also a haven for theme restaurant aficionados, featuring a Hard Rock Cafe, a NASCAR Café, a Motown Cafe, and an NBA-themed restaurant. Additionally, you'll find plenty of places to dance the night away to the sounds of jazz, reggae, hip-hop, and pop. See p. 521.
- **Pleasure Island** (Orlando; © **407/939-2648**): This 16-acre, all-in-one complex of clubs, restaurants, and shops runs the entertainment gamut from jazz to modern rock to dance music. Catch an improvisational comedy show or hustle along on the disco floor—there's something here for everyone. Big-name artists occasionally make special appearances on two outdoor stages, but a nightly fireworks display ensures that every night here ends with a bang. See p. 520.
- **Ocean Deck Restaurant & Beach Club** (Daytona Beach; © **386/253-5224**): Reggae rules at this hot, noisy, packed, and always-fun beach bar near Daytona Beach's municipal pier, the town's "happening" district. By contrast, the upstairs restaurant is suitable for children, and it has great ocean views to accompany its fine and inexpensive fare. See p. 543.
- **Seville Quarter** (Pensacola; © **850/434-6211**): In Pensacola's Seville Historic District, this restored antique brick complex with New Orleans–style wrought-iron balconies contains pubs and restaurants whose names capture the ambience: Rosie O'Grady's Goodtime Emporium, Lili Marlene's Aviator's Pub, Apple Annie's Courtyard, End o' the Alley Bar, Phineas Phogg's Balloon Works (a dance hall, not a balloon shop), and Fast Eddie's Billiard Parlor (which has electronic games for kids, too). Live entertainment ranges from Dixieland jazz to country and western. See p. 601.

- **Flora-Bama Lounge** (Perdido Key, near Pensacola; ☎ 850/492-0611): This slapped-together Gulf-side pub is almost a shrine to country music, with jam sessions from noon until way past midnight on Saturdays and Sundays. Flora-Bama is the prime sponsor and a key venue for the Frank Brown International Songwriters' Festival during the first week of November. Take in the great Gulf views from the Deck Bar, and, if you're coming in late April, don't miss the Interstate Mullet Toss and Beach Party. See p. 601.

- **Shuckums Oyster Pub & Seafood Grill** (Panama City Beach; ☎ 850/235-3214): "We shuck 'em, you suck 'em" is the motto of this extremely informal pub, which became famous when comedian Martin Short tried unsuccessfully to shuck oysters here during the making of an MTV spring-break special. The original bar is virtually papered over with dollar bills signed by old and young patrons who have been flocking here since 1967. See p. 626.

14 The Rest of the Best

- **Best Driving Route:** A1A, a gorgeous oceanfront route that runs north up Miami Beach, through Sunny Isles and Hollywood into Fort Lauderdale (starting at Ocean Dr. and 1st St. in Miami, and merging onto Collins Ave. before running north), embodies the essence that is Florida. From time-warped hotels steeped in Art Deco kitsch to multimillion-dollar modern high-rises, A1A is one of the most scenic, albeit heavily trafficked, roads in all of Florida.

- **Best Place for People-Watching:** Lunchtime at News Cafe on Ocean Drive is the quintessential South Beach experience—lunching at News Cafe is more of a spectator sport than a dining experience. What the Big Mac is to McDonald's, people-watching is to News Cafe, whose Ocean Drive location is one of the best sidewalk spots from which to observe the wacky, colorful mix of pedestrians on parade. See p. 119.

- **Best Place to Hear a Moonlight Concert:** The Barnacle State Historic Site hosts a once-monthly, on or near the full moon (except July–Aug), concert in the backyard of their charming 1908 Coconut Grove bungalow built on 5 acres of waterfront property. Listeners are welcome to picnic and bask in this sublime setting for a mere $5. See p. 145.

- **Best Place to Learn the Salsa:** If the only salsa you're familiar with is the kind you put on your tacos, get over to Bongo's Cuban Café, the hottest salsa club north of Havana, where Miami's most talented salsa dancers will teach you how to move your two left feet in the right direction. See p. 173.

- **Best Place to Discover Your Inner Flipper:** The Dolphin Research Center will teach you how to communicate with and touch, swim, or play with the mammals at the nonprofit Dolphin Research Center in Marathon Key, home to a school of approximately 15 dolphins. See p. 190.

- **Best Cemetery:** The Key West Cemetery is funky, picturesque, and the epitome of the quirky Key West image, as irreverent as it is humorous. Headstones reflect residents' lighthearted attitudes toward life and death. I TOLD YOU I WAS SICK is one of the more famous epitaphs, as is the tongue-in-cheek widow's inscription

AT LEAST I KNOW WHERE HE'S SLEEP-
ING TONIGHT. See p. 213.

- **Best Way to See the Everglades Without Breaking a Sweat:** Airboat rides through the outskirts of the Everglades are particularly wonderful, since the area is unfettered by jet skis, cruise ships, and neon bikinis. The Everglades is Florida's Outback, resplendent in its swampy nature, which is best explored either by slow-moving canoes that really get you acquainted with your surroundings, or via an airboat that can quickly navigate its way through the most stubborn of sawgrass, providing you with an up-close-and-personal (as well as fun) view of the land's inhabitants, from alligators and manatees to raccoons and Florida panthers. See p. 246.

- **Best Place for a Family Vacation:** With eight theme parks, 80 smaller attractions, and virtually everything with a kid-friendly touch, it's hard to top Orlando and Lake Buena Vista. See chapter 12.

- **Best Blending of Old South with the Modern Era:** There's as much Old South ambience in the state's capital, Tallahassee, as anywhere else in Florida. Here you'll find 19th-century homes nestled among towering pine trees and sprawling live oaks, historic plantations, ancient Native American settlement sites and mounds, gorgeous gardens, quiet parks with picnic areas, beautiful lakes and streams, and myriad outdoor activities, as well as the state legislature, two college football teams, and all the modern conveniences you could want. See p. 633.

- **Best Place for Sunsets:** Florida's panhandle is the Land of the Two-Way Sun. It offers spectacular sunrises to the east and equally gorgeous sunsets to the west. One of the best viewing places is Bud & Alley's rooftop restaurant in Seaside. See p. 618.

2

Planning Your Trip to Florida

Whether you plan to spend a day, a week, 2 weeks, or longer in Florida, you'll need to make many "where," "when," and "how" choices before you leave home. This chapter explains how best to plan your trip.

1 The Regions in Brief

The first decision you'll have to make is where to go in Florida. Contrary to popular belief, it's not all sun, sand, and hanging chads—there are countless cultural, culinary, and nocturnal diversions as well. Of course, you will find ample sun, sea, and sand all along the 800 miles of shoreline here, but not every place in the Sunshine State is warm all of the time. Many Florida beaches are lined with flashy hotels and condominiums, whereas others are pristinely preserved in their natural states. You can spend your days in busy cosmopolitan cities or wile them away in picturesque small towns steeped in history. You can take the kids to see Mickey Mouse, or you can find a romantic retreat far from the madding crowd. The choice is yours.

Here's a brief rundown of the state's regions to help get you started:

MIAMI & MIAMI BEACH Sprawling across the southeastern corner of the state, metropolitan Miami is a city that prides itself on benefiting from its multiple, vibrant personalities as well as its no-passport-necessary international flair. Here you will hear a cacophony of Spanish and many other languages, not to mention accents, spoken all around you, for this cosmopolitan area is a melting pot of immigrants from Latin America, the Caribbean, and, undeniably, the

northeastern United States in particular. Cross the causeways, and you'll come to the sands of Miami Beach, long a resort mecca and home to the hyper-trendy South Beach, famous for its Art Deco architecture, electric nightlife, and celebrity sightings. See chapters 4 and 5 for more information on the Miami area; see p. 68 for descriptions of the different districts within Miami.

THE KEYS From the southern tip of the Florida mainland, U.S. 1 travels through a 100-mile-long string of islands stretching from Key Largo to the famous, funky, and laid-back "Conch Republic" of Key West, only 90 miles from Cuba and the southernmost point in the United States (it's always warm down here). While some of the islands are crammed with strip malls and tourist traps, most are dense with unusual species of tropical flora and fauna. The Keys don't have the best beaches in Florida, but the waters here—all in a vast marine preserve—offer the state's best scuba diving and snorkeling, and some of its best deep-sea fishing. See chapter 6 for more information.

EVERGLADES & BISCAYNE NATIONAL PARKS This is not your B-movie swamp. In fact, no excessive Hollywood studio budget could afford to replicate the stunning beauty found in this national landmark. Encompassing more than 2,000 square miles and 1.5 million acres, Everglades National Park covers the entire southern tip of Florida. The park, along with nearby Big Cypress National Preserve, protects a unique and fragile "River of Grass" ecosystem teeming with wildlife that is best seen by canoe, by boat, or on long or short hikes. To the east of the Everglades is Biscayne National Park, which preserves the northernmost living-coral reefs in the continental United States. See chapter 7 for more information.

THE GOLD COAST North of Miami, the Gold Coast is aptly named, for here are booming Hollywood and Fort Lauderdale and ritzy Boca Raton and Palm Beach—sun-kissed, glitzy, glammy, and sandy playgrounds of the rich and famous. Beyond its dozens of gorgeous beaches, the area offers fantastic shopping, entertainment, dining, boating, golfing, and tennis, and many places to relax in beautiful settings. With some of the country's most famous golf courses and even more tennis courts, this area also attracts big-name tournaments. See chapter 8 for more information.

THE TREASURE COAST Despite gaining unprecedented numbers of new residents in recent years, the beach communities running from Hobe Sound north to Sebastian Inlet have successfully and blissfully managed to retain their small-town feel. In addition to a vast array of wildlife (not to be mistaken with nightlife, which is intentionally absent from these parts), the area has a rich and colorful history. Its name stems from a violent 1715 hurricane that sank an entire fleet of treasure-laden Spanish ships. The sea around Sebastian Inlet draws surfers to the largest swells in the state, and the area has some great fishing as well. See chapter 9 for more information.

SOUTHWEST FLORIDA Ever since inventor Thomas Alva Edison built a home here in 1885, some of America's wealthiest families have spent their winters along Florida's southwest coast. They're attracted by the area's subtropical climate, shell-strewn beaches, and intricate waterways winding among 10,000-plus islands. Many charming remnants of Old Florida co-exist with modern resorts in the sophisticated riverfront towns of Fort Myers and Naples, and on islands like Gasparilla, Useppa, Sanibel, Captiva, and Marco. And thanks to some timely preservation, the area has many wildlife refuges, including the "back door" to Everglades National Park. See chapter 10 for more information.

THE TAMPA BAY AREA Halfway down the west coast of Florida lies Tampa Bay, one of the state's most densely populated areas. A busy seaport and commercial center, the city of Tampa is home to Busch Gardens Tampa Bay, which is both a major theme park and one of the country's largest zoos. Boasting a unique pier and fine museums, St. Petersburg's waterfront downtown is one of Florida's most pleasant. Most visitors elect to stay near the beaches skirting the narrow barrier islands that run some 25 miles between St. Pete Beach and Clearwater Beach. Across the bay to the south lies Sarasota, one of Florida's prime performing-arts venues, the riverfront town of Bradenton, and another string of barrier islands with great beaches and resorts spanning every price range. See chapter 11 for more information.

WALT DISNEY WORLD & ORLANDO Walt Disney announced plans to build the Magic Kingdom in 1965, a year before his death and 6 years before the theme park opened, changing forever what was then a sleepy Southern town. Walt Disney World claims four distinct parks, two entertainment districts, enough hotels and restaurants to fill a small city, and several smaller attractions, including water parks and miniature-golf courses. And then there are the rapidly

Then&Now   **The Perfect Florida Vacation, Then and Now**

In 1961, Frommer's published *Miami and the Caribbean on 10 Dollars a Day*. Although prices have changed since then, the premise of a Florida vacation is still the same: "to lie on a sunlit beach reading a paperback novel; to hunt out [local] centers of entertainment and culture; to be free; to experience the life of other peoples."

expanding Universal Studios Orlando and SeaWorld, as well as many more non-Disney attractions. Orlando is Florida's most popular tourist destination, thanks not only to an animated rodent, but also to those enterprising entertainment venues that have risen to the mouse's challenge. See chapter 12 for more information.

NORTHEAST FLORIDA   The northeast section of the state contains the oldest permanent settlement in America— St. Augustine, where Spanish colonists arrived and settled more than 4 centuries ago. Today its history comes to life in a quaint historic district. St. Augustine is bordered to the north by Jacksonville, an up-and-coming Sunbelt metropolis with miles of oceanfront beach and beautiful marine views along the St. Johns River. Up on the Georgia border, Amelia Island has two of Florida's finest resorts and its own historic town of Fernandina Beach. To the south of St. Augustine is Daytona Beach, home of the Daytona International Speedway and a maddening spring-break mecca for the MTV generation. Another brand of excitement is offered down at Cape Canaveral, where the Kennedy Space Center launches all manned U.S. space missions. See chapter 13 for more information.

NORTHWEST FLORIDA: THE PANHANDLE   Historic roots run deep in Florida's narrow northwest extremity, and Pensacola's historic district, which blends Spanish, French, and British cultures, is a highlight of any visit to today's Panhandle. Despite that, the accents here are decidedly Deep South. So, too, are the powdery, dazzlingly white beaches that stretch for more than 80 miles past the resorts of Pensacola Beach, Fort Walton Beach, Destin, and Panama City Beach. The Gulf Islands National Seashore has preserved much of this beach and its wildlife, and inland are state parks that offer some of the state's best canoeing adventures. All this makes the area a favorite summertime vacation destination for residents of neighboring Georgia and Alabama, with whom Northwest Floridians share many Deep South traditions. Sitting in a pine and oak forest just 30 miles from the Georgia line, the state capital of Tallahassee has a moss-draped, football-loving charm all its own. See chapter 14 for more information.

2 Visitor Information

Your best sources for detailed information about specific destinations in Florida are the local visitor information offices. They're listed under "Orientation" or "Essentials" in the chapters that follow.

Contact **Visit Florida,** P.O. Box 1100, Tallahassee, FL 32302-1100 (© **888/7-FLA-USA;** www.flausa.com), the state's official tourism marketing agent, for a free comprehensive guide to the state. For information on Florida state parks, check out the new website at www.floridastateparks.org. Visit Florida also operates **welcome centers:** 16 miles west of Pensacola on I-10, 4 miles north of Jennings on

I-75, 7 miles north of Yulee on I-95, and 3 miles north of Campbellton on U.S. 231. There's also a walk-in information office in the west foyer of the New Capitol Building in Tallahassee (see chapter 14).

3 Money

How much money you spend on your Florida vacation will depend on your own desires and choices, when you go, and most definitely *where* you go.

The state has a wide range of accommodations, from some of the country's most luxurious and expensive beachfront resorts to no-frills but friendly mom-and-pop motels sitting right by the beach. If you can do without the luxuries, you needn't spend a fortune.

Tourism is Florida's biggest industry, and the economic law of supply and demand dictates that the prices of hotel rooms are highest during the seasons when tourists invade Florida: the winter months in the southern half of the state, the summer months up north.

See "When to Go," below, for details on Florida's high, low, and in-between seasons.

CREDIT CARDS & ATMS

The easiest way to pay for almost everything in Florida is with a credit card. MasterCard and Visa credit and debit cards are accepted almost everywhere.

American Express, Diners Club, and Discover cards are also accepted, although not as widely as MasterCard and Visa.

The best way to get cash while you're traveling in Florida is to use your debit or credit cards at ATMs. Of the big national banks, **First Union Bank** and **Bank of America** have offices with ATMs throughout Florida.

Most ATMs are linked to a national network that most likely includes your bank at home. **Cirrus** (② **800/424-7787;** www.mastercard.com/atmlocator) and **PLUS** (② **800/843-7587;** www.visa.com/atms) are the two most popular networks; check the back of your ATM card to see which network your bank belongs to. Use the toll-free numbers or go online to locate ATMs in your destination. Be sure to check your bank's daily withdrawal limit and your credit limits before leaving home.

Also be sure to have your personal identification number (PIN), which you will need to activate the cash-withdrawal functions at all ATMs.

4 When to Go

To a large extent, the timing of your visit will determine how much you'll spend—and how much company you'll have—once you get to Florida. That's because room rates can more than double during high seasons, when countless visitors flock to Florida.

The weather determines the high seasons (see "Climate," below). In subtropical South Florida, high season is in the winter, from mid-December to mid-April. On the other hand, you'll be rewarded with incredible bargains if you can stand the heat and humidity of a South Florida summer between June and early September. In North Florida, the reverse is true: Tourists flock here during the summer, from Memorial Day to Labor Day.

Hurricane season runs from June to November, and, as seen in 2004, when Florida was hit by four hurricanes in a row, you never know what can happen. Pay close attention to weather forecasts during this season and always be prepared.

Presidents' Day weekend in February, Easter week, Memorial Day weekend at the end of May, the Fourth of July, Labor Day weekend at the start of September,

Thanksgiving, Christmas, and New Year's are busy throughout the state, especially at Walt Disney World and the other Orlando-area attractions, which can be packed any time school's out (see chapter 12 for more information on these areas).

Northern and southern Florida share the same "shoulder seasons": April through May, and September through November, when the weather is pleasant throughout Florida and hotel rates are considerably lower than during the high seasons. If price is a consideration, these months of moderate temperatures and fewer tourists are the best times to visit.

See the accommodations sections in the chapters that follow for specifics on the local high, shoulder, and off seasons.

CLIMATE   Northern Florida has a temperate climate, and even in the warmer southern third of the state, it's subtropical, not tropical. Accordingly, Florida sees more extremes of temperatures than, say, the Caribbean islands.

Spring, which runs from late March to May, sees warm temperatures throughout Florida, but it also brings tropical showers.

Summer in Florida extends from May to September, when it's hot and very humid throughout the state. If you're in an inland city during these months, you may not want to do anything too taxing when the sun is at its peak. Coastal areas, however, reap the benefits of sea breezes. Severe afternoon thunderstorms are prevalent during the summer heat (there aren't professional sports teams here named Lightning and Thunder for nothing), so schedule your activities for earlier in the day, and take precautions to avoid being hit by lightning during the storms.

Autumn—about September through November—is a great time to visit, since the hottest days are gone and the crowds have thinned out. Unless a hurricane blows through, November is usually Florida's driest month. June through November is hurricane season here, but even if one threatens, the National Weather Service closely tracks the storms and gives ample warning if there's need to evacuate coastal areas.

Winter can get a bit nippy throughout the state, and sometimes downright cold in northern Florida. Although snow is rare, a flake or two has been known to fall as far south as Miami. The "cold snaps" usually last only a few days in the southern half of the state, however, and daytime temperatures quickly return to the 70s.

For up-to-the-minute weather info, tune in to cable TV's Weather Channel or check out its website at www.weather.com.

Average Temperatures in Select Florida Cities (°F/°C)

	Jan	Feb	Mar	Apr	May	June	July	Aug	Sept	Oct	Nov	Dec
Key West	69/21	72/22	74/23	77/25	80/27	82/28	85/29	85/29	84/29	80/27	74/23	72/22
Miami	69/21	70/21	71/22	74/23	78/26	81/27	82/28	84/29	81/27	78/26	73/23	70/21
Tampa	60/16	61/16	66/19	72/22	77/25	81/27	82/28	82/28	81/27	75/24	67/19	62/17
Orlando	60/16	63/17	66/19	71/22	78/26	82/28	82/28	82/28	81/27	75/24	67/19	61/16
Tallahassee	53/12	56/13	63/20	68/20	72/22	78/26	81/27	81/27	77/25	74/23	66/19	59/15

FLORIDA CALENDAR OF EVENTS

January

FedEx Orange Bowl Classic, Miami. Football fanatics flock down to the big Orange Bowl game (oddly, taking place not at the Orange Bowl in seedy downtown, but at the much more savory Pro Player Stadium) on New Year's Day, featuring two of the year's best college football teams. Call ℂ **305/341-4700** for tickets, but do so early—they sell out quickly.

The Boys of Spring

Major-league baseball fans can watch the Florida Marlins in Miami and the Tampa Bay Devil Rays in St. Petersburg throughout their seasons from April to September, but the entire state is a baseball hotbed from late February to the end of March, when many other major-league teams tune up for the regular season with Grapefruit League exhibition games.

Most of Florida's spring-training stadiums are relatively small, so fans can see their favorite players up close, and maybe even get a handshake or an autograph. Also, tickets are priced from $5 to $12, a bargain when compared to admission for regular-season games. Many games sell out by early March, so don't wait until you're in Florida to buy tickets.

The teams can move from year to year, so check with the **Florida Sports Foundation,** 2390 Kerry Forest Pkwy., Suite 101, Tallahassee, FL 32309 (© 850/488-8347; fax 850/922-0482; www.flasports.com), which usually posts the Grapefruit League schedules on its website late in January. The main office of **Major League Baseball,** 350 Park Ave., New York, NY 10022 (www.mlb.com), is another place to find out where your favorite teams will be playing.

Here's the latest on where the teams play (see the outdoor-activities sections in subsequent chapters for specifics):

Atlanta Braves, Lake Buena Vista, near Orlando (© 407/939-GAME; www.braves.mlb.com); **Baltimore Orioles,** Fort Lauderdale (© 954/776-1921; www.orioles.mlb.com); **Boston Red Sox,** Fort Myers (© 877/733-7699; www.redsox.mlb.com); **Cincinnati Reds,** Sarasota (© 941/954-4464; www.reds.mlb.com); **Cleveland Indians,** Winter Haven (© 863/293-3900; www.indians.mlb.com); **Detroit Tigers,** Lakeland (© 813/287-8844 or 407/839-3900; www.tigers.mlb.com); **Florida Marlins,** Jupiter (© 561/966-3309; www.marlins.mlb.com); **Houston Astros,** Kissimmee, near Orlando (© 407/839-3900; www.astros.mlb.com); **Kansas City Royals,** Davenport (© 800/326-4000; www.royals.mlb.com); **Los Angeles Dodgers,** Vero Beach (© 772/569-6858; www.dodgers.mlb.com); **Minnesota Twins,** Fort Myers (© 800/338-9467; www.twins.mlb.com); **New York Mets,** Port St. Lucie (© 772/871-2115; www.mets.mlb.com); **New York Yankees,** Tampa (© 813/879-2244; www.yankees.mlb.com); **Philadelphia Phillies,** Clearwater (© 727/442-8496; www.phillies.mlb.com); **Pittsburgh Pirates,** Bradenton (© 941/748-4610; www.pirates.mlb.com); **St. Louis Cardinals,** Jupiter (© 561/775-1818, ext. 7; www.cardinals.mlb.com); **Tampa Bay Devil Rays,** St. Petersburg (© 888/FAN-RAYS or 727/825-3250; www.devilrays.mlb.com); **Texas Rangers,** Port Charlotte (© 800/326-4000; www.rangers.mlb.com); **Toronto Blue Jays,** Dunedin (© 800/707-8269; www.bluejays.mlb.com); **Washington Nationals,** Melbourne (© 321/633-4487; www.nationals.mlb.com).

Key West Literary Seminar (© 888/293-9291; www.keywestliterary seminar.org), Key West. Literary types get a good reason to put down their books and head to Key West. This 3-day event features a different theme every year, along with a roster of incredible authors, writers, and other literary types. The event is so popular it sells out well in advance, so call early for tickets.

February

Gasparilla Pirate Fest (© 813/353-8108; www.gasparillapiratefest.com), Tampa. Hundreds of boats and rowdy "pirates" invade the city and then parade along Bayshore Boulevard, showering crowds with beads and coins. Early February.

Everglades City Seafood Festival (© 239/695-2561; www.everglades seafoodfestival.com), Everglades City. What seems like schools of fish-loving people flock down to Everglades City for a 2-day feeding frenzy in which Florida delicacies from stone crab to gator tails are served from shacks and booths on the outskirts of this quaint Old Florida town. Free admission, but you pay for the food you eat, booth by booth. First full weekend in February.

Miami Film Festival (© 877/888-MIFF; www.miamifilmfestival.com), Miami. Though not exactly Cannes, the Miami Film Festival, sponsored by the Film Society of America, is an impressive 10-day celluloid celebration, featuring world premieres of Latin American, domestic, and other foreign and independent films. Actors, producers, and directors show up to plug their films and participate in Q&A sessions with the audiences. Early to mid-February.

Speedweeks (© 386/254-2700; www.daytonaintlspeedway.com), Daytona. Nineteen days of events, with a series of races that draw the top names in NASCAR stock-car racing, culminate in the **Daytona 500.** All events take place at the Daytona International Speedway. Especially for the Daytona 500, tickets must be purchased as far as a year in advance; they go on sale January 1 of the prior year. First 3 weeks of February.

Miami International Boat Show (© 954/441-3231; www.discover boating.com), Miami Beach. If you don't like crowds, beware, as this show draws a quarter of a million boat enthusiasts to the Miami Beach Convention Center. Some of the world's priciest megayachts, speedboats, sailboats, and schooners are displayed for purchase or for gawking. Mid-February.

South Beach Wine & Food Festival (www.sobewineandfoodfest.com), South Beach. A 3-day celebration featuring some of the Food Network's best chefs, who do their thing in the kitchens of various restaurants and at events around town. In addition, there are tastings, lectures, seminars, and parties that are all open to the public—for a price, of course. Call © 877/762-3933. Last weekend in February.

March

Bike Week (© 800/854-1234; www.officialbikeweek.com), Daytona Beach. This international gathering of motorcycle enthusiasts draws a crowd of more than 200,000. In addition to major races held at Daytona International Speedway (featuring the world's best road racers, motorcrossers, and dirt trackers), there are motorcycle shows, beach parties, and the Annual Motorcycle Parade, with thousands of riders. First week in March.

Winter Party, Miami Beach. Gays and lesbians from around the world book trips to Miami as far as a year in advance to attend this weekend-long series of parties and events benefiting the Dade Human Rights Foundation. Travel arrangements can be made through Different Roads Travel, the event's official travel company, by calling © 888/ROADS-55, ext. 510. For information on specific events, call © 305/538-5908 or visit www.winterparty.com. Early March.

Spring Break, Daytona Beach, Miami Beach, Panama City Beach, Key West, and other beaches. College students from all over the United States and Canada flock to Florida for endless partying, wet T-shirt and bikini contests, free concerts, volleyball tournaments, and more. Three weeks in March.

Calle Ocho Festival (✆ 305/644-8888), Little Havana. What Carnivale is to Rio, the Calle Ocho Festival is to Miami. This 10-day extravaganza, also called Carnival Miami, features a lengthy block party spanning 23 blocks, with live salsa music, parades, and, of course, tons of savory Cuban delicacies. Those afraid of mob scenes should avoid this party at all costs. Mid-March.

April

Black College Reunion (✆ 800/854-1234; www.daytonabeach.com), Daytona Beach. Some 75,000 students from 115 predominantly African-American universities bring a sometimes-rowdy end to the spring-break season. Mid-April.

PGA Seniors Golf Championship (✆ 561/624-8400), Palm Beach Gardens. This is the oldest and most prestigious of the senior golf tournaments, in which aging swingers prove they've still got spunk in their swing. Mid-April.

July

World's Richest Tarpon Tournament (✆ 941/964-0568; www.bocagrande chamber.com), Boca Grande. Some $175,000 is at stake in the great tarpon waters off Southwest Florida. Second Wednesday and Thursday in July.

Lower Keys Underwater Music Fest (✆ 800/872-3722), Looe Key. When you hear the phrase "the music and the madness," you may want to think of this amusing aural aquatic event in which boaters head out to the underwater reef at the Looe Key Marine Sanctuary, drop speakers into the water, and pipe in all sorts of music, creating a disco-diving spectacular. Considering the heat at this time of year, underwater is probably the coolest place for a concert. Early July.

Blue Angels Air Show (✆ 800/874-1234 or 850/434-1234; www.visit pensacola.com or www.blueangels. navy.mil), Pensacola. World-famous navy pilots do their aerial acrobatics just 33 feet off Pensacola Beach. Early July.

September

Labor Day Pro-Am Surfing Festival (✆ 321/459-2200; www.space-coast. com), Cocoa Beach. One of the largest surfing events on the East Coast draws pros and amateurs from around the country. There are also rock-'n'-roll bands and swimsuit contests. Labor Day weekend.

October

Biketoberfest (✆ 386/253-RACE; www.biketoberfest.org), Daytona. Road-racing stars compete at the CCS Motorcycle Championship at Daytona International Speedway. There are parties, parades, concerts, and more. Mid-October.

Clearwater Jazz Holiday (✆ 727/461-5200; www.clearwaterjazz.com), Clearwater. Top jazz musicians play for 4 days and nights at bayfront Coachman Park in this free musical extravaganza. Mid-October.

Columbus Day Regatta, Miami. On the day that Columbus discovered America, the party-hearty discover their fellow Americans' birthday suits, as this bacchanalia encourages participants in the so-called regatta (there is a boat race at some point during the day, but most people are too preoccupied to notice) to strip down to their bare necessities and party at the sandbar in the middle of Biscayne Bay. You may not need a bathing suit, but you will need a boat to get out to where all the action is. Consider renting one on Key Biscayne, which is the closest to the sandbar. October 8, 2007.

Halloween Horror Nights (© 800/ 837-2273 or 407/363-8000; www. universalorlando.com), Orlando. Universal Studios transforms its grounds for 19 nights into haunted attractions with live bands, a psychopath's maze, special shows, and hundreds of ghouls and goblins roaming the streets. The studio closes at dusk, reopening in a new macabre form at 7pm. Full admission is charged for the event, which is geared toward adults. Mid-October to Halloween.

Mickey's Not-So-Scary Halloween Party (© 407/934-7639; www.disney world.com), Orlando. At Walt Disney World, guests are invited to trick or treat in the Magic Kingdom, starting at 7pm. The party includes parades, storytelling, live music, and a bewitching fireworks display. End of October.

Fantasy Fest (© 305/296-1817), Key West. Mardi Gras takes a Floridian holiday as the streets of Key West are overtaken by wildly costumed revelers who have no shame and no parental guidance. This weeklong, hedonistic, X-rated Halloween party is not for children under 18. Make reservations in Key West early, as hotels tend to book up quickly during this event. Last week of October.

November

American Sandsculpting Festival (© 239/454-7500; www.fmbchamber. com), Fort Myers Beach. Some 50,000 gather to sculpt and to see the world's finest sand castles. First weekend in November.

Miami Bookfair International (© 305/237-3258), Miami. Bibliophiles, literati, and some of the world's most prestigious and prolific authors descend upon downtown Miami for a weeklong homage to the written word, which also happens to be the largest book fair in the United States. The weekend street fair is the best attended of the entire event, in which regular folk mix with wordsmiths such as Tom Wolfe and Jane Smiley while indulging in snacks, antiquarian books, and literary gossip. All lectures are free but fill up quickly, so get there early. Mid-November.

Blue Angels Homecoming Air Show (© 800/874-1234 or 850/434-1234; www.visitpensacola. com or www.blue angels.navy.mil), Pensacola. World-famous navy pilots do their aerial acrobatics just 33 feet off the beach. Second weekend in November.

White Party Week, Miami and Fort Lauderdale. This weeklong series of parties to benefit AIDS research is built around the main event, the White Party, which takes place at Villa Vizcaya and sells out as early as a year in advance. Philanthropists and celebrities such as Calvin Klein and David Geffen join thousands of white-clad, mostly gay men (and some women) in what has become one of the world's hottest and hardest-to-score party tickets. Visit www.whiteparty week.com for a schedule of parties and events. Thanksgiving week.

December

Art Basel, Miami Beach/Design District. Switzerland's most exclusive art fair and the world's most prominent collectors fly south for the winter and sets up shop on South Beach and in the Design District with thousands of exhibitions, not to mention cocktail parties, concerts, and containers—as in shipping—that are set up on the beach and transformed into makeshift galleries.

Edison & Ford Winter Homes Holiday House (© 239/334-7419; www.edison-ford-estate.com), Fort Myers. Christmas music and thousands of lights hail the holiday season here. At the same time, candles create a spectacular Luminary Trail along the full length of Sanibel Island's Periwinkle Way. First week of December.

Christmas at Walt Disney World (www.disneyworld.com), Orlando. As you would imagine, all of the Disney properties get into the holiday spirit. In the Magic Kingdom, Main Street is lavishly decked out with lights and holly and an 80-foot glistening tree. Call © 407/824-4321 for holiday events, or 407/934-7639 for special travel packages. Throughout December.

British Night Watch & Grand Illumination Ceremony (© 800/OLD-CITY; www.visitoldcity.com), St. Augustine. A torchlight procession through the Spanish Quarter kicks off a month of Christmas festivities and the "Nights of Lights," in which 1.25 million twinkling bulbs bathe the Old City. First Saturday in December; Nights of Lights until January 31.

Winterfest Boat Parade (© 954/767-0686), Fort Lauderdale. People who complain that the holiday season just isn't as festive in South Florida as it is in colder parts of the world haven't been to this spectacular boat parade along the Intracoastal Waterway. Forget decking the halls. At this parade, the decks are decked out in magnificent holiday regalia as they gracefully—and boastfully—glide up and down the water. If you're not on a boat, the best views are from waterfront restaurants or anywhere you can squeeze in along the water. Mid-December.

5 Health & Safety

THE HEALTHY TRAVELER

Florida doesn't present any unusual health hazards for most people. Folks with certain medical conditions such as liver disease, diabetes, and stomach ailments, however, should avoid eating raw **oysters,** which can carry a natural bacterium linked to severe diarrhea, vomiting, and even fatal blood poisoning. Cooking kills the bacteria, so if in doubt, order your oysters steamed, broiled, or fried.

Florida has millions of **mosquitoes** and invisible biting **sand flies** (known as "no-see-ums"), especially in the coastal and marshy areas. Fortunately, neither insect carries malaria or other diseases. (Although there were a few cases of mosquitoes carrying West Nile virus in the Panhandle, it's really not a problem in Florida.) Keep these pests at bay with a good insect repellent.

It's especially important to protect yourself against **sunburn.** Don't underestimate the strength of the sun's rays down here, even in the middle of winter. Use a sunscreen with a high protection factor and apply it liberally.

Remember to pack **prescription medications** in your carry-on luggage, and carry them in their original containers with pharmacy labels—otherwise, they won't make it through airport security. Also bring along copies of your prescriptions, in case you lose your pills or run out. And don't forget sunglasses and an extra pair of contact lenses or prescription glasses.

Always bring your insurance ID card with you when you travel. In most cases, your existing health plan will provide the coverage you need. But double-check; you may want to buy **travel medical insurance** instead.

If you get sick while away from home, consider asking your hotel concierge to recommend a local doctor—even his or her own. You can also try the emergency room at a local hospital; many have walk-in clinics for emergency cases that are not life threatening. You may not get immediate attention, but you won't pay the high price of an emergency-room visit.

THE SAFE TRAVELER

While tourist areas in Florida are generally safe, you should always stay alert.

This is particularly true in the larger cities, such as Miami, Orlando, Tampa, and St. Petersburg. If you're in doubt about which neighborhoods are safe, ask your hotel's front-desk staff or the area's tourist office.

Remember also that hotels are open to the public, and in a large hotel, security may not be able to screen everyone entering. Always lock your room door. Don't assume that, once inside your hotel, you are automatically safe and no longer need to be aware of your surroundings.

6 Specialized Travel Resources

GAY & LESBIAN TRAVELERS

Florida is not without its intolerant contingent, but there are active gay and lesbian groups in most cities here. In fact, the editors of *Out and About,* a gay and lesbian newsletter, have described Miami's **South Beach** as the "hippest, hottest, most happening gay travel destination in the world." For many years, that could also be said of **Key West,** which still is one of the country's most popular destinations for gays. **Fort Lauderdale**—where gays own more than 20 motels, 40 bars, and numerous other businesses—is definitely also on the gay-friendly map.

You can contact the **Gay, Lesbian & Bisexual Community Services of Central Florida,** 946 N. Mills Ave., Orlando, FL 32803 (© **407/228-8272;** www.glbcc.org), whose welcome packets usually include the latest issue of the *Triangle,* a quarterly newsletter dedicated to gay and lesbian issues, and a calendar of events pertaining to the gay and lesbian community. Although not a tourist-specific packet, it includes information and ads for the area's gay and lesbian clubs.

Watermark, P.O. Box 533655, Orlando, FL 32853 (© **407/481-2243;** fax 407/481-2246; www.watermarkonline.com), is a biweekly tabloid newspaper covering the gay and lesbian scene, including dining and entertainment options, in Orlando, the Tampa Bay area, and Daytona Beach.

SENIOR TRAVEL

With one of the largest retired populations of any state, Florida offers a wide array of activities and benefits for seniors. Don't be shy about asking for discounts, but always carry some kind of identification, such as a driver's license, that shows your date of birth. Mention the fact that you're a senior when you make your travel reservations. In most cities, people over the age of 60 qualify for reduced admission to theaters, museums, and other attractions, as well as discounted fares on public transportation.

Members of **AARP** (formerly known as the American Association of Retired Persons), 601 E St. NW, Washington, DC 20049 (© **888/687-2277** or 202/434-2277; www.aarp.org), get discounts on hotels, airfares, and car rentals. AARP offers members a wide range of benefits, including *AARP: The Magazine* and a monthly newsletter. Anyone over 50 can join.

The **U.S. National Park Service** offers a **Golden Age Passport** that gives seniors 62 and over lifetime entrance to all properties administered by the National Park Service—national parks, monuments, historic sites, recreation areas, and wildlife refuges—for a one-time processing fee of $10. The pass can be purchased in person at any NPS facility that charges an entrance fee. For more information, go to www.nps.gov/fees_passes.htm or call ⓒ 888/467-2757.

FAMILY TRAVEL

Florida is a great family destination, with Walt Disney World leading the list of theme parks geared to young and old alike. Consequently, most Florida hotels and restaurants are willing, if not eager, to cater to families traveling with children.

Many hotels and motels let children 17 and under stay free in a parent's room (be sure to ask when you reserve).

At the beaches, it's the exception rather than the rule for a resort not to have a children's activities program (some will even mind the youngsters while the parents enjoy a night off!). Even if they don't have a children's program of their own, most will arrange babysitting services.

You may also want to consult *The Unofficial Guide to Florida with Kids* (Wiley Publishing, Inc.) as well as *The Unofficial Guide to Walt Disney World with Kids* (Wiley Publishing, Inc.). Additionally, *How to Take Great Trips with Your Kids* (Harvard Common Press) is full of good general advice that can apply to travel anywhere.

7 Planning Your Trip Online

SURFING FOR AIRFARES

The "big three" online travel agencies, **Expedia.com, Travelocity.com,** and **Orbitz.com,** sell most of the air tickets bought on the Internet. (Canadian travelers should try Expedia.ca and Travelocity.ca; U.K. residents can go to Expedia.co.uk and Opodo.co.uk.) Each has different business deals with the airlines and may offer different fares on the same flights, so it's wise to shop around. Expedia and Travelocity will also send you **e-mail notification** when a cheap fare becomes available to your favorite destination. Of the smaller travel agency websites, **SideStep** (www.sidestep.com) has gotten the best reviews from Frommer's authors. It's a browser add-on that purports to "search 140 sites at once," but in reality beats competitors' fares only as often as other sites do.

Also remember to check **airline websites,** especially those for low-fare carriers such as AirTran, Southwest, and JetBlue, whose fares are often misreported or simply missing from travel agency websites.

Even with major airlines, you can often shave a few bucks from a fare by booking directly through the airline and avoiding a travel agency's transaction fee. But you'll get these discounts only by **booking online:** Most airlines now offer online-only fares that even their phone agents know nothing about. For the websites of airlines that fly to and from your destination, see "Getting There" (p. 45).

Great **last-minute deals** are available through free weekly e-mail services provided directly by the airlines. Most of these are announced on Tuesday or Wednesday and must be purchased online. Most are valid only for travel that weekend, but some (such as Southwest's) can be booked weeks or months in advance. Sign up for weekly e-mail alerts at airline websites, or check megasites that compile comprehensive lists of last-minute specials, such as **SmarterTravel.com.** For last-minute trips, **site59.com** and **lastminutetravel.com** in the U.S. (and **lastminute.com** in Europe) often have better air-and-hotel package deals than the major-label sites. A website listing numerous bargain sites and airlines around the world is **www.itravelnet. com**.

If you're willing to give up some control over your flight details, use what is called an **"opaque" fare service,** like **Priceline** (www.priceline.com; www. priceline.co.uk for Europeans) or its smaller competitor, **Hotwire** (www. hotwire.com). Both offer rock-bottom prices in exchange for travel on a "mystery airline" at a mysterious time of day, often with a mysterious change of planes en route. The mystery airlines are all major, well-known carriers—and the possibility of being sent from Philadelphia to Chicago via Tampa is remote; the airlines' routing computers have gotten a lot better than they used to be. But your chances of getting a 6am or 11pm flight are pretty high. Hotwire tells you flight prices before you buy; Priceline usually has better deals than Hotwire, but you have to play its "name your price" game. If you're new at this, the helpful folks at **Bidding-ForTravel** (www.biddingfortravel.com) do a good job of demystifying Priceline's prices and strategies. Priceline and Hotwire are great for flights within North America and between the U.S. and Europe. *Note:* In 2004, Priceline added nonopaque service to its roster. You now have the option to pick exact flights, times, and airlines from a list of offers— or opt to bid on opaque fares as before.

For much more about airfares and savvy air-travel tips and advice, pick up a copy of *Frommer's Fly Safe, Fly Smart* (Wiley Publishing, Inc.).

SURFING FOR HOTELS

Shopping online for hotels is generally done one of two ways: by booking through the hotel's own website or by going through an independent booking agency (or a fare-service agency like Priceline; see below). These Internet hotel agencies have multiplied in mind-boggling numbers lately, competing for the business of millions of consumers surfing for accommodations around the world. This competitiveness can be a boon to consumers who have the patience and time to shop and compare the online sites for good deals—but shop they must, for prices can vary considerably from site to site. And keep in mind that hotels at the top of a site's listing may be there for no other reason than that they paid money to get the placement.

Of the "big three" sites, **Expedia** offers a long list of special deals and "virtual tours" or photos of available rooms so you can see what you're paying for (a feature that helps counter the claims that the best rooms are often held back from bargain-booking websites). **Travelocity** posts unvarnished customer reviews and ranks its properties according to the AAA rating system. Also reliable are **Hotels.com** and **Quikbook.com.** An excellent free program, **TravelAxe** (www.travelaxe.net), can help you search multiple hotel sites at once—even ones you may never have heard of—and conveniently lists the total price of the room, including the taxes and service charges. Another booking site, **Travelweb** (www.travelweb), is partly owned by the hotels it represents (including the Hilton, Hyatt, and Starwood chains) and is therefore plugged directly into the hotels' reservations systems— unlike independent online agencies, which have to fax or e-mail reservation requests to the hotel, a good portion of which get misplaced in the shuffle. More than once, travelers have arrived at their hotel only to be told that they have no reservation. To be fair, many of the major sites are undergoing improvements in service and ease of use, and Expedia will soon be able to plug directly into the reservations systems of many hotel chains—none of which can be bad news for consumers. In the meantime, it's a good idea to get a **confirmation number**

Frommers.com: The Complete Travel Resource

For an excellent travel-planning resource, we highly recommend **Frommers.com** (www.frommers.com), voted Best Travel Site by *PC Magazine*. We're a little biased, of course, but we guarantee that you'll find the travel tips, reviews, monthly vacation giveaways, bookstore, and online-booking capabilities thoroughly indispensable. Among the special features are our popular **Destinations** section, where you'll get expert travel tips, hotel and dining recommendations, and advice on the sights to see for more than 3,500 destinations around the globe; the **Frommers.com Newsletter**, with the latest deals, travel trends, and money-saving secrets; our **Community** area, featuring **Message Boards**, where Frommer's readers post queries and share advice (sometimes even our authors show up to answer questions); and our **Photo Center**, where you can share vacation tips. When your research is finished, the **Online Reservations System** (www.frommers.com/book_a_trip) takes you to Frommer's preferred online partners for booking your vacation at affordable prices.

and make a **printout** of any online booking transaction.

In the opaque website category, **Priceline** and **Hotwire** are even better for hotels than for airfares; with both, you're allowed to pick the neighborhood and quality level of your hotel before offering your money. For both Priceline and Hotwire, you pay upfront, and the fee is nonrefundable. Priceline is much better at getting five-star lodging for three-star prices than at finding anything at the bottom of the scale. On the downside, many hotels stick Priceline guests in their least desirable rooms. Be sure to go to the BiddingforTravel website (see above) before bidding on a hotel room on Priceline; it features a fairly up-to-date list of hotels that Priceline uses in major cities. Be aware that some hotels do not provide loyalty program credits or points, or other frequent-stay amenities when you book a room through opaque online services. Priceline has added the option of nonopaque hotel bookings to its website.

Note: When booking hotels in Florida, be sure to clarify what "water view" means: It's often used to describe even those rooms from which you need to crane your head to see a speck of water!

SURFING FOR RENTAL CARS

For booking rental cars online, the best deals are usually found at rental-car company websites, although all the major online travel agencies also offer rental-car reservations services. Priceline and Hotwire work well for rental cars, too; the only "mystery" is which major rental company you get, and for most travelers, the difference among Hertz, Avis, and Budget is negligible.

8 The 21st-Century Traveler

INTERNET ACCESS AWAY FROM HOME

Travelers have any number of ways to check their e-mail and access the Internet on the road. Of course, using your own laptop—or even a PDA (personal digital assistant) or electronic organizer with a modem—gives you the most flexibility.

But if you don't have a computer, you can access your e-mail and even your office computer from cybercafes.

WITHOUT YOUR OWN COMPUTER It's hard nowadays to find a city that *doesn't* have a few cybercafes. Although there's no definitive directory for cybercafes—these are independent businesses, after all—two places to start looking are **www.cybercaptive.com** and **www.cybercafe.com**.

Aside from formal cybercafes, most **youth hostels** nowadays have at least one computer you can get to the Internet on. And most **public libraries** across the world offer Internet access for free or a small charge. Avoid **hotel business centers** unless you're willing to pay exorbitant rates.

Most major airports now have **Internet kiosks** scattered throughout their gates. These rather clunky kiosks, which you'll also see in shopping malls, hotel lobbies, and tourist information offices around the world, give you basic Web access for a per-minute fee that's usually higher than cybercafe prices.

To retrieve your e-mail, ask your **Internet service provider (ISP)** if it has a Web-based interface tied to your existing e-mail account. If your ISP doesn't have such an interface, you can use the free **mail2web** service (www.mail2web.com) to view and reply to your home e-mail. For more flexibility, you may want to open a free, Web-based e-mail account with **Yahoo! Mail** (http://mail.yahoo.com). (Microsoft's Hotmail is another popular option, but Hotmail has severe spam problems.) Your home ISP may be able to forward your e-mail to the Web-based account automatically.

If you need to access files on your office computer, look into a service called **GoToMyPC** (www.gotomypc.com). The service provides a Web-based interface for you to access and manipulate a distant PC from anywhere—even a cybercafe—provided that your "target" PC is on and has an always-on connection to the Internet (such as with a cable modem). The service offers top-quality security, but if you're worried about hackers, use your own laptop rather than a cybercafe computer to access the GoToMyPC system.

WITH YOUR OWN COMPUTER Wi-fi (wireless fidelity) is the buzzword in computer access, and more hotels, cafes, and retailers are signing on as wireless "hot spots" where you can get high-speed connection without cable wires, networking hardware, or a phone line (see below). You can get wi-fi connection one of several ways. Many laptops sold in the last year have built-in wi-fi capability (an 802.11b wireless Ethernet connection). Mac owners have their own networking technology, Apple AirPort. For those with older computers, an 802.11b/**wi-fi card** (around $50) can be plugged into your laptop. You sign up for wireless access service much as you do cellphone service, through a plan offered by one of several commercial companies that have made wireless service available in airports, hotel lobbies, and coffee shops, primarily in the U.S. (followed by the U.K. and Japan). **T-Mobile Hotspot** (www.t-mobile.com/hotspot) offers wireless connections at more than a thousand Starbucks coffee shops nationwide. **Boingo** (www.boingo.com) and **Wayport** (www.wayport.com) have set up networks in airports and high-class hotel lobbies. IPass providers (see below) also give you access to a few hundred wireless hotel lobby setups. Best of all, you don't need to be staying at the Four Seasons to use the hotel's network; just set yourself up on a nice couch in the lobby. The companies' pricing policies can be byzantine, with a variety of monthly, per-connection, and per-minute plans, but in general you'll pay around $30 a month for limited access—and as more companies jump on the wireless bandwagon, prices are likely to get even more competitive.

There are also places that provide **free wireless networks** in cities around the world. To locate these free hot spots, go to www.personaltelco.net/index.cgi/WirelessCommunities.

If wi-fi is not available at your destination, most business-class hotels throughout the world offer dataports for laptop modems, and a few thousand hotels in the U.S. and Europe now offer free high-speed Internet access using an Ethernet network cable. You can bring your own cables, but most hotels rent them for around $10. **Call your hotel in advance** to see what your options are.

In addition, major Internet service providers (ISPs) have **local access numbers** around the world, allowing you to go online by simply placing a local call. Check your ISP's website or call its toll-free number, and ask how you can use your current account away from home, and how much it will cost.

If you're traveling outside the reach of your ISP, the **iPass** network has dial-up numbers in most of the world's countries. You'll have to sign up with an iPass provider, who will then tell you how to set up your computer for your destination(s). For a list of iPass providers, go to www.ipass.com and click on "Individual Purchase." One solid provider is **i2roam** (© **866/811-6209** or 920/235-0475; www.i2roam.com).

Wherever you go, bring a **connection kit** of the right power and phone adapters, a spare phone cord, and a spare Ethernet network cable—or find out whether your hotel supplies them to guests.

TRAVEL BLOGS & TRAVELOGUES

More travelers are using travel web logs, or **blogs,** to chronicle their journeys online. To read a few blogs about Florida, try **Travelblog.com,** or post your own travelogue at **Travelblog.org.** For blogs that cover general travel news and highlight various destinations, try **Writtenroad.com** or Gawker Media's snarky **Gridskipper.com.** For more literary travel essays, try Salon.com's travel section (**Salon.com/Wanderlust**) and **Worldhum.com,** which also has an extensive list of other travel-related journals, blogs, online communities, newspaper coverage, and bookstores.

Digital Photography on the Road

These days, when it comes to taking vacation photos, many travelers are going digital. Not only are digital cameras left relatively unscathed by airport X-rays, but with digital equipment, you don't have to lug armloads of film along. In fact, nowadays you don't even have to carry your laptop to download the day's images to make room for more. With a **media storage card,** sold by major camera dealers, you can store hundreds of images in your camera. These "memory" cards come in different configurations—from memory sticks to flash cards—and different storage capacities (the more megabytes of memory, the more images a card can hold); they range in price from $30 to over $200. (*Note:* Each camera model works with a specific type of card, so you'll need to determine which storage card is compatible with your camera.) When you get home, you can print the images on your own printer; take the card to a camera store, drugstore, or chain retailer; or have images developed online by a service like **Snapfish** (www.snapfish.com) for about 25¢ per photo.

Online Traveler's Toolbox

Veteran travelers usually carry some essential items to make their trips easier. Following is a selection of handy online tools to bookmark and use.

- **Airplane seating** (www.seatguru.com). Find out which seats to reserve and which to avoid (and more) on all major domestic airlines.
- **Citysearch** (www.jacksonville.citysearch.com; www.miami.citysearch.com; www.orlando.citysearch.com; www.tampa.citysearch.com). Browse listings and reviews for dining, nightlife, shopping, and more by neighborhood and date (with a handy interactive calendar).
- **Intellicast** (www.intellicast.com) and **Weather.com** (www.weather.com). These sites provide weather forecasts for all 50 states and for cities around the world.
- **Mapquest** (www.mapquest.com). This best of the mapping sites lets you choose a specific address or destination; in seconds, it will return a map and detailed directions.
- **Visa ATM Locator** (www.visa.com), for locations of PLUS ATMs worldwide; or **MasterCard ATM Locator** (www.mastercard.com), for locations of Cirrus ATMs worldwide.

USING A CELLPHONE ACROSS THE U.S.

Just because your cellphone works at home doesn't mean it'll work elsewhere in the country (thanks to our nation's fragmented cellphone system). It's a good bet that your phone will work in major cities. But take a look at your wireless company's coverage map on its website before heading out—T-Mobile, Sprint, and Nextel are particularly weak in rural areas. If you need to stay in touch at a destination where you know your phone won't work, try renting a phone that does from **InTouch USA** (© **800/872-7626;** www.intouchglobal.com) or a rental-car location, but be aware that you'll pay $1 a minute or more for airtime.

If you're venturing deep into a national park, you may want to consider renting a **satellite phone** ("satphone"), which is different from a cellphone in that it connects to satellites rather than ground-based towers. A satphone is more costly than a cellphone, but it works where there's no cellular signal and no towers.

Unfortunately, you'll pay at least $2 per minute to use the phone, and it works only where you can see the horizon (that is, usually not indoors). In North America, you can rent iridium satellite phones from **RoadPost** (© **888/290-1606** or 905/272-5665; www.roadpost.com). InTouch USA (see above) offers a wider range of satphones, but at higher rates.

If you're not from the U.S., you'll be appalled at the poor reach of our GSM (Global System for Mobiles) wireless network, which is used by much of the rest of the world. Your phone will probably work in most major U.S. cities; it definitely won't work in many rural areas. (To see where GSM phones work in the U.S., check out www.t-mobile.com/coverage/national_popup.asp). And you may or may not be able to send SMS (text messaging) home—something Americans tend not to do anyway, for various cultural and technological reasons. (International budget travelers like to send text messages home because it's much cheaper than making international calls.) Assume nothing—call your wireless provider and get the full scoop. In a worst-case scenario, you can always rent a phone; InTouch USA (see above) delivers to hotels.

9 Getting There

BY PLANE
Most major domestic airlines fly to and from many Florida cities. Choose from **American** (✆ 800/433-7300; www.aa.com), **Continental** (✆ 800/525-0280; www.continental.com), **Delta** (✆ 800/221-1212; www.delta-air.com), **Northwest/KLM** (✆ 800/225-2525; www.nwa.com), **United** (✆ 800/241-6522; www.united.com), and **US Airways** (✆ 800/428-4322; www.usairways.com). Of these, Delta and US Airways have the most extensive network of commuter connections within Florida (see "Getting Around," beginning on p. 52).

Several so-called no-frills airlines—with low fares but few, if any, amenities—also fly to Florida. The biggest and best is **Southwest Airlines** (✆ **800/435-9792;** www.southwest.com), which has flights from many U.S. cities to Fort Lauderdale, Jacksonville, Orlando, and Tampa.

Others flying to Florida include **Air-Tran** (✆ 800/AIR-TRAN; www.airtran.com); **American Trans Air** (✆ 800/435-9282; www.ata.com); **Carnival Air** (✆ 800/824-7386), an arm of the popular cruise line; **JetBlue** (✆ 800/538-2583; www.jetblue.com); **Midwest Express** (✆ 800/452-2022; www.midwestexpress.com); **PanAm** (✆ 800/FLY-PANAM; www.flypanam.com); and **Spirit** (✆ 800/722-7117; www.spiritair.com).

Internet resources such as **Travelocity** (www.travelocity.com) and **Microsoft Expedia** (www.expedia.com) make it easy to compare prices and purchase tickets.

BY CAR
Florida is reached by **I-95** along the East Coast, **I-75** from the Central States, and **I-10** from the west. The **Florida Turnpike,** a toll road, links Orlando, West Palm Beach, Fort Lauderdale, and Miami (it's a shortcut from Wildwood on I-75 north of Orlando to Miami). **I-4** cuts across the state from Cape Canaveral through Orlando to Tampa.

See "Getting Around," beginning on p. 52, for more information about driving in Florida and the car-rental firms that operate here.

If you're a member, your local branch of the **American Automobile Association** (**AAA;** ✆ **800/AAA-HELP;** www.aaa.com) can provide a free trip-routing

---

Tips **Don't Stow It—Ship It**

If ease of travel is your main concern and money is no object, you can ship your luggage and sports equipment with one of the growing number of luggage-service companies that pick up, track, and deliver your belongings (often through couriers such as Federal Express) with minimum hassle for you. Traveling luggage-free may be ultraconvenient, but it's not cheap: One-way overnight shipping can cost from $100 to $200, depending on what you're sending. Still, for some people, especially the elderly or the infirm, it's a sensible alternative to lugging heavy baggage. Specialists in door-to-door luggage delivery include **Virtual Bellhop** (www.virtualbellhop.com), **SkyCap International** (www.skycapinternational.com), **Sports Express** (www.sportsexpress.com), and **Luggage Express** (www.usxpluggageexpress.com).

Tips **Saving with Golf & Tennis Packages**

Many Florida hotels and resorts, and even some motels, offer golf and tennis packages, which bundle the costs of the room, greens and court fees, and sometimes equipment. These deals usually don't include airfare, but they do represent savings over paying for the room and golf or tennis separately. See the accommodations sections in the following chapters for hostelries offering special packages to their guests.

Summer, early fall, and the first 3 weeks of December are good times to search for discounted deals in South Florida. For example, the Naples Beach Hotel & Golf Club, in Naples (p. 379), has offered bed-and-breakfast specials for about $125 a night per room, including a full breakfast buffet, during September and December. Regular autumn room rates are more than twice that amount, without breakfast.

---

plan. AAA members also have access to nationwide emergency road service.

BY TRAIN

Amtrak (© **800/USA-RAIL;** www.amtrak.com) offers train service to Florida from both the East and West coasts. It takes some 26 hours from New York to Miami, and 68 hours from Los Angeles to Miami, Amtrak's fares aren't much less—if not more—than many of the airlines' lowest fares.

Amtrak's **Silver Meteor** and **Silver Star** both run twice daily between New York and either Miami or Tampa, with intermediate stops along the East Coast and in Florida. Amtrak's Thruway Bus Connections are available from the Fort Lauderdale Amtrak station and Miami International Airport to Key West; from Tampa to St. Petersburg, Treasure Island, Clearwater, Sarasota, Bradenton, and

Fort Myers; and from Deland to Daytona Beach. From the West Coast, the **Sunset Limited** runs three times weekly between Los Angeles and Orlando. It stops in Pensacola, Crestview (north of Fort Walton Beach and Destin), Chipley (north of Panama City Beach), and Tallahassee. Sleeping accommodations are available for an extra charge.

If you intend to stop along the way, you can save money with Amtrak's **Explore America** (or All Aboard America) fares, which are based on three regions of the country.

Amtrak's **Auto Train** runs daily from Lorton, Virginia (12 miles south of Washington, D.C.), to Sanford, Florida (just northeast of Orlando). You ride in a coach while your car is secured in an enclosed vehicle carrier. Make your train reservations as far in advance as possible.

10 Special-Interest Trips

Bird-watching, boating and sailing, camping, canoeing and kayaking, fishing, golfing, tennis—you name it, the Sunshine State has it. In fact, you'll find these activities almost everywhere you go in Florida. Of course, beach lovers and watersports enthusiasts can indulge their passions nearly anywhere along the state's

lengthy coastlines. Merely head east or west, and you'll easily find plenty to do—or, viewed another way, Florida's multitudinous watersports operators will find you.

These and other activities are described in the outdoor-activities sections of the following chapters, but here's a brief overview of some of the best places to move your muscles, with tips on how to get more detailed information.

The **Florida Sports Foundation,** 2390 Kerry Forest Pkwy., Suite 101, Tallahassee, FL 32309 (C **850/488-8347;** fax 850/922-0482; www.flasports.com), publishes free brochures, calendars, schedules, and guides to outdoor pursuits and spectator sports throughout Florida. I've noted some of its specific publications in the sections below.

For excellent color maps of state parks, campgrounds, canoe trails, aquatic preserves, caverns, and more, contact the **Florida Department of Environmental Protection,** Office of Communications, 3900 Commonwealth Blvd., Tallahassee, FL 32399 (C **850/245-2118;** www.dep.state.fl.us). Some of the department's publications are mentioned below.

ACTIVITIES A TO Z

BIKING & IN-LINE SKATING
Florida's relatively flat terrain makes it ideal for bicycling and in-line skating. You can bike right into **Everglades National Park** along the 38-mile-long Main Park Road, and bike or skate from St. Petersburg to Tarpon Springs on the 47-mile-long converted railroad bed known as the **Pinellas Trail.** Many towns and cities have designated routes for cyclists, skaters, joggers, and walkers, such as the paved pathways running the length of **Sanibel Island,** the lovely Bayshore Boulevard in **Tampa,** and the bike lanes from downtown **Sarasota** out to St. Armands, Lido, and Longboat keys.

BIRD-WATCHING
With hundreds of both land- and sea-based species, Florida is one of America's best places for bird-watching—if you're not careful, pelicans will even steal your picnic lunch on the historic **Naples Pier.** The **J. N. ("Ding") Darling National Wildlife Refuge** is great for watching birds, and it shares Sanibel Island with luxury resorts and fine restaurants.

With its Northeast Florida section now open, the **Great Florida Birding Trail** will eventually cover some 2,000 miles throughout the state. Fort Clinch State Park, on Amelia Island, and Merritt Island National Wildlife Refuge in Cape Canaveral are gateways to the northeast trail. Information is available from the Birding Trail Coordinator, Florida Fish & Wildlife Conservation Commission, 620 S. Meridian St., Tallahassee, FL 32399-1600 (C **850/922-0664;** fax 850/488-1961; www.floridabirdingtrail.com). You can download maps from the website.

Many of the state's wildlife preserves have gift shops that carry books about Florida's birds, including the *Florida Wildlife Viewing Guide,* in which authors Susan Cerulean and Ann Morrow profile 96 great parks, refuges, and preserves throughout the state. The guide is also available directly from the publisher, Falcon Press (C **888/922-0789;** www.falcbooks.com).

BOATING & SAILING   With some 1,350 miles of shoreline, it's not surprising that Florida is a boating and sailing mecca. In fact, you won't be anyplace near the water very long before you see flyers and other advertisements for rental boats and sailboat cruises. Many of them are mentioned in the following chapters.

The **Moorings** (C **888/952-8420** or 727/530-5651; www.moorings.com), the worldwide sailboat charter company, has its headquarters in Clearwater and its Florida yacht base nearby in St. Petersburg. From St. Pete, experienced sailors can take bareboats as far as the Keys and the Dry Tortugas, out in the Gulf of Mexico.

Key West keeps gaining prominence as a world sailing capital. *Yachting* magazine sponsors the largest winter regatta in America here each January, and smaller events take place regularly.

Even if you've never hauled on a halyard, you can learn the art of sailing at

Steve and Doris Colgate's Offshore Sailing School (www.offshore-sailing.com), headquartered at the South Seas Plantation Resort & Yacht Harbour on Captiva Island, with an outpost in St. Petersburg. The prestigious **Annapolis Sailing** (http://annapolissailing.com) has bases in St. Petersburg and on Marathon in the Keys.

Florida Boating & Fishing, available for free from the Florida Sports Foundation (see the introduction to this section, above), is a treasure trove of tips on safe boating; state regulations; locations of marinas, hotels, and resorts; marine products and services; and more.

CAMPING   Florida is literally dotted with RV parks (if you own such a vehicle, it's the least expensive way to spend your winters here). But for the best tent camping, look to Florida's national preserves and 110 state parks and recreation areas. Options range from luxury sites with hot-water showers and cable TV hookups, to primitive island and beach camping with no facilities whatsoever.

Regular and primitive camping in **St. George Island State Park,** near Apalachicola, is a bird-watcher's dream—plus you'll be on one of the nation's most magnificent beaches. Equally great are the sands at **St. Andrews State Park,** in Panama City Beach (with sites right beside the bay). Other top spots are **Fort DeSoto Park,** in St. Pete Beach (more gorgeous bayside sites); the remarkably preserved **Cayo Costa Island State Park,** between Boca Grande and Captiva Island in Southwest Florida; **Canaveral National Seashore,** near the Kennedy Space Center; **Anastasia State Park,** in St. Augustine; **Fort Clinch State Park,** on Amelia Island; and **Bill Baggs Cape Florida State Park,** on Key Biscayne in Miami. Down in the Keys, the oceanside sites in **Long Key State Park** are about as nice as they get.

In all these popular campgrounds, reservations are essential, especially during the high seasons. All Florida's state parks take bookings up to 11 months in advance.

The **Florida Department of Environmental Protection,** Division of Recreation and Parks, Mail Station 535, 3900 Commonwealth Blvd., Tallahassee, FL 32399-3000 (© **850/245-2118;** www.dep.state.fl.us), publishes an annual guide of tent and RV sites in Florida's state parks and recreation areas.

Pet owners, note: Pets are permitted at some—but not all—state park beaches, campgrounds, and food service areas. Before bringing your animal, check with the department or the individual park to see if your pet will be allowed. And bring your pet's rabies certificate, which is required.

For private campgrounds, the **Florida Association of RV Parks & Campgrounds,** 1340 Vickers Dr., Tallahassee, FL 32303 (© **850/562-7151;** fax 850/562-7179; www.floridacamping.com), issues an annual *Camp Florida* directory with locator maps and details about its member establishments in the state.

CANOEING & KAYAKING   Canoers and kayakers have almost limitless options for discovery here: picturesque rivers, sandy coastlines, marshes, mangroves, and gigantic Lake Okeechobee. Exceptional trails run through several parks and wildlife preserves, including **Everglades National Park,** Sanibel Island's **J. N. ("Ding") Darling National Wildlife Refuge,** and **Briggs Nature Center,** on the edge of the Everglades near Marco Island.

According to the Florida state legislature, however, the state's official "Canoe Capital" is the Panhandle town of **Milton,** on U.S. 90 near Pensacola. Up here, Blackwater River, Coldwater River, Sweetwater Creek, and Juniper Creek are perfect for tubing, rafting, and paddle-boating, as well as canoeing and kayaking.

Another good venue is the waterways winding through the marshes between **Amelia Island** and the mainland.

Many conservation groups throughout the state offer half-day, full-day, and overnight canoe trips. For example, the **Conservancy of Naples** (℗ **239/262-0304**; www.conservancy.org) has a popular series of moonlight canoe trips through the mangroves, among other programs.

Based during the winter at Everglades City, on the park's western border, **North American Canoe Tours, Inc.** (℗ **239/695-3299**; www.evergladesadventures.com), offers weeklong guided canoe expeditions through the Everglades.

Thirty-six creek and river trails, covering 950 miles altogether, are itemized in the excellent free *Canoe Trails* booklet published by the Florida Department of Environmental Protection, Office of Communications, 3900 Commonwealth Blvd., Tallahassee, FL 32399 (℗ **850/245-2118;** www.dep.state.fl.us).

Specialized guidebooks include *A Canoeing and Kayaking Guide to the Streams of Florida: Volume 1, North Central Florida and Panhandle,* by Elizabeth F. Carter and John L. Pearce; and *Volume 2, Central and Southern Peninsula,* by Lou Glaros and Doug Sphar. Both are published by Menasha Ridge Press (www.menasharidge.com).

ECOADVENTURES If you don't want to do it yourself, you can observe Florida's flora and fauna on guided field expeditions—and contribute to conservation efforts while you're at it.

The **Sierra Club,** the oldest and largest grassroots environmental organization in the U.S., offers ecoadventures through its Florida chapters. Recent outings have included canoeing or kayaking through the Everglades, hiking the Florida Trail in America's southernmost national forest, camping on a barrier island, and exploring the sinkhole phenomenon in North-Central Florida. You do have to be a Sierra Club member, but you can join at the time of the trip. Contact the club's national outings office at 85 Second St., 2nd Floor, San Francisco, CA 94105-3441 (℗ **415/977-5500;** www.sierraclub.org).

The Florida chapter of the **Nature Conservancy** has protected 578,000 acres of natural lands in Florida and presently owns and manages 36 preserves. For a small fee, you can join one of its field trips or work parties that take place periodically throughout the year; fees vary from year to year, event to event, so call for more information. Participants get a chance to learn about and even participate in the preservation of the ecosystem. For details on all the preserves and adventures, contact the Nature Conservancy, Florida Chapter, 222 S. Westmonte Dr., Suite 300, Altamonte Springs, FL 32714 (℗ **407/682-3664;** fax 407/682-3077; http://nature.org).

A nonprofit organization dedicated to environmental research, the **Earthwatch Institute,** 3 Clocktower Place, Suite 100 (P.O. Box 75), Maynard, MA 01754 (℗ **800/776-0188** or 978/461-0081; www.earthwatch.org), has excursions to survey dolphins and manatees around Sarasota and to monitor the well-being of the whooping cranes raised in captivity and released in the wilds of Central Florida.

Another research group, the **Oceanic Society,** Fort Mason Center, Building E, San Francisco, CA 94123 (℗ **800/326-7491** or 415/441-1106; fax 415/474-3395; www.oceanic-society.org), also has Florida trips among its expeditions, including manatee monitoring in the Crystal River area north of Tampa.

FISHING In addition to the amberjack, bonito, grouper, mackerel, mahi-mahi, marlin, pompano, redfish, sailfish, snapper, snook, tarpon, tuna, and wahoo running offshore and in inlets, Florida has countless miles of rivers and streams, plus about 30,000 lakes and springs stocked with more than 100 species of freshwater fish. Indeed, Floridians seem to fish everywhere: off canal banks and old bridges, from fishing piers and fishing fleets. You'll even see them standing alongside the Tamiami Trail (U.S. 41) that cuts across the Everglades—one eye on their line, the other watching for alligators.

Anglers 16 and older need licenses for any kind of saltwater or freshwater fishing, including lobstering and spear fishing. Licenses are sold at bait-and-tackle shops around the state and online at www.wildlifelicense.com/fl.

The **Florida Department of Environmental Protection,** 3900 Commonwealth Blvd., Tallahassee, FL 32399-3000 (© **850/245-2118;** www.dep.state.fl.us), publishes the annual *Fishing Lines,* a free magazine with a wealth of information about fishing in Florida, including regulations and licensing requirements. It also distributes free brochures with annual freshwater and saltwater limits. And the Florida Sports Foundation (see the introduction to this section, above) publishes *Florida Fishing & Boating,* another treasure trove of information.

HIKING Although you won't be climbing any mountains in this relatively flat state, there are thousands of beautiful hiking trails in Florida. The ideal hiking months are October through April, when the weather is cool and dry and mosquitoes are less prominent. Like anywhere else, you'll find trails that are gentle and short, and others that are challenging—some trails in the Everglades require you to wade waist-deep in water!

Most Florida snakes are harmless, but a few have deadly bites, so it's a good idea to avoid them all. If you're venturing into the backcountry, watch out for gators,

and don't ever try to feed them (or any wild animal). You risk getting bitten (they can't tell the difference between the food and your hand). You're also upsetting the balance of nature, since animals fed by humans lose their ability to find their own food.

The **Florida Trail Association,** 5415 SW 13th St., Gainesville, FL 32608 (© **877/HIKE-FLA** or 352/378-8823; www.florida-trail.org), maintains a large percentage of the public trails in the state and puts out an excellent book packed with maps, details, and color photos.

For a copy of *Florida Trails,* which outlines the many options, contact Visit Florida (p. 30). Another resource is *A Guide to Your National Scenic Trails,* from the Office of Greenways and Trails, Department of Environmental Protection, 3900 Commonwealth Blvd., Tallahassee, FL 32399 (© **850/245-2118;** www.dep.state.fl.us/gwt). You can also contact the office of **National Forests in Florida,** Woodcrest Office Park, 325 John Knox Rd., Suite F-100, Tallahassee, FL 32303 (© **850/523-8500;** www.southernregion.fs.fed.us/florida). Finally, *Hiking Florida,* by M. Timothy O'Keefe (Falcon Press; www.falcbooks.com), details 132 hikes throughout the state, with maps and photos.

GOLF   Florida is the unofficial golf capital of the United States—some say the world—since the **World Golf Hall of Fame** is located near St. Augustine. This state-of-the-art museum is worth a visit even if you're not in love with the game.

One thing's for certain: Florida has more golf courses than any other state—more than 1,150 at last count, and growing. I've picked the best in chapter 1, but suffice it to say that you can tee off almost anywhere, any time there's daylight. The highest concentrations of excellent courses are in Southwest Florida around Naples and Fort Myers (more than 1,000 holes!), in the Orlando area (Disney alone has 99 holes open to the public), and in the Panhandle around Destin and Panama City Beach. It's a rare town in Florida that doesn't have a municipal golf course—even Key West has 18 great holes.

Greens fees are usually much lower at the municipal courses than at privately owned clubs. Whether public or private, greens fees tend to vary greatly depending on the time of year. You could pay $150 or more at a private course during the high season, but less than half that when the tourists are gone. The fee structures vary so much that it's best to call ahead and ask, and always reserve a tee time as far in advance as possible.

You can learn the game or hone your strokes at one of several excellent golf schools in the state. **David Ledbetter** has teaching facilities in Orlando and Naples, **Fred Griffin** is in charge of the Grand Cypress Academy of Golf at Grand Cypress Resort in Orlando, and you'll find **Jimmy Ballard**'s school at the Ocean Reef Club on Key Largo. The Westin Innisbrook Resort at Tarpon Springs has its **Innisbrook Golf Institute,** while Amelia Island (near Jacksonville) is home to the **Amelia Island Plantation Golf School.**

You can get information about most Florida courses, including current greens fees, and reserve tee times through **Tee Times USA,** P.O. Box 641, Flagler Beach, FL 32136 (© **888/GOLF-FLO** or 386/439-0001; www.teetimesusa.com), which publishes a vacation guide with many stay-and-play golf packages.

Florida Golf, published by the Florida Sports Foundation (see the introduction to this section, above), lists every course in Florida. It's the state's official golf guide and is available from Visit Florida (p. 30).

Golfer's Guide magazine publishes monthly editions covering most of Florida. It is available free at local visitor centers and hotel lobbies, or you can contact the magazine at 2 Park Lane, Suite E,

Hilton Head Island, SC 29928 (© **800/ 864-6101** or 843/842-7878; fax 843/842-5743; www.golfersguide.com).

Northwest Florida is covered by *South Coast Golf Guide,* published by Tee and J's Ent., LLC, P.O. Box 11278, Pensacola, FL 32524-1278 (© **850/505-7553;** fax 850/505-0057; www.southcoastgolfguide. com).

You can also get more information from the **Professional Golfers' Association (PGA),** 400 Ave. of the Champions, Palm Beach Gardens, FL 33418 (© **800/ 633-9150;** www.pga.com); or from the **Ladies Professional Golf Association (LPGA),** 100 International Golf Dr., Daytona Beach, FL 32124 (© **904/254-6200;** www.lpga.com).

More than 700 courses are profiled in *Florida Golf Guide,* by Jimmy Shacky (Open Roads Publishing), available at bookstores for $20.

SCUBA DIVING & SNORKELING
Divers love the Keys, where you can see magnificent formations of tree-size elkhorn coral and giant brain coral, as well as colorful sea fans and dozens of other varieties, sharing space with 300 or more species of rainbow-hued fish. Reef diving is good all the way from Key Largo to Key West, with plenty of tour operators, outfitters, and dive shops along the way. Particularly worthy are **John Pennekamp Coral Reef State Park** in Key Largo, and **Looe Key National Marine Sanctuary** off Big Pine Key. *Skin Diver* magazine picked Looe Key as the number-one dive spot in North America. Also, the clearest waters in which to view some of the 4,000 sunken ships along Florida's coast are in the Middle Keys and the waters between Key West and the Dry Tortugas. Snorkeling in the Keys is particularly fine between Islamorada and Marathon.

In Northwest Florida, the 100-fathom curve draws closer to the white, sandy Panhandle beaches than to any other spot on the Gulf of Mexico. It's too far north here for coral, but you can see brilliantly colored sponges and fish and, in Timber Hole, discover an undersea "petrified forest" of sunken planes, ships, and even a railroad car. The battleship USS *Massachusetts* lies in 30 feet of water just 3 miles off Pensacola. Every beach town in Northwest Florida has dive shops to outfit, tour, or certify visitors.

In the Crystal River area, north of the St. Petersburg and Clearwater beaches, you can snorkel with the manatees as they bask in the warm spring waters of Kings Bay.

If you want to keep up with what's going on statewide, you can subscribe to the monthly magazine *Florida Scuba News* (© 904/783-1610; www.scuba news.com). You might also want to pick up a specialized guidebook. Some good ones include *Coral Reefs of Florida,* by Gilbert L. Voss (Pineapple Press; www. pineapplepress.com); and *The Diver's Guide to Florida and the Florida Keys,* by Jim Stachowicz (Windward Publishing).

TENNIS   Year-round sunshine makes Florida great for tennis. There are some 7,700 places to play throughout the state, from municipal courts to exclusive resorts. Some municipal facilities—Cambier Park Tennis Center in Naples leaps to mind—equal expensive resorts, except they're free or close to it.

If you can afford it, you can learn from the best in Florida. **Nick Bollettieri** has sports academies in Bradenton. Safety Harbor Resort and Spa near St. Petersburg hosts the **Phil Green Tennis Program.** Amateurs can hobnob with the superstars at **ATP Tour International Headquarters** in Ponte Vedra Beach, near Jacksonville. **Mary Jo Fernandez** is affiliated with the **Arthur Ashe Tennis**

Center at the Doral Golf Resort & Spa in Miami. And **Chris Evert, Robert Seguso,** and **Carling Basset** have their own center in Boca Raton.

The three hard courts and seven clay courts at the **Key Biscayne Tennis Association,** 6702 Crandon Blvd. (© 305/361-5263), get crowded on weekends, since they're some of Miami's most beautiful. You'll play on the same courts as Lendl, Graf, Evert, McEnroe, and other greats; this is the venue for one of the world's biggest annual tennis events, the NASDAQ 100 Open. There's a pleasant, if limited, pro shop, plus many good pros. Only four courts are lighted at night, but if you reserve at least 48 hours in advance, you can usually take your pick. They cost $6 per person per hour. The courts are open daily from 8am to 9pm.

Famous as the spot where Chris Evert got in her early serves, the **Jimmy Evert Tennis Center,** 701 NE 12th Ave. (off Sunrise Blvd.), Fort Lauderdale (© 954/828-5378), has 18 clay and 3 hard courts (15 lighted). Her coach and father, James Evert, still teaches young players here, though he is very picky about whom he'll accept. Nonresidents of Fort Lauderdale pay $6 an hour per person before 5pm and $7 an hour per person after 5pm.

Other top places at which to learn and play are **Amelia Island Plantation,** on Amelia Island; **Colony Beach and Tennis Resort,** on Longboat Key off Sarasota (which *Tennis* magazine picked as the number-two tennis resort in the nation); **Sanibel Harbour Resort & Spa,** in Fort Myers, whose 5,500-seat stadium has hosted Davis Cup matches; **South Seas Resort & Yacht Harbour,** on Captiva Island; and the **Registry Resort,** in Naples.

11 Getting Around

Having a car is the best and easiest way to see Florida's sights, or just to get to and from the beach. Public transportation is

available only in the cities and larger towns, and even there it may provide infrequent or inadequate service. When it comes to getting from one city to another, cars and planes are the ways to go.

BY PLANE

The commuter arms of **Continental** (© 800/525-0280; www. flycontinental. com), **Delta** (© 800/221-1212; www. delta.com), and **US Airways** (© 800/428-4322; www.usairways.com) provide extensive service between Florida's major cities and towns. Fares for these short hops tend to be reasonable.

Cape Air (© 800/352-0714; www.fly capeair.com) flies between Key West, Fort Myers, and Naples, which means you can avoid backtracking to Miami from Key West if you're touring the state. (You can also take a boat between Key West and Fort Myers Beach, Naples, or Marco Island during the winter months; see p. 334.) **Paradise Aviation** (© 305/743-4222; www.flyparadiseair.com) connects Fort Lauderdale with Marathon.

BY CAR

Jacksonville is about 350 miles north of Miami and 500 miles north of Key West, so don't underestimate how long it will take you to drive all the way down the state. The speed limit is either 65 mph or 70 mph on the rural interstate highways, so you can make good time between cities. Not so on U.S. 1, U.S. 17, U.S. 19, U.S. 41, and U.S. 301; although most have four lanes, these older highways tend to be heavily congested, especially in built-up areas.

Every major car rental company is represented here, including **Alamo** (© 800/327-9633; www.goalamo.com), **Avis** (© 800/331-1212; www.avis.com), **Budget** (© 800/527-0700; www.budgetrenta car. com), **Dollar** (© 800/800-4000; www.dollarcar.com), **Enterprise** (© 800/325-8007; pickenterprise.com), **Hertz** (© 800/654-3131; www.hertz.com), **National** (© 800/227-7368; www. nationalcar.com), and **Thrifty** (© 800/367-2277; www.thrifty.com).

If you decide to rent a car, shop around and ask a lot of questions. Reservations clerks are used to being asked for the lowest rate available, and most will find it in order to get your business. You may have to try different dates, different pickup and drop-off points, and different discount offers to find the best deal. Also, if you're a member of any organization (AARP, Costco, or AAA, for example), be sure to ask if you're entitled to discounts.

Check the rental firms' websites: Most will automatically bring up the lowest available rate, and there are boxes to click if you are an association member or have a discount coupon or ID number. You can comparison-shop on websites such as **Travelocity** (www.travelocity.com) and **Expedia** (www.expedia.com), which will make reservations for you once you've found the best deal.

State and local **taxes** will add as much as 20% to your final bill. You'll pay an additional $2.05 per day in statewide use tax, and local sales taxes will tack on at least 6% to the total, including the statewide use tax. Some airports add another 35¢ per day and as much as 10% in "recovery" fees. You can avoid the recovery fee by picking up your car in town rather than at the airport. Budget and Enterprise both have numerous rental locations away from the airports. But be sure to weigh the cost of transportation to and from your hotel against the amount of the fee.

Competition is so fierce among Florida rental firms that most have now stopped charging **drop-off fees** if you pick up a car at one place and leave it at another. For example, I recently picked up a car at Tampa and dropped it off at Fort Myers for the same price I would have paid had I returned it to Tampa. Be sure to ask in advance if there's a drop-off fee.

To rent a car, you must have a valid **credit card** (not a debit or check card) in your name, and most companies require you to be at least 25 years old. Some also set maximum ages and may deny cars to anyone with a bad driving record. Ask about requirements and restrictions when you book, in order to avoid problems once you arrive.

BY TRAIN & BY BUS

You'll find that train travel isn't terribly feasible within Florida, and it's not significantly less expensive than flying, if at all. See "Getting There," earlier in this chapter, for Florida towns served by **Amtrak** (© **800/USA-RAIL;** www.amtrak.com). For bus travel, see the "Essentials" and "Getting There" sections in the following chapters.

RECOMMENDED BOOKS

To help you get into the Florida mood, pick up Ernest Hemingway's 1937 classic, *To Have and Have Not,* which was set in Key West. Marjorie Kinnan Rawlings's Pulitzer Prize–winning *The Yearling,* published in 1938, is about a boy growing up in central Florida. For a more contemporary look at the state, and one that's brilliantly satirical, pick up any of Carl Hiaasen's novels, which are all set in Florida.

For nonfiction, check out Joan Didion's *Miami,* or Marjory Stoneman Douglas's *The Everglades: River of Grass.* The latter is a personal testament to the magnificence of the Everglades; it was the catalyst of the preservation program that began in the 1940s.

FAST FACTS: Florida

American Express There are a number of American Express offices in Florida. Call © **800/528-4800** or go to www.americanexpress.com for the location nearest you.

ATM Networks ATMs are as ubiquitous in Florida as palm trees. They're found at nearly every street corner, main shopping area, and, in most cases, supermarkets and even convenience stores.

Banks Banks are usually open Monday through Friday from 9am to 3 or 4pm, and most have automated teller machines (ATMs) for 24-hour banking. You won't have a problem finding a Cirrus or PLUS machine. See "Money," earlier in this chapter, for more information.

Car Rentals See "Getting Around," above.

Emergencies To reach the police, ambulance, or fire department, dial © **911** from any phone. No coins are needed. Emergency hot lines include **Crisis Intervention** (© **305/358-HELP** or 305/358-4357) and the **Poison Information Center** (© **800/222-1222**).

Liquor Laws You must be 21 to purchase or consume alcohol in Florida. This law is strictly enforced, so if you look young, carry photo identification that gives your date of birth. Minors can usually enter bars where food is served, but they are not allowed to drink alcohol.

Newspapers & Magazines Most cities of any size have a local daily paper. The well-respected *Miami Herald* is generally available all over the state, with regional editions available in many areas. In the major cities, you can also find coin-operated boxes for *USA Today,* the *Wall Street Journal,* and the *New York Times.*

Safety Whenever you're traveling in an unfamiliar city, stay alert. Be aware of your immediate surroundings. Always lock your car doors and the trunk when your vehicle is unattended, and don't leave any valuables in sight. See "Health & Safety," earlier in this chapter, for more information.

Taxes The Florida state sales tax is 6%. Many municipalities add 1% or more to that, and most levy a special tax on hotel and restaurant bills. In general, expect at least 9% to be added to your final hotel bill. There are also hefty taxes on rental cars here (see "Getting Around," above).

Time Zones The Florida peninsula observes Eastern Standard Time, but most of the Panhandle, west of the Apalachicola River, is on Central Standard Time, 1 hour behind the rest of the state.

Weather Hurricane season runs June through November. For an up-to-date recording of current weather conditions and forecasts, call © **305/229-4522.** Online, you can check www.intellicast.com or www.weather.com.

3

Suggested Itineraries in Florida

Ask anyone who lives here and they'll tell you: Florida is such a *long* state. If you drive from Jacksonville to the southernmost point in Key West, it'll take 10 hours at least—without traffic. Thankfully, there are flights throughout the state that make exploration much easier. Don't tear your hair out if you can't get from Disney to the Everglades in the same trip. Set your sights on what you want to do and see the most, and simply unwind—this is, after all, a holiday. You can always come back. In fact, return visits are highly encouraged!

The range of possible itineraries is endless; what we've suggested below is a very full program covering Florida over a **2-week period.** If possible, you should extend your time—2 weeks is not really enough time if you plan to actually explore the Sunshine State, but if you plan to veg out on a beach, then it's plenty of time—or cut out some of the destinations suggested. You can always

tack on one itinerary to the next. We've done our best to keep it geographically viable and logical. Ideally, you should use this book's "Best Of" chapter to work out a route that covers those experiences or sights that really appeal to you. Whatever you finally decide to do, we highly recommend that you at least include a stop at one of Florida's natural wonders, be it the beaches, the Everglades or the Keys.

Important: Should limited time force you to include only the most obvious stops in your itinerary, you will invariably make contact with only those who depend on you to make a living, which regrettably could leave you with a frustrated sense that Florida is one big, long tourist trap. This is why it is so important to *get off the beaten tourist track,* to experience the wacky, the kitschy, the stunning, the baffling, and the fascinating people, places, and things that make this state one of the most popular vacation destinations in the world.

1 South Florida in 2 Weeks

Consider this tour a South Florida sampler. There's not enough time in 2 weeks to see and do everything, but we've custom-built an itinerary that will provide you with a locals'-eye view of some of the best diversions So Flo is known for. Whether you're a beach bum or a beachcomber, a club hopper or someone who prefers to swing a club, a nature lover or people watcher—there's something for everyone on this tour.

Days ❶–❷: Arrive in Key West ✸✸✸
After arriving in the so-called Conch Republic (or Margaritaville, if you will), plan to spend a day or 2 at the most here. A full day on the 4-mile-by-2-mile island is plenty for exploring, but if you're into

doing the Duval Bar Crawl, you may want to leave yourself with a day to recover from that inevitable hangover. Focus most of your sightseeing energy on Old Town, where you'll see stunning, restored Victorian-style homes; lush, tropical greenery; and the old Bahama Village. Be sure not to miss the sunset celebration at Mallory Square, and, if possible, do dinner at **Blue Heaven** in Bahama Village. Then hit the Duval Street bars if you're so inclined. The next day, either spend the day relaxing at your hotel pool—we recommend the **Gardens Hotel** or for a true Key West experience—or explore the Historic Seaport and all its shops and Key West kitsch. See p. 223.

Day ❸: Miami: Coral Gables, Little Havana & South Beach 🐟🐟🐟

Take the 3-hour drive on the Overseas Highway to **Miami**—one of the most scenic drives you'll ever take, albeit sometimes a boring one. If you've seen it before, just fly. Make a pit stop in Coral Gables, where you can either get a bite to eat on **Miracle Mile** or cool off in the **Venetian Pool.** If you like what you see, check into the historic **Biltmore Hotel.** If not, make sure to at least see the hotel and then continue on to Southwest 8th Street, otherwise known as Calle Ocho, the heart of Little Havana. Peruse the cigar stores and the old men playing dominoes in Domino Park. Grab a Cuban coffee at Versailles and then head north to South Beach to spend the night at one of its trendy hotels.

Day ❹: South Beach 🐟🐟🐟

Wake up early and catch the sunrise on the beach. Have breakfast at the Front Porch Café. Stake your claim on the sand and spend the morning on the beach. Hit Lincoln Road for lunch. Shop along Lincoln and Collins Avenue before having a cocktail at the Beach Bar at the Delano Hotel. Return to your own hotel for a disco nap; wake up around 9pm. Have dinner at Prime 112 and then hit the clubs: Opium Garden, Prive, and Mansion. Grab a late-night snack and then crash at your hotel.

Day ❺: From South Beach to Fort Lauderdale 🐟🐟

Have breakfast and watch the club kids coming home from the night before at the Big Pink. Get in the car and take A1A north—the scenic route. Hit the Hollywood Beach Boardwalk, our version of Atlantic City without the casinos. If you're hungry for lunch, have the world's best burger at Le Tub. Continue along A1A until you reach the famous Fort Lauderdale strip. Take a break at the world-famous Elbo Room and watch the action on the beach. Spend the night at the Riverside Hotel on Las Olas Boulevard.

Day ❻: Sand, Seminoles & Santana 🐟🐟

Hit the famous Fort Lauderdale Beach, where Frankie and Annette used to play beach-blanket bingo. Then take a bit of a diversion and head west to the Seminole Hard Rock Hotel and Casino, where you may catch a concert by a Billboard-charting artist or even Jerry Seinfeld, hit the jackpot on one of the hundreds of slot machines (the hotel claims it pays out $12.9 million daily!), or relax by the pool, which is almost as nice as, if not nicer than, the one at the Hard Rock Hotel in Vegas. Also check out the Seminole Okalee Indian Village and Museum before heading over and out to spot signs of real wildlife in the Everglades. See p. 260.

Days ❼–❽: Seminole Indian Reservation & Everglades National Park 🐟🐟🐟

Travel 45 minutes west on I-75 to the Seminole Indian Reservation, which encompasses over 69,000 acres of the Everglades' Big Cypress Swamp. Hop on a swamp buggy at the Billie Swamp Safari to see hogs, bison, gators, and deer. Continue west to Everglades City, check into the Ivey House B&B, and ask owners Sandee and David if they can hook you up with a special, insiders' tour of the 'Glades.

Suggested Florida Itineraries

START: Beachy Keen Florida in 1 Week

■ START: South Florida in 2 Weeks
▲ START: Florida's Gulf Coast in 1 Week: AKA Relaxing Florida
● START: Florida, Family Style in 1 Week
◆ START: Old Historic Florida in 1 Week
★ START: Beachy Keen Florida in 1 Week

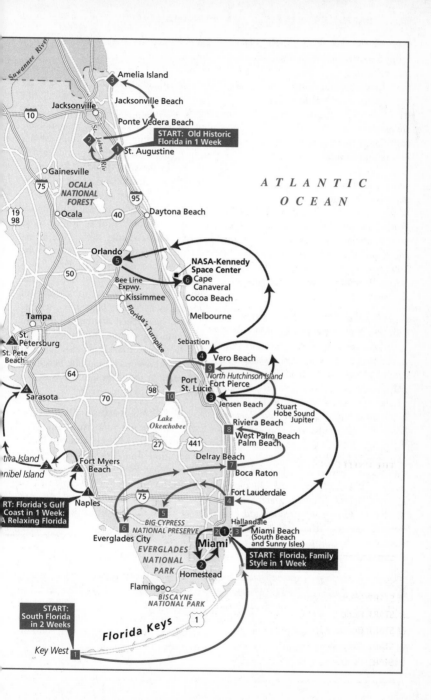

Days ❾–❿: The Palm Beaches ★★

From one extreme to another, after leaving charming and historic Everglades City, head east and north to the charming, historic, and bustling Delray Beach, where the only alligators you'll likely see are on the purses of the ladies who lunch and lounge there. Check into the Sundy House and peruse the hotel's Taru Gardens. The next day, do not miss the Morikami Museum and Japanese Gardens before moving on to West Palm Beach, where you should check into the Hotel Biba and do a little antiques shopping in downtown West Palm. At night, check out the clubs and restaurants in downtown West Palm, on Clematis Street. Be sure to have a beer and enjoy the view at Bradley's.

Day ⓫: From Mar-A-Lago to the Moon—Well, Jupiter, at Least ★★

Spend the morning driving around Palm Beach proper, making sure to stop and catch a glimpse of Donald Trump's palatial Mar-A-Lago. Stop by Worth Avenue to see the ladies with little dogs who lunch and shop. It's the Rodeo Drive of South Florida, truly, and you can't miss the people-watching there. For an actual glimpse inside a Palm Beach manse, go to the Flagler Museum, where you can explore Whitehall, Standard Oil tycoon Henry Flagler's wedding present to his third wife. Go back to reality and head toward Jupiter, the home of Burt Reynolds. Check into the PGA National Resort and Spa. See p. 309.

Days ⓬–⓭: The Treasure Coast

You may not find gold in your exploration of the Treasure Coast, but you will find Jonathan Dickinson State Park on Hutchinson Island, where you should rent a canoe and explore the plethora of botanical treasures. If you're into snorkeling and diving and feel like delving deeper, check out the most popular artificial reef in the area, the USS *Rankin,* an old WWII ship that was sunk in 1988, located 7 miles east-northeast of the St. Lucie Inlet. Check into the Hutchinson Island Marriott Beach Resort and Marina, and consider taking the Loxahatchee Queen for a 2-hour tour of the area. The next day, head to Vero Beach and Sebastian for a taste of Old Florida. Sports fans will want to check out Dodgertown, where the Los Angeles Dodgers spend their winters. Check into the completely unique Driftwood Resort and do dinner at Café du Soir, if your budget allows you. If not, The Beachside Restaurant at the Palm Court Resort is a great spot for blue-plate specials.

Day ⓮: Lake Okeechobee or Bust?

If you can't extend your trip to include a side trip to Lake Okeechobee, consider it for next time. In the meantime, fly home out of either Palm Beach International Airport, 35 miles south of Vero Beach, or the Melbourne International Airport, which is less than 35 miles north of Vero Beach.

2 Florida's Gulf Coast in 1 Week: aka Relaxing Florida

The beaches on the Gulf Coast are infinitely nicer than those in South Florida, with soft sand, stunning sunsets, and a sense of calm that often evades the hustle and bustle of So Flo. A week on the Gulf is akin to spending a month in a city spa. Refreshing and calming, the Gulf coast is an ideal spot for those looking to recharge their batteries.

Day ❶: Arrive in Fort Myers Beach 𝒓𝒓

Check into the Edison Beach House All Suite Hotel and take in the panoramic Gulf views. Waste no time making a dinner reservation at The Dragonfly Bistro, where you must, must try the jumbo lump-crab salad with aged cheddar and a corn blini with tomato vinaigrette. After dinner, consider hitting the rooftop bar at Beached Whale, a locals' fave. See p. 350.

Day ❷: Sanibel and Captiva Islands 𝒓𝒓𝒓

Just 14 miles west of Fort Myers are two of Florida's most beautiful islands. Before heading to the wildly kitschy Bubble Room restaurant, be sure to stop at the JN Ding Darling National Wildlife Refuge, home to alligators, raccoons, otters, and a dazzling array of bird life. Take your car down the Wildlife Drive for a Cliffs Notes version of the park. Then call Captiva Cruises and see if there's room for y'all on the next shuttle out to Boca Grande, sort of the Martha's Vineyard of Florida. After touring Boca Grande, return to Sanibel and check into the Casa Ybel Resort, if your budget allows you to; if not, we highly recommend the Tarpon Tale Inn on Sanibel, or the 'Tween Waters Inn on Captiva. Now you're ready for the Bubble Room! See p. 365.

Day ❸: To Naples 𝒓𝒓

Wake up early and do not miss breakfast and the biscuits at the Sanibel Café. Drive south for 40 or so miles, and you'll be in swanky, sleepy Naples. Take the Naples Trolley to get a feel for the place and then, without hesitation, hit the beach before sunset. For a ritzy experience, we recommend The Ritz-Carlton, Naples, one of the best in the entire chain. For a flip-flops-and-T-shirt experience with a hopping sunset bar scene, you'll love the Naples Beach Hotel and Golf Club. Both have fabulous beaches. After the beach, stroll down 5th Avenue, the city's main drag, where you'll find the only real semblance of nightlife, dining, and shopping. The next morning, head 70 miles north to Sarasota.

Days ❹–❺: Sarasota 𝒓𝒓𝒓

Sarasota's Siesta Key Beach is one of Florida's best. But if culture is your thing, don't miss the Ringling Museum of Art. If you can't stay at The Ritz-Carlton Sarasota, consider the Colony Beach and Tennis Resort on nearby Longboat Key. Do not miss dinner at Euphemia Haye. Just don't. For a fun diversion nearby in Bradenton, stop by the Gamble Plantation and the weird and wacky Solomon's Castle. Before heading to Tampa, have breakfast at the Blue Dolphin Café. See p. 457.

Days ❻–❼: Tampa Bay, St. Pete & Clearwater 𝒓𝒓

Because this is the relaxing Gulf Coast itinerary, we won't recommend Busch Gardens Tampa Bay unless you're really craving coasters. Same goes for Ybor City, the hub of Tampa's nightlife. It's rowdy and fun, but hardly relaxing. Therefore, we'd like to send you directly to the Saddlebrook Resort–Tampa, where the likes of Jennifer Capriati play tennis and aspiring Tiger Woods types play golf. If you prefer to be on the beach, however, head over to St. Pete Beach and Clearwater, where we recommend either the historic Don CeSar Beach Resort & Spa or the Clearwater Beach Marriott Suites on Sand Key. For arty types, the Salvador Dalí museum in downtown St. Pete is highly recommended. Fly home from Tampa International Airport.

3 Florida, Family Style

Florida is definitely a kid-friendly destination. And contrary to popular belief, not all diversions are animatronic or even remotely animated. Sure, there are the theme parks, the roller coasters, the talking mouse, and Cinderella Castle. We've got Flipper and Orca and parrots that play poker. And then there's the Playmobil Fun Park. But we've come up with another family-friendly itinerary you may not have experienced yet.

Day ❶: Key Biscayne ★★★
Both the Sonesta Beach Resort and The Ritz-Carlton Key Biscayne have fabulous children's programs, not to mention pretty cool diversions for adults. Spend a day checking out the resorts (skip the Miami Seaquarium unless the kids want to swim with the dolphins), and spend the day at the Marjory Stoneman Douglas Biscayne Nature Center, where the entire family can explore an ancient fossil tidal pool. If there's time left, check out the Bill Baggs Cape Florida State Park and rent a hydrobike. See p. 147.

Days ❷–❸: Coral Gables ★★★ & South Miami ★★
Get an early start and head south to Homestead's legendary Coral Castle. When the kids tire of seeing this wacky attraction, grab lunch at the family friendly, family-run Mexican mainstay, El Toro Taco. On your way to Coral Gables, make a stop at Miami Metrozoo or Monkey Jungle, depending on your preference in animals, and then clean off that stinky animal scent with a splash in Coral Gables's resplendent, refreshing Venetian Pool. If you're up for it, check out Vizcaya Museum and Gardens, and/or the Miami Museum of Science and Space Transit Planetarium. After working up an appetite, take the kids for a big dinner at Porcao, where they'll enjoy holding up their signs when they're ready to eat more meat!

Day ❹: Miami & Port St. Lucie ★★★
Before leaving Miami, be sure to stop at the Miami Children's Museum, where the kids can spend a few hours channeling their inner grown-up in a bona fide TV and recording studio. Grab a TV dinner at the G-rated Big Pink on South Beach, and then hit the road to Vero Beach. Check into the ClubMed- Sandpiper on the St. Lucie River, where there are four different children's clubs for ages 4 months all the way up to 13 years old. En route to Vero, you may want to take the kids to West Palm Beach's whimsical Playmobil Fun Park or on a safari through Lion Country Safari, and then grab lunch at Jupiter's legendary Nick's Tomato Pie. See chs. 4, 8, 9.

Day ❺: Vero Beach ★★★
As if Club Med doesn't have enough for the family to do—or not do—you may want to take the kids out to Dodgertown, the place where the LA Dodgers spend Spring Training, or to one of the beautiful beaches nearby.

Day ❻: Arrive in Lake Buena Vista ★★★
Okay, we lied. Sort of. We're sending you in the environs of Disney and friends, but only to check into the coolest kid-friendly hotel possibly in the entire world. The Nickelodeon Family Suites Resort, by Holiday Inn, is the first ever Nickelodeon-branded resort. There are Kids Suites with different themes featuring kids' favorite Nick characters. I know many a family that has traveled here just so the kids could stay in the hotel. If you choose, you can go to Disney or one of the theme parks. See p. 478.

Day ❼: Spacing Out at Cape Canaveral ✿✿✿

The John F. Kennedy Space Center is a must-see for everyone, but especially kids. You'll not only see where actual rockets and shuttles are launched, but you can also have lunch with an astronaut! Either spend the night here and fly out of the Melbourne International Airport, or make the 3-hour drive back to Miami International Airport.

4 Old Historic Florida

Many Floridians lament the loss of the days of the plastic pink flamingos, early-bird specials, cracker-style homes (as opposed to Cracker Barrel restaurants), and small, quaint towns. The thing is, they still exist! Old Florida begins in St. Augustine and doesn't end there at all. Here's a sample that promises to take you back to a Florida that would even seem ancient even to your grandparents.

Day ❶: St. Augustine ✿✿✿

The easiest way to hit America's oldest city is to fly into Daytona International Airport. But since this is a tour of Old Florida, we'll have you skip the Daytona Spring Break and NASCAR scene, and head an hour north into the 17th century.

Everything in St. Aug claims to be the Oldest whatever—and, in most cases, it's true: the Oldest Store, the Oldest Wooden Schoolhouse, the Oldest House, and more. Pop a multivitamin and skip the overrated Fountain of Youth. Instead, hit Anastasia State Park and see what a beach would look like if it were unfettered by modernization. To really keep with the old theme, we suggest a room at the Casablanca Inn on the Bay, a 1914 house listed on the National Register of Historic Places. See p. 545.

Days ❷–❹: North & South of the St. Johns River ✿✿

Despite its modern skyline, Jacksonville actually has some serious history. South of the St. Johns River, you will find the Fort Caroline National Memorial, a former 16th-century French Huguenot settlement that was wiped out by the Spanish but preserved in the form of archaeological relics. North of the river is the Zephaniah Kingsley Plantation, or at least the remains of what was once a 19th-century plantation complete with clapboard homes and slave cabins. Check into either the historic House on Cherry Street, also on the St. Johns, or the Plantation Manor Inn. See p. 561.

Days ❹–❻: Amelia Island ✿✿✿

With 13 miles of beachfront and bona fide, restored Victorian homes, Amelia Island is worth the 45-minute drive northeast of downtown Jacksonville. It's another world and, for many, out of this world. Also steeped in history, Amelia Island attracted Oprah Winfrey, who has promised to help restore American Beach, the only beach in the 1930s reserved for African Americans. Nearby is Fernandina Beach, which dates back to the post–Civil War period, where you'll swear you were somewhere else, with its Victorian, Queen Anne, and Italianate homes listed on the National Register. Nearby, the Palace Saloon claims to be Florida's oldest watering hole, challenging St. Augustine to an ongoing drinking contest! Check into the Amelia Island Plantation for a posh stay, or consider the Florida House Inn, once again, the oldest operating hotel in the entire state. See p. 575.

Day ❼: Back to the Future

Fly home and realize that new is not always better.

5 Beachy Keen Florida

The Panhandle may be known as the Redneck Riviera to some, but to those in the know, the area has some of Florida's best beaches, with undeveloped stretches of powder-white sand that's a hot commodity in the world these days.

Days ❶–❷: Gulf Islands National Seashore and Pensacola Beach ✪✪✪

This is, hands down, Florida's best beach. Not only are there 150 miles of protected beach, but there's also a 1,378-acre natural Live Oaks Area full of oaks, pines, and nature trails. Even the Clarion Suites Resort and Convention Center is pretty stunning, with tin-roofed pastel cottages that sit on the sand dunes. Do not leave without hitting the Flora-Bama Lounge, which prides itself on being the Last Great American Roadhouse. See p. 590.

Days ❸–❹: Destin Beach ✪✪

Grayton Beach State Park is a sublime white-sand paradise, with 356 acres of pine forests surrounding a lake. You can camp here to get back to nature, or you can choose to explore Destin's other fabulous beaches, such as Henderson Beach State Park and Fort Walton Beach's Okaloosa Island. You can't really go wrong with any. The Sandestin Golf and Beach Resort is good for a longer stay, a community unto itself with restaurants, shops, a private 5-mile beach, and, according to the experts, unparalleled golf. Don't get too marooned because you will want to go off property and check out AJ's Seafood and Oyster Bar, the hottest spot on Destin Harbor, famous for its rooftop bar and live music. See p. 603.

Days ❹–❺: Seaside & Rosemary Beach ✪✪✪

Live *The Truman Show* in this stunning, Victorian-style planned community with old-fashioned beach cottages set upon unfettered sand dunes. Just 8 miles east of Seaside is Rosemary Beach, a swanky community of Caribbean-style cottages and carriage houses with the most stunning private beach and Kodak-worthy Gulf views. Rent a cottage on the beach and enjoy the views. While in town, don't miss AJ's Seafood and Oyster Bar, Destin. See p. 612.

Day ❻: Panama City Beach ✪✪

St. Andrews State Park has 1,000 acres of white sand and dunes, a common theme in the Panhandle. Shell Island is pristine, uninhabited, and known for possessing shells that aren't available for purchase in those touristy souvenir shops. Spend the night at Marriott's Bay Point Village.

Day ❼: Apalachicola ✪✪

Florida's so-called Last Frontier happens to have one of the country's last amazing beaches, St. George Island State Park. Enjoy the 9 miles of nature before having to go back to reality. Spend your last night at the Apalachicola River Inn, the town's only waterfront stay, and home of the popular Frog Level Oyster Bar and Boss Oyster, where you'll be treated to some of the best crustaceans you've ever had.

4

Getting to Know Miami

A week in Miami is not unlike watching an episode of, say, *Access Hollywood* with a little CNN thrown in for good measure. Miami: the city to which J-Lo fled when she and Ben Affleck were on the outs, where the paparazzi camps out for days hoping to catch a glimpse of something or someone fabulous, where former U.S. president Bill Clinton kibitzes with the head of a top modeling agency at a St. Tropez-ish beach club, where Janet Reno throws a politically-driven dance party at a South Beach nightclub. And that's just a small sample of the surreal, Fellini-esque world that exists way down here at the bottom of the map. Nothing in Miami is ever what it seems.

What used to be a relatively sleepy beach vacation destination has awakened from its humid slumber, upped its tempo, and finally earned its place in the PDAs of cutting-edge jet-setters worldwide. But don't be fooled by the hipper-than-thou, celebrity-drenched playground known as South Beach. While the chic elite do, indeed, flock to Miami's coolest enclave, it is surprisingly accessible to the average Joe, Jane, or José. For every Philippe Starck–designed, bank account–busting boutique hotel on South Beach, there's a kitschy, candy-coated Art Deco one that's much less taxing on the pockets. For each Pan-Mediterranean-Asian haute cuisinerie,

there's always the down-home, no-nonsense Cuban bodega offering hearty food at ridiculously cheap prices.

Beyond the whole glitzy, *Entertainment-Tonight*-meets-beach-blanket-bacchanalia-as-seen-on-TV, Miami has an endless number of sporting, cultural, and recreational activities to keep you entertained. Its sparkling beaches are beyond compare. Plus, excellent shopping and nightlife activities include ballet, theater, and opera (as well as all the celebrity-saturated hotels, restaurants, bars, and clubs that have helped make Miami so famous).

Leave Miami, be it for the Keys, the Gold Coast, or the Treasure Coast, and you'll expose yourself not only to more UV rays, but to a world of cultural, historical, and sybaritic surprises where you can take in a spring baseball game, walk in the footsteps of Hemingway, get up close and personal with the area's sea life, soak up the serenity of unspoiled landscapes, catch the filming of *CSI: Miami* or a big-budget Hollywood flick, and much more.

Forget what you've heard about South Florida being Heaven's Waiting Room. That slogan is as passé as the concept of early-bird dinners (which you can still get—they just no longer define the region). In fact, according to some people, South Florida *is* heaven. So what are *you* waiting for?

1 Orientation

ARRIVING

Originally carved out of scrubland in 1928 by Pan American Airlines, **Miami International Airport (MIA)** has become 2nd in the United States for international passenger traffic and 10th in the world for total passengers. Despite the heavy traffic, the airport is quite user-friendly and not as much of a hassle as you'd think. You can change money or use your ATM card at Bank of America, located near the exit. Visitor information is available 24 hours a day at the **Miami International Airport Main Visitor Counter,** Concourse E, second level (© 305/876-7000). Information is also available at **www.miami-airport.com**. Because MIA is the busiest airport in South Florida, travelers may want to consider flying into the less crowded **Fort Lauderdale Hollywood International Airport (FLL)** (© 954/359-1200), which is closer to north Miami than MIA, or the **Palm Beach International Airport (PBI)** (© 561/ 471-7420), which is about 1½ hours from Miami.

GETTING INTO TOWN

Miami International Airport is located about 6 miles west of downtown and about 10 miles from the beaches, so it's likely you can get from the plane to your hotel room in less than half an hour. Of course, if you're arriving from an international destination, it will take more time to go through Customs and Immigration.

BY CAR   All the major car-rental firms operate off-site branches reached via shuttles from the airline terminals. See the "Rentals" section, under "Getting Around," on p. 73, for a list of major rental companies in Miami. Signs at the airport's exit clearly point the way to various parts of the city, but the car-rental firm should also give you directions to your destination. If you're arriving late at night, you might want to take a taxi to your hotel and have the car delivered to you the next day.

BY TAXI   Taxis line up in front of a dispatcher's desk outside the airport's arrivals terminals. Most cabs are metered, though some have flat rates to popular destinations. The fare should be about $20 to Coral Gables, $18 to downtown, and $24 to South Beach, plus tip, which should be about 15% (add more for each bag the driver handles). Depending on traffic, the ride to Coral Gables or downtown takes about 15 to 20 minutes, and to South Beach, 20 to 25 minutes.

BY VAN OR LIMO   Group limousines (multipassenger vans) circle the arrivals area looking for fares. Destinations are posted on the front of each van, and a flat rate is charged for door-to-door service to the area marked.

   SuperShuttle (© 305/871-2000; www.supershuttle.com) is one of the largest airport operators, charging between $10 and $40 per person for a ride within the county. Its vans operate 24 hours a day and accept American Express, MasterCard, and Visa. This is a cheaper alternative to a cab (if you are traveling alone or with one other person), but be prepared to be in the van for quite a while, as you may have to make several stops to drop passengers off before you reach your own destination. SuperShuttle also has begun service from Palm Beach International Airport to the surrounding communities. The door-to-door, shared-ride service operates from the airport to Stuart, Fort Pierce, Palm Beach, and Broward counties.

   Private limousine arrangements can be made in advance through your local travel agent. A one-way meet-and-greet service should cost about $50. Limo services include **City Limousine** (© 800/819-LIMO) and **DLS Limousine Service** (© 888/988-9567).

BY PUBLIC TRANSPORTATION   Public transportation in South Florida is a major hassle bordering on a nightmare. Painfully slow and unreliable, buses heading downtown leave the airport only once per hour (from the arrivals level), and connections are spotty, at best. It could take about an hour and a half to get to South Beach

via public transportation. Journeys to downtown and Coral Gables, however, are more direct. The fare is $1.50, plus an additional 25¢ for a transfer.

VISITOR INFORMATION

The most up-to-date information is provided by the **Greater Miami Convention and Visitor's Bureau,** 701 Brickell Ave., Suite 700, Miami, FL 33131 (© **800/933-8448** or 305/539-3000; fax 305/530-3113; www.tropicoolmiami.com). Several chambers of commerce in Greater Miami will send out information on their particular neighborhoods; for addresses and numbers, see "Visitor Information" in chapter 2.

If you arrive at the Miami International Airport, you can pick up visitor information at the airport's main visitor counter on the second floor of Concourse E: It's open 24 hours a day.

Always check local newspapers for special events during your visit. The city's only daily, the *Miami Herald,* is a good source for current-events listings, particularly the "Weekend" section in Friday's edition. Even better is the free weekly alternative paper the *Miami New Times,* available in bright red boxes throughout the city.

Information on everything from dining to entertainment in Miami is available on the Internet at www.miami.citysearch.com, www.digitalcity.com/southflorida, www.miaminewtimes.com, and www.herald.com.

CITY LAYOUT

Miami seems confusing at first but quickly becomes easy to navigate. The small cluster of buildings that makes up the downtown area is at the geographical heart of the city. In relation to downtown, the airport is northwest, the beaches are east, Coconut Grove is south, Coral Gables is west, and the rest of the city is north.

FINDING AN ADDRESS Miami is divided into dozens of areas with official and unofficial boundaries. Street numbering in the city of Miami is fairly straightforward, but you must first be familiar with the numbering system. The mainland is divided into four sections (NE, NW, SE, and SW) by the intersection of Flagler Street and Miami Avenue. Flagler divides Miami from north to south, and Miami Avenue divides the city from east to west. It's helpful to remember that avenues generally run north-south, while streets go east-west. Street numbers (1st St., 2nd St., and so forth) start from here and increase as you go farther out from this intersection, as do numbers of avenues, places, courts, terraces, and lanes. Streets in Hialeah are the exceptions to this pattern; they are listed separately in map indexes.

Getting around the barrier islands that make up Miami Beach is easier than moving around the mainland. Street numbering starts with 1st Street, near Miami Beach's southern tip, and goes up to 192nd Street, in the northern part of Sunny Isles. As in the city of Miami, some streets in Miami Beach have numbers as well as names. When listed in this book, both name and number are given.

The numbered streets in Miami Beach are not the geographical equivalents of those on the mainland, but they are close. For example, the 79th Street Causeway runs into 71st Street on Miami Beach.

STREET MAPS It's easy to get lost in sprawling Miami, so a reliable map is essential. The **Trakker Map of Miami** (www.trakkermaps.com) is a four-color accordion map that encompasses all of Dade County. Some maps of Miami list streets according to area, so you'll have to know which part of the city you are looking for before the street can be found.

THE NEIGHBORHOODS IN BRIEF

South Beach—The Art Deco District South Beach's 10 miles of beach are alive with a frenetic, circuslike atmosphere and are center stage for a motley crew of characters, from eccentric locals, seniors, snowbirds, and college students to gender benders, celebrities, club kids, and curiosity seekers: Individuality is as widely accepted on South Beach as Visa and MasterCard.

Bolstered by a Caribbean-chic cafe society and a sexually charged, tragically hip nightlife, people-watching on South Beach (1st St. to 23rd St.) is almost as good as a front-row seat at a Milan fashion show. And although the beautiful people do flock to South

Beach, the models aren't the only sights worth drooling over: The thriving Art Deco District within South Beach contains the largest concentration of Art Deco architecture in the world (in 1979, much of South Beach was listed in the National Register of Historic Places). The pastel-hued structures are supermodels in their own right—only *these* models improve with age.

Miami Beach In the fabulous '50s, Miami Beach was America's true Riviera. The stomping ground of choice for the Rat Pack and notorious mobsters such as Al Capone, its huge self-contained resort hotels were vacations unto themselves, providing a full day's worth of meals, activities, and entertainment. Then in the 1960s and 1970s, people who fell in love with Miami began to buy apartments rather than rent hotel rooms. Tourism declined, and many area hotels fell into disrepair.

However, since the late 1980s and South Beach's renaissance, Miami Beach has experienced a tide of revitalization. Huge beach hotels are finding their niche with new international tourist markets and are attracting large convention crowds. New generations of Americans are quickly rediscovering the qualities that originally made Miami Beach so popular, and they are finding out that the sand and surf now come with a thriving international city.

Before Miami Beach turns into Surfside, there's North Beach, where there are uncrowded beaches, some restaurants, and examples of Miami Modernism architecture. For information on North Beach and its slow renaissance, go to www.gonorthbeach.com.

Surfside, Bal Harbour, and **Sunny Isles** make up the north part of the beach (island). Hotels, motels, restaurants, and beaches line Collins Avenue and, with some outstanding exceptions,

the farther north one goes, the cheaper lodging becomes. Excellent prices, location, and facilities make Surfside and Sunny Isles attractive places to stay, although, despite a slow-going renaissance, they are still a little rough around the edges. A revitalization is in the works for these areas, and, while it's highly unlikely they will ever become as chic as South Beach, there is potential for this, especially as South Beach falls prey to the inevitable spoiler: commercialism. Keep in mind that beachfront properties are at a premium, so many of the area's moderately priced hotels have been converted to condominiums, leaving fewer and fewer affordable places to stay.

In exclusive and ritzy Bal Harbour, few hotels remain amid the many beachfront condominium towers. Instead, fancy homes, tucked away on the bay, hide behind gated communities, and the Rodeo Drive of Miami (known as the Bal Harbour Shops) attracts shoppers who don't flinch at four-, five-, and six-figure price tags.

Note that **North Miami Beach,** a residential area near the Dade-Broward County line (north of 163rd St.; part of N. Dade County), is a misnomer. It is actually northwest of Miami Beach, on the mainland, and has no beaches, though it does have some of Miami's better restaurants and shops. Located within North Miami Beach is the posh residential community of **Aventura,** best known for its high-priced condos, the Turnberry Isle Resort, and the Aventura Mall.

Note: South Beach, the historic Art Deco District, is treated as a separate neighborhood from Miami Beach.

Key Biscayne Miami's forested and secluded Key Biscayne is technically one of the first islands in the Florida Keys. However, this island is nothing like its southern neighbors. Located south of Miami Beach, off the shores of Coconut Grove, Key Biscayne is protected from the troubles of the mainland by the long Rickenbacker Causeway and its $1 toll.

Largely an exclusive residential community with million-dollar homes and sweeping water views, Key Biscayne also offers visitors great public beaches, some top (read: pricey) resort hotels, and several good restaurants. Hobie Beach, adjacent to the causeway, is the city's premier spot for windsurfing, sailboarding, and jet-skiing (see "Miami's Beaches" and "Watersports" in chapter 5). On the island's southern tip, Bill Baggs State Park has great beaches, bike paths, and dense forests for picnicking and partying.

Downtown Miami's downtown boasts one of the world's most beautiful cityscapes. Unfortunately, that's about all it offers—for now. During the day, a vibrant community of students, businesspeople, and merchants makes its way through the bustling streets, where vendors sell fresh-cut pineapples and mangos while young consumers on shopping sprees lug bags and boxes. However, at night, downtown is mostly desolate (except for NE 11th St., where there is a burgeoning nightlife scene) and not a place where you'd want to get lost. The downtown area does have a mall (Bayside Marketplace, where many cruise passengers come to browse), some culture (Metro-Dade Cultural Center), and a few decent restaurants, as well as the sprawling American Airlines Arena (home to the Miami Heat). A downtown revitalization project in the works promises a cultural arts center, urban-chic dwellings and lofts, and an assortment of hip boutiques, eateries, and bars, all to bring downtown back to a life it never really had. **The Downtown Miami Partnership** offers guided historic walking tours daily at 10:30am (© **305/379-7070**). For more information on Downtown, go to www.downtownmiami.com.

Design District With restaurants springing up between galleries and furniture stores galore, the Design District is, as locals say, the new South Beach, adding a touch of New York's SoHo to an area formerly known as downtown Miami's "Don't Go." The district, which is a hotbed for furniture-import companies, interior designers, architects, and more, has also become a player in Miami's ever-changing nightlife, with bars, lounges, clubs, and restaurants, ranging from uberchic and retro to progressive and indie, that have helped the area become hipster central for South Beach expatriates and artsy bohemian types. In anticipation of its growing popularity, the district has also banded together to create an up-to-date website, www.designmiami.com, which includes a calendar of events, such as the internationally lauded Art Basel, which attracts the who's who of the art world. The district is loosely defined as the area bounded by NE 2nd Avenue, NE 5th Avenue East and West, and NW 36th Street to the south.

Biscayne Corridor From downtown, near Bayside, to the 70s (affectionately known as the Upper East Side), where trendy curio shops and upscale restaurants are slowly opening, Biscayne Boulevard is aspiring to reclaim itself as a safe thoroughfare where tourists can wine, dine, and shop. Once known for sketchy, dilapidated 1950s- and 1960s-era hotels that had fallen on hard times, residents fleeing the high prices of the beaches in search of affordable housing are renovating Biscayne block by block, trying to make this famous boulevard worthy of a Sunday drive.

Little Havana If you've never been to Cuba, just visit this small section of Miami and you'll come pretty close. The sounds, tastes, and rhythms are very reminiscent of Cuba's capital city, and some say you don't have to speak a word of English to live an independent life here—even street signs are in Spanish and English.

Cuban coffee shops, tailor and furniture stores, and inexpensive restaurants line "Calle Ocho" (pronounced *Ka*-yey *O*-choh), SW 8th Street, the region's main thoroughfare. In Little Havana, salsa and merengue beats ring loudly from old record stores while old men in *guayaberas* (loose-fitting cotton short-sleeved shirts) smoke cigars over their daily game of dominoes. The spotlight focused on the neighborhood during the Elián González situation in 2000, but the area was previously noted for the groups of artists and nocturnal types who have moved their galleries and performance spaces here, sparking a culturally charged neobohemian nightlife.

Coral Gables "The City Beautiful," created by George Merrick in the early 1920s, is one of Miami's first planned developments. Houses here were built in a Mediterranean style along lush, tree-lined streets that open onto beautifully carved plazas, many with centerpiece fountains. The best architectural examples of the era have Spanish-style tiled roofs and are built from Miami oolite, native limestone commonly called "coral rock." The Gables's European-flaired shopping and commerce center is home to many thriving corporations. Coral Gables also has landmark hotels, great golfing, upscale shopping to rival Bal Harbour, and some of the city's best restaurants, headed by world-renowned chefs.

Coconut Grove An arty, hippie hangout in the psychedelic '60s, Coconut Grove has given way from swirls of tie-dyes to the uniform color schemes of the Gap. Chain stores, theme restaurants, a megaplex, and bars galore make Coconut Grove a commercial success, but this gentrification has pushed most alternative types out. Ritzier types have now resurfaced here, thanks, in part, to the anti-boho Ritz-Carlton Coconut Grove (p. 105). The intersection of Grand Avenue, Main Highway, and McFarlane Road pierces the area's heart. Right in the center of it all is Coco-Walk and the Shops at Mayfair, filled with boutiques, eateries, and bars. Sidewalks here are often crowded, especially at night, when University of Miami students come out to play.

Southern Miami–Dade County To locals, South Miami is both a specific area, southwest of Coral Gables, and a general region that encompasses all of southern Dade County, including Kendall, Perrine, Cutler Ridge, and Homestead. For the purposes of clarity, this book has grouped all these southern suburbs under the rubric "Southern Miami–Dade County." The area is heavily residential and packed with strip malls amid a few remaining plots of farmland. Tourists don't usually stay in these parts, unless they are on their way to the Everglades or the Keys. However, southern Miami–Dade County contains many of the city's top attractions (see chapter 5), meaning that you're likely to spend at least some of your time in Miami here.

2 Getting Around

Officially, Dade County has opted for a "unified, multimodal transportation network," which basically means you can get around the city by train, bus, and taxi. However, in practice, the network doesn't work very well. Things may improve when the city hopefully completes its long-awaited transportation center, but until then, unless you are going from downtown Miami to a not-too-distant spot, you are better off in a rental car or taxi.

With the exception of downtown Coconut Grove and South Beach, Miami is not a walker's city. Because it is so spread out, most attractions are too far apart to make walking between them feasible. In fact, most Miamians are so used to driving that they do so even when going just a few blocks.

BY PUBLIC TRANSPORTATION

BY RAIL   Two rail lines, operated by the **Metro-Dade Transit Agency** (© 305/ 770-3131 for information; www.co.miami-dade.fl.us/mdta), run in concert with each other.

Metrorail, the city's modern high-speed commuter train, is a 21-mile elevated line that travels north-south, between downtown Miami and the southern suburbs. Locals like to refer to this semi-useless rail system as Metro*fail*. If you are staying in Coral Gables or Coconut Grove, you can park your car at a nearby station and ride the rails downtown. However, that's about it. There are plans to extend the system to service Miami International Airport, but until those tracks are built, these trains don't go most places tourists go, with the exception of Vizcaya (p. 146) in Coconut Grove. Metrorail operates daily from about 6am to midnight. The fare is $1.25.

Metromover, a 4½-mile elevated line, circles the downtown area and connects with Metrorail at the Government Center stop. Riding on rubber tires, the single-car train winds past many of the area's most important attractions and its shopping and business districts. You may not go very far on the Metromover, but you will get a beautiful perspective from the towering height of the suspended rails. System hours are daily from about 6am to midnight, and the ride is free.

BY BUS   Miami's suburban layout is not conducive to getting around by bus. Lines operate and maps are available, but instead of getting to know the city, you'll find that relying on bus transportation will acquaint you only with how it feels to wait at bus stops. In short, a bus ride in Miami is grueling. You can get a bus map by mail, either from the Greater Miami Convention and Visitor's Bureau (see "Visitor Information," earlier in this chapter) or by writing the Metro-Dade Transit System, 3300 NW 32nd Ave., Miami, FL 33142. In Miami, call © **305/770-3131** for public-transit information. The fare is $1.25.

BY CAR

Tales circulate about vacationers who have visited Miami without a car, but they are very few indeed. If you are counting on exploring the city, even to a modest degree, a car is essential. Miami's restaurants, hotels, and attractions are far from one another, so any other form of transportation is relatively impractical. You won't need a car, however, if you are spending your entire vacation at a resort, are traveling directly to the Port of Miami for a cruise, or are here for a short stay centered on one area of the city, such as South Beach, where everything is within walking distance and parking is a costly nightmare.

When driving across a causeway or through downtown, allow extra time to reach your destination because of frequent drawbridge openings. Some bridges open about every half-hour for large sailing vessels to make their way through the wide bays and canals that crisscross the city, stalling traffic for several minutes.

RENTALS   It seems as though every car-rental company, big and small, has at least one office in Miami. Consequently, the city is one of the cheapest places in the world to rent a car. Many firms regularly advertise prices in the neighborhood of $150 per week for their economy cars. You should also check with your airline: There are often special discounts when you book a flight and reserve your rental car simultaneously. A minimum age, generally 25, is usually required of renters; some rental agencies have also set maximum ages! A national car-rental broker, **Car Rental Referral Service** (© **800/404-4482**), can often find companies willing to rent to drivers between the ages of 21 and 24 and can also get discounts from major companies as well as some regional ones.

National car-rental companies, with toll-free numbers, include **Alamo** (© 800/327-9633; www.goalamo.com), **Avis** (© 800/331-1212; www.avis.com), **Budget** (© 800/527-0700; www.budget.com), **Dollar** (© 800/800-4000 or 800/327-7607; www.dollar.com), **Hertz** (© 800/654-3131; www.hertz.com), **National** (© 800/328-4567; www.nationalcar.com), and **Thrifty** (© 800/367-2277; www.thrifty.com). One excellent company that has offices in every conceivable part of town and offers extremely competitive rates is **Enterprise** (© 800/325-8007; www.enterprise.com). Comparison-shop before you make any decisions—car-rental prices can fluctuate more than airfares.

Many car-rental companies also offer cellular phones or electronic map rentals. It might be wise to opt for these additional safety features (the phone will definitely come in handy if you get lost), although the cost can be exorbitant.

Finally, think about splurging on a convertible. Not only are convertibles one of the best ways to see the beautiful surroundings, but they're also an ideal way to perfect a tan!

PARKING   Always keep plenty of quarters on hand to feed hungry meters, most of which have been removed in favor of those pesky parking payment stations where you feed a machine and get a printed receipt to display on your dash. Or, on Miami Beach, stop by the chamber of commerce at 1920 Meridian Ave. or any Publix grocery store to buy a magnetic **parking card** in denominations of $10, $20, or $25. Parking is usually plentiful (except on South Beach and Coconut Grove), but when it's not, be careful: Fines for illegal parking can be stiff, starting at $18 for an expired meter and going way up from there.

In addition to parking garages, valet services are commonplace and often used. Because parking is such a premium in bustling South Beach as well as in Coconut Grove, prices tend to be jacked up—especially at night and when there are special events (day or night). You can expect to pay an average of $5 to $15 for parking in these areas.

LOCAL DRIVING RULES   Florida law allows drivers to make a right turn on a red light after a complete stop, unless otherwise indicated. In addition, all passengers are required to wear seat belts, and children under 3 must be securely fastened in government-approved car seats.

BY TAXI

If you're not planning on traveling much within the city (and especially if you plan on spending your vacation within the confines of South Beach's Art Deco District), an occasional taxi is a good alternative to renting a car and dealing with the parking hassles that come with renting your own car. Taxi meters start at $2.50 for the first quarter-mile and cost $2.40 for each additional mile. There are standard flat-rate charges for frequently traveled routes—for example, Miami Beach's Convention Center to Coconut Grove will cost about $20.

Major cab companies include **Yellow Cab** (✆ **305/444-4444**) and, on Miami Beach, **Central** (✆ **305/532-5555**).

BY BIKE

Miami is a biker's paradise, especially on Miami Beach, where the hard-packed sand and boardwalks make it an easy and scenic route. However, unless you are a former New York City bike messenger, you won't want to use a bicycle as your main means of transportation.

For more information on bicycles, including where to rent the best ones, see "More Ways to Play, Indoors & Out," in chapter 5.

FAST FACTS: Miami

Airport See "Orientation," earlier in this chapter.

American Express You'll find American Express offices in downtown Miami at 100 N. Biscayne Blvd. (✆ 305/358-7350; open Mon–Fri 9am–5pm); 9700 Collins Ave., Bal Harbour (✆ 305/865-5959; open Mon–Sat 10am–6pm); and 32 Miracle Mile, Coral Gables (✆ 305/446-3381; open Mon–Fri 9am–5pm and Sat 10am–4pm). To report lost or stolen traveler's checks, call ✆ 800/221-7282.

Area Code The original area code for Miami and all of Dade County was 305. That is still the code for older phone numbers, but all phone numbers assigned since July 1998 have the area code 786 (SUN). For all local calls, even if you're just calling across the street, you must dial the area code (305 or 786) first. Even though the Keys still share the Dade County area code of 305, calls to there from Miami are considered long distance and must be preceded by 1-305. (Within the Keys, simply dial the seven-digit number.) The area code for Fort Lauderdale is 954; for Palm Beach, Boca Raton, Vero Beach, and Port St. Lucie, it's 561.

Business Hours Banking hours vary, but most banks are open weekdays from 9am to 3pm. Several stay open until 5pm or so at least 1 day during the week, and most banks feature automated teller machines (ATMs) for 24-hour banking. Most stores are open daily from 10am to 6pm; however, there are many exceptions (noted in " Shopping," in chapter 5, beginning on p. 165). As far as business offices are concerned, Miami is generally a 9-to-5 town.

Car Rentals See "Getting Around," above.

Climate See "When to Go," in chapter 2.

Curfew Although not strictly enforced, there is an alleged curfew in effect for minors after 11pm on weeknights and midnight on weekends in all of Miami–Dade County. After those hours, children under 17 cannot be out on the streets or driving unless accompanied by a parent or on their way to work. Somehow, however, they still manage to sneak out and congregate in popular areas such as Coconut Grove and South Beach.

Dentists **A&E Dental Associates,** 11400 N. Kendall Dr., Mega Bank Building (✆ 305/271-7777), offers 'round-the-clock care and accepts MasterCard and Visa.

Doctors In an emergency, call an ambulance by dialing ℂ **911** (a free call) from any phone. The Dade County Medical Association sponsors a **Physician Referral Service** (ℂ **305/324-8717**), weekdays from 9am to 5pm. **Health South Doctors' Hospital,** 5000 University Dr., Coral Gables (ℂ **305/666-2111**), is a 285-bed acute-care hospital with a 24-hour physician-staffed emergency department.

Driving Rules See "Getting Around," above.

Drugstores See "Pharmacies," below.

Emergencies To reach the police, ambulance, or fire department, dial ℂ **911** from any phone. No coins are needed. Emergency hot lines include **Crisis Intervention** (ℂ **305/358-HELP** or 305/358-4357) and the **Poison Information Center** (ℂ **800/222-1222**).

Eyeglasses **Pearle Vision Center,** 7901 Biscayne Blvd. (ℂ **305/754-5144**), can usually fill prescriptions in about an hour.

Hospitals See "Doctors," above.

Information See "Visitor Information," earlier in this chapter.

Internet Access Internet access is available at **Kafka's Cyber Cafe,** 1464 Washington Ave., South Beach (ℂ **305/673-9669**); the **South Beach Internet Cafe,** 1106 Collins Ave. (ℂ **305/532-4331**); and, no joke, the swanky all-in-one **Mobil Station,** at 2500 NW 87th Ave., Doral (ℂ **305/477-2501**).

Laundry/Dry Cleaning For dry cleaning, self-service machines, and a wash-and-fold service by the pound, call **All Laundry Service,** 5701 NW 7th St. (ℂ **305/261-8175**); it's open daily from 7am to 10pm. **Clean Machine Laundry,** 226 12th St., South Beach (ℂ **305/534-9429**), is convenient to South Beach's Art Deco hotels and is open 24 hours a day. **Coral Gables Laundry & Dry Cleaning,** 250 Minorca Ave., Coral Gables (ℂ **305/446-6458**), has been dry cleaning, altering, and laundering since 1930. It offers a lifesaving same-day service and is open weekdays from 7am to 7pm and Saturday from 8am to 3pm.

Liquor Laws Only adults 21 or older may legally purchase or consume alcohol in the state of Florida. Minors are usually permitted in bars, as long as the bars also serve food. Liquor laws are strictly enforced; if you look young, carry identification. Beer and wine are sold in most supermarkets and convenience stores. The city of Miami's liquor stores are closed on Sunday. Liquor stores in the city of Miami Beach are open daily.

Lost Property If you lost something at the airport, call the **Airport Lost and Found** office (ℂ **305/876-7377**). If you lost something on the bus, Metrorail, or Metromover, call **Metro-Dade Transit Agency** (ℂ **305/770-3131**). If you lost something anywhere else, phone the **Dade County Police Lost and Found** (ℂ **305/375-3366**). You may also want to fill out a police report for insurance purposes.

Luggage Storage/Lockers In addition to the baggage check at Miami International Airport, most hotels offer luggage-storage facilities. If you are taking a cruise from the Port of Miami (see "Cruises & Other Caribbean Getaways," in chapter 5), bags can be stored in your ship's departure terminal.

Newspapers/Magazines The **Miami Herald** is the city's only English-language daily. It is especially known for its extensive Latin American coverage and has a decent Friday "Weekend" entertainment guide. The most respected alternative weekly is the giveaway tabloid called **New Times,** which contains up-to-date listings and reviews of food, films, theater, music, and whatever else is happening in town. Also free, if you can find it, is **Ocean Drive,** an oversize glossy magazine that's limited on text (no literary value) and heavy on ads and society photos. It's what you should read if you want to know who's who and where to go for fun; it's available at a number of chic South Beach boutiques and restaurants. It is also available on newsstands.

For a large selection of foreign-language newspapers and magazines, check with any of the large bookstores (see chapter 5) or try **News Cafe,** 800 Ocean Dr., South Beach (© 305/538-6397). Adjacent to the **Van Dyke Cafe,** 846 Lincoln Rd., South Beach (© 305/534-3600), is a fantastic newsstand with magazines and newspapers from all over the world. Also check out **Eddie's News,** 1096 Normandy Dr., Miami Beach (© 305/866-2661); and **Worldwide News,** 1629 NE 163rd St., North Miami Beach (© 305/940-4090).

Pharmacies **Walgreens Pharmacy** has dozens of locations all over town, including 8550 Coral Way (© 305/221-9271), in Coral Gables; 1845 Alton Rd. (© 305/531-8868), in South Beach; and 6700 Collins Ave. (© 305/861-6742), in Miami Beach. The branch at 5731 Bird Rd. at SW 40th Street (© 305/666-0757) is open 24 hours, as is **CVS,** 6460 S. Dixie Hwy., in South Miami (© 305/661-0778).

Photographic Needs **One Hour Photo,** in the Bayside Marketplace (© 305/377-FOTO), is pricey (about $20 to develop and print a roll of 36 pictures), but they're open Monday to Saturday from 10am to 10pm, and Sunday from noon to 8pm. Walgreens or Eckerd (see above, under "Pharmacies") will develop film for the next day for about $10.

Police For emergencies, dial © 911 from any phone. No coins are needed for this call. For other police matters, call © 305/595-6263.

Post Office The **Main Post Office,** 2200 Milam Dairy Rd., Miami, FL 33152 (© 800/275-8777), is located west of the Miami International Airport. Conveniently located post offices include 1300 Washington Ave. in South Beach and 3191 Grand Ave. in Coconut Grove. There is one central number for all post offices: © 800/275-8777.

Radio On the AM dial, 610 (WIOD), 790 (WNWS), 1230 (WJNO), and 1340 (WPBR) are all talk. There is no all-news station in town, although 940 (WINZ) gives traffic updates and headline news in between its talk shows. WDBF (1420) is a good big-band station, and WPBG (1290) features golden oldies. Switching to the FM dial, the two most popular R&B stations are WEDR/99 Jams (99.1) and Hot 105 (105.1). The best rock stations on the FM dial are WZTA (94.9), WBGG/Big 106 (105.9), and the progressive college station WVUM (90.5). WKIS (99.9) is the top country station. Top-40 music can be heard on WHYI (100.3), and hip-hop on Mega 103 (103.5). For more hip-hop and dance music, Power 96 (96.5) WPOW will help to get your groove on. WGTR (97.3) plays easy listening, WDNA (88.9) has the best Latin jazz and multiethnic sounds, and public radio can be heard either on WXEL (90.7) or WLRN (91.3).

Religious Services Miami houses of worship are as varied as the city's population and include St. Patrick Catholic Church, 3716 Garden Ave., Miami Beach (© 305/531-1124); Coral Gables Baptist Church, 5501 Granada Blvd. (© 305/665-4072); Temple Judea, 5500 Granada Blvd., Coral Gables (© 305/667-5657); Coconut Grove United Methodist, 2850 SW 27th Ave. (© 305/443-0880); Christ Episcopal Church, 3481 Hibiscus St., Coconut Grove (© 305/442-8542); Plymouth Congregational Church, 3400 Devon Rd., at Main Highway, Coconut Grove (© 305/444-6521); Masjid Al-Ansar (Muslim), 5245 NW 7th Ave., Miami (© 305/757-8741); and Buddhist Temple of Miami, 15200 SW 240th St., Homestead (© 305/245-2702).

Restrooms Stores rarely let customers use their restrooms, and many restaurants offer their facilities only for their patrons. However, most malls have restrooms, as do many fast-food restaurants. Public beaches and large parks often provide toilets, though in some places you have to pay or tip an attendant. Most large hotels have clean restrooms in their lobbies.

Safety As always, use your common sense and be aware of your surroundings at all times. Don't walk alone at night, and be extra wary when walking or driving though downtown Miami and surrounding areas.

Reacting to several highly publicized crimes against tourists several years ago, both local and state governments have taken steps to help protect visitors. These measures include special highly visible police units patrolling the airport and surrounding neighborhoods, and better signs on the state's most tourist-traveled routes.

Spas & Massage There are a number of great spa packages at some of the ritzier hotels, but those without spas often have relationships with on-call massage therapists, which can be arranged by asking the concierge to make an appointment for an in-room session. Popular day spas include the **Russian Turkish Baths,** 5445 Collins Ave. at the Castle Hotel (© 305/867-8313), otherwise known as "The Schvitz," where the old guard meets the new in eucalyptus-scented Turkish steam rooms and aroma baths bolstered by marble columns. **Browne's Beauty Lounge,** 841 Lincoln Rd., Miami Beach (© 305/532-8703), has expanded from a small second-floor salon into a full-service, 5,250-square-foot spa, offering massages, waxing, manicures, and a sublime signature hot-rock massage. **Le Spa Miami,** 150 8th St., Miami Beach (© 305/674-6744), is one of the best day spas in the area, exclusively using Lancôme products and featuring a laundry list of facials, body treatments, makeup applications, waxing, manicures, pedicures, and even photo shoots. **The Beauties Club Day Spa,** 919 W. 39th St., Miami Beach (© 786/276-9991), is a membership day spa that also caters to nonmembers, offering a series of treatments, including body detox and slim-and-firm treatments. Best known for introducing the uberpopular bare-it-all Brazilian bikini wax to the United States, the **J Sisters,** 663 Lincoln Rd., Miami Beach (© 305/672-7142), have finally brought their epilating expertise to Miami from New York so that the likes of Gwyneth and J-Lo can take care of business while in town.

As far as hotel spas go, my three favorites are at the Standard on South Beach; the Mandarin Oriental, Miami; and the Ritz-Carlton, Key Biscayne.

The Spa at Mandarin Oriental is where the likes of Cher, J-Lo, and P. Diddy are pampered with treatments such as the 4-hour Ultimate Spa Indulgence that includes a welcome foot ritual, purifying herbal linen wrap with hot stones, facial cleanse, body exfoliation, body wrap with fresh algae and nourishing mud, Ayurvedic holistic massage, heated volcanic stones or oil-pouring Shirodhara, herbal tea, two-course lunch, aromatherapy facial, holistic hand and nail treatment, foot and nail treatment, yoga, Oriental bath soak, and choice of Thai massage or Shiatsu. You needn't be a celebrity to experience this spa's stellar treatment.

The Ritz-Carlton, Key Biscayne's spa, has 20,000 square feet of space overlooking the Atlantic Ocean. It features unheard-of treatments such as the Rum Molasses Waterfall treatment (a combination massage/hair treatment), the Key Lime Coconut Body Scrub, and the Everglades Grass Body Wrap.

Hip hotelier Andre Balazs pulled out all the stops when renovating the old-school, Borscht Belt–style Lido Spa and transforming it into South Beach's very own branch of LA's hip **Standard Hotel**. While Tinseltown's Standards are high, the South Beach version breaks new ground in town as a bona fide spa hotel complete with hundreds of treatments, including an authentic Turkish hamam, the Wall of Sound Shower, a cedar sauna room, and more.

Taxes A 6% state sales tax (plus .5% local tax, for a total of 6.5% in Miami–Dade County [from Homestead to North Miami Beach]) is added on at the register for all goods and services purchased in Florida. In addition, most municipalities levy special taxes on restaurants and hotels. In Surfside, hotel taxes total 10.5%; in Bal Harbour, 9.5%; in Miami Beach (including South Beach), 11.5%; and in the rest of Dade County, a whopping 12.5%. In Miami Beach, Surfside, and Bal Harbour, the resort (hotel) tax also applies to hotel restaurants and restaurants with liquor licenses.

Taxis See "Getting Around," earlier in this chapter.

Television The local stations are channel 4, WFOR (CBS); channel 6, WTVJ (NBC); channel 7, WSVN (FOX); channel 10, WPLG (ABC); channel 17, WLRN (PBS); channel 23, WLTV (independent); and channel 33, WBFS (independent). Channel 39 is the WB (WBZL), and channel 33 is UPN (WBFS).

Time Zone Miami, like New York, is in the Eastern Standard Time (EST) zone. Between April and October, daylight saving time is adopted, and clocks are set 1 hour ahead. America's eastern seaboard is 5 hours behind Greenwich Mean Time. To find out what time it is, call ✆ **305/324-8811.**

Transit Information For Metrorail or Metromover schedule information, phone ✆ **305/770-3131** or surf over to www.co.miami-dade.fl.us/mdta/.

Weather Hurricane season in Miami runs June through November. For an up-to-date recording of current weather conditions and forecast reports, call ✆ **305/229-4522.** Also see the "When to Go" section in chapter 2 for more information on the weather.

3 Where to Stay in Miami

As much a part of the landscape as the palm trees, many of Miami's hotels are on display as if they were contestants in a beauty pageant. The city's long-lasting status on the destination A-list has given rise to an ever-increasing number of upscale hotels, and no place in Miami has seen a greater increase in construction than Miami Beach. Since the area's renaissance, which began in the late 1980s, the beach has turned what used to be a beachfront retirement community into a sand-swept hot spot for the Gucci and Prada set. Contrary to popular belief, however, the beach does not discriminate, and it's the juxtaposition of the chic elite and the hoi polloi that contributes to its allure.

While the increasing demand for rooms on South Beach means increasing costs, you can still find a decent room at a fair price. In fact, most hotels in the Art Deco District are less Ritz-Carlton than they are Holiday Inn, unless, of course, they've been renovated (many hotels in this area were built in the 1930s for the middle class). Unless you plan your vacation entirely in and around your hotel, most of the cheaper Deco hotels are adequate and a wise choice for those who plan to use the room only to sleep. Smart vacationers can almost name their price if they're willing to live without a few luxuries, such as an oceanfront view.

Many of the old hotels from the 1930s, 1940s, and 1950s have been totally renovated, giving way to dozens of "boutique" (small, swanky, and independently owned) hotels. Keep in mind that when a hotel claims that it was just renovated, it can mean that they've completely gutted the building—or just applied a coat of fresh paint. Always ask what specific changes were made during a renovation, and be sure to ask if a hotel will be undergoing construction while you're there. You should also find out how near your room will be to the center of the nightlife crowd; trying to sleep directly on Ocean Drive or Collins and Washington avenues, especially during the weekend, is next to impossible, unless your lullaby of choice happens to include throbbing salsa and bass beats.

The best hotel options in each price category and those that have been fully upgraded recently are listed below. You should also know that along South Beach's Collins Avenue, there are dozens of hotels and motels—in all price categories—so there's bound to be a vacancy somewhere. If you do try the walk-in routine, don't forget to ask to see a room first. A few dollars extra could mean all the difference between flea and fabu.

While South Beach may be the nucleus of all things hyped and hip, it's not the only place with hotels. The advantage to staying on South Beach as opposed to, say, Coral Gables or Coconut Grove, is that the beaches are within walking distance, the nightlife and restaurant options are aplenty, and, basically, everything you would need is right there. However, staying there is definitely not for everyone. If you're wary, don't worry: South Beach is centrally located and only about a 15- to 30-minute drive from most other parts of Miami.

For a less expensive stay that's only a 10-minute cab ride from South Beach, Miami Beach proper (the area north of 23rd St. and Collins Ave. all the way up to 163rd St. and Collins Ave.) offers a slew of reasonable stays, right on the beach, that won't cost you your kids' college education fund.

What *will* cost you a small fortune are the luxury hotels located in the city's financial Brickell Avenue district, the area of choice for expense-account business travelers and camera-shy celebrities trying to avoid the South Beach spotlight.

For a less frenetic, more relaxed, and more tropical experience, the resorts on Key Biscayne exude an island feel, even though, across the water, a cosmopolitan vibe beckons, thanks to the shimmering, spectacular Miami skyline.

Those who'd rather bag the beach in favor of shopping bags will enjoy North Miami Beach's proximity to the Aventura Mall. And for Miami with an Old World European flair, Coral Gables and its charming hotels and exquisite restaurants provide a more prim and proper, well-heeled perspective of Miami than the trendy boutique and condo hotels on South Beach.

SEASONS & RATES   South Florida's tourist season is well defined, beginning in mid-November and lasting until Easter. Hotel prices escalate until about March, after which they begin to decline. During the off season, hotel rates are typically 30% to 50% lower than their winter highs. But timing isn't everything. Rates also depend on your hotel's proximity to the beach and how much ocean you can see from your window. Small motels a block or two from the water can be up to 40% cheaper than similar properties right on the sand.

Rates below have been broken down into two broad categories: winter (generally, Thanksgiving through Easter) and off season (about mid-May through Aug). The months in between, the shoulder season, should fall somewhere in between the highs and lows, while rates always go up on holidays. Remember, too, that state and city taxes can add as much as 12.5% to your bill in some parts of Miami. Some hotels, especially those in South Beach, also tack on additional service charges, and don't forget that parking is a pricey endeavor.

PRICE CATEGORIES   The hotels below are divided first by area and then by price (**very expensive, expensive, moderate,** or **inexpensive**). Prices are based on published rates (or rack rates) for a standard double room during the high season. You should also check with the reservations agent, since many rooms are available above and below the category ranges listed below, and ask about packages, since it's often possible to get a better deal than these "official" rates. Most important, always call the hotel to confirm rates, which may be subject to change without notice because of special events, holidays, or blackout dates.

LONG-TERM STAYS   If you plan to visit Miami for a month, a season, or more, think about renting a condominium apartment or a room in a long-term hotel. Long-term accommodations exist in every price category, from budget to deluxe, and in general are extremely reasonable, especially during the off season. Check with the reservation services below, or write a short note to the chamber of commerce in the area where you plan to stay. In addition, many local real estate agents handle short-term rentals (meaning less than a year).

RESERVATION SERVICES   **Central Reservation Service** (© **800/950-0232** or 305/274-6832; www.reservation-services.com) works with many of Miami's hotels and can often secure discounts of up to 40%. It also gives advice on specific locales, especially in Miami Beach and downtown. During holiday time, there may be a minimum of a 3- to 5-day stay to use their services. Call for more information.

For bed-and-breakfast information throughout the state, contact **Florida Bed and Breakfast Inns** (© **800/524-1880;** www.florida-inns.com). For information on the ubiquitous boutique hotels, check out the Greater Miami Convention and Visitor's Bureau's new website, www.miamiboutiquehotels.com.

SOUTH BEACH

Choosing a hotel on South Beach is similar to deciding whether you'd rather pay $2 for french fries at Denny's or $10 for the same fries—but let's call them *pomme frites*—in a pricey haute cuisinerie. It's all about atmosphere. The rooms of some hotels may *look* ultrachic, but they can be as comfortable as sleeping on a concrete slab. Once you decide how much atmosphere you want, the choice will be easier. Fortunately, for every chichi hotel in South Beach—and there are many—there are just as many moderately priced, more casual options.

Prices mentioned here are rack rates—that is, the price you would be quoted if you walked up to the front desk and inquired about rates. The actual price you will end up paying will usually be less than this—especially if a travel agent makes the reservations for you. Many hotels on South Beach have chosen to go with a low-to-high rate representing the hotel's complete pricing range. It pays to try to negotiate the price of a room. In some of the trendier hotels, however, negotiating is highly unfashionable and not well regarded. In other words, your attempt at negotiation will either be met with a blank stare or a snippy refusal. It never hurts to try, though.

If status is important to you, as it is to many South Beach visitors, then you will be quite pleased with the number of haute hotels in the area. But the times may be a-changin': Not so long ago, Courtyard by Marriott (© **800/321-2211** or 305/604-8887) debuted a 90-room, moderately priced hotel on a seedy stretch of Washington Avenue, smack in the middle of Clubland, a horror to many a South Beach trendoid.

Note: Art Deco hotels, while pleasing to the eye, may be a bit run-down inside. Par for the course on South Beach, where appearances are, at times, deceiving.

To locate the hotels in this section, see the "South Beach" map (p. 83).

VERY EXPENSIVE

The Delano ✦ *Overrated* Before Ian Schrager revamped (emphasis on the *vamp*) the neighboring The Shore Club hotel, The Delano was the reigning force in the hierarchy of hip hotel royalty. But that was then. Today The Delano, a place where smiles from staffers were as rare as snow in Miami, is kinder and gentler, which, for some, takes away the whole cache of staying here. But it certainly still is amusing to look at—with 40-foot sheer white billowing curtains hanging outside, mirrors everywhere, Adirondack chairs, and faux fur–covered beds. The rooms are done up sanitarium style: sterile, yet terribly trendy, in pure white save for a perfectly crisp green Granny Smith apple in each room—the only freebie you're going to get here. A bathroom renovation recently took place in all of the rooms—but they remain small and spartan.

An attractive, white-clad staff looks as if they were hand-picked from last month's *Vogue.* While they may sigh if you ask for something, eventually they'll get it for you. The gym here is great (especially if you're looking for celebrities), and the powers that be finally waived the extra fee that guests had to pay to use it. The fantastic wading pool, thankfully, is free, but get out early to snag a chair. The Blue Door restaurant, formerly part-owned by Madonna, serves lots of attitude with its pricey haute cuisine, and for a quick bite of pricey sashimi, grab a seat at the communal eat-in-kitchen table at **Blue Sea,** the hotel's superb sushi bar. The lobby's **Rose Bar** is command central for the chic elite who don't flinch at paying in excess of $10 for a martini. At Agua, the rooftop spa, an hour massage while overlooking the ocean is blissful (if you can afford it).

1685 Collins Ave., South Beach, FL 33139. © **800/555-5001** or 305/672-2000. Fax 305/532-0099. www.delanohotel.com. 195 units, 1 penthouse. Winter $650–$925 standard, $1,050–$2,100 suite, $2,000–$3,000 bungalow or 2-bedroom, $2,900–$3,800 penthouse; off season $315–$795 standard, $950–$2,000 suite, $1,500–$3,000 bungalow or 2-bedroom, $2,400–$3,000 penthouse. Additional person $25. AE, DC, DISC, MC, V. Valet parking $25. **Amenities:** 3 restaurants (featuring the acclaimed Blue Door); bar; large outdoor pool; state-of-the-art David Barton gym; extensive watersports equipment; children's programs; concierge; business center; room service; in-room massage; same-day laundry and dry-cleaning services. *In room:* A/C, TV/VCR, CD player, Wi-Fi, minibar, hair dryer, safe.

Hotel Victor ★★★   This hotel is a victory for Ocean Drive, a street that hasn't seen a fabulous new hotel since The Tides. A sexy hotel with actual substance, Hotel Victor is a hyperluxe, 91-room boutique hotel designed by Parisian Jacques Garcia—this is his first hotel foray in the United States. Best known for his design work at Paris's tragically hip Hotel Costes and the discriminating Sultan of Brunei, Garcia has lent his exquisite taste to this hotel located on notoriously tacky Ocean Drive. Located directly across from the ocean and next to the legendary Versace mansion (now a private club), Hotel Victor stands apart from the rest of the cookie-cutter minimalist Miami hotels, breaking from bare minimalism and daring to go bold with color and rich fabrics. The opulent lobby is inviting and sceney, with lounges on two levels and an Asian motif, a large jellyfish tank, and hanging lamps resembling the stinging creatures. What also stings is the price tag here, but you're paying for the privilege of staying in a hotel that greets guests with personalized, wireless check-in, among other things. Deluxe rooms are just that, all with ocean views and with richly colored satin headboards and curtain trim, white marble, ebony-lacquered furniture, a full—not mini—bar, flat-screen plasma TVs and massive white-marbled bathrooms with infinity-edge bathtubs and rain-head shower heads. If you can afford it, choose a Pool Bungalow room, with private outdoor shower and terraces leading to the pool area. Ocean Suites feature infinity-edge tubs and panoramic views of the ocean. And if you think the inside is sexy, wait until you see the outdoor area, where the gorgeous second-level, oceanview pool is surrounded by oversize daybeds and cabana tents, which at night turn into a lush VIP lounge for those who rate. The hotel's upscale bistro, Vix, is also a magnet for the fabulati, but the Turkish Spa is the hottest spot, with its large unisex steam room, Turkish hammam, and heated marble slabs.

1144 Ocean Dr., South Beach, FL 33139. ⓒ **305/428-1234.** Fax 305/421-6281. www.hotelvictorsouthbeach.com. 91 units. Winter $470–$800 double; off season $330–$650 double. AE, DC, DISC, MC, V. Valet parking $25. **Amenities:** 2 restaurants; 4 bars; outdoor pool; 6,000-ft. fitness center, spa, and Turkish hammam; concierge; room service; book and music library. *In room:* A/C, TV/DVD, stereo system with CD players, Wi-Fi, minibar, hair dryer.

Loews Hotel ★ *Kids*   The Loews Hotel is one of the largest beach hotels to arrive in South Beach in almost 30 years, consuming an unprecedented 900 feet of oceanfront. This 800-room behemoth is considered an eyesore by many, an architectural triumph by others. However you perceive it, you can't miss the hotel's multitiered cone-shape 18-story tower perched high above the rest of South Beach. Rooms are a bit boxy and bland, nothing to rave about, but are clean and have new carpets and bedspreads to erase signs of early wear and tear from the hotel's heavy traffic.

The best rooms are those that do not face the very congested Collins Avenue, since those tend to be quite noisy. Though Loews attempts to maintain the intimacy of an Art Deco hotel while trying to accommodate business travelers, it is so large that it tends to feel like a convention hall. You're not going to get personal doting service here, but the staff does try, even if it takes them a while. If you can steer your way

South Beach

through all the name-tagged businesspeople in the lobby, which, thanks to a popcorn machine, smells much like a megaplex, you can escape to the pool (with an undisputedly gorgeous, landscaped entrance that's more Maui than Miami), which is large enough to accommodate families and conventioneers alike. In addition to children's fare such as the Loews Loves Kids program—featuring special menus, tours, welcome gifts for children under 10, supervised programs, free stays for children under 18, and the Generation G program for grandparents and grandkids traveling together—the hotel hosts fun activities for adults, such as Dive in Movies at the pool, salsa lessons, and bingo. Emeril Lagasse opened Miami's first-ever Emeril's restaurant here.

1601 Collins Ave., South Beach, FL 33139. © **800/23-LOEWS** or 305/604-1601. www.loewshotels.com. 800 units. Winter from $399 double; off season from $249 double. AE, DC, DISC, MC, V. Valet parking $19. Pets accepted. **Amenities:** 3 restaurants; 3 bars; coffee bar; sprawling outdoor pool; health club; Jacuzzi; sauna; watersports rentals; children's programs; concierge; business center; 24-hr. room service; babysitting; dry cleaning. *In room:* A/C, TV, dataport, minibar, coffeemaker, hair dryer.

The Regent South Beach ★★★

At press time, they were putting the finishing touches on this swank, $76 million, 80-suite, five-story hotel. With two entrances, one on Ocean Drive and one on Collins Avenue, the beach and nightlife are literally at your doorsteps. Best of all, a branch of LA hotspot Table 8, the restaurant helmed by celeb chef Govind Armstrong, is housed here in 8,000 square feet of indoor and outdoor space. Fifty-three suites all have about 500 square feet of indoor space and 225 of balcony space—27 spectacular penthouses have retractable awnings and spiral staircases leading to private rooftop terraces coming in at a whopping 600 square feet. All suites have Jerusalem stone floors and entertainment centers with wet bars, fully stocked private bars, and espresso machines. But that's not all. Every suite has floor-to-ceiling soundproof windows that provide spectacular views of the hustle and bustle of South Beach and, of course, the ocean. Bathrooms are huge, with marble floors, granite countertops, two vanity areas, and a huge shower with wall sprays and a rain shower. Feather beds, duvets, and goose-down pillows make it hard to leave the room, as does the Bose surround sound and two flat-screen TVs. A stunning glass-bottom pool provides prime viewing of the lounge scene at Table 8 below, and the open-air fitness center with all the latest equipment is a refreshing (temperature-controlled) change from the usual stuffy gyms. The Regent Spa provides services in the comfort of your own room, which is almost as convenient as the hotel's on-premises car service that will take you wherever you need to go at no additional cost. For those who insist on working, the wireless Internet connection is even available on your balcony.

1458 Ocean Dr., South Beach, FL 33139. © **800/545-4000** or 305/674-4554. Fax 305/674-4553. www.regenthotels. com. 83 units. Winter $355–$1,050 suite; off season $215–$595 suite. AE, DC, DISC, MC, V. Valet parking $20. **Amenities:** Restaurant; lounge; pool; spa and fitness center; 24-hour concierge; 24-hour room service. *In room:* A/C, TV, DVD, CD player, Wi-Fi, minibar, coffeemaker, hair dryer, iron, safe.

The Ritz-Carlton South Beach ★★★ *Kids*

The luxe life comes to a congested and somewhat seedy corner of South Beach in the form of this beachfront, lushly landscaped Ritz-Carlton. This Ritz has restored the landmark Morris Lapidus–designed 1950s DiLido Hotel to its original Art Moderne style and filled it with the hotel's signature five-star service. Far from ostentatious, The Ritz-Carlton's South Beach property moves away from gilded opulence in favor of the more soothing pastel-washed touches of Deco. An impressive $2 million art collection consisting of original works by Joan Miro, among others, will be on permanent loan to the hotel from Diana

Lowenstein Fine Art, which also happens to have a gallery in the hotel. (Mrs. Lowenstein is a principal owner of The Ritz-Carlton South Beach.) Though South Beach is better known for its trendy boutique hotels, The Ritz-Carlton offers comfort to those who might prefer 100% cotton Frette sheets and goose-down pillows to high-style minimalism. The best rooms, by far, are the 72 poolside and oceanview lanai rooms. Oh yeah, and there's also a tanning butler who will spritz you with SPF and water whenever you want.

With impeccable service, an elevated pool that provides unobstructed views of the Atlantic, an impressive stretch of sand with a fabulous beach club, and a world-class 13,000-square-foot spa and wellness center, The Ritz-Carlton kicks sand in the faces of some of the smaller hotels that think they're doing *you* a favor by allowing you to sleep there. Plus, for those with kids in tow, they have the Ritz Kids program for kids ages 5 through 12, which features supervised activities, movies, beach excursions, and more.

1 Lincoln Rd., South Beach, FL 33139. © **800/241-3333** or 786/276-4000. Fax 786/276-4001. www.ritzcarlton.com. 375 units. Winter $450–$720 double suite; off season $245–$545 double suite. AE, DISC, MC, V. Valet parking $30. **Amenities:** 3 restaurants; 3 bars; outdoor heated pool; health club; spa; extensive watersports rentals; children's program; 24-hr. business center; salon; 24-hr. room service; babysitting; overnight laundry service; beach service. *In room:* A/C, TV, dataport, minibar, hair dryer, iron, safe.

The Sagamore ☆☆☆

Located just two doors down from the hauter-than-thou Delano Hotel is The Sagamore, quietly fabulous in its own right, with an ultramodern lobby-cum-art-gallery that's infinitely warmer than your typical pop-art exhibit at the Museum of Modern Art. And although the lobby and its requisite bar and lounge areas have become command central for the international chic elite and celebrities such as Will Smith, The Sagamore's all-suite, apartment-like rooms are havens from the hype, with all the cushy comforts of home and then some. Once you hit those rooms or the sprawling outdoor lawn leading up to the pool and beachfront, you realize that this is yet another of South Beach's ways of making you realize that you're not in Kansas anymore. The hotel's new restaurant, Social Miami, just opened. It's the sister to Social Hollywood, a hipster haven of tapas, colorful cocktails, and celebrities.

1671 Collins Ave., South Beach, FL 33139. © **87/SAGAMORE** or 305/535-8088. Fax 305/535-8185. www.sagamore hotel.com. 93 units. Winter $355–$1,050 suite; off season $215–$595 suite. AE, DC, DISC, MC, V. Valet parking $20. **Amenities:** Bar; pool bar; pool; spa and fitness center; concierge; room service. *In room:* A/C, TV, VCR, DVD/CD player, dataport, full kitchen, minibar, coffeemaker, hair dryer, iron, safe.

The Sanctuary Hotel of South Beach ☆☆

Located a bit off the beaten path is this luxe, all-suite resident hotel (meaning people can actually rent or buy rooms and live here) that lives up to its name and then some. Flying into town? Let the Sanctuary's Bentley pick you up in pure bling-bling style. But don't mistake the flashy car as a sign that the hotel is tacky. It's just the opposite. Soothingly modern, all rooms have full state-of-the-art Italian kitchens, flat plasma-screen televisions, and Wi-Fi. In addition, bathrooms come with Jacuzzi tubs, and in-room fridges are stocked with everything you specify before checking into the hotel. A roof-deck "bedroom" allows you to relax in the sun, or slink around in the wading pool. At night, the roof is buzzing with hipsters convening at the small bar. The Sanctuary is almost too cool for words, and the hotel's delicious Italian restaurant, Sugo, is a hot spot situated smack in the middle of the very posh, very contemporary lobby. We think this hotel should be renamed the Swanktuary.

1745 James Ave., South Beach, FL 33139. © **305/673-5455.** Fax 305/673-3113. www.sanctuarysobe.com. 30 units. Winter $375–$1,500 suite; off season $215–$1,050 suite. AE, DC, DISC, MC, V. Valet parking $18. **Amenities:** Bar;

pool bar; rooftop pool; spa and fitness center; concierge; room service. *In room:* A/C, TV, VCR, DVD/CD player, dataport, full kitchen, minibar, coffeemaker, hair dryer, iron, safe.

The Setai 🎯🎯 This Zenlike, Asian-inspired hotel should have been built in the '80s, when people threw money around like Paris Hilton tosses fiancés. With rooms starting at upward of $1,000 a night, dinner tabs coming in at around $200 per person, martinis at $26, and a celebrity clientele who doesn't have to ask how much, The Setai is truly for that 1% of society who can afford it. That aside, if you want to splurge, the place is stellar, stunning, and all those superlatives. All suites—some of which are actually condos participating in the condo-hotel program, are gorgeous apartments with floor-to-ceiling windows, a full kitchen, and a Jacuzzi bathtub bigger than a small swimming pool. There are 75 regular hotel rooms that are a minute 550 square feet compared to the suites' 1,300 to 3,500 square feet. All are adorned in sleek Asian decor with all the usuals—plasma TV, comfy beds with real linen sheets, Lavazza espresso makers, Aqua di Parma bathroom amenities, and even Maytag washer-dryers. The hotel's designs are silently sleek, with lots of candlelight, sculptures, chocolate and honey tones, and stunning floral arrangements. The garden area with reflecting pools is lovely, but not as cool as the beach dune area with bar serving $26 burgers to a star-studded clientele. The Restaurant, its proper name, is exquisite and authentically Asian, with stainless-steel tandoori ovens and a star chef hailing from Australia. But with prices like the ones they charge—for small portions, no less—you may as well buy a ticket on Quantas. It's probably the same price! One last thing: The Setai also bought one of our longtime favorite hotels, The Abbey—to house all the staff they've imported from all over Asia!

2001 Collins Ave., South Beach, FL 33139. ✆ **305/520-6100.** Fax 305/520-6111. www.lhw.com/setaimiami. 125 units. Year round $900–$15,000. AE, DC, DISC, MC, V. Valet parking $30. **Amenities:** 2 restaurants; 3 bars; pool; spa and fitness center; concierge; 24-hour room service. *In room:* A/C, TV, DVD/CD player, dataport, full kitchen, minibar, coffeemaker, hair dryer, iron, safe.

The Shore Club 🎯 What used to be a concrete canyon, a mod-version of the eerily deserted hotel in *The Shining,* is now one of *the* hottest and hautest stays in South Beach, thanks to a constant cadre of celebrity appearances, among other things. That, not to mention Florida's first-ever Nobu sushi restaurant and cocktail lounge (a major hit in New York, Las Vegas, Paris, and London) and a celebrity clientele that would fill up an entire issue of *Us Weekly,* have made The Shore Club a sure thing. Because this hotel is infinitely more cavernous than its (not as) hipster neighbor, The Delano (see above), publicity-shy celebs such as Janet Jackson and Denzel Washington have been known to call this place their home away from home because there are indeed places for them to hide. Then again, publicity hog Leonardo DiCaprio also had no qualms slumber-partying with his posse here. Neither did Britney Spears, Beyonce Knowles, Jay-Z, and, well, you get the picture (and if you're lucky, you'll really get the picture and make a fortune from the tabloids, but beware of behemoth bodyguards). Stellar crowd aside, the hotel's interior still leaves a lot to be desired—the lobby here is sorely lacking in personality. But that's all forgotten once you reach the centerpiece of the place—the resplendent oasis of chic out back. A Miami outpost of L.A.'s celeb-laden SkyBar reigns supreme with a Marrakech-meets-Miami motif that stretches throughout the hotel's sprawling pool, patio, and garden areas. Beware of surly doormen if you're not a hotel guest. A branch of L.A. hot spot Ago (and its *extremely* pricey pasta) opened here with much fanfare and an appearance by co-owner Robert DeNiro, who hasn't been back since.

The Shore Club also boasts that 80% of its 325 rooms have an ocean view. Contrary to the cold, cavernous lobby, exquisite gardens draw guests toward the beach through courtyards and reflecting pools. A rooftop spa is a great respite from the hype and buzz down in the lobby and outdoor areas. Rooms are loaded with state-of-the-art amenities, not to mention 400-thread-count linen bedding, Mexican sandstone flooring in the bathroom, and an enclosed "wet area" with bathtub, shower, and teak bench. (Molton Brown bathroom amenities are worth bringing an extra bag for.) If you can't afford the penthouse or a poolside cabana, consider an Ocean View room, which is stellar in its own right, with its massive, two-nozzled tub/shower that's almost better than a day at the beach. If you are wondering whether to choose the still somewhat hip mainstay The Delano, over this hotel, consider that The Shore Club is much hungrier for the hipsters, and its rooms boast a bit more personality than The Delano's.

1901 Collins Ave., Miami Beach, FL 33139. ℂ 877/640-9500 or 305/695-3100. Fax 305/695-3299. www.shoreclub. com. 384 units, 8 cabanas. Winter $525–$775 double, $1,125 suite, $2,500 cabana; off season $425–$675 double, $1,025 suite, $1,500 cabana. AE, DC, MC, V. Valet parking $20. **Amenities:** 3 restaurants; 4 bars; outdoor reflecting pools with poolside health club with steam room and outdoor equipment; spa; concierge; 24-hr. room service. *In room:* A/C, TV, CD player, stereo, Intrigue System with digitally downloaded movies and high-speed Internet access, fax, dataport, minibar.

The Tides 🐟🐟🐟   This 12-story Art Deco masterpiece is reminiscent of a gleaming ocean liner, with porthole windows and lots of stainless steel and frosted glass. Rooms are starkly white but much more luxurious and comfortable than those at The Delano. Also, all rooms are at least twice the size of a typical South Beach hotel room and have a breathtaking panoramic view of the ocean. They feature king beds, spacious closets, large bathrooms, and even a telescope from which to view the vast ocean. The penthouses on the 9th and 10th floors are situated at the highest point on Ocean Drive, allowing for a priceless panoramic view of the ocean, the skyline, and the beach. Even if you can't afford it, you must ask for a tour of the Goldeneye Suite, a room suited for James Bond and his Bond girls, with a hot tub in the middle, a private deck, and high-tech toys. Although small, the freshwater pool is a welcome plus for those who aren't in the mood to feel the sand between their toes, but it really doesn't fit with the rest of the hotel, lacking in ambience and view (it overlooks an alley). At press time, however, the pool was undergoing renovations and landscaping to bring it up to posh par. The hotel's restaurant, Twelve Twenty, is located in the lobby, and is good, but for some reason always dead. The Terrace is a less expensive outdoor cafe. The Tides is a place where celebrities like Ben Affleck, Jennifer Lopez, and Bono come to stay for some R&R, but you won't find gawkers or paparazzi lurking in the lobby—just an elegant clientele and staff who are respectful of people's privacy and desire for peace and quiet.

1220 Ocean Dr., South Beach, FL 33139. ℂ 866/43-TIDES or 305/604-5070. Fax 305/604-5180. www.tidessouth beach.com. 45 units. Winter $550 suite, $3,000 penthouse; off season $420 suite, $3,000 penthouse. Additional person $25. Pets $150 one-time fee. AE, DC, DISC, MC, V. Valet parking $27. **Amenities:** 1 restaurant; lounge; bar; outdoor heated pool; fitness room; concierge; 24-hr. room service; in-room massage; laundry service; dry cleaning; beach lounge service. *In room:* A/C, TV/VCR, stereo/CD player with selection of music, video rentals, dataport, minibar, hair dryer, iron, safe.

EXPENSIVE
The Hotel 🐟🐟🐟   Kitschy fashion designer Todd Oldham whimsically restored this 1939 gem (formerly the Tiffany Hotel) as he would have a vintage piece of couture. He laced it with lush, cool colors; hand-cut mirrors; and glass mosaics from his ready-to-wear factory, then added artisan detailing, terrazzo floors, and porthole windows.

The small, soundproof rooms are very comfortable and incredibly stylish, though the bathrooms are a bit cramped. Nevertheless, the showers are irresistible, with fantastic rain-head shower heads. There's no need to pay more for an oceanfront view here—go up to the rooftop, where the hip and funky Spire Bar and pool are located, and you'll see an amazing view of the Atlantic. The hotel's restaurant, Wish (p. 112), is one of South Beach's best.

801 Collins Ave., South Beach, FL 33139. *C* 877/843-4683 or 305/531-2222. Fax 305/531-3222. www.thehotelof southbeach.com. 53 units. Winter $275–$325 double, $425 suite; off season $225–$255 double, $355 suite. AE, DC, DISC, MC, V. Valet parking $18. **Amenities:** Restaurant; bar; pool bar; small pool; health club; concierge; business center; room service. *In room:* A/C, TV/VCR, stereo system with CD and cassette players, video library, dataport, mini-bar, coffeemaker, hair dryer, Kiehl's products.

Hotel Astor 🌟🌟🌟   "Cozy-mod" best describes this diminutive Deco hotel built in 19 A 2002 renovation, which added a more urban, industrial feel to the place with dark woods, backlit glass, and very sleek contemporary furniture, continues to attract a lively local crowd to the small but sleek lobby bar and basement level hot spot, Metro Kitchen + Bar. Though the hotel hasn't been as sceney (a la The Delano) as it once was, it has already begun to experience a hipster revival, thanks to the fact that Metro, as it's more commonly known, is co-owned by Nicola Siervo, the owner of South Beach's celeb central Mynt (p. 169). Another plus is that what used to be a minute pool has been converted into an outdoor dining garden.

The hotel's rooms are still small but very soothing, featuring plush and luxurious details—brand-new Frette linens and towels, new carpeting, funky custom mood lighting with dimmer switches, and incredibly plush mattresses that are difficult to leave. I especially recommend the rooms overlooking the courtyard, for their views and for a bit more serenity than is afforded in rooms overlooking the street. Views are probably the worst thing about this hotel, as most rooms face the street or a neighboring seedy hotel. The hotel staff is known for its extreme attentiveness—especially Arturo, the hotel's *Cheers*-y bartender who actually knows everybody's names and their drinks of choice. Celeb alert: Justin Timberlake, Cameron Diaz, *American Idol*'s Ryan Seacrest, the irksome Hilton sisters, DMC from Run DMC, and dubious celeb O. J. Simpson have all been spotted hanging at Metro Kitchen + Bar.

956 Washington Ave., South Beach, FL 33139. *C* 800/270-4981 or 305/531-8081. Fax 305/531-3193. www.hotel astor.com. 40 units. Winter $155–$220 double, $340–$700 suite; off season $125–$170 double, $220–$500 suite. AE, DC, MC, V. Valet parking $20. **Amenities:** Restaurant; 2 bars; access to nearby health club; 24-hr. concierge service; secretarial services; room service; in-room massage; babysitting; laundry service; dry cleaning. *In room:* A/C, TV, data-port, minibar, fridge, hair dryer, safe.

Hotel Impala 🌟 *Finds*   This charming Mediterranean hideaway is one of the area's best, and it's just beautiful, from the Greco-Roman frescos and friezes to an intimate garden that is perfumed with the scents of hanging lilies and gardenias. Rooms have supercushy sleigh beds, sisal floors, wrought-iron fixtures, imported Belgian cotton linens, wood furniture, and fabulous-looking, but also incredibly small, bathrooms done up in stainless steel and coral rock. The two smallest rooms here are nos. 102 and 206; otherwise, they're pretty roomy and cushy. Adjacent to the hotel is Spiga (p. 117), an intimate, excellent Italian restaurant that is reasonably priced. Enclaves like this one are rare on South Beach. Rates also include complimentary continental breakfast.

1228 Collins Ave., South Beach, FL 33139. *C* 800/646-7252 or 305/673-2021. Fax 305/673-5984. www.hotel impalamiamibeach.com. 17 units. Winter $195–$425; off season $145–$325. AE, DC, MC, V. Valet parking $20 Small pets permitted. **Amenities:** Restaurant; concierge; room service. *In room:* A/C, TV/VCR, stereo, CD player, complimentary videos, high-speed Internet access, hair dryer.

Raleigh Hotel 🐬🐬   Upon entering the lobby of this oceanfront Art Deco hotel, you will feel like you've stepped back into the 1940s. Polished wood, original terrazzo floors, and an intimate martini bar add to the fabulous atmosphere that's favored by fashion photographers and production crews, for whom the hotel's fleur-de-lis pool is the favorite subject. In fact, one look at the pool and you'll expect Esther Williams to splash up in a dramatic, aquatic plié. Should you glance quickly inside the dimly lit lobby restaurant, you could swear Dorothy Parker and her fellow round-tablers took a detour from New York's Algonquin Hotel and landed here. Rooms are tidy and efficient (those overlooking the resplendent pool and ocean are the most peaceful), nothing too elaborate, but that's not why people stay here. It's the Raleigh's romantic Deco lure that has people skipping over from the chilly, antiseptic Delano a few blocks up for much needed warmth. And soon, you can expect the Raleigh to be even hotter— hip hotelier Andre Balazs (of Los Angeles's Chateau Marmont and Standard hotels fame), the high-profile new owner of the Raleigh, is implementing extensive renovations that will undoubtedly push the hotel back in the limelight as one of *the* places to be on South Beach yet again. A Sunday afternoon pool party known as Soiree Sunday, from noon until 10pm, has seen the likes of tennis tart Anna Kournikova, actor Mickey Rourke, and just about every hipster who has ever entered the 33139 zip code.

1775 Collins Ave., Miami Beach, FL 33139. ✆ **800/848-1775** or 305/534-6300. Fax 305/538-8140. www.raleighhotel. com. 111 units. Winter $395–$675 double, $895–$1,095 suite; off season $150–$295 double, $350–$650 suite. AE, DC, DISC, MC, V. Valet parking $20. **Amenities:** Restaurant; bar; coffee bar; fantastic large outdoor pool; small open-air fitness center; concierge; business services; 24-hr. room service; massage; overnight laundry service. *In room:* A/C, TV/VCR, CD player, dataport, minibar, fridge, hair dryer, iron, safe.

The Standard 🐬🐬   Another L.A. import, The Standard, owned by Raleigh Hotel owner Andre Balazs, is meant to be a shabby-chic spot, but is more chic than shabby. The quintessential spa resort a la Palm Springs, The Standard is housed in Miami Beach's legendary Lido Spa spot, a place that was swinging back in the days when women used to strap themselves into those machines to shake their fat off. Today the hotel is full of all the modern trappings of a swank spa resort, with a bay-front view and a serene location on the Venetian Causeway, a quiet and relaxing locale within walking distance of all the South Beach craziness. Unlike The Standard on the Sunset Strip in Hollywood, this one's meant for rejuvenation, not partying like rock stars. Remnants of the atomic age of the fabulous '50s still exist here—the lobby's white-marble walls, terrazzo floors, and stainless-steel elevators, to name a few. Add to that a touch of Scandinavian retro-modernism in the form of sconces from an old SAS Hotel in Stockholm and vintage Danish furniture, and you've got a photo spread in *Wallpaper* magazine. Nothing is typical here, especially the spa facilities, which come to you. Guest rooms—white-washed walls, clean and simple plywood floors, and macramé rugs—are serviced by roaming carts containing herbal teas and offering aromatherapy footbaths. There's a cedar sauna, a Turkish hammam with heated marble seats, and tongue-in-cheeky treatments such as the Standard Spanking, a $165 cellulite-fighting treatment—the 21st century version of that old 1950s machine we mentioned above. Then there's the chlorine-free plunge pool, with a 12-foot tall waterfall and DJ-spun music piped beneath the water. Nearby are clothing-optional mud baths. There's nothing standard about this hotel.

40 Island Ave., South Beach, FL 33139. ✆ **305/673-1717.** Fax 305/673-8181. www.standardhotel.com. 105 units. Year-round $150–$750 suite. AE, DC, DISC, MC, V. Valet parking $20. **Amenities:** Restaurant; bar; pool; spa; sauna; 24-hr. concierge; 24-hour room service. *In room:* A/C, TV/DVD, stereo system with CD player, free high-speed Internet access, minibar, coffeemaker, hair dryer, iron, safe.

MODERATE

The Catalina Hotel & Beach Club 🎀🎀   One of the newer boutique hotels on South Beach, the Catalina reminds me of something straight out of an Austin Powers movie. It's groovy, indeed! Stylish but not at all stuffy, the Catalina is perhaps the only hotel in the area that can pull off using red shag carpeting—which can use a good scrubbing, actually. The mod squad lobby decor gives way to rooms glazed in white with hints of bright colors featuring Tempur-Pedic Swedish Mattresses, 300-thread-count Mascioni sheets, goose-down comforters and pillows, and, of course, flat-screen TVs. The hotel's Spy Bar and Lounge debuted in late 2005 and fit right into the neighborhood with a jet-set vibe and world-renowned chef.

1732 Collins Ave., South Beach, FL 33139. ✆ 305/674-1160. Fax 305/672-8216. www.catalinahotel.com. 136 units. Winter $145–$250 double; off season $79–$250 double. Additional person $15. Rates include continental breakfast bar. AE, DC, MC, V. Valet parking $22; self-parking $6. **Amenities:** Bar; laundry services; wireless Internet ($15 a day); Japanese Koi fishpond; Zen garden. *In room:* A/C, TV/VCR, CD player, minibar, hair dryer, iron, safe.

Crest Hotel Suites 🎀 *Finds*   One of South Beach's best-kept secrets, the Crest Hotel is located next to the pricier, trendier Albion Hotel and features a quietly fashionable, contemporary, relaxed atmosphere with fantastic service. Built in 1939, the Crest was restored to preserve its Art Deco architecture, but the interior of the hotel is thoroughly modern, with rooms resembling cosmopolitan apartments. All suites have a living room/dining room area, kitchenette, and executive work space. An indoor/outdoor cafe with terrace and poolside dining isn't besieged with trendy locals but does attract a younger crowd. Crest Hotel Suites is conveniently located in the heart of the Art Deco Historic District, near all the major attractions. Around the corner from the hotel is Lincoln Road, with its sidewalk cafes, gourmet restaurants, theaters, and galleries. In an effort to expand its quiet trendiness, the Crest opened its second hotel, the **South Beach Hotel**, at 236 21st St., in an area that at present isn't so great (though it's on its way up). Until the neighborhood goes through more of a renaissance, this second hotel should probably be a last resort for you if you can't get a room elsewhere.

1670 James Ave., Miami Beach, FL 33139. ✆ 800/531-3880 or 305/531-0321. Fax 305/531-8180. www.crest grouphotels.com/cresthotelsuites.htm. 64 units. Winter $155 double, $235 suite; off season $115 double, $175 suite. Packages available and 10% discount offered if booked on website. AE, MC, V. **Amenities:** Restaurant; cafe; pool; laundry service; dry cleaning. *In room:* A/C, TV, dataport, kitchenette, fridge, coffeemaker (select units).

The Lily Leon Hotel 🎀 *Finds*   A great hotel with little attitude, which recently merged with the neighboring Lily Guesthouse, the Lily Leon Hotel (formerly known as the Hotel Leon) is like a reasonably priced high-fashion garment found hidden on a rack full of overpriced threads. This charismatic sliver of a property has won the loyalty of fashion industrialists and romantics alike. Built in 1929 and restored in 1996, the hotel still retains many original details, such as facades, woodwork, and even fireplaces (every room has one, not that you'll need to use it). The very central location (1 block from the ocean) is a plus, especially since the Leon lacks a pool. Most of the spacious and stylish rooms are immaculate and reminiscent of a loft apartment; spacious bathrooms with large, deep tubs are especially enticing. Wood floors and simple, pale furnishings are appreciated in a neighborhood where many others overdo the Art Deco motif. However, some rooms are dark and have not seen such upgrades (we have gotten complaints), and are to be avoided; do not hesitate to ask to change rooms. Service is warm, friendly, and accommodating. We've also gotten complaints about the music coming from the hotel next door, but you have to realize that if you're staying on Collins or Washington avenues, you're going to hear noise: South Beach isn't known for its quiet, peaceful demeanor! The lobby has an informal bar, not to mention a large communal table at which guests—production crews, fashion photographers, Europeans, and young hipsters—tend to mix and mingle. Because its entrance is not directly on pedestrian-heavy Collins Avenue, the Hotel Leon remains one of South Beach's most understated, yet coolest, stays.

841 Collins Ave., South Beach, FL 33139. © **305/673-3767.** Fax 305/535-9665. www.lilyleonhotel.com. 37 units. Winter $145–$245 suite, $395 penthouse; off season $100–$195 suite, $335 penthouse. Additional person $20. AE, DC, MC, V. Valet parking $20. "Well-behaved" pets accepted. **Amenities:** Lobby bar; reduced rates at local gym; concierge; business services. *In room:* A/C, TV, CD player, minibar, hair dryer, safe.

Pelican Hotel 🏵🏵 Owned by the same creative folks behind the Diesel Jeans company, the Pelican (whose brazen, albeit appropriate, motto is "A myth in its own limelight") is South Beach's only self-professed "toy-hotel," in which each of its 30 rooms and suites is decorated as outrageously as some of the area's more colorful drag queens. Each room has been designed daringly and rather wittily by Swedish interior decorator Magnus Ehrland, whose countless trips to antiques markets, combined with his wild imagination, have turned room no. 309, for instance, into the "Psychedelic(ate) Girl," room no. 201 into the "Executive Fifties" suite, and room no. Room 209 into the "Love, Peace, and Leafforest" room. But the most popular room is the tough-to-score room no. 215, or the "Best Whorehouse," which is said to have made even former Hollywood madam Heidi Fleiss red with envy. The Penthouse that occupies the top floor is almost more 007 than James Bond's own pad—very '60s in color and pattern, with a big aquarium built into a copper wall and a yellow Shultz table and chair. Very cool!

826 Ocean Dr., Miami Beach, FL 33139. © **800/7-PELICAN** or 305/673-3373. Fax 305/673-3255. www.pelicanhotel. com. 30 units. Winter $180–$250 double, $270–$440 oceanfront suite; off season $155–$195 double, $230–$310 oceanfront suite. Valet parking $20. AE, DC, MC, V. **Amenities:** Restaurant with a *Wine Spectator* award–winning wine list; bar; access to area gyms; concierge; business services; room service; same-day laundry service; dry cleaning; Wi-Fi throughout the property; movies and music "On Command." *In room:* A/C, TV, stereo/CD player, fridge, hair dryer, iron, safe.

Townhouse 🏵🏵 New York hipster Jonathan Morr felt that Miami Beach had lost touch with the bons vivants who gave the city its original cachet, so he decided to take matters into his own hands. His solution: this 67-room, five-story so-called shabby-chic hotel. The charm of this hotel is found in its clean and simple yet chic design with quirky details: exercise equipment that stands alone in the hallways, free laundry machines in the lobby, and a water bed–lined rooftop. Comfortable, shabby-chic rooms boast L-shape couches for extra guests (for whom you aren't charged). Though the rooms are all pretty much the same, consider the ones with the partial oceanview. The hotel's basement features the hot New York import, Bond St. Lounge (p. 115).

150 20th St., South Beach, FL 33139. © **877/534-3800** or 305/534-3800. Fax 305/534-3811. www.townhousehotel. com. 70 units. Winter $160–$225 double, $395 penthouse; off season $99–$155 double, $395 penthouse. Rates include Parisian-style (coffee and pastry) breakfast. AE, MC, V. Valet parking $18. **Amenities:** Restaurant; bar; workout stations; bike rental; free laundry service; rooftop terrace with water beds. *In room:* A/C, TV/VCR, CD player, dataport, fridge, hair dryer, safe.

Whitelaw Hotel 🏵 With a slogan that reads "Clean sheets, hot water, and stiff drinks," the Whitelaw Hotel stands apart from the other boutique hotels with a fierce sense of humor. Only half a block from Ocean Drive, this hotel, like its clientele, is full of distinct personalities, pairing such disparate elements as luxurious Belgian sheets with shag carpeting to create an innovative setting. All-white rooms manage to be homey and plush, and not at all antiseptic, but some guests have complained that their room looked more like a 1950s kitchen with linoleum floors than anything else. Bathrooms are pretty small and not that well stocked, and towels are sometimes in short supply, but those who stay here aren't really looking for luxe—they want to party. Complimentary cocktails in the lobby every night from 7 to 8pm contribute to a very social atmosphere.

808 Collins Ave., Miami Beach, FL 33139. ☎ **305/398-7000.** Fax 305/398-7010. www.whitelawhotel.com. 49 units. Winter $165–$225 double/king, $250-$300 mini-suite; off season $99–$145 double/king, $145–$250 mini-suite; during special events, rates are subject to change. Rates include complimentary continental breakfast and free cocktails in the lobby (7–8pm daily). AE, DC, MC, V. Parking $20. **Amenities:** Lounge; concierge; business services; free airport pickup (to and from MIA); laundry service; complimentary passes to area nightclubs. *In room:* A/C, TV, dataport, Wi-Fi ($15 per day), CD player, minibar, hair dryer, safe.

INEXPENSIVE
Hotel Shelley 𝒦 Newly renovated Hotel Shelley has a laid-back beach atmosphere, yet cutting-edge style. The architecturally sound boutique hotel built in 1931 in the heart of the Art Deco district in Miami Beach has reinvented itself with a complete $1.5-million renovation of its 49 guest rooms. Complete with Mascioni 300-thread-count linens, goose-down pillows and comforters, LCD plasma TVs, and custom-built cabinetry, the guest rooms at the Shelley allow you to chill out after a long day at the beach or rock out before a big night of partying. The subtle purple hues in the rooms and public areas lend to true Art Deco style. The bar in the lobby offers free drinks from 7 to 8pm every night and VIP passes to area nightclubs. Located on Collins and 1 block from Ocean Drive, you can reach beach, shopping, or nightlife within a few minutes' walk.

844 Collins Ave., Miami Beach, Florida 33139 ☎ **305/531.3341.** Fax 305/535.9665. www.hotelshelley.com. 49 units. Winter $95–$225 double, $125–$245 king, $165–$300 mini-suite; off-season $75–$125 double, $95–$145 king; $115–$165 mini-suite; during special events and holidays, rates are subject to change. Rates include complimentary continental breakfast and free cocktails in the lobby (7–8pm daily). AE, DC, MC, V. Parking $20. **Amenities:** Lounge; concierge; free airport pickup (to and from MIA); laundry service; complimentary passes to area nightclubs. *In room:* A/C, TV, CD player, dataport, minibar, hair dryer, safe.

MIAMI BEACH: SURFSIDE, BAL HARBOUR, SUNNY ISLES & NORTH BEACH

The area just north of South Beach, known as Miami Beach, encompasses Surfside, Bal Harbour, and Sunny Isles. Unrestricted by zoning codes throughout the 1950s, 1960s, and especially 1970s, area developers went crazy, building ever-bigger and more brazen structures, especially north of 41st Street, known as "Condo Canyon." Consequently, there's now a glut of medium-quality condos, with a few scattered holdouts of older hotels and motels casting shadows over the beach by afternoon.

To locate the hotels in this section, see the map "Where to Stay & Dine in Miami Beach, Surfside, Bal Harbour, Sunny Isles & North Beach" (p. 93).

VERY EXPENSIVE
Eden Roc Renaissance Resort and Spa 𝒦𝒦 Just next door to the mammoth Fontainebleau Hilton, this Morris Lapidus–designed flamboyant hotel, opened in 1956, seems almost intimate by comparison. The nautical Deco decor is a bit gaudy but nonetheless reminiscent of Miami Beach's Rat-Packed glory days of the '50s. The 55,000-square-foot modern Spa of Eden has excellent facilities and exercise classes,

Where to Stay & Dine in Miami Beach, Surfside, Bal Harbour, Sunny Isles & North Beach

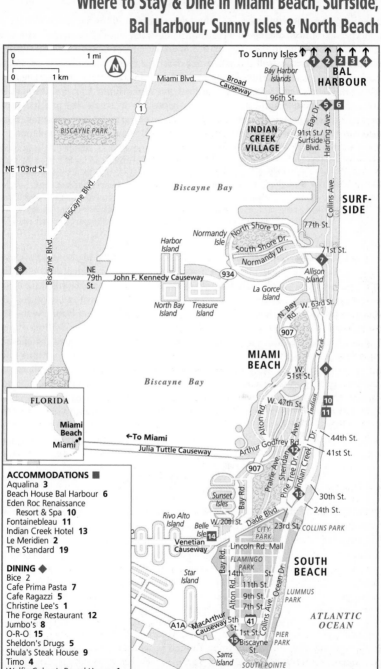

ACCOMMODATIONS ■
Aqualina **3**
Beach House Bal Harbour **6**
Eden Roc Renaissance
    Resort & Spa **10**
Fontainebleau **11**
Indian Creek Hotel **13**
Le Meridien **2**
The Standard **19**

DINING ◆
Bice **2**
Cafe Prima Pasta **7**
Cafe Ragazzi **5**
Christine Lee's **1**
The Forge Restaurant **12**
Jumbo's **8**
O-R-O **15**
Sheldon's Drugs **5**
Shula's Steak House **9**
Timo **4**
Wolfie Cohen's Rascal House **1**

including yoga. The big, open, and airy lobby is often full of name-tagged conventioneers and tourists looking for a taste of Miami Beach kitsch. The rooms, uniformly
outfitted with purple and aquatic-colored interiors and retouched 1930s furnishings,
are unusually spacious, and the bathrooms boast Italian marble bathtubs. Because of
the hotel's size, you should be able to negotiate a good rate unless there's a big event
going on. Harry's Grille specializes in seafood and steaks. From Aquatica, the poolside
bar and restaurant, bikini-clad patrons can enjoy casual meals and priceless ocean
views. At press time we heard that the new owners of the resort were planning to add
a 20-story tower with 300 rooms costing between $15 million and $20 million.

4525 Collins Ave., Miami Beach, FL 33140. (C) 800/327-8337 or 305/531-0000. Fax 305/674-5555. www.edenroc
resort.com. 349 units. Winter $339–$425 double, $394 suite, $2,500 penthouse; off season $199–$274 double,
$239 suite, $1,500 penthouse. Additional person $15. Packages available. AE, DC, DISC, MC, V. Valet parking $24. Pets
are accepted for a fee. **Amenities:** 2 restaurants; lounge; bar; 2 outdoor pools; squash courts; racquetball courts; basketball courts; rock-climbing arena; health club and spa; watersports equipment; concierge; tour desk; car-rental desk;
business center; salon; limited room service; in-room massage; babysitting; laundry service; dry cleaning. *In room:*
A/C, TV, VCRs for rent, dataport, kitchenettes (in suites and penthouse), minibar, coffeemaker, hair dryer, safe.

EXPENSIVE

Beach House Bal Harbour *★★* *Finds*   The Beach House Bal Harbour is the closest
thing the city has to a summer beach home—comfortable, unpretentious, and luxurious, yet decidedly low-key. In place of an elaborate hotel lobby, the public spaces of
the Beach House are divided into a series of intimate homey environments, from the
wicker-furnished screened-in porch to the Asian-inspired Bamboo Room, with overstuffed Ralph Lauren leather couches and Japanese bric-a-brac. The 24-hour Pantry,
inspired by Long Island's Sagaponack General Store, is packed with all the needs of
the hotel's "unplugged" urban clientele. The ultraspacious rooms (those ending in 04
are the most spacious) are brimming with the comforts of home. The Seahorse Bar
features a giant tank of—you guessed it—sea horses. The 200-foot private beach,
hammock grove, and topiary garden are so lush, they're said to have caused several
New York hipsters to renege on their summer shares in the Hamptons in favor of this
Beach House.

9449 Collins Ave., Surfside, FL 33154. (C) 800/327-6644 or 305/535-8606. Fax 305/535-8602. www.thebeachhouse
hotel.com. 170 units. Winter $150–$199 double, $209–$299 suite; off season $109–$124 double, $149–$199 suite.
AE, DC, DISC, MC, V. Valet parking $15. **Amenities:** Restaurant; pantry; bar (open until 11pm); heated pool; health
club and spa; watersports equipment; children's playground; business center. *In room:* A/C, TV, stereo/CD player, dataport, wireless TV Internet access, fridge, hair dryer, iron.

Fontainebleau Hotel and Resort *★★* *Kids*   Big changes are in store for what was
once the quintessential Miami Beach hotel. Also designed by the late and legendary
Morris Lapidus, who oversaw an expansion in 2000, this grand monolith symbolizes
old Miami decadence, especially with the debut of the hotel's all-suite tower, which
they appropriately bill as "a taller, thinner, sexier version of our old self." Since its
opening in 1954, the Fontainebleau has hosted presidents, pageants, and movie productions, including the James Bond thriller *Goldfinger*. This is where all the greats,
including Sinatra and his pals, performed in their prime, and to pay homage to the
Rat Pack, the hotel has redone its lobby bar to reflect the era of swagger, attitude, raff-
ish cool, and panache, featuring large, bordering on tacky but still swell silhouettes of
Frank, Sammy, Dino, Joey, and Peter, and the live music of The Pack, a really good
Rat Pack cover band. Drinks are named after all the greats, but the best one is Dino's
Martini—a classic, unfettered stiff one. Club Tropigala is reminiscent of Ricky

Then&Now **Hip Hotel, Then**

The Delano and The Shore Club may have the hippest hotel bars in Miami today, but when *Miami and the Caribbean on 10 Dollars a Day* was published, nothing was as cool as the **Fontainebleu** (p. 94): "If you feel that you have to trespass at least once in to the land of elegance and Cadillacs, then about the best you can do is the Boom Boom Room in the fanciest of all hotels, the **Fontainebleau.** This interesting club has the dubious distinction of being decorated like an enlarged African hut and yet casually serving Cantonese food. There's a two drink minimum at the tables (about $1.25 per drink)."

Ricardo's Tropicana and features a Las Vegas–style floor show with dozens of performers and two orchestras. The old rooms, which were luxurious and decorated in various styles from 1950s to ultramodern, are receiving a face-lift and will be just like every other luxury hotel room—flat-screen TVs, plush bedding, and, well, you get the idea. Adding to the Fontainebleau's opulence is the 7,000-square-foot Cookie's World water park; the water slide and river-raft ride bring a bit of Disney to Deco-land, which, along with supervised children's activities, is catered toward (though not reserved for) the little ones. At press time, the hotel's owner, Jeffrey Soffer, was planning a major reworking of the resort beginning in March 2006. He plans to bring celebrity chefs, big-name musical headliners, and other Vegas-style entertainment options. Rates will increase, too—up to 70%. He also plans to gut the hotel's main building and strip the walls, and to get rid of Cookie's World and turn it into a 40,000-square-foot spa. Ultimately, Soffer wants the hotel to return to its glory days, albeit in 21st-century style. We think it's a great idea, as long as the hotel doesn't turn into a clone of all the other resorts out there today.

4441 Collins Ave., Miami Beach, FL 33140. © **800/548-8886** or 305/538-2000. Fax 305/674-4607. www.fontaine bleau.com. 876 units. Winter $269–$349 double; off season $209–$259 double; year-round $525–$1,300 suite. Additional person $30. Packages available. AE, DC, DISC, MC, V. Overnight valet parking $17. Pets accepted at no extra cost. **Amenities:** 4 restaurants; 3 cocktail lounges; 2 large outdoor pools; 7 lighted tennis courts (after scheduled renovations); state-of-the-art health club; 3 whirlpool baths; watersports rentals; children's programs; game rooms; concierge; tour desk; car-rental desk; business center; shopping arcade; salon; room service; in-room massage; babysitting; laundry service; dry cleaning. *In room:* A/C, TV, fax, dataport, minibar, coffeemaker, hair dryer, iron, safe.

MODERATE

Indian Creek Hotel and Suites ★ *(Finds)*   Located off the beaten path, the Indian Creek Hotel is a meticulously restored 1936 building featuring one of the beach's first operating elevators. It's also the most charming hotel in the area. Besides that, the service is impeccable. Because of its location facing the Indian Creek waterway and its lush landscaping, this place feels more like an old-fashioned Key West bed-and-breakfast than a typical Miami Beach Art Deco hotel. The recently revamped rooms are outfitted in Art Deco furnishings, such as an antique writing desk, pretty tropical prints, and small but spotless bathrooms. Just 1 short block from a good stretch of sand, the hotel is also within walking distance of shops and restaurants, and has a landscaped pool area that is a great place to lounge in the sun. If you're looking for charm, friendly service, and peace and quiet, stay away from the South Beach hype and come here instead. A note of caution: One reader who stayed there complained that the staff was surly, the room was dirty, and the lush courtyard was overgrown. To each his own, but that doesn't excuse the fact that they had to get up at 7am to move their car from the street because the desk clerk didn't tell them about a parking permit—obtainable at the hotel, no less—that would exempt them from having to fill the meters. The good news is that there is new ownership and things seem to be running more smoothly. There's also a restaurant, finally—Creek 28—so you don't have to always run out for sustenance.

2727 Indian Creek Dr. (1 block west of Collins Ave. and the ocean), Miami Beach, FL 33140. ✆ **800/491-2772** or 305/531-2727. Fax 305/531-5651. www.indiancreekhotel.com. 61 units. Winter $69–$139 double, $269 suite; off season $69–$99double, $179 suite. Additional person $25. Group packages and summer specials available. AE, DC, DISC, MC, V. **Amenities:** Restaurant; bar; pool; concierge; car-rental desk; limited room service; laundry service; dry cleaning. *In room:* A/C, TV/VCR, CD player, dataport, fridge (in suites), hair dryer.

KEY BISCAYNE

Locals call it the Key, and technically, Key Biscayne is the northernmost island in the Florida Keys, even though it's located in Miami. A relatively unknown area until Richard Nixon bought a home here in the '70s, Key Biscayne, at 1¼ square miles, is an affluent but hardly lively residential and recreational island known for its pricey homes, excellent beaches, and actor Andy Garcia, who makes his home here. The island is far enough from the mainland to make it feel semiprivate, yet close enough to downtown for guests to take advantage of everything Miami has to offer.

To locate the hotels in this section, see the map "Where to Stay & Dine in Key Biscayne, Downtown Miami, West Miami, Airport Area, North Dade, Little Havana, Coral Gables & Coconut Grove" (p. 97).

VERY EXPENSIVE

The Ritz-Carlton Key Biscayne 🏨🏨🏨 *Kids*   Described by some as an oceanfront mansion, The Ritz-Carlton takes Key Biscayne to the height of luxury with 44 acres of tropical gardens, a 20,000-square-foot European-style spa, and a world-class tennis center under the direction of tennis pro Cliff Drysdale. Decorated in British colonial style, The Ritz-Carlton looks as if it came straight out of Bermuda, with its impressive flower-laden landscaping. The Ritz Kids programs provide children ages 5 to 12 with fantastic activities, and the 1,200-foot beachfront offers everything from pure relaxation to fishing, boating, or windsurfing. Spacious and luxuriously appointed rooms are elegantly Floridian, featuring large balconies overlooking the ocean or lush gardens. Unlike many behemoth hotels, The Ritz-Carlton is as much a part of the aesthetic value of the island as is its natural beauty, and its oceanfront Italian restaurant, Cioppino is excellent for formal dining, or, if you prefer casual dining, the ocean front Cantina Beach features great Mexican food and even a Tequlier—a sommelier for tequila. The best spa in Miami is also here, with 20,000 square feet of space overlooking the Atlantic Ocean. It features unheard-of treatments such as the Rum Molasses Waterfall treatment (a combination massage/hair treatment), the Key Lime Coconut Body Scrub, and the Everglades Grass Body Wrap.

455 Grand Bay Dr., Key Biscayne, FL 33149. ✆ **800/241-3333** or 305/365-4500. Fax 305/365-4501. www.ritzcarlton. com. 402 units. Winter $450–$590 double suite; off season $260–$490 double suite. AE, DC, DISC, MC, V. Valet parking (call for fees). **Amenities:** Restaurant; pool grill; spa cafe; 3 bars; 2 outdoor heated pools; tennis center with lessons available; spa and fitness center; watersports equipment; children's programs; concierge; business center; 24-hr. room service; overnight laundry service. *In room:* A/C, TV, dataport, minibar, hair dryer, safe.

Sonesta Beach Resort Key Biscayne 🏨🏨 *Kids*   Families and couples alike love this place for its oceanfront location and its many high-caliber amenities, which make

Where to Stay & Dine in Key Biscayne, Downtown Miami, West Miami, Airport Area, North Dade, Little Havana, Coral Gables & Coconut Grove

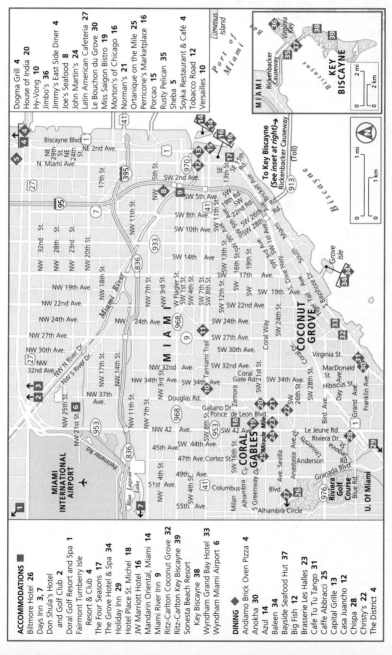

Dogma Grill **4**
House of India **20**
Hy-Vong **10**
Jimbo's **36**
Jimmy's East Side Diner **4**
Joe's Seafood **8**
John Martin's **24**
Latin American Cafeteria **27**
Le Bouchon du Grove **30**
Miss Saigon Bistro **19**
Morton's of Chicago **16**
Norman's **21**
Ortanique on the Mile **25**
Perricone's Marketplace **16**
Porcao **15**
Rusty Pelican **35**
Sheba **5**
Soyka Restaurant & Café **4**
Tobacco Road **12**
Versailles **10**

ACCOMMODATIONS ■
Biltmore Hotel **26**
Days Inn **3, 7**
Don Shula's Hotel
and Golf Club **2**
Doral Golf Resort and Spa **1**
Fairmont Turnberry Isle
Resort & Club **4**
The Four Seasons **17**
The Grove Hotel & Spa **34**
Holiday Inn **29**
Hotel Place St. Michel **18**
JW Marriott Hotel **16**
Mandarin Oriental, Miami **14**
Miami River Inn **9**
Ritz-Carlton Coconut Grove **32**
Ritz-Carlton Key Biscayne **39**
Sonesta Beach Resort
Key Biscayne **38**
Wyndham Grand Bay Hotel **33**
Wyndham Miami Airport **6**

DINING ◆
Andiamo Brick Oven Pizza **4**
Anokha **30**
Azul **14**
Baleen **34**
Bayside Seafood Hut **37**
Big Fish **12**
Brasserie Les Halles **23**
Cafe Tu Tu Tango **31**
Caffe Abbracci **25**
Capital Grille **13**
Casa Juancho **12**
Chispa **28**
Christy's **22**
The District **4**

it almost impossible to want to venture off the property. At press time, the hotel was scheduled to close September 2006 so it could start work on a $300-million redevelopment that will transform the hotel into an ultraluxe 350-room resort with oversize rooms, a full-service spa, a revamped pool and beach area, as well as restaurants and entertainment. Check back in mid-2007.

350 Ocean Dr., Key Biscayne, FL 33149. ℂ 800/SONESTA or 305/361-2021. Fax 305/361-3096. www.sonesta.com.

DOWNTOWN

If you've ever read Tom Wolfe's *Bonfire of the Vanities,* you may understand what downtown Miami is all about. If not, it's this simple: Take a wrong turn and you could find yourself in some serious trouble. Desolate and dangerous at night, downtown is trying to change its image, but it's been a long, tedious process. Recently, however, part of the area has experienced a renaissance in terms of nightlife, with several popular dance clubs and bars opening up in the environs of Northeast 11th Street off Biscayne Boulevard. If you're the kind of person who digs an urban setting, you may enjoy downtown, but if you're looking for shiny, happy Miami, you're in the wrong place (for now). As posh, pricey lofts keep going up faster than the nation's deficit, downtown is about to experience the renaissance it has been waiting for. Keep your eye on this area, and remember that you read it here first: Like orange—or pink, or white, or blue—being the new black, downtown Miami will be the new South Beach.

Most downtown hotels cater primarily to business travelers and cruise passengers. Although business hotels can be expensive, quality and service are of a high standard. Look for discounts and packages on weekends, when offices are closed and rooms often go empty.

To locate the hotels in this section, see the map "Where to Stay & Dine in Key Biscayne, Downtown Miami, West Miami, Airport Area, North Dade, Little Havana, Coral Gables & Coconut Grove" (p. 97).

VERY EXPENSIVE

The Four Seasons ★★★ *Kids*   Deciding between the hyperluxe Mandarin Oriental and the equally luxe, albeit somewhat museum-like (the artwork in the lobby, including originals by Fernando Botero, render most guests as silent as if they were examining the Mona Lisa) Four Seasons is almost like trying to tell the difference between Ava and Zsa Zsa Gabor. There are some obvious differences and some similarities, but they're kind of subtle. Flip a coin and decide where you prefer to stay because they are both spectacular in their own rights. While the architecturally striking Mandarin is located on the semiprivate Brickell Key, the equally striking, albeit in an office-building kind of way, 70-story Four Seasons is located on the more bustling Brickell Avenue, the thoroughfare of business transactions. Both have water views that are spectacular. The 221 rooms and 39 suites are luxuriously appointed, and, like the Mandarin, service here is paramount. It's much quieter here at the Four Seasons, the favored stay of camera-shy celebrities and business moguls. Most rooms overlook Biscayne Bay, and while all rooms are cushy, thanks to the hotel's signature "untucked" beds, the bland decor leaves little to be desired, really. The best rooms are the corner suites with views facing both south and east over the water. The hotel's restaurant, Acqua, serves fantastic, surprisingly affordable Italian fare, with floor-to-ceiling windows overlooking the pool area, but has yet to surpass the excellence coming out of the kitchen at the Mandarin's deservedly lauded Azul (p. 124). The 50,000-square-foot spa and Sports Club LA here are inimitable, but if you prefer a spa that's not as sprawling and a bit less harried, the Mandarin's got it beat. What the Four Seasons has over the Mandarin, however, are two more pools—a total of three gorgeous pools spread out on over 2 acres (this explains why the Mandarin Oriental recently debuted its sprawling beach club, an amenity the Four Seasons does not have). Bahia, the Latin American–influenced pool bar, is the scene for young, upscale movers and shakers. A phenomenal kids program makes the Four Seasons more desirable than the Mandarin, where kids are typically bored. It's hard to choose between the two uberluxurious properties, but one thing that remains consistent at both is that you won't be deprived of the lavish, luxe treatment that you're paying so dearly for. A celebrity clientele, including Tom Cruise and Britney Spears, is hard to spot because the hotel keeps them a well-guarded secret!

1435 Brickell Ave., Miami, FL 33131. © 305/358-3535. Fax 305/358-7758. www.fourseasons.com/miami. 221 units. Year-round $350 double; $725–$4,000 suite. AE, DC, DISC, MC, V. Valet parking $24. **Amenities:** 2 restaurants; martini bar; outdoor bar; 3 outdoor pools; Sports Club LA fitness center; full-service spa; outdoor Jacuzzi; concierge; 24-hr. business center. *In room:* A/C, TV, dataport, minibar, hair dryer, iron, safe.

Mandarin Oriental, Miami ✦✦✦   Corporate big shots and celebrities not in the mood for the South Beach spotlight have a high-end luxury hotel to stay in while wheeling and dealing their way through Miami. Catering to business travelers, conventioneers, big-time celebrities (J-Lo, Jacko, Will Smith, and so on), and the occasional leisure traveler who doesn't mind spending in excess of $500 a night for a room, the swank Mandarin Oriental features a waterfront location, residential-style rooms with Asian touches (most with balconies), and several upscale dining and bar facilities. The waterfront view of the city is the hotel's best asset, both priceless and absolutely stunning. Much of the hotel's staff was flown in from Bangkok and Hong Kong to demonstrate the hotel's unique brand of superattentive Asian-inspired service. The hotel's two restaurants, the high-end Azul (p. 124) and the more casual Café Sambal, are up to Mandarin standards and are both wonderful, as is the 15,000-square-foot The Spa at Mandarin Oriental, in which traditional Thai massages and Ayurvedic treatments are your tickets to nirvana. The Mandarin Oriental Miami is home to a 20,000-foot white-sand beach club with a fabulous Friday night happy hour, complete with beds with white cushions and canopies, beach butlers, and beachside cabana treatments, which is nice, considering that the hotel is 15 minutes from the beach. *Celeb tidbit:* Michael Jackson felt it necessary to autograph one of the paintings inside his suite, even though he didn't paint it.

500 Brickell Key Dr., Miami, FL 33131. © 305/913-8383. Fax 305/913-8300. www.mandarinoriental.com. 327 units. Year-round $415–$860; $1,250–$5,500 suites. AE, DC, DISC, MC, V. Valet parking $24 plus tax. **Amenities:** 2 restaurants; 3 bars; Oasis Beach Club; infinity pool; state-of-the-art fitness center; full-service holistic spa; outdoor Jacuzzi; concierge; business center; outdoor jogging trail. *In room:* A/C, TV, dataport, minibar, hair dryer, iron, safe, Aromatherapy Associates amenities.

MODERATE
JW Marriott Hotel ✦✦   Located smack in the middle of the business-oriented Brickell Avenue near downtown Miami, the JW Marriott is a *really* nice Marriott catering mostly to business travelers, but located conveniently enough between Coconut Grove and South Beach that it isn't a bad choice for vacationers, either. A small but elegant lobby features the classy, appropriately named Drake's Power Bar. The buzz of business deals being sealed amid clouds of cigar smoke contributes to the smoky but not staid atmosphere here. Rooms are equipped with every amenity you might need. A lovely outdoor pool, fitness center, sauna, and hot tub should become

everybody's business at this hotel. Next door is the area's bustling brewery, Gordon Biersch , which attracts well-heeled, young professional types who gather for post-work revelry.

1109 Brickell Ave., Miami, FL 33131. © **800/228-9290** or 305/374-1224. Fax 305/374-4211. www.marriott.com. Winter $259 deluxe room, $299 concierge room, $399 junior suite; off season $209 deluxe room, $249 concierge room, $349 junior suite. AE, DC, DISC, MC, V. Valet parking $18; self-parking $16. **Amenities:** 2 restaurants; bar; outdoor pool; health club; spa; sauna; concierge; tour desk; business center; laundry service. *In room:* A/C, TV, dataport with free Internet access, minibar, coffeemaker, hair dryer, iron, safe.

Miami River Inn 🌟🌟🌟 *(Finds)*   The Miami River Inn, listed on the National Register of Historic Places, is a quaint country-style hideaway (Miami's *only* bed-and-breakfast!), consisting of four cottages smack in the middle of downtown Miami. In fact, it's so hidden that most locals don't even know it exists, which only adds to its panache. Every room has hardwood floors and is uniquely furnished with antiques dating from 1908. In one room, you might find a hand-painted bathtub, a Singer sewing machine, and an armoire from the turn of the 20th century, restored to perfection. Thirty-eight rooms have private bathrooms—4 have a shower only, 6 have a tub only, and 28 have a splendid tub/shower. One- and two-bedroom apartments are available as well. In the foyer, you can peruse a library filled with books about old Miami, with histories of this land's former owners: Julia Tuttle, William Brickell, and Henry Flagler. It's close to public transportation, restaurants, and museums, and only 5 minutes from the business district.

118 SW South River Dr., Miami, FL 33130. © **800/468-3589** or 305/325-0045. Fax 305/325-9227. www.miamiriver inn.com. 40 units. Winter $89–$149 double; off season $69–$129 double. Rates include continental breakfast. Additional person $15. AE, DC, DISC, MC, V. Free parking. Pets accepted for $25 per night. **Amenities:** Small, lushly landscaped swimming pool; access to nearby YMCA facilities; Jacuzzi; babysitting; coin-op washers and dryers; laundry service; dry cleaning. *In room:* A/C, TV, hair dryer (upon request), iron (upon request).

WEST MIAMI/AIRPORT AREA

As Miami continues to grow at a rapid pace, expansion has begun westward, where land is plentiful. Several resorts have taken advantage of the space to build world-class tennis and golf courses. While there's no sea to swim in, a plethora of facilities can definitely make up for the lack of an ocean view.

To locate the hotels in this section, see the map "Where to Stay & Dine in Key Biscayne, Downtown Miami, West Miami, Airport Area, North Dade, Little Havana, Coral Gables & Coconut Grove" (p. 97).

EXPENSIVE

Doral Golf Resort and Spa 🌟 *(Kids)*   This sprawling 650-acre golf and tennis resort is in the middle of nowhere, and even though it still looks stuck in the '70s, it deserves a star just for its legendary golf course. If it weren't for the golf course, I'd never recommend anyone stay here. It's dull, and the area in which it's located is not one anyone needs to see while in Miami. While the pamperings in the spa are nothing to sneer at, the next-door golf resort hosts world-class tournaments and boasts the Blue Monster course as well as the Great White Course—the Southeast's first desertscape course, designed by The Shark himself, Greg Norman. Repeat guests usually book the season well in advance. Rooms here, like the hotel itself, are spacious, all with private balconies, many overlooking a golf course or garden. Much-needed renovations to the rooms reveal a plantation-style decor with lots of wicker and wood. Spacious bathrooms are done up in marble. Enhancements to the golf courses, spa suites, and driving range have also brought the resort up to speed with its competition. The spa's restaurant serves tasty, healthful fare—so good you won't realize it's health food, actually. And for kids, there's a phenomenal kids program and The Blue Lagoon water park featuring two 80,000-gallon pools with cascading waterfalls, a rock facade, and a 125-foot water slide. For a spa or golf vacation, the Doral is an ideal choice. Otherwise, consider investing your money in a hotel that's better located.

4400 NW 87th Ave., Miami, FL 33178. © **800/71-DORAL** or 305/592-2000. Fax 305/594-4682. www.doralresort. com. 693 units. Winter $270 double, $370 suite, $420 1-bedroom suite, $500 2-bedroom suite; off season $119 double, $280 suite, $400 1-bedroom suite, $480 2-bedroom suite. Additional person $35. Golf and spa packages available. AE, DC, DISC, MC, V. Valet parking $17. **Amenities:** 5 restaurants; 6 pools and a 125-ft. water slide; 5 golf courses and driving range; 10 tennis courts; health club and world-class spa; bike rental; concierge; business center; room service; babysitting; laundry service; dry cleaning. *In room:* A/C, TV, CD player, dataport, minibar, coffeemaker, hair dryer, iron, safe.

MODERATE

Don Shula's Hotel and Golf Club   Guests come to Shula's mostly for the golf, but there's plenty here to keep nongolfers busy, too. Opened in 1992 to much fanfare from the sports and business community, Shula's resort is an all-encompassing oasis in the middle of the planned, quaint residential neighborhood of Miami Lakes, complete with a Main Street and nearby shopping facilities—a good thing, since the site is more than a 20-minute drive from anything else. The guest rooms, located in the main building or surrounding the golf course, received a major, much-needed upgrade in 2005; even cooler, they opened a group of rooms with additional amenities designed specifically for the female travelers—meaning better and more shampoos, soaps, creams, etc. As expected, the hotel's Athletic Club features state-of-the-art equipment and is free to hotel guests. The newest addition to the resort is The Spa at Shula's, an Aveda Lifestyle Spa featuring massages, facials, and something called the Duija, which is a choreographed simultaneous facial and pedicure. The award-winning Shula's Steak House (p. 120) and the more casual Steak House Two get high rankings nationwide. They serve huge Angus beef steaks and seafood, which can be worked off with a round of golf the next day.

6842 Main St., Miami Lakes, FL 33014. © **800/24-SHULA** or 305/821-1150. Fax 305/820-8094. www.donshulahotel. com. 289 units. Winter $113–$201 suite; off season $108–$194 suite. Additional person $10. Business packages available. AE, DC, MC, V. **Amenities:** 2 restaurants; 1 bar; 2 pools; 2 golf courses (par 72 and par 3) and driving range; 9 tennis courts; sporting courts; health club; Jacuzzi; saunas; room service. *In room:* A/C, TV/VCR, dataport, coffeemaker, hair dryer, iron.

BARGAIN CHAINS

If you must stay near the airport, consider any of the dozens of moderately priced chain hotels. You'll find one of the cheapest and most recommendable options at either of the **Days Inn** locations at 7250 NW 11th St. and 4767 NW 36th St. (© **800/329-7466** for both, or 305/888-3661 or 305/261-4230, respectively), each about 2 miles from the airport. The larger property on 36th Street offers slightly cheaper rates, with singles starting as low as $49. The 11th Street locale may charge more for weekends, but prices usually start at $70. Prices include free transportation from the airport.

A more luxurious option is the **Wyndham Miami Airport,** at 3900 NW 21st St. (© **305/871-3800**), with rates from $100 to $225.

NORTH DADE

To locate the hotels in this section, see the map "Where to Stay & Dine in Key Biscayne, Downtown Miami, West Miami, Airport Area, North Dade, Little Havana, Coral Gables & Coconut Grove" (p. 97).

VERY EXPENSIVE

Aqualina, A Rosewood Resort 🐾🐾🐾   Some people are still scratching their heads as to why this over-the-top, luxurious resort decided to open across the street from a Denny's and T-shirt shops. That's because they haven't been inside. Once you enter Aqualina, you forget that you're even in Miami and feel as if you're somewhere on the Italian Riviera. In fact, it was Sophia Loren who gave this hotel its name when she was out kibitzing with the CEO of Rosewood. Located on 4½ beachfront acres with over 400 feet of Atlantic coastline, Aqualina is a massive Mediterranean-style resort towering over all the others with its Baroque fountains and just 97 impeccably appointed, insanely luxurious rooms and suites featuring the usual trimmings—flat-screen TVs, goose-down duvet and pillows—and some unusual ones as well. Among them: posh Lady Primrose's bath products, Rivolta Carmigani sheets, and, in some suites, full gourmet kitchens with Sub Zero fridge, granite countertops, and dishwasher—not that the people who can afford to stay here will be doing any cleaning. A branch of NYC's acclaimed Il Mulino restaurant is also here. Less fancy fare is offered at the beach bar and restaurant, Costa Grill, which is under the supervision of the resort's executive chef, Ted Peters, who honed his skills at the highly regarded The Mansion at Turtle Creek in Dallas. The spa, called ESPA, is a bi-level, 20,000-square-foot oceanfront Eden, featuring everything from massage and aromatherapy and a standard Welcome Foot Ritual, in which your own personal needs are assessed while your feet are caressed. There are three pools steps away from the beach—an adults-only known as the Tranquility pool, a heated jet pool, and a free-for-all pool. The hotel's fantastic AcquaMarine Program offers a splashy array of marine-biology activities for kids and adults. Beach cabanas offer the ultimate in luxurious lingering. All this luxury doesn't come cheap, so if you can afford it, go for it. It isn't nearly as pricey as South Beach's Setai, and the chance of Paris Hilton and Tara Reid partying here is unlikely. Aqualina caters more to the young, sophisticated, international jet-set crowd that's been there, done that, and doesn't need the T-shirt to remind them of where they are.

17875 Collins Ave., Sunny Isles Beach 33160. ☎ **888/767-3966** or 305/918-8000. Fax 305/918-8100. www.rose woodhotels.com. 97 units. Winter $675–$950 double, $1,075-$5,000 suite; off season $425–$675 double, $775–$5,000 suite. AE, DC, DISC, MC, V. Valet parking $25 **Amenities:** 3 restaurants; bar; 3 outdoor pools; state-of-the-art spa; extensive watersports equipment rental; 24-hour concierge; 24-hr. room service; babysitting. *In room:* A/C, TV, CD player, fax, Wi-Fi, minibar, coffeemaker, hair dryer, iron, safe.

Fairmont Turnberry Isle Resort & Club 🐾🐾🐾   One of Miami's classiest resorts (along the lines of the Mandarin Oriental), this gorgeous 300-acre compound has every possible facility for active guests, particularly golfers. You'll pay a lot to stay here—but it's worth it. The main attractions are two Trent Jones courses, available only to members and guests of the hotel. A new seven-story Jasmine wing looks like a Mediterranean village and is surrounded by tropical gardens that are joined by covered marble walkways to the other wings. Treat yourself to a "Turnberry Retreat" at the Turnberry Spa, which recently underwent a $10-million renovation. The spa comprises three levels of deluxe pampering and includes aerobics and fitness classes, stress reduction, massage therapy, and a juice bar designed for complete rejuvenation. Impeccable service from check-in to checkout consistently brings loyal fans back to this resort for more. Its location in the well-manicured residential and shopping area of North Miami Beach known as Aventura means you'll find excellent shopping and some of the best dining in Miami right in the neighborhood. Unless you're into boating, the higher-priced resort rooms (instead of the yacht club) are where you'll want to stay; you'll be steps from the spa facilities and the renowned Veranda restaurant. The well-proportioned rooms are gorgeously tiled to match the Mediterranean-style architecture. The huge bathrooms even have a color TV mounted within reach of the whirlpool bathtubs and glass-walled showers. The only drawback to this hotel is that you'll need to take a shuttle to the beach. *Celeb alert:* You never know who may stay here. Paul McCartney and his wife, Heather Mills, were here just before they tied the knot and allegedly had a huge enough fight that Mills threw her rock of an engagement ring out the window. A week later, Sir Paul paid for a staffer to personally fly the ring back to his estate in the U.K.

19999 W. Country Club Dr., Aventura, FL 33180. (✆ 800/327-7028 or 305/936-2929. Fax 305/933-6560. www. turnberryisle.com. 392 units. Winter $459–$589 double, $609–$899 suite; off season $175–$275 double, $140–$409 suite; year-round $4,000 grand presidential suite. AE, DC, DISC, MC, V. Valet parking $12; free self-parking. **Amenities:** 6 restaurants; numerous bars and lounges; 2 outdoor pools; 2 golf courses; 2 tennis complexes; state-of-the-art spa; extensive watersports equipment rental; concierge; secretarial services; 24-hr. room service; babysitting. *In room:* A/C, TV/VCR, CD player, fax, dataport, minibar, fridge (upon request), coffeemaker (upon request), hair dryer, iron, safe.

Le Meridien Sunny Isles Beach 🏵🏵 The latest in luxury hotels to open in the area, this 210-suite all-suite beachfront resort is Le Meridien's first oceanfront resort in the U.S. It brings a nice touch of European-style glitz and glamour to the area and, sorry Donald, trumps the nearby Trump resort in many ways. All rooms—there are 126 one-bedroom suites and 80 two-bedroom suites—feature king-size beds with Egyptian cotton linens and duvet covers, and the latest in technology, including full-size Italian kitchens, flat-screen TVs, Wi-Fi, a washer/dryer, and a spa-quality bathroom with amenities you'll want to take home with you. The gorgeous lobby has a bustling 30-seat bar where people usually hang out when waiting for a table at the delicious Bice Italian restaurant. Service throughout the hotel is impeccable. The hotel's 6,000-square-foot spa is also a hot spot for those seeking pampering, but I prefer the pool area, where an infinity-edged beachfront pool stands out like a supermodel in a crowd of circus clowns. A great spot for families looking for a bit more luxury than usual, Le Meridien has planned activities for both kids and families.

18683 Collins Ave., Miami Beach, FL 33140. (✆ 800/543-4300 or 305/503-6000. Fax 305/503-6001. www.miami. lemeridien.com. 210 units. Winter from $354 1-bedroom suite, from $559 2-bedroom suite; off season from $302 1-bedroom suite, from $507 2-bedroom suite. AE, DC, DISC, MC, V. Valet parking $25. **Amenities:** Restaurant; lounge; bar; outdoor pool spa; watersports equipment; 24-hour concierge; business center; 24-hour room service; in-room massage; babysitting; laundry service; dry cleaning. *In room:* A/C, TV/DVD, Wi-Fi, kitchen, minibar, coffeemaker, hair dryer, safe.

CORAL GABLES

Translated appropriately as "City Beautiful," the Gables, as it's affectionately known, was one of Miami's original planned communities and is still among the city's prettiest, most pedestrian-friendly, albeit preservation-obsessed neighborhoods. Pristine with a European flair, Coral Gables is best known for its wide array of excellent upscale restaurants of various ethnicities, as well as a hotly contested (the quiet city didn't want to welcome new traffic) mega shopping complex featuring upscale stores such as Nordstrom.

If you're looking for luxury, Coral Gables has a number of wonderful hotels, but if you're on a tight budget, you may be better off elsewhere. Two well-priced chains in the area are **Holiday Inn,** 1350 S. Dixie Hwy. (✆ **800/HOLIDAY** or 305/667-5611), with rates between $89 and $189; and **Terrace Inn,** 1430 S. Dixie Hwy. (✆ **305/665-7501**), with rates ranging from $59 to $89. Both are located directly across the street from the University of Miami and are popular with families and friends of students.

To locate the hotels in this section, see the map "Where to Stay & Dine in Key Biscayne, Downtown Miami, West Miami, Airport Area, North Dade, Little Havana, Coral Gables & Coconut Grove" (p. 97).

VERY EXPENSIVE

Biltmore Hotel ☆☆☆   A romantic sense of old-world glamour combined with a rich history permeate the Biltmore as much as the pricey perfume of the guests who stay here. Built in 1926, it's the oldest Coral Gables hotel and is a National Historic Landmark—one of only two operating hotels in Florida to receive that designation. Rising above the Spanish-style estate is a majestic 300-foot copper-clad tower, modeled after the Giralda bell tower in Seville and visible throughout the city. Over the years, the Biltmore has passed through many incarnations (including a post–World War II stint as a VA hospital), but it is now back to its original 1926 splendor. More intriguing than scary is the rumor that ghosts of wounded soldiers and even Al Capone, for whom the Everglades Suite is nicknamed, roam the halls here. But don't worry. The hotel is far from a haunted house. It is warm, welcoming, and extremely charming. Now under the management of the Seaway Hotel Corporation, the hotel boasts large Moorish-style rooms decorated with tasteful decor, European feather beds, Egyptian cotton duvets, writing desks, and some high-tech amenities. The enormous lobby, with its 45-foot vaulted ceilings, makes a bold statement of elegance. Always a popular destination for golfers, including former President Clinton (who stays in the Al Capone suite), the Biltmore is situated on a lush, rolling 18-hole course that is as challenging as it is beautiful. The spa is fantastic, and the enormous 23,000-square-foot winding pool (surrounded by arched walkways and classical sculptures) is legendary—it's where a pre-*Tarzan* Johnny Weismuller broke the world's swimming record. Even if you don't stay at the Biltmore Hotel, definitely take a tour of it (call ✆ **305/445-1926** for more information; p. 151) to learn about its fascinating history and mystery. The Sunday brunch here is legendary—book early.

1200 Anastasia Ave., Coral Gables, FL 33134. ✆ **800/727-1926** or 305/445-1926. Fax 305/442-9496. www. biltmorehotel.com. 276 units. Winter $294–$354 double; off season $254–$319 double; year-round specialty suites $394–$2,850. Additional person $20. Special packages available. AE, DC, DISC, MC, V. Overnight valet parking $16; free self-parking. **Amenities:** 4 restaurants; 4 bars; outdoor pool; 18-hole golf course; 10 lit tennis courts; state-of-the-art health club; full-service spa; sauna; concierge; car rental through concierge; elaborate business center and secretarial services; salon; 24-hr. room service; laundry service; dry cleaning; wine cellar. *In room:* A/C, TV, VCR on request, fax, dataport, kitchenette (in tower suite), minibar, hair dryer, iron, safe.

EXPENSIVE

Hotel Place St. Michel ☆☆☆   This European-style hotel, in the heart of Coral Gables, is one of the city's most romantic options. The accommodations and hospitality are straight out of old-world Europe, complete with dark wood–paneled walls, cozy beds, beautiful antiques, and a quiet elegance that seems startlingly out of place in trendy Miami. Everything here is charming—from the brass elevator and parquet floors to the paddle fans. One-of-a-kind furnishings make each room special. Bathrooms are on the smaller side but are hardly cramped. All have tub/showers except for two, which have one or the other. If you're picky, request your preference. Guests are treated to fresh fruit upon arrival and enjoy perfect service throughout their stay. The exceptional Restaurant St. Michel is a very romantic dining choice.

162 Alcazar Ave., Coral Gables, FL 33134. ✆ **800/848-HOTEL** or 305/444-1666. Fax 305/529-0074. www.hotel placestmichel.com. 27 units. Winter $179 double, $200 suite; off season $129 double, $160 suite. Additional person $10. Rates include continental breakfast and fruit basket upon arrival. AE, DC, MC, V. Self-parking $7. **Amenities:** Restaurant; lounge; access to nearby health club; concierge; room service; laundry service; dry cleaning; Wi-Fi in all public areas. *In room:* A/C, TV, dataport, hair dryer, iron (available upon request).

COCONUT GROVE

This waterfront village hugs the shores of Biscayne Bay, just south of U.S. 1 and about 10 minutes from the beaches. Once a haven for hippies, head shops, and artsy bohemian characters, the Grove succumbed to the inevitable temptations of commercialism and has become a Gap nation, featuring a host of themey restaurants, bars, a megaplex, and lots of stores. Outside the main shopping area, however, you'll find the beautiful remnants of Old Miami in the forms of flora, fauna, and, of course water.

To locate the hotels in this section, see the map "Where to Stay & Dine in Key Biscayne, Downtown Miami, West Miami, Airport Area, North Dade, Little Havana, Coral Gables & Coconut Grove" (p. 97).

VERY EXPENSIVE

Grove Isle Club and Resort ✷   Hidden away in the bougainvillea and lushness of the Grove, the Grove Isle Resort is off the beaten path on its own lushly landscaped 20-acre island, just outside the heart of Coconut Grove. The isolated exclusivity of this resort contributes to a country-club vibe, though, for the most part, the people here aren't snooty; they just value their privacy and precious relaxation time. Everyone dresses in white and pastels, and if they're not on their way to a set of tennis, they're not in a rush to get anywhere. You'll step into suites that are elegantly furnished with mosquito-netted canopy beds and a patio overlooking the bay. You'll need to reserve early here—rooms go very fast. Baleen (p. 131), a fantastic yet pricey haute cuisinerie, serves fresh seafood and other regional specialties in a spectacular, elegant dining room, or, better yet, outside on the water.

4 Grove Isle Dr., Coconut Grove, FL 33133. ✆ **800/88-GROVE** or 305/858-8300. Fax 305/854-6702. www.groveisle. com. 49 units (all suites). Winter $409 suite; off season $199–$219 suite. Rates include breakfast with certain packages only. AE, DC, MC, V. Valet parking $17. **Amenities:** Large outdoor heated pool; 12 outdoor tennis courts; deluxe health club; concierge; secretarial services; salon; room service; in-room massage; babysitting; laundry service; dry cleaning. *In room:* A/C, TV/VCR, dataport, minibar, hair dryer, iron, safe.

Ritz-Carlton Coconut Grove   The third and smallest of Miami's Ritz-Carlton hotels is, hands down, the most intimate of its properties, surrounded by 2 acres of tropical gardens and overlooking Biscayne Bay and the Miami skyline. Decorated in an Italian Renaissance design, the hotel's understated luxury is a welcome addition to an area known for its gaudiness. In addition to the usual Ritz-Carlton standard of service and comfort, the hotel has an excellent, extremely elegant restaurant (with footstools for women to put their purses on—how classy!), Biscaya Grill, and a sophisticated wine-tasting scene at the Amadeus Bar.

3300 SW 27th Ave., Coconut Grove, FL 33133. ✆ **800/241-3333** or 305/644-4680. Fax 305/644-4681. www.ritz carlton.com. 115 units. Winter $385–$650 double suite; off season $215–$400 double suite. AE, DC, DISC, MC, V. Valet parking. **Amenities:** Restaurant; pool grill; 3 bars; outdoor heated pool; fitness center; spa; concierge; business center; boutique; 24-hr. room service; babysitting; overnight laundry service. *In room:* A/C, TV, dataport, minibar, hair dryer, safe.

Wyndham Grand Bay Hotel ✷✷✷   Grand in size and stature, the Grand Bay Hotel looks like it belongs in Acapulco with its ziggurat structure and tropical landscaping, but once you see the massive bright red sculpture/structure done by late *Condé Nast* editorial director Alexander Lieberman in the driveway, you know you're not in Mexico. Ultraluxurious, the Grand Bay is quietly elegant and, as a result, has hosted the likes of privacy fanatics such as Michael Jackson. British singer George Michael filmed his "Careless Whisper" video here because of its sweeping views of Biscayne Bay. Rooms are superb, with views of the bay and the Coconut Grove Marina, and they're decorated in soft peach tones with a country French theme. Bathrooms are equally luxurious. Service is outstanding, and the clientele ranges from families to international jet-setters.

2669 S. Bayshore Dr., Coconut Grove, FL 33133. (*©* **305/858-9600**. Fax 305/859-2026. www.wyndham.com. 177 units. Winter $159–$909 suite; off season $120–$849 suite. Additional person $20. AE, DC, MC, V. Valet parking $18. **Amenities:** Restaurant; outdoor pool; 24-hr. health club; Jacuzzi; sauna; concierge; business center; babysitting. *In room:* A/C, TV, fax, CD player, dataport, minibar, coffeemaker, hair dryer, iron, safe.

4 Where to Dine in Miami

Don't be fooled by the plethora of superlean model types you're likely to see posing throughout Miami: Contrary to popular belief, dining in this city is as much a sport as the in-line skating on Ocean Drive. With over 6,000 restaurants to choose from, dining out in Miami has become a passionate pastime for locals and visitors alike. Our star chefs have fused Californian-Asian with Caribbean and Latin elements to create a world-class flavor all its own: *Floribbean.* Think mango chutney splashed over fresh swordfish or a spicy sushi sauce served alongside Peruvian ceviche.

Formerly synonymous with early-bird specials, Miami's new-wave cuisine now rivals that of San Francisco—or even New York. Nouveau Cuban chef Douglas Rodriguez has returned to South Beach and Coral Gables with two fantastic restaurants. In addition, other stellar chefs, such as the Food Network's own Michelle Bernstein, Mark Militello, Allen Susser, Norman van Aken, Govind Armstrong, Clay Conley, and Jonathan Eismann, remain firmly planted in the city's culinary scene, fusing local ingredients into edible masterpieces. Indulging in this New World cuisine is not only high in calories; it's high in price. But if you can manage to splurge at least once, it'll be worth it.

Thanks to a thriving cafe society in both South Beach and Coconut Grove, you can also enjoy a moderately priced meal and linger for hours without having a waiter hover over you. In Little Havana, you can chow down on a meal that serves about six for less than $10. And since seafood is plentiful, it doesn't have to cost you an arm and a leg to enjoy the appendages of a crab or lobster. Don't be put off by the looks of our recommended seafood shacks in places such as Key Biscayne—oftentimes these spots get the best and freshest catches.

Whatever you're craving, Miami's got it—with the exception of decent Chinese food and a New York–style slice of pizza. If you're craving a scene with your steak, then South Beach is the place to be. Like many cities in Europe and Latin America, it is fashionable to dine late in South Beach, preferably after 9pm, sometimes as late as midnight. Service on South Beach is notoriously slow and arrogant, but it comes with the turf. (Of course, it is possible to find restaurants that defy the notoriety and actually pride themselves on friendly service.) On the mainland—especially in Coral Gables, and, more recently, downtown and on Brickell Avenue—you can also experience fine dining without the pretense.

The biggest complaint when it comes to Miami dining isn't the haughtiness, but rather the dearth of truly moderately priced restaurants, especially in South Beach and

Coral Gables. It's either really cheap or really expensive; the in-between somehow gets lost in the culinary shuffle. Quick-service diners don't really exist here as they do in other cosmopolitan areas. I've tried to cover a range of cuisines in a range of prices. But with new restaurants opening on a weekly basis, you're bound to find a savory array of dining choices on every budget.

Many restaurants keep extended hours in season (roughly Dec–Apr) and may close for lunch and/or dinner on Monday when the traffic is slower. Always call ahead, since schedules do change. Also, always look carefully at your bill—many Miami restaurants add a 15% gratuity to your total due to the enormous influx of European tourists who are not accustomed to tipping. Keep in mind that this amount is the *suggested* amount and can be adjusted, either higher or lower, depending on your assessment of the service provided. Because of this tipping-included policy, South Beach waitstaff are best known for their lax or inattentive service. *Feel free to adjust it* if you feel your server deserves more or less.

SOUTH BEACH

The renaissance of South Beach started in the early '90s and is still continuing as classic cuisine gives in to mod-temptation by inevitably fusing with more chic, nouveau developments created by faithful followers and devotees of the Food Network school of cooking. The ultimate result has spawned dozens of first-rate restaurants. In fact, big-name restaurants from across the country have capitalized on South Beach's international appeal and opened, and continue to open, branches here with great success. A few old standbys remain from the *Miami Vice* days, but the flock of newcomers dominates the scene, with places going in and out of style as quickly as the tides.

On South Beach, new restaurants are opening and closing as frequently as Emeril says "Bam!" Since it's impossible to list them all, I recommend strolling and browsing. Most restaurants post a copy of their menu outside. With very few exceptions, the places on Ocean Drive are crowded with tourists and priced accordingly. You'll do better to venture a little farther onto the pedestrian-friendly streets just west of Ocean Drive.

To locate the restaurants in this section, see the "South Beach" map (p. 83).

VERY EXPENSIVE

BED 🐟🐟 ECLECTIC BED—that's Beverage, Entertainment, Dining —is one of the most gimmicky dining lounges to land in South Beach in a very long time. So gimmicky, in fact, that an episode of *Sex and the City* featured a then-fictional New York branch (now BED NY is in a West Chelsea penthouse) of the sexy South Beach establishment. When you walk inside, you'll feel as if you've entered a Buddhist temple. An array of inviting mosquito-netted beds awaits diners. You'll rest your head against soft, cushiony pillows. A DJ spins Euro mood music and some techno. You'll have no problem appreciating the taste and aroma of the exquisite (and exquisitely priced) cuisine, featuring dishes such as pan-seared foie gras with caramelized mango and cranberry with French toast, and Florida yellowtail snapper with garlic mash, matchstick asparagus (a fancy way of saying thin asparagus), and a choice of caper beurre noisette or Vermouth cream sauce. For dessert, try the Cloud Nine-Dulce de Leche Soufflé, or indulge in some Fire and Ice—molten chocolate cake with rum vanilla ice cream and caramel sauce. Sheets are always changed for the second seating, thank goodness, and were switched from white to dark brown to withstand stilettos and boots that eventually end up traipsing on them when the dancing begins. For the crowd-phobic, do not go to BED on a weekend or on its most popular Monday or

Wednesday nights—it's a nightmare. If you really want to enjoy the food, make sure you go to the 8pm seating or else you may be sharing that food with several hundred of your closest (by proxy) friends.

929 Washington Ave., South Beach. ℰ 305/532-9070. www.bedmiami.com. Reservations required, accepted only on the day you plan to dine here. Main courses $32–$40. AE, DC, MC, V. Mon–Sat first lay (no actual seats) 8pm; second lay 10:30pm. Lounge 11pm–5am.

Casa Tua ✿✿ *Finds* ITALIAN   The stunning Casa Tua is a sleek and chic country Italian-style establishment set in a refurbished 1925 Mediterranean-style house-cum-hotel. It has several dining areas, including a resplendent outdoor garden, comfy Ralph Lauren-esque living room, and a communal eat-in kitchen. The lamb chops are stratospheric in price ($42) but sublime in taste. Service is, as always with South Beach eateries, inconsistent, ranging from ultraprofessional to absurdly lackadaisical. For these prices, they should be wiping our mouths for us. What used to be a fabulous lounge upstairs is now a members' only club, so don't even try to get in.

1700 James Ave., South Beach. ℰ 305/673-1010. Reservations required. Main courses $24–$42. AE, DC, MC, V. Mon–Sat 7pm–midnight.

China Grill ✿✿ PAN-ASIAN   If ever a restaurant could be as cavernous as, say, the Asian continent, this would be it. Formerly a hub of hype and pompous circumstance, China Grill has calmed on the coolness meter despite the infrequent appearance of the likes of J-Lo and Enrique Iglesias (separately, of course), but its cuisine is still sizzling, if not better than ever. With an incomparable and dizzying array of amply portioned dishes (such as the outrageous crispy spinach, wasabi mashed potatoes, seared rare tuna in spicy Japanese pepper, broccoli rabe dumplings, lobster pancakes, and a sinfully delicious dessert sampler complete with sparklers), an epicurean journey into the world of near-perfect Pan-Asian cuisine is well worth a stop on any foodie's itinerary. Keep in mind that China Grill is a family-style restaurant and that dishes are meant to be shared. For those who can't stay away from sushi, China Grill recently introduced Dragon, a 40-seat "sushi den" in a private back room with one-of-a-kind rolls such as the Havana Roll, which consists of yellowtail snapper, rum, coconut, avocado, and red tobiko, and cocktails such as the Lemongrass Saketini.

404 Washington Ave., South Beach. ℰ 305/534-2211. Reservations strongly recommended. Main courses $25–$59. AE, DC, MC, V. Mon–Thurs 11:45am–midnight; Fri 11:45am–1am; Sat 6pm–1am; Sun 6pm–midnight.

Emeril's Miami Beach ✿ CREOLE   It was only a matter of time before, bam!, Emeril Lagasse set up shop in South Beach. If only it were a few years sooner. Not that we're knocking Emeril's culinary skills, but it just seems that amid a bunch of trendy, innovative restaurants, Emeril's is just an upscale cross between Red Lobster and TGI Friday's. At any rate, if you've never dined at Emeril's original restaurant(s) in New Orleans and you're craving Creole cuisine, dine here. Elaborately (bordering on gaudily) designed, the 8,000-square-foot restaurant replaces the much-lauded Gaucho Room at the Loews Hotel. Signature dishes include New Orleans barbecue shrimp with a petite rosemary biscuit; Niman Ranch double-cut pork chop with tamarind glaze, carmelized sweet potatoes, and green chili mole sauce; and banana cream pie with banana crust, caramel sauce, and chocolate shavings. Order a few of those, and, bam!, suddenly, your waistline is bigger and your wallet thinner.

In the Loews Hotel, 1601 Collins Ave., South Beach. ℰ 305/695-4550. Reservations required. Main courses $18–$30. AE, MC, V. Daily 11:30am–2pm; Sun–Thurs 5:30–10pm; Fri–Sat 5:30–11pm.

Escopazzo ⁢ ITALIAN   *Escopazzo* means "I'm going crazy" in Italian, but the only sign of insanity in this primo Northern Italian eatery is the fact that it seats only 90 and it's one of the best restaurants in town. The wine bottles have it better—the restaurant's cellar holds 1,000 bottles of various vintages. Should you be so lucky to score a table at this romantic local favorite (choose one in the back dining room that's reminiscent of an Italian courtyard complete with fountain and faux windows; it's not cheesy at all), you'll have trouble deciding between dishes that will have you swearing off the Olive Garden with your first bite. Standouts are squid-ink pasta with ragout of mussels, clams, and calamari in a crispy pasta basket, or Smithfield pork tenderloin filled with smoked mozzarella in a Madeira, sage, and amarene cherry sauce. The hand-rolled pastas and risotto are near perfection. Eating here is like dining with a big Italian family—it's never boring (the menu changes five or six times a year), the service is excellent, and nobody's happy until you are blissfully full.

1311 Washington Ave., South Beach. Ⓡ **305/674-9450.** Reservations required. Main courses $18–$32. AE, MC, V. Mon–Fri 6pm–midnight; Sat 6pm–1am; Sun 6–11pm.

Joe's Stone Crab Restaurant ⁢ SEAFOOD   Unless you grease the palms of one of the stone-faced maitre d's with some stone-cold cash, you'll be waiting for those famous claws for up to 2 hours—if not more. As much a Miami landmark as the beaches themselves, Joe's is a microcosm of the city, attracting everyone from T-shirted locals to a bejeweled Ivana Trump. Whatever you wear, however, will be eclipsed by a kitschy, unglamorous plastic bib that your waiter will tie on you unless you say otherwise. Open only during stone-crab season (Oct–May), Joe's reels in the crowds with the freshest, meatiest stone crabs and their essential accouterments: creamed spinach and excellent sweet-potato fries. The claws come in medium, large, and jumbo. Some say size doesn't matter; others swear by the jumbo (and more expensive) ones. Whatever you choose, pair them with a savory mustard sauce (a perfect mix of mayo and mustard) or hot butter. Not feeling crabby? The fried chicken and liver and onions on the regular menu are actually considered by many as far superior—they're definitely far cheaper—to the crabs. Oh yeah, and save room for dessert. The Key lime pie here is the best in town. If you don't feel like waiting, try Joe's Takeaway, which is located next door to the restaurant—it's a lot quicker and just as tasty.

11 Washington Ave. (at Biscayne St., just south of 1st St.), South Beach. Ⓡ **305/673-0365** or 305/673-4611 for take-out. www.joesstonecrab.com. Reservations not accepted. Market price varies but averages $63 for a serving of jumbo crab claws, $43 for large claws. AE, DC, DISC, MC, V. Daily 11:30am–2pm; Sun 4–10pm; Mon–Thurs 5–10pm; Fri–Sat 5–11pm. Open mid-Oct to mid-May.

Mark's South Beach ⁢ NEW WORLD/MEDITERRANEAN   Named after owner and chef Mark Militello, this is one of the best restaurants in all of Miami. But because celebrities don't go here, it's not on the A-list as far as scene is concerned, and for true foodies, this is a blissful thing. A cozy, contemporary restaurant nestled in the basement of the quietly chic Hotel Nash, Mark's New World and Mediterranean-influenced menu changes nightly. What doesn't change is the consistency and freshness of the restaurant's exquisite cuisine. The roasted rack of Colorado lamb with semolina gnocchi is exceptional and worth every bit of cholesterol it may have. Crispy-skin yellowtail snapper with shrimp, tomato, black olives, oregano, and crumbled feta cheese is in a school of its own. Desserts, including an impressive cheese cart, are outrageous, especially the pistachio cake with chocolate sorbet. Unlike many South Beach eating establishments, the knowledgeable servers are here because of their experience in the restaurant—not modeling—business. If you're expecting to spot celebs and be part of the "scene," then Mark's is not the place for you. For a few bucks extra and a trip over the causeway, go to Azul at the Mandarin Oriental Miami instead.

In the Hotel Nash, 1120 Collins Ave., South Beach. © **305/604-9050.** Reservations recommended. Main courses $26–$41. AE, DC, DISC, MC, V. Wed–Sun 7–11am and noon–3pm; Wed–Sat 7pm–midnight, Sun 7–11pm.

Metro Kitchen + Bar ✸ FUSION   Diehard foodies find it hard to accept that anything has replaced the Astor Place Bar and Grill, but hipsters welcome the change, thanks to the fact that club owner Nicola Siervo is a partner in the Hotel Astor's sizzling subterranean restaurant—and when he builds things, celebs come. Besides the fact that Cameron Diaz, Justin Timberlake, and even O. J. Simpson have been spotted dining here, it's not just about the scene. The decor is described as "tropical urban Art Deco," but I prefer to call it cosmopolitan chic, with its glass ceiling, plush banquettes, and rich wood accents. The outdoor garden, set up on what used to be the hotel's minipool, is gorgeous when it's not too hot out. Metro definitely looks as if it belongs in a metropolis. So does the smart-looking crowd. The cuisine is a combination of modern American, Asian, French, and Italian cuisines. For dinner, do not miss the tomato tartlette appetizer with Majorero cheese and aged sherry vinegar. For a main course, choose from strip steak with truffle fries—the best fries you'll ever eat, pan-cooked snapper with udon noodles, or duck breast with grilled apples and fresh spinach. On Tuesday nights, Metro becomes a big scene as local luminaries convene here for cocktails, kibitzing, and star-spotting.

In the Hotel Astor, 956 Washington Ave., South Beach. © **305/672-7217.** Reservations recommended. Main courses $26–$29. AE, DC, DISC, MC, V. Daily 11:30am–2:30pm; Sun–Thurs 7pm–midnight; Fri–Sat 7pm–1am.

Nobu ✸✸✸ SUSHI   When Madonna ate here, no one really noticed. Same thing happened when Justin Timberlake and Cameron Diaz canoodled here. Not because they were purposely trying not to notice, but because the real star at Nobu is the sushi. The raw facts: Nobu has been hailed as one of the best sushi restaurants in the world, with always-packed eateries in New York, London, and Los Angeles. The Omakase, or Chef's Choice—a multicourse menu entirely up to the chef for $70 per person and up—gets consistent raves. And although you won't wait long for your food to be cooked, you will wait forever to score a table here.

At The Shore Club Hotel, 1901 Collins Ave., South Beach. © **305/695-3232.** Reservations for parties of 6 or more. Main courses $26 and above. AE, MC, V. Sun 7–11pm; Mon–Thurs 7pm–midnight; Fri–Sat 7pm–1am.

Ola ✸✸ NUEVO LATINO   Star chef Douglas Rodriguez single-handedly created the nouveau Latino and Cubano cuisine in Miami when he founded Lincoln Road's Yuca restaurant in 1989. From there, he skyrocketed to fame (and left Yuca to rot in mediocrity) and became co-owner and executive chef at New York City's lauded Patria (leaving Miami restaurant-goers to wallow in their sorrows). But now Rodriguez is back in full force with Ola, housed in Deco landmark The Savoy, serving Spanish tapas and ceviches as well as Rodriguez's very own inimitable culinary concoctions. For those who are addicted to the low-carb craze, you'll find several items on the menu tailored to your diet. But why bother? Latin food is about flavor and carbs, so indulge here (like your wallet will have to). For a more meat-intensive Rodriguez experience, check out **Ola Steak**, 320 San Lorenzo Ave. (© **305/461-4442**), in Coral Gables.

455 Ocean Dr., Miami Beach © **305/695-9125.** Reservations recommended. Main courses $24–$40. AE, DC, MC, V. Mon–Thurs 5:30–11pm; Fri–Sat 5:30pm–midnight.

o-R-o ✿✿ CONTEMPORARY AMERICAN   This swank new spot above the rough-and-tumble Monty's Raw Bar is a welcome addition to the cadre of chichi restaurants in town. One thing it has that the others doesn't: a panoramic water view of the city skyline, Fisher Island, and Miami Beach Marina. The cavernous, chandelier-lit main 175-seat dining room features a black floor and all-white booths, tables, and chairs made of ostrich leather. It's over the top, just like the food. Steaks served on butcher blocks are no match for the old-school lobster thermidor, perched high on a massive platter, draped with a red-and-white-checked napkin and complete with mallet, cracker, roe picker, and more. Or you can have one of the stellar servers do it for you. Desserts are outrageous, ranging from make-your-own s'mores and a giant ice cream sandwich to a trio of custom minicakes from pastry superstar Cake Designs by Edda. Add to that the amusing juxtaposition of the fine Mikasa flatware and glassware, the black granite bar area, and the private champagne-tasting room with the disco soundtrack and fried chicken entree, and you've got one fantastic dining experience.

455 Ocean Dr., Miami Beach ✆ **305/673-3444.** Reservations recommended. Main courses $16–$38. AE, MC, V. Sun–Wed 5–11pm; Thurs–Sun 5pm–1am.

Pacific Time ✿✿ PAN-ASIAN   When Pacific Time opened on a desolate Lincoln Road in 1993, people thought former-model-turned-chef Jonathan Eismann was insane. Eleven years later, Lincoln Road is bustling and Pacific Time's dishes remain stunning hybrids of Chinese, Japanese, Korean, Vietnamese, Korean, Mongolian, and Indonesian flavors. Everything is fresh, and the restaurant prides itself on not owning a single can opener or microwave. One of the best appetizers is the Indochine beef salad, seared Angus beef with a spicy satay vinaigrette. For a main course, the ever-changing menu offers many locally caught fish specialties, such as Szechuan grilled mahimahi served on a bed of shredded shallots and ginger with a sweet sake-infused sauce and tempura-dunked sweet-potato slivers on the side. The famous chocolate bomb is every bit as decadent as they say, with hot bittersweet chocolate bursting from the cupcakelike center—order it as soon as you sit down. The wine list is quite extensive and includes red and white wines from Italy, France, the Napa Valley, Australia, Argentina, New Zealand, and South Africa. The restaurant's best deal is its pretheater menu, a three-course dinner for only $30, available nightly from 6 to 7:30pm—one good reason to go early bird. At the time of this writing, Eismann was revamping the Design District space formerly known as Grass.

915 Lincoln Rd. (between Jefferson and Michigan aves.), South Beach. ✆ **305/534-5979.** Reservations recommended. Main courses $24–$32. AE, DC, MC, V. Sun–Thurs 6–11pm; Fri–Sat 6pm–midnight.

Prime 112 ✿✿✿ STEAKHOUSE   Part of the ever-expanding culinary empire of Nemo, Big Pink, and Shoji Sushi, Prime 112 is the latest darling to join the exclusive group of restaurants in the hot South of Fifth Street area of South Beach. A sleek steakhouse ambience and bustling bar (complete with dried strips of bacon in lieu of nuts) play second fiddle to the beef, which is arguably the best in the entire city. The 12-ounce filet mignon is seared to perfection and can be enhanced with optional dipping sauces (for a price)—truffle, garlic herb, foie gras, and chipotle. The 22-ounce bone-in rib-eye is fabulous, as is the gigantic 48-ounce porterhouse. Prime 112 also features a Kobe beef burger, a $30 version of sheer ecstasy, although fries are extra at $8, as are all the side dishes (the broccoli rabe sautéed in garlic is outstanding, as are the scalloped potatoes)—typical in a steakhouse, but the prices here are hefty. A powerhouse crowd gathers here for lunch and dinner, and reservations are more rare than the yellowfin tuna tartare appetizer, but should you be lucky enough to score such a, um, prime reservation, take it without hesitation.

112 Ocean Dr. (in The Browns Hotel), South Beach. ⓒ **305/532-8112**. www.prime112.com. Reservations recommended. Main courses $28–$42. AE, DISC, MC, V. Daily 6:30pm–midnight; Mon–Fri 11:30am–3pm.

Table 8 ✹✹✹ CALIFORNIA CUISINE   Finally! After years of speculation, star chef Govind Armstrong, who got his start at the age of 13 with Wolfgang Puck at L.A.'s legendary Spago, opened a branch of this L.A. hot spot on South Beach. Housed in the swank Regent Hotel, Table 8 is a massive space of all things hip, groovy, swell, and sleek. With 255 seats, the restaurant consists of a main dining room, a private dining room for celeb and VIP clientele, and a wine room. Can't score reservations? Don't fret! There's also a 40-seat lounge situated beneath the Regent's fabulous glass bottom pool and featuring a delicious small-plate lounge menu. Among chef Armstrong's signature dishes: a salt-roasted porterhouse steak, which the *Robb Report* called the best of the best in one of their coveted "best of" issues.

1458 Ocean Dr. South Beach. ⓒ **305/695-4114**. www.table8southbeach.com. Reservations recommended. Main courses $20–$35. AE, DC, DISC, MC, V. Hours of operation not yet available at press time.

Tuscan Steak ✹✹ ITALIAN/STEAK   This excellent Northern Italian restaurant, a member of the China Grill scion, is all about meat served Italian style, in large family-style portions. With a rich wood interior, the atmosphere is reminiscent of the dining room of a well-connected family—ornate and very loud. The house salad is a massive undertaking of the classic antipasto, filled with shredded slices of salami and pepperoni, chunks of mozzarella, and a delicate vinaigrette. Be sure to order the sautéed spinach with garlic and the onion mashed potatoes with whichever steak you choose. All steaks are big enough for at least three people to share. The house specialty is a delicious T-bone steak served with pungent garlic purée. On any given weekend night, reservations are secondary to being friends with the ultratanned host, so expect a long wait for a table. The bar is the only place to wait if you can find a spot there, and drinks are rather pricey. The background music is straight out of Studio 54, and so is the flashy crowd. Despite the long waits, after one meal here, you'll likely want to kiss the ring of the true boss of this culinary mob scene—the chef.

433 Washington Ave., South Beach. ⓒ **305/534-2233**. Reservations strongly recommended on weekends. Main courses $20–$65. Family-style meals $50 per person, including appetizer and main course. AE, DISC, MC, V. Sun–Thurs 6–11pm; Fri–Sat 6pm–midnight.

Wish ✹✹✹ ECLECTIC   Wish, located in the stylish Todd Oldham–designed The Hotel, is one of the most beautiful, romantic outdoor restaurants in South Beach. Chef Michael Bloise has taken the restaurant to a new level of taste with a fabulous, funky cuisine that Bloise himself calls "unpretentious yet artful." He's spot on. Three of Wish's finest dishes are the five-spiced pork chop with roasted beets and a spicy sweet-potato-and-edamame hash, along with a crispy pastry cup filled with lemon-goat-cheese yogurt; short ribs braised in Guinness beer with mushroom and coconut risotto wrapped in a cigar-shape phyllo; and pan-seared foie gras staked on roasted banana slices with black pepper marshmallow. Sounds outrageous, right? It is—in a very, very good way!

801 Collins Ave., South Beach. ⓒ **305/531-2222**. Reservations suggested. Main courses $25-$33. AE, DC, MC, V. Daily 11:30am–3pm; Tues–Sun 6–11pm; Fri–Sat 6pm–midnight. Closed for dinner Mon.

EXPENSIVE

Barton G. The Restaurant ★★★ AMERICAN   For those who are jaded by pan-fusion, pan-everything cuisine these days, Barton G. The Restaurant is the culinary ticket to creative and delectable salvation. Located on a residential block on the west side of South Beach, Barton G., named after its owner, who happens to be one of Miami's best-known, most over-the-top event planners, is a place that looks like a trendy restaurant but eats like a show. Here, presentation is paramount. Take, for instance, the popcorn shrimp appetizer. This is not your average Red Lobster popcorn shrimp. Served on a plate full of, yes, popcorn, with field greens and the plump shrimp stuffed into an actual popcorn box, this dish is one of many awe-inspiring—and tasty—items you'll find in this, the most unique restaurant in Miami. A grilled sea bass that is light and flavorful is served in a brown paper bag with laundry clips keeping the steam in until your server unclips them and releases the flavor within. Desserts are equally outrageous, including 3 pints of homemade ice cream on a plate with all the toppings on the side, and a giant plume of cotton candy reminiscent of drag diva Dame Edna's hair surrounded by three white-, dark-, and milk chocolate–covered popcorn balls, which, when cracked, reveal a sinful chocolate truf-fle inside. Or, brace yourself for the Make A Shake dessert, which includes three syrups, multiple toppings, a mini blender, and cookies for dipping. There's nothing ordinary about this seemingly ordinary restaurant, which is why people like Tom Cruise and Will Smith are regulars. And as whimsical as it is, it's far from kitschy or even cheesy. An elegant, well-lit indoor dining room is popular with the members of the socialite set, for whom Barton G. has done many an affair, while the bar area and outdoor courtyard is the place to be for younger trendoids who appreciate what's on their plates as much as they do who's sitting next to them.

1427 West Ave., South Beach. © **305/672-8881.** Reservations suggested. Main courses $10–$50. AE, DC, DISC, MC, V. Daily 6pm–midnight.

Grazie ★★★ ITALIAN   Owned and operated by an Israeli and a Honduran, Grazie, go figure, is one of Miami's best-loved *Italian* restaurants. The warm and inviting din-ing room blissfully offsets the surrounding schmutz and schmaltz of Washington Avenue. The food is authentically Italian, with a variety of carpaccios—yellowtail and beef-cheek carpaccio rock—hot and cold antipasti, including an addictive bruschetta; and, the reason why you're here—homemade pastas from fusilli alla Bolognese with homemade sausage, angel hair with fresh garlic, and ravioli stuffed with lump crabmeat in a pink lobster sauce. There are not many places to get pasta as good as you'll have it here. Just ask Miami Heat giant Shaquille O' Neal, who is a regular pasta eater here.

701 Washington Ave., South Beach. © **305/673-1312.** www.graziesoutbeach.com. Reservations recommended. Main courses $15–$32. AE, MC, V. Sun–Thurs 6–11pm, Fri–Sat 6pm–midnight.

Madiba Miami ★★ *Kids* SOUTH AFRICAN   Making up for the dearth of ethnic restaurants in Miami besides Cuban, Italian, and Japanese is this hip Brooklyn, New York, import named after a term of endearment for Nelson Mandela. In addition to the very different, very tasty food, the offbeat, off-the-beaten-path place is a visual experience based on a traditional South African Shebeen, an informal social hall of sorts. Add a little South Beach splash to it, and you've got Madiba. In addition to a modern downstairs lounge and the very rustic main dining room, Madiba has a tiny boutique called Homesick?, featuring all sorts of South African food, arts, crafts, and music. Best of all, a portion of the proceeds goes to the Ubuntu Education Fund in

South Africa. The food is full of spice—not necessarily spicy, but full of flavor. Among the highlights are the prawns peri-peri—grilled prawns with yellow rice and a very zesty salad; baby back ribs char-grilled with "monkey gland sauce"—sounds vile but it's a traditional South African gravy that has nothing to do with monkeys; and Chaka-laka, a spicy mix of baked beans, carrots, tomato, and onions. Madiba also loves kids and has a special children's menu with prices ranging from $3 to $8, with free ice cream.

1766 Bay Rd., South Beach. ℰ **305/695-1566.** www.madibarestaurant.com. Reservations recommended. Main courses $14–$26. AE, MC, V. Sun–Thurs noon–midnight; Fri–Sat noon–1am. Lounge open nightly except Mon noon–5am. Closed Mon.

Nemo 🕸🕸 PAN-ASIAN   Located on the quickly developing South Beach area known as SoFi (for "south of Fifth St."), Nemo is a funky, high-style eatery with an open kitchen and an outdoor courtyard canopied by trees and lined with an eclectic mix of model types and foodies. Among the reasons to eat in this restaurant, whose name is actually *omen* spelled backward: grilled Indian-spiced pork chop; grilled local mahimahi with citrus and grilled sweet-onion salad, kimchi glaze, basil and crispy potatoes; and an inspired dessert menu by Hedy Goldsmith that's not for the faint of calories. Seating inside is comfy-cozy but borders on cramped. On Sunday mornings, the open kitchen is converted into a buffet counter for the restaurant's unparalleled brunch. Be prepared for a wait, however, which tends to spill out onto the street.

100 Collins Ave., South Beach. ℰ **305/532-4550.** Reservations recommended. Main courses $22–$36; Sun brunch $29. AE, MC, V. Mon–Sat noon–3pm and 6:30pm–midnight, Sun 11am–3pm and 6pm–midnight. Valet parking $10 or $20 for curbside.

Shoji Sushi 🕸 SUSHI   Despite the sushi saturation on South Beach, Shoji stands apart from the typical sashimi-and-California-roll routine with expertly prepared, exquisitely fresh, and innovative top-notch rolls. The sleek sister to its next-door neighbor Nemo, Shoji is known for its authentic Japanese box sushi technique, in which the sushi, rice, and ingredients are packed into a tidy, tasty cake that won't crumble into your lap. Among the rolls I can't seem to get enough of here are the hamachi jalapeño—cilantro, daikon sprout, asparagus, avocado, and jalapeños—and the spicy lobster roll, which consists of mango, avocado, scallion, shiso, salmon egg, and huge chunks of lobster. Wash it all down with the saketinis and my personal fave, the gingertini, which is made with ginger, vodka, triple sec, ginger ale, and pickled ginger juice.

100 Collins Ave., South Beach. ℰ **305/532-4245.** Reservations recommended. Main courses $20–$25. AE, MC, V. Mon–Fri noon–3pm; Mon–Thurs 6pm–midnight; Fri–Sun 6pm–1am. Valet parking $10.

Talula 🕸🕸🕸 CREATIVE AMERICAN   Take two star chefs and combine their epicurean efforts, and you've got Talula, one of the most creative, refreshing restaurants to come onto the South Beach scene since Barton G. The Restaurant (p. 113). Owned by husband-and-wife team Andrea Curto-Randazzo, formerly of Wish, and Frank Randazzo, formerly of the now-defunct Gaucho Room, Talula is a blissful marriage of many flavors, as seen in such signature dishes as grilled Sonoma foie gras with caramelized figs, blue-corn cakes, chile syrup, and candied walnuts; and grilled Atlantic salmon with royal trumpet mushroom, baby zucchini hash, and golden tomato salad and lemon vinaigrette. Chef Frank's chop-house specials are also hot ticket items, including the 14-ounce, 21-day dry-aged rib-eye, at a relatively decent price of $28, compared to other area steak joints. Daily specials always include a chopped salad, soup, risotto, and meat or fish dish. The wine list is well balanced, featuring 85 vintages from California, Italy, France, Australia, and South America. Wines by the glass are a reasonable, un–South Beach $6 to $9. As to be expected with any restaurant in South Beach, Talula is cool looking, with an unpretentious, warm decor and outdoor garden patio that is a popular spot for the fantastic buffet-style Sunday brunches. An exhibition kitchen is a tempting seating option, with five seats allowing a priceless view of the culinary action.

210 23rd St., South Beach. © 305/672-0778. Reservations recommended. Main courses $18–$32. AE, MC, V. Tues–Thurs 6:30–11pm; Fri–Sat 6:30–11:30pm; Sun 6–10pm; open for lunch Tues–Fri noon–2:30pm. Happy hour Tues–Sun 5–7pm.

MODERATE

Balan's ⚘ MEDITERRANEAN   Balan's provides undeniable evidence that the Brits actually do know a thing or two about cuisine. A direct import from London's Soho, Balan's draws inspiration from various Mediterranean and Asian influences, labeling its cuisine "Mediterrasian." With a brightly colored interior straight out of a mod '60s flick, Balan's is a favorite among the gay and arty crowds. The moderately priced food is rather good here—especially the sweet-potato soufflé with leeks and roasted garlic; fried goat cheese and portobello mushrooms; and Chilean sea bass with roasted tomato. When in doubt, the restaurant's signature lobster club sandwich is always a good choice. Adding to the ambience is the restaurant's people-watching vantage point on Lincoln Road.

1022 Lincoln Rd. (between Lenox and Michigan), South Beach. © 305/534-9191. Reservations accepted, except for weekend brunch. Main courses $7–$25 (breakfast and dinner specials weekdays). AE, DISC, MC, V. Sun–Thurs 8am–midnight; Fri–Sat 8am–1am; Sat–Sun brunch noon–3:30pm.

Big Pink ⚘ *Kids* AMERICAN   "Real Food for Real People" is the motto to which this restaurant strictly adheres. Located on what used to be a gritty corner of Collins Avenue, Big Pink—owned by the folks at the higher-end Nemo—is quickly identified by a whimsical Pippi Longstocking–type mascot on a sign outside. Scooters and motorcycles line the streets surrounding the place, which is a favorite among beach bums, club kids, and those craving Big Pink's comforting and hugely portioned pizzas, sandwiches, salads, and hamburgers. The fare is above average, at best, and the menu is massive, but it comes with a good dose of kitsch, such as their "gourmet" spin on the classic TV dinner, which is done perfectly, right down to the compartmentalized dessert. Televisions line the bar area, and family-style table arrangement (there are several booths, too) promotes camaraderie among diners. Outdoor tables are available. Even picky kids will like the food here, and parents can enjoy the family-friendly atmosphere (not the norm for South Beach) without worrying whether their kids are making too much noise.

157 Collins Ave., Miami Beach. © 305/532-4700. Main courses $13–$20. AE, DC, MC, V. Mon–Wed 8am–midnight; Thurs and Sun 8am–2am; Fri–Sat 8am–5am.

Bond St. Lounge ⚘ SUSHI   A New York City import, the sceney Bond St. Lounge is located in the basement of the shabby chic Townhouse Hotel and is packing in hipsters as tightly as the crabmeat in a California roll. Despite its tiny size, Bond St. Lounge's superfresh nigiri and sashimi, and funky sushi rolls such as the sun-dried tomato and avocado or the arugula crispy potato, are worth cramming in for. As the evening progresses, however, Bond St. becomes more of a bar scene than a restaurant, but sushi is always available at the bar to accompany your sake Bloody Mary.

Townhouse Hotel, 150 20th St., South Beach. © **305/398-1806**. Reservations recommended. Sushi $6–$15. AE, MC, V. Daily 6pm–2am.

El Rancho Grande ✿✿ MEXICAN   Hidden on a side street off of Lincoln Road, El Rancho Grande is a favorite local cantina that has attracted the likes of Cher and Matt Damon, thanks to its ultrafresh fare and unassuming ambience. With a "Pottery Barn meets Acapulco" decor, El Rancho Grande doesn't hold anything back when it comes to the cuisine. The Aztec Soup, a hot-and-spicy blend of chicken and tortilla strips, is some of the best I've had. The salsa here is not at all watery and is freshly made—a tongue-tickling blend of spices, cilantro, tomatoes, onions, and peppers, and the Mexican favorites of burritos, enchiladas, and fajitas are all very well represented. All portions are huge and can be shared or taken home for extra meal mileage. Margaritas are a little weak when frozen and better ordered on the rocks. Expect a wait at the small bar for your table, especially on weekends. Limited outdoor seating is also available.

1626 Pennsylvania Ave., South Beach. © **305/673-0480**. Main courses $10–$19. AE, DC, MC, V. Daily 11am–11pm.

Grillfish ✿✿ SEAFOOD   From the beautiful Byzantine-style mural and the gleaming oak bar, you'd think you were eating in a much more expensive restaurant, but Grillfish manages to pay the exorbitant South Beach rent with the help of a loyal local following who come for fresh, simple seafood in a relaxed but upscale atmosphere.

The servers are friendly and know the menu well. The barroom seafood chowder is full of chunks of shellfish, as well as some fresh whitefish filets in a tomato broth. The small ear of corn included with each entree is about as close as you'll get to any type of vegetable offering besides the pedestrian salad. Still, at these prices, it's worth a visit to try some local fare, including mako shark, swordfish, tuna, marlin, and wahoo.

1444 Collins Ave. (corner of Española Way), South Beach. © **305/538-9908**. www.grillfish.com. Reservations for 6 or more only. Main courses $9–$26. AE, DC, DISC, MC, V. Daily 11:30am–4pm and 5:30pm–midnight.

Joe Allen ✿ *Finds* AMERICAN   It's hard to compete in a city with haute spots everywhere you look, but Joe Allen, a restaurant that has proven itself in both New York and London, has stood up to the challenge by establishing itself off the beaten path in possibly the only area of South Beach that has remained impervious to trendiness and overdevelopment. Located on the bay side of the beach, Joe Allen is conspicuously devoid of neon lights, valet parkers, and fashionable pedestrians. Inside, however, one discovers a hidden jewel: a stark yet elegant interior and no-nonsense, fairly priced, ample-portioned dishes such as meatloaf, pizza, fresh fish, and salads. The scene has a homey feel favored by locals looking to escape the hype without compromising quality.

1787 Purdy Ave./Sunset Harbor Dr. (3 blocks west of Alton Rd.), South Beach. © **305/531-7007**. Reservations recommended, especially on weekends. Main courses $15–$25. MC, V. Daily 11:30am–11:30pm.

L'Entrecote de Paris ✿ FRENCH   New York's got the Statue of Liberty and Miami's got L'Entrecote de Paris. We don't complain. Everything in this little piece of Paris, a classy, albeit recently expanded, little bistro, is simple. For dinner, it's either steak, chicken, or seafood—I'd stick to the steaks, particularly the house special, L'Entrecote's French steak, with all-you-can-eat french fries (or *pommes frites,* rather). The salmon looks like spa cuisine, served with a pile of bald steamed potatoes and a salad with simple greens and an unmatchable vinaigrette. The steak, on the other hand, is the stuff cravings are made of, even if you're not a die-hard carnivore. Its salty sharp sauce is rich but not thick, and full of the beef's natural flavor. I loved the *profiteroles* *au chocolat,* a perfect puff pastry filled with vanilla ice cream and topped with a dark, bittersweet chocolate sauce. Most diners are very Euro and pack a petit attitude. If you want a quiet dinner, come early because, as the night grows long, L'Entrecote transforms itself into a lounge, with DJs who do *not* spin Edith Piaf's greatest hits.

413 Washington Ave., South Beach. © 305/673-1002. Reservations recommended on weekends. Main courses $16–$24. DC, MC, V. Sun–Thurs 6:30pm–midnight; Fri–Sat 6pm–1am.

Macaluso's ✰✰ ITALIAN   This restaurant epitomizes the Italians' love for—and mastery of—savory, plentiful, down-home Staten Island–style food. While the storefront restaurant is intimate and demure in nature, there's nothing delicate about the bold mix of flavors in every meat and pasta dish here. Catch the fantastic clam pie when in season—the portions are huge. Pricier items vary throughout the season but will likely feature fresh fish handpicked by chef (and owner) Michael, the don of the kitchen, who is so accommodating he'll take special requests or even bring to your table a complimentary signature meatball. If he doesn't, don't hesitate to ask your waiter for one; he'll be glad to bring it to you. Everyone will recommend favorites such as the rigatoni and broccoli rabe. There are also delicious desserts that range from homemade anisette cookies to gooey pastries. The wine list is also good. ***Celeb alert:*** Macaluso's is where Demi Moore and Ashton Kutcher made their official debut as a couple while in Miami. ***Note:*** One disappointed reader reported to us that service was surly and the pasta wasn't cooked to satisfaction. This is a first, really.

1747 Alton Rd., Miami Beach. © 305/604-1811. Main courses $14–$28; pizza $8–$13. MC, V. Tues–Sat 6pm–midnight; Sun 6–11pm. After 10:30pm, only pies are served. Closed Mon.

Spiga ✰✰ *(Finds)* ITALIAN   If you want a side of scene with your spaghetti, don't even think of dining at Spiga, a place that's so on the down low that many of South Beach's most ostentatious hipsters have never even heard of it, which is why people like Julia Roberts choose to eat here rather than Ago while in town. The complimentary bruschetta with grilled eggplant, served to you at one of the few tables inside or out, is the first of many culinary treats. The simple gnocchi with tomato and basil is a garlicky sensation, not to mention a most filling entree. The fresh asparagus baked in Parmesan cheese is so fresh that gourmands insist that Alice Waters, the queen of organic cooking, had something to do with it, and the red snapper with kalamata olives, fresh tomatoes, capers, and onions is a refreshingly simple departure from the fusion variety that can be found in almost any area restaurant. The place is extremely romantic and vaguely reminiscent of a Florentine trattoria.

Hotel Impala, 1228 Collins Ave., South Beach. © 305/534-0079. Reservations accepted. Main courses $7–$20. AE, DC, MC, V. Daily 6pm–midnight.

Van Dyke Cafe ✰ AMERICAN   News Cafe's younger, less harried sibling, Van Dyke is a locals' favorite, at which people-watching is also premium but attitude is practically nonexistent. Like News, the menu here is pretty cut and dried—sandwiches, salads, eggs, and so on, but the Van Dyke's warm, wood-floored interior, upstairs jazz bar, accessible parking, and intense chocolate soufflé make it a less taxing alternative. Also, unlike News, Van Dyke turns into a sizzling nightspot featuring live jazz nearly every night of the week (a $5 cover charge is added to your bill if you sit at a table; the bar's free). Outside there's a vast tree-lined seating area that provides a front-row seat to the people-watching. Those allergic to or afraid of dogs may want to reconsider eating here, as Van Dyke is also a canine hot spot.

846 Lincoln Rd., South Beach. (C) **305/534-3600.** Reservations recommended for dinner. Main courses $9–$17. AE, DC, MC, V. Daily 8am–2am.

INEXPENSIVE

11th Street Diner AMERICAN   The only real diner on the beach, the 11th Street Diner is the antidote to a late-night run to Denny's. Some of Miami's most colorful characters, especially the drunk ones, convene here at odd hours, and your greasy-spoon experience can quickly turn into a three-ring circus. Uprooted from its 1948 Wilkes-Barre, Pennsylvania, foundation, the actual structure was dismantled and rebuilt on a busy—and colorful (a gay bar is right next door, so be on the lookout for flamboyant drag queens) corner of Washington Avenue. Although it can use a good window cleaning, it remains a popular 'round-the-clock spot that attracts all walks of life. If you're craving french fries, order them smothered in mozzarella with a side of gravy—a tasty concoction that I call disco fries because of its popularity among starving clubbers.

1065 Washington Ave., South Beach. (C) **305/534-6373.** Items $8–$15. AE, MC. Daily 24 hr.

Front Porch Café ★ AMERICAN   Located in an unassuming, rather dreary-looking Art Deco hotel, the Front Porch Café is a relaxed local hangout known for cheap breakfasts. Some of the servers tend to be a bit attitudinal and lackadaisical (many are bartenders or club kids by night), so this isn't the place to be if you're in a hurry, especially on the weekends, when the place is packed all day long and lines are the norm. Enjoy home-style French toast with bananas and walnuts, omelets, fresh fruit salads, pizzas, and classic breakfast pancakes that put IHOP to shame. If you're looking to avoid the tourists and prefer to dine with the locals, Front Porch is where it's at for breakfast, lunch, and even dinner.

In the Penguin Hotel, 1418 Ocean Dr., South Beach. (C) **305/531-8300.** Main courses $5–$16. AE, DC, DISC, MC, V. Daily 8am–10:30pm.

La Sandwicherie SANDWICHES   You can get mustard, mayo, or oil and vinegar on sandwiches elsewhere in town, but you'd be missing out on all the local flavor. This gourmet sandwich bar, open until the crack of dawn, caters to ravenous club kids, biker types, and the body artists who work in the tattoo parlor next door. For many people, in fact, no night of clubbing is complete without capping it off with a turkey sub from La Sandwicherie.

229 14th St. (behind the Amoco station), South Beach. (C) **305/532-8934.** Sandwiches and salads $6–$12. AE, MC, V. Daily 9am–5am. Delivery 9:30am–11pm.

Lincoln Road Café ★ (Value) CUBAN   The Van Dyke Cafe (p. 117) is good for people-watching and reliable food, but if you're starving and not in the mood to wait for a table, and you don't want to spend more than $10 for breakfast, head over to the Lincoln Road Café. Harkening to the days of old South Beach, before the trendoids came and took over Lincoln Road with minimalist, ultramodern decor and uncomfortable chairs, Lincoln Road Café remains a local hot spot for cheap breakfasts, lunches, and dinners. Breakfast is the real bargain, however: For a mere $6, you can gorge yourself on eggs, bacon, ham, sausage, Cuban toast, and a mind-blowing, brain-buzzing café con leche. For lunch and dinner, there are hefty portions of Cuban faves from black beans and rice to arroz con pollo, all at low, low prices. Lincoln Road Café

THE TRAVELOCITY GUARANTEE

...THAT SAYS EVERYTHING YOU BOOK WILL BE RIGHT, OR WE'LL WORK WITH OUR TRAVEL PARTNERS TO MAKE IT RIGHT, RIGHT AWAY.

*To drive home the point,
we're going to use the word "right" in every single sentence.*

Let's get right to it. Right to the meat! Only Travelocity guarantees everything about your booking will be right, or we'll work with our travel partners to make it right, right away. Right on!

Here's a picture taken smack dab right in the middle of Antigua, where the Guarantee also covers you.

The Guarantee covers all but one of the items pictured to the right.

For example, what if the ocean view you booked actually looks out at a downright ugly parking lot? You'd be right to call – we're there for you. And no one in their right mind would be pleased to learn the rental car place has closed and left them stranded. Call Travelocity and we'll help get you back on the right track.

Now, you may be thinking, "Yeah, right, I'm so sure." That's OK; you have the right to remain skeptical. That is until we mention help is always right around the corner. Call us right off the bat, knowing our customer service reps are there for you 24/7. Righting wrongs. Left and right.

Now if you're guessing there are some things we can't control, like the weather, well you're right. But we can help you with most things – to get all the details in righting,* visit travelocity.com/guarantee.

*Sorry, spelling things right is one of the few things not covered under the Guarantee.

I'd give my right arm for a guarantee like this, although I'm glad I don't have to.

travelocity
You'll never roam alone.

If you think America's #1 Beach – 2005 is spectacular, imagine the memories you'll make here.

Stroll along 35 miles of award-winning beaches including Fort De Soto Park, rated America's #1 Beach in 2005. Then, enjoy championship golf, the world-class Salvador Dali Museum; sunset dining and unique shopping and entertainment at The Pier. Visit FloridasBeach.com or call 877.352.3224.

ST. PETERSBURG CLEARWATER
FloridasBeach.com

(*Then&Now* **Café Cardozo, Then and Now**

The **Café Cardozo**, at the Cardozo Hotel is a popular South Beach respite, much as it was when *Miami and the Caribbean on 10 Dollars a Day* was published: "Ever since Frank Sinatra played a hotel owner in the movie 'A Hole in the Head,' tourists have flocked to the (Cordozo) where the movie was filmed."

---

doesn't need Philippe Starck's designs to help bring in crowds: Thanks to cheap, good food, this unassuming eatery is a hot spot in its own right.

941 Lincoln Rd., South Beach. (**305/538-8066**. Items $6–$11. AE, DC, MC, V. Daily 8am–midnight.

News Cafe ☞ AMERICAN   This South Beach cafe-cum-landmark hasn't fallen off the radar as far as buzz and hype are concerned. The quintessential South Beach experience, News is still au courant, albeit swarming with mostly tourists. Unless it's appallingly hot or rainy out, you should wait for an outside table, which is where you need to be to fully appreciate the experience. Service is abysmal and often arrogant (perhaps because the tip is included), but the menu is reliable, running the gamut from sandwiches and salads to pasta dishes and omelets. My favorite here is the Middle Eastern platter, a dip lover's paradise, with hummus, tahini, tabouleh, babaganoush, and fresh pita bread. If it's not too busy, feel free to order just a cappuccino—your server may snarl, but that's what News is all about; creative types like to bring their laptops and sit here all day (or all night—this place is open 24 hr. a day). If you're by yourself and need something to read, there's an extensive collection of national and international newspapers and magazines at the in-house newsstand. News Cafe also opened another clone, **Café Cardozo,** at the Cardozo Hotel at 1300 Ocean Dr. on South Beach, in case 5 blocks is too much to walk to the original.

800 Ocean Dr., South Beach. (**305/538-6397**. Items $5–$20. AE, DC, MC, V. Open 24 hrs.

Pizza Rustica ☞ PIZZA   It's four in the morning and there's a line out the door at Pizza Rustica, not because they're short staffed, but because Pizza Rustica has become a nutritional mainstay for Miami's nocturnal set. Why wait in line at the crack of dawn when there are countless other late-night slice spots? The pizza here is *that* good. So good they had to open another Pizza Rustica just blocks away. Day or night—and morning, this place is always slammed with people who must fulfill their craving for meal-size slices of moan-inducing Tuscan-style pizza. Spinach and Gorgonzola cheese blend blissfully with a touch of olive oil and garlic that will last for a few hours to remind you of just how good their pizza is. Other designer varieties include four cheese, arugula, chicken, and rosemary-potato. Pizza Rustica's slices are made so that you can either scarf down an entire slab, which is the size of a floor tile, or ask them to cut the slice into fours, creating dainty, bite-size installments. If the original spot is too busy, try your luck at their other South Beach locations, at 1447 Washington Ave. (between 14th and 15th sts.; (**305/538-6009**) and 667 Lincoln Rd. ((**305/672-2334**). Whatever location, it's worth the wait.

863 Washington Ave., South Beach. (**305/674-8244**. Slice $3.75. No credit cards. Daily 11am–6am.

Puerto Sagua ☞ CUBAN/SPANISH   This brown-walled diner is one of the only old holdouts on South Beach. Its steady stream of regulars ranges from *abuelitos* (little old grandfathers) to hipsters who stop in after clubbing. It has endured because the food is good, if a little greasy. Some of the less heavy dishes are a superchunky fish soup with pieces of whole flaky grouper, chicken, and seafood paella, or marinated kingfish. Also good are most of the shrimp dishes, especially the shrimp in garlic sauce, which is served with white rice and salad.

This is one of the most reasonably priced places left on the beach for simple, hearty fare. Don't be intimidated by the hunched, older waiters in their white button-down shirts and black pants. Even if you don't speak Spanish, they're usually willing to do charades. Anyway, the extensive menu, which ranges from BLTs to grilled lobsters to yummy fried plantains, is translated into English. Hurry, before another boutique goes up in its place.

700 Collins Ave., South Beach. ☎ 305/673-1115. Main courses $6–$24; sandwiches and salads $5–$10. AE, DC, MC, V. Daily 7:30am–2am.

MIAMI BEACH, SURFSIDE, BAL HARBOUR & SUNNY ISLES
The area north of the Art Deco District—from about 21st Street to 163rd Street—had its heyday in the 1950s, when huge hotels and gambling halls blocked the view of the ocean. Now many of the old hotels have been converted into condos or budget lodgings, and the bayfront mansions have been renovated by and for wealthy entre-preneurs, families, and speculators. The area has many more residents, albeit seasonal, than visitors. On the culinary front, the result is a handful of superexpensive, tradi-tional establishments as well as a number of value-oriented spots.

To locate the restaurants in this section, see the map "Where to Stay & Dine in Miami Beach, Surfside, Bal Harbour, Sunny Isles & North Beach" (p. 93).

VERY EXPENSIVE
The Forge Restaurant ✸✸✸ STEAK/AMERICAN   English oak paneling and Tiffany glass suggest high prices and haute cuisine, and that's exactly what you get at The Forge. Each elegant dining room possesses its own character and features high ceilings, ornate chandeliers, and European artwork. The atmosphere is elegant but not too stuffy. On Wednesday night (the party night here), however, it's pandemonium as the who's who of Miami society gather for dinner, dancing, and schmoozing. Like the rest of the menu, appetizers are mostly classics, from Beluga caviar to baked onion soup to shrimp cocktail and escargot. When they're in season, order the stone crabs. For the main course, any of the seafood, chicken, or veal dishes are recommendable, but The Forge is especially known for its award-winning steaks. Its wine selection is equally lauded—ask for a tour of the cellar. *Celeb alert:* None other than Michael Jackson has dined here on numerous occasions and considers The Forge one of his favorite restaurants of all time. Same goes for Jennifer Lopez, Paris Hilton, Michael Jordan, and, well, you get the picture.

432 Arthur Godfrey Rd. (41st St.), Miami Beach. ☎ 305/538-8533. Reservations recommended. Main courses $25–$60. AE, DC, MC, V. Sun–Thurs 6pm–midnight; Fri–Sat 6pm–1am.

Shula's Steak House ✸✸ AMERICAN/STEAK   Climb a sweeping staircase in the Alexander All-Suite Luxury Hotel and go through the glass hallway—designed like an atrium, so exotic flora and fauna beckon from both within and without—and you'll find yourself in this magnificent restaurant that has been acclaimed as one of the greatest steakhouses in all of North America. If you're feeling adventurous, try the 48-ounce club (you can get your name engraved on a gold plaque if you can finish this absolutely *huge* piece of meat), or settle for the 20-ounce Kansas City strip or the 12-ounce filet mignon. Fresh seafood abounds when in season, and the oysters Rockefeller are a particularly good choice. The entertaining staff is very knowledgeable. The restaurant also has the No Name Lounge, where live piano music, premium spirits, and cigar smoking are available.

There's another branch of Shula's at 7601 NW 154th St. (in Don Shula's Golf Club off the Palmetto Expwy.; (© **305/820-8102**) in West Dade.

In the Alexander Hotel, 5225 Collins Ave., Miami Beach. (© **305/341-6565**. Reservations recommended. Main courses $23–$78. AE, DISC, MC, V. Daily 11am–3:30pm and 6–11pm. Free valet parking.

EXPENSIVE

Christine Lee's ☆☆ CHINESE This Cantonese restaurant is a 35-year-old Miami staple that serves excellent but overpriced Chinese-style dishes featuring steak, shrimp, and lobster sauce, as well as a good rendition of steak kew, a Cantonese dish with oyster sauce and hot bean paste. Considering the dearth of good Chinese restaurants in Miami, this is a good choice if you absolutely *must* satisfy your cravings for Chinese, but it will definitely cost you more than it should.

17082 Collins Ave. (1 block south of the Rascal House, in the RK strip mall, directly on Collins Ave.), Sunny Isles. (© **305/947-1717**. Reservations recommended. Main courses $8–$32. AE, DISC, MC, V. Daily 11:30am–3pm and 4–10:30pm (not open for lunch May–Sept).

Timo ☆☆☆ ITALIAN/MEDITERRANEAN Finally! A hip, haute restaurant in Sunny Isles, where, until recently, Tony Roma's was the hottest eatery. Owned by Tim Andriola, former executive chef of Mark's South Beach, Timo is a stylish Italian Mediterranean restaurant catering to mostly North Miami Beach locals who have been yearning for something else besides the fabulous Chef Allen's. Among the specialties, try the handcrafted pastas, including semolina gnocchi with braised oxtail; a traditional Sicilian pasta pie consisting of thin slices of eggplant wrapped around macaroni with crushed red pepper and buffalo mozzarella; and a phenomenal veal scaloppini. Less pricey, less heavy items are also available, such as a delicious ricotta-and-fontina wood-fired pizza with white truffle oil—perfect for lunch or a happy-hour snack. At Timo, a cool bistro-meets-lounge atmosphere gives way to a decidedly cool vibe, something that was always conspicuously lacking at Tony Roma's.

17624 Collins Ave., Sunny Isles. (© **305/936-1008**. Reservations required. Main courses $11–$24. AE, DC, MC, V. Daily 11:30am–3pm; Sun–Thurs 6–10:30pm; Fri–Sat 6–11pm.

MODERATE

Cafe Prima Pasta ☆☆ ITALIAN Once a small, unknown trattoria on a very trafficky, tacky street, Cafe Prima Pasta has expanded into a place to be for amazing Italian food and quite a bit of fanfare. Because there was always a massive wait that spilled out onto the street, the cafe has expanded to include ample outdoor seating that is set back from the street noise and traffic, thanks to some creative landscaping. The pasta here is homemade and the kitchen's choice ingredients include ripe, juicy tomatoes; imported olive oil that would cost you a boatload if you bought it in the store; fresh, drippy mozzarella; and fish that tastes as if it has just been caught right out back. The zesty, spicy garlic and oil that is brought out as dip for the bread is something you may want to keep with you during the course of your meal, as it doubles as extra seasoning for your food—not that it's necessary. Though tables are packed in, the atmosphere still manages to be romantic. Because of the chef's fancy for garlic, this is a three-Altoid restaurant, so be prepared to pop a few or request that they go light on the stuff.

414 71st St. (half a block east of the Byron movie theater), Miami Beach. ℭ 305/867-0106. Reservations not accepted (except for parties of 6 or more). Main courses $9–$19; pastas $12–$19. MC, V. Mon–Thurs noon–midnight; Fri noon–1am; Sat 1pm–1am; Sun 5pm–midnight.

Cafe Ragazzi ✦✦✦ ITALIAN   This diminutive Italian cafe, with its rustic decor and a swift, knowledgeable waitstaff, enjoys great success for its tasty, simple pastas. The spicy puttanesca sauce with a subtle hint of fish is perfectly prepared. Also recommended is the salmon with radicchio. You can choose from many decent salads and carpacci, too. Lunch specials are a real steal at $10, including soup, salad, and daily pasta. Unlike Cafe Prima Pasta (see above), Cafe Ragazzi is light on sceniness—people come here for the food only. Nevertheless, you can still expect to wait on weekend nights.

9500 Harding Ave. (on the corner of 95th St.), Surfside. ℭ 305/866-4495. Reservations accepted for 3 or more. Main courses $9–$18. MC, V. Mon–Fri 11:30am–3pm; daily 5–11:30pm.

Wolfie Cohen's Rascal House ✦ DELI   Although Jerry's Famous Deli on South Beach has taken away some of the Rascal House's younger patrons, the retro fabulous vibe at Wolfie's is inimitable. Open since 1954 and still going strong, this historic, nostalgic culinary extravaganza is one of Miami Beach's greatest traditions. Scooch into one of the vinyl booths, practically antique relics of the days when Frank Sinatra and his Rat Pack used to dine here after performances, and review the huge menu that's loaded with authentic Jewish staples. Consider the classic corned-beef sandwich, stuffed cabbage, brisket, or potato pancakes. Make sure to warm up to the servers, many of whom have been here since day one, and they will provide you with a coveted wax paper bag (a culinary souvenir, if you will) so you can take home your uneaten Danish and rolls. There is another Wolfie's in Boca Raton, at 2006 NW Executive Center Circle (ℭ 561/982-8899).

17190 Collins Ave. (at 163rd St.), Sunny Isles. ℭ 305/947-4581. Main courses $8–$30. AE, MC, V. Sun–Thurs 6:30am–1am; Fri–Sat 6:30am–2am.

INEXPENSIVE

Sheldon's Drugs ✦ 𝘝𝘢𝘭𝘶𝘦 AMERICAN   This typical, old-fashioned drugstore counter was a favorite breakfast spot of Isaac Bashevis Singer. Consider stopping into this historic site for a good piece of pie and a side of history. According to legend, the author was sitting at Sheldon's eating a bagel and eggs when his wife got the call in 1978 that he had won the Nobel Prize for Literature. The menu hasn't changed much since then. You can get eggs and oatmeal and a good tuna melt. A blue-plate special might be spaghetti and meatballs or grilled frankfurters. The food is basic, but you can't beat the prices.

9501 Harding Ave., Surfside. ℭ 305/866-6251. Main courses $4–$8; soups and sandwiches $2–$7. AE, DISC, MC, V. Mon–Sat 7am–7pm; Sun 7am–4pm.

NORTH MIAMI BEACH

Although there aren't many hotels in North Dade, the population in the winter months explodes due to the onslaught of seasonal residents from the Northeast. A number of exclusive condominiums and country clubs (including William's Island, Turnberry, and the Jockey Club) breed a demanding clientele, many of whom dine out nightly. That's good news for visitors, who can find superior service and cuisine at value prices.

To locate the restaurants in this section, see the map "Where to Stay & Dine in Miami Beach, Surfside, Bal Harbour, Sunny Isles & North Beach" (p. 93).

VERY EXPENSIVE

Chef Allen's ✿✿✿ NEW WORLD   If anyone deserves to have a restaurant named after him, it's chef Allen Susser, winner of the esteemed James Beard Award for Best American Chef in the Southeast—the Academy Award of cuisine—and practically every other form of praise and honor awarded by the most discriminating palates. Chef Allen, the man, is royalty around here. Chef Allen's, the restaurant, is his province, and foodies are his disciples. His platform? New World cuisine and the harmony of exotic tropical fruits, spices, and vegetables. It is under chef Allen's magic that ordinary Key limes and mangoes reappear in the forms of succulent salsas and sauces. A traditional antipasto is transformed into a Caribbean one, with papaya-pineapple barbecued shrimp, jerk calamari, and charred rare tuna. Whole yellowtail in coconut milk and curry sauce is a particularly spectacular entree. Unlike other restaurants where location is key, Chef Allen's, located at the rear of a strip mall, could be in the desert and hordes of people would still make the trek.

19088 NE 29th Ave. (at Biscayne Blvd.), North Miami Beach. ✆ 305/935-2900. Reservations recommended. Main courses $25–$40. AE, DC, MC, V. Sun–Thurs 6–10pm; Fri–Sat 6–11pm.

Bice ✿✿ ITALIAN   Although Bice moved from Coconut Grove's Wyndham Grand Bay Hotel to Sunny Isles's swanky Le Meridien, it hasn't changed the exquisite Milanese cuisine. Knowledgeable and friendly servers complement the comprehensive Italian menu. Every appetizer sounds so good that it's almost impossible to decide. Beef carpaccio is a delight, with hearts of palm and reggiano cheese; a colorful grilled-vegetable pyramid consists of gargantuan portions of meaty portobello mushrooms, fresh asparagus, and peppers with bursts of mouthwatering goat cheese lying within; Maryland crab cakes with the perfect hint of lemon are exceptional. For main courses, the pastas, homemade and extremely fresh, are eclipsed by a heavenly slab of Nebraska filet mignon with peppercorn sauce and a tower of french fries and onion rings. The veal chop is also sublime. For dessert, the crème brûlée and coffee gelato are delicious. Unlike many chichi restaurants, especially those found within swanky hotels, all dishes at Bice are generous in portion—huge, actually—and the only thing stuffy about dining here is how you'll feel after indulging.

18683 Collins Ave. (in Le Meridien), Sunny Isles. ✆ 305/503-6011. Reservations recommended. Main courses $15–$40. AE, MC, V. Daily 7am–noon; Mon–Fri noon–3pm; Mon–Sat 6–10pm.

Prime Grill ✿ KOSHER STEAKHOUSE   The only thing that's not entirely kosher about this place is the fact that it serves sushi in addition to the steaks for which it's known. This glatt kosher New York import has opened in the heavily Jewish neighborhood of Aventura to rave reviews from gourmands and grandmas alike. Upscale with a sleek, sophisticated interior, this 12,000-square-foot waterfront restaurant has an executive chef formerly of New York's legendary Windows on the World cooking up kosher New York rib steaks, T-bones, and Delmonico cuts hand-selected from the restaurant's private aging room. All steaks are served with béarnaise and red-wine shallot sauce and tobacco onion rings. Wait, tobacco onion rings? Since when is tobacco kosher? Anyway, if you're not into meat, there are several excellent fish dishes, such as oak-grilled tuna mignon. Side dishes are a la carte and include excellent garlic mashed potatoes and creamed spinach. And single people, beware: Some of the waitstaff have been known to play matchmaker.

3599 NE 207th St., North Miami Beach. Ⓒ **305/692-9392**. Reservations recommended. Main courses $19–$34. AE, DC, MC, V. Sun–Thurs 5–11pm; Sun brunch 11:30am–3pm.

EXPENSIVE

The Fish Joint 🐟🐟 SEAFOOD   People jonesing for an out-of-this-world high that won't get them arrested can usually be found lining up at this small neighborhood seafood spot where the frills are on the fish and not the decor. Industrial kitsch is the best description of The Fish Joint's interior, which tends to be on the loud side, but you don't go here for the decor: Simple, fresh fish is the draw, prepared in a multitude of ways, including the Chilean sea bass in sweet-and-sour glaze or the grouper oreganato. If you like shrimp, order the shrimp cocktail—the crustaceans are absolutely Jurassic size. Every meal comes with irresistible potato pancakes rather than your average boring baked potato. No matter what you order, however, you're guaranteed to experience a high of sorts, thanks to the stellar quality of this one-of-a-kind fish joint.

2570 NE Miami Gardens Dr., North Miami Beach. Ⓒ **305/936-8333**. Main courses $17–$24. AE, DC, MC, V. Sun–Thurs 5–10pm; Fri–Sat 5–11pm.

DOWNTOWN

Downtown Miami is a large, sprawling area divided by the Brickell Bridge into two distinct areas: Brickell Avenue and the bayfront area near Biscayne Boulevard. You shouldn't walk from one to the other—it's quite a distance and unsafe at night. Convenient Metromover stops do adjoin the areas, so it's better to hop on the scenic sky tram (even though it's closed after midnight).

To locate the restaurants in this section, see the map "Where to Stay & Dine in Key Biscayne, Downtown Miami, West Miami, Airport Area, North Dade, Little Havana, Coral Gables & Coconut Grove" (p. 97).

VERY EXPENSIVE

Azul 🐟🐟🐟 GLOBAL FUSION   Azul is one of the most upscale, prettiest—and priciest—waterfront restaurants in town. The views of the city skyline are stunning and rival the food—well, almost. Executive chef Clay Conley, who honed his skills with star chef Todd English, creates a tour de force of international cuisine, inspired by Caribbean, French, Argentine, Asian, and even American flavors. Like a stunning designer gown, the restaurant's decor, with its waterfront view, high ceilings, walls burnished in copper, and silk-covered chairs, is complemented by sparkling jewels—in this case, the food. Among the standouts: grilled chop and loin of Colorado lamb with harrisa, charred eggplant, braised shank bastila, and feta; and "A Study in Tuna Roll": raw tuna, tempura avocado, and Asian sauces with ossetra caviar. Downstairs is the Mandarin's more casual, less expensive **Café Sambal**, an Asian eatery serving breakfast, lunch, and dinner with the same priceless views.

At the Mandarin Oriental, 500 Brickell Key Dr., Miami. [tel **305/913-8254**. Reservations strongly recommended. Main courses $24–$38. AE, DC, DISC, MC, V. Mon–Fri noon–3pm; Mon–Sat 7–11pm.

Capital Grille 🐟🐟 STEAK   This place reeks of power. Seated among wine cellars filled with high-end classics, the dark wood paneling, pristine white tablecloths, chandeliers, and marble floors all contribute to the clubby atmosphere. For an appetizer, start with the lobster and crab cakes. If you're not in the mood for beef or lobster, try the pan-seared red snapper and asparagus covered with Hollandaise. The wine cellars you're surrounded by are filled with about 5,000 bottles of wine—too extensive and rare to list. While some people prefer the more stalwart style and service of Morton's up the block (see below), others find Capital to be a bit livelier. The food's pretty much the same between the two, though I find the steaks at Morton's to be a notch better; however, the atmosphere at the Capital Grille is *much* more inviting. Complimentary valet parking here, as opposed to Morton's, which charges a fee, is another reason to visit this carnivorous capital.

444 Brickell Ave., Miami. (C) **305/374-4500.** Reservations recommended. Main courses $21–$35. AE, DC, DISC, MC, V. Mon–Fri 11:30am–3pm; Mon–Thurs 5–10:30pm; Fri 5–11pm; Sat 6–11pm; Sun 5–10pm.

Morton's of Chicago ⚜ STEAK   A private, clublike ambience, with dark wood, leather booths, and tablecloths, makes Morton's of Chicago the preferred spot for major business transactions and quiet, romantic dinners. A vast menu includes a wide variety of excellent steaks and an award-winning menu consisting of shrimp Alexander, oysters on the half shell, sea scallops with apricot chutney, swordfish medallions with béarnaise sauce, and a dense, hot Godiva chocolate cake that's out of this world. Private dining rooms are perfect for carrying on clandestine conversations and romantic liaisons. The open kitchen is probably the only thing here that's not private. At lunchtime, the power is tangible as business deals are sliced and diced as often as the steak is. At night, the scene is more elegant, attracting older sophisticates and pre- and post-theater crowds.

1200 Brickell Ave., Miami. (C) **305/400-9990.** Reservations recommended. Main courses $30–$35. AE, DC, MC, V. Mon–Fri 11:30am–11pm; Sat 5:30–11pm; Sun 5–10pm.

Porcao ⚜⚜ BRAZILIAN   The name sounds eerily like "pork out," which is what you'll be doing at this exceptional Brazilian *churrascaria* (a Brazilian-style restaurant devoted mostly to meat—it's the Portuguese translation of "steakhouse"). For about $40, you can feast on salads and meat *after* you sample the unlimited gourmet buffet, which includes such fillers as pickled quail eggs, marinated onions, and an entire pig. Do not stuff yourself here, as the next step is the meaty part: Choose as much lamb, filet mignon, chicken hearts, and steak as you like, grilled, skewered, and sliced right at your table. Side dishes also come with the meal, ranging from beans and rice to fried yucca.

801 Brickell Bay Dr., Miami. (C) **305/373-2777.** Reservations accepted. Prix fixe $40 per person, all you can eat. AE, DC, MC, V. Daily noon–midnight.

EXPENSIVE

Big Fish ⚜⚜ *Finds* SEAFOOD/ITALIAN   This scenic seafood shack on the Miami River is a real catch—if you can find it. Hard to locate but well worth the search, Big Fish's remote location keeps many people biting. In fact, it added some Italian options to its all-seafood menu in the hopes of luring more people, and that worked, too. Big Fish has a sweeping view of the Miami skyline and some of the freshest catch around; the pasta served with it is only a starchy diversion. But the spectacular setting may be the real draw, right there on the Miami River where freighters, fishing boats, dinghies, and sometimes yachts slink by to the amusement of the faithful diners who no longer have to fish around for a charming, serene seafood restaurant. However, you should beware of Friday nights, when Big Fish turns into a big happy-hour scene.

55 SW Miami Ave. Rd. (C) **305/373-1770.** Main courses $15–$28. AE, DC, MC, V. Mon–Thurs noon–11pm; Fri–Sat noon–midnight. Cross the Brickell Ave. Bridge heading south and take the 1st right on SW 5th St. The road narrows under a bridge. The restaurant is just on the other side.

The District ✦ NEW AMERICAN   Housed in the beloved space formerly known as Picadilly Garden, the District isn't quaint or charming. It's modern, funky and, depending on what time you go, loud. Paris Hilton and O. J. Simpson—separately— have been spotted at this happening New American restaurant whose food rivals its scene. Specialties like citrus-dusted wild Alaska salmon, banana-leaf red snapper, and Japanese bread crumb–crusted crispy calamari truly rock. On weekend nights, the District kinda sorta turns into a club, so be prepared. Lunch hour gets more of a business crowd.

35 NE 40th St., Miami. ℭ **305/576-7242.** Reservations recommended. Main courses $15–$19. AE, DC, DISC, MC, V. Mon–Fri 11:30am–4:30pm; Mon–Wed 5–11pm; Thurs–Sat 6–11:30pm; Sun 11am–4pm. Late-night menu available.

Provence Grill ✦ FRENCH   This restaurant serves some of the tastiest French meals this side of Toulouse. The brothers Cormouls-Houles use their prodigious culinary skills to assemble an affordable menu that allows the rest of us to know just how the French really live—and they do it, dare we say, with incredible panache. The grilled specialties, from chicken to salmon, are imbued with only the best seasonings and sauces. Sautéed mussels with garlic and chives are fabulous as a meal and as a dipping sauce for the crusty bread. Canard lovers will enjoy the grilled duck filet in a red port sauce. Real culinary adventurers should try the dessert menu—crème brûlée spiced with lavender (a local French favorite) is just one selection—which is truly a delight. A full bar outside brings you back from your French delusions of grandeur and returns you to a delightful downtown Miami state of mind with beautiful views of the downtown skyline.

1001 South Miami Ave., Miami. ℭ **305/373-1940.** Main courses $14–$22; appetizers $4.95–$6.95. AE, MC, V. Mon–Fri 11am–3pm; Sun–Thurs 5:30–10:30pm; Fri–Sat 5:30–11pm.

Sheba Ethiopian Restaurant ✦✦ (Finds) ETHIOPIAN   This Design District find is a fantastic, funky place, not to mention an ideal opportunity to expand your palate. The authentic Ethiopian fare—D'Jaj Bi Zitoune: marinated chicken tenderloins sautéed with green olives and spices; Doro Wat, Ethiopia's national dish of chicken legs and thighs marinated and seasoned in garlic, ginger, and fenugreek (a Mediterranean-grown spice and herb), and stewed in a spicy Berbere (spicy Ethiopian sauce with cardamom, shallots, peppercorns, and fenugreek) sauce—is outstanding and bursting with flavor. If you like spicy food, you'll love Sheba, whose chefs are not afraid to use generous amounts of peppers, peppercorns, and African spices. The restaurant itself exudes a very cool vibe with dim lighting, authentic African masks and decor, and an awesome world-music soundtrack. The bar scene is abuzz here with local artists, hipsters, and those with more adventurous palates.

4029 N. Miami Ave. Rd. ℭ **305/573-1819.** Main courses $12–$26. AE, DC, MC, V. Mon–Sat 11:30am–midnight; Sun 5–11pm.

MODERATE
Joe's Seafood ✦ (Finds) SEAFOOD   A good catch on the banks of the Miami River, Joe's Seafood (not to be confused with Joe's Stone Crab) has a great waterfront setting and a fairly simple yet tasty menu of fresh fish cooked in a number of ways—grilled, broiled, fried, or, the best, in my opinion, in garlic or green sauce. Meals are quite the deal here, all coming with green salad or grouper soup, and yellow rice or french fries. The complimentary fish spread appetizer is also a nice touch. Because of this, not to mention the great, gritty ambience that takes you away from neon, neo-Miami in favor of the old seafaring days, there's usually a wait for a table.

400–404 NW N. River Dr., Miami. ☎ **305/381-9329.** Reservations recommended. Main courses $14–$23. AE, DC, DISC, MC, V. Sun–Thurs 11am–10pm; Fri–Sat 11am–11pm.

Perricone's Marketplace ⊛ ITALIAN   A large selection of groceries and wine, plus an outdoor porch and patio for dining, makes this one of the most welcoming spots downtown. Its rustic setting in the midst of downtown is a fantastic respite from city life. Sunday offers buffet brunches and all-you-can-eat dinners, too. But it's most popular weekdays at noon, when the suits show up for delectable sandwiches, quick and delicious pastas, and hearty salads.

15 SE 10th St. (corner of S. Miami Ave.), Miami. ☎ **305/374-9693.** Sandwiches $5.95 and up; pastas $13 and up. AE, MC, V. Sun and Mon 7am–10pm; Tues–Sat 7am–11pm.

Soyka Restaurant & Café ⊛ AMERICAN   Brought to us by the same man who owns the News and Van Dyke Cafes in South Beach, Soyka is a much-needed addition (though it's easy to miss) to the seedy area known as the Biscayne Corridor. The motif inside is industrial chic, reminiscent of a souped-up warehouse you might find in New York. Lunches focus on burgers, sandwiches, and wood-fired oven pizzas. Dinners include simple fare such as an excellent, massive Cobb salad or more elaborate dishes such as the delicious turkey Salisbury steak. The bar area offers a few comfy couches and bar stools and tables on which to dine, if you prefer not to sit in the open dining room. A children's menu is available for both lunch and dinner. A lively crowd of bohemian Design District types, professionals, and singles gathers here for a taste of urban life. On weekends, the place is packed and very loud. Do not expect an after-dinner stroll around the neighborhood—it's still too dangerous for pedestrian traffic. Head over the causeway to South Beach and stroll there.

5556 NE 4th Court (Design District, off Biscayne Blvd. and 55th St.), Miami. ☎ **305/759-3117.** Reservations recommended for 8 or more. Main courses $8–$26. AE, MC, V. Sun–Thurs 11am–11pm (bar open until midnight); Fri–Sat 11am–midnight (bar open until 1am). Happy hour Mon–Fri 4–7pm.

INEXPENSIVE

Andiamo Brick Oven Pizza ⊛ PIZZA   Leave it to visionary Mark Soyka (News Cafe, Van Dyke Cafe, Soyka) to turn a retro-style 1960s car wash into one of the city's best pizza places. The brick-oven pizzas are to die for, whether you choose the simple Andiamo pie (tomato sauce, mozzarella, and basil) or the designer combos of pancetta and caramelized onions; hot and sweet sausage with broccoli rabe; or portobello mushrooms with truffle oil and goat cheese. Pizzas come in three sizes—10-, 13-, and 16-inch. And while the pizza is undeniably delicious here, the most talked-about aspect of Andiamo is the fact that while you're washing down slice after slice, you can get your car washed and detailed at Leo's, the space's original and still-existing occupant out back—killing two birds with one, uh, slice.

5600 Biscayne Blvd., Miami. ☎ **305/762-5751.** Main courses $3–$15. MC, V. Sun–Thurs 11am–11pm; Fri–Sat 11am–midnight.

Dogma Grill ⊛⊛ HOT DOGS   A little bit of L.A. comes to a gritty stretch of Biscayne Boulevard in the form of this very tongue-and-cheeky hot dog stand whose motto is "A Frank Philosophy." Owned by a former MTV executive, Dogma will change the way you view hot dogs, offering a plethora of choices, from your typical chili dog to Chicago style with celery salt, hot peppers, onions, and relish. The tropical version with pineapple is a bit funky but fitting for this stand, which attracts a very colorful, arty crowd from the nearby Design District. The buns here are softer than feather pillows, and the hot dogs are grilled to perfection. Try the garlic fries and the lemonade, too.

7030 Biscayne Blvd., Miami. ⓒ 305/759-3433. Main courses $3–$4. Cash only. Daily 11am–9pm.

Jimmy's East Side Diner ⓖ DINER   The only thing wrong with this quintessential, consummate greasy-spoon diner is that it's not open 24 hours. Other than that, for the cheapest breakfasts in town, not to mention lunches and early dinners, Jimmy's is a dream come true. Try the banana pancakes, corned beef hash, roasted chicken, or Philly cheese steak. Located on the newly hip Upper East Side of Biscayne Boulevard, Jimmy's is a very neighborhood-y place at which late Bee Gee Maurice Gibb used to dine every Sunday. Adding to the aging regulars is a new, eclectic contingency of hungover hipsters for whom Jimmy's is a sweet—and cheap—morning-after salvation.

7201 Biscayne Blvd., Miami. ⓒ 305/759-3433. Main courses $3–$11. Cash only. Daily 7am–4pm.

Jumbo's ⭑⭑⭑ (Finds) SOUL FOOD   Open 24 hours daily, this Miami institution is the kind of place where you'll see everyone from Rastafarian musicians and cab drivers to Lenny Kravitz. Although it is in a shady neighborhood—Carol City—if you go there, you're going for only one reason—Jumbo's. Family-owned for over 50 years, Jumbo's is known for its world-famous fried shrimp, fried chicken, catfish fingers, and collard greens. Their motto—"Life is to be enjoyed, not to be endured . . . Making friends is our business" is spot on. The service is friendly and fun, and there's history here, too. Jimbo's is the first restaurant in Miami to integrate in 1966, and the first to hire African-American employees in 1967.

7501 NW 7th Ave., Miami. ⓒ 305/751-1127. Main courses $5–$15. AE, DC, MC, V. Daily 24 hr.

Tobacco Road AMERICAN   Miami's oldest bar is a bluesy Route 66–inspired institution favored by barflies, professionals, and anyone else who wishes to indulge in good and greasy bar fare—chicken wings, nachos, and so on—at reasonable prices in a down-home, gritty-but-charming atmosphere. The burgers are also good—particularly the Death Burger, a deliciously unhealthful combo of choice sirloin topped with grilled onions, jalapeños, and pepper-jack cheese (bring on the Tums!). Also a live-music venue, the Road, as it's known by locals, is well traveled, especially during Friday's happy hour and Tuesday's Lobster Night, when 100 1¼-pound lobsters go for only $13 apiece.

626 S. Miami Ave. ⓒ 305/374-1198. www.tobacco-road.com. Main courses $7–$10, nightly specials $12–$15. AE, DC, MC, V. Mon–Sat 11:30am–5am; Sun noon–5am. Cover $5 or $6 Fri–Sat nights.

LITTLE HAVANA

The main artery of Little Havana is a busy commercial strip called Southwest 8th Street, or Calle Ocho. Auto-body shops, cigar factories, and furniture stores line this street, and on every corner there seems to be a pass-through window serving superstrong Cuban coffee and snacks. In addition, many of the Cuban, Dominican, Nicaraguan, Peruvian, and other Latin American immigrants have opened full-scale restaurants ranging from intimate candlelit establishments to bustling stand-up lunch counters.

To locate the restaurants in this section, see the map "Where to Stay & Dine in Key Biscayne, Downtown Miami, West Miami, Airport Area, North Dade, Little Havana, Coral Gables & Coconut Grove" (p. 97).

EXPENSIVE

Casa Juancho ⭐⭐ SPANISH A generous taste of Spain comes to Miami in the form of the cavernous Casa Juancho, which looks like it escaped from a production of *Don Quixote.* The numerous dining rooms are decorated with traditional Spanish furnishings and enlivened nightly by strolling Spanish musicians who tend to be annoying and expect tips—do not encourage them to play at your table; you'll hear them loud and clear from other tables, trust me. Try not to be frustrated with the older staff that doesn't speak English or respond quickly to your subtle glance—the food's worth the frustration. Your best bet is to order lots of *tapas,* small dishes of Spanish finger food. Some of the best include mixed seafood vinaigrette, fresh shrimp in hot garlic sauce, and fried calamari rings. A few entrees stand out, like roast suckling pig, baby eels in garlic and olive oil, and Iberian-style snapper.

2436 SW 8th St. (just east of SW 27th Ave.), Little Havana. ℂ 305/642-2452. Reservations recommended but not accepted on Fri–Sat after 8pm. Main courses $15–$34; tapas $6–$10. AE, DC, DISC, MC, V. Sun–Thurs noon–midnight; Fri–Sat noon–1am.

MODERATE

Hy-Vong ⭐⭐ VIETNAMESE A must in Little Havana, expect to wait hours for a table, and don't even think of mumbling a complaint. Vietnamese cuisine combines the best of Asian and French cooking with spectacular results. Food at Hy-Vong is elegantly simple and superspicy. Appetizers include small, tightly packed Vietnamese spring rolls, and kimchi, a spicy, fermented cabbage (which they ran out of on my last visit here because I got there too late—get there early!). Star entrees include pastry-enclosed chicken with watercress cream-cheese sauce and fish in tangy mango sauce. Unfortunately, service here is not at all friendly or stellar—in fact, it borders on abysmal, but once you finally do get your food, all will be forgotten.

Enjoy the wait with a traditional Vietnamese beer and lots of company. Outside this tiny storefront restaurant, you'll meet interesting students, musicians, and foodies who come for the large, delicious portions.

3458 SW 8th St. (between 34th and 35th aves.), Little Havana. ℂ 305/446-3674. Reservations accepted for parties of 5 or more. Main courses $7–$19. AE, DISC, MC, V. Sun–Thurs 6–11pm; Fri–Sat 6–11:30pm. Closed Mon and 2 weeks in Aug.

INEXPENSIVE

Versailles ⭐⭐ CUBAN Versailles is the meeting place of Miami's Cuban power brokers, who meet daily over café con leche to discuss the future of the exiles' fate. A glorified diner, the place sparkles with glass, chandeliers, murals, and mirrors meant to evoke the French palace. There's nothing fancy here—nothing French, either—just straightforward food from the home country. The menu is a veritable survey of Cuban cooking and includes specialties such as Moors and Christians (flavorful black beans with white rice), *ropa vieja* (shredded beef stew), and fried whole fish. Versailles is the place to come for mucho helpings of Cuban kitsch. With its late hours, it's also the perfect place to come after spending your night in Little Havana.

3555 SW 8th St., Little Havana. ℂ 305/444-0240. Soup and salad $2–$10; main courses $5–$20. DC, DISC, MC, V. Mon–Thurs 8am–2am; Fri 8am–3am; Sat 8am–4:30am; Sun 9am–1am.

KEY BISCAYNE

Key Biscayne has some of the world's nicest beaches, hotels, and parks, yet it is not known for great food. Locals, or "Key rats," as they're known, tend to go off-island for meals or takeout, but here are some of the best on-the-island choices.

To locate the restaurants in this section, see the map "Where to Stay & Dine in Key Biscayne, Downtown Miami, West Miami, Airport Area, North Dade, Little Havana, Coral Gables & Coconut Grove" (p. 97).

EXPENSIVE

Rusty Pelican 𝒜 SEAFOOD   The Pelican's private tropical walkway leads over a lush waterfall into one of the most romantic dining rooms in the city, located right on beautiful blue-green Biscayne Bay. The restaurant's windows look out over the water onto the sparkling stalagmites of Miami's magnificent downtown. Inside, quiet wicker paddle fans whirl overhead and saltwater fish swim in pretty tableside aquariums. The restaurant's surf-and-turf menu features conservatively prepared prime steaks, veal, shrimp, and lobster. The food is good, but the atmosphere—the reason why you're here—is even better, especially at sunset, when the view over the city is magical.

3201 Rickenbacker Causeway, Key Biscayne. 📞 **305/361-3818.** Reservations recommended. Main courses $16–$30. AE, DC, MC, V. Daily 11:30am–4pm; Sun–Thurs 5–11pm; Fri–Sat 5pm–midnight.

INEXPENSIVE

Bayside Seafood Hut 𝒜 *Finds* SEAFOOD   Known by locals as "the Hut," this ramshackle restaurant and bar is a laid-back outdoor Tiki hut and terrace that serves pretty good sandwiches and fish platters on paper plates. A blackboard lists the latest catches, which can be prepared blackened, fried, broiled, or in a garlic sauce. The fish dip is wonderfully smoky and moist, if a little heavy on mayonnaise. Local fishers and yachties share this rustic outpost with equal enthusiasm and loyalty. A completely new air-conditioned area for those who can't stand the heat is a welcome addition, as are the new deck and spruced-up decor. But behind it all, it's nothing fancier than a hut— if it was anything else, it wouldn't be nearly as appealing.

3501 Rickenbacker Causeway, Key Biscayne. 📞 **305/361-0808.** Reservations accepted for 15 or more. Appetizers, salads, and sandwiches $5–$15; platters $7–$13. AE, MC, V. Daily 10am until closing (which varies).

Jimbo's *Finds* SEAFOOD   Locals like to keep quiet about Jimbo's, a ramshackle seafood shack that started as a gathering spot for fishermen and has since become the quintessential South Florida watering hole, snack bar, and hangout for those in the know. If ever Miami had a backwoods, this was it, right down to the smoldering garbage can, stray dogs, and chickens. Do *not* get dressed up to come here—you will get dirty. Go to the bathroom before you get here, too, because the Porta-Potties are absolutely rancid. Grab yourself a dollar can of beer (there's only beer, water, and soda, but you are allowed to bring your own choice of drink if you want) from the cooler and take in the view of the tropical lagoon where they shot *Flipper*. You may even see a manatee or two. Vacant shacks that served as backdrops for films such as *True Lies* surround this hidden enclave, which attracts everyone from shrimpers and politicians to well-oiled beach bums. Oddly enough, there's even a bocce court here, and the owner, Jimbo, may challenge you to a game. Play if you must, but word has it he never loses. Jimbo's smoked fish—marlin or salmon—is the best in town, but *be fore-warned:* There are no utensils or napkins. When I asked for some, the woman said, "Lady, this is a place where you eat with your hands." I couldn't have said it better.

Off the Rickenbacker Causeway at Sewerline Rd., Virginia Key. 📞 **305/361-7026.** Smoked fish about $8 a pound. No credit cards. Daily 6am–6:30pm, weekends until 7:30pm. Head south on the main road toward Key Biscayne, make a left just after the MAST Academy (there will be a sign that says VIRGINIA KEY); tell the person in the toll booth you're going to Jimbo's, and he'll point you in the right direction.

COCONUT GROVE

Coconut Grove was long known as the artists' haven of Miami, but the rush of developers trying to cash in on the laid-back charm of this old settlement has turned it into something of an overgrown mall. Still, there are several great dining spots both inside and outside the confines of Mayfair and CocoWalk.

To locate the restaurants in this section, see the map "Where to Stay & Dine in Key Biscayne, Downtown Miami, West Miami, Airport Area, North Dade, Little Havana, Coral Gables & Coconut Grove" (p. 97).

VERY EXPENSIVE

Baleen ☆☆☆ SEAFOOD/MEDITERRANEAN   While the prices aren't lean, the cuisine here is worth every pricey, precious penny. Oversize crab cakes, oak-smoked diver scallops, and steakhouse-quality meats are among Baleen's excellent offerings. The lobster bisque is the best on Biscayne Bay. Everything here is a la carte, so order wisely, as it tends to add up quicker than you can put your fork down. The restaurant's spectacular waterfront setting makes Baleen a true knockout. Request one of the few tables that are actually on the water's edge; lit with Tiki torches and an illuminated backdrop of Biscayne Bay, Baleen is the kind of restaurant that you'd expect a reality show like *The Bachelor* to use as the place where the happy couple expresses their love for each other.

4 Grove Isle Dr. (in the Grove Isle Hotel), Coconut Grove. ☎ 305/858-8300. Reservations recommended. Main courses $18–$46. AE, DC, MC, V. Sun–Wed 7am–10pm; Thurs–Sat 7am–11pm.

EXPENSIVE

Anokha ☆☆☆ INDIAN   This is the best Indian restaurant in Miami. Anokha's motto is "A guest is equal to God and should be treated as such," and they do stick to it. The food here is from the gods, with fantastic tandooris, curries, and stews. The restaurant's location at the end of a quiet stretch of Coconut Grove is especially enticing because it prevents the throngs of pedestrians from overtaking what some people consider a diamond in the rough.

3195 Commodore Plaza (between Main Hwy. and Grand Ave.), Coconut Grove. ☎ 786/552-1030. Main courses $12–$40. AE, DC, MC, V. Sun and Tues–Wed 6–10:30pm; Thurs–Sat 6–11:30pm; closed Mon.

Le Bouchon du Grove ☆☆ FRENCH   This very authentic, exceptional bistro is French right down to the waitstaff, who may speak only French to you, forgetting that they are in the heart of Coconut Grove, USA. But it matters not. The food, prepared by an animated French (what else?) chef, is superb. An excellent starter is the wonderful *gratinée Lyonnaise* (traditional French onion soup). Fish is brought in fresh daily; try the Chilean sea bass when in season *(filet de loup poele)*. Though it is slightly heavy on the oil, it is delivered with succulent artichokes, tomato confit, and seasoned roasted garlic that is a gastronomic triumph. The *carre d'agneau roti* (roasted rack of lamb with Provence herbs) is served warm and tender, with an excellent amount of seasoning. There is also an excellent selection of pricey but doable French and American red and white wines.

3430 Main Hwy., Coconut Grove. ☎ 305/448-6060. Reservations recommended. Main courses $18–$26. AE, MC, V. Mon–Fri 10am–3pm; Mon–Thurs 5–11pm; Fri 5pm–midnight; Sat 8am–3pm and 5pm–midnight; Sun 8am–3pm and 5–11pm.

INEXPENSIVE

Cafe Tu Tu Tango ☆ SPANISH/INTERNATIONAL   This restaurant, in the bustling CocoWalk, is designed to look like a disheveled artist's loft. Dozens of original paintings—some only half-finished—hang on the walls and on studio easels. Seating is either inside, among the clutter, or outdoors, overlooking the Grove's main drag. Flamenco and other Latin-inspired tunes complement a menu with a decidedly Spanish flair. Hummus spread on rosemary flat bread and baked goat cheese in marinara sauce are two good starters. Tapas items include roast duck with dried cranberries, toasted pine nuts, and goat cheese, plus Cajun chicken egg rolls filled with corn, cheddar cheese, and tomato salsa. Pastas, ribs, fish, and pizzas round out the eclectic offerings, and several visits have proved each consistently good. Try the sweet, potent sangria and enjoy the warm, lively atmosphere from a seat with a view.

3015 Grand Ave. (on the 2nd floor of CocoWalk), Coconut Grove. ☎ **305/529-2222.** Reservations not accepted. Tapas $3–$9.50. AE, MC, V. Sun–Wed 11:30am–midnight; Thurs 11:30am–1am; Fri–Sat 11:30am–2am.

CORAL GABLES & ENVIRONS

Coral Gables is a foodie's paradise—a city in which you certainly won't go hungry. What Starbucks is to most major cities, excellent gourmet and ethnic restaurants are to Coral Gables, where there's a restaurant on every corner and everywhere in between.

To locate the restaurants in this section, see the map "Where to Stay & Dine in Key Biscayne, Downtown Miami, West Miami, Airport Area, North Dade, Little Havana, Coral Gables & Coconut Grove" (p. 97).

VERY EXPENSIVE

Chispa ✿✿✿ CONTEMPORARY LATIN   Simply put, Chispa rocks. The brainchild of star chef Robin Haas (formerly of Baleen), this cavernous, stylish nouveau Latin restaurant will blow you away. If you've ever tasted the delicious, greasy croquetas at any Cuban bodega, wait until you try Chispa's gourmet version—a magnificent shrimp-and-black-eyed-pea croquetta that renders the greasy ones good for only hangovers. For a real Cuban experience, try Sergio's Spit Roasted Young Suckling Pig. A slew of fantastic seafood ceviches and an unparalleled mahimahi with sour orange aioli, those addictive shrimp-and-black-eyed-pea croquetas with wood-roasted mushrooms atop a seared cornmeal stew prove that there is indeed a way to be creative with Cuban food. A 40-foot bar and massive booths seating 8 to 10 people make Chispa a great place for large groups. The acoustics, however, need to be improved, as it's louder than a Celia Cruz tribute in here.

225 Altara Ave., Coral Gables. ☎ **305/648-2600.** Reservations strongly recommended. Main courses $17–$25. AE, DC, MC, V. Sun–Thurs 11:30am–2:30pm and 5:30–10:30pm; Fri–Sat 5:30–11:30pm.

Christy's ✿✿ STEAK/AMERICAN   Power is palpable at this elegant English-style restaurant where an ex-president could be sitting at one table and a rock star at another. But Christy's is the kind of place where conversations are at a hush and no one seems to care whom they're sitting next to. The selling point here, rather, is the corn-fed beef and calves' liver, not to mention the broiled lamb chops, prime rib of beef with horseradish sauce, teriyaki-marinated filet mignon, and perfectly tossed Caesar salad. Baked sweet potatoes and a sublime blackout cake are also yours for the taking. For a little drama, order the cruise ship-esque baked Alaska. It livens up the staid place. Just like a fine wine or the typical Christy's customer, the meat here is aged a long time. A landmark since 1978, Christy's has thrived amid the comings and goings of neighboring nouveau Coral Gables restaurants. Located on a nondescript corner, you know you've arrived at the right place if you can count the Rolls Royces parked out front.

3101 Ponce de León Blvd., Coral Gables. ☎ **305/446-1400.** Reservations recommended. Main courses $20–$37. AE, DC, MC, V. Mon–Thurs 11:30am–10pm; Fri 11:30am–11pm; Sat 5–11pm; Sun 5–10pm.

Norman's ✦✦✦ NEW WORLD CUISINE   *Gourmet* magazine called Norman's the best restaurant in South Florida, but many disagree: They think it's the best restaurant in the entire United States. Gifted chef and cookbook author Norman van Aken takes New World Cuisine (which, along with chef Allen Susser, he helped create) to another plateau with dishes that have landed him on such shows as the Discovery Channel's *Great Chefs of the South* and on the wish lists of gourmands everywhere. The open kitchen invites you to marvel at the mastery that lands on your plate in the form of pan-roasted swordfish with black-bean *muneta;* stuffed baby bell pepper in cumin-scented tomato broth with avocado *crema;* chargrilled New York strip steak with chimichurri sabayon, *pommes frites,* and Creole mustard–spiced caramelized red onions; plantain-crusted dolphin; or chicken and tiny shrimp paella with garbanzo beans and chorizo mojo, to name a few.

The staff is adoring and professional, and the atmosphere is tasteful without being too formal. The portions are realistic, but still, be careful not to overdo it. You'll want to try some of the funky, fantastic desserts.

21 Almeria Ave. (between Douglas and Ponce de León), Coral Gables. ☎ **305/446-6767.** Reservations highly recommended. Main courses $22–$38. AE, DC, MC, V. Mon–Thurs 6–10pm; Fri–Sat 6–10:30pm; closed Sun. Bar opens at 5:30pm.

EXPENSIVE

Caffe Abbracci ✦✦ ITALIAN   You'll understand why this restaurant's name means "hugs" in Italian the moment you enter the dark, romantic enclave: Your appetite will be embraced by the savory scents of fantastic Italian cuisine wafting through the restaurant. The homemade black and red ravioli filled with lobster in pink sauce, risotto with porcini and portobello mushrooms, and the house specialty—grilled veal chop topped with tricolor salad—are irresistible and perhaps the culinary equivalent of a warm, embracing hug. A cozy bar and lounge was added recently to further encourage the warm and fuzzy feelings.

318 Aragon Ave. (1 block north of Miracle Mile, between Salzedo St. and Le Jeune Rd.), Coral Gables. ☎ **305/441-0700.** Reservations recommended for dinner. Main courses $15–$30; pastas $15–$20. AE, DC, MC, V. Mon–Fri 11:30am–3pm; Sun–Thurs 6–11:30pm; Fri–Sat 6pm–12:30am.

MODERATE

Brasserie Les Halles ✦✦ FRENCH   Known especially for its fine steaks and delicious salads, this very welcome addition to the Coral Gables dining scene became popular as soon as it opened in 1997 and has continued to do a brisk business. The moderately priced menu is particularly welcome in an area of overpriced, stuffy restaurants. For starters, try the mussels in white-wine sauce and the escargot. For a main course, the duck confit is an unusual and rich choice. Pieces of duck meat wrapped in duck fat are slow-cooked and served on salad frissé with baby potatoes with garlic. Service by the French staff is polite but a bit slow. The tables tend to be a little too close, but there is a lovely private balcony space overlooking the long, thin dining room where large groups can gather.

2415 Ponce de León Blvd. (at Miracle Mile), Coral Gables. ☎ **305/461-1099.** Reservations recommended on weekends. Main courses $13–$26. AE, DC, DISC, MC, V. Daily 11:30am–midnight.

House of India ✿ INDIAN   House of India's curries, kormas, and kabobs are very good, but the restaurant's well-priced all-you-can-eat lunch buffet is unsurpassed. All the favorites are on display, including tandoori chicken, naan, various meat and vegetarian curries, as well as rice and dal (lentils). This place isn't fancy and could use a good scrub-down (in fact, I've heard it described as a "greasy spoon"), but the service is excellent and the food is good enough to keep you from staring at your surroundings.

22 Merrick Way (near Douglas and Coral Way, 1 block north of Miracle Mile), Coral Gables. ✆ 305/444-2348. Reservations recommended. Main courses $8–$17. AE, DC, DISC, MC, V. Daily 11:30am–3pm; Sun–Thurs 5–10pm; Fri–Sat 5–11pm.

John Martin's ✿ IRISH PUB   Forest green and dark wood give way to a very intimate publike atmosphere in which local businesspeople and barflies alike come to hoist a pint or two. The menu offers some tasty British specialties (not necessarily an oxymoron!), such as bangers and mash and shepherd's pie, as well as Irish lamb stew and corned beef and cabbage.

Of course, to wash it down, you'll want to try one of the ales on tap or one of the more than 20 single-malt scotches. The crowd is upscale and chatty, as is the young waitstaff. Check out happy hour on weeknights, plus the Sunday brunch with loads of hand-carved meats and seafood.

253 Miracle Mile, Coral Gables. ✆ 305/445-3777. Reservations recommended on weekends. Main courses $9–$20; sandwiches and salads $5–$16. AE, DC, DISC, MC, V. Sun–Thurs 11:30am–midnight; Fri–Sat 11:30am–2am.

Ortanique on the Mile ✿✿✿ NEW WORLD CARIBBEAN   You'll be greeted as you walk in by soft spiderlike lights and canopied mosquito netting that will make you wonder whether you're on a secluded island or inside one of King Tut's temples. Chef Cindy Hutson has truly perfected her tantalizing New World Caribbean menu that also graces the tables of her two other Ortaniques in D.C. and Vegas. For starters, an absolute must is the pumpkin bisque with a hint of pepper sherry. Afterward, move on to the tropical mango salad with fresh marinated Sable hearts of palm, julienne mango, baby field greens, toasted Caribbean candied pecans, and passion-fruit vinaigrette. For an entree, I recommend the pan-sautéed Bahamian black grouper marinated in teriyaki and sesame oil. It's served with an ortanique (an orangelike fruit) orange liqueur sauce and topped with steamed seasoned chayote, zucchini, and carrots on a lemon-orange boniato–sweet plantain mash. For dessert, try the chocolate mango tower—layers of brownie, chocolate mango mousse, meringue, and sponge cake, accompanied by mango sorbet and tropical-fruit salsa. Entrees may not be cheap, but they're a lot less than airfare to the islands, from where most, if not all, the ingredients used here hail.

278 Miracle Mile (next to Actor's Playhouse), Coral Gables. ✆ 305/446-7710. Reservations requested. Main courses $19–$36. AE, DC, MC, V. Mon–Tues 6–10pm; Wed–Sat 6–11pm; Sun 5:30–9:30pm.

INEXPENSIVE

Miss Saigon Bistro ✿✿ VIETNAMESE   Unlike Andrew Lloyd Webber's bombastic Broadway show, this Miss Saigon is small, quiet, and not at all flashy. Servers at this family-run restaurant—among them, Rick, the owners' son—will graciously offer to recommend dishes or even to custom-make something for you, and if you're lucky, he may even sing you an aria with a voice ironically tailored to Webber shows. The menu is varied and reasonably priced, and the portions are huge—large enough to share. Noodle dishes and soup bowls are hearty and flavorful; caramelized prawns are fantastic, as is the whole snapper with lemon grass and ginger sauce. Despite the fact that there are few tables inside and a hungry crowd usually gathers outside in the street, they will not rush you through your meal, which is worth savoring. There is also a new, much larger location at 9503 S. Dixie Hwy., in South Miami's Pinecrest (✆ **305/661-2911**), and one in the financial district at 600 Brickell Ave. (✆ **305/416-0337**).

148 Giralda Ave. (at Ponce de León and 37th Ave.), Coral Gables. ✆ **305/446-8006**. Main courses $9–$18. AE, DC, DISC, MC, V. Mon–Fri 11:30am–3pm; Sun–Mon and Wed–Thurs 5:30–10pm; Tues 6:30–10pm; Fri–Sat 5:30–11pm.

SOUTH MIAMI & WEST MIAMI

Though mostly residential, these areas nonetheless have several eating establishments worth the drive.

EXPENSIVE

Tropical Chinese ★★ CHINESE   This strip-mall restaurant, way out in West Miami–Dade, is hailed as the best Chinese restaurant in the city. While the food is indeed very good—certainly more interesting than at your typical beef-and-broccoli place—it still seems overpriced. Garlic spinach and prawns in a clay pot are delicious, with the perfect mix of garlic cloves, mushrooms, and fresh spinach, but it's not cheap, at $17. And unlike at most Chinese restaurants, the dishes here are not large enough to share. Sunday-afternoon dim sum is extremely popular, and lines often snake around the shopping center.

7991 Bird Rd., West Miami. ✆ **305/262-7576**. Reservations highly recommended on weekends. Main courses $10–$25. AE, DC, MC, V. Mon–Fri 11:30am–10:30pm; Sat 11am–11:30pm; Sun 10:30am–10pm. Take U.S. 1 to Bird Rd. and go west on Bird, all the way down to 78th Ave. The restaurant is between 78th and 79th on the north side of Bird Rd.

INEXPENSIVE

Crepe Maker Café ★ *Kids* CREPES/FRENCH   Create your own delicious crepes at this little French cafe. You can choose from ham, tuna, black olives, red peppers, capers, artichoke hearts, and pine nuts. Some of the best include a Philly cheesesteak with mushrooms, and a classic chicken *cordon bleu*. Delicious dessert crepes include ice cream, strawberries, peaches, walnuts, and pineapples. Enjoy your crepe fresh off the griddle at the counter or from a bar stool. The soups are delicious. Kids can run around in a small play area.

8269 SW 124th St., South Miami. ✆ **305/233-4458** or 305/233-1113. Crepes $1.50–$8.50. AE, DC, MC, V. Sun–Thurs 11:30am–9:30pm; Fri–Sat 11:30am–10:30pm. Take U.S. 1 south to 124th St. and make a left. The restaurant is on the north side of the street, across from the park.

El Toro Taco Family Restaurant ★★★ *Finds* MEXICAN   Until I discovered this Mexican oasis in the midst of South Florida farmland, I'd never had good enough reason to leave my quasicosmopolitan confines in Miami for rural Homestead, way down south. This 96-seat family-run restaurant has put major miles on my car since I first stumbled upon it a few years ago when I was lost and very hungry. Fabulous (and I mean fabulous) Mexican fare—tacos, enchiladas, and burritos drenched with the freshest and zestiest salsa this side of Baja—is what you'll find here in abundance. It may sound odd to travel from a big city with tons of restaurants to farm country for Mexican food, but trust me: It's so cheap and delicious, it's worth the trip.

1 S. Krome Ave., Homestead. ✆ **305/245-8182**. Main courses $1.75–$12. DISC, MC, V. Tues–Sun 10am–9pm (until 10pm Fri–Sat). Take 836 W. (Dolphin Expwy.) toward Miami International Airport. Take Florida Tpk. S. ramp toward Florida City/Key West. Take U.S. 41/SW 8th st. exit (exit 25) and turn left onto SW 8th St. Take SW 8th St. to Krome Ave. (½ mile) and turn left.

Kon Chau ✪ CHINESE/DIM SUM   Don't be put off by the rather unappealing shopping center in which this cheap dim-sum place is located. If you want fancy plastic chopsticks and fancy prices, go up the block to Tropical Chinese (see above). If you want delicious dim sum at ridiculously low prices, Kon Chau is where you'll find it. A simple checklist allows you to choose as many items as you want, from savory steamed shrimp dumplings to airy pork buns, for as little as $1 apiece, all day long. There are also regular dishes if you don't want dim sum.

8376 Bird Rd., West Miami. ☏ 305/553-7799. Items $1 and up. MC, V. Mon–Sat 11am–9:45pm; Sun 10am–9:30pm. Take Bird Rd. west to 83rd St. The restaurant is between 83rd and 84th sts. on the south side of the road, in a Dunkin' Donuts shopping center.

Shorty's ✪ BARBECUE   A Miami tradition since 1951, this honky-tonk of a log cabin still serves some of the best ribs and chicken in South Florida. People line up for the smoke-flavored, slow-cooked meat that's so tender it seems to fall off the bone. The secret, however, is to ask for your order with sweet sauce. The regular stuff tastes bland and bottled. All of the side dishes, including the coleslaw, corn on the cob, and baked beans, look commercial but complete the experience. This is a jeans-and-T-shirt kind of place, but you may want to wear jeans with an elastic waistband, as overeating is not uncommon.

9200 S. Dixie Hwy. (between U.S. 1 and Dadeland Blvd.), South Miami. ☏ 305/670-7732. Main courses $5–$9. DISC, MC, V. Sun–Thurs 11am–10pm; Fri–Sat 11am–11pm.

The Tea Room at Cauley Square ✪ ENGLISH TEA   Do stop in for a spot of tea at this recently rebuilt tearoom in historic Cauley Square, off U.S. 1. The little lace-curtained room is an unusual sight in this heavily industrial area better known for its warehouses than its doilies. Try one of the simple sandwiches, such as the turkey club with potato salad and a small lettuce garnish, or onion soup—rich brown broth and stringy cheese. The Ambrosia with finger sandwiches is an interesting choice: a blend of pineapple, mandarin oranges, miniature marshmallows, and sour cream served with finger sandwiches or banana-nut bread. Daily specials (such as spinach-and-mushroom quiche) and delectable desserts are musts before you begin your explorations of the old antiques and art shops in this little enclave of civility down south. Oh, and remember to put your pinky up while sipping your tea.

12310 SW 224th St. (at Cauley Sq.), South Miami. ☏ 305/258-0044. Sandwiches and salads $7–$12; soups $3–$4. AE, DISC, MC, V. Daily 11am–4pm. Take 836 W. (Dolphin Expwy.) toward Miami International Airport. Take Palmetto Expwy. S. ramp toward Coral Way. Merge onto 826 S. Follow signs to Florida Tpk. toward Homestead. Take Tpk. south and exit at Caribbean Blvd. (exit 12). Go about 1 mile on Caribbean Blvd. and turn left on S. Dixie Hwy. and then right at SW 224th St. Then turn left onto Old Dixie Hwy. and take a slight right onto SW 224th St. The restaurant is at Cauley Square Center.

5

What to See & Do in Miami

If there's one thing Miami doesn't have, it's an identity crisis. In fact, it's the city's vibrant, multifaceted personality that attracts millions each year from all over the world. South Beach may be on the top of many Miami to-do lists, but the rest of the city, a fascinating assemblage of multicultural neighborhoods, should not be overlooked. Once considered "God's Waiting Room," the Magic City now attracts an eclectic mix of old and young, celebs and plebes, American and international, and geek and chic with an equally varied roster of activities.

For starters, Miami boasts some of the world's most natural beauty, with blinding blue waters, fine sandy beaches, and lush tropical parks. The city's man-made brilliance, in the form of Crayola-colored architecture, never seems to fade in Miami's unique Art Deco District. And for cultural variation, you can experience the tastes, sounds, and rhythms of Cuba in Little Havana.

As in any metropolis, though, there are areas that aren't as great as others. Downtown Miami, for instance, is still in the throes of a major, albeit slow, renaissance, in which the sketchier warehouse sections of the city are being transformed into hubs of all things hip. In contrast to this

development, however, are the still poverty-stricken areas of downtown such as Overtown, Liberty City, and Little Haiti (though Overtown is striving to transform itself into the Overtown Historic Village, showcasing its landmarks such as the famous Lyric Theater and the home of D. A. Dorsey, Miami's first African-American millionaire). While it's obvious to advise you to exercise caution when exploring the less-traveled parts of the city, I would also be remiss in telling you to bypass them completely.

Lose yourself in the city's nature and its neighborhoods and, best of all, its people—a sassy collection of artists and intellectuals, beach bums and international transplants, dolled-up drag queens and bodies beautiful. No wonder celebrities love to vacation here—the spotlight is on the city and its residents. And unlike most stars, Miami is always ready for its close-up. With so much to do and see, Miami is a virtual amusement park that's bound to entertain all those who pass through its palm-lined gates.

You'll find a "Miami Area Attractions & Beaches" map in this chapter. For a map of South Beach's attractions, see the "South Beach" map on p. 83.

1 Miami's Beaches

Perhaps Miami's most popular attraction is its incredible 35-mile stretch of beachfront, which runs from the tip of South Beach north to Sunny Isles and circles Key Biscayne and the numerous other pristine islands dotting the Atlantic. The characteristics of Miami's many beaches are as varied as the city's population: There are beaches for swimming, socializing, or serenity; for family, seniors, or gay singles; some to make

---

Then&Now Miami, Then

When Frommer's published *Miami and the Caribbean on 10 Dollars a Day,* most of Florida wasn't a vacation destination, just the beaches of Miami. To writer Elliott Kanbar, it was a fantasy vacation land: "Miami Beach, Florida, is materialism run amok—and therein lies its utter fascination. For miles on end, there are giant seaside hotels whose splendor would rival the palaces of an Assyrian king. There are gleaming cars, resplendent women, cabana-dotted beaches and spotlighted palm trees. In even the lowest of Miami restaurants, the meat in the sandwiches is at least an inch thick."

---

you forget you're in the city, others darkened by huge condominiums. Whatever type of beach vacation you're looking for, you'll find it in one of Miami's two distinct beach areas: Miami Beach and Key Biscayne.

MIAMI BEACH'S BEACHES Collins Avenue fronts more than a dozen miles of white-sand beach and blue-green waters from 1st to 192nd streets. Although most of this stretch is lined with a solid wall of hotels and condos, beach access is plentiful. There are lots of public beaches here, wide and well maintained, complete with lifeguards, bathroom facilities, concession stands, and metered parking (bring lots of quarters). Except for a thin strip close to the water, most of the sand is hard packed— the result of a $10 million Army Corps of Engineers Beach Rebuilding Project meant to protect buildings from the effects of eroding sand.

In general, the beaches on this barrier island (all on the eastern, oceanside of the island) become less crowded the farther north you go. A wooden boardwalk runs along the hotel side of the beach from 21st to 46th streets—about 1½ miles—offering a terrific sun-and-surf experience without getting sand in your shoes. Miami's lifeguard-protected public beaches include 21st Street, at the beginning of the boardwalk; 35th Street, popular with an older crowd; 46th Street, next to the Fontainebleau Hilton; 53rd Street, a narrower, more sedate beach; 64th Street, one of the quietest strips around; and 72nd Street, a local old-timers' spot.

KEY BISCAYNE'S BEACHES If Miami Beach doesn't provide the privacy you're looking for, try Virginia Key and Key Biscayne. Crossing the Rickenbacker Causeway ($1 toll), however, can be a lengthy process, especially on weekends, when beach bums and tan-o-rexics flock to the Key. The 5 miles of public beach there, however, are blessed with softer sand and are less developed and more laid-back than the hotel-laden strips to the north.

2 The Art Deco District (South Beach)

"You know what they used to say? 'Who's Art?'" recalls Art Deco revivalist Dona Zemo. "You'd say, 'This is an Art Deco building,' and they'd say, 'Really, who is Art?' These people thought 'Art Deco' was some guy's name."

How things have changed. This guy Art has become one of the most popular Florida attractions since, well, that mouse named Mickey. The district is roughly bounded by the Atlantic Ocean on the east, Alton Road on the west, 6th Street to the south, and Dade Boulevard (along the Collins Canal) to the north.

Miami Area Attractions & Beaches

American Airlines Arena **11**
Barnacle State Historic Site **24**
Bayfront Park **19**
Bayside Marketplace **20**
Bill Baggs Cape Florida State
  Recreation Center **15**
Biltmore Hotel **31**
CocoWalk **23**
Coral Castle **27**
Crandon Park Golf Course **17**
Dolphins Stadium **1**
Doral Park Golf
  and Country Club **7**
Fairchild Tropical Garden **26**
Fisher Island **14**
Gulfstream Park **3**
Haulover Beach Park **5**
Haulover Marina **6**
Historical Museum
  of Southern Florida **21**

The Kampong **25**
Latin American Art Museum **22**
Lowe Art Museum **29**
Main Library **21**
Marjory Stoneman Douglas
  Biscayne Nature Center **16**
Miami Art Museum **21**
Miami Children's Museum **13**
Miami Jai Alai Fronton **8**
Miami Metrozoo **27**
Miami Museum of Science and
  Space Transit Planetarium **29**
Miami Seaquarium **18**
Miami-Dade Cultural Center
  (Miami Art Museum & the Historical
  Museum of Southern Florida) **21**
Miccosukee Indian Gaming **27**
Monkey Jungle **27**
Museum of Contemporary Art
  (MOCA) **4**

Oleta River State Recreation Area **3**
Parrot Jungle Island **12**
Preston B. Bird and Mary Heinlein
  Fruit and Spice Park **27**
Rubell Family Art Collection **9**
Sea Grass Adventures **16**
Spanish Monastery Cloisters **2**
Venetian Pool **30**
The Vizcaya Museum and Gardens **27**
World Erotic Art Museum **10**

Simply put, Art Deco is a style of architecture that, in its heyday of the 1920s and 1930s, used to be considered ultramodern. Today fans of the style consider it retro-fabulous. And while some people may not consider the style fabulous, it's undoubtedly retro. According to the experts, Art Deco made its debut in 1925 at an exposition in Paris in which it set a stylistic tone, with buildings based on early neoclassical styles with the application of exotic motifs like flora, fauna, and fountains based on geometric patterns. In Miami, Art Deco is marked by the pastel-hued buildings that line South Beach and Miami Beach. But it's a lot more than just color. If you look carefully, you will see the intricacies and impressive craftsmanship that went into each building back in Miami in the '20s, '30s, '40s, and today, thanks to intensive restoration.

Most of the finest examples of the whimsical Art Deco style are concentrated along three parallel streets—Ocean Drive, Collins Avenue, and Washington Avenue—from about 6th to 23rd streets.

After years of neglect and calls for the wholesale demolition of its buildings, South Beach got a new lease on life in 1979. Under the leadership of Barbara Baer Capitman, a dedicated crusader for the Art Deco region, and the Miami Design Preservation League, founded by Baer Capitman and five friends, an area made up of an estimated 800 buildings was granted a listing on the National Register of Historic Places. Designers then began highlighting long-lost architectural details with soft sherbet shades of peach, periwinkle, turquoise, and purple. Developers soon moved in, and the full-scale refurbishment of the area's hotels was underway.

Not everyone was pleased, though. Former Miami Beach commissioner Abe Resnick said, "I love old buildings. But these Art Deco buildings are 40, 50 years old. They aren't historic. They aren't special. We shouldn't be forced to keep them." But Miami Beach kept those buildings, and Resnick lost his seat on the commission.

Today hundreds of new establishments—hotels, restaurants, and nightclubs—have renovated these older, historic buildings, putting South Beach on the cutting edge of Miami's cultural and nightlife scene.

Finds Walking by Design

The Miami Design Preservation League offers several tours of Miami Beach's historic architecture, all of which leave from the Art Deco Welcome Center at 1001 Ocean Dr. in Miami Beach. A self-guided audio tour (available 7 days a week, from 10am–4pm) turns the streets into a virtual outdoor museum, taking you through Miami Beach's Art Deco district at your own leisure, with tours in several languages for just $15 for adults, $10 for seniors. Guided tours conducted by local historians and architects offer an in-depth look at the structures and their history. The 90-minute Ocean Drive and Beyond tour (offered every Wed and Sat at 10:30am) takes you through the district, pointing out the differences between Mediterranean Revival and Art Deco for $20 for adults, $15 for seniors. If you're not blinded by neon, the Thursday night Art Deco District Up-to-Date Tour (leaving at 6:30pm) will whisk you around for a 90-minute walk, making note of how certain local hot spots were architecturally famous way before the likes of Madonna and Co. entered the scene. The cost is $20 for adults, $15 for seniors. For more information on tours or reservations, call ℂ **305/672-2014.**

EXPLORING THE AREA

If you're touring this unique neighborhood on your own, start at the **Art Deco Welcome Center,** 1001 Ocean Dr. (© **305/531-3484**), which is run by the Miami Design Preservation League. The only beachside building across from the Clevelander Hotel and bar, the center gives away lots of informational material, including maps and pamphlets, and runs guided tours around the neighborhood. Art Deco books (including *The Art Deco Guide,* an informative compendium of all the buildings here), T-shirts, postcards, mugs, and other paraphernalia are for sale. It's open daily from 10am to 7:30pm.

Take a stroll along **Ocean Drive** for the best view of sidewalk cafes, bars, colorful hotels, and even more colorful people. Another great place for a walk is **Lincoln Road,** which is lined with boutiques, large chain stores, cafes, and funky art and antiques stores. The Community Church, at the corner of Lincoln Road and Drexel Avenue, was the neighborhood's first church and is one of its oldest surviving buildings, dating from 1921.

3 Miami's Museum & Art Scene

Miami has never been known as a cultural mecca as far as museums are concerned. Though several exhibition spaces have made forays into collecting nationally acclaimed work, limited support and political infighting have made it a difficult proposition. Recently, however, things have changed as museums such as the Wolfsonian, the Museum of Contemporary Art, the Bass Museum of Art, and the Miami Art Museum have gotten on the bandwagon, boasting collections and exhibitions high on the list of art aficionados. It's now safe to say that world-class exhibitions start here. Listed below are the most lauded museums that have become a part of the city's cultural heritage and are as diverse as the city itself. Art lovers should check local listings for periodic gallery walks.

IN SOUTH BEACH

The focal point of December's enormously popular Art Basel is **Collins Park Cultural Center,** which comprises a trio of arts buildings on Collins Park and Park Avenue (off Collins Ave.), bounded by 21st to 23rd streets—the newly expanded Bass Museum of Art (see below), the new Arquitectonica-designed home of the Miami City Ballet, and the Miami Beach Regional Library, an ultramodern building designed by architect Robert A. M. Stern, with a special focus on the arts. The Library Café is on the library's first floor, serving coffee and pastries and exuding that cafe society ambience. Collins Park, the former site of the Miami Beach Library, returned to its original incarnation as an open space extending to the Atlantic, but it is also now the site of large sculpture installations and cultural activities planned jointly by the organizations that share the space.

ArtCenter/South Florida ⍟ Not exactly a museum in the classic sense of the word, ArtCenter/South Florida is a multichambered space where local artists display their works in all media—from photography and sculpture to video and just about anything else that might exemplify their artistic nature. Admission is free, and it's quite fun to mosey through the space viewing the various artists at work in their studios. Of course, all the art is for sale, but there's no pressure to buy. If you call ahead, you can schedule a guided tour of all the studios, which will give you extra insight into the exhibits. Otherwise, just wander and enjoy.

800–924 Lincoln Rd. (at Meridian Ave.), South Beach. ✆ 305/674-8278. www.artcentersf.org. Free admission. Daily 11am–10pm.

Bass Museum of Art ✸✸✸   The Bass Museum of Art has expanded and received a dramatically new look, rendering it Miami's most progressive art museum. World-renowned Japanese architect Arata Isozaki designed the magnificent new facility, which has triple the former exhibition space, and added an outdoor sculpture terrace, a museum cafe and courtyard, and a museum shop, among other improvements. In addition to providing space in which to show the permanent collection, exhibitions of a scale and quality not previously seen in Miami will now be featured at the Bass. The museum's permanent collection includes European paintings from the 15th through the early 20th centuries, with special emphasis on Northern European art of the Renaissance and baroque periods, including Dutch and Flemish masters. Past exhibitions have included the works of Picasso, Frida Kahlo, and Francois Marie Banier. The museum also has a lab, The New Information Workshop, making it possible for all aspiring artists to create their own masterpieces on computers for free or a nominal charge.

2121 Park Ave. (1 block west of Collins Ave.), South Beach. ✆ 305/673-7530. www.bassmuseum.org. Admission $8 adults, $6 students and seniors, free for children 6 and under. Free 2nd Thurs of the month 6–9pm. Tues–Wed and Fri–Sat 10am–5pm; Thurs 10am–9pm; Sun 11am–5pm. Closed Mon.

Diaspora Vibe Art Gallery ✸✸   This culturally charged art complex is a funky artist hangout and is the home to some of the greatest artworks of Miami's diverse Caribbean, Latin American, and African-American cultures. The gallery has two seasons of shows, often focusing on emerging artists. During the winter, three artists are selected by the gallery to travel to and exhibit their works in Paris. On the last Friday of every month, from May through October, the gallery holds its fabulous cocktail-infused "Final Fridays." A new artist's work is spotlighted inside, while outside in the courtyard are live music performances and readings of poetry and folk tales. Delicious Caribbean cuisine is also served while the who's who of Miami's cognoscenti gather here to recharge their cultural batteries.

3938 N. Miami Ave., Miami. ✆ 305/573-4046. www.diasporavibe.com. Free admission. "Final Fridays" events $15. "Final Fridays" events May–Oct last Fri of the month 7–11pm. Open Tues–Sat 11am–6pm

Holocaust Memorial ✸✸✸   This heart-wrenching memorial is hard to miss and would be a shame to overlook. The powerful centerpiece, Kenneth Triester's *Sculpture of Love & Anguish,* depicts victims of the concentration camps crawling up a giant yearning hand stretching up to the sky, marked with an Auschwitz number tattoo. Along the reflecting pool is the story of the Holocaust, told in cut marble slabs. Inside the center of the memorial is a tableau that is one of the most solemn and moving tributes to the millions of Jews who lost their lives in the Holocaust I've seen. You can walk through an open hallway lined with photographs and the names of concentration camps and their victims. From the street you'll see the outstretched arm, but do stop and tour the sculpture at ground level.

1933 Meridian Ave. (at Dade Blvd.), South Beach. ✆ 305/538-1663. www.holocaustmmb.org. Free admission. Daily 9am–9pm.

Latin American Art Museum   In addition to the permanent collection of contemporary artists from Spain and Latin America, this 3,500-square-foot museum hosts monthly exhibitions of works from Latin America and the Caribbean Basin. Usually, the exhibitions focus on a theme, such as international women or surrealism. It's not a major attraction, but it's worth a stop if you're interested in Latin American art. On the same block, you'll find great design stores and a few other galleries.

2206 SW 8th St., Little Havana. (C) **305/644-1127**. Free admission (though donation suggested). Tues–Fri 11am–5pm; Sat 11am–4pm. Second Fri of every month 6:30–10pm. Closed major holidays.

Lowe Art Museum ★★ Located on the University of Miami campus, the Lowe Art Museum has a dazzling collection of 8,000 works that include American paintings, Latin American art, Navajo and Pueblo Indian textiles, and Renaissance and baroque art. Traveling exhibits such as *Rolling Stone* magazine's photo collection also stop here. For the most part, the Lowe is known for its collection of Greek and Roman antiquities, and, as compared to the more modern MOCA, Bass, and Miami Art Museum, features mostly European and international art hailing back to ancient times.

University of Miami, 1301 Stanford Dr. (at Ponce de León Blvd.), Coral Gables. (C) **305/284-3603**. www.lowe museum.org. Admission $5 adults, $3 seniors and student with ID. Donation day is first Tues of the month. Tues–Wed and Fri–Sat 10am–5pm; Thurs noon–7pm; Sun noon–5pm.

Miami Art Museum at the Miami–Dade Cultural Center ★★★ The Miami Art Museum (MAM) features an eclectic mix of modern and contemporary works by such artists as Eric Fischl, Max Beckmann, Jim Dine, and Stuart Davis. Rotating exhibitions span ages and styles, and often focus on Latin American or Caribbean artists. JAM at MAM is the museum's popular happy hour, which takes place the third Thursday of the month and is tied in to a particular exhibit. Almost as artistic as the works inside the museum is the composite sketch of the people—young and old—who attend these events.

The Miami–Dade Cultural Center, where the museum is housed, is a fortresslike complex designed by Phillip Johnson. In addition to the acclaimed Miami Art Museum, the center houses the main branch of the Miami–Dade Public Library, which sometimes features art and cultural exhibits, and the Historical Museum of Southern Florida, which highlights the fascinating history of the area. Unfortunately, the plaza onto which the complex opens is home to many of downtown Miami's homeless population, which makes it a bit off-putting but not dangerous.

101 W. Flagler St., Miami. (C) **305/375-3000**. www.miamiartmuseum.org. Admission $5 adults, $2.50 seniors and students, free for children under 12. Tues–Fri 10am–5pm; 3rd Thurs of each month 10am–9pm; Sat–Sun noon–5pm. Closed Mon and major holidays. From I-95 south, exit at Orange Bowl–NW 8th St. and continue south to NW 2nd St.; turn left at NW 2nd St. and go 1½ blocks to NW 2nd Ave.; turn right.

Miami Children's Museum ★★ *Kids* This brand-new museum, located across the MacArthur Causeway from Parrot Jungle Island, is a modern, albeit odd-looking, 56,500-square-foot facility that includes 12 galleries, classrooms, a parent/teacher resource center, a Kid Smart educational gift shop, a 200-seat auditorium, and a Subway restaurant. The museum offers hundreds of bilingual, interactive exhibits as well as programs and classes and learning materials related to arts, culture, community, and communication. Even as an adult, I have to say I was tempted to participate in some kids-only activities and exhibitions, such as the miniature Bank of America and Publix Supermarket, and a re-creation of the NBC 6 television studio. There's also a re-creation of a Carnival Cruise ship and even a port stop in a re-created Brazil. Perhaps the coolest thing of all is the World Music Studio in which aspiring Britneys, Justins, and Lenny Kravitzes can lay down a few tracks and play instruments.

980 MacArthur Causeway, Miami Beach. (C) **305/373-5437**. www.miamichildrensmuseum.org. $10 adults and children, $5 for city residents. Daily 10am–6pm.

Miami Museum of Science and Space Transit Planetarium ★★ (Kids)

The Museum of Science features more than 140 hands-on exhibits that explore the mysteries of the universe. Live demonstrations and collections of rare natural history specimens make a visit here fun and informative. Many of the demos involve audience participation, which can be lots of fun for willing and able kids and adults alike. There is also the Wildlife Center, with more than 175 live reptiles and birds of prey. The adjacent Space Transit Planetarium projects astronomy and laser shows as well as interactive demonstrations of upcoming computer technology and cyberspace features. Call or visit their website for a list of upcoming exhibits and laser shows.

3280 S. Miami Ave. (just south of the Rickenbacker Causeway), Coconut Grove. (℄ 305/646-4200 for general information. www.miamisci.org. $10 adults, $8 seniors and students, $6 children 3–12, free for children 2 and under; laser shows $7 adults, $4 seniors and children 3–12. $2 off admission for museum ticket holders. Call for laser show times. Ticket are half-price after 4:30pm. 10% discount for AAA members. Tickets cover entrance to all museum galleries, planetarium shows, and the Wildlife Center. Museum of Science daily 10am–6pm; call for show times (last show is at 4pm weekdays and 5pm on weekends). Closed Thanksgiving and Christmas.

Museum of Contemporary Art (MOCA) ★★★

MOCA boasts an impressive collection of internationally acclaimed art with a local flavor. It is also known for its forward thinking and ability to discover and highlight new artists. A high-tech screening facility allows for film presentations to complement the exhibitions. You can see works by Jasper Johns, Roy Lichtenstein, Larry Rivers, Duane Michaels, and Claes Oldenberg, plus there are special exhibitions by such artists as Yoko Ono, Sigmar Polke, John Baldessari, and Goya. Guided tours are offered in English, Spanish, French, Creole, Portuguese, German, and Italian. The MOCA Annex at the Goldman Warehouse in the Wynwood Arts District, 404 NW 26th St., is used to exhibit portions of the museum's permanent collection and projects by emerging artists.

770 NE 125th St., North Miami. (℄ 305/893-6211. Fax 305/891-1472. www.mocanomi.org. Admission $5 adults, $3 seniors and students with ID, free for children 12 and under. Tues by donation. Tues–Sat 11am–5pm; Sun noon–5pm. Closed Mon and major holidays.

Rubell Family Art Collection ★★★ (Finds)

This impressive collection, owned by the Miami hotelier family the Rubells, is housed in a two-story 40,000-square-foot former Drug Enforcement Agency warehouse in a sketchy area north of downtown Miami. The building looks like a fortress, which is fitting: Inside is a priceless collection of more than a thousand works of contemporary art by the likes of Keith Haring, Damien Hirst, Julian Schnabel, Jean-Michel Basquiat, Paul McCarthy, Charles Ray, and Cindy Sherman. But *be forewarned:* Some of the art is extremely graphic and may be off-putting to some. The gallery changes exhibitions twice yearly, and there is a seasonal program of lectures, artists' talks, and performances by prominent artists.

95 NW 29th St. (on the corner of NW 1st Ave. near the Design District), Miami. (℄ 305/573-6090. www.rubellfamily collection.com. Adults $5, students and seniors $2. Wed–Sun 10am–6pm.

Sanford L. Ziff Jewish Museum of Florida ★

Chronicling over 230 years of Jewish heritage and experiences in Florida, the Jewish Museum presents a fascinating look at religion and culture through films, lectures, and exhibits such as "Mosaic: Jewish Life in Florida," which features over 500 photos and artifacts documenting the Jewish experience in Florida since 1763. Housed in a former synagogue, the museum also delves into the Jewish roots of Latin America.

301 Washington Ave., South Beach. (℄ 305/672-5044. www.jewishmuseum.com. $5 adults, $4 seniors and students, $10 families. Free admission Sat. Tues–Sun 10am–5pm. Closed Mon and Jewish holidays.

Wolfsonian-Florida International University ✫✫✫ *Finds*   Mitchell Wolfson, Jr., heir to a family fortune built on movie theaters, was known as an eccentric, but I'd call him a pack rat. A premier collector of propaganda and advertising art, Wolfson was spending so much money storing his booty that he decided to buy the warehouse that was housing it. It ultimately held more than 70,000 of his items, from controversial Nazi propaganda to King Farouk of Egypt's match collection. Thrown in the eclectic mix are also zany works from great modernists such as Charles Eames and Marcel Duchamp. He then gave this incredibly diverse collection to Florida International University. The former 1927 storage facility has been transformed into a museum that is the envy of curators around the world. The museum is unquestionably fascinating and hosts lectures and rather swinging events surrounding particular exhibits. The Dynamo, the museum's new cafe and shop, is a fun and funky spot serving coffee, wine, beer, and nibbles, whose focal point is a large library shelving system from the late nineteenth century, donated by Samson Management, designed by Bernard R. Green, and crafted of iron by the Snead & Company Iron Works. The design represents the first modular book-stacking system ever created. Leave it to the Wolfsonian to make even its restaurant a piece of work!

1001 Washington Ave., South Beach. ✆ 305/531-1001. www.wolfsonian.org. Admission $7 adults, $5 seniors, students with ID, and children 6–12. Mon–Tues and Fri–Sat 11am–6pm; Thurs 11am–9pm; Sun noon–5pm.

The World Erotic Art Museum ✫   The Hustler store across the street's got nothing on this wacky, X-rated museum. Opened in 2005 by 70-year-old grandmother Naomi Wilzig, the museum features Wilzig's collection of more than 4,000 pieces of erotic art, including Kama Sutra temple carvings from India, peek-a-boo Victorian figurines that flash their booties, and a prop from the sexual thriller *A Clockwork Orange.* The 12,000-square-foot museum is located above Mansion, a club that's no stranger to erotic art—that is, performance art. This is a great place to spend an hour or two on a rainy day, and more than anything, the stuff is more amusing than sexy or racy.

1205 Washington Ave., South Beach. ✆ 305/532-9336. Admission $15; 18 and over. Daily 11am–midnight.

4 Historic Homes & Sites

South Beach's well-touted Art Deco District is but one of many colorful neighborhoods that can boast dazzling architecture. The rediscovery of the entire Biscayne Corridor (from downtown to about 80th St. and Biscayne Blvd.) has given light to a host of ancillary neighborhoods on either side that are filled with Mediterranean-style homes and Frank Lloyd Wright gems. Coral Gables is home to many large and beautiful homes, mansions, and churches that reflect architecture from the 1920s, 1930s, and 1940s. Some of the homes, or portions of their structures, have been created from coral rock and shells. The Biltmore Hotel is also filled with history; see p. 151 for information on touring it.

Barnacle State Historic Site ✫✫   The former home of naval architect and early settler Ralph Middleton Munroe is now a museum in the heart of Coconut Grove. It's the oldest house in Miami and it rests on its original foundation, which sits on 5 acres of hardwood and landscaped lawns. The house's quiet surroundings, wide porches, and period furnishings illustrate how Miami's first snowbird lived in the days before condomania and luxury hotels. Enthusiastic and knowledgeable state park employees offer a wealth of historical information to those interested in quiet, low-tech attractions like this one. Call for details on the fabulous monthly moonlight concerts during which folk, blues, or classical music is presented and picnicking is encouraged.

3485 Main Hwy. (1 block south of Commodore Plaza), Coconut Grove. © 305/448-9445. Fax 305/448-7484. Admission $1. Concerts $5, free for children under 10. Fri–Mon 9am–4pm. Tours Fri–Mon at 10am, 11:30am, 1pm, and 2:30pm. From downtown Miami, take U.S. 1 south to 27th Ave., make a left, and continue to S. Bayshore Dr.; then make a right, follow to the intersection of Main Hwy., and turn left.

Coral Castle 🔆 *Finds*   There's plenty of competition, but Coral Castle is probably the strangest attraction in Florida. In 1923, the story goes, a 26-year-old crazed Latvian, suffering from unrequited love of a 16-year-old who left him at the altar, immigrated to South Miami and spent the next 25 years of his life carving huge boulders into a prehistoric-looking roofless "castle." It seems impossible that one rather short man could have done all this, but there are scores of affidavits on display from neighbors who swear it happened. Apparently, experts have studied this phenomenon to help figure out how the Great Pyramids and Stonehenge were built. Rocker Billy Idol was said to have been inspired by this place to write his song "Sweet 16." An interesting 25-minute audio tour guides you through the spot, now in the National Register of Historic Places. Although Coral Castle is overpriced and under maintained, it's worth a visit when in the area, which is about 37 miles from Miami.

28655 S. Dixie Hwy., Homestead. © 305/248-6345. www.coralcastle.com. Admission $9.75 adults, $6.50 seniors, $5 children 7–12. Daily 7am–8pm. Take 836 West (Dolphin Expwy.) toward Miami International Airport. Merge onto 826 South (Palmetto Expwy.) and take it to the Florida Tpk. toward Homestead. Take the 288th St. exit (#5) and then take a right on South Dixie Hwy., a left on SW 157th Ave., and then a sharp left back onto South Dixie Hwy. Coral Castle is on the left side of the street.

Spanish Monastery Cloisters 🔆🔆🔆 *Finds*   Did you know that the alleged oldest building in the Western Hemisphere dates from 1133 and is located in Miami? The Spanish Monastery Cloisters were first erected in Segovia, Spain. Centuries later, newspaper magnate William Randolph Hearst purchased and brought them to America in pieces. The carefully numbered stones were quarantined for years until they were finally reassembled on the present site in 1954. It has often been used as a backdrop for weddings, movies, and commercials, and is a very popular tourist attraction.

16711 W. Dixie Hwy. (at NE 167th St.), North Miami Beach. © 305/945-1461. www.spanishmonastery.com. Admission $4.50 adults, $2.50 seniors and students with ID, $1 children 3–12. Mon–Fri 10am–4pm; Sun 1–5pm. Call ahead because the monastery closes for special events without being announced.

Venetian Pool 🔆🔆🔆 *Kids*   Miami's most beautiful and unusual swimming pool, dating from 1924, is hidden behind pastel stucco walls and is honored with a listing in the National Register of Historic Places. Underground artesian wells feed the free-form lagoon, which is shaded by three-story Spanish porticos and features both fountains and waterfalls. It can be cold in the winter months. During summer, the pool's 800,000 gallons of water are drained and refilled nightly, thanks to an underground aquifer, ensuring a cool, *clean* swim. Visitors are free to swim and sunbathe here, just as Esther Williams and Johnny Weissmuller did decades ago. For a modest fee, you or your children can learn to swim during special summer programs.

2701 DeSoto Blvd. (at Toledo St.), Coral Gables. © 305/460-5356. www.venetianpool.com. Admission and hours vary seasonally. Nov–Mar $6.25 for those 13 and older, $3.25 children under 13; April–Oct $9.50 for those 13 and older, $5.25 children under 13. Children must be 3 years old and provide proof of age with birth certificate, or 38 in. tall to enter. Hours are at least 11am–4:30pm but are often longer. Call for more information.

The Vizcaya Museum and Gardens 🔆🔆🔆   Sometimes referred to as the "Hearst Castle of the East," this magnificent villa is more Gatsby-esque than anything else you'll find in Miami. It was built in 1916 as a winter retreat for James Deering, co-founder and former vice president of International Harvester. The industrialist was fascinated by 16th-century art and architecture, and his ornate mansion, which took 1,000 artisans 5 years to build, became a celebration of that period. If you love antiques, this place is a dream come true, packed with European relics and works of art from the 16th to the 19th centuries. Most of the original furnishings, including dishes and paintings, are still intact. You will see very early versions of a telephone switchboard, central vacuum-cleaning system, elevators, and fire sprinklers. A free guided tour of the 34 furnished rooms on the first floor takes about 45 minutes. The second floor, which consists mostly of bedrooms, is open to tour on your own. The spectacularly opulent villa wraps itself around a central courtyard. Outside, lush formal gardens, accented with statuary, balustrades, and decorative urns, front an enormous swath of Biscayne Bay. Definitely take the tour of the rooms, but immediately thereafter, you will want to wander and get lost in the resplendent gardens.

3251 S. Miami Ave. (just south of Rickenbacker Causeway), North Coconut Grove. (℃ 305/250-9133. www.vizcaya museum.com. Admission $12 adults, $5 children 6–12, free for children 5 and under. Villa daily 9:30am–5pm (ticket booth closes at 4:30pm); gardens daily 9:30am–5:30pm.

5 Nature Preserves, Parks & Gardens

The Miami area is a great place for outdoors types, with beaches, parks, nature preserves, and gardens galore. For information on South Florida's two national parks, the Everglades and Biscayne National Park, see chapter 7.

The **Amelia Earhart Park,** 401 E. 65th St., Hialeah (℃ **305/685-8389**), is the only real reason to travel to industrial, traffic-riddled Hialeah. The park has five lakes stocked with bass and bream for fishing; playgrounds; picnic facilities; a skate park; and a big red barn that houses cows, sheep, and goats for petting and ponies for riding. There's also the Bill Graham Farm Village, a re-created Miami–Dade County homestead housing a country store and dozens of old-time farm activities like horseshoeing, sugarcane processing, and more. Parking is free on weekdays and $4 per car on weekends. The park is open daily from 9am to sunset, but all the attractions close at about 4pm. To drive here, take I-95 north to the NW 103rd Street exit, go west to East 4th Avenue, and then turn right. Parking is 1½ miles down the street. Depending on traffic, Hialeah is about a half-hour from downtown Miami.

At the historic **Bill Baggs Cape Florida State Park** ⊛, 1200 Crandon Blvd. (℃ **305/361-5811**), at the southern tip of Key Biscayne about 20 minutes from downtown Miami, you can explore the unfettered wilds and enjoy some of the most secluded beaches in Miami. There's also a historic lighthouse that was built in 1825, which is the oldest lighthouse in South Florida. The lighthouse was damaged during the Second Seminole War (1836) and again in 1861 during the Civil War. Out of commission for a while, in 1978 the U.S. Coast Guard restored it to working lighthouse condition. A rental shack leases bikes, hydrobikes, kayaks, and many more water toys. It's a great place to picnic, and a newly constructed restaurant serves homemade Latin food, including great fish soups and sandwiches. Just be careful that the raccoons don't get your lunch—the furry black-eyed beasts are everywhere. Wildlife aside, however, Bill Baggs has been consistently rated as one of the top 10 beaches in the U.S. for its 1¼ miles of wide, sandy beaches and its secluded, serene atmosphere. Admission is $5 per car with up to eight people (or $3 for a car with only one person; $1 to enter by foot or bicycle). Open daily from 8am to sunset. Tours of the lighthouse are available every Thursday through Monday at 10am and 1pm. Arrive at least half an hour early to sign up—there is room for only 10 people on each. Take I-95 to the Rickenbacker Causeway and take that all the way to the end.

Fairchild Tropical Garden ☆☆☆, at 10901 Old Cutler Rd. in Coral Gables (© 305/667-1651; www.ftg.org), is the largest of its kind in the continental United States. A veritable rainforest of both rare and exotic plants, as well as 11 lakes and countless meadows, are spread across 83 acres. Palmettos, vine pergola, palm glades, and other unique species create a scenic, lush environment. More than 100 species of birds have been spotted at the garden (ask for a checklist at the front gate), and it's home to a variety of animals. You should not miss the 30-minute narrated tram tour (tours leave on the hour 10am–3pm weekdays and 10am–4pm on weekends) to learn about the various flowers and trees on the grounds. There is also a museum, a cafe, a picnic area, and a gift shop with edible gifts and fantastic books on gardening and cooking. The 2-acre rainforest exhibit, *Windows to the Tropics,* will save you a trip to the Amazon. Expect to spend a minimum of 2 hours here.

Admission is $20 for adults, $15 for seniors, $10 for children 3 to 12, and free for children under 3. Open daily, except Christmas, from 9:30am to 4:30pm. Take I-95 south to U.S. 1, turn left onto Le Jeune Road, and follow it straight to the traffic circle; from there, take Old Cutler Road 2 miles to the park.

Located on Biscayne Bay in Coconut Grove (4013 Douglas Rd.; www.ntbg.org/kampong.html), the **Kampong** ☆☆ is a 7-acre botanical garden featuring a stunning array of flowering trees and tropical fruit trees, including mango, avocado, and pomelos. In the early 1900s, noted plant explorer David Fairchild traveled the world seeking rare plants of economic and aesthetic value that might be cultivated in the United States. In 1928, Fairchild and his wife, Marian—the daughter of Alexander Graham Bell—decided to build a residence here (now listed on the National Register of Historic Places) surrounded by some of his findings, and named it after the Malaysian word *kampong,* meaning "home in a garden." In the 1960s, the Fairchilds sold the Kampong to Catherine Hauberg Sweeney, who donated it to the National Tropical Botanical Garden to promote and preserve this South Florida treasure. It's a must-see for those interested in horticulture. Admission and tours are by appointment only, from Monday to Friday. For tour and price information, call © 305/442-7169 from 9am to 5pm Monday through Friday. Take U.S. 1 to Douglas Road (SW 37th Ave.). Go east on Douglas Road for about a mile. The Kampong will be on your left.

Named after the late champion of the Everglades, the **Marjory Stoneman Douglas Biscayne Nature Center** ☆, 6767 Crandon Blvd., Key Biscayne (© 305/361-6767; www.biscaynenaturecenter.org), is housed in a brand-new $4 million facility and offers hands-on marine exploration, hikes through coastal hammocks, bike trips, and beach walks. Local environmentalists and historians lead intriguing trips through the local habitat. Call to reserve a spot on a regularly scheduled weekend tour or program. Be sure to wear comfortable closed-toe shoes for hikes through wet or rocky terrain. Open daily 10am to 4pm. Admission to the park is $4 per person; admission to the nature center is free. Special programs and tours cost $10 per person. Call for weekend programs. To get there, take I-95 to the Rickenbacker Causeway Exit (#1) and take the causeway all the way until it becomes Crandon Boulevard. The center is on the east side of the street (the Atlantic Ocean side) and about 25 minutes from downtown Miami.

Because so many people are focused on the beach itself, the **Miami Beach Botanical Garden,** 2000 Convention Center Dr., Miami Beach (© 305/673-7256), remains a secret garden. The lush, tropical 4½-acre garden is a fabulous natural retreat from the hustle and bustle of the silicone-enhanced city. Open Tuesday through Sunday from 9am to 5pm; admission is free.

The **Oleta River State Recreation Area** 🐾🐾, 3400 NE 163rd St., North Miami (© **305/919-1846**), consists of 993 acres—the largest urban park in the state—on Biscayne Bay. The beauty of the Oleta River, combined with the fact that you're essentially in the middle of a city, makes this park especially worth visiting. With miles of bicycle and canoe trails, a sandy swimming beach, shaded picnic pavilions, and a fishing pier, Oleta River State Recreation Area offers an outstanding outdoor recreational experience cloistered from the confines of the big city. There are 14 air-conditioned cabins on the premises, sleeping four people. The cost is $51 per night, and guests are required to bring their own linens. Bathrooms and showers are outside, as is a fire circle with grill for cooking. For reservations, call © **800/326-3521.** Open daily from 8am to sunset. Admission for pedestrians and cyclists is $1 per person. By car: Driver plus car costs $3; driver plus one to seven passengers and car costs $5. Take 1-95 to exit 17 (S.R. 826 E.) and go all the way east until just before the causeway. The park entrance is on your right. Driving time from downtown Miami is about a half-hour.

A testament to Miami's unusual climate, the **Preston B. Bird and Mary Heinlein Fruit and Spice Park** 🐾, 24801 SW 187th Ave., Homestead (© **305/247-5727;** www.fruitandspicepark.org), harbors rare fruit trees that cannot survive elsewhere in the country. If a volunteer is available, you'll learn some fascinating things about this 30-acre living plant museum, where the most exotic varieties of fruits and spices— ackee, mango, Ugli fruits, carambola, and breadfruit—grow on strange-looking trees with unpronounceable names. There are also original coral rock buildings dating back to 1912. The Strawberry Folk Festival in February and an art festival here in January are among the park's most popular—and populated—events. The best part? You're free to take anything that has *naturally* fallen to the ground (no picking here). You'll also find samples of interesting fruits and jellies made from the park's bounty, as well as exotic ingredients and cookbooks in the gift store.

Admission to the spice park is $5 for adults and $1.50 for children under 12. It's open daily from 10am to 5pm; closed on Christmas. Tours are included in the price of admission and are offered at 11am, 1:30pm, and 3pm. Take U.S. 1 south, turn right on SW 248th Street, and go straight for 5 miles to SW 187th Avenue. The drive from Miami should take 45 minutes to an hour.

Tropical Park, 7900 SW 40th St. in West Miami (© **305/226-8315**), has it all. Enjoy a game of tennis or racquetball for a minimal fee, swim and sun yourself on the secluded little lake, rent bikes, or try horseback riding. You can use the fishing pond for free, and they'll even supply you with the rods and bait. If you catch anything, however, you're on your own. Open daily from 7am to 10pm; admission is free. To get there, go west on Bird Road until you reach the overpass for the Palmetto Expressway (826). The park is on the left side immediately after the overpass.

6 Sightseeing Cruises & Organized Tours
BOAT & CRUISE-SHIP TOURS
You don't need a boating license or a zillion-dollar yacht to explore Miami by boat. Thanks to several enterprising companies, boat tours are easy to find, affordable, and an excellent way to see the city from a more liquid perspective.

Bay Escape ⚘   This 1-hour air-conditioned cruise will take you past Millionaires' Row and the Venetian Islands (see the "Venice in Miami" box, above) for just $15. There's also a food stand and cash bar. Tours are bilingual.

Bayside Marketplace Marina, 401 Biscayne Blvd., Downtown. ℂ 305/373-7001. All tickets $15, free for children 12 and under. Millionaires' Row tour daily 1, 3, 5, and 7pm. Evening party cruise (music and cash bar) Fri–Sat 9–11pm.

Heritage Miami II **Topsail Schooner**   This relaxing ride aboard Miami's only tall ship is a fun way to see the city, since it's on a schooner (as opposed to the other tour company's cruising boats), which gives you more of a feel of the water. The 2-hour cruise passes by Villa Vizcaya, Coconut Grove, and Key Biscayne, and puts you in sight of Miami's spectacular skyline and island homes. Call ahead to confirm the ship's schedule. On Friday, Saturday, and Sunday evenings, there are 1-hour tours to see the lights of the city, for $15 per person.

Bayside Marketplace Marina, 401 Biscayne Blvd., Downtown. ℂ 305/442-9697. Fax 305/442-0119. Tickets for day tours $20 adults, $15 children 12 and under. Sept–May only. Tours leave daily at 1:30, 4, and 6:30pm, and Fri–Sun also at 9, 10, and 11pm.

Miami Duck Tours   Hands down, this is the corniest, kookiest tour in the entire city. In fact, the company prefers to call these tours the "Quackiest" way to visit Miami and the Beaches. Whatever you call it, it's weird. The *Watson Willy* is the first of several Miami Duck Tours "vesicles," not a body part, but a hybrid name that means part vessel, part vehicle (technical name: Hydra Terra Amphibious Vehicle). Each "vesicle" seats 49 guests, plus a captain and tour guide, and leaves from Watson Island behind Parrot Jungle Island, traveling through downtown Miami and South Beach. If you're image conscious, you may want to reconsider traveling down Ocean Drive in a duck. That's right, a duck, which is what the "vesicle" looks like. After driving the streets in the duck, you'll end up cruising Biscayne Bay, past all the swanky houses. Embarrassing or downright hilarious, Miami Duck Tours is definitely something unique.

1665 Washington Ave. South Beach. ℂ 877/DUCK-TIX. www.ducktoursmiami.com. Tickets $26 adults, $22 seniors and military, $18 children 12 and under.

Tropical Boat Tours   Private boat trips on 22-foot power boats are a fantastic way to explore the bay-ways and waterways of Miami, if you can afford it. There are also

---

Moments Venice in Miami

You don't have to endure jet lag and time-zone differences to enjoy the beauty of Italy. Located just off Miami Beach, Florida's own Venetian Islands (NE 15th St. and Dade Blvd.) were joined together in 1926 by a bascule bridge known as the **Venetian Causeway.** A series of 12 bridges connecting the Venetian Islands and stretching between Miami and Miami Beach features octagonal concrete entrance towers, which give you a great view of the water. The oldest causeway in metropolitan Miami, the Venetian is rickety in a charming way, with fantastic views of the city and the mammoth cruise ships docked at the port, not to mention glimpses of some of Miami's most beautiful waterfront homes. Bikers and joggers especially love the Venetian Causeway, thanks to its limited traffic and beautiful scenery.

beautiful yachts and catamarans for rent. Tour Biscayne Bay or even go as far as Bimini in the Bahamas. Among the best tours: "Islands of the Rich and Famous," in which you cruise past Star Island, Hibiscus Island, Fisher Island, and Palm Island. Keep your eyes open—Star Island resident Rosie O'Donnell always goes jet-skiing out by these boats. A sunset cruise of Miami is also highly recommended. We hear that Tropical Boat Tours are a popular activity among visiting celebrities who relish their privacy—even on the high seas.

© **786/218-3030.** www.tropicalboat.com. Trips $145–$1400.

SIGHTSEEING TOURS

Miami Nice Excursion Travel and Service *©*   Pick your destination and the Miami Nice tours will take you by bus to the Everglades, Fort Lauderdale, South Beach, the Seaquarium, Key West, Cape Canaveral, or wherever else you desire. The best trip for first-timers is the City Tour, a comprehensive tour of the entire city and its various neighborhoods. If you've got the time, you will definitely want to add on a side trip to the Everglades and/or Key West (though I suggest exploring the Everglades on your own). Included in most Miami trips is a fairly comprehensive city tour narrated by a knowledgeable guide. The company is one of the oldest in town.

18801 Collins Ave., Miami Beach. *©* **305/949-9180.** www.miaminicetours.com. Tours $32–$115 adults, $29–$100 children 3–9. Mon–Sat 7am–10pm. Closed Sun. Call ahead for directions to various pickup areas.

SPECIALIZED TOURS

In addition to those listed below, a great option for seeing the city is to take a tour led by **Dr. Paul George.** Dr. George is a history teacher at Miami–Dade Community College and a historian at the Historical Museum of Southern Florida. He also happens to be "Mr. Miami." There's a variety of tours (including the "Murder, Mystery, and Mayhem Bus Tour," detailed below), all fascinating to South Florida buffs. Tours focus on neighborhoods such as Little Havana, Brickell Avenue, or Key Biscayne, and on themes such as Miami cemeteries and the Miami River. The often-long-winded discussions can be a bit much for those who just want a quick look around, but Dr. George certainly knows his stuff. The cost is $15 to $39, and reservations are required (*©* **305/375-1621;** www.historical-museum.org/educate/tours/tours.htm). Tours leave from the Historical Museum at 101 W. Flagler St., Downtown. Call for a schedule.

Biltmore Hotel Tour *©©© Value*   Take advantage of these free Sunday walking tours to enjoy the hotel's beautiful grounds. The Biltmore is full of history and mystery, including a few ghosts. In addition, there are free weekly fireside sessions that are open to the public and presented by Miami Storytellers. Learn about the hotel's early days and rich stories of the city's past. These wonderful sessions are held in the main lobby by the fireplace and are accompanied by a glass of champagne. Call ahead to confirm.

1200 Anastasia Ave., Coral Gables. *©* **305/445-1926.** www.biltmorehotel.com. Free admission. Tours depart Sun at 1:30, 2:30, and 3:30pm. Storytelling sessions are held every Thurs at 7:30pm.

Eco-Adventure Tours *©©©*   For the ecoconscious traveler, the Miami–Dade Parks and Recreation Department offers guided nature, adventure, and historic tours involving biking, canoeing, snorkeling, hiking, and bird-watching all over the city. Contact them for more information.

© **305/365-3018.** www.miamidade.gov/parks.

Herencia Hispana Tour For those looking to immerse themselves in Miami's rich Latin-American culture, the Herencia Hispana Tour is the ideal way to explore it all. Hop on a bus and zoom past such hotbeds of Latin activity as downtown's Flagler Street, the unavoidable Elián González house, the Latin American Art Museum, and Little Havana's Domino Park and Tower Theater, among others. Not just a sightseeing tour, this one includes two very knowledgeable, albeit corny, guides who know just when to infuse a necessary dose of humor into the Elián saga, a segment of history that some people may not consider so amusing.

Tours depart at 9, 9:30, and 10am every Sat in Oct from the Steven P. Clark Government Center, 111 NW 1st St. ℭ 305/884-7567. Tours (which are in Spanish or English, but you must specify which one you require) are free, but advanced reservations are required.

Miami Design Preservation League ℛℛ On Thursday evenings and Saturday mornings, the Design Preservation League sponsors walking tours that offer a fascinating inside look at the city's historic Art Deco District. Tour-goers meet for a 1½-hour walk through some of America's most exuberantly "architectured" buildings. The league led the fight to designate this area a National Historic District and is proud to share the splendid locale with visitors. Also see p. 140 for more information.

Art Deco Welcome Center, 1001 Ocean Dr., South Beach. ℭ 305/672-2014. www.mdpl.org. Walking tours $15 per person. Tours leave Wed and Sat at 10:30am and Thurs at 6:30pm. Self-guided audio tours also available daily for $10. No reservations necessary, but arrive 15 minutes early. Call ahead for updated schedules.

Murder, Mystery, and Mayhem Bus Tour ℛℛℛ Visit the past by video and bus to Miami–Dade's most celebrated crimes and criminals from the 1800s to the present. From the murder spree of the Ashley Gang to the most notorious murders and crimes of our century, including the murder of designer Gianni Versace, historian Paul George conducts a most fascinating 3-hour tour of scandalous proportions.

Held twice a year, usually in April and Oct; leaves from the Dade Cultural Center, 101 W. Flagler St., Miami. Tickets $39. Advance reservations required; call ℭ 305/375-1621.

7 Watersports

There are many ways to get well acquainted with Miami's wet look. Choose your own adventure from the suggestions listed below.

BOATING Private rental outfits include **Boat Rental Plus,** 2400 Collins Ave., Miami Beach (ℭ **305/534-4307**), where 50-horsepower, 18-foot powerboats rent for some of the best prices on the beach. There's a 2-hour minimum, and rates go from $100 to $500, including taxes and gas. They also have great specials on Sunday. Cruising is permitted only in and around Biscayne Bay (ocean access is prohibited), and renters must be 21 to rent a boat. The rental office is at 23rd Street, on the inland waterway in Miami Beach. It's open daily from 10am to sunset. If you want a specific type of boat, call ahead to reserve. Otherwise, show up and take what's available.

Club Nautico of Coconut Grove, 2560 S. Bayshore Dr. (ℭ **305/858-6258;** www. clubnauticomiami.com), rents high-quality powerboats for fishing, water-skiing, diving, and cruising in the bay or ocean. All boats are Coast Guard–equipped, with VHF radios and safety gear. Rates start at $299 for 4 hours and $499 for 8 hours. Club Nautico is open daily from 8am to 6pm (weather permitting). Other locations include the Crandon Park Marina, 4000 Crandon Blvd., Key Biscayne (ℭ **305/361-9217**), with the same rates and hours as the Coconut Grove location; and the Miami Beach Marina, Pier E, 300 Alton Rd., South Beach (ℭ **305/673-2502**), where rates start at

$299 for 4 hours and $499 for 8 hours. Nautico on Miami Beach is open daily from 9am to 5pm. For money-saving coupons, log on to www.boatrent.com.

JET SKIS/WAVERUNNERS

Don't miss a chance to tour the islands on the back of your own powerful watercraft. Bravery is, however, a prerequisite, as Miami's waterways are full of speeding jet skiers and boaters who think they're in the Indy 500. Many beachfront concessionaires rent a variety of these popular (and loud) water scooters. The latest models are fast and smooth. **American Watersports**, at the Miami Beach Marina, 300 Alton Road (© **305/538-7549;** www.jetskiz.com), is the area's most popular spot for jet ski rental. Rates begin at $65 for a half-hour and $120 for an hour. They also offer fun jet-ski tours past celebrity homes for $140 for the first hour and $70 for the second, with a 2-hour minimum.

KAYAKING

The laid-back **Urban Trails Kayak Company** rents boats at 3400 NE 163rd St. in Oleta River Park (© **305/947-1302;** www.urbantrails.com). The outfitters here give explorers a map to take with them and quick instructions on how to work the paddles and boats. They also operate very scenic 4-hour guided tours through rivers with mangroves and islands—fewer than 10 people on the tour costs $45 per person; more than 10 people costs $35 per person. These must be booked in advance. Rates are $12 an hour, $20 for up to 4 hours, and $25 for the half-day. Tandems (for two people) are $17 an hour, $45 for the half-day. Canoes cost $20 per hour or $45 for the half-day. Guided ecotours are also available with advance reservation at $65 per person. While you are on the paddling route, make sure to stop at the Blue Marlin Fish House for some smoked fish. To keep the kayaks overnight is an extra $10. They also rent mountain bikes. Open daily from 9am to 5pm in the winter, and 9am to 6pm in the summer.

SAILING

You can rent sailboats and catamarans through the beachfront concessions desk of several top resorts, such as the Doral Golf Resort and Spa (p. 100).

Sailboats of Key Biscayne Rentals and Sailing School, in the Crandon Marina (next to Sundays on the Bay), 4000 Crandon Blvd., Key Biscayne (© **305/361-0328** days, 305/279-7424 evenings), can also get you out on the water. A 22-foot sailboat rents for $35 an hour, $110 for a half-day, and $175 for a full day. A Cat-25 or J24 is available for $35 an hour, $110 for a half-day, and $175 for a full day. If you've always had a dream to win the America's Cup but can't sail, the able teachers at Sailboats will get you started. They offer a 10-hour course over 5 days for $300 for one person, or $400 for you and a buddy.

SCUBA DIVING & SNORKELING

In 1981, the U.S. government began a wide-scale project designed to increase the number of habitats available to marine organisms. One of the program's major accomplishments has been the creation of nearby artificial reefs, which have attracted all kinds of tropical plants, fish, and animals. In addition, Biscayne National Park (see the park's section in chapter 7, beginning on p. 251) offers a protected marine environment just south of downtown.

Several dive shops around the city offer organized weekend outings, either to the reefs or to one of over a dozen old shipwrecks around Miami's shores. Check "Divers" in the Yellow Pages for rental equipment and for a full list of undersea tour operators.

Diver's Paradise of Key Biscayne, 4000 Crandon Blvd. (© **305/361-3483**), offers one dive expedition per day during the week and two per day on the weekends to the more than 30 wrecks and artificial reefs off the coast of Miami Beach and Key Biscayne. You can take a 3-day certification course for $450, which includes all the dives and gear. If you already have your C-card, a dive trip costs about $100 if you need equipment and $50 if you bring your own gear. It's open Tuesday through Friday from 10am to 6pm, and Saturday and Sunday from 8am to 6pm. Call ahead for times and locations of dives. For snorkeling, they will set you up with equipment and maps on where to see the best underwater sights. Rental for mask, fins, and snorkel is $50.

South Beach Divers, 850 Washington Ave., Miami Beach (© **305/531-6110;** www.southbeachdivers.com), will also be happy to tell you where to go under the sea and will provide you with scuba rental equipment as well for $40. You can rent snorkel gear for $15. They also do dive trips to Key Largo three times a week and do dives off Miami on Sunday at $100 for a two-tank dive.

WINDSURFING   Many hotels rent windsurfers to their guests, but if yours doesn't have a watersports concession stand, head for Key Biscayne. **Sailboards Miami,** Rickenbacker Causeway, Key Biscayne (© **305/361-SAIL;** www.sailboards miami.com), operates out of two big yellow trucks on Windsurfer Beach, the most popular (though our pick for best is Hobie Beach) windsurfing spot in the city. For those who've never ridden a board but want to try it, they offer a 2-hour lesson for $69 that's guaranteed to turn you into a wave warrior, or you get your money back. After that, you can rent a board for $25 to $30 an hour. If you want to make a day of it, a 10-hour prepaid card costs $180. These cards reduce the price by about $70 for the day. You can use the card year-round, until the time on it runs out. Open Tuesday through Sunday from 10am to 5:30pm. Make your first right after the tollbooth (at the beginning of the causeway—you can't miss it) to find the outfitters. They also rent kayaks.

8 More Ways to Play, Indoors & Out

The cement promenade on the southern tip of South Beach is a great place to ride. Biking up the beach (either on the beach or along the beach on a cement pathway—which is a lot easier!) is great for surf, sun, sand, exercise, and people-watching—just be sure to keep your eyes on the road, as the scenery can be most distracting. Most of the big beach hotels rent bicycles, as does the **Miami Beach Bicycle Center,** 601 5th St., South Beach (© **305/674-0150**), which charges $8 per hour or $20 for up to 24 hours. It's open Monday through Saturday from 10am to 7pm, Sunday from 10am to 5pm.

Bikers can also enjoy more than 130 miles of paved paths throughout Miami. The beautiful and quiet streets of Coral Gables and Coconut Grove (several bike trails are spread throughout these neighborhoods) are great for bicyclists, where old trees form canopies over wide, flat roads lined with grand homes and quaint street markers.

The terrain in Key Biscayne is perfect for biking, especially along the park and beach roads. If you don't mind the sound of cars whooshing by your bike lane, **Rickenbacker Causeway** is also fantastic, since it is one of the only bikeable inclines in Miami from which you get fantastic elevated views of the city and waterways. However, be warned that this is a grueling ride, especially going up the causeway. **Key Cycling,** 61 Harbor Dr., Key Biscayne (© **305/361-0061**), rents mountain bikes for $5 an hour or $20 a day, with a 2-hour minimum. It's open Tuesday through Friday

> **Tips** **A Fisherman's Friend**
>
> The Biscayne Bay area is prime tarpon-fishing country and a pretty good spot for a lot of other trophy sportfish: snook, bonefish, dolphin fish, swordfish, and sailfish. For a fee, local guides are happy to show you the hot spots and make sure you reel one in. One such guide is **Capt. David Parsons** (*C* **305/968-9603**), who owns a great 36-foot boat, *Hakuna Matada*. He knows where the fish are biting and will take you from Biscayne Bay to the Atlantic Ocean in search of the best catch of the day for $700 for four people (swordfish can be caught at nighttime only; those trips are also $700), including rods, gear, and bait. All you bring is food and drink. Capt. Parsons also leads trips to Bimini for those who want to explore the fishing in the Bahamas.

from 10am to 7pm, Monday and Saturday from 10am to 6pm, and Sunday from 10am to 3pm.

If you want to avoid the traffic altogether, head out to **Shark Valley** in the Everglades National Park—one of South Florida's most scenic bicycle trails and a favorite haunt of city-weary locals. For more information on Shark Valley and the Everglades, see chapter 7.

For a decent list of trail suggestions throughout South Florida, visit www.geocities.com/floutdoorzone/bike.html. *Biking note:* Children under the age of 16 are required by Florida law to wear a helmet, which can be purchased at any bike store or retail outlet selling biking supplies.

FISHING Fishing licenses are required in Florida. If you go out with one of the fishing charter boats listed below, you are automatically accredited because the companies are. If you go out on your own, however, you must have a Florida fishing license, which costs $17 for Florida residents and $32 for nonresidents. Call *C* **888/FISH-FLO** or visit www.wildlifelicense.com for more information.

Some of the best surf casting in the city can be had at **Haulover Beach Park** at Collins Avenue and 105th Street, where there's a bait-and-tackle shop right on the pier. **South Pointe Park,** at the southern tip of Miami Beach, is another popular fishing spot and features a long pier, comfortable benches, and a great view of the ships passing through Government Cut, the deep channel made when the port of Miami was dug.

You can also do some deep-sea fishing in the Miami area. One bargain outfitter, the **Kelley Fishing Fleet,** at the Haulover Marina, 10800 Collins Ave. (at 108th St.), Miami Beach (*C* **305/945-3801;** www.miamibeachfishing.com), has half-day, full-day, and night fishing aboard diesel-powered "party boats." The fleet's emphasis on drifting is geared toward trolling and bottom fishing for snapper, sailfish, and mackerel. Half-day and night-fishing trips are $31 for adults and $22 for children up to 10 years old, and full-day trips are $49 for adults and $39 for children; prices are $5 cheaper if you have your own rod. Daily departures are scheduled at 9am and 1:45 and 8pm; reservations are recommended.

Also at the Haulover Marina is the charter boat *Helen C* (10800 Collins Ave.; *C* **305/947-4081;** www.fishmiamibeach.com). Although there's no shortage of private charter boats here, Capt. Dawn Mergelsberg is a good pick, since she puts individuals together to get a full boat. Her *Helen* is a twin-engine 55-footer, equipped for big-game "monster" fish like marlin, tuna, dolphin fish, shark, and sailfish. The cost is $100 per person. Private, full-day trips are available for groups of six people per vessel and cost $900; half-days are $500. Group rates and specials are also available. Sailings are scheduled for 8am to noon and 1 to 5pm daily; call for reservations. Children are welcome.

Key Biscayne offers deep-sea fishing to those willing to get their hands dirty and pay a bundle. The competition among the boats is fierce, but the prices are basically the same, no matter which you choose. The going rate is about $400 to $450 for a half-day and $600 to $700 for a full day of fishing. These rates are usually for a party of up to six, and the boats supply you with rods and bait as well as instruction for first-timers. Some will also take you out to the Upper Keys if the fish aren't biting in Miami.

You might also consider the following boats, all of which sail out of the Key Biscayne marina and are in relatively good shape and nicer than most out there: **Sunny Boy** (© **305/361-2217**), **Top Hatt** (© **305/361-2528**), and **L & H** (© **305/361-9318**). Call for reservations.

Bridge fishing in Biscayne Bay is also popular in Miami; you'll see people with poles over almost every waterway. But look carefully for signs telling you whether it's legal to do so wherever you are: Some bridges forbid fishing.

GAMBLING   Although gambling is technically illegal in Miami, there are plenty of loopholes that allow all kinds of wagering. Gamblers can try their luck at offshore casinos or on shore at bingo, jai alai, card rooms, horse tracks, dog races, and Native-American reservations.

Especially popular is **Miccosukee Indian Gaming,** 500 SW 177th Ave. (off S.R. 41, in West Miami on the outskirts of the Everglades; © **800/741-4600** or 305/222-4600), where a touch of Vegas meets west Miami. This tacky casino isn't Caesar's Palace, but you can play tab slots, high-speed bingo (watch out for the serious blue-haired players who will scoff if you make too much noise or if you win before they do), and even poker (with a $10 maximum pot). With more than 85,000 square feet of playing space, the complex even offers overnight accommodations for those who can't get enough of the thrill and don't want to make the approximately 1-hour trip back to downtown Miami. Take the Florida Turnpike south toward Florida City/Key West. Take the SW 8th Street exit (#25) and turn left onto SW 8th Street. Drive for about 3½ miles and then turn left onto Krome Avenue, and left again at 177th Street; you can't miss it.

Recently, many of Miami's sketchier gambling-cruise operators have been shut down. The classiest and most legit gambling cruise still in business is the **Casino Princesa,** which docks behind the Hard Rock Cafe in Bayside Marketplace. This 200-foot $15-million yacht has more than 200 slot machines, 32 tables, a restaurant, and four lounges in 10,000 square feet of gaming space on two decks. It's also a major bargain (unless, of course, you lose), at $10 per person. Ships sail for 5 hours from 12:30 to 5:30pm and 7:30pm to 12:30am daily. They will also pick you up at your hotel. Call © **305/379-5825** or visit www.casinoprincesa.com for updated schedules. You must be 21 or older to sail.

GOLF   There are more than 50 private and public golf courses in the Miami area. Contact the **Greater Miami Convention and Visitor's Bureau** (© **800/933-8448;** www.miamiandbeaches.com) for a list of courses and costs.

The best hotel courses in Miami are found at the **Doral Golf Resort and Spa** (p. 100), home of the legendary Blue Monster course, as well as the Gold Course, designed by Raymond Floyd; the Great White Shark Course; and the Silver Course, refinished by Jerry Pate.

Other hotels with excellent golf courses include the **Fairmont Turnberry Isle Resort & Club** (p. 102), with two Robert Trent Jones, Sr.–designed courses for guests and members, and the **Biltmore Hotel** ☞☞ (p. 104), which is my pick for best public golf course because of its modest greens fees and an 18-hole par-71 course located on the hotel's spectacular grounds. It must be good: Despite his penchant for privacy, former President Bill Clinton prefers teeing off at this course over any other in Miami!

Otherwise, the following represent some of the area's best public courses. **Crandon Park Golf Course,** formerly known as the Links, 6700 Crandon Blvd., Key Biscayne (📞 **305/361-9129**), is the number-one-ranked municipal course in the state and one of the top five in the country. The park is situated on 200 bayfront acres and offers a pro shop, rentals, lessons, carts, and a lighted driving range. The course is open daily from dawn to dusk; greens fees (including cart) are $148 per person during the winter and $65 per person during the summer. Special twilight rates are also available.

One of the most popular courses among real enthusiasts is the **Doral Park Golf and Country Club,** 5001 NW 104th Ave., West Miami (📞 **305/591-8800**); it's not related to the Doral Hotel or spa. Call to book in advance, since this challenging, semiprivate 18-holer is extremely popular with locals. The course is open from 6:30am to 6pm during the winter and until 7pm during the summer. Cart and greens fees vary, so call 📞 **305/592-2000,** ext. 2104, for information.

Known as one of the best in the city, the **Country Club of Miami,** 6801 Miami Gardens Dr., at NW 68th Avenue, North Miami (📞 **305/829-8456**), has three 18-hole courses of varying degrees of difficulty. You'll encounter lush fairways, rolling greens, and some history, to boot. The west course, designed in 1961 by Robert Trent Jones, Sr., and updated in the 1990s by the PGA, was where Jack Nicklaus played his first professional tournament and Lee Trevino won his first professional championship. The course is open daily from 7am to sunset. Cart and greens fees are $40 to $75 per person during the winter, and $20 to $34 per person during the summer. Special twilight rates are available.

Golfers looking for some cheap practice time will appreciate **Haulover Beach Park,** 10800 Collins Ave., Miami Beach (📞 **305/940-6719**), in a pretty bayside location. The longest hole on this par-27 course is 125 yards. It's open daily from 7:30am to 6pm during the winter, and until 7:30pm during the summer. Greens fees are $7 per person during the winter and summer. Handcarts cost $2.

IN-LINE SKATING   Miami's consistently flat terrain makes in-line skating a breeze. Lincoln Road, for example, is a virtual skating rink as bladers compete with bikers and walkers for a slab of slate. But the city's heavy traffic and construction do make it tough to find long routes suitable for blading.

Because of the popularity of blading and skateboarding, the city has passed a law prohibiting skating on the west side (the cafe-lined strip) of Ocean Drive in the evenings, as well as a law that all bladers must skate slowly and safely. Also, if you're going to partake in the sport, remember to keep a pair of sandals or sneakers with you, since many area shops won't allow you inside with skates on.

Despite all the rules, you can still have fun, and the following rental outfit can help chart an interesting course for you and supply you with all the necessary gear. In South Beach, **Fritz's Skate Shop,** 730 Lincoln Rd. Mall (📞 **305/532-1954**), rents top-quality skates, including safety pads, for $8 per hour, $22 per day, and $34 overnight.

They provide free lessons at 10:30am on Sunday when you rent equipment, or they can hook you up with an instructor for private lessons. The shop also stocks lots of gear and clothing.

SWIMMING There is no shortage of water in the Miami area. See the Venetian Pool listing (p. 146) and the "Miami's Beaches" section on p. 137 for descriptions of good swimming options.

TENNIS Hundreds of tennis courts in South Florida are open to the public for a minimal fee. Most courts operate on a first-come, first-served basis and are open from sunrise to sunset. For information and directions, call the **City of Miami Beach Recreation, Culture, and Parks Department** (✆ 305/673-7730) or the **City of Miami Parks and Recreation Department** (✆ 305/575-5256). Of the 590 public tennis courts throughout Miami, the 3 hard courts and 7 clay courts at the **Key Biscayne Tennis Association,** 6702 Crandon Blvd. (✆ 305/361-5263), are the best and most beautiful. Because of this, they often get crowded on weekends. You'll play on the same courts as Lendl, Graf, Evert, McEnroe, and other greats; this is also the venue for one of the world's biggest annual tennis events, the Nasdaq 100 Open. There's a pleasant, if limited, pro shop, plus many good pros. Only four courts are lit at night, but if you reserve at least 24 to 48 hours in advance, you can usually take your pick. They cost $6 per person per hour. The courts are open Monday through Friday from 8am to 9pm, Saturday and Sunday until 6pm.

Other courts are pretty run of the mill and can be found in most neighborhoods. I do, however, recommend the **Miami Beach public courts at Flamingo Park,** 1001 12th St. in South Beach (✆ 305/673-7761), where there are 19 clay courts that cost $4 per person an hour for Miami Beach residents and $8 per person an hour for nonresidents. It's first come, first served. Open 8am to 9pm Monday through Friday, 8am to 8pm Saturday and Sunday.

Hotels with the best tennis facilities are the Biltmore, Fairmont Turnberry Isle Resort and Spa, Doral Resort and Spa, and Inn and Spa at Fisher Island.

9 Spectator Sports

Check the *Miami Herald*'s sports section for a daily listing of local events and the paper's Friday "Weekend" section for comprehensive coverage and in-depth reports. For last-minute tickets, call the venue directly, since many season ticket holders sell singles and return unused tickets. Expensive tickets are available from brokers or individuals listed in the classified sections of the local papers. Some tickets are also available through **Ticketmaster** (✆ 305/358-5885).

BASEBALL The 2003 World Champion **Florida Marlins** shocked the sports world in 1997 when they became the youngest expansion team to win a World Series, but then floundered as their star players were sold off by former owner Wayne Huizenga. They shocked the sports world again in 2003 by winning the World Series, and turned many of Miami's apathetic sports fans into major-league ball fans. They're not that good anymore after trading their best players, and rumor has it that the Marlins are looking to move to another state. The Maine Marlins? Sounds fishy. Anyway, if you're interested in catching a game, be warned: The summer heat in Miami can be unbearable, even in the evenings.

Home games are held at the **Dolphin Stadium,** 2267 Dan Marino Blvd., North Miami Beach (✆ 305/623-6200). Tickets cost from $4 to $50. Box office hours are

Monday to Friday from 8:30am to 5:30pm and before games; tickets are also available through Ticketmaster. The team currently holds spring training in Melbourne, Florida.

BASKETBALL The **Miami Heat** (© 786/777-1000), once again led by celebrity coach Pat Riley and featuring star player Shaquille O'Neal, is one of Miami's hottest tickets. Courtside seats are full of visiting celebrities, from P. Diddy to Madonna. The season lasts from October to April, with most games beginning at 7:30pm. They play in the brand-new waterfront **American Airlines Arena,** located downtown on Biscayne Boulevard. Tickets are $14 to $100 or much more. Box office hours are Monday through Friday from 10am to 5pm (until 8pm on game nights); tickets are also available through Ticketmaster (© **305/358-5885**).

FOOTBALL Miami's golden boys are the **Miami Dolphins,** the city's most recognizable team, followed by thousands of "dolfans." The team plays at least eight home games during the season, between September and December, at **Dolphin Stadium,** 2269 Dan Marino Blvd., North Miami Beach (© **305/620-2578**). Tickets cost between $20 and much, much more. The box office is open Monday through Friday from 8:30am to 5:30pm; tickets are also available through Ticketmaster (© **305/358-5885**).

HORSE RACING Located on the Dade–Broward County border in Hallandale (just north of North Miami Beach/Aventura) is **Gulfstream Park,** at U.S. 1 and Hallandale Beach Boulevard (© **305/931-7223;** www.gulfstreampark.com), South Florida's very own version of the Kentucky Derby, albeit not nearly as sceney. This horse track is a haven for serious gamblers and voyeurs alike. Large purses and important races are commonplace at this sprawling suburban course, and the track is typically crowded, especially during its amusing and entertaining concert series from January to April, which features has-beens and one-hit wonders such as Cindy Lauper, REO Speedwagon, and Bryan Adams on the front lawn for just $5. Call for schedules. Admission is $3 to the grandstand weekdays and $5 weekends, and $5 to the clubhouse; parking is free. Children under 17 are free. January through March, post times are 1:30pm on weekdays and 1pm on weekends. Closed Tuesday. At press time Gulfstream was closed for a massive-dollar renovation but should reopen in 2007.

ICE HOCKEY The young **Florida Panthers** (© 954/835-7000) have already made history. In the 1994–95 season, they played in the Stanley Cup finals, and they have amassed a legion of fans who love them. Much to the disappointment of Miamians, they moved to a new venue in Sunrise, the next county north of Miami–Dade, more than an hour from downtown Miami. Call for directions and ticket information.

JAI ALAI Jai alai, sort of a Spanish-style indoor lacrosse, was introduced to Miami in 1924 and is regularly played in two Miami-area frontons (the buildings in which jai alai is played). Although the sport has roots stemming from ancient Egypt, the game, as it's now played, was invented by Basque peasants in the Pyrenees Mountains during the 17th century. Players use woven baskets, called *cestas,* to hurl balls, called *pelotas,* at speeds that sometimes exceed 170 mph. Spectators, who are protected behind a wall of glass, place bets on the evening's players. The Florida Gaming Corporation owns the jai alai operations throughout the state, making betting on this sport as legal as buying a lottery ticket.

The **Miami Jai Alai Fronton,** 3500 NW 37th Ave., at NW 35th Street (© **305/ 633-6400**), is America's oldest fronton, dating from 1926. It schedules 13 games per

Jai Alai Explained

Jai alai originated in the Basque country of northern Spain, where players used church walls as their courts. The game looks very much like lacrosse, actually, with rules similar to handball or tennis. The game is played on a court with numbered lines. What makes the game totally unique, however, is the requirement that the ball must be returned in one continuous motion. The server must bounce the ball behind the serving line and, with the basket, must hurl the ball to the front wall, with the aim being that, upon rebound, the ball will bounce between lines four and seven. If it doesn't, it is an under- or overserve and the other team receives a point.

night, which typically last 10 to 20 minutes but can occasionally go much longer. Admission is $1 to the grandstand, $5 to the clubhouse. There are year-round games. On Wednesday, Thursday, and Sunday, there are matinees only, which run from noon to 5:30pm. Friday, Saturday, and Monday, there are matinees in addition to evening games, from 7pm to midnight. The fronton is closed on Tuesday. This is the main location where jai alai is played in Miami. The other South Florida jai alai venue is in Dania, near the Fort Lauderdale Hollywood International Airport. See p. 263 for more information on **Dania Jai Alai.**

10 Cruises & Other Caribbean Getaways

Cruising has come a long way since the days of bingo, shuffleboard, and even the delusional *Love Boat.* Whether you prefer megaships with rock-climbing walls or a smaller, less elaborate ship that just sails you to your destination, a floating vacation can be a very enticing option for people traveling to South Florida. The proximity to the Caribbean makes 3-, 4-, 6-, 7-, or 9-day cruises an excellent diversion from the hustle and bustle of the big city.

If you want to catch a weekend in the Caribbean while you're in South Florida but aren't enthralled with the idea of boat travel, there are a number of air packages available as well. Travel to Cuba is severely restricted from Miami (or anywhere in the United States) for all but those who have obtained licenses from the U.S. State Department (see details at www.destinationcuba.com/whocanvisit.htm), although many people choose to go there from Mexico, Jamaica, or the Bahamas.

The following sections aren't intended to be detailed descriptions of the cruising and package options available out of Miami and the Keys—that would fill up an entire book on its own—but they will give you a good overview of the cruising and package picture. At press time, there were deep discounts on all cruise lines, with prices as low as, and sometimes lower than, $50 a day, so be sure to check carefully and get the best deal out there.

CRUISES   The Port of Miami is the world's busiest cruise-ship port, with a passenger load of close to three million annually. The popularity of these cruises shows no sign of tapering off, and the trend in ships is toward bigger, more luxurious liners. Usually all-inclusive, cruises offer value and simplicity compared to other vacation options. Most of the Caribbean-bound cruise ships sail weekly out of the Port of Miami. They are relatively inexpensive, can be booked without advance notice, and make for an excellent excursion.

The Port of Miami is very close to downtown Miami, but the most popular pre- and post-cruise destination in Miami is South Beach (about a 10-min. ride from the port) because of its proximity to the port and the fact that it's a relatively small (and walkable) area full of nightlife, beaches, hotels, and restaurants (see the South Beach sections of this book). If you're just looking for a quick overnight stay, your best bet may be one of the downtown-area hotels, which are closest to the port. The Biscayne Bay Marriott is a good bet and located about 5 minutes away. For restaurants in this area, check the Downtown dining section of chapter 4, beginning on p. 124. Cabs are abundant at the port. A ride to the airport should cost about $25, and a ride to South Beach should be about $10.

All the shorter cruises (3 and 4 days) are well equipped for gambling. Their casinos open as soon as the ship clears U.S. waters—typically 45 minutes after leaving port. Usually, four full-size meals are served daily, with portions so huge they're impossible to finish. Games, movies, and other onboard activities ensure you're always busy. Passengers can board up to 2 hours before departure for meals, games, and cocktails.

There are dozens of cruises from which to choose—from 1-day excursions to a trip around the world. You can get a full list of options from the **Metro-Dade Seaport Department,** 1015 N. America Way, Miami, FL 33132 (© 305/371-7678). It's open Monday through Friday from 8am to 5pm.

The cruise lines and ships listed below offer 3-, 4-, and 7-night cruises to the Caribbean, Key West, and other longer itineraries that often change. If you want more information, contact the individual line, or, for Bahamas cruises, call the **Bahamas Tourist Office,** 1200 S. Pine Island, Suite 750, Plantation, FL 33234 (© 954/236-9292;** www.bahamas.com). All passengers must travel with a passport or proof of citizenship for reentry into the United States.

For detailed information on Caribbean cruises, pick up a copy of *Frommer's Caribbean Cruises & Ports of Call.*

Carnival Cruise Lines (© 800/327-9501 or 305/599-2200; www.carnival.com) has 3-, 4-, and 6-day cruises to Key West and the Caribbean, as well as 7- and 9-day excursions that include stops in Mexico, Jamaica, and the Cayman Islands. Carnival's ships are appropriately known as Fun Ships, catering to a young, party-hearty crowd. There's also a smoke-free ship called the *Paradise.* Cruises usually depart from Miami Friday through Monday. Prices range from $400 to $3,000 (lower rates are usually available, depending on season), not including port charges, which can be as high as $200 per person.

Cunard (© 800/528-6273 or 305/463-3000; www.cunardline.com), which moved here in late 1997, is known for its old-world elegance and caters to an older, sophisticated crowd. If you're looking for Internet cafes and ice-skating rinks, Cunard isn't for you. This line's Miami ships include the legendary throwback from the halcyon days of the mighty luxe ocean liner *Queen Elizabeth II,* as well as the *Queen Mary II.* Itineraries are usually at least 10 days long, though there are some that last 6 days, such as the jazz, fine arts, and big-band cruises. Prices start at $3,300 per person.

Norwegian Cruise Line (NCL) (© 800/327-7030 or 305/436-0866; www.ncl. com) has four ships based in Miami during the winter months and usually one in the summer. NCL is known for having the most flexible dining setup at sea, with open seating and casual dress codes. A mixture of young and older crowds can be found on their ships. Ships go to Key West, the Bahamas, and the Western Caribbean. Its short-est cruises are 3 days; the longest—from Miami to France—is 15 days. Rates range from $50 per person for an inside cabin on the shortest cruises to $4,500 per person for the very best cabin on the transcontinental journey.

Royal Caribbean International (RCI; ✆ 800/327-6700 or 305/539-6000; www.royalcaribbean.com), one of the premier lines in Miami, has about half a dozen ships departing Miami at any given time. The Port of Miami actually had to renovate three cruise terminals in 1999—at a price of $60 million—to accommodate Royal Caribbean's 142,000-ton ship *Voyager of the Seas,* which boasts an ice-skating rink and a rock-climbing wall, among other theme park–like diversions. *Mariner of the Seas, Navigator of the Seas, Explorer of the Seas,* and *Adventure of the Seas* are the line's four other theme parks at sea, totaling five *Voyager*-class ships also featuring extreme sports and an assortment of high-tech activities. As a result, RCI caters to a young and old(er) active crowd, as well as families with children. The line mostly offers Caribbean cruises and some Bahamas destinations. The *Legend of the Seas* and the *Splendor of the Seas* offer 3- and 4-night Bahamas trips for as low as $100 per person, per day, to as high as $7,500 per person for an 11-night cruise through the Caribbean.

FLIGHTS & WEEKEND PACKAGES   For those who want a quick getaway to the Caribbean without the experience of cruising, many airlines and hotels team up to offer extremely affordable weekend packages.

For example, the Bahamas' most entertaining and family-friendly resort, the **Atlantis** on Paradise Island (✆ 888/528-7155; www.atlantis.com), is a tropical theme park offering extensive watersports plus an active casino. Reasonably priced 3-day packages start at about $390, depending on departure date. (It's generally cheaper to fly midweek.) Flights on **Continental Airlines** (✆ 800/786-7202) depart at least twice daily from Miami International. You can also choose to stay in the company's other luxurious resorts: the **Paradise Beach Resort** and the **Ocean Club.** Book pack-age deals through **Paradise Island Vacations** (✆ 800/722-7466).

Other groups that arrange competitively priced packages include **American Fly-away Vacations,** operated by American Airlines (✆ 800/321-2121); **Bahamas Air** (✆ 800/222-4262), and **Chalks Ocean Airways** (✆ 305/371-8628). Call for rates, since they vary dramatically throughout the year and also depend on what type of accommodations you choose. Keep your eye on the travel section of the *Miami Her-ald* as well, as special deals and packages are almost always advertised.

11 Animal Parks

For a tropical climate, Miami's got a lot of nontropical animals to see, and we're not talking about the motorists on I-95. Everything from dolphins and alligators to lions, tigers, and bears call Miami home (most in parks, some in nature). Call the parks to inquire about discount packages or coupons, which may be offered at area retail stores or in local papers.

Miami Metrozoo 🐾🐾 *Kids*   This 290-acre, sparsely landscaped complex (it was devastated by Hurricane Andrew) is quite a distance from Miami proper and the beaches—about 45 minutes—but worth the trip. Isolated and never really crowded, it's also completely cageless—animals are kept at bay by cleverly designed moats. This is a fantastic spot to take younger kids (the older ones seem bored and unstimulated here); there's a wonderful petting zoo and play area, and the zoo offers several daily programs designed to educate and entertain. Mufasa and Simba (of Disney fame) were modeled on a couple of Metrozoo's lions. Other residents include two rare white Bengal tigers, a Komodo dragon, rare koala bears, a number of kangaroos, and an African meerkat. The air-conditioned Zoofari Monorail tour offers visitors a nice overview of the park. One of the zoo's newer and more fun exhibits is the interactive Wild Earth Jeep Simulator, in which you climb aboard an actual jeep and go on a virtual, simulated safari. Rides cost $5 per person. The zoo is always upgrading its facilities, including the impressive aviary. *Note:* The distance between animal habitats can be great, so you'll do *a lot* of walking here. There are benches and shaded gazebos strategically positioned throughout the zoo so you can rest when you need to. Also, because the zoo can be miserably hot during summer months, plan these visits in the early morning or late afternoon. Expect to spend about 3 hours here.

12400 SW 152nd St., South Miami. (C) 305/251-0400. www.miamimetrozoo.com. Admission $12 adults, $7 children 3–12. Daily 9:30am–5:30pm (ticket booth closes at 4pm). Free parking. From U.S. 1 south, turn right on SW 152nd St. and follow signs about 3 miles to the entrance.

Miami Seaquarium ✲ (Kids (Overrated   If you've been to Orlando's SeaWorld, you may be disappointed with Miami's version, which is considerably smaller and not as well maintained. It's hardly a sprawling seaquarium, but you will want to arrive early to enjoy the effects of its mild splash. You'll need at least 3 hours to tour the 35-acre oceanarium and see all four daily shows, starring a number of showy ocean mammals. You can cut your visit to 2 hours if you limit your shows to the better, albeit corny, *Flipper Show* and *Killer Whale Show.* The highly regarded Water and Dolphin Exploration Program (WADE) allows visitors to touch and swim with dolphins in the Flipper Lagoon. The program costs $140 per person participating, $32 per observer, and is offered twice daily, at noon and 3:30pm, 7 days a week. Children must be at least 52 inches tall to participate. Reservations are necessary for this program. Call (C) 305/365-2501 in advance for reservations. The Seaquarium took a major hit during 2005's Hurricane Wilma and reopened in early 2006, restoring all the damage to the park's most popular attractions, such as Discovery Bay and Shark Channel. The Seaquarium also debuted a new sea lion show.

4400 Rickenbacker Causeway (south side), en route to Key Biscayne. (C) 305/361-5705. www.miamiseaquarium. com. Admission $26 adults, $21 children 3–9, free for children under 3. Daily 9:30am–6pm (ticket booth closes at 4pm). Parking $6.

Monkey Jungle ✲ (Overrated   Personally, I think this place is disgusting. It reeks, the monkeys are either sleeping or in heat, and it's really far from the city, even farther than the zoo. But if primates are your thing and you'd rather pass on the zoo, you'll be in paradise. You'll see rare Brazilian golden lion tamarins and Asian macaques. There are no cages to restrain the antics of the monkeys as they swing, chatter, and play their way into your heart. Screened-in trails wind through acres of "jungle," and daily shows feature the talents of the park's most progressive pupils. People who go here are not monkeying around—many of the park's frequent visitors are scientists and anthropologists. In fact, an interesting archaeological exhibition excavated from a Monkey Jungle sinkhole displays 10,000-year-old artifacts, including human teeth and animal bones. A somewhat amusing attraction here, if you can call it that, is the Wild Monkey Swimming Pool, a show in which you get to watch monkeys diving for food. If you can stand the humidity, the smell, and the bugs (flies, mosquitoes, and so

on), expect to spend about 2 hours here. The park's website sometimes offers down-loadable discount coupons, so if you have Internet access, take a look before you visit.

14805 SW 216th St., South Miami. © 305/235-1611. www.monkeyjungle.com. Admission $20 adults, $17 seniors and active-duty military, $14 children 4–12. Daily 9:30am–5pm (tickets sold until 4pm). Take U.S. 1 south to SW 216th St., or from Florida Tpk., take exit 11 and follow the signs.

Parrot Jungle Island ✿ *Kids* *Overrated*   This Miami institution took flight from its lush, natural South Miami environment and headed north in the winter of 2003 to a new, overly fabricated, disappointing $46-million home on Watson Island, along the MacArthur Causeway near Miami Beach. While the island doubles as a protected bird sanctuary, the jungle's former digs (in a coral rock structure built around 1900 in the heart of South Miami) had a lot more charm and kitsch. The new, overpriced 19-acre park features an Everglades exhibit, a petting zoo, and several theaters, jungle trails, and aviaries. Watch your heads because flying above are hundreds of parrots, macaws, peacocks, cockatoos, and flamingos. Be sure to check out the Crocosaurus, a 20-foot-long saltwater crocodile who hangs out in the park's Serpentarium. Also a pleasant sur-prise here is the Ichimura Miami Japan Garden (see the "A Japanese Garden" box, below). Continuous shows star roller-skating cockatoos, card-playing macaws, and numerous stunt-happy parrots. There are also tortoises, iguanas, and a rare albino alli-gator on exhibit. The park's website sometimes offers downloadable discount coupons, so take a look before you visit because you definitely won't want to pay full price for this park. If you do get your money's worth and see all the shows and exhibits, expect to spend upward of 4 hours here. *Note:* The former South Miami site of Parrot Jun-gle is now known as **Pinecrest Gardens,** 11000 Red Rd. (© **305/669-6942**), which features a petting zoo, mini water park, lake, natural hammocks, and Banyan caves. Open daily from 8am until sunset; admission is $5 adults, $3 kids, and $4 seniors.

1111 Parrot Jungle Trail, Watson Island (on the north side of MacArthur Causeway/I-395). © 305/372-3822. www.parrotjungle.com. Admission $25 adults, $23 seniors and military, $20 children 3–10. Parking an additional $6 per vehi-cle. Daily 10am–6pm. From I-95, take I-395 E (MacArthur Causeway); make a right on Parrot Jungle Trail, which is the first exit after the bridge. Follow the road around and under the causeway to the parking garage on the left side.

Sea Grass Adventures ✿ *Value* *Kids*   Even better than the Seaquarium is Sea Grass Adventures, in which a naturalist from the Marjory Stoneman Douglas Biscayne Nature Center will introduce ($10 per person) kids and adults to an amazing variety

---

A Japanese Garden

If you ask someone what Japanese influences can be found in Miami, they'll likely point to Nobu, Sushi Siam, Sushi Rock Café, and even Benihana. But back in the '50s, well before sushi became trendy, Kiyoshi Ichimura became obsessed with Miami and started sending people and objects from Tokyo, including car-penters, gardeners, and a landscape architect to design and construct the San-Ai-An Japanese Garden. Originally located in the Parrot Jungle Island space, the garden was dismantled during construction and re-created adjacent to the park. The completed 1-acre garden was renamed Ichimura Miami Japan Garden in honor of its original benefactor, and its sculptures and Japanese artifacts are managed by a coalition of city organizations. Japanese holidays and festivals are celebrated here.

of creatures that live in the sea grass beds of the Bear Cut Nature Preserve near Crandon Beach on Key Biscayne. You will be able to wade in the water with your guide and catch an assortment of sea life in nets provided by the guides. At the end of the program, participants gather on the beach while the guide explains what everyone's just caught, passing the creatures around in miniature viewing tanks. Call for available dates, times, and reservations.

Marjory Stoneman Douglas Biscayne Nature Center, 6767 Crandon Blvd., Key Biscayne. *(C)* 305/361-6767. The center is free. Daily 10am–4pm.

12 Shopping

If you're not into sunbathing and outdoor activities, or you just can't take the heat, you'll be in good company in one of Miami's many malls—and you are not likely to emerge empty handed. In addition to the strip malls, Miami offers a choice of megamalls, from the upscale Village of Merrick Park and mammoth Aventura Mall to the ritzy Bal Harbour Shops and touristy yet scenic Bayside Marketplace (just to name a few).

Miami also offers more unique shopping spots, such as the up-and-coming Biscayne Corridor, where funky boutiques dare to defy the Gap, and Little Havana, where you can buy hand-rolled cigars and *guayabera* shirts.

You may want to order the Greater Miami Convention and Visitors Bureau's *Shop Miami: A Guide to a Tropical Shopping Adventure.* Although it is limited to details on the bureau's paying members, it provides some good advice and otherwise unpublished discount offers. The glossy little pamphlet is printed in English, Spanish, and Portuguese, and provides information on transportation from hotels, translation services, and shipping. Call *(C)* **800/283-2707** or 305/539-3000 for more information.

THE SHOPPING SCENE

Below you'll find descriptions of some of the more popular retail areas, where many stores are conveniently clustered together to make browsing easier.

As a general rule, shop hours are Monday through Saturday from 10am to 6pm, and Sunday from noon to 5pm. Many stores stay open late (until 9pm or so) 1 night of the week, usually Thursday. Shops in Coconut Grove are open until 9pm Sunday through Thursday, and even later on Friday and Saturday. South Beach's stores also stay open later—as late as midnight. Department stores and shopping malls keep longer hours as well, with most staying open from 10am to 9 or 10pm Monday through Saturday, noon to 6pm on Sunday. With all these variations, you may want to call specific stores to find out their hours.

The 6.5% state and local sales tax is added to the price of all nonfood purchases. Food and beverage in hotels and restaurants are subject to the resort tax, which is 3% in Miami/South Beach and Bal Harbour, 4% in Surfside, and 2% in the rest of Miami–Dade County.

SHOPPING AREAS

Most of Miami's shopping happens at the many megamalls scattered from one end of the county to the other. However, excellent boutique shopping and browsing can be found in the following areas (see "The Neighborhoods in Brief," on p. 68, for more information):

AVENTURA On Biscayne Boulevard between Miami Gardens Drive and the county line at Hallandale Beach Boulevard is a 2-mile stretch of major retail stores including Best Buy, Borders, Circuit City, Linens 'n Things, Marshall's, Sports Authority, and more. Also here is the mammoth Aventura Mall, housing a fabulous collection of shops and restaurants.

CALLE OCHO   For a taste of Little Havana, take a walk down 8th Street between SW 27th Avenue and SW 12th Avenue, where you'll find some lively street life and many shops selling cigars, baked goods, shoes, furniture, and record stores specializing in Latin music. For help, take your Spanish dictionary.

COCONUT GROVE   Downtown Coconut Grove, centered on Main Highway and Grand Avenue, and branching onto the adjoining streets, is one of Miami's most pedestrian-friendly zones. The Grove's wide sidewalks, lined with cafes and boutiques, can provide hours of browsing pleasure. Coconut Grove is best known for its chain stores (Gap, Banana Republic, and so on) and some funky holdovers from the days when the Grove was a bit more bohemian, plus excellent sidewalk cafes centered on CocoWalk and the Streets of Mayfair.

MIRACLE MILE (CORAL GABLES)   Actually only a half-mile long, this central shopping street was an integral part of George Merrick's original city plan. Today the strip still enjoys popularity, especially for its bridal stores, ladies' shops, haberdashers, and gift shops. Recently, newer chain stores, like Barnes & Noble, Old Navy, and Starbucks, have been appearing on the Mile. The hyperupscale Village of **Merrick Park,** a mammoth, 850,000-square-foot upscale outdoor shopping complex between Ponce de León Boulevard and Le Jeune Road, just off the Mile, houses Nordstrom, Neiman Marcus, Armani, Gucci, Jimmy Choo, and Yves St. Laurent, to name a few.

DOWNTOWN MIAMI   If you're looking for discounts on all types of goods—especially watches, fabric, buttons, lace, shoes, luggage, and leather—Flagler Street, just west of Biscayne Boulevard, is the best place to start. I wouldn't necessarily recommend buying expensive items here, as many stores seem to be on the shady side and do not understand the word *warranty.* However, you can still have fun here as long as you are a savvy shopper and don't mind haggling. Most signs are printed in English, Spanish, and Portuguese; however, many shopkeepers may not be entirely fluent in English. Mary Brickell Village, a 192,000-square-foot urban entertainment center west of Brickell Avenue and straddling South Miami Avenue between 9th and 10th streets downtown, is slated to open in late 2006. The $80-million complex will consist of a slew of trendy restaurants, boutiques, and the requisite Starbucks—a sure sign that a neighborhood has been revitalized.

BISCAYNE CORRIDOR ✦   Amid the ramshackle old motels of yesteryear exist several funky, kitschy, and arty boutiques along the stretch of Biscayne Boulevard from 50th Street to about 79th Street known as the Biscayne Corridor. Everything from hand-painted tank tops to expensive Juicy Couture sweat suits can be found here, but it's not just about fashion: Several furniture stores selling antiques and modern pieces exist along here as well, so look carefully, as you may find something here that would cause the appraisers on *Antiques Road Show* to lose their wigs.

SOUTH BEACH ✦   Slowly but surely, South Beach has come into its own as far as shopping is concerned. While the requisite stores—Gap, Banana Republic, et al.—have anchored here, several higher-end stores have also opened on the southern blocks of Collins Avenue, which has become the Madison Avenue of Miami. For the hippest clothing boutiques (including Armani Exchange, Ralph Lauren, Versace, Benetton,

Levi's, Barneys Co-Op, Diesel, Guess?, Club Monaco, Kenneth Cole, and Nicole Miller, among others), stroll along this pretty strip of the Art Deco District.

For those who are interested in a little more fun with their shopping, consider South Beach's legendary Lincoln Road. This pedestrian mall, originally designed in 1957 by Morris Lapidus, recently underwent a multimillion-dollar renovation, restoring it to its former glory. Here shoppers find an array of clothing, books, tchotchkes, and art, as well as a menagerie of sidewalk cafes flanked on one end by a multiplex movie theater and, at the other, the Atlantic Ocean.

13 Miami After Dark

With all the hype, you'd expect Miami to have long outlived its 15 minutes of fame by now. But you'd be wrong. Miami's nightlife, in South Beach *and,* slowly but surely, downtown, is hotter than ever before—and still getting hotter. Practically every club in the area has installed closely guarded velvet ropes to create an air of exclusivity. Don't be fooled or intimidated by them—*anyone* can go clubbing in the Magic City, and throughout this chapter, I've provided tips to ensure that you gain entry to the venue you want to go to.

South Beach is certainly Miami's uncontested nocturnal nucleus, but more and more diverse areas, such as the Design District, South Miami, and even Little Havana, are increasingly providing fun alternatives without the ludicrous cover charges, "fashionably late" hours of operation (things don't typically get started on South Beach until after 11pm), the lack of sufficient self-parking, and outrageous drink prices that come standard in South Beach.

And while South Beach dances to a more electronic beat, other parts of Miami dance to a Latin beat—from salsa and merengue to tango and cha cha. However, if you're looking for a less frenetic good time, Miami's bar scene offers something for everyone, from haute hotel bars to sleek, loungey watering holes.

Parts of downtown, such as the Biscayne Corridor, the Miami River, and the Design District, are undergoing a trendy makeover a la New York City's Meatpacking District. Cool lounges, bars, and clubs are popping up and providing the "in" crowds with a newer, more urban-chic nocturnal pasture.

But if the possibility of a celebrity sighting in one of the city's lounges, bars, or clubs doesn't fulfill your cultural needs, Miami also offers a variety of first-rate diversions in theater, music, and dance, including a world-class ballet (under the aegis of Edward Villella), a recognized symphony, and a talented opera company. The brand-new Cesar Pelli–designed, $446-million Miami Performing Arts Center is the focal point for the arts, created to prove to the world that Miami isn't as shallow and devoid of culture as people once thought.

For up-to-date listing information, and to make sure the club of the moment hasn't expired, check the *Miami Herald's* "Weekend" section, which runs on Friday, or the more comprehensive listings in *New Times,* Miami's free alternative weekly, available each Wednesday; or visit www.miami.citysearch.com online.

BARS & LOUNGES

There are countless bars and lounges in and around Miami (most require proof that you are over 21 to enter), with the highest concentration on trendy South Beach. The selection here is a mere sample. Keep in mind that many of the popular bars—and the easiest to get into—are in hotels (with a few notable exceptions—see below). For a clubbier scene, if you don't mind making your way through hordes of inebriated club kids, a stroll on Washington Avenue will provide you with ample insight into what's hot and what's not. Just hold on to your bags. It's not dangerous, but, occasionally, a few shady types manage to slip into the crowd. Another very important tip when in a club: *Never put your drink down out of your sight*—there have been unfortunate incidents in which drinks have been spiked with illegal chemical substances. For a less hard-core, more collegiate nightlife, head to Coconut Grove. Oh, yes, and when going out in South Beach, make sure to take a so-called disco nap, as things don't get going until at least 11pm. If you go earlier, be prepared to face an empty bar or club. Off of South Beach and in hotel bars in general, the hours are fashionably earlier, with the action starting as early as, say, 7pm.

The Abbey   Dark, dank, and hard to find, this local microbrewery is a favorite for locals looking to escape the $15 candy-flavored martini scene. Best of all, there's never a cover and it's always open until 5am, perfect for those pesky and insatiable hops cravings that pop up at 3 or 4 am. 1115 16th St., South Beach. ✆ **305/538-8110.**

Automatic Slim's   This is *the* bar where Ozzie and Harriet types become more like Ozzy and Sharon. As South Beach's most popular unpretentious bar, Automatic Slim's is indeed a slim space of bar, but it packs people in, thanks to an exhaustive list of cheap(er) drinks, lack of attitude, great rock music, and a decor that can only be described as white trash–chic. 1216 Washington Ave., South Beach. ✆ **305/695-0795.**

Blue   A very laid-back, very local scene set to a sultry soundtrack of deep soul and house music has Miami's hipsters feeling the blues here on a nightly basis from 10pm to 5am. Before you whip out the St. John's Wort, dive into this so-not-trendy-it's-trendy lounge, in which the pervasive color blue will actually heighten your spirits as an eclectic haze of models, locals, and lounge lizards gather to commiserate in their dreaded trendy status. 222 Española Way (between Washington and Collins aves.), South Beach. ✆ **305/534-1009.**

Clarke's   Ever since this classy Irish pub and restaurant opened in the chichi South of Fifth Street area in 2005, it became command central for everyone from Shaquille O'Neal and the Miami Beach police chief to local moguls and club kids looking for cold beer and, surprisingly, a gourmet menu consisting of Shepherd's Pie, seared scallops and the best burger in the 'hood. My personal fave, however, is the New York–style pretzel served on a spike with a side of mustard. 840 1st St., South Beach ✆ **305/538-9885.**

Clevelander   If wet-T-shirt contests and a fraternity party atmosphere are your thing, then this Ocean Drive mainstay is your kind of place. Popular with tourists and

---

Then&Now   **The Clevelander, Then and Now**

In *Frommer's Florida 2007* author Leslie Abravanel says the **The Clevelander Hotel** (p. 168) is the place to head for a "fraternity party atmosphere." The hotel was already working on its rowdy and youthful reputation when it appeared in *Miami and the Caribbean on 10 Dollars a Day:* "[The Clevelander is] a well-designed and attractive establishment that is appealing more and more to the budget-minded single crowd. In addition to the swimming pool, the hotel features a roof-top sun club. A third person can fit into most of the double rooms for $2 in winter and only $1 in summer."

Impressions
There are two shifts in South Beach. There's nine to five. And then there's nine to five.

—South Beach artist Stewart Stewart

locals who like to pretend they're tourists, the Clevelander attracts a lively, sporty, adults-only crowd (the burly bouncers *will* confiscate fake IDs) who have no interest in being part of a scene, but, rather, like to take in the very revealing scenery. A great time to check out the Clevelander is on a weekend afternoon, when beach Barbies and Kens line the bar for a post-tanning beer or frozen cocktail. 1020 Ocean Dr., South Beach. ℂ 305/531-3485.

Forge   The Forge bar hosts an unusual mix of the uptight and those who wear their clothes too tight. It's also where surgically altered ladies look for their cigar-chomping sugar daddies in a setting that somehow reminds me of *Dynasty.* Call well in advance if you want to watch the parade of characters from a dinner table (p. 120). The Forge owners also own **Glass**, a ritzier nightclub (which is attached to the club) that debuted in 2006 (they say it's a private club, but if you dine at the restaurant or are acquainted with someone in the know, you can get in). 432 41st St., Miami Beach. ℂ 305/538-8533. (Door policy tends to be a bit exclusive; dress up and you should have no problem.)

Mac's Club Deuce   Standing amid an oasis of trendiness, Mac's Club Deuce is the quintessential dive bar, with cheap drinks and a cast of characters ranging from your typical barfly to your atypical drag queen. It's got a well-stocked jukebox, friendly bartenders, and a pool table. Best of all, it's an insomniac's dream, open daily from 8am to 5am. 222 14th St., South Beach. ℂ 305/673-9537.

Mynt   A massive 6,000-square-foot place, Mynt is nothing more than a huge living room in which models, celebrities, and assorted hangers-on bask in the green glow to the beats of very loud lounge and dance music. If you want to dance—or move, for that matter—this is not the place in which to do so. It's all about striking a pose in here. And unless you know the person at the door, be prepared to be ridiculed, emasculated, and socially shattered, as you may be forced to wait outside upward of an hour. If that's the case, forget it; it's not worth it. Wait next door at the Greek place for a celebrity sighting, since you'll have a better chance seeing people from there than actually waiting in the melee at the door. 1921 Collins Ave., South Beach. ℂ 786/276-6132. Cover $10–$20.

Playwright Irish Pub   Bono came here once when U2 was in town, not because it's such an authentic Irish pub, but because the bar was showing some European soccer match—and serves pints of Guinness. A great pre- or post-club spot, Playwright is one of the few places in town that also features live music from time to time. 1265 Washington Ave, South Beach. ℂ 305/534-0667.

Post   It's hard to imagine a friendly, inviting place opened by the same person who used to inflict a reign of nocturnal terror and rejection at the now defunct Design District spot Grass, but it's true. Post is a fabulous, modern lounge owned by ex-Grass owner Laurent Bourgade, who learned that nasty isn't necessarily nice in nightlife. The food's great, the loungey DJ-ed music kicks you know what, and on Thursday's hip-hop night, women *eat* free at this off-Brickell hot spot. 1777 SW 3rd St., Miami. ℂ 305/856-8585.

Moments **Stargazing**

The most popular places for celebrity sightings include Mynt, Opium Garden, Skybar, poolside at the Shore Club or the Delano, and, when it comes to J-Lo, somewhere on the beach around 20th Street. Miami Heat basketball games are also star magnets.

The Purdy Lounge   With the exception of a wall of lava lamps, Purdy is not unlike your best friend's basement, featuring a pool table and a slew of board games such as Operation to keep the attention-deficit-disordered from getting bored. Because it's a no-nonsense bar with relatively cheap cocktails (by South Beach standards), Purdy gets away with not having a star DJ or fancy bass-heavy Bose sound system. A CD player somehow does the trick. With no cover and no attitude, a line is inevitable (it gets crowded inside), so be prepared to wait. Saturday night has become the preferred night for locals, while Friday night's happy hour draws a young professional crowd on the prowl. 1811 Purdy Ave./Sunset Harbor, South Beach. (C) 305/531-4622.

Rok Bar   Larger-than-life rocker Tommy Lee has assembled a motley Miami crew at this paradox of a bar that combines down-'n'-dirty rock 'n' roll with the swank comforts of a chic lounge. The place is claustrophobic, with limited seating (unless you're Pamela Anderson, forget about scoring a table), high-priced drinks, and an oxymoronic soundtrack of Lynyrd Skynyrd, Michael Jackson, and Kid Rock. 1905 Collins Ave., South Beach. (C) 305/538-7171.

The Room   It's beer and wine only at this South of Fifth hideaway where locals and NY expats (there are a few Rooms in NYC) come to get away from the insanity of just a few blocks away. The beer selection is comprehensive and features brews from almost everywhere in the world. The wine's not so great, but there's no whining here at this tiny, industrial-style, candlelit spot that doesn't have a DJ—just a CD player spinning indie tunes—or those pesky Paris Hilton sightings. 100 Collins Ave, South Beach. (C) 305/531-6061.

Rose Bar at the Delano   If every rose has its thorn, the thorn at this painfully chic hotel bar is the excruciatingly high-priced cocktails. Otherwise, the crowd here is full of the so-called glitterati, fabulatti, and other assorted poseurs who view life through (Italian-made) rose-colored glasses. 1685 Collins Ave., South Beach. (C) 305/672-2000.

Segafredo Espresso   Although Segafredo is technically a cafe, it has become an integral part of Miami's nightlife as command central for Euros who miss that very special brand of European cafe society. Not in the mood for a club or bar but want to hear great music, sip a few cocktails, snack on delicious sandwiches and pizza, and sit outside and people-watch? This is the place. European lounge music, tons of outdoor tables on a prime corner of Lincoln Road, and always a mob scene make 'Fredo one of my—and many other Miamians'—favorite nocturnal diversions. 1040 Lincoln Rd., South Beach. (C) 305/673-0047.

Skybar at The Shore Club   Skybar lives up to its name in terms of loftiness; something this place has perfected better than anyone else, whether at its original L.A. location or the sprawling South Beach location at The Shore Club. If you're not a hotel guest, not Beyonce, or not on the "list," or if you're a guy with several other guys and no girls, fugghedaboutit. For those of you who can't get in, the Skybar is basically the entire backyard area of The Shore Club, consisting of several areas, including the Moroccan-themed garden area, the hip-hop-themed indoor Red Room, the Sand Bar by the beach, and the Rum Bar by the pool. Popular on any given night, Sky Bar is yet another brilliant example of how hotelier Ian Schrager has managed to control the hipsters in a most Pavlovian way. At The Shore Club, 1901 Collins Ave., South Beach. (*) 305/695-3100.

Taverna Opa   Although this Greek taverna (also located in Hollywood and Ft. Lauderdale) calls itself a restaurant, I consider it more of a raucous dance club that just happens to serve excellent Greek food. How many restaurants do you know of that allow patrons to dance suggestively with waiters on tables, throw napkins in the air as if they were confetti, and guzzle ouzo straight from the bottle, all to the tune of some very loud jazzed-up Greek dance music? Get here early, as the place is always packed— and I mean *packed* as in Standing Room Only. Although there is an outdoor bar, the real fun and scenery is indoors in the dining room, where the tables double as dance floors and some very animated characters channel their best Zorbas. Be prepared for a big, fat Greek hangover the next day. 36 Ocean Dr., South Beach. (*) 305/673-6730.

Transit Lounge   It's hard to find, but once you do find Transit Lounge, you'll be happy you did. Reminiscent of what locals describe as "a real big-city lounge," Transit is cavernous, featuring a huge bar, tons of cozy couches and tables, board games, a funky crowd, and, hallelujah, live music. 1729 SW 1st Ave. Miami. (*) 305/377-4628.

Vino Miami   Vino is the city's *only* bona fide wine bar, with a collection of over 300 bottles and 60 wines by the glass, mostly from boutique and unheard-of wineries around the world. Decorated as if it came straight out of a West Elm catalogue, this chic, Manhattan-esque wine bar is known for many things, especially the fact that it's a chill lounge in which the 30-and-over set can hang out, have audible conversations, sip wine, and even enjoy cheeses, fondues, and delicious desserts. Vino also has monthly wine-tasting events with experts hailing from around the world. 1601 Washington Ave., South Beach. (*) 305/532-1860.

Wet Willie's   With such telling drinks as Call a Cab, this beachfront oasis is not the place to go if you have a long drive ahead of you. A well-liked pre- and post-beach hangout, Wet Willie's inspires serious drinking. Popular with the Harley-Davidson set, tourists, and beachcombers, this bar is best known for its rooftop patio (get there early if you plan to get a seat) and its half-nude bikini beauties. 760 Ocean Dr., South Beach. (*) 305/532-5650.

DANCE CLUBS, LIVE MUSIC, THE GAY & LESBIAN SCENE & LATIN CLUBS
DANCE CLUBS

Clubs are as much a cottage industry in Miami as is, say, cheese in Wisconsin. Clubland, as it is known, is a way of life for some. On any given night in Miami, there's something going on—no excuses are needed to throw a party here. Short of throwing a glammy event for the grand opening of a new gas station, Miami is very party hearty, celebrating everything from the fact that it's Tuesday night to the debut of a hot new DJ. Within this very bizarre after-dark community, a very colorful assortment of characters emerges, from (a)typical nine-to-fivers to shady characters who have reinvented themselves as hot shots on the club circuit. While this "see and be seen" scene may not be your cup of Absolut, it's certainly never boring.

The club music played on Miami's ever-evolving social circuit is good enough to get even the most rhythmically challenged wallflowers dancing. To keep things fresh in Clubland, local promoters throw one-nighters, which are essentially parties with various themes or motifs, from funk to fashion. Because these change so often, we can't possibly list them here. Word of mouth, local advertising, and listings in the free weekly *New Times,* www.miami.citysearch.com, or the "Weekend" section of the *Miami Herald* are the best ways to find out about these ever-changing events.

Before you get all decked out to hit the town as soon as the sun sets, consider the fact that Miami is a very late town. Things generally don't get started here before 11pm. The Catch-22 is that if you don't arrive on South Beach early enough, you may find yourself driving around aimlessly for parking, as it is very limited outside of absurd $20 valet charges. Municipal lots fill up quickly, so your best bet is to arrive on South Beach somewhat early and kill time by strolling around, having something to eat, or sipping a cocktail in a hotel bar. Another advantage of arriving a bit earlier than the crowds is that some clubs don't charge a cover before 11pm or midnight, which could save you a wad of cash over time. Most clubs are open every night of the week, though some are open only Thursday to Sunday and others are open only Monday though Saturday. Call ahead to get the most up-to-date information possible: Things change very quickly around here, and a call in advance can help you make sure that the dance club you're planning to go to hasn't become a video arcade. Cover charges are very haphazard, too. If you're not on the ubiquitous guest list (ask your concierge to put you on the list— he or she usually has the ability to do so, which won't help you with the wait to get in,

---

Tips **Ground Rules: Stepping Out in Miami**

- Nightlife on South Beach doesn't really get going until after 11pm. As a result, you may want to consider taking what is known as a disco nap so that you'll be fully charged until the wee hours.
- If you're unsure of what to wear out on South Beach, your safest bet will be anything black.
- Do *not* try to tip the doormen manning the velvet ropes. That will only make you look desperate, and you'll find yourself standing outside for what will seem like an ungodly amount of time. Instead, try to land your name on the ever-present guest lists by calling the club early in the day yourself or, better yet, having the concierge at your hotel do it for you. If you don't have connections and you find yourself without a concierge, then act assertive, not surly, at the velvet rope, and your patience will usually be rewarded with admittance. If all else fails—for men, especially—surround yourself with a few leggy model types and you'll be noticed quicker.
- If you are a man going out with a group of men, unless you're going to a gay bar, you will most likely not get into any South Beach hot spot unless you are with women.
- Finally, have fun. It may look like serious business when you're on the outside, but once you're in, it's another story. Attacking Clubland with a sense of humor is the best approach to a successful, memorable evening out.

Winter Music Conference

Every March, Miami is besieged by the most unconventional conventioneers the city has ever seen. These fiercely dedicated souls descend upon the city in a very audible way, with dark circles under their eyes and bleeps, blips, and scratches that can wake the dead. No, we're not talking about a Star Trek convention, but, rather, the Winter Music Conference, the world's biggest and most important gathering of DJs, remixers, agents, artists, and pretty much anyone who makes a dime off of the booming electronic music industry hailing from over 60 countries from all over the world. But unlike most conventions, this one is completely interactive and open to the paying public as South Beach and Miami's hottest clubs transform into showcases for the various audio wares. For 5 consecutive days and nights, DJs, artists, and software producers play for audiences comprised of A&R reps, talent scouts, and locals just along for the ride. Parties take place everywhere, from hotel pools to street corners. There's always something going on every hour on the hour, and most people who really get into the throes of the WMC get little or no sleep. Energy drinks become more important than water, and, for the most part, if you see people popping pills, they're not likely to be vitamins. At any rate, the WMC is worth checking out if you get ecstatic over names such as Hex Hector, Paul Oakenfold, Ultra Nate, Chris Cox, and Mark Ronson, among many, many others. For more information on WMC events, go to www.wmcon.com. And for those who just yearn to be the next big DJ, the **Scratch DJ Academy,** 642 6th St., South Beach (℃ **305/ 535-2599;** www.scratch.com) is now open and ready to teach you the turntables for a whopping $300 per 70-minute course. But just think, top DJs these days make in excess of $300,000 per gig, so it may be worth the investment!

but will eliminate the cover charge), you may have to fork over a ridiculous $20 to walk past the ropes. Don't fret, though. There are many clubs and bars that have no cover charge—they just make up for it by charging $13 for a martini!

Bongo's Cuban Café   Gloria Estefan's latest hit in the restaurant business pays homage to the sights, sounds, and cuisine of pre-Castro Cuba. Bongo's is a mammoth restaurant attached to the American Airlines Arena in downtown Miami. On Friday after 11pm and Saturday after 11:30pm, it's transformed from a friendly family restaurant into the city's hottest 21-and-over salsa nightclub. Cover charges can be hefty, but consider it your ticket to what happens to be an astounding show of some of the best salsa dancers in the city. Prepare yourself for standing room only. At the American Airlines Arena, 601 Biscayne Blvd., Downtown Miami. ℃ **786/777-2100.** Cover Fri, ladies free, guys $10; Sat $20 for all.

Club Space ✿   Clubland hits the mainland with this cavernous downtown warehouse of a club. With over 30,000 square feet of dance space, you can spin around a la Stevie Nicks (albeit to a techno beat) without having to worry about banging into someone. On Saturday and Sunday nights, the party usually extends to the next morning, sometimes as late 10am. It's quite a sight to see club kids rushing off to work

---

Impressions

Working the door teaches you a lot about human nature.

—A former South Beach doorman

---

straight from Space on a Monday morning. Known as the venue of choice for world-renowned DJs, Club Space sometimes charges ludicrous admission fees to cover their hefty price tags. *Note:* Club Space doesn't really get going until around 3am. Call for more information, as it doesn't have a concrete schedule. 34 NE 11th St., Miami. ✆ 305/372-9378. Cover $0–$20.

crobar ✭ Still haunted by the ghost of clubs past, the space formerly known as the Cameo Theatre is now possessed by the mod, millennial, industrial spirit that is cro-bar. With its intense, dance-heavy sound system, an industrially chic ambience, and crowds big enough to scare away any memories of a sadly abandoned Cameo, this Chicago import has raised the bar on South Beach nightlife with crazy theme nights (the monthly Sex Night is particularly, uh, stimulating), top-name DJs, and the occasional celebrity appearance. On Sunday, the club hosts an extremely popular gay night known as Anthem (p. 177). Open Thursday through Monday from 10pm to 5am. 1445 Washington Ave., South Beach. ✆ 305/531-8225. www.crobarmiami.com. Cover Thurs, Sun, Mon $20; Fri–Sat $25.

I/O Although I'd like to call this new warehouse-y club "ghetto fabulous," I don't want to give out mixed messages. I/O is the club for that funky, arty/hipster set that listens to music by the likes of Belle and Sebastian and other groups that your Britney-loving sister probably never heard of. The club is composed of three areas—a bar area in which Japanese anime is played, a dance area with live music where cool kids do their best breakdancing (or whatever they're calling it these days), and an outdoor bar area, which is cool during winter months but brutally hot in the summer. The best nights here are Thursday night's Latin-flavored Fuacata! and Saturday night's Pop Life, an homage to the Depeche Mode era of New Wave. 30 NE 14th St., Downtown Miami. ✆ 305/358-8007. Cover $5–$10.

Mansion Housed in the space formerly known as Level, this latest nocturnal venture from the same team behind the utterly addictive Opium Garden (see below) is a massive multilevel lounge that, according to the owners and promoters, is entirely "VIP," meaning you'd best know someone to get in or else you'll be among the masses outside and not even close to the manse. Live DJs, models, and celebrities galore—ubiquitous Paris Hilton, Tara Reid, Shannen Doherty, N*Sync, and more—not to mention high ceilings, wood floors, brick walls, and a decidedly nonsmoky interior make this Mansion, despite its cheesy name, a *must* on the list of see-and-be-scen-esters. Open Tuesday through Sunday from 11pm to 5am. 1235 Washington Ave., South Beach. ✆ 305/531-5535. Cover varies, $10–$40.

Nikki Beach Club *Finds* What the Playboy Mansion is to L.A., the Nikki Beach Club is to South Beach. This place is the product of local nightlife royalty Tommy Pooch and Eric Omores. Half-naked ladies and men actually venture into the daylight on Sunday (around 4pm, which is ungodly in this town) to see, be seen, and, at times, be obscene. At night, it's very "Brady Bunch goes to Hawaii" seeming, with a sexy Tiki hut/Polynesian theme style, albeit rated R. The Sunday-afternoon beach party is almost legendary and worth a glimpse—that is, if you can get in. Egos are easily shattered, as surly doormen are known to reject those who don't drive up in a Ferrari. Also located within this bastion of hedonism is the super-hot **Pearl,** a modish, 380-seat, orange-hued restaurant and lounge that features a Continental menu created by Nikki chef Brian Rutherford. But you'd do better to forget the food and go for the eye candy. 101 Ocean Dr., South Beach. 🕐 **305/538-1111.** Cover $10–$20.

Opium Garden   Housed in a massive open-air space, Opium Garden is a highly addictive nocturnal habit for those looking for a combination of sexy dance music; scantily clad dancers; celebrities such as J-Lo, Janet Jackson, Lenny Kravitz, and P. Diddy; and, for the masochists out there, an oppressive door policy in which two sets of velvet ropes are set up to keep those deemed unworthy out of this see-and-be-sceney den of inequity. Opium has a sushi restaurant (decent) and an ultra-VIP, celeb-saturated lounge, Prive, whose own separate door policy makes the aforementioned seem like a romp in the sand. 136 Collins Ave., South Beach. 🕐 **305/531-5535.** Cover $20.

Pawn Shop Lounge   This former Pawn Shop is far from shabby or schlocky, but it is, perhaps, the kitschiest spot in Miami in which *Sanford and Son* meets South Beach. In addition to a full-blown big yellow school bus that doubles as a cocktail lounge, Pawn Shop boasts an Airstream Trailer in which the likes of Colin Farrell and Paris Hilton have kicked back on the couch and looked out the window at the ensuing insanity on the dance floor. Or relax in a seat located in the jetliner fuselage—actual plane seats that are surprisingly more comfy than in cattle class. Pawn Shop throws unusual parties such as the one when they featured an impersonator of Larry Wilcox, "The white guy from CHiPs," and the one when Hilton debuted her album by taking over the DJ booth and screaming "I hate techno, so turn this *&* off." Alan T., the door personality—there's no other word for him—is one of the club's best attractions. Be sure to tell him we say hello. 1222 NE 2nd Ave. 🕐 **305/373-3511.** Cover $10-$20.

SoHo Lounge *(Finds*   This multilevel, multifaceted Design District club is tons of fun if you are into either '80s music or electroclash. Cheap drinks, a sprawling outdoor patio, and several different nooks, crannies, bars, and dance areas are available for perusal. The best area in the entire club is the two-story dance floor in which a big screen shows everything from *Tron* to anime. Music ranges from the '80s greatest hits to more obscure music from Europe. One of the best venues in town for live music, SoHo Lounge has hosted the likes of Peaches and Electro-cute, and if those names don't ring a bell, consider going to SoHo to become acquainted with them. 175 NE 36th St., Design District. 🕐 **305/576-1988.** Cover $0–$10.

Rock 'n' Bowl

A new kind of nightlife debuted in South Beach in 2005 in the form of **Lucky Strike Lanes,** 1691 Michigan Ave. South Beach (🕐 **305/532-0307;** www.bowl luckystrike.com), which keeps you off the streets but in the gutters. Low lighting, glow-in-the-dark pins, and loud music keep things rolling day and night from 11am until 2 am. If you're not in the mood to bowl, the restaurant and bar are always hopping, too. Games are $4.95 to $7.95 depending on the time you're there, or $55 to $75 an hour; shoes are an extra $4. After 9pm, you have to be 21 and older to enter.

LIVE MUSIC

Unfortunately, Miami's live music scene is not thriving. Instead of local bands garnering devoted fans, local DJs are more admired, skyrocketing much more easily to fame—thanks to the city's lauded dance-club scene. However, there are still several places that strive to bring Miami up to speed as far as live music is concerned. You just have to look—and listen—for it a bit more carefully. The following is a list of places where you can, from time to time, catch some live acts, be it a DJ or an aspiring Nirvana.

Churchill's Hideaway *(Finds* British expatriate Dave Daniels couldn't live in Miami without a true English-style pub, so he opened Churchill's Hideaway, the city's premier space for live rock music. Filthy and located in a rather unsavory neighborhood, Churchill's is committed to promoting and extending the lifeline of the lagging local music scene. A fun no-frills crowd hangs out here. Bring earplugs with you, as it is deafening once the music starts. Monday is open-mic night, while Wednesday is reserved for ladies' wrestling. 5501 NE 2nd Ave., Little Haiti. (ℭ 305/757-1807. www.churchillspub.com. Cover $0–$6.

Jazid *(Finds* Smoky, sultry, and illuminated by flickering candelabras, Jazid is the kind of place where you'd expect to hear Sade's "Smooth Operator" on constant rotation. Instead, however, you'll hear live jazz (sometimes acid jazz), soul, and funk. An eclectic mix of mellow folk convenes here for a much-necessary respite from the surrounding Washington Avenue mayhem. 1342 Washington Ave., South Beach. (ℭ 305/673-9372. Cover $10.

Tobacco Road Al Capone used to hang out here when it was a speakeasy. Now locals flock here to see local bands perform, as well as national acts such as George Clinton and the P-Funk All-Stars, Koko Taylor, and the Radiators. Tobacco Road (the proud owner of Miami's very first liquor license) is small and gritty, and meant to be that way. Escape the smoke and sweat in the backyard patio, where air is a welcome commodity. The downright cheap nightly specials, such as the $11 lobster on Tuesday, are quite good and are served until 2am; the bar is open until 5am. 626 S. Miami Ave. (over the Miami Ave. Bridge near Brickell Ave.), Downtown. (ℭ 305/374-1198. Cover $5–$10 Thurs–Sat.

Upstairs at the Van Dyke Cafe *(Finds* The cafe's jazz bar, located on the second floor, resembles a classy speakeasy in which local jazz performers play to an intimate, enthusiastic crowd of mostly adults and sophisticated young things, who often huddle at the small tables until the wee hours. 846 Lincoln Rd., South Beach. (ℭ 305/534-3600. Cover Sun–Thurs $5, Fri–Sat $10 for a seat; no cover at the bar.

THE GAY & LESBIAN SCENE

Miami and the beaches have long been host to what is called a "first-tier" gay community. Similar to the Big Apple, the Bay Area, or LaLa land, Miami has had a large alternative community since the days when Anita Bryant used her citrus power to boycott the rise in political activism in the early '70s. Well, things have changed and Miami–Dade now has a gay-rights ordinance.

Newcomers intending to party in any bar, whether downtown or certainly on the beach, will want to check ahead for the schedule, as all clubs must have a gay or lesbian night to pay their rent. Miami Beach, in fact, is a capital of the gay circuit party scene, rivaling San Francisco, Palm Springs, and even the mighty Sydney, Australia, for tourist dollars. However, ever since South Beach got bit by the hip-hop bug, many of Miami's gays have been crossing county lines into Fort Lauderdale, where there are, surprisingly, many more gay establishments.

Anthem   Sunday nights at crobar (see above) sing the gay anthem with this hyper-popular one-nighter featuring Miami's own superstar DJ Abel. 1445 Washington Ave., South Beach. ℂ **877/CRO-SOBE** or 305/531-5027. Cover $20.

O-Zone   This is the zone of choice for gay men with an aversion to South Beach's cruisy, scene-heavy vibes. It's known for a heavily Latin crowd (mixed with a few college boys from the nearby University of Miami) and fantastic, outlandish drag shows on the weekends. 6620 SW 57th Ave. (Red Rd.), South Miami. ℂ **305/667-2888**. No cover for men on Sat; other nights $5–$10.

Score   There's a reason this Lincoln Road hotbed of gay activity is called Score. In addition to the huge pick-up scene, Score offers a multitude of bars, dance floors, lounge areas, and outdoor tables, in case you need to come up for air. Sunday-afternoon Tea Dances are legendary. 727 Lincoln Rd., South Beach. ℂ **305/535-1111**.

Twist   One of the most popular bars (and hideaways) on South Beach, this recently expanded bar (which is literally right across the street from the police station) has a casual yet lively atmosphere. 1057 Washington Ave., South Beach. ℂ **305/538-9478**.

LATIN CLUBS

Considering that Hispanics make up a large part of Miami's population and that there's a huge influx of Spanish-speaking visitors, it's no surprise that there are some great Latin nightclubs in the city. Plus, with the meteoric rise of the international music scene based in Miami, many international stars come through the offices of MTV Latino, SONY International, and a multitude of Latin TV studios based in Miami—and they're all looking for a good club scene on weekends. Most of the Anglo clubs also reserve at least 1 night a week for Latin rhythms.

Casa Panza *(Finds)*   This *casa* is one of Little Havana's liveliest and most popular nightspots. Every Tuesday, Thursday, and Saturday night, Casa Panza, in the heart of Little Havana, becomes the House of Flamenco, with shows at 8 and 11pm. You can either enjoy a flamenco show or strap on your own dancing shoes and participate in the celebration. Enjoy a fantastic Spanish meal before the show, or just a glass of sangria before you start stomping. Open until 4am, Casa Panza is a hot spot for young Latin club kids and, occasionally, a few older folks who are so taken by the music and the scene that they've failed to realize that it's well past their bedtime. 1620 SW 8th St. (Calle Ocho), Little Havana. ℂ **305/643-5343**.

Hoy Como Ayer   Formerly known as Cafe Nostalgia, the Little Havana hangout dedicated to reminiscing about Old Cuba, Hoy Como Ayer is like the Brady Bunch of Latin hangouts—while it was extremely popular with old timers in its Cafe Nostalgia incarnation, it is now experiencing a resurgence among the younger generation, seeking their own brand of Nostalgia. Its Thursday night party, Fuacata (slang for "Pow!"), is a magnet for Latin hipsters, featuring classic Cuban music mixed in with modern DJ-spun sound effects. Open Thursday to Sunday from 9pm to 4am. 2212 SW 8th St. (Calle Ocho), Little Havana. ℂ **305/541-2631**. Cover $10 Thurs–Sun.

La Covacha *(Finds)*   This hut, located virtually in the middle of nowhere (West Miami), is the hottest Latin joint in the entire city. Sunday features the best in Latin rock, with local and international acts. But the shack is really jumping on weekend

The Rhythm Is Gonna Get You

Are you feeling shy about hitting a Latin club because you fear your two left feet will stand out? Then take a few lessons from one of the following dance companies or dance teachers. They offer individual and group lessons to dancers of any origin who are willing to learn. These folks have made it their mission to teach merengue and flamenco to non-Latinos and Latino left-foots, and are among the most reliable, consistent, and popular ones in Miami. So what are you waiting for?

Thursday and Friday nights at **Bongo's Cuban Café** (American Airlines Arena, 601 Biscayne Blvd., Downtown; ✆ 786/777-2100) are an amazing showcase of some of the city's best salsa dancers, but amateurs need not be intimidated, thanks to the instructors at Latin Groove Dance Studios, who are on hand to help you with your two left feet. Lessons are free.

At **Ballet Flamenco La Rosa** (in the Performing Arts Network building, 13126 W. Dixie Hwy., North Miami; ✆ 305/899-7730), you can learn to flamenco, salsa, or merengue. This is the only professional flamenco company in the area. If you're feeling shy, $50 will buy you a private lesson; otherwise, it's $10 for a group lesson.

Nobody salsas like **Luz Pinto** (✆ 305/868-9418), and she teaches the basics with patience and humor. She charges between $40 and $55 for a private lesson for up to four people, and $10 per person for a group lesson. A good introduction is her multilevel group class at 7pm Sunday evenings at the PAN building. Although she teaches everything from ballroom to merengue, her specialty is Casino-style salsa, popularized in the 1950s in Cuba, Luz's homeland. A mix of disco and square dancing, Casino-style salsa is all the rage in Latin clubs in town. Good students may be able to convince Luz, for an extra fee, to chaperone a trip to a nightclub to show off their moves. Ask her for more information.

Angel Arroya has been teaching salsa to the clueless out of his home (at 16467 NE 27th Ave., North Miami Beach; ✆ 305/949-7799) for the past 10 years. Just $10 will buy you an hour's time. He traditionally teaches Monday and Wednesday nights, but call ahead to check for any schedule changes.

nights, when the place is open until 5am. Friday is *the* night here, so much so that the owners had to place a red velvet rope out front to maintain some semblance of order. It's an amusing sight—a velvet rope guarding a shack—but once you get in, you'll understand the need for it. Do not wear silk here, as you *will* sweat. 10730 NW 25th St. (at NW 107th Ave.), West Miami. ✆ 305/594-3717. Cover $0–$10.

Mango's Tropical Café   Claustrophobic types do not want to go near Mango's. Ever. One of the most popular spots on Ocean Drive, this outdoor enclave of Latin liveliness shakes with the intensity of a Richter-busting earthquake. Mango's is *Cabaret,* Latin style. Nightly live Brazilian and other Latin music, not to mention scantily clad male and female dancers, draw huge gawking crowds in from the sidewalk. But pay attention to the music, if you can: Incognito international musicians often lose their anonymity and jam with the house band on stage. Open daily from 11am to 5am. 900 Ocean Dr., South Beach. ℭ 305/673-4422. Cover $5–$15.

THE PERFORMING ARTS

Highbrows and culture vultures complain that there is a dearth of decent cultural offerings in Miami. What do locals tell them? Go back to New York! In all seriousness, however, in recent years Miami's performing arts scene has improved greatly. The city's Broadway Series features Tony Award–winning shows (the touring versions, of course), which aren't always Broadway caliber, but they are usually pretty good and not nearly as pricey. Local arts groups such as the Miami Light Project, a not-for-profit cultural organization that presents live performances by innovative dance, music, and theater artists, have had huge success in attracting big-name artists such as Nina Simone and Philip Glass to Miami. In addition, a burgeoning bohemian movement in Little Havana has given way to performance spaces that have become nightclubs in their own right.

THEATER

The **Actors' Playhouse,** a musical theater at the newly restored Miracle Theater at 280 Miracle Mile, Coral Gables (ℭ **305/444-9293;** www.actorsplayhouse.org), is a grand 1948 Art Deco movie palace with a 600-seat main theater and a smaller theater/rehearsal hall that hosts a number of excellent musicals for children throughout the year. In addition to these two rooms, the Playhouse recently added a 300-seat children's balcony theater. Tickets run from $27 to $40.

The **Coconut Grove Playhouse,** 3500 Main Hwy., Coconut Grove (ℭ **305/442-4000;** www.cgplayhouse.org), is also a former movie house, built in 1927 in an ornate Spanish rococo style. Today this respected venue is known for its original and innovative staging of both international and local dramas and musicals. The house's second, more intimate Encore Room is well suited to alternative and experimental productions. Tickets run from $35 to $45.

The **Gables Stage,** at the Biltmore Hotel (p. 104), Anastasia Avenue, Coral Gables (ℭ **305/445-1119**), stages at least one Shakespearean play, one classic, and one contemporary piece a year. This well-regarded theater usually tries to secure the rights to a national or local premiere as well. Tickets cost $35 for adults, and $15 and $32, respectively, for students and seniors.

The **Jerry Herman Ring Theatre** is on the main campus of the University of Miami in Coral Gables (ℭ **305/284-3355**). The University's Department of Theater Arts uses this stage for advanced-student productions of comedies, dramas, and musicals. Faculty and guest actors are regularly featured, as are contemporary works by local playwrights. Performances are usually scheduled Tuesday through Saturday during the academic year. In the summer, don't miss "Summer Shorts," a selection of superb one-acts. Tickets sell for $14 to $16.

The **New Theater,** 4120 Laguna St., Coral Gables (ℭ **305/443-5909**), prides itself on showing renowned works from America and Europe. As the name implies, you'll find mostly contemporary plays, with a few classics thrown in. Performances are staged Thursday through Sunday year-round. Tickets are $35 on Thursday, $40 on Friday and Saturday, and $35 to $40 on Sunday. If tickets are available on the day of the performance—and they usually are—students pay half-price.

CLASSICAL MUSIC

In addition to a number of local orchestras and operas (see below), which regularly offer quality music and world-renowned guest artists, each year brings a slew of classical-music special events and touring artists to Miami. The **Concert Association of Florida (CAF;** C **877/433-3200)** produces one of the most important and longest-running series. Known for more than a quarter of a century for its high-caliber, star-packed schedules, CAF regularly arranges the best "serious" music concerts for the city. Season after season, the schedules are punctuated by world-renowned dance companies and seasoned virtuosi like Itzhak Perlman, Andre Watts, and Kathleen Battle. Since CAF does not have its own space, performances are usually scheduled in the Miami–Dade County Auditorium or the Jackie Gleason Theater of the Performing Arts (see the "Major Venues" section below). The season lasts October through April, and ticket prices range from $20 to $70.

Florida Philharmonic Orchestra   South Florida's premier symphony orchestra, under the direction of James Judd, presents a full season of classical and pops programs interspersed with several children's and contemporary popular music performances. The Philharmonic performs downtown in the Gusman Center for the Performing Arts and at the Miami–Dade County Auditorium (see the "Major Venues" section below). 4120 Leguna St., Coral Gables. C **800/226-1812.** Tickets $15–$60. When extra tickets are available, students are admitted free on day of performance.

Miami Chamber Symphony   This professional orchestra is a small, subscription-series orchestra that's not affiliated with any major arts organizations and is therefore an inexpensive alternative to the high-priced classical venues. Renowned international soloists perform regularly here. The season runs October to May, and most concerts are held in the Gusman Concert Hall, on the University of Miami campus. 5690 N. Kendall Dr., Kendall. C **305/284-6477.** Tickets $12–$30.

New World Symphony   This organization, led by artistic director Michael Tilson Thomas, is a stepping stone for gifted young musicians seeking professional careers. The orchestra specializes in innovative, energetic performances, and often features renowned guest soloists and conductors. The season lasts from October to May, during which time there are many free concerts. 541 Lincoln Rd., South Beach. C **305/673-3331.** www.nws.org. Tickets free–$58. Rush tickets (remaining tickets sold 1 hr. before performance) $20. Students $10 (1 hr. before concerts; limited seating).

OPERA

Florida Grand Opera   Around for more than 60 years, this company regularly features singers from top houses in both America and Europe. All productions are sung in their original language and staged with projected English supertitles. Tickets become scarce when Placido Domingo or Luciano Pavarotti (who made his American debut here in 1965) comes to town. The season runs roughly from November to April, with five performances each week. In 2007, the opera may move into more upscale headquarters opposite the Miami Performing Arts Center. Until then, performances take place at the Miami–Dade County Auditorium and the Broward Center for the Performing Arts, about 40 minutes from downtown Miami. Box office: 1200 Coral Way, Southwest Miami. C **800/741-1010.** www.fgo.org. Tickets $19–$145. Student discounts available.

DANCE

Several local dance companies train and perform in the Greater Miami area. In addition, top traveling troupes regularly stop at the venues listed below. Keep your eyes open for special events and guest artists.

Ballet Flamenco La Rosa   For a taste of local Latin flavor, see this lively troupe perform impressive flamenco and other styles of Latin dance on Miami stages. (They also teach Latin dancing—see the "The Rhythm Is Gonna Get You" box above.) 13126 W. Dixie Hwy., North Miami, ✆ **305/899-7729.** Tickets $25 at door, $20 in advance, $18 for students and seniors.

Miami City Ballet   This artistically acclaimed and innovative company, directed by Edward Villella, features a repertoire of more than 60 ballets, many by George Balanchine, and has had more than 20 world premieres. The company's three-story center features eight rehearsal rooms, a ballet school, a boutique, and ticket offices. The City Ballet season runs from September to April. Ophelia and Juan Jr. Roca Center, Collins Ave. and 22nd St., South Beach. ✆ **305/929-7000** or 305/929-7010 for box office. Tickets $17–$50.

MAJOR VENUES

The **Colony Theater,** on Lincoln Road in South Beach (✆ **305/674-1040**), which has become an architectural showpiece of the Art Deco District, is open in 2006 after a $4.3-million renovation that will add wing and fly space, improve access for those with disabilities, and restore the lobby to its original Art Deco look.

At the **Miami–Dade County Auditorium,** West Flagler Street at 29th Avenue, Southwest Miami (✆ **305/547-5414**), performers gripe about the lack of space, but for patrons, this 2,430-seat auditorium is the only Miami space in which you can hear the opera—for now. A multimillion-dollar performing arts center downtown has been in the works for years (see below), but for now, the Auditorium is home to the city's Florida Grand Opera, and it also stages productions by the Concert Association of Florida, many programs in Spanish, and a variety of other shows.

At the 1,700-seat **Gusman Center for the Performing Arts,** 174 E. Flagler Street, downtown Miami (✆ **305/372-0925**), seating is tight, and so is funding, but the sound is superb. In addition to hosting the Florida Philharmonic Orchestra and the Miami Film Festival, the elegant Gusman Center features pop concerts, plays, film screenings, and special events. The auditorium was built as the Olympia Theater in 1926, and its ornate palace interior is typical of that era, complete with fancy columns, a huge pipe organ, and twinkling "stars" on the ceiling.

Not to be confused with the Gusman Center (above), the **Gusman Concert Hall,** 1314 Miller Dr. at 14th Street, Coral Gables (✆ **305/284-6477**), is a roomy 600-seat hall that gives a stage to the Miami Chamber Symphony and a varied program of university recitals.

The elegant **Jackie Gleason Theater of the Performing Arts,** located in South Beach at Washington Avenue and 17th Street (✆ **305/673-7300;** www.gleason theater.com), is the home of the Miami Beach Broadway Series, which has recently presented *Rent, Phantom of the Opera,* and *Les Misérables.* This 2,705-seat hall also hosts other big-budget Broadway shows, classical music concerts, and dance performances.

And last, but definitely not least, **The Performing Arts Center**, 1444 Biscayne Blvd. (✆ **305/372-1220**), opens in late 2007 after a whopping $446 million tab. The 2,400-seat **Sanford and Dolores Ziff Ballet Opera House** and the 2,200-seat **Carnival Concert Hall** will be Miami venues for the **Concert Association of Florida**, **Florida Grand Opera**, **Miami City Ballet**, and **New World Symphony**, as well as premier venues for a wide array of local, national, and international performances, ranging from Broadway musicals and visiting classical artists to world and urban music, Latin concerts, and popular entertainment from many cultures. The **Studio**

Theater, a flexible black-box space designed for up to 200 seats, will host intimate performances of contemporary theater, dance, music, cabaret, and other entertainment. The **Peacock Education Center** will act as a catalyst for arts education and enrichment programs for children and adults. Finally, the **Plaza for the Arts** will be a magnificent setting for outdoor entertainment, social celebrations, and informal community gatherings.

Designed by world-renowned architect Cesar Pelli, it is the focal point of a planned Arts, Media, and Entertainment District in mid-Miami. The complex is wrapped in limestone, slate, decorative stone, stainless steel, glass curtain walls, and tropical landscaping, and was completed in mid-2006. For more information, check out their website at www.pacfmiami.org.

CINEMAS

In addition to the annual Miami Film Festival in February and other, smaller film events, Miami has nearly as many multiplex cinemas as it does palm trees. And for good reason. When it rains in Miami, what else is there to do besides go to the movies, a museum, or the mall? But if 40 screens of *Jurassic Park III* aren't your idea of a day at the movies, consider the following artsy theaters, known for showing lots of subtitled, foreign films as well as those that get bumped off the big screen by the *Jurassic Parks* of the celluloid world.

Bill Cosford Cinema, at the University of Miami, is located on the second floor of the memorial building off Campo Sano Avenue (© **305/284-4861**). This well-endowed little theater was recently revamped and boasts high-tech projectors, air-conditioning, and a new decor. It sponsors independent films as well as lectures by visiting filmmakers and movie stars. Andy Garcia and Antonio Banderas are a few of the big names this theater has attracted. It also hosts the African American Film Festival, a Student Film Festival, and collaborations with the Fort Lauderdale Festival (a very small film festival). Admission is $6; seniors pay $3.

Miami Beach Cinematheque, 508 Española Way (© **305/673-4567**; www.mb cinema.com), is the kind of place where people who call movies "films" like to hang out, with comfy couches and very arty, foreign, domestic, and classic flicks. Admission ranges from $8 to $10.

6

The Keys & the Dry Tortugas

The drive from Miami to the Keys is a slow descent into an unusual but breathtaking American ecosystem: On either side of you, for miles ahead, lies nothing but emerald waters. (On weekends, however, you will also see plenty of traffic.) Strung out across the Atlantic Ocean like loose strands of cultured pearls, more than 400 islands make up this 150-mile-long necklace.

Despite the usually calm landscape, these rocky islands can be treacherous, as tropical storms, hurricanes, and tornadoes are always possibilities. The exposed coast poses dangers to those on land as well as at sea.

When Spanish explorers Juan Ponce de León and Antonio de Herrera sailed amid these craggy, dangerous rocks in 1513, they and their men dubbed the string of islands Los Martires (The Martyrs) because they thought the rocks looked like men suffering in the surf. It wasn't until the early 1800s that rugged and ambitious pioneers, who amassed great wealth by salvaging cargo from ships sunk nearby, settled the larger islands (legend has it that these shipwrecks were sometimes caused by "wreckers," who removed navigational markers from the shallows to lure unwitting captains aground). At the height of the salvaging mania (in the 1830s), Key West boasted the highest per-capita income in the country.

However, wars, fires, hurricanes, mosquitoes, and the Depression took their toll on these resilient islands in the early part of the 20th century, causing wild swings between fortune and poverty. In 1938, the spectacular Overseas Highway (U.S. 1) was finally completed atop the ruins of Henry Flagler's railroad (which was destroyed by a hurricane in 1935, leaving only bits and pieces still found today), opening the region to tourists, who had never before been able to drive to this sea-bound destination. These days, the highway connects more than 30 of the populated islands in the Keys. The hundreds of small, undeveloped islands that surround these "mainline" keys are known locally as the "backcountry" and are home to dozens of exotic animals and plants. Therein lie some of the most renowned outdoor sporting opportunities, from bonefishing to spear fishing and—at appropriate times of the year—diving for lobsters and stone crab. To get to the backcountry, you must take to the water—a vital part of any trip to the Keys. Whether you fish, snorkel, dive, or cruise, include some time on a boat in your itinerary; otherwise, you haven't truly seen the Keys.

Of course, people go to the Keys for the peaceful waters and the year-round warmth, but the sea and the teeming life beneath and around it are the main attractions here: Countless species of brilliantly colored fish can be found swimming above the ocean's floor, and you'll discover a stunning abundance of tropical and exotic plants, birds, and reptiles.

The warm, shallow waters (deeper and rougher on the eastern/Atlantic side of the Keys) nurture living coral that supports a

---

> (*Tips*　**Don't Be Fooled**
>
> Avoid the many "tourist information centers" that dot the main highway. Most are private companies hired to lure visitors to specific lodgings or outfitters (anything that says FREE DISNEY TICKETS or something like that is probably a scam or timeshare racket). You're better off sticking with the official, not-for-profit centers (the legit ones usually don't advertise on the turnpike) that are extremely well located and staffed.

---

complex, delicate ecosystem of plants and animals—sponges, anemones, jellyfish, crabs, rays, sharks, turtles, snails, lobsters, and thousands of types of fish. This vibrant underwater habitat thrives on one of the only living tropical reefs on the entire North American continent. As a result, anglers, divers, snorkelers, and watersports enthusiasts of all kinds come to explore.

Heavy traffic has taken its toll on this fragile ecoscape, but conservation efforts are underway (traffic laws are strictly enforced on Deer Key, for example, due to deer crossings that have been contained, thanks to newly installed fences). In fact, environmental efforts in the Keys exceed those in many other high-traffic visitor destinations.

Although the atmosphere throughout the Keys is that of a laid-back beach town, don't expect many impressive beaches here, especially after the damaging effects of recent hurricane seasons. Beaches are mostly found in a few private resorts, though there are some small, sandy strips in John Pennekamp Coral Reef State Park, Bahia Honda State Park, and Key West. One great exception is Sombrero Beach, in Marathon (p. 188), which is well maintained by Monroe County and is larger and considerably nicer than other beaches in the Keys. Sombrero Beach features a beachfront park, picnic facilities, a playground, and a protected cove for children.

The Keys are divided into three sections, both geographically and in this chapter. The Upper and Middle Keys are closest to the Florida mainland, so they are popular with weekend warriors who come by boat or car to fish or relax in towns like Key Largo, Islamorada, and Marathon. Farther on, just beyond the impressive Seven-mile Bridge (which actually measures 6½ miles), are the Lower Keys, a small, unspoiled swath of islands teeming with wildlife. Here, in the protected regions of the Lower Keys, is where you're most likely to catch sight of the area's many endangered animals—with patience, you may spot the rare eagle, egret, or Key deer. You should also keep an eye out for alligators, turtles, rabbits, and a huge variety of birds.

Key West, the most renowned—and last—island in the Lower Keys, is literally at the end of the road. The southernmost point in the continental United States (made famous by Ernest Hemingway), this tiny island is the most popular destination in the Florida Keys, overrun with cruise-ship passengers and day-trippers, as well as franchises and T-shirt shops. More than 1.6 million visitors pass through it each year. Still, this "Conch Republic" has a tightly knit community of permanent residents who cling fiercely to their live-and-let-live attitude—an atmosphere that has made Key West famously popular with painters, writers, and free spirits.

The last section in this chapter is devoted to the Dry Tortugas, a national park located 68 nautical miles from Key West.

The Florida Keys

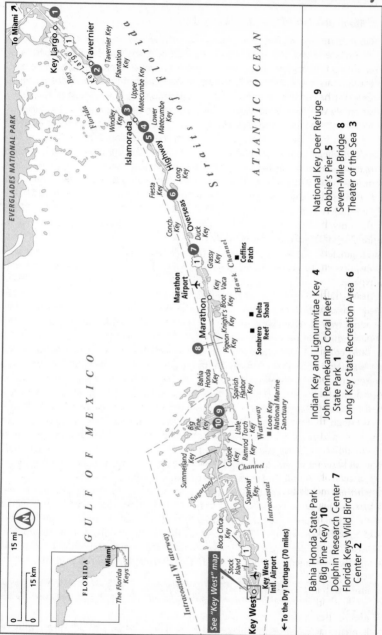

Bahia Honda State Park
(Big Pine Key) **10**
Dolphin Research Center **7**
Florida Keys Wild Bird
Center **2**

Indian Key and Lignumvitae Key **4**
John Pennekamp Coral Reef
State Park **1**
Long Key State Recreation Area **6**

National Key Deer Refuge **9**
Robbie's Pier **5**
Seven-Mile Bridge **8**
Theater of the Sea **3**

⌒Moments **No Place Like Card Sound**

On its own, there's not much to the waterfront shack that is **Alabama Jack's,** 5800 Card Sound Rd., Card Sound (ⓒ **305/248-8741**). The bar serves beer and wine only, and the restaurant specializes in delicious, albeit greasy, bar fare. But this quintessential Old Floridian dive, located in a historic fishing village called Card Sound between Homestead and Key Largo, is a colorful must on the drive south, especially on Sunday, when bikers mix with barflies, anglers, line dancers, and Southern belles who look as if they just got off the *Hee Haw* set in all their fabulous frills. Live country music resurrects the legendary Johnny Cash and Co. Pull up a bar stool, order a cold one, and take in the sights—in the bay and at the bar. The views of the mangroves are spectacular. To get here, pick up Card Sound Road (the old Rte. 1) a few miles after you pass Homestead, heading toward Key Largo. Alabama Jack's is on the right side and can't be missed.

EXPLORING THE KEYS BY CAR

After you have gotten off the Florida Turnpike and landed on U.S. 1, which is also known as the Overseas Highway (see "Getting There" under "Essentials," below), you'll have no trouble negotiating these narrow islands, since only one main road connects the Keys. The scenic, lazy drive from Miami can be very enjoyable if you have the patience to linger and explore the diverse towns and islands along the way. If you have the time, I recommend allowing at least 2 days to work your way down to Key West, and 3 or more days once there.

Most of U.S. 1 is a narrow two-lane highway, with some wider passing zones along the way. The speed limit is usually 55 mph (35–45 mph on Big Pine Key and in some commercial areas). Despite the protests of island residents, there has been talk of expanding the highway, but plans have not been finalized. Even on the narrow road, you can usually get from downtown Miami to Key Largo in just over an hour. If you're determined to drive straight through to Key West, allow at least 3½ hours. Weekend travel is another matter entirely: When the roads are jammed with travelers from the mainland, the trip can take upward of 5 to 6 hours (when there's an accident, traffic is at an absolute standstill). If at all possible, I strongly urge you to avoid driving anywhere in the Keys on Friday afternoon or Sunday evening.

To find an address in the Keys, don't bother looking for building numbers; most addresses (except in Key West and parts of Marathon) are delineated by mile markers (MM), small green signs on the roadside that announce the distance from Key West. The markers start at no. 127, just south of the Florida mainland. The zero marker is in Key West, at the corner of Whitehead and Fleming streets. Addresses in this chapter are accompanied by a mile marker (MM) designation when appropriate.

---

1 The Upper & Middle Keys: Key Largo ★★ to Marathon ★

58 miles SW of Miami

The Upper Keys are a popular year-round refuge for South Floridians, who take advantage of the islands' proximity to the mainland. This is the fishing and diving capital of America, and the swarms of outfitters and billboards never let you forget it.

Key Largo, once called Rock Harbor but renamed to capitalize on the success of the 1948 Humphrey Bogart film (which wasn't actually filmed here), is the largest key and is more developed than its neighbors to the south. Dozens of chain hotels, restaurants, and tourist information centers service the water enthusiasts who come to explore the nation's first underwater state park, **John Pennekamp Coral Reef State Park,** and its adjacent marine sanctuary. **Islamorada,** the unofficial capital of the Upper Keys, offers the area's best atmosphere, food, fishing, entertainment, and lodging. It's an unofficial "party capital" for mainlanders seeking a quick tropical excursion. Here (Islamorada is actually composed of four islands) nature lovers can enjoy walking trails, historic explorations, and big-purse fishing tournaments. For a more tranquil, less party-hearty Keys experience, all other keys besides Key West and Islamorada are better choices. **Marathon,** smack in the middle of the Florida Keys, is known as the heart of the Keys and is one of the most populated. It is part fishing village, part tourist center, and part nature preserve. This area's highly developed infrastructure includes resort hotels, a commercial airport, and a highway that expands to four lanes.

ESSENTIALS

GETTING THERE   From Miami International Airport (there is also an airport in Marathon), take Le Jeune Road (NW 42nd Ave.) to Route 836 West. Follow signs to the Florida Turnpike South, about 7 miles. The turnpike extension connects with U.S. 1 in Florida City. Continue south on U.S. 1. For a scenic option, take Card Sound Road south of Florida City, a backcountry drive that reconnects with U.S. 1 in upper Key Largo. The view from Card Sound Bridge is spectacular and well worth the $1 toll.

If you're coming from Florida's west coast, take Alligator Alley to the Miami exit and then turn south onto the turnpike extension. The turnpike ends in Florida City, at which time you will be dumped directly onto the two-lane U.S. 1, which leads to the Keys. Have plenty of quarters (at least $10 worth, round-trip) for the tolls.

The newly inaugurated **TransFloridianStarCraft Vehicle** (© **954/523-0859**) transports up to 14 people in a 26-foot luxury car that features reclining leather seats, plenty of legroom, wireless Internet service, in-seat power ports for electronic devices, personal headphone jacks, multichannel audio entertainment, overhead DVD monitors, and service by on-board attendants. Transportation from Miami, Fort Lauderdale, or Orlando to and from the Florida Keys ranges from $500 to $850.

Greyhound (© **800/231-2222;** www.greyhound.com) has three buses leaving Miami for Key West every day, with stops in Key Largo, Tavenier, Islamorada, Marathon, Big Pine Key, Cudjoe Key, Sugarloaf, and Big Coppit on the way south. Prices range from $13 to $36 one-way and $26 to $67 round-trip; the trip takes from 1 hour and 40 minutes to 4 hours and 40 minutes, depending on how far south you're going. Seats fill quickly in season, so come early. It's first come, first served.

Once you've arrived in the Keys, pilot **Dan Baker** (© **305/731-0000**) offers 18- to 20-minute helicopter tours of the Middle Keys and Marathon areas, departing from Florida Keys Marathon Airport, MM 52.2 bayside. Up to four passengers can be accommodated on each tour, depending on weight. Cost is $75 per person for four, $100 per person for three, and $150 per person for two.

VISITOR INFORMATION   Make sure you get your information from an official not-for-profit center. The **Key Largo Chamber of Commerce,** U.S. 1 at MM 106, Key Largo, FL 33037 (© **800/822-1088** or 305/451-1414; fax 305/451-4726; www. keylargo.org), runs an excellent facility, with free direct-dial phones and plenty of brochures. Headquartered in a handsome clapboard house, the chamber operates as an information clearinghouse for all of the Keys and is open daily from 9am to 6pm.

The **Islamorada Chamber of Commerce,** housed in a little red caboose, U.S. 1 at MM 82.5, P.O. Box 915, Islamorada, FL 33036 (© **800/322-5397** or 305/664-4503; fax 305/664-4289; www.islamoradachamber.com), offers maps and literature on the Upper Keys.

You can't miss the big blue visitor center at MM 53.5, **Greater Marathon Chamber of Commerce,** 12222 Overseas Hwy., Marathon, FL 33050 (© **800/262-7284** or 305/743-5417; fax 305/289-0183; www.floridakeysmarathon.com). Here you can receive free information on local events, festivals, attractions, dining, and lodging.

OUTDOOR SIGHTS & ACTIVITIES

Anne's Beach (MM 73.5, on Lower Matecumbe Key, at the southwest end of Islamorada) is really more picnic spot than full-fledged beach, but die-hard tanners still congregate on this lovely but tiny strip of coarse sand that was damaged beyond recognition during the series of storms in 1998. The place has been spruced up a bit, but the public bathrooms there are rancid and need some attention.

A better choice for real beaching is **Sombrero Beach** 𝒦𝒦, in Marathon at the end of Sombrero Beach Road (near MM 50). This wide swath of uncluttered beachfront actually benefited from Hurricane George in 1998, with generous deposits of extra sand and a face-lift courtesy of the Monroe County Tourist Development Council. More than 90 feet of sand is dotted with palms, Australian pines, and royal poincianas, as well as with grills, clean restrooms, and Tiki huts for relaxing in the shade. It's also a popular nesting spot for turtles that lay their eggs at night.

If you're interested in seeing the Keys in their natural, pre–modern development state, you must venture off the highway and take to the water. Two backcountry islands that offer a glimpse of the "real" Keys are **Indian Key** and **Lignumvitae Key** 𝒦𝒦𝒦. Visitors come here to relax and enjoy the islands' colorful birds and lush hammocks (elevated pieces of land above a marsh).

Named for the lignum vitae ("wood of life") trees found there, Lignumvitae Key supports a virgin tropical forest, the kind that once thrived on most of the Upper Keys. Over the years, human settlers imported "exotic" plants and animals to the Keys, irrevocably changing the botanical makeup of many backcountry islands and threatening much of the indigenous wildlife. Over the past 25 years, however, the Florida Department of Natural Resources has successfully removed most of the exotic vegetation from this key, leaving the 280-acre site much as it existed in the 18th century. The island also holds the Matheson House, a historic structure built in 1919 that has survived numerous hurricanes. You can go inside, but it's is interesting only if you appreciate the coral rock of which the house is made. It's now a museum dedicated to the history, nature, and topography of the area. More interesting are the Botanical Gardens, which surround the house and are a state preserve. Lignumvitae Key has a visitor center at MM 88.5 (© **305/664-2540**).

Indian Key, a much smaller island on the Atlantic side of Islamorada, was occupied by Native Americans for thousands of years before European settlers arrived. The 10-acre historic site was also the original seat of Dade County before the Civil War. Interestingly, from an archaeological standpoint, you can see the ruins of the previous settlement and tour the lush grounds on well-marked trails (off Indian Key Fill, Overseas Hwy., MM 79). For information on Indian Key, call the Florida Park Service (© **305/664-4815**) or check out www.abfla.com/parks/indiankey/indiankey.html.

If you want to see both islands, plan to spend at least half a day. You can rent your own powerboat from **Robbie's Rent-A-Boat,** U.S. 1 at MM 77.5 (on the bay side), on Islamorada. It's then a $1 admission fee to each island, which includes an informative hour-long guided tour by park rangers. This is a good option if you're a confident boater. I also recommend Robbie's **ferry service.** A visit to one island costs $15 for adults and $10 for kids 12 and under, which includes the $1 park admission; trips to both islands cost $25 per person. (If you have time for only one island, make it Lignumvitae.) The ferry is a more economical, easier way to enjoy the beauty of the islands when you aren't negotiating the shallow reefs along the way. The runabouts, which carry up to six people, depart from Robbie's Pier (p. 191) Thursday through Monday at 9am and 1pm for Indian Key, and at 10am and 2pm for Lignumvitae Key. In high season, you may need to book 2 days before departure. Call © **305/664-4815** for information from the park service, or © **305/664-9814** for Robbie's.

Crane Point Hammock ☆☆ *Finds Kids*   Crane Point Hammock is a little-known but worthwhile stop, especially for those interested in the rich botanical and archaeological history of the Keys. This privately owned 64-acre nature area is considered one of the most important historic sites in the Keys. It contains what is probably the last virgin thatch palm hammock in North America, as well as a rainforest exhibit and an archaeological site with prehistoric Indian and Bahamian artifacts.

Also headquarters for the Florida Keys Land and Sea Trust, the hammock's impressive nature museum has simple, informative displays of the Keys' wildlife, including a walk-through replica of a coral-reef cave and life-size dioramas with tropical birds and Key deer. Kids can participate in art projects, see 6-foot-long iguanas, climb through a scaled-down pirate ship, and touch a variety of indigenous aquatic and landlubbing creatures.

5550 Overseas Hwy. (MM 50), Marathon. © 305/743-9100. www.cranepoint.org. Admission $7.50 adults, $6 seniors over 64, $4 students, free for children under 6. Mon–Sat 9am–5pm; Sun noon–5pm.

Pigeon Key ☆☆   At the curve of the old bridge on Pigeon Key is an intriguing historic site that has been under renovation since late 1993. This 5-acre island was once the camp for the crew that built the old railway in the early 20th century, and later served as housing for the bridge builders. From here, the vista includes the vestiges of Henry Flagler's old Seven-mile Bridge and the one on which traffic presently soars, as well as many old wooden cottages and a truly tranquil stretch of lush foliage and sea. If you miss the shuttle tour from the Pigeon Key visitor center or would rather walk or bike to the site, it's about 2½ miles. Either way, you may want to bring a picnic to enjoy after a brief self-guided walking tour of the Key and museum visit to what has become an homage to Flagler's railroad, featuring artifacts and photographs of the old bridge. An informative 28-minute video of the island's history is offered every hour starting at 10am. Parking is available at the Knight's Key end of the bridge, at MM 48, or at the visitor center at MM 47, on the ocean side.

East end of the Seven-mile Bridge near MM 47, Marathon. © 305/743-5999. Admission $8.50 adults, $5 children under 13. Prices include shuttle transportation from the visitor center. Daily 10am–3pm; shuttle tours run hourly 10am–4pm.

Seven-mile Bridge ☆☆☆   A stop at the Seven-mile Bridge is a rewarding and relaxing break on the drive south. Built alongside the ruins of oil magnate Henry Flagler's incredible Overseas Railroad, the "new" bridge (between MMs 40 and 47) is considered an architectural feat. The apex of the wide-arched span, completed in 1985

Fun Fact **Bridge Mix**

The Seven-mile Bridge is the longest fragmented (unconnected pieces) bridge in the world. Completed in 1985, it was constructed parallel to the original bridge, part of Henry Flagler's Florida East Coast Railroad, which served as the original link to the Lower Keys. Some people may recognize the remnants of the old bridge from the Arnold Schwarzenegger movie *True Lies*. Others fearfully contemplate a wrong turn leading them to the old bridge instead of the new one. Not to worry: The old bridge is closed to cars and has been transformed into the world's longest fishing pier.

---

at a cost of more than $45 million, is the highest point in the Keys. The new bridge and its now-defunct neighbor provide excellent vantage points from which to view the stunning waters of the Keys. In the daytime, you may want to walk, jog, or bike along the scenic 4-mile stretch of old bridge. Or you may join local anglers, who catch barracuda, yellowtail, and dolphin (the fish, not the mammal) on what is known as "the longest fishing pier in the world." Parking is available on both sides of the bridge.

Between MMs 40 and 47 on U.S. 1. ✆ **305/289-0025.**

VISITING WITH THE ANIMALS

Dolphin Research Center ✹✹✹ *Kids*   If you've always wanted to touch, swim, or play with dolphins, this is the place to do it. Of the three such centers in the continental United States (all located in the Keys), the Dolphin Research Center is the most organized and informative. Although some people argue that training dolphins is cruel and selfish, this is one of the most respected of the institutions that study and protect the mammals. Knowledgeable trainers at the center will also tell you that the dolphins need stimulation and enjoy human contact. They certainly seem to. They nuzzle and seem to smile and kiss the lucky few who get to swim with them in the daily program. The "family" of 15 dolphins swims in a 90,000-square-foot natural saltwater pool carved out of the shoreline.

If you can't get into the swim program, you can still watch the frequent shows, sign up for a class in hand signals, or feed the dolphins from docks. Because the Dolphin Encounter swimming program is the most popular, reservations must be made at least a month in advance. The cost is $155 per person. If you're not brave enough to swim with the dolphins or if you have a child under 12 (not permitted to swim with dolphins), try the Dolphin Splash program, in which participants stand on an elevated platform from which they can "meet and greet" the critters. A height requirement of 44 inches is enforced, and an adult must hold up children under the required height. Cost for this program is $100 per person (free for children under 3).

Note: Swimming with dolphins has both its critics and its supporters. You may want to visit the Whale and Dolphin Conservation Society's website at www.wdcs.org. For more information about responsible travel in general, check out www.treadlightly. org and www.ecotourism.org.

U.S. 1 at MM 59 (on the bay side), Marathon. ✆ **305/289-1121.** www.dolphins.org. Admission $20 adults, $17 seniors, $14 children 4–12. Daily 9am–4pm. Educational walking tours 5 times daily: 10am, 11am, 12:30pm, 2pm, and 3:30pm.

Florida Keys Wild Bird Center ⍟   Wander through lush canopies of mangroves on wooden walkways to see some of the Keys' most famous residents—the large variety of native birds, including broad-wing hawks, great blue and white herons, roseate spoonbills, cattle egrets, and pelicans. This not-for-profit center operates as a hospital for the many birds that have been injured by accident or disease. In 2002, the World Parrot Mission was established here, focusing on caring for parrots and educating the public about the birds. Visit at feeding time, usually about 3:30pm, when you can watch the dedicated staff feed the hundreds of hungry birds.

U.S. 1 at MM 93.6 (bay side), Tavernier. © 305/852-4486. www.fkwbc.org. Donations suggested. Daily 8:30am–6pm.

Robbie's Pier ⍟⍟⍟ *(Value)*   One of the best and definitely one of the cheapest attractions in the Upper Keys is the famed Robbie's Pier. Here the fierce steely tarpons, a prized catch for backcountry anglers, have been gathering for the past 20 years. You may recognize these prehistoric-looking giants that grow up to 200 pounds; many are displayed as trophies and mounted on local restaurant walls. To see them live, head to Robbie's Pier, where tens and sometimes hundreds of these behemoths circle the shallow waters waiting for you to feed them. Robbie's Pier also offers ranger-led boat tours and guided kayak tours to Indian Key, where you can go snorkeling or just bask in the glory of your surroundings.

U.S. 1 at MM 77.5, Islamorada. © 305/664-9814. Admission $1. Bucket of fish $2. Daily 8am–5pm. Look for the HUNGRY TARPON restaurant sign on the right after the Indian Key channel.

Theater of the Sea ⍟ *(Kids)*   Established in 1946, the Theater of the Sea is one of the world's oldest marine zoos. Recently refurbished, the park's dolphin and sea-lion shows are entertaining and informative, especially for children. If you want to swim with dolphins and you haven't booked well in advance, you may be able to get into this place with just a few hours' notice, as opposed to the more rigid Dolphin Research Center in Marathon (see above). While the Dolphin Research Center is a legitimate, scientific establishment, this is more theme-parky attraction. That's not to say the dolphins are mistreated, but it's not as educational and professional as the Dolphin Research Center. Theater of the Sea also permits you to swim with sea lions and stingrays. (Children under 5 cannot participate.) There are twice-daily 4-hour adventure and snorkel cruises, which cost $65 for adults and $40 for children 3 to 12, in which you can learn about the history and ecology of the marine environment.

U.S. 1 at MM 84.5, Islamorada. © 305/664-2431. www.theaterofthesea.com. Admission $24 adults, $16 children 3–12. Dolphin swim $150; sea-lion swim $100; stingray swim $50. Reservations are a must. Daily 10am–5pm (ticket office closes at 4pm).

TWO EXCEPTIONAL STATE PARKS

One of the best places to discover the diverse ecosystem of the Upper Keys is its most famous park, **John Pennekamp Coral Reef State Park** ⍟⍟⍟, located on U.S. 1 at MM 102.5, in Key Largo (© 305/451-1202; www.pennekamppark.com). Named for a former *Miami Herald* editor and conservationist, the 188-square-mile park is the nation's first undersea preserve: It's a sanctuary for part of the only living coral reef in the continental United States. The original plans for Everglades National Park included this part of the reef within its boundaries, but opposition from local homeowners made its inclusion politically impossible.

Because the water is extremely shallow, the 40 species of coral and more than 650 species of fish here are accessible to divers, snorkelers, and glass-bottomed-boat passengers. To experience this park, visitors must get in the water—you can't see the reef from the shore. Your first stop should be the visitor center, which features a mammoth 30,000-gallon saltwater aquarium that re-creates a reef ecosystem. At the adjacent dive shop, you can rent snorkeling and diving equipment and join one of the boat trips that depart for the reef throughout the day. Visitors can also rent motorboats, sailboats, windsurfers, and canoes. The 2-hour glass-bottomed-boat tour is the best way to see the coral reefs if you don't want to get wet. Watch for the lobsters and other sea life residing in the fairly shallow ridge walls beneath the coastal waters. ***Remember:*** These are protected waters, so you can't remove anything from them.

Canoeing around the park's narrow mangrove channels and tidal creeks is also popular. You can go on your own in a rented canoe or, in winter, sign up for a tour led by a local naturalist. Hikers have two short trails from which to choose: a boardwalk through the mangroves, and a dirt trail through a tropical hardwood hammock. Ranger-led walks are usually scheduled daily from the end of November to April. Call ✆ **305/451-1202** for schedule information and reservations.

Park admission is $3.50 per vehicle for one occupant; for two or more, it's $6 per vehicle, plus 50¢ per passenger. Pedestrians and bicyclists pay $1.50 each. On busy weekends, there's often a line of cars waiting to get into the park. On your way in, ask the ranger for a map. Glass-bottomed-boat tours cost $22 for adults and $15 for children 11 and under. Snorkeling tours are $29 for adults and $24 for children 17 and under, including equipment. Sailing and snorkeling tours are $34 for adults and $29 for children 17 and under, including equipment. Canoes rent for $12 per hour. For experienced boaters only, four different sizes of reef boats (powerboats) rent for $135 to $210 for 4 hours, and $210 to $359 for a full day; call ✆ **305/451-6325** for information. A minimum $400 deposit (more, depending on boat size) is required. The park's boat-rental office is open daily from 8am to 5pm (last boat rented at 3pm); phone for tour and dive times. Reservations are recommended for all of the above. Also see below for more options on diving, fishing, and snorkeling these reefs.

Long Key State Recreation Area ♠♠♠, U.S. 1 at MM 68, Long Key (✆ **305/664-4815;** www.abfla.com/parks/longkey/longkey.html), is one of the best places in the Middle Keys for hiking, camping, snorkeling, and canoeing. This 965-acre site is situated atop the remains of an ancient coral reef. At the entrance gate, ask for a free flyer describing the local trails and wildlife.

Three nature trails can be explored via foot or canoe. The Golden Orb Trail is a 40-minute walk through mostly plants, the Layton Trail is a 15-minute walk along the bay, and the Long Key Canoe Trail glides along a shallow-water lagoon. The excellent 1½-mile canoe trail is short and sweet, allowing visitors to loop around the mangroves in about an hour. Long Key is also a great spot to stop for a picnic if you get hungry on your way to Key West. Campsites are available along the Atlantic Ocean. The swimming and saltwater fishing (license required) are top-notch here, as is the snorkeling, which is shallow and on the shoreline of the Atlantic. For novices, educational programs on the aforementioned are available, too.

Railroad builder Henry Flagler created the Long Key Fishing Club here in 1906, and the waters surrounding the park are still popular with game fishers. In summer, sea turtles lumber onto the protected coast to lay their eggs. Educational programs are available to view this phenomenon.

Admission is $4 per car, plus 50¢ per person (except for the Layton Trail, which is free). The recreation area is open daily from 8am to sunset. You can rent canoes at the

The 10 "Keymandments"

The Keys have always attracted independent spirits, from Ernest Hemingway and Tennessee Williams to Jimmy Buffett, Zane Grey, and local hero Mel Fisher. Writers, artists, and freethinkers have long drifted down here to escape.

Although you'll generally find a very laid-back and tolerant code of behavior in the Keys, some rules do exist. Be sure to respect the 10 "Keymandments" while you're here, or suffer the consequences.

- Don't anchor on a reef. (Reefs are alive.)
- Don't feed the animals. (They'll want to follow you home.)
- Don't trash our place (or we'll send Bubba to trash yours).
- Don't touch the coral. (After all, you don't even know them. Some pose a mild risk of injury to you as well.)
- Don't speed (especially on Big Pine Key, where deer reside and tar-and-feathering is still practiced).
- Don't catch more fish than you can eat. (Better yet, let them go. Some of them support schools.)
- Don't collect conch. (This species is protected by Bubba.)
- Don't disturb the bird nests. (They find it very annoying.)
- Don't damage the sea grass. (And don't even think about making a skirt out of it.)
- Don't drink and drive on land or sea. (There's nothing funny about it.)

trail head for about $5 per hour. The nearest place to rent snorkel equipment is **Holiday Isle,** 84001 U.S. 1, Islamorada (© **800/327-7070**).

WATERSPORTS FROM A TO Z

There are literally hundreds of outfitters in the Keys who will arrange all kinds of water activities, from cave dives to parasailing. If those recommended below are booked up or unreachable, ask the local chamber of commerce for a list of qualified members.

BOATING   In addition to the rental shops in the state parks, you'll find dozens of outfitters along U.S. 1 offering a range of runabouts and skiffs for boaters of any experience level. **Captain Pip's,** U.S. 1 at MM 47.5, Marathon (© **800/707-1692** or 305/743-4403; www.captainpips.com), charges $145 to $330 per day. Overnight accommodations are available and include a free boat rental: 2-night minimum $235 to $309; weekly $1,115 to $2,258. Rooms are Key West comfortable and charming, with ceiling fans, tile floors, and pine paneling. But the best part is that every room comes with an 18- to 21-foot boat for your use during your stay. **Robbie's Rent-a-Boat,** U.S. 1 at MM 77.5, Islamorada (© **305/664-9814**; www.robbies.com), rents 14- to 27-foot motorboats with engines ranging from 15 to 200 horsepower. Boat rentals are $70 to $205 for a half-day, and $90 to $295 for a full day.

CANOEING & KAYAKING   I can think of no better way to explore the uninhabited backcountry on the Gulf side of the Keys than by kayak or canoe, since you can reach places big boats just can't get to because of their large draft. Manatees will sometimes cuddle up to the boats, thinking them another friendly species.

Many area hotels rent kayaks and canoes to guests, as do the outfitters listed here. **Florida Bay Outfitters,** U.S. 1 at MM 104, Key Largo (© **305/451-3018**; www. kayakfloridakeys.com), rents canoes and sea kayaks for use in and around John Pennekamp Coral Reef State Park for $35 to $45 for a half-day, $50 to $60 for a full day. At **Coral Reef Park Co.,** U.S. 1 at MM 102.5, Key Largo (© **305/451-1621**), you can rent canoes and kayaks for $12 per hour; most canoes are sit-on-tops. **Florida Keys Kayak and Sail,** U.S. 1 at MM 75.5, Islamorada (© **305/664-4878**), at Robbie's Pier, offers backcountry tours, botanical-preserve tours of Lignumvitae Key, historic-site tours of Indian Key, and sunset tours through the mangrove tunnels and saltwater flats. Tour rates are from $39 to $49; rental rates range from $15 per hour to $45 per day for a single kayak, and $20 per hour to $60 per day for a double kayak. **Reflections Nature Tours** (© **305/872-4668**; www.floridakeyskayaktours.com) is a small mobile company that specializes in kayak tours through the Lower Keys. Guided kayak excursions cost $50 per person for a 3-hour tour, $33 per person for a 2-hour full-moon tour. The 3-hour custom tours start at $125 for one person and $195 for two people. All tours are by appointment only.

DIVING & SNORKELING Located just 6 miles off Key Largo is a U.S. Navy Landing Ship Dock, the latest artificial wreck site to hit the Keys—or, rather, to be submerged 130 feet *below* the Keys.

The **Florida Keys Dive Center,** U.S. 1 at MM 90.5, Tavernier (© **305/852-4599**; www.floridakeysdivectr.com), takes snorkelers and divers to the reefs of John Pennekamp Coral Reef State Park and environs every day. PADI (Professional Association of Diving Instructors) training courses are available for the uninitiated. While some people have complained that employees are rude here, others disagree; I suggest you decide for yourself. Tours leave at 8am and 12:30pm; the cost is $30 per person to snorkel (plus $9 rental fee for mask, snorkel, and fins), and $65 per person to dive (plus an extra $20 if you need to rent all the gear).

At **Hall's Dive Center & Career Institute,** U.S. 1 at MM 48.5, Marathon (© **305/743-5929**; www.hallsdiving.com), snorkelers and divers can dive at Looe Key, Sombrero Reef, Delta Shoal, Content Key, or Coffins Patch. Tours are scheduled daily at 9am and 1pm. You'll spend 1 hour at each of two sites per tour. If you mention this book, you'll get a special discounted rate ($5–$10 off) of $35 per person to snorkel (additional gear $11) and $45 per person to dive (tanks $8.50 each).

FISHING **Robbie's Partyboats & Charters,** U.S. 1 at MM 84.5, Islamorada (© **305/664-8070** or 305/664-4196), located at the south end of the Holiday Isle Resort's docks (p. 199), offers day and night deep-sea and reef-fishing trips aboard a 65-foot party boat. Big-game fishing charters are also available, and "splits" are arranged for solo fishers. Party-boat fishing costs $33 for a half-day morning tour ($3 for rod and reel rental); it's $15 extra if you want to go back out on an afternoon tour. Charters run about $400 for a half-day, $600 for a full day; splits begin at $65 per person. Phone for information and reservations.

Bud n' Mary's Fishing Marina, U.S. 1 at MM 79.8, Islamorada (© **800/742-7945** or 305/664-2461; www.budnmarys.com), one of the largest marinas between Miami and Key West, is packed with sailors offering backcountry fishing charters. This is the place to go if you want to stalk tarpon, bonefish, and snapper. If the seas

Acquaint Yourself

Fans of stone crabs can get further acquainted with the seasonal crustaceans on 3-hour tours offered by **Keys Fisheries,** aboard 40- to 50-foot vessels that leave from Marathon. The tour includes views of fishermen as they collect crabs from traps and process their claws. The $450 cost includes up to six passengers and up to 6 pounds of fresh claws iced for travel or prepared at a dockside restaurant. Stone-crab season is October 15 to May 15. Call © **305/743-4353** or check www.keysfisheries.com for more information.

are not too rough, deep-sea and coral fishing trips can also be arranged. Charters cost $500 to $550 for a half-day, $750 to $800 for a full day; splits begin at $125 per person.

The **Bounty Hunter,** 15th Street at Burdine's Marina, Marathon (© **305/743-2446**), offers full- and half-day outings. For 28 years, Capt. Brock Hook's huge sign has boasted, NO FISH, NO PAY: You're guaranteed to catch something, or your money back! Choose your prey from shark, barracuda, sailfish, or whatever else is running. Prices are $400 for a half-day, $500 for three-quarters of a day, and $600 for a full day. Rates are for groups of no more than six people.

WHERE TO STAY

U.S. 1 is lined with chain hotels in all price ranges. In the Upper Keys, the best moderately priced option is the **Key Largo Ramada,** off U.S. 1 at MM 100, Key Largo (© **800/THE-KEYS** or 305/451-3939), which has three pools and a casino boat, and is just 3 miles from John Pennekamp Coral Reef State Park. Another good Upper Keys option is **Days Inn Oceanfront Resort,** U.S. 1 at MM 82.5 (© **800/DAYS-INN** or 305/664-3681). In the Middle Keys, the **Wellesley Inn,** 13351 Overseas Hwy., MM 54 in Marathon (© **305/743-8550**), offers reasonably priced oceanside rooms.

Since the real beauty of the Keys lies mostly beyond the highways, there is no better way to see this area than by boat. So why not stay in a floating hotel? Especially if you're traveling with a group, houseboats can be economical. To rent a houseboat, call Ruth and Michael Sullivan at **Smilin' Island Houseboat Rentals,** MM 99.5, Key Largo (© **305/451-1930**). Rates are from $750 to $1,350 for 3 nights. Boats accommodate up to six people.

For land options, consider the recommendations below.

VERY EXPENSIVE

Cheeca Lodge & Spa, A RockResort ★★★ (Kids)   Relaxing Cheeca has been hosting celebrities, royalty, and politicians since its opening in 1949. Guests can now enjoy the luxury of the Cheeca's freshly renovated rooms. Note that some of the on-site accommodations have been converted to uber-expensive condos that are part of the new Cheeca Lodge and Club, a private club in which owners have the options of renting their units as hotel rooms. Each of the 199 units here offers all the amenities of units in a world-class resort—like flat-screen plasma TVs—in a very laid-back setting. You may not feel compelled to leave the sprawling grounds, but it's good to know that the hotel is conveniently situated near the best restaurants and nightlife. Located on 27 lush acres of beachfront property (the 1,100-ft. palm-lined beach is truly idyllic) with gorgeous beachfront bungalows that have private gardens and balconies, this rambling resort is known for its excellent sports facilities, including one of the only golf courses in the Upper Keys. All rooms are spacious, and many have balconies; the nicer ones overlook the ocean and have large marble bathrooms. Units by the golf course have showers, not tubs, and overlook man-made lagoons.

The Atlantic's Edge (p. 201) is one of the best restaurants in the Upper Keys. In addition to all the sporty amenities, Cheeca has the luxurious Avanyu Spa, with a state-of-the-art fitness studio. Children 6 to 12 can have their own customized vacation with Camp Cheeca's organized activities and events. The $39 daily resort fee may seem steep at first, but the value is insurmountable. It includes tennis, golf, fishing rods (bait extra), pool floats, beach cabanas, kayaks and paddleboats (subject to availability), valet parking, Internet access, spa exercise classes, in-room Starbucks coffee and bottled water, housekeeping gratuity, local calls, daily newspaper, and fax services.

U.S. 1 at MM 82 (P.O. Box 527), Islamorada, FL 33036. ℂ 866/591-ROCK or 305/664-4651. Fax 305/664-2893. www.rockresorts.com. 199 units. Winter $469–$599 deluxe double, $659–$1,428 deluxe suite; off season $249–$369 deluxe double, $359–$878 deluxe suite. AE, DC, DISC, MC, V. **Amenities:** 2 restaurants; 2 lounges (1 poolside); 2 outdoor heated pools; saltwater lagoon; 9-hole golf course; 6 lighted hard tennis courts; access to nearby health club; Jacuzzi; 5 hot tubs; watersports equipment rental; bike rental; children's nature programs; concierge; tour desk; car-rental desk; limited room service; in-room massage; babysitting; laundry services; dry cleaning; nature trails. *In room:* A/C, TV/DVD, CD player, dataport, kitchenette (in suites), minibar, coffeemaker, hair dryer, iron, robe.

Hawk's Cay Resort 🏖🏖🏖 *Kids*   Located on its own 60-acre island in the Middle Keys, this resort has a relaxed and casual atmosphere. If it's recreation you're looking for, Hawk's Cay is far superior to the more luxurious Cheeca Lodge. It offers an impressive array of activities—sailing, fishing, snorkeling, and water-skiing, to name a few—plus the unique opportunity to interact directly with dolphins in the resort's natural saltwater lagoon. (You'll need to reserve a spot well in advance for this.) Guest rooms are large and newly renovated, with island-style furniture and private balconies with ocean or tropical views. The large bathrooms are well appointed and have granite counters. There are also 295 hyperposh villas—each with full kitchen, washer/dryer, and living room with water views—modeled after the kitschy 1950s concept of the "boatel." The 7,000-square-foot Indies Spa offers stellar treatments and a blissful steam room that'll clear even the most stubborn of sinuses. In addition to a lagoon and several pools for families, the resort boasts a secluded pool for adults only. Organized children's activities, including special marine- and ecology-inspired programs, will keep your little ones busy while you relax.

61 Hawk's Cay Blvd. at MM 61, Duck Key, FL 33050. ℂ 888/814-9104 or 305/743-7000. Fax 305/743-5215. www. hawkscay.com. 177 rooms and suites, 295 2- and 3-bedroom villas. Winter $260–$410 double, $460–$1,300 suite, $450–$1,500 villa; off season $220–$340 double, $380–$1,200 suite, $390–$1,300 villa. Packages available. AE, DC, DISC, MC, V. **Amenities:** 4 restaurants; lounge; outdoor heated pool; adults-only private pool; nearby golf course (transportation available); 8 tennis courts (6 hard, 2 clay; 2 lighted); small exercise room; Jacuzzi; watersports equipment rental; bike rental; children's programs ($28–$35 per child); game room; concierge; limited room service; in-room massage. *In room:* A/C, TV/VCR, DVD (villas only), fridge, coffeemaker, hair dryer, iron.

Dol-fans Beware

Swimming with dolphins has both its critics and its supporters. You may want to visit the Whale and Dolphin Conservation Society's website at www.wdcs. org. For more information about responsible travel in general, check out www. treadlightly.org and www.ecotourism.org.

EXPENSIVE

Casa Morada ✦✦✦ (Finds)   The closest thing to a boutique hotel in the Florida Keys, Casa Morada is the brainchild of a trio of New York women with major experience in the hotel business—at Ian Schrager Hotels, of all places—but who were no longer in the mood to deal with brutal winters. This 16-suite property is tucked away off a sleepy street and radiates serenity and style in an area where serenity is aplenty but style elusive. Originally built in the 1950s, Casa Morada sits on 1.7 acres of prime bayfront land, which has been upgraded with gorgeous landscaping, a limestone grotto, a freshwater pool, and a waterside terrace for breakfast, lunch, and poolside beverage service. Each of the cool rooms features either a private garden or a terrace—request the one with the open-air Jacuzzi that faces the bay. While the decor is decidedly island, think St. Barts rather than, say, Gilligan's. Although the hotel doesn't have a restaurant, a complimentary breakfast is served daily, and if you order out from one of the area's excellent eateries, the hotel will re-plate the food on Casa Morada china. Because of the boutiquey nature of the place, expect a young crowd of hipsters. Free use of bikes, bocce, and board games, as well as arrangements for snorkeling, diving, and fishing, are available. Families with kids should avoid Casa Morada, since it's such an adults-oriented place and is quiet, with few distractions for the little ones.

136 Madeira Rd., Islamorada, FL 33036. ✆ 888/881-3030 or 305/664-0044. Fax 305/664-0674. www.casamorada. com. 16 units. Winter $289–$649; off season $229–$519. Rates include continental breakfast. AE, DISC, MC, V. From U.S. 1 S., at MM 82.2, turn right onto Madeira Rd. and continue to the end of the street. The hotel is on the right. **Amenities:** Freshwater pool; complimentary bike use; bocce ball; snorkeling; diving; fishing. *In room:* A/C, TV, DVD, CD player, minibar, hair dryer, safe.

Jules' Undersea Lodge ✦✦✦ (Finds)   Staying here is certainly an experience of a lifetime—if you're brave enough to take the plunge. Originally built as a research lab, this small underwater compartment, which rests on pillars on the ocean floor, now operates as a two-room hotel. As expensive as it is unusual, Jules' is most popular with diving honeymooners. To get inside, guests swim 21 feet under the structure and pop up into the unit through a 4×6-foot "moon pool" that gurgles soothingly all night long. The 30-foot-deep underwater suite consists of two separate bedrooms that share a common living area. Room service will deliver your meals, daily newspapers, and even a late-night pizza in waterproof containers, at no extra charge.

51 Shoreland Dr., Key Largo, FL 33037. ✆ 305/451-2353. Fax 305/451-4789. www.jul.com. 2 units. $295–$395 per person. Rates include breakfast and dinner, as well as all equipment and unlimited scuba diving in the lagoon for certified divers. Packages available. AE, DISC, MC, V. From U.S. 1 S., at MM 103.2, turn left onto Transylvania Ave., across from the Central Plaza shopping mall. **Amenities:** Entertainment center; dining area. *In room:* A/C, kitchenette.

The Moorings ✦✦✦ (Finds)   The Moorings is more like a secluded beach house than a hotel. You'll never see another soul on this 18-acre resort, a former coconut plantation, if you choose not to. There isn't even maid service unless you request it. The romantic whitewashed units, from cozy cottages to three-bedroom houses, are spacious and modestly decorated. Most have washers and dryers, and all have CD players and DVD players; ask when you book. The real reason to come to this resort is to relax on the 1,000-plus-foot beach (one of the only real beaches around). You'll also find a hard tennis court and a few kayaks and windsurfers, but no motorized water vehicles in the waters surrounding the hotel, making it completely tranquil. There's no room service or restaurant, but Morada Bay and Pierres across the street are excellent. This is a place for people who like each other a lot. Leave the kids at home unless they're extremely well behaved and not easily bored.

123 Beach Rd. near MM 81.5 on the ocean side, Islamorada, FL 33036. ℂ **305/664-4708.** Fax 305/664-4242. www.themooringsvillage.com. 18 cottages. Winter $275 small cottage, $425 1-bedroom house, $4,975–$8,875 weekly oceanfront house; off season $250 small cottage, $395 1-bedroom house, $3,000–$7,000 weekly oceanfront house. 2-night minimum for smaller cottages; 1-week minimum for larger cottages. MC, V. **Amenities:** Large outdoor heated pool; tennis court; watersports equipment rental. *In room:* A/C, TV, DVD, CD player, kitchen, coffeemaker, hair dryer, microwave.

MODERATE

Banana Bay Resort & Marina ✹✹ *Finds* It doesn't look like much from the sign-cluttered Overseas Highway, but once you enter the lush grounds of Banana Bay, you'll realize you're in one of the most bucolic and best-run properties in the Upper Keys. Built in the early 1950s as a place for fishermen to stay during extended fishing trips, the resort is a beachfront maze of two-story buildings hidden among banyans and palms. The rooms are moderately sized, and many have private balconies where you can enjoy your complimentary coffee and newspaper every morning. Recent additions include a recreational-activity area with horseshoe pits, a bocce court, picnic areas with barbecue grills, and a giant lawn chessboard. The kitschy restaurant serves three meals a day, indoors and poolside. The hotel also offers rentals of bikes, boats, WaveRunners, kayaks, day-sailing dinghies, and bait and tackle. Another surprising amenity is Pretty Joe Rock, the hotel's private island, which is available for long weekends and weekly rentals. This island has a Keys-style, two-bedroom, two-bathroom cottage that's ideal for romantic escapes. Banana Bay is family-friendly, but if you're looking for an adults-only resort, there's also a **Banana Bay Resort** at 2319 N. Roosevelt Blvd., in Key West (ℂ **305/296-6925**), that doesn't allow children.

U.S. 1 at MM 49.5, Marathon, FL 33050. ℂ **800/BANANA-1** or 305/743-3500. Fax 305/743-2670. www.bananabay. com. 60 units. Winter $135–$225 double; off season $95–$175 double. Rates include continental breakfast. 3- and 7-night honeymoon and wedding packages available. AE, DC, DISC, MC, V. **Amenities:** Restaurant; 3 bars; pool; tennis courts; health club; Jacuzzi; watersports equipment rental; self-service laundry, small beach and snorkeling area; charter fishing; sailing; diving. *In room:* A/C, TV, dataport, fridge, hair dryer, iron.

Conch Key Cottages ✹ *Finds* Here's your chance to play castaway in the Keys. Occupying its own private micro-island just off U.S. 1, Conch Key Cottages is a comfortable hideaway run by live-in owners Ron Wilson and Wayne Byrnes, who are constantly fixing and adding to their unique property. This is a place to get away from it all. The cottages offer solitude, with the exception of one or two interesting eateries. The units, which were built at different times over the past 40 years, overlook their own stretch of natural, but very small, private beach. They have screened-in porches, cozy bedrooms, bathrooms, hammocks, barbecue grills, and two-person kayaks. The two-bedroom cottages are the most spacious and are well designed, practically tailor-made for couples or families. On the other side of the pool is a handful of efficiency apartments that are similarly outfitted but enjoy no beach frontage.

Near U.S. 1 at MM 62.3, Marathon, FL 33050. ℂ **800/330-1577** or 305/289-1377. Fax 305/743-8207. www.conchkey cottages.com. 12 cottages. Dec 15–Sept 8 $110–$288 for up to 6 people; Sept 9–Dec 14 $74–$215 for up to 4 people. DISC, MC, V. **Amenities:** Pool; complimentary kayaks; laundry facilities. *In room:* A/C, TV, kitchen, coffeemaker, no phone.

Faro Blanco Marine Resort ✹ Spanning both sides of the Overseas Highway and located entirely on waterfront property, this huge, two-shore marina-and-hotel complex is undergoing a complete renovation and thus will remain closed into 2006. When it reopens, it will offer something for every taste. The free-standing camp-style cottages were the resort's least expensive accommodations. The houseboats were the best choice and value: Permanently tethered in a tranquil marina, these white rectangular boats look like floating mobile homes and feature four hotel rooms each, fully equipped kitchenettes, porches, and water, water everywhere. The condo units have three bedrooms, two bathrooms, and terraces. Finally, two unusual rental units, located in a lighthouse on the pier, have circular staircases, unusually shaped rooms and showers, and nautical decor—they're unique places to stay, but some guests might find them claustrophobic.

1996 Overseas Hwy., U.S. 1 at MM 48.5, Marathon, FL 33050. (C) 800/759-3276 or 305/743-9018. Fax 305/866-5235. www.faroblanco.com. 123 units, 31 houseboats with 4 units each. Winter $89–$150 cottage, $109–$200 houseboat, $185 lighthouse, $267–$327 condo; off season $79–$119 cottage, $99–$178 houseboat, $145 lighthouse, $215–$263 condo. AE, DISC, MC, V. **Amenities:** 4 restaurants; 2 lounges; Olympic-size pool; fully equipped dive shop; barbecue and picnic areas; playground. In room: A/C, TV.

Holiday Isle Resort

A huge complex encompassing five restaurants, several lounges, Tiki huts, a large marina, many shops, and four distinct (if not distinctive) hotels, the Holiday Isle is one of the biggest resorts in the Keys. It attracts a spring-break kind of crowd year-round, a crowd that tends not to care about the rooms themselves—and has no qualms cramming an entire fraternity into a single unit for budget reasons. The famous Tiki Bar claims to have invented the Rum Runner drink (151-proof rum, blackberry brandy, banana liqueur, grenadine, and lime juice), and there's no reason to doubt it. It's the Tiki Bar that brings the people, really. Hordes of partiers are attracted to the resort's nonstop merrymaking, live music, and beachfront bars. As a result, some of the accommodations can be noisy. Rooms tend to be bare-bones; despite the ocean views, they're pretty awful and need a good scrub-down—especially the units that lead to the filthy, sandy Tiki Bar. El Captain and Harbor Lights, two of the least expensive hotels on the property, are both austere and could use a thorough rehab. Howard Johnson, another Holiday Isle property, is a little farther from the action and a tad more civilized, in case you should have one too many drinks and can't drive farther to a nicer hotel. Some renovations to the on-site restaurants have been made, so hopefully that will spread to the rooms.

U.S. 1 at MM 84, Islamorada, FL 33036. (C) 800/327-7070 or 305/664-2321. Fax 305/664-2703. www.holidayisle.com. 178 units. Winter $135–$265 double, $295–$485 suite; off season $115–$199 double, $245–$415 suite. AE, DISC, MC, V. **Amenities:** 5 restaurants; 12 bars; 3 outdoor heated pools; kids' pool; Jacuzzi; watersports equipment rentals; kids' programs; laundry facilities. In room: A/C, TV, fridge, hair dryer.

Kona Kai Resort & Gallery 🐠🐠

Unique to the Upper Keys, this little haven is both casual and elegant, a romantic, adults-only waterfront property that is located right on Florida Bay—a choice location that offers a stunning sunset view overlooking Everglades National Park. Quaint rooms and suites dot the lush 2-acre property, which boasts a variety of native vegetation such as palms, bougainvillea, and ferns, plus an impressive collection of fruit-bearing trees like carambola, passion fruit, banana, Key lime, guava, and coconut, which you can sample. An orchid house has over 350 beautiful flowers. Lounge chairs, hammocks, a freshwater pool (heated in winter and cooled in summer), a Jacuzzi, and a private beach that's larger than the Marriott's are available for those who want to relax. For the more adventurous, the owners will organize excursions to the Everglades, the backcountry, or wherever you want to go. Kayaks, paddleboats, and tennis are included at no extra charge. All of the rooms are very private and simply furnished; bathroom amenities are fabulous, with lotions, soaps, and shampoos made from tropical fruits. Smoking is not permitted indoors. For meals, you'll need to visit a nearby restaurant—there are three within walking distance. A gallery featuring work by American and international painters, photographers, and sculptors doubles as the property's office and lobby. Even if you aren't staying here, stop in to see the art.

97802 Overseas Hwy. (U.S. 1 at MM 97.8), Key Largo, FL 33037. © 800/365-7829 or 305/852-7200. Fax 305/852-4629. www.konakairesort.com. 11 units. Winter $296–$331 double, $339–$962 1- to 2-bedroom suite; off season $189–$228 double, $236–$736 1- to 2-bedroom suite. AE, DISC, MC, V. Closed Sept. Children under 16 not permitted. **Amenities:** Heated pool; lighted tennis court; spa; Jacuzzi; watersports equipment; concierge; in-room massage and facials; Ping Pong on the beach; shuffleboard; boat dockage. *In room:* A/C, TV, DVD, DVD library, CD player with a selection of CDs by local recording artists, full kitchen (suites only), fridge, hair dryer, no phone.

Lime Tree Bay Resort Motel ⚜ The Lime Tree Bay Resort is the only place to stay in the tiny town of Layton (pop. 183). Midway between Islamorada and Marathon, the hotel is steps from Long Key State Recreation Area. It's situated on a very pretty piece of waterfront graced with hundreds of mature palm trees and lots of other tropical foliage. It prides itself on its promise of no hustle, no valets and, most amusingly, no bartenders in Hawaiian shirts! Motel rooms and efficiencies have tiny bathrooms with showers, but are clean and well maintained. The best deal is the two-bedroom bay-view cottage: A spacious living area with new furnishings leads to a large private deck where you can enjoy a view of the Gulf from your hammock. The full kitchen and two full bathrooms make it a comfortable space for up to six people. Fifteen efficiencies and suites have kitchenettes. Pretty cool in its own right is the Zane Grey Suite (named after the famous author and screenwriter, who lived right around the corner), a two-bedroom, one-bathroom unit with the best views and a second-story location with private stairs.

U.S. 1 at MM 68.5, Layton, Long Key, FL 33001. © 800/723-4519 or 305/664-4740. Fax 305/664-0750. www.limetreebayresort.com. 30 units. Winter $105–$159 double, $165–$345 suite, $155–$215 cottage; off season $79–$115 double, $125–$285 suite, $125–$200 cottage. AE, DC, DISC, MC, V. **Amenities:** Restaurant; small outdoor pool; tennis court; Jacuzzi; watersports equipment rental. *In room:* A/C, TV, dataport, kitchenette (in some units).

Pines and Palms ⚜⚜⚜ *Finds* Looking for a beachfront cottage or, better yet, an oceanfront villa, but don't want to spend your future child's college fund? This is the place. Cheery, cozy cottages; Atlantic views; and a private beachfront with hammocks and a pool give way to a relaxed, tropical paradise. Service is friendly and accommodating. All rooms and cottages have full kitchens and balconies, and are ideal for extended stays. Although there's no restaurant on site, the staff will be happy to bring a Weber barbecue to your patio so you can grill out by the beach. Because of its popularity, Pines and Palms usually has a 2-night minimum.

MM 80.4, oceanside Islamorada, FL 33036. © 800/624-0964 or 305/664-4343. www.pinesandpalms.com. 25 units. Year-round $99–$219 double; $129–$219 suite; $139–$459 cottage; $399–$549 villa. AE, MC, V. **Amenities:** Oceanfront heated freshwater pool; bikes and kayaks available for rent; laundry. *In room:* A/C, kitchen (most units), fridge, coffeemaker.

INEXPENSIVE

Ragged Edge Resort ⚜⚜ This small oceanfront property's Tahitian-style units are spread along more than half a dozen gorgeous, grassy waterfront acres. All are immaculately clean and comfortable, and most are outfitted with full kitchens and tasteful furnishings. There's no bar, restaurant, or staff to speak of, but the retreat's affable owner is happy to lend bicycles and offer advice on the area's offerings. A large dock attracts boaters and a variety of local and migratory birds. An outdoor heated fresh-water pool is a bonus for those months when the temperature gets a bit chilly.

243 Treasure Harbor Rd. (near MM 86.5), Islamorada, FL 33036. ✆ **800/436-2023** or 305/852-5389. www.ragged-edge.com. 11 units. Year-round $79–$139 double; $209 suite. AE, MC, V. **Amenities:** Outdoor pool; free use of bikes; laundry. *In room:* A/C, kitchen (most units), fridge, coffeemaker.

CAMPING

John Pennekamp Coral Reef State Park 🌟🌟 One of Florida's best parks (p. 191), Pennekamp offers 47 well-separated campsites, half of which are available by advance reservation. The tent sites are small but equipped with restrooms, hot water, and showers. Note that the local environment provides fertile breeding grounds for insects, particularly in late summer, so bring repellent. Two man-made beaches and a small lagoon nearby attract many large wading birds. Reservations are held until 5pm; the park must be notified of late arrival by phone on the check-in date. Pennekamp opens at 8am and closes around sundown.

U.S. 1 at MM 102.5 (P.O. Box 487), Key Largo, FL 33037. ✆ **305/451-1202.** www.pennekamppark.com. 47 camp-sites. Reservations can be made in advance by calling Reserve America (✆ 800/326-3521). $26 (with electricity) per site. Park entry $4 per vehicle (50¢ for each additional person). Yearly permits and passes available. AE, DISC, MC, V. No pets.

Long Key State Park 🌟 The Upper Keys' other main state park is more secluded than its northern neighbor—and more popular. All sites are located oceanside and sur-rounded by narrow rows of trees and nearby restroom facilities. Reserve well in advance, especially in winter.

U.S. 1 at MM 67.5 (P.O. Box 776), Long Key, FL 33001. ✆ **305/664-4815.** www.abfla.com/parks/longkey/longkey. html. 60 sites. $26 per site for 1–4 people; $3.25 per vehicle. AE, DISC, MC, V. No pets.

WHERE TO DINE

Although not known as a culinary hot spot (though always improving), the Upper and Middle Keys do offer some excellent restaurants, most of which specialize in seafood. Often visitors (especially those who fish) take advantage of accommodations that have kitchen facilities and cook their own meals. Some restaurants will even clean and cook your catch, for a fee.

VERY EXPENSIVE

Atlantic's Edge 🌟🌟🌟 SEAFOOD/REGIONAL Ask for a table by the oceanfront window to feel really privileged at this restaurant, the most elegant in the Keys. Although the service and food are generally first rate, don't get dressed up—sports coats for men are fine but not necessary. You can choose from an innovative menu that offers fresh fish, steak, chicken, and pastas. The crab cakes, made with stone crab when in season, are the very best in the Keys; served on a warm salad of baby greens with a mild sauce of red peppers, they're the stuff cravings are made of. Other excel-lent dishes include a Thai-spiced fresh baby snapper and the vegetarian angel-hair pasta with mushrooms, asparagus, and peppers in a rich broth. Service can sometimes be less than efficient but is always courteous and professional.

In the Cheeca Lodge, U.S. 1 at MM 82, Islamorada. ✆ **305/664-4651.** Reservations recommended. Main courses $20–$46. AE, DC, DISC, MC, V. Daily 6–10pm.

Kaiyo 🌟🌟🌟 JAPANESE/SUSHI This funky, colorful restaurant looks out of place in an area where most eateries are housed in shanty shacks, and its exquisite, modern sushi is a first for Islamorada—but the food is so good, people from all over South Florida plan trips around a meal at Kaiyo. The brainchild of chef Dawn Sieber, former executive chef at Cheeca Lodge, Kaiyo isn't your typical sushi restaurant, but rather one that fuses Florida's fine ingredients with some of the freshest raw fish this side of Tokyo. Signature sushi items such as the Spicy Volcano Conch roll and the Key Lime Lobster roll are outstanding, as are the farm-raised raw oysters and farmed baby-conch tempura. A hip, modern interior is an amusing contrast to the casually dressed, Key-ed up diners, and service here is of five-star caliber—something not typically found in the laid-back Keys. Before you say that you came to the Keys not for trendy sushi, but for fresh fish and conch fritters, do have a meal at Kaiyo. It *will* change the way you view Keys cuisine.

81701 Old Hwy., U.S. 1 at MM 82, Islamorada. (✆ **305/664-5556**. www.kaiyokeys.com Reservations recommended. Main courses $12–$20; sushi $4.50–$15. AE, DC, MC, V. Mon–Sat noon–10pm.

EXPENSIVE

Barracuda Grill ✦✦ SEAFOOD   Owned by Lance Hill and his wife, Jan, a former sous-chef at Little Palm Island (p. 206), this small, casual spot serves excellent seafood, steaks, and chops. Some favorites here are the Caicos gold conch and mangrove snapper and mango. Try the appetizer of Tipsy Olives, marinated in gin or vodka, to kick-start your meal. For fans of spicy food, go for the red-hot calamari. Decorated with barracuda-themed art, the restaurant also features a well-priced American wine list with lots of California vintages.

U.S. 1 at MM 49.5 (bay side), Marathon. (✆ **305/743-3314**. www.barracudagrill.com. Main courses $10–$26. AE, MC, V. Mon–Sat 6–10pm.

Marker 88 ✦✦✦ SEAFOOD/REGIONAL   An institution in the Upper Keys, Marker 88 has been pleasing locals and visitors since it opened in the 1970s. New chefs and owners have infused a new life into the place and the menu, which still utilizes fresh fruits, local ingredients, and fish caught in the Keys' waters. Among the menu highlights are the yellowtail Rangoon, sautéed and topped with black current gelee and cinnamon, and served with fresh tropical fruits; yellowtail Martinique, sautéed and topped with sweet basil, grilled bananas, and garlic butter. The waitresses, who are pleasant enough, require a bit of patience, but the food—not to mention the spectacular Gulf views—is worth it.

U.S. 1 at MM 88 (bay side), Islamorada. (✆ **305/852-9315**. Reservations suggested. Main courses $14–$33. AE, DC, DISC, MC, V. Tues–Sun 5–11pm. Closed Sept.

MODERATE

Lorelei Restaurant and Cabana Bar ✦ SEAFOOD/BAR FOOD   Don't resist the siren call of the enormous roadside mermaid—you won't be dashed onto the rocks. This big old fish house and bar, with excellent views of the bay, is a great place for a snack, a meal, or a beer. A good-value menu focuses mainly on seafood; in season, lobster is the way to go. Other fare includes the standard clam chowder, fried shrimp, and doughy conch fritters. Salads and soups are hearty and satisfying. For those tired of fish, the menu offers a few beef options. The outside bar has live music every evening, and you can order snacks and light meals from a limited menu.

U.S. 1 at MM 82, Islamorada. (✆ **305/664-4656**. Reservations not usually required. Main courses $12–$24. AE, DC, DISC, MC, V. Daily 7am–10:30pm. Outside bar serves breakfast 7–11am; lunch/appetizer menu 11am–9pm. Bar closes at midnight.

INEXPENSIVE

Calypso's Seafood Grill ⊛ SEAFOOD   The awning still bears the name of the former restaurant, Demar's, but the food here is all that of Todd Lollis, an inspired young chef who looks like he might be more comfortable at a Grateful Dead concert than in a kitchen—but who turns out inventive seafood dishes in a casual and rustic waterside setting. If it's available, try the butter-pecan sauce over whatever fish is freshest. Don't miss the white-wine sangria, full of tangy oranges and limes, and served in a children's beach bucket. The prices are surprisingly reasonable, but the service may be a little more laid back than you're used to.

1 Seagate Blvd. (near MM 99.5), Key Largo. ℂ **305/451-0600.** Main courses $9–$18. MC, V. Wed–Mon 11:30am–10pm (Fri–Sat until 11pm). From the south, turn right at the blinking yellow lights near MM 99.5 to Ocean Bay Dr. and then turn right. Look for the blue vinyl-sided building on the left.

Islamorada Fish Company ⊛⊛ SEAFOOD   Pick up a cooler of stone crab claws in season (mid-Oct to Apr), or try the great fried-fish sandwiches. A few hundred yards up the road (at MM 81.6) is Islamorada Fish Company Restaurant & Bakery, the newer establishment, which looks like an average diner but has fantastic seafood, pastas, and breakfasts. Locals gather here for politics and gossip as well as delicious grits, oatmeal, omelets, and pastries. Keep your eyes open while dining outside—the last time I was here, baby manatees were floating around, waiting for their close-ups.

U.S. 1 at MM 81.5 (up the street from Cheeca Lodge), Islamorada. ℂ **800/258-2559** or 305/664-9271. www. islamoradafishco.com. Reservations not accepted. Main courses $8–$27; appetizers $4–$7. DISC, MC, V. Sun–Thurs 11am–9pm; Fri–Sat 11am–10pm.

THE UPPER & MIDDLE KEYS AFTER DARK

Nightlife in the Upper Keys tends to start before the sun goes down, often at noon, since most people—visitors and locals alike—are on vacation. Also, many anglers and sports-minded folk go to bed early.

Hog Heaven, MM 85.3, just off the main road on the ocean side, Islamorada (ℂ **305/664-9669**), opened in the early 1990s, the joint venture of young locals tired of tourist traps. This whitewashed biker bar is a welcome respite from the neon-colored cocktail circuit. It offers a waterside view and diversions such as big-screen TVs and video games. The food isn't bad, either. The atmosphere is cliquish since most patrons are regulars, so start up a game of pool to break the ice. Open daily from 11am to 4am.

No trip to the Keys is complete without a stop at the **Tiki Bar at the Holiday Isle Resort** (p. 199), U.S. 1 at MM 84, Islamorada (ℂ **305/664-2321**). Hundreds of revelers visit this oceanside spot for drinks and dancing at any time of day, but the live rock starts at 8:30pm. The thatched-roof Tiki Bar draws a mix of thirsty people, all in pursuit of a good time. In the afternoon and early evening (when everyone is either sunburned, drunk, or just happy to be dancing to live reggae), head for **Kokomo's,** next door. It often closes at 7:30pm on weekends (5:30pm on weekdays), so arrive early. For information, call the Holiday Isle Resort.

Locals and tourists mingle at the outdoor cabana bar at **Lorelei** (see "Where to Dine," above). Most evenings after 5pm, you'll find local bands playing on a thatched-roof stage—mainly rock, reggae, and sometimes blues.

Woody's Saloon and Restaurant, U.S. 1 at MM 82, Islamorada (ℂ **305/664-4335**), is a lively, wacky, loud, raunchy, local legend of a place serving up mediocre pizzas, buck-naked strippers, and live bands almost every night. The house band, Big Dick and the Extenders, showcases a 300-pound Native American who does a lewd, rude, and crude routine of politically incorrect jokes and songs starting at 9pm Tuesday through Sunday. He is a legend. By the way, don't think you're lucky if you're offered the front table: It's the target seat for Big Dick's haranguing. Avoid the lame karaoke performance on Sunday and Monday evenings. There's a small cover most nights. Drink specials, contests, and the legendary Big Dick keep this place packed until 4am almost every night. *Note:* This place is not for the faint of heart, but more for those from the Howard Stern school of nightlife.

For a more subdued atmosphere, try the handsome stained-glass and mahogany-wood bar and club at **Zane Grey's,** on the second floor of World Wide Sportsman, MM 81.5 (✆ **305/664-4244**). Outside, enjoy a view of the calm waters of the bay; inside, soak up the history of real longtime anglers. It's open from 11am to at least 11pm (later on weekends). Call to find out who's playing on Friday and Saturday nights, when there's live entertainment and no cover.

2 The Lower Keys: Big Pine Key to Coppitt Key

128 miles SW of Miami

Unlike their neighbors to the north and south, the Lower Keys (including Big Pine, Sugarloaf, and Summerland) are devoid of rowdy spring-break crowds, boast few T-shirt and trinket shops, and have almost no late-night bars. What they do offer are the very best opportunities to enjoy the vast natural resources on land and water that make the area so rich. Stay overnight in the Lower Keys, rent a boat, and explore the reefs—it might be the most memorable part of your trip.

ESSENTIALS

GETTING THERE   See "Essentials" for the Upper and Middle Keys (p. 187) and continue south on U.S. 1. The Lower Keys start at the end of the Seven-mile Bridge. There are also airports in Marathon and Key West.

VISITOR INFORMATION   **Big Pine and Lower Keys Chamber of Commerce,** ocean side of U.S. 1 at MM 31 (P.O. Box 430511), Big Pine Key, FL 33043 (✆ **800/ 872-3722** or 305/872-2411; fax 305/872-0752; www.lowerkeyschamber.com), is open Monday through Friday from 9am to 5pm, and Saturday from 9am to 3pm. The pleasant staff will help with anything a traveler may need. Call, write, or stop in for a comprehensive, detailed information packet.

WHAT TO SEE & DO

Once the centerpiece (these days, it's Big Pine Key) of the Lower Keys and still a great asset is **Bahia Honda State Park** ✍, U.S. 1 at MM 37.5, Big Pine Key (✆ **305/872-2353;** www.bahiahondapark.com), which, even after the violent storms of 2005, has one of the most beautiful coastlines in South Florida. Bahia (pronounced *Bah*-ya) Honda is a great place for hiking, bird-watching, swimming, snorkeling, and fishing. The 524-acre park encompasses a wide variety of ecosystems, including coastal mangroves, beach dunes, and tropical hammocks. There are miles of trails packed with unusual plants and animals, plus a small white-sand beach. Shaded seaside picnic areas are fitted with tables and grills. Although the beach is never wider than 5 feet, even at low tide, this is the Lower Keys' best beach area.

True to its name (Spanish for "deep bay"), the park has relatively deep waters close to shore—perfect for snorkeling and diving. Easy offshore snorkeling here gives even novices a chance to lie suspended in warm water and simply observe diverse marine life passing by. Or else head to the stunning reefs at Looe Key, where the coral and fish are more vibrant than anywhere else in the United States. Snorkeling trips go from the Bahia Honda concessions to Looe Key National Marine Sanctuary (4 miles offshore). They depart twice daily March through September and cost $29 for adults, $24 for children 6 to 14 and $6 for equipment rental. Call © 305/872-3210 for a schedule.

Entry to the park is $5 per vehicle (plus 50¢ per person), $1.50 per pedestrian or bicyclist, free for children 5 and under. If you're alone in a car, you'll pay only $2.50. Open daily from 8am to sunset.

The most famous residents of the Lower Keys are the tiny Key deer. Of the estimated 300 existing in the world, two-thirds live on Big Pine Key's **National Key Deer Refuge** ⚲. To get your bearings, stop by the rangers' office at the Winn-Dixie Shopping Plaza, near MM 30.5 off U.S. 1. They'll give you an informative brochure and map of the area. The refuge is open Monday through Friday from 8am to 5pm.

If the office is closed, head out to the **Blue Hole,** a former rock quarry now filled with the fresh water that's vital to the deer's survival. To get there, turn right at Big Pine Key's only traffic light onto Key Deer Boulevard (take the left fork immediately after the turn) and continue 1½ miles to the observation-site parking lot, on your left. The ½-mile **Watson Hammock Trail,** about ³⁄₁₀-mile past the Blue Hole, is the refuge's only marked footpath. The deer are more active in cool hours, so try coming out to the path in the early morning or late evening to catch a glimpse of these gentle dog-size creatures. There is an observation deck from which you can watch and photograph the protected species. Refuge lands are open daily from half an hour before sunrise to half an hour after sunset. Don't be surprised to see a lazy alligator warming itself in the sun, particularly in outlying areas around the Blue Hole. If you do see a gator, do not go near it, do not touch it, and do not provoke it. Keep your distance; if you must get a photo, use a zoom lens. Also, whatever you do, do not feed the deer—it will threaten their survival. Call the **park office** (© **305/872-2239**) to find out about the infrequent free tours of the refuge, scheduled throughout the year.

OUTDOOR ACTIVITIES

BIKING The Lower Keys are a great place to get off busy U.S. 1 to explore the beautiful back roads. On Big Pine Key, cruise along Key Deer Boulevard (at MM 30). Those with fat tires can ride into the National Key Deer Refuge. Many lodgings offer bike rentals.

BIRD-WATCHING A stopping point for migratory birds on the Eastern Flyway, the Lower Keys are populated with many West Indian bird species, especially in spring and fall. The small, vegetated islands of the Keys are the only nesting sites in the U.S. for the white-crowned pigeon. They're also some of the few breeding places for the reddish egret, roseate spoonbill, mangrove cuckoo, and black-whiskered vireo. Look for them on Bahia Honda Key and the many uninhabited islands nearby.

BOATING Dozens of shops rent powerboats for fishing and reef exploring. Most also rent tackle, sell bait, and have charter captains available. For instance, **Jaybird's Powerboats,** U.S. 1 at MM 33, Big Pine Key (© **305/872-8500**), is an excellent option but rents for full days only. Prices start at $155 for a 19-footer.

CANOEING & KAYAKING The Overseas Highway (U.S. 1) touches on only a few dozen of the many hundreds of islands that make up the Keys. To really see the Lower Keys, rent a kayak or canoe—perfect for these shallow waters. **Reflections Kayak Nature Tours,** operating out of Parmer's Resort, U.S. 1 at MM 28.5, Little

Torch Key (*©* **305/872-4668**), offers fully outfitted backcountry wildlife tours, either on your own or with an expert. The expert, Mike Wedeking, a former U.S. Forest Service guide, keeps up an engaging discussion describing the area's fish, sponges, coral, osprey, hawks, eagles, alligators, raccoons, and deer. The 3-hour tours cost $50 per person and include spring water, fruit, granola bars, and use of binoculars. Bring a towel and sea sandals or sneakers.

FISHING A day spent fishing, either in the shallow backcountry or in the deep sea is a great way to ensure yourself a fresh-fish dinner, or you can release your catch and just appreciate the challenge. Whichever you choose, **Strike Zone Charters,** U.S. 1 at MM 29.5, Big Pine Key (*©* **305/872-9863**), is the charter service to call. Prices for fishing boats start at $450 for a half-day and $595 for a full day. If you have enough anglers to share the price, it isn't too steep. The outfitter may also be able to match you with other interested visitors.

HIKING You can hike throughout the flat, marshy Keys on both marked trails and meandering coastlines. The best places to trek through nature are **Bahia Honda State Park,** at MM 29.5, and **National Key Deer Refuge,** at MM 30 (for more information on both, see "What to See & Do," above). Bahia Honda Park has a free brochure describing an excellent self-guided tour along the Silver Palm Nature Trail. You'll traverse hammocks, mangroves, and sand dunes, and cross a lagoon. The walk (less than a mile) explores a great cross-section of the natural habitat in the Lower Keys and can be done in under half an hour.

SNORKELING & SCUBA DIVING Snorkelers and divers should not miss the Keys' most dramatic reefs at the **Looe Key National Marine Sanctuary.** Here you'll see more than 150 varieties of hard and soft coral—some centuries old—as well as every type of tropical fish, including gold and blue parrotfish, moray eels, barracudas, French angels, and tarpon. **Looe Key Dive Center,** U.S. 1 at MM 27.5, Ramrod Key (*©* **305/872-2215**), offers a mind-blowing 5-hour tour aboard a 45-foot catamaran with two shallow 1-hour dives for snorkelers and scuba divers. Snorkelers pay $30; divers with their own equipment pay $40. On Wednesday and Saturday, you can do a fascinating dive to the *Adolphus Busch, Sr.,* a shipwreck sunk off Looe Key in 100 feet of water, for $45. (See "What to See & Do," above, for other diving options.)

WHERE TO STAY

There are a number of cheap, fairly unappealing fish shacks along the highway for those who want bare-bones accommodations. So far, there are no national hotel chains in the Lower Keys. For information on lodging in cabins or trailers at local campgrounds, see "Camping," below.

VERY EXPENSIVE

Little Palm Island Resort & Spa 🐠🐠🐠 This exclusive island escape—host to presidents, royalty, and even Howard Stern—is not just a place to stay while in the Lower Keys; it is a destination all its own. Built on a private 5½-acre island, it's accessible only by boat or seaplane. Guests stay in thatched-roof duplexes amid lush foliage and flowering tropical plants. Many villas have ocean views and private decks with hammocks. Inside, the romantic suites have all the comforts of a luxurious contemporary beach cottage, but without phones, TVs, or alarm clocks. As if its location weren't idyllic enough, the award-winning SpaTerre offers Indonesian-inspired spa experiences. Note that on the breezeless south side of the island, mosquitoes can be a problem, even in winter. (Bring spray and lightweight, long-sleeved clothing.) Known for its innovative and pricey food, Little Palm also hosts visitors just for dinner, brunch, or lunch. If you're staying on the island, opt for the full American plan, which includes three meals a day.

Launch is on the ocean side of U.S. 1 at MM 28.5, Little Torch Key, FL 33042. © **800/343-8567** or 305/872-2524. Fax 305/872-4843. www.littlepalmisland.com. 28 bungalows, 2 deluxe suites. Winter $795–$1,695 double; off season $695–$1,595 double. Rates include transportation to and from the island and unlimited (nonmotorized) watersports. Meal plans include 2 meals daily for $125 per person per day, 3 meals at $140 per person. AE, DC, DISC, MC, V. No children under 16. **Amenities:** Restaurant; bar; 2 pools (1 outdoor with small waterfall, 1 indoor); health club and spa; extensive watersports equipment rental; concierge; courtesy van from Key West or Marathon airport; ferry service to and from the mainland; limited room service; in-room massage; laundry service; dry cleaning; jogging trail. *In room:* A/C, dataport, minibar, coffeemaker, hair dryer, Jacuzzi, no phone.

INEXPENSIVE

Parmer's Resort ⚓   Parmer's, a fixture here for more than 20 years, is well known for its charming hospitality and helpful staff. This downscale resort offers modest but comfortable cottages, each of them unique. Some are waterfront, many have kitchenettes, and others are just a bedroom. The Wahoo room (no. 26), a one-bedroom efficiency, is especially nice, with a small sitting area that faces the water. All units have been recently updated and are very clean. Many can be combined to accommodate families. The hotel's waterfront location, not to mention the fact that it's only a half-hour from lively Key West, almost makes up for the fact that you must pay extra for maid service.

565 Barry Ave. (P.O. Box 430665), near MM 28.5, Little Torch Key, FL 33043. © **305/872-2157.** Fax 305/872-2014. www.parmersresort.com. 45 units. Winter $109–$169 double; off season $89–$119 double, from $119 efficiency. Rates include continental breakfast. AE, DISC, MC, V. From U.S. 1, turn right onto Barry Ave. Resort is ½ mile down on the right. **Amenities:** Heated pool; kayak rental; bike rental; coin-op washers and dryers; boat ramp. *In room:* A/C, TV.

CAMPING

Bahia Honda State Park ⚓⚓⚓ (© **800/326-3521;** www.abfla.com/parks/bahia honda/bahiahonda.html) offers some of the best camping in the Keys. It is as loaded with facilities and activities as it is with campers. But don't be discouraged by its popularity—this park encompasses more than 500 acres of land, 80 campsites spread throughout three areas, and three spacious and comfortable duplex cabins. Cabins hold up to eight guests each and come complete with linens, kitchenettes, wraparound terraces, barbecue pits, and rocking chairs. For one to four people, camping costs about $25 per site without electricity and $26 with electricity. Depending on the season, cabin prices range from $50 to $110. Additional people (over four) cost $6 each.

Another excellent value can be found at the **KOA Sugarloaf Key Resort** ⚓⚓, near MM 20. This oceanside facility has 200 fully equipped sites, with water, electricity, and sewer, which rent for about $85 a night (no-hookup sites cost about $45). Or you can pitch a tent on the 5 acres of waterfront property. This place is especially nice because of its private beaches and access to diving, snorkeling, and boating; its grounds are also well maintained. In addition, the resort rents travel trailers: The 25-foot Dutchman sleeps six and costs about $120 a day. For details, contact the resort at P.O. Box 420469, Summerland Key, FL 33042 (© **800/562-7731** or 305/745-3549; fax 305/745-9889; www.koa.com).

WHERE TO DINE

There aren't many fine-dining options in the Lower Keys, with the exception of the **Dining Room at Little Palm Island** (p. 206), MM 285, Little Torch Key (© **305/ 872-2551**), where you'll be wowed with gourmet French Caribbean fare that looks like a meal but eats like a vacation. You need to take a ferry to this chichi private island, where you can indulge at the exquisite oceanside restaurant even if you're not staying over.

MODERATE

Mangrove Mama's Restaurant   SEAFOOD/CARIBBEAN   As the dedicated locals who come daily for happy hour will tell you, this is a true Lower Keys institution and a dive in the best sense of the word (the restaurant is a shack that used to have a gas pump as well as a grill). Guests share the property with stray cats and some miniature horses out back. A handful of simple tables, inside and out, are shaded by banana trees and palm fronds. Fish is the menu's mainstay, although soups, salads, sandwiches, and omelets are also good. Grilled-chicken and club sandwiches are tasty alternatives to fish, as are meatless chef's salads and spicy barbecued baby back ribs.

U.S. 1 at MM 20, Sugarloaf Key. © 305/745-3030. Main courses $10–$20; lunch $6–$9; brunch $5–$7. MC, V. Daily 11am–3pm and 5:30–10pm.

Monte's   SEAFOOD   Certainly nobody goes to this restaurant/fish market for its atmosphere: Plastic place settings rest on picnic-style tables in a screen-enclosed dining patio. But Monte's doesn't need great atmosphere, since it has survived for more than 20 years on its very good and incredibly fresh food. The day's catch may include shark, tuna, lobsters, stone crabs, or shrimp.

U.S. 1 at MM 25, Summerland Key. © 305/745-3731. Main courses $13–$17; lunch $6–$10. No credit cards. Mon–Sat 9am–10pm; Sun 10am–9pm.

INEXPENSIVE

Coco's Kitchen ☞ CUBAN/AMERICAN   This tiny storefront has been dishing out black beans, rice, and shredded beef for more than 10 years. The owners, who are actually from Nicaragua, cook not only superior Cuban food, but local specialties, Italian dishes, and Caribbean choices. Specialties include fried shrimp, whole fried yellowtail, and Cuban-style roast pork (available only on Sat). The best bet is the daily special, which may be roasted pork or fresh grouper, served with rice and beans or salad and crispy fries. Top off the huge, cheap meal with a rich caramel-soaked flan.

283 Key Deer Blvd. (in the Winn-Dixie Shopping Center), Big Pine Key. © 305/872-4495. Main courses $6–$15; breakfast $2–$5. MC, V. Mon–Sat 7am–7:30pm. Turn right at the traffic light near MM 30.5; stay in the left lane.

No Name Pub   PUB FOOD/PIZZA   This funky old bar out in the boonies serves snacks and sandwiches until 11pm on most nights, and drinks until midnight. Pizzas are tasty—try one topped with local shrimp. Or consider a bowl of chili with all the fixings. Everything is served on paper plates. Locals hang out at the rustic bar, one of the Keys' oldest, drinking beer and listening to a jukebox heavy with 1980s tunes.

¼ mile south of No Name Bridge on N. Watson Blvd., Big Pine Key. © 305/872-9115. Pizzas $6–$18; subs $5. MC, V. Daily 11am–11pm. Turn right at Big Pine's only traffic light (near MM 30.5) onto Key Deer Blvd. Turn right on Watson Blvd. At the stop sign, turn left. Look for a small wooden sign on the left marking the spot.

THE LOWER KEYS AFTER DARK

Although the mellow islands of the Lower Keys aren't exactly known for wild nightlife, there are some friendly bars and restaurants where locals and tourists gather to hang out and drink. One of the most scenic is **Sandbar,** on Barry Avenue near MM 28.5 (© **305/872-9989**), a wide-open, breezy wooden house built on slender stilts and overlooking a wide channel. It attracts an odd mix of bikers and blue-hairs daily from 11am to 10pm, and is a great place to overhear local gossip and colorful metaphors. Pool tables are the main attraction, but there's also live music some nights. The drinks are reasonably priced, and the food isn't too bad, either. For another fun bar scene, see the **No Name Pub,** listed above in "Where to Dine."

3 Key West ★★★

159 miles SW of Miami

There are two schools of thought on Key West—one is that it has become way too commercial, and the other is that it's still a place where you don't have to worry about being prim, proper, or even well groomed. I think it's a bizarre fusion of both—a fascinating look at small-town America where people truly live by the (off)beat of their own drum, albeit one with a Coach outlet, Banana Republic, and, most recently, Starbucks, thrown in to bring you back to reality. The locals, or "conchs" (pronounced *conks*), and the developers here have been at odds for years. This once low-key island has been thoroughly commercialized—there's a Hard Rock Cafe smack in the middle of Duval Street, and thousands of cruise-ship passengers descend on Mallory Square each day. It's definitely not the seedy town Hemingway and his cronies once called their own. Or is it?

Laid-back Key West still exists, but it's now found in different places: the backyard of a popular guesthouse, for example, or an art gallery, a secret garden, a clothing-optional bar, or the hip hangouts of Bahama Village. Fortunately, there are plenty of these, and Key West's greatest historic charm is found just off the beaten path. Don't be afraid to explore these residential areas, as conchs are notoriously friendly. In fact, exploring the side streets always seems to yield a new discovery. Of course, there are always the calm waters of the Atlantic and the Gulf of Mexico all around.

The heart of town offers party people a good time—that is, if your idea of a good time is the smell of stale beer, loud music, and hardly shy revelers. Here you'll find good restaurants, fun bars, live music, rickshaw rides, and lots of shopping. Key West is still very gay-centric, except during spring break. Same-sex couples walking hand in hand are the norm here, and if you're not open-minded and would prefer to avoid this scene, look for the ubiquitous rainbow flag hanging outside gay establishments and you'll know what to expect. For the most part, however, the scene is extremely mixed and colorful. If partying isn't your thing, then avoid Duval Street—the Bourbon Street of South Florida—at all costs. Instead, take in the scenery at a dockside bar or oceanside Jacuzzi. Whatever you do, don't bother with a watch or tie—this is the home of the perennial vacation.

ESSENTIALS

GETTING THERE   For directions by car, see "Essentials" for the Upper and Middle Keys (p. 187) and continue south on U.S. 1. When entering Key West, stay in the far-right lane onto North Roosevelt Boulevard, which becomes Truman Avenue in Old Town. Continue for a few blocks and you'll find yourself on **Duval Street** ★, in the heart of the city. If you stay to the left, you'll also reach the city center after passing the airport and the remnants of historic houseboat row, where a motley collection of boats once made up one of Key West's most interesting neighborhoods.

Several regional airlines fly nonstop (about 55 min.) from Miami to Key West; fares are about $120 to $300 round-trip. **American Eagle** (© 800/433-7300), **Continental** (© 800/525-0280), **Delta** (© 800/221-1212), and **US Airways Express** (© 800/428-4322) land at **Key West International Airport,** South Roosevelt Boulevard (© 305/296-5439), on the southeastern corner of the island.

Greyhound (© **800/231-2222;** www.greyhound.com) has buses leaving Miami for Key West every day for about $30 to $32 one-way and $57 to $67 round-trip. Seats fill up in season, so come early. The ride takes about 4½ hours.

GETTING AROUND   With limited parking, narrow streets, and congested traffic, driving in Old Town Key West is more of a pain than a convenience. Unless you're staying in one of the more remote accommodations, consider trading in the car for a bicycle. The island is small and as flat as a board, which makes it easy to negotiate, especially away from the crowded downtown area. Many tourists choose to cruise by moped, an option that can make navigating the streets risky, especially since there are no helmet laws in Key West. Hundreds of visitors are seriously injured each year; be careful and spend the extra few bucks to rent a helmet.

Rates for simple one-speed cruisers start at about $10 per day. Mopeds start at about $12 for 2 hours, $25 per day, and $100 per week. The best shops include the **Bicycle Center,** 523 Truman Ave. (© **305/294-4556**); the **Moped Hospital,** 601 Truman Ave. (© **305/296-3344**); and **Tropical Bicycles & Scooter Rentals,** 1300 Duval St. (© **305/294-8136**). The **Bike Shop,** 1110 Truman Ave. (© **305/294-1073**), rents cruisers for $10 per day; a $150 deposit is required.

PARKING   Parking in Key West's Old Town is particularly limited, but there is a well-placed **municipal parking lot** at Simonton and Angela streets, just behind the firehouse and police station. If you've brought a car, you may want to stash it here while you enjoy the very walkable downtown part of Key West.

VISITOR INFORMATION   The **Key West Chamber of Commerce,** 402 Wall St., Key West, FL 33040 (© **800/527-8539** or 305/294-2587; www.keywestchamber.com), offers both general and specialized information. The lobby is open daily from 8:30am to 6pm; phones are answered from 8am to 8pm. The **Key West Visitor Center** (© **800/LAST-KEY**) is the area's best for information on accommodations, goings-on, and restaurants; it's open Monday through Friday from 8am to 5:30pm, Saturday and Sunday from 8:30am to 5pm. Gay travelers may want to call the **Key West Business Guild** (© **305/294-4603**), which represents more than 50 guesthouses and B&Bs, as well as many other gay-owned businesses (ask for its color brochure); or call **Good Times Travel** (© **305/294-0980**), which will set up lodging and package tours on the island.

While you're in one of the above offices, be sure to pick up a free copy of *Sharon Wells' Walking & Biking Guide to Historic Key West.* Though I still couldn't find all the spots I wanted to in the Key West Cemetery (p. 213) while using her guide, it was helpful for historic descriptions throughout town. She also leads guided walking tours around the island. For information, call her at © **305/294-8380** or go to www.seekeywest.com.

ORIENTATION   A mere 2×4-mile island, Key West is simple to navigate, even though there is no real order to the arrangement of streets and avenues. As you enter town on U.S. 1 (Roosevelt Blvd.), you will see most of the moderate chain hotels and fast-food restaurants. The better restaurants, shops, and outfitters are crammed onto

Key West

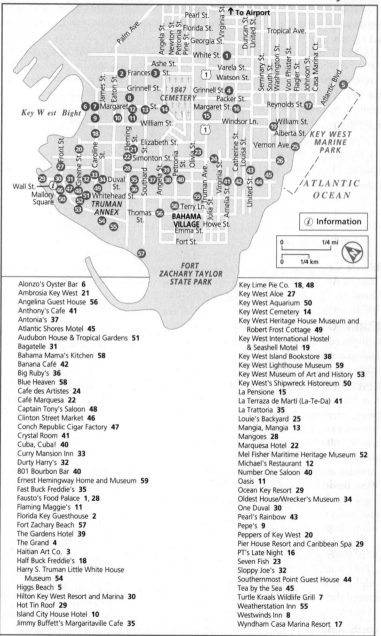

Alonzo's Oyster Bar **6**
Ambrosia Key West **21**
Angelina Guest House **56**
Anthony's Cafe **41**
Antonia's **37**
Atlantic Shores Motel **45**
Audubon House & Tropical Gardens **51**
Bagatelle **31**
Bahama Mama's Kitchen **58**
Banana Café **42**
Big Ruby's **36**
Blue Heaven **58**
Cafe des Artistes **24**
Café Marquesa **22**
Captain Tony's Saloon **48**
Clinton Street Market **46**
Conch Republic Cigar Factory **47**
Crystal Room **41**
Cuba, Cuba! **40**
Curry Mansion Inn **33**
Durty Harry's **32**
801 Bourbon Bar **40**
Ernest Hemingway Home and Museum **59**
Fast Buck Freddie's **35**
Fausto's Food Palace **1, 28**
Flaming Maggie's **11**
Florida Key Guesthouse **2**
Fort Zachary Beach **57**
The Gardens Hotel **39**
The Grand **4**
Haitian Art Co. **3**
Half Buck Freddie's **18**
Harry S. Truman Little White House
   Museum **54**
Higgs Beach **5**
Hilton Key West Resort and Marina **30**
Hot Tin Roof **29**
Island City House Hotel **10**
Jimmy Buffett's Margaritaville Cafe **35**

Key Lime Pie Co. **18, 48**
Key West Aloe **27**
Key West Aquarium **50**
Key West Cemetery **14**
Key West Heritage House Museum and
   Robert Frost Cottage **49**
Key West International Hostel
   & Seashell Motel **19**
Key West Island Bookstore **38**
Key West Lighthouse Museum **59**
Key West Museum of Art and History **53**
Key West's Shipwreck Historeum **50**
La Pensione **15**
La Terraza de Martí (La-Te-Da) **41**
La Trattoria **35**
Louie's Backyard **25**
Mangia, Mangia **13**
Mangoes **28**
Marquesa Hotel **22**
Mel Fisher Maritime Heritage Museum **52**
Michael's Restaurant **12**
Number One Saloon **40**
Oasis **11**
Ocean Key Resort **29**
Oldest House/Wrecker's Museum **34**
One Duval **30**
Pearl's Rainbow **43**
Pepe's **9**
Peppers of Key West **20**
Pier House Resort and Caribbean Spa **29**
PT's Late Night **16**
Seven Fish **23**
Sloppy Joe's **32**
Southernmost Point Guest House **44**
Tea by the Sea **45**
Turtle Kraals Wildlife Grill **7**
Weatherstation Inn **55**
Westwinds Inn **8**
Wyndham Casa Marina Resort **17**

Duval Street, the main thoroughfare of Key West's Old Town. Surrounding streets contain many inns and lodges in picturesque Victorian/Bahamian homes. On the southern side of the island is the coral-beach area and some of the larger resort hotels.

The area called Bahama Village has only recently become known to tourists. With several newly opened, trendy restaurants and guesthouses, this hippie-ish neighborhood, complete with street-roaming chickens and cats, is the roughest and most urban you'll find in the Keys. You might see a few drug deals on street corners, but they're nothing to be overly concerned about: It looks worse than it is, and resident business owners tend to keep a vigilant eye on the neighborhood. The area is actually quite funky and should be a welcome diversion from the Duvalian mainstream.

SEEING THE SIGHTS

Key West's newest attraction, the Florida Keys Eco-Discovery Center, is set to open in summer 2006, but be sure to call ahead is you plan to visit. Overlooking the waterfront at the Truman Annex (*Ⓒ* **301/608-3040**), the Center features 6,000 square feet of interactive exhibits depicting Florida Keys underwater and upland habitats—with emphasis on the ecosystem of North America's only living contiguous barrier coral reef, which parallels the Keys.

Before shelling out big bucks for any of the dozens of worthwhile attractions in Key West, I recommend getting an overview on either of the two comprehensive island tours, the **Conch Tour Train** or the **Old Town Trolley** (see p. 216 for both). There are simply too many attractions and historic houses to list. I've highlighted my favorites below, but I encourage you to seek out others.

Audubon House & Tropical Gardens *ⓕⓕ*   This well-preserved 19th-century home stands as a prime example of early Key West architecture. Named after renowned painter and bird expert John James Audubon, who is said to have visited the house in 1832, the graceful two-story structure is a peaceful retreat from the bustle of Old Town. Included in the price of admission is a self-guided, half-hour audio tour that spotlights rare Audubon prints, gorgeous antiques, historic photos, and lush tropical gardens. With voices of several characters from the house's past, the tour never gets boring—though it is a bit hokey at times. Even if you don't want to explore the grounds and home, check out the impressive gift shop, which sells a variety of fine mementos at reasonable prices.

205 Whitehead St. (between Greene and Caroline sts.). *Ⓒ* **305/294-2116**. www.audubonhouse.com. Admission $10 adults, $5 children 6–12. Daily 9:30am–5pm (last entry at 4:30pm).

East Martello Museum and Gallery   Adjacent to the airport, the East Martello Museum is located in a Civil War–era brick fort that itself is worth a visit. The museum contains a bizarre variety of exhibits that collectively do a thorough job of interpreting the city's intriguing past. Historic artifacts include model ships, a deep-sea diver's wooden air pump, a crude raft from a Cuban "boat lift," a supposedly haunted doll, and a horse-drawn hearse. Exhibits illustrate the Keys' history of salvaging, sponging, and cigar making. After seeing the galleries (which should take 45–60 min.), climb a steep spiral staircase to the top of the lookout tower for good views over the island and ocean. A member of the Key West Art and Historical Society, East Martello has two cousins: the **Key West Museum of Art and History,** 281 Front St. (*Ⓒ* **305/295-6616**), and the **Key West Lighthouse Museum** (p. 214).

3501 S. Roosevelt Blvd. *Ⓒ* **305/296-3913**. www.kwahs.com/martello.htm. Admission $6 adults, $5 seniors, $3 children 8–12. Daily 9:30am–4:30pm (last entry at 4pm).

Ernest Hemingway Home and Museum ☆

Hemingway's particularly handsome stone Spanish Colonial house, built in 1851, was one of the first on the island to be fitted with indoor plumbing and a built-in fireplace. It also has the first swimming pool built on Key West (look for the penny he pressed into the cement near the pool). The author owned the home from 1931 until his death in 1961, and lived here with about 50 cats, whose descendants, including the famed six-toed felines, still roam the premises. It was during those years that the Nobel Prize–winning author wrote some of his most famous

> **Impressions**
> I've a notion to move the capitol to Key West and just stay.
> —President Harry S Truman

works, including *For Whom the Bell Tolls, A Farewell to Arms,* and *The Snows of Kilimanjaro.* Fans may want to take the optional half-hour tour to see his study as well as rooms in his house with glass cabinets that store certain artifacts, books, and pieces of mail addressed to him. It's interesting (to an extent) and included in the price of admission. If you don't take the tour or have no interest in Hemingway, the price of admission is really a waste of money, except for the lovely architecture and garden. If you're feline phobic, beware: There are cats everywhere.

907 Whitehead St. (between Truman Ave. and Olivia St.). ☎ **305/294-1136.** Fax 305/294-2755. www.hemingway home.com. Admission $11 adults, $6 children. Daily 9am–5pm. Limited parking.

Harry S Truman Little White House ☆☆

President Truman used to refer to the White House as the "Great White Jail." On temporary leave from the Big House, Truman discovered the serenity of Key West and made his escape to what became known as the Little White House, which is open to the public for touring. The house is fully restored; the exhibits document Truman's time in the Keys. Tours run every 15 minutes and last between 45 and 50 minutes. For fans of all things Oval Office–related, there's a presidential gift shop on the premises.

111 Front St. ☎ **305/294-9911.** www.trumanlittlewhitehouse.com. Admission $11 adults, $5 children under 12. Daily 9am–4:30pm.

Key West Aquarium ☆☆ *Kids*

The oldest attraction on the island, the Key West Aquarium is a modest but fascinating place. A long hallway of eye-level displays showcases dozens of varieties of fish and crustaceans. Kids can touch sea cucumbers and sea anemones in a shallow tank. If possible, catch one of the free guided tours—you can witness the dramatic feeding frenzy of the sharks, tarpon, barracudas, stingrays, and turtles. Expect to spend 1 to 1½ hours here.

1 Whitehead St. (at Mallory Sq.). ☎ **305/296-2051.** www.keywestaquarium.com. Admission $10 adults, $5 children 4–12. Tickets good for 2 consecutive days. Look for discount coupons at local hotels, at Duval St. kiosks, and from trolley and train tours. Daily 10am–6pm; tours at 11am and 1, 3, and 4pm.

Key West Cemetery ☆☆☆ *Finds*

This funky cemetery is the epitome of quirky Key West: irreverent and humorous. Many tombs are stacked several high, condominium style—the rocky soil made digging 6 feet under nearly impossible for early settlers. Epitaphs reflect residents' lighthearted attitudes toward life and death. I TOLD YOU I WAS SICK is one of the more famous, as is the tongue-in-cheek widow's inscription AT LEAST I KNOW WHERE HE'S SLEEPING TONIGHT. Pick up a copy of *Sharon Wells' Walking & Biking Guide to Historic Key West* (p. 210). Some of the inscriptions are hard to find even with the free walking-tour guide, but this place is fun to explore.

Entrance at the corner of Margaret and Angela sts. Free admission. Daily dawn–dusk.

Going, Going, Gone: Where to Catch the Famous Key West Sunset

A tradition in Key West, the Sunset Celebration can be relaxing or overwhelming, depending on your vantage point. If you're in town, you must check out this ritual at least once. Every evening, locals and visitors gather at the docks behind Mallory Square (at the westernmost end of Whitehead St.) to celebrate the day gone by. Secure a spot on the docks early to experience the carnival of portrait artists, acrobats, food vendors, animal acts, and other performers trading on the island's bohemian image. But the carnival atmosphere isn't for everyone: In season, the crowd can be overwhelming, especially when the cruise ships are in port. Also, hold on to your bags and wallets, as the tight crowds make Mallory Square at sunset prime pickpocketing territory.

A more refined choice is the Hilton's **Sunset Deck** (© 305/294-4000), a luxurious second-floor bar on Front Street, right next door to Mallory Square. From the civilized calm of a casual bar, you can look down on the mayhem with a drink in hand.

Also near the Mallory madness is the bar at the **Ocean Key Resort,** at the very tip of Duval Street (© 800/328-9815 or 305/296-7701). This long open-air pier serves drinks and decent bar food against a dramatic pink-and-yellow-streaked sky.

For the very best potent cocktails and great bar food on an outside patio or enclosed lounge, try **Pier House Resort and Caribbean Spa's Havana Docks,** 1 Duval St. (© 305/296-4600). There's usually live music and a lively gathering of visitors enjoying this island's bounty. The bar is right on the water and makes a prime sunset-viewing spot.

Key West Heritage House Museum and Robert Frost Cottage ✮ (Finds)   For a glimpse into one of the oldest houses in Key West, check out the Heritage House Museum, the former 1834 home of Jesse Porter, a Key West preservationist who hosted the likes of Robert Frost, Tennessee Williams, Gloria Swanson, and Tallulah Bankhead in his home-cum-salon. Furnished with 19th-century antiques, the house is a fascinating look at 19th- and early-20th-century Key West. Guided tours are informative and entertaining, sort of an antique version of an *E! True Hollywood Story.*

410 Caroline St. © 305/296-3573 for tour reservations. www.heritagehousemuseum.org. Free admission. Mon–Sat 10am–4pm.

Key West Lighthouse Museum ✮   When the Key West Lighthouse opened in 1848, it signaled the end of a profitable era for the pirate salvagers who looted reef-stricken ships. The story of this and other area lighthouses is illustrated in a small museum that was formerly the keeper's quarters. It's worth mustering the energy to climb the 88 claustrophobic steps to the top, where you'll be rewarded with magnificent panoramic views of Key West and the ocean.

938 Whitehead St. © 305/294-0012. Admission $8 adults, $7 seniors and locals, $4 children 7–12. Daily 9:30am–4:30pm.

Key West's Shipwreck Historeum   You'll see more impressive artifacts at nearby Mel Fisher's museum, but for the morbidly curious, shipwrecks should rank right up there with car wrecks. For those of you who can't help but look, this museum is the place to be for everything you ever wanted to know about shipwrecks and more. See movies, artifacts, and a real-life wrecker, who will be more than happy to indulge your curiosity about the wrecking industry that preoccupied the early pioneers of Key West. Depending on your level of interest, you can expect to spend up to 2 hours here.

1 Whitehead St. (at Mallory Sq.). (C) **305/292-8990.** Fax 305/292-5536. www.shipwreckhistoreum.com Admission $10 adults, $5 children 4–12. Shows daily every half-hour 9:45am–4:45pm.

Mel Fisher Maritime Heritage Museum 🐟🐟   This museum honors local hero Mel Fisher, whose death in 1998 was mourned throughout South Florida and who, along with a crew of other salvagers, found a multimillion-dollar treasure trove in 1985 aboard the wreck of the Spanish galleon *Nuestra Señora de Atocha.* If you're into diving, pirates, and sunken treasures, check out this small museum, full of doubloons, pieces of eight, emeralds, and solid-gold bars (one of them you can lift!). A 1700 English merchant slave ship, the only tangible evidence of the transatlantic slave trade, is on view on the museum's second floor. An exhibition telling the story of more than 1,400 African slaves captured in Cuban waters and brought to Key West for sanctuary is the museum's latest, most fascinating one to date.

200 Greene St. (C) **305/294-2633.** www.melfisher.org. Admission $11 adults, $9.50 seniors, $6 children 6–12. Daily 9:30am–5pm. Take U.S. 1 to Whitehead St. and turn left on Greene.

Oldest House/Wrecker's Museum 🐟   Dating from 1829, this old New England Bahama House has survived pirates, hurricanes, fires, warfare, and economic ups and downs. The 1½-story home was designed by a ship's carpenter and incorporates many features from maritime architecture, including portholes and a ship's hatch designed for ventilation before the advent of air-conditioning. Especially interesting is the detached kitchen building outfitted with a brick "beehive" oven and vintage cooking utensils. Although not a must-see on the Key West tour, history and architecture buffs will appreciate the finely preserved details and the glimpse of a slower, easier time in the island's life.

322 Duval St. (C) **305/294-9502.** Admission $5 adults, $1 children 6–12. Daily 10am–4pm.

(*Moments* **A Great Escape**

Many people complain that Key West's quirky, quaint panache has been lost to the vulture of capitalism, evidenced by the glut of T-shirt shops and tacky bars. But that's not entirely so. For a quiet respite, visit the **Key West Botanical Gardens,** a little-known slice of serenity tucked between the Aqueduct Authority plant and the Key West Golf Course. The 11-acre gardens—maintained by volunteers and funded by donations—contain the last hardwood hammock in Key West, plus a colorful representation of wildflowers, butterflies, and birds. A genetically cloned tree is the latest addition. Although the gardens received a terrible blow from the storms of 2005, the calm remains within them. Located at Botanical Garden Way and College Road, Stock Island. Free admission. Open daily from 8am to sunset. Follow College Road; then turn right just past Bayshore Manor.

ORGANIZED TOURS

BY TRAM & TROLLEY-BUS   Yes, it's more than a bit hokey to sit on this 60-foot tram of yellow cars, but it's worth it—at least once. The city's whole story is packed into a neat, 90-minute package on the **Conch Tour Train,** which covers the island and all its rich, raunchy history. In operation since 1958, the cars are open-air, which can make the ride uncomfortable in bad weather. The engine of the "train" is a propane-powered Jeep disguised as a locomotive. Tours depart from both Mallory Square and the Welcome Center, near where U.S. 1 becomes North Roosevelt Boulevard, on the less-developed side of the island. For information, call © 305/294-5161 or go to www.conchtourtrain.com. The cost is $25 for adults, $12 for children 4 to 12. Daily departures are every half-hour from 9am to 4:30pm.

The **Old Town Trolley** is the choice in bad weather or if you're staying at one of the hotels on its route. Humorous drivers maintain a running commentary as the enclosed trolley loops around the island's streets past all the major sights. Trolley buses depart from Mallory Square and other points around the island, including many area hotels. For details, call © **305/296-6688** or visit www.trolleytours.com. Tours are $22 for adults, $11 for children 4 to 12. Departures are daily every half-hour (though not always on the half-hour) from 9am to 4:30pm.

Whichever you choose, both of these historic trivia-packed tours are well worth the price of admission.

BY AIR   Proclaimed by the mayor as "the official air force of the Conch Republic," **Island Airplane Tours,** at Key West Airport, 3469 S. Roosevelt Blvd. (© **305/294-8687**), offers windy rides in its open-cockpit 1940 Waco biplanes that take you over the reefs and around the islands. Thrill seekers will also enjoy a spin in the company's S2-B aerobatics airplane, which does loops, rolls, and sideways figure-eights. Company owner Fred Cabanas was "decorated" in 1991, after he spotted a Cuban airman defecting to the United States in a Russian-built MIG fighter. Sightseeing flights cost $50 to $200, depending on duration.

BY BOAT   The catamaran *The Pride of Key West* and the glass-bottom boat *Fireball,* both at Zero Duval St. (© **305/296-6293;** fax 305/294-8704), depart on daytime

---

Chucky Lives in Key West!

The original "Chucky," Robert the Doll, has been said to resemble everything from Michael Jackson to Curious George. Residing at The East Martello Museum, Robert is not your typical doll. His original home was at The Artist House Bed & Breakfast, where he lived with his owner, Gene Otto. Robert was given to Gene by a Bahamian girl who was the daughter of ill-treated servants of the Otto family. Speculation as to his creation says that the doll contains a crystal or was made much like a voodoo doll, thereby creating his evil entity. Whatever his method of creation, Robert is allegedly possessed. One of Robert's favorite activities is to prevent his photo from being taken. Visitors have reported a variety of camera malfunctions, and Robert's favorite trick is to black out his own photo while leaving the remaining film unharmed. He frequently creates electric and electronic fluctuations, and has been said to move his toy lion from one knee to the other and to tap on his glass display case. Creepy!

Literary Key West

Counting Ernest Hemingway and Tennessee Williams among your denizens would give any city the right to call itself a literary mecca. But over the years, tiny Key West has been home—or at least home away from home—to dozens of literary types who are drawn to some combination of its gentle pace, tropical atmosphere, and lighthearted mood (not to mention its lingering reputation for an oft-ribald lifestyle). Writers have long known that more than a few muses prowl the tree-laden streets of Key West.

Robert Frost first visited Key West in 1934 and wintered here for the remainder of his life. In the early 20th century, writers like John Dewey, Archibald MacLeish, John Dos Passos, Wallace Stevens, and S. J. Perelman were drawn to the island. Even as Key West boomed and busted and boomed again, and despite the island's growing popularity with world travelers, writers continued to move to Key West or to visit it with such regularity that they were deemed honorary "conchs." Novelists Phil Caputo, Tom McGuane, Jim Harrison, John Hershey, Alison Lurie, and Robert Stone were among these.

Of course, one of Key West's favorite sons also earned a spot in the annals of local literary history. Famous for his good-time, tropical-laced music, Jimmy Buffett was also a surprisingly well-received novelist in the 1990s. Although Buffett now makes the infinitely ritzier Palm Beach his Florida home, his presence is still felt in virtually every corner of Key West.

But it is Nobel Prize winner and avid outdoorsman Ernest Hemingway who is most identified with Key West. Much of the island has changed since he lived here from 1931 to 1961. Even the famous Sloppy Joe's bar, which Hemingway frequented mostly from 1933 to 1937, has changed locations (reportedly without closing—customers picked up their drinks and whatever else from the bar they could carry and brought it all down the block to the new location, and service resumed with barely a blink!). Fortunately, the Ernest Hemingway Home and Museum (p. 213) has been lovingly preserved. But to get the best feel for what Hemingway loved most about Key West, visit the docks at Garrison Bight. It is from here that Hemingway and his many famous (and infamous) friends and contemporaries departed for Caribbean ports of call and for sport upon the sea.

Key West pays homage to its literary legacy with the annual Key West Literary Seminar in January. For information, call © **888/293-9291** or visit www. keywestliteraryseminar.org.

coral-reef tours and evening sunset cruises (call for times). Reef trips cost $30 per person; sunset cruises are $35 per person. Kids 5 through 12 sail all cruises for $15.

The schooner *Western Union* (© **305/292-9830;** www.schoonerwesternunion. com) was built in 1939 and served as a cable-repair vessel until it was designated the flagship of the city of Key West and began day, sunset, and charter sailings. Sunset sailings are especially memorable and include entertainment, cocktails, and a cannon fire. Prices vary; inquire for details.

Parrotheads on Parade

For Jimmy Buffett fans, or Parrotheads, as they're also known, there's **Trails of Margaritaville** (© 305/292-2040), an amusing 90-minute walking tour providing fans with an officially sanctioned peek at the stamping grounds of Buffett's carefree days in Key West back in the 1970s. Decked out in full Parrothead regalia—Hawaiian shirts and parrot hats—the informative and often hilarious guides lead you past the hangouts and other high points of Buffett's Key West, spinning yarns about the musician and Key West in general. The tour departs daily at 4pm from **Captain Tony's Saloon,** 428 Greene St., where Buffett used to hang out and perform, and ends at—you guessed it—Margaritaville Cafe, on Duval Street. Tickets are $20 for adults, $15 for locals with ID, and $10 for children 6 to 10. Bring cash or traveler's checks; no credit cards are accepted. Reservations are required at least 2 days in advance. *Note:* If you're not a huge fan of Jimmy Buffett, you might want to skip this tour, as the price is relatively steep and you probably won't be as interested in these attractions as diehard types.

M/V *Heritage* (© 305/295-8687) is a 45-foot custom-designed schooner that offers 1-hour tours of the town's historic harbor. Sites of interest on this tour include Fort Zachary Taylor, a Civil War–era fortification; the Truman Naval Station; the Key West National Wildlife Preserve; and Mallory Square. Tours are fully narrated to highlight the island's pirates, wreckers, spongers, fishermen, and the U.S. Navy and Coast Guard. Departures are daily at 9am, 11am, 1pm, 3pm, and 5pm from the Hilton Marina, 245 Front St. The cost is $12 per person.

A new boat tour combines Florida Keys sunsets with delectable Keys cuisine. **Sunset Culinaire Tours** (© 305/296-0982) is a cruise aboard the vessel RB's Lady and includes a tour of Key West Harbor as the sun sinks below the horizon, and a gourmet dinner prepared by Chef Brian Kirkpatrick. The vessel departs from Sunset Marina, off U.S. 1 at 5555 College Road, at 5:30 p.m. nightly. Boarding time is 5 p.m. and cost is $65 per person.

OTHER TOURS   Sharon Wells (© 305/294-8380; www.seekeywest.com) leads a slew of great tours throughout the island, focusing on things as diverse as literature, architecture, and places connected with the island's gay and lesbian culture.

Key West Tour Association offers two tours. For a lively look at Key West, try the **Key West Pub Crawl,** a tour of the island's most famous bars. It starts daily at 8pm, lasts 2½ hours, costs $38, and includes four drinks. Another fun option is the 1-mile, 90-minute **ghost tour,** leaving daily at 8pm from the Holiday Inn La Concha, 430 Duval St. Cost is $18 for adults and $12 for children under 12. This spooky and interesting tour gives participants insight into many old island legends.

Since the early 1940s, Key West has been a haven for gay luminaries such as Tennessee Williams and Broadway legend Jerry Herman. A new tour of **Gay Key West,** created by the Key West Business Guild, showcases the history, contributions, and landmarks associated with the island's flourishing gay and lesbian culture. Highlights include Williams's house, the art gallery owned by Key West's first gay mayor, and a variety of guesthouses whose gay owners fueled the island's architectural-restoration movement. The 70-minute tours take place Saturday at 11am, starting and ending at 511 South St. The cost is $20. Call © **305/294-4603.**

OUTDOOR ACTIVITIES

BEACHES   Unlike the rest of the Keys, Key West actually has a few small beaches, although they don't compare with the state's wide natural wonders up the coast; the Keys' beaches are typically narrow and rocky. Here are your options: Smathers Beach, off South Roosevelt Boulevard west of the airport; Higgs Beach, along Atlantic Boulevard between White Street and Reynolds Road; and Fort Zachary Beach, located off the western end of Southard Boulevard.

A magnet for partying teenagers, **Smathers Beach** is Key West's largest and most overpopulated. Despite the number of rowdy teens, the beach is actually quite clean and looks lovely since its renovation in the spring of 2000. If you go early enough in the morning, you may notice people sleeping on the beach from the night before.

Higgs Beach is a favorite among Key West's gay crowds, but what many people don't know is that beneath the sand is an unmarked cemetery of African slaves who died while waiting for freedom. Higgs has a playground and tennis courts, and is near the minute Rest Beach, which is actually hidden by the White Street Pier.

Although there is an entrance fee ($3.75 per car, plus more for each passenger), I recommend **Fort Zachary Beach,** since it includes a great historic fort, a Civil War museum, and a large picnic area with tables, barbecue grills, restrooms, and showers. Large trees scattered across 87 acres provide shade for those who are reluctant to bake in the sun.

BIKING & MOPEDING   A popular mode of transportation for locals and visitors, bikes and mopeds are available at many rental outlets in the city (p. 210). Escape the hectic downtown scene and explore the island's scenic side streets by heading away from Duval Street toward South Roosevelt Boulevard and the beachside enclaves along the way.

DIVING   One of the area's largest scuba schools, **Dive Key West, Inc.,** 3128 N. Roosevelt Blvd. (© **800/426-0707** or 305/296-3823; www.divekeywest.com), offers instruction at all levels; its dive boats take participants to scuba and snorkel sites on nearby reefs.

Key West Marine Park (© **305/294-3100**), the newest dive park along the island's Atlantic shore, incorporates no-motor "swim-only" lanes marked by buoys, providing swimmers and snorkelers with a safe way to explore the waters around Key West. The park's boundaries stretch from the foot of Duval Street to Higgs Beach.

Wreck dives and night dives are two of the special offerings of **Lost Reef Adventures,** 261 Margaret St. (© **800/952-2749** or 305/296-9737). Regularly scheduled runs and private charters can be arranged. Phone for departure information.

Also see **Mosquito Coast Outfitters,** under "Kayaking," below.

FISHING   As any angler will tell you, there's no fishing like Keys fishing. Key West has it all: bonefish, tarpon, dolphin, tuna, grouper, cobia, and more. Sharks, too.

Tips Reel Deals

When looking for the best deals on fishing excursions, know that the bookers from the kiosks in town generally take 20% of a captain's fee in addition to an extra monthly fee. You can usually save yourself money by booking directly with a captain or by going straight to one of the docks.

Step aboard a small exposed skiff for an incredibly diverse day of fishing. In the morning, you can head offshore for sailfish or dolphin (the fish, not the mammal), and then by afternoon get closer to land for a shot at tarpon, permit, grouper, or snapper. Here in Key West, you can probably pick up more cobia—one of the best fighting and eating fish around—than anywhere else in the world. For a real fight, ask your skipper to go for the tarpon—the greatest fighting fish there is, famous for its dramatic "tail walk" on the water after it's hooked. Shark fishing is also popular.

You'll find plenty of competition among the charter-fishing boats in and around Mallory Square. You can negotiate a good deal at **Charter Boat Row,** 1801 N. Roosevelt Ave. (across from the Shell station), home to more than 30 charter-fishing and party boats. Just show up to arrange your outing, or call **Garrison Bite Marina** (② 305/292-8167) for details.

The advantage of the smaller, more expensive charter boats is that you can call the shots. They'll take you where you want to go, to fish for what you want to catch. These "light tackles" are also easier to maneuver, which means you can go to backcountry spots for tarpon and bonefish, as well as out to the open ocean for tuna and dolphin. You'll really be able to feel the fish, and you'll get some good fights, too. Larger boats, for up to six or seven people, are cheaper and are best for kingfish, billfish, and sailfish. Consider Capt. Vinnie Argiro's **Heavy Hitters Charters** (② 305/745-6665) if you want a light-tackle experience. For a larger boat, try Capt. Henry Otto's 44-foot *Sunday,* docked at the Hyatt in Key West (② 305/294-7052).

The huge commercial party boats are more for sightseeing than serious angling, though you can be lucky enough to get a few bites at one of the fishing holes. One especially good deal is the *Gulfstream III* (② 305/296-8494), an all-day charter that goes out daily from 9:30am to 4:30pm. You'll pay $40 for adults, $30 for kids under 12, plus $3 for a rod and reel. This 65-foot party boat usually has at least 30 other anglers. Bring your own cooler or buy snacks onboard. Beer and wine are allowed.

Serious anglers should consider the light-tackle boats that leave from **Oceanside Marina,** on Stock Island at 5950 Peninsula Ave., 1½ miles off U.S. 1 (② 305/294-4676). It's a 20-minute drive from Old Town on the Atlantic side. There are more than 30 light-tackle guides, which range from flatbed, backcountry skiffs to 28-foot open boats. There are also a few larger charters and a party boat that goes to the Dry Tortugas. Call for details.

For a light-tackle outing with a very colorful Key West flair, call **Capt. Bruce Cronin** (② 305/294-4929) or **Capt. Kenny Harris** (② 305/294-8843), two of the more famous (and pricey) captains working these docks for over 20 years. You'll pay from $650 for a full day, usually about 8am to 4pm, and from $450 for a half-day.

GOLF   A relative newcomer in terms of local recreation, golf is gaining in popularity here, as it is in many visitor destinations. The area's only public golf club is **Key West Golf Club** (② 305/294-5232), an 18-hole course located at the entrance to the island of Key West at MM 4.5 (turn onto College Rd. to the course entrance). Designed by Rees Jones, the course has plenty of mangroves and water hazards on its 6,526 yards. It's open to the public and has a new pro shop. Call ahead for tee-time reservations. Rates are $150 per player or $85 after 2:30pm, including cart.

KAYAKING   Housed in a woodsy wine bar, **Mosquito Coast Outfitters,** 1017 Duval St. (② 305/294-7178), operates a first-rate kayaking and snorkeling tour every day as long as the weather is mild. The tours depart at 9am sharp and return around

3pm. Included in the $55 price are snacks, soft drinks, and a guided tour of the mangrove-studded islands of Sugar Key or Geiger Key, just north of Key West. The tour is primarily for kayaking, but you will have the opportunity to get in the water for snorkeling, if you're interested.

SHOPPING

You'll find all kinds of unique gifts and souvenirs in Key West, from coconut postcards to Key lime pies. On Duval Street, T-shirt shops outnumber almost any other business. If you must get a wearable memento, be careful of unscrupulous salespeople. Despite efforts to curtail the practice, many shops have been known to rip off unwitting shoppers. It pays to check the prices and the exchange rate before signing any sales slips. You are entitled to a written estimate of any T-shirt work before you pay for it.

At Mallory Square, you'll find the **Clinton Street Market,** an overly air-conditioned mall of kiosks and stalls designed for the many cruise-ship passengers who never venture beyond this super-commercial zone. Amid the dreck are some delicious coffee and candy shops, and some high-priced hats and shoes. There's also a free and clean restroom.

Once the main industry of Key West, cigar making is enjoying renewed success at the handful of factories that survived the slow years. Stroll through "**Cigar Alley**" (while on Green St., go 2 blocks west and you'll hit Cigar Alley, also known as Pirate's Alley), where you will find *viejitos* (little old men) rolling fat stogies just as they used to do in their homeland across the Florida Straits. Stop at the **Conch Republic Cigar Factory,** 512 Greene St. (© **305/295-9036**), for an excellent selection of imported and locally rolled smokes, including the famous El Hemingway. Remember, buying or selling Cuban-made cigars is illegal. Shops advertising "Cuban cigars" are usually referring to domestic cigars made from tobacco grown from seeds that were brought from Cuba decades ago. To be fair, though, many premium cigars today are grown from Cuban seed tobacco—only it is grown in Latin America and the Caribbean, not Cuba.

If you're looking for local or Caribbean art, you'll find nearly a dozen galleries and shops clustered on Duval Street between Catherine and Fleming streets. There are also some excellent shops scattered on the side streets. One worth seeking out is the **Haitian Art Co.,** 600 Frances St. (© **305/296-8932**), where you can browse through room upon room of original paintings from well-known and obscure Haitian artists in a range of prices, from a few dollars to a few thousand. Also check out **Cuba, Cuba!** at 814 Duval St. (© **305/295-9442**), where you'll see paintings, sculpture, and photos by Cuban artists, as well as books and art from the island.

A favorite stop in the Keys is the deliciously fragrant **Key West Aloe,** 524 Front St., between Simonton and Duval streets (© **305/294-5592**). Since 1971, this shop has been selling a simple line of bath products—including lotions, shampoos, and soothing balms—for those who want a reminder of the tropical breezes once they're back home. At the main shop (open until 8pm), you can find great gift baskets, tropical perfumes, and candies and cookies, too. In addition to frangipani, vanilla, and hibiscus scents, sample Key West for Men, a unique and alluringly musky best-seller.

For foodies, the **Key Lime Pie Co.** (© **305/294-6567**) is so popular for its pies, cookies, and pretty much anything you can think of made with Key lime (candles, soaps, lotions) that there are two locations on the tiny island. One is at 701 Caroline St.; the other is at 424 Greene St. From sweet to spicy, **Peppers of Key West,** 602 Greene St. (© **305/295-9333**), is a hot-sauce-lover's heaven, with hundreds of variations, from mild to brutally spicy. Grab a seat at the tasting bar and be prepared to let your taste buds sizzle.

Literature and music buffs will appreciate the many bookshops and record stores on the island. **Key West Island Bookstore,** 513 Fleming St. (© **305/294-2904**), carries new, used, and rare books, and specializes in fiction by residents of the Keys, including Ernest Hemingway, Tennessee Williams, Shel Silverstein, Ann Beattie, Richard Wilbur, and John Hersey. The bookstore is open daily from 10am to 9pm. **Flaming Maggie's,** 830 Fleming St. (© **305/294-3931**), carries a wide selection of gay books. It's open Monday through Saturday from 10am to 6pm.

For anything else, from bed linens to candlesticks to clothing, go to downtown's oldest and most renowned department store, **Fast Buck Freddie's,** 500 Duval St. (© **305/294-2007**). For the same merchandise at reduced prices, try **Half Buck Freddie's** ☆, 726 Caroline St. (© **305/294-2007**), where you can shop for out-of-season bargains and "rejects" from the main store.

Also check out **KW Light Gallery,** 534 Fleming St. (© **305/294-0566**), for high-quality contemporary photography as well as historic images and other artwork that relate to the Keys or exemplify the concept of light and its varied interpretations. The gallery is open Thursday through Tuesday from 10am to 6pm (10am–4pm in summer).

WHERE TO STAY

You'll find a wide variety of places to stay in Key West, from resorts with all the amenities to seaside motels, quaint bed-and-breakfasts, and clothing-optional guesthouses. Unless you're in town during Key West's most popular holidays—Fantasy Fest (around Halloween), where Mardi Gras meets South Florida for the NC-17 set; Hemingway Days (in July), where Papa is seemingly and eerily alive and well; and Christmas and New Year's—or for a big fishing tournament (many are held Oct–Dec) or boat-racing tourney, you can almost always find a place to stay at the last minute. However, you may want to book early, especially in winter, when prime properties fill up and many require 2- or 3-night minimum stays. Prices at these times are extremely high. Finding a decent room for under $100 a night is a real trick.

Another suggestion, and my recommendation, is to call **Vacation Key West** (© **800/595-5397** or 305/295-9500; www.vacationkw.com), a wholesaler that offers discounts of 20% to 30% and is skilled at finding last-minute deals. It represents mostly larger hotels and motels, but can also place visitors in guesthouses. The phones are answered Monday through Friday from 9am to 6pm, and Saturday from 11am to 2pm. **Key West Innkeepers Association** (© **800/492-1911** or 305/292-3600) can also help you find lodging in any price range from among its members and affiliates.

Gay travelers may want to call the **Key West Business Guild** (© **305/294-4603**), which represents more than 50 guesthouses and B&Bs in town, as well as many other gay-owned businesses. Be advised that most gay guesthouses have a clothing-optional policy. One of the most elegant and popular is **Big Ruby's,** 409 Applerouth Lane (© **800/477-7829** or 305/296-2323; www.bigrubys.com), located on a little alley just off Duval Street. Rates start at $147 double in peak season and $102 off season. A low cluster of buildings surrounds a lush courtyard where a hearty breakfast is served each morning and wine is poured at dusk. The all-male guests hang out by the pool, tanning in the buff. Also popular is **Oasis,** 823 Fleming St. (© **305/296-2131;** www.keywest-allmale.com), which is superclean and friendly, with a central location and a 14-seat hot tub. Rates are $169 to $229 in winter and $109 to $169 in summer.

Another luxurious property is the **Florida Key Guesthouse,** 412 Frances St. (© **305/296-4719**), which is more romantic and traditionally decorated, and welcomes many lesbian travelers as well. *Out and About* gave it a five-star rating. Rates are $225 in season and $125 off season. For women only, **Pearl's Rainbow,** 525 United St. (© **800/74-WOMYN** or 305/292-1450; www.pearlsrainbow.com), is a large, fairly well-maintained guesthouse with lots of privacy and amenities, including two pools and two hot tubs. Rates in season range from $99 to $229.

VERY EXPENSIVE
The Gardens Hotel ★★★ *Finds*   At last, the true garden of Eden has been located—and it's on Angela Street in Key West. Once a private residence, the Gardens Hotel (whose main house is listed on the National Register of Historic Places) is hidden amid the exotic Peggy Mills tropical botanical gardens. Behind the greenery is a Bahamian-style hideaway featuring luxuriously appointed rooms in the main house, garden and courtyard rooms in the carriage house, and one uber-secluded cottage. I stayed in a courtyard room and didn't want to leave, even though the place is within walking distance of frenetic Duval Street. A gorgeous free-form pool is centered in the courtyard, where a Tiki bar serves libations. The Jacuzzi is hidden behind beautiful landscaping. Guest rooms are resplendent, with hardwood floors, brass and iron beds, marble bathrooms, Aveda products, and a sense of serenity that words can't describe. Winding brick pathways leading to secluded seating areas in the private gardens make for an idyllic getaway that's the quintessence of paradise. *Note:* If you plan to party, do not stay here—guests tend to be on the quieter, more sophisticated side.

526 Angela St., Key West, FL 33040. © **800/526-2664** or 305/294-2661. Fax 305/292-1007. www.gardenshotel. com. 17 units. Winter $155–$295 double, $295–$575 suite; off season $130–$175 double, $245–$385 suite. Rates include continental breakfast. AE, DC, MC, V. **Amenities:** Bar; pool. *In room:* A/C, TV, hair dryer, safe.

Hilton Key West Resort and Marina ★★   Ideally situated at the very end of Duval Street in the middle of all of Old Town's action, the Hilton Key West is a prime spot from which to enjoy sunsets as well as that hard-to-find, quietly elegant ambience that's so lacking in most big resorts here. The rooms are large and well appointed, with all the modern conveniences. Choose a suite in the main building if you want a Jacuzzi in your living room. Otherwise, the marina building has great views. The secluded beach is great for an escape from the Duval Street frenzy. For just $10 per person (free for children under 18), you can also enjoy the Hilton's private Sunset Key beach, accessible only by the hotel's launch at the marina. Bistro 245, the elegant dining room, offers ample breakfasts and a huge Sunday brunch.

Hilton's gorgeous **Sunset Key Guest Cottages** ★★★, with whitewashed interiors and fabulous views, are located 500 yards offshore on Sunset Key and are accessible only by private launch. Check in at the Hilton and take a 10-minute cruise to the island, where there are no cars—only a beach, restaurant, bar, and free-form pool with whirlpool jets. Cottages are equipped with full kitchens, high-tech entertainment centers, and one, two, or three massive bedrooms. Sunset Key guests have access to all watersports at the Hilton.

245 Front St. (at the end of Duval St.), Key West, FL 33040. © **800/221-2424** or 305/294-4000. Fax 305/294-4086. www.hilton.com. 215 units. Winter $369–$529 double, $459–$1,149 suite; off season $229–$459 double, $359–$1,059 suite. 37 Sunset Key Cottages, up to 5 people: winter $745–$2,000; off season $625-$1,545. Private chef: $75 per person plus additional chef/hotel fees, tax, and gratuities. AE, DC, DISC, MC, V. Self-parking $7, valet parking $10. **Amenities:** 2 restaurants; pool bar; outdoor heated pool; health club; Jacuzzi; watersports equipment rental; bike rental; game room; concierge; business center; limited room service; in-room massage; self-service laundry; dry cleaning; full-service marina. *In room:* A/C, TV, dataport, minibar, coffeemaker, hair dryer, iron.

Ocean Key Resort and Spa ⭑   You can't beat the location of this 100-room resort, at the foot of Mallory Square, the epicenter of the sunset ritual. Ocean Key also features a Gulf-side heated pool and the lively Sunset Pier, where guests can wind down with cocktails and live music. Guest rooms are huge and luxuriously appointed, with living and dining areas, oversize Jacuzzis, and views of the Gulf, the harbor, or Mallory Square and Duval Street. The two-bedroom suite is 1,200 square feet and has a full kitchen, three beds, and a large private balcony. The property is adorned in classic Key West decor, from the tile floors and hand-painted furniture to the pastel art. The brand-new Indonesian-inspired Spa Terre is perhaps the best in town. The resort's restaurant, Hot Tin Roof (p. 229), is one of Key West's best.

Zero Duval St. (near Mallory Docks), Key West, FL 33040. ② 800/328-9815 or 305/296-7701. Fax 305/292-2198. www.oceankey.com. 100 units. Winter $379–$679 double, $479–$1,149 suite; off season $239–$439 double, $319–$639 suite. AE, DC, MC, V. **Amenities:** 2 restaurants; 3 bars; heated pool; watersports equipment rental; moped/bike rental; concierge; room service; in-room massage; babysitting; laundry services. *In room:* A/C, TV, wireless Internet access, minibar, coffeemaker, hair dryer, iron.

Pier House Resort and Caribbean Spa ⭑   If you're looking for something a bit more intimate than the Wyndham Reach (see below), Pier House is an ideal choice. Its location—at the foot of Duval Street and just steps from Mallory Docks—is the envy of every hotel on the island. Set back from the busy street, on a short strip of private beach, this place is a welcome oasis of calm. The accommodations vary tremendously, from simple business-style rooms to romantic quarters complete with stereos and whirlpool tubs. Although every unit has either a balcony or a patio, not all overlook the water. My favorites, in the two-story spa building, don't have any view at all. But what they lack in scenery, they make up for in opulence: Each well-appointed spa room has a sitting area and a huge Jacuzzi bathroom.

1 Duval St. (near Mallory Docks), Key West, FL 33040. ② 800/327-8340 or 305/296-4600. Fax 305/296-9085. www.pierhouse.com. 142 units. Winter $290–$460 double, $485–$1,800 suite; off season $200–$355 double, $355–$1,400 suite. AE, DC, MC, V. **Amenities:** 3 restaurants; 3 bars; heated pool; full-service spa and fitness center; 2 Jacuzzis; sauna; watersports equipment rental; moped/bike rental; concierge; limited room service; in-room massage; babysitting; laundry services. *In room:* A/C, TV, dataport, minibar, coffeemaker, hair dryer, iron.

Wyndham Reach Resort ⭑⭑   Unlike Wyndham's Casa Marina resort, the Reach is better suited to adults and not families. The location here can be either a highlight or a drawback; it's a 5-minute walk from the center of the Duval Street action. Supported by stilts that leave the entire ground floor for parking, the hotel offers four floors of rooms designed around atriums. The wonderful guest rooms are large and feature tile floors and sturdy wicker furnishings. All have sliding-glass doors that open onto balconies, and some have ocean views. There's also a private pier for fishing and tanning. The protected waters are tame and shallow. For steak lovers, Shula's on the Beach is a Keys sibling to Miami's lauded Shula's Steak House (p. 120).

1435 Simonton St., Key West, FL 33040. ② 800/874-4118, or 800/996-3426 for reservations. Fax 305/296-2830. www.wyndham.com/hotels/EYWRR/main.wnt. 150 units. Winter $309–$469 double; off season $169–$369 double. AE, DC, DISC, MC, V. **Amenities:** 2 restaurants; bar; outdoor heated pool; nearby tennis and golf; health club and spa; watersports equipment rental; bike rental; concierge; tour desk; business center; salon; 24-hr. room service; in-room massage; babysitting; dry cleaning. *In room:* A/C, TV, dataport, minibar, fridge, coffeemaker, hair dryer, iron.

EXPENSIVE

Curry Mansion Inn ⭑⭑ *Finds*   This charismatic inn is the former home of the island's first millionaire, a once-penniless Bahamian immigrant who made a fortune as a pirate. Owned today by Al and Edith Amsterdam, the Curry Mansion is now on the National Register of Historic Places, but you won't feel like you're staying in a museum—it's rather like a wonderfully warm home. Rooms are very sparsely decorated, with wicker furniture, four-poster beds, and pink walls—call it Key West minimalism meets Victorian. The dining room is reminiscent of a Victorian dollhouse, with elegant table settings and rich wood floors and furnishings. Every morning, there's a delicious European-style breakfast buffet; at night, cocktail parties are held. There's also a really nice patio, on which, from time to time, there's live entertainment.

511 Caroline St., Key West, FL 33040. ℂ 800/253-3466 or 305/294-5349. Fax 305/294-4093. www.currymansion. com. 28 units. Winter $200–$240 double, $260–$325 suite; off season $145–$195 double, $220–$245 suite. Rates include breakfast buffet. AE, DC, MC, V. No children under 12. **Amenities:** Dining room; pool; bike rental; concierge. *In room:* A/C, TV, minibar.

Island City House Hotel 🌟🌟   A small resort unto itself, the Island City House consists of three separate buildings that share a common junglelike patio and pool. The first building, unimaginatively called the Island City House building, is a historic three-story wooden structure with wraparound verandas on every floor. The warmly outfitted interiors here include wood floors and many antiques. The tile bathrooms could use more counter space, but eccentricities are part of this hotel's charm. The unpainted wooden Cigar House has particularly large bedrooms, similar in ambience to those in the Island City House. The Arch House is the least appealing of the three buildings, but still recommended. Built of Dade County pine, this house's cozy bedrooms are furnished in wicker and rattan, and come with small kitchens and bathrooms.

411 William St., Key West, FL 33040. ℂ 800/634-8230 or 305/294-5702. Fax 305/294-1289. www.islandcityhouse. com. 24 units. Winter $190–$240 1-bedroom suite, $285–$350 2-bedroom suite; off season $120–$185 1-bedroom suite, $195–$250 2-bedroom suite. Rates include breakfast. AE, DC, DISC, MC, V. **Amenities:** Outdoor heated pool; access to nearby health club; Jacuzzi; bike rental; concierge; in-room massage; babysitting; laundry service and self-service laundry; dry cleaning. *In room:* A/C, TV, kitchen, coffeemaker, hair dryer.

Marquesa Hotel 🌟🌟🌟 *Finds*   The Marquesa offers the charm of a small historic hotel coupled with the amenities of a large resort. It encompasses four buildings, two pools, and a three-stage waterfall that cascades into a lily pond. Two of the hotel's buildings are luxuriously restored Victorian homes outfitted with plush antiques and contemporary furniture. The rooms in the two newly constructed buildings are even more opulent; many have four-poster wrought-iron beds with bright floral spreads. The bathrooms in the new buildings are lush and spacious; those in the older buildings are also nice, but not nearly as huge and luxe. The decor is simple, elegant, and spotless. The hotel also boasts one of Key West's most elegant restaurants, Cafe Marquesa.

600 Fleming St. (at Simonton St.), Key West, FL 33040. ℂ 800/869-4631 or 305/292-1919. Fax 305/294-2121. www.marquesa.com. 27 units. Winter $285–$450 double; off season $185–$320 double. AE, DC, MC, V. No children under 12. **Amenities:** Restaurant; 2 outdoor pools (1 heated); access to nearby health club; bike rental; concierge; limited room service. *In room:* A/C, TV, CD player, dataport, minibar, hair dryer, iron, safe.

Weatherstation Inn 🌟 *Finds*   Originally built in 1912 as a weather station, this beautifully restored, meticulously maintained Renaissance-style inn is just 2 blocks from Duval Street but seems worlds away. It's situated on the tropical grounds of the former Old Navy Yard, now an exclusive and private gated community. Truman, Eisenhower, and JFK all visited the station. Spacious and uncluttered, each guest room is uniquely furnished to complement the interior architecture: hardwood floors, tall sash windows, and high ceilings. The large, modern bathrooms are especially appealing. The staff is both friendly and accommodating.

57 Front St., Key West, FL 33040. ⓒ **800/815-2707** or 305/294-7277. Fax 305/294-0544. www.weatherstationinn. com. 8 units. Winter $215–$325 double; off season $170–$235 double. Rates include continental breakfast. AE, DISC, MC, V. **Amenities:** Outdoor pool; concierge. *In room:* A/C, TV/VCR, hair dryer.

MODERATE

Ambrosia Key West ★★ *Finds*   Even after making countless visits a year to the tiny island of Key West, I discover yet another hidden treasure every time I go back. Ambrosia is one of them, a private compound set on 2 lush acres just a block from Duval Street. Three lagoon-style pools, suites, townhouses, and a cottage are spread around the grounds. Townhouses have living rooms, kitchens, and spiral staircases leading to master suites with vaulted ceilings and private decks. The cottage, overlooking a dip pool, is a perfect family retreat, with two bedrooms, two bathrooms, a living room, and a kitchen. All rooms have private entrances, most with French doors opening onto a variety of intimate outdoor spaces, including private verandas, patios, and gardens with sculptures, fountains, and pools. Fantastic service, bolstered by the philosophy that it's better to have high occupancy than high rates, explains why Ambrosia has a 90% year-round occupancy—a record in seasonal Key West.

622 Fleming St., Key West, FL 33040. ⓒ **800/535-9838** or 305/296-9838. Fax 305/296-2425. www.ambrosiakey west.com. 19 units. Winter $139–$189 double, $154–$499 suite; off season $120–$135 double, $145–$325 suite. Rates include breakfast. AE, DISC, MC, V. Off- and on-street parking. Pets accepted. **Amenities:** 3 outdoor heated pools; hot tub. *In room:* A/C, TV, CD player, kitchens (in some units), fridge, coffeemaker, hair dryer, iron.

Doubletree Grand Key Resort ★ *Finds*   If you don't mind staying on the quiet "other" side of the island, a 10-minute cab ride away from Duval Street, the Doubletree is an excellent choice, not to mention excellent value. An ecologically conscious resort, the hotel has been renovated with ecosensitive materials as well as an interior created to conserve energy, reduce waste, and preserve the area's natural resources. Rooms are clean and comfortable, with some looking onto the spacious pool area, which is surrounded by an unsightly empty lot of mangroves and marshes. The newest addition is a welcome one—a Beach Club located off-property at Smathers Beach, where the hotel has established a hut with chairs, towels, and umbrellas. Watersports are available here, as is a free shuttle to transport guests back and forth. The hotel's restaurant is very good—but for excitement, look elsewhere.

3990 S. Roosevelt Blvd., Key West, FL 33040. ⓒ **888/310-1540** or 305/293-1818. Fax 305/296-6962. www.double treekeywest.com. 216 units. Winter $112–$275 double, $195–$315 suite; off season $89–$139 double, $115–$299 suite. Rates include continental breakfast. AE, DISC, MC, V. Free parking. **Amenities:** Restaurant; Tiki bar and lounge; pool; concierge; meeting rooms; limited room service. *In room:* A/C, TV/Web TV, PlayStation, dataport, minibar, coffee-maker, hair dryer, iron, safe.

La Pensione ★★   This classic B&B, located in a stunning 1891 home, is a total charmer. The comfortable rooms all have air-conditioning, ceiling fans, and king-size beds. Many also have French doors opening onto spacious verandas. Although the rooms have no TVs, the distractions of Duval Street, only steps away, should keep you adequately occupied. Breakfast, which includes Belgian waffles, fresh fruit, and a variety of breads or muffins, can be taken on the wraparound porch or at the communal dining table. Recent guests, however, have informed us that service here is not as friendly as it used to be and that the inn's location on U.S. 1 isn't so hot when it comes to the noise and traffic levels.

809 Truman Ave. (between Windsor and Margaret sts.), Key West, FL 33040. ⓒ **800/893-1193** or 305/292-9923. Fax 305/296-6509. www.lapensione.com. 9 units. Winter $178–$188 double; off season $118–$128 double. Rates include

breakfast. 10% discount for readers who mention this book. AE, DC, DISC, MC, V. No children. **Amenities:** Outdoor pool; access to nearby health club; bike rental. *In room:* A/C.

Southermost Point Guest House ★★ *Finds* *Kids*   One of the few inns that actually welcomes children and pets, this romantic guesthouse is a real find. The antiseptically clean rooms are not as fancy as the house's ornate 1885 exterior, but each is unique and includes some combination of basic beds and a hodgepodge of furnishings, such as futon couches and high-back wicker chairs. Room no. 5 is best, with a private porch, ocean view, and windows that let in lots of light. Every unit comes with fresh flowers, wine, and a full decanter of sherry. Mona Santiago, the kind, laid-back owner, provides chairs and towels for the beach, which is just a block away. Guests can help themselves to free wine as they soak in the 14-seat hot tub. Kids will enjoy the backyard swings and the pet rabbits.

1327 Duval St., Key West, FL 33040. © **305/294-0715.** Fax 305/296-0641. www.southernmostpoint.com. 6 units. Winter $115–$175 double, $235–$265 suite; off season $75–$110 double, $155–$165 suite. Rates include breakfast. AE, MC, V. Pets accepted ($5 in summer, $10 in winter). **Amenities:** Garden pool; hot tub; laundry facilities; barbecue grills. *In room:* A/C, TV/VCR, fridge, coffeemaker, hair dryer, iron.

Westwinds Inn ★   A close second to staying in your own private 19th-century, tin-roofed clapboard house is this tranquil inn, just 4 blocks from Duval Street in the historic Seaport district. Lush landscaping keeps the place extremely private and secluded; at times, you'll feel as if you're alone. Two pools, one heated in winter, are offset by alcoves, fountains, and the well-maintained whitewashed inn, which is actually composed of five separate buildings. Rooms are Key West comfortable, with private bathrooms, wicker furnishings, and fans. All are nonsmoking.

914 Eaton St., Key West, FL 33040. © **800/788-4150** or 305/296-4440. Fax 305/293-0931. www.westwindskeywest.com. 22 units. Winter $145–$205 double, $205–$225 suite; off season $75–$110 double, $135-$150 suite. Rates include continental breakfast. DISC, MC, V. No children under 12. **Amenities:** 2 pools (1 heated); bike rental; self-service laundry. *In room:* A/C (some rooms have TVs and kitchenettes).

INEXPENSIVE

Angelina Guest House ★★   This former bordello and gambling hall–turned–youth hostel type guesthouse is about the cheapest in town—and it's conveniently located near a hot hippie restaurant called Blue Heaven (p. 231). Though the neighborhood is definitely urban, it's generally safe and full of character. Accommodations are furnished uniquely in a modest style. Two rooms have full kitchens, one has a microwave and small fridge, and all but three have private bathrooms. A gorgeous lagoon-style heated pool with waterfall and tropical landscaping was an excellent addition. Even better are the poolside hammocks—get out there early, as they go quickly! Even though the Angelina is sparse (perfect for bohemian types who don't mind a little grit), it's a great place to crash if you're traveling on the cheap.

302 Angela St. (at Thomas St.), Key West, FL 33040. © **888/303-4480** or 305/294-4480. Fax 305/272-0681. www.angelinaguesthouse.com. 14 units. Winter $89–$159 double; off season $59–$109 double. Rates include continental breakfast. DISC, MC, V. **Amenities:** Outdoor heated pool; concierge. *In room:* A/C, hair dryer, iron, no phone.

The Grand ★★ *Finds*   Don't expect cabbies or locals to know about this well-kept secret, located in a modest residential section of Old Town, about 5 blocks from Duval Street. It's got almost everything you could want, including a very moderate price tag. Proprietor Elizabeth Rose goes out of her way to provide any and all services for her appreciative guests. All units have private bathrooms, air-conditioning, and private entrances. The best deal is room no. 2; it's small and lacks a closet, but it has a porch

and the most privacy. Suites are a real steal, too: The large two-room units come with full kitchens. This place is undoubtedly the best bargain in town.

1116 Grinnell St. (between Virginia and Catherine sts.), Key West, FL 33040. ℭ **888/947-2630** or 305/294-0590. Fax 305/294-0477. www.thegrandguesthouse.com. 11 units. Winter $108–$158 double, $148–$188 suite; off season $88–$98 double, $108–$118 suite. Rates include continental breakfast. AE, DISC, MC, V. **Amenities:** Bike/scooter rental; concierge. *In room:* A/C, TV, fridge.

Key West International Hostel & Seashell Motel   This well-run hostel is a 3-minute walk to the beach and Old Town. Very busy with European backpackers, it's a great place to meet people. The dorm rooms are dark, grimy, and sparse, but livable if you're desperate for a cheap stay. The higher-priced motel rooms are a good deal, especially those equipped with kitchens. Amenities include a pool table under a Tiki roof; bike rentals; cheap food at breakfast, lunch, and dinner; and discounted prices for snorkeling, diving, and sunset cruises.

718 South St., Key West, FL 33040. ℭ **800/51-HOSTEL** or 305/296-5719. Fax 305/296-0672. www.keywesthostel. com. 96 units, 10 private rooms, 1 2-bedroom suite with Jacuzzi. Year-round $28 members, $31 nonmembers. Motel units $75–$105 in season; $55–$85 off season. MC, V. Free parking. **Amenities:** Bike rental; kitchen. *In room:* Motel rooms: A/C, TV, fridge, coffeemaker, hair dryer. Dorm rooms: A/C only.

WHERE TO DINE

With its share of the usual drive-through fast-food franchises—mostly up on Roosevelt Boulevard—and Duval Street succumbing to the lure of a Hard Rock Cafe, you might be surprised to learn that, over the years, an upscale and high-quality dining scene has begun to thrive in Key West. Just wander Old Town or the newly spruced-up Bahama Village and browse menus after you've exhausted my list of picks below.

If you don't feel like venturing out, call **We Deliver** (ℭ **305/293-0078**), a service that will bring anything you want from any of the area's restaurants or stores for a small fee ($3–$6); it's available from 3 to 11pm. If you're staying in a condominium or efficiency, you may want to stock your fridge with groceries, beer, wine, and snacks from the area's oldest grocer, **Fausto's Food Palace.** Open since 1926, there are now two locations: 1105 White St. and 522 Fleming St. The Fleming Street location will deliver with a minimum $25 order (ℭ **305/294-5221** or 305/296-5663).

VERY EXPENSIVE

Cafe des Artistes 🌟🌟🌟 FRENCH   Open for nearly 2 decades, the Cafe des Artistes' impressive longevity is the result of its winning combination of food and atmosphere. The fact that it was once part of a hotel built in 1935 by Al Capone's bookkeeper adds to its allure, but it's the food that's the draw. Traditional French meals benefit from a subtle tropical twist. Start with the duck-liver pâté, made with fresh truffles and old cognac, or Maryland crabmeat served with a confit of artichoke heart and herbed tomato. Nouvelle and traditional French entrees include lobster flambé with mango and basil, and wine-basted lamb chops rubbed with rosemary and ginger.

1007 Simonton St. (near Truman Ave.). ℭ **305/294-7100.** Reservations recommended. Main courses $25–$38. AE, MC, V. Daily 6–11pm.

Café Marquesa 🌟🌟🌟 CONTEMPORARY AMERICAN   If you're looking for fabulous dining (and service) in Key West, this is the place. The intimate, 50-seat restaurant is something to look at, but it's really the food that you'll want to admire. Specialties include peppercorn-dusted yellowfin tuna with saffron risotto; grilled Florida lobster tail and diver sea scallops with Thai basil sauce, black Thai rice, and Asian vegetables; and an almost perfect feta and pine nut–crusted rack of lamb with rosemary demiglace, creamy polenta, and eggplant caponata. If you're looking to splurge, this is the place.

In the Marquesa Hotel, 600 Fleming St. ✆ **305/292-1919.** Reservations highly recommended. Main courses $20–$36. AE, DC, MC, V. Summer daily 7–11pm; winter daily 6–11pm.

Hot Tin Roof 𝒢𝒢𝒢 FUSION Ever hear of conch fusion cuisine? Neither did I until I experienced it firsthand—or -mouth, rather—at Hot Tin Roof, Ocean Key Resort's chichi restaurant where CIA graduate Jesse Van Rossum takes South American, Asian, French, and Keys cuisine and transforms it into an experience unlike any other in this part of the world. The vibrant 3,000-square-foot space features both indoor and outdoor deck seating overlooking the harbor. Live jazz/fusion adds to the stunning environment—it's the epitome of casual elegance. Signature dishes include an irresistible lobster and roasted corn quesadilla, seafood paella, and chocolate-lava cake that makes this tin roof very hot, to say the least, especially for Key West.

In the Ocean Key Resort, Zero Duval St. ✆ **305/296-7701.** Reservations highly recommended. Main courses $18–$35. AE, DC, MC, V. Daily 7:30–11am and 5–10pm.

Louie's Backyard 𝒢𝒢 CARIBBEAN Nestled amid blooming bougainvillea on a lush slice of the Gulf, Louie's remains one of the most romantic restaurants on earth. Famed chef Norman Van Aiken of Norman's in Miami brought his talents farther south and started what has become one of the finest dining spots in the Keys. As a result, this is one of the hardest places to score a reservation: Either call way in advance or hope that your hotel concierge has some pull. After dinner, sit at the dockside bar and watch the waves crash, almost touching your feet, while enjoying a cocktail at sunset. You can't go wrong with the fresh catch of the day, or any seafood dish, for that matter. The weekend brunches are also great. If you can't stay for dinner, go for lunch; this is one dining experience you won't want to miss.

700 Waddell Ave. ✆ **305/294-1061.** Reservations highly recommended. Main courses $25–$30; lunch $8–$15. AE, DC, MC, V. Daily 11:30am–3pm and 6–10:30pm.

One Duval 𝒢𝒢𝒢 CARIBBEAN The waterfront setting of this restaurant at the Pier House Resort is beautiful, but you may be too distracted to notice the views when you taste the food, which executive chef Will Greenwood describes as New Calypso Harvest. One of the best restaurants in Key West, One Duval blends the ingredients of the Caribbean and Florida with an innovative twist. For starters, the crabmeat stuffed in phyllo is outstanding, and the goat-cheese soufflé is incredibly hedonistic. For main courses, smoked cured pork chop with Captain Morgan–spiced rum sauce is a best bet, as is ponzu-marinated yellowfin tuna tartare and avocado mousse timbale. The Key lime pie with meringue is a must-have. Service is friendly and professional; this is not the kind of restaurant that will rush you. Eat first, then sit back and digest the views so you don't miss any of this fine restaurant's offerings.

In the Pier House Resort, 1 Duval St. ✆ **305/296-4600.** Reservations highly recommended. Main courses $25–$30. AE, DC, MC, V. Daily 6–10:30pm.

EXPENSIVE

Antonia's 𝒢𝒢 REGIONAL ITALIAN The food is great, but the atmosphere a bit fussy for Key West. If you don't have a reservation in season, don't even bother. Still, if you don't mind paying high prices for dishes that go for much less elsewhere, try this old favorite. From the perfectly seasoned homemade focaccia to an exemplary crème brûlée, this elegant little standout is amazingly consistent. The menu includes a small selection of classics, such as *zuppa di pesce* and veal Marsala. But go for one of the nightly specials. You can't go wrong with any of the handmade pastas. And the owners, Antonia Berto and Phillip Smith, travel to Italy every year to research recipes, so you can be sure you're getting an authentic taste of Italy in small-town Key West.

615 Duval St. ✆ 305/294-6565. Fax 305/294-3888. Reservations suggested. Main courses $20–$28; pastas $13–$18. AE, DC, MC, V. Daily 6–11pm.

Bagatelle ✪✪✪ SEAFOOD/TROPICAL   Reserve a seat at the elegant second-floor veranda overlooking Duval Street's mayhem. From the calm above, you may want to start your meal with the excellent herb-and-garlic-stuffed whole artichoke or the sashimi-like seared tuna rolled in black peppercorns. The best chicken and beef dishes are given a tropical treatment: grilled with papaya, ginger, and soy.

115 Duval St. ✆ 305/296-6609. Reservations recommended. Main courses $14–$21; lunch $5–$10. AE, DISC, MC, V. Sun–Thurs 11:30am–10pm; Fri–Sat 11:30am–11pm.

La Trattoria ✪ ITALIAN   Have a true Italian feast in a relaxed atmosphere. Each dish here is prepared and presented according to old Italian tradition. Try the delicious bread-crumb-stuffed mushroom caps; they're firm yet tender. The stuffed eggplant with ricotta and roasted peppers is light and flavorful. Or have the seafood salad of shrimp, calamari, and mussels, fish-market fresh and tasty. The pasta dishes are also great—go for the penne Venezia, with mushrooms, sun-dried tomatoes, and crab-meat. For dessert, don't skip the homemade tiramisu; it's light yet full-flavored. The dining room is spacious but still intimate, and the waiters are friendly. Before you leave, visit Virgilio's, a cocktail lounge with live jazz until 2am.

524 Duval St. ✆ 305/296-1075. Pasta $10–$17; main courses $17–$22. AE, DC, DISC, MC, V. Daily 5:30–11pm.

Mangoes ✪✪✪ FLORIBBEAN   This restaurant's large brick patio, shaded by over-grown banyan trees, is so alluring to passersby that it's packed almost every night of the week. Many people don't realize how pricey the meals can be here because, upon first glance, it looks like a casual Duval Street cafe. Appetizers include grilled shrimp cocktail with spicy mango chutney. Crispy curried chicken and local snapper with pas-sion-fruit sauce are typical among the entrees, but the Garlic and Lime Pinks—a half-pound of Key West pink shrimp seasoned and grilled with a roasted garlic and Key lime glaze—is the menu's best offering by far. Even though it's right on touristy Duval Street, Mangoes enjoys a good reputation among locals and stands out from the rest of the places here offering greasy bar fare.

700 Duval St. (at Angela St.). ✆ 305/292-4606. Reservations recommended for parties of 6 or more. Main courses $12–$26; pizzas $10–$13; lunch $7–$14. AE, DC, DISC, MC, V. Daily 11am–midnight; pizza until 1am.

Michael's ✪✪✪ *(Finds* STEAK   Tucked away in a residential neighborhood, Michael's is a meaty oasis in a big sea of fish. With steaks flown in daily from Chicago, this is *the* steakhouse to be at when you're craving meat. Unlike most steakhouses, Michael's exudes a relaxed, tropical ambiance with a fabulous indoor/outdoor setting that's romantic but not stuffy. A fantastic fondue menu makes for a tasty snack or even meal, complimented by an excellent, reasonably priced wine list. Sure, Michael's is on the pricier side, but it's not every day that you can enjoy slabs of beef from Chicago in a warm, tropical setting.

532 Margaret St. ✆ 305/295-1300. Reservations recommended. Main courses $15–$35. AE, DC, DISC, MC, V. Daily 5-11pm.

Seven Fish ★★★ *Finds* SEAFOOD "Simple, good food" is Seven Fish's motto, but this hidden little secret is much more than simple. One of the most popular locals' restaurants, Seven Fish is a chic seafood spot serving some of the best fish dishes on the island. Crab and shiitake-mushroom pasta, fish of the day, and gnocchi with blue cheese and sautéed fish are among the dishes to choose from. For dessert, do not miss the Key lime cake over tart lime curd with fresh berries.

632 Olivia St. ℭ 305/296-2777. Reservations recommended. Main courses $12–$23. AE, MC, V. Wed–Mon 6–10pm.

MODERATE

Alonzo's Oyster Bar ★ SEAFOOD Alonzo's offers good seafood in a casual setting. It's located on the ground floor of the A&B Lobster House, at the end of Front Street in the marina; if you want to dress up, go upstairs for the "fine dining." To start your meal, try the steamed beer shrimp—tantalizingly fresh jumbo shrimp in a sauce of garlic, Old Bay, beer, and cayenne pepper. A house specialty is white-clam chili, a delicious mix of tender clams, white beans, and potatoes served with a dollop of sour cream. The staff is cheerful and informative, and the service is very good.

231 Margaret St. ℭ 305/294-5880. Appetizers $5–$8; main courses $11–$17. MC, V. Daily 11am–11pm.

Banana Café ★★★ *Finds* FRENCH Although neither as elaborate as Cafe des Artistes nor as casual as Blue Heaven, Banana Café is open for three meals a day and benefits from a French-country-cafe look and feel. The upscale local eatery discovered by savvy visitors on the less-congested end of Duval Street has retained its loyal clientele with affordable prices and delightful, light preparations. The crepes are legendary on the island for breakfast or lunch; the fresh ingredients and French-themed menu bring daytime diners back for the casual, classy, tropical-influenced dinner menu. There's live jazz every Thursday night.

1211 Duval St. ℭ 305/294-7227. Main courses $4.80–$23; breakfast and lunch $2–$8.50. AE, DC, MC, V. Daily 8am–11pm.

Blue Heaven ★★ *Finds* SEAFOOD/AMERICAN/NATURAL This hippie-run restaurant has become the place to be in Key West—and with good reason. Be prepared to wait in line. The food here is some of the best in town—especially at breakfast, which features homemade granola, tropical-fruit pancakes, and seafood Benedict. Dinners are just as good and run the gamut from fresh-caught fish and Jamaican jerk chicken to curried soups and vegetarian stews. Some people are put off by the dirt floors and roaming cats and birds, but frankly, it adds to the charm. The building used to be a bordello, where Hemingway was said to hang out watching cockfights. It's still lively here, but not *that* lively!

305 Petronia St. ℭ 305/296-8666. Main courses $10–$30; lunch $6–$14; breakfast $5–$11. DISC, MC, V. Daily 8–11:30am, noon–3pm, and 6–10:30pm; Sun brunch 8am–1pm. Closed mid-Sept to early Oct.

Mangia, Mangia ★ *Value* ITALIAN/AMERICAN Locals appreciate that they can get good, inexpensive food here in a town filled with tourist traps. Off the beaten track, this great Chicago-style pasta place serves some of the best Italian food in the Keys. The family-run restaurant offers superb homemade pastas of every description, including one of the tastiest marinaras around. The simple grilled chicken breast brushed with olive oil and sprinkled with pepper is another good choice. You wouldn't know it from the front, but there's a fantastic little patio dotted with twinkling pepper lights and lots of plants. While you wait for your table, relax out back with a glass of wine—this place is said to have the largest selection in the Keys—or homemade beer.

900 Southard St. (at Margaret St.). ℂ 305/294-2469. Reservations not accepted. Main courses $9–$15. AE, MC, V. Daily 5:30–10pm.

Pepe's ℛ *(Finds)* AMERICAN   This old dive has been serving good, basic food for nearly a century. Steaks and Apalachicola Bay oysters are the big draw for regulars, who appreciate the rustic barroom setting and historic photos on the walls. Look for original scenes of Key West in 1909, when Pepe's first opened. If the weather is nice, choose a seat on the patio under a stunning mahogany tree. Burgers, fish sandwiches, and standard chili satisfy hearty eaters. Buttery sautéed mushrooms and rich mashed potatoes are the best comfort foods in Key West. There's always a wait, so stop by early for breakfast, when you can get old-fashioned chipped beef on toast and all the usual egg dishes. In the evening, reasonably priced cocktails are served on the deck.

806 Caroline St. (between Margaret and Williams sts.). ℂ 305/294-7192. Main courses $13–$22; breakfast $2–$9; lunch $5–$9. DISC, MC, V. Daily 6:30am–10:30pm.

Turtle Kraals Wildlife Grill ℛ *(Finds)* *(Kids)* SOUTHWESTERN/SEAFOOD   You'll join lots of locals in this out-of-the-way converted warehouse with indoor and dockside seating that serves innovative seafood at great prices. Try the twin lobster tails stuffed with mango and crabmeat, or any of the big quesadillas or fajitas. Kids will like the wildlife exhibits and the very cheesy menu. Blues bands play most nights.

213 Margaret St. (at Caroline St.). ℂ 305/294-2640. Main courses $10–$20. DISC, MC, V. Mon–Thurs 11am–10:30pm; Fri–Sat 11am–11pm; Sun noon–10:30pm. Bar closes at midnight.

INEXPENSIVE

Anthony's Cafe ℛ ITALIAN DELI/ROTISSERIE   Although owned and operated by a Greek import, this rustic Italian-style trattoria is a welcome addition to an area crowded with more expensive and less delicious options. Fragrant roasted chicken and overstuffed sandwiches on fresh-baked bread are the best choices. Also good are the many salads and daily specials.

1111 Duval St. (at Amelia St.). ℂ 305/296-8899. Breakfast $2–$5; sandwiches and salads $5.50–$7 with a side; hot plates $8–$13. No credit cards. Daily 8am–10pm.

Bahama Mama's Kitchen ℛ BAHAMIAN   Sit outside under an umbrella and enjoy the authentic Bahamian fare made from recipes that have been handed down for the past 150 years. Try the coconut shrimp: butterflied, soaked in coconut oil, battered with egg, and then rolled in fresh shredded coconut and deep-fried. The fresh catch comes blackened, broiled, or fried, and is served with island plantains, shrimp hash cakes, and crab rice. The service is good and the staff is friendly.

In the Bahama Village Market, 324 Petronia St. ℂ 305/294-3355. Appetizers $4–$7; main courses $9–$13. MC, V. Daily 11am–10pm.

PT's Late Night ℛ *(Finds)* AMERICAN   This place is worth knowing about, not just because it's one of the only places in town serving food past 10pm, but also because it happens to serve good food at extremely reasonable prices. PT's is more sports bar than restaurant, and service can be a bit slow and brusque, but you'll enjoy the heaping plates of nachos, sizzling fajitas, and super-fresh salads—so big they can be meals in themselves.

920 Caroline St. (at Margaret St.). © **305/296-4245.** Main courses $6.95–$15. DISC, MC, V. Daily 11am–4am.

KEY WEST AFTER DARK

Duval Street is the Bourbon Street of Florida. Amid the T-shirt shops and clothing boutiques, you'll find bar after bar serving neon-colored frozen drinks to revelers who bounce from bar to bar from noon 'til dawn. Bands and crowds vary from night to night and season to season. Your best bet is to start at Truman Avenue and head up Duval to check them out for yourself. Cover charges are rare, except in gay clubs (see the "The Gay Scene," below), so stop into a dozen and see which you like. For the most part, Key West is a late-night town, and bars and clubs don't close until around 3 or 4am.

Captain Tony's Saloon   Just around the corner from Duval's beaten path, this smoky old bar is about as authentic as you'll find. It comes complete with old-time regulars who remember the island before cruise ships docked here; they say Hemingway drank, caroused, and even wrote here. The owner, Capt. Tony Tarracino, a former controversial Key West mayor—"immortalized" in Jimmy Buffett's "Last Mango in Paradise"—has recently capitalized on the success of this once-quaint tavern by franchising the place. 428 Greene St. © **305/294-1838.**

Durty Harry's   This large complex features live rock bands almost every night. You can wander to one of the many outdoor bars or head to Upstairs at Rick's, an indoor/outdoor dance club that gets going late. For racy singles or couples, there is the Red Garter, a pocket-size strip club. The hawker outside reminds couples, in case they've forgotten, that "the family that strips together sticks together." 208 Duval St. © **305/296-4890.**

Sloppy Joe's   You'll have to stop in here just to say you did. Scholars and drunks debate whether this is the same Sloppy Joe's that Hemingway wrote about, but there's no argument that this classic bar's early-20th-century wooden ceiling and cracked-tile floors are Key West originals. There's live music nightly, as well as a cigar room and martini bar. 201 Duval St. © **305/294-5717,** ext. 10. www.sloppyjoes.com.

THE GAY SCENE

Key West's bohemian live-and-let-live atmosphere extends to its thriving and quirky gay community. Before and after Tennessee Williams, Key West has provided the perfect backdrop to a gay scene unlike that of many large urban areas. Seamlessly blended with the prevailing culture, there is no "gay ghetto" in Key West, where alternative lifestyles are embraced and even celebrated.

Although restaurants and businesses welcome visitors without discrimination, nightlife *is* inevitably nightlife. In Key West, the best music and dancing can be found at the predominantly gay clubs. While many of the area's other hot spots are geared toward tourists who like to imbibe, the gay clubs are for those who want to rave, gay or not. Covers vary but are rarely more than $10.

Two popular adjacent late-night spots are the **801 Bourbon Bar/Number One Saloon** (801 Duval St. and 514 Petronia St.; © **305/294-9349** for both), featuring great drag and lots more disco. A mostly male clientele frequents this hot spot from

9pm until 4am. Another Duval Street favorite is **Aqua,** 711 Duval St. (© **305/292-8500**), where you might catch drag queens belting out torch songs or judges voting on the best package in the wet-jockey-shorts contest.

Sunday nights are fun at two local spots. **Tea by the Sea,** on the pier at the Atlantic Shores Motel, 510 South St. (© **800/520-3559**), attracts a faithful following of regulars and visitors alike. The clothing-optional pool is always an attraction. Show up after 7:30pm. Sometime in 2008, the Shores will be demolished to make way for swank condos, to the dismay of many. Better known around town as La-Te-Da, **La Terraza de Martí,** 1125 Duval St. (© **305/296-6706**), the former Key West home of Cuban exile José Martí, is a great spot to gather poolside for the best martini in town—but don't bother with the food. Just upstairs is the **Crystal Room** (© **305/296-6706**), with a high-caliber cabaret performance featuring the popular Randy Roberts in winter.

4 The Dry Tortugas ★★

70 miles W of Key West

Few people realize that the Florida Keys don't end at Key West, since about 70 miles west is a chain of seven small islands known as the Dry Tortugas. Since you've come this far, you might wish to visit them, especially if you're into bird-watching, their primary draw.

Ponce de León, who discovered this far-flung cluster of coral keys in 1513, named them Las Tortugas because of the many sea turtles, which still flock to the area during nesting season in the warm summer months. Oceanic charts later carried the preface "dry" to warn mariners that fresh water was unavailable here. Modern intervention has made drinking water available, but little else.

These undeveloped islands make a great day trip for travelers interested in seeing the natural anomalies of the Florida Keys—especially the birds. The Dry Tortugas are nesting grounds and roosting sites for thousands of tropical and subtropical oceanic birds. Visitors will also find a historic fort, good fishing, and terrific snorkeling around shallow reefs.

GETTING THERE

BY BOAT   The **Yankee Fleet,** based in Key West (© **800/634-0939** or 305/294-7009; www.yankeefleet.com/keywest.cfm), offers day trips from Key West for sightseeing, snorkeling, or both. Cruises leave daily at 7:30am for the 3-hour journey from Land's End Marina at Margaret Street to Garden Key. Breakfast is served onboard. Once on the island, you can join a guided tour of Fort Jefferson or explore it on your own. Boats return to Key West by 7pm. Tours cost $139 for adults; $129 for seniors, students, and military personnel; and $94 for children 16 and under. Prices include breakfast, lunch, dinner, and snorkeling equipment. Call for reservations.

Sunny Days Catamarans (© **800/236-7937** or 305/292-6100) operates the *Fast Cat,* which is faster, quieter, and more high-tech than the loud Yankee fleet, as well as a better value. The round-trip fare ($110 for adults, $105 for seniors, $80 for children) includes a continental breakfast; a buffet lunch with cold cuts, fresh veggies, fruits, salads, and unlimited sodas and water; an island tour; and a snorkeling excursion to a shipwreck in 5 to 20 feet of water. The high-speed cat leaves Key West for Garden Key at 8am and returns by 6pm.

BY PLANE   Seaplanes of Key West, based at Key West Airport (📞 **800/950-2-FLY** or 305/294-0709; www.seaplanesofkeywest.com), offers daily excursions. Weather permitting, flights depart at 8am, 10am, noon, and 2pm. The 40-minute trip at about 500 feet offers a great introduction to the Dry Tortugas. Fares include snorkeling equipment and a cooler for use on the island. A half-day costs $189 for adults, $139 for kids 7 to 12, and $109 for kids 6 and under; a full day costs $325 for adults, $245 for kids 7 to 12, and $190 for kids 6 and under. Bring a bathing suit, snorkeling equipment, and snacks to enjoy on these remote and beautiful islands.

EXPLORING THE DRY TORTUGAS

Of the seven islands that make up the Dry Tortugas, Garden Key is the most visited because it is where Fort Jefferson and the visitor center are located. Loggerhead Key, Middle Key, and East Key are open only during the day and are for hiking. Bush Key is for the birds—literally! It's a nesting area for birds only, though it is open from October to January for special excursions. Hospital and Long Keys are closed to the public.

Fort Jefferson, a huge six-sided, 19th-century fortress, is set almost at the water's edge of Garden Key, so it appears to float in the middle of the sea. The monumental structure is surrounded by formidable 8-foot-thick walls that rise from the sand to a height of nearly 50 feet. Impressive archways, stonework, and parapets make this 150-year-old monument a grand sight. With the invention of the rifled cannon, the fort's masonry construction became obsolete and the building was never completed. For 10 years, however, from 1863 to 1873, Fort Jefferson served as a prison, a kind of "Alcatraz East." Among its prisoners were four of the "Lincoln Conspirators," including Samuel A. Mudd, the doctor who set the broken leg of fugitive assassin John Wilkes Booth. In 1935, Fort Jefferson became a national monument administered by the National Park Service. Today, however, Fort Jefferson is struggling to resist erosion from the salt and sea, as iron used in gun openings and shutters in the fort's walls has accelerated the deterioration, and the structure's openings need to be rebricked. As a result, the National Park Service has designated the fort the recipient of a $15-million face-lift, a project that may take up to a decade to complete.

For more information on Fort Jefferson and the Dry Tortugas, call the **Everglades National Park Service** (📞 **305/242-7700**) or visit www.fortjefferson.com. Fort Jefferson is open during daylight hours on Garden Key. A self-guided trail describes the history of the human presence in the Dry Tortugas while leading visitors through the fort.

OUTDOOR ACTIVITIES

BIRD-WATCHING   Bring your binoculars and your bird books: Bird-watching is *the* reason to visit this little cluster of tropical islands. The Dry Tortugas, uniquely situated in the middle of the migration flyway between North and South America, serve as an important rest stop for the more than 200 winged varieties that pass through here annually. The season peaks from mid-March to mid-May, when thousands of birds show up, but many species from the West Indies can be found here year-round.

DIVING & SNORKELING   The warm, clear, shallow waters of the Dry Tortugas produce optimum conditions for snorkeling and scuba diving. Four endangered species of sea turtles—green, leatherback, Atlantic ridley, and hawksbill—can be found here, along with myriad marine species. The region just outside the seawall of

Fort Jefferson is excellent for underwater touring; an abundant variety of fish, coral, and more live in just 3 to 4 feet of water.

FISHING In July 2001, a federal law closed off all fishing in a 90-square-mile tract of open ocean called the Tortugas North and a 61-square-mile tract of open ocean called the Tortugas South, which basically prohibits all fishing in order to preserve the dwindling population of fish (a result of commercial fishing and environmental factors). Instead, head to Key West.

CAMPING

The rustic beauty of tiny Garden Key (the only island of the Dry Tortugas where campers are allowed to pitch tents) is a camper's dream. Don't worry about sharing your site with noisy RVs or motor homes; they can't get there. The abundance of birds doesn't make it quiet, but the camping—a stone's throw from the water—is as picturesque as it gets. Picnic tables, cooking grills, and toilets are provided, but there are no showers. All supplies must be packed in and out. Sites are $3 per person per night and are available on a first-come, first-served basis. The 10 sites book up fast. For more information, call the **National Park Service** (© **305/242-7700**).

7

The Everglades & Biscayne National Park

President Harry S Truman once declared the Everglades "an irreplaceable primitive area." And while those words don't exactly do the Everglades and its surrounding Biscayne National Park justice, he clarified what he said: "Here are no lofty peaks seeking the sky, no mighty glaciers or rushing streams wearing away the uplifted land. Here is land, tranquil in its quiet beauty, serving not as the source of water, but as the last receiver of it. To its natural abundance we owe the spectacular plant and animal life that distinguishes this place from all others in our country."

There's no better reality show than the one that exists in the Everglades. Up-close-and-personal views of alligators, crocodiles, and bona fide wildlife—not the kind you'd find on, say, South Beach, after midnight—make for an interesting, photo-opportunistic experience that even the Crocodile Hunter would find hard to mimic on his show.

Tourists who come to South Florida shouldn't leave the area without taking time to see some of the wild plant and animal life in the swampy Everglades and the underwater treasures of Biscayne National Park.

1 A Glimpse of Everglades National Park ★★

35 miles SW of Miami

Before going there, my conception of the Everglades was that it was one big swamp swarming with ominous creatures, sort of like that creepy TV show *Invasion*. For someone who'd rather endure an endless series of root canals than audition for a role on *Survivor* (the closest I'd ever been to nature was sleep-away camp), the Everglades may as well have been the *Never*glades. That is, until I finally decided to venture there. To my surprise, and contrary to popular belief, the Everglades isn't really a swamp at all, but one of the country's most fascinating natural resources.

For first-timers or those with dubious athletic skills, the best way to see the 'glades is probably via airboats, which aren't actually allowed in the park proper, but cut through the saw grass on the park's outskirts, taking you past countless birds, alligators, crocodiles, deer, and raccoons. A walk on one of the park's many trails will provide you with a different vantage point: up-close interaction with an assortment of tame wildlife. But the absolutely best way to see the 'glades is via canoe, which allows you to get incredibly close to nature. Whichever method you choose, I guarantee that you will marvel at the sheer beauty of the Everglades. Despite the multitude of mosquito bites (the bugs seem to be immune to repellent—wear long pants and cover your arms), an Everglades experience will definitely contribute to a newfound appreciation for Florida's natural (and beautiful) wonderland.

Everglades National Park

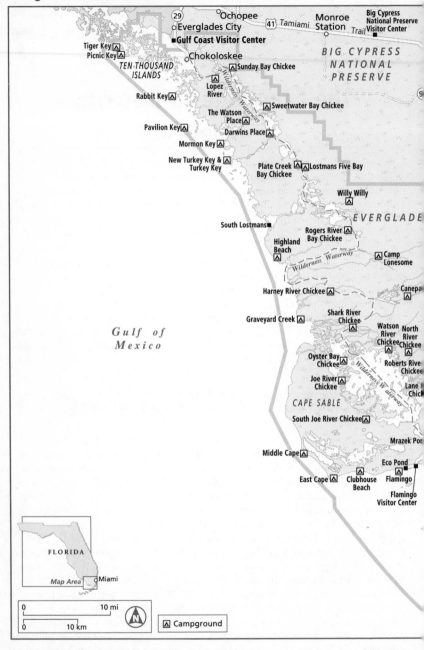

Ochopee
Everglades City
Gulf Coast Visitor Center
29
41 Tamiami Trail
Monroe Station
Big Cypress National Preserve Visitor Center

Tiger Key
Picnic Key
TEN THOUSAND ISLANDS
Chokoloskee

BIG CYPRESS NATIONAL PRESERVE

Sunday Bay Chickee
Lopez River
Rabbit Key
Sweetwater Bay Chickee
The Watson Place
Pavilion Key
Darwins Place
Mormon Key
New Turkey Key & Turkey Key
Plate Creek Bay Chickee
Lostmans Five Bay
Willy Willy
South Lostmans
Rogers River Bay Chickee
Highland Beach
Wilderness Waterway
Camp Lonesome
EVERGLADE
Harney River Chickee
Graveyard Creek
Shark River Chickee
Canepa
Watson River Chickee
North River Chickee
Oyster Bay Chickee
Roberts Rive Chickee
Joe River Chickee
Wilderness Waterway
Lane Chick
CAPE SABLE
South Joe River Chickee
Mrazek Por
Middle Cape
Eco Pond
Flamingo
East Cape
Clubhouse Beach
Flamingo Visitor Center

Gulf of Mexico

Wilderness Waterway

FLORIDA
Map Area
Miami

0   10 mi
0   10 km

N

⬜ Campground

238

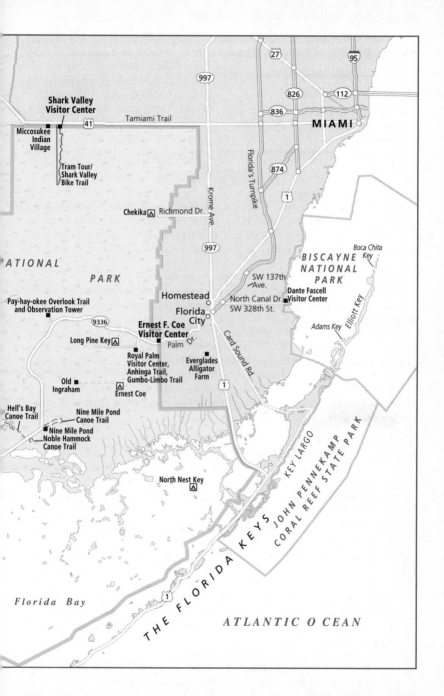

Shark Valley
Visitor Center

Miccosukee
Indian
Village

Tamiami Trail

(41)

(27)

(997)

(826)

(112)

(95)

(836)

MIAMI

Florida's Turnpike

(874)

(1)

Tram Tour/
Shark Valley
Bike Trail

Chekika △ Richmond Dr.

Krome Ave.

(997)

BISCAYNE
NATIONAL
PARK

Boca Chita
Key

ATIONAL

PARK

Pay-hay-okee Overlook Trail
and Observation Tower

SW 137th
Ave.

Dante Fascell
Visitor Center

Elliott Key

Adams Key

(9336)

Long Pine Key △

Homestead

Florida
City

Ernest F. Coe
Visitor Center

North Canal Dr.
SW 328th St.

Palm Dr.

Card Sound Rd.

Old
Ingraham

Royal Palm
Visitor Center,
Anhinga Trail,
Gumbo-Limbo Trail

△
Ernest Coe

Everglades
Alligator
Farm

(1)

Hell's Bay
Canoe Trail

Nine Mile Pond
Canoe Trail

Nine Mile Pond
Noble Hammock
Canoe Trail

North Nest Key
△

KEY LARGO

JOHN PENNEKAMP
CORAL REEF STATE PARK

THE FLORIDA KEYS

(1)

Florida Bay

ATLANTIC OCEAN

This vast and unusual ecosystem is actually a shallow, 40-mile-wide, slow-moving river. Rarely more than knee deep, the water is the lifeblood of this wilderness, and the subtle shifts in water level dictate the life cycle of the native plants and animals. In 1947, 1.5 million acres—less than 20% of the Everglades' wilderness—were established as Everglades National Park. At that time, few lawmakers understood how neighboring ecosystems relate to each other. Consequently, the park is heavily affected by surrounding territories and is at the butt end of every environmental insult that occurs upstream in Miami.

> **Fun Fact Lazy River**
>
> It takes a month for 1 gallon of water to move through Everglades National Park.

While there has been a marked decrease in the indigenous wildlife here, Everglades National Park nevertheless remains one of the few places where you can see dozens of endangered species in their natural habitat, including the swallowtail butterfly, American crocodile, leatherback turtle, southern bald eagle, West Indian manatee, and Florida panther.

Take your time on the trails, and a hypnotic beauty begins to unfold. Follow the rustling of a bush, and you might see a small green tree frog or tiny brown anole lizard, with its bright-red spotted throat. Crane your neck to see around a bend, and discover a delicate, brightly painted mule-ear orchid.

The slow and subtle splendor of this exotic land may not be immediately appealing to kids raised on video games and rapid-fire commercials, but they'll certainly remember the experience and thank you for it later. Your kids will find plenty of dramatic fun around the park, such as airboat rides, hiking, and biking, to keep them satisfied for at least a day.

Note: As of the writing of this book, wicked Hurricane Wilma made a mess of the Glades, but thanks to clean-up crews, things will be restored to normal by the time this book is in your hands.

JUST THE FACTS

GETTING THERE & ACCESS POINTS   Although the Everglades may seem overwhelmingly large and unapproachable, it's easy to get to the park's two main areas—the northern section, which is accessible via Shark Valley and Everglades City; and the southern section, accessible through the Ernest F. Coe Visitor Center, near Homestead and Florida City.

Northern Entrances   A popular day trip for Miamians, **Shark Valley,** a 15-mile paved loop road (with an observation tower in the middle of the loop) overlooking the pulsating heart of the Everglades is the easiest and most scenic way to explore the national park. Just 25 miles west of the Florida Turnpike, Shark Valley is best reached via the Tamiami Trail, South Florida's pre-turnpike, two-lane road, which cuts across the southern part of the state along the park's northern border. Roadside attractions (boat rides and alligator farms, for example) along the Tamiami Trail are operated by the Miccosukee Indian Village and are worth a quick, fun stop. An excellent tram tour (leaving from the Shark Valley Visitor Center) goes deep into the park along a trail that's also terrific for biking. Shark Valley is about an hour's drive from Miami.

A little less than 10 miles west along the Tamiami Trail from Shark Valley, you'll discover **Big Cypress National Preserve,** in which stretches of vibrant green cypress and pine trees make for a fabulous Kodak moment. If you pick up S.R. 29 and head south from the Tamiami Trail, you'll hit a modified version of civilization in the form of

Everglades City (where the Everglades meet the Gulf of Mexico), where there's another entrance to the park and the **Gulf Coast Visitor Center.** From Miami to Shark Valley: Go west on I-395 to S.R. 821 South (the Florida Tpk.). Take the U.S. 41/Southwest 8th Street (Tamiami Trail) exit. The Shark Valley entrance is just 25 miles west. To get to Everglades City, continue west on the Tamiami Trail and head south on S.R. 29. Everglades City is approximately a 2½-hour drive from Miami, but because it is scenic, it may take longer if you stop or slow down to view your surroundings.

Southern Entrance (via Homestead & Florida City)   If you're in a rush to hit the 'glades and don't care about the scenic route, this is your best bet. Just southeast of Homestead and Florida City, off S.R. 9336, the southern access to the park will bring you directly to Ernest F. Coe Visitor Center. Right inside the park, 4 miles beyond Ernest F. Coe Visitor Center, is Royal Palm Visitor Center, which is the starting point for the two most popular walking trails, Gumbo Limbo and Anhinga, where you'll witness a plethora of birds and wildlife roaming freely, unperturbed by human voyeurs. Thirteen miles west of Ernest F. Coe Visitor Center, you'll hit Pa-hay-okee Overlook Trail, which is worth a trek across the boardwalk to reach the observation tower, over which vultures and hawks hover protectively amid a resplendent, picturesque, bird's-eye view of the Everglades. From Miami to the southern entrance: Go west on I-395 to S.R. 821 South (Florida Tpk.), which will end in Florida City. Take the first right through the center of town (you can't miss it) and follow signs to the park entrance on S.R. 9336. Ernest F. Coe Visitor Center is about 1½ hours from Miami.

VISITOR CENTERS & INFORMATION   General inquiries and specific questions should be directed to **Everglades National Park Headquarters,** 40001 S.R. 9336, Homestead, FL 33034 (© **305/242-7700**). Ask for a copy of *Parks and Preserves,* a free newspaper that's filled with up-to-date information about goings-on in the Everglades. Headquarters is staffed by helpful phone operators daily from 8:30am to 4:30pm. You can also try www.nps.gov/ever/visit/index.htm.

Note that all hours listed are for the high season, generally November through May. During the slow summer months, many offices and outfitters keep abbreviated hours. Always call ahead to confirm hours of operation.

Ernest F. Coe Visitor Center, located at the Park Headquarters entrance, west of Homestead and Florida City, is the best place to gather information for your trip. In addition to details on tours and boat rentals, and free brochures outlining trails, wildlife, and activities, you will find state-of-the-art educational displays, films, and interactive exhibits. A gift shop sells postcards, film, an impressive selection of books about the Everglades, unusual gift items, and a supply of your most important gear: insect repellent. The shop is open daily from 8am to 5pm.

The **Royal Palm Visitor Center,** a small nature museum located 3 miles past the park's main entrance, is a smaller information center. The museum is not great (its

Glades in the Spotlight

ABC's hit television series *Invasion* may be shot mostly on a set in Los Angeles, but its creator, Shaun Cassidy, a Florida resident and, yes, that Shaun Cassidy, has been to the Everglades and is as intrigued as the rest of us. "It's a very primordial place," Cassidy said in a magazine interview. "There are a lot of species that have existed there that have not existed anywhere else. It's a place that was cut off from the rest of the world for a very long time."

displays are equipped with recordings about the park's ecosystem), but the center is the departure point for the popular Anhinga and Gumbo Limbo trails. The center is open daily from 8am to 4pm.

Knowledgeable rangers, who provide brochures and personal insight into the park's activities, also staff **Flamingo Visitor Center,** 38 miles from the main entrance, at the park's southern access, which has natural-history exhibits and information on visitor services; and the **Shark Valley Visitor Center,** at the park's northern entrance. Both are open daily from 8:30am to 5pm.

ENTRANCE FEES, PERMITS & REGULATIONS   Permits and passes can be purchased only at the main park or Shark Valley entrance station. Even if you are just visiting the park for an afternoon, you'll need to buy a 7-day permit, which costs $10 per vehicle. Pedestrians and cyclists are charged $5 each. An Everglades Park Pass, valid for a year's worth of unlimited admissions, is available for $20. You may also purchase a 12-month National Parks Pass for $50, which is valid for entrance into any U.S. national park. U.S. citizens 62 and older pay only $10 for a Golden Age Passport that's valid for life. A Golden Access Passport is available free to U.S. citizens with disabilities.

Permits are required for campers to stay overnight either in the backcountry or at the primitive campsites. See "Camping in the Everglades," on p. 248.

Those who want to fish without a charter captain must obtain a standard State of Florida saltwater fishing license. These are available in the park at Flamingo Lodge or at any tackle shop or sporting goods store nearby. Nonresidents pay $17 for a 7-day license or $7 for a 3-day license. Florida residents pay $14 for an annual fishing license. Snook and crawfish licenses must be purchased separately at a cost of $2 each.

Charter captains carry vessel licenses that cover all paying passengers, but ask to be sure. Freshwater fishing licenses are available at various bait-and-tackle stores outside the park at the same rates as those offered inside the park. A good one nearby is **Don's Bait & Tackle,** 30710 S. Federal Hwy., right on U.S. 1 in Homestead (© **305/247-6616**). *Note:* Most of the area's freshwater fishing, limited to murky canals and artificial lakes near housing developments, is hardly worth the trouble when so much good saltwater fishing is available.

SEASONS   There are two distinct seasons in the Everglades: high season and mosquito season. High season is also dry season and lasts from late November to May. Most winters here are warm, sunny, and breezy—a good combination for keeping the bugs away. This is the best time to visit because low water levels attract the largest variety of wading birds and their predators. As the dry season wanes, wildlife follows the receding water; by the end of May, the only living things you are sure to spot will make you itch. The worst, called "no-see-ums," are not even swattable. If you choose to visit during the buggy season, be vigilant in applying bug spray. Also, realize that many establishments and operators either close or curtail offerings in summer, so always call ahead to check schedules.

RANGER PROGRAMS   More than 50 ranger programs, free with entry, are offered each month during high season and give visitors an opportunity to gain an expert's perspective. Ranger-led walks and talks are offered year-round from Royal Palm Visitor Center, and at the Flamingo and Gulf Coast visitor centers, as well as Shark Valley Visitor Center during winter months. Park rangers tend to be helpful, well informed, and good humored. Some programs occur regularly, such as Royal Palm Visitor Center's Glade Glimpses, a walking tour on which rangers point out flora and fauna, and discuss issues affecting the Everglades' survival. Tours are scheduled at

Warning!

High levels of mercury have been found in Everglades bass and in some fish species in northern Florida Bay. Do not eat bass caught north of the Main Park Road. Do not eat bass caught south of the Main Park Road more than once a week. Children and pregnant women should not eat any bass. The following salt-water species caught in northern Florida Bay should not be consumed more than once per week by adults or once per month by women of child-bearing age and children: spotted seatrout, gafftopsail, catfish, bluefish, crevalle jack, or ladyfish.

1:30pm daily. The Anhinga Amble, a similar program that takes place on the Anhinga Trail, starts at 10:30am daily. Since times, programs, and locations vary from month to month, check the schedule, available at any of the visitor centers.

SAFETY   There are many dangers inherent in this vast wilderness area. *Always* let someone know your itinerary before you set out on an extended hike. It's mandatory that you file an itinerary when camping overnight in the backcountry (which you can do when you apply for your overnight permit at either the Flamingo Visitor Center or the Gulf Coast Visitor Center). When you're on the water, watch for weather changes; severe thunderstorms and high winds often develop rapidly. Swimming is not recommended because of the presence of alligators, sharks, and barracudas. Watch out for the region's four indigenous poisonous snakes: diamondback and pygmy rattlesnakes, coral snakes (identifiable by their colorful rings), and water moccasins (which swim on the surface of the water). Bring insect repellent to ward off mosquitoes and biting flies. First aid is available from park rangers. The nearest hospital is in Homestead, 10 miles from the park's main entrance.

SEEING THE HIGHLIGHTS

Shark Valley, a 15-mile paved road (ideal for biking) through the Everglades, provides a fine introduction to the wonders of the park, but don't plan on spending more than a few hours here. Bicycling and taking a guided tram tour (p. 247) are fantastic ways to cover the highlights.

If you want to see a greater array of plant and animal life, make sure that you venture into the park through the main entrance, pick up a trail map, and dedicate at least a day to exploring from there.

Stop first along the Anhinga and Gumbo Limbo trails, which start right next to each other, 3 miles from the park's main entrance. These trails provide a thorough introduction to Everglades flora and fauna and are highly recommended to first-time visitors. Each is a ½-mile round-trip. **Gumbo Limbo Trail** (my pick for best walking trail in the Everglades) meanders through a gorgeous, shaded, junglelike hammock of gumbo limbo trees, royal palms, ferns, orchids, air plants, and a general blanket of vegetation, though it doesn't put you in close contact with much wildlife. **Anhinga Trail** is one of the most popular trails in the park because of its abundance of wildlife: There's more water and wildlife in this area of the park than in most parts of the Everglades, especially during dry season. Alligators, lizards, turtles, river otters, herons, egrets, and other animals abound, making this one of the best trails for seeing wildlife. Arrive early to spot the widest selection of exotic birds, like the Anhinga bird, the trail's namesake, a large black fishing bird so accustomed to humans that many of them build their nests in plain view. Take your time—at least an hour is recommended for each trail. Both are wheelchair accessible. If you treat the trails and modern boardwalk as pathways to get through quickly, rather than destinations to experience and savor, you'll miss out on the still beauty and hidden treasures that await you.

To get closer to nature, a few hours in a canoe along any of the trails allows paddlers the chance to sense the park's fluid motion and to become a part of the ecosphere. Visitors who choose this option end up feeling more like explorers than observers. (See "Sports & Outdoor Activities," below.)

No matter which option you choose (and there are many), I strongly recommend staying for the 7pm program, available during high season at the Long Pine Key Amphitheater. This ranger-led talk and slide show will give you a detailed overview of the park's history, natural resources, wildlife, and threats to its survival.

SPORTS & OUTDOOR ACTIVITIES

BIKING   The relatively flat 38-mile paved **Main Park Road** is great for biking because of the multitude of hardwood hammocks (treelike islands or dense stands of hardwood trees that grow only a few inches above land) and a dwarf cypress forest (stunted and thinly distributed cypress trees, which grow in poor soil on drier land).

Shark Valley, however, is the best biking trail by far. If the park isn't flooded from excess rain (which it often is, especially in spring), this is South Florida's most scenic bicycle trail. Many locals haul their bikes out to the 'glades for a relaxing day of wilderness-trail riding. You'll share the flat, paved road only with other bikers, trams, and a menagerie of wildlife. (Don't be surprised to see a gator lounging in the sun or a deer munching on some grass. Otters, turtles, alligators, and snakes are common companions in the Shark Valley area.) There are no shortcuts, so if you become tired or are unable to complete the entire 15-mile trip, turn around and return on the same road. Allow 2 to 3 hours to bike the entire loop.

Those who love to mountain-bike and who prefer solitude might check out the **Southern Glades Trail,** a 14-mile unpaved trail lined with native trees and teeming with wildlife such as deer, alligators, and the occasional snake. The remote trail runs along the C-111 canal, off S.R. 9336 and Southwest 217th Street.

You can rent bikes at **Flamingo Lodge, Marina, and Outpost Resort** (p. 247) for $17 per 24 hours, $14 per full day, $8 per half-day (any 4-hr. period), or $3 per hour. A $50 deposit is required for each rental. Rentals can be picked up from 7am and must be returned by 5pm. Bicycles are also available from **Shark Valley Tram Tours,** at the park's Shark Valley entrance (© **305/221-8455**), for $5.25 per hour; rentals can be picked up anytime between 8:30am and 3pm and must be returned by 4pm.

BIRD-WATCHING   More than 350 species of birds make their home in the Everglades. Tropical birds from the Caribbean and temperate species from North America can be found here, along with exotics that have flown in from more distant regions. Eco and Mrazek ponds, located near Flamingo, are two of the best places for birding, especially in early morning or late afternoon in the dry winter months. Pick up a free birding checklist from one of the visitor centers (p. 241) and ask there what's been spotted in recent days.

CANOEING   Canoeing through the Everglades may be one of the most serene, surprisingly diverse adventures you'll ever have. From a canoe (where you're incredibly close to the water level), your vantage point is priceless. Canoers in the 'glades can coexist with the gators and birds in a way no one else can; they behave as if you're part of the ecosystem—something that won't happen on an airboat. A ranger-guided boat tour is your best bet and costs $20, plus a required deposit. As always, a ranger will help you understand the surroundings and what you're seeing.

Everglades National Park's longest "trails" are designed for boat and canoe travel, and many are marked as clearly as walking trails. The **Noble Hammock Canoe Trail,** a 2-mile loop, takes 1 to 2 hours and is recommended for beginners. The **Hell's Bay Canoe Trail,** a 3- to 6-mile course for hardier paddlers, takes 2 to 6 hours, depending on how far you choose to go. Fans of this trail like to say, "It's hell to get in and hell to get out." Park rangers can recommend other trails that best suit your abilities, time limitations, and interests.

You can rent a canoe at the **Flamingo Lodge, Marina, and Outpost Resort** (p. 247) for $50 for 24 hours, $40 per full day (any 8-hr. period), $30 per half-day (any 4-hr. period), or $12 per hour. Skiffs, kayaks, and tandem kayaks are also available. The concessionaire will shuttle your party to the trail head of your choice and pick you up afterward. Rental facilities are open daily from 6am to 8pm.

Overnight canoe rentals are available for $50 to $60. During ideal weather conditions (stay away during bug season!), you can paddle right out to the Gulf and camp on the beach. However, Gulf waters at beach sites can be extremely rough, and people in small watercraft such as a canoe should exercise caution.

You can also take a canoe tour from the Parks Docks on Chokoloskee Causeway on S.R. 29, ½ mile south of the traffic circle at the ranger station in Everglades City. Call **Everglades National Park Boat Tours** (© **800/445-7724**) for information.

FISHING   About a third of Everglades National Park is open water. Freshwater fishing is popular in brackish **Nine-mile Pond** (25 miles from the main entrance) and other spots along the Main Park Road, but because of the high mercury levels found in the Everglades, freshwater fishers are warned not to eat their catch. Before casting, check in at a visitor center, as many of the park's lakes are preserved for observation only. Fishing licenses are required; see p. 242 for more information.

Saltwater anglers will find snapper and sea trout plentiful. Charter boats and guides are available at Flamingo Lodge, Marina, and Outpost Resort (p. 247). Phone for information and reservations.

MOTORBOATING   Motorboating around the Everglades seems like a great way to see plants and animals in remote habitats, and, indeed, it's an interesting and fulfilling experience as you throttle into nature. However, environmentalists are taking stock of the damage inflicted by motorboats (especially airboats) on the delicate ecosystem. If you choose to motor, remember that most of the areas near land are "no wake" zones and that, for the protection of nesting birds, landing is prohibited on most of the little mangrove islands. Motorboating is allowed in certain areas, such as Florida Bay, the backcountry toward Everglades City, and the Ten Thousand Islands area. In all the freshwater lakes, however, motorboats are prohibited if they're above 5 horsepower. There's a long list of restrictions and restricted areas, so get a copy of the park's boating rules from Park Headquarters before setting out.

The Everglades' only marina—accommodating about 50 boats with electric and water hookups—is **Flamingo Lodge, Marina, and Outpost Resort** (p. 247). The well-marked channel to the Flamingo is accessible to boats with a maximum 4-foot draft and is open year-round. Reservations can be made through the marina store (© **239/695-3101,** ext. 304). Skiffs with 15-horsepower motors are available for rent. These low-power boats cost $90 per day, $65 per half-day (any 5-hr. period), and $22 per hour. A $125 deposit is required.

ORGANIZED TOURS

AIRBOAT TOURS   Shallow-draft, fan-powered airboats were invented in the Everglades by frog hunters who were tired of poling through the brushes. Airboats cut through the saw grass and are sort of like hydraulic boats; at high-enough speeds, a boat actually rises above the saw grass and into the air. Even though airboats are the most efficient (not to mention fast and fun!) way to get around, they are not permitted in the park—these shallow-bottom runabouts tend to inflict severe damage on animals and plants. Just outside the boundaries of the Everglades, however, you'll find a number of outfitters offering rides. *Tip:* Consider bringing earplugs, as these high-speed boats are loud.

One of the best airboat outfitters is **Gator Park,** 12 miles west of the Florida Turnpike at 24050 SW 8th St. (*©* **305/559-2255;** www.gatorpark.com), which, despite its touristy name, happens to be one of the most informative and entertaining around, not to mention one of the only airboat-tour operators that gives out free earplugs. Request Rick, who deserves a medal for getting out into the water and poking around a massive alligator even though he's not really supposed to. After the boat ride, there's a free interactive wildlife show that features alligator wrestling and several other frightening acts involving scorpions. Take note of the gorgeous peacocks that live in the trees here. Admission for the boat ride and show is $19 for adults, $11 for children 6 to 11; prices are cheaper if you purchase tickets online. Airboats depart every 20 minutes. Gator Park is open daily from 9am to 7pm.

Another outfitter I recommend is **Coopertown Airboat Tours** (*©* **305/226-6048;** www.coopertownairboats.com), located about 11 miles west of the Florida Turnpike on the Tamiami Trail (U.S. 41) in a town that boasts a total population of eight humans! The superfriendly staff has helped the company garner the title of "Florida's Best" by the *Miami Herald* for 40 years in a row. You never know what you're going to see, but with great guides, you're sure to see *something* of interest on the 40-minute, 9-mile round-trip tours. There's also a restaurant and a small gator farm on the premises. Airboat rides cost $14 for adults, $8 for children 7 to 11. The company is open daily from 8am to 6pm; tours leave frequently.

Airboat rides are also offered at the **Miccosukee Indian Village,** just west of the Shark Valley entrance on U.S. 41/Tamiami Trail and MM 70 (*©* **305/223-8380;** www.miccosukeetours.com). The price is $10 per person, with cheaper rates online. However, *be warned and advised:* I am not recommending this particular outfit over others—it's merely the one closest to the Shark Valley entrance. As always, the quality of your tour is going to be only as good as the quality of your tour guide, and, unfortunately, I've gotten some complaints about the Miccosukee tours.

The **Everglades Alligator Farm,** 4 miles south of Palm Drive on Southwest 192nd Avenue (*©* **305/247-2628;** www.everglades.com), offers half-hour guided airboat tours daily from 9am until 6pm. The price, which includes admission to the park, is $17 for adults and $10 for children 4 to 11.

Another reputable company is **Captain Doug's,** located 35 miles south of Naples and 1 mile past the bridge in Everglades City (*©* **800/282-9194**).

CANOE TOURS   A fabulous way to explore the Everglades backcountry is via canoe. Slink through the mangroves, slide across saw-grass prairies, and even walk the sands of the unfettered Ten Thousand Islands. Expert guides will lead you in the right direction. Contact **North American Canoe Tours** (*©* **239/695-3299**), at the Ivey House B&B (p. 249).

ECOTOURS   Although it's fascinating to explore on your own, it would be a shame for you to tour the Everglades without a clue as to what you're seeing. It's a lot more than saw grass and alligators in the backcountry, which is why **Everglades Rentals and Eco Adventures** (© 239/695-3299), located within the Ivey House B&B (p. 249), is there to guide and entertain you, as well as explain key issues like the differences between alligators and crocodiles, or between swamps and the Everglades.

MOTORBOAT TOURS   Both Florida Bay and backcountry tours are offered at the **Flamingo Lodge, Marina, and Outpost Resort** (p. 247). Florida Bay tours cruise nearby estuaries and sandbars, while six-passenger backcountry boats visit smaller sloughs. Passengers can expect to see birds and a variety of other animals (I once saw a raccoon and some wild pigs). Both are available in 1½- and 2-hour versions that cost $12 or $18 for adults, $7 or $12 for children 6 to 13. Tours depart throughout the day; reservations are recommended. Charter-fishing and sightseeing boats can also be booked through the resort's main reservation number (© 239/695-3101).

TRAM TOURS   At the park's Shark Valley entrance, open-air tram buses take visitors on 2-hour naturalist-led tours that delve 7½ miles into the wilderness and make the best quick introduction you can get to the Everglades. At the trail's midsection, passengers can disembark and climb a 65-foot observation tower that offers good views of the 'glades (though the tower on the Pa-hay-okee Trail is better). Visitors will see plenty of wildlife and endless acres of saw grass. Tours run December through April, daily on the hour between 9am and 4pm, and May through November at 9:30am, 11am, 1pm, and 3pm. They're sometimes stalled by flooding or particularly heavy mosquito infestation. Reservations are recommended from December to March. The cost is $13 for adults, $11 for seniors, and $7.75 for children 12 and under. For further information, contact **Shark Valley Tram Tours** (© 305/221-8455).

WHERE TO STAY

The only lodging in the park proper is Flamingo Lodge, a fairly priced and very recommendable option. However, a few accommodations just outside the park are even cheaper. A $45-million casino hotel, **Miccosukee Resort** (© 877/242-6464; www.miccosukee.com), was built adjacent to the Miccosukee bingo and gaming hall on the northern edge of the park. And although bugs can be a major nuisance, especially in the warm months, camping (the best way to fully experience South Florida's wilderness) is really the way to go in this very primitive environment.

LODGING IN THE NATIONAL PARK

Flamingo Lodge, Marina, and Outpost Resort ★★   The Flamingo Lodge is the only lodging actually located within the boundaries of Everglades National Park. This woodsy, sprawling complex offers a few houseboats, and rooms overlooking the Florida Bay in either a two-story plain motel or the lodge. Either option feels very much like being at summer camp, with a few more amenities. Unfortunately, it was heavily damaged in 2005 by Hurricanes Katrina and Wilma, and will be closed until at least late 2006. Check back periodically to see if the lodge has reopened.

1 Flamingo Lodge Hwy., Flamingo, FL 33034. © **800/600-3813** or 239/695-3101. Fax 239/695-3921. www.flamingo lodge.com. 97 units. Winter $82–$98 double, $113–$148 suite, $102–$138 cottage; off season $68–$85 double, $102–$116 suite, $92–$105 cottage. Rates for cottages or suites are for 1–4 people. Children under 17 stay free in parent's room. AE, DC, DISC, MC. Take Florida Tpk. south to Florida City; exit on U.S. 1. At 4-way intersection, turn right onto Palm Dr.; continue for 3 miles and turn left at Robert Is Here fruit stand. Turn right at the 3-way intersection. The park entrance is 3 miles ahead. Continue about 38 miles to reach lodge. **Amenities:** Waterside bar and

restaurant; freshwater pool; bike, canoe, and kayak rental; marina with boat tours; boat rental; houseboat and fishing charters; coin-op washers and dryers; convenience store. *In room:* A/C, TV (in standard rooms and suites but not in cottages), kitchen (in cottages and suites).

CAMPING IN THE EVERGLADES

Campgrounds are available year-round in Flamingo and Long Pine Key. Both have drinking water, picnic tables, charcoal grills, restrooms, and tent and trailer pads, and welcome RVs (Flamingo allows up to 40-ft. vehicles, while Long Pine Key accepts up to 60-footers), though there are no electrical hookups. Flamingo has cold-water showers; Long Pine Key does not have showers or hookups for showers. Private ground fires are not permitted, but supervised campfire programs are conducted during winter months. Long Pine Key and Flamingo are popular and require reservations in advance, which can be made through the National Park Reservations Service (© **800/ 365-CAMP;** www.nps.gov/ever/visit/camping.htm). Campsites are $14 per night with a 14-day consecutive-stay limit, and a maximum of 30 days a year.

Camping is also available year-round in the **backcountry** (those remote areas accessible only by boat, foot, or canoe—basically most of the park), on a first-come, first-served basis. Campers must register with park rangers and get a free permit in person or by phone no less than 24 hours before the start of their trip. For more information, contact the **Gulf Coast Visitor Center** (© **239/695-3311**) or the **Flamingo Visitor Center** (© **239/695-2945**), which are the only two places that give out these permits. Once you have one, camping sites cost $14 (with a maximum of 8 people per site), or $28 for a group site (maximum of 15 people). Campers can use only designated campsites, which are plentiful and well marked on visitor maps.

Many backcountry sites are *chickee* **huts**—covered wooden platforms (with toilets) on stilts. They're accessible only by canoe and can accommodate free-standing tents (without stakes). Ground sites are located along interior bays and rivers, and beach camping is also popular. In summer especially, mosquito repellent is necessary gear.

LODGING IN EVERGLADES CITY

Since Everglades City is 35 miles southeast of Naples and 83 miles west of Miami, many visitors choose to explore this western entrance to Everglades National Park, located off the Tamiami Trail, on S.R. 29. An annual seafood festival held the first weekend in February is a major event that draws hordes of people. Everglades City (the gateway to the Ten Thousand Islands), where the 'glades meet the Gulf of Mexico, is the closest thing you'll get to civilization in South Florida's swampy frontier, with a few tourist traps—er, shops—a restaurant, and two bed-and-breakfasts.

Everglades Spa and Lodge ★★★ (Finds)   This very cute B&B is right on the money, as far as kitsch is concerned—it's a fabulous retreat from the lush greenery of the swampy Everglades to the even more lush greenery of money. Located in a building that was formerly the first bank established, in 1923, in Collier County, money is this place's premise, but it won't cost you too much to stay here. Rooms such as the Trust Department, the Savings Department, and the Mutual Funds Department, all with bathrooms, are clean and comfortable; they're located on the floor where banking used to be done until 1962. Perhaps the best things about the place, besides the congenial service, are that breakfast is served in the bank's fully restored vault and that original artifacts from the bank are still visible, such as the 3,000-pound cannonball safe. Unlike a real bank, however, the knowledgeable staff at the inn is happy to give free advice on what to do in the area. A new day spa on the premises provides all the necessary pampering after a long day exploring the swamps.

201 W. Broadway, Everglades City, FL 34139. © 239/695-3151. Spa © 239/695-1006. Fax 239/695-3335. www.banksoftheeverglades.com. 7 units. $75–$150 double. Rates include continental breakfast delivered to your door. AE, DISC, MC, V. **Amenities:** Free use of bikes; Everglades excursions available. *In room:* A/C, TV.

Ivey House B&B ★★ *Finds*

Housed in what used to be a recreational center for the men who built the Tamiami Trail, the Ivey House offers three types of accommodations. In the original house, 10 small rooms share communal bathrooms (one each for women and men). There are no TVs or phones in these rooms. One private cottage consists of two bedrooms, a full kitchen, a private bathroom, and a screened-in porch. The Ivey's newer inn (opened in 2001) adds 18 rooms—with private bathrooms, TVs, and phones—that face a courtyard with a screened-in shallow "conversation" pool. During the summer, however, the mosquitoes are out in full force, so a trip to the pool could leave you with multiple bites, as it did me (screens or not). Bring bug spray!

Owners Sandee and David Harraden are extremely knowledgeable about the Everglades, and the guests usually are as well. A living-room area offers guests the opportunity to mingle. Rates include a full hot breakfast served from 6:30 to 11am. The Ghost Orchid Grill is the inn's full-service restaurant serving breakfast from November until the end of April. Box lunches, stored in a cooler so you can bring them along for your Everglades excursions, are offered for $9.50 each. *Note:* There is no smoking in any of the buildings.

107 Camellia St., Everglades City, FL 34139. © **239/695-3299.** Fax 239/695-4155. www.iveyhouse.com. 28 units. Winter $70–$200 double in main houses, $125–$175 cottage (2-night minimum); off season $50—100 double in main houses, cottage closed. MC, V. 2-night minimum during Everglades Seafood Festival in Feb. Closed Sept. **Amenities:** Restaurant; small pool; free use of bikes; Everglades excursions available. *In room:* A/C, TV, kitchen (cottage only), fridge (inn and cottage).

Rod & Gun Lodge ★

This rustic old white-clapboard house has plenty of history and all kinds of activities for sports enthusiasts, including a pool, bike rentals, a tennis center, and nearby boat rentals and private fishing guides. Set on the banks of the sleepy Barron River, the Rod & Gun Lodge was originally built as a private residence nearly 170 years ago, but Barron Collier turned it into a cozy hunting lodge in the 1920s. Hoover vacationed here after his 1928 election victory, and Truman flew in to sign Everglades National Park into existence in 1947 and stayed over as well. Other guests have included Richard Nixon, Burt Reynolds, and Mick Jagger. The public rooms are beautifully paneled and hung with tarpon, wild boar, deer antlers, and other trophies. Guest rooms in this single-story building are unfussy but perfectly comfortable. All have porches looking out on the river. Out by the pool, a screened veranda with ceiling fans offers a pleasant place for a libation. The excellent seafood restaurant serves breakfast, lunch, and dinner. The entire property is nonsmoking.

Riverside Dr. and Broadway (P.O. Box 190), Everglades City, FL 34139. © 239/695-2101. 17 units. Winter $125 double; off season $85 double. No credit cards. Closed after July 4 for the summer. **Amenities:** Restaurant; pool; tennis courts; bicycle rental. *In room:* A/C, TV.

LODGING IN HOMESTEAD & FLORIDA CITY

Homestead and Florida City, two adjacent towns that were almost blown off the map by Hurricane Andrew in 1992, have come back better than before. Located about 10 miles from the park's main entrance, along U.S. 1, 35 miles south of Miami, these somewhat rural towns offer several budget options, including a handful of chain hotels. There is a **Days Inn** (© **305/245-1260**) in Homestead and a **Hampton Inn** (© **800/426-7866** or 305/247-8833) right off the turnpike in Florida City. However, the best options are listed below.

Best Western Gateway to the Keys   This standard two-story motel offers contemporary style and comfort about 10 miles from the park's main entrance. A decent-size pool and a small spa make it an attractive option to some. Each standard room has bright, tropical bedspreads and oversize picture windows. The suites offer convenient extras like a microwave, coffeemaker, extra sink, and small fridge. Clean and conveniently located, the only drawback is that, in season, there is often a 3-day minimum-stay requirement. You'd do best to call the local reservation line instead of the toll-free number—on several occasions, the hotel has made an exception to the rule, while the central reservation line was not able to do the same.

411 S. Krome Ave. (U.S. 1), Florida City, FL 33034. © 800/528-1234 or 305/246-5100. Fax 305/242-0056. www.best western.com. 114 units. Year-round $109–$119 double. Rates include continental breakfast. During races and the very high season, there may be a 3-night minimum stay. AE, DC, DISC, MC, V. **Amenities:** Pool; spa; laundry service; dry cleaning. *In room:* A/C, TV, dataport, fridge, coffeemaker, hair dryer.

Everglades International Hostel 🏕   This is what a hostel *should* be. Sure, I've seen cleaner, more modern ones, but the feeling of camaraderie here is what hostels are all about. Located in a 1930s boardinghouse, this hostel has dorm rooms as well as doubles (all with shared bathrooms), a great kitchen, a washer/dryer, high-speed Internet access, bike rentals, and a garden (with tents, forts, and an outdoor chess board). The friendly, amazingly accommodating staff here offers tons of helpful information and runs sightseeing/canoe trips to the Everglades. *Note:* There are rooms here that are cheaper than the rates listed below, but these do not have air-conditioning.

20 SW 2nd Ave., Florida City, FL 33034. © 800/372-3874 or 305/248-1122. www.evergladeshostel.com. Dorm beds $14; private doubles $35; nonmember fee $3. MC, V. **Amenities:** Bike rental; tours; laundry facilities; Internet access; kitchen. *In room:* A/C (in some).

WHERE TO DINE IN & AROUND THE PARK

You won't find fancy nouvelle cuisine in this suburbanized farm country, but there are plenty of fast-food chains along U.S. 1 and a few old favorites worth a taste.

Here for nearly a quarter of a century, **El Toro Taco Family Restaurant,** 1 S. Krome Ave., near Mowry and Campbell drives, Homestead (© **305/245-8182**), opens daily at 9:30am and stays crowded until at least 9pm most days. The fresh grilled meats, tacos, burritos, salsas, guacamole, and stews are all mild and delicious. No matter how big your appetite, it's hard to spend more than $12 per person at this Mexican outpost. Bring your own beer or wine. See p. 135 for a full review.

Housed in a one-story, windowless building that looks something like a medieval fort, the **Capri Restaurant,** 935 N. Krome Ave., Florida City (© **305/247-1542**), has been serving hearty Italian-American fare since 1958. Great pastas and salads complement a menu of meat and fish dishes; portions are big. Lunch and dinner are served Monday through Friday until 9:30pm and Saturday until 10:30pm. The **White Lion Café,** 146 NW 7th St., Homestead (© **305/248-1076**), is a quaint home and gardens cum cafe with live blues, jazz, and swing music at night, and a tongue-in-cheeky menu with items like Dirty Little Shrimp and Poor Man's Steak, which is actually delicious meatloaf with mushrooms, gravy, mashed potatoes, and veggies for just $11. Dinner is served Tuesday through Saturday from 5pm until "the fat lady sings."

The **Miccosukee Restaurant,** just west of the Shark Valley entrance on the Tamiami Trail/U.S. 41 (© **305/223-8380**), serves authentic pumpkin bread, fry bread, and fish, and not-so-authentic Native American interpretations of tacos and fried chicken. It's worth a stop for brunch, lunch, or dinner.

Near the Miccosukee reservation is the **Pit Bar-B-Q,** 16400 SW 8th St. (© **305/ 226-2272**), a total pit of a place known for some of the best smoked ribs, barbecued chicken, and corn bread this side of the Deep South. It's open daily from 11am to 8pm.

In Everglades City, the **Oyster House,** on Chokoloskee Causeway, S.R. (the locals call it Hwy.) 29 South (© **239/695-2073**), is a large but homey seafood restaurant with modest prices, excellent service, and a fantastic view of the Ten Thousand Islands. Try the hush puppies.

Once inside the Everglades, you'll want to eat at the only restaurant within the boundaries of this huge park, the **Flamingo Restaurant** (© **239/695-3101**). Located in the Flamingo Lodge, Marina, and Outpost Resort (p. 247), this is a very civilized and affordable establishment. All of Flamingo took a beating from 2005's ruthless hurricanes Katrina and Wilma, and the restaurant, like the lodge, was closed at the time of this writing. The restaurant was slated to reopen in late 2006—call first to be sure.

2 Biscayne National Park ⁄★

35 miles S of Miami, 21 miles E of Everglades National Park

With only about 500,000 visitors each year (mostly boaters and divers), the unusual Biscayne National Park is one of the least-crowded parks in the country. Perhaps that's because the park is a little more difficult than most to access—more than 95% of its 181,500 acres is underwater.

The park's significance was first formally acknowledged in 1968 when, in an unprecedented move (and despite intense pressure from developers), President Lyndon B. Johnson signed a bill to conserve the barrier islands off South Florida's east coast as a national monument—a protected status just a rung below national park. After being twice enlarged, once in 1974 and again in 1980, the waters and land surrounding the northernmost coral reef in North America became a full-fledged national park—the largest of its kind in the country.

To be fully appreciated, Biscayne National Park should be thought of as more preserve than destination. I suggest using your time here to explore underwater life, of course, but also to relax.

The park's small mainland mangrove shoreline and keys are best explored by boat. Its extensive reef system is renowned by divers and snorkelers worldwide.

The park consists of 44 islands, but only a few of them are open to visitors. The most popular is **Elliott Key,** which has campsites and a visitor center plus freshwater showers (cold water only), restrooms, trails, and a buoyed swim area. It's located about 9 miles from **Convoy Point,** the park's official headquarters on land. During Columbus Day weekend, there is a very popular regatta in which a lively crowd of party people gathers—sometimes in the nude—to celebrate the long weekend. If you'd prefer to rough it a little more, the 29-acre island known as **Boca Chita Key,** once an exclusive haven for yachters, has now become a popular spot for all manner of boaters. Visitors can camp and tour the island's restored historic buildings, including the county's second-largest lighthouse and a tiny chapel.

JUST THE FACTS

GETTING THERE & ACCESS POINTS   Convoy Point, the park's mainland entrance, is 9 miles east of Homestead. To reach the park from Miami, take the Florida Turnpike to the Tallahassee Road (SW 137th Ave.) exit. Turn left, then left again at North Canal Drive (SW 328th St.), and follow signs to the park. Another option is to rent a speedboat in Miami and cruise south for about 1½ hours. If you're coming from U.S. 1, whether you're heading north or south, turn east at North Canal Drive (SW 328th St.). The entrance is approximately 9 miles away. The rest of the park is accessible only by boat.

Because most of Biscayne National Park is accessible only to boaters, mooring buoys abound, since it is illegal to anchor on coral. When no buoys are available, boaters must anchor on sand or on the docks surrounding the small harbor off Boca Chita. Boats can also dock here overnight for $15. Even the most experienced boaters should carry updated nautical charts of the area, which are available at Convoy Point's Dante Fascell Visitor Center. The waters are often murky, making the abundant reefs and sandbars difficult to detect—and there are more interesting ways to spend a day than waiting for the tide to rise. There's a boat launch at adjacent Homestead Bayfront Park and 66 slips on Elliott Key, available free on a first-come, first-served basis.

Round-trip transportation to and from the visitor center to Elliott Key costs $27 (plus tax) per person and takes about an hour. This is a convenient option, ensuring that you don't get lost on some deserted island by boating there yourself. Call ☎ **305/ 230-1100** for the seasonal schedule.

VISITOR CENTERS & INFORMATION   **Dante Fascell Visitor Center,** often referred to by its older name, **Convoy Point Visitor Center,** 9700 SW 328th St., Homestead, FL 33033-5634, at the park's main entrance (☎ **305/230-7275;** fax 305/ 230-1190; www.nps.gov/bisc), is the natural starting point for any venture into the park without a boat. It provides comprehensive information about the park; on request, rangers will show you a short video on the park, its natural surroundings, and what you may see. The center is open daily from 9am to 5pm.

For information on transportation, glass-bottom-boat tours, and snorkeling and scuba-diving expeditions, contact the park concessionaire, **Biscayne National Under- water Park, Inc.,** P.O. Box 1270, Homestead, FL 33030 (☎ **305/230-1100;** fax 305/ 230-1120; www.nps.gov/bisc). It's open daily from 8:30am to 5pm.

ENTRANCE FEES & PERMITS   Entering Biscayne National Park is free. There is a $15-per-night overnight docking fee at both Boca Chita Key Harbor and Elliott Key Harbor ($7.50 per night for holders of Golden Age or Golden Access passports), which includes a campsite. Campsites are $10 for those staying without a boat. Group camping costs $25 a day and covers up to 6 tents and 25 people. See p. 242 for information on fishing permits. Backcountry camping permits are free and can be picked up from the Dante Fascell Visitor Center. For more information on fees and permits, call the park ranger at ☎ **305/230-1144.**

SEEING THE HIGHLIGHTS

Since the park is primarily underwater, the only way to truly experience it is with snorkel or scuba gear. Beneath the surface of Biscayne National Park, the aquatic universe pulses with multicolored life: Bright parrotfish and angelfish, gently rocking sea fans, and coral labyrinths abound. See the "Snorkeling & Scuba Diving" section below for more information.

Afterward, take a picnic out to Elliott Key and taste the crisp salt air blowing off the Atlantic. Or head to Boca Chita, an intriguing island that was once the private playground of wealthy yachters.

SPORTS & OUTDOOR ACTIVITIES

CANOEING & KAYAKING   Biscayne National Park offers excellent canoeing, both along the coast and across the open water to nearby mangroves and artificial islands that dot the longest uninterrupted shoreline in the state of Florida. Since tides can be strong, only experienced canoeists should attempt to paddle far from shore. If you do plan to go far, first obtain a tide table from the visitor center and paddle with the current. Free ranger-led canoe tours are scheduled from 9am to noon on the second and fourth Saturdays of the month between January 10 and April 24; phone for information. You can rent a canoe at the park's concession stand for $12 an hour. Two-person kayaks go for $16 an hour. Call © **305/230-1100** for reservations, information, ranger tours, and boat rentals.

FISHING   Ocean fishing is excellent year-round at Biscayne National Park; many people cast their lines from the breakwater jetty at Convoy Point. A fishing license is required (see p. 242 for information). Bait is not available in Biscayne National Park but is sold in adjacent Homestead Bayfront Park. Stone crabs and Florida lobsters can be found here, but you're allowed to catch these only on the ocean side when they're in season. There are strict limits on size, season, number, and method of take (including spear fishing) for both fresh- and saltwater fishing. The latest regulations are available at most marinas, bait-and-tackle shops, and the park's visitor centers. Or you can contact the **Florida Fish and Wildlife Conservation Commission,** Bryant Building, 620 S. Meridian St., Tallahassee, FL 32399-1600 (© **850/488-0331**).

HIKING & EXPLORING   Since the majority of this park is underwater, hiking is not the main attraction here, but there are some interesting sights and trails nonetheless. At Convoy Point, you can walk along the 370-foot boardwalk and along the ½-mile jetty that serves as a breakwater for the park's harbor. From here, you can usually see brown pelicans, little blue herons, snowy egrets, and a few exotic fish.

Elliott Key is accessible only by boat, but once you're there, you have two good trail options. True to its name, the Loop Trail makes a 1.5-mile circle from the bayside visitor center, through a hardwood hammock and mangroves, to an elevated oceanside boardwalk. It's likely that you'll see purple and orange land crabs scurrying around the mangrove roots.

Reopened in 1998, Boca Chita Key was once a playground for wealthy tycoons, and it still offers the peaceful beauty that attracted elite anglers from cold climates. Many of the historic buildings are still intact, including an ornamental lighthouse that was never put into use. Take advantage of the tours, usually led by a park ranger and available every Sunday in winter only at 1:30pm. The tour, including the boat trip, takes about 3 hours. The price is $26 for adults, $21 for seniors, and $16 for children under 12. However, call in advance to see if the sea is calm enough for the trip—the boats won't run in rough waters. See "Glass-Bottom-Boat Tours," below, for information about the daily 10am excursions.

SNORKELING & SCUBA DIVING   The clear, warm waters of Biscayne National Park are packed with colorful tropical fish that swim in the offshore reefs. If you don't have your own gear, or if you don't want to lug it to the park, you can rent or buy snorkeling and scuba gear at the full-service dive shop at Convoy Point. Rates are in line with those at mainland dive shops.

The best way to see the park from underwater is to take a snorkeling or diving tour operated by **Biscayne National Underwater Park, Inc.** (© **305/230-1100;** www.nps.gov/bisc). Snorkeling tours depart at 1:30pm daily, last about 3 hours, and cost

$37 per person, including equipment. There are also weekend two-tank dives for certified divers; the price is $54, including two tanks and weights. Make your reservations in advance. The shop is open daily from 9am to 5pm.

Before entering the water, be sure to apply waterproof sunblock—once you begin to explore, it's easy to lose track of time, and the Florida sun is brutal, even during winter.

SWIMMING   You can swim at the protected beaches of Elliott Key, Boca Chita Key, and adjacent Homestead Bayfront Park, but none of these matches the width or softness of other South Florida beaches. Check the water conditions before heading into the sea: The strong currents that make this a popular destination for windsurfers and sailors can be dangerous, even for strong swimmers. Homestead Bayfront Park is really just a marina located next to Biscayne National Park, but it does have a beach and picnic facilities as well as fishing areas and a playground. It's located at Convoy Point, 9698 SW 328th St., Homestead (© **305/230-3034**).

GLASS-BOTTOM-BOAT TOURS

If you prefer not to dive, the best way to see the sights is on a glass-bottom boat. **Biscayne National Underwater Park, Inc.** (© **305/230-1100;** www.nps.gov/bisc), offers daily trips to view some of the country's most beautiful coral reefs and tropical fish. Boats depart year-round from Convoy Point at 10am and stay out for about 3 hours. At $26 for adults, $21 for seniors, and $19 for children 12 and under, the scenic and informative tours are well worth the price. Boats carry fewer than 50 passengers; reservations are almost always necessary.

WHERE TO STAY

Besides campsites, there are no facilities available for overnight guests to this watery park. Most noncamping visitors come for an afternoon, on their way to the Keys, and stay overnight in nearby Homestead, where there are many national chain hotels and other affordable lodgings (see p. 249 for more information).

Although you won't find hotels or lodges in Biscayne National Park, it does have some of the state's most pristine campsites. Since they are inaccessible by motor vehicle, you'll be sure to avoid the mass of RVs so prevalent in many of the state's other campgrounds. The sites on Elliott Key and Boca Chita can be reached only by boat. If you don't have your own, call © **305/230-1100** to arrange a drop-off. Transportation to and from the visitor center costs $27 (plus tax) per person. Boca Chita has only saltwater toilets (no showers or sinks); Elliot Key has freshwater, cold-water showers and toilets, but is otherwise no less primitive. If you didn't pay for the overnight docking fee, campsites are $10.

With a backcountry permit, available free from the visitor center, you can pitch your tent somewhere even more private. Ask for a map and be sure to bring plenty of bug spray. Sites cost $10 a night for up to six persons staying in one or two tents. Backcountry camping is allowed only on Elliott Key, which is a very popular spot (accessible only by boat) for boaters and campers. It is approximately 9 miles from the Dante Fascell Visitor Center and offers hiking trails, fresh water, boat slips, showers, and restrooms. While there, don't miss the Old Road, a 7-mile tropical hammock trail that runs the length of Elliott Key. This trail is one of the few places left in the world to see the highly endangered Schaus' swallowtail butterfly, recognizable by its black wings with diagonal yellow bands. They're usually out from late April to July.

8

The Gold Coast: Hallandale to the Palm Beaches

Named not for the sun-kissed skin of the area's residents, but for the gold salvaged from shipwrecks off its coastline, the Gold Coast embraces more than 60 miles of beautiful Atlantic shoreline—from the pristine sands of Jupiter in northern Palm Beach County to the legendary strip of beaches in Fort Lauderdale.

If you haven't visited the cities along Florida's southeastern coast in the last few years, you'll be amazed at how much has changed. Miles of sprawling grassland and empty lots have been replaced with luxurious resorts and high-rise condominiums. Taking advantage of their proximity to Miami, the cities that make up the Gold Coast have attracted millions looking to escape crowded sidewalks, traffic jams, and the everyday routines of life.

Fortunately, amid all the building, much of the natural treasure of the Gold Coast remains. There are 300 miles of Intracoastal Waterway, not to mention Fort Lauderdale's Venetian-inspired canals. And the unspoiled splendor of the Everglades is just a few miles inland.

The most popular areas in the Gold Coast are Fort Lauderdale, Boca Raton, and Palm Beach. While Fort Lauderdale is a favored beachfront destination, Boca Raton and Palm Beach are better known for their country-club lifestyles and excellent shopping. Farther north is the quietly popular Jupiter, best known for spring training at the Roger Dean Stadium and for former resident Burt Reynolds. In between these better-traveled destinations are a few things worth stopping for, but not much. Driving north along the coastline is one of the best ways to fully appreciate what the Gold Coast is all about—it's a perspective you certainly won't find in a shopping mall.

Tourists come here by the droves, but they aren't the only people coming; thousands of transplants, fleeing the increasing population influx in Miami and the frigid winters up north, have made this area their home. As a result, there has been a construction boom in the existing cities and even westward, into the swampy areas of the Everglades. More than 20 homes per day are being built in Broward County alone. There has also been a great revitalization of several downtown areas, including Hollywood, Fort Lauderdale, and West Palm Beach. These once-desolate urban centers have been spruced up and now attract more young travelers and families than ever.

Unfortunately, like its neighbors to the south, the Gold Coast can be prohibitively hot and buggy in summer. The good news is that bargains are plentiful May through October, when many locals take advantage of package deals and uncrowded resorts.

For the purposes of this chapter, the Gold Coast will consist of the towns of Hallandale, Hollywood, Pompano Beach, Fort Lauderdale, Dania, Deerfield, Boca Raton, Delray Beach, Boynton Beach, Jupiter, and the Palm Beaches.

EXPLORING THE GOLD COAST BY CAR

Like most of South Florida, the Gold Coast consists of a mainland and adjacent barrier islands. You'll have to check maps to keep track of the many bridges that allow access to the islands where most tourist activity is centered. Interstate 95, which runs north-south, is the area's main highway. Farther west is the Florida Turnpike, a toll road that can be worth the expense since the speed limit is higher and it's often less congested than I-95. Also on the mainland is U.S. 1, which generally runs parallel to I-95 (to the east) and is a narrower thoroughfare mostly crowded with strip malls and seedy hotels.

I recommend taking Florida A1A, a slow oceanside road that connects the long, thin islands of Florida's entire east coast. Although the road is narrow, it is the most scenic and, thus, ushers you into the relaxed atmosphere of these resort towns.

1 Broward County: Hallandale & Hollywood ★ to Fort Lauderdale ★★

23 miles N of Miami

Less exposed than the highly hyped Miami, Broward County is a lot calmer and, according to some, a lot friendlier than the Magic City. In fact, a friendly rivalry exists between residents of Miami–Dade County and those of Broward County. Miamians consider themselves more sophisticated and cosmopolitan than their northern neighbors, who, in turn, dismiss the alleged sophistication as snobbery and actually prefer their own county's gentler pace.

With more than 23 miles of beachfront and 300 miles of navigable waterways, Broward County is also a great outdoor destination. Scattered amid the shopping malls, condominiums, and tourist traps is a beautiful landscape lined with hundreds of parks, golf courses, tennis courts, and, of course, beaches.

The City of Hallandale Beach is a small, peaceful oceanfront town located just north of Dade County's Aventura. Condos are the predominant landmarks in Hallandale, which is still pretty much a retirement community, although the revamped multimillion-dollar Westin Diplomat Resort (p. 268) is slowly trying to revitalize and liven up the area.

Just north of Hallandale is the more energetic, burgeoning city of Hollywood. Once a sleepy community wedged between Fort Lauderdale and Miami, Hollywood is now a bustling area of 1.5 million people belonging to an array of ethnic and racial identities: from white and African American to Jamaican, Chinese, and Dominican. (*Money* magazine trumpeted the self-described "City of the Future" as having an ethnic makeup that mirrors what the U.S. will look like by the year 2022.) 2004 saw the debut of the $300-million Seminole Hard Rock Hotel & Casino (p. 271), with a 500-room hotel, spa, and 130,000-square-foot casino. This was exactly what the city needed to kick its slow renaissance up a notch. A spate of redevelopment has made the pedestrian-friendly center along Hollywood Boulevard and Harrison Street, east of Dixie Highway, a popular destination for travelers and locals alike. Some predict Hollywood will be South Florida's next big destination—South Beach without the attitude and traffic jams. While the prediction is a dubious one, Hollywood is definitely awakening from its long slumber. Prices are a fraction of those at other tourist areas, and a quasibohemian vibe is apparent in the galleries, clubs, and restaurants that dot the new "strip." Its gritty undercurrent, however, prevents it from becoming too trendy.

Fort Lauderdale, with its well-known strip of beaches, restaurants, bars, and souvenir shops, has also undergone a major transformation. Once famous (or infamous)

The Gold Coast

for the annual mayhem it hosted during spring break, this area is now attracting a more affluent, better-behaved yachting crowd. Starwood Hotels has announced plans for a W Fort Lauderdale, a 346-room boutique hotel originally slated to open in South Beach but instead opening here the fall of 2007.

In addition to beautiful wide beaches, Fort Lauderdale, known as the Venice of America, has more than 300 miles of navigable waterways and innumerable canals, which permit thousands of residents to anchor boats in their backyards. Boating is not just a hobby here; it's a lifestyle. Visitors can easily get on the water, too, by renting a boat or by hailing a moderately priced water taxi.

Huge cruise ships also take advantage of Florida's deepest harbor, Port Everglades. The seaport is located on the southeastern coast of the Florida peninsula, near the Fort Lauderdale–Hollywood International Airport on the outskirts of Hollywood and Dania Beach. Port Everglades is the second-busiest cruise-ship base in Florida, after Miami, and one of the top five in the world. For further information on cruises, see p. 160 and consult *Frommer's Caribbean Cruises & Ports of Call* (Wiley Publishing, Inc.).

ESSENTIALS

GETTING THERE   If you're driving from Miami, it's a straight shot north to Hollywood or Fort Lauderdale. Visitors on their way to or from Orlando should take the Florida Turnpike to exits 53, 54, 58, or 62, depending on the location of your accommodations.

The **Fort Lauderdale–Hollywood International Airport** is small, easy to negotiate, and located just 15 minutes from both of the downtown areas it services. But its user-friendliness may not last much longer: Because of its popularity, the airport is undergoing a $650-million expansion and renovation that often renders it just as maddening as any other major metropolitan airport. The airport has wireless Internet access and a fantastic car-rental center in which 10 rental companies are located under one roof—very convenient. Levels 1 through 4 are home to Alamo, Avis, Budget, Dollar, Enterprise, E-Z, Hertz, National, Royal, and Thrifty. Levels 5–9 provide 5,500 spaces for public parking.

Amtrak (© 800/USA-RAIL) stations are at 200 SW 21st Terrace (Broward Blvd. and I-95), Fort Lauderdale (© 954/587-6692), and 3001 Hollywood Blvd. (northwest corner of Hollywood Blvd. and I-95; © 954/921-4517).

VISITOR INFORMATION   The **Greater Fort Lauderdale Convention & Visitors Bureau,** 1850 Eller Dr., Suite 303 (off I-95 and I-595 E), Fort Lauderdale, FL 33316 (© 954/765-4466; fax 954/765-4467; www.sunny.org), is an excellent resource for area information in English, Spanish, and French. Call in advance to request a free comprehensive guide covering events, accommodations, and sightseeing in Broward County. In addition, once you're in town, you can call the 24-hour **information line** (© 954/527-5600; www.activityline.net) to get easy-to-follow directions, travel advice, and assistance from multilingual operators.

Also available for brochures, information, and vacation packages in Fort Lauderdale are operators at **Greater Than Ever Fort Lauderdale** (© 800/22-SUNNY).

The **Greater Hollywood Chamber of Commerce,** 330 N. Federal Hwy. (at U.S. 1 and Taylor St.), Hollywood, FL 33020 (© 954/923-4000; fax 954/923-8737; www.hollywoodchamber.org), is open Monday through Friday from 9am to 5pm. Here you'll find the lowdown on all of Hollywood's events, attractions, restaurants, hotels, and tours.

Fort Lauderdale, Hollywood & Pompano Beach Area

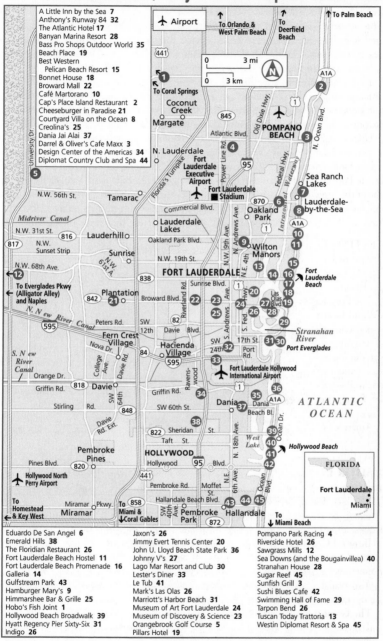

A Little Inn by the Sea **7**
Anthony's Runway 84 **32**
The Atlantic Hotel **17**
Banyan Marina Resort **28**
Bass Pro Shops Outdoor World **35**
Beach Place **19**
Best Western
  Pelican Beach Resort **15**
Bonnet House **18**
Broward Mall **22**
Café Martorano **10**
Cap's Place Island Restaurant **2**
Cheeseburger in Paradise **21**
Courtyard Villa on the Ocean **8**
Creolina's **25**
Dania Jai Alai **37**
Darrel & Oliver's Cafe Maxx **3**
Design Center of the Americas **34**
Diplomat Country Club and Spa **44**

✈ **Airport**

To Orlando &
West Palm Beach

To
Deerfield
Beach

To Palm Beach

0 ____ 3 mi
0 ____ 3 km

N

To Coral Springs

Coconut
Creek
Margate

Atlantic Blvd.

**POMPANO
BEACH**

N. Lauderdale
Fort
Lauderdale
Executive
Airport

Fort Lauderdale
■ Stadium

Sea Ranch
Lakes

Lauderdale-
by-the-Sea

N.W. 56th St.   Tamarac

Commercial Blvd.

Oakland
Park

Lauderdale
Lakes

Oakland Park Blvd.

Midriver Canal

N.W. 31st St.

N.W.
Sunset Strip

Lauderhill

Sunrise

N.W. 19th St.

Wilton
Manors

N.W. 68th Ave.

FORT LAUDERDALE

To Everglades Pkwy
(Alligator Alley)
and Naples

N. New River Canal

Plantation

Sunrise Blvd.

Broward Blvd.

Las
Olas
Blvd.

**Fort
Lauderdale
Beach**

Peters Rd.

Fern Crest
Village

Nova Dr.

SW
12th

Davie Blvd.

Hacienda
Village

SW
24th

*Stranahan
River*

Port
Rd.

Port Everglades

*S. New
River
Canal*

Orange Dr.

Griffin Rd.   Davie

Stirling   Rd.

Griffin Rd.

SW 60th St.

Dania

Dania
Beach Bl.

**ATLANTIC
OCEAN**

*Davie
Rd. Ext.*

Sheridan   St.

Taft   St.

*West
Lake*

Hollywood Beach

Pembroke
Pines

Pines Blvd.

HOLLYWOOD

Hollywood   Blvd.

FLORIDA

Hollywood North
Perry Airport

Pembroke Rd.

Moffet
St.

Fort Lauderdale

Miami

To
Homestead
& Key West

Miramar   Pkwy.

Miramar

To
Miami &
Coral Gables

Hallandale Beach Blvd.

Pembroke
Park   Hallandale

To
Miami Beach

Eduardo De San Angel **6**
Emerald Hills **38**
The Floridian Restaurant **26**
Fort Lauderdale Beach Hostel **11**
Fort Lauderdale Beach Promenade **16**
Galleria **14**
Gulfstream Park **43**
Hamburger Mary's **9**
Himmarshee Bar & Grille **25**
Hobo's Fish Joint **1**
Hollywood Beach Broadwalk **39**
Hyatt Regency Pier Sixty-Six **31**
Indigo **26**

Jaxon's **26**
Jimmy Evert Tennis Center **20**
John U. Lloyd Beach State Park **36**
Johnny V's **27**
Lago Mar Resort and Club **30**
Lester's Diner **33**
Le Tub **41**
Mark's Las Olas **26**
Marriott's Harbor Beach **31**
Museum of Art Fort Lauderdale **24**
Museum of Discovery & Science **23**
Orangebrook Golf Course **5**
Pillars Hotel **19**

Pompano Park Racing **4**
Riverside Hotel **26**
Sawgrass Mills **12**
Sea Downs (and the Bougainvillea) **40**
Stranahan House **28**
Sugar Reef **45**
Sunfish Grill **3**
Sushi Blues Cafe **42**
Swimming Hall of Fame **29**
Tarpon Bend **26**
Tuscan Today Trattoria **13**
Westin Diplomat Resort & Spa **45**

HITTING THE BEACH

The southern part of the Gold Coast, Broward County, has the region's most popular and amenities-laden beaches, which stretch for more than 23 miles. Most do not charge for access, though all are well maintained. Here's a selection of some of the county's best from south to north:

Hollywood Beach, stretching from Sheridan Street to Georgia Street, is a major attraction in the city of Hollywood, a virtual carnival of young hipsters, big families, and sunburned French Canadians who dodge bicyclers and skaters along the rows of tacky souvenir shops, T-shirt shops, game rooms, snack bars, beer stands, hotels, and miniature-golf courses. **Hollywood Beach Broadwalk,** modeled after Atlantic City's legendary boardwalk, is the town's popular beachfront pedestrian thoroughfare, a cement promenade that's 30 feet wide and stretches along the shoreline for 3 miles. A recent makeover added, among other things, a concrete bike path, a crushed-shell jogging path, new trash receptacles, and the relocation of beach showers to each street end (all of are them are handicap accessible). Popular with runners, skaters, and cruisers, the Broadwalk is also renowned as a hangout for thousands of retirement-age snowbirds who get together for frequent dances and shows at a faded outdoor amphitheater. Despite efforts to clear out a seedy element, the area remains a haven for drunks and scammers, so keep alert.

If you tire of the hectic diversity that defines Hollywood's Broadwalk, enjoy the natural beauty of the beach itself, which is wide and clean. There are lifeguards, showers, restroom facilities, and public areas for picnics and parties.

The **Fort Lauderdale Beach Promenade,** along the beach, underwent a $26-million renovation and looks fantastic. It's especially peaceful in the mornings, when there's just a smattering of joggers and walkers; but even at its most crowded on weekends, the expansive promenade provides room for everyone. Note, however, that the beach is hardly pristine; it is across the street from an uninterrupted stretch of hotels, bars, and retail outlets. Also nearby is a retail-and-dining megacomplex, Beach Place (p. 278), on Florida A1A, midway between Las Olas and Sunrise boulevards.

On the sand just across the road, most days you'll find hard-core volleyballers who always welcome anyone with a good spike, and you'll find an inviting ocean welcoming swimmers of any level. The unusually clear waters are under the careful watch of some of Florida's best-looking lifeguards. Freshen up afterward in any of the clean showers and restrooms conveniently located along the strip. Pets have been banned from most of the beach in order to maintain the impressive cleanliness; a designated area for pets exists away from the main sunbathing areas.

Especially on weekends, parking at the oceanside meters is nearly impossible. Try biking, skating, or hitching a ride on the water taxi instead. The strip is located on Florida A1A, between SE 17th Street and Sunrise Boulevard.

Dania Beach's **John U. Lloyd Beach State Park,** 6503 N. Ocean Dr., Dania (© 954/923-2833), consists of 251 acres of barrier island between the Atlantic Ocean and the Intracoastal Waterway, from Port Everglades on the north to Dania on the south. Its natural setting contrasts sharply with the urban development of Fort Lauderdale. Lloyd Beach, one of Broward County's most important nesting beaches for sea turtles, produces some 10,000 hatchlings a year. The park's broad, flat beach is popular for both swimming and sunning. Self-guided nature trails are great for those too restless to sunbathe. The park and beach received significant damage during 2005's Hurricane Wilma, but by the time this book hits the shelves, all will be well again. We hope.

Turtle Trail

In June and July, the John U. Lloyd Beach is crawling with nature lovers who come for the spectacular **Sea Turtle Awareness Program.** Park rangers begin the evening with a lecture and slide show while scouts search the beach for nesting loggerhead sea turtles. If a turtle is located—plenty of them usually are—a beach walk allows participants to see the turtles nesting and, some-times, their eggs hatching. The program begins at 9pm on Wednesday and Fri-day from mid-May to mid-July. Call ✆ **954/923-2833** for reservations. Walks last between 1 and 3 hours. Comfortable walking shoes and insect repellent are a must. The park entrance fee of $3 to $5 per carload applies.

OUTDOOR ACTIVITIES & SPECTATOR SPORTS

BOATING   Often called the "yachting capital of the world," Fort Lauderdale pro-vides ample opportunity for visitors to get out on the water, either along the Intra-coastal Waterway or on the open ocean. If your hotel doesn't rent boats, try **Aloha Watersports,** Marriott's Harbor Beach Resort, 3030 Holiday Dr., Fort Lauderdale (✆ **954/462-7245**). It can outfit you with a variety of craft, including jet skis, WaveRunners, and catamarans. Rates start at $65 per half-hour for WaveRunners ($15 each additional rider; doubles and triples available), $70 to $125 for sailboats, $60 to $70 for catamarans, $20 per person per hour for ocean kayaks, and $60 per person for a 10- to 12-minute parasailing ride. Aloha also offers Coast Guard classes at 9am daily, through which adults can obtain their Florida Boaters License for $3.

CRUISES   The *Jungle Queen,* 801 Sea Breeze Blvd. (3 blocks south of Las Olas Blvd. on Fla. A1A), in the Bahia Mar Yacht Center, Fort Lauderdale (✆ **954/462-5596**), is a Mississippi River–style steamer and one of Fort Lauderdale's best-known attractions, cruising up and down the New River. All-you-can-eat 4-hour dinner cruises (departing nightly at 7pm and costing $32 for adults and $18 for children 2–10) and 3-hour sightseeing tours (scheduled daily at 10am and 2pm, and costing $14 for adults and $9.95 for children 2–10) take visitors past Millionaires' Row, Old Fort Lauderdale, and the new downtown. There's also a seasonal 8-hour cruise that goes down to Miami (Bayside), leaving Wednesday and Saturday at 9:15am and cost-ing $18 for adults and $13 for children.

If you're interested in gambling, several casino-boat companies operate day cruises out of Port Everglades and offer blackjack, slots, and poker. **Discovery Cruise Lines** (✆ **800/937-4477**) has daily 7:45am departures to the Bahamas, where you can gam-ble, eat, and party for 10 to 12 hours (you have about 3 hr. in the Bahamas to go to the Straw Market or to do even more gambling) for about $129 Monday through Thursday, $145 Friday through Sunday. The price includes breakfast, lunch, and din-ner, but drinks cost extra.

Sea Escape (✆ **800/327-2005** or 954/453-3333) also launches daily casino cruises 15 times a week, and traveling a few miles offshore. Trips "to nowhere" are offered Monday through Sunday from 11am to 4:30pm, Monday through Friday from 7:30pm to 12:30am, and Saturday from 7:30pm to 1:30am. Daytime cruises cost $35 for adults ($25 if you purchase in advance) and $13 for children 2 to 12 (who are not allowed on the evening cruises). Evening cruises have the same prices, except on Fri-day and Saturday, when adults pay $30 in advance, $40 at the dock. Party cruises offer buffet meals and full casinos for $30 to $40 per person. I recommend spending an additional $20 for a cabin ($25 per cabin on the evening cruises) so you can stretch out and relax between hands. Even though the cruises don't go far from the coast, 5 or 6 hours is a long time to spend at sea, especially if the weather is rough.

FISHING   The **IGFA (International Game Fish Association) World Fishing Center,** 300 Gulf Stream Way, Dania Beach (© **954/922-4212;** www.igfa.org), is an angler's paradise. One of the highlights of this museum, library, and park is the virtual-reality fishing simulator, which allows visitors to actually reel in their own computer-generated catch. Also included in the 3-acre park are displays of antique fishing gear, record catches, famous anglers, various vessels, and a wetlands lab. To get a list of local captains and guides, call **IGFA headquarters** (© **954/927-2628**) and ask for the librarian. Admission is $6 for adults, $5 for seniors and children 3 to 16. The museum and library are open daily from 10am to 6pm. On the grounds is also **Bass Pro Shops Outdoor World,** a huge retail complex set on a 3-acre lake.

GOLF   More than 50 golf courses in all price ranges compete for players. Among the best is **Emerald Hills,** 4100 N. Hills Dr., Hollywood, (© **954/961-4000;** www.the clubatemeraldhills.com), just west of I-95 between Sterling Road and Sheridan Street. This beauty consistently lands on the "best of" lists of golf writers nationwide. The 18th hole, on a two-tier green, is the course's signature; it's surrounded by water and is more than a bit rough. The course is pricey—Friday through Sunday, greens fees start at $125 for tee times after 1pm, and $165 for tee times before noon during high season; Monday through Friday, the fees are $125 before noon and $100 after 1pm. Rates are cheaper during the brutally hot summers.

The **Diplomat Country Club and Spa,** 501 Diplomat Pkwy., Hallandale Beach (© **954/602-6000;** www.diplomatcountryclub.com), is located across the Intracoastal from the Westin Diplomat Resort. It has fabulous golf facilities, with 8 acres of lakes and rolling fairways, plus a fantastic delivery service that brings lunch and drinks to your cart. You pay for the services, however, with greens fees of about $205 during high season and $85 to $159 off season. Twilight fees at 2pm cost from $50 to $95.

For one of Broward's best municipal challenges, try the 18-holer at the **Orange-brook Golf Course,** 400 Entrada Dr., Hollywood (© **954/967-GOLF**). Built in 1937, this is one of the state's oldest courses and one of the area's best bargains. Morning and noon rates are $17 to $22. After 2pm, you can play for about $15, including a cart. Men must wear collared shirts to play here, and no spikes are allowed.

SCUBA DIVING   In Broward County, the best dive wreck is the *Mercedes I,* a 197-foot freighter that washed up in the back yard of a Palm Beach socialite in 1984 and

---

Fun Fact **Remnants of the Past**

Any diving outfit in Jupiter Beach will take you to the spot where remnants of a shipwreck from a 16th- or 17th-century Spanish galleon lie. Discovered in 1988 by Jupiter lifeguard Peter Leo, who on his morning swim came across an anchor and a cannon, the wreck has since produced 10 more cannons and more than 10,000 gold and silver coins. However, if you come across more coins, you won't be able to throw them in your piggy bank—Leo owns the rights to the wreck. This is a more historic dive than the *Mercedes I,* since it's an actual wreck and not one that was intentionally submerged for divers.

was sunk for divers the following year off Pompano Beach. The artificial reef, filled with colorful sponges, spiny lobsters, and barracudas, is located 97 feet below the surface, a mile offshore between Oakland Park and Sunrise boulevards. Dozens of reputable dive shops line the beach. Ask at your hotel for a nearby recommendation, or contact **Neil Watson's Undersea Adventures,** 1525 S. Andrews Ave., Fort Lauderdale (© **954/462-3400;** www.nealwatson.com).

SPECTATOR SPORTS   Baseball fans can get their fix at the **Fort Lauderdale Stadium,** 5301 NW 12th Ave. (© **954/828-4980**), where the Baltimore Orioles play spring-training exhibition games starting in early March; call © **954/776-1921** for tickets. General admission is $8, a spot in the grandstand $12, and box seats $18; kids 14 and under pay $4. During the season, the Florida Marlins play just south of Hallandale at **Dolphin Stadium,** near the Dade–Broward County line. Tickets go on sale in January for $4 to $50; call **Ticketmaster** (© **305/358-5885**) to purchase them.

Pompano Park Racing, 1800 SW 3rd St., Pompano Beach (© **954/972-2000**), features parimutuel harness racing from October to early August. Admission is free to both grandstand and clubhouse.

Wrapped around an artificial lake, **Gulfstream Park,** at U.S. 1 and Hallandale Beach Boulevard, Hallandale (© **954/454-7000**), is pretty and popular. Large purses and important horse races are commonplace at this recently refurbished suburban course, and the track is often crowded. The most recent renovation has transformed it into a world-class, state-of-the-art facility with four higher-end restaurants, 20 luxury suites, private accommodations for top players, and more. It hosts the Florida Derby each March. Call for schedules. Admission is $3 Monday through Friday, $5 Saturday and Sunday to the grandstand, and always $5 to the clubhouse. Parking is free. From January 3 to April 25, post times are 1:30pm weekdays and 1pm weekends, and the doors open at 11:30am. Many weekends feature concerts by well-known musicians.

Jai alai, a sort of Spanish-style indoor lacrosse, was introduced to Florida in 1924 and still draws big crowds, who bet on the fast-paced action. Broward's only fronton, **Dania Jai Alai,** 301 E. Dania Beach Blvd., at Florida A1A and U.S. 1 (© **954/920-1511**), is a great place to spend an afternoon or evening.

In the sport of ice hockey, the young **Florida Panthers** (© **954/835-7000**) play in Sunrise at the **BankAtlantic Center,** 2555 NW 137th Way (© **954/835-8000**). Tickets range from $15 to $100. Call for directions and ticket information.

TENNIS   There are hundreds of courts in Broward County, and plenty are accessible to the public. Many are at resorts and hotels. If yours has none, try the **Jimmy Evert Tennis Center,** 701 NE 12th Ave. (off Sunrise Blvd.), Fort Lauderdale (© **954/828-5378**), famous as the spot where Chris Evert got in her early serves. Her coach and father, James Evert, still teaches young players here, though he is very picky about whom he'll accept. There are 18 lighted clay and 3 hard courts here. Nonresidents of Fort Lauderdale pay $6 per hour before 4pm and $7 after. Reservations are accepted after 2pm for the following day but cost an extra $3.

SEEING THE SIGHTS

Billie Swamp Safari   Billie Swamp Safari is an up-close-and-personal view of the Seminole Indians' 2,200-acre Big Cypress Reservation. There are daily tours into reservation wetlands, hardwood hammocks, and areas where wildlife (seemingly strategically placed deer, water buffalo, bison, wild hogs, ornery ostriches, rare birds, and alligators) reside. Tours are provided aboard swamp buggies, customized motorized

One If by Land, Taxi If by Sea

Plan to spend at least an afternoon or evening cruising Fort Lauderdale's 300 miles of waterways in the only way you can: by boat. The **Water Bus of Fort Lauderdale** (✆ 954/467-6677; www.watertaxi.com) is one of the greatest innovations for water lovers since those cool Velcro sandals. A trusty fleet of older port boats serves the dual purpose of transporting and entertaining visitors as they cruise through the "Venice of America." Because of its popularity, the water taxi fleet has welcomed several sleek, 70-passenger "water buses" (featuring indoor and outdoor seating with an atrium-like roof).

Taxis operate on demand and also along a fairly regular route, carrying up to 48 passengers to 20 stops. If you're staying at a hotel on the route, you can be picked up there, usually within 15 minutes of calling, and then be shuttled to any of the dozens of restaurants, bars, and attractions on or near the waterfront. If you aren't sure where you want to go, ask one of the personable captains, who can point out historic and fun spots along the way.

Starting daily at 8am, boats run until midnight 7 days a week, depending on the weather. Check the website for exact times of pickup. The cost is $5 for a day pass, $4 for a one-way trip, $10 for a 3-day pass, and $25 for a weeklong pass. Tickets are available onboard; no credit cards are accepted.

vehicles specially designed to provide visitors with an elevated view of the frontier while you comfortably ride through the wetlands and cypress heads. The more adventurous may want to take a fast-moving airboat ride or trek a nature trail. Airboat rides run about 20 minutes, while swamp-buggy tours last about an hour. A stop at an alligator farm reeks of Disney, but the kids won't care. You can stay overnight in a native Tiki hut if you're really looking to immerse yourself in the culture.

Big Cypress Reservation, 1½-hr. drive west of Fort Lauderdale. ✆ 800/949-6101. Free admission. Swamp-buggy tours $22 adults, $20 seniors 62 and over, $12 children 4–12; airboat tours $14 for all ages. Daily 8:30am–6pm. Airboats depart every 30 min. beginning at 9:30am; last ride at 4:30pm. Swamp-buggy tours leave on the hour (except 4pm) between 11am and 5pm.

Bonnet House 🐾🐾🐾   This historic 35-acre plantation home and estate, accessible by guided tour only, will provide you with a fantastic glimpse of Old Florida. Built in 1921, the sprawling two-story waterfront home (surrounded by formal tropical gardens) is really the backdrop of a love story, which the very chatty volunteer guides will share with you if you ask. Some have actually lunched with the former resident of the house, the late Evelyn Bartlett, wife of world-acclaimed artist Frederic Clay Bartlett. The worthwhile 1¼-hour tour brings you quirky people, whimsical artwork, lush grounds, and interesting design.

900 N. Birch Rd. (1 block west of the ocean, south of Sunrise Blvd.), Fort Lauderdale. ✆ 954/563-5393. www.bonnet house.org. Admission $15 adults, $13 seniors, $11 students under 18, free for children 6 and under. Call for hours and tour times.

International Swimming Hall of Fame 🐾🐾🐾   Any aspiring Olympic swimmer or those who appreciate the sport will love this splashy homage to the best backstrokers, frontstrokers, and divers in the world The museum houses the world's largest collection of aquatic memorabilia and is the single largest source of aquatic books, manuscripts, and literature. Among the highlights are Johnny Weissmuller's Olympic medals, Mark Spitz's starting block used to win six of his seven 1972 Olympic gold medals, and over 60 Olympic, national, and club uniforms, warm-ups, and swimsuits. For those who don't mind getting their feet wet, the ISHOF Aquatic Complex is the only one of its kind in the world that offers two 50m pools, a diving well, and a swimming flume.

1 Hall of Fame Dr. Fort Lauderdale. © 954/462-6536. www.ishof.org. Admission $10 per family or $5 adults, $2 students and seniors. Call for hours and tour times.

Museum of Art Fort Lauderdale ★ (Kids)

A fantastic modern-art facility, the Museum of Art Fort Lauderdale features permanent collections, including those from William Glackens; the CoBrA Movement in Copenhagen, Brussels, and Amsterdam with over 200 paintings; 50 sculptures; 1,200 works on paper from 1948 to 1951, including the largest repository of Asger Jorn graphics outside the Silkeborg Kunstmuseum in Denmark; stunning Picasso ceramics; and contemporary works from over 90 Cuban artists in exile around the world. Traveling exhibits and continuing art classes make the museum a great place to spend a rainy day.

1 E. Las Olas Blvd., Fort Lauderdale. © 954/525-5500. www.moafl.org. Admission $6 adults, $5 seniors, $3 students, free for children under 6. Wed–Mon 11am–7pm (Thurs until 9pm).

Museum of Discovery & Science ★★ (Kids)

This museum's high-tech, interactive approach to education proves that science can equal fun. Adults won't feel as if they're in a kiddie museum, either. Kids 7 and under enjoy navigating their way through the excellent explorations in the Discovery Center. Florida Ecoscapes is particularly interesting, with a living coral reef, bees, bats, frogs, turtles, and alligators. Most weekend nights, you'll find a diverse crowd ranging from hip high-school kids to 30-somethings enjoying a rock film in the IMAX theater, which also shows short science-related films daily. Out front in the atrium, see the 52-foot-tall *Great Gravity Clock*, the largest kinetic-energy sculpture in the state.

401 SW 2nd St., Fort Lauderdale. © 954/467-6637. www.mods.org. Museum admission (includes admission to IMAX film) $14 adults, $13 seniors, $12 children 3–12. Mon–Sat 10am–5pm; Sun noon–6pm. Movie theater closes later. From I-95, exit on Broward Blvd. E. Continue to SW 5th Ave., turn right; garage is on the right.

Stranahan House ★★★

In a town whose history is younger than many of its residents, visitors may want to take a minute to see Fort Lauderdale's very oldest standing structure and a prime example of classic "Florida Frontier" architecture. Built in 1901 by the "father of Fort Lauderdale," Frank Stranahan, this house once served as a trading post for Seminole trappers, who came here to sell pelts. It's been a post office, town hall, and general store, and now serves as a worthwhile little museum of South Florida pioneer life, containing turn-of-the-last-century furnishings and historic photos of the area. It is also the site of occasional concerts and social functions; call for details.

335 SE 6th Ave. (Las Olas Blvd. at the New River Tunnel), Fort Lauderdale. © 954/524-4736. www.stranahanhouse. com. Admission $6 adults, $5 seniors, $3 students and children. Wed–Sat 10am–3pm; Sun 1–3pm. Tours are on the hour; last tour at 3pm. Accessible by water taxi.

SHOPPING & BROWSING

It's all about malls in Broward County. And while most of the best shopping is located within Fort Lauderdale proper, other areas in the county are also worth browsing.

Dania is known as the antiques capital of the South because within 1 square mile of Federal Highway, the city has more than 100 dealers selling everything from small collectibles to fine antiques. Parking is best along Federal Highway, on the "row," where Federal Highway meets U.S. 1. For information on "Antique Row," call ℰ **954/924-3627.** Also in Dania is the **Design Center of the Americas (DCOTA),** at the intersection of I-95 and Griffin Road (ℰ **954/920-7997;** www.designcenter oftheamericas.com), a 775,000-square-foot interior-design center with furniture showrooms (featuring everything from ultramod to classic), designer studios, and, from time to time, fabulous sample sales. Last time we were there, Matt Damon and his fiancée were there furnishing their zillion-dollar Miami Beach manse.

For bargain mavens, there's a strip of "fashion" stores on Hallandale Beach Boulevard's "Schmatta Row," east of Dixie Highway and the railroad tracks, where off-brand shoes, bags, and jewelry are sold at deep discounts. Hollywood Boulevard also offers some interesting shops, with everything from Indonesian artifacts to used and rare books, leather bustiers, and handmade hats. Dozens of shops line the pedestrian-friendly strip just west of Young Circle. The art galleries are clustered along Harrison Street, just east of Dixie Highway.

The area's only beachfront mall, **Beach Place,** is in Fort Lauderdale on Florida A1A just north of Las Olas Boulevard. This 100,000-square-foot giant sports the usual chains, like Sunglass Hut, Limited Express, Banana Republic, and Gap, as well as lots of popular bars and restaurants. While it used to be all the rage with the spring-break set, Beach Place is now aiming for a much more upscale clientele, adding many new higher-end stores and restaurants. Still, we think it's just one big tourist trap.

Other more traditional malls include the upscale **Galleria,** at Sunrise Boulevard near the Fort Lauderdale Beach, and **Broward Mall,** west of I-95 on Broward Boulevard, in Plantation.

If you're looking for unusual boutiques, especially art galleries, head to quaint **Las Olas Boulevard** 🦖, located west of A1A and a block east of Federal Highway/U.S. 1, off SE 8th Street, where there are hundreds of shops with alluring window decorations (like kitchen utensils posing as modern-art sculptures) and intriguing merchandise such as mural-size oil paintings. On the edge of the Arts and Science District is **Las Olas Riverfront,** a retail complex with 260,000 square feet of restaurants, clothing stores, arcades, and a multiplex movie theater.

The **Fort Lauderdale Swap Shop,** 3291 W. Sunrise Blvd. (ℰ **954/791-SWAP**), is one of the world's largest flea markets. I think it's rather schlocky. In addition to endless acres of vendors hawking everything from electronics to underwear, there's a miniature amusement park, a 13-screen drive-in theater, weekend concerts, and even a free daily circus complete with elephants, horse shows, high-wire acts, and clowns.

The monster of all outlet malls is **Sawgrass Mills,** 12801 W. Sunrise Blvd., Sunrise (ℰ **800/FL-MILLS** or 954/846-2350; fax 954/846-2312). Since the most recent expansion, completed in mid-1999, which added more than 30 new designer outlets, this behemoth (shaped like a Florida alligator) now holds more than 300 shops, kiosks, a 24-screen movie theater, and many restaurants and bars, including a Hard Rock Cafe. **Wanadoo City,** a $50-million education-and-amusement center for kids, is a tot-spot, giving them something to do while Mom shops the day away. The enclosed mall area covers nearly 2.5 million square feet over 50 acres—there's no way to see it all in a day. 2006 saw the opening of the Colonnade Outlets—an outlet of luxury stores within the outlet. Among the stores in the new open-air, Mediterranean-style center: Barney's New York, Coach, Cole Haan, Crate & Barrel, Escada Company Store, Salvatore Ferragamo, Hugo Boss Factory Store, MaxMara, Miss Sixty, and St.

John Knits. To get here, take I-95 to I-595 West to the Flamingo Road exit, turn right, and drive 2 miles to Sunrise Boulevard; you'll see the large complex on the left. From the Florida Turnpike, exit Sunrise Boulevard West.

Fishing enthusiasts won't want to miss **Bass Pro Shops Outdoor World,** 200 Gulfstream Way, Dania Beach (*(C)* **954/929-7710**), a sprawling retail complex just west of I-95 where you can buy anything from yachts to lures.

For those who like to turn an ordinary shopping trip into an extraordinary event, **Activity Planners** (*(C)* **954/525-9194**) will do just that, arranging a water taxi, limo, or Town Car for your own shopping tour through the Greater Fort Lauderdale area.

WHERE TO STAY

The Fort Lauderdale beach has a hotel or motel on nearly every block, ranging from the run-down to the luxurious. Both the **Howard Johnson,** 700 N. Atlantic Blvd., on Florida A1A south of Sunrise Boulevard (*(C)* **800/327-8578** or 954/563-2451); and the **Fort Lauderdale Beach Resort Hotel and Suites,** 4221 N. Ocean Blvd. (*(C)* **800/ 329-7466** or 954/563-2521), offer clean oceanside rooms starting at about $150. For a cushier stay, look into the **St. Regis Resort** (*(C)* **954/568-4623**), featuring 197 suites, a gourmet restaurant, and a spa; at press time, it was slated to open in April 2006. And projected to open in the fall of 2006 is the $220-million **W Fort Lauderdale Hotel & Residences** (*(C)* **954/525-8133**), a boutique-hotel-slash-condominium with ocean views and a very hip and happening bar.

In Hollywood, where prices are generally cheaper, the **Holiday Inn,** 101 N. Ocean Blvd. (*(C)* **954/923-8700**), operates a full-service hotel right on the ocean. With prices starting at around $110 in season and discounts for AAA members, it's a great deal. **Howard Johnson,** 2501 N. Ocean Dr. (I-95 to Sheridan St. E. to Fla. A1A S.; *(C)* **800/ 423-9867** or 954/925-1411), has a good location right on the beach.

Extended Stay America/Crossland Economy Studios (*(C)* **800/398-7829**) has four super-clean properties in Fort Lauderdale and offers year-round rates as low as $49 a night and $159 per week. The studios are designed with business travelers in mind: Each includes free local calls, a dataport, a kitchenette, and a well-lit desk.

For rentals for a few weeks or months, call **Florida Sunbreak** (*(C)* **800/SUN-BREAK**) or check the annual list of small lodgings compiled by the **Greater Fort Lauderdale Convention & Visitors Bureau** (*(C)* **954/765-4466**). The latter is especially helpful if you're looking for privately owned, charming, affordable lodgings.

VERY EXPENSIVE

The Atlantic 🐶🐶🐶   Luxe hit Fort Lauderdale beach with this Starwood Luxury Hotel property. Sitting on 23 miles of white sand, The Atlantic is a study in minimal modernity—soothing colors, and comfortable, stylish decor. Besides the usual high-tech amenities found in all rooms of this category of luxe—flat-screen TVs, wireless Internet—The Atlantic boasts something other hotels do not: a star chef hailing from NYC's Tribeca Grill and a five-star restaurant. Trina Restaurant and Lounge comes to Ft. Lauderdale, thanks to celebrated restaurateurs Don Pintabona, former executive chef of Tribeca Grill in New York City, and Nick Mautone, former managing partner of Gramercy Tavern. And the 6,000-square-foot spa isn't too shabby, either. Service is usually stellar, though we've had some complaints of a bit of attitude, but for some die hard New Yorkers who stay here, that's a plus!

601 N. Ft. Lauderdale Beach Blvd, Fort Lauderdale, FL 33316. *(C)* **800/325-3589** or 954/567-8020. Fax 954/567-8040. www.starwoodhotels.com. 180 units. Winter $509–$619 double, $969–$999 suite; off season $209–$319 double,

$669 suite. AE, DC, DISC, MC, V. Valet parking $27. **Amenities:** 2 restaurants, bar; outdoor heated pool; spa; water-sports equipment rental; bike rental; 24-hour concierge; business center; salon; 24-hr. room service; laundry service; dry cleaning. *In room:* A/C, TV, dataport, minibar, microwave, coffeemaker, hair dryer, iron, safe.

Hyatt Regency Pier Sixty-Six ★★ Located on 22 tropical acres on the Intracoastal Waterway, this resort is best known for its world-class marina and a rooftop lounge that spins every 66 minutes. If you experience vertigo after sitting in the revolving lounge, an invigorating body- or skin-care treatment at the hotel's intimate, exquisite European Spa LXVI will help you relocate your sense of balance. Equally invigorating are the Hyatt Regency's recreational amenities, which include a three-pool complex with a 40-person hydrotherapy pool, tennis courts, and an aquatic center with every watersport imaginable. The hotel transformed its uberpopular California Cafe into Grille 66 and Bar, a classy, upscale steakhouse. Tropical-style guest rooms have cherrywood furnishings and bathrooms with marble floors and granite vanities. All units have flat-screen televisions, wireless Internet access, and balconies with views of the Intracoastal Waterway and the hotel's lushly landscaped gardens. Designer suites come with a Jacuzzi, wet bar, living room, dining room, and exceptional views.

2301 SE 17th St. Causeway, Fort Lauderdale, FL 33316. ℂ **800/233-1234** or 954/525-6666. Fax 954/728-3541. www.hyatt.com. 380 units. Winter $259–$359 double; off season $130–$250 double; year-round from $1,000 suite. Rates are cheaper online. AE, DC, DISC, MC, V. Valet parking $14; self-parking $10 maximum per day. **Amenities:** 5 restaurants; 2 bars; 3 pools; 2 lighted clay tennis courts; spa; watersports equipment rental; bike rental; concierge; business center; salon; 24-hr. room service; laundry service and self-service laundry; dry cleaning. *In room:* A/C, TV, dataport, minibar, coffeemaker, hair dryer, iron, safe.

Marriott's Harbor Beach ★★ This recently renovated resort is loaded with the same amenities as Pier Sixty-Six but has a more secluded setting on 16 oceanfront acres just south of Fort Lauderdale's "strip." Everything in this place is huge—from the guest rooms and suites to the 8,000-square-foot pool, to the $8-million, 24,000-square-foot European spa. Accommodations feature marble, crown molding, and bathrooms with granite vanities, marble flooring, and wraparound mirrors. All units open onto private balconies overlooking either the ocean or the Intracoastal Waterway. The hotel's 3030 Ocean is an excellent seafood restaurant and raw bar; the Riva, a Mediterranean-style oceanfront eatery, is also top notch. Return guests include many convention groups and families who enjoy the space and the great location.

3030 Holiday Dr., Fort Lauderdale, FL 33316. ℂ **800/222-6543** or 954/525-4000. Fax 954/766-6193. www.marriott harborbeach.com. 637 units. Winter $429–$669 double; off season $259–$609 double; year-round from $600 suite. AE, DC, DISC, MC, V. Valet parking $18, self-parking $14. From I-95, exit on I-595 E. to U.S. 1 N.; proceed to SE 17th St.; make a right and go over the Intracoastal bridge past 3 traffic lights to Holiday Dr.; turn right. **Amenities:** 3 restaurants; 2 bars; outdoor heated pool; 4 clay tennis courts; basketball court; health club; European-style spa; extensive watersports equipment; bike rental; children's center and programs; game room; concierge; tour desk; courtesy car; business center; salon; 24-hr. room service; in-room massage; babysitting; laundry service and self-service laundry. *In room:* A/C, TV, PlayStation, dataport, minibar, coffeemaker, hair dryer, iron, safe.

Westin Diplomat Resort & Spa The Diplomat is a 1,060-room, full-service beach resort loaded with amenities. The main building is a 39-story oceanfront tower surrounded by 8 acres of man-made lakes. A gorgeous bridged, glass-bottomed swimming pool with cascading waterfalls, private cabanas, and a slew of watersports and activities adds a tropical touch. Rooms are a cross between those in a subtle boutique hotel and those in an Art Deco throwback, with dark woods, hand-cut marble and the 10-layer Heavenly Bed, a Westin trademark, with custom-designed pillow-top mattresses and very cushy down blankets (crank up the air-conditioning!).

Dining options are resortlike in quantity and quality, from the fine-dining steakhouse to several more casual options. Diplomat Landing, the hotel's shopping-and-entertainment complex across the street, features nocturnal hotspots—such as Nikki Marina, an offshoot of South Beach's Nikki Beach Club, as well as an art gallery, clothing boutique, and gelato shop.

The Diplomat's Country Club and Spa is modeled after an Italian villa, with 60 luxurious guest rooms, yacht slips, a 155-acre golf course, and a world-class spa and tennis club. The 30,000-square-foot spa has 17 treatment rooms, a spa pool, a spa menu, and an extensive selection of treatments.

3555 S. Ocean Dr. (Fla. A1A), Hollywood, FL 33019. © 800/327-1212 or 954/602-6000. Fax 954/602-7000. www. diplomatresort.com. 1,060 units. Winter $255–$400 double, $450–$540 suite; off season $210–$250 double, $280–$320 suite. AE, DC, DISC, MC, V. Valet parking $16. **Amenities:** 6 restaurants; 3 lounges; 2 pools; golf course; 10 clay tennis courts; health club and spa; watersports equipment rental; 24-hr. room service. In room: A/C, TV/Web TV, fax, dataport, minibar, coffeemaker, hair dryer.

EXPENSIVE

Lago Mar Resort and Club 🌟🌟 (Kids)   A charming lobby with a rock fireplace and saltwater aquarium sets the tone of this utterly inviting resort, a casually elegant piece of Old Florida that occupies its own little island between Lake Mayan and the Atlantic. Guests have access to the broadest and best strip of beach in the entire city, not to mention a wonderful bougainvillea-lined, 9,000-square-foot swimming lagoon. Lago Mar is very family oriented, with lots of facilities and supervised activities for children. Service is spectacular. The rooms and suites have Mediterranean or Key West influences and are well appointed. A full-service spa offers a wide array of pampering treatments and steam rooms, while the 1,000-square-foot exercise facility may come in handy after you indulge in the hotel's Northern Italian restaurant, Acquario, which is worth a visit even if you don't stay here.

1700 S. Ocean Lane, Fort Lauderdale, FL 33316. © 800/524-6627 or 954/523-6511. Fax 954/524-6627. www.lago mar.com. 212 units. Winter $285 double, from $355 suite; off season $165 double, from $190 suite. AE, DC, MC, V. Free valet parking. From Federal Hwy. (U.S. 1), turn east onto SE 17th St. Causeway; turn right onto Mayan Dr.; turn right again onto S. Ocean Dr.; turn left onto Grace Dr.; then turn left again onto S. Ocean Lane to the hotel. **Amenities:** 4 restaurants; bar; wine room; outdoor pool and lagoon; 2 tennis courts; exercise room; watersports equipment rental; children's programs during holiday periods; game room; concierge; tour desk; business center; 24-hr. room service; laundry service; dry cleaning. In room: A/C, TV, dataport, kitchenette, coffeemaker (in some units), hair dryer.

Pillars Hotel 🌟🌟🌟 (Finds)   It took me a while to discover this hotel—and apparently that's exactly the point. One of Fort Lauderdale's best-kept secrets, if not the best, the Pillars transports you from the neon-hued flash and splash of Fort Lauderdale's strip and takes you to a two-story British Colonial, Caribbean-style retreat tucked away on the bustling Intracoastal Waterway. Since it has just 23 rooms, you'll feel as if you have the grand house all to yourself—albeit a house with white-tablecloth room service, an Eden-istic courtyard with a free-form pool, lush landscaping, access to a water taxi, and signing privileges at nearby restaurants and spa. Rooms are luxurious and loaded with amenities such as private-label bath products, ultraplush bedding, and, if you're so inclined, a private masseuse to iron out your personal kinks. Upon arrival, you will be greeted with a welcome cocktail, and there's always free iced tea at the pool. A library area (with a grand piano and over 500 books and videos) is at your disposal, as is pretty much anything else you request here. The quintessential Fort Lauderdale retreat, the Pillars is the zenith of Fort Lauderdale accommodations.

111 N. Birch Rd., Fort Lauderdale, FL 33304. © 954/467-9639. Fax 954/763-2845. www.pillarshotel.com. 23 units. Winter $199–$269 double, $299–$499 suite; off season $129–$209 double, $199–$409 suite. AE, DC, DISC, MC, V.

Complimentary off-street parking. **Amenities:** Waterfront pool; 24-hr. concierge; business services; 24-hr. room service; same-day laundry service; signing privileges at Max's Beach Place restaurant; water-taxi service; preferred rates at beachfront and downtown health clubs. *In room:* AC, TV/VCR, dataport, minibar, hair dryer, iron, safe.

Riverside Hotel ★★ A touch of New Orleans hits Fort Lauderdale's popular Las Olas Boulevard in the form of this charming six-story 1936 hotel. There's no beach here, but the hotel is located on the sleepy and scenic New River, capturing the essence of that ever-elusive Old Florida. Guest rooms, outfitted in Mexican tile and wicker furnishings, are spacious and well maintained. Details like intricately tiled bathrooms and old-style furniture enhance the charm of the otherwise stark building. The best units face the river, but it's hard to see the water past the parking lot and trees. Twelve rooms offer king-size beds with mirrored canopies and flowing drapes. There are also seven elegantly decorated suites with wet bars and French doors that lead to private balconies. The hotel has two restaurants worth trying: Indigo, a fantastic Asian/Indonesian establishment (p. 275), and the Grill Room, for old-world elegance.

620 E. Las Olas Blvd., Fort Lauderdale, FL 33301. ✆ **800/325-3280** or 954/467-0671. Fax 954/462-2148. www.riverside hotel.com. 217 units. Winter $225–$275 suite; off season $139–$185 suite. Special packages available. Discount for online bookings. AE, DC, MC, V. Valet parking $8–$10. From I-95, exit onto Broward Blvd.; turn right onto Federal Hwy. (U.S. 1); turn left onto Las Olas Blvd. **Amenities:** 2 restaurants; outdoor pool; concierge; secretarial services; limited room service; laundry service; dry cleaning. *In room:* A/C, TV, dataport, minibar, fridge, coffeemaker, hair dryer, iron.

MODERATE
Banyan Marina Resort ★★ These fabulous waterfront apartments, located on a beautifully landscaped residential island, may have you vowing never to stay in a hotel again. They're intimate, charming, *and* reasonably priced. Built around a stunning 75-year-old banyan tree, the Banyan Marina Resort is situated directly on the active canals halfway between Fort Lauderdale's downtown and the beach. When available, you'll choose between one- and two-bedroom apartments, which have been recently renovated. All are comfortable and spacious, with French doors, full kitchens, and living rooms. The best part of staying here, besides your gracious and knowledgeable hosts, Dagmar and Peter Neufeldt, is that the convenient water taxi will find you here and take you anywhere you want to go, day or night. There is a small outdoor heated pool and a marina for those with boats in tow.

111 Isle of Venice, Fort Lauderdale, FL 33301. ✆ **954/524-4430**. Fax 954/764-4870. www.banyanmarina.com. 10 units. Winter $95–$200 apt; off season $73–$150 apt. Weekly and monthly rates available. MC, V. Free parking. From I-95, exit Broward Blvd. E.; cross U.S. 1 and turn right on SE 15th Ave. At the 1st traffic light (Las Olas Blvd.), turn left. Turn left at the 3rd island (Isle of Venice). **Amenities:** Restaurant; pool; dock. *In room:* A/C, TV, dataport, kitchen, coffeemaker, hair dryer.

Best Western Pelican Beach Resort ★ Not bad for a Best Western, the Pelican Beach Resort sits on 500 feet of sand, features 180 rooms (including 117 with balconies), and has a sublimely relaxing wraparound oceanfront veranda and sun deck with rocking chairs. What also rocks about this place is the heated outdoor pool, complete with lazy river raft ride. On the north end of the property is the older Sun Tower, which has 24 oceanfront rooms and suites. Stick to the newer part, however.

2000 N. Atlantic Blvd., Fort Lauderdale, FL 33301. ✆ **800/525-OCEAN** or 954/568-9431. Fax 954/565-2662. www. pelicanbeach.com. 180 units. Winter $275–$349 double, $420 suite; off season $190–$239 double, $299 suite. Rates include continental breakfast. AE, DC, MC, V. Free parking. **Amenities:** Restaurant; heated outdoor pool; sun deck. *In room:* A/C, TV, dataport, fridge, microwave, coffeemaker, hair dryer.

Courtyard Villa on the Ocean ★★ Nestled between a bunch of larger hotels, this small historic hotel offers a romantic getaway right on the beach. Courtyard Villa offers spacious oceanfront efficiencies with private balconies, larger suites overlooking the pool, and full two-bedroom apartments. Accommodations are plush, with chenille bedspreads and carved four-poster beds; fully equipped kitchenettes are an added convenience. The tiled bathrooms have strong, hot showers to wash off the beach sand. Room no. 8 is especially nice, with French doors that open to a private balcony overlooking the ocean. Relax in the hotel's unique heated pool/spa or on the second-floor sun deck. You can also swim from the beach to a living reef just 50 feet offshore. Scuba-diving instruction is available on the premises.

4312 El Mar Dr., Lauderdale-by-the-Sea, FL 33308. ℂ 800/291-3560 or 954/776-1164. Fax 954/491-0768. www. courtyardvilla.com. 10 units. Winter $179 double, $272 2-bedroom; off season $115 double, $167 2-bedroom. Rates include full breakfast. AE, MC, V. Pets under 35 lb. accepted with a $200 deposit; must be caged while outside; no pit bulls, Dobermans, or Rottweilers. **Amenities:** Outdoor heated pool; Jacuzzi; free use of bikes; limited room service; scuba instruction; free laptop use with Internet access. *In room:* A/C, TV/VCR, kitchenette, coffeemaker, hair dryer.

Seminole Hard Rock Hotel & Casino ✦✦✦   Welcome to Casino City—Florida. That's right, the Seminole Indians have managed to create a miniature Vegas within Hollywood, Florida, and it's doing a booming business. Although the massive 130,000-square-foot casino doesn't have typical bet-against-the-house Vegas games (such as blackjack, roulette, or craps), it does have thousands of video slot machines and poker tables, and they're always packed. The main draw here is the casino, but the guest rooms are surprisingly cushy and swank, with flat-screen TVs, Egyptian-cotton linens, and big bathrooms with massive shower heads; the suites are hyperluxurious. Equally impressive is the 4½-acre lagoon-style pool very similar to the one at the Hard Rock in Vegas, with waterfalls, hot tubs, wireless access for those who insist on working, and, of course, a bar. In fact, there are lots of bars here, especially at the attached entertainment complex, with two clubs open 24/7, as well as restaurants and stores. The food court within the casino isn't a bad choice for a quick bite, or you can choose from several on-site, full-service restaurants, including a swanky steakhouse. The 22,000-square-foot spa isn't too shabby, either.

1 Seminole Way, Hollywood, FL 33314. ℂ **800/937-0156** or 954/797-5440. Fax 954/797-2376. www.seminole hardrock.com. 500 units. Winter $189–$259 double, $550–$1500 suite (year round rate); off season $135–$180 double. AE, DC, DISC, MC, V. **Amenities:** 8 restaurants; a million bars; pool; spa; Jacuzzi; watersports; 24-hr. room service. *In room:* A/C, TV, CD player, Internet access, coffeemaker, hair dryer.

INEXPENSIVE

A Little Inn by the Sea ✦   It's not fancy, but A Little Inn by the Sea sits on a primo piece of oceanfront, and most rooms have private balconies overlooking the ocean. There's also 300 feet of private, palm-tree-lined beach. The accommodations are hardly worthy of a spread in an interior-design magazine, but the views make up for the lackluster decor. A free breakfast buffet, a rooftop terrace, and a heated freshwater pool are lovely perks.

4546 El Mar Dr., Lauderdale-by-the-Sea, FL 33308. [tel **800/492-0311** or 954/772-2450. Fax 954/938-9354. www. alittleinn.com. 29 units. Winter $139–$149 double, $169–$199 suite, $358 2-bedroom apt; off season $89–$109 double, $129–$159 suite, $248–$268 2-bedroom apt. MC, V. Free parking. **Amenities:** Heated pool; access to nearby tennis court; nearby children's playground; coin laundry. *In room:* A/C, TV.

Fort Lauderdale Beach Hostel   For the young, or for backpackers on a budget, this hostel is a great option, with both dorm beds and private rooms at bargain-basement prices. Clean and conveniently located, the hostel is just 654 feet from the ocean. It features free parking, free phones, free self-cook food, free breakfast buffet, and, if you're lucky, free use of the surfboards or in-line skates lying around.

2115 N. Ocean Blvd., Fort Lauderdale, FL 33305. © 954/567-7275. www.fortlauderdalehostel.com. 12 units. Dorm beds $20 per night, $130 per week; private rooms $40 for 1 person, $50 double. Rates include breakfast buffet. MC, V. **Amenities:** Ping Pong; free Internet access; sun deck; garden. *In room:* A/C, TV, iron.

Sea Downs (and the Bougainvillea) ★★   This bargain lodging is often booked months in advance by return guests who want to be directly on the beach without paying a fortune. The hosts of this superclean 1950s motel, Claudia and Karl Herzog, live on the premises and keep things running smoothly. Many rooms have been redecorated here and at the Herzogs' other, even less expensive property next door, the 11-unit Bougainvillea. Guests at both hotels share the Sea Downs' pool.

2900 N. Surf Rd., Hollywood, FL 33019. © 954/923-4968. Fax 954/923-8747. www.seadowns.com or www.bougainvilleahollywood.com. 12 units. Winter $68–$105 studio, $93–$155 1-bedroom apt; off season $65–$78 studio, $90–$110 1-bedroom apt. No credit cards. From I-95, exit Sheridan St. E. to Fla. A1A and go south; drive ½ mile to Coolidge St.; turn left. **Amenities:** Freshwater outdoor pool; concierge; laundry facilities. *In room:* A/C, TV, dataport, kitchen, fridge, coffeemaker.

WHERE TO DINE

It took a while for a more sophisticated, varied epicurean scene to reach these shores, but Fort Lauderdale—and, to some extent, Hollywood—finally has several fine restaurants. Increasingly, ethnic options are joining the legions of surf-and-turferies that have dominated the area for so long. **Las Olas Boulevard** has so many eateries that the city has put a moratorium on the opening of new restaurants on the 2-mile street.

VERY EXPENSIVE

Café Martorano ★★ ITALIAN   This small storefront eatery doesn't win any awards for decor or location, but when it comes to food that's good enough to feed an entire Italian family, Café Martorano is one of the best. People wait for a table for upward of 2 hours because the restaurant accepts no reservations and can get away with it. An almost-offensive sound system (playing disco tunes and Sinatra) has a tendency to turn off many a diner, but you don't go to Café Martorano for an intimate dinner. Coming here is like being at a big, fat, Italian wedding, where eating, drinking, and dancing are paramount. The menu changes daily, but regulars can request special off-the-menu items. If you don't ask, you don't get, so open your mouth. Also keep your eyes wide open for celebrities such as Liza Minelli, James Gandolfini, and Steven Van Zandt, among others, who make it a point to stop here for a meal while in town.

3343 E. Oakland Park Blvd., Fort Lauderdale. © 954/561-2554. Reservations not accepted. Main courses $13–$29. MC, V. Daily 5–11pm.

Darrel & Oliver's Cafe Maxx ★★ FLORIDIAN/NEW WORLD   Despite its bleak location in an unassuming storefront, Darrel & Oliver's Cafe Maxx is one of the best restaurants in Broward County. When it opened in 1984, it was the first restaurant to have an open kitchen, and what a stir that caused! Now, instead of the kitchen, the marvel is what comes out of it. Consider crispy yucca-scallion Florida grouper with vanilla-rum butter, sweet mash, asparagus, and Parisienne vegetables; sweet-onion-crusted yellowtail snapper with Madeira sauce; or veal chop with truffled-mushroom butter and wild-mushroom risotto.

2601 E. Atlantic Blvd., Pompano Beach. © 954/782-0606. Fax 954/782-0648. Reservations recommended. Main courses $18–$39. AE, DC, DISC, MC, V. Mon–Thurs 5:30–10:30pm; Fri–Sat 5:30–11pm; Sun 5:30–10pm. From I-95, exit at Atlantic Blvd. E. The restaurant is 3 lights east of Federal Hwy.

Mark's Las Olas ★★★ NEW WORLD   Before star chef Mark Militello hit Las Olas Boulevard, there was really no reason to dine here. However, once he opened the doors to his sleek, modern restaurant, he opened the eyes and mouths of discriminating Fort Lauderdale gourmands to his excellent New World cuisine. Roasted-garlic-stuffed grilled tenderloin of beef with caramelized sweet onion, Swiss chard, marrow toast, and red-wine short-rib sauce is possibly the best item on the menu. Everything else on offer, from the hot-pepper pizza with chorizo to the crab-crusted black grouper with wild-mushroom/salsify ragout, is delicious. Save room for a chocolate dessert—any one will do.

1032 E. Las Olas Blvd., Fort Lauderdale. © 954/463-1000. Reservations suggested. Main courses $14–$30. AE, DC, MC, V. Mon–Fri 11:30am–2:30pm; Mon–Thurs 6–10:30pm; Fri–Sat 6–11pm; Sun 6–10pm.

EXPENSIVE

Anthony's Runway 84 ★★★ ITALIAN   Meet Anthony, the youthful, gregarious owner of this Fort Lauderdale restaurant whose interior is all about jet-setting—albeit in the mid- to late '70s—and whose bar is crafted out of a plane fuselage. Once you meet him, he will introduce you to your server, whose name is likely to be Tony. Same goes for the bartender. The quintessential, convivial Italian vibe in here (think Travolta in *Saturday Night Fever*) is conducive to one of the most enjoyable meals you'll ever have. The best way to go is—what else?—family style, in which you'll be able to share lots of dishes like mussels marinara, fried clams, roasted red peppers in garlic, shrimp parmigiana, an out-of-this-world rigatoni with cauliflower (although it sounds boring, order it no matter what!), and stellar meat and poultry dishes that frequent fliers to Anthony's rave about each time, as if it were their last meal. For the best pizza, try nearby **Anthony's Coal Fired Pizza,** 2203 S. Federal Hwy. (© 954/462-5555).

330 S.R. 84, Fort Lauderdale. © 954/467-8484. Reservations not accepted. Main courses $11–$25. AE, DC, DISC, MC, V. Tues–Thurs and Sun noon–10pm; Fri–Sat 5–11pm.

Eduardo De San Angel ★★★ MEXICAN   Gourmet Mexican is *not* an oxymoron, and for those who don't believe that, take one meal at the sublime Eduardo De San Angel and you'll see how true it is. Chef Eduardo Pria has a masterful way with food, as seen in dishes such as Jaibas Rellenas (fresh Florida blue crab, plum tomatoes, onions, jalapeños, and Spanish green olives baked in a shell with melted jack cheese au gratin and mole poblano). Fresh flowers and candlelight, not to mention the fact that the restaurant resembles an intimate hacienda, also drive home the fact that this isn't your mom's Old El Paso taco dinner.

2822 E. Commercial Blvd., Fort Lauderdale. © 954/772-4731. Reservations essential. Main courses $18–$29. AE, DC, DISC, MC, V. Mon–Thurs 11:30am–10:30pm; Fri–Sat 5:30–10:30pm.

Himmarshee Bar & Grille ★ AMERICAN   Located on a popular street of bars frequented by Fort Lauderdale's young professionals, Himmarshee Bar & Grille is known for its scene and its cuisine. A mezzanine bar upstairs is ideal for people-watching; outdoor tables are tight but strategically situated in front of all the street's action. On weekend nights, in particular, it's difficult to get a table. However, if you can deal with cramming into the bar, it's worth a cocktail or two. The wine list is impressive, and the grilled sirloin burger with creamy basil Gorgonzola is a delicious meal in itself for only $7.50. Also try the wasabi-crusted salmon or the pan-roasted baramundi (Australian sea bass). Check out Side Bar, the restaurant's very ski-lodgey bar next door featuring live music and a bustling crowd of young hipsters.

210 SW 2nd St. (south of Broward Blvd., west of U.S. 1), Fort Lauderdale. ✆ **954/524-1818.** Reservations recommended. Main courses $12–$24. AE, MC, V. Mon–Fri 11:30am–2:30pm; Sun–Thurs 6–10:30pm; Fri–Sat 6–11:30pm.

Hobo's Fish Joint ⭐⭐ SEAFOOD   Huge portions of extremely fresh fish are prepared in more than a dozen ways at this steakhouse-style restaurant with wood floors and white tablecloths. Despite the fact that it's located away from the ocean in the utterly suburban enclave of Coral Springs, this joint is worth the trip. Some even say it offers the best seafood in Broward County. I say it's a tough call between here and the Sunfish Grill (see below). See for yourself with the littleneck clams in garlic bouillon or the Chilean sea bass oreganato on a bed of orzo.

10317 Royal Palm Blvd. (at Coral Springs Dr.), Coral Springs. ✆ **954/346-5484.** Reservations accepted for groups of 6 or more. Main courses $17–$27. AE, MC, V. Mon–Thurs 5:30–9:30pm; Fri–Sat 5:30–10:30pm; Sun 5:30–9pm. From I-95, exit at Commercial Blvd., go west to University Dr., turn right, and, about a mile up, take a left on Royal Palm Blvd.

Sunfish Grill ⭐⭐⭐ SEAFOOD   Unlike its fellow contemporary seafood restaurants, the Sunfish Grill chooses to focus on fish, not fusion. Chef Anthony Sindaco is content to leave the spotlight on his fantastic fish dishes, which are possibly the freshest in town, thanks to the fact that he buys his fish at local markets and often from well-known local fishermen who appear at his back door with their catches of the day. The shrimp bisque cappuccino is a deliciously rich soup served in a demitasse cup— because it's that rich. Conch fritters are purely spectacular and not full of filler. Chilean sea bass, expertly cooked with roasted fennel, saffron potatoes, and a caramelized-onion broth, is wonderful. The best dish, in my opinion, is the seared tuna resting on a bed of mushroom and oxtail ragout with garlic mashed potatoes. In fact, almost everything at the Sunfish Grill is better than at most seafood restaurants.

2771 E. Atlantic Blvd., Pompano Beach. ✆ **954/788-2434.** Reservations recommended. Main courses $17–$28. AE, MC, V. Mon–Thurs 6–9:30pm; Fri–Sat 6–10:30pm.

Trina Restaurant ⭐⭐⭐ MEDITERRANEAN   A bona fide dining hot spot like this is one is a novelty to the area because restaurants this hot usually open in Miami, not Fort Lauderdale. Thanks to the collaborative efforts of Don Pintabona, former executive chef of Tribeca Grill in New York City and Nick Mautone, formerly of Gramercy Tavern, Miami's got some competition. Yes, it's expensive, but the Mediterranean-infused seafood dishes are worth every penny. Reservations here are hard to come by, especially in season, but the Trina Lounge is also a great option, offering lighter—and cheaper fare—in a high-style ambiance. Although we love the buzz of the indoor dining room, request a table outside overlooking the ocean.

601 N. Ft. Lauderdale Beach Blvd., Fort Lauderdale. ✆ **954/567-8070.** Reservations recommended. Main courses $29–$45. AE, DC, DISC, MC, V. Sun–Thurs 5:30–10pm; Fri–Sat 5:30–10:30pm. Lounge open later.

MODERATE

Cap's Place Island Restaurant ⭐⭐⭐ *(Finds)* SEAFOOD   Opened in 1928 by a bootlegger who ran in the same circles as gangster Meyer Lansky, this barge-turned-restaurant is one of the area's best-kept secrets. Although it's no longer a rum-running restaurant and casino, its illustrious past (FDR and Winston Churchill dined here together) landed it a spot on the National Register of Historic Places. To get here, you have to take a ferryboat, provided by the restaurant. The short ride across the Intracoastal definitely adds to the Cap's Place experience. And the food's good, too! Traditional seafood dishes such as Florida or Maine lobster, clams casino, and oysters Rockefeller will take you back to the days when a soprano was just an opera singer.

2765 NE 28th Court, Lighthouse Point. ℂ **954/941-0418**. Reservations recommended. Main courses $20–$25. MC, V. Daily 5:30pm–midnight. To get to Cap's Place, motor-launch from I-95, exit at Copan's Rd. and go east to U.S. 1 (Federal Hwy.). At NE 24th St., turn right and follow the double lines and signs to the Lighthouse Point Yacht Basin and Marina (8 miles north of Fort Lauderdale). From here, follow the CAP'S PLACE sign pointing you to the shuttle.

Creolina's 🐾🐾 CREOLE   You'll find authentic Louisiana Creole cuisine at this small but very popular restaurant situated along the Riverwalk. Try shrimp jambalaya with shrimp, sausage, and vegetables in a rich Cajun sauce served over rice; or perhaps the étouffée with crayfish tail simmered in a mellow Cajun sauce served over rice. The mashed potatoes are homemade, and the delicious lemonade is fresh-squeezed daily. There is also a terrific New Orleans Sunday brunch. Ask to sit in sassy Rosie's section.

209 SW 2nd St., Fort Lauderdale. ℂ **954/524-2003**. Appetizers $4–$9; main courses $13–$18. AE, MC, V. Mon–Fri 11am–2:30pm; Sun–Mon 5–9pm; Tues–Thurs 5–10pm; Fri–Sat 5–11pm.

Indigo 🐾🐾 SOUTHEAST ASIAN/ECLECTIC   It seems a little strange to chow down on Southeast Asian food in an utterly New Orleans–style hotel, but this is South Florida—the wackier, the better. The not-so-traditional meal begins with a basket of pappadams, puffy naan bread, and shrimp-puff bread. Next might be a super-rich grilled vegetable cassoulet au gratin and a fried-rice dish with shallots, corn, and asparagus; or pizzas baked on top of naan covered with such toppings as onions, shiitake mushrooms, goat cheese, spinach, eggplant, garlic, curried tomato, and pine nuts. Particularly good is the meaty soy-and-portobello-mushroom combination wrapped in fluffy puff pastry and served with a delicate broccoli sauce. Sounds like a lot of activity going on in one dish, but like the restaurant itself, somehow it all works.

In the Riverside Hotel, 620 E. Las Olas Blvd., Fort Lauderdale. ℂ **954/467-0671**. Reservations accepted for groups of 6 or more. Main courses $12–$22. AE, DC, DISC, MC, V. Daily 7am–9:45pm.

Sugar Reef 🐾🐾 FRENCH VIETNAMESE/CARIBBEAN   I could go on about the restaurant's priceless ocean view, but the menu of Mediterranean, Caribbean, and French-Vietnamese dishes is just as outstanding. A pleasant tropical decor is bolstered by the fresh air wafting in from the Atlantic. Seafood bouillabaisse in green curry and coconut broth, and pork loin Benedict—layers of jerk-spiced pork and hollandaise sauce—are among the restaurant's most popular dishes. The kitchen puts a savory spin on duck, roasted and topped with sweet-chile-and-papaya salsa. This is not a place you'd expect to find on a beach boardwalk, which makes it all the more delightful.

600 N. Surf Rd. (on the Broadwalk just north of Hollywood Blvd.), Hollywood. ℂ **954/922-1119**. Reservations accepted for groups of 6 or more. Main courses $10–$24; sandwiches and salads $4–$9. AE, DISC, MC, V. Mon 4–10:30pm; Tues–Thurs 11am–10:30pm; Fri–Sun 11am–11pm (sometimes later in winter).

Sushi Blues Cafe 🐾 SUSHI   Before Hollywood was "hot," Sushi Blues Cafe was singing the blues—in a good way, as the only game in town. Now that the area is bustling, it's singing the blues in an even better way, serving up live music 4 nights a week along with raw fish that's quite good. Garlic- and ginger-studded tuna steak is also fantastic for those who are bored with sushi. Even better, however, is the fact that, for once, a meal at a sushi restaurant in an area where such restaurants are a dime a dozen actually seems like a unique experience.

600 N. Surf Rd. (on the Broadwalk just north of Hollywood Blvd.), Hollywood. ℂ **954/922-1119**. Reservations accepted for groups of 6 or more. Sushi rolls $3–$10; main courses $7–$21. AE, DISC, MC, V. Daily 11:30am–2am.

Tarpon Bend 🐾🐾 SEAFOOD/AMERICAN   This restaurant is one of the few places where the fishermen still bring the fish to the back door. The oysters from the raw bar are shucked to order and are incredible. Try the house specialty, "smoked fish dip"—a kingfish smoked on premises. The steamed clambake, with half a Maine lobster, clams, potatoes, mussels, and corn on the cob, is scrumptious and served in its own pot. For chocolate lovers, the chocolate-brownie sundae is a must. There's live entertainment Wednesday through Saturday and a full bar. A new Tarpon Bend opened in Coral Gables at 65 Miracle Mile (② **305/444-3210**).

200 SW 2nd St., Fort Lauderdale. ② **954/523-3233**. Reservations accepted for groups of 6 or more. Main courses $12–$15. AE, MC, V. Mon–Thurs 11:30am–1am; Fri–Sat 11:30am–3am.

Tuscan Today Trattoria *★★ Finds* ITALIAN   For classic Tuscan food in a charming atmosphere, Tuscan Today is something you should not put off until tomorrow. Inspired by the peasant origins of the original trattoria, the restaurant consistently turns out outstanding pizzas and flavorful meat and fish from a customized woodburning brick oven imported from Tuscany. A reasonable and excellent wine list provides you with a difficult choice in two affordable price ranges: $19 and $23. Tagliatelle Arometto St. David is an elaborate name for an elaborate dish of fresh herbs marinated in extra-virgin olive oil and lightly tossed with flat semolina pasta and Parmigiano Reggiano cheese, then garnished with diced sweet peppers, olives, and tomatoes. It's outstanding. Grilled thin-crusted pizzas are prepared as the Italians prefer them—light on sauce and cheese but heavy on flavor. For pasta lovers, the powerful but surprisingly light gnocchi with spinach is a good way to go. And if you order a meat or fish entree, be sure to try the rosemary roast potatoes.

1161 N. Federal Hwy., Fort Lauderdale. ② **954/566-1716**. Reservations accepted for groups of 6 or more. Main courses $8.95–$15. AE, DC, DISC, MC, V. Sun–Thurs 11am–10pm; Fri–Sat 11am–11pm.

INEXPENSIVE

Cheeseburger in Paradise *★* AMERICAN/DINER   If you're a Jimmy Buffet fan, it's worth the schlep into the suburbs to eat at this fun, TGI Friday's–ish restaurant featuring, of course, burgers, and assorted New Orleans– and Caribbean-style island fare. The Tiki Bar features a huge drink menu, and beer lovers can't get enough of the draft beer, which is served at a chilly 29°. The Key West–style restaurant has karaoke on Thursday nights, when you can belt out your best version of *Margaritaville*.

321 N. University Dr., Plantation. ② **954/474-2174**. Sandwiches $5–$10. AE, DC, DISC, MC, V. Mon–Wed 4–11pm; Thurs–Sat 4pm–1am; Sun 4–10pm.

The Floridian Restaurant *★ Value* AMERICAN/DINER   The Floridian has been filling South Florida's diner void for over 63 years, serving breakfast, lunch, and dinner, 24/7. It's especially busy on weekend mornings when locals and tourists come in for huge omelets, fresh oatmeal, sausage, and biscuits.

1410 E. Las Olas Blvd., Fort Lauderdale. ② **954/463-4041**. Fax 954/761-3930. Sandwiches $3–$7; breakfast combos $3.50–$8; hot platters $7–$14. No credit cards. Daily 24 hr.

Hamburger Mary's *★★* AMERICAN   For fans of kitsch, Hamburger Mary's is a place to tell your friends about. For one thing, the check is presented to you in a stiletto heel from Frederick's of Hollywood. Second, the hamburgers are fabulous and full of tongue-in-cheeky names such as Buffy the Hamburger Slayer (a garlic-and-Swiss burger), Mary's Breast, and Mary Tyler S'mores. Located in the gay-friendly hamlet of Wilton Manors, Mary's is the neon spot in an already colorful neighborhood, with its shabby-chic decor that consists of lamps made from galvanized-steel buckets, beads and feather boas, speakers covered by wigs, and shoes on the ceiling. An outdoor lanai area provides a fabulous setting for events such as Monday's Martini

Movie Night, in which campy classics are shown on a big screen, and Tuesday's Mary's House of Blues, featuring live jazz and blues and $3 Tarantula Margaritas. On Sunday, live reggae and $3 Absolut Peppar Bloody Marys bring in the crowds.

2449 Wilton Dr., Wilton Manors. ⓒ 954/567-1320. Main courses $6–$10. AE, DC, MC, V. Sun–Thurs 11:30am–11pm; Fri–Sat 11:30am–midnight. Bar stays open 2 hr. later.

Jaxon's 𝔯 *Kids* ICE CREAM   South Florida's best and only authentic old-fashioned ice-cream parlor and country store attracts sweet tooths from all over the area looking to satisfy their cravings with an unabridged assortment of homemade ice cream served any which way. Kids love the candy store in the front of the restaurant, and adults love the pre–Ben & Jerry's authenticity. For the calorie conscious, the sugar-free and fat-free versions are pretty good. Jaxon's most famous everything-but-the-kitchen-sink sundae features countless scoops and endless toppings.

128 S. Federal Hwy., Dania Beach. ⓒ 954/923-4445. Sundaes $2.75–$7.95. AE, DISC, MC, V. Mon–Thurs 11:30am–11pm; Fri–Sat 11:30am–midnight; Sun noon–11pm.

Lester's Diner 𝔯 AMERICAN   Since 1968, Lester's Diner has been serving swarms of South Floridians large portions of great greasy-spoon fare until the wee hours. Try the eggs Benedict and the 14-ounce "cup" of classic coffee, or sample one of Lester's many homemade desserts. The place serves breakfast 24 hours a day and is a Fort Lauderdale institution that attracts locals, club crowds, city officials, and a generally motley, friendly crew of hungry people craving no-nonsense food served by seasoned waitresses, whose beehive hairdos contribute to the campy atmosphere.

250 S.R. 84, Fort Lauderdale. ⓒ 954/525-5641. Main courses $5–$12. AE, MC, V. Daily 24 hr.

Le Tub 𝔯𝔯 *Finds* AMERICAN   Hands down, this is one of the coolest, most unpretentious, quintessential pre-swanky South Florida restaurants, if not one of the coolest restaurants, period. Established in 1959 as a Sunoco gas station, Le Tub was purchased in 1974 by a man who personally transformed the place into this waterfront restaurant, made out of flotsam, jetsam, and ocean-bone treasures gathered over 4 years of jogging on Hollywood Beach. But the waterfront location and unique building aren't the only things to marvel at. As you walk in, take note of the hand-painted bathtubs and toilet bowls (it's not at all gross; they're used as planters) lining the walkway. Inside is a divey bar complete with pool table and jukebox; outside seating on the deck is the real gem. Le Tub is famous for its burgers, chili, and seafood, but more appealing than the food is the peaceful, easy feeling exuded by the place.

1100 N. Ocean Dr., Hollywood. ⓒ 954/931-9425. Main courses $6–$17. No credit cards. Daily 10:30am–4am.

THE HOLLYWOOD & FORT LAUDERDALE AREA AFTER DARK

Fort Lauderdale no longer mimics the raucous antics of *Animal House* as far as nightlife is concerned. It has gotten hip to the fact that an active nightlife is vital to the city's desire to distract sophisticated, savvy visitors from the magnetic lure of South Beach. And while Lauderdale is no South Beach, it has vastly improved the quality of its nightlife by welcoming places that wouldn't dare host wet T-shirt or beer-chugging contests. It also lacks the South Beach attitude, which is part of the attraction.

Hollywood's nightlife seems to be in the throes of an identity crisis, touting itself as the next South Beach, while at the same time hyping its image as an attitude-free nocturnal playground. Here's the real deal: At press time, Hollywood nightlife was barely awake, with the exception of a few bars and one struggling dance club. If you're looking for a quiet night out, it's probably your best bet. But don't come too late—after midnight, the city is absolutely deserted.

For information on clubs and events, pick up a free copy of Fort Lauderdale's weekly newspaper *City Link,* or the Fort Lauderdale edition of the *New Times.*

Beach Place   This outdoor shopping-and-entertainment complex, modeled after Coconut Grove's hugely successful CocoWalk, landed on the legendary "strip" with several franchised bars and restaurants. It's the beachy version of a mall and is popular with a very young set at night. The view of the ocean makes it worth a stop for a drink. Hours vary by establishment; some places are open until 2 or 3am, while others close around 11pm. 17 S. Fort Lauderdale Beach Blvd., Fort Lauderdale. ℂ 954/760-9570.

The Culture Room   If you consider rock and heavy metal to be culture, visit the Culture Room and bang your head to local bands. Open nightly from 8pm to 3am. 3045 N. Federal Hwy. (at Oakland Park Blvd.), Fort Lauderdale. ℂ 954/564-1074. Cover varies.

Elbo Room   Formerly spring-break central, the Elbo Room has actually managed to maintain its rowdy and divey reputation by serving up frequent drink specials and live bands. Open daily from 10am to 2am. 241 S. Atlantic Blvd. (corner of Las Olas Blvd. and Fla. A1A), Fort Lauderdale. ℂ 954/463-4615.

Harrison's Wine Gallery   Dark, cozy, and so comfy that it's hard to get up from the big leather couches, Harrison's attracts a hip crowd that mulls over, sniffs, and sips from more than 100 kinds of vino at reasonable prices. There are also 40 bottled beers. Cheese platters, hummus platters, and panini are available. Open daily from 4pm to 2am. 1916 Harrison St., Hollywood. ℂ 954/922-0074.

Karma Lounge   Almost too hip for Fort Lauderdale, Karma Lounge boasts a British resident DJ, which, if you know anything about DJs or club music, is a big deal. Progressive house music is the soundtrack for this glammy, orange-and-white ultramod spot that's frequented by the dolled-up over-25 set. Open Wednesday though Thursday from 10pm to 3am, Friday and Saturday from 10pm to 4am. 4 W. Las Olas Blvd., Fort Lauderdale. ℂ 954/523-7159. Cover varies.

Mai Kai *(Moments*   Immerse yourself in this fabulous vestige of Polynesian kitsch: hula dancers, fire eaters, and potent drinks served in coconuts. The food, an ambiguous blend of Chinese, Polynesian, and other Asian cuisines, is tasty but overpriced. No matter; it's bound to get cold as you watch the hilarious show, which includes everything from Tahitian classics to Polynesian versions of American hits. A trip to undeniably fun Mai Kai is a must. *Note:* The cocktails cost almost as much as a meal. Open daily from 5pm until midnight. 3599 N. Federal Hwy. (between Commercial and Oakland Park blvds.), Fort Lauderdale. ℂ 954/563-3272. Reservations required. Shows (2 nightly) are $9.95 for adults, free for children 12 and under.

O'Hara's   What used to be a mediocre jazz club has turned into a premier venue for excellent live R&B, pop, and funk music. Two locations: 1905 Hollywood Blvd., Hollywood (ℂ 954/925-2555, or 24-hr. Jazz & Blues Hot Line 954/524-2801); and 722 E. Las Olas Blvd., Fort Lauderdale (ℂ 954/524-1764).

Pangaea and Gryphon   The two hottest dance clubs and lounges at the Seminole Hard Rock Hotel and Casino opened by a NYC nightlife impresario, Pangaea and Gryphon attract an A-list of club kids spanning the tricounty area. Open 24 hours. 5707 Seminole Way, Hollywood ℂ 954/581-5454. Cover $20 Fri −Sat nights.

Where the Boys Are: Gay Fort Lauderdale

While South Beach is a magnet for the so-called circuit boys—gay men who party on a continual basis—Fort Lauderdale has a more low-key, small-town scene similar to that of, say, Provincetown. Here local gay-owned bars, clubs, and restaurants are the choice for those who find South Beach's scene too pretentious and drug infested. Fort Lauderdale's Wilton Manors is the hub of gay life, but there is a smattering of gay establishments throughout the city.

The **Copa**, 2800 S. Federal Hwy. (east on I-595, near the airport; ✆ 954/463-1507), is the hottest gay spot north of South Beach—the granddaddy of Fort Lauderdale's gay club scene. Patrons of **Cathode Ray**, 1105 E. Las Olas Blvd. (✆ 954/462-8611), call this bar their "Cheers." **Georgie's Alibi**, 2266 Wilton Dr. (✆ 954/565-2526), is the most popular gay bar in Wilton Manors. Two great dance clubs are the **Coliseum**, 2520 S. Miami Rd. (✆ 954/832-0100), and **Club 84**, 1000 W. S.R. 84 (✆ 954/525-7883).

The Parrot   Fort Lauderdale's most famous dive bar, The Parrot is a local's and out-of-towner's choice for an evening of beer (16 kinds on tap), bonding, and browsing of the bar's gallery of photos of almost everyone who's ever imbibed here since its opening in 1970. Open Sunday through Thursday from 11am to 2am, and Friday and Saturday from 11am to 3am. 911 Sunrise Lane, Fort Lauderdale. ✆ 954/563-1493.

The Poor House   There's nothing poor about this microbrew hangout, where excellent live music from local bands starts at midnight and goes on well into the wee hours. A friendly, lively mixed crowd composes a generational cross-section where the gap is bridged by a common love of music, cold beer, and good times. Open nightly from 5pm to 2am. 110 SW 3rd Ave., Fort Lauderdale. ✆ 954/522-5145.

Revolution   Some of today's hottest indie bands play here, but if you're not into live music, fret not because this cavernous place is a dance club, too. Open Thursday to Sunday until 4am. Opening hours and cover charges vary, depending on what band is playing. 200 W. Broward Blvd., Fort Lauderdale. ✆ 954/727-0950.

Riverwalk   You'll find this outdoor shopping-and-entertainment complex in the heart of downtown Fort Lauderdale, on the sleepy yet scenic New River—as a result of its river site, it's got more charm than most such complexes. In fact, if you've got a boat, you can sail here. A host of bars, restaurants, and shops, not to mention a high-tech virtual-reality arcade, the Escape, and a multiplex cinema, are enough to keep you occupied for at least a few hours. On weekends, this place is packed. 400 SW 2nd St. (along the New River from NE 6th Ave. to SW 6th Ave.), Fort Lauderdale.

Shooters   This waterfront bar is quintessential Fort Lauderdale. Inside you'll find nautical types, families, and young professionals mixed in with a good dose of sun-burned tourists enjoying the live reggae, jazz, or Jimmy Buffett–style tunes, with the gorgeous backdrop of the bay and marinas all around. Open Monday through Friday from 11:30am to 2am, Saturday from 11:30am to 3am, and Sunday from 10am to 2am. 3033 NE 32nd Ave., Fort Lauderdale. ✆ 954/566-2855.

2 Boca Raton ★★ & Delray Beach ★

26 miles S of Palm Beach, 40 miles N of Miami, 21 miles N of Fort Lauderdale

Boca Raton is one of South Florida's most expensive, well-maintained cities—home to ladies who lunch and SUV-driving yuppies. The city's name literally translates as "rat's mouth," but you'd be hard-pressed to find rodents in this area's fancy digs.

If you're looking for funky, wacky, and eclectic, look elsewhere. Boca is a luxurious resort community and, for some, the only place worth staying in South Florida. Although Jerry Seinfeld's TV parents retired to the fictional Del Boca Vista, Boca's just too pricey to be a retirement community. With minimal nightlife, entertainment in Boca is restricted to leisure sports, excellent dining, and upscale shopping. The city's residents and vacationers happily comply.

Delray Beach, named after a suburb of Detroit, is a sleepy-yet-starting-to-awaken beachfront community that grew up completely separate from its southern neighbor. Because of their proximity, Boca and Delray can easily be explored together. Budget-conscious travelers would do well to eat and sleep in Delray and dip into Boca for sightseeing and beaching only. The 2-mile stretch of beach here is well maintained and crowded, though not mobbed. Delray's "downtown" area is confined to Atlantic Avenue, which is known for restaurants from casual to chic, quaint shops, and art galleries. During the day, Delray is slumbering, but thanks to the recent addition of trendy restaurants and bars, nighttime is a much more animated hotbed of hipster activity. Still, compared to Boca, Delray is much more laid back, hardly as chichi, and more cute little beach town than sprawling, swanky, suburban Boca.

ESSENTIALS

GETTING THERE   Like the rest of the cities on the Gold Coast, Boca Raton and Delray are easily reached from I-95 or the Florida Turnpike. Both the Fort Lauderdale–Hollywood International Airport and the Palm Beach International Airport are about 20 minutes away. **Amtrak** (© **800/USA-RAIL;** www.amtrak.com) trains make stops in Delray Beach at an unattended station at 345 S. Congress Ave.

VISITOR INFORMATION   Contact or stop by the **Palm Beach County Convention and Visitors Bureau,** 1555 Palm Beach Lakes Blvd., Suite 800, West Palm Beach, FL 33401 (© **800/554-PALM** or 561/233-3000; fax 561/471-3990; www.palmbeachfl.com). It's open Monday through Friday from 8:30am to 5:30pm and has excellent coupons and discounts. Monday through Friday from 8:30am until at least 4pm, stop by the **Greater Boca Raton Chamber of Commerce,** 1800 N. Dixie Hwy., 4 blocks north of Glades Road, Boca Raton, FL 33432 (© **561/395-4433;** fax 561/392-3780; www.bocaratonchamber.com), for information on attractions, accommodations, and events in the area. You can also try the **Greater Delray Beach Chamber of Commerce,** 64 SE 5th Ave., half a block south of Atlantic Avenue on U.S. 1, Delray Beach, FL 33483 (© **561/278-0424;** fax 561/278-0555; www.delraybeach.com), but I recommend the Palm Beach County Convention and Visitors Bureau since it has information on the entire county.

BEACHES & OUTDOOR ACTIVITIES

BEACHES   Thankfully, Florida had the foresight to set aside some of its most beautiful coastal areas for the public's enjoyment. Many of the area's best beaches are located in state parks and are free to pedestrians and bikers, though most do charge for parking. Among the beaches I recommend are Delray Beach's **Atlantic Dunes**

Boca Raton & Delray Beach

Beach, 1600 S. Ocean Blvd., which charges no admission to access a 7-acre developed beach with lifeguards, restrooms, changing rooms, and a family park area; and Boca Raton's **South Beach Park,** 400 N. Ocean Blvd., with 1,670 feet of beach, 25 acres, lifeguards, picnic areas, restrooms, showers, and 955 feet of developed beach south of the Boca Inlet, accessible for an admission charge of $15 Monday through Friday, and $17 Saturday and Sunday. The two beaches below are also very popular.

Delray Beach, on Ocean Boulevard at the east end of Atlantic Avenue, is one of the area's most popular hangouts. Weekends especially attract a young and good-looking crowd of active locals and tourists. Refreshments, snack shops, bars, and restaurants are just across the street. Families enjoy the protection of lifeguards on the clean, wide strip. Gentle waters make it a good swimming beach, too. Restrooms and showers are available, and there's limited parking at meters along Ocean Boulevard.

Spanish River Park Beach, on North Ocean Boulevard (Fla. A1A), 2 miles north of Palmetto Park Road in Boca Raton, is a huge 95-acre oceanfront park with a ½-mile-long beach with lifeguards as well as a large grassy area, making it one of the best choices for picnicking. Facilities include picnic tables, grills, restrooms, showers, and a 40-foot observation tower. You can walk through tunnels under the highway to access nature trails that wind through fertile grasslands. Volleyball nets always have at least one game going on. The park is open from 8am to 8pm. Admission is $16 for vehicles Monday through Friday; $18 on Saturday, Sunday, and major holidays.

Also see the description of **Red Reef Park** under "Scuba Diving & Snorkeling," below.

GOLF   This area has plenty of good courses. The best ones that are not located in a gated community are **Boca Raton Resort & Club** (p. 284) and the **Inn at Ocean Breeze Golf and Country Club** (p. 286), formerly known as the Inn at Boca Teeca. Another great place to swing clubs is at the **Deer Creek Golf Club,** 2801 Country Club Blvd., Deerfield Beach (© **954/421-5550**), a 300-plus-yard driving range where a large bucket of balls costs $7 and a small one costs $4. Rates at the Deer Creek Golf Club are seasonal and range from $45 to $95. However, from May to October or November, about a dozen private courses open their greens to visitors staying in Palm Beach County hotels. This "Golf-A-Round" program is free or severely discounted (carts are additional), and reservations can be made through most major hotels. Ask at your hotel or contact the **Palm Beach County Convention and Visitors Bureau** (© **561/471-3995**) for information on which clubs are available for play.

The semiprivate, 18-hole, par-61 course at the **Boca Raton Executive Country Club,** 7601 E. Country Club Blvd. (© **561/997-9410**), is usually open to the public and is an excellent choice for those looking to improve their game in a professional setting. A driving range is on-site, as well as a restaurant and a pro shop that rents clubs. If you like, take lessons from a PGA pro. Greens fees are $20 per person.

The **Boca Raton Municipal Golf Course,** 8111 Golf Course Rd. (© **561/483-6100**), is the area's best public golf course. There's an 18-hole, par-72 course covering approximately 6,200 yards, as well as a 9-hole, par-30 course. Facilities include a snack bar and a pro shop where clubs can be rented. Greens fees are $11 to $25 for 9 holes, and $19 to $36 for 18 holes. Ask about special summer discounts.

SCUBA DIVING & SNORKELING   **Moray Bend,** a 58-foot dive spot located about ¾ mile off Boca Inlet, is the area's most popular. It's home to three moray eels that are used to being fed by scuba divers. The reef is accessible by boat from **Force E**

Dive Center, 877 E. Palmetto Park Rd., Boca Raton (© **561/368-0555**). Phone for dive times. Dives cost $40 to $50 per person.

Red Reef Park, 1400 N. Ocean Park Blvd. (© **561/393-7974**), a 67-acre ocean-front park in Boca Raton, has good swimming and year-round lifeguard protection. There's snorkeling around the shallow rocks and reefs that lie just off the beach. The park has restrooms and a picnic area with grills. Located ½ mile north of Palmetto Park Road, it's open daily from 8am to 10pm. The cost is $10 per car Monday through Friday, $12 on Saturday and Sunday; walkers and bikers get in free.

TENNIS   The snazzy **Delray Beach Tennis Center,** 201 W. Atlantic Ave. (© **561/243-7360;** www.delraytennis.com), has 14 lighted clay courts and 5 hard courts available by the hour. Phone for rates and reservations.

The 17 public lighted hard courts at **Patch Reef Park,** 2000 NW 51st St. (© **561/997-0881;** www.ci.boca-raton.fl.us/parks/patchreef.cfm), are available by reservation. The fee for nonresidents is $5.75 per person per 1½ hours. Courts are available Monday through Saturday from 7:30am to 10pm, and Sunday from 7:30am to dusk; you can call ahead to see if a court is available. To reach the park from I-95, exit at Yamato Road West and continue past Military Trail to the park.

SEEING THE SIGHTS

Boca Raton Museum of Art 🐾🐾

In addition to a relatively small but well-chosen permanent collection that's strongest in 19th-century European oils (Degas, Klee, Matisse, Picasso, Seurat), the museum stages a wide variety of excellent temporary exhibitions by local and international artists. Lectures and films are offered on a fairly regular basis, so call ahead for details.

Mizner Park, 501 Plaza Real, Boca Raton. © 561/392-2500. www.bocamuseum.org. Admission $8 adults, $6 seniors, $4 students, free for children under 12. Additional fees may apply for special exhibits and performances. Free on Wed except during special exhibitions. Tues, Thurs, and Sat 10am–5pm; Wed and Fri 10am–9pm; Sun noon–5pm.

Daggerwing Nature Center 🐾

Seen enough snowbirds? Head over to this 39-acre swampy splendor where birds of another feather reside, including herons, egrets, woodpeckers, and warblers. The trails come complete with a soundtrack provided by songbirds hovering above (watch your head). The park's Night Hikes will take you on a nocturnal wake-up call for owls at 6pm. Bring a flashlight.

South County Regional Park, 11200 Park Access Rd., Boca Raton. © 561/488-9953. Free admission. Tues–Fri 1–4:30pm; Sat 9am–4:30pm. Call for tour and activity schedule.

Gumbo Limbo Environmental Complex 🐾🐾🐾

If manicured lawns and golf courses aren't your idea of communing with nature, then head to Gumbo Limbo. Named for an indigenous hardwood tree, the 20-acre complex protects one of the few surviving coastal hammocks, or forest islands, in South Florida. Walk through the hammock on a ½-mile-long boardwalk that ends at a 40-foot observation tower, from which you can see the Atlantic Ocean, the Intracoastal Waterway, and much of Boca Raton. From mid-April to September, sea turtles come ashore here to lay eggs.

1801 N. Ocean Blvd. (on Fla. A1A between Spanish River Blvd. and Palmetto Park Rd.), Boca Raton. © 561/338-1473. Fax 561/338-1483. Free admission. Mon–Sat 9am–4pm; Sun noon–4pm.

Morikami Museum and Japanese Gardens 🐾🐾🐾

Slip off your shoes and enter a serene Japanese garden that dates from 1905, when an entrepreneurial farmer, Jo Sakai, came to Boca Raton to build a tropical agricultural community. The Yamato Colony, as it was known, was short lived; by the 1920s, only one tenacious colonist remained: George Sukeji Morikami. But Morikami was quite successful, eventually running one of the largest pineapple plantations in the area. The 200-acre Morikami Museum and Japanese Gardens, which opened to the public in 1977, was Morikami's gift to Palm Beach County and the state of Florida. A stroll through the garden is almost a mile long. An artificial waterfall that cascades into a koi- and carp-filled moat; a small rock garden for meditation; and a large bonsai collection with miniature maple, buttonwood, juniper, and Australian pine trees are all worth contemplation. There's also a cafe with an Asian-inspired menu if you want to stay for lunch.

4000 Morikami Park Rd., Delray Beach. © 561/495-0233. www.morikami.org. Museum $10 adults, $9 seniors, $6 children 6–18. Museum Tues–Sun 10am–5pm; gardens Tues–Sat 10am–5pm. Closed major holidays.

SHOPPING & BROWSING

Even if you don't plan to buy anything, a trip to Boca Raton's **Mizner Park** is essential for capturing the essence of the city. Mizner is the place to see and be seen, where Rolls-Royces and Ferraris are parked curbside, freshly coiffed women sit amid shopping bags at outdoor cafes, and young movers and shakers chat on their constantly buzzing cellphones. Beyond the human scenery, however, Mizner Park is scenic in its own right, with beautiful landscaping. It's really an outdoor mall, with 45 specialty shops, seven good restaurants, and a multiplex. Each shop front faces a grassy island with gazebos, potted plants, and garden benches. Mizner Park is located on Federal Highway, between Palmetto Park and Glades roads (© **561/362-0606**).

Boca's **Town Center Mall,** located on the south side of Glades Road, just west of I-95, has seven huge department stores, including Nordstrom, Bloomingdale's, Burdines, Lord & Taylor, and Saks Fifth Avenue. Add to that the hundreds of specialty shops, an extensive food court, and a range of other restaurants, and you have the area's most comprehensive shopping center.

On Delray Beach's Atlantic Avenue, especially east of Swinton Avenue, you'll find a few antiques shops, clothing stores, and galleries shaded by palm trees and colorful awnings. Pick up the *Downtown Delray Beach* map and guide at almost any of the stores on this strip, or call © **561/278-0424** for more information.

WHERE TO STAY

A number of national chain hotels worth considering include the moderately priced **Holiday Inn Highland Beach Oceanside,** 2809 S. Ocean Blvd., on Florida A1A, southeast of Linton Boulevard (© **800/234-6835** or 561/278-6241). Although you won't find rows of cheap hotels as in Fort Lauderdale and Hollywood, a handful of mom-and-pop motels have survived along Florida A1A between the towering condominiums of Delray Beach. Look along the beach just south of Atlantic Boulevard. Especially noteworthy is the pleasant little two-story, shingle-roofed **Bermuda Inn,** 64 S. Ocean Blvd. (© **561/276-5288**).

Even more economical options can be found in Deerfield Beach, Boca's neighbor, south of the county line. A number of beachfront efficiencies offer great deals, even in the winter months. Try the **Panther Motel and Apartments,** 715 S. A1A (© **954/427-0700**), a clean and convenient motel with rates starting as low as $45 (in season, you may have to book for a week at a time; rates then start at $250).

VERY EXPENSIVE

Boca Raton Resort & Club ★★ *Kids* This famous and often-photographed property shows that Boca's country-club lifestyle is alive and well. Built in 1926 by Addison Mizner, the posh resort now comprises three oddly matched buildings: the original building; the somewhat drab, pink 27-story Tower; and the more modern, airier Beach Club, which is accessible by water shuttle. Fans of the old-school resort may be disappointed with the increasing modernization of the hotel; others will be happy things have been dusted off and spruced up. Everything at this resort, which straddles the Intracoastal Waterway and encompasses over 350 acres of land, is at your fingertips but may sometimes require a little effort to reach since the place is so huge. Amenities here include two 18-hole championship golf courses, a $10-million tennis and fitness center, indoor basketball and racquetball courts, a 25-slip marina with fishing and boating facilities, and a private beach with watersports equipment. With a choice of 10 places to dine, five pools, and an excellent children's program, the place is ideal for families. Upon check-in, see if Harry the bellman is available to take you to your room—he's been at the resort for more than 46 years and has a photographic memory of the hotel's previous guests, from Joseph Cotton and Charlton Heston to Bill Gates, who became a partner in the hotel after spending enough time there.

501 E. Camino Real (P.O. Box 5025), Boca Raton, FL 33431. ✆ **800/327-0101** or 561/395-3000. Fax 561/447-3183. www.bocaresort.com. 963 units, 120 golf villas. Winter $290–$760 double; off season $190–$495 double. Reasonable seasonal packages available. AE, DC, DISC, MC, V. From I-95 N., exit onto Palmetto Park Rd. E. Turn right onto Federal Hwy. (U.S. 1), then left onto Camino Real. **Amenities:** 8 restaurants; 6 bars; 5 pools; 2 18-hole championship golf courses; 34 clay tennis courts; indoor basketball court; 4 indoor racquetball courts; 3 fitness centers; Mediterranean spa; watersports equipment rental; extensive children's programs; concierge; business center; 24-hr. room service; laundry; 25-slip marina. *In room:* A/C, TV, minibar, hair dryer.

Sundy House 🐾🐾🐾   One of the few properties in South Florida that hasn't given way to the faux-Mediterranean, Mizner-esque style of architecture, Sundy House is the oldest residence in Delray Beach and is a bona fide 1902 Queen Anne house that has been restored to its Victorian glory—on the outside, at least. Inside, however, the four one- and two-bedroom apartments are in a style that is best described as Caribbean funky, adorned in brilliant colors and outfitted with state-of-the-art audiovisual equipment, full modern kitchens, and laundry facilities. Six new guest rooms known as the Stables are equestrian chic, with more rustic appointments in dark woods. While the rooms here are comfortable and gorgeous in their own right, it's the surrounding property that garners the most oohs and aahs. Set on an acre of lush gardens, the Sundy House is surrounded by over 5,000 species of exotic plants, gently flowing streams, and colorful parrots, making an escape here seem more like something you'd find in Hawaii rather than South Florida. In the hotel's swimming pond, guests can swim with the fish (in a good way!). The on-site restaurant, De La Tierra, is equally awe inspiring, featuring exquisite New Florida cuisine, oftentimes using fresh fruits and herbs straight from Sundy House's botanical Taru Garden (see below for full review). The Roux Bamboux Lounge oozes a caviar-and-martini sophistication. One of South Florida's best-kept secrets (though not for much longer), Sundy House is paradise rediscovered.

106 S. Swinton Ave., Delray Beach, FL 33444. ✆ **877/439-9601** or 561/272-5678. Fax 561/272-1115. www.sundy house.com. 11 units. Winter $250–$500 1- or 2-bedroom or cottage; off season $175–$500 1- or 2-bedroom or cottage. AE, DC, DISC, MC, V. **Amenities:** Restaurant; bar; swimming pond; limited room service. *In room:* A/C, TV, DVD player, CD player, minibar, kitchen, coffeemaker, hair dryer, safe, washer/dryer.

EXPENSIVE

Crane's BeachHouse 🐾🐾   If you can't afford your own South Florida beach house—and why bother with all the maintenance, anyway?—Crane's BeachHouse, meticulously run and maintained by husband and wife Cheryl and Michael Crane, is a haven away from home, located just 1 block from the beach and right in the middle of historic Delray Beach. The main draws here are the whimsical, tropical suites, in which every piece of furniture and bric-a-brac is completely original and oftentimes crafted by local artists. Although each unit has its own theme—Hawaii, Amazon, Anacapri, and Capetown, for instance—the beds are all the same, in that they are downright heavenly. Lush gardens, a Tiki bar, and a swimming pool leave you with little reason to flee the premises, but when you do, you'll want to return as quickly as possible.

82 Gleason St., Delray Beach, FL 33483. (©) **866/372-7263** or 561/278-1700. Fax 561/278-7826. www.cranesbeach house.com. 27 units. Winter $185–$485 suite; off season $136–$299 suite. AE, DC, DISC, V. Free parking. **Amenities:** 2 small outdoor pools. *In room:* A/C, TV, VCR, dataport, minibar, full kitchen, coffeemaker, hair dryer, iron, safe.

MODERATE

The Inn at Ocean Breeze Golf and Country Club ★★★   For over 3 decades, this

lodging, formerly known as the Inn at Boca Teeca, has attracted golf fanatics who could care less about the small but comfortable rooms because they're too busy out on the superb 27-hole golf course, open only to members and guests. For the golf widow(er)s, most of the rooms in this three-story building have balconies or patios from which to watch or signal to their significant others that it's time for dinner.

5800 NW 2nd Ave., Boca Raton, FL 33487. (©) **561/994-0400.** Fax 561/998-8279. 46 units. Winter from $130 double; off season $80–$120 double. AE, DC, MC, V. **Amenities:** Restaurant; small pool; golf course; 6 tennis courts; fitness center. *In room:* A/C, TV.

INEXPENSIVE

Ocean Lodge ★   Situated around a small heated pool and sun deck, this two-story

motel is a particularly well-kept property in an area of run-down or overpriced options. The large rooms offer furnishings and decor that are clean but a bit impersonal. A recent renovation that added modern Formica and floral wallpaper lifts this a notch above a basic motel. Ask for a room in the back since the street noise can be a bit loud, especially in season. The bonus is that you're across the street from the ocean and in one of Florida's most upscale resort towns.

531 N. Ocean Blvd. (just north of Palmetto Park Rd. on Fla. A1A), Boca Raton, FL 33432. (©) **800/STAY-BOCA** or 561/395-7772. Fax 561/395-0554. 18 units. Winter $99–$125 double; off season $75–$99 double. AE, MC, V. **Amenities:** Pool. *In room:* A/C, TV.

WHERE TO DINE

Boca Raton and its surrounding area is the kind of place where you discuss dinner plans at the breakfast table. Nightlife in Boca means going out to a restaurant. But who cares? This is some of the best dining in South Florida.

VERY EXPENSIVE

The Addison ★★★ CONTINENTAL   Located in Addison Mizner's 1925 office

building near his famous Boca Raton Resort, The Addison is one of Boca's most popular—and romantic—restaurants, with a stunning courtyard and a setting straight out of a swank Spanish village. The menu ranges from steaks and chops to more nouveau dishes such as corn-crusted soft-shell crab with roasted garlic mash and fennel salad. Service is swift and professional, but it's the ambiance people come here for.

2 East Camino Real., Boca Raton. (©) **561/395-9335** Reservations recommended. Main courses $20–$50; fixed-price dinners $26-$36. AE, DC, DISC, MC, V. Sun–Thurs 5–10pm; Fri–Sat 5–11pm.

La Vieille Maison ★★★ FRENCH   The luxurious setting in a Mediterranean-

inspired home filled with a variety of antique French furnishings and paintings gives you the feeling of walking into a small château. Culinarily speaking, however, this place is a castle. Begin with lobster bisque, gratin of escargot with fennel and pistachio nuts, or pan-seared foie gras. The many enticing entrees range from red snapper in black- and green-olive potato crust, to medallions of beef, lamb, and venison over three sauces. You have to try at least a few of the gorgeous cheeses the server offers after your main course—the most extensive selection I've seen in this country. The lemon crepe soufflé with raspberry sauce is the dessert of choice—remember to order it early.

770 E. Palmetto Park Rd., Boca Raton. (C) **561/391-6701** or 561/737-5677. Reservations recommended. Main courses $20–$50; fixed-price dinners $45-$70. AE, DC, DISC, MC, V. Daily 6–9:30pm (call for seating times).

New York Prime ✿ STEAKHOUSE   This South Florida outpost of a South Carolina–based chain is the prime spot for carnivores looking to satisfy their cravings for big, succulent steaks. Fish dishes are also available, including lobsters ranging from 3 to 13 pounds. But excess does not come cheap. In fact, the restaurant brazenly states its case on the menu: "We strive to be the Mercedes of steak houses by offering the very best . . . but you can't drive a Mercedes for the same price as a Buick." Cute motto, but in terms of consistency, New York Prime is a Pinto. On one night the food and service are exquisite, while on another, abysmal. Take your chances, though, because if you do hit it on a good night, you won't be disappointed.

2350 Executive Center Dr., Boca Raton. (C) **561/998-3881.** Reservations recommended. Main courses $25–$65. AE, MC, V. Daily 5–11pm.

EXPENSIVE

De La Tierra ✿✿✿ FLORIBBEAN   This restaurant is a stunning experience that combines elegant indoor dining and lush tropical outdoor settings with a gastronomic wizardry of fresh fruits, vegetables, and spices grown on the Sundy House's 5-acre farm. Each dish is prepared with a palpable precision. Consider the following: Smoked-tomato soup is served with tiny grilled Brie sandwiches and cilantro sour cream; leg of duck confit cakes are accompanied by mango coleslaw; diver scallops are caramelized and served with truffle-braised oyster mushrooms, corn broth, caviar, and microgreens; and slightly smoked salmon is served with chive/potato latkes, papaya/apple chutney, and dill/shallot sour cream. Save room for dessert, which includes a phenomenal blueberry cobbler and mango-and-jackfruit shortcake. A decadent Sunday brunch buffet makes the day before going back to work infinitely more bearable. De La Tierra may mean "of the earth," but in my book, it's from the gods. On the negative side, the service here can be surly and spotty.

In the Sundy House, 106 S. Swinton Ave., Delray Beach. (C) **561/272-5678.** Reservations essential. Main courses $15–$30. AE, DC, DISC, MC, V. Daily 11:30am–2:30pm and 6–10pm; Sun brunch 10:30am–2:30pm.

Max's Grille ✿✿ AMERICAN   Max's Grille is a very popular, very good option in Mizner Park, but you will have to wait to be seated. With an exhibition kitchen occupying the back wall of the restaurant, those lucky enough to score a table can watch as their yellowfin tuna steak or filet mignon is seared on a flaming oak grill. There's also a large selection of chicken, meatloaf, pastas, and main-course salads.

404 Plaza Real, in Mizner Park, Boca Raton. (C) **561/368-0080.** Reservations accepted for groups of 6 or more. Main courses $14–$26; pastas $11–$17. AE, DC, DISC, MC, V. Mon–Sat 11:30am–3pm; Mon–Thurs 5–10:30pm; Fri–Sat 5–11pm; Sun 11:30am–10pm.

32 East ✿✿ NEW AMERICAN   The menu changes every day at this popular people-watching outpost of tasty, contemporary American food that has added a little hipness to the Delray Beach scene. Among the standouts are crispy Key West shrimp in lemon-mint butter with endive and spicy melon coulis; Oregon porcini, corn, and lobster risotto with herb salad in a Vidalia vinaigrette; and mesquite-grilled skirt steak and radicchio di Treviso on fontina polenta with horseradish gremolata. The abuzz-with-activity ambience makes 32 East a popular hangout spot for the cocktail set.

32 E. Atlantic Ave., Delray Beach. ℂ **561/276-7868**. Reservations recommended. Main courses $10–$16. AE, DC, MC, V. Sun–Thurs 5:30–10pm; Fri–Sat 5:30–11pm; bar until 2am.

Uncle Tai's ✦✦✦ CHINESE   Not your average egg-roll-and-lo-mein place, Uncle Tai's, Boca's best upscale Chinese restaurant, offers a savory spin on classics such as garlic chicken and duck with plum sauce. A family-run restaurant, Uncle Tai's is the product of Wen Dah Tai, who studied with master chefs in China, Japan, and the Philippines. Tai wants to make sure you emerge from his restaurant satisfied, and he'll go the extra mile to discourage you from ordering a dish that's less suited to Western palates because it was specially created for the restaurant's many Chinese diners.

5250 Town Center Circle (between Glades and Palmetto Park roads), Boca Raton. ℂ **561/368-8806**. Reservations suggested. Main courses $12–$32. AE, DISC, MC, V. Sun–Thurs 11:30am–2:30pm and 5–10pm; Fri–Sat 11:30am–2:30pm and 5–10:30pm.

MODERATE

Bistro Zenith ✦ NEW AMERICAN   At the height of innovative cuisine, Bistro Zenith's consistently changing menu keeps local foodies coming back for its tasty offerings of traditional American dishes graced with Asian, Mediterranean, or Southwestern influences.

In the Regency Court, 3011 Yamato Rd., Boca Raton. ℂ **561/997-2570**. Reservations recommended. Main courses $9–$15. AE, MC, V. Mon–Fri 11:30am–2:30pm; Sun–Thurs 5:30–10pm; Fri–Sat 5:30–11pm.

Mario's of Boca ✦ ITALIAN   This extremely popular, bustling Italian bistro keeps Boca's biggest mouths busy with massive portions of great homemade Italian food. The garlic rolls and the pizza are especially worth piping down for. If you're really hungry, there's an all-you-can-eat buffet 7 days a week.

1901 N. Military Trail (at the Holiday Inn, opposite Kings Market), Boca Raton. ℂ **561/392-5595**. Reservations not accepted. Main courses under $15. AE, MC, V. Daily 7–10:30am; Mon–Thurs 11:30am–10pm; Fri–Sat 11:30am–11pm; Sun noon–9:30pm.

INEXPENSIVE

Baja Cafe ✦ MEXICAN   A jeans-and-T-shirt kind of place with wooden tables, Baja Cafe serves fantastic Mexican food at even better prices. It's located right by the Florida East Coast Railway tracks, so don't be surprised if you feel a little rattling. Live music and entertainment make this place a hot spot for an unpretentious crowd.

201 NW 1st Ave., Boca Raton. ℂ **561/394-5449**. Reservations not accepted. Main courses $6–$10. No credit cards. Mon–Thurs 11:30am–10pm; Fri–Sat 11:30am–11pm; Sun 5–10pm.

The Tin Muffin Cafe ✦ BAKERY/SANDWICH SHOP   Popular with the downtown lunch crowd, this excellent storefront bakery keeps them lining up for big sandwiches on fresh bread, plus muffins, quiches, and good homemade soups like split-pea or lentil. The curried-chicken sandwich is stuffed with chunks of white meat doused in a creamy curry dressing and fruit. There are a few cafe tables inside and even one outside on a tiny patio. Be warned, however, that service is forgivably slow and parking is a nightmare. Try looking for a spot a few blocks away at a meter.

364 E. Palmetto Park Rd. (between Federal Hwy. and the Intracoastal Bridge), Boca Raton. ℂ **561/392-9446.** Sandwiches and salads $6.50–$11. No credit cards. Mon–Fri 11am–5pm; Sat 11am–4pm.

BOCA RATON & DELRAY BEACH AFTER DARK

THE BAR, CLUB & MUSIC SCENE

Atlantic Avenue in Delray Beach has finally gotten quite hip to nightlife and is now lined with sleek and chic restaurants, lounges, and bars that attract the Palm Beach County "in crowd," along with a few randoms such as Yanni, who has a house nearby. Although it's hardly South Beach or Fort Lauderdale's Las Olas and Riverfront, Atlantic Avenue holds its own as far as a vibrant nightlife is concerned. In Boca Raton, **Mizner Park** is the nucleus of nightlife, with restaurants masking themselves as nightclubs or, at the very least, sceney bars, such as **Gigi's Tavern,** 346 Plaza Real (ℂ **561/ 368-4488**), and **Mark's Mizner Park,** 334 Plaza Real (ℂ **561/395-0770**).

Boston's on the Beach   This is a family restaurant with a somewhat lively bar scene. It's a good choice for post-sunbathing, supercasual happy hours Monday through Friday from 4 to 8pm, or live reggae on Monday. With two decks overlooking the ocean, Boston's is an ideal place to mellow out and take in the scenery. Open daily from 7am to 2am. 40 S. Ocean Blvd., Delray Beach. ℂ **561/278-3364.**

Dada   Dada is a nocturnal outpost of food, drink, music, art, culture, and history. In other words, here you can expect to find neobohemian, arty types lingering in their dark glasses and berets on one of the living room's cozy couches, listening to music, poetry, or dissertations on the latest in life. Live music, great food, a bar, an outdoor patio area, and a very eclectic crowd make Dada the coolest hangout in Delray. Open daily from 5:30pm to 2am. 52 N. Swinton Ave., Delray Beach. ℂ **561/330-DADA.**

Delux   Believe it or not, this red-hued dance club on Atlantic Avenue is cooler than some of South Beach's big-shot clubs, thanks to a soundtrack of sexy house music, bedlike seating, and a beautiful crowd in which someone as striking as past patron Gwen Stefani can actually blend in without being noticed. Open Wednesday through Sunday from 7pm to 2am. 16 E. Atlantic Ave., Delray Beach. ℂ **561/279-4792.**

Elwood's   Over the train tracks just steps from the chic bars and restaurants on Atlantic Avenue is this fabulous blues-themed biker bar housed in a former gas station and garage. No fancy martinis here, just cold beer and good tunes. Open Monday through Friday from 5pm to 2am, Saturday from 11am to 2am, and Sunday from 11am to midnight. 301 E. Atlantic Ave., Delray Beach. ℂ **561/272-7427.**

Falcon House   A cozy wine and tapas bar located on a side street off the Atlantic Avenue bustle, Falcon House is reminiscent of a bar you'd find in Napa Valley, with an impressive selection of wines and a hip, well-heeled crowd. It's a haven for those who are over the whole hip-hop scene on Atlantic. Open Monday through Saturday from 5pm to 2am. 116 NE 6th Ave., Delray Beach. ℂ **561/243-9499.**

Gatsby's   This always-busy bar is singles central, featuring big-screen TVs, microbrews, and martinis. Thursday college nights are especially popular, as are Friday happy hours. Open Monday, Tuesday, and Thursday from 4pm to 2am; Wednesday from 4pm to 3am; Friday from 4pm to 4am; Saturday from 6pm to 4am; and Sunday from 4pm to 3am. 5970 SW 18th St., Boca Raton. ℂ **561/393-3900.**

THE PERFORMING ARTS

For details on upcoming events, check the *Boca News* or the *Sun-Sentinel,* or call the **Palm Beach County Cultural Council** information line at ℂ **800/882-ARTS.**

During business hours, a staffer can give details on current performances. After hours, a recorded message describes the week's events.

The **Florida Symphonic Pops,** a 70-piece professional orchestra, performs jazz, swing, rock, big-band, and classical music throughout Boca Raton. This musical force has entertained audiences for nearly 50 years. Call ℂ **561/393-7677** for a schedule.

Boca's best theater company is the **Caldwell Theatre,** and it's worth checking out. Located in a strip shopping center at 7873 N. Federal Hwy., this equity showcase does well-known dramas, comedies, classics, off-Broadway hits, and new works throughout the year. Ticket prices are reasonable—usually $29 to $38. Full-time students with ID will be especially interested in the little-advertised student rush: When available, tickets are sold for $5 if you arrive at least an hour early. Call ℂ **561/241-7432** for details.

3 Palm Beach ★★ & West Palm Beach ★

65 miles N of Miami, 193 miles E of Tampa, 45 miles N of Fort Lauderdale

Palm Beach County encompasses cities from Boca Raton in the south to Jupiter and Tequesta in the north. But it is Palm Beach, the small island town across the Intracoastal Waterway, that has been the traditional winter home of America's aristocracy—the Kennedys, the Rockefellers, the Pulitzers, the Trumps, titled socialites, and plenty of CEOs. For a perspective on what it means to put on the ritz, there is no better place than Palm Beach, where teenagers cruise around in their parents' Rolls-Royces while socialites seem to jump out of the glossy pages of society magazines and into an even glitzier real life. It's something to be seen, despite the fact that some may consider it all over the top and, frankly, obscene. But this is not only a city of upscale resorts and chic boutiques. In fact, Palm Beach holds some surprises, from a world-class art museum to one of the top bird-watching areas in the state.

Across the water from Palm Beach proper, or the "island" as locals call it, is downtown West Palm Beach, which is where everybody else lives. Clematis Street is the area's nightlife hub, with a great selection of bars, clubs, and restaurants. City Place is West Palm's version of Mizner Park; shops, restaurants, and other entertainment options liven up this once-dead area. In addition to good beaching, boating, and diving, you'll find great golf and tennis throughout the county. *Note:* Palm Beach's population swells from 20,000 in the summer to 40,000 in the winter. Book early if you plan to visit during the winter months.

ESSENTIALS

GETTING THERE If you're driving up or down the Florida coast, you'll probably reach the Palm Beach area by way of I-95. Exit at Belvedere Road or Okeechobee Boulevard, and head east to reach the most central part of Palm Beach.

Visitors on their way to or from Orlando or Miami should take the Florida Turnpike, a toll road with a speed limit of 65 mph. Tolls are pricey, though; you may pay upward of $9 from Orlando and $4 from Miami. If you're coming from Florida's west coast, you can take either S.R. 70, which runs north of Lake Okeechobee to Fort Pierce, or S.R. 80, which runs south of the lake to Palm Beach.

All major airlines fly to the **Palm Beach International Airport,** at Congress Avenue and Belvedere Road (ℂ **561/471-7400**). **Amtrak** (ℂ **800/USA-RAIL;** www.amtrak.com) has a terminal in West Palm Beach, at 201 S. Tamarind Ave. (ℂ **561/832-6169**).

GETTING AROUND Although a car is almost a necessity in this area, a recently revamped public transportation system is extremely convenient for getting to some

Palm Beach & West Palm Beach

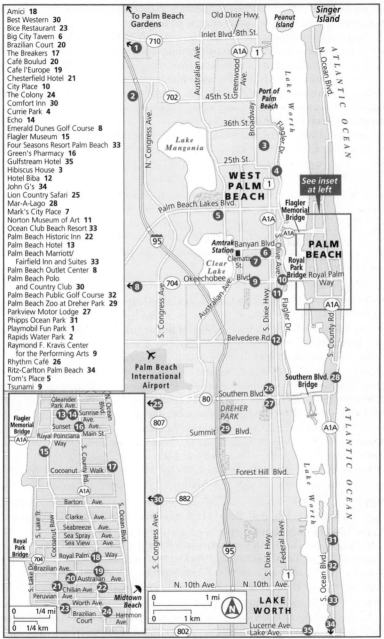

Amici **18**
Best Western **30**
Bice Restaurant **23**
Big City Tavern **6**
Brazilian Court **20**
The Breakers **17**
Café Boulud **20**
Cafe l'Europe **19**
Chesterfield Hotel **21**
City Place **10**
The Colony **24**
Comfort Inn **30**
Currie Park **4**
Echo **14**
Emerald Dunes Golf Course **8**
Flagler Museum **15**
Four Seasons Resort Palm Beach **33**
Green's Pharmacy **16**
Gulfstream Hotel **35**
Hibiscus House **3**
Hotel Biba **12**
John G's **34**
Lion Country Safari **25**
Mar-A-Lago **28**
Mark's City Place **7**
Norton Museum of Art **11**
Ocean Club Beach Resort **33**
Palm Beach Historic Inn **22**
Palm Beach Hotel **13**
Palm Beach Marriott/
    Fairfield Inn and Suites **33**
Palm Beach Outlet Center **8**
Palm Beach Polo
    and Country Club **30**
Palm Beach Public Golf Course **32**
Palm Beach Zoo at Dreher Park **29**
Parkview Motor Lodge **27**
Phipps Ocean Park **31**
Playmobil Fun Park **1**
Rapids Water Park **2**
Raymond F. Kravis Center
    for the Performing Arts **9**
Rhythm Café **26**
Ritz-Carlton Palm Beach **34**
Tom's Place **5**
Tsunami **9**

attractions in both West Palm and Palm Beach. **Palm Tran** covers 32 routes with over 140 buses. The fare is $1 for adults, 50¢ for children 3 to 18, seniors, and riders with disabilities. Free route maps are available by calling © **561/233-4-BUS.** Information operators are available Monday through Saturday from 6am to 7pm.

In downtown West Palm, free shuttles from City Place to Clematis Street operate Monday through Friday from 9am until 4pm, with plans to expand operations to evenings and weekends, too. Allegedly, the shuttles come every 5 minutes, but I'd count on them taking longer. Look for the bubble-gum-pink minibuses throughout downtown. Call © **561/833-8873** for details.

For a more nostalgic route, consider the stately wicker chariots that run in the downtown area, especially on weekends and during special events. Rates vary according to the time of day but average $1 to $2 per block, plus a per-person charge of $1. Call © **561/835-8922** for pickup or information.

VISITOR INFORMATION   The **Palm Beach County Convention and Visitors Bureau,** 1555 Palm Beach Lakes Blvd., Suite 204, West Palm Beach, FL 33401 (© **800/554-PALM** or 561/471-3995; www.palmbeachfl.com), distributes an informative brochure and answers questions about visiting the Palm Beaches. Ask for a map as well as a copy of the *Arts and Attractions Calendar,* a day-to-day guide to art, music, stage, and other events in the county.

BEACHES & OUTDOOR ACTIVITIES

BEACHES   Public beaches are a rare commodity here in Palm Beach. Most of the island's best beaches are fronted by private estates and are inaccessible to the general public. However, there are a few notable exceptions, including **Midtown Beach,** east of Worth Avenue, on Ocean Boulevard between Royal Palm Way and Gulfstream Road, which boasts more than 100 feet of undeveloped sand. This newly widened coast is now a centerpiece and a natural oasis in a town dominated by commercial glitz. There are no restrooms or concessions here, though a lifeguard is on duty until sundown. A popular hangout for locals lies about 1½ miles north of here, near Dunbar Street; they prefer it to Midtown Beach because of the relaxed atmosphere. Parking is available at meters along Florida A1A. At the south end of Palm Beach, there's a less-popular but better-equipped beach at **Phipps Ocean Park.** On Ocean Boulevard, between the Southern Boulevard and Lake Avenue causeways, there's a lively public beach encompassing more than 1,300 feet of groomed oceanfront. With picnic and recreation areas and plenty of parking, the area is especially good for families.

BIKING   Rent anything from an English single-speed to a full-tilt mountain bike at the **Palm Beach Bicycle Trail Shop,** 223 Sunrise Ave. (© **561/659-4583**). Rates are $8 per hour, $20 per half-day (9am–5pm), and $26 for 24 hours, and include a basket and lock (not that a lock is necessary in this fortress of a town). The most scenic route is called the Lake Trail, running the length of the island along the Intracoastal Waterway. On it, you'll see some of the most magnificent mansions and grounds, and enjoy the views of downtown West Palm Beach as well as some great wildlife.

GOLF   There's good golfing in the Palm Beaches, but many private-club courses are maintained exclusively for members' use. Ask at your hotel or contact the **Palm Beach County Convention and Visitors Bureau** (© **561/471-3995**) for information on which clubs are available for play. In the off season, some private courses open to visitors staying in Palm Beach County hotels. This "Golf-A-Round" program offers free greens fees; reservations can be made through most major hotels.

The Sport of Kings

The posh **Palm Beach Polo and Country Club** and the **International Polo Club** are two of the world's premier polo grounds and host some of the sport's top-rated players. Even if you're not a sports fan, you must attend a match at one of these fields, which are on the mainland in a rural area called Wellington. Rest assured, however, that the spectators, and many of the players, are pure Palm Beach. After all, a day at the pony grounds is one of the only good reasons to leave Palm Beach proper. You need not be a Vanderbilt or a Kennedy to attend—matches are open to the public and are surprisingly affordable.

Even if you haven't a clue how the game is played, you can spend your time people-watching. In recent years, stargazers have spotted Prince Charles, Sylvester Stallone, Tommy Lee Jones, Bo Derek, and Ivana Trump, among others. Dozens of lesser-known royalty keep box seats right on the grounds.

Dress is casual; a navy or tweed blazer over jeans or khakis is the standard for men, while neat-looking jeans or a pantsuit is the norm for women. On warmer days, shorts and, of course, a polo shirt are fine, too.

General admission is $10 to $20; box seats cost $75 to $100. Matches are held throughout the week. Schedules vary, but the big names usually compete on Sunday at 3:30pm from January to April.

The fields are located at 11809 Polo Club Rd. and 3667 120th Ave. South Wellington, 10 miles west of the Forest Hill Boulevard exit of I-95. Call ✆ 561/793-1440 or 561/204-5687 for tickets and a detailed schedule of events.

The best hotel for golf in the area is the **PGA National Resort & Spa** (p. 309; ✆ 800/633-9150), which features a whopping 90 holes of golf.

One of the state's best public courses is **Emerald Dunes Golf Course** ✸, 2100 Emerald Dunes Dr., West Palm Beach (✆ 561/687-1700). Designed by Tom Fazio, this dramatic 7,006-yard, par-72 course was voted "One of the Best 10 You Can Play" by *Golf* magazine. It is located just off the Florida Turnpike at Okeechobee Boulevard. Bookings are taken up to 30 days ahead. Fees are $45 to $135, including carts.

The **Palm Beach Public Golf Course,** 2345 S. Ocean Blvd. (✆ 561/547-0598), a popular public 18-hole course, is a par-54. The course opens at 8am on a first-come, first-served basis. Club rentals are available. Greens fees start at $16 to $35 per person.

SCUBA DIVING   Year-round warm waters, barrier reefs, and plenty of wrecks make South Florida one of the world's most popular places for diving. One of the best-known artificial reefs in this area is a vintage Rolls-Royce Silver Shadow, which was sunk offshore in 1985. Nature has taken its toll, however, and divers can no longer sit in the car, which has been ravaged by time and saltwater. For gear and excursions, call **Ocean Sports Scuba Center,** 1736 S. Congress Ave., West Palm Beach (✆ 561/641-1144); or **Jim Abernaethy's Scuba Adventures,** 2116 Ave. B, Riviera Beach (✆ 561/691-5808).

TENNIS   There are hundreds of tennis courts in Palm Beach County. Wherever you are staying, you're bound to be within walking distance of one. In addition to the many hotel tennis courts (see "Where to Stay," below), you can play at **Currie Park,** 2400 N. Flagler Dr., West Palm Beach (℗ **561/835-7025**), a public park with three lighted hard courts. They're free and available on a first-come, first-served basis.

WATERSPORTS   Call the **Seaside Activities Station** (℗ **561/835-8922**) to arrange sailboat, jet-ski, bicycle, kayak, water-ski, and parasail rentals.

SEEING THE SIGHTS

Flagler Museum 🜲🜲🜲   The Gilded Age is preserved in this luxurious mansion commissioned by Standard Oil tycoon Henry Flagler as a wedding present to his third wife. Whitehall, also known as the "Taj Mahal of North America," is a classic Edwardian-style mansion containing 55 rooms, including a Louis XIV music room and art gallery, a Louis XV ballroom, and 14 guest suites outfitted with original antique European furnishings. Out back, climb aboard the *Rambler,* Mr. Flagler's private restored railroad car. Allow at least 1½ hours to tour the stunning grounds and interior. Group tours are available, but for the most part, this is a self-guided museum.

1 Whitehall Way (at Cocoanut Row and Whitehall Way), Palm Beach. ℗ 561/655-2833. www.flaglermuseum.us. Admission $10 adults, $3 children 6–12. Tues–Sat 10am–5pm; Sun noon–5pm.

Norton Museum of Art 🜲🜲🜲   The Norton is world famous for its prestigious permanent collection and top temporary exhibitions. The museum's major collections are divided geographically. The American galleries contain major works by Hopper, O'Keeffe, and Pollock. The French collection contains Impressionist and post-Impressionist paintings by Cézanne, Degas, Gauguin, Matisse, Monet, Picasso, Pissarro, and Renoir. And the Chinese collection contains more than 200 bronzes, jades, and ceramics, as well as monumental Buddhist sculptures. Allow about 2 hours to see this museum, depending on your level of interest.

1451 S. Olive Ave., West Palm Beach. ℗ 561/832-5196. Fax 561/659-4689. www.norton.org. Admission $8 adults, $3 ages 13–21. Mon–Sat 10am–5pm; Sun 1–5pm. Closed Mon May–Oct and all major holidays. Take I-95 to exit 52 (Okeechobee Blvd. E.). Travel east on Okeechobee to Dixie Hwy., then south ½ mile to the Norton. Access parking through entrances on Dixie Hwy. and S. Olive Ave.

Unreal Estate

No trip to Palm Beach is complete without at least a glimpse of **Mar-A-Lago,** the stately residence of Donald Trump, the 21st century's answer to Jay Gatsby. In 1985, Trump purchased the estate of cereal heiress Marjorie Merriweather Post for a meager $8 million (for a fully furnished beachfront property of this stature, it was a relative bargain), to the great consternation of locals, who feared that he would turn the place into a casino. Instead, Trump, who sometimes resides in a portion of the palace, opened the house to the public—for a price, of course—as a tony country club (membership fee: $100,000).

While there are currently no tours open to the public, you can glimpse the gorgeous manse as you cross the bridge from West Palm Beach into Palm Beach. It's located at 1100 S. Ocean Blvd., Palm Beach.

Playmobil Fun Park *★★* *Kids*   For a child, it doesn't get any better than this. The 17,000-square-foot Playmobil Fun Park is housed in a replica castle and loaded with themed areas for imaginative play: a medieval village, a Western town, a fantasy doll-house, and more. Kids can play with the Playmobil boats on two water-filled tables. Tech-minded youths may get bored, but tots up to age 5 or so will love this place. You *could* spend hours here and not spend a penny, but parents, beware: Everything is available for purchase. There's another Playmobil park in Orlando.

8031 N. Military Trail, Palm Beach Gardens. © 800/351-8697 or 561/691-9880. Fax 561/691-9517. www.playmobil. com. Admission $1. Mon–Sat 10am–6pm; Sun noon–5pm. From I-95, go north to Palm Beach Lakes Blvd., then west to Military Trail. Turn left; the park is about a mile down on the right.

NATURE PRESERVES & ATTRACTIONS

Lion Country Safari *★★* *Kids*   More than 1,300 animals on this 500-acre preserve (the nation's first cageless drive-through safari) are divided into their indigenous regions, from the East African preserve of the Serengeti to the American West. Elephants, lions, wildebeest, ostriches, American bison, buffalo, watusi, pink flamingos, and many other unusual species roam the preserve. When I visited, most of the lions were asleep; when awake, they travel freely throughout the cageless grassy landscape (this can be very scary). In fact, you're the one who's confined in your own car without an escort (no convertibles allowed). You're given a detailed pamphlet with photos and descriptions, and are instructed to obey the 15 mph speed limit—unless you see the rhinos charge (a rare occasion), in which case you're encouraged to floor it. Driving the loop takes just over an hour, though you could make a day of just watching the chimpanzees play on their secluded islands. Included in the admission is Safari World, an amusement park with paddleboats, a carousel, miniature golf, and a baby animal nursery. Picnics are encouraged, and camping is available. The best time to go is late afternoon, right before the park closes; it's much cooler then, so the lions are more active. Though some may consider this a tourist trap, I had a great time.

Southern Blvd. W. at S.R. 80, West Palm Beach. © 561/793-1084, or 561/793-9797 for camping reservations. www. lioncountrysafari.com. Admission $20 adults, $18 seniors, $16 children 3–9. Van rental $8 per hour. Daily 9:30am–5:30pm (last vehicle admitted at 4:30pm). From I-95, exit on Southern Blvd. Go west for about 18 miles.

Palm Beach Zoo at Dreher Park *★*   If you want animals, go to Lion Country Safari. Unlike big-city zoos, this intimate 23-acre attraction is more like a stroll in the park than an all-day excursion. It features about 500 animals representing more than 100 different species. The monkey exhibit and petting zoo are favorites with kids. Stroller and wagon rentals are available. The newest attraction is the Tropics of the Americas, a 3-acre jungle path and complex that will immerse guests in the animals, plants, and culture of a New World rainforest. You'll encounter animals such as jaguars, monkeys, giant anteaters, tapirs, bats, birds, snakes, and more. A new Siamang Habitat opened in 2005 and is home to a pair of primates known to be the largest species of lesser apes in the world. Allow at least 2 hours to see all of the sights here.

1301 Summit Blvd. (east of I-95 between Southern and Forest Hill boulevards). © 561/547-WILD. Fax 561/ 585-6085. www.palmbeachzoo.org. Admission $13 adults, $10 seniors, $9 children 3–12. Daily 9am–5pm. Closed Thanksgiving.

Rapids Water Park *★* *Kids*   It may not be on the same grand scale as the theme parks in Orlando, but Rapids is a great way to cool off on a hot day. There are 12 acres of water rides, including a children's area and miniature golf course. Check out the Superbowl, a tubeless water ride that spins and swirls before dumping you into the pool below, and the Big Thunder, a giant funnel that plunges you down 50 feet in a four-person tube. Claustrophobia, anyone?

6566 N. Military Trail, West Palm Beach (1 mile west of I-95 on Military between 45th St./exit 54 and Blue Heron Blvd./exit 55 in West Palm Beach). ✆ 561/842-8756. www.rapidswaterpark.com. Admission $28 plus tax; free for children 2 and under. Parking $5. Mid-Mar to Sept Mon–Fri 10am–5pm; Sat–Sun 10am–6pm.

SHOPPING & BROWSING

No matter what your budget, be sure to take a stroll down Worth Avenue, the "Rodeo Drive of the South" and a window-shopper's dream. Between South Ocean Boulevard and Cocoanut Row, there are more than 200 boutiques, posh shops, art galleries, and upscale restaurants. If you want to fit in, dress as if you are going to an elegant luncheon and not to the mall down the street.

Despite the presence of the usual suspects (**Gucci, Chanel, Armani, Hermès,** and **Louis Vuitton,** among others), Worth Avenue is not impervious to the mainstream. Several chains such as **Victoria's Secret** and **Limited Express** have snuck in here, but so have a good number of unique boutiques. **History Buff,** 32 Via Mizner (✆ **561/ 366-8255**), is a virtual museum selling every genre of original historic autographs, some dating back to the 1600s, as well as vintage signed photos, first-edition books, and memorabilia. **Treasures Autograph Gallery,** 217 Worth Ave. (✆ **561/835- 1891**), sells a priceless collection of John Hancocks, including those of Joe DiMaggio, Mickey Mantle, Andrew Jackson, Abraham Lincoln, Howard Hughes, and hundreds more, all displayed in beautiful frames. For privileged feet, **Stubbs & Wooton,** 4 Via Parigi (✆ **561/655-4105**), sells velvet slippers that are a favorite of the loofahed locals. The **Purple Turtle,** 150 Worth Ave. (✆ **561/655-1625**), in the Esplanade promenade, outfits infants in designer clothes, including Baby Dior and Baby Armani. For rare and estate jewelry, **Richter's of Palm Beach,** 224 Worth Ave. (✆ **561/655- 0774**), has been specializing in priceless gems since 1893. Just off Worth Avenue is the **Church Mouse,** 374 S. County Rd. (✆ **561/659-2154**), a great consignment/thrift shop with antique furnishings and tableware, as well as lots of good castaway clothing and shoes. This shop usually closes for 2 months during the summer; call to be sure.

City Place, Okeechobee Road (at I-95), West Palm Beach (✆ **561/820-9716**), is a $550-million, Mediterranean-style shopping, dining, and entertainment complex that's responsible for revitalizing what was once a lifeless downtown West Palm Beach. Among the 78 mostly chain stores are **Macy's, FAO Schwarz, Benetton** (which contains an in-line skating track), **Armani Exchange, Pottery Barn,** and **SEE** eyewear. Restaurants include a Ghirardelli ice-cream shop, Legal Seafoods, City Cellar Wine Bar and Grill, and Cheesecake Factory. Best of all is the Muvico Parisian, a 20-screen movie theater where you can wine and dine while watching a feature.

Elsewhere, downtown West Palm Beach has a scant number of interesting boutiques along Clematis Street. In addition to the large and well-organized **Clematis Street Books,** 206 Clematis St. (✆ **561/832-2302**), there are a few used-record stores, clothing shops, and several art galleries.

As if there weren't enough shopping malls in South Florida, enter the newest one, the **Mall at Wellington Green,** 10300 W. Forest Hill Blvd., Wellington (✆ **561/227- 6900**), featuring 140 specialty shops and department stores such as Nordstrom, Lord & Taylor, and Dillard's.

WHERE TO STAY

The island of Palm Beach is the epitome of *Lifestyles of the Rich and Famous,* oozing with glitz, glamour, and the occasional scandal. Royalty and celebrities come to winter here, and there are plenty of lavishly priced options to accommodate them. Happily, there are also a few special inns that offer reasonably priced rooms in elegant settings. But most of the more modest places to lay your straw hat surround the island.

A few of the larger hotel chains operating in Palm Beach include the **Palm Beach Marriott/Fairfield Inn and Suites,** 2870 S. Ocean Blvd. (© **800/228-2800** or 561/582-2581), across the street from the beach. Also beachside is the pricey **Ocean Club Beach Resort,** formerly known as the Palm Beach Hilton, 2842 S. Ocean Blvd. (© **561/586-6542**). An excellent and affordable alternative right in the middle of Palm Beach's commercial section is a condominium that operates as a hotel, too: the **Palm Beach Hotel,** 235 Sunrise Ave., between County Road and Bradley Place, across the street from the Publix supermarket (© **561/659-7794**). With winter prices starting at about $155, this clean and comfortable place for accommodations is a great option for those looking for the rare bargain in Palm Beach.

In West Palm Beach, chain hotels are located mostly on the main arteries close to the highways and a short drive from downtown. They include **Best Western,** 1800 Palm Beach Lakes Blvd. (© **800/331-9569** or 561/683-8810), and, just down the road, **Comfort Inn,** 1901 Palm Beach Lakes Blvd. (© **800/221-2222** or 561/689-6100). Farther south is **Parkview Motor Lodge,** 4710 S. Dixie Hwy., just south of Southern Boulevard (© **561/833-4644**). This 28-room motel is the best of many along Dixie Highway (U.S. 1). With rates starting at $75 for a room with TV, air-conditioning, and phone (don't laugh, some don't have any), you can't ask for more.

For other options, contact **Palm Beach Accommodations** (© **800/543-SWIM**).

VERY EXPENSIVE

Brazilian Court ✸✸✸   This elegant, old-world, Mediterranean-style hotel dates from the 1920s and almost looks like a Beverly Hills bungalow. No two rooms are the same as far as decor, but all are elegant and luxurious, with mahogany crown molding, Provence-style wood shutters, imported fabrics, individual climate controls, and stunning bathrooms adorned in limestone with Ultra Air Jet tubs and frameless shower enclosures. Service is doting, though a bit aloof—you won't always be received by smiling faces, but you will get whatever you want. There's even room service exclusively for pets (you know the type: held hostage in Mummy's Gucci bag). A large hotel by Palm Beach standards (the Breakers notwithstanding), Brazilian Court sprawls over half a block and features fountains and private courtyards. Celebrity stylist Frederick Fekkai offers the hotel's premier salon and spa. With the recent addition of renowned chef Daniel Boulud's hauter-than-thou Café Boulud (which provides stellar 24-hr. room service), Brazilian Court has replaced the Italian mainstay Bice Restaurant (p. 303) as Palm Beach's number-one place to see and be seen.

301 Australian Ave., Palm Beach, FL 33480. © 800/552-0335 or 561/655-7740. Fax 561/655-0801. www.thebrazilian court.com. 103 units. Winter $335–$525 double, $550–$875 suite; off season $165–$315 double, $350–$525 suite. Special packages available. AE, DC, DISC, MC, V. **Amenities:** Restaurant; private dining room (up to 12); heated outdoor pool; exercise room; spa treatments; concierge; salon; 24-hr. room service; library. *In room:* A/C, TV, minibar, coffeemaker, hair dryer, iron.

The Breakers ✸✸✸ *(Kids)*   This 140-acre beachfront hotel is what Palm Beach is all about. Elaborate, stately, and resplendent in all its Italian Renaissance–style glory, it's where old money mixes with new money, and the Old World gives way, albeit reluctantly, to a bit of modernity.

The Breakers consists of a seven-story building with a frescoed lobby and long, majestic hallways reminiscent of a palace. Elegant guest rooms feature plush furnishings, huge bathrooms, and views of the ocean or of the hotel's magnificently manicured grounds. If you can afford it, the Flagler Club is the Breakers' exclusive, hyperluxe hotel within a hotel, featuring private entry, 28 rooms, butlers, concierges, and doting service, as well as tea, cocktails, hors d'oeuvres, and desserts all day and night. Delightful chief concierge Bernard Nicole has a wealth of local lore.

The indulgent oceanfront spa and beach club features a spectacular fitness center (the ocean view makes workouts a lot less grueling), four pools, cabanas, and saunas. Treatments at the sublime spa are aplenty, filling up a 16-page book. Ask for one upon arrival and marvel at the spa-portunities. A revamp of Florida's oldest existing golf course, led by Brian Silva, transformed the Ocean Course into a 6,200-yard, championship-level par-70. For those who need a few lessons before hitting the greens, **Todd Anderson Golf Academy** (© **561/659-8474**; www.tagolf.com) will assist you in finding your zone with world-class instruction by PGA members and apprentices. While Daddy and Mommy are playing golf, the kids can hang out at the Family Entertainment Center, a 6,160-square-foot space filled with video games, air hockey, board games, a movie room, Xbox games, and several supervised camps. I have to say that, despite the magnificence of the adult facilities, the kids' area is most impressive.

Each of the resort's five restaurants holds its own, especially the oceanfront Seafood Bar and signature French restaurant L'Escalier. Do not miss the decadent Sunday brunch at the Circle, the magnificent dining room with to-die-for ocean views.

1 S. County Rd., Palm Beach, FL 33480. © **800/833-3141**, 888/BREAKERS, or 561/655-6611. Fax 561/659-8403. www.thebreakers.com. 560 units. Winter $420–$675 double, $700–$3,000 suite; off season $270–$425 double, $500–$1,950 suite. Special packages available. AE, DC, DISC, MC, V. Valet parking $17. From I-95, exit Okeechobee Blvd. E., head east to S. County Rd., and turn left. **Amenities:** 5 restaurants; 3 bars; 4 outdoor pools; golf course; 14 tennis courts; health club and spa; croquet; shuffleboard; beach volleyball courts; watersports equipment (including scuba and sailing); bike rental; children's programs; game rooms; concierge; business center; shopping arcade; salon; 24-hr. room service; in-room massage; babysitting; laundry service; dry cleaning. *In room:* A/C, TV, CD player, PlayStation, dataport, minibar, hair dryer, iron.

Four Seasons Resort Palm Beach 👫👫 (Kids)   Built in 1989 on the pristine Palm Beach oceanfront, this elegant resort has gained accolades from around the world. An incredibly hospitable staff works hard to be sure this beachfront gem lives up to its reputation. The elegant marble lobby is replete with a diverse collection of art, artifacts, and dramatic flower arrangements. Guest rooms are spacious, with private balconies and lavish bathrooms with color TVs. The full-service spa is excellent, and don't miss experiencing an incredible massage at a poolside cabana. The main dining room, known simply as The Restaurant, features the Southeastern regional cuisine of executive chef Hubert Des Marais. Two other less-formal restaurants, The Ocean Bistro and The Atlantic Bar & Grill, round out the dining options. The resort offers a complimentary kids program, and teens will enjoy the game room with Xbox, a pool table, and a large-screen TV. Meanwhile, parents can entertain themselves in The Living Room, a swank lounge featuring live jazz on weekends.

2800 S. Ocean Blvd., Palm Beach, FL 33480. © **800/432-2335** or 561/582-2800. Fax 561/547-1557. www.four seasons.com/palmbeach. 210 units. Winter $445–$775 double, from $1,900 suite. Off season $290–$550 double, from $1,125 suite. AE, DC, DISC, MC, V. Valet parking $21. From I-95, take the 6th Ave. exit east and turn left onto Dixie Hwy. Turn east onto Lake Ave. and north onto A1A (S. Ocean Blvd.); the resort is just ahead on your right. Pets under 20 lbs. accepted. **Amenities:** 3 restaurants; lounge; outdoor heated pool and whirlpool; 2 tennis courts; spa and fitness center; watersports equipment rentals; complimentary children's programs; concierge; business center; salon; 24-hr. room service; in-room massage; babysitting; laundry service; dry cleaning; monthly cooking classes. *In room:* A/C, TV/VCR/DVD, CD/MP3 player, high-speed Internet access, minibar, fridge, hair dryer, iron, safe, robes.

Ritz-Carlton Palm Beach ⭐⭐⭐   If the Breakers is too mammoth for your taste, consider the Ritz-Carlton. A lot warmer than the Four Seasons, The Ritz, though hyperluxurious, manages to lack pretension. Located on a beautiful beach in a tiny town about 8 miles from Palm Beach's shopping and dining area, the resort offers tennis courts with pros, a creative Ritz Kids program, and an extensive watersports facilities onsite. It is so discreet, in fact, that Palm Beach's luminaries often escape here for a rare weekend of anonymity. The hotel's French 18th- and 19th-century antique furnishings give no hint that the property is not even 15 years old. Each guest room has a private balcony and at least a glimpse of the ocean below. All are spacious, and the large marble bathrooms are extremely inviting. The specialty restaurant, The Grill, is open for dinner only; a casual oceanfront restaurant called Soleil features contemporary American fare with fresh seafood. There's also a poolside cafe and bar. Cocktails are served in the lobby lounge, where you can find live entertainment on weekends. Afternoon tea is available most days but is best on Friday, when guests can enjoy the hotel's Art Tour as well. The Ritz completed a $15-million guest room renovation in December 2005, including the introduction of 32-inch LCD HDTV flat-screens, bedside electronic control panels, new mahogany furniture, and sleeper chairs and sofas in guest rooms and suites.

100 S. Ocean Blvd., Manalapan, FL 33462. © **800/241-3333** or 561/533-6000. Fax 561/588-4202. www.ritzcarlton. com. 284 units. Winter $559–$789 double, $939 suite, $4,000 Presidential suite; off season $239–$359 double, $459 suite, $4,000 Presidential suite. AE, DISC, MC, V. Valet parking $20. From I-95, take exit for Lantana Rd., heading east. After 1 mile, turn right onto Federal Hwy. (U.S. 1- Dixie). Continue south to the next light and turn left onto Ocean Ave. Cross the Intracoastal Waterway and turn right onto Fla. A1A. **Amenities:** 4 restaurants; bar; outdoor pool; fitness and massage center; Jacuzzi; sauna; watersports equipment rental; bike rental; children's center/programs; concierge; business center; salon; 24-hr. room service; in-room massage; laundry service; dry cleaning. *In room:* A/C, TV, wireless dataport, minibar, hair dryer, iron, safe.

EXPENSIVE

Chesterfield Hotel ⭐⭐⭐   Reminiscent of an English country manor, the Chesterfield in all its flowery, Laura Ashley–inspired glory is a magnificent, charming hotel with exceptional service. Warm and inviting, the Chesterfield is one of the only places in South Florida in which the idea of a fireplace (there's one in the hotel's library) doesn't seem ridiculous. Traditional English tea is served every afternoon, featuring fresh-baked scones, petit fours, and sandwiches. Rooms are decorated with antiques and with bright fabrics and wallpaper. The roomy marble bathrooms are stocked with an array of luxurious toiletries. A small heated pool and courtyard are nice, and the beach is only 3 blocks away, but the real action is inside: The hotel's retro-elegant Leopard Lounge (p. 305) serves decent Continental cuisine, but is better as a late-night hangout for live music, schmoozing, and staring at the local cognoscenti.

363 Cocoanut Row, Palm Beach, FL 33480. © **800/243-7871** or 561/659-5800. Fax 561/659-6707. www.chesterfield pb.com. 65 units. Winter $395–$500 double, $750 suite; off season $230–$295 double, $350 suite. Rollaway bed $15 extra. Packages available. AE, DC, DISC, MC, V. Free valet parking. From I-95, exit onto Okeechobee Blvd. E., cross the Intracoastal Waterway, and turn right onto Cocoanut Row. **Amenities:** Restaurant; lounge; small heated pool; access to nearby health club; Jacuzzi; bike rental; concierge; business center; 24-hr. room service; in-room massage; babysitting; dry cleaning. *In room:* A/C, TV, VCR on request, dataport, hair dryer, iron, safe.

MODERATE

The Colony ⭐⭐   The sign outside of this Palm Beach mainstay should read ROXANNE PULITZER SLEPT HERE. She did, actually, for quite a while after her 7-week marriage went bust. For years, the Colony has been a favorite hangout—hideout, perhaps—for old-timers, socialites, and mysterious luminaries. Beyond that, this Georgian-style hotel is known for its attentive staff, floral-decorated guest rooms, and, unfortunately, really small bathrooms. The 39 suites and apartments, not to mention the seven two-bedroom villas with Jacuzzis, are much more lavish—and lavishly priced.

155 Hammon Ave., Palm Beach, FL 33480. ℂ 800/521-5525 or 561/655-5430. Fax 561/659-8104. www.thecolony palmbeach.com. 85 units, 7 villas. Winter $290–$450 double, $475–$695 suite; off season $169–$225 double, $225–$575 suite. AE, DC, MC, V. From I-95, exit onto Okeechobee Blvd. E. and cross the Intracoastal Waterway. Turn right on S. County Rd. and then left onto Hammon Ave. **Amenities:** Restaurant; bar; heated Florida-shape pool; spa; concierge; limited seasonal room service. In room: A/C, TV, dataport, hair dryer, iron.

Palm Beach Historic Inn 𝒶𝒶   Built in 1923, the Palm Beach Historic Inn is an area landmark within a block's walking distance of the beach (chairs and towels are provided for guests of the hotel), Worth Avenue, and several good restaurants. The small lobby is filled with antiques, books, magazines, and an old-fashioned umbrella stand, all of which add to the homey feel of this intimate B&B. In-room wine, fruit, snacks, tea, and cookies ensure that you won't go hungry—never mind the excellent continental breakfast that is brought to you daily. All bedrooms are uniquely deco-rated and feature hardwood floors, down comforters, Egyptian-cotton linens, fluffy bathrobes, and plenty of good-smelling toiletries. Here you'll find a casual elegance that's comfortable for everyone. In addition, a baby grand piano and guitars for the musically inclined, as well as videotapes to keep the kids entertained, have been added to the hotel's amenities. *Note:* Smoking is not permitted.

365 S. County Rd., Palm Beach, FL 33480. ℂ 561/832-4009. Fax 561/832-6255. www.palmbeachhistoricinn.com. 13 units. Winter $200–$235 double, $315–$405 suite; off season $110–$135 double, $195–$225 suite. Rates include continental breakfast. Children stay free in parent's room. AE, MC, V. Small pets accepted. In room: A/C, TV/VCR, fridge, hair dryer, iron.

INEXPENSIVE
Gulfstream Hotel 𝒶   Just over the bridge from glitzy, glammy Palm Beach is Lake Worth, not exactly a hotbed of activity; nonetheless, this sleepy enclave is peaceful and very popular for no-frills relaxation. The only game in town is the Gulfstream Hotel, a historic property on the Intracoastal Waterway whose rooms are comfortable but nothing to look at. The pool here is functional but, again, nothing to look at. Perhaps the most appealing feature is the lobby, reminiscent of an old Deep South hotel with high ceilings, paddle fans, and free cookies at the check-in desk. The focal point of activity is the restaurant, Daniel's Lake Ave. Grill, a comfortable wood-floored dining room serving excellent seafood, meat, and pasta dishes; it transforms itself into a ver-itable disco on Friday and Saturday—the only form of nightlife in town. If you're looking to experience the Palm Beaches casually and comfortably without feeling like you have to get decked out to leave your hotel room, the Gulfstream is a great option—not to mention a bargain compared to the ritzier hotels over the bridge.

1 Lake Ave., Lake Worth, FL 33460. ℂ 888/540-0669 or 561/540-6000. Fax 561/582-6904. www.thegulfstreamhotel. com. 106 units. Winter $149 double, $259–$339 suite; off season $99 double, $259–$339 suite. AE, DC, DISC, V. Free self-parking. **Amenities:** Restaurant; bar; pool bar; outdoor pool; concierge; limited room service. In room: A/C, TV, dataport, coffeemaker, hair dryer, iron.

Hibiscus House 𝒶𝒶 *(Finds)*   Inexpensive bed-and-breakfasts are rare in Southeast Florida, making the Hibiscus House, one of the area's firsts, a true find. Located a few miles from the coast in a quiet residential neighborhood, this 1920s-era B&B is filled with handsome antiques and tapestries. Every room has a private terrace or balcony. The Red Room has a fabulous bathroom with Jacuzzi. The peaceful backyard retreat has been transformed into a tropical garden, with a heated pool and lounge chairs.

There are pretty indoor areas for guests to enjoy; one little sitting room is wrapped in glass and is stocked with playing cards and board games. Huge gourmet breakfast portions are as filling as they are beautiful. Make any special requests in advance; owners Raleigh Hill and Colin Rayer will be happy to oblige.

501 30th St., West Palm Beach, FL 33407. (© 800/203-4927 or 561/863-5633. Fax 561/863-5633. www.hibiscus house.com. 8 units. Winter $125–$210 double; off season $95–$150 double. Rates include breakfast. AE, DC, DISC, MC, V. From I-95, exit onto Palm Beach Lakes Blvd. E. and continue 4 miles. Turn left onto Flagler Dr. and continue for about ½ mile; then turn left onto 30th St. Pets accepted. **Amenities:** Heated pool; concierge. *In room:* A/C, TV, hair dryer.

Hotel Biba ★★ *(Finds)*   As West Palm Beach came into its own in terms of nightlife, it was only a matter of time before a boutique hotel made its appearance in the historic El Cid neighborhood, located 1 mile from City Place and nightlife-heavy Clematis Street. The very cool Biba answers the call for an inexpensive, chic hotel that young hipsters can call their own. Housed in a renovated Colonial-style 1940s motor lodge, Biba has been remarkably updated by de rigueur designer Barbara Hulanicki and now features a sleek lobby with the requisite hip hotel bar, a gorgeously landscaped outdoor pool area with Asian gardens, and a reflection pond. Guest rooms are equally fabulous, with private patios, mosaic-tile floors, custom-made mahogany furniture, Egyptian-cotton linens, down pillows, exquisite bathroom products, and high-tech amenities. The bold color schemes mix nicely with the high-fashion crowd that convenes here. *A word of advice:* This place is not exactly soundproof. Rooms may be cloistered by fence and gardens, but they're still extremely close to a major thoroughfare. Ask for a room that's on the quieter Belvedere Road, as opposed to those facing South Olive Avenue.

320 Belvedere Rd., West Palm Beach, FL 33405. (© **561/832-0094.** Fax 561/833-7848. www.hotelbiba.com. 43 units. Year-round $109–$170 double; $130–$190 suite. Online rates are cheaper. AE, DC, MC, V. **Amenities:** Lounge; outdoor pool; concierge. *In room:* A/C, TV, CD player, dataport, hair dryer.

WHERE TO DINE

Palm Beach has some of the area's swankiest restaurants. Thanks to the development of downtown West Palm Beach, however, there is also a great selection of trendier, less expensive spots. Dress here is slightly more formal than in most other areas of Florida: Men wear blazers, and women generally put on modest dresses or chic suits when they dine out, even on the oppressively hot days of summer.

In addition to the listings below, you may want to check out City Place's new **Coach Schnellenberger's Original Steakhouse & Sports Theater,** 700 S. Rosemary Ave., West Palm Beach (© **561/833-1400**), which features an exhibition kitchen, a mesquite grill, beef aged and cut on the premises, rotisserie chicken, lobster and fresh fish, and hand-spun ice cream in a sports fanatic–friendly environment.

VERY EXPENSIVE

Café Boulud ★★★ FRENCH   Snowbird socialites rejoiced over the opening of star chef Daniel Boulud's eponymous restaurant in the Brazilian Court hotel. Nonsocialites said, "Figures, another restaurant where we can't afford even a bread crumb." If you're out to splurge, Boulud is ideal, with an exquisite menu divided into four sections—La Tradition (French and American classics), La Saison (seasonal dishes), Le Potager (dishes inspired by the vegetable market), and Le Voyage (world cuisine). Grilled Colorado lamb with wilted romaine, Greek yogurt, coriander, and cumin is spectacular and almost worth all $38 you'll pay for it. The chickpea fries are a bargain at $6, but you'll be frowned upon if you snag a coveted table and just order those. If star chefs, stuffy socialites, and froufrou cuisine aren't your thing, don't even bother.

In the Brazilian Court, 301 Australian Ave., Palm Beach. ✆ 561/655-6060. Reservations essential. Main courses $17–$40. AE, DC, MC, V. Daily 9am–10pm.

Cafe l'Europe ✦✦✦ CONTINENTAL   One of Palm Beach's finest and most popular, this award-winning, romantic, and formal restaurant gives you a good reason to get dressed up. The enticing appetizers served by a superb staff might include Chinese spring rolls, baked-goat-cheese salad with raspberry-walnut dressing, poached salmon, or chilled gazpacho with avocado. Main courses run the gamut from sautéed potato-crusted Florida snapper to roast Cornish game hen. Seafood dishes and steaks in sumptuous but light sauces are always exceptional.

331 S. County Rd. (at Brazilian Ave.), Palm Beach. ✆ 561/655-4020. Reservations recommended. Main courses $18–$34. AE, DC, DISC, MC, V. Tues–Sat noon–3pm; Tues–Sun 6–10pm.

Echo ✦✦ ASIAN   Don't think that because this hyperstylish, New York–ish restaurant is located by the overly commercial City Place that it's either commercial or affordable. When I ate here with a group of eight, we ordered a sushi platter that ended up costing $300. Outrageous! The ridiculously expensive sushi is, indeed, delicious, as is the Peking duck and pretty much every Thai, Vietnamese, Indonesian, Japanese, and Chinese dish, but there are other places to go for those. Instead, check out the groovy bar area, have cocktails, and share a few pieces of sushi to get the vibe without breaking the bank and hearing those echoes in your empty wallet.

230 Sunrise Ave., Palm Beach. ✆ 561/802-4222. Reservations essential. Main courses $25–$50. AE, DC, MC, V. Tues–Sun 5:30–9:30pm.

Mark's City Place ✦✦✦ NEW AMERICAN   Star chef Mark Militello of Mark's Las Olas and South Beach has landed at West Palm's bustling entertainment-and-dining complex to the delight of foodies in Palm Beach. Wood-burning ovens churn out Militello's specialty pizzas, trendy versions of the thin-crusted classic with toppings such as shrimp, pesto, fontina cheese, and sun-dried tomatoes. The sushi bar here is, frankly, out of place. Focus on entrees that range from risotto with wild mushroom and truffle oil to a seared, black peppercorn–crusted yellowfin tuna. For dessert, try the double-chocolate bread pudding with white-chocolate-chip ice cream.

700 S. Rosemary Ave., West Palm Beach. ✆ 561/514-0770. www.chefmark.com. Reservations recommended. Main courses $17–$38. AE, DC, MC, V. Mon–Thurs 5–11pm; Fri–Sat 5pm–midnight; Sun 5–10:30pm.

Tsunami ✦✦✦ SUSHI   If you're a sushi lover, this place is worth every precious penny you'll pay. One of West Palm's hot spots, Tsunami is reminiscent of a New York City eatery, where the reservations book reads like *Hollywood Reporter*. Instead of celebrities, this place caters to the chichi crowds of Palm Beach, who actually cross the bridge for some of the freshest fish this side of Japan. Although we thought they'd change the name after the 2005 disaster in Thailand, they stuck it out with excellent food and drink to make people forget the unfortunate connection.

651 Okeechobee Blvd., West Palm Beach. ✆ 561/835-9696. Reservations required. Main courses $6–$75. AE, DISC, MC, V. Sun–Wed 5–10pm; Thurs–Sat 5–11:30pm.

EXPENSIVE

Amici ✦ *Overrated* ITALIAN   This is one of those restaurants whose scene is tastier than its cuisine. An upper-crusty Palm Beach set convenes here and consistently raves about above-average, overpriced Italian food. The best item on the menu is gnocchi with white truffle oil, fontina cheese, and spinach. Everything else is fairly standard: grilled sandwiches, pastas with rustic sauces, pizzas, grilled shrimp, and fish. Despite its less-than-stellar food, Amici is always crowded and very noisy.

288 S. County Rd. (at Royal Palm Way), Palm Beach. ✆ **561/832-0201**. Reservations strongly recommended on weekends. Main courses $18–$27; pastas and pizzas $8–$19. AE, DC, MC, V. Mon–Thurs 11:30am–3pm and 5:30–10:30pm; Fri–Sat 11:30am–3pm and 5:30–11pm; Sun 5:30–10:30pm.

Bice Restaurant ★★ NORTHERN ITALIAN Bice's cuisine far surpasses that of Amici's, but as far as atmosphere, the air in here is a bit haughty, bordering on rude. Servers and diners alike have attitudes, but you'll forget all that with one bite of the juicy veal cutlet with tomato salad or the *pasta e fagioli* (pasta with beans).

313½ Worth Ave., Palm Beach. ✆ **561/835-1600**. Reservations essential. Main courses $20–$32. AE, DC, MC, V. Daily noon–10pm.

MODERATE

Big City Tavern ★★ AMERICAN If the Palm Beach–proper dining scene is too stuffy, head over the bridge to Clematis Street to find this yuppie brick-and-pressed-tin enclave where people-watching is at a premium. Despite its all-American appearance, Big City Tavern offers a varied menu, including coconut-shrimp tempura with a salmon inside-out sushi roll and a delicious bowl of littleneck clams in wine broth with roasted garlic and escarole. The place is mobbed on weekends, so plan for a long wait that's best spent at the action-packed bar.

224 Clematis St., West Palm Beach. ✆ **561/659-1853**. Reservations suggested. Main courses $7.95–$28. AE, MC, V. Daily 10:30am–2pm; Sun–Tues 5:30–10:30pm; Wed–Sat 5:30pm–midnight.

Rhythm Café ★ *Finds* ECLECTIC AMERICAN This funky hole-in-the-wall is where those in the know come to eat some of West Palm Beach's most laid-back gourmet food. On the handwritten, photocopied menu (which changes daily), you'll always find a fish specialty accompanied by a hefty dose of greens and garnishes. Reliably outstanding is the sautéed medallion of beef tenderloin, served on arugula with a tangy rosemary vinaigrette. Salads and soups are a great bargain, since portions are relatively large. The kitschy decor of this tiny cafe comes complete with vinyl tablecloths and a changing display of paintings by local amateurs. Young, handsome waiters are attentive but not solicitous. The old drugstore where the restaurant recently relocated features an original 1950s lunch counter and stools.

3800 S. Dixie Hwy., West Palm Beach. ✆ **561/833-3406**. Reservations recommended on weekends. Main courses $12–$31. AE, DISC, MC, V. Tues–Sat 6–10pm; Sun (Dec–Mar) 5:30–9pm. Closed in early Sept. From I-95, exit east on Southern Blvd. Go 1 block north of Southern Blvd.; restaurant is on the right.

INEXPENSIVE

Green's Pharmacy ★ *Value* AMERICAN This neighborhood pharmacy offers one of the best meal deals in Palm Beach. Both breakfast and lunch are served coffee-shop style, either at a Formica bar or at tables on a black-and-white checkerboard floor. Breakfast specials include eggs and omelets served with home fries and bacon, sausage, or corned-beef hash. The grill serves burgers and sandwiches, as well as ice-cream sodas and milkshakes, to a loyal crowd of pastel-clad Palm Beachers.

151 N. County Rd., Palm Beach. ✆ **561/832-0304**. Fax 561/832-6502. Breakfast $2–$5; burgers and sandwiches $3–$6; soups and salads $2–$7. AE, DISC, MC, V. Mon–Sat 7am–5pm; Sun 7am–3pm.

John G's ★ AMERICAN This coffee shop is the most popular in the county. For decades, John G's has been attracting huge breakfast crowds; lines run out the door (on weekends, all the way down the block). Stop in for good, greasy-spoon food served in heaping portions right on the beachfront. This place is known for fresh and tasty fish and chips, and its selection of creative omelets and grill specials.

10 S. Ocean Blvd., Lake Worth. ℂ 561/585-9860. www.johngs.com. Reservations not accepted. Breakfast $3–$8.50; lunch $5–$14. No credit cards. Daily 7am–3pm. From the Florida Tpk., take the Lake Worth exit and head toward the ocean.

Tom's Place 🕸🕸 *Finds* BARBECUE There are two important factors in a successful barbecue: the cooking and the sauce. Tom and Helen Wright's no-nonsense shack wins on both counts, offering flawlessly grilled meats paired with well-spiced sauces. Beef, chicken, pork, and fish are served soul-food style, with your choice of sides such as rice with gravy, collard greens, black-eyed peas, coleslaw, or mashed potatoes. There's another very popular branch of Tom's in Boca Raton at 7251 N. Federal Highway (ℂ **561/997-0920**).

1225 Palm Beach Lakes Blvd., West Palm Beach. ℂ 561/832-8774. Reservations not accepted. Main courses $8–$15; sandwiches $5–$6; early-bird special $7.95. AE, MC, V. Tues–Thurs 11:30am–10:30pm; Fri 11:30am–10pm; Sat noon–10pm.

THE PALM BEACHES AFTER DARK
THE BAR, CAFE & MUSIC SCENE

A decade-old project to revitalize downtown West Palm Beach has finally become a reality, with **Clematis Street** at its heart. Artists' lofts, sidewalk cafes, bars, restaurants, consignment shops, and galleries dot the street from Flagler Drive to Rosemary Avenue, creating a hot spot for a night out, especially on weekends, when yuppies mingle with stylish Euros and disheveled artists. Every Thursday night is a mob scene of 20- and 30-somethings who come out for "Clematis by Night." Each week features a different rock, blues, or reggae band, plus an art show. Vendors sell food and drinks, and the street's bars and restaurants are packed. Most of the nightspots listed below are open until about 3 or 4am.

Over the bridge, it's a completely different world. Palm Beach is much quieter and better known for its rather private society balls and estate parties. With the exception of some restaurants that are more of a scene (such as **Amici,** described above, or **Ta-boo,** reviewed below), Palm Beach nightlife is more likely to entail sipping port at one of the finer hotels like the Breakers, Colony, Ritz-Carlton, Four Seasons, or Chesterfield.

West Palm Beach

E. R. Bradley's What used to be a swank saloon on the island of Palm Beach is now a friendly, very casual indoor/outdoor bar in downtown West Palm, attracting a mixed crowd. The later-night bar scene is a real draw. If you're hungry, try the "crab bomb," Maryland lump crabmeat baked in a light cream sauce with steamed vegetables. Open Sunday through Wednesday from 8am to 3am, Thursday through Saturday from 8am to 4am. 104 Clematis St. ℂ 561/833-3520.

Monkey Club This tacky yet trendy Caribbean-inspired dance club is 7,500 square feet of wall-to-wall, well-dressed revelers. Theme nights are popular here, from ladies' night to the classier version of the wet T-shirt contest—the Miss Hawaiian Tropic Model Search. Open Thursday through Saturday from 9pm to 3am. 219 Clematis St. ℂ 561/833-6500. Cover $0–$10.

Respectable Street Café This is one of the premier live-music venues in South Florida. In addition to the requisite DJs, the grungy bar features a lineup of alternative-music acts. The plain storefront exterior belies a funky, high-ceilinged interior, decorated with large black booths, psychedelic wall murals, and a checkerboard-tile dance floor. Open Wednesday and Thursday from 9pm to 3am, Friday and Saturday from 9pm to 4am. 518 Clematis St. ℂ 561/832-9999. Cover $5–$20.

Palm Beach
Leopard Lounge *(finds)*   *The Flintstones* meets *Dynasty* at this spotty lounge in the Chesterfield Hotel, in which the carpeting, tablecloths, and waitstaff's waistcoats are all in leopard print. There's live music every night, ranging from Cole Porter to swing. The crowd's a bit older, but younger couples and a celebrity or two often find their way here, which makes for an amusing scene. Open daily from 6pm to 1:30am. 363 Cocoanut Row. ℂ 561/659-5800.

Ta-boo   Ta-boo is reminiscent of an upscale TGI Friday's (with food that's about on the same level). It caters to a well-heeled crowd, with lots of greenery, a fireplace, and a somewhat cheesy Southwestern decor. But make no mistake, Ta-boo is not about the food: This stellar after-dinner spot is where bejeweled socialites spill out of fancy cars to salsa and show off their best Swarovski. Find someplace else to eat first. Open Sunday through Thursday from 11:30am to 10pm, and Friday and Saturday from 11:30am to 11pm. 221 Worth Ave., Palm Beach. ℂ 561/835-3500.

GAMBLING
The ***Palm Beach Princess*** (ℂ 800/841-7447 or 561/845-7447) is a 421-foot cruise ship offering affordable casino gambling cruises out of the Port of Palm Beach (U.S. 1 between 45th St. and Blue Heron Blvd.) every day and evening. Choose from craps, roulette, poker, blackjack, and slots. Cruises offer a large buffet with food like spaghetti, chicken, Greek salad, and vegetables; best is the prime rib at the carving board. Cruises sail daily between 11am and 4:30pm, and 6:30 and 11:45pm. Friday and Saturday evening cruises run from 6:30pm to 12:30am. Sunday cruises sail from 11am to 5pm and 6:30 to 11:30pm. Prices are $20 per person Monday through Friday, $25 Saturday and Sunday. Florida-resident, AARP, and AAA discounts are available.

THE PERFORMING ARTS
With a number of dedicated patrons and enthusiastic supporters of the arts, this area happily boasts many good venues for those craving culture. Check the *Palm Beach Post* or the *Palm Beach Daily News* for up-to-date listings and reviews.

The **Raymond F. Kravis Center for the Performing Arts,** 701 Okeechobee Blvd., West Palm Beach (ℂ **561/832-7469;** www.kravis.org), is the area's largest and most active performance space. With a huge curved-glass facade and more than 2,500 seats in two lushly decorated indoor spaces, plus a new outdoor amphitheater, the Kravis stages more than 300 performances each year. Phone or check the website for a current schedule of Palm Beach's best music, dance, and theater.

4 Jupiter ⍟ & Northern Palm Beach County ⍟

20 miles N of Palm Beach, 81 miles N of Miami, 60 miles N of Fort Lauderdale

While Burt Reynolds is Jupiter's hometown hero (and Celine Dion just built a sprawling manse here, too), the stars of quaint Jupiter are its beautiful beaches. In the spring, you can also catch the St. Louis Cardinals during their spring-training season. North Palm Beach County's other towns—Tequesta, Juno Beach, North Palm Beach, Palm Beach Gardens, and Singer Island—invite tourists who want to enjoy the outdoor activities that make this area so popular with retirees, seasonal residents, and families.

ESSENTIALS

GETTING THERE   The quickest route from West Palm Beach to Jupiter is on the Florida Turnpike or the sometimes-congested I-95. You can also take a slower but more scenic coastal route, U.S. 1 or Florida A1A. Since Jupiter is so close to Palm Beach, it's easy to fly into **Palm Beach International Airport** (© **561/471-7420**) and rent a car there. The drive should take less than half an hour.

VISITOR INFORMATION   A **visitor center** located between I-95 and the Florida Turnpike at 8020 Indiantown Rd., Jupiter (© **561/575-4636;** www.jupiterfloridausa. com), is open Monday through Friday from 8:30am to 5:30pm.

BEACHES, OUTDOOR ACTIVITIES & SPECTATOR SPORTS

BASEBALL   The **Roger Dean Stadium,** 4751 Main St. (© **561/775-1818**), hosts spring training for the St. Louis Cardinals, along with minor-league action from Florida's state league, the Hammerheads. Tickets range in price from $8 to $20. Call for schedules and information.

BEACHES   The farther north you head from populated Palm Beach, the more peaceful and pristine the coast becomes. Just a few miles north of the bustle, castles and condominiums give way to wide-open space and public parkland. There are dozens of recommendable spots. The following are a few of the best.

John D. MacArthur Beach is a spectacular beach that preserves the subtropical coastal habitat that once covered Southeast Florida. This state park has a remarkable 4,000-square-foot Nature Center with exhibits, displays, and a video interpreting the barrier island's plant and animal communities. Dominating a large portion of Singer Island, the barrier island just north of Palm Beach, this beach has frontage on both the Atlantic Ocean and Lake Worth Cove. It's great for hiking, swimming, and sunning. Restrooms and showers are available. To reach the park from the mainland, cross the Intracoastal Waterway on Blue Heron Boulevard and turn north on Ocean Boulevard.

Jupiter Inlet meets the ocean at **Dubois Park,** a 29-acre beach that's popular with families. The shallow waters and sandy shore are perfect for kids, while adults can play in the rougher swells of the lifeguarded inlet. A footbridge leads to **Ocean Beach,** an area popular with windsurfers and surfers. There's a short fishing pier and plenty of shaded barbecue grills and picnic tables. Explore the Dubois Pioneer Home, situated atop a shell mound built by the Jaega Indians. The home was built of cypress in 1898 by Harry Dubois, a citrus worker, as a wedding gift to his wife, Susan, whose pictures are still in the house. The butter churn, the pump sewing machine in the living room, and the dining room and bedroom are straight out of *Little House on the Prairie.* The park entrance is on Dubois Road, about a mile south of the junction of U.S. 1 and Florida A1A.

BIKING   Bike enthusiasts will enjoy exploring this flat and uncluttered area. North Palm Beach has hundreds of miles of smooth, paved roads. Loggerhead Park in Juno Beach and Florida A1A along the ocean also have great trails for starters. You'll find many more scenic routes over the bridges and west of the highway. Rent a bike at **Jupiter Outdoor Center,** 18095 Coastal A1A, in Jupiter (© **561/747-9666**).

CANOEING   You can rent a boat at several outlets throughout northern Palm Beach County, including **Canoe Outfitters,** 9060 W. Indiantown Rd. (west of I-95), in North Jupiter (© **561/746-7053;** www.canoes-kayaks-florida.com), which provides access to one of the area's most beautiful natural waterways. Canoers start at Riverbend Park along an 8-mile stretch of Intracoastal Waterway, where the lush foliage supports dozens of exotic birds and reptiles. Keep your eyes open for gators, who love to sunbathe on the shallow shores of the river. You'll end up, exhausted, at Jonathan Dickinson Park about 5 or 6 hours later. A pamphlet describing local flora and fauna is available for $1. Trips run Thursday through Monday and cost $40 for two people in a double canoe. Guided trips are also available for $35 per person.

CRUISES   Several sightseeing cruises offer tours of the magnificent waterways that make up northern Palm Beach County. Water taxis conduct daily narrated tours through the scenic waters. One interesting excursion that will take you past the mansions of the rich and famous, and possibly past the manatees swimming off the port of Palm Beach, departs from **Panama Hatties,** at PGA Boulevard and the Intracoastal Waterway. Prices for the 2-hour ride are $17 for adults, $15 for seniors, and $9 for children under 12. Call *©* **561/775-2628** for information. The *Manatee Queen,* 1065 N. Ocean Blvd. (at the Crab House), Jupiter (*©* **561/744-2191**), is a 40-foot catamaran with bench seating for up to 49 people. Two-hour tours of Jupiter Island depart daily at 2:30pm, passing Burt Reynolds's and Perry Como's former mansions, among other spots of historic and natural interest. There's also a daily sunset cruise from 5 to 6:30pm. Reservations are highly recommended, especially in season; call for the current schedule. Prices are $19 for adults and $12 for children 6 to 12. Bring your own lunch, or purchase chips and sodas at the snack bar.

FISHING   Before you leave, order an information-packed fishing kit with details on fish camps, charters, and tournament and tide schedules; it's distributed by the **West Palm Beach Fishing Club** (*©* **561/832-6780**). The cost is $10 and well worth it. Allow at least 4 weeks for delivery.

   In town, several outfitters along U.S. 1 and Florida A1A rent vessels and equipment if your hotel doesn't. One of the most complete facilities is **Sailfish Marina & Resort,** 98 Lake Dr. (off Blue Heron Blvd.), Palm Beach Shores (*©* **561/844-1724**). Call for equipment, bait, guided trips, or boat rentals.

GOLF   Even if you're not lucky enough to be staying at the **PGA National Resort & Spa** (p. 309), you may still be able to play on its award-winning courses. If you or someone in your group is a member of another golf or country club, have the head pro write a note on club letterhead to Jackie Rogers at PGA to request a play date. Be sure the pro includes his PGA number and contact information. Allow at least 2 weeks for a response. Also ask about the "Golf-A-Round" program, in which selected private clubs open their doors to nonmembers for free or discounted rates. Contact **Palm Beach County Convention and Visitors Bureau** (*©* **561/471-3995**) for details.

   Dotting the area are plenty of other great courses, including the **Golf Club of Jupiter,** 1800 Central Blvd., Jupiter (*©* **561/747-6262**), where a well-respected 18-hole, par-70 course is situated on more than 6,200 yards of narrow fairways and fast greens. Fees are $31 until noon, $27 after noon, and $22 after 2pm; they include a mandatory cart. The course borders I-95, so watch your swing.

HIKING   In an area that's not particularly known for extraordinary natural diversity, **Blowing Rocks Preserve** has a terrific hiking trail along a dramatic limestone outcropping. You won't find hills or scenic vistas, but you will see Florida's unique and varied tropical ecosystem. The well-marked, mile-long trail passes oceanfront dunes, mangrove wetlands, and a coastal hammock. The preserve, owned and managed by the Nature Conservancy, 574 South Beach Rd., Hobe Sound, FL 33455 (*©* **561/744-6668**), also protects an important habitat for West Indian manatees and loggerhead

Discovering a Remarkable Natural World

North Palm Beach is well known for the giant sea turtles that lay their eggs on the county's beaches from May to August. These endangered marine animals return here annually, from as far away as South America, to lay their clutches of about 115 eggs each. Nurtured by the warm sand, but targeted by birds and other predators, only about one or two babies from each nest survive to maturity.

Many environmentalists recommend that visitors take part in an organized turtle-watching program (rather than go on their own), to minimize disturbance to the turtles. **Jupiter Beach Resort** (p. 309) sponsors free guided expeditions to the egg-laying sites from May to August (call to reserve), as does the Marinelife Center of Juno Beach (below).

Located just south of Jupiter is the **Marinelife Center of Juno Beach,** Loggerhead Park, 14200 U.S. 1, in Juno Beach (© **561/627-8280**). Combining a science museum and nature trail, this small center is dedicated to the coastal ecology of northern Palm Beach County. Hands-on exhibits teach visitors about wetlands and beach areas, as well as offshore coral reefs and local sea life. Visitors are encouraged to walk the center's sand-dune nature trails, all of which are marked with interpretive signs. This is one place where you're guaranteed to see live sea turtles year-round. During the peak of breeding season (June–July), the center conducts narrative walks along a nearby beach; reservations are a must. The booking list opens on May 1 and is usually full by midmonth. Admission to the center is free, though donations are accepted. Open Monday through Saturday from 10am to 4pm, and Sunday from noon to 3pm.

turtles. Located along South Beach Drive (Fla. A1A), north of the Jupiter inlet, Blowing Rocks is about a 10-minute drive northeast of Jupiter. Free guided tours are available Friday at 1pm and Sunday at 11am; no reservations are necessary. From U.S. 1, head east on S.R. 707 and cross the Intracoastal Waterway to the park. Admission is $3 for adults and free for kids 12 and under.

SCUBA DIVING & SNORKELING   Year-round warm, clear waters make northern Palm Beach County great for both diving and snorkeling. The closest coral reef is located ¼ mile from shore and can be reached easily by boat. Three popular wrecks are clustered near one another, less than a mile offshore of the Lake Worth Inlet at about 90 feet. The best wreck, however, is the 16th- or 17th-century Spanish galleon discovered by lifeguard Peter Leo just off Jupiter Beach (see p. 262 for more information). If your hotel doesn't offer dive trips, call **South Florida Dive Headquarters,** 101 N. Riverside Dr., Pompano Beach (© **800/771-DIVE** or 954/783-2299); or **Seafari Dive and Surf,** 75 E. Indiantown Rd., Suite 603, Jupiter (© **561/747-6115**).

TENNIS   In addition to the many hotel tennis courts (see "Where to Stay," below), you can swing a racquet at a number of local clubs. The **Jupiter Bay Tennis Club,** 353 U.S. 1, Jupiter (© **561/744-9424**), has seven clay courts (three lighted) and charges $16 per person per day. Reservations are highly recommended. More economical options are available at relatively well-maintained municipal courts. Call ℂ **561/966-6600** for locations and hours. Many are available free on a first-come, first-served basis.

A HISTORIC LIGHTHOUSE

Jupiter Inlet Lighthouse ✫   Completed in 1860, this redbrick structure is the oldest extant building in Palm Beach County. Still owned and maintained by the U.S. Coast Guard, the lighthouse is now home to a small historical museum, located at its base. The Florida History Museum sponsors tours of the lighthouse, enabling visitors to explore the cramped interior, which is filled with artifacts and photographs illustrating the rich history of the area. A 15-minute video explains the shipwrecks, Indian wars, and other events that helped shape this region. Helpful volunteers are eager to tell colorful stories to highlight the 1-hour tour.

500 S.R. 707, Jupiter. ℂ **561/747-8380**. Admission $6. Sat–Wed 10am–4pm (last tour departs at 3:15pm). Children must be 4 ft. or taller to climb. No open-backed shoes.

SHOPPING

Northern Palm Beach County may not have the glitzy boutiques of Worth Avenue, but it does have an impressive indoor mall, the **Gardens of the Palm Beaches,** 3101 PGA Blvd. (ℂ **561/775-7750**), where you can find department stores such as Bloomingdale's, Burdines, Macy's, and Saks Fifth Avenue, as well as more than 100 specialty shops. A large, diverse food court and fine sit-down restaurants in this 1.3-million-square-foot facility make a shopping excursion an all-day affair.

WHERE TO STAY

The northern part of Palm Beach County is much more laid back and less touristy than the rest of the Gold Coast. There are relatively few fancy hotels or attractions here.

VERY EXPENSIVE

Jupiter Beach Resort ✫✫   The only resort located directly on Jupiter's beach, this unpretentious retreat is popular with families and seems a world away from the more luxurious resorts just a few miles to the south. A multimillion-dollar renovation to guest rooms, public areas, and restaurants in 2004–05 transformed the place from shabby-chic to simply chic Caribbean. The guest rooms are furnished in a comfortable island style, and every unit has a private balcony with ocean or sunset views overlooking the beachfront. Excursions to top-rated area golf courses are available.

5 N. A1A, Jupiter, FL 33477. ℂ **800/228-8810** or 561/746-2511. Fax 561/747-3304. www.jupiterbeachresort.com. 153 units. Winter $350–$450 double, $485–$583 suite, $900–$1,200 penthouse suite; off season $129–$179 double, $189–$219 suite, $600–$850 penthouse suite. AE, DC, DISC, MC, V. Valet parking $5. From I-95, take exit 59A, going east to the end of Indiantown Rd. at A1A. The resort is at this intersection, on the ocean. **Amenities:** 2 restaurants; 2 bars; outdoor heated pool; tennis court; exercise room; extensive watersports equipment rental; bike rental; children's programs; concierge; business center; limited room service; in-room massage; dry cleaning. *In room:* A/C, TV, VCR and DVD ($10 additional charge), dataport, kitchenette (in suites only), minibar, coffeemaker, iron.

PGA National Resort & Spa ✫✫✫   This rambling resort, the national headquarters of the PGA, is a premier golf-vacation spot—but its top-rated Mediterranean spa could be a destination in itself. With five 18-hole courses on more than 2,300 acres, golfers and other sports-minded travelers will find plenty to keep them occupied— like croquet, tennis, sailing, a health and fitness center, and that sublime spa. Constant updating has kept the grounds and buildings in like-new condition. The par-72 Champion Course, redesigned in 1990 by Jack Nicklaus, is the resort's most valuable asset. More than 100 sand bunkers and plenty of water on 6,400-square-foot greens keep golfers of all levels alert. Guest rooms are spacious and comfortable, bordering on residential, with immense bathrooms. Club cottages are especially nice, offering great privacy and serenity. This is not a beach resort, however. Six outdoor therapy pools known as "Waters of the World" are surrounded by mineral pools, which are so amazing, they make the ocean look like a kiddie pool. Don Shula's award-winning steakhouse is the hotel's best and most popular restaurant.

400 Ave. of the Champions, Palm Beach Gardens, FL 33418. ✆ 800/633-9150 or 561/627-2000. Fax 561/225-2595. www.pga-resorts.com. 339 units, 59 club cottages. Winter $299–$339 double, $369–$829 suite; off season $144–$169 double, $174–$659 suite. Children 16 and under stay free in parent's room. Special packages available. AE, DC, DISC, MC, V. From I-95, take exit 57B (PGA Blvd.) going west and continue for approximately 2 miles to the resort entrance on the left. **Amenities:** 7 restaurants and lounges; 9 pools; 5 18-hole tournament courses plus the PGA National's Academy of Golf; 19 clay tennis courts; aerobics studio; 5 tournament croquet lawns; 5 indoor racquetball courts; Mediterranean spa; watersports equipment rental; concierge; car-rental desk; salon; limited room service; babysitting; laundry. *In room:* A/C, TV, dataport, minibar, hair dryer, safe.

MODERATE/INEXPENSIVE

Baron's Landing Motel & Apartments ✸ *Value*   This charming family-run inn is a perfect little beach getaway. It's not elegant, but it is cozy. The single-story motel fronting the Intracoastal Waterway is often full in winter with snowbirds who dock their boats at the hotel's marina for weeks or months at a time. Nearly all rooms, which are situated around a small pool, have small kitchenettes. Each unit has a funky mix of used furniture; some have pullout sofas. Bathrooms have been remodeled. Considering that you're a few blocks from some of the most expensive real estate in the country, this is a good deal. Dock rentals are available as well.

18125 Ocean Blvd. (Fla. A1A at Clemens St.), Jupiter, FL 33477. ✆ 561/746-8757. 8 units. Winter $75–$125 double, $1,350–$1,700 monthly; off season $45–$75 double, $700–$900 monthly. No credit cards. **Amenities:** Small pool. *In room:* A/C, TV, fax, dataport, kitchen, fridge, coffeemaker, iron.

WHERE TO DINE

In addition to the national fast-food joints that line Indiantown Road and U.S. 1, you'll find a number of touristy fish restaurants serving battered and fried everything. There are only a few really exceptional eateries in North Palm Beach and Jupiter. Try those listed below for guaranteed good food at reasonable prices.

MODERATE

Capt. Charlie's Reef Grill ✸✸ SEAFOOD/CARIBBEAN   The trick here is to arrive early, ahead of the crowd of local foodies who come for the more than a dozen daily local-catch specials prepared in myriad styles. Imaginative appetizers include Caribbean chili (a rich, chunky stew filled with fresh seafood) and a tuna spring roll big enough for two. The enormous Cuban crab cake is perfectly browned without tasting fried and is served with homemade mango chutney and black beans and rice. Sit at the bar to watch the hectic kitchen turn out perfect dishes on the 14-burner stove. Somehow, the pleasant waitresses keep their cool even when the place is packed. In addition to the terrific seafood, this little dive offers an extensive, affordable wine and beer selection—more than 30 of each from around the world.

12846 U.S. 1 (behind O'Brian's and French Connection), Juno Beach. ✆ 561/624-9924. Reservations not accepted. Main courses $9.95–$22. MC, V. Sun–Fri 11:30am–3pm and 5–9:30pm.

Nick's Tomato Pie ✸ ITALIAN   A fun family restaurant, Nick's is a popular attraction that's known to bring folks even from Miami for a piece of this pie. With a huge menu of pastas, pizzas, fish, chicken, and beef, this cheery (and noisy) spot has something for everyone. On Saturday night, you'll see lots of couples on dates, and families leaving with doggie bags of leftovers from the impossibly generous portions. The homemade sausage is a delicious treat, served with sautéed onions and peppers. The *pollo Marsala* (chicken in Marsala sauce), too, is good and authentic.

1697 W. Indiantown Rd. (1 mile east of I-95, exit 59A), Jupiter. ⓒ **561/744-8935.** Reservations accepted for groups of 6 or more. Main courses $12–$20; pastas $10–$15. AE, DC, DISC, MC, V. Mon–Thurs and Sun 5–9:30pm; Fri–Sat 5–10:30pm.

Sinclair's Ocean Grill & Rotisserie ✮✮ CARIBBEAN   As close to upscale as Jupiter gets, Sinclair's, recently renovated along with the entire hotel, is the Jupiter Beach Resort's excellent restaurant overlooking the pool. It features fresh, locally caught fish as well as an excellent filet mignon. Especially popular are the Sunday brunches.

In the Jupiter Beach Resort, 5 N. Fla. A1A. ⓒ **561/745-7120.** Reservations recommended. Main courses $18–$27. AE, MC, V. Daily 6:30am–2pm and 8–10pm.

9

The Treasure Coast:
Stuart to Sebastian

The area north of Palm Beach is known as the Treasure Coast for the same reason that the area from Fort Lauderdale to Palm Beach is known as the Gold Coast—it was the site of a number of shipwrecks that date back more than 300 years, which led to the discovery of priceless treasures in the water (some historians believe that treasures *still* lie buried deep beneath the ocean floor).

The difference, however, is that while the Gold Coast is a bit, well, tarnished as far as development is concerned, the Treasure Coast remains, for the most part, an unspoiled, quiet natural jewel. Miles of uninterrupted beaches and aquamarine waters attract swimmers, boaters, divers, anglers, and sun worshippers. If you love the great outdoors and prefer a more understated environment than hyperdeveloped Miami and Fort Lauderdale, the Treasure Coast is a real find.

For hundreds of years, Florida's east coast was a popular stopover for European explorers, many of whom arrived from Spain with full coffers with gold and silver. Rough weather and poor navigation often took a toll on their ships, but in 1715, a violent hurricane stunned the northeast coast and sank an entire fleet of Spanish ships laden with gold. Although Spanish salvagers worked for years to collect the lost treasure, much of it remained buried beneath the shifting sand. Workers hired to excavate the area in the 1950s and 1960s discovered centuries-old coins under their tractors.

Today you can still see shipwrecks and incredible barrier reefs in St. Lucie County, which can be reached from the beaches of Fort Pierce and Hutchinson Island. On these same beaches, you'll also find an occasional treasure hunter trolling the sand with a metal detector, alongside swimmers and sunbathers who come to enjoy the stretches of beach that extend into the horizon. The sea, especially around Sebastian Inlet, is a mecca for surfers, who find some of the largest swells in the state.

Along with the pleasures of the talcum-powder sands, the Treasure Coast offers good shopping, sporting, and numerous other opportunities to take a reprieve from the hubbub of the rat race. Visitors to this part of South Florida should not miss the extensive array of wildlife, which includes the endangered West Indian manatee, loggerhead and leatherback turtles, tropical fish, alligators, deer, and exotic birds. Sports enthusiasts will find boundless opportunities here—from golf and tennis to polo, motorcar racing, the New York Mets during spring training, and the best freshwater fishing around.

The downtown areas of the Treasure Coast have been experiencing a very slow rebirth in the past few years, along with an unprecedented influx of new residents. Fortunately, growth has occurred at a

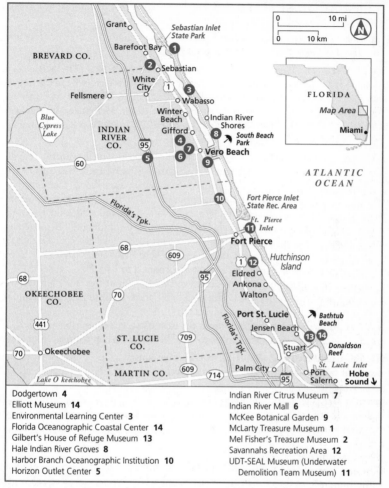

The Treasure Coast

Dodgertown **4**
Elliott Museum **14**
Environmental Learning Center **3**
Florida Oceanographic Coastal Center **14**
Gilbert's House of Refuge Museum **13**
Hale Indian River Groves **8**
Harbor Branch Oceanographic Institution **10**
Horizon Outlet Center **5**

Indian River Citrus Museum **7**
Indian River Mall **6**
McKee Botanical Garden **9**
McLarty Treasure Museum **1**
Mel Fisher's Treasure Museum **2**
Savannahs Recreation Area **12**
UDT-SEAL Museum (Underwater
    Demolition Team Museum) **11**

reasonable pace, allowing the neighborhoods to retain their small-town feel. The result is a batch of freshly spruced-up accommodations, shops, and restaurants from Stuart to Sebastian.

Southern Martin County's well-to-do Hobe Sound, in particular, is a Treasure Coast hot spot with its pristine beaches, banyan-tree-canopied streetscapes, one-of-a-kind antiques shops, and art galleries. Hobe Sound rests at the front door of the Gold Coast and the back door of the Treasure Coast, and it has access to both the Atlantic Ocean and the Intracoastal Waterway. Real estate here is at a premium, with million-dollar waterfront mansions lining the shores.

While the Treasure Coast took a major hit during the brutal 2004 hurricane season, all's still golden here.

For the purposes of this chapter, the Treasure Coast runs roughly from Hobe Sound in the south to Sebastian Inlet in the north, encompassing some of Martin, St. Lucie, and Indian River counties, and all of Hutchinson Island.

TREASURE COAST ESSENTIALS
GETTING THERE
Since virtually every town described in this chapter runs along a straight route along the Atlantic Ocean, I've given all directions below.

BY PLANE   The **Palm Beach International Airport** (✆ **561/471-7420**), located about 35 miles south of Stuart, is the closest gateway to this region if you're flying. See the "Getting There" section on Palm Beach, on p. 290, for complete information. If you're traveling to the northern part of the Treasure Coast, **Melbourne International Airport,** off U.S. 1 in Melbourne (✆ **321/723-6227**), is less than 25 miles north of Sebastian and about 35 miles north of Vero Beach.

BY CAR   If you're driving up or down the Florida coast, you'll probably reach the Treasure Coast via I-95. If you're heading to Stuart or Jensen Beach, take exits 61 (Rte. 76/Tanner Hwy.) or 62 (Rte. 714); to Port St. Lucie or Fort Pierce, take exits 63 or 64 (Okeechobee Rd.); to Vero Beach, take exit 68 (S.R. 60); to Sebastian, take exit 69 (County Rd.). You can also take the Florida Turnpike; this toll road is the fastest (but not the most scenic) route, especially if you're coming from Orlando. If you're heading to Stuart or Jensen Beach, take exit 133; to Fort Pierce, take exit 152 (Okeechobee Rd.); to Port St. Lucie, take exits 142 or 152; to Vero Beach, take exit 193 (S.R. 60); to Sebastian, take exit 193 to S.R. 60 east and connect to I-95 N.

If you're staying in Hutchinson Island, which runs almost the entire length of the Treasure Coast, you should check with your hotel or see the listings below to find the best route to take.

Finally, if you're coming directly from the west coast, you'll probably take S.R. 70, which runs north of Lake Okeechobee to Fort Pierce, located up the road from Stuart.

BY RAIL   Amtrak (✆ **800/USA-RAIL;** www.amtrak.com) stops in West Palm Beach, at 201 S. Tamarind Ave.; and in Okeechobee, at 801 N. Parrot Ave., off U.S. 441 North.

BY BUS   Greyhound (✆ **800/231-2222;** www.greyhound.com) serves the area with bus terminals in Stuart, at 1308 S. Federal Hwy.; in Fort Pierce, at 7005 Okeechobee Rd. (✆ **772/461-3299**); and in Vero Beach, at U.S. 1 and S.R. 60 (✆ **772/562-6588**).

GETTING AROUND
A car is a necessity in this large and rural region. Although heavy traffic is not usually a problem here, on the smaller coastal roads, like A1A, expect to travel at a slow pace, usually between 25 and 40 mph.

1 Hobe Sound ★★★, Stuart (North Hutchinson Island ★★) & Jensen Beach

Once just a stretch of pineapple plantations, the towns of Martin County, which include Hobe Sound, Stuart, and Jensen Beach, retain much of their rural character. Dotted between citrus groves and mangroves are modest homes and an occasional high-rise condominium. Although the area is definitely still, the atmosphere is pure small town. Even in historic downtown Stuart, the result of a successful, ongoing restoration, expect the storefronts to be dark and the streets abandoned after 10pm. Martin County did suffer some damage in 2004 and 2005 due to hurricanes Frances, Jeanne, Charley, Katrina, and Wilma, and parks like Jonathan Dickinson State Park were closed for a bit, but by now everything should be open and fully functional.

Wildlife Exploration: From Gators to Manatees to Turtles

One of the most scenic areas on this stretch of the coast is **Jonathan Dickinson State Park** ☆, 12 miles south of Stuart at 16450 S. Federal Hwy. (U.S. 1), Hobe Sound (© **772/546-2771**). The park intentionally receives less maintenance than other, more meticulously maintained parks in order to resemble the rough-around-the-edges, wilderness-like environment of hundreds of years ago, before Europeans started chopping, dredging, and "improving" the area. Dozens of species of Florida's unique wildlife, including alligators and manatees, live on the park's more than 11,300 acres. Bird-watchers will be delighted by glimpses of rare and endangered species such as the bald eagle, the Florida scrub-jay, and the Florida sandhill crane, which still call this park home. You can rent canoes from the concessions stand to explore the Loxahatchee River on your own. Admission is $4 per car of up to eight adults. Day hikers, bikers, and walkers pay $1 each. The park is open from 8am until sundown. See p. 318 for details on camping.

Close to Jonathan Dickinson State Park is **Hobe Sound Wildlife Refuge,** on North Beach Road off S.R. 708, at the north end of Jupiter Island (© **772/546-6141**). This is one of the best places to spot sea turtles that nest on the shore in the summer months, especially in June and July. Because it's home to a large variety of other plant and animal species, the park is worth visiting the rest of the year as well. Admission is $4 per car, and the preserve is open daily from sunrise to sunset. Exact times are posted at each entrance and change seasonally.

For turtle walks on Hutchinson Island, call © **877/375-4386.** These walks take place from May 22 to July 22 at 9pm on Friday and Saturday. Reservations are necessary and should be made well in advance (they're accepted as of May 1), since each walk is limited to 50 people.

ESSENTIALS

The **Stuart/Martin County Chamber of Commerce,** 1650 S. Kanner Hwy., Stuart, FL 34994 (© **800/524-9704** or 772/287-1088; fax 772/220-3437; www.goodnature.org), is the region's main source for information. The **Jensen Beach Chamber of Commerce,** 1901 NE Jensen Beach Blvd., Jensen Beach, FL 34957 (© **772/334-3444;** fax 772/334-0817; www.jensenchamber.com), also offers visitors information about its simple beachfront town.

BACK TO NATURE: THE BEACHES & BEYOND

BEACHES   Hutchinson Island, one of the most popular beach destinations of the Treasure Coast, is the area just north of Palm Beach on the Atlantic Ocean. Some 70 miles of excellent beaches and laid-back, Old Florida ambience make for an idyllic, frozen-cocktail-on-the-beach resort vacation. The best of them is **Bathtub Beach,** on North Hutchinson Island. The calm waters here are protected by coral reefs, and visitors can explore the region on dune and river trails. Pick a secluded spot on the wide stretch of sand, or enjoy marked nature trails across the street. Facilities include showers and toilets open during the day. To reach Bathtub Beach from the northern tip of

Hutchinson Island, head east on Ocean Boulevard (Stuart Causeway) and turn right onto MacArthur Boulevard. The beach is about a mile ahead on your left, just north of the Hutchinson Island Marriott Beach Resort and Marina. Parking is plentiful.

CANOEING   **Jonathan Dickinson State Park** (see "Wildlife Exploration: From Gators to Manatees to Turtles," below) is the most popular area for canoeing. Although the park experienced a major blow with 2005's Hurricane Wilma, by the time this book is in your hands, all will have been repaired and restored. The route winds through a variety of botanical habitats. You'll see lots of birds and the occasional manatee. Canoes rent for $10 for 2 hours and $4 for each additional hour, available through the concessions stand (© **561/746-1466**) located in the back of the park; it's open Monday through Friday from 9am to 5pm, and Saturday and Sunday from 8am to 5pm.

FISHING   Several charter captains operate on Hutchinson Island and Jensen Beach. One of the largest operators is the **Sailfish Marina,** 3565 SE St. Lucie Blvd., Stuart (© **772/221-9456**), which maintains half a dozen charter boats for fishing excursions year-round. Also on-site are a bait-and-tackle shop and a knowledgeable, helpful staff. Other reputable charter operators include **Hungry Bear Adventures, Inc.,** docked at Indian River Plantation Marriott Resort, 4730-1 SE Teri Place, Stuart (© **772/285-7552;** www.hungrybear.net); and **Bone Shaker Sportfishing,** 3585 SE St. Lucie Blvd., Stuart (© **772/286-5504;** veejay4842@aol.com).

GOLF   Try the **Champions Club at Summerfield,** on U.S. 1, south of Cove Road in Stuart (© **772/283-1500**), a somewhat challenging championship course designed by Tom Fazio. This rural course, the best in the area, offers great glimpses of wildlife amid the wetlands. Winter greens fees are around $65; carts are mandatory. Reservations are a must and are taken 4 days in advance.

SCUBA DIVING & SNORKELING   Three popular artificial reefs off Hutchinson Island provide excellent scenery for both novice and experienced divers. The **USS Rankin** lies 7 miles east-northeast of the St. Lucie Inlet. The *Rankin* is a 459-foot ship that lies on its port side in 80 feet of water. This ship was used in World War II for troop transportation and was sunk in 1988. Deck hatches on the wreck are open and allow exploration. Inside there are thousands of Atlantic Spiny oysters, and a cannon is attached to the bow. The **Donaldson Reef** consists of a cluster of steel tanks and barrels sunk in 58 feet of water to create an artificial reef. It's located due east of the Gilbert's House of Refuge Museum (see below). The **Ernst Reef,** made from old tires, is a 60-foot dive located 4½ miles east-southeast of the St. Lucie Inlet. Local dive shops have tips on the best spots, along with rules and regulations for safe diving.

SEEING THE SIGHTS

Balloons Over Florida 🌟🌟🌟 *(Finds*   For a lofty view of Martin County's wildlife, take a hot-air balloon ride above the animals' natural habitat. Two fully licensed and insured balloons and pilots will take a maximum of four people up, up, and away for about an hour, depending on wind and weather conditions. After you've landed, drink in the sights over a glass of complimentary champagne and a continental breakfast. The entire experience takes about 3 hours.

Tours begin at approximately 6:30am from a takeoff point to be determined. © **772/334-9393.** $195 per person, including continental breakfast and champagne.

Elliott Museum 🌟🌟   A treasure trove of wacky artifacts that really personify Americana, the Elliott Museum is a tribute to inventors, sports heroes, and collectors. The museum was created by the son of turn-of-the-20th-century inventor Sterling Elliott to display the genius of the American spirit. Among the things you'll see here are displays of an apothecary, ice-cream parlor, barbershop, and other old-fashioned commercial enterprises, as well as an authentic hand-carved miniature circus. Sports fans will appreciate the baseball memorabilia, including an autographed item from every player in the Baseball Hall of Fame. A gallery of patents and models of machines, invented by the museum's founder and his son, provides an intriguing glimpse into the business of tinkering. Their collection of restored antique cars is also impressive. Expect to spend at least an hour seeing the highlights.

825 NE Ocean Blvd. (north of Indian River Plantation Resort), Hutchinson Island, Stuart. ⓒ 772/225-1961. www. elliotmuseumfl.org Admission $8 adults, $4 children 6–13, free for children 5 and under. Mon–Sat 10am–4pm, Sun 1-4pm.

Florida Oceanographic Coastal Center ⭑⭑
This is a nature lover's Disney World. Opened by the South Florida Oceanographic Society in 1994, the 44-acre site (surrounded by coastal hammock and mangroves) is its own little ecosystem and serves as an outdoor classroom, teaching visitors about the region's flora and fauna. The modest main building houses saltwater tanks, and wet and dry "discovery tables" with small indigenous animals. The incredibly eager staff of volunteers encourages visitors to wander the lush, well-marked nature trails.

890 NE Ocean Blvd. (across the street from the Elliott Museum), Hutchinson Island, Stuart. ⓒ 772/225-0505. www.floridaoceanographic.org. Admission $8 adults, $4 children 3–12. Mon–Sat 10am–5pm; Sun noon–4pm.

Gilbert's House of Refuge Museum ⭑
Gilbert's, the oldest structure in Martin County, dates from 1875, when it functioned as one of 10 rescue centers for shipwrecked sailors. After a thorough rehab to its original condition along the rocky shores, the house now displays marine artifacts and turn-of-the-20th-century lifesaving equipment and photographs. It's worth a visit to get a feel for the area's early days.

301 SE MacArthur Blvd. (south of Indian River Plantation Resort), Hutchinson Island, Stuart. ⓒ 772/225-1875. Admission $4 adults, $2 children 6–13. Daily 10am–4pm.

A BOAT TOUR

The *Loxahatchee Queen* ⭑⭑⭑ (ⓒ 561/746-1466), a 35-foot, 44-passenger pontoon boat in Jonathan Dickinson State Park in Hobe Sound, makes daily tours of the area's otherwise inaccessible backwater, where curious alligators, manatees, eagles, and tortoises often peek out to see who's in their yard. Catch the 2-hour tour, given Wednesday through Sunday as the tide permits, when it includes a stop at Trapper Nelson's home. Known as the "Wildman of Loxahatchee," Nelson lived in primitive conditions on a remote stretch of the water in a log cabin he built himself, now preserved for visitors. Tours leave four times daily—at 9am, 11am, 1pm, and 3pm—and cost $15 for adults and $9.50 for children 6 to 12. See "Wildlife Exploration: From Gators to Manatees to Turtles" (p. 315) for more information on the state park.

SHOPPING

Downtown Stuart's historic district, along Flagler Avenue between Confusion Corner and St. Lucie Avenue, offers shoppers diversity and quality in an old small-town setting. Shops offer a range of goods: antique bric-a-brac, old lamps and fixtures, books, gourmet foods, furnishings, and souvenirs. For bargains, check out the **B & A Flea Market** (ⓒ 772/288-4915), the Treasure Coast's oldest and largest flea market.

WHERE TO STAY

Although the area boasts some beautiful beaches, the bulk of the hotel scene is downtown, where the nicer (and more reasonably priced) accommodations can be found among the shops and restaurants. There are, however, a few excellent beachfront hotels and inns. One of the bigger chain hotels in the area is the **Hutchinson Island Inn,** 3793 NE Ocean Blvd., on Hutchinson Island in Jensen Beach (© **800/992-4747** or 772/225-3000). At press time, its stunning beachfront property was closed due to Hurricane Wilma and slated to reopen in fall 2007. There's also a **Holiday Inn Downtown Stuart,** at 1209 S. Federal Hwy. (© **772/287-6200**). This simple two-story building on a busy main road is kept in very good shape and is convenient to Stuart's historic district. Rates range from $159 to $179. *Note:* A 2% tax is added to accommodations rates in the Stuart–Hutchinson Island area.

VERY EXPENSIVE

Hutchinson Island Marriott Beach Resort and Marina ★★★ *Kids* This sprawling 200-acre compound offers many diversions for active (or not-so-active) vacationers, and families in particular. This is definitely Hutchinson Island's best resort, occupying the lush grounds of a former pineapple plantation. Activities include tennis, golf, boating, sport fishing, scuba diving, and other watersports. Rooms overlook either the Intracoastal and the resort's marina, the ocean, or gardens. All are generously sized and have full kitchens. Be sure to sign up for a summer "turtle watch" so you can observe turtles crawling onto the sand to lay their eggs. Another great activity, offered at an extra cost, is a sightseeing cruise along the St. Lucie and Indian rivers. The Baha Grill seafood restaurant is a great choice on property.

555 NE Ocean Blvd., Hutchinson Island, Stuart, FL 34996. © **800/775-5936** or 772/225-3700. Fax 772/225-0003. www.marriott.com. 298 units. Winter $179–$289 double, $309–$499 suite; off season $169–$189 double, $199–$299 suite. AE, MC, V. From downtown Stuart, take E. Ocean Blvd. over 2 bridges to NE Ocean Blvd.; turn right. Pets accepted with $50 deposit. **Amenities:** Restaurant; coffee shop; lounge; 4 large pools; 18-hole golf course; 13 tennis courts; fitness center and spa; extensive watersports; bike rental; children's programs; game room; concierge; on-property transportation; limited room service; babysitting; laundry services; dry cleaning. *In room:* A/C, TV, high-speed Internet access, kitchenette, minibar, coffeemaker, hair dryer, iron.

CAMPING

There are comfortable campsites (rustic cabins and sites for your tent or camper) in **Jonathan Dickinson State Park,** in Hobe Sound (see "Wildlife Exploration: From Gators to Manatees to Turtles," on p. 315). The River Camp area of the park offers the benefit of the nearby Loxahatchee River, while the Pine Grove site has beautiful shade trees. There are concession areas for daytime snacks and 135 campsites with showers, clean restrooms, water, optional electricity, and open-fire pits for cooking. Overnight rates in winter are $22 with electricity. In summer, rates are about $14 for four people.

For a cushier camping experience, reserve a cabin with furnished kitchen, bathroom with shower, heat and air-conditioning, and outdoor grill. Cabins rent for $85 (one bed and a pullout couch), $95 (two beds and a pullout couch), and up per night. They sleep four people comfortably, or up to six if your group is really into togetherness. Call © **772/546-2771** Monday through Friday between 9am and 5pm, well in advance, to reserve a spot. A $50 key deposit is required. Bring your own linens.

WHERE TO DINE
EXPENSIVE

The Courtyard Grill ★★ CONTINENTAL Although this restaurant faces railroad tracks and a station that was never fully built, the Courtyard Grill is the essence of charm, with the warm and inviting vibe of a place where no railroad would ever go. Old-school fare such as clams casino and escargot are juxtaposed with nouveau cuisine such as duck-stuffed ravioli, but old standards like Dover sole are best. An impressive wine list, a gorgeous garden room, and homemade desserts assure you that you're on the right track as far as fine food in Hobe Sound is concerned, train or no train.

11970 SE Dixie Hwy., Hobe Sound. © **772/546-2900**. Reservations recommended. Main courses $11–$18. MC, V. Mon–Fri 11am–3pm; daily 5:30–9:30pm.

11 Maple Street 𝕏𝕏𝕏 AMERICAN   The most highly rated restaurant in Jensen Beach, 11 Maple Street occupies a converted old house. Dining is both indoors and out, in any one of a series of cozy dining rooms or on a covered patio surrounded by gardens. Interesting dishes not typically found in these parts of Florida include wood-grilled venison with French green lentils, broccoli rabe, caramelized turnip, hazelnut and white-bean purée with grilled tomato sauce; and braised Moulard duck leg with wood-grilled Oregon quail, Tuscan cabbage, butternut squash, and chestnut tart with a balsamic pear reduction. The restaurant uses organic produce from its own garden, and poultry and meats that are farm raised and free of chemical additives.

11 Maple St., Jensen Beach. © **772/334-7714**. Reservations recommended. Main courses $20–$32. MC, V. Wed–Sun 6–10pm. Head east on Jensen Beach Blvd. and turn right after the railroad tracks.

Flagler Grill 𝕏𝕏 AMERICAN/FLORIDA REGIONAL   In the heart of historic downtown, this seemingly out-of-place Manhattan-style bistro serves up classics with a twist. Dishes are fresh and light enough to quench the appetites of the adventurous—for example, Maryland jumbo lump crabmeat and rock shrimp cake served with a Key-lime aioli and spicy Cajun aioli. For a main course, the grilled double-stuffed pork chop filled with pecan-apple corn-bread stuffing with cranberry-orange chutney, fresh vegetables, and smashed garlic potatoes gives meaning to the term "comfort food." It's hard to go wrong with any of the many salads, pastas, fish dishes, or delectable beef choices. The desserts, too, are worth the calories. Ask the bartender to make you the Big Apple martini—apple vodka, apple schnapps, and a wedge of apple—dessert with a kick! No smoking is allowed in the restaurant or bar.

47 SW Flagler Ave. (just before the Roosevelt Bridge), downtown Stuart. © **772/221-9517**. Reservations strongly suggested in season. Main courses $18–$28. AE, DC, DISC, MC, V. Winter daily 5–10pm; off season Tues–Sat 5:30–9:30pm. Lounge and bar until 11:30pm. Special sunset menu offered 5–6pm.

Rottie's 𝕏𝕏 SEAFOOD   Ocean views and fabulous seafood make you forget the name of this romantic Jensen Beach eatery. It's expensive, yes, but worth it. Try the pan-seared Florida snapper and the jumbo lump crab cakes, and share an appetizer of sautéed calamari and mussels, which is super-heavy on the garlic. Live music almost nightly and a lively Tiki bar help set the mood for a delightful dining experience here.

10900 S. Ocean Dr., Jensen Beach. © **772/229-7575**. Main courses $25–$35. AE, DC, DISC, MC, V. Sun, Tues, Thurs 11:30am–2:30pm and 5:30–10pm; Fri–Sat 5:30–11pm.

MODERATE

Black Marlin 𝕏 FLORIDA REGIONAL   Although it looks and feels like a dank English pub, the Black Marlin offers full Floridian flavor. The salmon BLT is typical of the dishes here—grilled salmon on a toasted bun topped with bacon, lettuce, tomato, and coleslaw. Pizzas are adorned with shrimp, roasted red peppers, and the like; main dishes, served with vegetables and potatoes, range from lobster tail with honey-mustard sauce to grilled chicken breast on radicchio with caramelized onions.

53 W. Osceola St., downtown Stuart. © 772/286-3126. Reservations not accepted. Salads and sandwiches $4–$8; full meals $9–$24. AE, MC, V. Mon–Thurs 5–10pm; Fri–Sat 5–11pm (bar open later).

Conchy Joe's Seafood ✦✦ *Finds* SEAFOOD   Known for fresh seafood and Old Florida hospitality, Conchy Joe's enjoys an excellent reputation that's far bigger than the restaurant itself. Shorts and flip-flops are the attire of choice here, and dining is either indoors or out on a covered patio overlooking the St. Lucie River. The menu features a variety of freshly shucked shellfish and daily-catch selections that are baked, broiled, or fried; the conch chowder is sublime. Beer is the drink of choice here, though other beverages are available. Conchy Joe's has been the most active place in Jensen Beach since it opened in 1983. The large bar is popular at night and during weekday happy hours.

3945 NE Indian River Dr. (½ mile from the Jensen Beach Causeway), Jensen Beach. © 772/334-1130. Reservations not accepted. Main courses $12–$20. AE, DISC, MC, V. Daily 11:30am–2:30pm and 5–10pm.

INEXPENSIVE

Harry and the Natives ✦✦ AMERICAN   When you dine at this wild and wacky, kitschy Old Florida institution (to which both Harleys and Bentleys flock), you'll get decent bar fare (try the venison burger) with a fabulous dish of humor on the side. The menu is hysterical, especially "Acceptibles: Visa, MasterCard, our gift certificates, cash, oceanfront homes, table dancing, honeydripping, and dishwashing." No offense to our Canadian friends, but the menu also jokingly has a "Canadian Breakfast—(no tip) $20." The food ranges from omelets and pancakes to the "President Bush Omelet—$1,000,000,000; Profits go to the Palm Beach County Election Supervisor to buy more butterfly ballots, voting machines, and incompetent help." I won't spoil it all, so be sure to read the entire menu. There's live music Wednesday, Friday, and Saturday; request the Harry and the Natives theme song.

11910 S. Federal Hwy., Hobe Sound. © 772/546-3061. Main courses $5–$10. MC, V. Daily 6:30am–2:30am.

Nature's Way Cafe ✦ HEALTH FOOD   This lovely dining room has dozens of little tables, a few bar stools, and some sidewalk seating, too. A sort of health-food deli, Nature's Way excels in serving quick and nutritious meals such as huge salads, vegetarian sandwiches, and frozen yogurts. Try some of the homemade baked goods. Sit outside on quaint Osceola Street or get your lunch packed up to take to the beach.

25 SW Osceola St., in the Post Office Arcade, Stuart. © 772/220-7306. Sandwiches and salads $4–$7; juices and shakes $1–$3. No credit cards. Mon–Fri 10am–4pm; Sat 11am–3pm.

STUART & JENSEN BEACH AFTER DARK

Nightlife on the Treasure Coast may as well be called night*dead* because there really isn't any! This is not the place if you're looking for active nightlife. That said, Stuart and Jensen Beach are the closest to nightlife in the region; local restaurants serve as the centers of after-dark happenings. "Night" ends pretty early here, even on weekends.

The bar at the **Black Marlin** (see "Where to Dine," above) is popular with locals and out-of-towners alike. And no list of Jensen nightlife would be complete without mention of **Conchy Joe's Seafood** (see "Where to Dine," above), one of the region's most active spots. Inside, locals chug beer and watch a large-screen TV, while outside on the waterfront patio, live bands perform a few nights a week for a raucous crowd of dancers. Happy hours, Monday through Friday from 3 to 6pm, draw large crowds.

The centerpiece of Stuart's slowly expanding cultural offerings is the newly restored **Lyric Theater,** 59 SW Flagler Ave. (© 772/286-7827). This beautiful 1920s-era theater hosts a variety of shows, readings, concerts, and films throughout the year.

2 Port St. Lucie & Fort Pierce

Port St. Lucie and Fort Pierce are two true Old Florida towns—reminiscent of the pre-neon, pre-condo-maniacal Florida, a sleepy world apart from the Gold Coast and Miami. Both towns thrive on sport fishing, and a seemingly endless row of piers juts out along the Intracoastal Waterway and the Fort Pierce Inlet for both river and ocean runs. Visitors can dive, snorkel, beachcomb, and sunbathe in an area that has been left untouched by the overdevelopment that has altered its neighbors to the south and north.

Most sightseeing takes place along the main beach road (the strip across from the Ocean/A1A). Driving along Florida A1A on Hutchinson Island, you'll discover several secluded beach clubs interspersed with 1950s-style homes, a few small inns, grungy raw bars, and a few high-rise condominiums. Much of this island is government owned and kept undeveloped for the public's enjoyment.

ESSENTIALS

The **St. Lucie County Chamber of Commerce,** 2200 Virginia Ave., Fort Pierce, FL 34982 (© 772/595-9999; www.stluciechamber.org), is the region's main source of information. There's another branch at 1626 SE Port St. Lucie Blvd., in Port St. Lucie. Both spots are open Monday through Friday from 9am to 5pm.

BEACHES & NATURE PRESERVES

North Hutchinson Island's beaches are the most pristine in this area. You won't find restaurants, hotels, or shopping; instead, you'll spend your time swimming, surfing, fishing, and diving. Most of the beaches along this stretch of the Atlantic Ocean are private, but thankfully the state has set aside some of the best areas for the public.

Fort Pierce Inlet State Recreation Area (© 772/468-3985) is a stunning 340-acre park with almost 4,000 feet of sandy shores that were once the training ground for the original Navy frogmen. A short nature trail leads through a canopy of live oaks, cabbage palms, sea grapes, and strangler figs. The western side of the area has swamps of red mangroves that are home to fiddler crabs, osprey, and a multitude of wading birds. **Jack Island State Preserve,** in the state recreation area, is popular with bird-watchers and offers hiking trails. Jutting into the Indian River, the mangrove-covered peninsula contains several marked trails, varying in distance from ½ mile to over 4 miles. The trails through mangrove forests lead to a short observation tower.

The best beach in the state recreation area, **Jetty Park,** lies in the northern part. Families will enjoy the picnic areas and barbecue grills here. There are also restrooms and outdoor showers, and lifeguards look after swimmers. The park is located at 905 Shorewinds Dr., north of Fort Pierce Inlet. To get here from I-95, take exit 66 E. (Rte. 68) and turn left onto U.S. 1 North; in about 2 miles, you will see signs to Florida A1A and the North Bridge Causeway. Turn right on A1A and cross over to North Hutchinson Island. Admission is $4 per vehicle; the park is open daily from 8am to sunset.

SPECTATOR SPORTS & OUTDOOR PURSUITS

BASEBALL   The **New York Mets** hold spring training in Port St. Lucie from late February to the end of March at **Tradition Field,** 525 NW Peacock Blvd. (© 772/871-2115). Tickets for games and practices cost $6 to $25. From April to August, their farm team, the Port St. Lucie Mets, plays home games in the stadium.

FISHING   The **Fort Pierce City Marina,** 1 Ave. A, Fort Pierce (© 772/464-1245), has more than a dozen charter captains who keep their motors running for anglers anxious to catch a few. Brochures available at the marina list all of the privately owned charter operators, who organize trips on an as-desired basis. The price usually starts at $150 per person for half-day tours, depending on the season.

GOLF   The most notable courses in Port St. Lucie are at the **PGA Golf Club at the Reserve,** 1916 Perfect Dr. (© **772/467-1300**). The club's first of three 18-hole public golf courses opened in 1996 and was designed by Tom Fazio; another course was designed by Pete Dye. The South Course, a classic Old Florida–style course, is set on wetlands, offers views of native wildlife, and is the most popular. The center also offers lessons for amateurs. The club is open daily from 7am to 6pm. Greens fees are usually $59, but after 2pm they go down to $49. Reserve at least 9 days in advance.

SEEING THE SIGHTS

Harbor Branch Oceanographic Institution ☆☆   Harbor Branch is a working nonprofit scientific institute that studies oceanic resources and welcomes visitors on scheduled tours. Stops include the J. Seward Johnson Marine Education Center, which houses submersibles used to conduct research at depths of up to 3,000 feet. A video details current projects, and several large aquariums simulate the environments of the Indian River Lagoon and a saltwater reef. Visitors see the Aqua-Culture Farming Center, a research facility that contains tanks growing seaweed and other oceanic plants. The 90-minute Lagoon Wildlife Tour examines the Indian River Lagoon from a pontoon boat. The boat tours are offered Monday through Saturday at 10am, 1pm, and 3pm; the cost is $17 for adults, $12 for children 6 to 12. The bus tour of the 600-acre campus costs $10 and leaves Monday through Saturday at 10am, noon, and 2pm.

5600 U.S. 1 N., Fort Pierce. © 772/465-2400. www.hboi.edu. Admission $10 adults, $6 children 6–12. Mon–Fri 8am–5pm; visitor center gift shop Mon–Sat 9am–5pm. Arrive at least 20 min. before tour.

Savannahs Recreation Area ☆☆☆ *Finds*   A 550-acre former reservoir, Savannahs is one of the most interesting places in these parts—it's a veritable wilderness, with botanical gardens, nature trails, campsites, a petting zoo, and scenery reminiscent of the Florida Everglades, but in a much more contained environment.

1400 E. Midway Rd., Fort Pierce. © 772/464-7855. Admission $1 per car. Daily 8am–6pm.

UDT-SEAL Museum (Underwater Demolition Team Museum)   Florida is full of unique museums, but none more curious than the UDT-SEAL Museum, an interesting tribute to the secret forces of the U.S. Navy frogmen and their successors, the SEAL teams. Chronological displays trace the history of these clandestine divers and detail their most important achievements. The best exhibits are those on the intricately detailed equipment used by the Navy's most elite members. Expect to spend about an hour here, depending on your interests.

3300 N. S.R. A1A, Fort Pierce. © 772/595-5845. www.navysealmuseum.com. Admission $5 adults, $2 children 6–12. Mon–Sat 10am–4pm; Sun noon–4pm. Closed Mon in off season.

WHERE TO STAY

The Port St. Lucie mainland is pretty run-down, but there are a number of inexpensive hotel options on scenic Hutchinson Island that are charming and well priced. Probably the best choice is the **Hampton Inn,** 2831 Reynolds Dr. (© **800/426-7866** or 772/460-9855), which is beautifully maintained. If you want to be closer to the water, try the **Days Inn Hutchinson Island,** 1920 Seaway Dr. (© **800/325-2525** or 772/461-8737), a simple, very well-kept motel that sits along the Intracoastal Inlet.

Budget travelers will be glad to know about the **Edgewater Motel and Apartments,** 1160 Seaway Dr. (next door to and under the same ownership as the Dockside–Harborlight Inn and Resort), Fort Pierce (☎ **800/286-1745** or 772/468-3555). Rooms start at less than $70 in high season; efficiencies are also available from $80. Guests can enjoy a private pool, shuffleboard courts, and a nearby fishing pier.

EXPENSIVE

Club Med–Sandpiper 🏖🏖 🅚🅘🅓🅢   This 400-acre, all-inclusive resort isn't your typical bacchanalian Club Med, but rather a fabulous getaway for families with kids. The hotel markets itself to Europeans looking for a Florida getaway. They come in droves (Americans, too) with all the kids and nannies for an active vacation with lavish meals, from buffets to sit-downs, for a package price. Thanks to tailored programs for kids— there's Baby Club Med, Petit Club Med, Mini Club Med, and Junior's Club Med— the resort is all about families with kids. Rooms are so-so and retro, but not in a cool way. The drawback is that guests are 20 minutes from the nearest beach. The buildings could use an overhaul, but there are plenty of diversions on-site, such as golf, tennis, water-skiing, sailing, and boating on the Indian River, and even a circus school!

4500 SE Pine Valley, Port St. Lucie, FL 34952. ☎ **800/CLUB-MED** or 772/398-5100. Fax 772/398-5101. www.club med.com. 338 units. Winter $800–$1,700 per week; off season $700–$1,000 per week (prices are per adult; reduced rates are offered for children). Rates include accommodations; all meals; unlimited wine, beer, and soft drinks with lunch and dinner; sports equipment and instruction; and nightly entertainment. Transport from your city of departure to the village, as well as transfers to and from the village, is available. AE, MC, V. Closed Nov–Mar. From U.S. 1 S., turn left onto Westmoreland Blvd. Make another left onto Pine Valley Rd.; the resort entrance is straight ahead. **Amenities:** 2 restaurants; bar; 4 pools; 3 golf courses; 19 tennis courts (9 lighted); fitness center; watersports equipment; game rooms; coin-op washers and dryers. *In room:* A/C, TV, hair dryer.

MODERATE

Dockside–Harborlight Inn and Resort 🏖   Fronting the Intracoastal Waterway, the Harborlight is a great choice for boating and fishing enthusiasts, offering 15 boat slips and two private fishing piers. The hotel itself carries on the nautical theme with pierlike wooden stairs and rope railings. While not exactly captain's quarters, the rooms (straight out of Rooms to Go, albeit with a bit of a nautical flair) are attractive enough. Higher-priced units have either waterfront balconies or small kitchenettes.

1160 Seaway Dr., S. Hutchinson Island, FL 34949. ☎ **800/286-1745** or 772/468-3555. Fax 772/489-9848. www. docksideinn.com. 64 units. Winter $79 standard room, $95–$130 efficiency; off season $70–$105 standard room or efficiency. AE, DC, DISC, MC, V. From I-95, exit at 66A E. to U.S. 1 N. to Seaway Dr. **Amenities:** 2 outdoor heated pools; self-service laundry; 5 lighted fishing docks; boat dockage; grilling areas. *In room:* A/C, TV, dataport, kitchenette (in higher-priced rooms), minibar, coffeemaker.

WHERE TO DINE

There are a number of good seafood restaurants in the Fort Pierce and St. Lucie areas, but it's also easy to drive to Stuart for more diverse dining options. See p. 318 for recommendations in Stuart.

MODERATE

Le Brittany's 🏖🏖 FRENCH   Strip-mall dining never tasted so good. At this French Continental find, seafood is paramount and prix-fixe bargains make haute cuisine an accessible reality. Try the smoked salmon, duck pâté, Dover sole, and Grand Marnier. Chef Denis Floch and his wife, Françoise, definitely know their French food.

899 Prima Vista Blvd., Port St. Lucie. ☎ **772/871-2231.** Reservations recommended. Main courses $12–$20. MC, V. Wed–Sun 4:30–9pm.

Mangrove Mattie's ✿✿ SEAFOOD   A rustic restaurant on the Fort Pierce Inlet, Mangrove Mattie's is the best place for outdoor dining, thanks to both its priceless location—right on the inlet, affording panoramic views of the Atlantic—and its excellent fresh seafood. Happy hours, Monday through Friday from 4 to 7pm, are especially popular and feature a free buffet.

1640 Seaway Dr., Fort Pierce. (℃ **772/466-1044**. Reservations not necessary. Main courses $11–$18. AE, DISC, MC, V. Daily 11:30am–10pm.

PORT ST. LUCIE & FORT PIERCE AFTER DARK
ArtWalk, an event to showcase the galleries, restaurants, and shops of Fort Pierce, is held the second Wednesday of every month from 5 to 8pm and costs $5 per person. It begins in front of the Sunrise Theater (℃ **772/466-3880**). All galleries are usually open for this event, and they supply free beverages and cheese. The free **Friday Fest Street Festival** (www.mainstreetfortpierce.org), on the first Friday of every month at the Historic Downtown Riverfront, features live music and refreshments for sale. The **St. Lucie Blues Club,** 338 Port St. Lucie Blvd. (℃ **772/873-1111**), has jazz, blues, and rock music Tuesday through Sunday nights; reservations are recommended.

3 Vero Beach ✶ & Sebastian ✶✶

Old Florida is thriving in these remote and tranquil villages. Vero Beach, known for its exclusive and affluent winter population, and Sebastian, known as one of the last remaining fishing villages, are located at the northern tip of the Treasure Coast region in Indian River County. These two beach towns are populated with folks who appreciate the area's small-town feel, and that's exactly the appeal for visitors: a laid-back atmosphere, friendly people, and friendlier prices.

A crowd of well-tanned surfers from all over the state descends on the region, especially the Sebastian Inlet, to catch some of the state's biggest waves. Other watersports enthusiasts enjoy the area's fine diving and windsurfing. Anglers are also in heaven here. In spring, baseball buffs can catch some action from the L.A. Dodgers as they train in exhibition games.

ESSENTIALS
The **Indian River County Tourist Council,** 1216 21st St., Vero Beach, FL 32961 (℃ **772/567-3491;** fax 772/778-3181; www.vero-beach.fl.us/chamber), will send visitors a detailed information packet on the county (which includes Vero Beach and Sebastian), with a full-color map, a list of upcoming events, a hotel guide, and more.

BEACHES & OUTDOOR ACTIVITIES
BEACHES   You'll find plenty of free and open beachfront along the coast—most areas are uncrowded and are open from 7am until 10pm.

South Beach Park, on South Ocean Drive, at the end of Marigold Lane, is a busy, developed, lifeguarded beach with picnic tables, restrooms, and showers. It's known as one of the best swimming beaches in Vero Beach and attracts a young crowd that plays volleyball in a tranquil setting. A nature walk takes you onto beautiful secluded trails.

At the very north tip of the island, **Sebastian Inlet State Park** ✿, 9700 S. Fla. A1A, Melbourne (℃ **321/984-4852**), has flat, sandy beaches with lots of facilities, including kayak, paddleboat, and canoe rentals; a well-stocked surf shop; picnic tables; and a snack shop. The winds seem to stir up the surf with no jetty to stop their swells, to the delight of surfers and boarders, who come here to catch the big waves. Campers enjoy fully equipped sites in a woody area. At press time, the park was readying itself for the arrival of cozy, 1,150- to 1,600-square-foot cabins with high-tech amenities, such as Internet access, as well as woodsy ones, such as rocking chairs, porches, and fireplaces. Entry fees to the park are $5 per car and $1 for those who walk or bike in.

FISHING   Capt. Terry Lamielle has been fishing the area for more than 40 years and will teach you all about fly-fishing for red fish, snook, and tarpon. His **Indian River Adventures** (② 321/725-7255; www.indianriveradventures.com) takes anglers on his Sterling Flats fishing boat for private river excursions. Half-day jaunts on the Indian River cost $300 for one or two people (the minimum required for a charter), tackle, rigs, and everything included; it's $50 extra for a third person.

Many other charters, guides, party boats, and tackle shops operate in this area. Consult your hotel for suggestions, or call the **Vero Beach Chamber of Commerce** (② 772/567-3491). You can also contact **Captain Hiram's** (② 772/589-4345; www. hirams.com), a restaurant/bar/hotel/marina that houses many charter boats.

GOLF   Hard-core golfers insist that of the dozens of courses in the area, only a handful are worth their plot of grass. Set on rolling hills with uncluttered views of sand dunes and sky, the **Sandridge Golf Club,** 5300 73rd St., Vero Beach (② 772/770-5000), offers two par-72 18-holers. The Dunes is a long course with rolling fairways, while the newer Lakes course has lots of water. Both charge $26 to $35, including cart. Reservations are recommended and are taken 2 days in advance.

Although less challenging, the **Sebastian Municipal Golf Course,** 1010 E. Airport Dr. (② 772/589-6801), is a good 18-hole par-72. It's scenic, well maintained, and a relative bargain. Greens fees are $18 to $29 per player, with cart.

Golfers who are also baseball fans will be pleased to know there are two golf courses at **Dodgertown** (p. 326).

TENNIS   Many of the tennis courts around Vero Beach and Sebastian are at hotels and resorts, and are thus closed to nonguests. Instead, try **Riverside Racket Complex,** 350 Dahlia Lane, at Royal Palm Boulevard at the east end of Barber Bridge, Vero Beach (② 772/231-4787). This popular park has 10 hard courts (6 lighted) that can be rented for $3 per person per hour if you're a county resident, and $4 if not. Reservations are accepted up to 24 hours in advance.

SEEING THE SIGHTS

Environmental Learning Center *Kids*   The Indian River is not really a river at all, but a large, brackish lagoon that's home to a greater variety of species than any other estuary in North America—it has thousands of species of plants, animals, fish, and birds, including 36 species on the endangered list. The privately funded Environmental Learning Center was created to educate visitors about the Indian River area's environment. Situated on 51 island acres, the center features a 600-foot boardwalk through the mangroves and dozens of hands-on exhibits that are geared to both children and adults. There are touch tanks, exhibits, and microscopes for viewing the smallest sea life up close. The best thing to do is join one of the center's interpretive canoe trips, offered by reservation only ($10 for adults, $5 for children 6–12).

255 Live Oak Dr. (just off the 510 Causeway), Wabasso Island (a 51-acre island in the Indian River Lagoon). ② 772/589-5050. www.elcweb.org. Free admission. Tues–Fri 10am–4pm; Sat 9am–noon; Sun 1–4pm.

Indian River Citrus Museum   The tiny Indian River Citrus Museum exhibits artifacts relating to the history of the citrus industry, from its initial boom in the late

1800s to the present; a small grove displays several varieties. The gift shop sells citrus-themed items along with, of course, ready-to-ship fruit.

2140 14th Ave., Vero Beach. ℂ **772/770-2263**. Admission $1 donation. Tues–Fri 10am–4pm.

McKee Botanical Garden ⭐⭐   This impressive 18-acre attraction was originally opened in 1932 and featured a virtual jungle of orchids, exotic and native trees, monkeys, and birds. After years of neglect, it was placed on the National Register of Historic Places in 1998 and renovated; you can now again experience the full charms of this little Eden.

350 U.S. 1, Vero Beach. ℂ **772/794-0601**. Fax 772/794-0602. www.mckeegarden.org. Admission $6 adults, $5 seniors, $3.50 children 5–12. Tues–Sat 10am–5pm; Sun noon–5pm.

McLarty Treasure Museum ⭐   If you're unsure of why this area is called the Treasure Coast, then this is a must-see. Built on the site of a salvage camp from a 1715 shipwreck, this little museum is full of interesting history. It may not have the treasures of the nearby Mel Fisher museum (see below), but it offers an engaging 45-minute video describing the many aspects of treasure hunting. You'll also see household items salvaged from the Spanish fleet and dioramas of life in the 18th century.

13180 N. Fla. A1A, Sebastian Inlet State Recreation Area, Vero Beach. ℂ **772/589-2147**. Admission $1, free for children under 6. Daily 10am–4:30pm.

Mel Fisher's Treasure Museum ⭐⭐   This museum—where you can see millions of dollars in treasures from the doomed Spanish fleet that went down in 1715—is truly priceless. Although not as extensive as the museum in Key West (p. 215), the exhibits here include gold coins, bars, and Spanish artifacts that are worth a look. The preservation lab shows how the goods are extricated, cleaned, and preserved.

1322 U.S. 1, Sebastian. ℂ **772/589-9874**. www.melfisher.com. Admission $6.50 adults, $5 seniors over 55, $2 children 6–12. Mon–Sat 10am–5pm; Sun noon–5pm.

DODGERTOWN

Vero is the winter home of the **Los Angeles Dodgers** (at least for the time being; there's been talk of a move), and the town hosts the team in grand style. The 450-acre compound, **Dodgertown,** at 3901 26th St. (ℂ **772/569-4900;** www.dodgertownvero beach.com), encompasses spring-training camp, two golf courses, a conference center, a country club, a movie theater, a recreation room, citrus groves, and a residential community. It is a city unto its own for baseball fanatics. You can watch afternoon exhibition games between mid-February and the end of March in the comfortable 6,500-seat outdoor stadium. Even if the game sells out, you can sprawl on the lawn for just $8 (the stadium has never turned away an eager fan). And when spring training is over, you can still catch a game: The Dodgers' farm team, the Vero Beach Dodgers, has a full season of minor-league baseball in summer. Admission to the complex is free; tickets to games are $15 for a reserved seat. The complex is open daily from 9am to 5pm, with game time usually at 1pm. From I-95, take the exit for S.R. 60 East to 43rd Avenue and turn left; continue to 26th Street and turn right.

SHOPPING

Ocean Boulevard and Cardinal Drive are Vero's two main shopping streets. Both are near the beach and lined with boutiques, including antiques and home-decor shops.

   If you want to send fruit back home, the local source is **Hale Indian River Groves,** 615 Beachland Blvd. (ℂ **800/562-4502;** www.halegroves.com), a shipper of local citrus and jams since 1947, with four locations in Vero Beach. The grove is closed 2 to 3 months a year, usually from summer to early fall, depending on the crops; the season generally runs from November to Easter.

The **Horizon Outlet Center,** at S.R. 60 and I-95, Vero Beach (© **877/GO-OUT-LET** or 772/770-6171), contains more than 80 discount stores selling name-brand shoes, kitchenware, clothing, and more. The center is open Monday through Saturday from 9am to 8pm, and Sunday from 11am to 6pm.

Indian River Mall, 6200 20th St. (S.R. 60), about 5 miles east of I-95 (© **772/770-6255**), is a monster mall with the big chains and several department stores. It's open Monday through Saturday from 10am to 9pm, and Sunday from noon to 6pm.

WHERE TO STAY

You can choose to stay on the mainland or on the beach. As you might expect, the beachfront accommodations are a bit more expensive—but, I think, worth it. A great spot to know, especially if you're planning to fish, is the **Key West Inn at Captain Hiram's,** 1580 U.S. Hwy. 1, Sebastian (© **772/388-8588;** www.hirams.com), where 70 rooms are available adjacent to the restaurant and overlooking the water. (Also see "Fishing," above, and "Vero Beach & Sebastian After Dark," below.)

Comfortable and inexpensive chain options near the Horizon Outlet Center, off S.R. 60, include **Holiday Inn Express** (© **800/465-4329** or 772/567-2500) and **Hampton Inn** (© **800/426-7866** or 772/770-4299). Rates for both run between $70 and $80, and include breakfast and local calls.

MODERATE

Driftwood Resort ★★ *Finds*   Originally planned in the 1930s as a private estate by eccentric entrepreneur Waldo Sexton, the Driftwood was opened to the public in the late '30s after several travelers stopped by to inquire about renting a room here, since it was the largest property in Vero Beach and people assumed it was an attraction or, at least, a hotel. All of the guest rooms were renovated in 2000, and each is unique. Some feature terra-cotta floors and lighter furniture, while others have a more rustic feel with hardwoods and antiques. Some of the rooms contain Jacuzzis, and all are equipped with full kitchens. Two of the best units are the Captain's Quarters, which overlooks the ocean with a private staircase to the pool; and the town house located in the breezeway building, featuring a spiral staircase as well as living-room and bedroom views of the ocean. The resort is listed on the National Register of Historic Places and, to say the least, has lots of quirky charm. *Note:* The resort is currently undergoing rebuilding due to damage by Hurricane Wilma; it's slated to fully reopen by mid-2007. Check the website for the latest details.

3150 Ocean Dr., Vero Beach, FL 32963. © **772/231-0550.** Fax 772/234-1981. www.thedriftwood.com. 100 units. Winter $130–$160 double; off season $79–$120 double. AE, DISC, MC, V. **Amenities:** 2 outdoor heated pools; dry-cleaning service. *In room:* A/C, TV, kitchen (in most 1-bedroom and all 2-bedroom units), coffeemaker, Jacuzzi (in some rooms).

Islander Inn ★   This is one of the most comfortable and welcoming inns in the area. Well located in downtown Vero Beach, the small, quaint Key-West-meets-Old-Florida-style motel is just a short walk to the beach, restaurants, and shops. Every breezy guest room has a small refrigerator, either a king-size bed or two double beds, paddle fans, wicker furniture, and vaulted ceilings. They open onto a pretty courtyard and sparkling pool. Efficiencies have full kitchens.

3101 Ocean Dr., Vero Beach, FL 32963. © **800/952-5886** or 772/231-4431. 16 units. Winter $105–$120 double; off season $72–$99 double. Efficiencies cost $10 extra. AE, MC, V. **Amenities:** Cafe; pool. *In room:* A/C, TV, fridge.

Sea Turtle Inn & Apartments ℛ This two-part, smoke-free property offers the best value on the beach (just 2 blocks from the ocean). The 1950s motel and an adjacent apartment building have been fully renovated and outfitted with understated yet efficient furnishings. You won't find any fancy amenities, but its price and location make up for what it lacks in frills. The properties share a small pool and sun deck. Book early, especially in season, since they fill up quickly with long-term visitors.

835 Azalea Lane, Vero Beach, FL 32963. ℂ 877/998-8785 or 772/234-0788. www.seaturtleinn.net. 20 units. $99–$135 double; $145–$215 apt. Weekly and monthly rates available. MC, V. From I-95, go east on S.R. 60; it's about 10 miles to Cardinal Dr. Turn right onto Azalea Lane. **Amenities:** Small pool; bike rental; laundry facilities. *In room:* A/C, TV, small fridge, coffeemaker.

CAMPING

The Vero Beach and Sebastian areas of the Treasure Coast are popular with campers, who choose from nearly a dozen camping locations. If you aren't camping at the scenic and popular **Sebastian Inlet State Park** (p. 324), then try the **Vero Beach RV Park,** 8850 U.S. 1, Wabasso (ℂ **772/589-5665**). This 120-site campground is 2 miles from the ocean and the Intracoastal Waterway, and ¼ mile from the Indian River, a big draw for fishing fanatics. There's access to running water and electricity, as well as showers, a shop, and hookups for RVs. Rates are $40 per site and $32 for tents. To get here, take I-95 to exit 69 East; at U.S. 1, turn left.

WHERE TO DINE
EXPENSIVE
Café du Soir ℛℛℛ FRENCH/CONTINENTAL Exquisite country French cooking, a comprehensive wine list, and white-glove service complement the fine linens and imported china at this romantic standout owned and operated by Yannick Martin. Excellent starters include Louisiana sausage with sautéed apples, foie gras with caramelized raisins, and exceptional escargot. Main courses include sautéed Dover sole and filet mignon stuffed with Roquefort cheese. Desserts might include raspberry and strawberry Napoleons and country apple tartes.

21 Royal Palm Pointe., Vero Beach. ℂ **772/569-4607.** www.cafedusoir.com. Reservations recommended. Main courses $22–$35; fixed-price dinner $36 available in off season. AE, MC, V. Mon–Sat from 6pm; closing time varies based on last reservation.

MODERATE
Ocean Grill ℛℛ *(Finds)* STEAKS/SEAFOOD The Ocean Grill attracts faithful devotees with its simple but rich cooking and its stunning locale, right on the ocean's edge; ask for a table along the wall of windows that open onto the sea. Built over 60 years ago by Vero Beach eccentric Waldo Sexton, the restaurant was once an officers' club for residents of the nearby naval airbase during World War II. All fish can be prepared Cajun style, wood-grilled, or deep-fried. Indian River crab cakes make for a memorable meal, deep-fried with fresh backfin and claw meat rolled in cracker meal. Try stone crab claws when they're in season, the house shrimp scampi baked in butter and herbs and served with a tangy mustard sauce, or any of the big servings of meats. I especially recommend the Cajun rib-eye, featuring a béarnaise sauce that's delightfully jolting to the taste buds. Dinners are uniformly good here; the only tacky element of this place is the gift shop.

1050 Sexton Plaza (by the ocean at the end of S.R. 60), Vero Beach. ℂ **772/231-5409.** Reservations accepted only for large parties. Main courses $17–$30. AE, DC, DISC, MC, V. Mon–Fri 11:30am–2:30pm and 5:30–10pm; Sat–Sun 5:30–10pm. Closed Thanksgiving, Super Bowl Sun, and July 4.

INEXPENSIVE

Nino's Cafe ✧ ITALIAN   This little beachside cafe looks like a stereotypical pizza joint, complete with fake brick walls, murals of the Italian countryside, and red-and-white checked tablecloths. The atmosphere is pure cheese and so is much of the food—pizza and parmigiana dishes are smothered in the stuff. Still, the thin crust and fresh toppings make pizzas here a cut above the rest. Entrees and pastas are also tasty.

1006 Easter Lily Lane (off Ocean Dr., next to Humiston Park), Vero Beach. ✆ 772/231-9311. Main courses $9–$13. No credit cards. Mon–Thurs 11am–9pm; Fri–Sat 11am–10pm; Sun 4–9pm.

VERO BEACH & SEBASTIAN AFTER DARK

More than half the residents in this area are retirees, so it shouldn't be a surprise that, even on weekends, this town retires relatively early. Hotel lounges often have live music and a good bar scene, however, especially in high season, and sometimes stay open as late as 1am, if you're lucky. For beachside drinks, go to the **Driftwood Resort** (p. 327).

A mostly 30-something and younger crowd goes to **Bombay Louie's,** 398 21st St., Vero Beach (✆ **772/978-0209**), where a DJ spins dance music after 9pm Wednesday through Saturday.

Vero Beach is also known as an artsy enclave, hosting galleries such as the **Art Works,** 2855 Ocean Dr., Vero Beach (✆ 772/231-4688); and the **Bottalico Gallery,** 3121 Ocean Dr., Vero Beach (✆ 772/231-0414). The **Civic Arts Center,** at Riverside Park, is a hub of culture; it includes the **Riverside Theatre** (✆ 772/231-6990), the **Agnes Wahlstrom Youth Playhouse** (✆ 772/234-8052), and the **Center for the Arts** (✆ 772/231-0707), known for films and an excellent lecture series.

In Sebastian, you'll find live music every weekend (and daily in season) at **Captain Hiram's,** 1606 N. Indian River Dr. (✆ 772/589-4345), a salty outdoor restaurant and bar on the Intracoastal Waterway that locals and tourists love at all hours of the day and night (well, until it closes at 11pm, that is). The feel is tacky Key West, complete with a sand floor and thatched-roof bar.

North of the inlet, head for the tried-and-true **Sebastian Beach Inn** (SBI to locals), 7035 S. Fla. A1A (✆ **321/728-4311**), for live music on weekends. Jazz, blues, or sometimes rock 'n' roll starts at 9pm on Friday and Saturday. On Sunday, it's old-style reggae after 2pm. The inn is open daily for drinks from 11am until anytime between midnight and 2am.

4 A Side Trip Inland: Fishing at Lake Okeechobee ✧✧✧

60 miles SW of West Palm Beach

Many visitors to the Treasure Coast come to fish, and they certainly get their fill off the miles of Atlantic shore and on the inland rivers. But if you want to fish freshwater and nothing else, head for "The Lake"—**Lake Okeechobee,** that is. The state's largest, it's chock-full of good eating fish. Only about a 1½-hour drive from the coast, it makes a great day or weekend excursion.

ESSENTIALS

GETTING THERE   From Palm Beach, take I-95 S. to Southern Boulevard (U.S. 98 W.) in West Palm Beach, which merges with S.R. 80 and S.R. 441. Follow signs for S.R. 80 West through Belle Glade to South Bay. In South Bay, turn right onto U.S. 27 North, which leads directly to Clewiston.

VISITOR INFORMATION   Contact the **Clewiston Chamber of Commerce,** 544 W. Sugarland Hwy., Clewiston, FL 33440 (📞 **863/983-7979;** www.clewiston.org), for maps, business directories, and the names of numerous fishing guides throughout the area. In addition, you might contact the **Pahokee Chamber of Commerce,** 115 E. Main St., Pahokee, FL 33476 (📞 **772/924-5579;** fax 772/924-8116; www. pahokee.com), which will send a complete package of magazines, guides, and accommodations listings.

OUTDOOR ACTIVITIES

FISHING   See "Going After the Big One," below.

SKY DIVING   Besides fishing, the biggest sport in Clewiston is jumping out of planes, due to the area's limited air traffic and vast areas of flat, undeveloped land. **Air Adventures** (📞 **800/533-6151** or 863/983-6151; www.skydivefl.com) operates a year-round program from the Airglades Airport. If you've never jumped before, you can go on a tandem dive, where you'll be attached to a "jumpmaster." For the first 60 seconds, the two of you free-fall from about 12,500 feet. Then a quick pull of the chute turns your rapid descent into a gentle, balletlike cruise to the ground, with time to see the whole majestic lake from a privileged perspective. Dive packages start at $175; group rates start at $150.

WHERE TO STAY

If you aren't camping, book a room at the **Clewiston Inn** 🌟🌟, 108 Royal Palm Ave., Clewiston (📞 **800/749-4466** or 863/983-8151; www.clewistoninn.com). Built in 1938, this allegedly haunted Southern plantation–inspired hotel is the oldest in the Lake Okeechobee region. Its 52 rooms are simply decorated and nondescript. The lounge area sports a 1945 mural depicting the animals of the region. Double rooms start at $99 a night; suites begin at $129. All have air-conditioning and TVs.

Another choice, especially if you're here to fish, is **Roland Martin,** 920 E. Del Monte (📞 **800/473-6766** or 863/983-3151), the "Disney of fishing." This RV park (no tent sites) offers modest motel rooms, efficiencies, condominiums, apartments, and sites for your RV, with two heated pools, gift and marina shops, and a restaurant. The modern complex, dotted with prefab buildings, is clean and well manicured. Rooms rent for $68; efficiencies cost $88. Condominiums are about $150 a night, with a 3-night minimum. RV sites go for about $25 with TV and cable hookup.

CAMPING

During the winter, campers own the Clewiston area. Campsites are jammed with regulars who come year after year for the simple pleasures of the lake and, of course, the warm weather. Every manner of RV, from simple pop-top Volkswagens to Winnebagos to fully decked-out mobile homes, finds its way to the many campsites along the lake.

Okeechobee Landings, U.S. 27 E. (📞 **863/983-4144**), is one of the best; it has every conceivable amenity included in the price of a site. More than 250 sites are situated around a lake, clubhouse, snack bar, pool, Jacuzzi, horseshoe pit, shuffleboard court, and tennis court. Full hookup includes a sewage connection, which is not the case throughout the county. RV spots are sold to regulars, but there are usually some spots available for rental to one-time visitors. Rates start at $25 a day or $150 a week, plus tax, including hookup. Year-round rates for trailer rentals, which sleep two people, start at $32 Sunday through Thursday and from $37 on Friday and Saturday.

Also see **Roland Martin,** described above.

Going After the Big One

Fishing on Lake Okeechobee is a year-round affair, though the fish tend to bite a little better in the winter, perhaps for the benefit of the many snowbirds who flock here (especially Feb–Mar). RV camps are mobbed almost year-round with fish-frenzied anglers who come down for weeks at a time for a decent catch.

You'll need a fishing license to go out with a rod and reel. It's a simple matter to apply. The chamber of commerce and most fishing shops can sign you up on the spot. The cost for non-Florida residents is $17 for 7 days or $32 for the year.

You can rent, charter, or bring your own boat to Clewiston; just be sure to schedule your trip in advance. You don't want to show up during one of the frequent fishing tournaments only to find you can't get a room, campsite, or fishing boat. All tournaments are held at Roland Martin's marina (see below). For more information on tournaments, check out www.roland martinmarina.com.

There are several marinas where you can rent or charter boats. If it's your first time on the lake, I suggest chartering a boat with a guide who can show you the most fertile spots and help you handle your tackle. **Roland Martin,** 920 E. Del Monte (© **863/983-3151;** www.rolandmartinmarina.com), is the one-stop spot where you can find a guide, tackle, rods, bait, coolers, picnic supplies, and a choice of boats. Rates for a guided fishing tour are $200 for a half-day and $300 for a full day, for one or two people. You need a fishing license, which is available here for $17. There are also boat rentals: A 16-foot johnboat goes for $40 half-day and $60 full day, with a $40 deposit.

Another reputable boat-rental spot is **Angler's Marina,** 910 Okeechobee Blvd. (© **800/741-3141** or 863/983-BASS). Rentals for a 14-footer start at $40 half-day, for a maximum of four people. A full day costs $60. If you want a guide, rates start at $150 (for two people) for a half-day, though in the summer (June–Oct), when it's slow, you can usually get a cheaper deal.

WHERE TO DINE

If you aren't frying up your own catch for dinner, you can find a number of good eating spots in town. At the **Clewiston Inn** (see "Where to Stay," above), you can get catfish, beef stroganoff, ham hocks, fried chicken, and liver and onions in a setting as Southern as the food. The dining room is open daily from 6am to 2pm and 5 to 9pm; entrees cost $10 to $18. **L&L Restaurant,** 265 N. Devils Garden Rd. (© **863/983-6666**), is a good Spanish restaurant, with entrees ranging from $8 to $12. **Pinky's On the Green Pub,** Highway 80 (© **863/983-8464**), is a no-frills diner, with entrees under $10.

10

Southwest Florida

Although there are no adobe houses, cacti, or deserts, and, as far as we know, no John Edwards's *Crossing Over*–esque mystics hawking crystals here, Southwest Florida is definitely the Southwest in terms of serenity, golf, retirees, and expensive homes. While the area itself may be staid, and the ride here, through the Everglades, may be the closest thing to adventure you're going to get in this neck of the SoFlo woods, it's definitely an area worth exploring.

As primitive as it gets, Alligator Alley (I-75) is the closest thing to a dirt road that South Florida's got. Once a desolate two-lane road connecting Southeast Florida with the Gulf Coast, Alligator Alley is still pretty quiet, but hardly lifeless, thanks to the presence of the egrets, wood storks, owls, herons, osprey, red-shouldered hawks, belted kingfishers, and, of course, alligators that call the area behind the fenced-in, protected shoulders home. As you go through Alligator Alley, en route to or from Southwest Florida, your cellphone will not work and your only option for refueling will be at the Miccosukee Indian Reservation. Driving through Alligator Alley is like entering a time warp. When you reach the end, you will enter another world, where million-dollar mansions, posh resorts, golf courses, and all the signs of the good life are juxtaposed with nature.

Bordered on the east and south by the Everglades and on the west by an intriguing island-studded coast, Southwest Florida traces its nature-loving roots to

inventor and amateur botanist Thomas A. Edison, who was so enamored of it that he spent his last 46 winters in Fort Myers. His friend Henry Ford liked it, too, and built his own winter home next door. The world's best tarpon fishing lured President Theodore Roosevelt and his buddies to the 10,000 or so islands dotting this coast. Some of the planet's best shelling helped entice the du Ponts of Delaware to Gasparilla Island, where they founded the village of Boca Grande. The unspoiled beauty of Sanibel and Captiva islands so entranced Pulitzer Prize–winning political cartoonist J. N. "Ding" Darling that he campaigned to preserve much of those islands in their natural states. And the millionaires who built Naples make their town one of the most alluring—and expensive—in Florida.

Note: Southwest Florida took a beating during the brutal 2004 and 2005 hurricane seasons. The Category-4 storm Charlie hit hardest in the areas surrounding Fort Myers—Sanibel and Captiva islands, Fort Myers Beach, Punta Gorda, and Arcadia. While hotels on Sanibel and Captiva endured mostly landscaping damage, Fort Myers Beach suffered the worst in terms of erosion. At press time, the areas were awaiting funds from FEMA to repair damages.

Southwest Florida International Airport, on the eastern outskirts of Fort Myers, is this region's major airport (see "Essentials," in section 1, below). From here it's only 20 miles to Sanibel Island,

Southwest Florida

765
767
767
78
767
867
765
78
31
41
Olga
78
Bay Shore Rd.
Beach Blvd.
Tice
Orange River
Orange River Blvd.
Pondella Rd.
North Fort Myers
867
Palm
80
Ortiz Ave.
M.L. King Blvd.
FORT MYERS
867
Colonial Blvd.
82
75
Cleveland Ave.
Six Mile Cypress Pkwy.
Commerce Lakes Dr.
Cape Coral
Cape Coral Pkwy.
College Pkwy.
Cypress Lake Dr.
Daniels Pkwy.
Southwest Florida International Airport
Gladiolus Dr.
865
869
41
Alico Rd.
San Carlos Blvd.
McGregor Blvd.
Hendry Creek
San Carlos Park
J.N. "Ding"-Darling National Wildlife Refuge
Punta Rassa
Sanibel
Fort Myers Beach
Estero Blvd.
Mound Key State Park
Estero
SANIBEL ISLAND
Estero Bay
Tamiami Trail
887
Gulf of Mexico
865
41
Bonita Springs
Bonita Beach
Bonita Beach Rd.
901
75
Vanderbilt Beach
846
951
Cocohatchee River
862
Pine Ridge Rd.
896
31
851
41
Golden Gate Pkwy.
Naples
Naples Municipal Airport
84
Davis Blvd.
41
951
FLORIDA
Fort Myers
Map Area
MARCO ISLAND
Collier Blvd.
San Marco Rd.
GOODLAND
92
Everglades City
Ten Thousand Islands

Usseppa Island
Bokeelia
Charlotte Harbor
Pineland
Cabbage Key
Matlacha
Pine Island
PINE ISLAND
Cayo Costa
CAPTIVA ISLAND
Pine Island Sound
Intracoastal Waterway
Santa Barbara Blvd.
Chiquita Blvd.
Burnt Store Rd.
Pine Island Rd.
Del Prado Pkwy.
Caloosahatchee River

0   2 mi
0   2 km
N

ATTRACTIONS
Briggs Nature Center   **9**
Edison and Ford
   Winter Estates   **2**
Fort Myers
   Historical Museum   **3**
Koreshan State Historic Site   **5**
Lover's Key State Park   **7**
Olde Naples   **8**
Mound Key State
   Archaeological Park   **6**
Sanibel Lighthouse   **4**
Shell Factory   **1**
Tigertail Public Beach   **10**

35 miles to Naples, and 46 miles to Marco Island. If you have a car, you can see the area's sights and participate in most of its activities easily from one base of operations.

EXCURSIONS TO THE EVERGLADES & KEY WEST You won't be in Southwest Florida for long before you see advertisements for excursions to the Everglades. Naples is only 36 miles from Everglades City, the "back door" to wild and wonderful Everglades National Park, so it's easy to combine a visit to the national park with your stay in Southwest Florida. See chapter 7 for full details on the Everglades.

From Southwest Florida, you can also easily make a day trip to Key West by air or sea. **Cape Air** (© 800/352-0714; www.flycapeair.com) shuttles its small planes several times a day between Key West and both Southwest Florida International Airport and the Naples Municipal Airport. The same-day round-trip fare is about $180. The **Key West Shuttle** (© 888/539-2628 or 239/732-7744; www.keywestshuttle.com) runs to Key West from both Fort Myers Beach and Marco Island between November and May, departing in the morning, arriving in Key West about midday, and beginning the return voyage about 5pm. That gives you about 5 hours in Key West, so you may want to stay there overnight in order to more thoroughly explore the town. Round-trip fare is about $129 for adults and $109 for children 6 to 12. Contact the shuttle for schedules and reservations. See chapter 6 for full details on Key West and the rest of the Keys.

1 Fort Myers

148 miles NW of Miami, 142 miles S of Tampa, 42 miles N of Naples

You know how there are two schools of martini drinkers—one whose students consider themselves shaken-not-stirred purists and the other whose students believe in candy-colored cocktails, with the brighter and sweeter, the better? The purists usually shudder at the candy-cocktailers, and vice versa. Now replace those opposing martini camps with fans of technological progress and those who thought things were just fine the way they were, and you're on your way to understanding the dual mindset of historic Fort Meyers. You see, inventor Thomas Alva Edison came here in 1885 to regain his health after years of incessant toil and the death of his first wife. But unlike most new arrivals, he didn't just merge quietly into the population. Rather, his presence turned the city into one big light bulb: The cows didn't know what hit 'em. Some regret the light bulb ever making its way into Fort Myers. Others couldn't care less.

Today, however, the debate is moot, and the city's prime attractions are the homes Edison and Henry Ford built on the banks of the Caloosahatchee. Edison planted lush tropical gardens around the two homes and royal palms in front of the properties along McGregor Boulevard, once a cow trail leading from town to the docks at Punta Rassa. Had those two never showed up, Fort Myers would probably have been yet another Denny's-lined truck stop. Now lining McGregor Boulevard for miles, the trees give Fort Myers its nickname: the City of Palms.

After you've seen the Edison and Ford homes, you'll want to hightail it to the sands of nearby Fort Myers Beach or Sanibel or Captiva islands (see sections 2 and 3, later in this chapter). You also can venture inland and observe incredible numbers of wildlife in their river and swamp habitats, including those at the Babcock Ranch, largest of the surviving cattle producers and now a major game preserve.

Impressions
There is only one Fort Myers and 90 million people are going to find out.

—Thomas Edison

ESSENTIALS

GETTING THERE   This entire region is served by **Southwest Florida International Airport,** off Daniels Parkway east of I-75 (© 239/768-1000; www.swfia.com). You can get here on **Air Canada** (© 888/247-2262), **AirTran** (© 800/247-8726), **American** (© 800/433-7300), **American Trans Air** (© 800/225-2995), **America West** (© 800/235-9292), **Continental** (© 800/525-0280), **Delta** (© 800/221-1212), **JetBlue** (© 800/538-2583), **LTU International** (© 800/888-0200), **Midwest Express** (© 800/452-2022), **Northwest/KLM** (© 800/225-2525), **Royal** (© 800/667-7692), **Spirit** (© 800/772-7117), **Sun Country** (© 800/359-5786), **United** (© 800/241-6522), and **US Airways** (© 800/428-4322). The two baggage-claim areas have information booths (with maps) and free phones to various hotels in the region.

Alamo (© 800/327-9633), **Avis** (© 800/331-1212), **Budget** (© 800/527-0700), **Dollar** (© 800/800-4000), **Enterprise** (© 800/325-8007), **Hertz** (© 800/654-3131), **National** (© 800/CAR-RENT), and **Thrifty** (© 800/367-2277) have rental cars here.

Vans and **taxis** are available at a booth across the street from baggage claim. The maximum fares for one to three passengers are $26 to downtown Fort Myers, $38 to Fort Myers Beach, $40 to $47 to Sanibel Island, $60 to Captiva Island, $60 to Naples, and $75 to Marco Island. Each additional passenger pays $8.

Amtrak (© **800/USA-RAIL;** www.amtrak.com) provides bus connections between Fort Myers and its nearest station, in Tampa. The Amtrak buses arrive at and depart from **Greyhound/Trailways** (© **800/231-2222;** www.greyhound.com) bus station, at 2275 Cleveland Ave.

VISITOR INFORMATION   For advance information on Fort Myers, Fort Myers Beach, and Sanibel and Captiva islands, contact the **Lee Island Coast Visitor and Convention Bureau,** 2180 W. 1st St., Suite 100, Fort Myers, FL 33901 (© **800/237-6444** or 239/338-3500; fax 239/334-1106; www.leeislandcoast.com).

Volunteers staff information booths in the baggage-claim areas at Southwest Florida International Airport. Once you're in town, drop by the **Greater Fort Myers Chamber of Commerce** (© **800/366-3622** outside Florida, or 239/332-3624; fax 239/332-7276; www.fortmyers.org), which has a walk-in visitor center at Edwards Drive and Lee Street, on the waterfront. It's open Monday through Friday from 9am to 4:30pm. There's also an information booth at the Edison and Ford Winter Estates (see "Exploring the Area," below).

GETTING AROUND   LeeTran (© **239/275-8726;** www.rideleetran.com) operates public buses. System maps are available from the Greater Fort Myers Chamber of Commerce (see above). There's no public bus service to Sanibel and Captiva islands, but you can connect to the **Fort Myers Beach Trolleys** (p. 343).

For a taxi, call **Yellow Cab** (© **239/332-1055**), **Bluebird Taxi** (© **239/275-8294**), or **Admiralty Taxi** (© **239/275-7000**).

EXPLORING THE AREA
TOURING THE ESTATES

Edison and Ford Winter Estates 🎭🎭   Thomas Edison and his second wife, Mina, brought their family to this Victorian retreat—they called it Seminole Lodge—in 1886 and wintered here until the inventor's death, in 1931. Mrs. Edison gave the 14-acre estate to the city of Fort Myers in 1947, and today it's Southwest Florida's top historic attraction. It looks exactly as it did during Edison's lifetime. Costumed actors portraying the Edisons, the Fords, and their friends such as Harvey S. Firestone give living-history accounts of how the wealthy lived in those days.

An avid amateur botanist, Edison experimented with the exotic foliage he planted in the lush tropical gardens surrounding the mansion (he turned goldenrod into rubber and used bamboo for light-bulb filaments). Some of his light bulbs dating from the 1920s still burn in the laboratory where he and his staff worked on some of his 1,093 inventions. The monstrous banyan tree that shades the laboratory was 4 feet tall when Firestone presented it to Edison in 1925; today, it's the largest specimen in Florida. A museum displays some of Edison's inventions as well as his unique Model-T Ford, a gift from friend Henry Ford.

In 1916, Ford and his wife, Clara, built Mangoes, the bungalow-style house next door, so they could winter with the Edisons. Like Seminole Lodge, Mangoes is furnished as it appeared in the 1920s. The Fords' home is not as interesting as the Edisons', but when you go to the Edison House, you go through the Ford House, too, since the only way to see either one is on a guided tour, which includes both.

Allow an extra hour here to take a scenic ride on the river in a replica of Edison's electric boat, *Reliance.*

2350 McGregor Blvd. 🕿 **239/334-3614** for a recording, or 239/334-7419. www.edison-ford-estate.com. Admission $16 adults, $8.50 children 6–12. Boat rides $5.50 per person. Homes open Mon–Sat 9am–5:30pm, Sun noon–5:30pm (1½-hr. tours depart continuously; last tour departs at 4pm daily). Boat rides Mon–Fri 9am–3pm (weather permitting). Closed Thanksgiving, Christmas Eve, and Christmas Day.

OTHER DOWNTOWN ATTRACTIONS

A good way to explore downtown Fort Myers during the winter season is on a leisurely, 2-hour guided walking tour hosted by the **Fort Myers Historical Museum,** 2300 Peck St., at Jackson Street (🕿 **239/332-5955;** www.cityftmyers.com/attractions/historical. htm). The tours are held on Wednesday from 10am to noon and cost $5 for adults, $3 for children. Reservations are required.

The museum itself is housed in the restored Spanish-style depot served by the Atlantic Coast Line from 1924 to 1971. Inside you'll see exhibits depicting the city's history from the ancient Calusa peoples and the Spanish conquistadors to the first settlers. The remains of a P-39 Aircobra helps explain the town's role in training fighter pilots in World War II. Outside stands a replica of an 1800s "cracker" home and the *Esperanza,* the longest and one of the last of the plush Pullman private cars. Admission is $9.50 for adults, $8.50 for seniors, and $4 for children 3 to 12. Open Tuesday through Saturday from 10am to 5pm, and Sunday from noon to 4pm.

The Georgian Revival **Burroughs Home,** 2505 1st St., at Fowler Street (🕿 **239/ 332-6125;** www.cityftmyers.com/attractions/burroughs.aspx), was built on the banks of the Caloosahatchee River in 1901 by cattleman John Murphy and later sold to the Burroughs family. At press time, the home was under renovation and closed until further notice, so call before you go to make sure it's open.

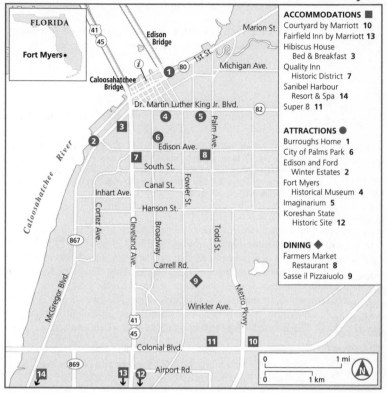

ACCOMMODATIONS ■
Courtyard by Marriott **10**
Fairfield Inn by Marriott **13**
Hibiscus House
  Bed & Breakfast **3**
Quality Inn
  Historic District **7**
Sanibel Harbour
  Resort & Spa **14**
Super 8 **11**

ATTRACTIONS ●
Burroughs Home **1**
City of Palms Park **6**
Edison and Ford
  Winter Estates **2**
Fort Myers
  Historical Museum **4**
Imaginarium **5**
Koreshan State
  Historic Site **12**

DINING ◆
Farmers Market
  Restaurant **8**
Sasse il Pizzaiuolo **9**

To avoid the kids going batty on a rainy day, head for the **Imaginarium,** 2000 Cranford Ave., at Martin Luther King, Jr., Boulevard (© **239/337-3332;** www.cityft myers.com/Attractions/imaginarium.htm), a hands-on museum in the old city water plant. A host of toylike exhibits explains basic scientific principles such as gravity and the weather. Admission is $8 for adults, $7 for seniors, and $5 for children 3 to 12. Open Monday through Saturday from 10am to 5pm, Sunday noon to 5pm. Closed Thanksgiving and Christmas.

A NEARBY HISTORIC ATTRACTION

Koreshan State Historic Site   Worth a 15-mile drive south of downtown Fort Myers if you're into canoeing or quirky gurus, these 300 acres on the narrow Estero River were home to the Koreshan Unity Movement (pronounced Ko-*resh*-en), a sect led by Chicagoan Cyrus Reed Teed. The Koreshans—who should not be confused with the late, disturbing Branch Davidian leader David Koresh—believed that humans lived *inside* the earth and—ahead of their time—that women should have equal rights. They established a self-sufficient settlement here in 1894. You can visit their garden and several of their buildings, plus view photos from the archives.

Canoeists will find marked trails winding down the slow-flowing river to **Mound Key,** an islet made of the shells discarded by the Calusa Indians (see "Canoeing &

Playing in the Sand

At the **American Sandsculpting Festival,** held each November on Fort Myers Beach, sand sculptors from around the world compete for prize money in two competitions, one for amateurs and one for pros.

Kayaking" under "Outdoor Activities & Spectator Sports," below). There's also a picnic and camping area with 60 wooded sites for tents and RVs. For information, contact the park superintendent at P.O. Box 7, Estero, FL 33928.

U.S. 41 at Corkscrew Rd., Estero (15 miles south of downtown Fort Myers). (©) **239/992-0311.** www.floridastate parks.org/koreshan/default.cfm. Admission $4 per vehicle for up to 8 people, $3 for a single-occupant vehicle, $1 per pedestrian or biker; tours $2 adults, $1 children 6–12. Canoes $5.30 per hour, $27 per day. Camping $22 year-round. Park daily 8am to sunset; settlement buildings daily 8am–5pm; 1-hr. tours Sat–Sun 1pm. From I-75, take Corkscrew Rd. (exit 19), go 2 miles west, and cross U.S. 41 into the site.

AN OLD-FASHIONED TRAIN RIDE

For those who claim there's little excitement or intrigue to be had in these parts, consider a ride on the **Seminole Gulf Railway** (© **800/736-4853** or 239/275-8487; www.semgulf.com), the original railroad that ran between Fort Myers and Naples. Today it chugs on daytime sightseeing trips and evening dinner/murder-mystery excursions south to Bonita Springs and north across the river. Call for the schedule and reservations, which are required for the dinner trips. The trains depart Fort Myers from its Colonial Station, a small, coral-colored building on Colonial Boulevard at Metro Parkway. The Bonita Springs station is on Old U.S. 41 at Pennsylvania Avenue.

SHOPPING

A kitschy (read: tacky) tourist attraction, the **Shell Factory and Nature Park,** 5 miles north of the Caloosahatchee River Bridge on U.S. 41 (© **800/282-5805** or 239/995-2141; www.shellfactory.com), not only carries one of the world's largest collections of shells, corals, sponges, and fossils, but also has bumper-boat rides, a light show, a gallery of African art, a small zoo, and two restaurants. Inside the store, entire sections are devoted to shell jewelry and shell lamps; many items cost under $10, some under $1. The Shell Factory is good for a rainy day, but if it's sunny, why pay for shells when you can collect them for free on the beach? Open daily from 9am to 9pm.

Outlet shoppers will find a large Levi's store, among other major-brand shops, at the **Sanibel Tanger Factory Stores,** on the way to the beaches at Summerlin Road and McGregor Boulevard (© **888/SHOP-333** or 239/454-1616; www.tangeroutlet. com). Another Levi's, plus Brooks Brothers, Donna Karan, Dockers, Fila, Nike, Reebok, Nautica, and many more stores, are at the much larger **Miromar Outlets,** on Corkscrew Road at I-75, Estero (© **239/948-3766;** www.miromar.com), about halfway between Fort Myers and Naples. Both outlet malls are open Monday through Saturday from 10am to 9pm, Sunday from 11am to 6pm.

OUTDOOR ACTIVITIES & SPECTATOR SPORTS

CANOEING & KAYAKING   The area's slow-moving rivers and quiet, island-speckled inland waters offer fine canoe and kayak adventures; you'll visit with birds and manatees along the way. Two popular local venues are the winding waterways around Pine Island west of town and the Estero River south of Fort Myers. The Estero

River route is an official Florida canoe trail and leads 3½ miles from U.S. 41 to Estero Bay, which is itself a state aquatic preserve (p. 343). Near the mouth of the river lies **Mound Key State Archaeological Park,** one of the largest Calusa shell middens. Scholars believe that this mostly artificial island dates back some 2,000 years and was the capital of the Calusa chief who ruled all of South Florida when the Spanish arrived. There's no park ranger on the key, but signs explain its history.

Koreshan State Historic Site, ½ mile south of the bridge at the intersection of U.S. 41 and Corkscrew Road (© 239/992-0311), rents canoes (see "A Nearby Historic Attraction," above). Less than a mile from the site, at the Estero River bridge, **Estero River Tackle & Canoe Outfitters,** 20991 S. Tamiami Trail (U.S. 41), Estero (© 239/ 992-4050; www.all-florida.com/swestero.htm), offers guided historic and nature tours (call for schedule and prices) and rents canoes and kayaks from 8am to 4pm for $18 to $30 a day. Open daily from 8am to sunset.

In addition to its cruises described below, **Tropic Star Cruises,** based at Pineland Marina, 3921 Waterfront Dr., Pineland on Pine Island (© 239/283-0015; www.tropic starcruises.com), rents kayaks and has guided tours over 18 miles of paddling trails. Rentals cost $35 a day for single-seaters, $45 for doubles. Call for schedule and prices of guided tours. The company also has a ferry service to Cayo Costa State Park, where it rents kayaks (p. 369).

CRUISES   J. C. Boat Cruises (© 239/334-7474; www.modernsurf.com/jccruises) presents a variety of year-round cruises on the Caloosahatchee River and its tributaries, including lunch and dinner voyages on the stern-wheeler *Captain J. P.* The 3-hour Everglades Jungle Cruise is a good way to observe the area's wildlife, with lots of manatees to be seen from November to April. Once a week, a full-day cruise goes all the way up the Caloosahatchee to Lake Okeechobee and back. The ticket office is at the Fort Myers City Yacht Basin, Edwards Drive at Lee Street, opposite the chamber of commerce. Prices range from $15 to $83 for adults. Schedules change and reservations are required, so call ahead.

"Buggy" Rides through a Mysterious Swamp

One of the easiest and most informative ways to see Southwest Florida's abundant wildlife is on a swamp-buggy ride with **Babcock Wilderness Adventures** 🌟🌟, 8000 S.R. 31, Punta Gorda, about 11 miles northeast of Fort Myers (© **800/500-5583** or 239/338-6367; www.babcockwilderness. com). Experienced naturalists lead 90-minute tours through the Babcock Ranch, the largest contiguous cattle operation east of the Mississippi River, and home to countless birds and wildlife as well as domesticated bison and quarter horses.

Unlike most wildlife tours in the region, this one covers five different ecosystems, from open prairie to cypress swamp. Admission is $18 for adults, $11 for children 3 to 12. The tours usually leave on the hour from 9am to 3pm November through April, and from 9am to noon May through October. Reservations are required, so call ahead.

If you're headed out to Cabbage Key, Cayo Costa State Park, or Boca Grande (see "Nearby Island Hopping," on p. 367), **Tropic Star Cruises** (© **239/283-0015;** www.tropicstarcruises.com) provides a faster way to get there from Fort Myers than driving to Captiva Island and taking a boat from there. Tropic Star's nature cruises on Pine Island Sound depart daily at 9:30am from Pineland Marina (see above) on Pine Island. They include a stop at Cayo Costa and Cabbage Key, and cost $29 for adults, $17 for kids under 12. The company also runs daily ferries to Cayo Costa State Park ($23 for adults, $17 for kids under 12) and to Boca Grande ($35 adults, $25 kids under 12). The ferries take less than 30 minutes to cross the sound. Call for departure times.

Much more luxurious, the sleek, 100-foot-long yacht *Sanibel Harbour Princess* (© **239/466-2128**) goes on sunset dinner cruises from its base at Sanibel Harbour Resort & Spa (p. 341). Evening cruises start at $53 for adults and $33 for children 6 to 12, including tax and gratuity. A 2-hour Sunday-brunch cruise costs $33 for adults, $23 for children. Call ahead for departure times and reservations.

GOLF & TENNIS   For an excellent rundown of Southwest Florida golf courses, pick up a free copy of *Golfer's Guide,* available at the visitor centers and many hotel lobbies, as well as online at www.golfersguide.com. See p. 375 for information on subscribing or ordering the current edition. And don't forget that you can call **Tee Times USA** (© **800/374-8633** or 888/465-3356; www.teetimesusa.com) to book starting times at Florida courses.

Although it looks like an exclusive private enclave, the **Fort Myers Country Club,** McGregor Boulevard at Hill Avenue (© **239/936-2457**), is a municipal course. Designed in 1917 by Donald Ross, it's flat and uninteresting by today's standards, but it's right in town. A steak-and-seafood restaurant now occupies the fine old clubhouse. The municipal course is the more challenging **Eastwood Golf Club,** on Ortiz Avenue between Colonial Boulevard and Dr. Martin Luther King, Jr., Boulevard (© **239/ 275-4848**), in the eastern suburbs. Greens fees at both courses range from $25 in summer to $60 in winter. Nonresidents must book tee times 24 hours in advance.

Other area courses open to the public include the Tom Fazio–designed **Gateway Golf & Country Club,** on Daniels Parkway east of the airport (© **239/561-1010**); and the two nationally acclaimed **Pelican's Nest** courses in Bonita Springs (© **239/ 947-4600**).

SPECTATOR SPORTS   While many baseball teams have jumped around Florida for spring training, the Red Sox and the Twins have worked out in Fort Myers for years. The **Boston Red Sox** play at the 6,500-seat **City of Palms Park,** Edison Avenue and Broadway (© **877/733-7699** or 239/334-4799; www.redsox.mlb.com). Tickets range from $10 to $44. The **Minnesota Twins** work out at the 7,500-seat **Bill Hammond Stadium** in the Lee County Sports Complex, on Six Mile Cypress Parkway between Daniels Parkway and Metro Parkway (© **800/338-9467** or 239/768-4200; www.twins.mlb.com). The Twins' minor-league affiliate, the **Fort Myers Miracle** (© **239/768-4210;** www.miraclebaseball.com), play in the stadium April through August.

The **Florida Everblades** (© **239/948-7825;** www.floridaeverblades.com) play minor-league professional hockey October through March at **Germain Arena,** at exit 19 off I-75 in Estero. Tickets range from $10 to $31.

WHERE TO STAY

If you're looking for a stay in a hotel with personality in Fort Myers proper, you're not going to find it. For that, you'll have to head to Fort Myers Beach (p. 343). But if you're looking for bargains and don't mind driving to the beach, Fort Myers has just about every chain hotel imaginable. Most are quite clean and reliable.

As in the rest of South Florida, winter room rates here are highest, and reservations essential, from mid-December to April. Even the chain hotels and motels along U.S. 41 in Fort Myers—most brands are represented along this thoroughfare—charge premium rates then. During the off season, however, prices drop by as much as 50% or more.

If you can't get a room at the properties mentioned below, the **Lee Island Coast Visitor and Convention Bureau** operates a free reservations service (℃ **800/733-7935**), covering many more accommodations in Fort Myers, Fort Myers Beach, and Sanibel and Captiva islands.

A few blocks from the Edison and Ford homes, the **Hibiscus House Bed & Breakfast,** 2135 McGregor Blvd., at Clifford Street (℃ **239/332-2651;** fax 239/332-8922; www.thehibiscushouse.net), is a must-stay for B&B fans, with five comfortable rooms, each with private bathroom, in a charming 100-year-old wooden house built in North Fort Myers. The building was later split in two, floated across the river, and nailed back together. The inn's owner brings 20-plus years of culinary experience (as the former owner of haute caterer A Moveable Feast in New York's tony Hamptons). Rates are $133 to $159 in winter, $119 to $139 off season, including breakfast.

Chain lodgings in the area include **Courtyard by Marriott,** 4455 Metro Pkwy., at Colonial Boulevard (℃ **800/321-2211** or 239/275-8600; www.marriott.com); **Fairfield Inn by Marriott,** 7090 Cypress Terrace, off U.S. 41 a block south of Daniels Parkway (℃ **800/228-2800** or 239/437-5600; www.marriott.com); and **Super 8,** 2717 Colonial Blvd. (℃ **800/800-8000** or 239/275-3500; www.super8.com).

Many business travelers opt for the Art Deco **Quality Inn Historic District,** 2431 Cleveland Ave. (U.S. 41), at Edison Avenue (℃ **800/998-0466** or 239/332-3232). Its location, a 2-block walk to the Red Sox training facility and a short drive to the Edison and Ford homes, is a plus for vacationers, too. Minor-league hopefuls stay here during spring training, so you could meet a future major-leaguer.

All hotel bills in Southwest Florida are subject to a 9% tax.

The only campground with tent sites near here is **Koreshan State Historic Site** (p. 338).

Sanibel Harbour Resort & Spa 𝓕𝓕𝓕 *(Kids*   This completely updated (2005) seaside resort is nestled on a tranquil 85-acre peninsula overlooking San Carlos Bay and Sanibel Island (a resort shuttle offers guests complimentary transportation to the island's beaches and to a bike-rental shop daily). The resorts 400 accommodations include the hotel tower, the pampering, concierge-style **Grande Bay at Sanibel Harbour,** and two condominium towers, all modern and luxurious throughout. All resort guest rooms and condominiums have balconies with wonderful water and island views, including spectacular sunsets over Sanibel. Five attractive outdoor pools and a delightful bayside beach offer relaxing sunning areas at the resort. The spa features over 60 sublime treatments, including the incredible and almost indescribable BETAR bed, one of only 16 such systems in the world, in which the body is bathed in sound waves to create a state of total relaxation. If fitness is your passion, the resort offers a world-class fitness center, five clay tennis courts, and an assortment of classes and clinics daily. And although this place exudes romance, it is also a fabulous vacation destination for families. The resort's award-wining Kids Klub offers fun-filled, educational adventures for children 5 to 12, daily from 10am to 4pm (night programs are added on weekends). Souvenirs, prizes, and lunch are included in the daily fee.

17260 Harbour Pointe Rd., Fort Myers, FL 33908. ℂ 800/767-7777 or 239/466-4000. Fax 239/466-2150. www. sanibel-resort.com. 400 units, including 53 condo apts. Winter from $359–$509 double, $429–$569 suite, $529–$729 condo apt; off season from $179–$449 double, $229–$519 suite, $329–$499 condo apt. Daily resort fee is $15 per unit, per day. Packages available. AE, DC, DISC, MC, V. Valet parking $13; free self-parking. Take the last exit off Summerlin Rd. before the Sanibel Causeway toll plaza. **Amenities:** 6 restaurants and lounges; 5 heated outdoor pools and 1 indoor pool; 5 clay tennis courts; health club and spa; watersports rentals; concierge; children's programs; activities desk; business center; room service; laundry service; dry cleaning. *In room:* A/C, TV, high-speed Internet access, kitchen (condos only), minibar (hotel only), minifridge (Grande Bay only), coffeemaker, hair dryer, iron, safe.

WHERE TO DINE

Fort Myers's main commercial strip, Cleveland Avenue (U.S. 41), is where you'll find most of the national fast-food and family chain restaurants, especially near College Parkway.

Farmers Market Restaurant ★★ *(Finds* SOUTHERN Cabbage, okra, green beans, and tomatoes at the retail Farmers Market next door provide the fodder for some of the best country-style cooking in Florida at this plain and simple restaurant, frequented by everyone from business executives to truck drivers. Specialties are beef and pork barbecue from the tin smokehouse out by Edison Avenue, plus other Southern favorites like country-fried steak, fried chicken livers and gizzards, and smoked ham hocks with a bowl of lima beans. Yankees can order fried chicken, roast beef, or pork chops, and hash browns instead of grits with the big breakfast. But forget about Southern Comfort: No alcohol is served, nor is smoking permitted.

2736 Edison Ave. (at Cranford Ave.). ℂ 239/334-1687. Breakfast $3–$7.50; sandwiches $3–$6; meals $7.50. No credit cards. Mon–Sat 6am–8pm; Sun 6am–7pm.

Sasse il Pizzaiuolo ★★ *(Finds* CONTINENTAL/ITALIAN In a small shopping strip north of the Edison Mall, this informal, often-noisy spot (pronounced Sassy's) offers one of the area's most unusual and reasonably priced dining experiences. Aromas waft from the wood-fired oven in the open kitchen, from which come enormous slabs of pizzalike bread (served with seasoned olive oil for dipping). The selections change daily, though you can usually count on braised lamb shank served over polenta, as well as veal scallopini stuffed with prosciutto, roasted peppers, and mozzarella. It's all of a quality rarely found at these prices, and the portions are so huge that most patrons carry home doggie bags. Note that reservations are not accepted (and preference is sometimes given to regulars), so be prepared to wait for a table, especially on weekends. I've gotten complaints about the service here, though I've never personally had a bad experience.

3651 Evans Ave., in Carrell Corner shopping center (between Carrell Rd. and Winkler Ave.). ℂ 239/278-5544. Reservations not accepted. Main courses $8–$18. No credit cards. Tues–Fri 11:30am–1:15pm; Wed–Sat 5:30–8:15pm.

FORT MYERS AFTER DARK

For the most part, Fort Myers shuts down after dark, and the pay-per-view on your hotel room's TV may be your best bet for entertainment. But some activities do take place when the sun goes down. For entertainment ideas and schedules, consult the daily *News-Press* (www.news-press.com), especially Friday's "Gulf Coasting" section. Also be on the lookout for *Happenings,* a tabloid-size entertainment guide distributed free at the visitor centers and in some hotel lobbies. Tickets for most events are available from **Ticketmaster** (© **239/334-3309**).

The city's showcase performing-arts venue is the **Barbara B. Mann Performing Arts Hall** ⟨×⟩, 8099 College Pkwy., at Summerlin Road (© **800/440-7469,** or 239/ 481-4849 for tickets; www.bbmannpah.com), on the campus of Edison College. It features world-famous performers and Broadway plays.

Originally a downtown vaudeville playhouse, the 1908-vintage **Arcade Theater,** 2267 1st St., between Bay and Hendry streets (© **239/332-4488**), presents a variety of performances.

2 Fort Myers Beach ⟨×⟩⟨×⟩

13 miles S of Fort Myers, 28 miles N of Naples, 12 miles E of Sanibel Island

Often overshadowed by trendy Sanibel and Captiva islands to the north and by ritzy Naples to the south, down-to-earth Fort Myers Beach, which occupies all of skinny Estero Island, offers just as much sun and sand as its affluent neighbors, both a half-hour drive away, but more moderate prices. In fact, if you're looking for that Jimmy Buffet style of slacking, Fort Myers Beach is where it's at.

Droves of families and young singles flock to the busy intersection of San Carlos Boulevard and Estero Boulevard, an area so packed with bars, beach-apparel shops, restaurants, and motels that the locals call it "Times Square." That Coney Island image certainly doesn't apply to the rest of Estero Island, where old-fashioned beach cottages, manicured condominiums, and quiet motels beckon couples and families in search of more sedate vacations. In fact, promoters of the southern end of the island don't even say they're in Fort Myers Beach; rather, they're on Estero Island. It's their way of distinguishing their part of town from congested Times Square.

Narrow Matanzas Pass leads into broad Estero Bay, which separates the island from the mainland. While the pass is the area's largest commercial fishing port (when they say "fresh off the boat" here, they aren't kidding), the bay is an official state aquatic preserve inhabited by a host of birds as well as manatees, dolphins, and other sea life. Nature cruises go forth onto this lovely protected bay, which is dotted with islands.

A few miles south of Fort Myers Beach, a chain of pristine barrier islands includes unspoiled Lover's Key, a state park where a tractor-pulled tram runs through a mangrove forest to one of Florida's best beaches.

ESSENTIALS

GETTING THERE   See section 1 on Fort Myers, beginning on p. 334, for information about Southwest Florida International Airport, car-rental firms, Amtrak trains, and Greyhound/Trailways bus service to the area.

VISITOR INFORMATION   You can get advance information from the **Lee Island Coast Visitor and Convention Bureau** (p. 335) and from the **Fort Myers Beach Chamber of Commerce,** 17200 San Carlos Blvd., Fort Myers Beach, FL 33931 (© **800/782-9283** or 239/454-7500; fax 239/454-7910; www.fmbchamber.com), which also sells a detailed street map ($2) and operates a visitor center on the mainland portion of San Carlos Boulevard, just south of Summerlin Road. The chamber is open Monday through Friday from 8am to 5pm, Saturday from 10am to 5pm, and Sunday from 11am to 5pm.

GETTING AROUND   Estero Island is absolutely inundated with traffic during the peak winter months, but you can get around on the **Beach Trolley,** which runs every

15 minutes, daily from 7am to 9:30pm, along the length of Estero Boulevard from Bowditch Regional Park at the north end south to Lover's Key. In winter, the **Beach Park & Ride Trolley** runs daily from 6:30am to 9:30pm between Summerlin Square Shopping Center, on the mainland at Summerlin Road and San Carlos Boulevard, to Bowditch Regional Park. Both trolleys cost $1 per person. Ask your hotel staff or call **LeeTran** (© 239/275-8726; www.rideleetran.com) for more info.

For a cab, call **Local Motion Taxi** (© 239/463-4111).

There are no bike paths, per se, although many folks ride along the paved shoulders of Estero Boulevard. A variety of rental bikes, scooters, and in-line skates are available at **Fun Rentals,** 1901 Estero Blvd., at Ohio Avenue (© 239/463-8844). Rates start at $55 a day for one-passenger scooters, $18 a day for bikes.

HITTING THE BEACH

A prime attraction for both beachgoers and nature lovers is the gorgeous **Lover's Key State Park** ☆☆☆, 8700 Estero Blvd. (© 239/463-4588; www.floridastateparks.org/loverskey/default.cfm), on the totally preserved Lover's Key, south of Estero Island. Although the highway runs down the center of the island, access to this unspoiled beach from the parking lot is restricted to footpaths and a tractor-pulled tram through a bird-filled forest of mangroves. The beach itself is known for its multitude of shells. Facilities include a snack shop and bathhouses with outdoor showers. The park is open daily from 8am to sunset. Admission is $5 per vehicle with two to eight occupants, $3 for vehicles with a single occupant, and $1 for pedestrians and bicyclists. No alcohol is allowed, nor are pets permitted on the beach or in the water (you must keep them on a leash elsewhere in the park).

On Estero Island, **Lynn Hall Memorial Park** features a fishing pier and beach in the middle of Times Square. It has changing rooms, restrooms, and one of the few public parking lots in the area; the meter costs 75¢ per hour, so keep it fed—there's a $35 fine if your time runs out. At the island's north end, **Bowditch Regional Park** has picnic tables, showers, and changing rooms. Parking is only for drivers with disabilities permits, but the park is also the turnaround point for the Beach Connection Trolley.

Several beach locations are hotbeds of parasailing, jet-skiing, sailboating, and other beach activities. **Times Square,** at San Carlos and Estero boulevards, and the **Best Western Beach Resort,** about ¼ mile north, are popular spots on Estero's busy north end. Other hot spots are **Diamond Head All Suite Beach Resort** (p. 346), just south of Times Square, and the **Junkanoo Beach Bar** (p. 350), in the midbeach area. Down south, activities are centered on the **Outrigger Beach Resort** (p. 347).

OUTDOOR ACTIVITIES

BOATING & BOAT RENTALS   Powerboats are available from the **Mid Island Marina** (© 239/765-4371), the **Fort Myers Beach Marina** (© 239/463-9552), the **Fish Tale Marina** (© 239/463-3600), and **Salty Sam's Marina** (© 239/463-7333). **Dockside Boat Rentals** (© 239/765-4433) rents them at the Best Western Pink Shell Beach Resort, on Estero Island's northern end. Boat rental costs about $125 for a half-day, $200 for a full day.

For canoers and kayakers, the big news is that the beaches of Fort Myers and Sanibel have rolled out the **Great Calusa Blueway** (© 800/296-0249; www.greatcalusablueway.com), a new 40-mile paddling trail that covers the waters of Lovers Key State Recreation Area; Mound Key State Archaeological Site; Koreshan State Historic Site; Fort Myers Beach; and Sanibel, Captiva, and Pine islands, ending at Cayo Costa. Even

0   1 Mi

0   1 Km

(i) **Information**

Bowditch
Point

Estero
Pass

Hurricane
Bay

San Carlos
Island

Main St.

San Carlos
Blvd.

TIMES
SQUARE

Mantanza Pass

Hell
Peckney
Bay

Dog
Key

FLORIDA

Fort Myers •

865

Estero Blvd.

Julies
Island

ESTERO
ISLAND

Starvation
Key

Gulf of
Mexico

Estero Bay

Ostego
Bay

Coon
Key

The Fish House 10

Lover's
Key

Carlos
Point

Big Carlos Pass

ACCOMMODATIONS ■
Best Western Pink Shell
   Beach Resort **2**
Diamond Head All Suite
   Beach Resort **6**
Edison Beach House
   All Suite Hotel **3**
Island House Motel **3**
Outrigger Beach Resort **9**
Palm Terrace Apartments **7**
Sandpiper Gulf Resort **8**

DINING ◆
Beach Pierside Grill **4**
Channel Mark **1**
The Dragonfly Bistro **1**
The Fish House **10**
Francesco's Italian Deli
   & Pizzeria **10**
Gulf Shore Grill **4**
Loggerheads **10**
Pappa Mondo Ristorante
   Italiano **5**

cooler, the Blueway utilizes GPS technology, marking key points along the trail to aid navigation.

CRUISES   A good way to get out on the water and see some of this area's wildlife is on a nature cruise aboard the *Island Princess* ((*C*) **239/765-4433**), an open pontoon boat based at the Best Western Pink Shell Beach Resort marina, on the north end of the island (p. 347). The boat usually goes on 1½-hour nature cruises Monday through Saturday afternoons. Prices are $13 for adults, $7 for children 6 to 12. The *Island Princess* also has bay fishing trips departing at 9am on Monday, Wednesday, Friday, and Saturday ($25 adults, $23 children), plus shelling trips departing at 9am on Tuesday and Thursday ($25 adults, $12 children). Reservations are required.

FISHING   You can surf-cast, throw your line off the pier at Times Square, or venture offshore on a number of charter-fishing boats here. The staff at **Getaway Marina,** 18400 San Carlos Blvd., about ½ mile north of the Sky Bridge ((*C*) **239/466-3600**), is adept at matching clients with skilled charter-boat skippers. Expect to spend about $65 for a full day's fishing for up to six persons, $45 for a half-day.

No reservations are required on party boats that take groups out. Operating year-round, the *Great Getaway* and *Great Getaway II* ((*C*) **239/466-3600**) sail from the Getaway Marina, about ½ mile north of the bridge. The *Island Lady* ((*C*) **239/482-2005**) is docked at Fisherman's Wharf, virtually under the San Carlos Island end of

43546

the Skyway Bridge. All depart between 8 and 9:30am, cost $70 per person, and have air-conditioned lounges with bars. Call for details and reservations.

SCUBA DIVING & SNORKELING   Scuba diving is available at **Seahorse Scuba,** 15600 San Carlos Blvd. (© **239/454-3111**). Two-tank dives start at $75. In business since 1989, the company also teaches diver-certification courses.

The live-aboard dive boat *Ultimate Getaway,* based at Getaway Marina, 18400 San Carlos Blvd. (© **239/466-3600;** fax 239/644-7529; www.ultimategetaway.net), makes 4-day voyages to the Dry Tortugas (70 miles west of Key West). This 100-foot vessel carries a maximum of 20 divers and is equipped with a dive platform, chase boat, and TV/VCR. Trips cost about $500 per person, including meals, beer, air, and weights, but bring your own regulator, mask, and fins. Reservations are essential.

WHERE TO STAY

The hostelries recommended below are removed from the crowds of Times Square, but three chain motels offer comfortable accommodations right in the center of the action: **Ramada Inn** (© **800/544-4592** or 239/463-6158), **Days Inn** (© **800/544-4592** or 239/463-9759), and **Howard Johnson Inn** (© **800/544-4592** or 239/463-9231). The midrise **Best Western Beach Resort** (© **800/336-4045** or 239/463-6000) is ¼ mile north, just far enough to escape the noise but still have a lively beach.

Sunstream Resorts, 6640 Estero Blvd., Fort Myers Beach (© **800/625-4111;** fax 239/463-3060; www.sunstream.com), manages "condominium hotels" that include the plush **Casa Playa,** 510 Estero Blvd. (© **800/569-4876** or 239/765-0510; www.casaplayaresort.com), and the **Lover's Key Beach Club & Resort,** 8771 Estero Blvd. (© **877/798-4879** or 239/765-1040; www.loverskey.com). The latter is on the north end of Lover's Key. The 60 spacious apartments in the older, 16-story **Pointe Estero Island Resort,** 6640 Estero Blvd. (© **239/765-1155**), all have whirlpool tubs and screened balconies with gorgeous Gulf or bay views. The less expensive **Santa Maria,** 7317 Estero Blvd. (© **239/765-6700**), is on the bay side of the island.

For campers, the somewhat-cramped **Red Coconut RV Resort,** 3001 Estero Blvd. (© **239/463-7200;** fax 239/463-2609; www.redcoconut.com), has sites for RVs and tents both on the Gulf side of the road and right on the beach. They start at $60 a night in winter and $31 off season.

EXPENSIVE

Diamond Head All Suite Beach Resort &   This luxurious 12-story beachside building sports large, comfortable one-bedroom apartments. Sliding-glass doors lead from both the living quarters and the bedrooms to screened balconies. The beachfront apartments are the most appealing, but every unit has a view (spectacular from the upper floors). Each room was renovated in 2006 and has a private 700-square-foot balcony, a sleeper sofa, two TVs, and a kitchen area. There's a full-service restaurant indoors, and Cabana's Beach Bar provides libation and light lunches beside the pool. During the winter season, evidence of nightlife can be found at the hotel's lounge, which has live music. If it's summer, however, you're on your own.

2000 Estero Blvd. (at Palm Ave.), Fort Myers Beach, FL 33931. © **888/765-5002** or 239/765-7654. Fax 239/765-1694. www.diamondheadfl.com. 124 units. Winter $238–$355 double; off season $160–$222 double. AE, DISC, MC, V. **Amenities:** 2 restaurants; 2 bars; heated outdoor pool; exercise room; Jacuzzi; watersports equipment rental; children's programs; limited room service; laundry service; coin-op washers and dryers. *In room:* A/C, TV, dataport, kitchen, fridge, microwave, coffeemaker, hair dryer, iron.

Edison Beach House All Suite Hotel 🌟🌟 No standardized list of amenities does justice to this obsessive-compulsively clean, intimate, five-story, nonsmoking beachside inn; when owner Larry Yax built it in 1999, he equipped every unit as if he were going to live in it. Each of the light and airy rooms has a balcony, ceiling fan, fully equipped kitchen (look for your complimentary bag of popcorn in the microwave oven), writing desk stocked with office supplies, and linen closet packed with extra towels. Most recently they added 47-inch HDTVs and high-speed Internet access to every room. Most of the bathrooms also have washer/dryers. The freshly laundered bedspreads provided to each new guest are but one example of the premium Larry puts on cleanliness. The beachfront units have the best view, but much more romantic are the "A" suites, whose queen-size beds are almost surrounded by windows formed by a turret on one corner of the building—you'll wake up to a panoramic view.

830 Estero Blvd., Fort Myers Beach, FL 33931. ℂ **800/399-2511** or 239/463-1530. Fax 239/765-9430. www.edison beachhouse.com. 24 units. Winter $145–$375 double; off season $125–$195 double. AE, DISC, MC, V. **Amenities:** Heated outdoor pool; laundry service. *In room:* A/C, TV, dataport, kitchen, coffeemaker, hair dryer, iron.

Pink Shell Beach Resort 🌟 This popular, family-oriented establishment fronts 12 acres of the Gulf and the Matanzas Pass from its perch on Estero's quiet northern end. It has efficiencies, suites, and one- and two-bedroom fully equipped apartments in three midrise, Gulf-front buildings with lovely views of Sanibel Island from screened balconies. The standard efficiencies are the least expensive units here. Old Florida–style cottages on stilts are pure kitsch. For a more luxurious stay, choose one of the beachfront White Sand Villas. More oceanfront villas—called Captiva Villas—should be completed in 2007. Sailboats and nature and sightseeing cruises pick up guests at the bayside marina, which rents boats and bikes. One of the coolest aspects of this hotel is its spa and the fact that it has a program called Aquateen, featuring a menu of spa and salon services for kids from 5 to 15. The scenic Hungry Pelican Cafe, on a covered deck overlooking the channel, is a great spot for breakfast or lunch.

275 Estero Blvd., Fort Myers Beach, FL 33931. ℂ **800/554-5454** or 239/463-6181. Fax 239/463-1229. www.pink shell.com. 234 units. Winter $205–$515 condo or cottage; off season $145–$500 condo or cottage. Packages and weekly rates available. AE, DC, DISC, MC, V. **Amenities:** Restaurant; bar; 4 heated outdoor pools; lighted tennis courts; watersports equipment rental; bike rental; babysitting; laundry service; coin-op washers and dryers. *In room:* A/C, TV, dataport, kitchen, fridge, microwave, coffeemaker, hair dryer, iron, safe.

MODERATE

Outrigger Beach Resort Well known for its beachside Tiki bar, this clean, pleasant motel has been owned and operated by the same family since 1965. The "garden efficiencies" in the original building have the feel of small cottages, with excellent ventilation through both front and rear windows, and doors opening to backyard decks. Other buildings here are two-story blocks containing motel-style rooms and efficiencies, which have views of the large parking lot. The beachside bar is one of the best places in Fort Myers Beach to watch the sun set.

6200 Estero Blvd., Fort Myers Beach, FL 33931. ℂ **800/749-3131** or 239/463-3131. Fax 239/463-6577. www.out riggerfmb.com. 144 units. Winter $130–$235 double; off season $95–$195 double. AE, MC, V. **Amenities:** Restaurant; bar; heated outdoor pool; exercise room; game room; coin-op washers and dryers. *In room:* A/C, TV, dataport, kitchen (efficiencies only), fridge, coffeemaker (efficiencies only), hair dryer, safe.

Sandpiper Gulf Resort Reminiscent of a private condo right on Fort Myers Beach, the Sandpiper Gulf Resort comprises two low-rise buildings, both with front-row access to the beach and to two tropical garden courtyards, in case the sand should get too hot. Suites are the beachfront apartments you always wanted to own but could never afford, although they could benefit from a little remodeling and updating (they're a bit like a beachy-keen Holiday Inn dating around 1975). Shuffleboard courts are delightfully retro, as are the guests (who tend to be on the AARP side).

5550 Estero Blvd., Fort Myers Beach, FL 33931. (℃ 800/584-1449 or 239/463-5721. Fax 239/765-0039. www.sand pipergulfresort.com. 63 units. Winter $160–$225 double; off season $90–$125 double. Additional person $8. AE, DC, DISC, MC, V. **Amenities:** 2 heated pools; Jacuzzi. In room: A/C, TV, dataport, kitchen, coffeemaker.

INEXPENSIVE

Island House Motel ✶ Value   Sitting on stilts in the Old Florida fashion, but with modern furnishings, Ken and Sylvia Lachapelle's clapboard-sided Island House enjoys a quiet location along a bayside channel, directly across the boulevard from the Best Western Beach Resort and within walking distance of busy Times Square. Four of the units have screened porches; all have kitchens and ceiling fans. Ken and Sylvia maintain an open-air lounge with a small library beneath one of the units; they also provide free beach chairs and bikes. Book as early as possible for February and March.

The Lachapelles also operate the three-story **Edgewater Inn,** less than a block away at 781 Estero Blvd. (same phone, fax, and website). The two one-bedroom and four two-bedroom apartments here all have screened lanais. They're available on a weekly basis in winter and for 3-day minimum stays off season.

701 Estero Blvd., Fort Myers Beach, FL 33931. (℃ 800/951-9975 or 239/463-9282. Fax 239/463-2080. 5 units. Winter $119–$149 double; off season $59–$79 double. Weekly rates available. MC, V. **Amenities:** Heated outdoor pool; access to nearby health club; free use of bicycles; coin-op washers and dryers. In room: A/C, TV, kitchen, coffeemaker, hair dryer, iron, free local calls.

Palm Terrace Apartments ✶ Value   Many European guests stay in these comfortable apartments about midway down the beach. In fact, between them, husband-and-wife owners Peter Piazza and Deborah Bowers speak fluent German and French and passable Italian. Their smaller, less-expensive units are on the ground level, with sliding-glass doors opening to a grassy yard, but even these rooms have cooking facilities that include microwave ovens. Most units are upstairs, with screened porches or decks overlooking a courtyard with a heated pool, a shuffleboard court, and a charcoal grill for barbecuing. Public access to the beach is across Estero Boulevard. There's no daily maid service, but you'll have an ample supply of clean linens.

3333 Estero Blvd., Fort Myers Beach, FL 33931. (℃ 800/320-5783 or 239/765-5783. Fax 239/765-5783. www. palm-terrace.com. 8 units. Winter $103–$156 double; off season $58–$96 double. 3-day minimum stay required in winter. Weekly rates available. AE, DISC, MC, V. **Amenities:** Heated outdoor pool; access to nearby health club; coin-op washers and dryers. In room: A/C, TV/VCR, dataport, WiFi access, kitchen, coffeemaker.

WHERE TO DINE

The busy area around Times Square has fast-food joints to augment several local restaurants catering to the beach crowd. The best of these is the **Beach Pierside Grill,** directly on the beach at the foot of Lynn Hall Memorial Pier (℃ 239/765-7800), a lively pub with blond-wood trim and vivid colors reminiscent of establishments in Miami's South Beach. It opens onto a large beachside patio with dining at umbrella tables, outstanding sunsets, and live bands playing at night. The reasonably priced fare is a catch-all of conch fritters, shrimp and fish baskets, burgers, and seafood main courses. Reservations are accepted; food is served daily from 11am to 11pm.

EXPENSIVE

The Dragonfly Bistro ✶✶ AMERICAN   Chef Preston Dishman (what better name for a chef?), graduate of New York City's French Culinary Institute, set his sights on this sleek restaurant after working at New York's famed Le Bernadin, and Fort Myers couldn't be luckier. Rich-red banquettes contribute to the coolness of the restaurant, but the menu, which changes with the seasons (even though Florida doesn't really experience seasons), is even cooler and richer. Everything but the sorbet is made from scratch here. Salivate over local hand-picked jumbo lump crab salad with aged cheddar and corn blini with tomato vinaigrette; seared fresh Maine sea scallops with roasted cauliflower, Yukon Gold potatoes, sweet garlic greens, and mustard butter; and chargrilled prime steak with Yukon Gold fries and caramelized onion aioli.

13499 U.S. 41 (in the Bell Tower Shops), Fort Myers Beach. (C) 239/415-9463. Reservations recommended. Main courses $21–$30. AE, DC, MC, V. Mon–Sat 7:30–9am; Sun 7:30–10am; Mon–Fri 11:15am–3pm; Sat 11:15am–4pm; Mon–Sat 5pm until "the customers stop coming in the door."

MODERATE

Channel Mark ✦✦ SEAFOOD   The crab cakes, delicately seasoned with Old Bay spice in true Maryland fashion, are enough to make this the beach's best place for seafood. Nestled by the "Little Bridge" leading onto San Carlos Island's northern end, every table here looks out on a maze of channel markers on Hurricane Bay. A dock with palms growing through it makes this a tranquil place for a waterside lunch. At night, a relaxed tropical ambience is ideal for kindling romance. The adjacent lounge offers the same menu and has live entertainment on weekends.

19001 San Carlos Blvd. (at north end of San Carlos Island). (C) 239/463-9127. Reservations recommended on major holidays; not accepted other times. Main courses $10–$25. AE, DISC, MC, V. Sun–Thurs 11am–10pm; Fri–Sat 11am–11pm.

Gulf Shore Grill SEAFOOD/AMERICAN   On the southern fringes of Times Square, this old clapboard building offers splendid views of the Gulf and the beach. It began life in the 1920s as the Crescent Beach Casino and has seen various incarnations as a bathhouse, gambling casino, dance hall, and rooming house. Traditional Florida-style main courses include baked grouper imperial, grilled mahimahi, and shrimp wrapped in bacon and coated with honey. This is one of the best breakfast spots on the beach, with items ranging from biscuits and gravy to eggs on a muffin with Alaskan crabmeat and a charon sauce. The kitchen also provides the pub fare for the **Cottage Bar,** an open-air drinking establishment next door with daily hours from 11am to 2am.

1270 Estero Blvd. (on the beach at Ave. A). (C) 239/765-5440. Reservations recommended for dinner. Main courses $10–$25; breakfast $5–$15; sandwiches and burgers $6–$13. AE, DISC, MC, V. Daily 8am–3pm and 5–10pm.

Loggerheads SEAFOOD/AMERICAN   The motto "The Local's Nest" accurately describes this friendly storefront restaurant, the best bet on the island's south end. Charter-boat captains and other locals congregate around a big square bar on one side of the knotty pine–accented dining room. The menu offers a wide range of appetizers, big salads, sandwiches, burgers, and entrees from both land and sea. Grouper prepared in a number of satisfying ways leads the main courses, but you can order traditionally fried, grilled, broiled, or blackened seafood, as well as pastas, steaks, and jerk chicken.

In Santini Marina Plaza, 7205 Estero Blvd. (at Lennel Rd.). (C) 239/463-4644. Reservations recommended on weekends. Main courses $13–$20; sandwiches and burgers $7–$8. AE, DISC, MC, V. Sun–Thurs 11am–11pm; Fri–Sat 11am–midnight.

Pappa Mondo Ristorante Italiano ✦✦ (Value) NORTHERN ITALIAN   Pasquale Riso (he's the chef) and Andrea Mazzonetto hail from Italy, and the fare they present in their attractive dining room—or out on their roadside patio—is authentic old-country cooking. They make everything from scratch—you can watch them producing pasta at a big machine behind a large picture window. Especially tasty is the ravioli, either ricotta-and-cheese-topped with butter-and-sage sauce, or stuffed with veal and served with a cream sauce tinged with balsamic vinegar.

1821 Estero Blvd. (at Ohio Ave.). © **239/765-9660**. Reservations recommended. Main courses $11–$16. AE, MC, V. Daily 3:30–10pm. Closed Christmas.

INEXPENSIVE

The Fish House SEAFOOD   You'll find the beach's least-expensive outdoor dining at the dockside tables of this friendly, no-frills pub. You'll also see charter-boat skippers slaking their thirst at a large wooden bar occupying about half the open-air screened dining room. Go for the fried or grilled grouper and other fish the captains have just landed. Sandwiches are available all day, including a tasty grouper version.

7225 Estero Blvd. (at Fish Tale Marina, behind Santini Marina Plaza). © **239/765-6766**. Main courses $7–$20; sandwiches $6.50–$9. AE, DISC, MC, V. Winter daily 11am–11pm; off season daily 11am–10pm. Closed Thanksgiving and Christmas.

Francesco's Italian Deli & Pizzeria ♣ ITALIAN   Wonderful aromas of baking pizzas, cannoli, breads, cookies, and fabulous calzones waft from this New York–style Italian deli. Order at the counter over a chiller packed with fresh deli meats, Italian sausage, and cheeses; then devour your goodies at tables inside or out on the covered walkway, or picnic on the beach. You can also take "heat-and-eat" meals of spaghetti, lasagna, eggplant parmigiana, manicotti, and ravioli to your hotel or condominium oven. The shelves are loaded with Italian wines, pastas, cookies, and anisette toast.

In Santini Marina Plaza, 7205 Estero Blvd. (at Lennel Rd.). © **239/463-5634**. Subs and sandwiches $5.50–$8; pizzas $12–$14; ready-to-cook meals $9–$11. No credit cards. Mon–Sat 8am–7pm.

FORT MYERS BEACH AFTER DARK

To find out what's going on during your stay, pick up a copy of the daily *News-Press* (www.news-press.com). The two local tabloids, *Beach Bulletin* and *Fort Myers Beach Observer,* are available at the chamber of commerce (p. 343).

The area around Times Square is always active, every day in winter and on weekends in the off season. At the foot of Lynn Hall Memorial Pier, the **Beach Pierside Grill,** 1000 Estero Blvd. (© **239/765-7800**), has live entertainment on its beachside patio. Facing due west, **Jimmy's Beach Bar,** in the Days Inn at 1130 Estero Blvd. (© **239/463-9759**), has live music nightly for the "best sunsets on the island" (actually, you can say that of all the beachside establishments here). It's not directly on the beach, but locals in the know head for the rooftop bar at **Beached Whale,** 1249 Estero Blvd. (© **239/463-5505**), which supplies free chicken wings during its nightly happy hour. Rock and reggae music are played downstairs for dancing.

Away from the crowds in the "middle beach" area, the **Junkanoo Beach Bar,** under Anthony's on the Gulf, 3040 Estero Blvd. (© **239/463-2600**), attracts a more affluent crowd for its bohemian-style parties that run from 11:30am to 1:30am daily. Live bands here specialize in reggae and other island music. The menu offers inexpensive subs, sandwiches, burgers, and pizzas, and a concessionaire rents beach cabanas and watersports toys, making it a good place for a lively day at the beach.

On Sunday afternoons, revelers jam the docks for the famous outdoor reggae parties at the **Bridge Waterfront Restaurant,** 708 Fisherman's Wharf (© **239/765-0050**), which is under the Sky Bridge on San Carlos Island.

3 Sanibel & Captiva Islands (★(★(★

14 miles W of Fort Myers, 40 miles N of Naples

Sanibel and Captiva are Florida's unfussy cousins. They don't need lip gloss and eye shadow to make them pretty. Leave the Tammy Faye makeup for Miami and Orlando. Here you'll find none of the neon signs, amusement parks, and high-rise condominiums that clutter most beach resorts in the state. Indeed, Sanibel's main drag, Periwinkle Way, runs under a canopy of whispery pines and gnarled oaks so thick they almost obscure the small signs for chic shops and restaurants. This wooded ambience is the work of local voters, who have saved their trees and tropical foliage, limited the size and appearance of signs, and permitted no building higher than the tallest palm and no WaveRunner or other noisy beach toy within 300 yards of their gorgeous, shell-strewn beaches. And although they haven't yet banned cacophonous cellphones, don't be surprised if they eventually do. It's *that* peaceful here.

Nevertheless, the islands have wildlife: More than half of the islands are preserved in their natural state as wildlife refuges. You can ride, walk, bike, canoe, or kayak through the J. N. ("Ding") Darling National Wildlife Refuge, one of Florida's best.

Legend says that Ponce de León named the larger of these two barrier islands San Ybel, after Queen Isabella of Spain. Another legend claims that Captiva's name comes from the captured women kept here by the pirate Jose Gaspar. The modern era of the islands dates from 1892, when a few farmers settled here. One of them, Clarence Chadwick, started an unsuccessful Key lime and copra plantation on Captiva; many of his towering coconut palms still stand, adding to the little island's tropical luster.

ESSENTIALS

GETTING THERE   See section 1 on Fort Myers, beginning on p. 334, for information on air, train, bus, and rental-car services. The Amoco station at 1015 Periwinkle Way, at Causeway Road, is the Sanibel agent for **Enterprise Rent-a-Car** (© **800/ 325-8007** or 239/395-2880).

VISITOR INFORMATION   The **Sanibel & Captiva Islands Chamber of Commerce,** 1159 Causeway Rd., Sanibel Island, FL 33957 (© **239/472-1080;** fax 239/ 472-1070; www.sanibel-captiva.org), maintains a visitor center on Causeway Road as you drive onto Sanibel from Fort Myers. The chamber gives away an island guide and sells a detailed street map for $3. Also for sale are books such as a comprehensive shelling guide and a helpful collection of menus from the islands' restaurants. Phones are available for making hotel and condominium reservations; check the brochure racks for discounts in summer and the month of December. Open Monday through Saturday from 9am to 7pm, Sunday from 10am to 5pm.

GETTING AROUND   Neither Sanibel nor Captiva has public transportation. No parking is permitted on any street or road on Sanibel. Free beach parking is available on the Sanibel Causeway. Other municipal lots either are reserved for local residents or have a 75¢ hourly fee. Accordingly, many residents and visitors get around by bicycle (see "More Ways to Enjoy the Outdoors," below). If you need a cab, call **Sanibel Taxi** (© **239/472-4160**).

PARKS & NATURE PRESERVES

Named for the *Des Moines Register* cartoonist who was a frequent visitor here and who started the federal Duck Stamp program, the outstanding **J. N. ("Ding") Darling**

National Wildlife Refuge ✸✸✸ (www.dingdarlingsociety.org), on Sanibel-Captiva Road, is home to alligators, raccoons, otters, and hundreds of species of birds. Occupying more than half of Sanibel Island, this 6,000-plus-acre area of mangrove swamps, winding waterways, and uplands has a 2-mile boardwalk nature trail and a 5-mile, one-way **Wildlife Drive.** The visitor center shows brief videos on the refuge's inhabitants every half-hour and sells a map keyed to numbered stops along the Wildlife Drive. The best times for viewing wildlife are early morning, late afternoon, and at low tide (tables are posted at the visitor center and are available at the chamber of commerce). Mosquitoes and "no-see-ums" (tiny, biting sand flies) are especially prevalent at dawn and dusk, so bring repellent.

Admission to the visitor center is free. The Wildlife Drive costs $5 per vehicle, $1 for hikers and bicyclists (free to holders of current federal Duck Stamps and National Park Service access passports). The visitor center is open November through April daily from 9am to 5pm; off season, daily from 9am to 4pm. It's open on federal holidays January through May, but closed on holidays the rest of the year. The Wildlife Drive is open year-round Saturday through Thursday from 1 hour after sunrise to 1 hour before sunset. For more information, contact the refuge at 1 Wildlife Dr., Sanibel Island, FL 33957 (✆ **239/472-1100**).

You'll get a lot more from your visit by taking a naturalist-narrated tram tour operated by **Tarpon Bay Explorers,** at the north end of Tarpon Bay Road (✆ **239/472-8900;** www.tarponbayexplorers.com). The tours last 2 hours and cost $10 for adults, $7 for children 12 and under. Schedules are seasonal, so call ahead.

Tarpon Bay Explorers also offers a variety of guided **canoe and kayak tours,** with an emphasis on the historical, cultural, and environmental aspects of the refuge (call for schedule and reservations, which are required). It also rents canoes, kayaks, and small boats with electric trolling motors (see "More Ways to Enjoy the Outdoors," below).

A short drive from the visitor center, the nonprofit **Sanibel/Captiva Conservation Foundation,** 3333 Sanibel-Captiva Rd. (✆ **239/472-2329;** www.sccf.org), maintains a nature center, a native-plant nursery, and 4.5 miles of nature trails on 1,100 acres of wetlands along the Sanibel River. You can learn more about the islands' unusual ecosystems through environmental workshops, guided 1½-hour trail walks, beach walks, and a 2-hour natural-history boat cruise (call for seasonal schedules and reservations). Various items are for sale, including native plants and publications on the islands' birds and other wildlife. Admission is $3 for adults, free for children 16 and under. The nature center is open from November 15 to April 14, Monday through Friday from 8:30am to 4pm, Saturday from 10am to 3pm; off season, Monday through Friday from 8:30am to 3pm.

Also nearby, the **Clinic for the Rehabilitation of Wildlife (C.R.O.W.),** 3883 Sanibel-Captiva Rd. (✆ **239/472-3644;** www.crowclinic.org), is dedicated to the care of sick, injured, and orphaned wildlife. Tours usually take place year-round Monday through Friday at 11am, but call to make sure. The cost is $3 per person.

Fun Fact **Did You Know?**

Captiva Island was the inspiration for the best-selling book *A Gift from the Sea,* by Anne Morrow Lindbergh, wife of the famous aviator. She described in detail the stunning island but never revealed its name.

Sanibel & Captiva Islands

ACCOMMODATIONS ■
Beachview Cottages **32**
Captiva Island Inn
 Bed & Breakfast **5**
Casa Ybel Resort **30**
Gulf Breeze Cottages **28**
Island Inn **31**
Jensen's on the Gulf **5**
Palm View Motel **27**
Sanibel Inn **26**

Sanibel's Seaside Inn **24**
Song of the Sea **25**
South Seas Resort **1**
Sundial Beach Resort **32**
Tarpon Tale Inn **23**
'Tween Waters Inn **6**

ATTRACTIONS ●
Bailey-Matthews
 Shell Museum **10**
J. N. (Ding) Darling
 National Wildlife
 Refuge **8**
Sanibel/Captiva
 Conservation
 Foundation **9**
Sanibel Historical Village
 & Museum **14**
Sanibel Lighthouse **22**
Tarpon Bay Recreation **11**

DINING ◆
The Bubble Room **2**
Captiva Sunshine Cafe **2**
Grandma Dot's
 Seaside Saloon **20**
The Green Flash **4**
Hungry Heron **13**
Jacaranda **18**
Jerry's Family
 Restaurant **16**
The Lazy Flamingo II **19**
Lighthouse Cafe **21**
Mad Hatter **7**
McT's Shrimp House
 & Tavern **17**
Morgan's Forest **29**
Mucky Duck **3**
R. C. Otter's Island Eats **2**
Sanibel Cafe **15**
The Timbers Restaurant
 & Fish Market **12**

HITTING THE BEACH: SHELLING & SEA LIFE

BEACHES   Sanibel has four public beach-access areas with metered parking: the eastern point around **Sanibel Lighthouse,** which has a fishing pier; **Gulfside City Park,** at the end of Algiers Lane, off Casa Ybel Road; **Tarpon Bay Road Beach,** at the south end of Tarpon Bay Road; and **Bowman's Beach,** off Sanibel-Captiva Road. **Turner Beach,** at Blind Pass between Sanibel and Captiva, is highly popular at sunset since it faces due west; there's a small free parking lot on the Captiva side, but parking on the Sanibel side is limited to holders of local permits. All except Tarpon Bay Road Beach have restrooms. *Be forewarned:* Although nude bathing is illegal, the north end of Bowman's Beach often sees more than its share of bare straight and gay bodies.

   Another popular beach on Captiva is at the end of Andy Rosse Lane in front of the Mucky Duck Restaurant. It's the one place here where you can rent motorized watersports equipment (see "More Ways to Enjoy the Outdoors," below), but you'll have to use the Mucky Duck's restrooms if you need to go. There's limited free parking just north of here, at the end of Captiva Drive (go past the entrance to South Seas Resort to the end of the road).

SHELLING   Sanibel and Captiva are famous for their seashells, and local residents and visitors alike can be seen in the "Sanibel stoop" or the "Captiva crouch" while searching for some 200 species. Only if you're a hard-core shell fanatic should you

> ## (Tips Don't Take Live Shells
>
> Florida law prohibits taking live shells (those with living creatures inside them) from the beaches, and federal regulations prevent them from being removed from the J. N. ("Ding") Darling National Wildlife Refuge.

check out the **Bailey-Matthews Shell Museum** ✹✹, 3075 Sanibel-Captiva Rd. (© **888/679-6450** or 239/395-2233; www.shellmuseum.org), the only museum in the United States devoted solely to saltwater, freshwater, and land shells (yes, snails are included). The museum is a far cry from the tourist-trappy shell factories you'll see throughout the state. Shells from as far away as South Africa surround a 6-foot globe in the middle of the main exhibit hall, thus showing their geographic origins. A spinning wheel–shaped case identifies shells likely to wash up on Sanibel. Other exhibits are devoted to shells in tribal art, fossil shells found in Florida, medicinal qualities of various mollusks, the endangered Florida tree snail, and "sailor's Valentines"—shell crafts made by natives of Barbados for sailors to bring home to their loved ones. The library attracts serious malacologists—for the uninitiated, those who study mollusks—and a shop purveys clever shell-themed gifts. The museum is open Tuesday through Sunday from 10am to 4pm; admission is $6 for adults and $3 for children 8 to 16.

The months from February to April, or after any storm, are the prime times of the year to look for whelks, olives, scallops, sand dollars, conch, and many other varieties of shells. Low tide is the best time of day. The shells can be sharp, so wear Aqua Socks or old running shoes whenever you go walking on the beach.

With so many shellers scouring Sanibel, you may have better luck finding that rare shell on the nearby islands, such as Upper Captiva and Cayo Costa (see "Nearby Island Hopping," beginning on p. 367). **Captiva Cruises** ✹✹ (© **239/472-5300;** www.captivacruises.com) runs shelling trips from the South Seas Resort on Captiva, daily at 9am and noon. They cost $45 for adults and $25 for children; reservations are required. Captiva Cruises also offers popular dolphin-watching and wildlife cruises, with narration by a naturalist from the Sanibel-Captiva Conservation Foundation, daily from 4 to 5:30pm. The cruises cost $20 for adults, $13 for kids. All of Captiva Cruises' boats are air-conditioned and have restrooms and snack bars.

At least 15 charter-boat skippers also offer to take guests on shelling expeditions to these less-explored areas. Their half-day rates are about $200 for up to four people, so get a group to go. Several operate from the **'Tween Waters Inn Marina,** on Captiva (© **239/472-5161**), including **Capt. Mike Fuery** (© **239/466-3649**). Others are based at **Jensen's Twin Palms Marina** on Captiva (© **239/472-5800**), and at the **Sanibel Marina** on North Yachtsman Drive, off Periwinkle Way east of Causeway Boulevard (© **239/472-2723**). Charter-boat brochures are available at the chamber of commerce's visitor center (p. 351), as well as listed in the free tourist publications.

MORE WAYS TO ENJOY THE OUTDOORS

BIKING, WALKING, JOGGING & IN-LINE SKATING   On Sanibel, paved bike paths run alongside most roads, including the length of Periwinkle Way and along Sanibel-Captiva Road to Blind Pass, making the island a paradise for cyclists, walkers, joggers, and in-line skaters. You can also walk or bike the 5-mile, one-way nature trail through the J. N. ("Ding") Darling National Wildlife Refuge. There are no bike paths on Captiva, where trees next to the narrow roads can make for dangerous riding.

The chamber of commerce's visitor center has bike maps, as do Sanibel's rental firms: **Finnimore's Cycle Shop,** 2353 Periwinkle Way (© 239/472-5577); the **Bike Rental,** 2330 Palm Ridge Rd. (© 239/472-2241); **Billy's Rentals,** 1470 Periwinkle Way (© 239/472-5248); **Boats, Bikes & Beach Stuff,** 2427 Periwinkle Way (© 239/472-8717); and **Tarpon Bay Explorers,** at the north end of Tarpon Bay Road (© 239/472-8900). On Captiva, **Jim's Bike & Skate Rentals,** on Andy Rosse Lane (© 239/472-1296), rents bikes and beach equipment. Bike rates range from $7 for 4 hours to $15 a day for basic models. Both Finnimore's and Jim's also rent in-line skates.

BOATING & FISHING   On Sanibel, rental boats and charter-fishing excursions are available from the **Boat House,** at the Sanibel Marina, North Yachtsman Drive (© **239/472-2531**), off Periwinkle Way east of Causeway Road. **Tarpon Bay Explorers,** at the north end of Tarpon Bay Road (© **239/472-8900**), rents boats with electric trolling motors and tackle for fishing.

On Captiva, check with **Sweet Water Rentals,** at the 'Tween Waters Inn Marina (© **239/472-6376**); **Jensen's Twin Palms Marina** (© **239/472-5800**); and **McCarthy's Marina** (© **239/472-5200**), all on Captiva Road. Rental boats cost about $125 for a half-day, $200 for a full day.

Many charter-fishing captains are docked at these marinas. Half-day rates are about $300 for up to four people. The skippers leave free brochures at the chamber of commerce's visitor center (p. 351), and they're also listed in the free tourist publications found there.

CANOEING & KAYAKING   As noted under "Parks & Nature Preserves," above, **Tarpon Bay Explorers** (© **239/472-8900;** www.tarponbayexplorers.com) has guided canoe and kayak trips in the J. N. ("Ding") Darling National Wildlife Refuge. Do-it-yourselfers can rent canoes and kayaks here. They cost $20 for the first 2 hours, $10 for each additional hour. **Captiva Kayak Co./WildSide Adventures,** at McCarthy's Marina (© **877/395-2925** or 239/395-2925), rents canoes and kayaks on Captiva, as does **'Tween Waters Inn Marina** (© **239/472-5161**).

Naturalist, avid environmentalist, and former Sanibel mayor Mark "Bird" Westall of **Canoe Adventures** ✿✿ (© **239/472-5218;** fax 239/472-6833) takes visitors on canoe trips through the wildlife refuge and on the Sanibel River. His excursions are timed for low tide and cost $45 for adults, $25 for children under 18. He will tailor shorter trips to accommodate children or anyone else not up to 2½ to 3 hours in a canoe. Naturalist **Brian Houston** leads kayaking trips from 'Tween Waters Inn Marina, on Captiva, but make your reservations at Tarpon Bay Recreation, on Sanibel (© **239/472-8900**). Brian charges $45 per person. **Captiva Kayak Co./WildSide Adventures,** based at McCarthy's Marina, on Captiva (© **877/395-2925** or 239/395-2925), has day and night back-bay ecology trips for $35 adults, $25 teens, and $20 children (add $10 to each price for night trips). The company will customize tours, including camping on Cayo Costa (see "Nearby Island Hopping," beginning on p. 367) for advanced kayakers. Reservations are essential for all operators.

For information on the new 40-mile **Great Calusa Blueway** paddling trail, see p. 344.

GOLF & TENNIS   Golfers may view a gallery of wild animals while playing the 5,600-yard, par-70, 18-hole course at the **Dunes Golf and Tennis Club,** 949 Sandcastle Rd., Sanibel (© **239/472-2535;** www.dunesgolfsanibel.com), whose back 9 runs across a wildlife preserve. Call a day in advance for seasonal greens fees and a tee time. The Dunes also has seven tennis courts.

Don't Take the Bait

If you plan on fishing, keep the following information in mind:

- Fees start at $200 for a half-day (4-hour) trip; 6-hour and 8-hour trips are also available.
- The guide will provide the boat, license, fishing gear, equipment, and bait.
- Many guides will clean and fillet the catches, and can recommend places that will mount the big ones.
- Licensed guides are required to know CPR and first aid—and are periodically retested.
- Virtually all guides have ship-to-shore radios on their boats in the event of an emergency.
- If a meal is planned at a restaurant after the trip, usually the client buys the guide's lunch.
- Clients usually tip guides after a successful fishing experience, ranging from $20 to $50 per trip.

You can also play nine water-bordered holes at **Beachview Golf Club,** 1100 Par View Dr., Sanibel (© 239/472-2626).

The **South Seas Resort,** on Captiva (p. 360), has tennis courts and a nine-hole golf course, but they're for guests only.

SAILING   If you want to learn how to sail or simply polish your skills, noted yachties Steve and Doris Colgate have a branch of their **Offshore Sailing School** at the South Seas Resort on Captiva (© **888/454-9002** or 239/472-5111, ext. 7141; www.offshore-sailing.com). Clinics range from a half-day to a full week. Also ask about the popular women-only, father-son, and mother-daughter programs.

Also based on Captiva are two sailboats that take guests out on the waters of Pine Island Sound: the *Adventure* (© **239/472-5300**) and the *New Moon* (© **239/395-1782**). They cost $95 per hour with a 2-hour minimum. Reservations are required.

Do-it-yourselfers can rent small sailboats from **Captiva Kayak Co./WildSide Adventures,** based at McCarthy's Marina (© **877/395-2925** or 239/395-2925). Prices range from $25 to $55 an hour, depending on the size of the craft.

WATERSPORTS   Sanibel may prohibit motorized watersports equipment on its beaches, but Captiva doesn't. **Yolo Watersports** (© **239/472-9656**) offers parasailing and WaveRunner rentals on the beach in front of the Mucky Duck Restaurant, at the Gulf end of Andy Rosse Lane.

MORE TO SEE & DO

Worth a brief stop after you've done everything else here, the **Sanibel Historical Village & Museum,** 950 Dunlop Rd. (© **239/472-4648**), includes the 1913-vintage Rutland home and the 1926 versions of Bailey's General Store (complete with Red Crown gasoline pumps), the post office, and Miss Charlotta's Tea Room. Displays highlight the islands' prehistoric Calusa, as well as old photos from pioneer days, turn-of-the-20th-century clothing, and a variety of memorabilia. It's open from November to May Wednesday through Saturday from 10am to 4pm; from June to mid-August Wednesday through Saturday from 10am to 1pm. Admission is by $3 donation.

At the east end of Periwinkle Way, the **Sanibel Lighthouse** has marked the entrance to San Carlos Bay since 1884. The light keepers used to live in the cottages at the base of the 94-foot tower. The now-automatic lighthouse makes for a lovely Kodak moment, but it isn't open to visitors, though the grounds and beach are.

The best way to get the lay of the land and learn all about the islands' history is on a 2-hour **Sanibel Island Eco-History Trolley Tour,** staged by Adventures in Paradise (© 239/472-8443; www.adventureinparadiseinc.com). Tours depart the chamber of commerce (p. 351) Monday through Saturday at 10:30am and 1pm. They're $20 for adults, $15 for children, and free for kids 3 and under. Call for reservations.

In addition to its other trips, **Captiva Cruises** (© 239/472-5300; www.captiva cruises.com) goes on daily sunset cruises from South Seas Resort, on Captiva. The cruise costs $20 adults, $10 children 6 to 12. Call for times and reservations.

SHOPPING

Most shops are open Monday through Saturday from 9am to 6pm, Sunday from noon to 5pm. You can burn up a rainy day and lots of credit at Sanibel's numerous upscale boutiques carrying expensive jewelry, apparel, and gifts. Many are in **Periwinkle Place** and **Tahitian Gardens,** the main shopping centers along Periwinkle Way. The larger Periwinkle Place sports mostly high-end men's and women's clothiers, while Tahitian Gardens has some excellent gift shops, including the **Cheshire Cat** (© 239/482-8697), which sells nature toys and other unique items for kids.

More than a dozen Sanibel galleries feature original works of art; pick up a gallery guide at the chamber of commerce's visitor center (p. 351). On Captiva, the treehouse-like **Jungle Drums,** on Andy Rosse Lane (© 239/395-2266), has the area's most unique collection of wildlife art.

Founded in 1899, **Bailey's General Store,** Periwinkle Way and Tarpon Bay Road (© 239/472-1516), is still going strong, with a supermarket, deli, salad bar, hardware store, beach shop, shoe repair, and Western Union all under one roof. Bailey's is open daily from 7am to 9pm.

WHERE TO STAY

Sanibel & Captiva Central Reservations, Inc. (© 800/325-1352 or 239/472-0457; fax 239/472-2178; www.sanibel-captivarent.com) and **1-800-SANIBEL** (© 800/726-4235 or 239/472-1800; fax 239/395-9690; www.1-800-sanibel.com) are reservations services that can book you into most condominiums and cottages here.

In general, Sanibel and Captiva room and condominium rates are highest during the shelling season, February through April. January is usually somewhat less expensive. But note that most rates fall drastically during the off season; don't hesitate to ask for a discount or special deal then. Since most properties on the islands are geared to 1-week vacations, you can save by purchasing a package for stays of 7 nights or longer.

The islands' sole campground, the **Periwinkle Trailer Park,** 1119 Periwinkle Way, Sanibel Island (© 239/472-1433), is so popular it doesn't even advertise. No other camping is permitted on either Sanibel or Captiva.

SANIBEL ISLAND
Very Expensive
Casa Ybel Resort ✿✿✿   One of the best resorts on Sanibel, this all-condo property sits on 23 acres beside the beach on the historic site of the island's first beachfront

hotel, the Thistle Lodge. The present-day Casa Ybel's turn-of-the-20th-century central building houses a restaurant of that name, where both guests and nonguests can enjoy wonderful cuisine—butter-poached lobster tail, pan-steamed Maine lobster, crackling coconut prawns with Thai orange-chile sauce—and magnificent Gulf views. The swimming pool in front of the restaurant is one of Florida's most picturesque. There are also 14 miles of seashell-studded white sand. This is bliss. The spacious one- and two-bedroom condominiums, housed in gray four-story buildings on the island's most beautifully landscaped grounds, all have screened porches (complete with outdoor gas grills facing the Gulf). With upstairs bedrooms, the town house–style units provide more privacy than most condominiums on Sanibel.

2255 W. Gulf Dr., Sanibel Island, FL 33957. ℂ 800/276-4753 or 239/472-3145. Fax 239/472-2109. www.casaybelresort.com. 114 units. Winter $315–$495 condo; off season $275–$315 condo. Packages and weekly rates available. AE, DISC, MC, V. **Amenities:** Restaurant; bar; heated outdoor pool; tennis courts; Jacuzzi; watersports equipment rental; bike rental; children's programs; concierge; massage; babysitting; laundry service. *In room:* A/C, TV, kitchen, coffeemaker, hair dryer, iron.

Sanibel Inn 🅵 *Kids*   A back-to-nature theme prevails at this beachside inn, in both the room decor and the grounds planted with native Florida foliage specifically designed to attract butterflies and hummingbirds. In fact, back-to-nature children's programs make this a great choice for ecofriendly families. Kids can go on shell safaris, nature walks, and dolphin watches. The hotel rooms and fully equipped two-bedroom, two-bathroom condominium apartments (the latter are some of Sanibel's most luxurious) were recently renovated to look like a modern—but warm—beach house with bamboo floors, wicker furnishing, and great lighting. All units have screened porches to keep the relentless mosquitoes out. The award-winning restaurant Ellington's Jazz Bar and Restaurant offers seafood, steaks, pasta, and live music.

937 E. Gulf Dr., Sanibel Island, FL 33957. ℂ 800/237-1491 or 239/472-3181. Fax 239/472-5234. www.sanibelinn.com. 94 units. Winter $329–$539 double; off season $165–$275 double. Packages available. AE, DC, DISC, MC, V. **Amenities:** Restaurant; bar; heated outdoor pool; tennis courts; access to nearby health club; watersports equipment rental; bike rental; children's programs; limited room service; babysitting; laundry service. *In room:* A/C, TV, dataport, kitchen, fridge, coffeemaker, hair dryer, iron.

Sanibel's Seaside Inn 🅵🅵   This comfortable, friendly Key West–style establishment enjoys a tranquil location near the island's southeastern tip. The 1960s-style, fully renovated cottage duplexes are spacious, brightly furnished one-bedroom apartments decorated in what I like to call retro-cal—a combo of '50s retro and tropical, but if you can do without a kitchen, the choice units here are the beachfront hotel rooms, whose screened porches face the Gulf. All units have ceiling fans and open-air balconies or decks. No smoking is permitted indoors. Guests receive special privileges at the nearby Dunes Golf and Tennis Club.

541 E. Gulf Dr., Sanibel Island, FL 33957. ℂ 800/831-7384 or 239/472-1400. Fax 239/472-6518. www.seasideinn.com. 32 units. Winter $239–$539 double; off season $165–$279 double. Rates include continental breakfast. Packages available. AE, DC, DISC, MC, V. **Amenities:** Heated outdoor pool; access to nearby health club; free use of bikes; babysitting; coin-op washers and dryers. *In room:* A/C, TV/VCR, dataport, kitchen (some units), fridge, coffeemaker, hair dryer, iron.

Song of the Sea 🅵🅵   Popular with Europeans, this beachside inn offers efficiencies and one-bedroom suites with plantation-style shutters behind sliding-glass doors opening to screened porches. Don't expect a lot of extra space in the suites, whose bedrooms are barely large enough to hold their king-size beds; still, the decor is quite lovely. Furnished in French-country style, the rooms feature oak tables and chairs, and pine Bahamian shutters on patio doors and windows. A pathway leads to the next-door Sanibel Inn (see above), where guests can use the facilities. An extensive continental breakfast is served in the public building and eaten at umbrella tables on a brick patio. Guests get discounts on the facilities at Sundial Beach Resort (see below).

863 E. Gulf Dr., Sanibel Island, FL 33957. (C) 800/231-1045 or 239/472-2220. Fax 239/472-8569. www.songofthe sea.com. 30 units. Winter $263–$399 double; off season $179–$229 double. Rates include continental breakfast. Packages available. AE, DC, DISC, MC, V. **Amenities:** Heated outdoor pool; access to nearby health club; Jacuzzi; free use of bikes; babysitting; coin-op washers and dryers. *In room:* A/C, TV, fax, dataport, kitchen, fridge, coffeemaker, hair dryer, iron, safe.

Sundial Beach Resort 🏖🏖 *Kids*   The largest resort on Sanibel, this condominium complex lacks intimacy, but it has lots to keep families occupied (even jogging strollers are provided so you don't have to schlep your own), from a palm-studded, beachside pool area to a free marine-biology program and a small ecology center with touch tank. The one-, two-, and three-bedroom condominiums are housed in two- and three-story buildings (as high as they get on Sanibel) and have screened balconies overlooking the beach or landscaped gardens. Rooms have gone from pleasantly decorated in a *Golden Girls* kind of way to a more tropical, modern vibe.

Among the several dining options here, the award-winning **Windows on the Water** offers glorious Gulf views at breakfast, lunch, and dinner. Master chefs put on a show as they prepare delicious steak, chicken, and seafood dishes right by your table in **Noopie's Japanese Seafood & Steakhouse** ((C) **239/395-6014**), where dinner reservations are required. Overlooking the pool and the Gulf, the relaxing **Beaches Grill & Bar** is popular at sunset and has nightly entertainment.

1451 Middle Gulf Dr., Sanibel Island, FL 33957. (C) 800/237-4184 or 239/481-3636. Fax 239/481-4947. www. sundialresort.com. 270 units. Winter $263–$519 condo apt; off season $169–$429 condo apt. Packages available. AE, DC, DISC, MC, V. **Amenities:** 4 restaurants; 2 bars; 5 heated outdoor pools; 12 tennis courts; exercise room; Jacuzzi; watersports equipment rental; bike rental; children's programs; game room; concierge; activities desk; business center; limited room service; massage; babysitting; laundry service; coin-op washers and dryers. *In room:* A/C, TV/VCR, kitchen, coffeemaker, hair dryer, iron.

Moderate

Island Inn 🏖🏖   It's difficult to get accommodations here during winter season, but it's worth trying because this classic beach resort situated on 550 feet of Gulf beach has been in business for more than a century. Its original central building houses a genteel dining room (closed Apr 15–Oct 16), a spacious lounge, and a library brightly furnished with old-style bentwood and wicker sofas and chairs. This is the kind of place where guests dress for dinner—jackets and collared shirts are required (and ties recommended) for men at dinner—and seating is assigned (some guests have had the same table for years). Don't oversleep and miss the sticky buns served at breakfast. You will thank me for this later (although your waistline won't). Motel rooms (with or without kitchens) are fine, and most have screened porches or balconies, but I say go for a private cottage. They aren't luxurious, but are certainly private and give off that beach-house vibe.

3111 W. Gulf Dr., Sanibel Island, FL 33957. (C) 800/851-5088 or 239/472-1561. Fax 239/472-0051. www.islandinn sanibel.com. 57 units, including 9 cottages. Winter $165–$560 double; off season $150–$300 double. Winter rates include breakfast and dinner. AE, DISC, MC, V. **Amenities:** Restaurant (seasonal); bar; small heated outdoor pool; tennis court; croquet area; coin-op washers and dryers. *In room:* A/C, TV, kitchen (some units), fridge, coffeemaker, hair dryer, iron.

Tarpon Tale Inn ✦ *Finds*   Owners Dawn and Joe Ramsey preside over this low-slung gray building in Sanibel's Old Town, the island's first settlement, where the ferries from Fort Myers used to dock near the lighthouse. White walls and tile floors make the comfortable units bright; French doors lead to gardens dense with sea grape, palm, and ficus trees, which provide privacy for a large outdoor hot tub. Three of the five units (which are attached yet completely private bungalows hidden amid palms, bougainvillea, hibiscus, ferns, sea grape, gumbo limbo, and Key lime) have separate bedrooms, while two other "deluxe studios" are actually two-bedroom suites. All units have shower-only bathrooms. The makings for a continental breakfast are delivered the night before. Smoking is not permitted inside the inn's rooms. There is no daily maid service, though towels and linens are exchanged every 3 days or as needed.

367 Periwinkle Way, Sanibel Island, FL 33957. ✆ **888/345-0939** or 239/472-0939. Fax 239/472-6202. www.tarpon tale.com. 5 units. $99–$199 double (depending on room and length of stay). Rates include continental breakfast. AE, DC, DISC, MC, V. Some pets accepted for a fee; call first. **Amenities:** Jacuzzi; free use of bikes; coin-op washers and dryers; free use of beach chairs and umbrellas; free local calls. *In room:* A/C, TV/VCR, CD player, kitchen, coffeemaker, hair dryer (upon request), iron (upon request), no phone (though guest phones are in common room and laundry room).

Inexpensive
Palm View Motel   In a quiet residential area less than a block from the Holiday Inn Beach Resort and Morgan's Forest restaurant, this little property is one of Sanibel's few inexpensive motels. The best choices here are the spacious, well-ventilated one- and two-bedroom apartments, but even the smaller efficiencies have kitchens and separate living and sleeping areas. There's a hot tub in the backyard plus fire pits and barbecues, and pets are allowed.

706 Donax St., Sanibel Island, FL 33957. ✆ **239/472-1606.** Fax 239/472-6733. www.palmviewsanibel.com. 5 units. Winter $145–$185 efficiency or apt; off season $85–$135 efficiency or apt. Weekly rates available. MC, V. Pets accepted ($10 per day). **Amenities:** Jacuzzi; free loan of bikes, beach chairs, and umbrellas; free guest laundry. *In room:* A/C, TV/VCR, kitchen, microwave, coffeemaker, hair dryer, iron.

CAPTIVA ISLAND
Captiva Island Inn Bed & Breakfast ✦   This B&B complex sits virtually surrounded by restaurants, art galleries, and boutiques along Captiva's block-long commercial street. That can make it a bit busy for some eyes and ears, but it has its charms. Two suites in the Key West–style main building open to porches overlooking the lane, while four Dutch clapboard cottages sit out back on the fringes of a gravel parking lot (you get just enough yard here for hammocks and a gas grill). The ceiling in one cottage that once housed aviator Charles Lindbergh has clouds painted against a blue sky. All units have ceiling fans, kitchens, large bathrooms, queen-size sofa beds in the living rooms, cool tile floors, and designer bed linens (including down comforters for the occasional chilly night). Some rooms have shower-only bathrooms. Guests get free use of towels and chairs for the beach (a block away), as well as a complimentary full breakfast at the **Keylime Bistro,** which has good American-style food and superb Key lime cheesecake; it's open daily from 8am to 10pm.

11509 Andy Rosse Lane (P.O. Box 848), Captiva Island, FL 33924. ✆ **800/454-9898** or 239/395-0882. Fax 239/395-0862. www.captivaislandinn.com. 12 units; 1 5-bedroom, 5-bathroom house. Winter $150–$300 double; off season $99–$160 double. Rates include full breakfast. AE, DISC, MC, V. **Amenities:** Access to nearby spa; free use of bikes. *In room:* A/C, TV, fridge, coffeemaker.

South Seas Island Resort ✦ *Kids*   Formerly Clarence Chadwick's 330-acre copra plantation, this exclusive establishment is the premier property on these two islands. It's one of the best choices in South Florida for serious tennis buffs. Its Gulf-side golf course is one of the most picturesque 9-holers anywhere, and its two marinas host scuba-dive operators. The resort occupies all of Captiva's northern third, making it ideal if you want to step from your luxury house or condominium right onto 2½ miles of gorgeous beach. The resort is so spread out that a free trolley shuttles back and forth through the mangrove forests. In 2005 it underwent a whopping $140-million reno-vation in which rooms—from standard hotel rooms to one-, two-, and three-bedroom beach villas and private homes—were done up in a soothingly swank West Indies decor. Other enhancements include a souped-up pool area with two new lagoon-style pools, private luxury cabanas with DVD players, plasma TVs, and cabana stewards, a redesigned golf course, and new bars and restaurants. The resort's no-cash, charge-to-your-room policy prevents gate-crashers from entering the resort proper.

P.O. Box 194, Captiva Island, FL 33924. © 800/CAPTIVA or 239/472-5111. Fax 239/481-4947. www.south-seas-resort.com. 660 units. Winter $369–$489 double, $350–$1,800 condo or house; off season $199–$259 double, $165–$1,300 condo or house. $8 per person per day added to room bills, 18%–20% to food and bar bills, in lieu of tipping. Packages available. AE, DC, DISC, MC, V. **Amenities:** 3 restaurants; 2 bars; 18 heated outdoor pools; 9-hole golf course; 18 tennis courts; health club; Jacuzzis; watersports equipment rental; bike rental; children's programs; game room; concierge; activities desk; business center; shopping arcade; salon; limited room service; massage; babysitting; laundry service; coin-op washers and dryers. *In room:* A/C, TV, dataport, kitchen (larger units only), coffeemaker, hair dryer, iron.

'Tween Waters Inn ✮✮   Wedged between the Gulf beach and the bay on the nar-rowest part of Captiva, this venerable establishment was the regular haunt of cartoon-ist J. N. ("Ding") Darling. Anne Morrow Lindbergh also dined here often while writing *A Gift from the Sea.* Situated in a sandy palm grove, these pink cottages have been upgraded but still capture that Old Florida spirit. Some face the Gulf; others, the bay. Themed to honor their famous guests, they range in size from the honeymoon cottage, with barely enough room for its king-size bed and a tiny kitchen, to the three-bedroom, two-bathroom house. The spacious hotel rooms and apartments are in three modern buildings on stilts; all have screened balconies facing the Gulf or the bay.

The Old Captiva House restaurant appears very much as it did in Ding Darling's days (note his cartoons adorning the dining-room walls), and the Canoe & the Kayak restaurant provides inexpensive lunches on its bayside deck. The popular Crow's Nest Lounge has live entertainment and snacks and light evening meals from 9pm to 1am.

Charter captains dock at the full-service marina here.

15951 Captiva Rd., Captiva Island, FL 33924. © 800/223-5865 or 239/472-5161. Fax 239/472-0249. www.tween-waters.com. 138 units. Winter $185–$295 double, $280–$620 suite, $300–$630 cottage; off season $165–$215 dou-ble, $255–$470 suite, $215–$510 cottage. Rates include continental breakfast. Packages available. AE, DC, MC, V. Pets accepted in some units ($15 per day). **Amenities:** 2 restaurants; 2 bars; outdoor pool; 3 tennis courts; exercise room; massage room; Jacuzzi; watersports equipment rental; bike rental; coin-op washers and dryers. *In room:* A/C, TV, dataport, kitchen (suites and cottages), fridge, coffeemaker, hair dryer, iron (suites only), safe.

COTTAGES

The islands have several Old Florida–style cottages that offer charming, often afford-able alternatives to hotels and condos. Some of the best are members of the **Sanibel-Captiva Small Inns & Cottages Association.** Contact the association (via its website only) at www.sanibelsmallinns.com for a listing of properties.

Sitting between two condominium complexes off Middle Gulf Drive, **Gulf Breeze Cottages** ✮✮, 1081 Shell Basket Lane, Sanibel (© 800/388-2842 or 239/472-1626; www.gbreeze.com), is a collection of clapboard cottages separated from the beach by a lawn with covered picnic area and outdoor shower. One two-story building is divided into four efficiencies (the pick is no. 7, with a view of the Gulf from its big picture windows). Rates are $230 to $320 per day in winter, $130 to $260 off season.

Barely updated since the 1950s are the 32 pink-clapboard structures at **Beachview Cottages,** 3325 W. Gulf Dr., Sanibel (✆ **800/860-0532** or 239/472-1202; fax 239/ 472-4720; www.beachviewsanibel.com). None of the cottages has a phone, and some have shower-only bathrooms. The outdoor pool is heated. Rates are $175 to $255 in winter, $139 to $219 off season.

On Captiva, **Jensen's on the Gulf,** 15300 Captiva Dr. (✆ **239/472-4684;** www. jensen-captiva.com), rents cottages, homes, apartments, and studios ranging from $250 to $600 in winter, $150 to $425 off season. **Jensen's Twin Palm Resort & Marina** (✆ **239/472-5800;** www.jensen-captiva.com), on the bay near Andy Rosse Lane, has cottages ranging from $130 to $200 in winter, from $130 to $160 off season.

WHERE TO DINE

No restaurant can survive on these affluent islands without serving good food, so you're assured of getting a fine meal wherever you go. Oddly, only a handful of establishments offer dining with water views.

SANIBEL ISLAND

Much of the "help" on this affluent island dines at **Jerry's Family Restaurant,** 1700 Periwinkle Way, at Casa Ybel Road (✆ **239/472-9300**), which offers wholesome and inexpensive diner fare (ingredients come fresh from the adjacent Jerry's Supermarket). Both the restaurant and the supermarket are open daily from 6am to 11pm. Breakfast is served from 6am to 4pm, and you can usually get a table quickly here (which can't be said of Sanibel's other popular breakfast spots).

You'll find very reasonably priced pub fare at Sanibel's sports bars, such as the **Lazy Flamingo II** (p. 364) and **Sanibel Grill,** 703 Tarpon Bay Rd., near Palm Ridge Road (✆ **239/472-3128**), which actually serves as the bar for Timbers (p. 363), the fine seafood restaurant next door.

For picnics at Sanibel's beaches or on a canoe, the deli and bakery in **Bailey's General Store,** at Periwinkle Way and Tarpon Bay Road (✆ **239/472-1516**), carries a gourmet selection of breads, cheeses, and meats. **Huxter's Deli and Market,** 1203 Periwinkle Way, east of Donax Street (✆ **239/472-6988**), has sandwich fixings and "beach box" lunches to go.

Very Expensive

Mad Hatter ✻✻ ECLECTIC   One of Sanibel's best choices for a romantic dinner, this New American Gulf-front restaurant has only 12 tables, but each has a view that's perfect at sunset. The ever-changing menu features flavors from around the world, such as Thai-style peanut sauce over a seared, sesame-encrusted yellowfin tuna steak. The jumbo shrimp Wellington is a fascinating twist on the classic beef dish, while the stuffed crab served with a lobster velouté is another winner.

6467 Sanibel-Captiva Rd., at Blind Pass. ✆ 239/472-0033. Reservations highly recommended. Main courses $26–$34. AE, MC, V. Dec 15–Jan 31 daily 5–9pm; Feb 1–Easter Sun–Mon 5–9:30pm, Tues–Sat 11:30am–2pm and 5–9:30pm; Easter–May 31 daily 5–9:30pm; June 1–Dec 14 Mon–Sat 5–9:30pm. Closed Sept after Labor Day.

Moderate

Jacaranda SEAFOOD/PASTA/STEAKS   With live music nightly, the Patio Lounge attracts an affluent over-40 crowd to this friendly and casual restaurant named for the purple-flowered jacaranda tree. Although the Jacaranda is best known as a local gathering spot, it has also received several dining awards. Fish is well prepared here, or

---

---

you can choose steaks or prime rib. The linguine with a dozen littleneck clams tossed in a piquant red or white clam sauce is excellent. For dessert, the turtle pie—ice cream, caramel, fudge sauce, chopped nuts, and whipped cream—will send you away stuffed.

1223 Periwinkle Way (east of Donax St.). (€ **239/472-1771.** Reservations recommended. Main courses $12–$30. AE, MC, V. Daily 5–10pm. Lounge daily 4pm–12:30am. Closed Christmas.

McT's Shrimp House & Tavern SEAFOOD   Shrimp reigns at this casual Old Florida–style establishment, where at 4pm you'll see a line of people waiting outside for the early-bird specials served to the first 100 in the door. Shrimp here is prepared in at least a dozen ways, from steamed to fried in a coconut-and-almond batter. There are also grouper and swordfish, plus steaks and chicken for the land-minded, but I recommend sticking to the shrimp here. (The Timbers Restaurant & Fish Market, described below, does a much better job of cooking fish.) McT's Tavern offers an extensive choice of appetizers and light dinners. All-you-can-eat peel-and-eat shrimp and stone crabs are available nightly, though if it's not stone-crab season (Oct–May), the crab will likely be frozen.

1523 Periwinkle Way (at Fitzhugh St.). (€ **239/472-3161.** Main courses $13–$22; early-bird specials $10. AE, DC, DISC, MC, V. Shrimp House daily 4:45–10pm. McT's Tavern daily 4pm–midnight. Closed Thanksgiving and Christmas.

Morgan's Forest *(Kids* SEAFOOD   The kids will love dining in this miniature jungle patterned after the Rainforest Cafes elsewhere. Parents, on the other hand, will suffer for the love of their children. Almost hidden among all the foliage are mechanical but lifelike moving jaguars, monkeys, birds, and a huge python entangled in vines above the bar. Squawking bird sounds, strobe lightning bolts followed by claps of thunder, and an occasional faux fog rolling across the floor are as pleasant as the sound of fingernails scratching a chalkboard. The owner of Fort Myers Beach's excellent Channel Mark restaurant is in charge here, which means that the food makes up for the harassing ambience. The fine crab cakes are the pick of a menu otherwise accented with South and Central American seasonings. A children's menu is available.

1231 Middle Gulf Dr., adjacent to the Holiday Inn Beach Resort. (€ **239/472-3351.** Main courses $14–$23. AE, DC, DISC, MC, V. Mon–Sat 7–11am and 5–10pm; Sun 7am–noon and 5–10pm.

The Timbers Restaurant & Fish Market *(Kids* SEAFOOD/STEAK   This casual upstairs restaurant, with bamboo railings, oversize canvas umbrellas, and paintings of tropical scenes through faux windows, is consistently Sanibel's best place for fresh fish and aged beef hot off the charcoal grill. It's true what they say—"We serve it fresh or we don't serve it at all." In the fish market out front, you can view the catch and have the chef charcoal-grill or blacken it to order. The steaks, cut on the premises, are the island's best. You can order a drink from the adjoining Sanibel Grill sports bar and wait for a table out on the shopping center's porch.

703 Tarpon Bay Rd. (between Periwinkle Way and Palm Ridge Rd.). (€ **239/472-3128.** Main courses $15–$23; early birds get $2.50 off regular price. AE, MC, V. Winter daily 4:30–9:30pm; off season daily 5–9:30pm.

Inexpensive

Grandma Dot's Seaside Saloon SEAFOOD One of Sanibel's most popular lunch spots, this open-air but screened cafe on the docks of Sanibel Marina offers excellent salads (try the seafood Caesar) and fine sandwiches, plus a few main courses led by broiled grouper in a sauce of lemon, dill, butter, and white wine.

At Sanibel Marina, 634 N. Yachtsman Dr. ⓒ **239/472-8138.** Reservations not accepted. Main courses $6–$23; salads and sandwiches $6–$12. MC, V. Daily 11:30am–7:30pm.

Hungry Heron ⭐⭐ *Kids* AMERICAN This tropically decorated eatery is Sanibel's most popular family restaurant. There's something for everyone on the huge, tabloid-size menu—from hot and cold appetizers and overstuffed "seawiches" to pasta and steamed shellfish. And if the 280 regular items aren't enough, there's a list of nightly specials. Seafood, steaks, and stir-fries from a sizzling skillet are popular with local residents, who bring the kids here for fun and the children's menu. An all-you-can-eat breakfast buffet on Saturday and Sunday mornings is an excellent value.

In Palm Ridge Place, 2330 Palm Ridge Rd. (at Periwinkle Way). ⓒ **239/395-2300.** Reservations not accepted, but call for preferred seating. Main courses $9–$18; sandwiches, burgers, and snacks $6–$11; weekend breakfast buffet $9 adults, $5 children under 10. AE, DISC, MC, V. Mon–Fri 11am–9pm; Sat–Sun 7:30am–9pm (breakfast buffet to 11am Sat, to noon Sun).

The Lazy Flamingo II *Value* SEAFOOD/PUB FARE The Lazy Flamingo is a down-homey type of place where the food is consistently good. Locals and visitors alike become repeat customers, flocking here for the reasonably priced food, a wide choice of beers iced down in a huge box behind the bar, and the sports TVs. Some of that beer is used to steam shrimp and a collection of oysters, clams, and spices known as "The Pot." Best pick, however, is grouper from the charcoals, as either a main course or a sandwich. The flamingo-pink menu has sandwiches, burgers, fish platters, and very spicy "Dead Parrot Wings." Fillet your own catch, and the chef will cook it to order for you. Happy-hour prices prevail whenever football games are on.

 A sister institution, the **Lazy Flamingo I,** 6520-C Pine Ave., at Sanibel-Captiva Road, ¼ mile south of Blind Pass (ⓒ **239/472-5353**), has the same menu and hours.

1036 Periwinkle Way, west of Causeway Blvd. ⓒ **239/472-6939.** Reservations not accepted. Main courses $11–$15; sandwiches and snacks $5–$9. Cook your catch $8. AE, DISC, MC, V. Daily 11:30am–1am.

Lighthouse Cafe ⭐ *Value* AMERICAN This casual storefront establishment dishes up breakfast omelets that are meals in themselves, especially the ocean frittata containing delicately seasoned scallops, crabmeat, shrimp, broccoli, and mushrooms, and crowned with an artichoke-heart-and-creamy-Alfredo sauce. Seafood Benedict is one of the more decadent offerings. For the light(er) eater, a slew of creative sandwiches is served after 11am. Reasonably priced cafe-style dinners are served during winter only. For the best pancakes ever, the Lighthouse Cafe has cornered the market, using a special recipe that draws up to 700 people a day in season. For just $3.95, you can go nuts on malted-blueberry or banana pancakes, or pretend to be healthy with granola-nut whole-wheat hot cakes with sliced bananas.

In Seahorse Shops, 362 Periwinkle Way (at Buttonwood Lane, east of Causeway Rd.). ⓒ **239/472-0303.** Call ahead to get on waiting list. Main courses $10–$15; breakfast $3.50–$7.50; sandwiches and salads $4.50–$8.50. MC, V. Mid-Dec to Easter daily 7am–3pm and 5–9pm; Easter to mid-Dec daily 7am–3pm.

Sanibel Cafe ⭐ *Value* AMERICAN Seashells are the not-so-original theme at Lynda and Ken Boyce's pleasant cafe, whose tables are museum-like glass cases containing delicate fossilized specimens from the Miocene and Pliocene epochs. Fresh-squeezed

orange and grapefruit juice, Danish Havarti omelets, and homemade muffins and biscuits highlight the breakfast menu. Lunch features specialty sandwiches; shrimp,
Greek, and chicken-and-grape salads made with a light, fat-free dressing; and a limited
list of main courses such as grilled or blackened chicken breast. At dinner, there's homemade meatloaf, crunchy grouper, and certified Angus steaks. Fatten up on Lynda's
homemade red-raspberry jam, apple or cherry crisp, and terrific Key lime pie.

In the Tahitian Gardens, 2007 Periwinkle Way. 🕐 **239/472-5323.** Call ahead for preferred seating. Main courses
$7.50–$17; breakfast $3.50–$9; salads, sandwiches, and burgers $4.50–$13. MC, V. Daily 7am–9pm.

CAPTIVA ISLAND

Big deli sandwiches and picnic fare are available at the **Captiva Island Store,** Captiva
Road at Andy Rosse Lane (🕐 **239/472-2374**); and at gourmet-oriented **C. W.'s Market and Deli,** at the entrance to the South Seas Resort (🕐 **239/472-5111**). The beach
is a block from these stores.

See the review for the Captiva Island Inn Bed & Breakfast (p. 360) for information
on the **Keylime Bistro.**

The Bubble Room ★★★ *Kids* STEAK/SEAFOOD   Imagine Walt Disney on acid,
and you'll understand where The Bubble Room is coming from. The kitschiest restaurant you'll probably ever find, The Bubble Room's tongue-in-cheeky American cuisine
is complemented by a decor that's filled with Christmas and Hollywood memorabilia
from the '30s, '40s, and '50s. Distracting, to say the least—but in a very good way—
The Bubble Room makes it hard to decide which is cooler, the Henny Young-One
boneless breast of young chicken, the prime ribs Weissmuller, or the thousands of
movie stills, puppets, antique jukeboxes, and toy trains. *Note:* I've gotten complaints
about the "awful" food here, but I still think The Bubble Room is fun, with good
(though admittedly not fabulous) food and a great atmosphere.

15001 Captiva Rd. (at Andy Rosse Lane). 🕐 **239/472-5558.** www.bubbleroomrestaurant.com. Reservations not
accepted, but call for preferred seating. Main courses $17–$30. AE, DC, DISC, MC, V. Daily 11:30am–2:30pm and
5–10pm. Closed Christmas.

The Cabbage Key Restaurant ★★★ AMERICAN   You can get here only by
boat, but there are constant shuttles from Captiva, so get onboard and experience the
true meaning of cheeseburgers in paradise. Jimmy Buffet allegedly wrote his famous
song here, and when you arrive, you'll understand why. The cheeseburgers rock, the
setting is sublime, and there are no fried foods or microwaves in sight. It's a place rich
in history, and in money: Thousands of dollar bills are signed and stuck to the walls
and ceiling with masking tape.

Intracoastal Water Marker 60, N. Fort Myers. 🕐 **239/283-2278.** Main courses $5–$15. MC, V. Mon–Sat 7:30–9am;
Sun 7:30–10am; Mon–Fri 11:15am–3pm; Sat 11:15am–4pm; Mon–Sat 6–8:30pm; Sun 6–7pm.

Captiva Sunshine Cafe ★ ECLECTIC   This friendly, open-kitchen cafe has only
12 tables—5 of them inside, 7 on the front porch. Everything except the bread is prepared on the premises; all of it is available for takeout. Specialties are steak, fish, and
shrimp from a wood-fired grill. The portions are as big as the prices are high; in fact,
appetizers such as black beans and rice can make a meal for lighter appetites. Various
desserts are offered daily; the apple crisp is a winner.

In Captiva Village Sq., Captiva Rd. at Laika Lane. 🕐 **239/472-6200.** Reservations recommended. Main courses
$23–$33; burgers $10. AE, MC, V. Daily 11:30am–3:30pm and 5–9pm.

The Green Flash ✦ SEAFOOD   You can't miss this restaurant, which sits at the infamous "curve" where Captiva Road takes a sharp turn to the north. You won't see the real "green flash" as the sun sets here because this modern building looks eastward across Pine Island Sound, but it does make for a nice view at lunch. And seeing the full moon turn the sound into glistening silver is worth having at least an evening drink here. The quality of the cuisine is very good, and the prices reasonable for Captiva. Start with oysters Rockefeller or shrimp bisque. Both are house specialties, as is the garlicky grouper "café de Paris" and the salmon with a dill-accented béarnaise sauce.

15183 Captiva Rd. ✆ **239/472-3337.** Reservations recommended. Main courses $13–$22. AE, DC, DISC, MC, V. Daily 11:30am–3:30pm and 5:30–9:30pm (bar open 11:30am–9:30pm).

Mucky Duck ✦ SEAFOOD/PUB FARE   A Captiva institution since 1976, this lively, British-style pub, named after a pub of the same name in Shakespeare's Stratford-upon-Avon in the U.K., is the only place on either island where you can dine right by the beach. If you don't get a seat with this great view, the humorous staff will gladly roll a fake window over to appease you. The menu offers a selection of fresh seafood items, plus English fish and chips, steak-and-sausage pie, and a ploughman's lunch. There's also a vegetarian platter. No smoking is allowed inside. You can't make a reservation, but you can order drinks, listen to live music (Mon–Sat), and bide your time at beachside picnic tables out front (come early for sunset).

Andy Rosse Lane (on the Gulf). ✆ **239/472-3434.** Reservations not accepted. Main courses $5.50–$11 lunch, $13–$19 dinner. AE, DC, DISC, MC, V. Mon–Sat 11am–2:30pm and 5–9:30pm.

R. C. Otter's Island Eats ✦✦ *Value* AMERICAN   Occupying an old clapboard-sided island cottage, this Key West–style cafe brings informality and good, inexpensive food to Captiva. In contrast to the island's 15 or so formal restaurants, you can dine here in your bare feet and not spend a fortune for an excellent breakfast, snack, lunch, or full meal. The choice seats are under ceiling fans on the front porch or umbrellas on the brick patio. In hot weather, opt for the air-conditioned dining room. The wide-ranging menu includes salads, hot dogs, burgers, sandwiches, stir-fries, meatloaf, country-fried steak, broiled fish, and soft-shell crabs, plus delicious nightly specials. The island's best breakfasts are equally varied, from bacon and eggs to a seafood quesadilla. Musicians perform out in the yard every day—you might find yourself dancing on the front porch.

11506 Andy Rosse Lane. ✆ **239/395-1142.** Reservations not accepted, but call for preferred seating. Main courses $10–$20; breakfast $6–$12; salads, sandwiches, and burgers $6–$12. AE, DISC, MC, V. Daily 7:30am–10pm (breakfast to 11:30am).

SANIBEL & CAPTIVA ISLANDS AFTER DARK

You won't find glitzy nightclubs on these family-oriented islands, but night owls do have places to roost at the resorts and restaurants listed above. Here's a brief recap:

SANIBEL ISLAND   The Sundial Beach Resort's **Beaches Bar & Grill,** 1451 Middle Gulf Dr. (✆ **239/472-4151**), features entertainers during dinner, then live bands for dancing from 9pm on. The **Patio Lounge,** in the Jacaranda, 1223 Periwinkle Way (✆ **239/472-1771**), attracts an affluent crowd of middle-agers and seniors to its live music every evening. **McT's Tavern,** 1523 Periwinkle Way (✆ **239/472-3161**), has darts, video games, and a large-screen TV for sports fans. Other popular sports bars are the **Sanibel Grill,** 703 Tarpon Bay Rd. (✆ **239/472-4453**); and the two **Lazy Flamingo** branches, at 1036 Periwinkle Way (✆ **239/472-6939**) and 6520-C Pine Ave. (✆ **239/472-5353**).

The Pirate Players, a group of professional actors, perform Broadway dramas and comedies from November to April in Sanibel's state-of-the-art, 150-seat **J. Howard Wood Theatre,** 2200 Periwinkle Way (© **239/472-4109**). The **Old Schoolhouse Theater,** 1905 Periwinkle Way (© **239/472-6862;** www.oldschoolhousetheater. com), complements its neighbor by offering Broadway musicals and revues from December to April. Call for the current schedule and prices.

CAPTIVA ISLAND   Local songwriters perform their works nightly at **R. C. Otter's Island Eats,** 11500 Andy Rosse Lane (© **239/395-1142**). The **Crow's Nest Lounge,** in the 'Tween Waters Inn on Captiva Road (© **239/472-5161**), is Captiva's top nightspot for dancing. **Chadwick's Lounge,** at the entrance to the South Seas Resort (© **239/472-5111**), has a large dance floor and music from 9pm on.

NEARBY ISLAND HOPPING

Sanibel and Captiva are jumping-off points for island-hopping boat trips to barrier islands and keys teeming with ancient legends and *Robinson Crusoe*–style beaches. You don't have to get completely lost out here, however, because several islets have comfortable inns and restaurants. The trip across shallow Pine Island Sound is itself a sightseeing adventure, with playful dolphins surfing on the boats' wakes and a variety of cormorants, egrets, frigate birds, and (in winter) rare white pelicans flying above.

Captiva Cruises (© **239/472-5300;** www.captivacruises.com) makes daily trips from the South Seas Resort on Captiva Island. One vessel goes to Cabbage Key, departing at 10:30am and returning at 3:30pm. It stops at Useppa Island going and coming Tuesday through Sunday. During the winter months, another vessel goes to Boca Grande by way of Cayo Costa State Park, departing Tuesday through Saturday at 10:30am and returning at 4pm. These day trips cost $30 for adults, $15 for children 6 to 12 to Cabbage Key or Useppa; $45 for adults, $25 for children 6 to 12 to Boca Grande or Cayo Costa. Reservations are required.

From Pine Island off Fort Myers, **Tropic Star Cruises** (© **239/283-0015;** www. tropicstarcruises.com) operates daily ferry service to Cayo Costa (p. 369).

CABBAGE KEY ⟨⟨

You never know who's going to get off a boat at 100-acre Cabbage Key and walk unannounced into the funky **Cabbage Key Inn** ⟨⟨, a rustic house built in 1938. Ernest Hemingway liked to hang out here in the early days, and novelist John D. MacDonald was a frequent guest 30 years later. Today you could find yourself rubbing elbows at the bar with the likes of Walter Cronkite, Ted Koppel, Sean Connery, or Julia Roberts. Singer and avid yachtie Jimmy Buffett likes Cabbage Key so much that it inspired his hit song "Cheeseburger in Paradise."

⟨ Fun Fact   Where Chocolate Grows on Trees

From December to February, the area's Black Sapote trees bear a most interesting fruit. Known as the "chocolate pudding fruit," it is round with thin olive-green skin and contains a mass of glossy, chocolate-colored pulp that's soft, sweet, and mild, very much like pudding. It makes a tasty and healthy dessert, a delicious pie filling, or an exotic tropical beverage when mixed with pineapple juice. The **Sunburst Tropical Fruit Company,** on Pine Island (© **239/283-1200**), has the fruit for sale, so you needn't pick from the trees.

Fishing with the Bushes

Former president George Bush, present President George W. Bush, Florida Gov. Jeb Bush—indeed, the entire Bush clan—like to retreat to **Boca Grande** ✦✦ for a little rest and relaxation every now and then. And well they should, for this charming village on Gasparilla Island is a head-of-state's kind of place. The du Ponts, the Astors, the Morgans, the Vanderbilts, and other moneyed folk started coming here in the 1920s and still turn the island into a Florida version of Nantucket during their winter "social season." In addition to the warm weather, the lure was then, and still is, some of the world's best tarpon fishing. Descendants of the watermen who were here first still guide the rich and famous. They live in modest homes on streets named Dam-If-I-Know, Dam-If-I-Care, and Dam-If-I-Will. You can see their backyards full of boats and fishnets, but high hedges hide the mani-cured "beachfronter" mansions over by the Gulf. **The Boca Grande Club**, 5000 Gasparilla Rd. (✆ **941/964-2211**), offers 80 condos for rent from $110 to $600 and features a beautiful beach, pool, tiki bar, lounge, restaurant, and fitness center.

You can explore the little village in a few hours on foot or by rental bike from **Island Bike 'n' Beach,** 333 Park Ave. (✆ **941/964-0711**). The pink-brick **Railroad Depot,** at Park Avenue and 4th Street, has been restored to the turn-of-the-20th-century grandeur it enjoyed when the rich arrived by train. It now houses a cluster of upscale boutiques and the **Loose Caboose** (✆ **941/964-0440**) restaurant and ice-cream parlor, where movie stars have been seen satiating their sweet tooths. **Banyan Street** (actually 2nd St.) is canopied with tangled banyan trees and is one of the prettiest places for a stroll. The **Johann Fust Community Library,** at Gasparilla Road and 10th Street (✆ **941/964-2488**), contains the extraordinary **Du Pont Shell Collec-tion,** gathered by Henry Francis du Pont during nearly 50 years of combing the island's beaches. At the island's south end, **Boca Grande Lighthouse Museum and Visitor's Center** (✆ **941/964-0060**) occupies the wood-frame lighthouse that began marking the pass into Charlotte Harbor in 1890. Exhibits explain the island's history, its tarpon fishing, and its wildlife and seashells. The white-sand beaches of **Gasparilla Island State Recreation Area** (✆ **941/964-0375;** www.floridastateparks.org/gasparillaisland) trim the lighthouse.

Captiva Cruises (✆ **239/472-5300**) has daily trips here during the winter season (see "Nearby Island Hopping," above). The fare is $45 for adults, $25 for children under 7; reservations are required. **Tropic Star Cruises** (✆ **239/283-0015;** www.tropicstarcruises.com) comes here daily from Pine Island off Fort Myers (p. 339). Fares are $35 for adults and $15 for children 6 to 12. Call for departure times.

For more information, contact the **Boca Grande Area Chamber of Com-merce,** 5800 Gasparilla Rd. (P.O. Box 704), Boca Grande, FL 33921 (✆ **941/964-0568;** fax 941/964-0620; www.bocagrandechamber.com).

A path leads from the tiny marina across a lawn dotted with coconut palms to this white-clapboard house that sits atop an ancient Calusa shell mound. Guests dine in the comfort of two screened porches and seek libations in the library-turned-bar, its pine-paneled walls now plastered with dollar bills left by visitors. The straight-back chairs and painted wooden tables show their age, but that's part of Cabbage Key's laid-back, don't-give-a-you-know-what charm.

In addition to the famous thick, juicy cheeseburgers so loved by Jimmy Buffett, the house specialties are fresh broiled fish and shrimp steamed in beer. Lunches range from $5 to $10; main courses at dinner, $15 to $25.

Most visitors come out here for the day, but if you want to stay overnight, the Cabbage Key Inn has six rooms and six cottages. The more expensive cottages, four of which have kitchens, are preferable to the rooms. Although the units have private bathrooms and air conditioners, they are very basic by today's standards, and some of their original 1920s furnishings have seen better days. Service for overnight guests can leave a lot to be desired, and there's no place on the islet to buy snacks or sundries. If you do decide to rough it, rates are $99 single or double for rooms, $145 to $289 for cottages. For information and reservations, contact Cabbage Key Inn, P.O. Box 200, Pineland, FL 33945 (© 239/283-2278; fax 239/283-1384; www.cabbage-key.com).

Captiva Cruises (© 239/472-5300; www.captivacruises.com) goes to Cabbage Key daily from Captiva Island, charging $30 for adults and $15 for kids 6 to 12 (reservations required). You can also get here from Pine Island via **Tropic Star Cruises** (© 239/283-0015; www.tropicstarcruises.com), which departs from Pineland Marina daily (p. 339). Fares are $29 for adults, $17 for children under 7. Call for departure times. Finally, one additional way to get here from Pine Island is with **Island Charters** (© 800/340-3321 or 239/283-1113).

CAYO COSTA ⚘⚘⚘

Short of Tom Hanks in *Castaway*, you can't get any more deserted than at **Cayo Costa State Park** ⚘⚘⚘ (pronounced *Kay*-oh *Cos*-tah), which occupies a 2,132-acre, completely unspoiled barrier island with miles of white-sand beaches, pine forests, mangrove swamps, oak-palm hammocks, and grasslands. Other than natural wildlife, the only permanent residents here are park rangers.

Day-trippers can bring their own supplies and use a picnic area with pavilions. A free tram carries visitors from the sound-side dock to the Gulf beach. The state maintains 12 very basic cabins and a primitive campground on the northern end of the island near Johnson Shoals, where the shelling is spectacular. Cabins cost $30 a day, and campsites are $18 a day year-round. For camping or cabin reservations, call © 800/326-3521 or go to www.reserveamerica.com. There's running water on the island, but no electricity.

The park is open daily from 8am to sundown. There's a $1-per-person honor-system admission fee for day visitors. You can rent single-seat kayaks for $35 a day, two-seaters for $45 a day; for reservations, call **Tropic Star Cruises,** on Pine Island (© 239/283-0015; www.tropicstarcruises.com).

For more information, contact **Cayo Costa State Park,** P.O. Box 1150, Boca Grande, FL 33921 (© 941/964-0375; www.floridastateparks.org/cayocosta). Office hours are Monday through Friday from 8am to 5pm.

UPPER (NORTH) CAPTIVA

Cut off by a pass from Captiva, its northern barrier-island sibling is occupied by the upscale resort of **North Captiva Island Club,** P.O. Box 1000, Pineland, FL 33945

Bokeeli-huh?

In Spanish, it means "little mouth," but in terms of traveling through Southwest Florida, *Bokeelia* means heaven. Located west of Fort Myers on the northern tip of Charlotte Harbor, Bokeelia joins Pine Island and St. James City as peaceful places where they've yet to pave paradise and put up a Starbucks. The **Bokeelia Tarpoon Inn,** 8241 Main St. (© 866/TARPON2 or 239/283-8961), is located in the historic Poe Johnson House, whose lineage dates back to 1914. Revamped without ruining its historic charm, the six-room inn features pine floors and walls, a fireplace, Indonesian wicker furniture, and spacious rooms with louvered shutters and plush queen-size beds. Because the waters around here are swimming with tarpon, among other fish, the inn has a fly-tying room where a local fisherman demonstrates the finer points of fly-fishing. The inn can also arrange boat charters. Complimentary breakfast, wine, and hors d'oeuvres, as well as the stunning views of Boca Grande and Charlotte Harbor, mean there's absolutely no reason to leave this unfettered little piece of Starbucks-free paradise.

(© **800/576-7343** or 239/395-1001; fax 239/472-5836; www.northcaptiva.com). Despite the development, however, about 750 of the island's 1,000 acres are included in a state preserve. The club rents accommodations ranging from efficiencies to luxury homes. There's scheduled water-taxi service from **Jensen's Twin Palms Marina,** on Captiva (© **239/472-5800**), or you can get here from Matson Marine on Pine Island with **Island Charters** (© **800/340-3321** or 239/283-1113). Both charge $25 per person round-trip.

USEPPA ISLAND

Useppa was a refuge of President Theodore Roosevelt and his tarpon-loving industrialist friends at the turn of the 20th century. New York advertising magnate Barron G. Collier bought the island in 1906 and built a lovely wooden home overlooking Pine Island Sound. His mansion is now the **Collier Inn,** where day-trippers and overnight guests can partake of lunches and seafood dinners in a country-club ambience. You can also visit the **Useppa Museum,** which explains the island's history and displays 4,000-year-old Calusa artifacts. Admission is by $2 donation.

The Collier Inn is the centerpiece of the **Useppa Island Club,** an exclusive development with more than 100 luxury homes, all in the clapboard-sided, tin-roofed style of Old Florida. For information, rates, and reservations, contact **Collier Inn & Cottages,** P.O. Box 640, Bokeelia, FL 33922 (© **888/735-6335** or 239/283-1061; fax 239/283-0290; www.useppa.com).

4 Naples ✫✫✫

42 miles S of Fort Myers, 106 miles W of Miami, 185 miles S of Tampa

Ah, sleepy, swanky Naples. A place that may have defined the meaning of R&R, considering the fact that there's not much to do here besides linger on the beach, play golf, and dream that this isn't a vacation but a way of life. Naples is also easily Southwest

Naples

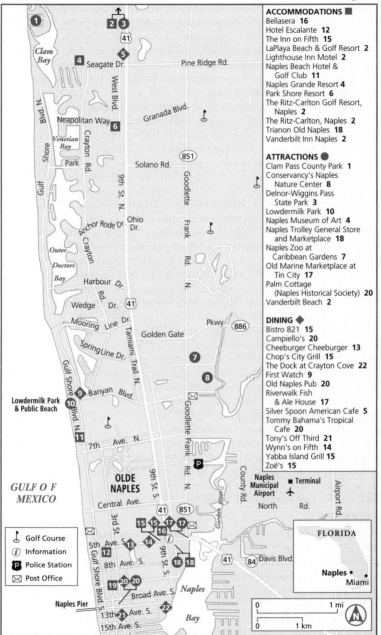

ACCOMMODATIONS ■
Bellasera **16**
Hotel Escalante **12**
The Inn on Fifth **15**
LaPlaya Beach & Golf Resort **2**
Lighthouse Inn Motel **2**
Naples Beach Hotel & Golf Club **11**
Naples Grande Resort **4**
Park Shore Resort **6**
The Ritz-Carlton Golf Resort, Naples **2**
The Ritz-Carlton, Naples **2**
Trianon Old Naples **18**
Vanderbilt Inn Naples **2**

ATTRACTIONS ●
Clam Pass County Park **1**
Conservancy's Naples Nature Center **8**
Delnor-Wiggins Pass State Park **3**
Lowdermilk Park **10**
Naples Museum of Art **4**
Naples Trolley General Store and Marketplace **18**
Naples Zoo at Caribbean Gardens **7**
Old Marine Marketplace at Tin City **17**
Palm Cottage (Naples Historical Society) **20**
Vanderbilt Beach **2**

DINING ◆
Bistro 821 **15**
Campiello's **20**
Cheeburger Cheeburger **13**
Chop's City Grill **15**
The Dock at Crayton Cove **22**
First Watch **9**
Old Naples Pub **20**
Riverwalk Fish & Ale House **17**
Silver Spoon American Cafe **5**
Tommy Bahama's Tropical Cafe **20**
Tony's Off Third **21**
Wynn's on Fifth **14**
Yabba Island Grill **15**
Zoë's **15**

Clam Bay

Seagate Dr.

Pine Ridge Rd.

West Blvd.

N. Blvd.

Neapolitan Way

Granada Blvd.

Venetian Bay

Crayton Rd.

Park

9th St. N.

Solano Rd.

Goodlette Frank Rd. N.

Gulf Shore

Anchor Rode Dr.

Ohio Dr.

Outer Doctors Bay

Crayton

Harbour Dr.

Rd.

Wedge Dr.

Mooring Line Dr.

Pkwy

Golden Gate

SpringLine Dr.

Tamiami Trail N.

Lowdermilk Park & Public Beach

Banyan Blvd.

7th Ave. N.

GULF O F MEXICO

OLDE NAPLES

Central Ave.

3rd St.

5th Ave. S.

8th Ave. S.

9th St. S.

Gulf Shore Blvd. N.

Gulf Shore Blvd. S.

Naples Pier

19 20 20

Broad Ave. S.

13th Ave. S.

15th Ave. S.

Naples Bay

Naples Municipal Airport ■ Terminal

North Rd.

County Rd.

Golden River

Airport Rd.

Davis Blvd.

FLORIDA

Naples ●

Miami

| Golf Course
| Information
| Police Station
| Post Office

0 — 1 mi
0 — 1 km

Florida's most sophisticated city. And while Naples has its requisite waterfront mansions, sprawling country-club fairways, and a thoroughfare of pricey boutiques and restaurants, it's not nearly as upper-crusty as, say, Palm Beach or Beverly Hills. Although the people are indeed very Ralph Lauren types, heavy on the starch, the snobbery factor and upper-tax-bracket lockjaw are conspicuously absent here—unlike how people usually characterize the east coast of Florida, which is just as moneyed, but nowhere near as friendly or laid back.

Don't even think of thumbing your nose at the long-bearded man dressed in ratty shorts and a Hawaiian T-shirt until you make sure he doesn't hop into a Bentley or zillion-dollar yacht. Therein lies the beauty of Naples. People are wealthy here but have no need to flaunt it—what they do flaunt are St. Tropez tans and a general joie de vivre. And leave the kids at home—even though there's a zoo here, it's not a place where the little ones will have fun. Your relaxation *will* be disturbed when little Johnny and Jane start tugging at your shirt whining of boredom. Naples is a romantic spot for couples; it's not a swinging singles scene whatsoever. In fact, this is the kind of city where the young singles need to try out for reality shows in order to find a mate. But you never know if the Mr. or Ms. Howell sitting at the bar is recently divorced and looking for a companion with whom to share their wealth. The median age in Naples can't be much lower than 45, but Naples itself isn't a spring chicken, either.

Naples was born in 1886, when a group of 12 Kentuckians and Ohioans bought 8,700 acres fronted by a gorgeous beach, laid out a town, and started selling lots. They built a pier and the 16-room Naples Hotel, whose first guest was President Grover Cleveland's sister Rose. She and other notables soon built a line of beach homes known as "Millionaires' Row." Today the area is known as Olde Naples and is carefully protected by its modern residents. Despite a building boom that has expanded the city, the original settlement still retains the air of that time a century ago.

Although high-rise buildings now line the beaches north of the old town, the newer sections of Naples still have their charm, thanks to Ohio manufacturer Henry B. Watkins, Sr. In 1946, Watkins and his partners bought the old hotel and all the town's undeveloped land, and laid out the Naples Plan, which created the very wealthy but environmentally conscious city you see today.

About 4 miles north of Olde Naples, Vanderbilt Beach has a more traditional beach-resort character than the historic district. Lined with high-rise hotels and condominiums, the main beach here sits like an island of development between two preserved areas: Delnor-Wiggins Pass State Park to the north, and a county reserve fronting the expensive Pelican Bay golf-course community to the south.

ESSENTIALS

GETTING THERE   Most visitors arrive at the **Southwest Florida International Airport,** 35 miles north of Naples in Fort Myers (p. 335). **Naples Municipal Airport,** on North Road off Airport-Pulling Road (© 239/643-6875; www.flynaples.com), is served by the commuter arms of **American** (© 800/433-7300) and **United/US Airways** (© 800/428-4322), which means you'll have to change planes in Miami, Tampa, or Orlando.

Taxis await all flights outside the small terminal building. **Avis** (© 800/331-1212), **Budget** (© 800/527-0700), **Hertz** (© 800/654-3131), and **National** (© 800/CAR-RENT) have booths at the airport. **Enterprise** (© 800/325-8007) is located in town.

VISITOR INFORMATION   The most comprehensive source of information is the **Naples Area Chamber of Commerce,** which maintains a visitor center at 895 5th

Ave. S. (at U.S. 41), Naples, FL 34102 (✆ **239/262-6141;** fax 239/435-9910; www. napleschamber.org). The center has a host of free information and phones for making hotel reservations; it also sells a detailed street map for $2. By mail, it will send you a free list of accommodations and other basic information, or you can order a complete Naples vacation packet for $8 ($12 to Canada and other countries) and the street map for $5. The center is open Monday through Saturday from 9am to 5pm.

GETTING AROUND   The **Naples Trolley** (✆ **239/262-7300;** www.naplestrolley tours.com) clangs around 25 stops between the Naples Trolley General Store and Welcome Center, 1010 6th Ave. S., at 10th Street South (2 blocks west of Tin City in Olde Naples), and Vanderbilt Beach. It runs Monday through Saturday from 8:30am to 5:15pm, and Sunday from 10:15am to 5:15pm. Daily fares are $19 for adults and $8 for children 4 to 12, with free reboarding. Schedules are available in brochure racks in the lobbies of most hotels and motels. The drivers provide narration, so the entire loop makes a good 2-hour sightseeing tour.

For a taxi, call **Yellow Cab** (✆ **239/262-1312**), **Checker Cab** (✆ **239/455-5555**), **Maxi Taxi** (✆ **239/262-8977**), or **Naples Taxi** (✆ **239/775-0505**).

HITTING THE BEACH

Unlike many Florida cities, where you have to drive over to a barrier island to reach the beach, this city's beach is right in Olde Naples. And rather than being fronted by tall condominium buildings, the backdrop here is the mansions along Millionaires' Row. Access to the gorgeous white sand is at the Gulf end of each avenue, although parking in the neighborhood can be brutal. Try the metered lots on 12th Avenue South near the **Naples Pier,** the town's most popular beaching spot (see "Exploring the Town," below), where there are also restrooms and food concessions. Families gather on the beach north of the pier, while bored local teens congregate on the south side.

Also popular, the very Norman Rockwellian **Lowdermilk Park,** on Millionaires' Row at Gulf Shore and North Banyan boulevards, has a pavilion, restrooms, showers, a refreshment counter, professional-quality volleyball courts (the area's best players practice here), a duck pond, and picnic tables. There's also metered parking, so bring quarters. A few blocks farther north is another metered parking lot with beach access, beside the Naples Beach Hotel & Golf Resort, 851 Gulf Shore Blvd. N., at Golf Drive.

Nature lovers head to the Pelican Bay development north of the historic district and the popular **Clam Pass County Park** ✦✦ (✆ **239/353-0404**). A free tram takes you along a 3,000-foot boardwalk winding through mangrove swamps and across a back bay to a beach of fine white sand. It's strange to see high-rise condominiums standing beyond the mangrove-bordered backwaters, but this is actually a miniature wilderness. Some 6 miles of canoe and kayak trails—with multitudes of birds and an occasional alligator—run from Clam Pass into the winding streams. The beach pavilion here has a bar (drinking is a sport in Naples), restrooms with foot showers only, picnic tables, and beach equipment rentals, including one- and two-person kayaks and 12-foot canoes. Entry is from a metered parking lot beside the Naples Grande Resort and Club, at the end of Seagate Drive. There's a $4-per-vehicle parking fee. You can push, but not ride, bicycles on the boardwalk.

At Vanderbilt Beach, about 4 miles north of Olde Naples, the **Delnor-Wiggins Pass State Park** ✦✦✦, at the west end of Bluebill Avenue–111th Avenue North (✆ **239/597-6196;** www.floridastateparks.org/delnor-wiggins), has been listed among America's top 10 stretches of sand. It has bathhouses, a boat ramp, and the area's best picnic facilities. A concessionaire sells hot dogs, sandwiches, and ice cream, and rents beach chairs, umbrellas, kayaks, canoes, and snorkeling gear. Fish viewing is great over a small reef under 12 feet of water about 150 feet offshore. Fishing from the beach is excellent, too. Rangers provide nature tours throughout the year, with the most interesting during the loggerhead turtle nesting season from June to October (call or check the park's website for the schedule). The park is open daily from 8am to sunset. Admission is $2 per vehicle with one occupant, $5 per vehicle with two to eight occupants, and $1 per pedestrian or biker. To get here from Olde Naples, go north on U.S. 41 about 4 miles and take a left onto 111th Avenue, which turns into Bluebill Avenue before it reaches the beach. Note that 111th Avenue is known as Immokalee Road east of U.S. 41.

OUTDOOR ACTIVITIES

BOATING   Powerboat and WaveRunner rentals are available from **Club Nautico,** at the Boat Haven Marina, 1484 E. Tamiami Trail (© **239/417-3474**), on the east bank of the Gordon River behind Kelly's Fish House; and from **Port-O-Call Marina,** also behind Kelly's Fish House (© **239/774-0479**).

CRUISES   Day Star Charters features the double-decked ***Double Sunshine*** (© **239/263-4949**), which sallies forth onto the river and bay daily from Tin City, where it has a ticket office. The 1½-hour cruises leave at 10am, noon, 2pm, and an hour before sunset. They cost $28 for adults and $14 for children under 12.

The ***Sweet Liberty*** (© **239/793-3525;** www.sweetliberty.com), a 53-foot sailing catamaran, makes 3-hour morning shelling cruises to Keewaydin Island. The vessel then spends the afternoon on 2-hour sightseeing cruises (you'll usually see dolphins playing in the river on this one) and 2-hour sunset cruises on Naples Bay before docking at Naples City Dock, 880 12th Avenue South. Shelling cruises cost $38 for adults, $15 for children 12 and under; sightseeing and sunset cruises cost $27 for adults, $15 for children 12 and under.

For a good deal more luxury, the 83-foot ***Naples Princess*** (© **800/728-2970** or 239/649-2275) has narrated breakfast, lunch, and sunset dinner cruises from Port-O-Call Marina, on the eastern shore of the Gordon River. With their extensive buffets, the sightseeing, sunset, and shelling cruises are good values, ranging from $25 to $50 per person. Children 12 and under pay $15 on all cruises. Call for schedules and reservations.

FISHING   The locals like to fish from the **Naples Pier** (see "Exploring the Town," below). The pier has tables on which to clean your catch, but watch out for the ever-present pelicans, which are master thieves. You can buy tackle and bait from the local marinas (see "Boating," above). The pier is open around the clock, and admission is free. No fishing license is required.

The least expensive way for singles, couples, and small families to fish without paying for an entire boat is on the 45-foot ***Lady Brett*** (© **239/263-4949**), which makes two daily half-day trips from Tin City for $50 for adults, $45 for kids under 12. Rod, reel, bait, and fishing license are included, but bring your own drinks and lunch. Its sister boat, the ***Captain Paul,*** goes on half-day backcountry fishing trips, departing daily at 9am. These cost $45 for adults, $40 for kids 12 and under.

A number of charter boats are based at the marinas mentioned under "Boating," above; call or visit them for booking information and prices.

GOLF   For a city its size, Naples has an extraordinary number of fine golf courses. Most are out in the suburbs, but not the flat but challenging 18 holes at the **Naples Beach Hotel & Golf Club** *** (p. 379), which are right in the middle of town. Nonguests can play here but should call ahead for a tee time.

Two of the best-known courses are the **Lely Flamingo Island Club** *** and the **Lely Mustang Golf Club,** both on U.S. 41 between Naples and Marco Island (© **800/ 388-GOLF** or 239/793-2223). Robert Trent Jones, Sr., designed the Lely Flamingo course; its hourglass fairways and fingerlike bunkers present many challenges. The Lee Trevino–designed Lely Mustang course is more forgiving but still fun. Former PGA Tour player Paul Trittler has his golf school at these courses. You'll pay a price here in winter, when 18-hole fees are about $135 at Lely Flamingo and $150 at Lely Mustang, including cart and range balls, but they drop progressively after Easter to about $40 and $50, respectively, in the muggy summer months.

Boyne South, on U.S. 41 between Florida 931 and Florida 92 (© **239/732-5108**), is another winner, with lots of wildlife inhabiting its many lakes (a 16-ft. alligator reportedly resides near the 17th hole). On-site are a driving range, practice facility, and restaurant; instruction is available. Wintertime fees are about $70, but in the off season they drop to $45 or less. Tee times are taken up to 4 days in advance.

Another local favorite is the player-friendly **Hibiscus Golf Club,** ½ mile east of U.S. 41 off Rattlesnake Hammock Road, East Naples (© **239/774-0088**). A pro shop and teaching professional are available. Fees are about $70 in winter, cart included, and drop to about $30 in summer.

At the intersection of Vanderbilt Beach and Airport-Pulling roads, the Greg Norman–designed 27 championship holes at the **Tiburón Golf Club** ***, 2620 Tiburón Dr. (© **877/WCI-PLAY** or 239/594-2040), play like a British Open course—but without the thick-thatch rough. Fees reach $200 in winter but drop as low as $70 in summer. The course is home to the **Rick Smith Golf Academy** (© **877/464-6531** or 239/593-1111) and the **Ritz-Carlton Golf Resort** (p. 381).

The area also has several other courses worth playing, most described in the Naples–Fort Myers edition of the *Golfer's Guide,* available at the chamber of commerce's visitor center (or check the magazine's website at www.golfersguide.com). Online, www.naplesgolf.com is also a good source of information about area courses.

SCUBA DIVING   Kevin Sweeney's **SCUBAdventures,** 971 Creech Rd., at Tamiami Trail (© **239/434-7477;** www.scubadventureslc.com), which also has a base on Marco Island (see section 5, later in this chapter), takes divers into the Gulf, teaches diver-certification courses, and rents watersports equipment.

TENNIS   In Olde Naples, the city's **Cambier Park Tennis Center** ***, 755 8th Ave. S., at 9th Street South (© **239/213-3060;** www.cambiertennis.com), is one of the country's finest municipal facilities. In fact, it matches those found at many luxury resorts. Play on its 12 lighted clay courts costs $25 an hour. Book at the pro shop in the modern building, which has restrooms but no showers. The shop is open Monday through Friday from 8am to 9pm, Saturday and Sunday from 8am to 5pm.

WATERSPORTS   **Naples Watersports,** 550 Port A Call Way (© **239/774-0479**), will hook you up with WaveRunners, jet skis, and the requisite water toys. Hobie Cats and windsurfers can also be rented on the beach at the **Naples Beach Hotel & Golf Club,** 851 Gulf Shore Blvd. N. (© **239/261-2222**); and at **Clam Pass County Park,** at the end of Seagate Drive (© **239/353-0404**). See p. 373 for more about Clam Pass.

EXPLORING THE TOWN

OLDE NAPLES ✸✸✸

Its history may go back only to 1886, but the beach skirting **Olde Naples** still has the charm of that Victorian era. The heart of the district lies south of 5th Avenue South (that's where U.S. 41 takes a 45-degree turn). The town docks are on the bay side, the stunning **Naples Beach** along the Gulf. Laid out on a grid, the tree-lined streets run between many houses, some dating from the town's beginning, and along Millionaires' Row between Gulf Shore Boulevard and the beach. With these gorgeous homes virtually hidden in the palms and casuarinas, Naples Beach seems a century removed from the high-rise condominiums found farther north.

The **Naples Pier,** at the Gulf end of 12th Avenue South, is a focal point of the neighborhood. Built in 1888 to let steamers land potential real-estate customers, the original 600-foot-long, T-shape structure was destroyed by hurricanes and damaged by fire. Local residents have rebuilt it because they like strolling its length to catch fantastic Gulf sunsets—and to get a glimpse of Millionaires' Row from the Gulf side. The pier is now a state historic site. It's open 24 hours a day, but parking in the nearby lots is restricted between 11pm and 7am.

Nearby **Palm Cottage,** 137 12th Ave. S., between 1st Street and Gordon Drive (✆ **239/261-8164**), was built in 1885 by one of Naples's founders, *Louisville Courier-Journal* publisher Walter Haldeman, as a winter retreat for his chief editorial writer. After World War II, its socialite owners hosted many galas attended by Hollywood stars such as Hedy Lamarr, Gary Cooper, and Robert Montgomery. One of the few remaining Southwest Florida houses built of tabby mortar (made by burning shells), Palm Cottage today is the home of the Naples Historical Society, which maintains it as a museum filled with authentic furniture, paintings, photographs, and other memorabilia. Tours are given in winter Monday through Friday from 1 to 3:30pm. Admission is $5 for adults, $3 for children 12 and under.

Near the Gordon River Bridge on 5th Avenue South, the old corrugated waterfront warehouses are now a shopping-and-dining complex known as the **Old Marine Marketplace at Tin City,** to which tourists throng and which local residents assiduously avoid. It does, however, look cool from the outside.

MUSEUMS & ZOOS

Naples Museum of Art ✸✸   The first full-scale art museum in Southwest Florida, the Naples Museum of Art features an impressive 15 galleries highlighting paintings, sculptures, and drawings, with major permanent collections concentrating on both the American Modern and Ancient Chinese genres. Touring shows and exhibitions bring a welcome element of eclecticism to the museum, whose very structure, including a 90×45-foot glass dome and 14-foot-high entrance gates, is a dramatic work of art on its own. October through May, free guided tours are given at 11am and 2pm Tuesday through Saturday.

5833 Pelican Bay Blvd. (at West Blvd.). ✆ 239/597-1900. www.thephil.org. Admission $8 adults, $4 students. Tues–Sat 10am–4pm; Sun noon–4pm. Closed Memorial Day, July 4, Thanksgiving, Christmas Eve, Christmas Day, New Year's Eve, New Year's Day, and Aug 1 to Labor Day.

Naples Zoo at Caribbean Gardens ✸ *Kids*   The only zoo in Florida to have rare, Indochinese tigers and a supporting cast of lions, leopards, spotted hyenas, and African wild dogs, Caribbean Gardens is an oasis of animal activity. In addition to the standard caged animals, the zoo has boat rides, primate islands, a large display of flora, and close encounters with kangaroos, alligators, and pythons. You can see them on a boat safari that slinks through spectacular tropical gardens and the islands of Lake Victoria, which monkeys, lemurs, and apes call home. The Safari Canyon presentation is a cool multimedia combination of video, music, and live animals that swim, leap, stalk, and slither around the natural rock-work theater that's only a splash away from the audience. You will easily fill 3 to 4 hours here. If you have kids with you, you may want to divide the zoo into several days of sightseeing so that you have something to do with the kids when they get antsy after swimming at the beach or the pool. Should all this animal activity make you hungry, a Subway branch sells sandwiches, and there are picnic facilities on the premises.

1590 Goodlette-Frank Rd. (at Fleischmann Blvd.). (℃ 239/262-5409. www.napleszoo.com. Admission $16 adults, $15 seniors, $10 children 4–15. Daily 9:30am–5:30pm. Closed Easter, Thanksgiving, and Christmas.

A NATURE PRESERVE

You can experience Southwest Florida's abundant natural life—and we don't mean those without silicone—without leaving town at the **Conservancy of Southwest Florida's Naples Nature Center** ✸, 14th Avenue North, east of Goodlette-Frank Road (℃ **239/262-0304;** www.conservancy.org), one of two preserves operated by the Conservancy (see p. 388 for the Briggs Nature Center). Here you'll find nature trails and an aviary (with bald eagles and other birds). You can take guided boat rides on the hour, between 10am and 3pm, weather permitting. The naturalist guides will explain the vegetation along the Gordon River, which isn't all that interesting unless you're a plant fanatic. However, the wildlife is interesting—including an occasional monkey escapee from the Caribbean Gardens next door (see "Museums & Zoos," above). You can also rent a canoe or kayak and see the area by yourself. An excellent nature store carries gift items. Admission fees of $7.50 for adults and $2 for children 3 to 12 include the boat rides. Canoes and kayaks cost $15 for 2 hours, $7.50 for each additional hour. The center is open year-round Monday through Saturday from 9am to 4:30pm; February through April, it's also open Sunday from 1 to 5pm. Closed July 4, Labor Day, Thanksgiving, Christmas Eve, and Christmas Day.

SHOPPING

A 2-block stretch of **3rd Street South** ✸✸, at Broad Avenue, aspires to be the Rodeo Drive of Naples, but with the conspicuous absence of Gucci, Prada, and Tiffany, it remains an ordinary (albeit lovely), pricey place for browsing. This collection of jewelers, clothiers, and galleries may be too rich for many wallets, but the window-shopping here is unmatched. Pick up a free brochure from the chamber of commerce's visitor center (p. 372); it lists the merchants and has a map of the area.

Nearby, the **5th Avenue South** ✸ shopping area, between 3rd and 9th streets south, is Naples's hottest wining-and-dining spot, complete with the requisite Starbucks. The avenue is longer and a bit less chic than 3rd Street South, with its stock brokerages and real-estate offices thrown into the mix of boutiques and antiques dealers.

Also in Olde Naples, the rustic, tacky **Old Marine Marketplace at Tin City,** 1200 5th Ave. S., at the Gordon River (℃ **239/262-4200**), has 50 boutiques selling everything from souvenirs to avant-garde resort wear and imported statuary. There are more boutiques in the **Dockside Boardwalk,** a half-block west on 6th Avenue South.

Even the malls in Naples have their charms. And if it rains, you'll definitely want to head to the mall—there's not much to do otherwise. **The Village at Venetian Bay,** 4200 Gulf Shore Blvd., at Park Shore Drive (℃ **239/643-0835**), evokes images of its Italian namesake, with 50 canalside shops featuring high-fashion men's and women's clothiers and fine-art galleries. Ornate Mediterranean architecture and a tropical waterfall highlight the open-air **Waterside Shops at Pelican Bay,** Seagate Drive at North Tamiami Trail (U.S. 41; ℂ **239/598-1605**), where the anchor store is Saks Fifth Avenue. There's also a huge Barnes & Noble bookstore across Seagate Drive.

Discount shoppers can head to **Prime Outlets Naples,** on Florida 951, about a mile south of U.S. 41 on the way to Marco Island (ℂ **888/545-7196** or 239/775-8083; www.primeoutlets.com). The 43 shops are open Monday through Saturday from 10am to 8pm, and Sunday from 11am to 6pm.

WHERE TO STAY

Branches of most chain hotels sit along U.S. 41, but these tend to be of higher quality and better value than their counterparts elsewhere in Southwest Florida.

One of the most reasonably priced condominium complexes, **Park Shore Resort,** 600 Neapolitan Way, Naples (ℂ **800/548-2077** or 239/263-2222; fax 239/263-0946; www.parkshorefl.com), has 156 attractive one- and two-bedroom condominiums surrounding an artificial lagoon with waterfalls cascading on its own island. Guests can walk across a bridge to the artificial island, where they can swim in the heated pool, barbecue on gas grills, or order a meal from the restaurant or a drink from the bar. There's also once-a-day (11am) complimentary transport to the beach. (To return from the beach, make a reservation at the front desk to catch a ride back at 2pm.) The condominiums range from $154 to $275 in winter, but drop to $106 to $159 off season.

One of the biggest condominium-rental agents here is **Bluebill Properties,** 26201 Hickory Blvd., Bonita Springs (ℂ **800/237-2010** or 239/992-6620; www.naples vacation.com).

The accommodations below are organized geographically in Olde Naples and north of the historic district, including Vanderbilt Beach.

IN OLDE NAPLES
Very Expensive
Bellasera 𝕶𝕶𝕶 The newest luxury property to hit Naples, Bellasera is the quintessence of swank. Inspired by the villas of Tuscany, the hotel's rooms are all suites that feature crown molding, gorgeous bathrooms with marble tubs, granite counters, and beds you may never want to leave. An outdoor heated pool has private cabanas as well as an Italian-style courtyard with fountain. ZiZi Restaurant and Lounge serves excellent Tuscan fare. Although the hotel's not on the beach, judging by the service here, they'd probably bring the beach to you if you asked. The top-notch service makes this one of Naples's best, and if you have to make a short walk to get to the beach (or take the hotel's complimentary beach shuttle), trust me, it's worth it.

221 9th St. S., Naples, FL 34102. ℂ **888/612-1115** or 239/649-7333. Fax 239/649-6233. www.bellaseranaples.com. 100 units. Winter $207–$695 double; off season $124–$225 double. AE, DC, DISC, MC, V. **Amenities:** Restaurant; heated outdoor pool; fitness center; Jacuzzi; limited room service. *In room:* A/C, TV, dataport, minibar, fridge, coffeemaker, hair dryer, iron.

Hotel Escalante 𝕶𝕶 On the western end of the 5th Avenue shopping district and 1½ blocks from the beach, this romantic boutique hotel is perfect for couples who want convenience, no crowds, and a bit of pampering. The closest thing to Italy that you'll find in Naples, *Florida,* this Mediterranean villa–style hotel is only blocks away from the beach and worlds away from the hustle and bustle of the real world, ensconced in 4 acres of private gardens with over 300 species of plants, walkways of old brick from Chicago, and fountains from France. The large rooms and one-bedroom suites are in eight one- and two-story buildings. The cottage-like suites have private patios opening to the lush courtyards. All units are luxuriously appointed, and the bathrooms come with two hand basins, ample vanity space, and big shower heads (the majority of bathrooms have walk-in showers as opposed to tubs). Special services include facials and massages from the day spa, lunch served on the beach, an evening wine reception, and an honor bar and complimentary cookies in the library. Now with a new restaurant, Fonteneda's Grill, that can cater to your every need.

290 5th Ave. S., Naples, FL 34102. (C) **239/659-3466.** Fax 239/262-8748. www.hotelescalante.com. 71 units. Winter $195–$655 double; off season $165–$400 double. Rates include continental breakfast. AE MC, V. **Amenities:** Bar; heated outdoor pool; exercise room; day spa; Jacuzzi; sauna; 24-hr. room service; massage; laundry service. In room: A/C, TV, dataport, minibar, fridge, coffeemaker, hair dryer, iron.

The Inn on Fifth ﴾ This former bank building still exudes that old-money, old-world European charm, but it's hardly stuffy. Located ideally on the closest thing to "happening" 5th Avenue South, the Inn features large guest rooms elegantly decorated in rich, warm tones—the antithesis of Florida decor, frankly. French doors opening onto a balcony or terrace may not reveal the ocean, but you will see either the lovely pool or the action on the Avenue. McCabe's Irish Pub downstairs is a hotbed of activity, featuring live music, a fabulous beer selection, and a youngish contingency of revelers. The Inn on Fifth is extremely relaxing, although the hotel's concierge could use a few lessons in service, being of no help whatsoever when my car ran out of gas out front. That aside, it's a charming, mostly quiet (the 3rd-floor rooms facing the street can get a tad noisy between 8 and 11pm), ideally located spot that's perfect for those looking for a romantic stay with little or no fuss.

699 5th Ave. S., Naples, FL 34102. (C) **888/403-8778** or 239/403-8777. Fax 239/403-8778. www.naplesinn.com. 87 units. Winter $190–$400 double; off season $190–$290 double. Rates include continental breakfast. AE, DC, DISC, MC, V. **Amenities:** Restaurant; bar; heated outdoor pool; fitness center; spa/salon; Jacuzzi; concierge; business services; room service; laundry service. In room: A/C, TV, dataport, coffeemaker, hair dryer, iron, safe.

Naples Beach Hotel & Golf Club ﴾﴾﴾ *Kids* In contrast to The Ritz-Carlton, Naples, and the Naples Grande Resort and Club (see below for both), which could be anywhere, this beachy-keen retro-resort definitely belongs in Olde Naples. In fact, the beachside setting on Millionaires' Row couldn't be better for carrying on the friendly and relaxed Old Florida ambience installed by Henry B. Watkins 60 years ago and continued by his family today. This is also Southwest Florida's only resort with its own 18-hole golf course, tennis center, and full-service spa right on the premises.

A stunning new building, across Gulf Shore Boulevard from reception, houses the spa, the golf club, and a restaurant and bar. Since the hotel predates the city's strict historic-district zoning laws, it also has Olde Naples's only restaurants and bar directly on the beach. Of these, the **Sunset Beach Bar** is one of the region's most famous beachside open-air bars; it's always crammed as the sun sets over the Gulf, and when live bands perform nightly and at the very popular Sunday evening pool parties. The semicircular Everglades Dining Room, which faces the Gulf, emphasizes traditional Florida cuisine, and offers a reasonably priced breakfast buffet to guests and nonguests alike. Complimentary afternoon tea and cookies are served in the lobby, and guests can hang shopping lists on their doorknobs at night for staff delivery of breakfast goodies from the Seminole Store, which sells inexpensive pastries, pizzas, salads, and sandwiches.

Rooms and suites are in several buildings spread over lush gardens hung with more than 5,000 orchids. The least expensive are in the Florida Wing, a two-story relic from 1948, whose recently updated units open to a long porch with views across a manicured lawn to the pool by the Gulf. Units in the Tower are over the main dining room and directly across the boulevard from the golf course, tennis center, and spa. The Watkins Wing houses the most spacious suites. Rooms in the Penthouse Wing, removed from the action at the north end of the property, directly face the beach and are the best choice for couples, especially during holidays and summer, when many families stay here (the clientele is mostly couples at other times).

851 Gulf Shore Blvd., Naples, FL 34102. (℃) **800/237-7600** or 239/261-2222. Fax 239/261-7380. www.naplesbeach hotel.com. 318 units. Winter $275–$485 double, $375–$775 suite; off season $145–$375 double, $220–$595 suite. Packages available. AE, DC, DISC, MC, V. **Amenities:** 4 restaurants; 3 bars; heated outdoor pool; 18-hole golf course; 6 tennis courts; fitness center; full-service spa; watersports equipment rental; bike rental; complimentary children's programs; game room; concierge; activities desk; salon; room service; massage; babysitting; laundry service; free valet parking; 4 shops. *In room:* A/C, TV, wireless Internet access, fridge, hair dryer, iron, safe.

Expensive

Trianon Old Naples *⋆* Located in a quiet (read: no activity) residential neighborhood, this elegant Mediterranean-style building with a classical European interior offers convenience and comfort without a lot of frills. The spacious rooms are equipped with Ritz-Carlton–quality furniture, including mahogany armoires, chairs, and writing desks. All have seating areas and extra-large bathrooms. Some units have balconies spacious enough for chairs, but others are for standing only. There's no restaurant, but continental breakfast is served on silver in a refined lounge. Wine, beer, champagne, and ports are served at a wine bar in the evenings.

955 7th Ave. S., Naples, FL 34102. (℃) **877/482-5228** or 239/435-9600. Fax 239/261-0025. www.trianon.com. 58 units. Rates include continental breakfast. AE, DC, DISC, MC, V. **Amenities:** Heated outdoor pool; laundry service. *In room:* A/C, TV, dataport, fridge (in some units), coffeemaker, hair dryer, iron, safe.

Moderate

LaPlaya Beach & Golf Resort *⋆⋆* There is certainly no dearth of beach resorts in Naples, but what is conspicuously missing—that is, until now—has been a more intimate resort directly on the beach, where you don't feel underdressed or socially inappropriate when walking through the lobby in a bathing-suit cover-up. Located on pristine Vanderbilt Beach, LaPlaya Beach & Golf Resort has filled the void with plush, beautifully decorated rooms overlooking the Gulf and bay (each with private balcony), a spectacular 4,500-square-foot spa, and a sprawling, scenic, and challenging Bob Cupp–designed golf club and the David Leadbetter Golf Academy for novices. But let's get back to the rooms for a minute. The French-country decor and goose-down pillows are hardly what you'd expect at a beach resort, but there's the rub! You'll find none of that cookie-cutter, as-seen-in-*Martha-Stewart-Living* stuff here. Bathrooms are spacious and luxurious, decked out in marble and overflowing with phenomenal products that are tempting to take home. Everything at this resort has a distinct personality, especially the impressive staff that will go to any lengths to accommodate you without being overly doting. The house restaurant also happens to be Baleen, a la the acclaimed Miami restaurant at The Grove Isle Hotel and Spa. Executive chef Jeffrey Bowles works his culinary magic on local seafood to produce a mesmerizing dining experience.

9891 Gulf Shore Dr., Naples, FL 34108. (℃) **800/237-6883** or 239/597-3123. Fax 239/597-6278. www.laplayaresort. com. 189 units. Winter $559–$769 double, $1,300–$1,475 suite; off season $269–$389 double, $419–$500 suite. AE, DC, DISC, MC, V. Valet parking $18 (no self-parking). **Amenities:** Restaurant; bar; pool bar; 4 outdoor pools; golf course; spa; watersports equipment rental (parasailing, kayaking, paddleboats, jet skis); concierge; room service. *In room:* A/C, TV, CD player, dataport, minibar, coffeemaker, hair dryer, iron, safe.

NORTH OF OLDE NAPLES
Very Expensive
The Naples Grande Resort & Club ✿   This sports-minded luxury high-rise formerly known as The Registry is not directly on the beach: Guests must ride the free Clam Pass County Park shuttle along a 3,000-foot boardwalk through mangroves to the Gulf (see the Clam Pass County Park section on p. 373). Once there, you can charge lounge chairs, cabanas, watersports equipment, and drinks to your room. To compensate for the lack of a beachside setting, the resort has a big outdoor complex with two swimming pools, a water slide, and a waterfall. Plus there's the 15-court tennis center, one of the main draws here. Inside its architecturally nondescript modern tower, The Naples Grande radiates a more relaxed ambience than the traditional Ritz-Carlton, but none of the Old Florida charm of its other chief rival, the Naples Beach Hotel & Golf Club (see above). Dining here is at least on a par with that at The Ritz, with the excellent **Brass Pelican** offering some of the city's finest seafood. As for nightlife (and, yes, there is some semblance of it here), the hotel's Luna—one of the city's few and far between dance clubs—is an ultra-mod haute spot reminiscent of South Beach. There's a full-service spa here, too, but treatment rooms are on the cramped side. A complete lobby renovation in 2006 added a more open, modern vibe to the hotel.

475 Seagate Dr., Naples, FL 34103. ✆ 800/422-6177 or 239/597-3232. Fax 239/597-3147. www.naplesgrande resort.com. 474 units. Winter $395–$475 double, $460–$715 suite; off season $160–$395 double, $205–$499 suite. Amenities fee $12 per day. Packages available. AE, DC, DISC, MC, V. From Olde Naples, go about 1½ miles north on U.S. 41 and turn left on Seagate Dr. Hotel is on the right. **Amenities:** 6 restaurants; 4 bars; 5 heated outdoor pools; access to golf course; 15 tennis courts; health club; spa; Jacuzzi; sauna; watersports equipment rental; bike rental; children's programs; game room; concierge; business center; salon; 24-hr. room service; massage; babysitting; laundry service. In room: A/C, TV, fax, dataport, kitchen (some suites), minibar, coffeemaker, hair dryer, iron, safe.

The Ritz-Carlton Golf Resort, Naples ✿✿✿   This Mediterranean-style resort opened in 2001 at the 36-hole (two 18-hole courses), Greg Norman–designed Tiburón Golf Club, in an exclusive residential enclave at the intersection of Vanderbilt Beach and Airport-Pulling roads. This is a golf-lover's version of its sister resort, The Ritz-Carlton, Naples (see below), and guests here can use the spa, beach, and other facilities at its older sibling, a 5-minute drive away. Each of the spacious, luxuriously appointed guest units has a private balcony overlooking the gorgeously landscaped course.

2600 Tiburón Dr., Naples, FL 34109. ✆ 888/856-4372 or 239/593-2000. Fax 239/254-3300. www.ritzcarlton.com. 295 units. Winter $479–$729 double, $829–$1,649 suite; off season $229–$489 double, $389–$1,099 suite. Packages available. AE, DC, DISC, MC, V. From Olde Naples, go north 3½ miles on U.S. 41. Turn right on Vanderbilt Beach Rd. (C.R. 862) to Airport-Pulling Rd. Hotel is on the left. **Amenities:** 2 restaurants; 2 bars; heated outdoor pool; 36-hole golf course; 4 tennis courts; health club; Jacuzzi; sauna; bike rental; children's programs; game room (billiards, cards); concierge; business center; 24-hr. room service; massage; babysitting; laundry service; concierge-level rooms. In room: A/C, TV, dataport, minibar, hair dryer, iron, safe.

The Ritz-Carlton, Naples ✿✿✿   This opulent 14-story Mediterranean-style hotel, one of Florida's finest, is a favorite among affluent guests who like standard Ritz amenities such as imported marble floors, antique art, Oriental rugs, Waterford-crystal chandeliers, British-style afternoon tea, and a staff that starts fawning over you from the moment you arrive. Still, it lacks the wonderful, unfabricated Old Florida charm of the Naples Beach Hotel & Golf Club (see above). Nor is it as close to the beach, for guests must walk through a narrow mangrove forest to reach the sands. The beach here is part of a public park, but hotel staff is out there to answer phones, deliver drinks and snacks, and rent cabanas, boats, and other toys (only towels, chairs, and ice water are complimentary). The plush, fully equipped guest rooms and suites overlook the Gulf, but not all have balconies.

The **Dining Room,** the hotel's signature restaurant, prepares seafood with an Asian flair, while the wood-paneled **Grill Room** is a beef emporium reminiscent of a British private club. Together they serve some of Naples's finest and most expensive cuisine. A $50-million, 51,000-square-foot full-service spa offers a host of pampering treatments. Guests here can play the golf course and use the other amenities at The Ritz-Carlton Golf Resort, Naples (see above).

280 Vanderbilt Beach Rd., Naples, FL 34108. (C) **888/856-4372** or 239/598-3300. Fax 239/598-6690. www.ritzcarlton. com. 463 units. Winter $449–$899 double, $769–$969 suite; off season $200–$439 double, $365–$625 suite. AE, DC, DISC, MC, V. Valet parking $18; self-parking $10 in winter, free off season. From Olde Naples, go north 3½ miles on U.S. 41. Turn left on Vanderbilt Beach Rd. (C.R. 862) to hotel on the left. **Amenities:** 5 restaurants; 2 bars; 5 heated outdoor pools; access to golf course; 4 tennis courts; spa; Jacuzzi; sauna; watersports equipment rental; bike rental; children's programs; game room; concierge; business center; salon; 24-hr. room service; massage; babysitting; laundry service. *In room:* A/C, TV, dataport, minibar, hair dryer, iron.

Expensive

Vanderbilt Inn Naples (F)   Beach-casual decor in the accommodations and public areas sets the tempo for a casual, fun vacation at this two-story motel right on Vanderbilt Beach, where you can go parasailing and rent boats and watersports equipment. Nature lovers can walk along the beach and into Delnor-Wiggins Pass State Park (p. 373). The 16 efficiencies (with kitchens) at the ends of the building open onto the beach. About half of the standard motel-style rooms face a magnificently landscaped courtyard with a kidney-shape pool surrounded by a brick terrace, while the other, less-expensive units open to parking lots. Although the rooms are entered from exterior walkways, their big windows are darkly tinted to provide privacy. A thatched-roof bar and full-service outdoor restaurant serve lunches and dinners by the beach and draw a crowd for sunset happy hour. The indoor dining room, Splash, serves breakfast and dinner. Another restaurant turns lively when bands play on Friday and Saturday nights. Kids 12 and under dine free when accompanied by adults here.

11000 Gulf Shore Dr., Naples, FL 34108. (C) **800/643-8654** or 239/597-3151. Fax 239/597-3099. www.vanderbiltinn. com. 147 units. Winter $145–$370 double; off season $110–$340 double. Weekly rates available. AE, DC, DISC, MC, V. From Olde Naples, go 4 miles north on U.S. 41; take a left on 111th Ave. (which becomes Bluebill Ave.) to hotel on the left. **Amenities:** 2 restaurants; 2 bars; heated outdoor pool; Jacuzzi; watersports equipment rental; business center. *In room:* A/C, TV, dataport, fridge, microwave (efficiencies only), coffeemaker (efficiencies only), safe.

Inexpensive

Lighthouse Inn Motel   A relic from decades gone by, Judy and Buzz Dugan's no-frills but spotlessly clean motel sits across the street from other, more expensive Gulfside properties on Vanderbilt Beach and within walking distance of The Ritz-Carlton, Naples. The efficiencies and apartments are simple, with cinder-block walls and small kitchens. The one kitchenless room has a small fridge and coffeemaker, but note that no units have phones, and four have shower-only bathrooms. Most guests take advantage of weekly and monthly rates in winter, when the motel is heavily booked. The Dugans also operate Buzz's Lighthouse Cafe next door, a pleasant place for an inexpensive dockside breakfast, lunch, or dinner.

9140 Gulf Shore Dr. N., Naples, FL 34108. (C) **239/597-3345.** Fax 239/597-5541. 15 units. Winter $105 double, $110 efficiency, $120 apt; off season $49 double, $59 efficiency, $69 apt. MC, V. From Olde Naples, go 3½ miles north on U.S. 41; take a left on Vanderbilt Beach Rd. (C.R. 862). Turn right on Gulf Shore Dr. to hotel on the right. **Amenities:** Restaurant; bar; heated outdoor pool. *In room:* A/C, TV, kitchen, fridge, coffeemaker, no phone.

WHERE TO DINE

Naples's beaches are ideal for picnics. In Olde Naples, you can get freshly baked breads and pastries, gourmet sandwiches, and fruit plates at **Tony's Off Third,** 1300 3rd St. S. (© **239/262-7999**). Stop by **Wynn's on Fifth,** 745 5th Ave. S., between 8th and Park streets (© **239/261-0901**), for high-quality deli items, sandwiches, salads, take-out meals, and gourmet pastries at very reasonable prices. Both have a few sidewalk tables and are fine places for coffee or a snack while window-shopping on 3rd and 5th avenues South.

IN OLDE NAPLES
Expensive
Campiello's ✸ ITALIAN   It's not about the homemade pasta at this see-and-be-scene spot in Naples, where the open-air bar is command central for local Naples luminaries and suntanned socialites. Par for the Naples course, the martini menu is impressive, featuring over 20 creative concoctions. Daily specials are the most interesting here: Chef Andrew Wicklander comes up with fabulous wood-oven pizzas and delicious pastas that you've never heard of before.

1177 3rd St. (at Broad Ave.). © 239/435-1166. Reservations recommended. Main courses $10–$15. AE, DC, DISC, MC, V. Daily 11:30am–2:30pm; Sun–Thurs 5–10:30pm; Fri–Sat 5–11pm.

Chop's City Grill ✸✸ STEAK/SEAFOOD   The smells of steak and money waft through this urbane bistro that's more Miami hip than Naples nautical. Aged, top-quality steaks and lamb chops are the house specialties, either chargrilled to perfection and served with thick onion rings and mashed potatoes, or peppered and served with a blackberry-and-cabernet-wine sauce. Fresh fish from the grill is another good choice. Asian influences appear here, too, such as sea scallops "shocked" in a wok with Thai curry sauce and served over noodles with wild mushrooms and stir-fried vegetables.

837 5th Ave. S. (between 8th and 9th sts. S.). © 239/262-4677. Reservations recommended. Main courses $15–$30. AE, DC, DISC, MC, V. Sun–Thurs 5–10pm; Fri–Sat 5–11pm.

Zoë's ✸✸ ECLECTIC   This dimly lit, modish bistro draws a lively crowd of young professionals who preen at the big bar to one side or at a raised, English pub–style drinking table. The eclectic menu changes every week or so to take advantage of fresh produce. Meatloaf, macaroni and cheese, and pot roast are regulars. They sound on the menu like those your mother made, but they're seasoned to be as lively as Zoë's patrons. If they are offered, opt for the homemade veal meatloaf; the pecan-crusted sea bass; or the seared, sesame-coated yellowfin tuna served with cucumber relish, a horseradish-tinged mayonnaise drizzle, and spicy soba noodles. Zoë's turns into a *Saturday Night Fever*–esque disco ($5 cover) on Friday and Saturday nights.

720 5th Ave. S. (between 7th and 8th sts. S.). © 239/261-1221. Reservations recommended. Main courses $15–$34. AE, MC, V. Sun–Thurs 5–10pm; Fri–Sat 5–10:30pm (music and dancing Fri–Sat 11pm–2am).

Moderate
Bistro 821 ✸ FUSION   This South Beach-y bistro is an excellent choice for Mediterranean-influenced fusion cuisine. Although the quarters are too close for private conversations, small ceiling spotlights romantically illuminate each table. The house specialty is rotisserie chicken, and a daily risotto leads a menu featuring penne in vodka sauce and a seasonal vegetable plate with herb couscous. But in my opinion, the best dishes on the menu are the rock-lobster satay with spicy ginger-and-lime dipping sauce, farfalle with Alaskan king crabmeat, and seafood risotto. Dishes are huge, but you can order either full or half portions. There's sidewalk dining here, too.

821 5th Ave. S. (between 8th and 9th sts. S.). ✆ 239/261-5821. Reservations recommended. Main courses $13–$26. AE, DC, MC, V. Daily 5–10pm.

The Dock at Crayton Cove ✷ ⱽᵃˡᵘᵉ SEAFOOD   Located right on the City Dock, this locals' hangout is the best place in town for a supercasual open-air meal or a cool drink while watching the boats go back and forth across Naples Bay. Servers are friendly and conversational. The chow ranges from hearty chowders by the mug to seafood with a Floribbean fare, with Jamaican-style jerk shrimp thrown in for spice; main courses are moderately priced. Grilled seafood Caesar salad and a good selection of sandwiches, hot dogs, and other pub-style fare also appear on the menu. "Margarita Madness" happy hour and a half-price raw bar (don't miss the steamed mussels with French bread for dipping into the garlic sauce) run daily from 9:30 to 11:30pm. The Great Dock Canoe Race draws thousands on the second Saturday in May.

12th Ave. S. (at the City Dock in Olde Naples). ✆ 239/263-9940. Reservations not accepted. Main courses $11–$26; sandwiches $9–$13. AE, DISC, MC, V. Daily 11am–midnight.

Tommy Bahama's Tropical Cafe ✷✷ CARIBBEAN   Walk through a thatch gateway into this lively, island-style watering hole (or upscale Margaritaville, if you will)—an incongruous sight in the middle of the staid 3rd Street South shopping enclave. If not in Tommy Bahama's *Indiana Jones*–meets–Florida threads, diners look as if they've stepped right out of a Ralph Lauren or Abercrombie catalog. They gather on a large front patio under shade trees, where a musician performs, or inside, where a large back-wall mural creates a Polynesian scene. An open kitchen is on one side of the dining room, a bar dispensing drinks on the other. In between, cane chairs and classic ceiling fans add to the exotic mood. Although the Jamaican pork, salmon St. Croix, and other Caribbean-style cuisine don't quite live up to the ambience, you'll have too much fun here to care whether it's gourmet—and the huge portions will satisfy any appetite. They don't appear on the dinner menu, but sandwiches are served if you ask (the meal-size grouper sandwich is a bargain, at $10).

1220 3rd St. S. (between 12th and 13th aves. S.). ✆ 239/643-6889. Reservations recommended. Main courses $17–$27; sandwiches $8–$14. AE, MC, V. Daily 11am–10pm.

Yabba Island Grill ✷ ⱽᵃˡᵘᵉ CARIBBEAN   Perhaps the noisiest, most crowded spot on 5th Avenue, Yabba Island Grill attempts to channel the Caribbean with loud music, a massive bar, and a tropical decor—and does a very decent job. The food makes as loud a statement as Yabba's pastel color scheme, with most items providing a riot of flavors from across the Caribbean. And if the party-hearty crowd that convenes here isn't enough to entice you, consider the St. Croix Sizzler, a terrific combination of small lobster tail, a chunk of mahimahi, and mussels over a bed of peppers, onions, and sweet mango-curry sauce. If you're looking for a peaceful and quiet meal, get here superearly—in fact, at 4:30pm, right at opening time—before all the antsy vacationers looking for some action start piling in.

711 5th Ave. S. (between 8th St. S. and Park Ave. S.). ✆ 239/262-5787. Reservations recommended. Main courses $10–$24; sandwiches $8–$10. AE, DISC, MC, V. Daily 4:30–11pm (bar to 2am Fri–Sat).

Inexpensive
Cheeburger Cheeburger ✷✷ AMERICAN   Though this is a chain restaurant, with no decor to speak of, if you're hankering for a good—no, make that great—burger with a side of fries or onion rings and a milkshake, this is definitely the place

to go. Choose the size you want (5 oz.–1 lb.!) and any of more than a dozen toppings, and enjoy. There are also salads for those who want to be healthy.

505 5th Ave. S. (between 5th and 6th sts.). © 239/435-9796. Burgers $4.25–$10. AE, DISC, MC, V. Daily 11am–9pm.

First Watch *Value* AMERICAN   Just like its siblings elsewhere in Florida, this diner is a favorite local haunt for breakfast, brunch, or a midday meal. You may have to wait for a table, but once you're seated, a young staff will provide quick and friendly service. The menu leans heavily on healthful selections, but you can still get your cholesterol from a sizzling skillet of fried eggs served over potatoes, vegetables, and melted cheese. Lunch features large salads, sandwiches, and quesadillas. In addition to the dining room, there's more seating at umbrella tables in the courtyard.

In Gulf Shore Sq., 1400 Gulf Shore Blvd. (at Banyan Rd.). © 239/434-0005. Most items $3.50–$8. AE, DISC, MC, V. Daily 7am–2:30pm. Closed Christmas.

Old Naples Pub *Finds* *Value* AMERICAN/PUB FARE   You would never guess that the person sitting next to you at the bar here is a mogul of some sort, so relaxed is this small, somewhat-cramped pub in the middle of the fabulous 3rd Street South shops. Diners fortunately find more room at tables on the shopping center's patio. The menu features very good pub fare (and at extraordinarily inexpensive prices for Olde Naples), including homemade soups, nachos, burgers, and sandwiches ranging from charcoal-grilled bratwurst to fried grouper. Only six main courses are offered: platters with New York strip steak, grilled tuna, the catch of the day, fried grouper or clam strips, and baby back ribs. Best bets are the chicken salad with grapes and walnuts, along with the burgers, steaks, and fish from the charcoal grill. You can catch live entertainment here nightly during winter, Wednesday through Saturday off season.

255 13th Ave. S. (between 3rd and 4th sts. S.). © 239/649-8200. Main courses $11–$15; salads, sandwiches, and burgers $5–$9. AE, DISC, MC, V. Mon–Sat 11am–10pm; Sun noon–9pm.

NORTH OF OLDE NAPLES
Silver Spoon American Cafe *Value* AMERICAN/ITALIAN/SOUTHWEST   Even though this member of the American Cafe chain is in the Waterside Shops complex and immediately screams TGI Friday's, it happens to be one of Naples's best dining bargains and makes the perfect spot for lunch. The food is high-quality chain-restaurant cuisine. Thick sandwiches are served with fries, spicy pecan rice, or black beans. The tomato-basil soup is worth a try, and the bruschetta appetizer—served on toasted French bread—is nearly a meal in itself. Gourmet pizzas and pasta dishes are also popular, especially with the after-theater crowds from the nearby Philharmonic Center for the Arts. Main courses, such as Cajun or herb-grilled chicken, are both tasty and an excellent value. Shoppers love to lunch here, so come early or be prepared for a wait.

In the Waterside Shops at Pelican Bay, 5395 N. Tamiami Trail (at Seagate Dr.). © 239/591-2123. Reservations not accepted, but call ahead for preferred seating. Main courses $9.50–$15; pizza and pasta $8–$12; soups, salads, and sandwiches $7–$9. AE, DC, DISC, MC, V. Sun–Thurs 11am–10pm; Fri–Sat 11am–11pm. From Olde Naples, go north on U.S. 41 and left on Seagate Dr. right into the shopping center. Proceed right at the dead-end to the restaurant on the left.

NAPLES AFTER DARK
For entertainment ideas, check the *Naples Daily News* (www.naplesnews.com), especially the "Neapolitan" section in Friday's edition.

THE PERFORMING ARTS   Known locally as "The Phil," the impressive **Philharmonic Center for the Arts** *Finds*, 5833 Pelican Bay Blvd., at West Boulevard

(© **800/597-1900** or 239/597-1900; www.thephil.org), is the home of the Naples Philharmonic, but its year-round schedule is also filled with cultural events, concerts by celebrated artists and internationally known orchestras, and Broadway plays and shows aimed at families. Call or check the website for the seasonal calendar.

A fine local theater group, the **Naples Players,** holds its winter-season performances in the new Sugden Community Theatre, 701 5th Ave. S. (© **239/263-7990;** www. naples.net/presents/theatre). Tickets can be hard to come by, so call well in advance.

THE CLUB & BAR SCENE   Remember: Naples is not South Beach, nor does it pretend to be. It does, however, realize that some people like to party well past early-bird hours, and, as a result, there are a few good spots here to get your groove on.

The restaurants and bistros along 5th Avenue South are popular watering holes, especially for young professional singles who make this their meat market on Friday nights. **Zoë's,** 720 5th Ave. S. (© **239/261-1221;** p. 383), turns into a high-energy nightclub Friday and Saturday from 10:30pm to 2am. Nearby, **McCabe's Irish Pub,** 699 5th Ave. S. (© **239/403-7170**), features traditional Irish music nightly. For a lot of camp with your cabaret, the **Ridgway Bar and Grill,** 3rd Street South and 13th Avenue (© **239/262-5500**), is a hot spot, thanks to pianist Jim Badger, whose bawdy shows bring in crowds of all ages (not recommended for those under 18).

In the 3rd Street South shopping area, **Old Naples Pub,** 255 13th Ave. S. (© **239/ 649-8200;** p. 385), has live music nightly during winter, Wednesday through Saturday nights off season.

The touristy **Old Marine Marketplace at Tin City,** which comprises the restored waterfront warehouses on 5th Avenue South on the west side of the Gordon River, comes alive in winter, when visitors flock to its shops and the **Riverwalk Fish & Ale House** (© **239/262-2734**), which has live entertainment during the season.

The beachside *chickee* hut bar at the **Naples Beach Hotel & Golf Club** (© **239/ 261-2222**) is always popular, has live entertainment many nights, and is *the* place to go on Sunday afternoon and early evening. So is the beachside bar at the **Vanderbilt Inn Naples** (© **239/597-3151**).

5 Marco Island

15 miles SE of Naples, 53 miles S of Fort Myers, 100 miles W of Miami

Marco Island is reminiscent of a sleepy, albeit swanky, beachfront retirement community. When the sun goes down, you can hear a pin drop, though. There is absolutely no life after dark here, but Capt. William Collier would still hardly recognize Marco Island if he were to come back from the grave today. No relation to Collier County founder Barron Collier, the captain settled his family on the north end of this island, the largest of Florida's Ten Thousand Islands, back in 1871. He traded pelts with the Native Americans, caught and smoked fish to sell to Key West and Cuba, and charged fishermen and other guests $2 a day for a room in his home. A few turn-of-the-20th-century buildings still stand here, but Collier would be shocked to come across the high-rise bridge to the island and see it now sliced by man-made canals and virtually covered by resorts, condominiums, shops, restaurants, and winter homes. These are the products of an extensive real-estate development begun in 1965, which means that Marco lacks any of the charm found in Naples and on Sanibel and Captiva islands. Much of the sales effort here was aimed at the northeastern states, so the island smacks more of New York and Massachusetts than of the laid-back Midwestern style of its neighbors. Marco's only real attractions are its crescent-shape beach and access to the nearby waterways running through a maze of small islands, its excellent boating and fishing, and the island's proximity to acres of wildlife preserves.

ESSENTIALS

GETTING THERE   See p. 335 and 372, respectively, for information on the **Southwest Florida International Airport** and the **Naples Municipal Airport.** Also see p. 335 for details on Amtrak train service and Greyhound/Trailways bus service to Fort Myers.

VISITOR INFORMATION   The **Marco Island Area Chamber of Commerce,** 1102 N. Collier Blvd., Marco Island, FL 34145 (© **800/788-6272** or 239/394-7549; fax 239/394-3061; www.marcoislandchamber.org), provides free information on the island. A message board and a phone are located outside the office for making hotel reservations even outside of operating hours. In winter, the chamber is open Monday through Friday from 9am to 5pm, and Saturday from 10am to 3pm.

GETTING AROUND   **Marco Island Trolley Tours** (© **239/394-1600**) makes four loops around the island and into the wacky, shacky fishing village of Goodland Monday through Saturday from 10am to 3:15pm. The conductors sell tickets and give a narration on the island's history. Daily fare is $21 for adults and $10 for children 11 and under, with free reboarding. The loop takes about 1 hour and 45 minutes. Make sure to ask for a free reboarding pass, in case you want to get off and tool around.

    Enterprise Rent-a-Car (© **800/325-8007** or 239/642-4488) has an office here. For a cab, call **A-Action Taxi** (© **239/394-4400**), **Classic Taxi** (© **239/394-1888**), or **A-Okay Taxi** (© **239/394-1113**).

    Depending on the type, rental bicycles cost from $5 an hour to $65 a week at **Scootertown,** 845 Bald Eagle Dr. (© **239/394-8400**), north of North Collier Boulevard near Olde Marco. Scooters go for about $50 for 24 hours.

HITTING THE BEACH

The sugar-white **Crescent Beach** curves for 3½ miles down the entire western shore of Marco Island. Its southern 2 miles are fronted by an unending row of high-rise condominiums and hotels, but the northern 1½ miles are preserved in **Tigertail Public Beach** (© **239/642-8414**), at the end of Hernando Drive. Restrooms, cold-water outdoor showers, a children's playground, watersports rentals, and a snack bar are available here. The park is open daily from dawn to dusk. There's no admission charge for the beach, but parking in the lot costs $3 per vehicle. The beaches in front of the Marriott, Hilton, and Radisson resorts have parasailing, windsurfing, and other watersports activities, all for a fee.

    If you're not staying at the big resorts, Collier County maintains a $3-per-vehicle parking lot and access to the developed beach on the southern end of the island, on Swallow Avenue at South Collier Boulevard.

OUTDOOR ACTIVITIES

Marco River Marina, 951 Bald Eagle Dr. (© **239/394-2502;** www.marcoriver.com), is the center for boat rentals, fishing, and cruises. Operating from a booth on the marina's dock, **Sunshine Tours** (© **239/642-5415;** www.sunshinetoursmarcoisland. com) will book offshore fishing charters and arrange back-bay fishing ($50 for adults, $40 for children under 10), shelling excursions to the small islands ($40 adults, $30 children under 10), sunset cruises ($33 adults, $15 children), and dinner cruises

($46–$49 per person). The back-bay fishing trips go at high tide, the shelling trips at low tide; call for the schedule and reservations.

SCUBAdventures, based at 845 Bald Eagle Dr., Olde Marco (© **239/389-7889**), charges $65 to $85 for two-tank dives, depending on the distance offshore.

Naples's Lely and Boyne South golf courses are a short drive away (see p. 375 for details). The closest public courses are the **Marco Shores Golf Club,** 1450 Mainsail Dr. (© **239/394-2581**), and **Marriott's Golf Club at Marco** (© **239/353-7061**), both in the marshlands off Florida 951 north of the island. A sign at the Marriott's course ominously warns: PLEASE DON'T DISTURB THE ALLIGATORS. Fees range from about $120 in winter down to $75 in summer.

A NATURE PRESERVE

Operated by the Conservancy and part of the Rookery Bay National Estuarine Research Reserve, the **Briggs Nature Center** ✦, on Shell Island Road, off Florida 951 between U.S. 41 and Marco Island (© **239/775-8569;** www.conservancy.org), has a ½-mile boardwalk through a pristine example of Florida's disappearing scrublands, home to threatened scrub jays and gopher tortoises. Rangers lead a variety of nature excursions, and there is a self-guided canoe trail, with canoes for rent Tuesday through Saturday mornings (you must return them by 1pm) at $13 for the first 2 hours, $5 for each additional hour. The center is open Monday through Saturday from 9am to 4:30pm. Admission to the boardwalk is $4 for adults, $2 for children 3 to 12. For information, contact the **Conservancy of Southwest Florida,** 1450 Merrihue Dr., Naples, FL 34102 (© **239/262-0304;** fax 239/262-0672; www.conservancy.org).

WHERE TO STAY

There are no chain hotels on Marco Island other than the large Marriott, Hilton, and Radisson properties listed below, which stand in a row along Crescent Beach on the island's southwestern corner. **Century 21 First Southern Trust** (© **800/523-0069** or 239/394-7653; fax 239/394-8048; www.c21marco.com) is one of the largest agents representing rental-property owners.

As elsewhere in South Florida, the high season here is from mid-December to mid-April. Rates drop precipitously in the off season.

Boat House Motel *Value*   One of the best bargains in these parts, this pleasant little motel is a throwback to the '50s and sits beside the Marco River in Olde Marco, on the island's northern end. The rooms are in an old-school, two-story, lime-green-and-white building that ends at a wooden dock with a small heated pool, lounge furniture, picnic tables, and barbecue grills. Two rooms on the end have their own decks, and all open to tiny courtyards. Bright paint, ceiling fans, and louvered shutters add a tropical ambience throughout. The one-bedroom condominiums next door open onto a riverside dock, upon which is built a two-bedroom cottage named The Gazebo, whose peaked roof is supported by umbrella-like spokes from a central pole.

1180 Edington Place, Marco Island, FL 34148. © **800/528-6345** or 239/642-2400. Fax 239/642-2435. www.the boathousemotel.com. 25 units. Winter $99–$155 double, $170–$260 apt or cottage; off season $83–$130 double, $125–$220 apt or cottage. MC, V. Pets accepted ($15 fee plus $5 per day). **Amenities:** Heated outdoor pool; coin-op washers and dryers. *In room:* A/C, TV, fridge, iron.

Marco Beach Ocean Resort ✦✦   Making up for the lack of a Ritz-y resort on Marco Island is this posh, all-suite place with full-service spa. The suites are definitely comfortable, complete with full kitchens and patios overlooking the Gulf. Although the marble lobby is mausoleum-like with little or no activity, it is a sight to see. I'm happy to report that ever since we criticized the hotel's strict dress code, management wisened up and got rid of it! Neither golf nor tennis courts are on the premises, but the concierge can arrange both at nearby clubs. While the pool features private cabanas and butlers rocks, the beach and its beach butlers are what really matters. Pristine and private, the Marco Beach Ocean Resort features beach service all day long.

480 S. Collier Blvd., Marco Island, FL 34145. ✆ 800/260-5089 or 239/393-1400. Fax 239/393-1401. www.marcoresort. com. 103 units. $199–$1200 suite. Valet parking $15 (no self-parking). AE, DC, DISC, MC, V. **Amenities:** 4 restaurants; 2 bars; heated outdoor pool; golf and tennis at nearby facilities; fitness center; spa; Jacuzzi; sauna; watersports equipment rental; concierge; business center; sundry shop; limited room service; massage; laundry service. *In room:* A/C, TV, dataport, full kitchen, minibar, fridge, coffeemaker, hair dryer, iron, safe.

Marco Island Hilton Beach Resort 🎇🎇   About half the size of the nearby Marco Island Marriott Resort & Golf Club (see below), but nevertheless a group-oriented hotel, this 11-story beachside tower overlooks the Gulf and a courtyard with a multi-angled pool wrapped around four coconut palms. The spacious units have curved balconies angled to give water views. One-bedroom units have cooking facilities. One kitchen here serves two outlets: the elegant Sandcastles for dinner and the adjacent Paradise Cafe for casual breakfasts, lunches, and dinners. The Beach Club by the pool serves lunches, snacks, and drinks. Sandcastles Lounge has a piano bar with nightly entertainment. *Note:* The hotel is 100% nonsmoking—outside and inside.

560 S. Collier Blvd., Marco Island, FL 34145. ✆ 800/HILTONS or 239/394-5000. Fax 239/394-8410. www.marcoisland. hilton.com. 298 units. Winter $199–$359 double; off season $130–$189 double. Resort amenities fee $9 per unit per day (includes local calls). Packages available. AE, DC, DISC, MC, V. Free parking. **Amenities:** 2 restaurants; 2 bars; heated outdoor pool; 3 tennis courts; exercise room; Jacuzzi; sauna; watersports equipment rental; children's programs; game room; concierge; activities desk; business center; salon; limited room service; massage; babysitting; laundry service; concierge-level rooms. *In room:* A/C, TV, dataport, kitchen (in suites only), minibar, fridge, coffeemaker, hair dryer, iron, safe.

Marco Island Marriott Resort & Golf Club 🎇🎇 *Kids*   Marco Island is far from Disney World, so if you plan to bring the kids while you experience the utmost in R&R, the sprawling Marco Island Marriott will make sure they're entertained with activities, from watersports and Everglades excursions to bingo, Frisbee, and dive-in movies (watch from the pool). Parents can play, too, or they can opt for the hotel's convenient nanny service. A $55-million renovation has spruced up the guest rooms, restaurants, and lounges and added a par-72 golf course located 7 minutes away, as well as a 24,000-square-foot Balinese spa. Luxuriously furnished and decorated, the spacious accommodations range from hotel rooms to two-bedroom suites. All have balconies or patios with indirect views of the Gulf. If you don't want to be bored during your Marco Island stay (a common affliction after too much pool or beach), definitely stay here, where there actually are things to do off—and on—the beach.

400 S. Collier Blvd., Marco Island, FL 34145. ✆ 800/438-4373 or 239/394-2511. Fax 239/642-2672. www.marco marriottresort.com. 797 units. Winter $275–$385 double, from $520 suite; off season $149–$340 double, from $320 suite. Packages available. AE, DC, DISC, MC, V. Valet parking $11; free self-parking. **Amenities:** 5 restaurants; 4 bars; 3 heated outdoor pools; golf course; tennis court; exercise room; Jacuzzi; watersports equipment rental; children's programs; game room; concierge; activities desk; car-rental desk; business center; shopping arcade; salon; limited room service; massage; babysitting; laundry service; concierge-level rooms. *In room:* A/C, TV, dataport, minibar, fridge, coffeemaker, hair dryer, iron, safe.

Olde Marco Inn & Suites 🎇🎇🎇   Considered by many to be one of Florida's most romantic resorts, the Victorian-style Olde Marco Inn & Suites dates from 1883, when Capt. Bill Collier built it on the Calusa Indian Grounds. While maintaining its historic charm, the place has been remodeled and updated, and now offers 51 new one- and two-bedroom, two-bathroom suites decorated with a tropical flair. Six penthouses on the fifth floor overlooking the Gulf are worth the splurge, ranging in size from 1,300 to 6,000 square feet. Lush gardens almost make you feel as if you're not even close to the beach, but you are. In addition to stellar service, the inn offers one of the area's nicest restaurants, Cafe de Marco, serving up fine seafood. For further relaxation, a spa and fitness center are also available. But the best amenity, hands down, is the private 38-foot catamaran that sails guests to serene, unspoiled beaches on and around Marco Island. These trips are complimentary and include beach chairs and towels. While on the boat, keep your eyes open for dolphins and manatees. Evening cruises with wine, beer, soft drinks, and appetizers are also available, but at a nominal fee. Couples looking for a first, second, or third honeymoon should stay here, without question.

100 Palm St., Marco Island, FL 34145. ℭ **877/475-3466.** Fax 239/394-4485. www.oldemarco.com. 329 units. Winter $129–$239 1- and 2-bedroom suites; penthouses $400—3,500; off season $119–$309 1-bedroom, $129–$339 2-bedroom; penthouses $350–$2,500. AE, DC, DISC, MC, V. **Amenities:** Restaurant; bar; outdoor pool; fitness center; concierge; limited room service. *In room:* A/C, TV, VCR, dataport, full kitchen, hair dryer, iron.

WHERE TO DINE

Cafe de Marco 𝒜𝒜 SEAFOOD   Purveyor of some of the island's finest cuisine, this homelike establishment at the Marco Village shops was originally constructed as housing for maids at Capt. William Collier's Olde Marco Inn. The chef specializes in excellent treatments of fresh seafood, from your choice of shrimp or baked fish with mushrooms, seasoned shallots, and garlic butter, to his own luscious creation of seafood and vegetables combined in a lobster sauce and served over linguine. If your waistline can stand it, finish with a Cafe Puff, an almond-praline ice-cream ball rolled in chocolate cookie crumbs, placed in a puff-pastry shell, and served with whipped cream. Early-bird specials here are a very good value. You can dine inside or on a screened patio.

244 Palm St., Olde Marco. ℭ **239/394-6262.** Reservations recommended. Main courses $16–$30; early-bird specials $13. Minimum charge $13 per adult, $4.50 per child. AE, MC, V. Winter daily 5–10pm; off season Mon–Sat 5–10pm. Early-bird specials 5–6pm.

Kahuna Restaurant AMERICAN   With fanciful Hawaiian themes highlighted by a small steaming volcano and a mural of porpoises playing underwater, Kahuna is the least expensive choice here. You can sit outside in the shopping center's parking lot or inside at colored booths and round tables under ceiling fans. The burgers are some of Marco's best (there's a condiments bar with a variety of fixings). Main courses include several fried seafood selections, baked crab cakes, and charcoal-grilled tuna, but your best bet is the nightly special, which might be salmon in a light dill sauce. Don't expect gourmet dining here; still, the quality is good for the price.

1035 N. Collier Blvd., in Town Center Mall (at Bald Eagle Dr.). ℭ **239/394-4300.** Reservations not accepted. Main courses $8.50–$15; sandwiches and burgers $3.50–$7.50; breakfast $3–$8. MC, V. Winter daily 8:30am–9pm; off season daily 11:30am–9pm.

Kretch's 𝒜𝒜 *Value* SEAFOOD/CONTINENTAL   Noted pastry chef Bruce Kretschmer rules this shopping-center roost, Marco's best all-around restaurant. Bruce has created a sinfully rich seafood strudel by combining shrimp, crab, scallops, cheeses, cream, and broccoli in a flaky Bavarian pastry and serving it all under a lobster sauce. It's available as either an appetizer or an entree. Cholesterol-counters can choose from broiled or charcoal-grilled fish, while the rest of us can indulge in shrimp, Florida lobster tail, steaks, or lamb chops. Bruce's popular Mexican Friday lunches feature delicious tacos and other inexpensive south-of-the-border selections. In winter, Sunday is home-cooking night, with chicken and dumplings, Yankee pot roast, and braised lamb shanks.

527 Bald Eagle Dr. (south of N. Collier Blvd.). © 239/394-3433. Reservations recommended in winter. Main courses $14–$25. DISC, MC, V. Mon–Fri 11am–3pm and 5–9pm; Sat–Sun 5–9pm. Closed Sun off season and Easter, July 4, Thanksgiving, Christmas Eve, and Christmas Day.

Snook Inn SEAFOOD   The choice dinner seats at this Old Florida establishment are in an enclosed dock right beside the scenic Marco River, but for lunch or libation (such as a fabulous Bloody Mary with pickled okra), head to the dockside Chickee Bar, a fun place anytime, but especially at sunset. The new garden courtyard isn't a bad place to be, either, as long as it's not mosquito season, in which case avoid all outdoor areas unless you've bathed in Off!. Live entertainment is featured both day and night during the winter season, nightly the rest of the year. Although seafood is the specialty, tasty steaks, chicken, burgers, and sandwiches are among the choices. Even the sandwiches come with a trip to the salad bar at dinner, making them a fine bargain. Bring a filet of that fish you caught today, and the chef will cook it up for you. Call A-Okay Taxi (p. 387) for a free ride from anywhere on Marco Island to Snook Inn.

1215 Bald Eagle Dr. (at Palm St.), Olde Marco. © 239/394-3313. Reservations not accepted. Main courses $12–$21; sandwiches $8–$10; cook-your-catch $11. AE, DC, DISC, MC, V. Daily 11am–4pm and 4:30–10pm. Closed Thanksgiving and Christmas.

MARCO ISLAND AFTER DARK
Marco Island nightlife is an oxymoron. When the sun sets, so does everything else here, for the most part. With the exception of the island's movie theater and a few hotel bars, there's not much doing after dark. A drive to Naples is necessary for those looking to burn the midnight oil.

To find out what is going on, check the *Naples Daily News* (www.naplesnews.com), especially the "Neapolitan" section in Friday's edition and its weekly "The Marco Islander" section, available at the chamber of commerce (p. 387).

It's not after dark, but one of the biggest parties in Florida takes place every Sunday afternoon at **Stan's Idle Hour Seafood Restaurant,** on C.R. 892, in Goodland (© 239/394-3041), where owner Stan Gober—an Ernest Hemingway look-alike—plays host and fires up the barbecue grills. Bands crank out the country music for dancing the "Buzzard Lope," and men compete to see who has the best legs. Stan's Goodland Mullet Festival, always the weekend before the Super Bowl, is the mother of all parties. Also in Goodland is the delightfully divey waterfront **Little Bar Restaurant,** 205 Harbor Dr. (© 239/294-5663), featuring a jukebox, bar, and surprisingly good menu.

Marco Island's much tamer but nevertheless entertaining version is the **Snook Inn** (see "Where to Dine," above), where bands play in the dockside Chickee Bar. Much more sedate are the lounges in the **Marriott** and **Hilton** resorts (see "Where to Stay," above), which provide pianists every evening.

It seems like everyone turns out for the free outdoor entertainment at the shopping malls: every Tuesday night year-round at the **Mission San Marco Plaza,** South Collier Boulevard at Winterberry Drive, and every Thursday night at the **Town Center Mall,** at North Collier Boulevard and Bald Eagle Drive.

11

The Tampa Bay Area

San Francisco isn't the country's only Bay Area. In fact, when some people hear the word *Tampa,* they typically think of Busch Gardens and never even mention its bay area. They'd be missing out: Tampa is a stunning, picturesque city, and while it may not have a red bridge, it does have an array of colors reflecting off its sparkling waters. If you haven't had a chance to explore Florida's bay area, do so now. There's so much more to the Tampa Bay area than beer and amusement parks. Sure, you can chug as much Busch Beer as you want, but you can also do (and see, eat, and experience) much more here.

Florida's very own city by the bay, Tampa has its own vibrant culture, with roots firmly planted in Cuban and American history.

The city of Tampa is the commercial center of Florida's west coast—a growing seaport and center of banking and high-tech manufacturing. You can come downtown during the day to see the sea life at the Florida Aquarium and stroll through the Henry B. Plant Museum, housed in an ornate, Moorish-style hotel built more than a century ago to lure tourists to the city. A short trolley ride will take you from downtown Tampa to Ybor City, the historic Cuban enclave, now a bustling, often rowdy nightlife and dining hot spot.

Two bridges and a causeway will whisk you west across Old Tampa Bay to St. Petersburg, Pinellas Park, Clearwater, Dunedin, Tarpon Springs, and other cities on the Pinellas Peninsula, one of Florida's most densely packed urban areas. Over here on the bay, photo-ready downtown St. Petersburg is famous for wintering seniors, a shopping and dining complex built on a pier, and, surprisingly, the world's largest collection of Salvador Dalí's surrealist paintings.

Keep driving west and you'll come to a line of barrier islands, where St. Pete Beach, Clearwater Beach, and other Gulf-side communities boast 28 miles of sunshine, surf, and white sand.

Heading south, I-275 will take you across the mouth of Tampa Bay to Sarasota and another chain of barrier islands that stretches 42 miles along the coast south of Tampa Bay. One of Florida's cultural centers, affluent Sarasota is the gateway to St. Armands and Longboat keys, two playgrounds of the rich and famous, and to Lido and Siesta keys, both attractive to families of more modest means.

1 Tampa

200 miles SW of Jacksonville, 85 miles SW of Orlando, 254 miles NW of Miami

Even if you stay on the beaches 20 miles to the west, you should consider driving into Tampa for a mild taste of metropolis. If you have children in tow, they may *demand* that you go into the city so they can ride the rides and see the animals at Busch Gardens. Once there, you can also educate them (and yourself) at the Florida Aquarium

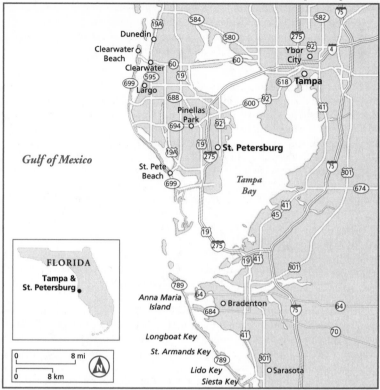

and the city's other fine museums. Additionally, historic Ybor City has the bay area's liveliest and hottest nightlife.

Tampa was a sleepy little port when Cuban immigrants founded Ybor City's cigar industry in the 1880s. A few years later, Henry B. Plant put Tampa on the tourist map by building a railroad that ran into town and by constructing bulbous minarets atop his garish Tampa Bay Hotel, now a museum named in his honor. During the Spanish-American War, Teddy Roosevelt trained his Rough Riders here and walked the Ybor City streets with Cuban revolutionary José Martí. A land boom in the 1920s gave the city its charming, Victorian-style Hyde Park suburb, now a gentrified redoubt for the baby boomers just across the Hillsborough River from downtown.

Today's downtown skyline is the product of the 1980s and 1990s booms, when banks built skyscrapers and the city put up an expansive convention center, a performing-arts center, and the St. Pete Times Forum (formerly the Ice Palace), a 20,000-seat bayfront arena that is home to professional hockey's Tampa Bay Lightning. The renaissance hasn't been as rapid as planned, given the recent economic recession, but it is continuing into the 21st century with redevelopment of the seaport area east of downtown. There the existing Florida Aquarium and the Garrison Seaport Center (a major home port for cruise ships bound for Mexico and the Caribbean) are joined by office buildings, apartment complexes, and a major shopping-and-dining center known as Channelside (in the Channel District) at Garrison Seaport.

You won't want to spend your entire Florida vacation in Tampa, but everything it offers adds up to a somewhat fast-paced, modern city on the go.

ESSENTIALS

GETTING THERE   **Tampa International Airport** (© 813/870-8770; www.tampa airport.com), 5 miles northwest of downtown Tampa, is the major air gateway to this area (**St. Petersburg–Clearwater International Airport** has limited service; see section 2, "St. Petersburg," later in this chapter). Most major and many no-frills airlines serve Tampa International, including **Air Canada** (© 800/268-7240 in Canada, or 800/776-3000 in the U.S.), **AirTran** (© 800/247-8726), **American** (© 800/433-7300), **America West** (© 800/235-9292), **British Airways** (© 800/247-9297), **Continental** (© 800/525-0280), **Delta** (© 800/221-1212), **JetBlue** (© 800/538-2583), **Lufthansa** (© 800/824-6200), **MetroJet** (© 800/428-4322), **Midway** (© 800/446-4392), **Midwest Express** (© 800/452-2022), **Northwest** (© 800/225-2525), **Southwest** (© 800/435-9792), **Spirit** (© 800/722-7117), **United** (© 800/241-6522), and **US Airways** (© 800/428-4322).

Alamo (© 800/327-9633), **Avis** (© 800/331-1212), **Budget** (© 800/527-0700), **Dollar** (© 800/800-4000), **Enterprise** (© 800/325-8007), **Hertz** (© 800/654-3131), **National** (© 800/227-7368), and **Thrifty** (© 800/367-2277) all have rental-car operations here.

The **Limo/SuperShuttle** (© **800/282-6817** or 727/527-1111; www.supershuttle. com) operates van services between the airport and hotels throughout the Tampa Bay area. Fares for one person range from $35 to $48 round-trip, depending on your destination. **Taxis** are plentiful at the airport; the ride to downtown Tampa takes about 15 minutes and costs $15 to $20.

Amtrak trains arrive downtown at the **Tampa Amtrak Station,** 601 Nebraska Ave. N. (© **800/872-7245;** www.amtrak.com).

VISITOR INFORMATION   Contact the **Tampa Bay Convention & Visitors Bureau,** 400 N. Tampa St., Tampa, FL 33602-4706 (© **800/448-2672,** 800/368-2672, or 813/223-2752; www.visittampabay.com), for advance information. If you're downtown, you can head to the bureau's **visitor information center** at 400 N. Tampa St. (Channelside), Suite 2800 (© **813/223-1111**). It's open Monday through Saturday from 9:30am to 5:30pm.

Operated by the Ybor City Chamber of Commerce, the **Centro Ybor Museum and Visitor Information Center,** in Centro Ybor, 1514½ E. 8th Ave. (between 15th and 16th sts. E.), Tampa, FL 33605 (© **813/248-3712;** www.ybor.org), distributes information and has exhibits on the area's history. A 7-minute video will orient you to this area—an 8-block stretch of Seventh Avenue. The center is open Monday through Saturday from 10am to 6pm, Sunday from noon to 6pm.

GETTING AROUND   Like most other Florida destinations, it's virtually impossible to see Tampa's major sights and enjoy its best restaurants without a car. You can get around downtown via the free **Uptown-Downtown Connector Trolley,** which runs north-south between Harbor Island and the city's North Terminal bus station on Marion Street at I-275. The trolleys run every 10 minutes from 6am to 6pm Monday through Friday. Southbound, they follow Tampa Street between Tyler and Whiting streets, and Franklin Street between Whiting Street and Harbor Island. Northbound trolleys follow Florida Avenue from the St. Pete Times Forum to Cass Street. The trolleys are operated by the Hillsborough Area Regional Transit/HARTline (© 813/254-4278; www.hartline.org), the area's transportation authority, which also provides scheduled **bus service** ($1.30–$3) between downtown Tampa and the suburbs. Pick up a route map at the visitor center (see above).

The transportation situation has gotten somewhat better, not to mention nostalgic, with the **TECO Line Street Car System,** a new but old-fashioned 2⅓-mile streetcar system, complete with overhead power lines, which hauls passengers between downtown and Ybor City via the St. Pete Times Forum, Channelside, Garrison Seaport, and the Florida Aquarium. The cars run every 30 minutes; one-way fares are $1.80. Check with the visitor center or call HARTline for schedules.

Taxis in Tampa don't normally cruise the streets for fares, but they do line up at public places, such as hotels, the performing-arts center, and bus and train depots. If you need a taxi, call **Tampa Bay Cab** (© 813/251-5555), **Yellow Cab** (© 813/253-0121), or **United Cab** (© 813/253-2424). Fares are $1.75 at flag fall, plus $1.75 for each mile.

EXPLORING THE THEME & ANIMAL PARKS

Adventure Island *(Kids)*   If the summer heat gets to you before one of Tampa's famous thunderstorms brings late-afternoon relief, you can take a waterlogged break at this 25-acre outdoor water theme park near Busch Gardens Tampa Bay (see below). You can also frolic here during the cooler days of spring and fall, when the water is heated. The Key West Rapids, Tampa Typhoon, Gulf Scream, and other exciting water rides will drench the teens, while other, calmer rides are geared toward younger kids. Wahoo Run plunges up to five riders more than 15 feet per second as the half-enclosed tunnel corkscrews more than 600 feet to a waiting splash pool. There are also places to picnic and sunbathe, an arcade, a volleyball complex, and an outdoor cafe. Although some people tend to go barefoot here, I suggest you wear shoes at all times—it gets kind of nasty after a while.

10001 Malcolm McKinley Dr. (between Busch Blvd. and Bougainvillea Ave.). © 813/987-5600. www.4adventure. com. Admission at least $33 adults, $31 children 3–9, plus tax; free for children 2 and under. Combination tickets with Busch Gardens Tampa Bay (1 day each) $100 adults, $90 children 3–9, free for children under 3. Website sometimes offers discounts. Parking $5. Mid-Mar to Labor Day daily 10am–5pm; Sept–Oct Fri–Sun 10am–5pm (extended hours in summer and on holidays). Closed Nov to late Feb. Check website for exact opening dates. Take exit 50 off I-275 and go east on Busch Blvd. for 2 miles. Turn left onto McKinley Dr. (N. 40th St.); entry is on the right.

Big Cat Rescue *(Kids)*   Not your typical animal theme park, this one bills itself as an educational sanctuary in which visitors can get up close and "purrsonal" (groan) with over 150 big wild cats. The world's largest accredited sanctuary for exotic cats, this one is definitely a unique experience for animal lovers because not only can you view and visit with bobcats and tigers, but you can feed them, take photo safaris, or even spend a night in one of the sanctuary's cabins. Something different, for sure.

12802 Easy Street © 813/920-4130. www.bigcatrescue.org.com. Day tours $20 per person ages 10 and over only Mon–Fri 9am–3pm; special kids tours for all ages, $10 Sat 9am; night tours $20 (ages 18 and over only), last Fri of the month at dusk; feeding tours $50 per person (ages 18 and over only), reservations required; Keeper for a Day tour $150 per person (ages 18 and over only), reservations required.

Busch Gardens Tampa Bay 🎭🎭 *(Kids)*   Although its heart-stopping thrill rides get much of the ink, this venerable theme park (it predates Disney World) ranks among the largest zoos in the country. It's a don't-miss attraction for children and adults, who

Tampa & St. Petersburg

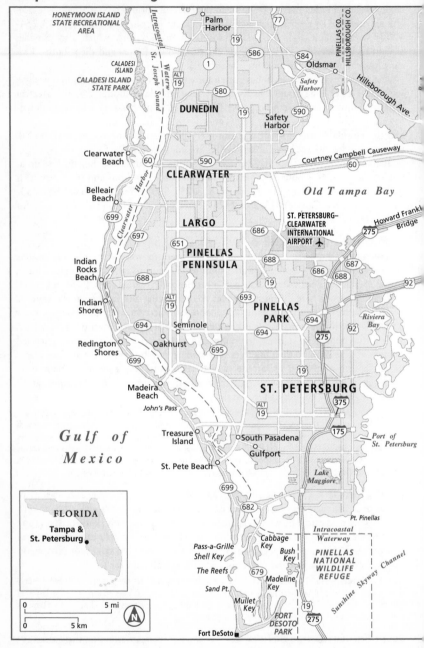

HONEYMOON ISLAND
STATE RECREATIONAL
AREA

Intracoastal

77

Palm
Harbor

19

586

St. Joseph Sound

CALADESI
ISLAND

CALADESI ISLAND
STATE PARK

1

ALT
19

584

Oldsmar

PINELLAS CO.
HILLSBOROUGH CO.

Hillsborough Ave.

580

Safety
Harbor

DUNEDIN

19

Safety
Harbor

590

Clearwater
Beach

60

590

Courtney Campbell Causeway

60

CLEARWATER

Clearwater Harbor

Belleair
Beach

Old Tampa Bay

699

LARGO

686

ST. PETERSBURG–
CLEARWATER
INTERNATIONAL
AIRPORT ✈

Howard Frankl
Bridge

275

697

651

688

Indian
Rocks
Beach

688

PINELLAS
PENINSULA

686

687

688

92

ALT
19

693

19

Indian
Shores

694

Seminole

PINELLAS
PARK

694

Riviera
Bay

Oakhurst

694

275

92

Redington
Shores

695

699

Madeira
Beach

19

John's Pass

ST. PETERSBURG

375

Gulf of
Mexico

Treasure
Island

ALT
19

South Pasadena

175

Port of
St. Petersburg

Gulfport

St. Pete Beach

Lake
Maggiore

699

682

Pt. Pinellas

FLORIDA

Tampa &
St. Petersburg

Intracoastal
Waterway

Cabbage
Key

Bush
Key

PINELLAS
NATIONAL
WILDLIFE
REFUGE

Sunshine Skyway Channel

Pass-a-Grille
Shell Key

The Reefs

679

Madeline
Key

Sand Pt.

Mullet
Key

0   5 mi

0   5 km

N

FORT
DESOTO
PARK

19

275

Fort DeSoto

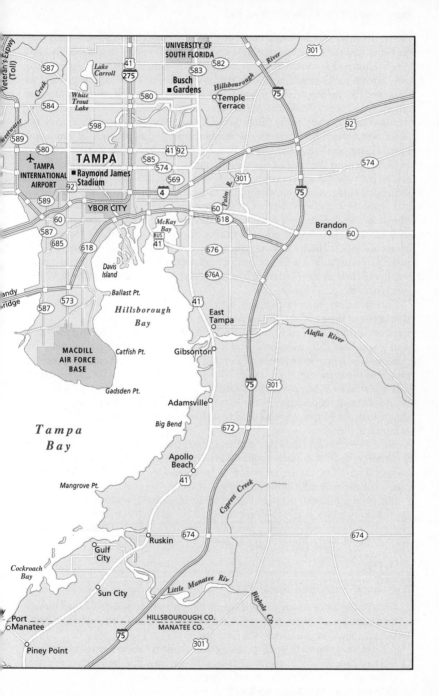

can see, in person, all those wild beasts they've watched on *Animal Planet*—and they'll get better views of them here than at Disney's Animal Kingdom in Orlando (p. 506). Busch Gardens has thousands of animals living in natural environments that help carry out the park's overall African theme. Most authentic is the 80-acre plain, reminiscent of the real Serengeti of Tanzania and Kenya, upon which zebras, giraffes, and other animals graze. Unlike the animals on the real Serengeti, however, these grazing creatures have nothing to fear from lions, hyenas, crocodiles, and other predators, which are confined to enclosures—as are the hippos and elephants. The park's sixth roller coaster, SheiKra, is the nation's first dive coaster that carries riders up 200 feet at 45 degrees and then hurtles them 70 mph back at a 45-degree angle. Yikes.

The park has eight areas, each with its own theme, animals, live entertainment, thrill rides, kiddie attractions, dining, and shopping. A Skyride cable car soars over the park, offering a bird's-eye view of it all. Turn left after the main gate and head to **Morocco,** a walled city with exotic architecture, crafts demonstrations, a sultan's tent with snake charmers, and an exhibit featuring alligators and turtles. The Moorish-style Moroccan Palace Theater features an ice show that many families consider to be the park's best entertainment for both adults and children. You can also attend a song-and-dance show in the Marrakech Theater. Overlooking it all is the Crown Colony Restaurant, the park's largest.

After watching the snake charmers, walk east past Anheuser-Busch's fabled Clydesdale horses to **Egypt,** where you can visit King Tut's tomb with its replicas of the real treasures and listen to comedian Martin Short narrate "Akbar's Adventure Tours," a wacky simulator that "transports" one and all across Egypt via camel, biplane, and mine car. The whole room moves on this ride, which lasts only 5 minutes—much less time than the usual wait to get inside. Youngsters can dig for their own ancient treasures in a sand area. Adults and kids 54 inches or taller can ride Montu, the tallest and longest inverted roller coaster in the world, with seven upside-down loops. Your feet dangle loose on Montu, so make sure your shoes are tied tightly and your lunch has had time to digest.

From Egypt, walk to the **Edge of Africa,** the most unique of the park's eight areas, and home of most of the large animals. Go immediately to the Expedition Africa Gift Shop and see if you can get on one of the park's zoologist-led wildlife tours (see the box "How to See Busch Gardens," below).

Next stop is **Nairobi,** the most beautiful part of the park, where you can see gorillas and chimpanzees in their lush rainforest habitat in the Myombe Reserve. Nairobi also has a baby-animal nursery, a petting zoo, turtle and reptile displays, an elephant exhibit (alas, the magnificent creatures seem to be bored to the point of madness), and

---

Tips **If You Need Another Day**

Once you're inside Busch Gardens Tampa Bay and decide you really need more time to see it all, check to see if the park has (frequently offered) **Next-Day Tickets,** which let you back in the next day for about $16 per person.

If you're going to Orlando as well, Busch Gardens Tampa Bay is included in the five-park version of the **FlexTicket,** a 14-day pass that also admits you to Universal Studios Florida, SeaWorld, Islands of Adventure, and Wet 'n' Wild, for $225 adults and $190 children 3 to 9.

Curiosity Caverns, where bats, reptiles, and small mammals that are active in the dark are kept in cages (it's the most traditional zoolike area here). The entry to Rhino Rally, the park's safari adventure, is at the western end of Nairobi.

Now head to **The Congo,** where the highlights are the rare white Bengal tigers that live on Claw Island. The Congo is also home to two roller coasters: Kumba, the largest and fastest coaster in the Southeastern United States (54-in. minimum height); and the Python (48-in. minimum), which twists and turns for 1,200 feet. You will get drenched—and refreshed on a hot day—by riding the Congo River Rapids, where you're turned loose in round boats that float down the swiftly flowing "river" (42-in. minimum). Bumper cars and kiddie rides can be found here, too.

From The Congo, walk south into **Stanleyville,** a prototype African village, with a shopping bazaar, orangutans living on an island, and the Stanleyville Theater, featuring shows for children. Two more water rides here are the Tanganyika Tidal Wave (48-in. minimum height), where you'll come to a very damp end, and the Stanley Falls Flume (an aquatic version of a roller coaster). Also, the picnic-style Stanleyville Smokehouse serves ribs and chicken that are among the best chow in the park.

Up next is **Land of the Dragons,** the most entertaining area for small children. They can spend the day enjoying a variety of elements in a fairy-tale setting, plus just-for-kids rides. The area is dominated by Dumphrey, a whimsical dragon who interacts with visitors and guides children around a three-story treehouse with winding stairways, tall towers, stepping stones, illuminated water geysers, and an echo chamber.

The next stop is **Bird Gardens,** the park's original core, offering rich foliage, lagoons, and a free-flight aviary for hundreds of exotic birds, including golden and American bald eagles. Be sure to see the Florida flamingos and Australian koalas while you're here.

Then you're off to take a break at the **Hospitality House,** which offers piano entertainment and free samples of Anheuser-Busch's famous beers. You must be 21 to imbibe (there's a limit of two free mugs per seating), but soft drinks are also available.

If your stomach can take another hair-raising ride, try **Gwazi** (48-in. minimum), an adrenaline-pumping attraction in which a pair of old-fashioned wooden roller coasters (named the Lion and the Tiger) start simultaneously and whiz within a few feet of each other six times as they roar along at 50 mph and rise to 90 feet. If you want to experience the park's fifth roller coaster, head to **Timbuktu** and climb aboard the **Scorpion,** a high-speed number with a 60-foot drop and 360-degree loop (42-in. height minimum).

Added attractions are a $350, 6-hour zookeeper-for-a-day program, and a 4-D multisensory R. L. Stine film. You can exchange foreign currency in the park, and interpreters are available. *Note:* You can get to Busch Gardens from Orlando via shuttle buses, which pick up at area hotels between 8 and 10:15am for the 1½- to 2-hour ride, with return trips starting at 5pm and continuing until the park closes. Round-trip fares are $5 per person. Call © **800/511-2450** for schedules, pickup locations, and reservations.

3000 E. Busch Blvd. (at McKinley Dr./N. 40th St.). © **888/800-5447** or 813/987-5283. www.buschgardens.com. **Note:** Admission and hours vary, so call ahead, check website, or get brochure at visitor centers. Admission single-day ticket $58 adults, $48 children 3–9, plus tax; free for children 2 and under. Daily 10am–6pm (extended hours to 7 and 8pm in summer and on holidays). Parking $8 for cars; $9 for trucks and campers. Take I-275 north of downtown to Busch Blvd. (exit 50) and go east 2 miles. From I-75, take Fowler Ave. (exit 54) and follow the signs west.

Florida Aquarium 🐠🐠 *Kids* See more than 5,000 aquatic animals and plants that call Florida home at this entertaining attraction. The exhibits follow a drop of water from the springs of the Florida Wetlands Gallery, through a mangrove forest in the

Tampa

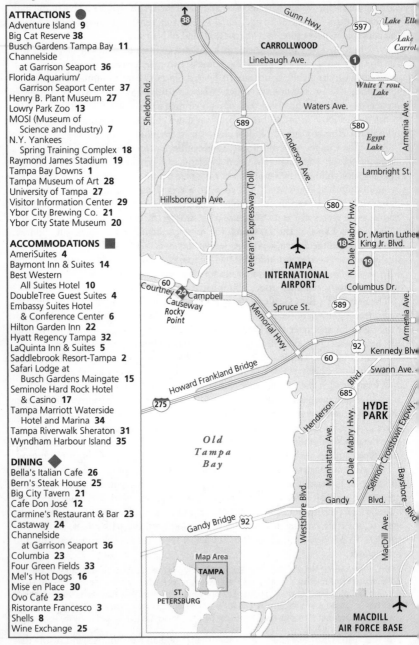

ATTRACTIONS ●
Adventure Island **9**
Big Cat Reserve **38**
Busch Gardens Tampa Bay **11**
Channelside
    at Garrison Seaport **36**
Florida Aquarium/
    Garrison Seaport Center **37**
Henry B. Plant Museum **27**
Lowry Park Zoo **13**
MOSI (Museum of
    Science and Industry) **7**
N.Y. Yankees
    Spring Training Complex **18**
Raymond James Stadium **19**
Tampa Bay Downs **1**
Tampa Museum of Art **28**
University of Tampa **27**
Visitor Information Center **29**
Ybor City Brewing Co. **21**
Ybor City State Museum **20**

ACCOMMODATIONS ■
AmeriSuites **4**
Baymont Inn & Suites **14**
Best Western
    All Suites Hotel **10**
DoubleTree Guest Suites **4**
Embassy Suites Hotel
    & Conference Center **6**
Hilton Garden Inn **22**
Hyatt Regency Tampa **32**
LaQuinta Inn & Suites **5**
Saddlebrook Resort-Tampa **2**
Safari Lodge at
    Busch Gardens Maingate **15**
Seminole Hard Rock Hotel
    & Casino **17**
Tampa Marriott Waterside
    Hotel and Marina **34**
Tampa Riverwalk Sheraton **31**
Wyndham Harbour Island **35**

DINING ◆
Bella's Italian Cafe **26**
Bern's Steak House **25**
Big City Tavern **21**
Cafe Don José **12**
Carmine's Restaurant & Bar **23**
Castaway **24**
Channelside
    at Garrison Seaport **36**
Columbia **23**
Four Green Fields **33**
Mel's Hot Dogs **16**
Mise en Place **30**
Ovo Café **23**
Ristorante Francesco **3**
Shells **8**
Wine Exchange **25**

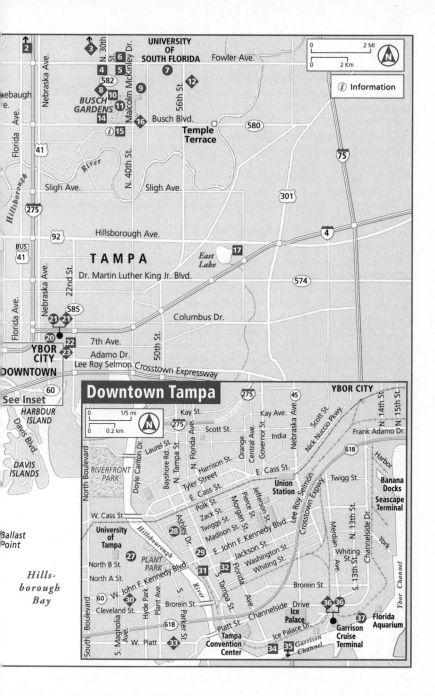

UNIVERSITY OF SOUTH FLORIDA

Fowler Ave.

Nebraska Ave.

N. 30th St.

Malcolm McKinley Dr.

56th St.

BUSCH GARDENS

Busch Blvd.

Temple Terrace

i Information

Hillsborough River

N. 40th St.

Sligh Ave.

Sligh Ave.

Hillsborough Ave.

TAMPA

Dr. Martin Luther King Jr. Blvd.

East Lake

Columbus Dr.

Nebraska Ave.

22nd St.

Florida Ave.

YBOR CITY

DOWNTOWN

7th Ave.

Adamo Dr.

Lee Roy Selmon Crosstown Expressway

50th St.

See Inset

HARBOUR ISLAND

DAVIS ISLANDS

Ballast Point

Downtown Tampa

YBOR CITY

Kay St.

Kay Ave.

Scott St.

Scott St.

Nick Nuccio Pkwy.

Frank Adamo Dr.

India

N. 14th St.

N. 15th St.

North Boulevard

RIVERFRONT PARK

Doyle Carlton Dr.

Laurel St.

Bayshore Rd.

N. Tampa St.

N. Florida Ave.

Orange

Central Ave.

Governor St.

Nebraska Ave.

Scott St.

Harbor

Harrison St.

Tyler Street

E. Cass St.

E. Cass St.

Union Station

Banana Docks

Seascape Terminal

W. Cass St.

Polk St.

Zack St.

Pierce St.

Jefferson St.

Lee Roy Selmon Crosstown Expwy.

Twigg St.

University of Tampa

PLANT PARK

Ashley Dr.

Twiggs St.

Madison St.

Morgan St.

E. John F. Kennedy Blvd.

Jackson St.

Washington St.

Whiting St.

Merdian Ave.

N. 13th St.

Channelside Dr.

York

Ybor Channel

North B St.

North A St.

Hillsborough River

S. Tampa St.

Florida Ave.

Whiting St.

Brorein St.

S. 13th St.

Hills- borough Bay

South Boulevard

S. Magnolia Ave.

Hyde Park Ave.

Plant Ave.

Brorein St.

S. Parker St.

Channelside Drive

Ice Palace

Ice Palace Dr.

Garrison Cruise Terminal

Florida Aquarium

Cleveland St.

W. Platt

Platt St.

Tampa Convention Center

Garrison Channel

Ybor Channel

Tips   How to See Busch Gardens

You can save a few dollars and avoid waiting in long lines by buying your tickets to Busch Gardens Tampa Bay at the privately owned **Tampa Bay Visitor Information Center,** opposite the park at 3601 E. Busch Blvd., at North Ednam Place (© **813/985-3601;** www.hometown.aol.com\tpabayinfoctr). Owner Jim Boggs worked for the park for 13 years and gives expert advice on how to get the most out of your visit. He sells slightly discounted tickets (buying here will also save you from the ticket line at the parks) to Busch Gardens, Adventure Island, and other attractions, and he will book hotel rooms and car rentals for you, often at a discount. The center is open Monday through Saturday from 10am to 5:30pm, Sunday from 10am to 2pm (closed Christmas).

Arrive early and allow at least a day to see the park. Try not to come when it's raining, since some rides may not be operating. Bring comfortable shoes, and, remember, you will get wet on some of the rides, so wear or bring appropriate clothing (shops near the rides sell plastic ponchos for $5 or $6, but they're cheaper in the outside world). There are lockers throughout the park where you can stash your gear.

As soon as you're through the turnstiles, pick up a map and the day's activity schedule, which tells you what's showing and when, at the 14 entertainment venues in the park. Then take a few minutes to carefully plan your time—it's a big park with lots to see and do.

Although you'll get close to Busch Garden's predators, hippos, and elephants in their glass-walled enclosures, the only way to mingle with the grazers is on a tour. The best is the **VIP Elite Adventure Tour,** which lets you roam the plains in the company of a zoologist. The 8-hour excursion costs $200 per person, regardless of age, unless a child is under 5, in which case it's free (in addition to the park's entry fee), and usually leaves at about 1:30pm daily. You won't have to wait in line, and you'll receive a complimentary continental breakfast and lunch at the park's Crown Colony Restaurant. The tours can fill up fast, and you can't call ahead for reservations, so as soon as you enter the park, go to the Expedition Africa Gift Shop, opposite Crown Colony Restaurant in the Edge of Africa, to reserve a spot. An option (though less attractive) is the 30-minute, zoologist-led **Serengeti Safari Special Tour,** in which you ride among the grazers on the back of a flatbed truck. This is worth the extra $34 per person, regardless of age. You can make reservations for the morning tour at the Expedition Africa Gift Shop, but the midday and afternoon tours are first come, first served. Note that children under 5 are not allowed on either tour.

Bays and Beaches Gallery, and out onto the Coral Reefs, where an impressive 43-foot-wide, 14-foot-tall panoramic window lets you look out at schools of fish and lots of sharks and stingrays. Also worth visiting are the educational Explore a Shore playground, a deepwater exhibit, and a tank housing moray eels. You can look for birds and sea life on 90-minute Eco Tour cruises in the *Bay Spirit,* a 64-foot catamaran. The aquarium also offers a **Dive with the Sharks** program (© 813/367-4005) that gives certified divers the chance to swim with blacktip reef, sand tiger, and nurse sharks for 30 minutes. The $150 price tag includes a souvenir photo and T-shirt.

701 Channelside Dr. © 813/273-4000. www.flaquarium.net. Admission $18 adults, $15 seniors, $12 children 3–11, free for children under 3. Eco Tour $19 adults, $18 seniors, $14 children 3–11, free for children under 3. Combination aquarium admission and Eco Tour $30 adults, $27 seniors, $20 children 3–11, free for children under 3. Website sometimes offers discounts. Parking $5. Daily 9:30am–5pm. Dolphin Quest Mon–Fri 2pm; Sat–Sun 1 and 3pm. Eco Tour daily 2 and 4pm, plus Sat noon. Closed Thanksgiving and Christmas.

Lowry Park Zoo *Kids*   The opportunity to watch 3,000-pound manatees, Komodo dragons, Persian leopards, and rare red pandas makes this a worthwhile excursion after the kids have seen the plains of Africa at Busch Gardens. With lots of greenery, bubbling brooks, and waterfalls, this 24-acre zoo displays animals in settings similar to their natural habitats. Exhibits include the Florida wildlife display, Asian Domain, Primate World, Aquatic Center, free-flight aviary with a birds-of-prey show, hands-on Discovery Center, and endangered-species carousel ride. The Wallaroo Station has kids' rides, a small water park, a kangaroo walk-about, and a petting zoo. Lowry Park has one of Florida's three manatee hospitals and rehabilitation centers. The Eco Tour is very popular, featuring a cruise on the Hillsborough River, where you'll see turtles, herons, and manatees. The cost is $10 for adults, $9 for seniors, and $7 for children 3 to 11. The zoo is also a sanctuary for Florida panthers and red wolves.

1101 W. Sligh Ave. © 813/935-8552, or 813/932-0245 for recorded information. www.lowryparkzoo.com. Admission $15 adults, $14 seniors, $11 children 3–11, free for children 2 and under. Daily 9:30am–5pm. Closed Thanksgiving and Christmas. Take I-275 to Sligh Ave. (exit 48) and follow the signs.

VISITING THE MUSEUMS

Henry B. Plant Museum   Originally built in 1891 by railroad tycoon Henry B. Plant as the superchichi 511-room Tampa Bay Hotel, this ornate building is worth a short trip across the river from downtown to the University of Tampa campus. Its 13 silver minarets and distinctive Moorish architecture, modeled after the Alhambra in Spain, make this National Historic Landmark a focal point of the Tampa skyline. Although the building is the highlight of a visit, don't skip its contents: art and furnishings from Europe and Asia, plus exhibits that explain the history of the original railroad resort, Florida's early tourist industry, and the hotel's role as a staging point for Theodore Roosevelt's Rough Riders during the Spanish-American War.

401 W. Kennedy Blvd. (between Hyde Park and Magnolia aves.). © 813/254-1891. www.plantmuseum.com. Free admission; suggested donation $5 adults, $2 children 12 and under. Tues–Sat 10am–4pm; Sun noon–4pm. Closed Thanksgiving, Christmas Eve, and Christmas Day. Take Kennedy Blvd. (Fla. 60) across the Hillsborough River.

MOSI (Museum of Science and Industry) *Kids*   A great place to take the kids, MOSI is the largest science center in the Southeast, with more than 450 interactive

---

Tips A Free Attraction

The Tampa Electric Company is a hot spot, not just because it provides the juice that makes the city tick, but also because the warm waters surrounding the plant are a haven for manatees—they need to be in temperatures of at least 68°F. The **Manatee Viewing Center** (© 813/228-4289; www.tampaelectric.com) is open November 1 to April 15 from 10am to 5pm.

exhibits. Step into the Gulf Hurricane to experience 74 mph winds, explore the human body in "The Amazing You," and, if your heart is up to it, ride a bicycle across a 98-foot-long cable suspended 30 feet above the lobby (don't worry: you'll be harnessed to the bike). You can also watch stunning movies in Florida's first IMAX dome theater. Outside, trails wind through a nature preserve with a butterfly garden.

4801 E. Fowler Ave. (at N. 50th St.). ☏ 813/987-6100. www.mosi.org. Admission $16 adults, $14 seniors, $12 children 2–12, free for children under 2. Admission includes IMAX movies. Daily 9am–5pm or later. From downtown, take I-275 N. to the Fowler Ave. E. exit (no. 51). Take this 2 miles east to museum on right.

Tampa Museum of Art Located on the east bank of the Hillsborough River, next to the round Bank of America building (locals facetiously call it the Beer Can), this fine-arts complex offers eight galleries with changing exhibits ranging from classical antiquities to contemporary Floridian art. There's also a 7-acre riverfront park and sculpture garden. Call or check the website for the schedule of temporary exhibits. However, if you have time for only one art museum on your trip, skip this one and head to St. Petersburg for the more innovative Salvador Dalí Museum.

600 N. Ashley Dr. (at Twiggs St.), downtown. ☏ 813/274-8130. www.tampamuseum.com. Admission $7 adults, $6 seniors, $3 children 6–18 and students with ID, free for children under 6, by donation Thurs 5–8pm and Sat 10am–noon. Tues–Sat 10am–5pm (Thurs to 8 pm); Sun 11am–5pm. Parking 90¢ per hour. Take I-275 to exit 44 (Ashley Dr.).

YBOR CITY

Northeast of downtown, the city's historic Latin district takes its name from Don Vicente Martinez Ybor (*Eeee*-bore), a Spanish cigar maker who arrived here in 1886 via Cuba and Key West. Soon his and other Tampa factories were producing more than 300,000 hand-rolled stogies a day.

It may not be the cigar capital of the world anymore, but Ybor is still a smokin' part of Tampa, and it's one of the best places in Florida to buy hand-rolled cigars. It's not on a par with New Orleans's Bourbon Street, Washington's Georgetown, or Miami's South Beach, but good food and great music dominate the scene, especially on weekends when the streets bustle until 4am (note to claustrophobes: avoid it at all costs then). Live-music offerings run the gamut from jazz and blues to rock.

At the heart of it all is **Centro Ybor,** a dining-shopping-entertainment complex that sprawls between 7th and 8th avenues and 16th and 17th streets (☏ **813/242-4660;** www.centroybor.com). Here you'll find a multiscreen cinema, a comedy club, several restaurants, and a large open-air bar. The Ybor City Chamber of Commerce has its visitor center here (see "Essentials," earlier in this chapter), and the Ybor City State Museum's gift shop is here as well (see below).

Check with the visitor center about walking tours of the historic district. **Ybor City Ghost Walks** (☏ 813/242-4660) will take you to the spookier parts of the area. The tours cost $10 per person, last 75 minutes, and are by reservation only. For those who enjoy an even darker side, **Secret Ybor: Scandals, Crimes, and Shady Ladies,** explores the more scandalous side of the city. Tours depart Saturday at 6pm from **Gaspar's Grotto**, 1805 E. 7th Ave. (☏ **813/831-5214;** www.gasparsgrotto.com), a wacky, pirate-themed entertainment venue, bar, and restaurant. Cost is $10 per person.

Even if you're not a cigar smoker, you'll enjoy a stroll through the **Ybor City State Museum** *★*, 1818 9th Ave., between 18th and 19th streets (☏ **813/247-6323;** www.ybormuseum.org), housed in the former Ferlita Bakery (1896–1973). You can take a self-guided tour to see the collection of cigar labels, cigar memorabilia, and works by local artisans. Admission is free. Walking tours of Ybor City are every Saturday morning at 10:30 am, cost $6, and start at the Ybor City Museum State Park. Depending on the availability of volunteer docents, admission includes a 15-minute guided tour of **La Casita,** a renovated cigar worker's cottage adjacent to the museum; it's furnished as it was at the turn of the last century. The museum is open daily from 9am to 5pm, but you have the best chance for the guided tour if you visit between 11am and 3pm. Better yet, plan to catch a cigar-rolling demonstration (ongoing; no specific schedule), held Friday through Sunday from 10am to 3pm.

Housed in a 100-year-old, three-story former cigar factory, **Ybor City Brewing Company,** 2205 N. 20th St., facing Palm Avenue, produces Ybor Gold and other brews, none with preservatives.

Like any area with trendy bars and restaurants, things are always changing, opening, and going out of business, so you may want to check www.ybortimes.com for the latest in Ybor City.

ORGANIZED TOURS

Swiss Chalet Tours, 3601 E. Busch Blvd. (© **813/985-3601;** www.hometown.aol. com\tpabayinfoctr), opposite Busch Gardens in the privately run Tampa Bay Visitor Information Center (see the box "How to See Busch Gardens," earlier in this chapter), operates guided bus tours of Tampa, Ybor City, and environs. The 4-hour tours of Tampa are given from 10am to 3pm daily, with a stop for lunch at the Columbia Restaurant in Ybor City. They cost $45 for adults and $40 for children 12 and under. The full-day tours (10am–5pm) of both Tampa and St. Petersburg give a good overview of the two cities and the beaches; these cost $70 for adults and $65 for children. Reservations are required at least 24 hours in advance; passengers are picked up at major hotels and various other points in the Tampa/St. Petersburg area. The company also books bus tours to Orlando, Sarasota, Bradenton, and other regional destinations (call for schedules, prices, and reservations).

OUTDOOR ACTIVITIES & SPECTATOR SPORTS

BIKING, IN-LINE SKATING & JOGGING   Bayshore Boulevard, a 7-mile-long promenade, is famous for its sidewalk right on the shores of Hillsborough Bay and is a favorite with runners, walkers, and in-line skaters. The route goes from the western edge of downtown in a southward direction, passing stately old homes in Hyde Park, a few high-rise condominiums, retirement communities, and houses of worship, ending at Ballast Point Park. The view from the promenade across the bay to the downtown skyline is matchless. (Bayshore Blvd. is also great for a drive.)

FISHING   For charters, try **Captain Jim's Inshore Sportfishing Charters,** 512 Palm Ave., Palm Harbor (© **727/ 439-9017;**   www.captainhud.com), which offers private sport-fishing trips for tarpon, redfish, trout, and snook. Rates are $300 to $525 for two anglers. Call for schedule and reservations.

> ### Cruise Control
> The **Port of Tampa** (© **800/741-2297** or 813/905-7678; www.tampaport. com) is home to four cruise lines and a changing cast of ships that travel the Caribbean and Latin America. At press time, the players were Celebrity Cruise Line, Royal Caribbean Cruise Lines, Holland America Cruise Lines, and Carnival Cruise Line.

GOLF   Tampa has three municipal golf courses where you can play for about $30 to $35, a relative pittance compared to fees at privately owned courses here and elsewhere in Florida. The **Babe Zaharias Municipal Golf Course,** 11412 Forest Hills Dr., north of Lowry Park (© **813/631-4374**), is an 18-hole, par-70 course with a pro shop, putting greens, and a driving range. It is the shortest of the municipal courses, but its small greens and narrow fairways present ample challenges. Water provides obstacles on 12 of the 18 holes at **Rocky Point Golf Course,** 4151 Dana Shores Dr. (© **813/673-4316**), located between the airport and the bay. It's a par-71 course with a pro shop, practice range, and putting greens. On the Hillsborough River in north Tampa, the **Rogers Park Golf Course,** 7910 N. 30th St. (© **813/673-4396**), is an 18-hole, par-72 championship course with a lighted driving and practice range. All of the courses are open daily from 7am to dusk, and lessons and club rentals are available.

You can book starting times and get information about these and the area's other courses by calling **Tee Times USA** (© **800/374-8633;** www.teetimesusa.com).

If you want to do some serious work on your game, the **Arnold Palmer Golf Academy World Headquarters** is at Saddlebrook Resort, 5700 Saddlebrook Way, Wesley Chapel, 12 miles north of Tampa (© **800/729-8383** or 813/973-1111; www.saddle brookresort.com). Half-day and hourly instruction is available, as well as 2-, 3-, and 5-day programs for adults and juniors. You have to stay at the resort or enroll in the golf program to play at Saddlebrook. See p. 411 for more information.

For course information online, go to www.golf.com or www.floridagolfing.com; or call the **Florida Sports Foundation** (© **850/488-8347**) or **Florida Golfing** (© **866/833-2663**).

SPECTATOR SPORTS   National Football League fans can catch the **Tampa Bay Buccaneers** at the modern, 66,000-seat Raymond James Stadium, 4201 N. Dale Mabry Hwy., at Dr. Martin Luther King, Jr., Boulevard (© **813/879-2827;** www.buccaneers.com) August through December. Single-game tickets (starting at $30) are very hard to come by, as they are usually sold out to the plethora of season ticket owners. This is a huge football city!

The National Hockey League's **Tampa Bay Lightning,** winners of the 2004 Stanley Cup, play in the St. Pete Times Forum starting in October (© **813/301-6500;** www.tampabaylightning.com). You can usually get single-game tickets ($8–$155) on game day.

New York Yankees fans can watch the Bronx Bombers during baseball's spring training, from mid-February to the end of March, at Legends Field (© **813/879-2244** or 813/875-7753; www.yankees.mlb.com), opposite Raymond James Stadium. This scaled-down replica of Yankee Stadium is the largest spring-training facility in Florida, with a 10,000-seat capacity. Tickets are $10 to $16. The club's minor-league team, the **Tampa Yankees** (same contact into), plays at Legends Field April through August.

The only thoroughbred racecourse on Florida's west coast is **Tampa Bay Downs,** 11225 Racetrack Rd., Oldsmar (© **800/200-4434** in Florida, or 813/855-4401; www.tampadowns.com), home of the Tampa Bay Derby. Races are held from December to May ($2 general admission, $3 clubhouse), and the track presents simulcasts year-round. Call for post times.

TENNIS   Sharpen your game at the **Hopman Tennis Program,** at the Saddlebrook Resort (p. 411). You must be a member or a guest to play here.

SHOPPING

Hyde Park and Ybor City are two areas of Tampa worth some window-shopping, perhaps sandwiched around lunch at one of the fine restaurants (see "Where to Dine," later in this chapter).

Fun Fact Did You Know?

Tampa used to be called Tanpa. No, this is not a spelling error. In the early days, when the place was an Indian fishing village, that's what it was called. Loosely translated, *Tanpa* means "land by the water." Early explorers had illegibly written Tanpa on the maps. In 1539, gold-searching explorers mistakenly changed the name to Tampa.

On the mall front, there's the upscale **International Plaza** (© **813/342-3790;** www.shopinternationalplaza.com), near Tampa International Airport, where the headliners include Neiman Marcus, Nordstrom, and Lord & Taylor.

CIGARS Ybor City is no longer a major producer of hand-rolled cigars, but you can still watch artisans making stogies at the **Gonzalez y Martinez Cigar Factory,** 2025 7th Ave., in the Columbia Restaurant building (© **813/247-2469**). Gonzalez and Martinez are recent arrivals from Cuba and don't speak English, but the staff does at the adjoining **Columbia Cigar Store** (it's best to enter here). Rollers are on duty Monday through Saturday from 10am to 6pm. You can stock up on fine domestic and imported cigars at **El Sol,** 1728 E. 7th Ave. (© **813/247-5554**), the city's oldest cigar store; **King Corona Cigar Factory,** 1523 E. 7th Ave. (© **813/241-9109**); and **Metropolitan Cigars & Wine,** 2014 E. 7th Ave. (© **813/248-3304**).

SHOPPING CENTERS **Old Hyde Park Village,** 1507 W. Swann Ave., at South Dakota Avenue (© **813/251-3500;** www.oldhydeparkvillage.com), is a terrific alternative to cookie-cutter suburban malls. Walk around the little boutiques in the sunshine and simultaneously check out Hyde Park, one of the city's most historic neighborhoods. The cluster of 50 upscale shops is set in a village layout. The selection includes Williams-Sonoma, Pottery Barn, Restoration Hardware, Brooks Brothers, Crabtree & Evelyn, and Godiva, to name a few. There's a free parking garage on South Oregon Avenue behind Jacobson's department store. Most shops are open Monday through Saturday from 10am to 7pm and Sunday from noon to 5pm. A farmers' market (at Swan and Dakota aves.) is held every Saturday from 9am to 2pm, offering local produce, seafood, and assorted tchotchkes.

The centerpiece of the downtown seaport renovation is the massive mall known as **Channelside at Garrison Seaport,** on Channelside Drive between the Garrison Seaport and the Florida Aquarium (© **813/223-4250;** www.channelside.com). It has stores, restaurants, a dance club, and a multiscreen cinema with an IMAX screen.

In Ybor City, **Centro Ybor,** on 7th Avenue East at 16th Street (© **813/242-4660;** www.centroybor.com), is primarily a dining and entertainment complex, but you'll find a few chains here, like American Eagle, Urban Outfitters, and Victoria's Secret.

WHERE TO STAY

The listings below are organized into three geographic areas: near Busch Gardens, downtown, and Ybor City. If you're going to Busch Gardens, Adventure Island, Lowry Park Zoo, or the Museum of Science and Industry (MOSI), the motels near Busch Gardens are much more convenient than those downtown, about 7 miles to the south. The downtown hotels are geared to business travelers, but staying there will put you near the Florida Aquarium, the Tampa Museum of Art, the Henry B. Plant Museum, the Tampa Bay Performing Arts Center, scenic Bayshore Boulevard, and the dining

---

Tips **Discount Packages**

Many Tampa hotels combine tickets to major attractions such as Busch Gardens in their packages, so always ask about special deals.

---

and shopping opportunities in the Channelside and Hyde Park districts. Staying in Ybor City will put you within walking distance of numerous restaurants and the city's hottest nightspots.

The Westshore area, near the bay, west of downtown and south of Tampa International Airport, is another commercial center, with a wide range of chain hotels catering to business travelers and conventioneers. It's not far from Raymond James Stadium and the New York Yankees' spring-training complex. Check with your favorite chain for a Westshore-Airport location.

Room rates at most hotels in Tampa vary little from season to season. This is especially true downtown, where the hotels do a brisk convention business year-round. Hillsborough County adds 12% tax to your hotel bill.

NEAR BUSCH GARDENS

The nearest chain motel to the park is a former Howard Johnson's that's now **Safari Lodge at Busch Gardens Maingate,** 4139 E. Busch Blvd. (© 813/988-9191), a motor lodge with very cheap rooms. It's 1½ blocks east of the main entrance. A bit farther away, the 500-room **Embassy Suites Hotel and Conference Center,** 3705 Spectrum Blvd., facing Fowler Avenue (© 800/362-2779 or 813/977-7066; fax 813/977-7933), is the plushest and most expensive establishment near the park. Almost across the avenue stands **LaQuinta Inn & Suites,** 3701 E. Fowler Ave. (© 800/687-6667 or 813/910-7500; fax 813/910-7600). Just south of Fowler Avenue are side-by-side branches of **AmeriSuites,** 11408 N. 30th St. (© 800/833-1516 or 813/979-1922; fax 813/979-1926), and **DoubleTree Guest Suites,** 11310 N. 30th St. (© 800/222-8733 or 813/971-7690; fax 813/972-5525).

Baymont Inn & Suites *Value*   Fake banana trees and a parrot cage welcome guests to the terra-cotta-floored lobby of this comfortable and convenient member of the small chain of cost-conscious but amenity-rich motels. All rooms are spacious and have ceiling fans and desks. Rooms with king-size beds also have recliners, business rooms sport dataport phones, and suites have refrigerators and microwaves. Outside, a courtyard with an unheated pool has plenty of space for sunning. There's no restaurant on the premises, but many are within walking distance.

9202 N. 30th St. (at Busch Blvd.), Tampa, FL 33612. © 800/428-3438 or 813/930-6900. Fax 813/930-0563. www.baymontinns.com. 146 units. Winter $79–$149 double; off season $70–$134 double. Rates include continental breakfast and local phone calls. AE, DC, DISC, MC, V. **Amenities:** Outdoor pool; game room; coin-op washers and dryers. *In room:* A/C, TV, free high-speed Internet access in all rooms, fridge, coffeemaker, hair dryer, iron.

Best Western All Suites Hotel *Finds* *Value*   This three-story all-suite hotel is the most beachlike vacation venue you'll find close to the park. Whimsical signs lead you around a lush tropical courtyard with a heated pool, hot tub, and lively, sports-oriented Tiki bar. The place prides itself on being "so close" to Busch Gardens that "the parrots escape to our trees," hence the hotel's nickname: "that parrot place." The bar can get noisy before closing at 9pm, and ground-level units are musty, so ask for an upstairs suite away from the action. Suite living rooms are well equipped; the separate bedrooms have narrow screened patios or balconies. The 11 "family suites" with bunk beds are great for those with kids.

Behind Busch Gardens, 3001 University Center Dr. (faces N. 30th St. between Busch Blvd. and Fowler Ave.), Tampa, FL 33612. *C* **800/786-7446** or 813/971-8930. Fax 813/971-8935. www.thatparrotplace.com. 150 units. Winter $99–$159 suite for 2; off season $79–$99 suite for 2. Rates include hot and cold breakfast buffet. AE, DC, DISC, MC, V. **Amenities:** Restaurant (breakfast and dinner only); bar; heated outdoor pool; access to nearby health club; Jacuzzi; game room; limited room service; laundry service; coin-op washers and dryers. *In room:* A/C, TV, dataport, fridge, coffeemaker, hair dryer, iron.

DOWNTOWN TAMPA

Hyatt Regency Tampa *&*   Just off the Franklin Street pedestrian mall, and in the heart of the business district, the Hyatt has lost its place as downtown's premier hotel to the newer Tampa Marriott Waterside (see below), but still attracts a corporate crowd. The spacious, recently renovated contemporary rooms lack balconies, and the higher office towers that now surround the hotel restrict views from the windows. Office workers congregate at the Avanzare restaurant for inexpensive light lunches.

2 Tampa City Center (corner of Tampa and E. Jackson sts.), Tampa, FL 33602. *C* **813/225-1234.** Fax 813/273-0234. www.tamparegency.hyatt.com. 521 units. $139–$359 double. Weekend packages available in summer. AE, DC, DISC, MC, V. Valet parking $12. **Amenities:** 2 restaurants; bar; heated outdoor pool; exercise room; Jacuzzi; concierge; business center; limited room service; laundry service; coin-op washers and dryers; concierge-level rooms. *In room:* A/C, TV, dataport/wireless Internet access, coffeemaker, hair dryer, iron.

Sheraton Tampa Riverwalk Hotel *&*   Set on the east bank of the Hillsborough River, this six-story hotel has gone through several chain-oriented hands, but no matter which parent company seems to own it, it remains one of Tampa's better stays. Half the rooms face west and have lovely views from their (unlighted) balconies of the Arabesque minarets atop the Henry B. Plant Museum and the University of Tampa across the river—quite a scene at sunset. These rooms cost more but are preferable to units on the east side of the building, which face downtown's skyscrapers and lack balconies. Rooms here are clean and of moderate size, but are rather tired, impersonal, and decorated in Drexel Heritage furniture. Set beside the river, the Ashley Drive Grill serves indoor-outdoor breakfasts and lunches, then offers fine dining in the evenings. The Boulanger bakery and deli, open from 5am to midnight, purveys fresh pastries, soups, sandwiches, and snacks. Unless you're here on business or are intent on staying downtown to be close to a specific attraction such as the performing-arts center, there's not much here to entice a mainstream traveler.

200 N. Ashley Dr. (at Jackson St.), Tampa, FL 33602. *C* **800/333-3333** or 813/223-2222. Fax 813/221-5929. www.tampariverwalkhotel.com. 282 units. Winter $219–$235 double; off season $139–$179 double. AE, DC, DISC, MC, V. Valet parking $10; self-parking $7. **Amenities:** 2 restaurants; bar; heated outdoor pool; exercise room; access to nearby health club; sauna; concierge; limited room service; laundry service; coin-op washers and dryers; concierge-level rooms. *In room:* A/C, TV, dataport, coffeemaker, hair dryer, iron.

Tampa Marriott Waterside Hotel and Marina *&&*   This luxurious 22-story hotel occupies downtown's most strategic location in the area's emerging Channel District—beside the river and between the Tampa Convention Center and the St. Pete Times Forum. Opening onto a riverfront promenade, the towering three-story lobby is large enough to accommodate the many conventioneers drawn to the two neighboring venues and to the hotel's own 50,000 square feet of meeting space. The third floor has a fully equipped spa, modern exercise facility, and outdoor heated pool. About half of the guest quarters have balconies overlooking the bay or city (choice views are high up on the south side). Although spacious, the regular rooms are dwarfed by the 720-square-foot suites. For those interested in boating the bay, there's also a 32-slip marina.

700 S. Florida Ave. (at St. Pete Times Forum Dr.), Tampa, FL 33602. (C) **800/228-9290** or 813/221-4900. Fax 813/221-0923. www.marriott.com. 717 units. Winter $239–$265 double, $379–$575 suite; off season $209–$239 double, $350–$500 suite. AE, DC, DISC, MC, V. Weekend rates available. Valet parking $14; no self-parking. **Amenities:** 3 restaurants; 3 bars; heated outdoor pool; health club; spa; Jacuzzi; concierge; activities desk; car-rental desk; business center; salon; limited room service; massage; babysitting; laundry service; coin-op washers and dryers; concierge-level rooms. *In room:* A/C, TV, fax, dataport (with high-speed Internet access), fridge, coffeemaker, hair dryer, iron.

Wyndham Harbour Island 🏵🏵🏵 Close enough to downtown but still worlds away on its own 177-acre island, this tropical-flair Wyndham insists that you're here on vacation and not stuck in some insipid downtown convention hotel. Rooms overlook the harbor and are hypercomfortable, with pillowtop mattresses and large bathrooms with Golden Door products. Luna di Mare is the hotel's exquisite Italian restaurant, overlooking the water and offering an extensive wine list, seafood, and chops. Guest privileges at the Harbour Island Athletic Club include full workout facilities, tennis courts, racquetball courts, and full-service spa. Stroll the boardwalk to fully appreciate your surroundings.

725 S. Harbour Island Blvd., Tampa, FL 33602. (C) **877/999-3223** or 813/229-5000. Fax 813/229-5322. www.wyndham.com/hotels/TPAHI/main.wnt. 299 units. $199–$289 double; $495–$895 suite. Weekend rates available. AE, DC, DISC, MC, V. Valet parking $12; no self-parking. **Amenities:** Restaurant; 3 bars; heated outdoor pool; access to nearby health club; access to spa; Jacuzzi; concierge; activities desk; car-rental desk; business center; salon; limited room service; massage; babysitting; laundry service. *In room:* A/C, TV, fax, high-speed Internet access, coffeemaker, hair dryer, iron.

YBOR CITY

Hilton Garden Inn 🏵 This modern, four-story hotel stands just 2 blocks north of the heart of Ybor City's dining and entertainment district. A one-story brick structure in front houses the bright lobby, a comfy relaxation area with a fireplace, a dining area providing cooked and continental breakfasts, and a small 24-hour pantry selling beer, wine, soft drinks, and frozen dinners. You can heat up the dinners in your comfortable guest room's microwave or store them in your fridge. Since Hilton's Garden hotels are aimed primarily at business travelers, your room will also have a large desk and two phones. If you opt for a suite, you'll get a separate living room and a larger bathroom.

1700 E. 9th Ave. (between 17th and 18th sts.), Tampa, FL 33605. (C) **800/445-8667** or 813/769-9267. Fax 813/769-3299. www.hiltongardeninn.com. 95 units. $119–$289 double. AE, DC, DISC, MC, V. **Amenities:** Restaurant (breakfast only); heated outdoor pool; exercise room; Jacuzzi; business center; laundry service; coin-op washers and dryers. *In room:* A/C, TV, dataport (w/high-speed Internet access), fridge, coffeemaker, hair dryer, iron.

Seminole Hard Rock Hotel & Casino 🏵🏵 Not quite as flashy as its South Florida sibling, Tampa's Seminole Hard Rock Hotel & Casino is still full of nonstop action. The 12-story building has 250 rooms, all of which feature modern amenities such as a flat-screen TV, a large bathroom with excellent lighting, and a fully stocked minibar. The casino offers 90,000 square feet of video slots and poker—no Sin City gaming such as blackjack, roulette, or craps. Several restaurants and bars keep the nongamblers entertained, especially when big-name talent performs here. The pool area is large, but not as nice as those at the Hard Rocks in Vegas or Hollywood, Florida. The fitness center is top-notch and even does outdoor treatments in its Zen garden.

5223 Orient Rd., Tampa, FL 33605. (C) **866/502-PLAY** or 813/627-7625. Fax 813/623-6862. www.hardrockhotelcasinotampa.com. 250 units. Winter $179–$549 double; off season $169–$219 double. AE, DC, DISC, MC, V. **Amenities:** 10 restaurants and bars; heated outdoor pool; full-service spa; Jacuzzi. *In room:* A/C, TV, CD player, dataport (w/high-speed Internet access), fridge, hair dryer, iron.

A NEARBY SPA & SPORTS RESORT

Saddlebrook Resort–Tampa *Kids* Set on 480 rolling acres of priceless countryside, Saddlebrook is a landlocked condominium development off the beaten path (30 min. north of Tampa International Airport). But if you're interested in spas, tennis, or golf, we recommend this resort, which offers complete spa treatments, the Hopman Tennis Program (Jennifer Capriati pitches a tent here), and the Arnold Palmer Golf Academy (see "Outdoor Activities & Spectator Sports," earlier in this chapter). Guests are housed in hotel rooms (all renovated to the tune of $8.5 million in 2005) or one-, two-, or three-bedroom suites. Much more appealing than the rooms, the suites come with a kitchen and either a patio or balcony overlooking lagoons, cypress and palm trees, and the resort's two 18-hole championship golf courses. There are shops, restaurants, a stunning pool, and a kids' club with supervised activities.

5700 Saddlebrook Way, Wesley Chapel, FL 33543. © 800/729-8383 or 813/973-1111. Fax 813/973-4504. www. saddlebrookresort.com. 800 units. Winter $242–$402 per person; off season $147–$234 per person. Rates include breakfast and dinner. Packages available. AE, DC, DISC, MC, V. Valet parking $10 overnight; free self-parking located 1 mile east of I-75 at exit 279. **Amenities:** 3 restaurants; 2 bars; heated outdoor pool; 2 golf courses; 45 grass, clay, and hard tennis courts; health club; spa; Jacuzzi; sauna; bike rental; children's activities program; concierge; activities desk; car-rental desk; business center; limited room service; massage; laundry service; washers and dryers. *In room:* A/C, TV, dataport, kitchen, minibar, fridge, coffeemaker, hair dryer, iron.

WHERE TO DINE

The restaurants that follow are organized by geographic area: near Busch Gardens, in or near Hyde Park (across the Hillsborough River from downtown), and in Ybor City. Although Ybor City is better known, Tampa's trendiest dining scene is along South Howard Avenue—"SoHo" to the locals—between West Kennedy Boulevard and the bay in affluent Hyde Park.

NEAR BUSCH GARDENS

You'll find the national fast-food and family restaurants east of I-275 on Busch Boulevard and Fowler Avenue.

Amish Country South?

Twelve miles east of Tampa, you'll find **Behind the Fence**, 1400 Viola Dr., at Country Side Street (© 813/685-8201), a fabulous and secluded country-style B&B in Brandon, Florida. Innkeeper Larry Yoss, raised in an Amish home in Ohio, brought his heritage to Florida by encouraging traveling artisans to frequent the inn's backyard, where they'd demonstrate their skills in soap making, candle dipping, basket weaving, looming, and open-hearth cooking. This became a yearly August-to-September weekend trip into the past, which is often carried over to Christmas, during which time Behind the Fence re-creates itself as an homage to Christmas in the 1800s. The inn itself is as charming as it sounds, with a porch overlooking a pool and breakfasts that include Amish sweet rolls. The three rooms in the main house are usually rented by friends or families traveling together because they share a single bathroom. The two cottage rooms by the pool are stunning and have their own facilities, including claw-foot tubs. Rates are Amishly reasonable, from $79 to $89.

Moderate

Cafe Don José SPANISH/AMERICAN   It's not nearly on a par with the Columbia in Ybor City (see below), but this Spanish-themed restaurant is among the best there is within a short drive of Busch Gardens. High-back chairs, dark-wood floors, and Spanish posters and paintings set an appropriate scene for the house specialties of traditional paella (allow 30 min. for preparation) and Valencia-style rice dishes. Don José also offers non-Spanish fare such as red snapper baked in parchment.

11009 N. 56th St. (in Sherwood Forest Shopping Center, ¼ mile south of Fowler Ave.). ✆ 813/985-2392. www.cafe donjose.com. Main courses $15–$59. AE, DC, MC, V. Mon–Fri 11:30am–4:30pm and 5–10pm; Sat 5–9pm.

Ristorante Francesco 𝄢 NORTHERN ITALIAN   This landmark Italian eatery has been kept just as it was, thanks to the fact that new owner Jay Lanier was original owner Frankie's right-hand man in the kitchen. The pasta remains homemade and shows up in more traditional fare such as seafood over linguine with a choice of marinara or white-wine sauce. The Tris di Pasta is a carbo-loader's delight, offering homemade gnocchi, tortellini, and ravioli in three different sauces. Yum.

In La Place Village Shopping Center, 1441 E. Fletcher Ave. (between 14th and 15th sts.). ✆ 813/971-3649. Reservations recommended. Main courses $11–$23. AE, DC, DISC, MC. V. Mon–Fri 11:30am–2:30pm and 5:30–10pm; Sat 5:30–10pm; Sun 5–9pm.

Shells 𝄢 (Value) SEAFOOD   You'll see Shells restaurants in many parts of Florida, and with good reason, as this casual, award-winning chain consistently provides excellent value. Particularly good are the spicy Jack Daniel's buffalo shrimp and scallop appetizers. Main courses range from the fried seafood platters to pastas, to grilled shrimp, fish, steaks, and chicken.

11010 N. 30th St. (between Busch Blvd. and Fowler Ave.). ✆ 813/977-8456. Main courses $9–$20 (most $10–$12). AE, DISC, MC, V. Sun–Thurs 11:30am–10pm; Fri–Sat 11:30am–11pm.

Inexpensive

Mel's Hot Dogs (Kids) AMERICAN   Catering to everyone from businesspeople to hungry families craving all-beef hot dogs, Mel Lohn's red-and-white cottage offers everything from "bagel-dogs" to bacon/cheddar Reuben-style hot dogs. All choices are served on poppy-seed buns and can be ordered with fries and a choice of coleslaw or baked beans. Even the decor is dedicated to wieners: The walls and windows are lined with hot-dog memorabilia, and a wiener-mobile is usually parked out front. Mel's chili is outstanding, too. And just in case hot-dog mania hasn't won you over, there are a few alternatives (chicken, beef, and veggie burgers, and terrific onion rings).

4136 E. Busch Blvd., at 42nd St. ✆ 813/985-8000. Most items $4–$9. No credit cards (but there's an ATM on the premises). Sun–Thurs 11am–8pm; Fri–Sat 11am–9pm.

HYDE PARK

Expensive

Bern's Steak House 𝄢𝄢 STEAKHOUSE   The exterior of this famous steakhouse looks like a factory. Inside, however, some say it looks like a brothel, containing eight ornate dining rooms with themes such as Rhône, Burgundy, and Irish Rebellion. However you perceive the decor, this is a carnivore's paradise, one to which I actually drove from Miami and back just for dinner. At Bern's, you order and pay for grilled steaks of perfectly aged beef according to the thickness and weight (the 60-oz., 3-in.-thick Porterhouse can feed four adults). The phone book–size wine list—one of the restaurant's most famous attributes—offers more than 7,000 selections, many available by the

Dining on the Bay

One of the newest additions to Tampa's dining scene is the 180-foot-long *StarShip* Dining Yacht (© 877/744-7999 or 813/223-7999; www.starship dining.com), which makes 2-hour lunch and dinner cruises from the Channelside out onto Tampa Bay. The ship's four dining rooms serve exceptional cruise fare. A house band plays during dinner and then moves to the top deck for dancing under the stars. Lunch cruises cost $40 per person with a meal, $16 for sightseers. Dinner cruises cost $70. There's also a Sunday brunch for $40. Call for the schedule.

glass. Ask your server for a sampling before you purchase a bottle. Upstairs, the restaurant's other most famous attribute—the dessert quarters—has 50 romantic booths paneled in aged California redwood; each can privately seat from 2 to 12 guests. All of these little chambers are equipped with phones for placing your order and closed-circuit TVs for watching and listening to a resident pianist. The dessert menu offers almost 100 selections, plus some 1,400 after-dinner drinks. It's possible to reserve a booth for dessert only, but preference is given to those who dine.

The big secret here is that steak sandwiches are available at the bar but are not mentioned on the menu. Smaller versions of the chargrilled steaks served in the dining rooms, they come with a choice of french fries or crispy onion rings. Add a salad, and you have a terrific meal for about half the price of the least-expensive main course.

Sidebern's, 2208 W. Morrison Ave., at South Howard Avenue (© **813/258-2233**), is the restaurant's New American offshoot. It's also quite good, but choose the original: Missing Bern's would be like watching the remake of *Psycho* without ever seeing the original.

1208 S. Howard Ave. (at Marjory Ave.). © **813/251-2421.** www.bernssteakhouse.com. Reservations recommended. Main courses $17–$59; sandwiches $9–$12. AE, DC, DISC, MC, V. Daily 5–11pm. Closed Christmas. Valet parking $5.

Moderate

Castaway ✮ SEAFOOD   Gorgeous ocean views trump the inconsistent seafood at Castaway, where crab legs, coconut shrimp, and daily catches reel in a steady crowd of locals and visitors alike. Insist on sitting on the deck and time your meal around sundown; the vantage point for sunsets here is the kind that makes developers drool and diners delight in the fact that this Castaway isn't going anywhere anytime soon.

7720 Courtney Campbell Causeway. © **813/281-0770.** Reservations recommended. Main courses $13–$40. AE, DC, DISC, MC, V. Mon–Sat 11:30am–10:30pm; Sun brunch 10:30am–2:30pm; Sun dinner 4–10pm.

Mise en Place ✮✮ ECLECTIC   Look around at all those happy, stylish people soaking up the trendy ambience, and you'll know why chef Marty Blitz and his wife, Maryann, have been among the culinary darlings of Tampa since 1986. They present the freshest of ingredients in a creative, award-winning menu that changes weekly. Main courses often include choices such as Creole-style mahimahi served with chili-cheese grits and a ragout of black-eyed peas, andouille sausage, and rock shrimp.

In Grand Central Place, 442 W. Kennedy Blvd. (at S. Magnolia Ave., opposite the University of Tampa). © **813/254-5373.** www.miseonline.com. Reservations recommended. Main courses $16–$35; tasting menu $53 with wine, $38 without. AE, DC, DISC, MC, V. Tues–Thurs 11:30am–2:30pm and 5:30–10pm; Fri 11:30am–2:30pm and 5:30–11pm; Sat 5–11pm.

Wine Exchange ☞☞ MEDITERRANEAN   This Tampa hot spot is an oenophile's dream come true, in which each dish is paired with a particular wine available by the bottle or the glass. The menu is rather simple, featuring pizzas, pastas, salads, and sandwiches, but daily specials are more elaborate, including grilled Delmonico steak, blackened pork tenderloin, or Dijon-crusted salmon. The outdoor patio is a great place to sit. There's almost always a wait at this buzzworthy eatery.

1611 W. Swan Ave. ⓒ 813/254-9463. Reservations not accepted. Main courses $10–$22. AE, DC, DISC, MC, V. Mon–Fri 11:30am–10pm; Sat 11am–11pm; Sun 11am–9pm; brunch Sat–Sun 11am–3pm.

Inexpensive

Bella's Italian Cafe ☞ 𝒱alue ITALIAN   Creative dishes and very reasonable prices make this sophisticated yet informal cafe one of SoHo's most popular neighborhood hangouts. Although you can go for wood-fired pizzas or homemade pasta under traditional Bolognese or Alfredo sauces, the stars here feature the tasty likes of blackened chicken in a creamy tomato sauce over fettuccine, or shrimp and scallops in a roasted tomato sauce over bow-tie pasta. Finish with the house version of tiramisu. Local professionals flock to the friendly bar during two-for-one happy hours, nightly from 4 to 7pm and from 11pm until closing. After 11pm, the open kitchen provides only appetizers, salads, pizzas, and desserts.

1413 S. Howard Ave. (at Mississippi Ave.). 813/254-3355. www.bellasitaliancafe.com Reservations not accepted. Main courses $12–$20; pizza $7–$10. AE, DC, DISC, MC, V. Mon–Tues 11:30am–11:30pm; Wed–Thurs 11:30am–12:30am; Fri 11am–1:30am; Sat 4pm–1:30am; Sun 4–11:30pm.

Four Green Fields IRISH/AMERICAN   Just across the bridge from the downtown convention center, this thatched-roof Irish pub may be surrounded by palm trees instead of potato fields, but it still offers the ambience and tastes of Ireland. Staffed by Irish immigrants, the large room with a square bar in the center smells of Bass and Harp ales. The Gaelic stew is predictably bland, but the salads and sandwiches are passable. The live Irish music Thursday through Saturday nights and Sunday afternoon draws a fun crowd, ranging from postcollege to early retirees.

205 W. Platt St. (between Parker St. and Plant Ave.). ⓒ 813/254-4444. www.fourgreenfields.com. Reservations not necessary. Main courses $9.50–$15; sandwiches $6–$7. AE, MC, V. Daily 11am–3am.

YBOR CITY
Moderate

Big City Tavern ☞ NEW AMERICAN   Although this restaurant is a chain, with additional locations in West Palm Beach and Fort Lauderdale, Ybor City's Big City Tavern takes the prize for best decor: It's housed in a converted ballroom and features columns, floor-to-ceiling windows, and wrought-iron balconies. The food's pretty good, too, especially the roasted duck with mango and basil risotto. The bar scene is a people-watching paradise in which a youngish, well-heeled, hip clientele gathers to trade tales of life in the big city.

1600 E. 8th Ave. ⓒ 813/247-3000. Reservations recommended. Main courses $11–$20. AE, MC, V. Sun–Thurs 11:30am–1am; Fri–Sat 11:30am–2am.

Columbia ☞☞☞ SPANISH   Celebrating 100 years in 2005, this tile building occupies an entire city block in the heart of Ybor City. Tourists flock here to soak up the ambience, and so do the locals because it's so much fun to clap along during fire-belching Spanish flamenco floor shows Monday through Saturday evenings ($6 per person additional charge besides dinner charge). You can't help coming back time after time for the famous Spanish bean soup and original "1905" salad. The *paella a la Valenciana* is outstanding, with more than a dozen ingredients ranging from Gulf grouper and Gulf pink shrimp to calamari, mussels, clams, chicken, and pork. Another favorite is *boliche* (eye of round stuffed with chorizo), accompanied by plantains and black beans and rice. Entrees come with a crispy hunk of Cuban bread with butter. Lighter appetites can choose from a limited menu of tapas, including "Cuban caviar" (a spicy black-bean dip). The decor throughout is graced with hand-painted tiles, wrought-iron chandeliers, dark woods, rich red fabrics, and stained-glass windows.

2117 E. 7th Ave. (between 21st and 22nd sts.). (✆ 813/248-4961. www.columbiarestaurant.com. Reservations recommended. Main courses $14–$28. AE, DC, DISC, MC, V. Mon–Thurs 11am–10pm; Fri–Sat 11am–11pm; Sun noon–9pm.

Inexpensive

Carmine's Restaurant & Bar ✸ CUBAN/ITALIAN/AMERICAN   Bright blue poles hold up an ancient pressed-tin ceiling above this noisy corner cafe. It's not the cleanest joint in town, but a great variety of loyal local patrons gather here for genuine Cuban sandwiches—smoked ham, roast pork, Genoa salami, Swiss cheese, pickles, salad dressing, mustard, lettuce, and tomato on crispy Cuban bread. There's a vegetarian version, too. The combination of a half-sandwich and choice of black beans and rice or a bowl of Spanish soup made with sausages, potatoes, and garbanzo beans makes a hearty meal for just $7 at lunch, $8 at dinner. Main courses are led by Cuban-style roast pork, thin-cut pork chops with mushroom sauce, spaghetti with a blue-crab tomato sauce, and a few seafood and chicken platters.

1802 E. 7th Ave. (at 18th St.). (✆ 813/248-3834. Reservations not accepted. Main courses $7–$17; sandwiches $4–$8. No credit cards. Mon–Tues 11am–11pm; Wed–Thurs 11am–1am; Fri–Sat 11am–3am; Sun 11am–6pm.

TAMPA AFTER DARK

The Tampa/Hillsborough Arts Council maintains an **Artsline** (✆ **813/229-2787**), a 24-hour information service providing the latest on current and upcoming cultural events. Racks in many restaurants and bars have copies of *Weekly Planet* (**www.weeklyplanet.com**), *Focus,* and *Accent on Tampa Bay,* three free publications detailing what's going on in the entire bay area. You can also check the "BayLife" and "Friday Extra" sections of the *Tampa Tribune* (**www.tampatrib.com**), as well as the Thursday "Weekend" section of the *St. Petersburg Times* (**www.sptimes.com**). The visitor center usually has copies of the week's newspaper sections (see "Essentials," earlier in this chapter).

THE CLUB & MUSIC SCENE   Ybor City is Tampa's favorite nighttime venue. All you have to do is stroll along 7th Avenue East between 15th and 20th streets, and you'll hear music blaring from the clubs. On Friday and Saturday from 9pm to 3am, the avenue is packed with people, a majority high schoolers and early 20-somethings;

The Hub of Tampa's Bar Scene

Ybor City and Bern's Steak House are command central for the boozy sophisticates of Tampa, but if you go downtown, you'll find the true hub of Tampa's bar scene in the form of, well, **The Hub**, 719 N. Franklin St. (✆ **813/229-1553**). It's a classic dive bar in which judges, lawyers, and the over-21 set shake and stir overstiff libations and a fabulous jukebox.

Tips **Careful Where You Park**

Parking can be scarce at night in Ybor City, and the area has seen an occasional robbery in the late hours. Play it safe and use the municipal parking lots behind the shops on 8th Avenue East, or the new parking garages near Centro Ybor, on 7th Avenue East at 16th Street.

---

but you'll also find something going on Tuesday through Thursday, and even on Sunday. The clubs change names frequently, so you don't need names, addresses, or phone numbers; your ears will guide you along 7th Avenue East. With all of the sidewalk seating, it's easy to judge what the clientele is like and make your choice from there.

The center of the action these days is **Centro Ybor,** on 7th Avenue East at 16th Street (℡ **813/242-4660;** www.centroybor.com), the district's large dining-and-entertainment complex. The restaurants and pubs in this family-oriented center tend to be tamer than many of those along 7th Avenue, at least on nonweekend nights. You don't have to pay to listen to live music in the center's patio on weekend afternoons.

THE PERFORMING ARTS With a prime downtown location on 9 acres along the east bank of the Hillsborough River, the huge **Tampa Bay Performing Arts Center** *✦*, 1010 N. MacInnes Place, next to the Tampa Museum of Art (℡ **800/955-1045** or 813/229-7827; www.tampacenter.com), is the largest performing-arts venue south of the Kennedy Center in Washington, D.C. Accordingly, this four-theater complex is the focal point of Tampa's performing-arts scene, presenting a wide range of Broadway plays, classical and pop concerts, operas, improv, and special events.

A sightseeing attraction in its own right, the restored **Tampa Theatre,** 711 Franklin St., between Zack and Polk streets (℡ **813/274-8286;** www.tampatheatre.org), dates from 1926 and is on the National Register of Historic Places. It presents a varied program of classic, foreign, and alternative films, as well as concerts and special events. (And it's said to be haunted!)

The 66,321-seat **Raymond James Stadium,** 4201 N. Dale Mabry Hwy. (℡ **813/673-4300;** www.raymondjames.com/stadium), is sometimes the site of headliner concerts. The **USF Sun Dome,** 4202 E. Fowler Ave. (℡ **813/974-3111;** www.sundome.org), on the University of South Florida campus, hosts major concerts by touring pop stars, rock bands, jazz groups, and other contemporary artists.

Bars featuring live music include **Whiskey Joe's,** 2500 N. Rocky Point Dr. (℡ **813/281-0557**), a bayfront shack with plenty of visual and audible color; Ybor City's **Twilight,** 1507 E. 7th Ave. (℡ **813/247-4225**), an industrial-chic soundstage for the likes of local bands and national acts such as Third Eye Blind; and **Skipper's Smokehouse,** 910 Skipper Rd. (℡ **813/971-0666**), a Key West–style former smokehouse turned blues, jazz, zydeco, ska, and reggae hot spot.

Ticketmaster (℡ **813/287-8844**) sells tickets to most events and shows.

---

2 St. Petersburg *✦*

20 miles SW of Tampa, 289 miles NW of Miami, 84 miles SW of Orlando

On the western shore of the bay, St. Petersburg stands in contrast to Tampa, much as San Francisco compares to Oakland in California. Whereas Tampa is the area's business, industrial, and shipping center, St. Petersburg was conceived and built a century

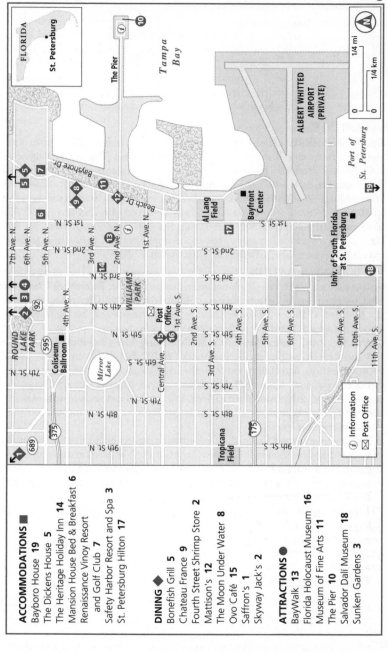

ACCOMMODATIONS ■
Bayboro House **19**
The Dickens House **5**
The Heritage Holiday Inn **14**
Mansion House Bed & Breakfast **6**
Renaissance Vinoy Resort
   and Golf Club **7**
Safety Harbor Resort and Spa **3**
St. Petersburg Hilton **17**

DINING ◆
Bonefish Grill **5**
Chateau France **9**
Fourth Street Shrimp Store **2**
Mattison's **12**
The Moon Under Water **8**
Ovo Café **15**
Saffron's **1**
Skyway Jack's **2**

ATTRACTIONS ●
BayWalk **13**
Florida Holocaust Museum **16**
Museum of Fine Arts **11**
The Pier **10**
Salvador Dalí Museum **18**
Sunken Gardens **3**

ago primarily for tourists and wintering snowbirds. Here you'll find one of the most picturesque and pleasant downtowns of any city in Florida, with a waterfront promenade and the famous inverted pyramid-shape Pier offering great views across the bay, plus quality museums, interesting shops, and a few good restaurants. Thanks to an urban redevelopment program, St. Pete has awoken from its slumber and actually resembles a city that could be considered hip, with renewed, restored streetscapes full of punk'd-out skateboarders, clubs, bars, and a vibrancy that goes well beyond the excitement surrounding bingo night at the "adult" communities in town.

ESSENTIALS

GETTING THERE   **Tampa International Airport,** approximately 16 miles northeast of St. Petersburg, is the prime gateway to the area (see "Essentials" in section 1, earlier in this chapter). The primary carrier at **St. Petersburg–Clearwater International Airport,** on Roosevelt Boulevard (Fla. 686) about 10 miles north of downtown St. Petersburg (© 727/453-7800; www.fly2pie.com), is **American Trans Air (ATA;** © 800/435-9282; www.ata.com). The Canadian carrier **Air Transat** (© 877/872-6728; www.airtransat.com) flies here during the winter months. **Amtrak** (© 800/ USA-RAIL; www.amtrak.com) has bus connections from its Tampa station to downtown St. Petersburg (see "Getting There" in section 1, above).

VISITOR INFORMATION   For advance information on St. Petersburg and the beaches (see section 3, later in this chapter), contact the **St. Petersburg/Clearwater Area Convention & Visitors Bureau,** 14450 46th St. N., Clearwater, FL 34622 (© 800/345-6710, or 727/464-7200 for hotel reservations; fax 727/464-7222; www.floridasbeach.com for information specific to the beaches).

After you arrive, you can head to the **St. Petersburg Area Chamber of Commerce,** 100 2nd Ave. N. (at 1st St.), St. Petersburg (© 727/821-4069; fax 727/895-6326; www.stpete.com). Across the street from the BayWalk shopping-and-dining complex, this downtown main office and visitor center is open Monday through Friday from 8am to 5pm, Saturday from 10am to 4pm, and Sunday from noon to 4pm. Ask for a copy of the chamber's visitor guide, which lists hotels, motels, condominiums, and other accommodations.

Also downtown, you'll find walk-in **information centers** on the first level of the Pier and in the lobby of the Florida International Museum. The chamber also operates the **Suncoast Welcome Center** (© 727/573-1449), on Ulmerton Road at exit 31B southbound off I-275 (there's no exit here for northbound traffic). The center is open daily from 9am to 5pm except New Year's Day, Easter, Thanksgiving, and Christmas.

GETTING AROUND   The **Pinellas Suncoast Transit Authority/PSTA** (© 727/ 530-9911; www.psta.net) operates regular bus service throughout St. Petersburg and the rest of the Pinellas Peninsula. Rides cost $1.25 for adults, 60¢ for seniors, and 75¢ for students.

Fun Fact Sunny Days

St. Petersburg is listed in the *Guinness Book of World Records* as the city with the longest number of days of consecutive sunshine—768, to be exact. From February 9, 1967, to March 17, 1969, the city experienced not a drop of rain, no clouds—just pure, unadulterated, tan-friendly sunshine!

> **Fun Fact Open-Air Mail**
>
> St. Petersburg residents don't have to go inside to get mail out of their boxes at St. Petersburg's open-air **post office,** at the corner of 1st Avenue North and 4th Street North. Built in 1917, this granite, arcaded Spanish Colonial structure is a popular local landmark and is often photographed by those enchanted by its charm.

If you need a cab, call **Yellow Cab** (© 727/821-7777) or **Independent Cab** (© 727/327-3444). Fares are $2.25 at flag fall, plus $2 for each additional mile.

SEEING THE TOP ATTRACTIONS

Florida Holocaust Museum ✦   This thought-provoking museum (the fourth-largest such museum in the U.S.) has exhibits about the Holocaust (Jewish life before the Holocaust, the rise of the Nazi party, and so on), including a boxcar used to transport human cargo to Auschwitz and a gallery of art relating to the Holocaust. Its main focus, however, is to promote tolerance and understanding in the present. It was founded by Walter P. Loebenberg, a local businessman who escaped Nazi Germany in 1939 and fought with the U.S. Army in World War II.

55 5th St. S. (between Central Ave. and 1st Ave. S.). © 800/960-7448 or 727/820-0100. www.flholocaustmuseum. org. Admission $8 adults, $7 seniors and college students, $3 children 6–18, free for kids under 6. Mon–Fri 10am–5pm; Sat–Sun noon–5pm (last admission at 4pm). Closed Easter, Rosh Hashanah, Yom Kippur, Thanksgiving, and Christmas.

Museum of Fine Arts ✦✦   Resembling a Mediterranean villa on the waterfront, this museum houses an excellent collection of European, American, pre-Columbian, and Far Eastern art, with works by such artists as Fragonard, Monet, Renoir, Cézanne, and Gauguin. Other highlights include period rooms with antique furnishings, plus a gallery of Steuben crystal, a new decorative-arts gallery, and world-class rotating exhibits. The best way to see it all is on a guided tour, which takes about 1 hour. Ask about classical-music performances from October to April.

255 Beach Dr. NE (at 3rd Ave. N.). © 727/896-2667. www.fine-arts.org. Admission $8 adults, $7 seniors 65 and over, $4 students with ID, free for children under 6 (special exhibits cost extra). Admission includes guided tour. Tues–Sat 10am–5pm; Sun 1–5pm. Guided tours Tues–Sat 11am and 1, 2, and 3pm; Sun 1 and 2pm. Closed New Year's Day; Martin Luther King, Jr., Day; Thanksgiving; and Christmas.

The Pier ✦ *Kids*   The Pier is a festive waterfront dining-and-shopping complex overlooking Tampa Bay. Originally built as a railroad pier in 1889, today it's capped by a spaceshiplike inverted pyramid offering five levels of shops, three restaurants, a tourist information desk, an observation deck, catwalks for fishing, boat docks, miniature golf, boat and watersports rentals, sightseeing boats, a food court, plus an aquarium. Cruise boats often operate from the Pier during the winter months, and you can rent fishing gear and drop your line into the bay year-round. There's valet parking at the end of the Pier, or you can park on land and ride a free trolley out to the complex.

800 2nd Ave. NE. © 727/821-6443. www.stpete-pier.com. Free admission to all public areas and decks; donations welcome at the Pier Aquarium. Valet parking $6; self-parking $3. Pier Mon–Thurs 10am–9pm; Fri–Sat 10am–10pm; Sun 11am–7pm. Aquarium Mon–Sat 10am–8pm; Sun 11am–6pm.

Salvador Dalí Museum ✦✦✦   This starkly modern museum houses the world's most comprehensive (and most valuable, at $125 million) collection of works by the

---

Tips **Car Smarts**

You can spend a small fortune in a parking garage or by feeding the meters in St. Petersburg, or you can cut costs substantially by parking at the **Pier** ($3 all day) and taking the **Looper,** the city's trolley service, which operates between the Pier and all major downtown attractions.

---

renowned Spanish surrealist—and for art lovers is reason enough to visit downtown St. Petersburg. Housing six of the artist's masterworks, the museum was given three stars by the Michelin Guide—the highest-ranked museum in the entire South. It includes oil paintings, watercolors, drawings, and more than 1,000 graphics, plus posters, photos, sculptures, objets d'art, and a 5,000-volume library on Dalí and surrealism. Take one of the free docent-led tours to get the most out of the museum.

1000 3rd St. S. (near 11th Ave. S.). (℃ 727/823-3767. www.salvadordalimuseum.org. Admission $14 adults, $12 seniors, $9 students, $3.50 children 5–9, free for children 4 and under; Thurs 5–8pm $5 for all. Mon–Wed and Fri–Sat 9:30am–5:30pm; Thurs 9:30am–8pm; Sun noon–5:30pm. Closed Thanksgiving and Christmas.

Sunken Gardens   Dating from 1935, this former tourist attraction is now operated as a 7-acre botanical garden by the city of St. Petersburg. It contains a vast array of 5,000 plants, flowers, and trees; a butterfly aviary; a display of snakes, spiders, and scorpions; and a rainforest information center. There's also a daily wildlife show. Call for a schedule of exhibits and tours.

1825 4th St. N. (between 18th and 19th aves. NE). (℃ 727/551-3100. www.stpete.org/fun/parks/sunken.htm. Admission $8 adults, $6 seniors, $4 children 3–16, free for children 2 and under. Mon–Sat 10am–4:30pm; Sun noon–4:30pm.

OUTDOOR ACTIVITIES & SPECTATOR SPORTS

You can get information about the city's parks and leisure activities online at **www.stpete.com/leisure.htm**.

BIKING, IN-LINE SKATING & HIKING   With miles of flat terrain, the St. Petersburg area is ideal for bikers, in-line skaters, and hikers. The **Pinellas Trail** is especially good, since it follows an abandoned railroad bed 47 miles from St. Petersburg north to Tarpon Springs (℃ 727/464-8201; www.pinellascounty.org/trailgd/default.htm). The **St. Pete trail head** is on 34th Street South (U.S. 19), between 8th and Fairfield avenues south. It's packed on weekends. Free strip maps of the trail are available at the St. Petersburg Area Chamber of Commerce (see "Visitor Information," above). The 2½-mile-long **Friendship TrailBridge** (www.friendshiptrail.org/index.html), linking Tampa and St. Petersburg, is another popular venue for hikers, bikers, bicyclists, anglers, and in-line skaters, but be careful going up and down the steep center span, especially if you're on skates.

GOLF   One of the nation's top 50 municipal courses, the **Mangrove Bay Golf Course** , 875 62nd Ave. NE (℃ 727/893-7800), hugs Old Tampa Bay and offers 18-hole, par-72 play. Facilities include a driving range. Lessons and golf-club rental are also available. Fees are about $30 in winter, slightly lower off season.

In Largo, the **Bardmoor Golf & Tennis Club,** 8001 Cumberland Rd. (℃ 727/392-1234), is often the venue for major tournaments. Lakes punctuate 17 of the 18 holes on this par-72 championship course. Lessons and rental clubs are available, as is a Tom Fazio–designed practice range. Call the clubhouse for seasonal greens fees. The course is open daily from 7am to dusk.

Call **Tee Times USA** (© 800/374-8633; www.teetimesusa.com) to reserve times at these and other area courses.

For course information online, go to www.golf.com or www.floridagolfing.com; or call the **Florida Sports Foundation** (© 850/488-8347) or **Florida Golfing** (© 866/833-2663).

SAILING   Both Steve and Doris Colgate's **Offshore Sailing School** (© 888/454-8002 or 239/454-1700; www.offshore-sailing.com) and the **Annapolis Sailing School** (© 800/638-9192 or 727/867-8102; www.annapolissailing.com) have operations here. Various courses lasting from 2 days to a week are offered. Contact the schools for prices and schedules.

SPECTATOR SPORTS   St. Petersburg has always been a baseball town, and **Tropicana Field,** a 45,000-seat domed stadium alongside I-175 between 9th and 16th streets (© 727/825-3100), is the home of the American League's **Tampa Bay Devil Rays** (© 888/326-7297 or 727/825-3137; www.devilrays.mlb.com). Baseball season runs April through October. Single-game tickets are $3 to $75 and are usually available on game days. Call or check the website for the schedule. The Devil Rays move outdoors to **Progress Energy Park at Al Lang Field,** on 2nd Avenue South at 1st Street South, for spring-training workouts and games from mid-February through March.

The **Philadelphia Phillies** now play their spring-training season in new digs in Clearwater, at Bright House Networks Field, 601 Old Coachman Rd. (© 727/442-8496). Their minor-league affiliate, the **Clearwater Phillies** (© 727/441-8638; www.clearwaterphillies.com; $3–$8), plays in the stadium April through August. The **Toronto Blue Jays** do their spring thing at Knology Park, 311 Douglas Ave., in Dunedin (© 800/707-8269 or 813/733-9302; www.bluejays.mlb.com; $13–$15), which is also home to their minor-league affiliate, the **Dunedin Blue Jays** (© 727/733-9302; www.dunedinbluejays.com), April through August.

TENNIS   You can learn to play or hone your game at the **Phil Green Tennis Academy,** at Safety Harbor Resort and Spa (p. 425).

SHOPPING

The Pier, at the end of 2nd Avenue Northeast (see "Seeing the Top Attractions," above), houses more than a dozen boutiques and crafts shops; but nearby **Beach Drive,** running along the waterfront, is one of the most fashionable downtown strolling and shopping venues. Here you'll find the **Glass Canvas Gallery,** at 4th Avenue NE (© 727/821-6767), featuring a dazzling array of glass sculpture, tableware, art, and crafts items by local, national, and international artists. **Red Cloud,** between 1st and 2nd avenues (© 727/821-5824), is an oasis for Native American crafts, including jewelry, headdresses, and art.

Downtown's new commercial showplace is **BayWalk** (© 727/895-9277; www.stpete.org/baywalk.htm), an open-air shopping, dining, and entertainment complex bordered by 1st and 2nd streets and 2nd and 3rd avenues North. It has a branch of Ann Taylor and some small boutiques.

Haslam's Book Store, 2025 Central Ave. (© 727/822-8616; www.haslams.com), is a favorite place to browse. Dating from 1933, its collection holds more than 350,000 volumes, making it Florida's largest bookstore. (As a perk, it is said to be haunted.)

Ancient Burial Mounds & Manatees

Drive north of St. Petersburg for an hour on congested U.S. 19, and you'll come to one of Florida's original tourist attractions, the famous **Weeki Wachee Springs** (© **877/469-3354** or 352/596-2062; www.weekiwachee. com). "Mermaids" have been putting on acrobatic swimming shows here every day since 1947. It's a sight to see them doing their dances in waters that come from one of America's most prolific freshwater springs, pouring some 170 million gallons of 72°F (22°C) water each day into the river. There's more than mermaids here; you can also take a Wilderness River Cruise across the Weeki Wachee River and send the kids on the flume ride at Buccaneer Bay, the waterpark part of the attraction. Admission is $14 for adults, $11 for children 3 to 10. Weeki Wachee Springs is open Monday through Thursday from 10am to 3pm, Friday through Sunday from 10am to 4pm. Buccaneer Bay waterpark is open only on Friday from 10am to 4pm, Saturday and Sunday from 10am to 5pm.

You can rent canoes on the Weeki Wachee River for $27 for a one-person kayak and $35 for a two-person kayak per day (© **352/597-0360**; www.florida canoe.com).

From Weeki Wachee, travel 21 miles north to the **Homosassa Springs Wildlife State Park**, 4150 S. Suncoast Blvd. (U.S. 19), in Homosassa Springs (© 352/628-5343; www.floridastateparks.org/homosassasprings). The highlight here is a floating observatory where visitors can "walk" underwater and watch manatees in a rehabilitation facility, as well as see thousands of fresh- and saltwater fish. You'll also spot deer, a bear, bobcats, otters, egrets, and flamingos along unspoiled nature trails. The park is open daily from 9am to 5:30pm (last tickets sold at 4pm). Admission is $9 for adults and $5 for children 3 to 12; it includes a 20-minute narrated boat ride.

About 7 miles north of Homosassa Springs, more than 300 manatees spend the winter in Crystal River. You can **swim or snorkel with the manatees** 🐾🐾 in the warm-water natural spring of Kings Bay. **American Pro Diving Center**, 821 SE Hwy. 19, Crystal River (© **800/291-3483** or 352/563-0041;

Central Avenue is another shopping area, featuring the **Gas Plant Antique Arcade,** between 12th and 13th streets (© **727/895-0368**), the largest antiques mall on Florida's west coast, with more than 100 dealers displaying their wares. (Downtown has several antiques-and-collectibles dealers; get a list and map from the chamber of commerce.) The **Florida Craftsmen Gallery,** at 5th Street (© **727/821-7391;** www. floridacraftsmen.net), is a showcase for the works of more than 150 Florida artisans and craftspeople specializing in jewelry, ceramics, woodwork, fiberwork, glassware, paper creations, and metalwork.

WHERE TO STAY

The **St. Petersburg/Clearwater Area Convention & Visitors Bureau** (see "Essentials," earlier in this section) operates a free **reservations service** (© **800/345-6710**), fax 352/563-5230; www.americanprodive.com), offers daily swimming and snorkel tours. Early morning is the best time to see the manatees, so try to take the 6:30am departure. The trips range from $30 to $50 per person. Call for schedule and reservations. American Pro Diving also rents cottages on the Homosassa River.

Also check out the **Weedon Island Preserve,** 4801 37th St. S. (© **727/893-2627**), located in the upper Tampa Bay waters of Pinellas County, on the western shore of the entrance to Old Tampa Bay and directly west of Port Tampa. The island was named for Dr. Leslie Weedon, a renowned authority on yellow fever, who acquired the 1,250-acre island in 1898 in what is now north St. Petersburg. Weedon had a fascination with Indian culture and developed a weekend retreat on the island, from which he began excavations that first revealed the importance of the site as an Indian burial mound. A Smithsonian expedition to the island in 1923 and 1924 further documented the importance of the site, which is now managed as a county preserve. Today it's home to an assortment of fish, snakes, raccoons, and dolphins. Rent a canoe to explore, and find yourself easily "becoming one" with nature.

Baseball fans won't want to miss the **Ted Williams Museum & Hitters Hall of Fame,** 2455 N. Citrus Hills Blvd., off C.R. 486 west of Hernando (© **352/527-6566**; www.twmuseum.com). Built in the shape of a baseball diamond, the museum holds the great hitter's personal memorabilia, including his two Triple Crown batting titles. It's open Tuesday through Sunday from 10am to 4pm. Admission is $6 for adults, $2 for children.

For more information about the area, contact the **Citrus County Chamber of Commerce,** 28 NW Hwy. 19, Crystal River, FL 34428 (© **352/795-3149**; fax 352/795-4260; www.citruscountychamber.com). The chamber's visitor center is open Monday through Friday from 8:30am to 4:30pm, Saturday from 9am to 1pm.

through which you can book rooms at most hotels and motels in St. Petersburg and at the beaches. The bureau also publishes a brochure that lists members of its Superior Small Lodgings program; these establishments have fewer than 50 rooms and have been inspected and certified for cleanliness and value.

Other than the Renaissance Vinoy Resort and Golf Club (see below), the only chain hotel downtown is the **St. Petersburg Hilton,** 333 1st St. S., between 3rd and 4th avenues South (© **800/445-8667** or 727/894-5000; fax 727/823-4797; www. stpetehilton.com), a 15-story convention hotel within steps of the Salvador Dalí Museum, Florida Power Park at Al Lang Field, and the Bayfront Center's theaters. Otherwise, views from the upper-floor rooms are its main draw for leisure travelers.

Note: Sales and hotel taxes will add 11% to your bill.

VERY EXPENSIVE

Renaissance Vinoy Resort and Golf Club ☆☆☆ For the swankiest digs in the area, the Renaissance Vinoy is it. Built as the grand Vinoy Park in 1925, this elegant Spanish-style establishment has hosted everyone from Jimmy Stewart to Bill Clinton, and is on the National Register of Historic Places after a total and meticulous $93-million restoration that made it once again the city's finest hotel. Dominating the northern part of downtown, it overlooks Tampa Bay and is within walking distance of the Pier, Central Avenue, and other attractions. All guest rooms, many of which enjoy lovely views of the bayfront, offer the utmost in comfort and include three phones, an additional TV in the bathroom, and bath scales. Some rooms in the original building have standing-room-only balconies; if you need enough room to sit outside, request a balconied unit in the new Tower Wing (some of these have whirlpool tubs, too). Overlooking the bay, the Mediterranean-style **Marchand's Grill** is the city's most elegant dining room and serves some of the best steaks and chops in town. The Vinoy also has 12 tennis courts and an 18-hole golf course.

501 5th Ave. NE (at Beach Dr.), St. Petersburg, FL 33701. ℂ 800/468-3571 or 727/894-1000. Fax 727/822-2785. www.renaissancehotels.com. 360 units. Winter $209–$429 double; off season $169–$369 double. Packages available. AE, DC, DISC, MC, V. Valet parking $13; self-parking $9. **Amenities:** 4 restaurants; 2 bars; 2 heated outdoor pools (connected by a waterfall); golf course; 12 tennis courts; health club and spa; Jacuzzi; concierge; activities desk; car-rental desk; business center; salon; 24-hr. room service; massage; laundry service; coin-operated washers and dryers; concierge-level rooms. In room: A/C, TV, dataport, minibar, coffeemaker, hair dryer, iron.

MODERATE

Bayboro House ☆☆ *Finds* A huge departure from the area's monstrous resorts, this four-room Victorian mansion, located on Tampa Bay, is a well-kept secret run by innkeepers Antonia and Gordon Powers, who have managed to preserve the home's early-1900s ambience with heart-of-pine flooring, a wooden mantelpiece, a fireplace, and a 1926 player piano. Each of the rooms has a private bathroom and other modern amenities. The Charles Harvey Room has a bay window and four-poster Jenny Lind bed. The Audubon Suite features a kitchen, living room, and wing chairs tucked into an alcove; and the Williams Room boasts a fabulous view of the bay. The last room, the Sarah Armistead Room, has twin beds. Complimentary wine and cheese, served every afternoon in the parlor or on the veranda, features the inn's own citrus wine, bottled at the Florida Orange Groves, Inc., and Winery. The house has a large front porch, complete with rocking chairs and a swing, and a sunny breakfast room.

1719 Beach Dr. SE, St. Petersburg, FL 33701. ℂ 877/823-4955. Fax 727/823-2341. www.bayborohousebandb.com. 8 units. Winter $129–$179 double, $199–$215 suite; off season $149 double, $189 suite; cottage $275. Rates include breakfast. MC, V. In room: A/C, TV/VCR.

The Dickens House ☆☆☆ No relation to British author Charles Dickens, this Dickens House once belonged to Henry and Sadie Dickens, early St. Pete settlers who built this home in 1912 in the heart of the city's growing northeast residential district. Purchased in 1995 by mural artist Ed Caldwell, a graduate of the prestigious Rhode Island School of Design, the Dickens House has been restored to its original Craftsman-style architecture. The charming inn has five guest rooms: The Cracker Suite has a custom-made bent-willow bed, while the Orange Blossom Room, the smallest but cutest in the house, has a Jenny Lind bed and a tiny bathroom that just happens to have a whirlpool. My personal fave, however, is the second-floor Cottage Suite, which resembles a Victorian-age beach cottage with white wicker, sea-grass carpet, roll-up awnings, and nightstands displaying shells. The Dickens Room isn't too shabby, either, with a two-person shower and a four-poster cherry canopy bed—*tres* romantic. All rooms have Egyptian cotton linens. Complimentary breakfasts are served on the veranda, while afternoon wine, soft drinks, and snacks are served in the Arts and Crafts–style living room.

335 8th Ave. NE, St. Petersburg, FL 33701. ℂ 727/822-8622. No fax. www.dickenshouse.com. 5 units. Winter $120–$210 double; off season $96–$168 double. AE, DC, DISC, MC, V. **Amenities:** Laundry service; library. *In room:* A/C, TV, dataport (w/high-speed Internet access), fridge, coffeemaker, hair dryer, iron.

The Heritage Holiday Inn ℱ When it comes to Holiday Inns, most people complain about the old, musty decor, or lack thereof. This hotel has that feel, for sure, but it also has atypical qualities that may appeal to some (though the rooms are still pretty basic). No ordinary Holiday Inn, the Heritage dates from the early 1920s, and although significantly updated, it retains the ambience of an old-fashioned hotel, with tall, double-hung windows and hardwood floors that creak as you walk down the long central hallway. A lovely sweeping veranda, French doors, and a tropical courtyard help attract an eclectic clientele, from business travelers to seniors.

234 3rd Ave. N. (between 2nd and 3rd sts.), St. Petersburg, FL 33701. ℂ 800/283-7829 or 727/822-4814. Fax 727/823-1644. www.ichotelsgroup.com. 71 units. $100–$150 double. AE, DC, DISC, MC, V. **Amenities:** Restaurant; bar; heated outdoor pool; Jacuzzi; limited room service; laundry service. *In room:* A/C, TV, dataport, coffeemaker, hair dryer, iron.

Mansion House Bed & Breakfast ℱℱ Mirror images of each other, these two houses separated by a landscaped courtyard were built between 1901 and 1912. The comfortable living room in the main house, which has 6 of the 10 units, opens to a sunroom, off which a small screened porch provides mosquito-free lounging and the only place where guests can smoke. Both houses have upstairs front parlors with TVs, VCRs, and libraries. Tall, old-fashioned windows let lots of light into the attractive guest rooms. The pick of the litter is the Pembroke Room, upstairs over the carriage house. It has a four-poster bed with mosquito netting, along with its own whirlpool tub in an outdoor screened hut. The brick courtyard garden between the two houses (there's a heated pool and Jacuzzi out there) is a popular spot for weddings and receptions.

105 5th Ave. NE (at 1st St. NE), St. Petersburg, FL 33701. ℂ 800/274-7520 or 727/821-9391. Fax 727/821-6909. www.mansionbandb.com. 10 units. $90–$220 double. Rates include full breakfast. AE, DC, DISC, MC, V. **Amenities:** Heated outdoor pool; access to nearby health club; Jacuzzi; bicycle rentals; laundry service. *In room:* A/C, TV, dataport, hair dryer.

A NEARBY SPA

Safety Harbor Resort and Spa ℱℱ *Value* Hernando de Soto thought he had found Ponce de León's fabled Fountain of Youth when, in 1539, he happened upon five mineral springs in what is now Safety Harbor on the western shore of Old Tampa Bay (see the "Tampa & St. Petersburg" map on p. 396). You may not recover your youth at this venerable spa, which is an Aveda Concept Spa and has been in operation since 1926, but you will be rejuvenated by such services as massage, hydrotherapy, and a full menu of fitness classes, from boxing to yoga. The mineral springs enable it to offer acclaimed water-fitness programs, and this is a good place to work on your games at the Quinzi Golf Academy and the Phil Green Tennis Academy (see "Outdoor Activities & Spectator Sports" on p. 421). The complex of beige-stucco buildings, with Spanish-tile roofs and lame, old-fogie-style rooms, sits on 22 waterfront acres in the sleepy town of Safety Harbor, north of St. Petersburg. The grounds make up for what the rooms lack. Moss-draped Safety Harbor has a charming small-town ambience, with a number of shops and restaurants just outside the spa's entrance. Given the reasonable off-season rates and packages available, this is one of Florida's better spa values.

105 N. Bayshore Dr., Safety Harbor, FL 34695. (C) 888/237-8772 or 727/726-1161. Fax 727/724-7749. www.safety harborspa.com. 189 units. Winter $205–$235 double; off season $129–$205 double; year-round from $325 suites. Packages available. AE, DC, DISC, MC, V. Valet parking $12; free self-parking. Pets accepted ($35 per night). **Amenities:** 1 restaurant; bar; heated indoor and outdoor pools; driving range; 7 tennis courts; full-service spa; bicycle rentals; concierge; activities desk; car-rental desk; business center; limited room service; laundry service; coin-op washers and dryers. *In room:* A/C, TV, dataport (w/high-speed Internet access), coffeemaker, hair dryer, iron.

WHERE TO DINE

Don't overlook the food court at the **Pier,** where the inexpensive chow is accompanied by a very rich, but quite free, view of the bay. Among the Pier's restaurants is a branch of Tampa's famous **Columbia** ((C) **727/822-8000;** p. 414).

EXPENSIVE

Chateau France 🍴🍴 CLASSICAL FRENCH   Chef Antoine Louro provides St. Petersburg's most romantic setting in this charming Victorian house built in 1910. He specializes in French classics such as homemade pâté, Dover sole meunière, filet mignon au poivre, coq au vin, and rich seafood bouillabaisse. Fresh baby vegetables, Gruyère-cheese potatoes, and Antoine's special Eiffel Tower salad accompany all main courses. The wine list is excellent, as are the bananas flambé and crêpes suzette.

136 4th Ave. N. (between Bayshore Dr. and 1st St. N.). (C) 727/894-7163. Reservations recommended. Main courses $20–$38. AE, DC, DISC, MC, V. Daily 5–11pm.

Saffron's 🍴🍴 CARIBBEAN   It may seem a bit odd to hear reggae music emanating from this historic building, but once you enter Saffron's, beckoned by the savory scents of jerk chicken, curried goat, conch fritters, and roasted pork, you'll think you're somewhere floating in the Caribbean and immediately thirst for an ice-cold Red Stripe and an encore of your favorite Bob Marley tune. Don't expect much in the way of decor—Saffron's looks like it could have been a Denny's—but when it comes to food and entertainment, Denny's has nothing on this place.

1700 Park St. N. (C) 727/345-6400. Reservations recommended. Main courses $13–$32. MC, V. Mon–Thurs 11am–9pm; Fri 11am–9:30pm ; Sat 4–9:30pm; late-night menu Fri–Sat 9:30pm–1:30am; Sun brunch 10:30am–4pm.

MODERATE

Bonefish Grill 🍴 SEAFOOD   Although this noisy seafood spot has become part of the Outback Steakhouse family, it hardly resembles a chain, with its fresh-fish dishes served in massive portions, not to mention a very happening martini bar. Swordfish with spinach and feta cheese is a favorite, but feel free to mix and match from five choices of fish and three sauces. The rock shrimp appetizer is delicious—South Beach's swank sushi spot to the stars, Nobu, has the same dish for about five times the price. Because of this, expect long lines.

5901 4th St. N. (C) 727/521-3434. Main courses $13–$18. AE, MC, V. Mon–Thurs 4–10:30pm; Fri–Sat 4–11:30pm; Sun 4–10pm.

Mattison's AMERICAN   Chef Paul Mattison's cozy bistro near the bay is a hit with travelers as well as locals, thanks to a menu brimming with seafood (crab-stuffed salmon, grouper piccata, and basil-pesto-crusted Idaho trout) and red meat (veal medallions with prosciutto and Parmesan butter, grilled rib-eye with roasted onions and cabernet sauce, and rack of lamb with rosemary paste and stewed veggies). A small vegetarian menu includes a grilled portobello stack with Brie and roasted tomatoes, and penne pasta tossed with spinach, shiitake mushrooms, veggies, and tomatoes.

111 2nd Ave. NE (between Beach Dr. and 1st St. in the Plaza Tower in the Republic Bank building). (C) 727/895-2200. www.mattisons.com. Reservations recommended. Main courses $10–$29. AE, DC, DISC, MC, V. Mon–Thurs 11am–10pm; Fri–Sat 11am–11pm.

INEXPENSIVE

Fourth Street Shrimp Store *Value* SEAFOOD   If you're anywhere in the area, at least drive by to see the colorful, cartoonlike mural on the outside of this eclectic and casual establishment just north of downtown. On first impression, it looks like graffiti, but it's actually a gigantic drawing of people eating. Inside it gets even better, with paraphernalia and murals on two walls that make the main dining room seem like a warehouse with windows that look onto an early-19th-century seaport (one painted sailor permanently peers in to see what you're eating). You'll pass a seafood market counter when you enter, from which comes the fresh namesake shrimp, the star here. You can also pick from grouper, clam strips, catfish, or oysters fried, broiled, or steamed, all served in heaping portions. This is the best and certainly the most interesting bargain in town. There's limited outdoor seating.

1006 4th St. N. (at 10th Ave. N.). (C) 727/822-0325. Main courses $5–$14; sandwiches $2.50–$7. MC, V. Daily 11am–9pm.

The Moon Under Water ASIAN/MIDDLE EASTERN/ AMERICAN   Tables on the veranda or sidewalk in front of this pub are a great place to take a break during your downtown stroll. The British Raj rules supreme inside the dark-paneled dining room with its slowly twirling ceiling fans and colonial artifacts, including obligatory pith helmets. Your taste buds are in for a treat here. The bill of fare covers a number of former British outposts, including America (burgers and Philly cheesesteaks), but the emphasis is on mild, medium, or blazing-hot Indian curries—with a recommended Irish, British, or Australian beer to slake the resulting thirst. For lighter fare, consider Mideastern tabbouleh. There's live music on weekends.

332 Beach Dr. NE (between 3rd and 4th aves.). (C) 727/896-6160. Main courses $7.50–$17; sandwiches and salads $6–$8. AE, DC, DISC, MC, V. Sun–Thurs 11:30am–11pm; Fri–Sat 11:30am–midnight. Closed New Year's Day, Thanksgiving, and Christmas.

Ovo Cafè INTERNATIONAL   This cafe, popular with the business set by day and the club crowd on weekend nights, features a mélange of sophisticated offerings. Pirogies and pasta pillows come with taste-tempting sauces and fillings, and there are several creative salads and unusual individual-size pizzas as well. Strawberries or blackberries and a splash of liqueur cover the thick waffles. Portions are substantial, but be careful of the strictly a la carte pricing here. The big bar dispenses a wide variety of martinis, plus some unusual liqueur drinks.

515 Central Ave. (C) 727/895-5515. Reservations strongly recommended Fri–Sat. Main courses $10–$15; sandwiches $7–$8.50; pizza $8.50–$10. AE, DC, DISC, MC, V. Mon–Tues 11am–3pm; Wed–Thurs 11am–10pm; Fri–Sat 11am–1am.

Skyway Jack's BREAKFAST   This is the restaurant that Cracker Barrel aspires to be, a down-home country kitchen with kitsch *and* outstanding breakfast fare. Start the day off with eggs Florentine, stuffed French toast, even sweetbreads and eggs; or go old school with eggs, grits, hash browns, and biscuits 'n' gravy. For early risers or late-night partiers, Skyway Jack's greases its griddle starting at 5am.

2795 34th St. S. © 727/867-1907. Main dishes $2.75–$6.50. No credit cards (but there's an ATM on the premises). Daily 5am–3pm.

ST. PETERSBURG AFTER DARK

Good sources of nightlife information are the Thursday "Weekend" section of the *St. Petersburg Times* (www.sptimes.com), the "BayLife" and "Friday Extra" sections of the *Tampa Tribune* (www.tampatrib.com), and the *Weekly Planet* (www.weeklyplanet. com), a tabloid available at visitor centers and in many hotel and restaurant lobbies.

The heart of downtown's nighttime scene is **BayWalk** (© 727/895-9277; www.st pete.org/baywalk.htm), the shopping-dining-entertainment complex bordered by 1st and 2nd streets and 2nd and 3rd avenues North. Its 20-screen cinema and several restaurants and bars will keep you busy.

THE BAR, CLUB & MUSIC SCENE   Ever since St. Pete started upping its hipster quotient, cool bars began appearing as quickly as Madonna changes her accent. Among them are **A Taste for Wine,** 241 Central Ave. (© 727/895-1623), an upscale spot with polished woods and a granite bar offering terrific by-the-glass vintages, appetizers, and a gorgeous outdoor balcony; the **Haymarket Pub,** 8308 4th St. N. (© 727/577-9621), the gay-friendly "Cheers" of St. Pete, where audible conversation and reasonably priced drinks aren't implausible demands; **Janus Landing,** 200 1st Ave. N. (© 727/896-1244), a fantastic outdoor concert venue and bar where mostly alternative and rock bands perform; **Ringside Cafe,** 2742 4th St. N. (© 727/894-8465), a laid-back jazz and blues bar; and **Martini Bar,** 131 2nd Ave. N. (© 727/895-8558), where a crowd that looks as if it stepped off the set of *Sex and the City* or *Friends* convenes for serious seeing and being seen.

A historic attraction, the Moorish-style **Coliseum Ballroom,** 535 4th Ave. N. (© 727/892-5202; www.stpete.org/coliseum.htm), has been hosting dancing, big bands, boxing, and other events since 1924 (it even made an appearance in the 1985 movie *Cocoon*). Come out and watch the town's many seniors jitterbug just like it was 1945 again! Call for schedule and prices.

THE PERFORMING ARTS   The **Bayfront Center,** 400 1st St. S. (© 727/892-5767, or 727/892-5700 for information), houses the 8,100-seat Bayfront Arena (www.stpete.org/bayfront.htm) and the 2,000-seat Mahaffey Theater (www.stpete. org/mahaffey.htm). The schedule includes a variety of concerts, Broadway shows, big bands, ice shows, and circus performances. **Ticketmaster** (© 813/287-8844) sells tickets to most events and shows.

Tropicana Field, 1 Stadium Dr. (© 727/825-3100; www.stpete.org/dome.htm), has a capacity of 50,000, but it also hosts a variety of smaller events when the Devil Rays aren't playing baseball.

3 St. Pete & Clearwater Beaches ★★★

If you're looking for sun and sand, you'll find plenty of both on the 28 miles of slim barrier islands that skirt the Gulf shore of the Pinellas Peninsula. With some one million visitors coming here every year, don't be surprised if you have lots of company. But you'll also discover quieter neighborhoods and some of the nation's finest beaches, among them ones protected from development by parks and nature preserves.

At the southern end of the strip, St. Pete Beach is the granddaddy of the area's resorts: Visitors started coming here a century ago, and they haven't quit. Today St. Pete Beach is heavily developed and often overcrowded during the winter season.

St. Pete & Clearwater Beaches

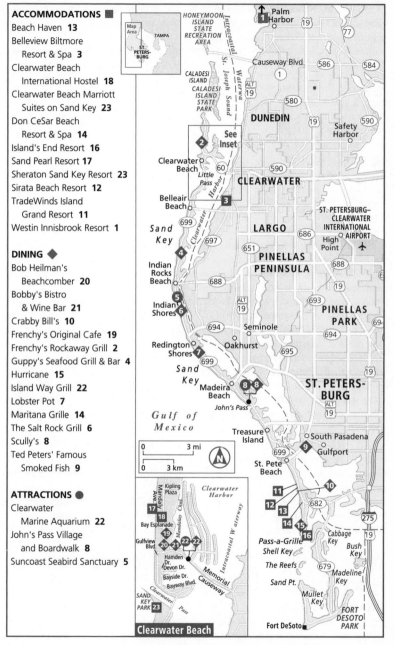

ACCOMMODATIONS ■

Beach Haven **13**
Belleview Biltmore
  Resort & Spa **3**
Clearwater Beach
  International Hostel **18**
Clearwater Beach Marriott
  Suites on Sand Key **23**
Don CeSar Beach
  Resort & Spa **14**
Island's End Resort **16**
Sand Pearl Resort **17**
Sheraton Sand Key Resort **23**
Sirata Beach Resort **12**
TradeWinds Island
  Grand Resort **11**
Westin Innisbrook Resort **1**

DINING ◆

Bob Heilman's
  Beachcomber **20**
Bobby's Bistro
  & Wine Bar **21**
Crabby Bill's **10**
Frenchy's Original Cafe **19**
Frenchy's Rockaway Grill **2**
Guppy's Seafood Grill & Bar **4**
Hurricane **15**
Island Way Grill **22**
Lobster Pot **7**
Maritana Grille **14**
The Salt Rock Grill **6**
Scully's **8**
Ted Peters' Famous
  Smoked Fish **9**

ATTRACTIONS ●

Clearwater
  Marine Aquarium **22**
John's Pass Village
  and Boardwalk **8**
Suncoast Seabird Sanctuary **5**

429

If you like high-rises and mile-a-minute action, St. Pete Beach is for you. But even here, Pass-a-Grille, on the island's southern end, is a quiet residential enclave with eclectic shops and a fine, though crowded, public beach.

A more gentle lifestyle begins just to the north on the 3½-mile-long Treasure Island. From here, you cross famous John's Pass to Sand Key, a 12-mile-long island occupied primarily by residential Madeira Beach, Redington Shores, Indian Shores, Indian Rocks Beach, and Belleair Beach. Finally, the road crosses a soaring bridge to Clearwater Beach, whose silky sands attract active families and couples.

If you like your great outdoors unfettered by development, the jewels here are Fort Desoto Park, south of St. Pete Beach at the mouth of Tampa Bay, and Caladesi Island State Park, north of Clearwater Beach. They are consistently rated among America's top beaches. Sand Key Park, on the southern shores of Little Pass (which separates Clearwater Beach from Belleair Beach), is one of Florida's finest local beach parks.

ESSENTIALS

GETTING THERE   See "Getting There" in section 1 (p. 394) for information on getting to the beaches.

VISITOR INFORMATION   See "Visitor Information" in section 2 (p. 394) for the St. Petersburg/Clearwater Area Convention & Visitors Bureau and the St. Petersburg Area Chamber of Commerce. The visitors bureau's website, at www.floridasbeach. com, has information specific to the beaches.

Once you're here, you can get beach information at the **Gulf Beaches of Tampa Bay Chamber of Commerce,** 6990 Gulf Blvd. (at 70th Ave.), St. Pete Beach (© 800/ 944-1847 or 727/360-6957; fax 727/360-2233; www.gulfbeaches-tampabay.com). It's open Monday through Friday from 9am to 5pm.

For advance information on Clearwater Beach, contact the **Clearwater Regional Chamber of Commerce,** 1130 Cleveland St., Clearwater, FL 33755 (© 727/461-0011; fax 727/449-2889; www.clearwaterflorida.org). You can also walk into the **Clearwater Visitor Information Center,** on Causeway Boulevard in the lobby of the Clearwater Beach Marina Building (© 727/462-6531). It's open Monday through Saturday from 9am to 5pm, Sunday from 1 to 5pm.

GETTING AROUND   The **Pinellas Suncoast Transit Authority/PSTA** (© 727/ 530-9911) operates motorized trolley service along Gulf Boulevard (Fla. 699) between the Hurricane restaurant (p. 394) in St. Pete Beach and the Sheraton Sand Key Resort (the one-way trip takes about an hour), where it connects with the **Jolly Trolley** (© 727/445-1200), which continues on Gulf Boulevard through Clearwater Beach. The PSTA trolley runs daily, every 20 minutes from 5am to 10pm, until midnight on Friday and Saturday. Rides cost $1.25, or you can buy a daily pass for $3. One-ride fares on the Jolly Trolley are 50¢ per person, 25¢ for seniors. Call for schedules, or pick up printed copies at the Gulf Beaches of Tampa Bay Chamber of Commerce.

Along the beach, the major cab company is **BATS Taxi** (© 727/367-3702). Fares are $2 at flag fall, plus 20¢ for each ½ mile.

HITTING THE BEACH

This entire stretch of coast is one long beach, but since hotels, condominiums, and private homes occupy much of it, you may want to sun and swim at one of the area's public parks. The very best are described below, but there's also the fine **Pass-a-Grille Public Beach,** on the southern end of St. Pete Beach, where you can watch the boats going in and out of Pass-a-Grille Channel and quench your thirst at the Hurricane restaurant (p. 439). This and all other Pinellas County public beaches have metered parking lots, so bring a supply of quarters. There are public restrooms along the beach.

Sand Key Park ✪, on the northern tip of Sand Key facing Clearwater Beach, sports a wide beach and gentle surf, and is relatively off the beaten path in this commercial area. It's a great place to go for a morning walk or jog. The park is open from 8am to dark and has restrooms. Admission is free, but the parking lot has meters. For more information, call ℂ **727/464-3347.**

Clearwater Public Beach (also known as Pier 60) has beach volleyball, watersports rentals, lifeguards, restrooms, showers, and concessions. The swimming is excellent, and there's a fishing pier with a bait-and-tackle shop, plus a children's playground. Gated municipal parking lots here cost $1 per hour or $7 a day. The lots are right across the street from the Clearwater Beach Marina, a prime base for boating, cruises, and other water activities (see "Outdoor Activities," below). A somewhat less crowded spot in Clearwater Beach is at the Gulf end of Bay Esplanade.

CALADESI ISLAND STATE PARK ✪✪✪

Occupying a 3½-mile-long island north of Clearwater Beach, **Caladesi Island State Park** boasts one of Florida's top beaches—a lovely, relatively secluded stretch with fine, soft sand edged in sea grass and palmettos. Dolphins often cavort in the waters offshore. In the park itself is a nature trail where you might see rattlesnakes, raccoons, armadillos, or rabbits. A concession stand, a ranger station, and bathhouses (with restrooms and showers) are available. Caladesi Island is accessible only by ferry from **Honeymoon Island State Recreation Area,** which is connected by Causeway Boulevard (Fla. 586) to Dunedin, north of Clearwater.

You'll first have to pay the admission to Honeymoon Island: $5 per vehicle with two to eight occupants, $2 per single-occupant vehicle, $1 for pedestrian or bicyclist. Beginning daily at 10am, the ferry (ℂ **727/734-5263**) departs Honeymoon Island every hour. Round-trip rides cost $8 for adults, $4.50 for kids.

Neither Caladesi nor Honeymoon allows camping, but pets are permitted in the inland and on South Beach (bring a leash and use it at all times). The two parks are open daily from 8am to sunset and are administered by Gulf Islands Geopark, 1 Causeway Blvd., Dunedin, FL 34698 (ℂ **727/469-5918;** www.floridastateparks.org/caladesiisland and www.floridastateparks.org/honeymoonisland).

FORT DESOTO PARK ✪✪

South of St. Pete Beach at the very mouth of Tampa Bay, **Fort DeSoto Park** encompasses all of Mullet Key, set aside by Pinellas County as a 900-acre bird, animal, and plant sanctuary. Besides the stunning white-sugar sand, it is best known for a Spanish-American War–era fort, which has a museum that's open daily from 9am to 4pm. Other diversions include fishing from piers, large playgrounds for kids, and 4 miles of trails winding through the park for in-line skaters, bicyclists, and joggers. Park rangers conduct nature and history tours, and you can rent canoes and kayaks to explore the winding mangrove channels along the island's bay side. The park has changing rooms and restrooms as well.

Sitting by itself on a heavily forested island, the park's **campground** ✪✪ is one of Florida's most picturesque (many sites are beside the bay). It's such great camping that the 233 tent and RV sites usually are sold out, especially on weekends, so it's best to reserve well in advance. But there are a few catches: You must appear in person no more than 30 days in advance at the campground office, at 631 Chestnut St. in Clearwater, or at 150 5th St. N. in downtown St. Petersburg. You must pay when you make your reservation, in cash or by traveler's check (no credit cards or personal checks). And you must reserve for at least 2 nights, but you can stay no more than 14 nights in any 30-day period. Sites cost $33 a night January through July, $28 a night the rest of the year. All sites have water and electricity hookups.

Entry to the park is free. It's open daily from 8am to dusk, although campers and persons fishing from the piers can stay later. To get here, take the Pinellas Byway (50¢ toll) east from St. Pete Beach and follow Florida 679 (35¢ toll) and the signs south to the park. For more information, contact the park at 3500 Pinellas Byway, Tierra Verde, FL 33715 (© **727/582-2267;** www.fortdesoto.com).

OUTDOOR ACTIVITIES

BOATING, FISHING & OTHER WATERSPORTS   You can indulge in parasailing, boating, deep-sea fishing, wave running, sightseeing, dolphin watching, waterskiing, and just about any other waterborne diversion your heart could desire in the St. Pete and Clearwater Beaches area. All you have to do is head to one of two beach locations: **Hubbard's Marina,** at John's Pass Village and Boardwalk (© **800/755-0677** or 727/393-1947; www.hubbardsmarina.com), in Madeira Beach on the southern tip of Sand Key; or **Clearwater Beach Marina,** at Coronado Drive and Causeway Boulevard (© **800/772-4479** or 727/461-3133), which is at the beach end of the causeway leading to downtown Clearwater. Agents in booths there will give you the schedules and prices (expect to pay $35–$45 for a half-day of fishing on a large party boat, $65–$70 for a full day), answer any questions you have, and make reservations, if necessary.

CRUISES   The top nature cruise here is the **Sea Life Safari** *ππ* (© **888/239-9414** or 727/441-1790; www.cmaquarium.org), operated by the Clearwater Marine Aquarium (p. 433). These 2½-hour safaris are available at 11am, 1:30pm, and 4pm, and are more like field trips than pleasure cruises. Aquarium biologists go along to explain what they pull up in trawl nets (don't worry—they throw it all back). You'll also see birds and other wildlife on a visit to a bird sanctuary. Dolphin sightings are likely, too. The cruises are well worth the $19 for adults, $12 for kids 3 to 12. You can combine the cruise with aquarium admission and save $3. Call for the schedule and to reserve. Ask about sunset nature cruises from mid-April to mid-October.

Hubbard's Sea Adventures, based at John's Pass Village and Boardwalk in Madeira Beach (© **800/755-0677** or 727/393-1947; www.hubbardsmarina.com), offers a 2-hour dolphin-watching and sightseeing cruise. It costs $12 for adults, $6 for kids 11 and under. There's also a 3-hour shelling tour ($20 for adults, $10 for kids), but the best outings are cruises to fascinating **Egmont Key State Park** *π*, on historic Egmont Key at the mouth of Tampa Bay (www.floridastateparks.org/egmontkey). This uninhabited island is the site of a lighthouse, of now-crumbling Fort Dade (built in 1900 during the Spanish-American War), and of endangered gopher tortoises. Sea turtles come ashore here to nest. You can go snorkeling and shelling, so bring your swimsuit (snorkel gear is available). The half-day cruises leave from St. Pete Beach Tuesday through Sunday and cost $15 for adults, $7.50 for children.

Another popular cruise destination is lovely **Shell Key,** one of Florida's last completely undeveloped barrier islands. Shell Key is great for bird-watchers, who can try to spot a remarkable 88 different species, including some of North America's rarest shorebirds. Hubbard's Shell Key beachcombing trips usually depart at 9am Monday through Saturday, at a cost of $20 for adults and $10 for kids 12 and under. You can rent beach chairs, umbrellas, snorkeling gear, and other equipment once you get there. Call to confirm the schedule and make reservations, which are recommended.

You can also get there on the **Shell Key Shuttle,** Merry Pier, on Pass-a-Grille Way at the eastern end of 8th Avenue in southern St. Pete Beach (© **727/360-1348;** www. shellkeyshuttle.com). Boats leave daily at 10am, noon, and 2pm. Prices are $16 for adults, $8 for children 12 and under. The ride takes 15 minutes, and you can return on any shuttle you wish.

The most unusual outings here are with **Captain Memo's Pirate Cruise,** at Clearwater Beach Marina (© 727/446-2587; www.captmemo.com). It sails the *Pirate's Ransom,* a reproduction of a pirate ship with a pirate crew, on 2-hour daytime cruises, as well as sunset and evening champagne cruises ($30–$32 adults, $25 seniors and children 13–17, $20 kids under 13).

Two paddle-wheel riverboats also operate here: The *Show Queen* offers lunch, sunset-dinner, and Sunday-brunch cruises from Clearwater Beach Marina (© **800/772-4479** or 727/461-3113; www.showqueen.com); while the *Starlite Princess* does likewise from 3400 Pasadena Ave. S. (© **800/444-4814** or 727/462-2628; www.starlite cruises.com), at the eastern side of the Corey Causeway linking St. Pete Beach to the mainland. Call for prices, schedules, and reservations.

SCUBA DIVING   You can dive on reefs and wrecks with **Dive Clearwater** (© **800/875-3483** or 727/443-6731; www.diveclearwater.com), which also operates the liveaboard boat *Plunger V.* Call for schedule and prices.

ATTRACTIONS ON LAND

Clearwater Marine Aquarium && *Kids*   This little jewel of an aquarium on Clearwater Harbor is very low key and friendly; it's dedicated to the rescue and rehabilitation of marine mammals and sea turtles. Exhibits include otters, sea turtles, sharks, stingrays, mangroves, and sea grass.

249 Windward Passage, Clearwater Beach. © 888/239-9414 or 727/441-1790. www.cmaquarium.org. Admission $9 adults, $6.50 children 3–11, free for children 2 and under. Mon–Fri 9am–5pm; Sat 9am–4pm; Sun 11am–4pm. The aquarium is off the causeway between Clearwater and Clearwater Beach; follow the signs.

John's Pass Village and Boardwalk   Casual and charming, albeit too touristy, this Old Florida, turn-of-the-last-century fishing village on John's Pass consists of a string of simple wooden structures topped by tin roofs and connected by a 1,000-foot boardwalk. Most buildings have been converted into shops, art galleries, restaurants, and saloons. The focal points are the boardwalk and marina, where many watersports are available for visitors (see "Outdoor Activities," above). If you don't go out on the water, this is a great place to enjoy an alfresco lunch—**Scully's** (© **727/393-7749**) is the best restaurant here—and watch the boats go in and out of the pass.

12901 Gulf Blvd. (at John's Pass), Madeira Beach. © **800/944-1847** or 727/394-0756. www.johnspass.com. Free admission. Shops and activities daily 9am–6pm or later.

Suncoast Seabird Sanctuary &   At any one time, there are usually more than 500 sea and land birds living at this sanctuary, from cormorants, white herons, and birds of prey to the ubiquitous brown pelican. The nation's largest wild-bird hospital, dedicated to the rescue, repair, recuperation, and release of sick and injured wild birds, is also here.

18328 Gulf Blvd., Indian Shores. © **727/391-6211**. www.seabirdsanctuary.org. Free admission; donations welcome. Daily 9am–sunset. Free tours Wed and Sun 2pm.

SHOPPING

John's Pass Village and Boardwalk, on John's Pass in Madeira Beach (see "Attractions on Land," above), has an unremarkable collection of beach souvenir shops, but the atmosphere makes it worth a stroll. The pick of the lot is the **Bronze Lady** (© 727/ 398-5994; www.bronzelady2000.com), featuring a collection of works by the late comedian/artist Red Skelton, best known for his numerous clown paintings. The shops are open daily from 9am to 6pm or later.

If you're in the market for one-of-a-kind jewelry, try **Evander Preston Contemporary Jewelry,** 106 8th Ave., Pass-a-Grille (© 727/367-7894), a gallery/workshop housed in a 75-year-old building in Pass-a-Grille's block-long 8th Avenue business district. Open Monday through Saturday from 10am to 5:30pm. There's a branch at TradeWinds Island Grand Resort (see "Where to Stay," below), too.

Among the shops in St. Pete Beach's Corey Landings Area, the town's original business strip along 75th Street east of Gulf Boulevard, **The Shell Store** (© 727/360-0586) specializes in corals and shells, with an on-premises mini-museum illustrating how they live and grow. There's a good selection of shell home decorations, hobbyist supplies, art, planters, and jewelry. The store is open Monday through Saturday from 9:30am to 5pm.

WHERE TO STAY

St. Pete Beach and Clearwater Beach have national chain hotels and motels of every name and description. You can also use the St. Petersburg/Clearwater Convention & Visitors Bureau's free **reservations service** (© 800/345-6710) to book rooms at most of them. The **St. Petersburg Area Chamber of Commerce** (p. 418) lists a wide range of hotels, motels, condominiums, and other accommodations in its annual visitor guide, and also publishes a brochure listing members of its Superior Small Lodgings program.

As is the case throughout Florida, there are more short- and long-term rental condominiums here than there are hotel rooms. Many of them are in high-rise buildings right on the beach. Among local rental agents, **JC Resort Management,** 17200 Gulf Blvd., North Redington Beach, FL 33708 (© 800/535-7776 or 727/397-0441; fax 727/397-8894; www.jcresort.com), has many from which to choose.

To many people's dismay, the longtime beachfront favorite **Clearwater Beach Hotel** was torn down in May 2005 to make way for the **Sandpearl Resort,** 470 Mandalay Ave. (© 800/572-1882 or 727/466-6785; www.sandpearl.com), a hyper luxurious 253-unit hotel with oversize oceanfront pool, luxury spa, and more. Completion is expected in February 2007.

ST. PETE BEACH
Very Expensive
Don CeSar Beach Resort A Loews Hotel ★★★ *(Kids)*   This Moorish-style "Pink Palace" was built to be a grand hotel (it's on the National Register of Historic Places), but its scheduled 1928 opening was derailed when Florida real estate went bust. The federal government used it as a rest-and-recreation center for soldiers during World War II and as an office building until 1967. Developer William Bowman, Jr., bought it in 1972 and restored it to its intended Gatsby-esque glory. Today it appeals to a wide range of clientele, from groups to families, from honeymooning couples to locals taking treatments in the full-service spa. Sitting majestically on 7½ acres of beachfront, this landmark sports a lobby of classic high windows and archways, crystal chandeliers,

marble floors, and original artwork. Some of the 275 rooms under the minarets of the original building may seem rather small by today's standards, but they do have high windows and offer views of the Gulf or Boca Ciega Bay. Some, but not all, of them have balconies. If you want more space but less charm, go for one of the resort's 70 spacious luxury condominiums in the Don CeSar Beach House, a midrise building ¾ mile to the north (there's 24-hr. complimentary transportation between the two). An excellent kids' program features supervised activities such as pizza parties, hermit-crab races, and T-shirt decorating. Most amusing, however, are the hotel's etiquette classes, instructing kids and adults on which fork to use and, most important, when and when not to use that irksome cellphone.

3400 Gulf Blvd. (at 34th Ave./Pinellas Byway), St. Pete Beach, FL 33706. © 866/728-2206 or 727/360-1881. Fax 727/367-6952. www.doncesar.com. 347 units. Winter $279–$428 double, $334–$1,731 suite; off season $209–$350 double, $269–$1,445 suite. $10 per person per day resort fee. Packages available. AE, DC, DISC, MC, V. Valet parking $10; free self-parking. **Amenities:** 4 restaurants; 3 bars; 2 heated outdoor pools; exercise room; spa; Jacuzzi; watersports equipment rental; children's programs; game room; concierge; business center; shopping arcade; salon; 24-hr. room service; massage; babysitting; laundry service; coin-op washers and dryers. *In room:* A/C, TV, dataport, minibar, hair dryer, iron.

Expensive

Sirata Beach Resort ⚐ A ton of money was spent a few years ago to completely renovate this older property and bring it up to second-tier status, on a par with its former sister hotel, the TradeWinds Island Grand Resort, but well below that of Don CeSar Beach Resort & Spa. A yellow-and-green Old Florida–style facade now disguises the eight-story main building, which houses hotel rooms and one-bedroom suites upstairs (upper-level units have nice views), and a convention center. Some guest rooms in this two-story building face the courtyard, but the choice quarters are the Gulf-side rooms, the only units with patios or balconies opening directly onto the beach. The most spacious units are efficiencies and one-bedroom suites in two-story buildings; they all have kitchenettes, but they look out primarily on parking lots.

5300 Gulf Blvd. (at 53rd Ave.), St. Pete Beach, FL 33706. © 800/360-4016 or 727/363-2212. Fax 727/363-2222. www.sirata.com. 380 units, including 170 suites. Winter $180–$385 double; off season $159–$327 double. Amenities fee of $12 per day per unit covers most activities. AE, DC, DISC, MC, V. **Amenities:** 2 restaurants; 2 bars; 3 heated outdoor pools; exercise room; Jacuzzi; watersports equipment rental; game room; concierge; business center; limited room service; babysitting; laundry service; coin-op washers and dryers. *In room:* A/C, TV, dataport, kitchen, fridge, coffeemaker, hair dryer, iron.

TradeWinds Island Grand Resort ⚐ *Kids* Don't be dismayed by the outward appearance of this six- and seven-story concrete-and-steel monstrosity, for underneath and beside it runs a maze of brick walkways, patios, and lily ponds connected by ¼ mile of streams. Many of the guest units, which look out on the Gulf or the 18 acres of grounds, have up-to-date kitchens or kitchenettes, and most have private balconies. Choice units directly face the Gulf, but this hotel has a great variety of accommodations, so consult the reservations clerk when booking. Although the resort draws large meetings and conventions, it's a big hit with families, too, especially Europeans, all of whom appreciate the children's program, ice-cream parlor, Pizza Hut outlet, and summer packages. One of the four heated pools is reserved for adults, and there's lots more to keep grown-ups busy, such as a unique beachside bar floating on one of the lily ponds, and the live entertainment nightly in one of the pubs.

5500 Gulf Blvd. (at 55th Ave.), St. Pete Beach, FL 33706. © 800/360-4016 or 727/363-2212. Fax 727/363-2222. www.justletgo.com. 585 units. Winter $219–$385 double; off season $189–$326 double. Resort amenities fee of $12 per day per unit covers most activities. Packages available summer and fall. AE, DC, DISC, MC, V. Valet parking $6;

free self-parking. **Amenities:** 4 restaurants; 4 bars; 4 heated outdoor pools; 4 tennis courts; health club; Jacuzzi; sauna; watersports equipment rental; children's programs; concierge; car-rental desk; business center; salon; limited room service; massage; babysitting; laundry service; coin-op washers and dryers. *In room:* A/C, TV, dataport, kitchen, fridge, microwave, coffeemaker, hair dryer, iron.

Moderate
Island's End Resort ΚΚΚ *Value*   A wonderful respite from the crowds, and a great bargain, to boot, this little all-cottage hideaway sits right on the southern tip of St. Pete Beach, smack-dab on Pass-a-Grille, where the Gulf of Mexico meets Tampa Bay. And since the island curves sharply here, nothing will block your view of the emerald bay. Strong currents run through the pass, but you can safely swim in the Gulf or grab a brilliant sunset at the Pass-a-Grille's public beach, just one door removed. Linked to one another by boardwalks, the comfortable one- and three-bedroom cottages have dining areas, living rooms, VCRs, and fully equipped kitchens. You will love the one monstrous unit with two living rooms (one can be converted to sleeping quarters), two bathrooms (one with a whirlpool tub and separate shower), and private bayside swimming pool. Maid service is available on request.

1 Pass-a-Grille Way (at 1st Ave.), St. Pete Beach, FL 33706. ℂ 727/360-5023. Fax 727/367-7890. www.islandsend. com. 6 units. Winter $155–$280 cottage; off season $125–$280 cottage. Weekly rates available. Complimentary breakfast served Tues, Thurs, and Sat. MC, V. **Amenities:** Coin-op washers and dryers. *In room:* A/C, TV/DVD, Internet access, kitchen, coffeemaker, hair dryer, iron.

Inexpensive
Beach Haven   Nestled on the beach between two high-rise condominiums, these low-slung, pink-with-white-trim structures look from the outside like the early 1950s motel they once were. But Jone and Millard Gamble, who used to own this motel and still have the charming Island's End Resort (see above), replaced the innards and installed bright tile floors, vertical blinds, pastel tropical furniture, and many modern amenities, including VCRs and refrigerators. Five of the original quarters remain motel rooms (with shower-only bathrooms), but the others are linked to make 12 one-bedroom units and 1 two-bedroom unit, all with kitchens. The top choice is the one-bedroom suite with sliding-glass doors opening onto a tiled patio beside an outdoor heated pool. There's also a sunning deck with lounge furniture by the beach. The 1950s rooms are smallish, but every unit is bright, airy, and comfortable.

4980 Gulf Blvd. (at 50th Ave.), St. Pete Beach, FL 33706. ℂ 727/367-8642. Fax 727/360-8202. www.beachhaven villas.com. 18 units. Winter $80–$150 double; off season $68–$122 double. AE, DISC, MC, V. **Amenities:** Heated outdoor pool; coin-op washers and dryers; concierge-level rooms. *In room:* A/C, TV, dataport, kitchen, coffeemaker, hair dryer, iron.

CLEARWATER BEACH
Moderate
Clearwater Beach Marriott Suites on Sand Key   You'll see the beauty of Sand Key Island from the suites in this boomerang-shape, 10-story, all-suite hotel located across the boulevard from the Sheraton Sand Key Resort (see below). Although the resort sits on the bay and not the Gulf, it has a large swimming-pool complex next to the water, and the beach and beautiful Sand Key Park are just a short walk or trolley ride away. The resort has a good children's program, and the whole family will enjoy exploring the adjacent boardwalk's 25 shops and restaurants, including a branch of Ybor City's excellent Columbia (p. 414). Each suite has a bedroom with a balcony offering water views, as well as a living room with sofa bed, wet bar, and entertainment

unit. The gorgeous heated pool with cascading waterfalls is reminiscent of an exotic resort in Mexico, Hawaii, or even Las Vegas.

1201 Gulf Blvd., Clearwater Beach, FL 33767. © **800/228-9290** or 727/596-1100. Fax 727/595-4292. www.clear waterbeachmarriottsuites.com. 220 units. Winter $199–$249 suite; off season $189–$239 suite. Packages available. AE, DC, DISC, MC, V. **Amenities:** 2 restaurants; 2 bars; heated outdoor pool; golf course; exercise room; Jacuzzi; sauna; children's programs; game room; car-rental desk; business center; shopping arcade; limited room service; massage; babysitting; laundry service; coin-op washers and dryers. *In room:* A/C, TV, dataport, minibar, coffeemaker, hair dryer, iron.

Sheraton Sand Key Resort   Set on 10 acres next to Sand Key Park, away from the honky-tonk of Clearwater, this nine-story Spanish-look hotel is a big favorite with groups and watersports enthusiasts. It's only a 450-foot walk across the broad beach in front of the hotel to the water's edge. The moderately spacious guest rooms here all have traditional dark-wood furniture and balconies or patios with views of the Gulf or the bay. The exercise room is on the top floor, affording great workout views. For those who love a little scandal, Room 538 was the one where infamous former PTL leader Jim Baker was busted with his then-assistant Jessica Hahn.

1160 Gulf Blvd., Clearwater Beach, FL 33767. © **800/325-3535** or 727/595-1611. Fax 727/596-1117. www.sheraton sandkey.com. 390 units. Winter $165–$336 double; off season $165–$259 double. AE, DC, DISC, MC, V. **Amenities:** 2 restaurants; 2 bars; heated outdoor pool; 3 tennis courts; exercise room; Jacuzzi; sauna; watersports equipment rental; children's programs (summer only); game room; concierge; business center; 24-hr. convenience store; limited room service; babysitting; laundry service; concierge-level rooms. *In room:* A/C, TV, dataport, coffeemaker, hair dryer, iron.

Inexpensive
Barefoot Bay Resort and Marina   A small family-owned and -operated motel on the bay, Barefoot Bay offers clean, comfortable apartment-like accommodations at great prices. There are four types of rooms to choose from, including a two-bedroom apartment with full kitchen. But the best part about the place, besides its location, is its backyard pool deck, complete with tropical landscaping and heated pool. It's actually more like hanging out at a friend's house than a motel. Even better, the beach is directly across the street.

500 Mandalay Ave. (at Baymont St.), Clearwater Beach, FL 33767. © **800/292-2295** or 727/441-2425. Fax 727/449-2083. www.clearwaterbeachhotel.com. 157 units. Winter $145–$205 double; off season $125–$169 double. AE, DC, MC, V. Free valet parking. **Amenities:** Restaurant; bar; heated outdoor pool; access to nearby health club; concierge; limited room service; laundry service. *In room:* A/C, TV, kitchen (efficiencies only), fridge, coffeemaker.

TWO NEARBY GOLF RESORTS
Belleview Biltmore Resort & Spa   The Gulf Coast's oldest operating tourist hotel, this gabled clapboard structure was built in 1896 by Henry B. Plant as the Hotel Belleview to attract customers to his Orange Belt Railroad. Sited on a bluff overlooking the bay, it's the largest occupied wooden structure in the world. Today it

attracts mostly groups and serious golfers (guests play at the adjoining Belleview Country Club), but there's no denying its Victorian charm and old-fashioned ambience—once you get past the out-of-place glass-and-steel foyer added by more recent owners. Historic tours are given daily ($5 adults, $3 kids 12–17). The creaky hallways lead to several shops and a museum explaining the establishment's history. The hotel provides complimentary shuttle service to the country club and to Clearwater Beach, and features a new beach club on nearby Sand Key.

25 Belleview Blvd., Clearwater, FL 33756. © **800/237-8947** or 727/373-3000. Fax 727/441-4173 or 727/443-6361. www.belleviewbiltmore.com. 240 units. Winter $89–$139 double, $150–$302 suite; off season $93–$120 double, $141–$302 suite. AE, DC, DISC, MC, V. Valet parking $5; free self-parking. Resort is 1 mile south of downtown on Belleview Blvd., off Alt. U.S. 19. **Amenities:** Restaurant; 2 bars; heated indoor and outdoor pools; golf course; 4 clay tennis courts; health club; Jacuzzi; sauna; concierge; business center; shopping arcade; salon; limited room service; babysitting; laundry service. *In room:* A/C, TV, coffeemaker, hair dryer, iron.

The Westin Innisbrook Resort 𝒶𝒶 *Golf Digest, Golf,* and other magazines pick this as one of the country's best places to play golf (provided you also stay here, of course). Situated off U.S. 19 between Palm Harbor and Tarpon Springs, this 1,000-acre, all-condominium resort has 90 holes on championship courses that are more like the rolling links of the Carolinas than the usually flat courses found in Florida. Some golf magazines think the **Copperhead Course** 𝒶𝒶 is number one in Florida. If you want to learn, Innisbrook has the largest resort-owned and -operated golf school in North America. In addition, it boasts a tennis center with instruction. It's similar to the sports-oriented Saddlebrook Resort near Tampa (p. 411), except that the courses are more challenging here and you're much closer to the beach. A free shuttle runs around the property, and another goes to the beach three times a day. Ranging in size from suites to two-bedroom models, the quarters are privately owned condos spread all over the premises. The focal points are the golf and tennis clubhouses, all of which have restaurants and bars: This place is not for serious beachgoers.

36750 U.S. 19 N., Palm Harbor, FL 34684. © **877/752-1480** or 727/942-2000. Fax 727/942-5576. www.westin-innisbrook.com. 700 units. Winter $229–$485 suite; off season $145–$289 suite. Golf packages available. AE, DC, DISC, MC, V. **Amenities:** 7 restaurants; 7 bars; heated outdoor pools; 4 golf courses; 15 tennis courts; health club; Jacuzzis; sauna; children's programs; concierge; activities desk; car-rental desk; limited room service; massage; babysitting; laundry service; coin-op washers and dryers. *In room:* A/C, TV, dataport, kitchen, minibar, coffeemaker, hair dryer, iron.

WHERE TO DINE

The restaurants here are grouped by geographic location: St. Pete Beach, including Pass-a-Grille; Indian Rocks Beach, including Madeira Beach, Redington Beach, North Redington Beach, Redington Shores, and Indian Shores; and Clearwater Beach.

ST. PETE BEACH

Crabby Bill's *Kids* SEAFOOD   This member of a small local chain sits right on the beach in the heart of the hotel district. It has an open-air rooftop bar, as well as a large dining room enclosed by big glass windows. There are fine water views from picnic tables equipped with rolls of paper towels and buckets of Saltine crackers, the better with which to eat the blue, Alaskan, snow, and stone crabs that are the big draws here. The crustaceans fall into the moderate price category or higher, but most other main courses, such as fried fish or shrimp, are inexpensive—and they aren't overcooked or overbreaded. This is a very good place to feed the family.

5300 Gulf Blvd. (at 53rd Ave.), St. Pete Beach. © **727/360-8858.** Main courses $10–$24; market price for lobster and stone-crab claws; sandwiches $5.50–$8. AE, MC, V. Mon–Thurs 11:30am–10pm; Fri–Sat 11:30am–11pm; Sun noon–10pm.

Hurricane SEAFOOD   A longtime institution, across the street from Pass-a-Grille Public Beach, this three-level gray Victorian building with white gingerbread trim is a great place to toast the sunset, especially from the rooftop bar. It's more beach pub than restaurant, but the grouper sandwiches are excellent, and there's always fresh fish. Downstairs you can dine inside the knotty-pine-paneled dining room or on the sidewalk terrace, where bathers from across Gulf Way are welcome (there's a walk-up bar for beach libation). You must be at least 21 to go up to the Hurricane Watch rooftop bar or to join the revelry when the second level turns into Stormy's Nightclub, at 10pm Wednesday through Saturday.

807 Gulf Way (at 9th Ave.), Pass-a-Grille. ℭ **727/360-9558.** www.thehurricane.com. Main courses $15–$30; sandwiches $7–$14. AE, MC, V. Daily 8am–1am.

Maritana Grille ✿✿ SEAFOOD/FLORIBBEAN   If you're not staying at Don CeSar Resort, at least consider eating there, at this bastion of fabulous Floribbean cuisine that's known for elegant dinners of steaks and seafood, but even more so for its spectacular Sunday brunch. The dining room is adorned with 1,500 gallons of saltwater aquariums and Florida fish. A specialty that's one of the most innovative dishes I've ever had is the orange habañero barbecued Gulf fish with warm pineapple, vanilla-bean stew, glazed banana, and rum pepper paint. The chef's table is a *dégustation* that takes place in the kitchen, at a private table from which guests are able to interact directly with and observe the chef in action.

At Don CeSar Resort, 3400 Gulf Blvd. (at 9th Ave.), St. Pete Beach. ℭ **727/360-1882.** Reservations recommended. Main courses $27–$38. AE, MC, V. Sun–Thurs 5:30–10pm; Fri–Sat 5:30–11pm.

Ted Peters' Famous Smoked Fish ✿ _Value_ SEAFOOD   This open-air eatery is an institution in these parts: Ted's has been around since the '50s. Some folks bring their catches for the staff to smoke, while others figure fishing is a waste of time and come right to Ted's for mullet, mackerel, salmon, and other fish slowly cooked over red oak. Enjoy the aroma and sip a cold one while you wait for your order.

1530 Pasadena Ave. (just across St. Pete Beach Causeway), Pasadena. ℭ **727/381-7931.** Main courses $8–$18. No credit cards. Wed–Mon 11am–7:30pm.

INDIAN ROCKS BEACH AREA
Guppy's Seafood Grill & Bar ✿✿ SEAFOOD   Locals love this small bar and grill across from Indian Rocks Public Beach because they know they'll always get terrific chow (it's associated with the excellent Lobster Pot; see below). You won't forget the salmon coated with potatoes and lightly fried, then baked with a creamy leek-and-garlic sauce; it's fattening, yes, but also a bargain, at $10. Another good choice is the lightly cooked tuna with a peppercorn sauce. The atmosphere is casual beach-friendly, with a fun bar in the middle of it all. Try the upside-down apple-walnut pie topped with ice cream. You can dine outside on a patio beside the main road.

1701 Gulf Blvd. (at 17th Ave.), Indian Rocks Beach. ℭ **727/593-2032.** Main courses $10–$18; sandwiches $6–$7. AE, DC, DISC, MC, V. Sun–Thurs 11:30am–10:30pm; Fri–Sat 11:30am–11pm.

Lobster Pot ✿✿✿ SEAFOOD/STEAK   Step into this weathered-looking restaurant near the beach and experience some of the finest seafood in the area. The prices are high, but the variety of Maine lobster dishes is amazing. The lobster Cardinal is a blend of meat, cream, and cognac baked to succulent perfection. In addition to lobster, there's a wide selection of grouper, snapper, salmon, shrimp, scallops, crab, and steaks, most prepared with elaborate sauces. The children's menu here is definitely out of the ordinary: It features half a Maine lobster and a petite filet mignon.

17814 Gulf Blvd. (at 178th Ave.), Redington Shores. (℃) 727/391-8592. www.lobsterpotrestaurant.com. Reservations recommended. Main courses $17–$40. AE, DC, MC, V. Daily 4:30–10pm.

The Salt Rock Grill 🦀🦀 SEAFOOD/STEAK Affluent professionals and the so-called beautiful people pack this waterfront restaurant, making it *the* place to see and be seen on the beaches. The big urbane dining room is built on three levels, thus affording every table a view over the creeklike waterway out back. And in fair weather, you can dine out by the dock or slake your thirst at the lively Tiki bar (bands play Sat–Sun during the summer). Thick, aged steaks are the house specialties. Pan-seared peppered tuna and salmon cooked on a cedar board lead the seafoods. Avoid spending a fortune by showing up for the early-bird specials or by ordering the meatloaf topped with mashed potatoes and onion straws ($9), or the half-pound sirloin steak ($11).

19325 Gulf Blvd. (north of 193rd Ave.), Indian Shores. (℃) 727/593-7625. www.saltrockgrill.com. Reservations strongly advised. Main courses $8–$40 (early-bird specials $8–$10). AE, DC, DISC, MC, V. Sun–Thurs 4–10pm; Fri–Sat 4–11pm (early-bird specials daily 4–5:30pm). Tiki bar open Sat 2pm–midnight (or later); Sun 2–10pm.

CLEARWATER BEACH

Bobby's Bistro & Wine Bar 🦀 AMERICAN Son of Bob Heilman's Beachcomber (see below), this chic bistro draws a more urbane crowd than its parent. A wine-cellar theme is amply justified by the real thing: a walk-in closet with several thousand bottles kept at a constant 55°F (12°C). Walk through and pick your vintage, then listen to jazz while you dine inside at tall, bar-height tables or outside on a covered patio. The chef specializes in gourmet pizzas on homemade focaccia crust, plus charcoal-grilled lamb chops, filet mignon, fresh fish, and monstrous pork chops with caramelized Granny Smith apples and a Mount Vernon mustard sauce. Everything's served a la carte here, so watch your credit card. There's a less expensive sandwich menu featuring bronzed grouper and chicken with a spicy Jack cheese.

447 Mandalay Ave. (at Papaya St., behind Bob Heilman's Beachcomber). (℃) 727/446-9463. Reservations recommended. Main courses $8–$22; sandwiches and pizzas $6–$10. AE, DC, DISC, MC, V. Sun–Thurs 5–11pm; Fri–Sat 5pm–midnight; bar later.

Bob Heilman's Beachcomber 🦀 AMERICAN In a row of restaurants, bars, and T-shirt shops, this establishment has been popular with the locals since 1948. Each dining room here is unique: Large models of sailing crafts create a nautical theme in one, a pianist makes music in a second, works of art create a gallery in the third, and booths and a fireplace make for a cozy fourth. The menu presents a variety of well-prepared fresh seafood and beef, veal, and lamb selections. If you tire of fruits-of-the-sea, the "back to the farm" fried chicken—from an original 1910 Heilman family recipe—is incredible. The Beachcomber shares valet parking and an extensive wine collection with Bobby's Bistro & Wine Bar (see above).

447 Mandalay Ave. (at Papaya St.). (℃) 727/442-4144. Reservations recommended. Main courses $13–$29. AE, DC, DISC, MC, V. Mon–Sat 11:30am–11pm; Sun noon–10pm.

Frenchy's Original Cafe SEAFOOD Popular with locals and visitors in the know since 1981, this casual pub makes the best grouper sandwiches in the area and has all the awards to prove it. The sandwiches are fresh, thick, juicy, and delicious. The atmosphere is pure Florida casual. There can be a wait during winter and on weekends year-round. For a similarly relaxed setting, directly on the beach, **Frenchy's Rockaway**

The Sponge Capital of the World

One of Florida's most fascinating small towns and a fine day trip from Tampa, St. Petersburg, or the beaches (it's 30 miles north of St. Petersburg, 23 miles west of Tampa, and 13 miles north of Clearwater), **Tarpon Springs** calls itself the "Sponge Capital of the World." Greek immigrants from the Dodecanese Islands settled here in the late 19th century to harvest sponges, which grew in abundance offshore. By the 1930s, Tarpon Springs was producing more sponges than any other place in the world. A blight ruined the business in the 1940s, but the descendants of those early immigrants stayed on. Today they compose about a third of the population, making Tarpon Springs a center of transplanted Greek culture.

Sponges still arrive at the historic **Sponge Docks,** on Dodecanese Boulevard. With a lively, carnival-like atmosphere, the docks are a great place to spend an afternoon or early evening, poking your head into shops selling sponges and other souvenirs while Greek music comes from the dozen or so family restaurants purveying authentic Aegean cuisine. You can also venture offshore from here: Booths on the docks hawk sightseeing and fishing cruises. Make your reservations as soon as you get here; then go sightseeing ashore or grab a meal at one of the multitudinous Greek restaurants and bakeries.

You also can visit **Spongeorama** (510 Dodecanese Blvd.; no phone; daily 10am–5pm), a museum dedicated to sponges and sponge divers that sells a wide variety of sponges and shows a 30-minute video on sponge diving several times a day. Admission is free. A scuba diver feeds sharks in the **Konger Tarpon Springs Aquarium** (850 Dodecanese Blvd.; ✆ 727/938-5378; Mon–Sat 10am–5pm, Sun noon–5pm), at the western end of the boulevard. Admission is $4.75 for adults, $4 for seniors, and $2.75 for children 3 to 11.

South of the docks, the **Downtown Historic District** sports turn-of-the-last-century commercial buildings along Tarpon Avenue and Pinellas Avenue (Alt. U.S. 19). On Tarpon Avenue west of Pinellas Avenue, you'll come to the Victorian homes overlooking **Spring Bayou.** This creekside area makes for a delightfully picturesque stroll.

The **Tarpon Springs Chamber of Commerce,** 11 E. Orange St., Tarpon Springs, FL 34689 (✆ **727/937-6109;** fax 727/937-2879; www.tarponsprings. com), has an information office on Dodecanese Boulevard at the Sponge Docks; it's open Tuesday through Sunday from 10:30am to 4:30pm.

To get to Tarpon Springs from Tampa or St. Petersburg, take U.S. 19 North and turn left on Tarpon Avenue (C.R. 582). From Clearwater Beach, take Alt. U.S. 19 North through Dunedin. The center of the historic downtown district is at the intersection of Pinellas Avenue (Alt. U.S. 19) and Tarpon Avenue. To reach the Sponge Docks, go 10 blocks north on Pinellas Avenue and turn left at Pappas' Restaurant onto Dodecanese Boulevard.

Grill, at 7 Rockaway St. (© **727/446-4844**), has a wonderful outdoor setting and keeps a charcoal grill going to cook fresh fish.

41 Baymont St. © **727/446-3607.** www.frenchysonline.com. Sandwiches and burgers $5–$7.50. AE, MC, V. Mon–Thurs 11:30am–11pm; Fri–Sat 11:30am–midnight; Sun noon–11pm.

Island Way Grill ★★ SEAFOOD   Not your ordinary waterfront seafood shanty, the glass-encased and wood-enhanced sleek Island Way Grill prepares the daily catch Pan-Asian style in their open kitchen. Everything here is delicious, from the resulting fish to the sushi. The wine list is also superb. Sit out on the patio and then gravitate toward the outdoor bar, where the fabulous people—like members and owners of the Tampa Bay Buccaneers—hang out, talk shop, and scope the scene.

20 Island Way. © **727/461-6617.** Main courses $21–$30. AE, MC, V. Sun–Thurs 4–10pm; Fri–Sat 4–11pm.

THE BEACHES AFTER DARK

If you haven't already found it during your sightseeing and shopping excursions, the restored fishing community of **John's Pass Village and Boardwalk,** on Gulf Boulevard at John's Pass in Madeira Beach, has plenty of restaurants, bars, and shops to keep you occupied after the sun sets. Elsewhere, the nightlife scene at the beach revolves around rocking bars that pump out music until 2am. All of the places listed in this section are bars that feature live music.

Pass-a-Grille has the popular, always-lively lounge at **Hurricane,** on Gulf Way at 9th Avenue, opposite the public beach (p. 439). Up on the northern tip of Treasure Island, **Gators on the Pass** (© 727/367-8951) claims to have the world's longest waterfront bar, with a huge deck overlooking the waters of John's Pass. The complex also has a nonsmoking sports bar and a three-story tower with a top-level observation deck for panoramic views of the Gulf of Mexico. Live music, from acoustic to blues to rock, is featured most nights.

In Clearwater Beach, the **Palm Pavilion Grill & Bar,** on the beach at 18 Bay Esplanade (© **727/446-2742**), has live music Tuesday through Sunday nights in winter and on weekends in the off season. Nearby, **Frenchy's Rockaway Grill,** at 7 Rockaway St. (© **727/446-4844;** www.frenchysonline.com/rockaway.html), is another popular hangout.

If you're into laughs, **Coconuts Comedy Club,** at the Howard Johnson motel, Gulf Boulevard at 61st Avenue in St. Pete Beach (© 727/360-5653), has an ever-changing program of live stand-up funny men and women. Call for the schedule and prices.

For a more highbrow evening, go to the Clearwater mainland and the 2,200-seat **Ruth Eckerd Hall,** 1111 McMullen-Booth Rd. (© **727/791-7400;** www.rutheckerdhall.com), which hosts a varied program of Broadway shows, ballet, drama, symphonic works, popular music, jazz, and country music.

4 Sarasota ★★★

52 miles S of Tampa, 150 miles SW of Orlando, 225 miles NW of Miami

Far enough away from Tampa Bay to have an identity very much its own, Sarasota is, surprisingly, one of Florida's cultural centers. In fact, many retirees spend their winters here because there's so much to keep them entertained and stimulated, including the Van Wezel Performing Arts Hall and the FSU Center for the Performing Arts, home of the annual Asolo Theatre Festival. Sarasota also has an extensive array of first-class resorts, restaurants, and upscale boutiques.

Sarasota Area

TAMPA BAY

Sunshine Skyway

Tamiami Trail

679

FORT DeSoto

FORT DESOTO PARK

275

19

Gillette

683

Parrish

Edgemont Channel

EGMONT KEY STATE PARK

Southwest Channel

Terra Ceia

19

Rubonia

41

75

301

Anna Maria Island

Anna Maria

DeSoto National Memorial

Memphis

683

Ellenton

Holmes Beach

Manatee

Palmetto

70

River

Arcadia

64

Rd.

Manatee Ave.

64

BRADENTON

789

Bradenton Beach

Cortez

Samoset

684

Longbeach

Bayshore Gardens

41

Oneco

70

301

70

Sarasota Bay

Tallevast

Braden

River

Longboat Key

Whitfield Estates

Sarasota-Bradenton International Airport

University Parkway

789

Ringling Museums

301

75

41

Mote Aquarium

SARASOTA

St. Armands Key

780

Fruitville

780

Lido Key

773

GULF OF MEXICO

758

Siesta Village

Bee Ridge Road

Clark Road

72

Stickney Point

Gulf Gate

Siesta Key

789

Vamo

Osprey

FLORIDA

Tampa

Sarasota

Casey Key

41

681

Cow Pen Slough

Laurel

Nokomis

Venice

0   3 mi

0   3 km

N

Offshore, more than 40 miles of gloriously white beaches fringe a chain of long, narrow barrier islands stretching from Tampa Bay to Sarasota. To the south, **Siesta Key** is a residential enclave popular with artisans and writers, and is home to Siesta Village, this area's funky, laid-back, and often-noisy beach hangout. Shielded from the Gulf by **Lido Key,** which has a string of affordable hotels attractive to family vacationers, **St. Armands Key** sports one of Florida's ritziest shopping and dining districts, while adjacent **Longboat Key** is one of the country's swankiest islands.

ESSENTIALS

GETTING THERE You'll probably find a less-expensive airfare by flying into **Tampa International Airport** (p. 394), an hour's drive north of Sarasota, and you can save even more since Tampa's rental-car agencies usually offer some of the best deals in Florida. If you don't rent a car, **Sarasota-Tampa Express** (© **800/326-2800** or 941/727-1344) provides bus connections for $22 for adults, $11 for children 3 to 12. Call in advance for a schedule and pickup locations.

If you fly directly here, **Sarasota-Bradenton International Airport** (© 941/359-2770; www.srq-airport.com), north of downtown, off University Parkway between U.S. 41 and U.S. 301, is served by **American Trans Air** (© 800/225-2995), **Continental** (© 800/525-0280), **Delta** (© 800/221-1212), **Northwest** (© 800/225-2525), and **US Airways** (© 800/428-4322).

Alamo (© 800/327-9633), **Avis** (© 800/331-1212), **Budget** (© 800/527-0700), **Dollar** (© 800/800-4000), **Hertz** (© 800/654-3131), and **National** (© 800/227-7368) all have car-rental offices here.

Diplomat Taxi (© **941/355-5155**) has a monopoly on service from the airport to hotels in Sarasota and Bradenton. Look for the cabs outside baggage claim. Fares range from about $10 to downtown Sarasota to $35 to Longboat Key or Anna Maria Island.

Amtrak has bus connections to Sarasota from its Tampa station (© **800/872-7245;** www.amtrak.com).

VISITOR INFORMATION Contact the **Sarasota Convention and Visitors Bureau,** 655 N. Tamiami Trail (U.S. 41), Sarasota, FL 34236 (© **800/522-9799** or 941/957-1877; fax 941/951-2956; www.sarasotafl.org). The bureau and its helpful visitor center are in a blue pagoda-shape building on Tamiami Trail (U.S. 41) at 6th Street. Hours are Monday through Saturday from 9am to 5pm, Sunday from 11am to 3pm; closed holidays.

You can get a packet of advance information on Bradenton and surrounding Manatee County from the **Greater Bradenton Area Convention and Visitors Bureau,** P.O. Box 1000, Bradenton, FL 34206 (© **800/462-6283** or 941/729-9177; fax 941/729-1820; www.floridaislandbeaches.org).

If you're driving from the north via I-75, you can get off at U.S. 301 (exit 224) and head west if you want to go to the **Manatee County Tourist Information Center** (© **941/729-7040**), where volunteers are on hand to answer questions and sell excellent road maps for less than you'll pay elsewhere. It's open daily from 8:30am to 5pm except Easter Sunday, Thanksgiving, the day after Thanksgiving, and Christmas Day. The office also has an information kiosk at **Prime Outlets,** across I-75, which is open Monday through Saturday from 10am to 6pm, and Sunday from 11am to 6pm.

GETTING AROUND The **Sarasota Trolley,** operated by Sarasota County Area Transit (**SCAT;** © **941/861-1234;** www.co.sarasota.fl.us/public_works_scat/scat.asp), runs every 20 minutes from 9am to 5pm Monday through Friday, every 40 minutes on Saturday. The Scenic Loop Trolley operates from Island Park, Bayfront at Ringling Boulevard, through downtown Sarasota, north to the FSU Ringling Center for the Cultural Arts, and out to St. Armands and Lido keys (but not to Siesta or Longboat keys). The Main Street Trolley goes from Island Park through downtown and eastward along Main Street. Fares are $1 on the Scenic Loop and 25¢ on the Main Street line, or you can buy a daily pass to both lines for $2. SCAT also operates regularly scheduled bus service. The Sarasota Convention and Visitors Bureau distributes route maps (see "Visitor Information," above).

Sarasota taxi companies include **Diplomat Taxi** (© **941/355-5155**), **Green Cab Taxi** (© **941/922-6666**), and **Yellow Cab of Sarasota** (© **941/955-3341**).

HITTING THE BEACH

Many of the area's 40-plus miles of beaches are occupied by hotels and condominium complexes, but there are excellent public beaches as well. The area's most popular is **Siesta Key Public Beach,** with a picnic area, a 700-car parking lot, crowds of families, and quartz sand reminiscent of the blazingly white beaches in Northwest Florida. There's also beach access at **Siesta Village,** which has a plethora of casual restaurants and pubs with outdoor seating (see the "Where to Dine" section later). The more secluded and quiet **Turtle Beach** is at Siesta Key's south end. It has shelters, boat ramps, picnic tables, and volleyball nets. Both beaches have bathroom facilities.

Unless you're staying on Longboat Key, you won't be able to hit the beach there, since private houses and condos block access to the Gulf. However, do drive the length of Longboat Key and admire the luxury homes. Then take a right off St. Armands Circle onto Lido Key and **North Lido Beach.** The south end of the island is occupied by **South Lido Beach Park,** with plenty of shade—a good spot for picnics and walks.

OUTDOOR ACTIVITIES & SPECTATOR SPORTS

BIKING & IN-LINE SKATING   The flat terrain in this area makes for good in-line skating and for fine, though not challenging, bike riding. You can bike and skate from downtown Sarasota to Lido and Longboat keys, since paved walkways/bike paths run alongside the John Ringling Causeway and then up Longboat Key. **Siesta Sports Rentals,** 6551 Midnight Pass Rd., in the Southbridge Mall just south of Stickney Point Bridge on Siesta Key (© **941/346-1797;** www.siestasportsrentals.com), rents bikes of various sizes (including stroller attachments for kids), plus motor scooters, kayaks, and beach chairs and umbrellas. They can even arrange kayak tours, if you wish. Bike rentals range from about $14 a day to $50 a week; scooters go for $20 an hour, $55 a day, or $175 a week. The shop is open daily from 9am to 5pm.

BOAT RENTALS   **All Watersports,** in the Boatyard Shopping Village, on the mainland end of Stickney Point Bridge (© **941/921-2754**), rents personal watercraft such as jet skis, speedboats, runabouts, and bow riders. At the island end of the bridge, **C. B.'s Saltwater Outfitters,** 1249 Stickney Point Rd. (© **941/349-4400**), and **Dockside Marine,** 1265 Old Stickney Point Rd. (© **941/349-8880**), both rent runabouts, pontoon boats, and other craft. Bait and tackle are available at the marinas.

CRUISES   The area's best nature cruises depart from Mote Aquarium (see "Exploring the Area," below).

That paddle-wheeler you see going up and down the bay is the ***Seafood Shack Showboat,*** operated by the Seafood Shack restaurant, 4110 127th St. W., in Cortez (© **941/794-5048**). It has afternoon cruises to Sarasota Bay, Tampa Bay, and as far away as the Sunshine Skyway. Prices are $15 for adults, $14 for seniors, and $10 for children 4 to 10. The *Showboat* has a different destination each day, and its schedule is seasonal, so call a day ahead for information. Reservations are not accepted.

FISHING   Charter fishing boats dock at most marinas here; check out **www.sarasotaboating.com** for a list. In downtown Sarasota, the **Flying Fish Fleet,** at Marina Jack's Marina, U.S. 41 at Island Park Circle (© **941/366-3373;** www.flying fishfleet.com), offers party-boat charter-fishing excursions, with bait and tackle furnished. Prices for half-day trips are $35 for adults, $30 for seniors, and $25 for kids 4 to 12. All-day voyages cost $55, $50, and $45, respectively. Call for the schedule. Other charter boats also line up along the dock here.

GOLF   The **Bobby Jones Golf Complex** *, 1000 Circus Blvd. (© **941/365-4653**), is Sarasota's only municipal facility, but it has two 18-hole championship layouts—the American (par 71) and British (par 72) courses—and the 9-hole Gillespie executive course (par 30). Tee times are assigned 3 days in advance. Greens fees range from $25 to $35, including cart rental.

The semiprivate **Rolling Green Golf Club,** 4501 Tuttle Ave. (© **941/355-6620**), is an 18-hole, par-72 course. Facilities include a driving range, rental clubs, and lessons. Tee times are assigned 2 days in advance. Prices, including cart, are about $50 in winter and $30 off season. Also semiprivate, the **Sarasota Golf Club,** 7820 N. Leewynn Dr. (© **941/371-2431**), is an 18-hole, par-72 course. Facilities include a driving range, lessons, club rentals, a restaurant, a lounge, and a golf shop. Fees, including cart, are about $65 in winter, $45 off season.

If you have reciprocal privileges, **University Park Country Club,** west of I-75 on University Parkway (© **941/359-9999**), is Sarasota's only nationally ranked course. Fees, including cart, are about $55 year-round.

Bradenton is home to the well-known **David Leadbetter Golf Academy,** 1414 69th Ave., at U.S. 41 (© **800/872-6425** or 941/755-1000; www.leadbetter.com), a part of the Nick Bollettieri Sports Academy (see "Tennis," below). Presided over by one of golf's leading instructors, this facility offers practice tee instruction, video analysis, scoring strategy, and more.

For course information online, go to www.golf.com or www.floridagolfing.com; or call the **Florida Sports Foundation** (© **850/488-8347**) or **Florida Golfing** (© **866/833-2663**).

KAYAKING   Based at Mote Aquarium (see the "Exploring the Area" section below), **Sarasota Bay Explorers** ** (© **941/388-4200;** www.sarasotabayexplorers.com) uses a 38-foot pontoon boat to ferry novice and experienced kayakers and their craft to a marine sanctuary, where everyone paddles through tunnels formed by mangroves. The paddling is easy and the waters are shallow. Experienced naturalists serve as guides. Wear a swimsuit and tennis shoes or rubber-soled booties, and bring a towel and lunch. The 3-hour trip is $50 for adults, $40 for children 5 to 17, and free for kids under 5 (seats are provided for the youngsters). Reservations are required.

SAILING   Take a leisurely cruise on the waters of Sarasota Bay and the Gulf of Mexico aboard the 41-foot, 12-passenger *Enterprise,* docked at Marina Jack's Marina, U.S. 41 at Island Park Circle (© **888/232-7768** or 941/951-1833; www.sarasotaboating.com/sailingcharters.html). Cruises range from 3 hours for $45 per person to 4 hours for $55 a head, while 2-hour sunset excursions cost $35 each. Departure times vary, and reservations are required. **Siesta Key Sailing,** 1219 Southport Dr. (© **941/346-7245;** www.siestakeysailing.com), charges about the same for cruises in a 42-foot Morgan Outlander sloop. Call for rates and reservations.

You can also get to historic Egmont Key, 3 miles off the northern end of Anna Maria Island at the mouth of Tampa Bay (p. 432), on a 30-foot sloop-rigged sailboat with **Spice Sailing Charters** (© 941/778-3240), based at the Galati Yacht Basin on Bay Boulevard on northern Anna Maria Island. Rates start at $30 per person. The company has sunset cruises as well. Call for the schedule and reservations.

SPECTATOR SPORTS   **Ed Smith Stadium,** 2700 12th St., at Tuttle Avenue, east of downtown Sarasota (© 941/954-4464), is the winter home of the **Cincinnati Reds** (© 941/955-6501; www.cincinnatireds.com), who hold spring training here in February and March. Game tickets are $5 to $12. From April to August, the stadium is home to the **Sarasota Red Sox** (© 941/365-4460, ext. 2300; www.sarasox.com), a Class A minor-league affiliate of the Boston Red Sox. Tickets are $4 to $5.

The **Pittsburgh Pirates** (© 941/748-4610; www.pirateball.com) do their February-through-March spring training at 6,562-seat McKechnie Field, 9th Street West and 17th Avenue West, south of downtown Bradenton. Tickets are $6 to $9.

The **Sarasota Polo Club,** 8201 Polo Club Lane (© 941/907-0000), at Lakewood Ranch, a planned community midway between Sarasota and Bradenton, is the site of Sunday-afternoon polo matches from mid-December to early April. General admission is $6 for adults, free for children under 13. Call for the schedule.

TENNIS   The **Nick Bollettieri Sports Academy,** 5500 34th St. W., Bradenton (© 800/872-6425 or 941/755-1000; www.bollettieri.com), is one of the world's largest tennis training facilities, with more than 70 championship grass, clay, and hard courts, and a pro shop. It's open year-round; reservations are required for all activities.

WATERSPORTS   You'll find watersports activities in front of the major hotels on the keys (see "Where to Stay," beginning on p. 451). **Siesta Sports Rentals,** 6551 Midnight Pass Rd. on Siesta Key (© 813/346-1797; www.siestasportsrentals.com), rents kayaks and sailboats, plus beach chairs and umbrellas.

EXPLORING THE AREA
IN SARASOTA

Art Center Sarasota   In addition to the marvelous John and Mable Ringling Museum of Art (see below), Sarasota is home to more than 40 galleries and exhibition spaces, all open to the public. A convenient starting point is this downtown community art center, next to the Sarasota Convention and Visitors Bureau. It contains three galleries and a small sculpture garden, presenting the area's largest display of works by national and local artists, ranging from paintings and pottery to sculpture, cartoons, jewelry, and enamelware. There are also art demonstrations and special events.

707 N. Tamiami Trail (at 6th St.). © 941/365-2032. www.artsarasota.org. Free admission ($2 suggested donation). Tues–Sat 10am–4pm; Sun noon–4pm.

Florida Ever-Glides, Inc. 🐾🐾   Ride the future (and get some history at the same time) when you take a tour with this great company, the first in the U.S. to offer historic and scenic guided tours using Segway Human Transporters—you know, those cool electric scooter-type things you've seen on TV (and saw George W. Bush fall from). The friendly staffers here will have you up, riding, and comfortable (I swear) in a matter of minutes, with orientation, training, and as many practice runs as you need before you start off on your 2-hour 9am or 2pm tour of downtown Sarasota and the bayfront, including the vintage 1920s Towles Court Artist Colony.

200 S. Washington Blvd., no. 11 (on the corner of Adams Lane). © 941/363-9556. Fax 941/363-9557. www.florida ever-glides.com. $61 per person. AE, DISC, MC, V. Daily 8am–5pm.

FSU Ringling Center for the Cultural Arts ✮✮✮   By far the top attraction here, this 66-acre site is where showman and circus legend John Ringling and his wife, Mable, collected art and built a house on a grand scale. Now under the aegis of Florida State University, the **John and Mable Ringling Museum of Art** is the state's official art museum. It's filled with more than 500 years of European and American works, including one of the world's most important collections of 17th-century baroque paintings, collections of decorative arts, and traveling exhibits. The Old Masters collection includes five renowned tapestry cartoons by Peter Paul Rubens.

Built in 1924 and 1925 at a cost of $1.5 million and modeled after a Venetian palace, the Ringlings' spectacular 32-room palatial bayfront four-story winter residence, **Ca'd'Zan** ("House of John" in the Venetian dialect), has been recently restored. An 8,000-square-foot terrace leads down to the dock at which Mable Ringling moored her Venetian gondola. Don't miss a tour of this house to see the period furniture and stunning architecture and artwork; in fact, I'd make it the first stop on your Ringling itinerary.

The **Ringling Museum of the Circus** is devoted to circus memorabilia (which is, in a way, more fascinating than the circus itself), including parade wagons, calliopes, costumes, and colorful posters. The grounds include a classical courtyard, a rose garden, a museum shop, and the historic **Asolo Theater,** a 19th-century Italian court playhouse, which the Ringlings moved here in the 1950s. It's now the centerpiece of the Florida State University Center for the Performing Arts. You'll need most of a day to see everything here.

5401 Bay Shore Rd. at N. Tamiami Trail (U.S. 41). ℭ **941/359-5700,** or 941/351-1660 for recorded information. www.ringling.org. Admission $15 adults, $13 seniors, $5 out-of-state students, free for Florida students and children 12 and under. Daily 10am–5:30pm. Closed New Year's Day, Thanksgiving, and Christmas. From downtown, take U.S. 41 N. to University Pkwy. and follow signs to the museum.

G. Wiz (Gulfcoast Wonder & Imagination Zone)   This hands-on, state-of-the-art science center has two floors of fun exhibits that cover the physical, earth, and health sciences. The ExploraZone features rotating interactive exhibits from San Francisco's renowned Exploratorium. The 35 exhibits have themes ranging from sound and music to mathematics and motion, color and optics, sight and illusion, and more.

1001 Blvd. of the Arts (in the Blivas Science and Technology Center, 1 block west of U.S. 41). ℭ **941/9061851.** www. gwiz.org. Admission $9 adults, $6 seniors, $2 kids 2 and over; free 5–8pm the 1st Wed of the month. Tues–Sat 10am–5pm; Sun noon–5pm.

Marie Selby Botanical Gardens ✮✮   A must-see for serious plant lovers and a should-see for those looking for good photo ops, this peaceful retreat on the bay, just south of downtown, is said to be the only botanical garden in the world specializing in the preservation, study, and research of epiphytes—that is, "air plants" such as

---

⟨Tips⟩ How to See the Ringling Museums

It's best to visit the FSU Ringling Center for the Cultural Arts on a weekday, when the center offers guided tours of the art museum, house, and circus museum (included in the price of admission). For tour times, call ahead or check at the information desk as soon as you arrive. While you're waiting for the next tour, explore the gardens or have lunch at the Banyan Cafe.

orchids. It's home to more than 20,000 exotic plants, including more than 6,000 orchids, as well as a bamboo pavilion, a butterfly and hummingbird garden, a medicinal-plant garden, a waterfall garden, a cactus and succulent garden, a fernery, a hibiscus garden, a palm grove, two tropical-food gardens, and a native shore-plant community. Selby's home and the Payne Mansion (both on the National Registry) are also located here.

811 S. Palm Ave. (south of U.S. 41). ⓒ 941/366-5731. www.selby.org. Admission $12 adults, $6 children 6–11, free for children 5 and under accompanied by an adult. Daily 10am–5pm. Closed Christmas.

Sarasota Classic Car Museum In operation since 1953, this is now a nonprofit museum dedicated to preserving antique automobiles. But there's more to the place than its 90-plus classic and "muscle" autos, from Rolls-Royces and Pierce Arrows to the four cars used personally by circus czar John Ringling. Also here are more than 1,200 antique music boxes and several of Thomas Edison's early phonographs, including a 1909 diamond-tipped-needle model. Check out the Penny Arcade's antique games (with original prices), and grab a cone at the ice-cream and sandwich shop.

5500 N. Tamiami Trail (at University Pkwy.). ⓒ 941/355-6228. www.sarasotacarmuseum.org. Admission $8.50 adults, $7.65 seniors, $5.75 children 13–17, $4 children 6–12, free for children under 6. Daily 9am–6pm. Take U.S. 41 north of downtown; museum is 2 blocks west of the airport.

ON ST. ARMANDS KEY

Mote Aquarium ★★ *Kids* Kids get to touch cool stuff like a stingray (minus the stinger, of course) and watch sharks in the shark tank at this excellent aquarium. Part of the noted Mote Marine Laboratory complex, it is more broad-based than Tampa's Florida Aquarium, which concentrates primarily on local sea life. See manatees in the Marine Mammal Center, a block's walk from the aquarium, as well as many research-in-progress exhibits. Start by watching the aquarium's 12-minute film on the feeding habits of sharks; then allow at least 90 minutes to take in everything on land. Add another 2 hours for a narrated sea-life encounter cruise with the **Sarasota Bay Explorers** (ⓒ 727/388-4200; www.sarasotabayexplorers.com). These fun and informative cruises visit a deserted island, and the guides throw out nets and bring up sea life for inspection. It's a good idea to make reservations a day in advance. This company has unusual kayaking adventures, too (p. 446).

1600 Ken Thompson Pkwy. (on City Island). ⓒ 800/691-6683 or 941/388-2541. www.mote.org. Admission $15 adults, $10 children 4–12, free for children under 4. Nature cruises $24 adults, $20 children 4–12, free for kids under 4. Combination aquarium-cruise tickets $30 adults, $25 children. Daily 10am–5pm. Nature cruises daily 11am, 1:30pm, and 4pm. From St. Armands Circle, head north toward Longboat Key; turn right just before the Lido-Longboat bridge.

IN & NEAR BRADENTON

DeSoto National Memorial Nestled on the Manatee River, west of downtown, this park attracts history buffs by re-creating the look and atmosphere of the period when Spanish explorer Hernando de Soto landed here in 1539. It includes a restoration of de Soto's original campsite and a scenic half-mile nature trail that circles a mangrove jungle and leads to the ruins of one of the first settlements in the area. Start by watching the 21-minute film about de Soto in America. From December to March, park employees dress in 16th-century costumes and portray the early settlers' way of life, including cooking and the firing of an arquebus, one of the world's earliest firearms.

DeSoto Memorial Hwy. (north end of 75th St. W.). ⓒ 941/792-0458. www.nps.gov/desoto. Free admission. Daily 9am–5pm. Take Manatee Ave. (Fla. 64) west to 75th St. W. and turn right; follow the road to its end and the entrance to the park.

Gamble Plantation 🏛   Situated northeast of downtown Bradenton, this is the oldest structure on the southwestern coast of Florida, and a fine example of an antebellum plantation home—something that's quite rare in Florida. It was constructed over a 6-year period in the late 1840s by Maj. Robert Gamble, made primarily of "tabby mortar" (a mixture of oyster shells, sand, molasses, and water), with 10 rooms, verandas on three sides, 18 exterior columns, and eight fireplaces. Now maintained as a state historic site, it includes a fine collection of 19th-century furnishings. Entrance to the house is by tour only, although you can explore the grounds on your own.

3708 Patten Ave. (U.S. 301), Ellenton. ✆ **941/723-4536**. www.floridastateparks.org/gambleplantation. Free admission. Tour $5 adults, $3 children 6–12, free for children under 6. Thurs–Mon 9am–4:30pm; 30-min. guided house tour at 9:30 and 10:30am, and at 1, 2, 3, and 4pm. Take U.S. 301 north of downtown to Ellenton; the site is on the left, just east of Ellenton-Gillette Rd. (Fla. 683).

Solomon's Castle 🏛🏛   This attraction gets the award in the Weirdest and Wackiest (and, boy, are there many) of Florida category. In 1974, Howard Solomon began building what has become a 60-foot-tall, 12,000-square-foot castle in a Manatee County swamp. Solomon, a metal and wood sculptor by trade, built the huge structure (where he now lives) out of 22-by-34-inch offset aluminum printing plates discarded by a local newspaper. He and the other tour guides (try to get the tour led by Solomon, or at least talk with him about his work) lead guests on a pun-filled tour of the castle, which is decked out with some of his smaller artistic creations, mostly made of other people's "trash," including a chair made out of 86 beer cans, an elephant pieced together with seven oil drums, a unicorn fashioned out of coat hangers, and about 80 stained-glass windows. Howard is continually building new things—you never know what you'll find. If that's not enough to tempt you, you can have lunch in the restaurant, which is in a Spanish galleon that Howard built in his spare time. You *have* to experience this to believe it. Seriously.

4533 Solomon Rd., Ona. ✆ **863/494-6007**. www.solomonscastle.com. Admission $10 adults, $4 kids under 12. Tours Oct–June Tues–Sun 11am–4pm. Closed Mon and July–Sept. Take Hwy. 64 east of I-75 29 miles to Hwy. 665, go south 9 miles, and turn left at the sign to the castle.

South Florida Museum and Parker Manatee Aquarium *Kids*   The star at this downtown complex is Snooty, the oldest manatee born in captivity (1948) and Manatee County's official mascot. The South Florida Museum tells the story of Florida's history, from prehistoric times to the present; it includes a Native American collection with life-size dioramas, and a Spanish courtyard containing replicas of 16th-century buildings. The museum is midway through a $5-million renovation program.

201 10th St. W. (on the riverfront, at Barcarrota Blvd.). ✆ **941/746-4131**. www.southfloridamuseum.org. Admission $9.95 adults, $7.95 seniors, $6 students with ID, $5 children 5–12, free for children 4 and under. Jan–Apr and July

---

Milky-White Stallions

Horse lovers are drawn to the famous **Lipizzaner Stallions,** which do their spectacular leaps at the Ottomar Herrmann training grounds, 32755 Singletary Rd., Myakka City (✆ **941/322-1501**), from late December to March (they tour the country the rest of the year). Members of a now-rare breed, the parents of these milky-white stallions were brought here from Austria in the 1960s by Col. Ottomar Herrmann. Their *haute école* performances are straight from Vienna's famous Spanish Riding School. Call for schedule and directions.

> *Tips* **Finding the Elusive Parking Space**
>
> Parking on or near St. Armands Circle can be scarce, and even if you *can* find a spot, on-street parking is limited to 3 hours. Your best bets are the free, unrestricted lots on Adams Drive at Monroe and Madison drives.

Mon–Sat 10am–5pm; Sun noon–5pm. Rest of year Tues–Sat 10am–5pm; Sun noon–5pm. Closed New Year's Day, Thanksgiving, and Christmas. From U.S. 41, take Manatee Ave. west to 10th St. W. and turn right.

SHOPPING

Visitors come from all over the world to shop at **St. Armands Circle** ✸✸, on St. Armands Key. Wander around this outdoor circle of more than 150 international boutiques, gift shops, galleries, restaurants, and nightspots, all surrounded by lush landscaping, patios, and antiques. Pick up a map at the Sarasota Convention and Visitors Bureau (p. 444). Many shops here are comparable to those in Palm Beach and on Naples's Third Avenue South, so check your credit card limits—or resort to some great window-shopping. I love to browse through **Global Navigator** (✆ **813/388-4514**), a travel-equipment and apparel shop that reminds me of Banana Republic when it carried really cool stuff (daily 10am–10pm).

For discount shopping, the focal point of this area is the **Prime Outlets Ellenton,** on U.S. 301 at exit 43 off I-75 in Ellenton (✆ **941/723-1150;** www.primeoutlets. com), about a 15-minute drive northeast of downtown Bradenton. This outdoor center has more than 100 factory and outlet stores. Shops are open Monday through Saturday from 10am to 9pm, and Sunday from 11am to 6pm.

Anna Maria Island and Holmes Beach have jewelry, clothing, antiques, and specialty shops along or near Gulf Drive. Favorites include **Fur Kids & U2** (✆ **941/778-4460**), which sells gifts and gear for pets and their people; **Ginny's Antiques & Art** (✆ **941/779-1773**); **Island Gallery West** (✆ **941/778-6648**), featuring 2-D and 3-D art; and **Museum Shoppe** (✆ **941/779-0273**), which stocks English and American antiques as well as maritime art.

WHERE TO STAY

The beaches here are virtually lined with condominiums, many of which are actually all-condo projects operated as hotels. Among the rental agencies requiring stays of less than a month are **Argus Property Management,** 2477 Stickney Point Rd., Sarasota, FL 34231 (✆ **941/927-6464;** fax 941/927-6767; www.argusmgmt.com); and **Florida Vacation Accommodations,** 4030 Gulf of Mexico Dr., Longboat Key, FL 34228 (✆ **800/237-9505** or 941/364-9505; fax 941/364-1830; www.vacationinfl.com).

The hotels below are organized by geographic region: in downtown Sarasota, on Lido Key, on Longboat Key, and on Siesta Key. The high season is from January to April. The hotel tax here is 10%.

DOWNTOWN SARASOTA

Most visitors stay out at the beaches, but cost-conscious travelers will find some good deals on the mainland, such as the **Best Western Midtown,** 1425 S. Tamiami Trail (U.S. 41) at Prospect St. (✆ **800/722-8227** or 941/955-9841; fax 941/954-8948; www.bw midtown.com). This older but well-maintained motel is 2 miles in either direction from the main causeways leading to the keys. Winter rates are $119 for a double room, dropping to $79 off season.

Downtown's top hotel before the opening of The Ritz-Carlton (see below), the **Hyatt Sarasota,** 1000 Blvd. of the Arts (*©* **800/233-1234** or 941/953-1234; fax 941/952-1987; www.sarasota.hyatt.com), is adjacent to the Civic Center and the Van Wezel Performing Arts Hall, and within walking distance of downtown shops and restaurants.

Most other chain motels are near the airport, including **Comfort Inn** (*©* **800/ 228-5150** or 941/355-7091), **Days Inn** (*©* **800/329-7466** or 941/355-9271), and **Hampton Inn** (*©* **800/336-9335** or 941/351-7734). All of recent vintage and thoroughly modern, they stand side by side on Tamiami Trail (U.S. 41) near the FSU Ringling Center for the Cultural Arts and the Asolo Center for the Performing Arts.

The Cypress 🟊🟊🟊   A throwback to the 1940s, the Cypress is a two-story, tin-roofed inn tucked amid giant mango trees and hovering palms. Best of all, it overlooks the bay. You can't get accommodations much better than this, with its antiques, a grand piano, and guest rooms with private bathrooms, queen-size beds, hardwood floors, ceiling fans, and Oriental rugs. The best unit is the Essie Leigh Key West Room, which has its own side entrance, a front-porch view of the bay, a brass-and-pewter bed, an antique oak chest, and Spanish-pine side tables. Other rooms are distinctly "Victorian meets Ralph Lauren," some with French doors and others with neoclassical twists.

621 Gulfstream Ave. S., Sarasota, FL 34236. *©* **941/955-4683.** www.cypressbb.com. 4 units. Winter $230–$260 double; off season $160–$180 double. AE, DISC, MC, V. *In room:* A/C, TV.

The Ritz-Carlton Sarasota 🟊🟊🟊   Downtown's swankiest digs, just north of the Ringling Causeway and across a narrow creek from the Sarasota Quay shopping-and-dining complex (p. 460), The Ritz occupies the bottom 10 floors of an 18-story Mediterranean-style building (the top floors are private residences). It sits perpendicular to the bay, so most of the spacious guest units have views looking across the water to the keys and the Gulf. The rooms are luxuriously appointed in typical Ritz-Carlton fashion, including marble bathrooms. The hotel's four restaurants are led by Vernona, while the Bay View Bar & Grill offers casual dining both indoors and out. The elegantly appointed lobby opens to a bayside courtyard with a heated pool. There is no beach on-site, but a shuttle will take you to the hotel's private beach club on Lido Key. There's also a full-service spa and fitness center on-site.

1111 Ritz-Carlton Dr. (at Tamiami Trail/U.S. 41), Sarasota, FL 34236. *©* **800/241-3333** or 941/309-2000. Fax 941/ 309-2100. www.ritzcarlton.com. 266 units. Winter $309–$695 double; off season $289–$519 double. AE, DC, DISC, MC, V. **Amenities:** 4 restaurants; 3 bars; outdoor pool; golf course; 3 tennis courts; health club; Jacuzzi; sauna; children's programs; concierge; activities desk; car-rental desk; business center; 24-hr. room service; massage; babysitting; laundry service; concierge-level rooms. *In room:* A/C, TV, dataport, minibar, hair dryer, iron, safe.

The Villa at Raintree Gardens 🟊🟊🟊 *Value*   High trees that spray mist to alleviate the brutal summer heat hover above orchids lining this charming turn-of-the-last-century fishing-lodge-turned-inn, which is expertly run by Raymond Nick and Elizabeth Sanford. Located within the orchid garden is a free-form pool built from black lava and green river stones. A screened-in whirlpool tub and thermal spa are surrounded by lush greenery. Nearby is a pool you won't want to swim in—it's brimming with a family of koi and waterlilies, and heron love to hang out here. Bold colors bring the interior of the inn to life, as does the motley collection of antiques. The two guest rooms, with queen-size beds and private bathrooms, are distinctly and uniquely furnished. A giant dictionary on a stand in the entry hallway adds to the character of this stunning home. The made-from-scratch breakfast includes herb-sautéed potatoes and eggs Benedict with Key lime–infused hollandaise sauce. If you're in the market for a quiet, romantic getaway, the Villa at Raintree Gardens is the closest you'll get to Eden in these parts.

1758 Vamo Dr., Sarasota, FL 34236. © 800/862-8583. Fax 941/966-6977. 2 units. Winter $150 double; off season $85 double. MC, V. **Amenities:** Heated pool; whirlpool spa; bicycles. *In room:* A/C, in-room massage.

ON LIDO KEY

The Helmsley Sandcastle ☞   Set on 600 feet of private, white-sand beach on the Gulf of Mexico and only minutes from the upscale St. Armands Circle, this place has an incredibly friendly staff and a nice, resorty feel. The guest rooms here are nothing special, though they are large and most have great views of the water. Stay here if you want to relax in a fine location without dealing with the stuffiness of a fancier hotel.

1540 Ben Franklin Dr., Sarasota, FL 34236. © 800/225-2181 or 941/388-2181. Fax 941/388-2655. www.helmsley hotels.com. 179 units. Winter $199–$279 double; off season $119–$189 double. AE, DC, DISC, MC, V. **Amenities:** 3 restaurants; poolside bar; 2 outdoor heated pools; nearby golf and tennis; business center. *In room:* A/C, TV, fridge, coffeemaker, hair dryer, iron.

Holiday Inn Lido Beach   Conveniently located at the north end of Lido, this modern seven-story hotel is within walking distance of St. Armands Circle. The beach is right across the street. The motel-style rooms have balconies that face the Gulf or the bay, and the rooftop restaurant and lounge offer panoramic views of the Gulf of Mexico.

233 Ben Franklin Dr. (at Thoreau Dr.), Sarasota, FL 34236. © 800/465-4329, 800/892-9174, or 941/388-5555. Fax 941/388-4321. www.ichhotelsgroup.com. 135 units. Winter $119–$279 double; off season $135–$199 double. AE, DC, MC, V. **Amenities:** Restaurant; 2 bars; heated outdoor pool; access to nearby health club; exercise room; watersports equipment rental; bike rental; limited room service; babysitting; laundry service; coin-op washers and dryers; concierge-level rooms. *In room:* A/C, TV, dataport, fridge, coffeemaker, hair dryer, iron.

ON LONGBOAT KEY

Colony Beach & Tennis Resort ☞☞   Sitting 3 miles north of St. Armands Circle, this beachside facility is consistently rated one of the nation's finest tennis resorts. The Colony Restaurant and pool date from 1952, when this was a beach club, but today's accommodations are in modern one- and two-bedroom condominium apartments that come complete with living room, dining area, fully equipped kitchenette, sun balcony, whirlpool tub, and steam shower. The choice units are the three private cottages right on the superb beach. The condominiums are built around a 21-court tennis center, where a staff of professionals conducts highly acclaimed programs for both adults and children. The beachside Colony Restaurant offers fine Continental cuisine for lunch and dinner (jackets requested for men at dinner).

1620 Gulf of Mexico Dr., Longboat Key, FL 34228. © 800/282-1138 or 941/383-6464. Fax 941/383-7549. www. colonybeachresort.com. 235 units. Winter $275–$1,150 suite; off season $195–$975 suite. Packages available. AE, DC, DISC, MC, V. **Amenities:** 2 restaurants; 2 bars; heated outdoor pool; 21 clay and hard tennis courts; health club; Jacuzzi; sauna; watersports equipment rental; bike rental; children's programs; game room; concierge; activities desk; car-rental desk; business center; salon; limited room service; massage; babysitting; laundry service; coin-op washers and dryers. *In room:* A/C, TV, kitchen, coffeemaker, hair dryer, iron.

The Resort at Longboat Key Club ☞☞   Part of a 410-acre real-estate development at the southern end of Longboat Key, this award-winning condominium resort pampers the country-club set with upscale restaurants and a variety of recreational activities in a lush tropical setting. The spacious, luxurious rooms and suites have private balconies overlooking the Gulf, a lagoon, or golf-course fairways. All have custom-designed furnishings and neoclassical decor, and all but 20 have full kitchens. Among several dining options here, the Sands Pointe Restaurant has the feel of an informal but elegant supper club, serving classical Italian cuisine in a romantic setting by the Gulf, while the adjacent lounge offers casual dining and live entertainment.

301 Gulf of Mexico Dr. (P.O. Box 15000), Longboat Key, FL 34228. © 800/237-5545 or 941/383-8821. Fax 941/383-0359. www.longboatkeyclub.com. 232 units. Winter $240–$435 double, $320–$1,160 suite; off season $215–$275 double, $265–$595 suite. Packages available. AE, DISC, MC, V. From St. Armands Key, take Gulf of Mexico Dr. north; take 1st left after bridge. **Amenities:** 5 restaurants; bars; heated outdoor pool; 2 golf courses (45 holes); 38 tennis courts; health club with spa treatments; Jacuzzi; sauna; watersports equipment rental; bike rental; children's programs; concierge; activities desk; salon; limited room service; massage; babysitting; laundry service. *In room:* A/C, TV, dataport, kitchen, coffeemaker, hair dryer, iron.

ON SIESTA KEY

Captiva Beach Resort ☆ *Value*   Owners Robert and Jane Ispaso have owned the property for over 25 years and their substantial upgrades have earned them honors from Zagat and the Superior Small Lodging Association for 2005 and 2006. Located about half a block from the beach in a tropical oasis with other small resorts, they pride themselves on being the cleanest small resort in Sarasota by winning housekeeping awards for the past 6 years. It is said that if someone says "Good morning" to you here, it's considered rude if you don't respond. It's very popular with longer-term guests during winter, and international guests and families during the summer. Every one of the comfortable, sparkling-clean units here has some form of cooking facility and five-star queen pillow-top beds, and some have separate living rooms with sleeper sofas. These are older buildings, so you'll find window air conditioners mounted through the walls; however, the property has been upgraded for all the modern conveniences, such as high-speed Internet connection and bottle-quality water at every faucet. You'll get fresh linens and towels daily except Sunday. Daily maid service is available for a small fee. Guests get complimentary use of beach towels, chairs, and sand toys. Several restaurants and shops are a short walk away.

6772 Sara Sea Circle, Siesta Key, FL 34242. © 800/349-4131 or 941/349-4131. Fax 941/349-8141. www.captiva beachresort.com. 20 units. Winter $150–$245 double, $250–$335 bungalows and suites; off season $99–$140 double, $185–$205 bungalows and suites. Weekly and monthly rates available. See website for packages. AE, DISC, MC, V. **Amenities:** Heated outdoor pool; coin-op washers and dryers. *In room:* A/C, TV, VCR, satellite service, high-speed Internet service, kitchen, coffeemaker, hair dryer, beach amenities.

Turtle Beach Resort ☆☆☆   On Siesta Key's south end, 2½ miles south of the Stickney Point Bridge, this intimate little bayside charmer is one of Florida's most romantic retreats. It began life years ago as a ramshackle fishing camp, but owners Gail and Dave Rubinfeld renovated the five original clapboard cottages and added five more in three separate buildings to increase privacy. The complex is tightly packed; although some units are very close to a small bayside swimming pool, heavy tropical foliage provides a reasonable degree of privacy, and high wooden fences surround each unit's private outdoor hot tub. Sitting right on the bay, all units also have one-way mirror windows, allowing guests to look out at the water in complete privacy. The cottages are done in various styles, such as Caribbean and Nantucket, and have at least one bedroom each. Although they can accommodate small families, they're better suited as a terrific escape for couples. There's no restaurant on the grounds, but all units have kitchens—and the gourmet waterfront seafood restaurant Ophelia's on the Bay is right next door. Guests can use fishing poles, kayaks, canoes, and paddleboats for free. Turtle Beach is only a

5-minute walk; I suggest you take a canoe to the private beach from the resort's docks—it's spectacular.

Ten new studios and one-bedroom luxury units, called the **Inn at Turtle Beach,** have been added across the street on the Gulf side. All units have hot tubs with aromatherapy jets. Facilities include kitchenettes and bathrooms, two boat docks, fountains, and a heated pool.

9049 Midnight Pass Rd., Sarasota, FL 34242. *(C)* **941/349-4554.** Fax 941/312-9034. www.turtlebeachresort.com. 10 units. Winter $335–$420 double; off season $250–$340 double. Weekly rates available. AE, DISC, MC, V. Pets accepted at an extra charge. **Amenities:** Outdoor pool; hot tub in each unit; free watersports equipment. *In room:* A/C, TV, DVD/VCR, kitchen, coffeemaker, hair dryer, iron.

WHERE TO DINE

The restaurants below are organized geographically: in downtown Sarasota, in Southside Village (the city's hottest new dining scene), on St. Armands Key (next to Lido Key), on Longboat Key, and on Siesta Key.

IN DOWNTOWN SARASOTA

Downtown's best breakfast spot is the local branch of **First Watch,** 1395 Main St., at Central and Pineapple avenues (*(C)* **941/954-1395**). Like its siblings in Naples (p. 385) and elsewhere, First Watch offers a wide variety of breakfast and lunch fare. It's open daily from 7:30am to 2:30pm. If the wait's too long, walk south along Central Avenue; this block has several coffeehouses and cafes with sidewalk seating.

Bijou Cafe *✿✿* INTERNATIONAL   Chef Jean-Pierre Knaggs prepares award-winning cuisines from around the world in his cafe, a former gas station, in the heart of the theater district. Although the more casual Michael's on East (see below) bistro draws a hefty after-theater crowd, this is the best place to dine within walking distance of the downtown entertainment venues. Jean-Pierre artfully presents the likes of prime veal Louisville (with crushed pecans and bourbon-pear sauce), pan-seared crab cakes served under a rémoulade and over a bed of fresh greens, and gently simmered lamb shanks with rosemary and garlic. His outstanding wine list has won accolades from *Wine Spectator* magazine.

1287 1st St. (at Pineapple Ave.). *(C)* **941/366-8111.** Reservations recommended. Main courses $17–$30. AE, DC, MC, V. Mon–Sat 11:30am–2pm; daily 5–9:30pm. Closed Sun June–Dec. Free valet parking nightly in winter, on weekends off season.

Marina Jack's SEAFOOD/CONTINENTAL   Overlooking the waterfront with a wraparound 270-degree view of Sarasota Bay and both Siesta and Lido keys, this establishment has spectacular vistas and a carefree "on vacation" attitude, especially on the open-air raw-bar deck, which is often packed all afternoon on weekends and at sunset every day. The food is good but not the best in town, so come here for a fun time. You may have to wait for a table or bar stool down on the deck, but be sure to make reservations if you want to have a meal in the upstairs dining room. Fresh local seafood is the star both upstairs and down—grilled grouper is your best bet. The downstairs lounge and raw bar also serves sandwiches and burgers.

In Island Park, Bayfront at Central Ave. *(C)* **941/365-4232.** Reservations recommended in dining room. Dining-room main courses $16–$35; deck main courses $14–$17; sandwiches and salads $8–$11; Sun brunch $12–$24. AE, DISC, MC, V. Daily 11:30am–2am. Closed Christmas.

Michael's on East *✿✿* CREATIVE INTERNATIONAL   At the rear of the Midtown Plaza shopping center on U.S. 41 south of downtown, Michael Klauber's chic bistro is one of the top places here for fine dining—it's the locals' favorite after-theater haunt. Huge cut-glass walls create three intimate dining areas, one a piano bar for pre- or after-dinner drinks. Prepared with fresh ingredients and a creative flair, the offerings here will tempt your taste buds. House specialties are Dungeness crab cakes, pan-seared Chilean sea bass with couscous and artichoke hearts in a thyme-accented tomato coulis, and grilled duck breast with Bermuda onion, shiitake fondue, and pecan risotto.

1212 East Ave. S. (between Bahia and Prospect sts.). © 941/366-0007. Reservations recommended. Main courses $18–$36. AE, DC, DISC, MC, V. Lunch Mon–Fri 11:30am–2pm, dinner nightly 5:30–10pm. Free valet parking.

Morel 🟊🟊 NEW AMERICAN   A warm, sophisticated, bistrolike ambience and innovative menu created by chef/owner Fredy Mayer has made Morel one of Sarasota's hottest and hautest restaurants. Of all the excellent fare, I recommend the potato-and-leek latkes with house-smoked salmon, the grilled veal chop in tomato-basil coulis, and the glazed Chilean sea bass.

3809 S. Tuttle Ave. © **941/927-8716.** Reservations recommended. Main courses $11–$30. AE, MC, V. Tues–Sat 4:30–9:30pm.

Patrick's AMERICAN/PUB FARE   With a semicircular facade, this upscale, pol-ished-oak and brass-rail sports bar offers wide-windowed views of downtown's main intersection. The menu offers very good pub fare: steaks and chops, burgers, seafood, pastas, small pizzas, salads, sandwiches, and omelets. Other entrees include broiled salmon with dill-hollandaise sauce, sesame chicken, and veal done three ways—piccata, Française, or Marsala. There's a good happy hour here Monday through Friday between 5 and 7pm.

1400 Main St. (at Pineapple Ave.). © **941/952-1170.** Main courses $14–$21; sandwiches and burgers $7–$9. AE, DC, DISC, MC, V. Daily 11am–midnight; Sun brunch 11am–3pm. Closed Christmas.

Yoder's 🟊 *Value* AMISH/AMERICAN   Just 3 miles east of downtown is an award-winning, value eatery operated by an Amish family (Sarasota and Bradenton have siz-able Amish communities and several other Amish restaurants). Evoking the Pennsylvania Dutch country, the simple dining room displays handcrafts, photos, and paintings celebrating the Amish way. The menu emphasizes plain, made-from-scratch cooking such as home-style meatloaf, Southern fried chicken, country-smoked ham, and fried filet of flounder. Burgers, salads, soups, and sandwiches are also available. Leave room for Mrs. Yoder's traditional shoofly and other homemade pies, one of the restaurant's biggest draws. *Note:* Alcohol is neither served nor allowed here.

3434 Bahia Vista St. (west of Beneva Rd.). © **941/955-7771.** Main courses $6.25–$9.50; breakfast $2.50–$7; sand-wiches, burgers, and salads $3.25–$8. No credit cards (ATM on premises). Mon–Sat 6am–8pm.

Zoria 🟊🟊🟊 ECLECTIC   Sleek and stylish, Zoria is a trendsetter in terms of Sara-sota's innovative cuisine scene, with such interesting menu items as duck breast with French lentils, crispy pancetta, turnips, and cherry marmalade; duck foie gras, fig jam, pear purée, and 8-year-old balsamic; and, my favorite—from the bar menu, which also happens to be exquisite and much cheaper—a ground-beef burger with rosemary, roasted garlic, and goat cheese on focaccia bread.

1991 Main St. © **941/955-4457.** www.zoria.net. Reservations recommended. Main courses $18–$31. AE, DC, MC, V. Mon–Sat 5–10pm; Sun 5–9pm.

IN SOUTHSIDE VILLAGE

Sarasota's hottest dining area is **Southside Village,** centered on South Osprey Avenue between Hyde Park and Hillview streets, about 15 blocks south of downtown. Here you'll find several hip restaurants, including Fred's and Pacific Rim (see below). The village landmark is **Morton's Gourmet Market** ✦, 1924 S. Osprey Ave. (© **941/955-9856**), which offers a multitude of deli items, specialty sandwiches, a ton of fresh salads, freshly baked pastries and desserts, and cooked meals dispensed from a cafeteria-style steam table. You can dine picnic-fashion at sidewalk tables. Most ready-to-go items cost less than $7. The market is open Monday through Saturday from 8am to 8pm, Sunday from 10am to 5pm.

Fred's ✦ CONTINENTAL   A popular hangout for the 20- and 30-something sets, especially on Friday nights, Fred's is the quintessential neighborhood brasserie serving an eclectic mix of American, European, Asian, and Latin influences in a stunning setting reminiscent of a sleek New York City bistro with copper ceilings and black-and-white checked floor. The food is essentially comfort food—rib-eye with mashed potatoes and penne pasta with chicken—and is pretty inconsistent, but what is consistent is the scene here, especially in the restaurant's cigar-friendly Tasting Room, which is abuzz with activity late into the night.

1923 S. Osprey Ave. © 941/364-5811. Reservations recommended. Main courses $15–$30. AE, DC, MC, V. Mon–Thurs 11am–10pm; Fri–Sat 11am–1am; Sun 9am–10pm.

Pacific Rim ✦ *Value* JAPANESE/THAI   Sarasotans love this chic and very casual restaurant for exceptional cuisine at economical prices. Japanese influence is felt at the sushi bar along one side of the dining room, while Thai spices make a strong impact on the regular menu. The chargrilled shrimp with Thai curry and coconut-milk sauce is especially tasty, as is the combination of chicken and vegetables stir-fried in a wok. Here you can select your meat and vegetables separately from the sauce, and the chefs will combine them on the grill, in the wok, or in the bowl (as in rice dishes).

In Hillview Centre, 1859 Hillview St. (between Osprey Ave. and Laurent Place). © 941/330-8071. Main courses $7.50–$15. AE, DISC, MC, V. Mon–Thurs 11:30am–2pm and 5–9pm; Fri 11:30am–2pm and 5–10pm; Sat 5–10pm.

ON ST. ARMANDS KEY

While locals are hanging out in Southside Village, part-year residents and visitors flock to St. Armands Circle. Plan to spend at least one evening here: The nighttime scene is like a fair, with everyone strolling around the circle, poking heads into the few stores that stay open after dark, and window-shopping the others. It's fun and safe, so come early and plan to stay late. See "Shopping," earlier in this section, for parking tips.

The circle has a branch of Tampa's famous **Columbia** (p. 414), between John Ringling Boulevard and John Ringling Parkway (© **941/388-3987**). The Spanish food is excellent, there's outdoor seating, and the Patio Lounge is one of the liveliest spots here for evening entertainment Thursday through Sunday. Like its sibling in Naples (p. 384), the local edition of **Tommy Bahama's Tropical Cafe,** 300 John Ringling Blvd. (© **941/388-2446**), draws a lively crowd of young professionals for its moderately priced seafood. It's upstairs over the Tommy Bahama's clothing store.

At dinner, you may wish to forgo an expensive dessert and wander over to the local branch of **Kilwin's,** 312 John Ringling Blvd. (© **941/388-3200**), for some gourmet chocolate, Mackinac Island fudge, or ice cream or yogurt in a homemade waffle cone. Enjoy your sweets on one of the sidewalk park benches—everyone else does.

Blue Dolphin Cafe *Value* AMERICAN/DINER   On the John Ringling Boulevard spoke of St. Armands Circle, this informal diner is the affluent area's best inexpensive place to have breakfast (served anytime). The owners, Jill and Rob Ball, are fonts of free information, too. They serve standard breakfast fare as well as fresh crab or lobster

Benedict, raspberry pancakes, and pecan-peach waffles. Lunchtime highlights are the homemade soups and grouper sandwiches. The Blue Dolphin is open for dinner on Friday nights during the winter season, offering the likes of flaky-crust chicken potpie, slow-roasted prime rib, and spicy crab cakes.

470 John Ringling Blvd. (1 block off St. Armands Circle). ℂ 941/388-3566. Breakfast $4.50–$10; sandwiches, burgers, and salads $5–$10. AE, DC, DISC, MC, V. Daily 7am–3pm.

Café L'Europe ☆☆☆ CONTINENTAL   One of Sarasota's most lauded restaurants, Café L'Europe has been the recipient of countless awards and praise for its Continental fare that fuses French, Caribbean, and Spanish influences into what the chef prefers to call New European cuisine. An elegant ambience makes Café L'Europe the place to celebrate special occasions, whether over the classic Dover sole or an updated version of sweetbreads—crispy sweetbreads this time, with mixed lettuces, poached pear, and mustard sauce. Sea bass—steamed in papillote with spinach, zucchini, roasted garlic, fingerling potatoes, dill, and tomatoes—is a sublime choice as well, especially when matched with one of the restaurant's many vintages. Service, as to be expected in an establishment of this caliber, is outstanding.

431 St. Armands Circle (at John Ringling Blvd.). ℂ 941/388-4415. Reservations recommended. Main courses $10–$30. AE, DC, MC, V. Daily 11am–10:30pm.

Hemingway's ☆ FLORIDIAN/CARIBBEAN   For a casual spot with an eclectic Floribbean menu and a large bar with a friendly, laid-back Key West vibe, take the elevator or climb the winding stairs to this second-floor hideaway. Hemingway's is a charming and comfortable combination of good food and Old Florida tradition. You can dine inside or out on one of two second-floor balconies.

325 John Ringling Blvd. (½ block off St. Armands Circle). ℂ 941/388-3948. Reservations recommended on weekends. Main courses $16–$22. AE, DC, DISC, MC, V. Sun–Thurs 11:30am–10pm; Fri–Sat 11:30am–11pm.

Hungry Fox AMERICAN   This upstairs restaurant is the only place on St. Armands Circle offering three inexpensive meals a day year-round. It's not much to look at inside, with faux-marble tables and plastic lawn chairs—so wait for a table out on the veranda, especially next to the railing, where you can overlook all the action down below. Breakfast, which is served until noon, offers everything from lox and bagels to Virginia ham and eggs. Sandwiches and salads appear at lunch, followed by steaks, chicken, pastas, and spicy jambalaya for dinner. Most items are good values for the prices, but stay away from anything cooked in the deep fryer if you're concerned about your cholesterol.

419 St. Armands Circle (above Cha Cha Coconuts). ℂ 941/388-2222. Main courses $11–$17; sandwiches, burgers, and salads $4.50–$9; breakfast $4.50–$10. AE, DISC, MC, V. Mon–Sat 8am–9pm; Sun 8am–2:30pm.

ON LONGBOAT KEY
Euphemia Haye/The Haye Loft ☆☆☆ INTERNATIONAL   This area's most extraordinary restaurant, the romantically lit Euphemia Haye is best known for chef Raymond Arpke's crispy roast duck filled with bread stuffing and accompanied by a tangy fruit sauce. His prime strip steak rolled in cracked peppercorns and served with an orange, brandy, and butter sauce is another winner, as are his shrimp in a delightful curry and coconut-cream sauce. If all this sounds sweet, wait until you go upstairs to the Haye Loft, his casual dessert bar. Up here, you can take your pick from fabulous pies topped with thick whipped cream or Ben & Jerry's ice cream. You can also sample the kitchen's offerings because the loft has its own light-fare menu, including soups, appetizers, small pizzas, and sandwiches. If you're lucky, the night's special

sandwich will be steak topped with Raymond's peppercorn sauce. Served open-face and garnished with a field-greens salad, it's a meal for about $10. Add a glass of superb wine and a slice of pie a la mode, and you've got a wonderful dinner for under $20.

5540 Gulf of Mexico Dr. (at Gulfbay Rd.). ☎ 941/383-3633. www.euphemiahaye.com. Reservations recommended downstairs, not accepted in the Haye Loft. Main courses $18–$39; sandwiches, pizzas, and salads $7–$12. DC, DISC, MC, V. Restaurant Sun–Thurs 5–10pm; Fri–Sat 5–10:30pm. Haye Loft daily 6pm–midnight.

Moore's Stone Crab SEAFOOD   Located in Longbeach, the old fishing village on the north end of Longboat Key, this popular bayfront restaurant began in 1967 as an offshoot of a family seafood business established 40 years earlier. From the outside, in fact, it still looks a little like a packing house, but the view of the bay dotted with mangrove islands makes a fine complement to stone crabs fresh from the family's own traps from October 15 to May 15. Otherwise, the menu offers an incredibly large variety of seafood, most of it fried or broiled. Sandwiches and salads are served all day.

800 Broadway (at Bayside Dr.). ☎ 941/383-1748. Main courses $15–$23; stone crab market price (as much as $40–$45 in season, from mid-Oct to mid-May); sandwiches and salads $7–$13. AE, DISC, MC, V. Winter daily 11:30am–9:30pm; off season Mon–Fri 4:30–9:30pm; Sat–Sun 11:30am–9:30pm.

ON SIESTA KEY

Ocean Boulevard, which runs through **Siesta Village,** the area's funky, laid-back beach hangout, is virtually lined with restaurants and pubs. Most have bars and outdoor seating, which attracts the beach crowd during the day. At night, rock-'n'-roll bands draw teenagers and college students to this lively scene.

Blasé Café ★★ *Finds* INTERNATIONAL   Tongue-in-cheeky, to say the least, this restaurant doesn't take itself seriously, hence the ironic and oxymoronic name. One of Florida's most unusual restaurants, Ralph and Cindy Cole's supercasual establishment has tables indoors and a few under the cover of the Village Corner shopping center's walkway, but most are alfresco, on a wooden deck built around a palm tree in the center's asphalt parking lot. Never mind the cars pulling in and out virtually next to your chair: Ralph's food is so good that it draws droves of locals who don't mind waiting for a table. This is Siesta Key's best breakfast spot, offering Italian- and Louisiana-flavored frittatas as well as plain old bacon and eggs. Lunchtime brings burgers, big salads, and platters such as chicken Alfredo or Florentine crepes with shrimp. At night, Ralph puts forth the likes of pan-seared, sushi-quality yellowfin tuna with tangy wasabi and pickled ginger. You can while away the rest of the evening in the wine bar, where the Coles have installed the original bar from Don CeSar Beach Resort & Spa in St. Pete Beach. Live music is featured on weekends.

In Village Corner, 5263 Ocean Blvd. (at Calle Miramar), Siesta Village. ☎ 941/349-9822. Reservations recommended. Main courses $10–$23; breakfast and lunch $5–$9. MC, V. Mon–Thurs 8:30am–9:30pm; Fri–Sat 8:30am–10pm. Closed Mon June–Nov.

Turtles AMERICAN   With tropical overtones and breathtaking water vistas across from Turtle Beach, this informal restaurant on Little Sarasota Bay has tables indoors and on an outdoor deck. Unique seafood offerings include snapper New Orleans and potato-encrusted mahimahi. You can't go wrong ordering grouper grilled, broiled, blackened, or fried. A selection of pastas is also available. The economical early-bird specials offer several choices, such as spicy Szechuan shrimp.

8875 Midnight Pass Rd. (at Turtle Beach Rd.). ☎ 941/346-2207. Main courses $11–$20; salads and sandwiches $7–$15; early-bird specials $9–$11. AE, DISC, MC, V. Mon–Sat 11:30am–9:30pm; Sun 10am–9pm. Early-bird specials daily 4–6pm.

SARASOTA AFTER DARK

The cultural capital of Florida's west coast, Sarasota is home to a host of performing arts, especially during the winter season. To get the latest on what's happening any time of year, call the city's 24-hour **Artsline** (✆ **941/365-2787**). Also check the "Ticket" section in Friday's *Herald-Tribune* (www.newscoast.com), the local daily newspaper; copies are usually available at the Sarasota Convention and Visitors Bureau (p. 444).

THE PERFORMING ARTS   Located at the FSU Ringling Center for the Cultural Arts (p. 448), the Florida State University Center for the Performing Arts, 5555 N. Tamiami Trail (U.S. 41; ✆ **800/361-8388** or 941/351-8000; www.asolo.org), presents the winter-through-spring **Asolo Theatre Festival** 🎭🎭🎭. This annual program of ballet and Broadway-style musicals and drama is one of the state's finest. In addition to the Asolo Theatre, a 19th-century Italian court playhouse moved here from Asolo, Italy, in the 1950s by the Ringlings, the center uses the 487-seat Harold E. and Ethel M. Mertz Theatre, originally constructed in Scotland in 1900 and transferred piece by piece to Sarasota in 1987. The 161-seat Asolo Conservatory Theatre was later added as a smaller venue for experimental and alternative offerings. The complex is under the direction of Florida State University (FSU).

The city's other prime venue is the lavender, seashell-shape **Van Wezel Performing Arts Hall** 🎭🎭🎭, 777 N. Tamiami Trail (U.S. 41), at 9th Street (✆ **800/826-9303** or 941/953-3368; www.vanwezel.org). Recently renovated, it offers excellent visual and acoustic conditions, and a wide range of year-round programming, including touring Broadway shows and visiting orchestras and dance troupes. It and the FSU Center host performances by the **Florida West Coast Symphony** (✆ **941/953-4252;** www. fwcs.org), the **Jazz Club of Sarasota** (✆ **941/366-1552** or 941/316-9207; www.jazz clubsarasota.com), the **Sarasota Pops** (✆ **941/795-7677**), and the **Sarasota Ballet** (✆ **800/361-8388** or 941/351-8000; www.sarasotaballet.org).

Downtown Sarasota's theater district is home to the **Florida Studio Theatre,** 1241 N. Palm Ave., at Cocoanut Avenue (✆ **941/366-9000;** www.fst2000.org), which has contemporary performances from December to August, including a New Play Festival in May. Built in 1926 as the Edwards Theater, the **Opera House,** 61 N. Pineapple Ave., between Main and 1st streets (✆ **941/366-8450;** www.sarasotaopera.org), presents classical operas (in their original languages) as well as highbrow concerts. Next door to the Opera House, the **Golden Apple Dinner Theatre,** 25 N. Pineapple Ave. (✆ **941/366-5454**), presents cocktails, dinner, and a professional Broadway-style show year-round. The nonequity **Theatre Works,** 1247 1st St., at Cocoanut Avenue (✆ **941/952-9170**), presents musical revues and other works year-round.

THE CLUB & MUSIC SCENE   You can find plenty of music to dance to on the mainland at **Sarasota Quay,** the downtown waterfront dining-shopping-entertainment complex on Tamiami Trail (U.S. 41), a block north of John Ringling Causeway. Just walk around this brick building and your ears will take you to the action. The laser sound-and-light crowd gathers at **In Extremis** (✆ **941/954-2008**), where a high-energy DJ spins Top 40 tunes for 20-somethings. Michael's Mediterranean Grill turns into **Anthony's After Dark,** where disco starts at 10:30pm. An older but still energetic crowd dances to contemporary jazz at the **Downunder Jazz Bar** (✆ **941/ 951-2467**). In Siesta Key Village, the **Old Salty Dog,** 5023 Ocean Blvd. (✆ **941/349-0158**), offers a fabulous selection of British ales and a lovely outdoor patio.

The Neglected Island

Most people are familiar with Longboat Key, but what they don't know is that it's actually part of Old Florida collectively called Florida's Gulf Islands. In addition to Longboat, there's **Anna Maria Island,** a place where the streets are sand swept and the white beaches are dotted with pastel-colored cottages. It's the kind of community where the hottest spot in town is an ice-cream parlor. Hop on the Manatee Trolley, and you can explore the island at its highest speed limit—25 mph. Everything in Anna Maria is slow paced, which is just how the locals like it. There are no high-rises—the town won't allow anything to obstruct the million-dollar view of the Gulf. For peace and quiet, this is where it's at. No big hotels exist here, just mom-and-pop establishments like the **Anna Maria Beach Cottages,** 12 Oak Ave. (© **941/778-1503**), owned by Britisher Nigel Brown and his wife. Here you can disappear into your own world, relax by the pool, walk the beach, or retreat into your cozy cottage. It's spectacular—none of it should be neglected by visitors ever again.

For more information on the Gulf Islands, check out www.flagulfislands. com. Anna Maria, Longboat, and Bradenton (on the "Mainland") are connected by bridges.

Over on St. Armands Circle, the **Patio Lounge** in the Columbia restaurant (© **941/388-3987;** p. 457) is one of the liveliest spots along the beach strip, featuring live, high-energy dance music Tuesday through Sunday evenings. And on Siesta Key, the pubs and restaurants along Ocean Boulevard in Siesta Village have noisy rock-'n'-roll bands entertaining a mostly young crowd; or you can retire to the pleasant confines of the wine bar at **Blasé Café** (© **941/349-9822;** p. 459) for live jazz.

12

Walt Disney World & Orlando

by Laura Lea Miller

It's hard to believe that Walt Disney World first opened its gates to the public just 35 years ago. I doubt anyone could have imagined the incredible transformation that followed in its wake. Orlando, once known for its citrus groves and cattle ranches, has evolved into a bustling international vacation destination. An extraordinary and diverse array of recreational activities, shopping and dining experiences, and world-class accommodations await those who visit, and the bonus is that it's all set amid the natural beauty of Central Florida.

Walt Disney World (WDW), practically a city unto itself, at 47 square miles, is now home to four major theme parks; two water parks; an incredible shopping, dining, and entertainment complex; tens of thousands of hotel rooms; scores of restaurants; and, to top it all off, a cruise line all its own.

When **Universal Orlando** (consisting of two major theme parks; an entertainment, dining, and shopping complex; and three luxury resorts), **SeaWorld** (including Discovery Cove and a yet unnamed eco-themed water park that will open in 2007), and the handful of smaller players toss their wonders into Orlando's mix of diverse offerings, well, it can get quite overwhelming.

Note: For a more in-depth look at WDW as well as Orlando's other offerings, check out Frommer's *Walt Disney World® & Orlando,* as well as *Frommer's Walt Disney World® With Kids* (Wiley Publishing, Inc.).

1 Essentials

GETTING THERE

BY PLANE   Over 37 scheduled airlines and several more charter companies serve the more than 33 million Orlando-bound passengers who arrive at the **Orlando International Airport** (✆ **407/825-2001;** www.orlandoairports.net) each year. The best travel fares to Orlando are often available during the months of November, December, and January, excluding holidays (when fares go way up).

  Delta (✆ 800/221-1212; www.delta.com), which decreased the number of gates it owns at the airport from 24 to 8, is no longer the top player in the air market—that's **Southwest Airlines** (✆ 800/435-9792; www.southwest.com), which offers service from roughly 63 cities. Additional carriers include **Air Canada** (✆ 888/247-2262; www.aircanada.ca); **Airtran Airways** (✆ 800/247-8726; www.airtran.com); **American** (✆ 800/433-7300; www.americanair.com); **British Airways** (✆ 800/247-9297; www.british-airways.com); **Continental** (✆ 800/525-0280; www.continental.com); **Jet Blue Airways** (✆ 800/538-2583; www.jetblue.com); **Northwest** (✆ 800/225-2525; www.nwa.com); **United Airlines,** including **TED** (✆ 800/241-6522;

www.united.com); **US Airways** (© 800/428-4322; www.usairways.com); and **USA 3000** (© 877/USA-3000; www.USA3000.com), among others.

Located only 25 miles from Walt Disney World, Orlando International is a relatively easy drive from the area's most popular destinations. If you're not renting a car, **Mears Transportation** (© **407/423-5566;** www.mearstransportation.com) provides car and shuttle service to and from the airport; vans run 24 hours a day and depart every 15 to 25 minutes. Round-trip fares are $26 to $42 for adults and $22 to $33 for children ages 4 to 11 (actual price depends on your destination); children 3 and under ride free. **Quicksilver Tours and Transportation** (© **888/468-6939,** 407/299-1434; www.quicksilver-tours.com) provides car, shuttle, and limo service with extras like meet and greet, luggage assistance, safety seats for the kids, and a 30-minute grocery stop included in the price. One-way shuttle fares run $65 to $70, round-trip $110 to $115, for up to 10 passengers. Rates vary depending on the destination and the type of vehicle.

BY CAR   From Atlanta, take I-75 S. to the Florida Turnpike to I-4 W. From the northeast, take I-95 S. to I-4 W. From Chicago, take I-65 S. to Nashville, then I-24 S. to I-75, then south to the Florida Turnpike to I-4 W. From Dallas, take I-20 E. to I-49 S.; then head south to I-10, east to I-75, and south to the Florida Turnpike to I-4 W.

BY TRAIN   **Amtrak** trains (© **800/872-7245;** www.amtrak.com) pull into stations in both downtown Orlando (23 miles from WDW) and Kissimmee (15 miles from WDW). Winter Park (10 miles north of downtown) and Sanford (23 miles northeast of downtown Orlando) have stations as well; Sanford is the terminus for Amtrak's Auto Train.

PACKAGE TOURS

Finding a vacation package to Orlando is easy; it's picking the right one that can be difficult, given the assortment of services and options you have to choose from. Choosing wisely means you must determine exactly what you want ahead of time, whether that includes airline tickets, a rental car, accommodations, park tickets, dining arrangements, recreational activities, or all of the above.

If you plan to spend most of your time at Walt Disney World, contact **Walt Disney World Central Reservation Operations (CRO),** at © **407/934-7639,** for a wide assortment of packages. **AAA,** the American Automobile Association (© **800/222-6953**; www.aaa.com), is also a good source for WDW packages. Another good place to look for packages is **www.mousesavers.com**—it's an "unofficial" site, but it offers plenty of useful information and deals. **Universal Orlando** packages can be booked at © **800/801-9720;** information is available online at **www.universalorlando.com**. For **SeaWorld** package information, call © **800/557-4268** or go to **www.seaworld.com**.

Many of the major airlines also offer Orlando packages. **Delta Vacations** (© **800/872-7786;** www.deltavacations.com), **Continental Airlines Vacations** (© **800/301-3800;** www.coolvacations.com), **American Airlines Vacations** (© **800/321-2121;** www.americanair.com), **United Vacations** (© **888/854-3899;** www.unitedvacations.com), **Southwest Airlines Vacations** (© **800/423-5683;** www.southwest.com), **NWA WorldVacations** (© **800/800-1504;** www.nwaworldvacations.com), and **US Airways Vacations** (© **800/455-0123;** wwwusairways.com) are just a few of the available options.

Orlando

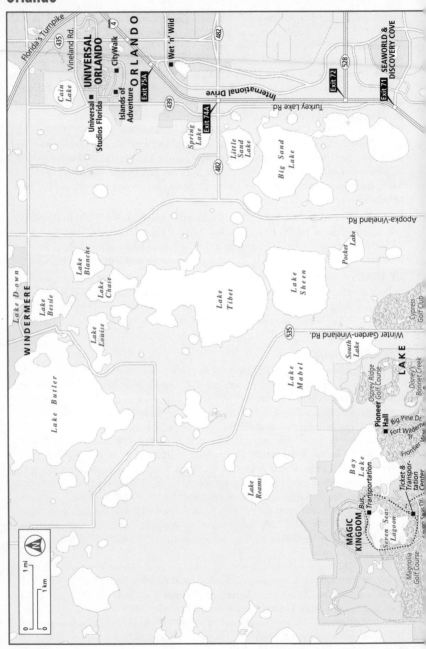

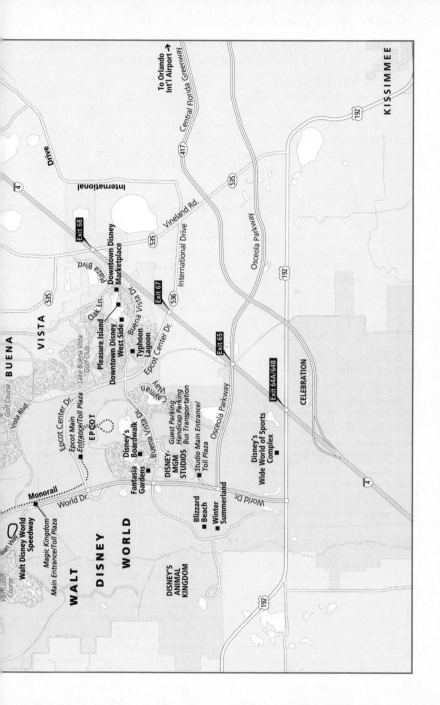

To Orlando
Int'l Airport →

Central Florida Greenway

417

KISSIMMEE

192

4

Drive

International

535

Vineland Rd.

International Drive

535

Exit 68

Downtown Disney
Marketplace

Plaza Blvd.

Oak Ln.

Pleasure Island

Downtown Disney
West Side

Typhoon
Lagoon

Buena Vista Dr.

Exit 67

536

Epcot Center Dr.

Exit 65

Osceola Parkway

192

U.S.
192

Exit 64A/64B

CELEBRATION

4

BUENA

VISTA

Lake Buena Vista
Golf Club

Golf Course

Vista Blvd.

Epcot Center Dr.

Epcot Main
Entrance/Toll Plaza

EPCOT

Disney's
Boardwalk

Cayman
Way

Buena Vista Dr.

Guest Parking
Handicap Parking
Bus Transportation

Studio Main Entrance/
Toll Plaza

DISNEY-
MGM
STUDIOS

Fantasia
Gardens

Osceola Parkway

Disney's
Wide World of Sports
Complex

Monorail

World Dr.

Walt Disney World
Speedway

Magic Kingdom
Main Entrance/Toll Plaza

WALT

DISNEY

WORLD

Blizzard
Beach

Winter
Summerland

World Dr.

DISNEY'S
ANIMAL
KINGDOM

192

Palm Golf
Course

an Way

American Express Travel (© **800/732-1991;** http://travel.americanexpress.com/ travel) offers packages that include special deals for their cardholders.

VISITOR INFORMATION

The **Orlando/Orange County Convention & Visitors Bureau,** 8723 International Dr., Suite 101, Orlando, FL 32819 (© **800/551-0181** or 407/363-5872; www.orlando info.com), will answer questions and send you an array of maps and brochures, including the *Official Visitors Guide.* The packet takes a few weeks to arrive—be sure to request it well in advance—and includes the Orlando Magicard, which is good for up to $500 in discounts on rooms, car rentals, and attractions. Order it by calling © **800/643-9492.**

For information about **Walt Disney World**—including vacation brochures, CDs and DVDs—contact Walt Disney World, Box 10000, Lake Buena Vista, FL 32830-1000 (© **407/934-7639** or 407/939-6244; www.disneyworld.com). The website is an especially good bet; it's easy to navigate and provides detailed information and photos of the Disney parks, restaurants, and resorts. A very comprehensive unofficial website worth checking out is **www.allearsnet.com**. Another site that offers a wealth of information, including timely updates, is **www.travel-insights.com**.

For information about **Universal Orlando,** call © **800/837-2273** or 407/363-8000; surf the Internet to **www.universalorlando.com**; or write to Universal Orlando, 1000 Universal Studios Plaza, Orlando, FL 32819.

You can obtain **SeaWorld** information online at **www.seaworld.com** or by calling © **407/351-3600.**

CITY LAYOUT

Interstate 4 (I-4) will take you everywhere you want to go in and around Orlando, with several exits along the way for Walt Disney World, SeaWorld, and Universal Studios Orlando, not to mention International Drive (or I-Dr.), Lake Buena Vista, and Kissimmee. *Note:* I-4 can often be jam-packed with traffic. Consult a detailed local map to find one of the many alternative routes best suited to your touring plans. If you must use the highway, it's least congested from late morning to mid-afternoon.

The Florida Turnpike crosses I-4 and links with I-75 to the north. U.S. 192, a major east-west highway, runs along Kissimmee's major motel area to U.S. 27, where it crosses I-4 near the Disney World entrance. The Bee Line Expressway goes east from I-4 past Orlando International Airport to Cape Canaveral.

NEIGHBORHOODS IN BRIEF

Walt Disney World WDW is located just southwest of the actual city of Orlando. Encompassing over 47 square miles, and practically a city unto itself, it includes within its boundaries four major theme parks, two smaller water parks, several resorts, and a plethora of restaurants and shops. It's also home of Downtown Disney (see below), Disney Quest, and the Wide World of Sports Complex.

Lake Buena Vista Lake Buena Vista encompasses all of WDW and includes much of the area bordering the resort. Here you'll find the "official" (but not Disney-owned) hotels along Hotel Plaza Boulevard. The area along Highway 535, or Apopka-Vineland, as it is also known, is home to many a resort and restaurant. Many of the resorts, restaurants, and shops are set far off the main thoroughfare to maintain a quieter atmosphere—making it one of the area's more popular places to stay.

Celebration This quaint 4,900-acre community of gingerbread-trimmed houses, some with white picket fences and shade trees in the front yard, evokes Disneyesque perfection. It should come as no surprise that Disney had a hand in its creation—experts as they are at creating the "perfect" vision of almost anything. The Market Street area, filled with a charming collection of upscale shops, restaurants, even its own boutique hotel, is a throwback to a bygone era when a stroll around town was fashionable and fun.

Downtown Disney Though not actually a neighborhood, Downtown Disney is certainly large enough to be distinguished as such. It encompasses Disney's two nighttime entertainment districts, Pleasure Island and West Side, as well as the shopping district known as Downtown Disney Marketplace. In Downtown Disney's clubs, entertainment venues, unique restaurants, and shopping experiences, you can celebrate New Year's Eve every night, shop till you drop, and tempt your taste buds all in one stop.

Kissimmee Brought back to life by a multimillion-dollar "Rebeautivacation" project, U.S. 192, Kissimmee's main tourist area, now sports extra-wide sidewalks, colorful (and plentiful) street lamps, landscaping, and location markers. Once home to mostly low-cost hotels, the area now features a handful of moderate hotels, some high-end luxury resorts, myriad eateries, and some minor attractions. That said, U.S. 192 remains frustratingly busy.

International Drive Area (Hwy. 536) This busy thoroughfare, better known as **I-Drive,** is home to more than 100 resorts and hotels, countless restaurants, attractions big and small, and some of the best shopping around. It's even got its own transportation system—the I Ride Trolley. This endless array offers something for every taste or budget.

Downtown Orlando Revitalized by the addition of ultrachic eateries, trendy nightclubs, eclectic shops, unique cultural venues (including theaters, museums, parks, and the visitor-friendly Orlando Science Center among others), downtown is reemerging as a center of new urbanism. Actually 25 miles or so northeast of Walt Disney World on I-4, the city is growing, almost exponentially, from within, something no other city in the U.S. can claim.

2 Getting Around

In a city that thrives on tourism, getting from point A to point B is easy enough, especially by car; it's the time it takes to get there that can wreak havoc on your schedule. What looks like a quick trip on a map can take forever. If you're traveling by highway, try to avoid the 7-day-a-week rush hour (7–9am and 4–6pm), if possible. But alternate routes can remain congested later in the evening, thanks to the dinner rush.

INTERNATIONAL DRIVE Traffic on I-Drive can be absolutely infuriating, compounded if you are visiting at one of the busier times of year (the 2 weeks surrounding the Easter holiday are among the busiest). Two of the best ways to conquer the traffic of I-Drive are to travel by foot (points of interest can be reasonably close together, but heavy traffic can be hazardous to pedestrians here) or by the **I-Ride Trolley** (© 407/248-9590; www.iridetrolley.com), which stops about every 2 blocks from one end of I-Drive to the other. The trolley runs from 8am to 10:30pm ($1 adults, 25¢ seniors, free for children under 12; *exact change is required*). Unlimited trolley passes covering between 1 and 14 days are available as well (the cost averages out to about a dollar a day for the latter). It's a fun and easy way to get around that's often a time saver when I-Drive is at a stand still.

BY THE DISNEY TRANSPORTATION SYSTEM   If you plan to stay at WDW and spend most of your time there, an extensive, free transportation network runs throughout the WDW property. Disney resorts and official hotels offer unlimited free transportation via bus, monorail, ferry, or water taxi to all WDW properties throughout the day and, at times, well into the evening. The free system saves you money on a rental car, insurance, and gas, as well as parking fees. The drawback, however, is that you're at the mercy of the Disney departure schedules and routes, which can often be slow and sometimes *very* indirect. Pick up a copy of the transportation map, found in the back of the *WDW Recreation, Dining and Shopping* guide, available at the guest services desks at any of the WDW resorts or theme parks, to determine the best route available.

BY SHUTTLE   Mears Transportation (✆ 407/423-5566) operates town cars, vans, and buses that go to all of the theme parks, as well as the Kennedy Space Center and Busch Gardens (yes, in Tampa). **Quicksilver Tours and Transportation (✆ 888/468-6939** or 407/299-1434) offers similar services but includes additional perks (free grocery stops, booster seats, etc.) in their prices.

BY TAXI   Taxis gather at the major resorts, and smaller properties will happily call a cab for you. **Yellow Cab (✆ 407/699-9999)** and **Ace Metro (✆ 407/855-0564)** are both good choices, though keep in mind that taxis are expensive, and charges may run as high as $3.25 for the first mile and $1.75 or more per mile thereafter.

FAST FACTS: Walt Disney World & Orlando

Babysitters Many Orlando hotels, including all of Disney's resorts, offer in-room babysitting services, usually from an outside service such as **Kids Night Out (✆ 800/696/8105** or 407/828-0920; www.kidsniteout.com) or **All About Kids (✆ 800/728-6506** or 407/812-9300; www.all-about-kids.com). Rates for in-room sitters usually run $10 to $15 per hour for the first child and $1 to $3 per hour more for each additional child. A transportation fee of $8 to $10 is usually charged as well. Several resorts offer child-care facilities with counselor-supervised activity programs right on the premises, including select Disney resorts (for kids ages 4–12; ✆ 407/939-3463). This type of child care usually costs between $10 and $15 per hour, per child. Reservations are highly recommended, often required for either type of service.

Business Hours Theme-park hours vary greatly depending on the time of year, even on the day of the week. While most open at 8 or 9am and close at 6 or 7pm, you should call or check a park's website for its most current schedule. Extended hours are usually in effect during summer and holiday periods. Other businesses are generally open from 9am to 5pm Monday through Friday.

Doctors & Dentists There are basic first-aid centers in all of the theme parks. There's also a 24-hour toll-free number for the **Poison Control Center (✆ 800/282-3171)**. To find a dentist, call **Dental Referral Service** at ✆ 800/235-4111 or go online to **www.dentalreferral.com**. **Doctors on Call Service** (℡ **407/399-3627**) makes house and room calls in most of the Orlando area (including the Disney resorts). **Centra-Care** lists several walk-in clinics in the Yellow Pages, including locations on Turkey Lake Road near Universal (℡ **407/351-6682**), and Lake Buena Vista, near Disney (℡ **407/934-2273**).

Emergencies Dial ℡ **911** for the police, the fire department, or an ambulance.

Hospitals **Sand Lake Hospital**, 9400 Turkey Lake Rd. (℡ **407/351-8500**), is about 2 miles south of Sand Lake Road. **Celebration Health** (℡ **407/303-4000**), located in the Disney town of Celebration, is at 400 Celebration Place.

Kennels The theme parks board pets for $6 per day. WDW also offers overnight boarding ($11 for the general public or $9 for Disney resort guests) at the Transportation and Ticket Center's kennel near the Polynesian Resort. Universal Orlando's resorts welcome pets, which can stay with you in your room.

Lost Children Every theme park has a designated spot where parents can reunite with lost children. Ask a park employee or guest services for details.

Pharmacies There's a **Walgreens** 24-hour pharmacy at 7650 W. Sand Lake Road (℡ **407/345-9497**). You can find additional locations (some open 24 hr.) near Disney, Universal Orlando, and in Kissimmee by logging on to **www.walgreens.com**. Numerous pharmacies are listed in the Yellow Pages.

Post Office The post office most convenient to Universal is at 10450 Turkey Lake Rd. (℡ **800/275-8777**). It's open Monday through Friday from 9am to 4:30pm and Saturday from 9am to noon. A smaller branch, closer to Disney, is at 12133 Apopka Vineland (S.R. 535) in Lake Buena Vista, just up the road from Hotel Plaza Boulevard (℡ **800/275-8777**).

Taxes In Florida, a 6.5% to 7% sales tax (depending on which county you happen to be in) is charged on all goods, with the exception of most edible grocery-store items and medicines. Hotels add an additional 2% to 5% in resort taxes to your bill, so the total tax on accommodations can run up to 12%.

Telephone If you make a local call in Orlando, even to someone just across the street, *you must dial the 407 area code followed by the number you wish to call,* for a total of 10 digits.

Weather Call ℡ **321/255-0212** for the local weather forecast; or check out the Weather Channel at **www.weather.com** for the most up-to-date information.

3 Where to Stay

There are more than 114,000 rooms in the Orlando area, with hundreds, sometimes thousands, added annually. Don't let that number fool you, as occupancy can be high much of the time. It's always a wise idea to book your room as far ahead as possible, but especially during peak season, generally around the holidays and in the summer. The lowest rates are available September through November (excluding the week of Thanksgiving) and January through April (excluding the weeks of spring break).

WALT DISNEY WORLD CENTRAL RESERVATIONS OFFICE

To reserve a room or book packages at Disney's resorts, villas, campgrounds, and official hotels, contact **Central Reservation Operations (CRO),** P.O. Box 10000, Lake Buena Vista, FL 32830-1000 (☏ **407/934-7639** or 407/939-6244; www.disneyworld. com). They'll recommend accommodations to fit your price range and needs, such as proximity to your favorite park or to those with supervised child-care centers. While Disney reservations folks are very helpful and knowledgeable, they usually won't volunteer information about better deals or specials, so be sure to *ask.*

DISNEY RESORTS
VERY EXPENSIVE
Disney's BoardWalk Inn & Villas ☆☆☆   Romantics and families alike will enjoy staying at this plush 1940s-style "seaside" resort. Here you will find an array of restaurants, shops, clubs, and carnival-style entertainment located along the ¼-mile boardwalk situated directly behind the resort, overlooking the water. The resort recaptures the spirit of Coney Island and Atlantic City back in their heyday but with Disney's own grand style. The Inn's Cape Cod–style rooms comfortably sleep four, some featuring balconies. The priciest rooms overlook the boardwalk (most provide a good view of Epcot's nightly fireworks) and the pool; the less expensive face the parking lot but are sheltered from the activity and noise of the boardwalk below. Hang on to your swimsuit if you hit the pool's famous—or infamous—200-foot "keister coaster" water slide. The BoardWalk's accommodations range from studios to grand villas that can comfortably sleep up to 12 people and offer all of the comforts of home. Epcot and MGM Studios are only minutes away by water taxi.

2101 N. Epcot Resorts Blvd. (off Buena Vista Dr.; P.O. Box 10000), Lake Buena Vista, FL 32830-1000. ☏ **407/934-7639** or 407/939-5100. Fax 407/934-5150. www.disneyworld.com. 372 units, 520 villas. $305–$710 double; $575–$2,460 suites; $305–$2,020 villa. Extra person $25. Children 17 and under stay free in parent's room. AE, DC, DISC, MC, V. Free self-parking; valet parking $7. Take I-4 to the Hwy. 536/Epcot Center Dr. exit and follow the signs. Pets $9 per night. **Amenities:** 4 restaurants; grill; 2 lounges; 3 clubs; 2 outdoor heated pools; kids' pool; 2 lighted tennis courts; health club; Jacuzzi; bike and sporting equipment rentals; playground; arcade; concierge; WDW Transportation System; transportation to non-Disney parks for a fee; business center; limited WiFi access (fee); shopping arcade; 24-hr. room service; babysitting; guest laundry; nonsmoking rooms; concierge-level rooms. *In room:* A/C, TV, dataport, high-speed Internet access (fee), kitchen (villas only), fridge (free upon request), hair dryer, iron, safe, portable crib, washer/dryer (villas only).

Disney's Grand Floridian Resort & Spa ☆☆☆ *Finds*   As an orchestra plays in the background, the elegance of this turn-of-the-20th-century Victorian resort transports guests back to a bygone era. The crystal chandeliers above the five-story domed lobby are just one example of the opulent touches you'll find throughout the resort, where high tea is served in the afternoon. If you prefer, you can spend the day luxuriating at the spa, the best in WDW. The Grand Floridian is one of the most romantic resorts for couples, especially honeymooners. Families will also appreciate the children's programs and recreational facilities. Victorian-style rooms sleep at least four; almost all overlook a garden, pool, courtyard, or the Seven Seas Lagoon. Located on the monorail system, the resort makes for a quick trip to the Magic Kingdom.

4401 Floridian Way (P.O. Box 10000), Lake Buena Vista, FL 32830-1000. ☏ **407/934-7639** or 407/824-3000. Fax 407/824-3186. www.disneyworld.com. 900 units. $359–$890 double; $940–$2,600 suite. Extra person $25. Children 17 and under stay free in parent's room. AE, DC, DISC, MC, V. Self-parking free; valet parking $7. Take I-4 to the Hwy. 536/Epcot Center Dr. exit and follow the signs. Pets $9 per night. **Amenities:** 5 restaurants; grill; 3 lounges; character meals; heated outdoor pool; kids' pool; beach; 2 lighted tennis courts; health club; spa; watersports equipment; children's club; arcade; concierge; car-rental desk; WDW Transportation System; transportation to non-Disney parks for a fee; business center; limited WiFi access (fee); shopping arcade; salon; 24-hr. room service; babysitting; guest laundry; nonsmoking rooms; concierge-level rooms; valet. *In room:* A/C, TV, dataport, high-speed Internet access (fee), minibar, fridge (free upon request), microwave (free upon request), hair dryer, iron, safe, portable crib (free upon request).

Disney's Polynesian Resort ⚡⚡ (Kids)   One of only three resorts found on the Disney monorail line, the 25-acre Polynesian features extensive recreational areas, including a stretch of beach along a lagoon dotted with hammocks and palm trees, a volcano-themed swimming pool, and watercraft rentals. An on-site child-care facility makes it a good choice for those traveling with kids. Its landscaped and torch-lit walkways, along with its longhouse-style thatched-roof buildings, give the resort a South Pacific ambience. At press time, the rooms were undergoing extensive renovations that include all new upscale and space-conscious furnishings, a muted earth-tone color scheme, and upscale amenities such as flat-screen TVs and refrigerators. Rooms can accommodate up to five people.

1600 Seven Seas Dr. (P.O. Box 10000), Lake Buena Vista, FL 32830-1000. ☎ **407/934-7639** or 407/824-2000. Fax 407/824-3174. www.disneyworld.com. 853 units. $315–$600 double; $440–$780 concierge level; $550–$2,640 suite. Extra person $25. Children 17 and under stay free in parent's room. AE, DC, DISC, MC, V. Self-parking free; valet parking $7. Take I-4 to the Hwy. 536/Epcot Center Dr. exit and follow the signs. Pets $9 per night. **Amenities:** Restaurant; cafe; 2 lounges; dinner show; character meals; 2 heated outdoor pools; kids' pool; watersports equipment; children's club; arcade; concierge; WDW Transportation System; transportation to non-Disney parks for a fee; shopping arcade; 24-hr. room service; babysitting; guest laundry; nonsmoking rooms; concierge-level rooms. *In room:* A/C, TV, dataport, high-speed Internet access (fee), fridge (free upon request), hair dryer, iron, safe, portable crib.

Disney's Yacht Club Resort ⚡⚡   The posh, upscale, and nautically themed Yacht Club shares its extensive recreational facilities with its sister resort, the Beach Club, located just next door. White, sandy beaches and an immense, beautifully landscaped swimming area (with sand-bottom pools, water slides, and a life-size shipwreck to explore) line the lagoon side of the resort. The atmosphere is geared more toward adults and families with older children, although young kids are certainly catered to (this *is* Disney). The turn-of-the-20th-century New England theme can be felt throughout, as the public areas are filled with brass accents, nautical instruments, and a lighthouse to help you find your way home. Rooms have space for up to five people, and most have balconies. Epcot is just a short walk away.

1700 Epcot Resorts Blvd. (off Buena Vista Dr.; P.O. Box 10000), Lake Buena Vista, FL 32830-1000. ☎ **407/934-7639** or 407/934-7000. Fax 407/924-3450. www.disneyworld.com. 630 units. $305–$545 double; $555–$2,440 suite; $435–$695 concierge level. Extra person $25. Children 17 and under stay free in parent's room. AE, DC, DISC, MC, V. Self-parking free; valet parking $7. Take I-4 to the Hwy. 536/Epcot Center Dr. exit and follow the signs. Pets $9 per night. **Amenities:** 3 restaurants; grill; lounge; 2 heated outdoor pools; kids' pool; 2 lighted tennis courts; Jacuzzi; watersports equipment; children's club; arcade; concierge; WDW Transportation System; transportation to non-Disney parks for a fee; business center; limited WiFi access (fee); shopping arcade; salon; 24-hr. room service; babysitting; guest laundry; nonsmoking rooms; concierge-level rooms. *In room:* A/C, TV, dataport, high-speed Internet access (fee), minibar, fridge (free upon request), microwave (free upon request), coffeemaker, iron, safe, portable crib.

Walt Disney World Dolphin and Swan ⚡⚡   If Antonio Gaudí and Dr. Seuss had teamed up on an architectural design, they might have created something like this Starwood resort and its adjacent sister, the Walt Disney World Swan. This hotel centers on a 27-story pyramid with two 11-story wings crowned by 56-foot twin dolphin sculptures (the Swan has—no surprise—45-ft. swans). Not nearly as theme intensive as the other Disney resorts, it's popular with business travelers and those who prefer their accommodations a little less sugary. Rooms were recently renovated and now feature a more contemporary decor and additional amenities. Rooms comfortably sleep

---

Tips **Wired to the Rest of the World**

By the end of 2006, all Disney resorts will be wired for high-speed Internet access. A fee of $9.95 per 24-hour period applies to use the service. Be sure to check whether your resort has a preselected "start" time, often the mid-afternoon, or you may find yourself being charged twice in a single day, depending on when you sign up for the service. Select Disney resorts (mostly in the Very Expensive range) offer limited Wi-Fi access (in public areas only) for a 24-hour period at a rate of $9.95, or 60 minutes at $4.99.

---

four (the Swan's are a tad smaller but are smoke-free). The resort has a grotto pool with waterfalls, a water slide, and whirlpools, as well as a small children's play area close by. The Swan and Dolphin share a stretch of beach, Body by Jake health club, Mandara Spa, and a handful of restaurants that includes Todd English's bluezoo, as well as other trimmings. Epcot and MGM studios are a water-taxi ride away. *Tip:* The beach next to the pool offers a great view of Epcot's IllumiNations fireworks.

1500 Epcot Resorts Blvd. (off Buena Vista Dr.; P.O. Box 22653), Lake Buena Vista, FL 32830-2653. *C* **800/227-1500** or 407/934-4000. Fax 407/934-4884. www.swandolphin.com. 1,509 units. $339–$499 double; $675–$4,300 suite. Extra person $25. Children 17 and under stay free in parent's room. AE, DC, DISC, MC, V. Self-parking $8; valet parking $14. Take I-4 to the Hwy. 536/Epcot Center Dr. exit and follow the signs. Pets $9 per night. **Amenities:** 4 restaurants; grill; 2 lounges; character meals; 4 heated outdoor pools; 4 lighted tennis courts; health club; spa; watersports equipment; children's club; 2 game rooms; concierge; car-rental desk; WDW Transportation System; transportation to non-Disney parks for a fee; business center; WiFi access (fee); shopping arcade; salon; 24-hr. room service; massage; babysitting; guest laundry; nonsmoking rooms; concierge-level rooms. *In room:* A/C, TV, Nintendo, dataport, high-speed Internet access (fee), minibar, fridge, hair dryer, iron, safe, portable crib (free upon request).

EXPENSIVE

Disney's Animal Kingdom Lodge *Finds*   Enter this resort's grand lobby, with its thatched roof and ornate shield chandeliers, and you'll feel like you've stepped into an African game-reserve lodge. The resort's *kraal* design (a semicircular layout), with many rooms overlooking a 33-acre savannah, allows guests occasional views of giraffes, zebras, and other African animals that roam the savannah. Families appreciate the array of activities, including fireside storytelling, sing-alongs, and more. Those in the mood for romance will appreciate the more remote and relaxed setting. Rooms are slightly smaller than at Disney's other "Deluxe" resorts, but the distinctive theme and spectacular surroundings are unparalleled, making it well worth the slightly tighter squeeze. Two of Orlando's best and most unique restaurants, Boma and Jiko, are a must, no matter where you end up staying. The lodge is adjacent to Animal Kingdom, but almost everything else on WDW property is quite a distance away.

2901 Osceola Pkwy., Bay Lake, FL 32830. *C* **407/934-7639** or 407/938-3000. Fax 407/939-4799. www.disneyworld. com. 1,293 units. $205–$525 double; $435–$625 concierge level; $655–$2,585 suite. Extra person $25. Children 17 and under stay free in parent's room. AE, DC, DISC, MC, V. Self-parking free; valet parking $7. Take I-4 to the Hwy. 536/Epcot Center Dr. exit and follow the signs. Pets $9 per night. **Amenities:** 3 restaurants; lounge; heated outdoor pool; kids' pool; health club; children's center; arcade; concierge; WDW Transportation System; transportation to non-Disney parks for a fee; shopping arcade; limited room service; babysitting; guest laundry; nonsmoking rooms; concierge-level rooms. *In room:* A/C, TV, dataport, fridge (free upon request), hair dryer, iron, safe, portable crib.

Disney's Saratoga Springs Resort and Spa * The first phase of the newest Disney Vacation Club resort opened in 2004, but construction is ongoing and its third phase is due to be completed in 2007. The resort transports guests back to the heyday of upstate New York's 19th-century resorts. The resort town of Saratoga Springs is evoked through lavish gardens, Victorian architecture, and bubbling springs. The resort's main pool brings to mind its namesake's natural springs, with "healing" waters spilling over the rocky landscaping. The renowned spa offers an array of services and treatments meant to invoke the healing powers of Saratoga's Springs themselves. Accommodations resemble those of the other Disney timeshare properties and range from studios that sleep 4 to villas that can sleep up to 12 people. Downtown Disney is a short ferry ride across the lake, but getting to the parks requires a bit more effort.

1960 Broadway St., Lake Buena Vista, FL 32830. © **407/827-1100** or 407/934-3400. Fax 407/827-1151. www. disneyworld.com. 828 units. $269–$389 studio; $360–$1,545 villa. Extra person no charge. Children 17 and under stay free in parent's room. AE, DC, DISC, MC, V. Free self-parking. Take I-4 to exit 67, make 3rd right, and follow signs to the resort. **Amenities:** Restaurant; lounge; barbecue areas; themed heated pool; kids' interactive pool area; golf; tennis; health club; spa; biking; boating; playground; arcade; free WDW transportation; limited room service; babysitting; guest laundry; limited grocery delivery. *In room:* A/C, TV, VCR (villas), full kitchen (villas), kitchenette (studios), fridge,microwave, hair dryer, iron, safe, portable crib, washer/dryer (villas).

Disney's Wilderness Lodge & Villas ⟨⟨⟨   The Wilderness Lodge is surrounded by a forest of towering pines, cypress, and oaks far away from the rest of Mickey's world. Beyond the "spring-fed" pool, set amid the rocky landscape, a spouting geyser erupts periodically. The log-framed lobby is adorned by a mammoth stone hearth, two gigantic totem poles, and four massive teepee chandeliers, giving the resort an old-time national park feel and making it a favorite of families and couples alike. Standard rooms at the lodge sleep 4, while the villas just next door can accommodate up to 12. The decor is among Disney's best, and the restaurants offer some of the most spectacular views in WDW. It's really not that far from the Magic Kingdom, but the bus ride to the park takes longer than you might expect.

901 W. Timberline Dr. (on the southwest shore of Bay Lake just east of the Magic Kingdom; P.O. Box 10000), Lake Buena Vista, FL 32830-1000. © **407/934-7639** or 407/938-4300. Fax 407/824-3232. www.disneyworld.com. 909 units. $205–$575 lodge; $370–$500 concierge level; $380–$1,250 suite; $295–$1,040 villa. Extra person $25. Children 17 and under stay free in parent's room. AE, DC, DISC, MC, V. Free self-parking; valet parking $7. Take I-4 to the Hwy. 536/Epcot Center Dr. exit and follow the signs. Pets $9 per night. **Amenities:** 2 restaurants; 2 lounges; heated outdoor pool; kids' pool; 2 Jacuzzis; watersports equipment; children's club; arcade; WDW Transportation System; transportation to non-Disney parks for a fee; limited room service; babysitting; guest laundry; nonsmoking rooms; concierge-level rooms. *In room:* A/C, TV, dataport, high-speed Internet access (fee), fridge (villas, upon request at the lodge), microwave (villas), hair dryer, iron, safe, portable crib.

MODERATE
Disney's Port Orleans Resort ⟨ *Value*   Run as two separate resorts, each with a distinctive Southern theme, Port Orleans has the best landscaping and coziest atmosphere of Disney's moderate resorts. The **French Quarter** reflects the charm of New Orleans at the turn of the 20th century, with accents of Mardi Gras, while **Riverside,** filled with grand mansions and back bayous, reflects the Old South. The dragon-themed Doubloon Lagoon pool, the Ol' Man Island swimming hole, and a nearby playground are a hit with kids. Guest rooms are large enough for four, but it'll be a tight fit. (Bayou Rooms have a trundle bed, offering room for an extra child.) Its central location is just east of Epcot and MGM; there's boat service to Downtown Disney. Recent renovations mean that the resort remains the best in its category.

2201 Orleans Dr. (off Bonnet Creek Pkwy.; P.O. Box 10000), Lake Buena Vista, FL 32830-1000. © **407/934-7639** or 407/934-5000. Fax 407/934-5353. www.disneyworld.com. 3,056 units. $139–$215 double. Extra person $15. Children 17 and under stay free in parent's room. AE, DC, DISC, MC, V. Free parking. Take I-4 to the Hwy. 536/Epcot Center Dr.

exit and follow the signs. Pets $9 per night. **Amenities:** 2 restaurants; grill/food court; 2 lounges; 6 heated outdoor pools; 2 kids' pools; Jacuzzi; watersports equipment rentals; playground; 2 arcades; WDW Transportation System; transportation to non-Disney parks for a fee; limited room service; babysitting; guest laundry; nonsmoking rooms. *In room:* A/C, TV, dataport, high-speed Internet access (Riverside, fee), fridge (free upon request), hair dryer, iron, safe, portable crib (free upon request), trundle bed (upon request at the French Quarter, fee).

INEXPENSIVE

Disney's All-Star Sports Resort *(Value)*   This resort sports surfing, basketball, football, and tennis themes, which explains the oversize equipment found throughout the grounds. The main pool is surrounded by shark fins, surfboards, and gigantic waves—all of which give it an ocean feel. The smaller baseball-diamond pool is a home run as well. As with all of the Disney value resorts, the rooms are on the small side and lack frills. Nevertheless, this is a good choice for the budget-conscious family that wants to stay on Disney property; kids love the larger-than-life themes.

Note: Disney has two additional All-Star resorts—the All-Star Movies Resort and the All-Star Music Resort—both identical to the Disney's All-Star Sports Resort where it counts (like room size and layout). The only major difference is the theme: One offers musical themes ranging from jazz to calypso, and the other features movies (of the Disney variety, of course). All three All-Star resorts are located out in the Disney boonies, and the closest park is Animal Kingdom.

1701 W. Buena Vista Dr. (at World Dr. and Osceola Pkwy.; P.O. Box 10000), Lake Buena Vista, FL 32830-1000. © 407/934-7639 or 407/939-5000. Fax 407/939-7333. www.disneyworld.com. 1,920 units. $79–$137 double. Extra person $10. Children 17 and under stay free in parent's room. AE, DC, DISC, MC, V. Free parking. Take I-4 to the Hwy. 536/Epcot Center Dr. exit and follow the signs. Pets $9 per night. **Amenities:** Food court; lounge; 2 heated outdoor pools; kids' pool; arcade; WDW Transportation System; transportation to non-Disney parks for a fee; limited room service; babysitting; guest laundry; nonsmoking rooms. *In room:* A/C, TV, dataport, fridge (upon request, fee), safe, portable cribs.

Disney's Pop Century Resort *(Value)*   Gigantic memorabilia from decades past—remember the eight-track and Rubik's Cube?—mark the exteriors at Disney's newest value resort. While there might not be a lot of frills, the price is right for families on a budget who want to bunk with Mickey. The guest rooms and bathrooms—just like those at Disney's All-Star properties—are tiny but will work for a family of four with a concerted bit of effort. The resort is closest to the Wide World of Sports Complex.

1050 Century Dr. (off Oceola Pkwy; P.O. Box 10000), Lake Buena Vista, FL 32830-1000. © 407/938-4000 or 407/939-6000. Fax 407/938-4040. www.disneyworld.com. 2,880 units. $79–$137 double. Extra person $10. Children 17 and under stay free in parent's room. AE, DC, DISC, MC, V. Free parking. Take I-4 to exit 65, make a right on Victory Way followed by a right onto Century Dr., which takes you to the resort. Pets $9 per night. **Amenities:** Food court; lounge; 2 heated outdoor pools; kids' pool; arcade; WDW Transportation System; transportation to non-Disney parks for a fee; limited room service; babysitting; guest laundry; nonsmoking rooms. *In room:* A/C, TV, dataport, fridge (upon request, fee), safe, portable crib (free upon request).

ROUGHING IT, DISNEY STYLE

Disney's Fort Wilderness Resort & Campground *(Kids)*   Pine trees, cypress trees, and fish-filled lakes and streams surround this woodsy 780-acre camping resort. The closest park is the Magic Kingdom, which you can reach by boat. If you're a true outdoors type, you'll enjoy the breath of fresh air away from the hustle and bustle of the parks. There are 110- and 220-volt outlets, grills, and comfort stations with private showers and restrooms. Tents and RVs are welcome. The 406 cabins sleep up to six and feature many of the comforts of home, with full kitchens and daily housekeeping service. The wide variety of outdoor recreational activities just adds to the appeal of this resort. It is also home to the Hoop De Doo Musical Review dinner show (p. 519).

Some sites are open to pets—at a cost of $3 per site, *not* per pet—which is cheaper than using the WDW overnight kennel, where you pay $9 per pet.

3520 N. Fort Wilderness Trail (P.O. Box 10000), Lake Buena Vista, FL 32830-1000. ℂ 407/934-7639 or 407/824-2900. Fax 407/824-3508. www.disneyworld.com. 784 campsites, 408 wilderness cabins. Campsite $39–$92 double; wilderness cabin $239–$349 double. Extra person $2 for campsite, $5 for cabin. Children 17 and under stay free in parent's room. AE, DC, DISC, MC, V. Free parking. Take I-4 to the Hwy. 536/Epcot Center Dr. exit and follow the signs. **Amenities:** 2 restaurants; grill; lounge; 2 heated outdoor pools; kids' pool; 2 lighted tennis courts; watersports equipment rentals; 2 game rooms; WDW Transportation System; transportation to non-Disney parks for a fee; babysitting; guest laundry; nonsmoking cabins; outdoor activities (fishing, horseback and hay rides, campfires). *In room:* A/C, TV, VCR, dataport (cabins only), kitchen, fridge, microwave, coffeemaker, hair dryer (cabins only), portable crib (cabins, free upon request), outdoor grill.

LAKE BUENA VISTA/OFFICIAL HOTELS

The "official" Disney hotels, though not owned or operated by Disney, are located along Hotel Plaza Boulevard, on the northeast side of Disney property and adjacent to Downtown Disney. Guests can enjoy some of the perks of staying in a WDW resort (including free transportation to Disney parks) while staying in a location somewhat more central to the rest of Orlando's offerings. You can reserve a room through **Central Reservations Operations** (ℂ **407/934-7639**), but it's best to call the individual hotel or parent chain to check for special deals and packages.

EXPENSIVE

Buena Vista Palace 👁️👁️   Formerly the Wyndham Palace Resort & Spa, this is the most upscale of the "official" properties and is popular with both business and leisure travelers. Rooms are comfortable, and many have balconies or patios; ask for one above the fifth floor with a "recreation view" facing the pools and Downtown Disney. Recreation Island is home to the resort's three pools (one partially indoors), game center, playground, tennis courts, and beach volleyball. The resort is well known for its full-service, European-style spa. Downtown Disney is just across the road.

1900 Buena Vista Dr. (just north of Hotel Plaza Blvd.; P.O. Box 22206), Lake Buena Vista, FL 32830. ℂ **866/397-6516** or 407/827-3228. Fax 407/827-6034. www.buenavistapalace.com or www.downtowndisneyhotels.com. 1,012 units. $169–$219 double; $249–$389 suite. $12 daily resort fee. Extra person $10. Children 17 and under stay free in parent's room. AE, DC, DISC, MC, V. Self-parking free; valet parking $15. From I-4, take the Hwy. 535/Apopka-Vineland Rd. exit north to Hotel Plaza Blvd. and go left. At 1st stoplight, turn right onto Buena Vista Dr. It's the 1st hotel on the right. **Amenities:** 3 restaurants; grill; 4 lounges; 3 heated outdoor pools; kids' pool; tennis; spa; Jacuzzi; sauna; arcade; playground; concierge; car-rental desk; free bus service to WDW parks; transportation to non-Disney parks for a fee; business center; minimarket; salon; 24-hr. room service; massage; babysitting; laundry; nonsmoking rooms; concierge-level rooms; valet. *In room:* A/C, TV w/pay movies, Playstation, dataport, high-speed and wireless Internet access (fee), minibar, fridge (suites), coffeemaker, hair dryer, iron, safe.

MODERATE

Note: Accommodations in this category are usually a step above the "moderate" resorts located inside WDW.

DoubleTree Guest Suites in the Walt Disney World Resort ⭐ 𝘒𝘪𝘥𝘴   Children get their own check-in desk and a gift upon arrival at this hotel, which is the best of the official hotels for families traveling with little ones. All of the accommodations in this seven-story hotel are two-room suites, large by most standards (with space for up to six), and include all the comforts of home. A recent $2 million renovation brought with it additional in-room amenities and improvements to the pool and landscaping. Don't forget the cookies given to guests at check-in, a tasty tradition at the Double-Tree properties. It's the farthest "official" hotel from Downtown Disney, but a bus is available for those not quite up to the lengthy though pleasant walk.

2305 Hotel Plaza Blvd. (just west of Hwy. 535/Apopka-Vineland Rd.), Lake Buena Vista, FL 32830. ℂ 800/222-8733 or 407/934-1000. Fax 407/934-1011. www.downtowndisneyhotels.com or www.doubletreeguestsuites.com. 229 units. $99–$299 double. Extra person $20. Children 17 and under stay free in parent's room. AE, DC, DISC, MC, V. Free parking. From I-4, take the Hwy. 535/Apopka-Vineland Rd. exit north to Hotel Plaza Blvd. and go left. It's the 1st hotel on the left. **Amenities:** Restaurant; 2 lounges; heated outdoor pool; kids' pool; 2 lighted tennis courts; volleyball; fitness center; playground; game room; arcade; concierge; car-rental desk; complimentary bus service to WDW parks; transportation to non-Disney parks for a fee; Disney gift shop; minimarket; limited room service; guest laundry; nonsmoking rooms; valet; theater. *In room:* A/C, 2 TVs w/pay movies and video games, dataport, fridge, microwave, coffeemaker, hair dryer, iron, safe.

The Hilton in the Walt Disney World Resort 🟊🟊

This resort's major claim to fame: It's the only official resort on Hotel Plaza Boulevard to offer guests Disney's Extra Magic Hour option (see p. 495 for details). The hotel's array of guest services, upscale yet friendly atmosphere, and prime location just across from Downtown Disney make it one of the best bets on the boulevard. Rooms sport a contemporary Shaker-style decor; junior suites, featuring sleeper sofas, are more spacious and a better option for families. The resort's two pools ensure plenty of space to lounge around. Rooms higher up on the front side of the resort offer a glimpse of Disney's nightly fireworks displays and a good view of Downtown Disney (just a short walk away).

1751 Hotel Plaza Blvd., Lake Buena Vista, FL 32830. ℂ 407/827-4000. Fax 407/827-6369. www.hilton.com. 814 units. $99–$299 double; concierge level additional $40. Resort fee $8 optional. Extra person $20. Children 17 and under stay free in parent's room. AE, DC, DISC, MC, V. Self-parking free; valet parking $10. From I-4 take exit 68, turn right onto S.R. 535, then left onto Hotel Plaza Blvd. Follow the boulevard, and the resort is near the end on the left. **Amenities:** 4 restaurants; 3 lounges; 2 outdoor heated pools; whirlpool; game room; concierge; car rental; complimentary bus service to WDW parks; transportation to non-Disney parks for a fee; business center; shops; minimarket; salon; 24-hr. room service; babysitting; valet laundry; concierge-level rooms; in-house doctor. *In room:* A/C, TV w/pay movies and video games, dataport, high-speed Internet access (fee), minibar, fridge (fee), microwave (fee), coffeemaker, hair dryer, iron.

Hotel Royal Plaza 🟊

The Royal Plaza is one of the boulevard's original hotels, but renovations over its 25-year history (including a multimillion-dollar upgrade in 2006) have ensured that it remains in excellent shape. A favorite with the budget-minded, its hallmark is a friendly staff, many of whom have been here since the hotel opened. The nicely decorated rooms, now sporting new furnishings and decor, are of good size, with enough space for five. Poolside rooms have balconies and patios. Tower rooms have separate sitting areas, and some offer whirlpool tubs in the bathrooms. If you want a view from up high, ask for a room facing west toward WDW.

1905 Hotel Plaza Blvd. (between Buena Vista Dr. and Hwy. 535/Apopka-Vineland Rd.), Lake Buena Vista, FL 32830. ℂ 800/248-7890 or 407/828-2828. Fax 407/827-6338. www.downtowndisneyhotels.com or www.royalplaza.com. 394 units. $160–$219 double; $180–$269 suite. $8 daily resort fee. No charge for extra person. AE, DC, DISC, MC, V. Self-parking free; valet parking $12. From I-4, take the Hwy. 535/Apopka-Vineland Rd. exit north to Hotel Plaza Blvd. and go left. It's the 2nd hotel on the left. **Amenities:** Restaurant; lounge; heated outdoor pool; 4 lighted tennis courts; fitness center; whirlpool; children's activity program; guest-services desk; complimentary bus service to WDW parks; transportation to non-Disney parks for a fee; Disney gift shop; limited room service; babysitting; guest laundry; nonsmoking rooms; valet. *In room:* A/C, TV w/pay movies, video games, dataport, high-speed Internet access (fee) minibar, coffeemaker, hair dryer, iron, safe.

OTHER LAKE BUENA VISTA HOTELS

The hotels in this section are within a few minutes' drive of the WDW parks, offering the location but not the privileges of staying at an "official" hotel.

VERY EXPENSIVE

Gaylord Palms 🟊🟊🟊 *Finds* It's the most extensively themed resort outside of Disney's not-so-little world. Practically a destination unto itself, the resort offers its own entertainment, fabulous themed dining, shops, recreational facilities, and a Canyon Ranch Spa Club to work out the kinks from the day's activities. The 4½-acre octagonal Grand Atrium, topped by an impressive glass dome, surrounds a replica of the Castillo de San Marcos, a real Spanish fort located in St. Augustine. Waterfalls, lush foliage, live alligators, cobblestone walkways, and a rocky landscape complete the feel. The Emerald Bay, a 362-room hotel within the hotel, has the most elegant air about it, while other themed areas include Key West, St. Augustine, and the Everglades. The spacious rooms are beautifully decorated and well appointed, each with a balcony overlooking the interior Floridian landscapes. Service is impeccable, friendly, and welcoming, not standoffish as with most other resorts of this class.

6000 Osceola Pkwy., Kissimmee, FL 34747. ℂ 877/677-9352 or 407/586-0000. Fax 407/239-4822. www.gaylord palms.com. 1,406 units. $199–$439 double; $635-$2,700 suite. $10 daily resort fee. Extra adult $20. Kids under 18 stay free in parent's room. AE, DC, DISC, MC, V. Self-parking $10; valet parking $12–$16. Take the I-4 Osceola Pkwy. exit east to the hotel. **Amenities:** 3 restaurants; 4 lounges; 2 outdoor heated pools; cabana rentals; fitness center; spa; children's center; concierge; tour desk; car-rental desk; free transportation to Disney parks; transportation to non-Disney parks for a fee; business center; shopping arcade; salon; 24-hr. room service; massage; babysitting; guest laundry; nonsmoking rooms; concierge-level rooms; valet. *In room:* A/C, TV w/pay movies, PlayStation, dataport, high-speed Internet access, coffeemaker, hair dryer, iron, safe.

Hyatt Regency Grand Cypress Resort ✹✹✹ (Finds)

Long a favorite of honeymooners, this upscale resort offers plenty for families as well. The lobby invites you in with its lush foliage, winding walkways, and soft music in the background. The 18-story atrium has inner and outer glass elevators (ride the outers to the roof for a panoramic rush) and a newly designed skylight to top it all off. The rooms, beautifully decorated with a Laura Ashley flair, are large enough to sleep four. The Hyatt shares a golf club and academy, racquet club, and equestrian center with its sister property, the Villas of Grand Cypress (see below); both offer excellent packages aimed at the sports set. The Hyatt's half-acre, 800,000-gallon pool is one of the best in Orlando and features caves, grottoes, waterfalls, rope bridges, and a 45-foot water slide. Be sure to make reservations at The Chef's Table for one of the most unique and impressive dining experiences in all of Orlando. *Tip:* Families in need of extra space can often get a great discount on the second room when booking connecting rooms.

1 N. Jacaranda (off Hwy. 535), Orlando, FL 32836. ℂ 800/233-1234 or 407/239-1234. Fax 407/239-3800. www. grandcypress.com. 750 units. $199–$385 double; $595–$5,750 suite. Optional $13 daily resort fee. Extra person $25. Children 17 and under stay free in parent's room. AE, DC, DISC, MC, V. Self-parking free; valet parking $18. Take I-4 to the Hwy. 535/Apopka-Vineland Rd. exit and go north; then turn left at the 2nd light (after the ramp light) onto Hwy. 535. **Amenities:** 4 restaurants; 4 lounges; large heated outdoor pool; 45 holes of golf; 12 tennis courts (5 lighted); 2 racquetball courts; health club; spa; watersports equipment; children's center; arcade; concierge; car-rental desk; free Disney shuttle; transportation to non-Disney parks for a fee; store; salon; 24-hr. room service; in-room massage; babysitting; guest laundry; nonsmoking rooms; concierge-level rooms; valet; equestrian center. *In room:* A/C, TV, dataport, high-speed Internet access (fee), minibar, hair dryer, iron, safe.

The Villas of Grand Cypress ✹✹✹ (Finds)

If you are willing to splurge—and I mean *splurge*—this is an exceptional place to retreat, with a remote location away from the buzz of the theme parks yet not too far off the beaten path. At its "modest" end, this Mediterranean-inspired resort has junior suites with beds for four, Roman tubs, and patios. Floor plans progress to elegant one- to four-bedroom villas, all with kitchens, dining rooms, and patios. The resort shares facilities with its sister property, Hyatt Regency Grand Cypress Resort (see above), located just down the road, but this very refined resort caters primarily to adults.

1 N. Jacaranda (off Hwy. 535), Orlando, FL 32836. ℂ **800/835-7377** or 407/239-4700. Fax 407/239-7219. www. grandcypress.com. 146 villas. $215–$500 club suite; $315–$2,000 villa. $12 daily resort fee. Extra person included. Children 17 and under stay free in parent's room. AE, DC, MC, V. Self-parking free. Take I-4 to the Hwy. 535/Apopka-Vineland Rd. exit and go north; then go left at the 2nd light (after the ramp light) onto Hwy. 535. The resort is on the right. **Amenities:** 2 restaurants; 2 lounges; heated outdoor pool; 45 holes of golf; 12 tennis courts (5 lighted); 2 racquetball courts; health club; spa; watersports equipment; kids' center (at the Hyatt); arcade (at the Hyatt); concierge; car-rental desk (at the Hyatt); free Disney shuttle; transportation to non-Disney parks for a fee; salon (at the Hyatt); 24-hr. room service; in-room massage; babysitting; guest laundry; nonsmoking rooms; concierge-level rooms; equestrian center. *In room:* A/C, TV, VCR, dataport, high-speed Internet access (fee), minibar, hair dryer, iron, safe.

EXPENSIVE

Marriott's Orlando World Center 🎖🎖 *Finds*　This upscale resort caters to both business and leisure travelers alike. Golf, tennis, and spa lovers will find plenty to do at this 230-acre Marriott, as will families, with the wide array of recreational activities it offers. The largest of its five pools has water slides and waterfalls surrounded by plenty of space to relax among the palm trees and tropical landscaping. The location, set back from the main thoroughfare and only 2 miles from the Disney parks, is a fabulous plus. The large, comfortable, and beautifully decorated rooms sleep four, and the higher poolside floors offer views of Disney.

8701 World Center Dr. (on Hwy. 536 between I-4 and Hwy. 535), Orlando, FL 32821. ℂ **800/621-0638** or 407/239-4200. Fax 407/238-8777. www.marriottworldcenter.com. 2,111 units. $199–$329 for up to 5; $750–$1,600 suite. Children 17 and under stay free in parent's room. AE, DC, DISC, MC, V. Self-parking free; valet parking $16. Take I-4 to the Hwy. 535/Apopka-Vineland Rd. exit, go south 1½ miles, proceed right/west on Hwy. 536, and continue ⅓ mile. **Amenities:** 4 restaurants; 2 lounges; 3 heated outdoor pools; heated indoor pool; kids' pool; 18-hole golf course; 8 lighted tennis courts; health club; spa; whirlpool; sauna; concierge; car-rental desk; transportation to all theme parks for a fee; business center; salon; 24-hr. room service; massage; babysitting; guest laundry; nonsmoking rooms. *In room:* A/C, TV w/pay movies, PlayStation, dataport, high-speed Internet access (fee), minibar, coffeemaker, hair dryer, iron, safe.

MODERATE

Embassy Suites Lake Buena Vista 🎖　Set near the end of Palm Parkway, just off Apopka-Vineland, this fun and welcoming all-suite resort is close to the action of Downtown Disney as well as the offerings along S.R. 535, yet remains a quiet retreat. Each suite sleeps five and includes separate living area (with pullout sofa) and sleeping quarters. The roomy accommodations make it a great choice for families.

8100 Lake Ave., Orlando, FL 32836. ℂ **800/257-8483** or 407/239-1144. Fax 407/238-0230. www.embassysuites orlando.com. 333 units. $109–$229 double. Extra person $15. Rates include breakfast and evening reception. AE, DC, DISC, MC, V. Self-parking free; valet parking $7. From I-4, take the Hwy. 535/Apopka-Vineland Rd. exit east to Palm Pkwy. Follow Palm ½ mile to Lake Ave. on the right. **Amenities:** Restaurant; cafe; lounge; indoor and outdoor heated pools; kids' pool and play area; tennis court; basketball court; fitness center; whirlpool and sauna; business center; high-speed Internet access; free shuttle to Disney parks; room service; guest laundry. *In room:* A/C, TV w/pay movies, dataport, fridge, microwave, hair dryer, iron, safe.

Nickelodeon Family Suites Resort by Holiday Inn 🎖🎖 *Finds* *Kids*　This all-suite property, the first-ever Nickelodeon-branded resort, is one of the best in the Orlando area for families. Its brightly colored Kid Suites feature second bedrooms for the kids (with either bunks or twin beds), mini-kitchens, and pullout sofas in the living areas. Three-bedroom suites include a second bathroom and a full kitchen. An all-new lobby and mall area, filled with restaurants, an arcade, shops, and nightly entertainment (including Studio Nick), have been added. Nickelodeon characters and color schemes (neon green and orange) run throughout the resort. The resort's two pool areas are veritable water parks, with extensive multi-level water slides, flumes, climbing nets, and water jets. "Nick After Dark," a supervised activity program for kids ages 5 to 12, allows parents to take a night off. Up to four kids eat free with a paying adult at the extensive breakfast buffet (not including the character breakfast).

14500 Continental Gateway (off Hwy. 536), Lake Buena Vista, FL 32821. (✆) **877/387-5437,** 407/387-5437, or 866/ GO2-NICK. Fax 407/387-1489. www.nickhotel.com. 789 units. $160–$275 suite. AE, DC, DISC, MC, V. Free self-parking. From I-4, take the Hwy. 536/International Dr. exit east 1 mile to the resort. **Amenities:** Restaurant; lounge; several fast-food counters; kids eat free program; character breakfast; 2 water park pools; minigolf course; fitness center; kids' spa; 2 Jacuzzis; 3 outdoor Ping-Pong tables; 2 shuffleboard courts; game room; complimentary recreation center for ages 4–12; tour desk; free shuttle to Disney, Universal Orlando, and SeaWorld parks; minimarket; coin-op washers and dryers. *In room:* A/C, TV w/pay movies and VCR (some with Nintendo), dataport, full kitchen (in select suites), fridge, coffeemaker, microwave, hair dryer, iron, safe.

Staybridge Suites Lake Buena Vista ✺✺   This recent edition to the Staybridge Suites chain is located just off Apopka-Vineland, close to the action of Downtown Disney and the theme parks, as well as many restaurants, shops, and smaller recreational venues. One- and two-bedroom suites come with full kitchens. The suites' separate living areas are larger and more comfortable than similar ones at other all-suite hotels. A nicely landscaped inner courtyard is where you'll find the resort's pool, along with plenty of space to soak up the sun. A unique plus is the complimentary grocery service, which allows you to select supermarket items for delivery to your room.

8751 Suiteside Dr., Orlando FL 32836. (✆) **800/866-4549** or 407/238-0777. Fax 407/238-2640. www.sborlando.com. 150 units. $119–$199 1-bedroom suite (up to 4 people); $149–$269 2-bedroom suite (up to 8 people). Rates include continental breakfast. Rollaway beds and cribs available at no charge. AE, DC, DISC, MC, V. Free self-parking. From I-4, take the 535 exit no. 68 and turn right. Follow the road to Vinings Way Rd. and turn right. The hotel is located on the left. **Amenities:** Deli; outdoor heated pool; children's pool; 24-hr. exercise room; Jacuzzi; 24-hr. game room; guest services desk; free shuttle to Disney parks; high-speed Internet access; convenience store; complimentary grocery delivery service; 24-hr. guest laundry; nonsmoking rooms; suites for those w/limited mobility. *In room:* A/C, TV/VCR, free high-speed Internet access, kitchen, hair dryer, iron/ironing board, safe.

ON U.S. 192/KISSIMMEE

This appealing stretch of highway, close to the Disney parks, is filled with restaurants, shops, and smaller attractions. The hotels and restaurants here generally cater to the budget-conscious traveler. However, a few luxury resorts are beginning to sprout just a few miles to the south of the highway, making the mix a bit more diverse.

EXPENSIVE
Celebration Hotel ✺✺   This hotel is as picture-perfect as the town that surrounds it. Its three-story, wood-frame design is straight out of 1920s Florida, as is its very charming interior. The hotel's public areas are filled with antiques and artwork, creating a warm and inviting atmosphere. The beautifully decorated rooms have incredibly comfortable beds. To enjoy a soothing view, ask for a lakefront room. The upscale ambience caters to adults, especially those seeking a romantic getaway. The only drawback: You'll have to deal with the traffic on U.S. 192 to get anywhere.

Tips **Prime Real Estate**

The Four Seasons is scheduled to open a 425-room luxury resort in the picturesque community of Celebration, complete with its own 18-hole golf course, in 2007. Also opening in 2007 is the **Sonesta Orlando Tierra Del Sol,** a luxe resort community located just 10 minutes from Disney.

700 Bloom St. (C) **888/499-3800** or 407/566-6000. Fax 407/566-6001. www.celebrationhotel.com. 115 units. $219–$359 for up to 4; $299–$459 suite. $10 daily resort fee. AE, DC, DISC, MC, V. Self-parking free; valet parking $14. Take I-4 to the U.S. 192 exit, go east to the 2nd light, then go right on Celebration Ave. and follow the signs. **Amenities:** Restaurant; lounge; outdoor heated pool; 18-hole golf course; state-of-the-art health-and-fitness center; spa; concierge; free shuttle to Disney parks; transportation to non-Disney parks for a fee; nearby shopping district; free WiFi (lobby). *In room:* A/C, TV, Nintendo, dataport, hair dryer, iron, safe.

The Omni at ChampionsGate ★★★ One of the newest luxury resorts to spring up just south of Disney in ChampionsGate, the Omni offers a comprehensive array of leisure facilities, including two championship golf courses designed by Greg Norman, a vast Grecian-style pool area with its very own lazy river, and a 10,000-square-foot European spa. The beautifully decorated rooms feature 9-foot ceilings and plush amenities, including bathrobes and free Wi-Fi access. There's a program especially geared to youngsters so parents can get some relaxation time on their own.

8390 ChampionsGate Blvd. (C) **888/444-6664** or 407/390-6664 . Fax 321/677-6600. www.omnihotels.com. 730 units. $199–$350 standard; $450–$2,500 suite. $10 daily resort fee. AE, DC, DISC, MC, V. Self-parking free; valet parking $12. Take I-4 to exit 58, and bear right to the main entrance. Pets under 25 lb. ($50 fee). **Amenities:** 5 restaurants; grill; 3 lounges; 2 outdoor heated pools; 2 18-hole gold courses; tennis courts; volleyball; health and fitness center; spa; lazy river; video arcade; Omni Kids Program; concierge; free shuttle to WDW parks; transportation to non-Disney parks for a fee; 24-hr. business center; retail gallery; salon; 24-hr. room service; laundry; valet. *In room:* A/C, TV w/pay movies and Nintendo, CD player, free Wi-Fi Internet access, minibar, hair dryer, iron/ironing board, safe, bathrobe.

MODERATE
Comfort Suites Maingate East ★ *Value* Set back from the main drag, this welcoming hotel is one of the nicest in the area. The lobby and accommodations—consisting of studio and one-bedroom suites—are bright and inviting. Nonsmoking suites are available upon request. The main pool and the children's pool, with an umbrella fountain to keep everyone cool, are open around the clock. For entertainment, Old Town (a small-scale shopping, dining, and entertainment complex) is next door, and a great miniature-golf course is located just in front of the property.

2775 Florida Plaza Blvd., Kissimmee, FL 34746. (C) **888/782-9772** or 407/397-7848. Fax 407/396-7045. www.comfortsuitesfl.com. 198 units. $69–$175 double. Extra person $10. Rates include continental breakfast. Children 17 and under stay free in parent's room. AE, DC, DISC, MC, V. Free self-parking. From I-4 take the US 192 E. exit; continue 1¾ miles, then turn right on Florida Plaza Blvd. **Amenities:** Outdoor heated pool; kids' pool; fitness center; game room; concierge; free shuttle to Disney, Universal, and Sea World parks; business center; guest laundry. *In room:* A/C, TV, dataport, free high-speed Internet access, fridge, microwave, coffeemaker, hair dryer, iron, safe.

INTERNATIONAL DRIVE AREA
The hotels and resorts listed here are 7 to 10 miles northeast of the Walt Disney World parks and 1 to 3 miles from Universal Orlando and SeaWorld, which makes this area the most centrally located for those who want to sample all that Orlando has to offer. The disadvantages: The northern end of International Drive is horribly congested (both on the road and off). The shops, motels, eateries, and attractions along this stretch can vary greatly in quality (some are decidedly tacky); as a general rule (with some exceptions), the closer to the convention center, the better the hotels and dining.

VERY EXPENSIVE
Peabody Orlando ★★★ *Finds* The five mallards that march into a lobby fountain every morning at 11am and back out at 5pm, accompanied by Sousa's *King Cotton March,* are just part of the appeal of this very upscale and service-oriented hotel. If your budget allows, you won't be disappointed with a stay here. Primarily a business

and convention destination, the Peabody also appeals to adults looking for a classy hotel that provides top-of-the-line service, amenities, and atmosphere. Rooms sleep up to five, and are tastefully decorated and well appointed. Those on the west side (sixth floor and higher) offer distant views of Disney and its fireworks displays.

9801 International Dr. (between Bee Line Expwy. and Sand Lake Rd.), Orlando, FL 32819. ✆ **800/732-2639** or 407/352-4000. Fax 407/354-1424. www.peabodyorlando.com. 891 units. $395–$490 standard room for up to 3; $550–$1,775 suite. Extra person $15. Children 17 and under stay free in parent's room. AE, DC, DISC, MC, V. Self-parking free; valet parking $14. From I-4, take the Sand Lake Rd./Hwy. 482 exit east to International Dr., then go south. Hotel is on the left across from the Convention Center. **Amenities:** 3 restaurants; deli; 3 lounges; outdoor heated pool; kids' pool; 4 lighted tennis courts; fitness center; spa; Jacuzzi; game room; concierge; guest-services desk; shuttle to WDW and other parks for a fee; business center; shopping arcade; salon; 24-hr. room service; massage; nonsmoking rooms; concierge-level rooms; valet. *In room:* A/C, TV, dataport, minibar, hair dryer.

Renaissance Orlando Resort at SeaWorld ✿✿ This resort just goes to show that you should never judge a book by its cover. A simple hotel exterior gives way to an absolutely beautiful and inviting interior, with luxurious touches throughout. A glass-covered atrium soars high above the stunning indoor courtyard area filled with lush gardens, cascading waterfalls, and an elegant free-flight aviary. The tastefully decorated rooms provide plenty of space to spread out and relax. Even after extensive renovations to the pool area, a $20-million makeover (that will include the installation of a full-service spa) is currently underway. SeaWorld fans will appreciate the location: just across the street from the park.

6677 Sea Harbour Dr., Orlando, FL 32821. ✆ **800/327-6677** or 407/351-5555. Fax 407/351-1991. www.renaissanceseaworld.com. 778 units. $119–$329 double. Extra person no charge. Children 17 and under stay free in parent's room. AE, DC, DISC, MC, V. Self-parking $7; valet parking $14. From I-4, take the Hwy. 528/Bee Line Expwy. exit east to International Dr., then go south to Sea Harbour Dr. and turn right. Small pets accepted. **Amenities:** 3 restaurants; grill; 3 lounges; outdoor heated pool; kids' pool; golf privileges (fee), 4 lighted tennis courts, tennis instruction (fee); basketball; volleyball; health club; spa; 2 Jacuzzis; sauna; arcade; playground; concierge; tour desk; car-rental desk; transportation to all the parks for a fee; business center; shopping arcade; salon; 24-hr. room service; massage; babysitting; guest laundry; nonsmoking rooms; valet. *In room:* A/C, TV w/pay movies, PlayStation, dataport, minibar, fridge (some rooms), hair dryer, safe.

MODERATE

La Quinta Inn & Suites Convention Center ✿ This is one of a handful of upscale, moderately priced motels on Universal Boulevard, which runs parallel to International Drive. The hotel is aimed at business travelers, but families with kids will find the rooms most comfortable. King rooms come with a fridge and microwave. A limited number of two-room suites offer separate living and sleeping areas.

8504 Universal Blvd., Orlando, FL 32819. ✆ **800/531-5900** or 407/345-1365. Fax 407/345-5586. www.laquinta.com. 184 units. $75–$125 double. Extra person $7. Rates include continental breakfast. Children 18 and under stay free in parent's room. AE, DC, DISC, MC, V. Free self-parking. Take I-4 to the Sand Lake Rd./Hwy. 482 exit; go east toward Universal, then right. Small pets accepted. **Amenities:** Outdoor heated pool; exercise room; Jacuzzi; transportation to all theme parks for a fee; guest laundry; nonsmoking rooms. *In room:* A/C, TV w/pay movies, Nintendo, dataport, free high-speed Internet access, fridge (some rooms), microwave (some rooms), coffeemaker, hair dryer, iron.

INEXPENSIVE

Fairfield Inn and Suites International Cove ✿ *Value* If you're looking for I-Drive's best value, it's hard to beat the Fairfield. It offers a quiet location off the main drag, earthly rates, and a clean motel in one package. The rooms are very comfortable and there are a number of restaurants within walking distance.

7495 Canada Ave. (off International Dr. near Sand Lake Rd.), Orlando, FL 32819. ✆ **407/351-7000.** Fax 407/351-0052. www.fairfieldinn.com. 200 units. $77–$119 for up to 4. Rates include continental breakfast. AE, DC, DISC, MC,

V. Free self-parking. From I-4, take the Sand Lake Rd./Hwy. 482 exit east, then turn east onto Canada Ave. **Amenities:** Outdoor heated pool; game room; guest-services desk; transportation to the parks for a fee; guest laundry; non-smoking rooms; valet. *In room:* A/C, TV w/pay movies, dataport, fridge (some rooms), microwave (some rooms), hair dryer, iron/ironing board, safe.

UNIVERSAL ORLANDO RESORTS

Universal Orlando has three unique and upscale themed properties of its own, all run by the Loews hotel group. Like the Disney resorts, Universal offers its resort guests additional privileges, including preferred access to the Universal parks' rides and attractions—show your room key and you will head right to the front of the line.

Portofino Bay Hotel ☆☆☆   Universal's first hotel has the stature and magnificence of Disney's Grand Floridian. This romantic, upscale resort is designed to look like the village of Portofino, Italy, complete with a harbor and canals that lead you via boat to the theme parks. The rooms sleep up to five and have beds with Egyptian-woven sheets and pillows so soft you'll want to take them home. Thanks to a recent multi-million-dollar renovation, rooms now feature additional amenities and a fresh, new sophisticated decor. Ask for a view overlooking the piazza and "bay" area. The Portofino doesn't just have swimming pools; its beach pool has a stone fort with a water slide, and the villa pool offers several cabanas with laptop hookups for the perfect mix of business and pleasure. The resort's Mandara Spa features a state-of-the-art fitness center and full-service spa. The drawbacks: There are stairs everywhere you turn, and the sheer size of the resort can make it difficult find your way around.

5601 Universal Blvd., Orlando FL 32819. ℂ **888/322-5541** or 407/503-1000. Fax 407/224-7118. www.loewshotels. com/hotels/orlando or www.universalorlando.com. 750 units. $264–$488 double; $459–$2,400 suites and villas. Extra person $25. Children 17 and under stay free in parent's room. AE, DC, DISC, MC, V. Self-parking $10; valet parking $17. From I-4, take the Kirkman Rd./Hwy. 435 exit and follow the signs to Universal. Small pets stay free. **Amenities:** 4 restaurants; deli; 3 lounges; 3 outdoor heated pools (1 for concierge-level and suite guests only); kids' pool; fitness center; spa; watersports equipment; kids' club; playground; arcade; salon; concierge; tour desk; free water-taxi and bus transportation to Universal Studios, Islands of Adventure, and CityWalk; free shuttle to SeaWorld; transportation to WDW parks for a fee; business center; shopping arcade; 24-hr. room service; babysitting; guest laundry; non-smoking rooms; concierge-level rooms; valet. *In room:* A/C, TV, CD and DVD players, video games (fee), high-speed Internet access (fee),minibar, fridge (suites), microwave (suites), hair dryer, iron, safe, crib (free), rollaway bed (fee).

EXPENSIVE

Hard Rock Hotel ☆☆☆ *Kids*   You can't get any closer than this to Universal Studios Florida. This California mission–style resort sports a rock-'n'-roll theme with rates a shade less expensive than the Portofino's (above). The atmosphere is slightly more casual than at other Universal resorts, though with an air of chic sophistication. Public areas abound with rock memorabilia, but it's the pool area that takes center stage—the large free-form pool's underwater sound system will make sure you don't miss a beat. The rooms are very comfortable, with a sophisticated modern decor. Unfortunately, though fairly soundproof, a few notes seep through the walls, so you may want to ask for one away from the lobby area. If you're bringing the school-age kids, it's the best bet among the three Universal resorts. *Tip:* The Hard Rock is a cut above some of Disney's comparable properties.

5000 Universal Blvd., Orlando, FL 32819. ℂ **800/232-7827** or 407/363-8000. Fax 407/224-7118. www.loewshotels. com/hotels/orlando or www.universalorlando.com. 650 units. $229–$466 double; $409–$2,040 suite. Extra person $25. Children 17 and under stay free in parent's room. AE, DC, DISC, MC, V. Self-parking $10; valet parking $17. From I-4, take the Kirkman Rd./Hwy. 435 exit and follow the signs to Universal. Small pets stay free. **Amenities:** 3 restaurants; grill; 2 lounges; outdoor heated pool; kids' pool; fitness center; kids' club; playground; arcade; concierge; free water-taxi or bus transportation to Universal Studios, Islands of Adventure, and CityWalk; free shuttle to SeaWorld;

transportation to WDW parks for a fee; shopping arcade; 24-hr. room service; babysitting; guest laundry; nonsmoking rooms; concierge-level rooms; valet. *In room:* A/C, TV, CD players, video games (fee), high-speed Internet access (fee), minibar, fridge (suites), microwave (suites), hair dryer, iron, safe, cribs (free), rollaway beds (fee).

Royal Pacific Resort ⭐⭐ *(Kids)*   The third of Universal Orlando's three resorts features a spectacular beachfront lagoon-style pool. It's lined with palm trees, winding walkways, waterfalls, and an exquisite orchid garden, all giving it a remote island feel (apart from the screams emanating from the nearby Islands of Adventure). The abandoned float plane (a scene that reminds more than a few people of *Gilligan's Island*) makes a great backdrop. The rooms, smaller than those at other Universal resorts, are decorated with wood accents and carvings, but are quite plain when compared to similar Disney resorts. The public areas are very impressive and well worth exploring. The addition of the Wantilan Luau Pavilion ensures that the resort's weekly luau is now held rain or shine. If you're traveling with young children, The Royal Pacific is the best choice at Universal.

6300 Hollywood Way, Orlando, FL 32819. *(C)* **800/232-7827** or 407/503-3000. Fax 407/503-3202. www.loewshotels. com/hotels/orlando or www.universalorlando.com. 1,000 units. $199–$428 double; $325–$1,875 suite. Extra person $25. Children 17 and under stay free in parent's room. AE, DC, DISC, MC, V. Self-parking $10; valet parking $17. From I-4, take Exit 75B, Kirkman Rd./Hwy. 435, and follow the signs to Universal. Small pets stay free. **Amenities:** 2 restaurants; 3 lounges; outdoor heated pool; kids' pool; Jacuzzi; sauna; kids' club; arcade; concierge; free water-taxi and bus transportation to Universal Studios, Islands of Adventure, and CityWalk; free shuttle to SeaWorld; transportation to WDW parks for a fee; babysitting; nonsmoking rooms; concierge-level rooms; valet. *In room:* A/C, TV, dataport, high-speed Internet access (fee), fridge (suites), microwave (suites), coffee maker, hair dryer, iron, safe, cribs (free), rollaway beds (fee).

PLACES TO STAY ELSEWHERE IN ORLANDO

There are three good reasons to choose accommodations away from the hustle and hassle of the attractions: Crowds are thinner; in some cases, prices are lower; and those traveling without children may appreciate the lack of them here. On the flip side, if you're heading to the theme parks, being located off the beaten path means you'll have to deal with a much longer drive and a great deal more traffic.

Westin Grand Bohemian ⭐⭐ *(Finds)*   Downtown's hotel jewel, the Grand Bohemian caters almost exclusively to the business and romance crowds, which means—much to the satisfaction of its adult guests—you'll find almost no children on the premises. The "Heavenly Beds" (firm mattresses, down blankets, comforters, five pillows) are among the best in Orlando. Upper floors on the east side overlook the pool; those on the north side face downtown. This smoke-free hotel's interior is adorned with more than 100 pieces of 19th- and 20th-century American fine art.

325 S. Orange Ave. (across from City Hall). *(C)* **866/663-0024** or 407/313-9000. Fax 407/313-6001. www.grand bohemianhotel.com. 250 units. $239–$439 for up to 4; $349–$549 suite. Extra person $25. AE, DC, DISC, MC, V. Valet parking $19. Take I-4 to the Washington St. exit, merge with W. Robinson/Hwy. 526, then head south on Orange St. The garage is 2 blocks west on Jackson St. **Amenities:** Restaurant; lounge; coffee shop; heated outdoor pool and spa; fitness center; concierge; shuttle to the theme parks for a fee; business center; 24-hr. room service; guest laundry and dry cleaning; concierge-level rooms. *In room:* A/C, TV w/pay movies, CD player, Nintendo (fee), dataport, high-speed Internet access (fee), minibar, coffeemaker, hair dryer, iron, safe.

4 Where to Dine

From family-style restaurants to fast-food to five-star dining, Orlando has restaurants to please every palate and to bend to every budget. As most Orlando visitors spend the majority of their time at Disney, most of the dining options I list below can be found there, too. I do, however, list plenty of other worthwhile restaurants, including some of the better places to eat at Universal Orlando and along International Drive.

ADVANCE RESERVATIONS AT DISNEY RESTAURANTS

"Advance Reservations" *aren't* really reservations at all. They are simply a way of claiming the first table that becomes available (and can accommodate your party) close to the time of your choosing. You'll be given priority over others who simply walked up in the hopes of getting a table without prior arrangements, though you may still have a 10- to 20-minute wait. And if you don't make Advance Reservations, especially for the most popular restaurants, of which there are many, you may miss out altogether, as they're usually booked well in advance, leaving little or no room at all for guests who decide to drop in. To make Advance Reservations at any WDW restaurant (in the parks or at the resorts), call ☎ **407/939-3463.** You can book as far as 180 days in advance of your arrival for most restaurants (which may be necessary during the busier times of year and is essential at the most popular restaurants).

Disney's **dinner shows** (by far the most popular dining experiences at WDW) can be booked only 180 days in advance (a far cry from the previous 2-year time frame) and now include Mickey's BBQ, but you must pay in full at the time of booking.

If you're staying on Disney property and haven't made arrangements prior to coming, you can make Advance Reservations right from your resort. At Epcot, you can do it at Guest Relations near Innoventions East; at the Magic Kingdom, head to City Hall or the guest relations counter near the park entrance; and at MGM, head to the Hollywood Junction for help. You can also go directly to the restaurant of your choice and make the arrangements in person.

TIPS ON WALT DISNEY WORLD RESTAURANTS

All park restaurants (as well as all restaurants in Florida) are **nonsmoking.**

Magic Kingdom restaurants don't serve alcohol, but those at Animal Kingdom, Epcot, and Disney–MGM Studios do.

Sit-down restaurants in WDW take American Express, Diners Club, Discover, MasterCard, Visa, and the Disney Card.

Unless otherwise noted, *restaurants in the parks require park admission.* Unless you're using WDW transportation, there is a $9 parking fee.

Nearly all WDW restaurants with sit-down or counter service offer children's menus with items ranging from $5 to $9.

INSIDE THE WALT DISNEY WORLD THEME PARKS

For the most part, the food offered throughout the parks is fairly decent, though, with few exceptions, you won't find Disney's park restaurants winning accolades from *Food & Wine* or *Bon Appétit.* And while the portions are generally on the large side, so are the prices. The following list includes Magic Kingdom, Epcot, Disney–MGM Studios, and Animal Kingdom. You can get information on all Disney restaurants by calling ☎ **407/939-3463** or visiting **www.disneyworld.com**.

EPCOT
World Showcase

The World Showcase has some of the best and most unique dining options inside the WDW theme parks, thanks to the cultural cuisine of its 11 nation pavilions. Although many consider a meal here an essential part of the park experience, I must point out that the food is priced higher than comparable fare in the free world, though no outside restaurants come close to matching the atmosphere you'll find here.

The restaurants below are arranged geographically, beginning at the Canada pavilion and proceeding counterclockwise around the World Showcase Lagoon. *Prices are for entrees only.*

CANADA   Le Cellier Steakhouse's vaulted archways, stone walls, and lanterns create a cozy and unique atmosphere much like that of a centuries-old wine cellar. While sandwiches and salads make for a meatier lunch than most, steaks are the main menu item for dinner, with a variety of cuts to choose from, including filet, porterhouse, and prime rib. Try one of the Canadian Ice Wines for a very sweet after-dinner treat. Lunch runs $10 to $22; dinner is $16 to $27.

UNITED KINGDOM   The **Rose & Crown** is a cozy English pub where folk music and saucy servers entertain as you dine. The menu features traditional British favorites, including fish and chips, prime rib, and Yorkshire pudding. Head over later in the evening for a pint of Bass or Guinness, as the patio is one of the best places to see the nightly fireworks display. Lunch is $13 to $16; dinner is $15 to $27.

FRANCE   One of Disney's priciest park restaurants, **Les Chefs de France** has a glass exterior that's among the prettiest around. The interior, agleam with mirrors and brass chandeliers, is impressive as well. Three renowned French chefs take credit for the menu, which includes such entrees as Mediterranean seafood casserole (grouper, scallops, and shrimp dusted with saffron, then enrobed in a mild garlic sauce) and a leg of lamb braised in tomatoes and wine. Lunch is $14 to $18; dinner is $16 to $28.

MOROCCO   Of all the Epcot restaurants, **Marrakesh** ☞ best exemplifies the spirit of the park. Guests often pass it by, worried the menu may be too exotic. The setting is grand; the interior is filled with tile mosaics, brilliantly colored carpets, and brass chandeliers. Belly dancers and Moroccan music often entertain guests as they feast on beef or chicken shish kabobs, and a host of seafood and lamb choices. Couscous accompanies most entrees. Lunch costs $15 to $18; dinner is $18 to $35.

JAPAN   If you've been to any of the Japanese steakhouse chains, you know what to expect at **Teppanyaki:** Guests sit around large grill tables while agile chefs dice, slice, stir-fry, and launch the occasional shrimp onto your plate with amazing skill. The culinary acrobatics here are a sight to see; the cuisine is average. Lunch is $14 to $35; dinner is $16 to $35. The adjoining **Yakitori House** is a rather small bamboo-roofed teahouse with fare like chicken with teriyaki sauce, beef in spicy sauce with Asian noodles, and ginger ice cream for dessert. Meals here are generally under $10.

ITALY   **L'Originale Alfredo di Roma,** set inside one of the most beautiful of the world pavilions, is Epcot's most popular restaurant. Singing waiters top off the dining experience at this elegant place. The most famous and popular item on the menu is the signature fettuccine Alfredo. For something on the meatier side of the menu, pan-seared veal in a wine sauce with wild mushrooms is a good choice. If you want a quieter setting, ask for a seat on the veranda overlooking the center courtyard. Lunch costs $11 to $23; dinner runs $19 to $30.

GERMANY ☞   The **Biergarten** feels like a Bavarian village at Oktoberfest. The lively mood is thanks in part to the Bavarian musicians who perform during the dinner hour, and quite possibly the beer—it's served in some rather tremendous steins. Diners are encouraged to join the fun by singing and dancing with the performers.

The all-you-can-eat buffet is heaped with traditional Bavarian fare (sausages, schnitzel, sauerbraten, seafood, roast chicken, sauerkraut, salads, and plenty of trimmings). The lunch buffet is $16 for adults, $8 for kids 3 to 11; dinner is $21 for adults, $9 for kids.

CHINA ✿ When it comes to decor, the **Nine Dragons** shines with carved rosewood furnishings and inlaid ceilings with plenty of dragon motifs. Some windows overlook the lagoon outside. Portions here, however, are small when compared with those at most Chinese restaurants. Lunch runs $11 to $19; dinners go for $13 to $40; samplers for two cost $30 to $44, and for four $60.

NORWAY **Akershus** is a re-created 14th-century castle complete with tremendous iron chandeliers above the large banquet hall. A smorgasbord of *smavarmt* (hot) and *koldtbord* (cold) dishes is on the menu here. While the Storybook breakfast features American fare, more traditional Norwegian fare, including cured salmon with spicy mustard; poached cod; braised lamb and cabbage; and venison stew are among the choices at lunch and dinner. Kids choose from grilled chicken, pasta, hot dogs, and turkey sandwiches. Several Disney princesses make their way around the hall, stopping at each table to say hello. Breakfast costs $23 for adults, $13 for kids 4 to 9; lunch is $25 for adults, $14 for kids 4 to 9; and dinner costs $29 for adults, $14 for kids.

MEXICO ✿ It's always night at the **San Angel Inn** ✿, where amid the marketplace, candlelit tables set a romantic mood under a faux star-lit sky. Reasonably authentic food, including the popular *mole poblano* (chicken simmered in spices, ground tortillas, and a hint of cocoa), is on the menu here. Lunch runs $11 to $19, and dinners around $18 to $24. The **Cantina de San Angel,** a cafeteria with outdoor seating at umbrella tables overlooking the lagoon, offers soft tacos, burritos, churros, and other items under $8.

Future World

Inside the Living Seas pavilion, the aptly named **Coral Reef** features tables scattered around a 5.6-million-gallon aquarium filled with tropical fish. Diners can watch Disney's denizens of the deep as they swim right by their tables; tiered seating ensures that everyone gets a decent view. The menu features mainly fresh seafood and shellfish with favorites such as Florida mahimahi, yellowtail snapper, and salmon. Try the lobster soup or corn chowder for starters. Lunch is $13 to $22; dinner is $17 to $31.

The **Sunshine Seasons Food Faire,** an upscale food court located just inside The Land, consists of six separate eateries, each offering a small menu of items, including Asian dishes; a variety of salads; chicken, fish, and beef entrees; sandwiches, and desserts. All new carpeting and a very contemporary earthy decor separate the large open seating area into smaller sections. Open to the second story, and with no real walls, it retains an airy feel. Most items cost between $4 and $10.

IN THE MAGIC KINGDOM

In addition to the restaurants listed below, there are plenty of fast-food outlets located throughout the park, of which Pecos Bill Cafe, Cosmic Ray's Starlight Cafe, and the Columbia Harbour House are your best choices. That said, you may find that a quiet, sit-down meal is an essential, if brief, getaway from the day's activities.

Fantasyland High atop the winding stone staircase inside Cinderella Castle awaits the medieval-themed **Cinderella's Royal Table** ✿. Stained-glass windows line the wall, and servers treat you like a lord or lady while fetching you such entrees as spice-crusted salmon, prime rib, and roasted chicken. Lunch costs $13 to $24; dinner is $23 to $29. Advanced Reservations are a must if you plan on dining here.

The **Crystal Palace,** named for its beautiful glass exterior, is a favorite with families because of its all-you-can eat character buffets (where kids and adults can choose from a decent variety of meats, veggies, and desserts). Breakfast costs $19 for adults and $11 for children ages 3 to 9. Lunch costs $21 for adults and $13 for children 3 to 9. Dinner runs $28 for adults and $13 for children 3 to 9. Advanced Reservations are a must.

AT DISNEY–MGM STUDIOS

There are more than a dozen unique places at which to refuel in this Hollywood-style theme park. Most of them feature more fun than fabulous food; the ones listed below are the best of the bunch. Again, Advanced Reservations are a must.

Modeled after the Los Angeles celebrity haunt where Louella Parsons and Hedda Hopper held court, the **Hollywood Brown Derby** re-creates the feel and atmosphere of a 1930s supper club. Caricatures of Hollywood's most famous line the walls. Highlights include the Cobb salad and spiced pan-roasted pork; the Derby's signature dessert, grapefruit cake with cream-cheese icing, is a perfect meal capper. Entrees go for $14 to $19 at lunch, $18 to $29 at dinner.

The **50's Prime Time Café** is like going home to Mom's for dinner—back in the 1950s. The atmosphere delivers with black-and-white TV sets showing *My Little Margie* and servers threatening to withhold dessert if you don't eat all your veggies. There are no elbows on the table here! The mainstays are the meatloaf and pot roast, though they aren't quite as good as Mom used to make. Come here for the atmosphere, not necessarily the food. Kids will get a kick out of the neon ice cubes glowing in their drinks. Lunch costs $11 to $17; dinner costs $11 to $18.

The best bets at the casual **Mama Melrose's Ristorante Italiano** are the wood-fired and brick-baked specialties, including the flat breads (pepperoni, portobello mushroom, and four cheeses). The warm and welcoming atmosphere makes you feel like you're at a mom and pop–run restaurant. Lunch and dinner run $15 to $29.

Take the above review for the 50's Prime Time Café, give it a science-fiction spin, and welcome to the **Sci-Fi Dine-In Theater Restaurant.** Diners sit in chrome-plated convertibles with the Hollywood Hills as a backdrop and are treated to newsreels, cartoons, and "B" horror flicks. Sandwiches, burgers, and salads make up the lunch menu; dinner features steak, pasta, ribs, and fish. Lunches run $12 to $18; dinners are $12 to $18. Eating here is a bit pricey, but the really unique atmosphere is worth it.

IN THE ANIMAL KINGDOM

You'll find only a few meal options in the Animal Kingdom, and most of those are of the grab-and-go style (of these, the Flame Tree BBQ is the best and the Chakranadi Chicken Shop the most unique). Nevertheless, there are two spots where you can sit yourself down for a spell.

Expect California fare with an island spin at the **Rainforest Cafe.** Menu offerings tend to be tasty and somewhat creative, but the prices run on the high side for what you get, and most people come for the junglelike tropical atmosphere. Lunch and dinner run anywhere from $9 to $40. ***Note:*** The restaurant is accessible from outside the park, so you don't have to pay park admission to eat here.

The thatched-roof **Tusker House** in Harambe village offers fast food with a bit of a flair. The slightly shaded patio out back, with a view over the trees, allows you to relax and enjoy your meal tucked away from the crowds. Out front the pavilion offers shade and, if timed right, a view of the live entertainment. Options include a grilled chicken salad, rotisserie or fried chicken, a turkey wrap with corn chowder, roasted-vegetable sandwiches, and grilled salmon. Prices run $7 to $8; kids' meals are $4.

IN THE WALT DISNEY WORLD RESORTS

Most of these restaurants continue the trend of being above market price, but the food is generally a few notches (or more, in certain cases) higher than what you find in the theme parks. Reservations are a must for dinner, but these restaurants can be far less crowded at lunch and during off hours, when most people are hitting at the parks.

VERY EXPENSIVE

Citricos ✦ NEW FRENCH   Eat here and you'll be treated to a fabulous view of the Seven Seas Lagoon, a warm Mediterranean atmosphere filled with orange and yellow hues, and a fine meal of French and Mediterranean cuisine with a Florida twist. The oft-changing menu might offer basil-crusted rack of lamb; sautéed shrimp with lemon, feta cheese, and white wine; or grilled salmon with roasted fennel and potatoes.

4401 Floridian Way, in Disney's Grand Floridian Resort & Spa. ✆ 407/939-3463. www.disneyworld.com. Advanced Reservations recommended. Main courses $23–$35. AE, DC, DISC, MC, V. Wed–Sun 5:30–10pm; Chef's Domain (Table) 6pm and 8:30pm Tues–Sat.

Victoria & Albert's ✦✦✦ *Finds* INTERNATIONAL   It's not often that dinner can be described as "an event," but Disney's most elegant restaurant earns that distinction. Dinner is next to perfect—if the portions seem small, it's simply so you can better enjoy all seven courses. The setting is exceptionally romantic; a violinist or harpist often plays in the background. Fare changes nightly, but you might find main events such as lamb seared with foie gras over brioche with Fuji apples, tamari-glazed blue-fin tuna over bok choy stir-fry, or Colorado lamb with corn risotto. The intimate dining room is crowned by a domed, chapel-style ceiling, 20 exquisitely appointed tables are lit softly by Victorian lamps, and your waitstaff (always named Victoria or Albert) provide service that will have you begging to take them home.

4401 Floridian Way, in Disney's Grand Floridian Resort & Spa. ✆ **407/939-3463.** www.disneyworld.com. Reservations required. Jackets required for men. Not recommended for children. Prix fixe $110 per person, $165 with wine pairing; $150 Chef's Table, $215 with wine. AE, DC, DISC, MC, V. 2 dinner seatings daily Sept–June, 5:45–6:30pm and 9–9:45pm; 1 seating July–Aug, 6:45–8pm. Chef's Table 6pm only. Valet parking $7.

Yachtsman Steakhouse ✦ SEAFOOD/STEAK   Even by outside-the-parks standards, this is a solid steakhouse with a cordial staff. In keeping with the resort, the atmosphere is nautical New England, with a slightly brighter decor than at most steakhouse-style restaurants. The exhibition kitchen provides a tantalizing peek at steaks, chops, and seafood being seared over oak and hickory. Options range from an 8-ounce filet to a 12-ounce strip to a belly-busting 24-ounce T-bone. The menu also has rack of lamb, salmon, and chicken.

1700 Epcot Resorts Blvd., in Disney's Yacht Club Resort. ✆ **407/939-3463.** Advanced Reservations recommended. Main courses $21–$55. AE, DC, DISC, MC, V. Daily 5:30–10pm. Free self- and valet parking.

EXPENSIVE

Artist Point ✦✦ *Finds* SEAFOOD/STEAKS   Enjoy a grand view of Disney's Wilderness Lodge in this rustically elegant establishment. Hand-painted murals of Southwestern scenery adorn the impressive raised ceiling, and ornate lanterns hang from tremendous timber columns. Select from a seasonally changing menu that might include grilled buffalo sirloin with a sweet-potato-and-hazelnut gratin, or cedar plank–roasted Silver Bay salmon with maple-whiskey glaze. *Note:* Artist Point has a more relaxed atmosphere than some of the busier WDW resort restaurants, but kids will have far more fun at the very lively **Whispering Canyon Café** just next door.

901 W. Timberline Dr., in Disney's Wilderness Lodge. *C* **407/939-3463** or 407/824-1081. www.disneyworld.com. Advanced Reservations recommended. Main courses $21–$49. AE, DC, DISC, MC, V. Daily 5:30–10pm. Free self- and valet parking.

Boma 🐾🐾 INTERNATIONAL   One of the Animal Kingdom Lodge's signature restaurants, Boma offers a nice diversion from the usual Disney fare. In front of the open kitchen lies an incredible buffet of international cuisine featuring authentic African dishes from over 50 different countries alongside a few more familiar favorites—including dishes especially for kids. A family atmosphere, similar to an African marketplace, is enhanced by colorful fabrics draped from above. A specialty of the house is the watermelon rind salad—very delicious. Everything is fresh and tasty. *Note:* An American buffet breakfast is served here daily.

2901 Osceola Pkwy., at Disney's Animal Kingdom Lodge. *C* **407/938-3000.** www.disneyworld.com. Advanced Reservations recommended. All You Can Eat Buffet $17–$26 for adults, $10–$12 for children 3–9. AE, DC, DISC, MC, V. Daily 7:30–11am and 5:30–10pm. Free self-parking.

California Grill 🐾🐾 CALIFORNIA   Make your way to the 15th floor of the Contemporary Resort and enjoy views of the Magic Kingdom—and its fireworks—while your meal is prepared in an exhibition kitchen. Headliners usually include wood-fired pizzas, smoked salmon, and grilled pork tenderloin with balsamic vinegar and cremini mushrooms. A vegetarian selection is available as well. The Grill features a sushi and sashimi menu. The upbeat atmosphere is enhanced by the contemporary and colorfully artistic decor. Reservations are required to ride the elevator to the restaurant, so be sure to make arrangements well ahead of time—this is a tough spot to get a table. *Note:* This is one of the few spots in WDW that isn't particularly well suited to kids.

4600 N. World Dr., at Disney's Contemporary Resort. *C* **407/939-3463** or 407/824-1576. www.disneyworld.com. Reservations required. Main courses $21–$34; sushi and sashimi $13–$24. AE, DC, DISC, MC, V. Daily 5:30–10pm. Free self-parking.

Todd English's bluezoo 🐾🐾🐾 SEAFOOD   Here's the hippest, hottest place in town, with a sophisticated marine-themed decor, an impressive exhibition kitchen, and a lounge where live music is often featured. Acclaimed chef Todd English has created an amazing menu of fresh seafood and coastal dishes served with creative flair. Don't miss the amazing "Olive's" *classico* flat bread. Entrees include lobster Bolognese, and grilled fish with a choice of three unique sauces. Portions are large, so do note that side dishes will run you an extra $5 to $7. Dress is casual, but the upscale atmosphere is chic and adult (though a children's menu is available—this is Disney).

1500 Epcot Resort Blvd., at the WDW Dolphin. *C* **407/934-1111.** www.disneyworld.com. Advanced Reservations recommended. Main courses $18–$52. AE, DISC, MC, V. Daily 3:30–11pm. Free self- and validated valet parking.

MODERATE

ESPN Club 🐾 AMERICAN   If you are a sports enthusiast, this is *the* place to dine. Upon entering, you will be surrounded by monitors showing every possible sporting event. The all-American fare includes such choices as "Boo-Yeah" chili, hot wings, and burgers. Sandwiches and salads are available as well. The service is impeccable—never have I had a waiter so quick on his feet. While the food is quite good, it's really the atmosphere that draws the crowds here.

2101 N. Epcot Resorts Blvd. At Disney's BoardWalk. ☎ **407/939-1177**. www.disneyworld.com. Advanced Reservations not available. Lunch and dinner $8–$21. AE, DC, MC, V. Mon–Thurs 11:30am–1am; Fri–Sat 11:30am–2am. Valet or free self-parking.

'Ohana ☆ *Kids* PACIFIC RIM   Its star is earned on the fun front, but the decibel level here may turn off those without children in tow. As your luau is prepared exhibition style over an 18-foot-wide fire pit, the staff keeps you busy with coconut races, hula lessons, and other shenanigans. Servers come around the tables with three-foot skewers of pork, turkey, steak, and vegetables, while starters and sides are all served family style. More kid-friendly fare can be requested. *Note:* A daily character breakfast with Lilo, Stitch, Mickey, and Pluto is served here, too.

1600 Seven Seas Dr., at Disney's Polynesian Resort. ☎ **407/939-3463** or 407/824-2000. www.disneyworld.com. Advanced Reservations strongly encouraged. $19–$26 adults; $11–$12 children 3–11. AE, DC, DISC, MC, V. Daily 7:30–11am and 5–10pm. Valet or free self-parking.

DOWNTOWN DISNEY
VERY EXPENSIVE
Fulton's Crab House ☆☆ SEAFOOD   Oysters and stone-crab claws are the specialties of this upscale eatery, located in a replica of a 19th-century Mississippi riverboat. Outdoor decks offer the best views of the lake and Downtown Disney. It's one of the area's best seafood houses, so bring along some extra cash. The menu changes often; however, with over 50 fresh seafood selections to choose from you won't be disappointed. And though you may not see many of them, kids are welcome.

1670 Buena Vista Dr., aboard the riverboat docked at Downtown Disney. ☎ **407/934-2628**. www.levyrestaurants.com. Advanced Reservations recommended. Main courses $10–$52 lunch, $26–$52 dinner. AE, DC, DISC, MC, V. Daily 11:30am–4pm and 5–11pm. Self-parking free; valet parking $7.

MODERATE
Rainforest Cafe ☆ CALIFORNIA   Don't arrive starving (or expecting a peaceful meal—the extensively themed jungle atmosphere entertains most kids but can be distractingly noisy). Waits here average 2 hours if you fail to call ahead to make Advance Reservations, and you'll still wait longer than at Animal Kingdom's Rainforest Cafe (p. 487). The menu can be tasty and creative, though somewhat overpriced. The choices seem endless, but a few of the more fun dishes include Mogambo Shrimp (sautéed in olive oil and served with penne pasta) and Maya's Mixed Grill (ribs, chicken breast, and shrimp).

Downtown Disney Marketplace, near the smoking volcano. ☎ **407/827-8500**. www.rainforest.com. Advanced Reservations. Main courses $11–$40 at lunch and dinner (most under $25). AE, DISC, MC, V. Sun–Thurs 10:30am–11pm; Fri–Sat 10:30am–midnight. Free self-parking.

Wolfgang Puck Café ☆☆ CALIFORNIA   The wait can be distressing, but this restaurant's energized atmosphere, along with an eclectic mix of menu choices, makes it worth the effort. An eye-catching exhibition kitchen in the casual downstairs cafe allows you to watch as your food is prepared. A favorite stop is the sushi bar, an artistic copper-and-terrazzo masterpiece that delivers some of the best sushi in Orlando. The upstairs room offers a more refined atmosphere—and a menu to match. Puck's is noisy, making conversation difficult no matter which level you choose.

1482 Buena Vista Dr., at Disney's West Side. ☎ **407/938-9653**. www.wolfgangpuck.com/myrestaurants or www.levyrestaurants.com. Reservations not accepted on lower level; Advanced Reservations for upstairs dining room. Main courses upstairs $22–$37; main courses cafe $11–$36; pizza and sushi $11–$27; Express $9–$15. AE, DC, DISC, MC, V. Daily 11am–1am. Free self-parking.

ELSEWHERE IN LAKE BUENA VISTA
MODERATE

The Crab House SEAFOOD   Decent seafood (as well as other options for landlubbers) at decent prices is what you get at this casual restaurant. The all-you-can-eat seafood-and-salad bar is a great way to sample all the tasty offerings. On the menu you'll find a variety of fish and shrimp dishes, Maine lobster, and, of course, crab—from Alaskan and king to Maryland Blue. The service is friendly and prompt.

8496 Palm Pkwy., Orlando, FL 32836 (just off Apopka-Vineland across and up from Hotel Plaza Blvd.) ℭ 407/239-1888. www.landrysrestaurants.com. Reservations accepted. Lunch $9–$22, dinner $14–$45. AE, DC, DISC, MC, V. Daily 11:30am–11pm. Free self-parking. Take I-4 to exit 68 (Hwy. 535), turn right, follow the road past the Crossroads to Palm Pkwy., and turn right. The restaurant is back a bit on the right.

Pebbles Island Grill ★★ *Finds* FLORIDIAN   If you want to dine like a gourmet without the hefty price, this is the restaurant for you. This local chain has a reputation for great food and creative appetizers. Its pleasant Key West style is casual and comfortable, and the generous portions are presented with artistic flair. The delicious Ybor Gold twin filets are seared, then bathed in the namesake lager and delivered with caramelized onions and three-cheese potatoes.

12551 Apopka-Vineland Rd., in the Crossroads Shopping Center. ℭ **407/827-1111.** www.pebblesworldwide.com. Reservations not accepted. Main courses $8–$28. AE, DC, DISC, MC, V. Mon–Thurs 11am–11pm; Fri 11am–midnight; Sat noon–midnight; Sun noon–11pm. Free self-parking. Take the I-4 Hwy. 535/Apopka-Vineland Rd. exit north to the Crossroads Shopping Center on the right.

INEXPENSIVE

Romano's Macaroni Grill ★ *Value* NORTHERN ITALIAN   Though it's part of a multistate chain, Romano's has the down-to-earth cheerfulness of a mom-and-pop joint. The laid-back atmosphere makes it a good place for families or those looking for a casual dinner. The menu offers thin-crust pizzas made in a wood-burning oven and topped with such items as barbecued chicken. The grilled chicken Portobello (with smoked mozzarella and spinach orzo pasta) alone is worth the visit.

12148 Apopka–Vineland Rd. (just north of Hwy. 535/Palm Pkwy.). ℭ **407/239-6676.** www.macaronigrill.com. Main courses $6–$21 lunch, $8–$20 dinner (most under $12). AE, DC, DISC, MC, V. Sun–Thurs 11am–10pm; Fri–Sat 11am–11pm. Free self-parking. Take I-4 exit 68, Hwy. 535/Apopka–Vineland Rd. N., and continue straight when Hwy. 535 goes to the right. Romano's is about 2 blocks on the left.

PLACES TO DINE IN UNIVERSAL ORLANDO

Universal Orlando's CityWalk and resorts are home to a number of good dining spots.

VERY EXPENSIVE

Emeril's ★★ NEW ORLEANS   It's next to impossible to get short-term reservations for dinner here unless you're willing to take your chances with no-shows. If you do get in, you'll find the dynamic, Creole-inspired cuisine worth the struggle. Best bets are the andouille-crusted redfish (a moist white fish with roasted pecan-vegetable relish and meunière sauce) and the rib-eye steak dusted with kosher salt and cracked black pepper, served with wild-mushroom bread pudding and grilled vegetables. If you want a show, we recommend one of eight counter seats, where you can watch chefs work their magic; but to get one, reservations are required *excruciatingly* early (2–3 months, at least).

Note: Lunch costs about half what you'll spend on dinner, and the menu and portions are almost the same. It's also easier to get a midday reservation. No matter when you come, leave the kids at home—this restaurant caters to adults.

Value **Bring On the Barbecue**

Finally, **Bubbalou's Bodacious BBQ** ✈, 5818 Conroy Rd., Orlando (© **407/423-1212**; www.bubbalous.com), has opened a location not too far off the beaten path. Come here for some of the best barbecue in Florida. Go for the full pork platter that comes with a heaping helping and all the fixin's. The uninitiated should stay away from the "Killer" sauce if you value your taste buds; you might even taste-test the mild sauce before moving up to the hot. Main courses run $4 to $13. Hours are Monday through Saturday from 10am to 9pm. To get here, take exit 75B off of I-4, follow Kirkman, then make a left onto Conroy Road and follow your nose; Bubbalou's is on the left.

6000 Universal Studios Blvd., in CityWalk. © **407/224-2424**. www.emerils.com/restaurants/index_orlando.htm. Reservations necessary. Main courses $18–$28 lunch, $18–$45 dinner. Daily 11:30am–2pm and 5:30–10pm (until 11pm Fri–Sat). AE, DISC, MC, V. Parking $9 (free after 6pm). From I-4, take the Kirkman Rd./Hwy. 435 exit and follow the signs to Universal.

EXPENSIVE

Tchoup Chop ✪✪✪ PACIFIC RIM   Culinary perfection is pronounced "chop chop." Emeril Lagasse's second restaurant in Orlando is named for the location of his original restaurant, Tchoupitoulous Street in New Orleans. Think bluezoo (see above) with an Asian Pacific twist—very chic, contemporary, and impressive. The service is impeccable and the relaxing atmosphere, stunning decor, and excellent food ensure that the experience is unmatched. Polynesian- and Asian-influenced dishes such as macadamia nut–crusted Atlantic salmon, Polynesian crab cakes with mango habanero butter sauce and papaya salsa, and ahi tuna lettuce wraps are just a sampling of the tasty offerings.

6300 Hollywood Way, in Universal's Royal Pacific Hotel. © **407/503-2467**. www.emerils.com/restaurants/index_ orlando.htm. Reservations strongly recommended. Main courses $13–$34. AE, DISC, MC, V. Daily 11:30am–2pm; Sun–Thurs 5:30–10pm; Fri–Sat 5:30–11pm. Valet parking $5. From I-4, take the Kirkman Rd./Hwy. 435 exit and follow the signs to Universal.

MODERATE

Pastamore Ristorante SOUTHERN ITALIAN   The *antipasto primo* here is a meal unto itself and includes bruschetta, eggplant caponata, melon with prosciutto, grilled portobello mushrooms, Italian cold cuts, olives, plum tomatoes, and mozzarella. This casual eatery features Italian classics, seafood, pastas, and grilled specialties. Options include veal Marsala, chicken piccata, fettuccine Alfredo, and pizza, among several others. An open kitchen allows diners a view of the chefs at work. You can also eat in a cafe where lighter fare is served from 8am to 2am.

1000 Universal Studios Plaza, in CityWalk. © **407/363-8000**. www.universalorlando.com. Reservations accepted. Main courses $8–$28. AE, DISC, MC, V. Daily 5pm–midnight. Parking $9 (free after 6pm). From I-4, take the Kirkman Rd./Hwy. 435 exit and follow the signs to Universal.

PLACES TO DINE IN THE INTERNATIONAL DRIVE AREA

International Drive has one of the area's larger collections of fast-food joints, but the midsection and southern third also have some of this region's better restaurants. International Drive is 10 minutes by car from the Walt Disney World parks.

VERY EXPENSIVE

Atlantis ✸ SEAFOOD/STEAK/CHOPS   This intimate dining room, adorned with hand-painted murals, has a warm, elegant feel, especially in the booths separated by etched-glass panels. Chef's specials such as a Mediterranean seafood medley (Florida lobster, grouper, shrimp, and scallops) frequently complement menu standards such as grilled sea bass or pan-seared duck and rock shrimp. Sunday's champagne brunch is served in the beautifully landscaped atrium. Themes change, but the menu often has treats such as quail, duck, lamb chops, Cornish hen, mussels, snapper, sea bass, sushi, and more. Although pricey, it's one of Orlando's more popular brunches.

6677 Sea Harbour Dr., in the Renaissance Orlando Resort. ✆ 407/351-5555. www.renaissanceseaworld.com or www.atlantisorlando.com. Reservations recommended. Main courses $27–$35; Sun brunch $35 adults, $18 children. AE, DC, DISC, MC, V. Daily 6–10pm. Self-parking free; valet parking $14 (complimentary for the brunch). From I-4, take the 417/Central Florida Pkwy. exit and follow the signs to SeaWorld.

EXPENSIVE

Ran-Getsu of Tokyo JAPANESE   Its authentic cuisine and sushi bar have made Ran-Getsu a popular haunt for moneyed Asian tourists, though some diners find the prices too high. *Tekka-don,* tender slices of tuna mild enough for first-timers, is a refreshing sushi choice. *Yosenabe* is a bouillabaisse with a savory twist—duck and chicken are added to the seafood mix. A traditional Japanese drum show is performed Thursday through Saturday evenings.

8400 International Dr., near Orlando Convention Center. ✆ 407/345-0044. www.rangetsu.com. Reservations recommended. Main courses $14–$70 (most under $25); sushi entrees $15–$45 (most under $25). AE, DC, DISC, MC, V. Daily 5–11:30pm. From I-4, take the Sand Lake Rd./Hwy. 528 exit east to International Dr., then head south. Restaurant is on the right.

MODERATE

Café TuTu Tango ✸ *Finds* INTERNATIONAL/TAPAS   Authentic cuisine and the eclectic atmosphere of a Mediterranean artist's loft are the main draws to this interesting eatery. The portions are small, but the tastes are big. The roasted pears on pecan crisps—topped with Spanish blue cheese and a balsamic reduction, and served with arugula—are a must. The service is fabulous; your server will be happy to educate you about the menu as well as offer some great suggestions to tempt your taste buds.

8625 International Dr. ✆ 407/248-2222. www.cafetututango.com. Reservations accepted but not required. Tapas (small portions) $4–$20. AE, DC, DISC, MC, V. Sun–Thurs 11:30am–11pm; Fri–Sat 11:30am–1am. Free self-parking. From I-4, take exit 74A, Sand Lake Rd./Hwy. 528, east to International Dr., then head south. It is on the left.

Ming Court ✸✸ CHINESE   Its diverse menu and tasty dishes make this one of Orlando's most popular Chinese restaurants. The deep-fried chicken breast gets zip from a delicate lemon-tangerine sauce. If you're in the mood for beef, try the filet mignon Szechuan style. Portions are sufficient and the service is excellent. The 250-foot carved dragons that greet you at the entrance hint at what awaits you inside. Kids get their own menu, featuring beef, shrimp, chicken, and pork served with Asian flair.

9188 International Dr., between Sand Lake Rd. and Bee Line Expwy. ✆ 407/351-9988. www.ming-court.com. Reservations recommended. Dim sum mostly $3–$6; main courses $7–$14 lunch, $13–$36 dinner. AE, DC, DISC, MC, V. Daily 11am–2:30pm and 4:30–11:30pm. Free self-parking. From I-4, take the Sand Lake Rd./Hwy. 528 exit east to International Dr., then south. Ming Court is on the right opposite Pointe Orlando.

Siam Orchid ✸ *Finds* THAI   Tim and Krissnee Martsching grow the mint, chiles, cilantro, lemon grass, and wild lime that go into their entrees. Star attractions include Pad Thai (noodles tossed with ground pork, garlic, shrimp, crab, and peanuts in a sweet sauce) and Royal Thai (chicken, potatoes, and onion in yellow curry sauce). Siam Orchid serves sake, plum wine, and Thai beers from a full bar.

7575 Universal Blvd. (between Sand Lake Rd. and Carrier Dr.). © **407/351-0821**. Reservations recommended. Main courses $12–$24. AE, DC, DISC, MC, V. Mon–Fri 11am–2pm; daily 5–11pm. Free self-parking. From I-4, take the Sand Lake Rd./Hwy. 528 exit east to Universal, then go north to the restaurant (on the left).

ONLY IN ORLANDO: DINING WITH DISNEY CHARACTERS

Dining with Disney characters is a treat for almost any Disney fan, but it's a special one for those under the age of 10. The characters will greet you, sign autographs, pose for photos, and interact with the entire family. These dining experiences are extremely popular, so make Advanced Reservations (© **407/939-3463**) as early as possible (up to 180 days in advance), and call for schedules. Prices vary, but generally expect breakfast (most serve it) to be $17 to $32 for adults, and $11 to $22 for kids 3 to 9. Restaurants that serve dinner charge $28 to $40 for adults and $13 to $25 for kids.

Character meals are offered at **Cape May Café** (in Disney's Beach Club Resort), **Chef Mickey's** (at Disney's Contemporary Resort), **Cinderella's Royal Table** (in Cinderella Castle, Magic Kingdom), **Crystal Palace Buffet** (at the Crystal Palace, Magic Kingdom), **Donald's Prehistoric Breakfastosaurus** (in Dinoland U.S.A., Animal Kingdom), **Garden Grill** (in the Land Pavilion, Epcot), **Liberty Tree Tavern** (in Liberty Square, Magic Kingdom), **'Ohana** (at Disney's Polynesian Resort), **Akershus Castle** (in Epcot's Norway Pavilion), **1900 Park Fare** (at Disney's Grand Floridian Resort & Spa), and the **Garden Grove Café** and **Gulliver's Grill** (at the WDW Swan).

5 Tips for Visiting Walt Disney World Attractions

Walt Disney World, home to the four major theme parks of Magic Kingdom, Epcot, Disney–MGM Studios, and Animal Kingdom, welcomes around 43 million guests in a typical year. Besides its larger theme parks, Disney has an assortment of other venues, including Downtown Disney (Cirque du Soleil, DisneyQuest, Pleasure Island, West Side, and the Marketplace), Blizzard Beach, and Typhoon Lagoon, just to name a few.

Parking   Cars, light trucks, and vans pay $9. Visitors with disabilities can park in special areas near the entrances. *Don't forget* to write down where you parked (area and row number) because after a long day at the parks, Minnie, Mickey, Goofy, and Donald all start to look and sound alike.

When You Arrive   Grab a printed park guide. It tells you not only where the fun is (including current ride-restriction information), but when and where to eat and shop. Pick up a copy of the daily entertainment schedule, too. If you want to see certain shows or parades, you will need to know when to go. And don't forget to arrive early (usually about 20–30 min., depending on the season) to get a good seat.

Best Times to Visit   There isn't really an off season in Orlando, but crowds are thinner from early January to mid-March and from mid-September until the week before Thanksgiving. The busiest days at all theme parks are generally Saturday and Sunday, when the locals visit. Monday, Thursday, and Saturday are pretty frantic in the Magic Kingdom; Tuesday and Friday are hectic at Epcot; Sunday and Wednesday are crazy at Disney–MGM Studios; and Monday, Tuesday, and Wednesday are a zoo at Animal Kingdom. Major holidays attract scores of visitors: Christmas to New Year's is the busiest of time of year; the week preceding and following Easter comes in a very close second. *Note:* Summer, though one of the least expensive times to visit, can also be the worst. The crowds are heavy, and the heat and humidity can be intolerable.

Operating Hours Park hours vary and are influenced by special events as well as the economy. Call ahead or go to **www.disneyworld.com** to check for operating times; otherwise, you could find yourself expecting to stay all night when, in reality, the park closes at 6pm. Hours vary not only from park to park, but also from week to week, and even day to day. This can greatly affect your plans, so don't just assume that a park is open; check the schedule ahead of time or once you arrive.

Tip: If you are a WDW resort guest (or are staying at the WDW resort's Hilton, the WDW Swan, or the WDW Dolphin), you can take advantage of Disney's **Extra Magic Hour** program. This allows WDW resort guests early entry (or extended evening hours) at select theme parks (including the water parks) on select days. The Extra Magic Hour schedule can change frequently, so it's best to check with your resort upon arrival for the most up-to-date information.

Tickets Disney's Magic Your Way ticketing structure now gives visitors who stay here for a few days far better deals than those who come for just a day. The system allows guests to customize tickets by first purchasing a base ticket for a set fee, and then purchasing add-ons, including a Park Hopper option, a no-expiration option, and the option to include admission to some of Disney's smaller venues, such as Pleasure Island, the water parks, and DisneyQuest (the Magic Plus Pack option). There is even a Premium ticket that includes both the Park Hopper and Magic Plus options.

Ticket durations can vary from a single day to 10 days (after 7 days, an annual pass is a wise purchase), and the more you stay, the less you pay per day. Note that unless you purchase a no-expiration add-on to your ticket, it will now expire within 14 days of the first day of use (but you don't have to use your tickets on consecutive days).

The following prices don't include 6.5% sales tax unless noted. *Note:* Price hikes are frequent occurrences, so call (© **407/824-4321**) or visit WDW's website (**www.disneyworld.com**) for the most up-to-the-minute pricing.

One-day/one-park Base Tickets, for admission to the Magic Kingdom, Epcot, Animal Kingdom, or Disney–MGM, are $63 for adults, $52 for children 3 to 9. (Ouch!) **Multiday Base Tickets** allow you to visit *one park per day.* A 7-day ticket costs $204 for adults (about $29 a day), $165 for kids (about $24 a day).

A **Park Hopper** add-on ($40 *per ticket,* per person) allows visitors unlimited admission to the Magic Kingdom, Epcot, Animal Kingdom, and Disney–MGM Studios for the length of their ticket. A 1-day adult Park Hopper ticket costs $103, while the 7-day version costs $244—making the latter a far better deal. Because the $40 fee applies per ticket and not per day, the longer you stay, the better deal you get.

Water Park Fun & More tickets are a different add-on that allows visitors a choice of two to six admissions (the number depends on the length of your pass) to Typhoon Lagoon, Blizzard Beach, Pleasure Island, DisneyQuest, or Disney's Wide World of Sports. Prices range from an obscene $113 for a 1-day adult pass to $254 for a 7-day

---

Tips **Advance Ticket Purchase Discounts**

Purchasing your 4- to 10-day Disney tickets (which must also include the Park Hopper and/or Water Park Fun & More option) ahead of time can result in substantial savings. You can save $2 to $18 with an advance ticket for a guest age 10 or up, and save $2 to $12 by purchasing an advance ticket for a child 3 to 9 years old. This can add up to $60 in savings for a family of four.

pass (a good deal). *Note:* If you wish to park-hop and visit some of Disney's lesser attractions, you'll have to tack on $90 in add-ons to a Base Ticket; that's not a huge added expense if you're staying at Disney for 7 days (total ticket price: $294 per adult), but it's ridiculous if you're there for only 2 (total ticket price: $215).

A **1-day ticket** to **Typhoon Lagoon, Blizzard Beach,** or **DisneyQuest** is $34 for adults, $28 for children.

A **1-day ticket** to **Pleasure Island** is $21. Because this is primarily an 18-and-over entertainment complex, there's no bargain price for children.

If you're planning an extended stay or are going to visit Walt Disney World more than once during the year, **annual passes** ($415–$539 adults, $365–$475 children 3–9) are another great option.

6 The Magic Kingdom

The Magic Kingdom is by far the most enchanting of all the Disney parks. Taking center stage is Cinderella Castle, the best known and most recognized symbol of Disney. From the minute you look down Main Street U.S.A., you're transported to a world of fantasy, ostensibly free from all the cares and worries of the outside world. The park's **seven "lands"** surround the castle to form the most magical place on earth.

MAIN STREET, USA

The gateway to the Kingdom, Main Street resembles the perfect turn-of-the-20th-century American street (okay, so it leads to a 13th-century European castle—nobody complains). It features shops, restaurants, and outdoor entertainment. Main Street, however, is best left for the end of the day when you're heading back to your hotel.

As soon as you arrive at Main Street, you can board the **Walt Disney World Railroad,** an authentic 1928 steam-powered train, for a 20-minute trip around the perimeter of the park. It's a good way to travel if you're headed to one of its three stations—the park entrance, Frontierland, and Mickey's Toontown Fair—or if you want to go for a relaxing ride that has shorter lines.

ADVENTURELAND

Cross a bridge and stroll through an exotic jungle of foliage, thatched roofs, and totems. Amid dense vines and stands of bamboo, drums are beating and swashbuckling adventures are beginning.

On the 10-minute **Jungle Cruise,** you sail through the Congo, an Amazon rainforest, and the Nile River in Egypt, among other locales. Dozens of animatronic creatures inhabit the hanging vines, cascading waterfalls, and tropical foliage.

The first major ride added to Adventureland since 1971, the **Magic Carpets of Aladdin** ✿ delights wee ones and some older kids. Its 16 four-passenger carpets circle a giant genie's bottle while the camels spit water at the passengers. The flying carpets spin and move up, down, forward, and back.

In the classic **Pirates of the Caribbean** ✿✿, the pirates chase "wenches" as your boat passes audio-animatronic figures that include "yo-ho-ho-ing" pirates raiding a Caribbean town. Spurred by the popularity of the first and release of the second *POTC* movie (with a third still to come), Jack Sparrow, Barbossa, and Davy Jones have joined the set. A tweak in the storyline to better mirror the movie, and a mix of new and updated special effects have been added, too. Still, the ride might be a bit scary for kids under 5 due to the unexpected (but small) drops and moments of darkness.

Tips **FASTPASS**

Don't want to stand in long lines? Disney parks use a system in which you go to the most popular rides, feed your theme-park ticket into a small ticket-taker machine, and get an assigned time to return. When you return at the appointed time, head to the reasonably short FASTPASS line and hop aboard. Here's the drill:

Hang on to your ticket when you enter, and head to the hottest ride of your choosing. If it's a FASTPASS attraction (they're noted in the park guide you get when you enter) and there's a line, feed your ticket stub into the FASTPASS ticket taker. Retrieve both your ticket stub and the FASTPASS stub that comes with it. Look at the two times stamped on the FASTPASS. Come back during that 1-hour window, and you can enter the ride with almost no wait. In the interim, venture on out and experience another attraction or show.

Note: Early in the day, your window may begin as close as only 40 minutes after you feed the FASTPASS machine, but later in the day it could be hours. Initially, Disney allowed you to do this on only one ride at a time; however, now you can get a pass for a second attraction 2 hours after your first assigned time (a time frame that's subject to change). Note, however, that the passes go quickly at times and the system can max out, sometimes by noon, so be sure to head to the rides most important to you earliest in the day.

The Enchanted Tiki Room Under New Management is a very upbeat and enchanting show featuring a slew of tropical birds singing and telling jokes. It is a bit loud on the decibel front but is otherwise cute and entertaining.

FRONTIERLAND

From Adventureland, step into the wild and woolly past of the American frontier. The landscape is straight out of the Wild West, complete with log cabins and rustic saloons.

The low-key **Big Thunder Mountain Railroad** 🎠🎠 roller coaster has tight turns and dark descents rather than sudden, steep drops. It's situated in a 200-foot-high red-stone mountain with 2,780 feet of track through caves and canyons. Your train careens through the ribs of a dinosaur, under a thundering waterfall, past geysers and bubbling mud pots, and over a bottomless volcanic pool. It's tailor-made for kids and grown-ups who want a thrill but aren't quite up to tackling the big coasters. *Note:* You must be 40 inches or taller to ride.

The **Country Bear Jamboree** 🎠🎠 is a hoot. It's a 15-minute show featuring audio-animatronic bears belting out rollicking country tunes and crooning plaintive love songs. It's a great place to cool off, too.

Based on Disney's 1946 film *Song of the South,* **Splash Mountain** 🎠🎠🎠 takes you flume-style past 26 colorful scenes that include swamps, bayous, caves, and waterfalls. Riders are caught up in the schemes of Brer Fox and Brer Bear as they chase the ever-wily Brer Rabbit. Your hollow-log vehicle twists, turns, and splashes, sometimes plummeting in darkness as the ride leads to a 52-foot-long, 40-mph splashdown in a briar-filled pond. *Note:* You must be at least 40 inches tall to ride.

LIBERTY SQUARE

Step back into 18th-century America. Thirteen lanterns, symbolizing the colonies, hang from the Liberty Tree, an immense live oak in the center of the courtyard. You may even encounter a fife-and-drum corps on the cobblestone streets.

Every American president is represented by a lifelike audio-animatronic figure in the **Hall of Presidents** 🎟. Look closely, and you'll see them fidget and whisper. The show begins with a film, and then the curtain rises on America's leaders. Each president's costume reflects his period's fashion, fabrics, and tailoring techniques.

Once you're inside the **Haunted Mansion** 🎟🎟, darkness, spooky music, howling, and screams enhance the ambience. After a brief and somewhat ominous welcome, the slow-motion ride takes you past a host of bizarre scenes, including a ghostly banquet and ball, a graveyard band, a talking head in a crystal ball, and weird flying objects. At the end, a ghost will "hitch" a ride with you in your car. It's a classic that's more amusing than terrifying for anyone over the age of 5.

FANTASYLAND

The attractions in this happy land are themed after classics such as *Snow White, Peter Pan,* and *Dumbo.* If your kids are 8 and under, you may want to make this and Mickey's Toontown your primary stops in the Magic Kingdom.

There's not a lot to do at **Cinderella Castle** 🎟, but its status as the Magic Kingdom's icon makes it a must (not that you can really miss it, as it stands 185 ft. tall). The namesake character appears daily in the new *Cinderellabration* show on the castle stage, and Cinderella's Royal Table restaurant is located inside.

The elaborate and beautiful **Cinderella's Golden Carousel** 🎟🎟 was constructed by Italian carvers in 1917 and refurbished by Disney artists, who added 18 hand-painted scenes from the Cinderella story on a wooden canopy above the horses. Kids of all ages will enjoy this ride.

Dumbo the Flying Elephant 🎟 is a very tame kids' ride, in which the Dumbos go around in a circle, gently rising and dipping. If you can stand the lines (and they are usually quite long), it's very exciting for wee ones.

Built for the 1964 New York World's Fair, **It's a Small World** 🎟 takes you to countries inhabited by appropriately costumed audio-animatronic dolls singing "It's a small world after all," in tiny doll voices. Every adult who has ever ridden this in the past will remember the tune, as it can be difficult to get out of your mind.

Mad Tea Party is a traditional amusement park ride with an *Alice in Wonderland* theme that's always a hit with the younger set. Riders sit in big pastel-hued teacups on saucers that careen around a circular platform at the same time that they, too, are spinning. Adults may want to ground themselves when they get off, as the kids tend to spin as fast as physically possible.

Mickey's PhilharMagic 🎟🎟🎟 is the most amazing 3-D film I've ever seen. Covering one of the largest screens ever made for a 3-D movie, the production's special effects (similar in style to those in **Jim Henson's Muppet*Vision 3D,** but even better, p. 504) are incredible. Many of Disney's most beloved characters make an appearance to help (or, in some cases, hinder) the attempts of Donald Duck to retrieve Mickey's magical sorcerer's hat. This is a must-see for absolutely everyone.

On **Peter Pan's Flight** 🎟, you'll ride in airborne versions of Captain Hook's ship and take a calm flight over nighttime London to Never-Never Land. You will fly above the mermaids, the ticking crocodile, the Lost Boys, Princess Tiger Lily, Tinker Bell,

Hook, and Smee. This is a fun ride for younger kids and Peter Pan fans of all ages. Just be prepared for one of the longest waits in the park.

Though it may still scare kids under 5, contrary to its name, **Snow White's Scary Adventures'** storyline is bright (though the witch puts in an appearance or two), and the title heroine appears in pleasant scenes, such as one at a wishing well.

MICKEY'S TOONTOWN FAIR

Where's Mickey? This 2-acre site is a great place for small children to find him and his pals. Toontown offers you and your kids a chance to meet Disney characters, including Mickey, Minnie, Donald, and Goofy. You can even have your photo taken with them (if you can make it through the sometimes endless lines).

The Barnstormer at Goofy's Wiseacre Farm ⚘⚘ is a mini–roller coaster likely inspired by Woody Woodpecker's Nuthouse Coaster at Universal Orlando (p. 511). It looks and feels like a crop duster that flies off-course and through Goofy's barn. The ride has very little in the dip-and-drop department, but a bit of zip on the spin-and-spiral front. The 60-second corkscrew ride has a 35-inch height minimum.

Donald's Boat (S.S. *Miss Daisy*) ⚘ offers a lot of interactive fun, and the "waters" around it feature fountains of water snakes and other wet fun things that earn squeals of joy (and relief on hot days). Bring extra clothes or a swimsuit for this one.

Mickey's & Minnie's Country Houses ⚘ are separate cottages that offer a lot of visual fun and some marginal interactive areas for youngsters. Mickey's place features garden and garage playgrounds. Minnie's lets kids play in her kitchen, where popcorn goes wild in a microwave and a cake comes to life in the oven as the utensils play melodies. Head behind his house and through the garden, and you'll find Mickey available for photos and autographs throughout the day.

TOMORROWLAND

The reasonably cute **Stitch's Great Escape** debuted in 2004, recruiting riders to help capture and contain the infamous "experiment 626," who is wreaking havoc on the galaxy. Disney animatronics bring the friendly characters to life, and sensory effects and overhead restraints help provide atmosphere. *Tip:* Younger kids who reach the 38-inch height restriction may not care for the long periods of darkness and silence.

On **Buzz Lightyear's Space Ranger Spin** ⚘⚘⚘, join Buzz and try to save the universe while flying your cruiser through a world you'll recognize from the original *Toy Story* movie. Kids enjoy using the dashboard-mounted laser cannons as they spin through the sky. If they're good shots, they can set off sight and sound gags with their lasers. You may be riding this more than once if you have kids.

The cosmic coaster, **Space Mountain** ⚘ usually has *long* lines (if you don't use FASTPASS), even though it's years past its prime. Once aboard a "rocket," you'll climb and dive through the inky, starlit blackness of outer space. The hairpin turns and plunges make it seem as if you're going at breakneck speed, but your car doesn't go any faster than 28 mph. *Note:* Riders must be at least 44 inches tall.

The Timekeeper is hosted by a robot/mad scientist (Robin Williams) and his assistant, 9-EYE, a flying, camera-headed droid that moonlights as a time-machine test pilot. In this jet-speed escapade, the audience hears Mozart as a young prodigy playing for French royalty, watches da Vinci work, and floats in a hot-air balloon over Red Square. It appeals more to adults than kids.

Younger kids love **Tomorrowland Indy Speedway,** especially if their adult companion lets them drive (without a big person, there's a 52-in. height minimum for driving a lap). Teens and other fast starters find it just too slow—the cars go only 7 mph and are loosely locked into lanes.

PARADES, FIREWORKS & MORE

For up-to-the-moment information, see the entertainment schedule in the park guide map as well as the *Times Guide & New Information* card that you can (and should) pick up when entering the park.

The Magic Kingdom's first new fireworks display in over 30 years, **Wishes** 👁👁👁 debuted in 2003 to lots of acclaim. Its precise mix of choreographed bursts, music, and story is just amazing and has to be experienced to be appreciated. It's absolutely the best way to end your day in the Magic Kingdom. The fireworks go off nightly during peak periods, but only on selected nights the rest of the year.

A 20-minute after-dark display, **SpectroMagic** 👁👁, combines fiber optics, holographic images, old-fashioned twinkling lights, and a soundtrack featuring classic Disney tunes. The parade runs on a *very limited basis.*

7 Epcot

Epcot is an acronym for Experimental Prototype Community of Tomorrow, and it was Walt Disney's dream for a planned residential community. However, long after his death, Epcot opened in 1982 as Central Florida's second Disney theme park.

The 260-acre park has two very distinct sections: **Future World** and **World Showcase.** It's so large that hiking World Showcase (1⅓ miles) can be exhausting. That's why some say Epcot really stands for "Every Person Comes Out Tired." Depending on how long you linger at the 11 countries in World Showcase, this park can be seen in 1 day, but it's better to do it over 2 days to take it all in properly.

FUTURE WORLD

Future World is centered on Epcot's icon, a giant geosphere known as Spaceship Earth. Major corporations sponsor most themed areas, with a focus on discovery, scientific achievements, and tomorrow's technologies in areas running from energy to undersea exploration. Here are the headliners:

The fountains at the **Imagination** 👁👁 pavilion are magical—they fire "water snakes" that arch in the air and dare kids to avoid their "bite." The 3-D *Honey I Shrunk the Audience* 👁👁 show shrinks you, then terrorizes you with giant mice, a cat, and a 5-year-old who gives you a sound shaking (less scary than it sounds). **Journey into Your Imagination** 👁 features a park favorite, Figment the dragon.

Innoventions 👁 is divided into two sections (both constantly updated, so it's always worth stopping in). House of Innoventions in **Innoventions East** heralds a smart house equipped with a refrigerator that can make your grocery list, and a picture frame that can send photos to other smart frames. The exhibits in **Innoventions West** are led by Sega's Video Games of Tomorrow. Good luck getting the kids out.

The largest of Future World's pavilions, **The Land** 👁 looks at human relationships with food and nature. **Living with the Land** 👁 is a 13-minute boat ride through a rainforest, an African desert, and the windswept American plains. **Circle of Life** 👁 blends spectacular live-action footage with animation in a 15-minute, 70mm motion picture based on *The Lion King* that delivers a cautionary environmental message. **Soarin'** 👁👁👁, a popular transplant from Disney's California Adventure park, allows guests a bird's-eye view of the diverse California landscape. Lifted 40 feet into the air by immense hang gliders, your feet freely dangling, you'll soar above spectacular scenery projected onto the gigantic domed screen. Sensory elements and gentle winds add realism to the experience. There's a 40-inch height minimum.

The Living Seas ⚓ pavilion's 5.7-million-gallon aquarium has a reef and 4,000 sea creatures, such as sharks, barracudas, parrotfish, rays, and dolphins. A 2½-minute multimedia preshow about today's ocean technology is followed by a 7-minute film on the formation of the earth and seas as a means to support life. After the films, you enter "hydrolators" for a hokey "descent" to the simulated ocean floor, where you get close-up views through acrylic windows of the denizens in a natural coral-reef habitat. Kids and adults will get a kick out of the newest addition—**Turtle Talk with Crush** ⚓⚓, in which the sea turtle from *Finding Nemo* engages guests in conversation from his movie-screen tank.

Blast off on **Mission: Space** ⚓⚓⚓, Epcot's most intense pavilion. Simulator technology developed with NASA launches you on an amazing ride through space that feels a lot like the real deal (so some NASA astronauts have claimed). This one is not for the faint at heart. ***Note:*** Riders must be at least 44 inches tall.

Spaceship Earth is the large, silvery geosphere that is Epcot's icon, but all that awaits inside is a boring audiovisual history lesson. The slow-moving cars take you on a 15-minute-journey through time depicting the history of communications.

Test Track ⚓⚓ is a marvel that combines GM engineering and Disney Imagineering. The line for this one can be more than an hour long, so consider FASTPASS. Once you're in your six-passenger convertible, the 5-minute ride follows what looks like a real highway and includes a brake test, climb, and tight S-curves. There's also a 12-second burst of speed that reaches 65 mph on the straightaway. ***Note:*** Riders must be at least 40 inches tall.

Sponsored by Exxon, the **Universe of Energy** ⚓⚓ pavilion is home to a 32-minute ride, **Ellen's Energy Adventure,** which features comedian Ellen DeGeneres being tutored by Bill Nye the Science Guy to be a *Jeopardy!* contestant. You'll learn about energy from fossil fuels and take a ride through the age of the dinosaurs.

Housed in a vast geodesic dome fronted by a 75-foot-tall replica of a DNA strand, **Wonders of Life** ⚓⚓ offers some of Future World's most engaging shows and attractions. The *Making of Me* is a captivating 15-minute motion picture combining live action (starring Martin Short) with animation and spectacular in-utero photography to create the sweetest introduction imaginable to the facts of life. (Be aware that if your kids are under 8, this show may prompt certain questions about reproduction that you may or may not be ready for.) In **Body Wars,** you're "reduced" to the size of a cell in order to join a medical rescue team inside the immune system of a human body. The motion simulator takes you on a wild ride through gale-force winds in the lungs and pounding heart chambers. This one isn't a smart choice for those prone to motion sickness or who generally prefer to be stirred rather than shaken. ***Note:*** Riders must be at least 40 inches tall. In the hilarious, multimedia **Cranium Command** ⚓⚓, you tag along with Buzzy, an audio-animatronic brain-pilot-in-training charged with a seemingly impossible task—controlling the brain of a typical 12-year-old boy. Celebrities play the boy's body parts as he encounters preadolescent traumas such as meeting a girl and having a run-in with the principal.

WORLD SHOWCASE

Surrounding the nearly 40-acre lagoon at the north end of the park is this community of 11 miniaturized nations, re-created with meticulous detail and featuring indigenous architecture, landscaping, restaurants, and shops. The nations' cultural facets are

---

Moments **A Grand Nightcap**

IllumiNations ✦✦ is a blend of fireworks, lasers, and fountains in a display that's signature Disney. The show is worth the crowds that flock to the parking lot when it's over—don't miss it! *Tip:* Stake your claim to the best viewing areas a half-hour before show time (listed in your entertainment schedule). The ones near Showcase Plaza have a head start for the exits. The Rose & Crown Pub in the U.K. pavilion (see below), offers a great view of the proceedings.

---

explored in art, dance and live performances, or innovative films. The cast members working at each pavilion are natives of that country, making the experience that much more authentic. The World Showcase opens at 11am or noon and remains open up to 2 hours after Future World closes, so plan on heading there after Future World.

The architecture in **Canada** ✦✦ ranges from a mansard-roofed replica of Ottawa's 19th-century, French-style Château Laurier (here called Hôtel du Canada) to a stone building modeled after a landmark near Niagara Falls. But the highlight is *O Canada!* ✦, a dazzling 22-minute, 360-degree CircleVision film of Canada's scenic splendor, from a dog-sled race to the thundering flight of thousands of snow geese.

The **China** ✦✦ pavilion is entered via a triple-arched ceremonial gate inspired by the Temple of Heaven in Beijing. Passing through the gate, you'll see a half-size replica of this ornately embellished red-and-gold circular temple, built in 1420 during the Ming Dynasty. Inside, the CircleVision film *Reflections of China* shows off China's greatest cities. Gardens simulate those in Suzhou, with waterfalls, lotus ponds, bamboo groves, corkscrew willows, and weeping mulberry trees. Outside, the amazing **Dragon Legend Acrobats** provide live thrills.

The **France** pavilion focuses on La Belle Epoque, a period from 1870 to 1910 during which French art, literature, and architecture flourished. It's entered via a replica of the Pont des Arts footbridge over the Seine and leads to a ¹⁄₁₀-scale model of the Eiffel Tower constructed from Gustave Eiffel's original blueprints. The big attraction here is *Impressions du France* ✦✦, a 20-minute film featuring the country's top sights and scenery set to the music of famous French composers.

Enclosed by castle walls and towers, the festive **Germany** pavilion is centered on a cobblestone square with pots of colorful flowers girding a fountain statue of St. George and the Dragon. The adjacent clock tower's glockenspiel figures herald each hour with quaint melodies. Sixteenth-century facades replicate a merchant's hall in the Black Forest and the town hall in Römerberg Square. Model-train enthusiasts and kids shouldn't miss the detailed **miniature German village** ✦.

One of the prettiest World Showcase pavilions, **Italy** ✦ lures visitors over an arched footbridge to a replica of Venice's pink-and-white Doge's Palace. Other highlights include an 83-foot-tall bell tower, Venetian bridges, and a central piazza enclosing a version of Bernini's Neptune Fountain.

At **Japan** ✦✦, a flaming-red *torii* (gate of honor) leads the way to the Goju No To pagoda, inspired by a shrine built at Nara in A.D. 700. In a Japanese garden, cedars, yews, bamboos, willows, and flowering shrubs frame pebbled footpaths, rustic bridges, waterfalls, rock landscaping, and a pond of koi. The Yakitori House is based on the 16th-century Katsura Imperial Villa in Kyoto, considered the crowning achievement of Japanese architecture. Another highlight is the moated **White Heron Castle,** a replica of the Shirasagi-Jo, a 17th-century fortress overlooking the city of Himeji. The drums of **Matsuriza** 👑👑—one of the best performances in the World Showcase— entertain guests daily. There's also a gallery featuring exhibitions on various themes.

You'll hear marimbas and mariachi bands (including **Mariachi Cobre**) as you approach the **Mexico** 👑 showcase, fronted by a towering Mayan pyramid modeled on the Aztec temple of Quetzalcoatl (God of Life) and surrounded by dense Yucatán jungle landscaping. Upon entering the pavilion, you'll find yourself in a museum of pre-Columbian art and artifacts. Down a ramp, after you have passed through the marketplace and its shops, **El Rio del Tiempo (River of Time)** 👑 offers an 8-minute cruise through Mexico's past and present. For a more contemporary perspective, **Casa Mexicana** shows guests what a modern Mexican home is like.

When you enter **Morocco** 👑👑, note the imperfections in the mosaic tile in the Koutoubia Minaret, the prayer tower of a 12th-century mosque in Marrakech. They were put there in accordance with the belief that only Allah is perfect. The **Medina (Old City),** entered via a replica of an arched gateway in Fez, leads to Fez House (a traditional Moroccan home) and the winding streets of the *souk,* a bustling market-place where all manner of authentic merchandise is sold. **Treasures of Morocco** is a daily 35-minute tour that highlights this country's culture, architecture, and history.

Inside **Norway** 👑, a *stavekirke* (stave church), styled after the 13th-century Gol Church of Hallingdal, features changing exhibits. A replica of Oslo's 14th-century **Akershus Castle,** next to a cascading waterfall, is the setting for the pavilion's restaurant (p. 486). **Maelstrom** 👑, a ride in a dragon-headed Viking vessel, traverses fjords before you crash through a gorge into the North Sea, where you're hit by a storm (albeit a relatively calm one). Passengers disembark at a 10th-century Viking village to view the 70mm film *Norway,* which documents Norwegian history.

The **United Kingdom** 👑 pavilion beckons you with **Britannia Square,** a formal London-style park complete with gazebo bandstand, red phone booth, and statue of the Bard. Four centuries of architecture are represented along quaint cobblestone streets. A formal garden with low box hedges in geometric patterns, flagstone paths, and a stone fountain replicate the landscaping of 16th- and 17th-century palaces. *Tip:* Don't miss the **British Invasion** 👑, a group that impersonates the Beatles every day except Sunday, and pub pianist Pam Brody (Tues, Thurs–Fri, and Sun).

Housed in a Georgian-style structure, the 29-minute **U.S.A.—The American Adventure** 👑 is a dramatization of U.S. history using video, music, and a cast of animatronic figures, including Mark Twain and Ben Franklin. You'll see Jefferson writing the Declaration of Independence, Matthew Brady photographing a family being divided by the Civil War, the stock market crash of 1929, the attack on Pearl Harbor, and the *Eagle* heading for the moon. Entertainment includes the **Spirit of America Fife & Drum Corps** and **Voices of Liberty,** singing patriotic songs.

8 Disney–MGM Studios

Disney bills this park as "the Hollywood that never was and always will be." Hollywood's golden era of the 1940s, and done up a la Disney, surrounds you with Art Deco–style buildings accented with pastel colors and neon lights. You'd be hard-pressed to miss Mickey's giant sorcerer's hat looming ahead on Hollywood Boulevard, or the Tower of Terror and the Earful Tower—the latter is a water tower outfitted with giant mouse ears—rising above the landscape. This park is also home to two of Disney's most pulse-quickening rides, a variety of movie- and TV-themed shows, and some of the most uniquely themed restaurants in all of WDW.

MAJOR ATTRACTIONS & SHOWS

The 35-minute **Disney–MGM Studios Backlot Tour** ✾ takes you behind the scenes via tram for a look at the vehicles, props, costumes, sets, and special effects used in movies and TV shows. But the real fun begins once you reach **Catastrophe Canyon,** where an earthquake causes canyon walls to rumble. A raging oil fire, massive explosions, torrents of rain, and flash floods threaten you and other riders before you're taken behind the scenes to see how filmmakers use special effects to make such disasters. Over at soundstage 4, on Mickey Avenue, the frozen world of Narnia comes alive. At **Journey into Narnia: Creating the Lion, the Witch, and the Wardrobe,** guests walk through a gigantic wardrobe and into a wintery landscape reminiscent of the movie. Filling the gallery just beyond the set are elaborate creatures along with actual costumes, armory, and props used in the making of the film.

Producers adapted the 30-minute show **Beauty and the Beast Live on Stage** ✾ from the movie of the same name. The sets and costumes are lavish, and the production numbers are pretty spectacular. Arrive early to get a good seat.

On **The Great Movie Ride,** film footage and 50 audio-animatronic replicas of movie stars re-create some of the most famous scenes in film, including clips from *Casablanca, Mary Poppins,* and *Alien.* The ride is longer than most, at 22 minutes, but true movie buffs will find this ride down memory lane sheer bliss.

Peek into the world of movie stunts at the 30-minute **Indiana Jones Epic Stunt Spectacular** ✾✾✾, which re-creates major scenes from the Indiana Jones films. Arrive early and sit near the stage for your shot at being an audience participant. Alas, this is a job for adults only.

Kermit and Miss Piggy star in **Jim Henson's Muppet*Vision 3D** ✾✾, a must-see film that marries Jim Henson's puppets with Disney audio-animatronics, special effects, and 3-D technology. The coming-at-you action includes flying Muppets, cream pies, and cannonballs, as well as high winds, fiber-optic fireworks, bubble showers, even an actual spray of water. This comical 25-minute show runs continuously.

Younger kids will appreciate the nearby *Honey, I Shrunk the Kids* **Movie Set Adventure,** as they can crawl and climb their way through the larger-than-life set filled with 30-foot blades of grass and gigantic spider webs, among other features.

⟮Moments⟯ A Nighttime Spectacle

The fireworks, laser lights, and choreography of **Fantasmic!** ✾✾✾ make it a spectacular 25-minute end-of-day experience. The extravaganza features shooting stars, fireballs, a cast of 50, a giant dragon, a king cobra, and 1 million gallons of water. And everything is orchestrated by a familiar sorcerer mouse. Throughout, music and characters from Disney classics entertain you.

Tip: If you want to eat at Disney–MGM and see the show, make Advanced Reservations for the Hollywood Brown Derby, Mama Melrose's Ristorante Italiano, or Hollywood & Vine. When you do, ask for the Fantasmic! package ($23–$36 for adults, depending on your dinner selection, $11 for kids 3-9; ✆ 407/939-3463). After dinner you'll get preferred seating at the show. Be aware that the number of packages available per evening is limited.

The **Magic of Disney Animation** features Mushu the dragon from Disney's *Mulan,* who co-hosts a theater presentation in which secrets behind the creation of Disney's animated characters are revealed. The Q & A session that follows allows guests to ask questions about the animation process before attempting their own Disney character drawings while under the supervision of a working animator. You'll also get the chance to meet and greet a variety of Disney characters.

Younger audiences (ages 2–5) love the 20-minute **Playhouse Disney—Live on Stage!,** where they meet characters from *Bear in the Big Blue House, The Book of Pooh,* and others. It encourages preschoolers to dance, sing, and play along with the cast. It shows several times a day. Check your schedule.

Want the best thrill ride WDW has to offer? Then tackle the **Rock 'n' Roller Coaster** ✿✿✿. You sit in a 24-passenger "stretch limo" with 120 speakers that blare Aerosmith as you blast from 0 to 60 mph in 2.8 seconds, then fly into the first gut-tightening inversion at 5Gs. Then you're off on a wild ride through a California freeway system in the semidarkness. *Note:* Riders must be at least 48 inches tall.

Cutting-edge when it opened, **Star Tours,** based on the original *Star Wars* trilogy, is now a couple of rungs below the latest technology but is still fun. After boarding a 40-seat "spacecraft," you're off in a whoosh on a journey that takes you through some of the more famous *Star Wars* scenes, full of sudden drops, crashes, and oncoming laser blasts as you career out of control. *Note:* Riders must be at least 40 inches tall.

Disney continues to fine-tune **The Twilight Zone Tower of Terror** ✿✿✿, making it one of the most exciting rides at WDW. As legend has it, during a violent storm on Halloween night 1939, lightning struck the Hollywood Tower Hotel, causing an entire wing and an elevator full of people to disappear. And you're about to meet them as you star in a special episode of *The Twilight Zone.* The ride features random drop sequences, allowing for a real sense of the unknown. Because it offers a different experience every time you dare to ride, it's far better than any other attraction of its kind. Be prepared, though, as your stomach may need a few minutes to find its way back to where it belongs. *Note:* You must be at least 40 inches tall to ride.

Hazy lighting and special effects create an underwater effect in a reef-walled theater, helping set the mood for the charming musical show **Voyage of the Little Mermaid** ✿✿, which combines live performers with puppets, film clips, and more. Many of the movie's major songs, including the theme, "Under the Sea," are featured. The 17-minute show is a great place to rest, cool off, and sing along.

Lights, Motors, Action! Extreme Stunt Show debuted in 2005. Taking its cue from the original show at Disneyland Resort Paris, the show features high-flying, high-speed movie stunts full of pyrotechnic effects and more. It's similar to the Indiana Jones Stunt Spectacular, but more fast-paced and action-packed.

Contestants can't win $1 million on *Who Wants to Be a Millionaire—***Play It!** ✿, but they can win points used to buy prizes ranging from a collectible pin to a leather jacket to a 3-night Disney cruise (including airfare) for four. Based on Disney-owned ABC TV's game show, the theme-park version features "lifelines" (such as asking the audience or calling a stranger on two phones set up in the park). Games run continuously in the 600-seat studio. Audience members play along on keypads. The fastest to answer qualifying questions become contestants.

9 Animal Kingdom

Disney's fourth major park combines the elaborate and impressive landscapes of Asia and Africa, including the exotic creatures that inhabit these distant lands, with the prehistoric lands of the dinosaur. A conservation venue as much as an attraction ensures that you won't find the animals blatantly displayed throughout the 500-acre park. Instead, naturalistic habitats blend seamlessly into the spectacular surroundings. This unfortunately means that, at times, you'll have to search a bit to find the inhabitants. Your experience here will be far different than at Disney's other parks, as the focus is on the surroundings, meticulously recreated architecture, and intricate detailing, not so much on the attractions sprinkled throughout (even though Expedition Everest is pretty impressive). *A bonus:* This is one of Disney's less ride-intensive parks, allowing for it to easily be enjoyed in a single day (usually less) and making it a good choice when you need to cut back and take it a bit slower and easier.

DISCOVERY ISLAND

Like Cinderella Castle in the Magic Kingdom, the 14-story **Tree of Life** ☆☆ is the park's central landmark. WDW artisans built the tree, which has 8,000 limbs, 103,000 leaves, and 325 mammals, reptiles, amphibians, bugs, birds, Mickeys, and dinosaurs carved into its trunk, limbs, and roots. Teams of artisans worked for a year creating its sculptures, and it's worth a walk around its roots, especially on the way to see **It's Tough to Be a Bug!** ☆☆, a 3-D movie with impressive special effects. Grab your glasses and settle into a creepy-crawly seat. It's not a good one for very young kids (it's dark and loud, with a few buzzing sensory effects) or bug haters, but for others it's a fun, sometimes poignant look at life from a smaller perspective.

DINOLAND U.S.A.

Enter beneath "Olden Gate Bridge," a 40-foot Brachiosaurus reassembled from fossils. You'll also find a replica of "Sue," a 67-million-year-old Tyrannosaurus Rex skeleton that was worked on by paleontologists here before being shipped to her new home at Chicago's Field Museum.

Kids love the chance to slip, slither, slide, and slink through the **Boneyard** ☆☆, a giant playground where they can discover and uncover the realistic-looking remains of Triceratops, T-Rex, and other vanished giants. It's also a great place for parents to take a break from the pavement pounding of a day in the park.

Dinosaur ☆ hurls you through the darkness in a CTX Rover "time machine" to the time when dinosaurs ruled Earth. The expedition takes you past an array of snarling and ferocious-looking dinosaurs, one of which thinks that you would make a great lunchtime treat. Young children may find the dinos and darkness a bit frightening and the ride a bit jarring. *Note:* You must be 40 inches or taller to climb aboard.

In **Primeval Whirl,** a spinning, free-style twin roller coaster, you control the action through its wacky maze of curves, peaks, and dippity-do-dahs. This is a modern version of those old carnival roller coasters of the '50s and '60s. *Note:* It carries a 48-inch height minimum.

TriceraTop Spin is a mini-thrill for youngsters. Friendly-looking dinosaur "cars" circle a hub while moving up and down and all around, much like Dumbo and the Magic Carpets of Aladdin (p. 496) at the Magic Kingdom.

CAMP MINNIE-MICKEY

A character meet-and-greet zone and one of the best theme-park shows in town are the main attractions in this small area of Animal Kingdom.

If your kids are hooked on getting every character autograph possible, the **Character Greeting Trails** should be your first stop (though lines can get excruciatingly long). Disney characters, from Winnie the Pooh and Pocahontas to Timon and Baloo, have separate trails where you can meet and mingle, snap photos, and get autographs. Mickey, Minnie, Goofy, and Pluto make periodic appearances.

Everyone in the audience comes alive when the music starts at the rousing, 28-minute **Festival of the Lion King** ⚜⚜⚜ in the Lion King Theater. The festival celebrates nature's diversity with a talented troupe of singers, dancers, and life-size critters; they lead the way to an inspiring sing-along that gets the crowd caught up in the fun. The action is onstage as well as offstage in the audience. It is a sight-and-sound spectacular that shouldn't be missed. Make sure to arrive at least 20 minutes early.

AFRICA

Enter through Harambe, a re-creation of an African coastal village at the edge of the 21st century. A central marketplace is surrounded by structures built of coral stone, aged for an authentic look, and thatched with reed by African craftsman.

Animal Kingdom has expanded its collection of rides, but the **Kilimanjaro Safaris** ⚜⚜⚜ is still one of the most popular. As you bump along through a simulated African savannah in a large truck, you may spot black rhinos, hippos, crocodiles, antelopes, wildebeests, zebras, giraffes, and lions. *The downside:* If the animals aren't feeling cooperative at the time you're riding, you may not see much. They're scarce at midday most of the year (in cooler months, you may get lucky), so *ride this one as close to the park's opening or closing as you can.*

Hippos, tapirs, ever-active mole rats, and other critters are often on the **Pangani Forest Exploration Trail** ⚜⚜ for your viewing, but the real prize is getting a look at the gorillas. Don't expect full cooperation, however, because in hot weather, they spend most of the day in shady areas and out of view. Those who come early, stay late, are patient, or make return visits should be rewarded with a close-up look.

ASIA

Disney's Imagineers did an amazing job of creating the mythical kingdom of **Anandapur.** The intricately painted artwork is just another example of the lengths Disney has gone to in order to transport you from the real world to the places of your imagination.

Kali River Rapids ⚜ is a good raft ride, though not as wild as Popeye & Bluto's Bilge-Rat Barges at Islands of Adventure (p. 513). Its churning waters and optical illusions will have you wondering if you're about to drop over the falls. Expedition Everest makes a brief but impressive appearance along the way. You *will* get wet (okay, soaked). *Note:* There's a 38-inch height minimum.

Impressively detailed surroundings and up-close views of the animals make **Maharajah Jungle Trek** ⚜⚜ an often overlooked jewel. If you don't show up in the midday heat, you may see Bengal tigers through the thick glass, while nothing but air divides you from dozens of giant fruit bats (with wingspans up to 6 ft.) and other smaller inhabitants. Be sure to pick up one of the guides that lists the many unusual and often rare inhabitants to look for along the way.

Expedition Everest ⚜⚜⚜, the newest and most impressive attraction in the park, transports guests to the small and meticulously detailed Himalayan village of Serka

Zong. Guests board the Anandapur Rail Service bound for Mount Everest; after passing bamboo forests and waterfalls, diving through fields of glaciers, and climbing snow-capped peaks, the train suddenly veers "out of control," sending riders careening down Mount Everest's rough and rugged terrain. You'll be thrust forward and backward, in and out of the darkness. And that's not the end—a close encounter with the legendary Yeti will have your hair standing on end before it's all over.

10 Other WDW Attractions

TYPHOON LAGOON ✹✹✹

A storm-stranded fishing boat—*Miss Tilly*—teeters atop 95-foot-high Mount Mayday overlooking this tropically themed and seemingly typhoon-tossed Disney water park. Guests can be tossed about on a number of twisting and turning wild rides and slides here. There are more relaxing activities as well.

Castaway Creek's rafts and inner tubes glide along a 2,100-foot-long river that circles most of the park, passing through a rainforest, caves, and grottoes. At **Water Works,** jets of water spew from shipwrecked boats.

Ketchakiddie Creek is for the 2- to 5-year-old set. An innovative water playground, it has bubbling fountains in which to frolic, mini–water slides, a pint-size "white-water" tubing run, spouting whales and squirting seals, rubbery crocodiles to climb on, grottoes to explore, and waterfalls to loll under.

At **Shark Reef,** guests get free equipment and receive a few instructions—and then you're off for a 15-minute swim through a snorkeling area that's home to a simulated reef and sunken shipwreck, and populated by parrotfish, rays, and small sharks.

The Surf Pool ✹✹, the park's 2.75-million-gallon wave pool, is one of the world's largest. Every 90 seconds, a foghorn sounds, warning you of the impending and crashing waves, just in case you want to head for cover. Young children appreciate wading in the lagoon's more peaceful tidal pools of **Blustery Bay** and **Whitecap Cove;** the bigger waves of the Surf Pool would most likely sweep them away.

Humunga Kowabunga consists of three 214-foot Mount Mayday slides that send you plummeting down the mountain on a serpentine route through waterfalls and bat caves, and past nautical wreckage before depositing you into a bubbling catch pool. *Note:* You must be 48 inches or taller to ride this. **White-Water Rides** at Mount Mayday is the setting for three white-water rafting adventures—**Keelhaul Falls, Mayday Falls,** and **Gangplank Falls**—all offering steep and drenching drops coursing through caves and passing lush scenery.

The newest thrill to splash onto the scene is the **Crush 'n' Gusher,** a first-of-its-kind water coaster with three separate experiences to choose from: The **Banana Blaster, Coconut Crusher,** and **Pineapple Plunger** each offer steep drops, twists, and turns of varying degrees.

Typhoon Lagoon is open from 10am to 5pm, with extended hours during holiday periods and summer (✆ **407/560-4141;** www.disneyworld.com). A 1-day ticket is $35 for adults, $29 for children 3 to 9.

BLIZZARD BEACH ✹✹✹

Snowcapped mountaintops in the middle of sunny Orlando—who else but Disney could have created this 66-acre "ski resort," set in the midst of a tropical lagoon and centered on the 90-foot Mount Gushmore? *Note:* The majority of this park's attractions are geared to thrill-seekers, making it a better choice for families with kids at least 8 years of age.

The 2,900-foot-long **Cross Country Creek** is a lazy river ride that runs the perimeter of the park, but watch out for the brisk though refreshing melting "ice" as you pass through the Polar Caves. The waves of Melt-A-Way Bay offer another relaxing and less heart-pounding option. **Runoff Rapids** will send you and your inner tube careening down one of three twisting, turning runs through semidarkness.

Ski-Patrol Training Camp, designed for 'tweens and teens, features a rope swing, a T-bar hanging over the water, the wet and slippery **Mogul Mania** slide, and an ice-floe walk along slippery floating icebergs.

Snow Stormers has three flumes descending from the top of Mount Gushmore, following a switchback course through slalom-type gates.

Summit Plummet *⚲⚲* is one of the most breath-defying adventures in any water park. Read every speed, motion, vertical-dip, wedgie, and hold-on-to-your-breastplate warning before hopping on. This starts slow, with a lift ride to the 120-foot summit. But it finishes as the world's fastest body slide—a test of your courage and swimsuit—that virtually goes straight down and has you moving sans vehicle at 60 mph into the catch pool. *Note:* It has a 48-inch height minimum.

Teamboat Springs is this world's longest whitewater raft ride, twisting down a 1,200-foot series of rushing waterfalls.

Tike's Peak is a kid-friendly version of Mount Gushmore. It has short water slides, animals to climb aboard, a snow castle, a squirting ice pond, and a fountain play area for young guests.

Blizzard Beach is open from 10am to 5pm, with extended hours during some holiday periods and summer (© 407/560-3400; www.disneyworld.com). A 1-day ticket is $35 for adults, $29 for children 3 to 9.

MINIATURE GOLF *⚲*

Hippos, ostriches, and alligators decorate the **Fantasia Gardens** course, a good bet for beginners and kids. Seasoned minigolfers will most likely prefer the second 18-hole course, **Fantasia Fairways,** filled with sand traps, water hazards, and rather tricky putting greens. With holes ranging from 40 to 75 feet, and no whimsical characters in sight, this one's definitely not for novices—unless you appreciate frustration.

Santa Claus and his elves provide the theme for **Winter Summerland,** which offers two additional 18-hole courses, appropriate for all ages and abilities. The summer course is pure Florida, from sand castles to surfboards; the other course offers a touch of the North Pole and a visit with Santa on the "Winternet."

Tickets are about $11 for adults and $9 for kids 3 to 9. The courses are open from 10am to 10 or 11pm daily. For information about Fantasia Gardens, call © 407/560-4582. For information on Winter Summerland, call © 407/560-3000. Find both on the Internet at **www.disneyworld.com**.

11 What to See & Do Beyond Disney: Universal Orlando, SeaWorld & Other Orlando Attractions

There are so many attractions in Orlando (over 95) that it's impossible to see half of them unless you're here for a month. The following should help you finish picking your must-see list.

UNIVERSAL STUDIOS FLORIDA

Lights, camera, and action, action, action. Universal is touted as the park where you can "Ride the Movies," and that boast isn't far off the mark. It's filled with fast-paced, high-intensity attractions such as Revenge of the Mummy and *Men in Black* Alien Attack. As a plus, it's a working movie and TV studio, so occasional filming goes on at Nickelodeon's sound stages. And there's a lot for kids here as well, including plenty of characters on hand to meet and greet visitors throughout the park.

TICKET PRICES   A **1-day, 1-park ticket** costs $63 for adults, $52 for children 3 to 9. A 2-day, two-park Unlimited-Access Pass is $108 for all ages. A two-park preferred annual pass will run $180 (any age). This includes free parking and has no blackout dates. The two-park annual power pass is less expensive, at $120 (any age); however, most holidays and many weekends are blacked out, and parking is not included.

As with Disney, Universal offers savings on ticket purchases if you purchase them before you leave home. Buy your 2-day, two-park tickets online ($107.95), and you can choose from three bonus options: a 5-day ticket (good for both Universal parks and select CityWalk clubs), a non-expiration option, or "kids free plus 3 days free" (good for one free children's ticket per paying adult). Pick up your tickets at the front gate of either park, or have them sent (for a delivery charge) to your home.

THE FLEXTICKET   The least expensive way to see Universal, SeaWorld, *and* Wet 'n Wild is with a **FlexTicket.** This pass lets you pay one price for unlimited admission to participating parks during a 14-day period. A four-park pass to Universal Studios Florida, Islands of Adventure, Wet 'n Wild, and SeaWorld is $189.95 for adults and $155.95 for children 3 to 9. A five-park pass, which adds Busch Gardens in Tampa (p. 395), is $234.95 for adults and $199.95 for kids. The FlexTicket can be ordered through Universal (ⓒ 800/711-0080 or 407/363-8000; www.universalorlando.com) or the other participating parks. Free shuttle service among all of the parks, even Busch Gardens, is included in the ticket price.

PARKING   Parking is $9 for cars, light trucks, and vans. Valet parking is $16.

MAJOR ATTRACTIONS

On *Back to the Future:* **The Ride** 𝕬𝕬𝕬, you blast through the space-time continuum in a flight simulator built to look like the movie's famous DeLorean car. You twist, turn, dip, and dive—all the while feeling like you're really flying. *Note:* The ride is bumpy and might not be a good idea if you're prone to dizziness or motion sickness. Riders must be at least 40 inches tall.

Set in a parklike theater-in-the-round, the 25-minute musical *A Day in the Park with Barney* stars that big purple dinosaur, Baby Bop, and BJ. It uses song, dance, interactive play, and unique special effects to entertain younger guests. It's a must for preschoolers, though parents will need strength to endure it.

Not long after you climb on a San Francisco BART train at **Earthquake—the Big One** 𝕬𝕬, there's an earthquake that's 8.3 on the Richter scale! As you sit helplessly, concrete slabs collapse around you, a propane truck bursts into flames, a runaway train hurtles your way, and the station begins to flood with no way out.

Universal's newest thrill ride, **Revenge of the Mummy** 𝕬𝕬𝕬, is a high-speed, twisting, turning, pulsating adventure through Egyptian tombs, with creepy skeletal warriors in hot pursuit. This one's packed full of amazing pyrotechnic effects, a state-of-the-art propulsion system, and hair-raising robotic creatures.

Soar with E.T. on a mission to save his ailing planet at **E.T. Adventure** 𝕬; you'll pass through the dense forest and gently glide into space aboard a bicycle.

The $45-million *Jaws* 𝕬𝕬 begins calmly enough, a seemingly leisurely boat ride through New England coastal waters, when suddenly a 3-ton, 32-foot-long great white shark is spotted lurking about. You can pretty much figure out what happens next. There are plenty of special effects, including a rather heated wall of flame that surrounds your boat as you chargrill the fish before landing safely back at the dock.

Buckle up for **Jimmy Neutron's Nicktoon Blast** ✦✦, one of Universal's newer rides. Jimmy's Rocket Pod hurtles you through hyperspace, thanks to sophisticated computer graphics, state-of-the-art ride technology, animation, and programmable motion-based seats. The attraction also features other popular characters, including SpongeBob SquarePants and Rugrats.

In *Men in Black* **Alien Attack** ✦✦✦, you board a six-passenger cruiser, buzz the streets of New York, and use your "zapper" to splatter up to 120 bug-eyed targets. You have to contend with return fire as well as light, noise, and clouds of liquid nitrogen (aka fog) that can spin you out of control. Your laser tag gun fires infrared bullets. The 4-minute, $70-million ride relies on 360-degree spins rather than speed for its thrill factor. *Note:* Guests must be at least 42 inches tall for this ride.

Another newer ride, *Shrek* **4-D** ✦, is a 20-minute show that can be seen, heard, felt, and smelled, thanks to motion-simulator technology, OgreVision glasses, and special effects such as water spritzers. The theater's seats are pneumatic air-propulsion nodules that can turn and tilt. I expected more from Universal in the seating-effects department, but the preshow and the movie are definitely worthwhile.

James Cameron, who directed *T2,* supervised the $60-million **Terminator 2: 3-D Battle Across Time** ✦✦, which features Arnie and other original cast members (on film). It combines three huge screens with technical effects and live action on stage, including a custom-built Harley and six 8-foot-tall cyberbots. The 3-D effects are among the best in any Orlando park. *Note:* Universal gives this show a PG-13 rating.

Two million cubic feet of air per minute (enough to fill four full-size blimps) create a funnel cloud five stories tall at *Twister* **. . . Ride It Out** ✦✦. The roar of a freight train, at rock-concert decibel level, fills the theater as cars, trucks, and a cow fly by while the audience watches just 20 feet away. Crowds sometimes applaud when it's all over. *Note:* This show has a PG-13 rating.

Woody Woodpecker's Nuthouse Coaster ✦✦ is a kiddie coaster that will thrill moms and dads, too. Although only 30 feet at its peak, it offers quick, banked turns. The ride lasts only about 60 seconds, and waits can be 30 minutes or more, but few kids will want to miss the experience. *Note:* The coaster has a 36-inch height minimum.

For a good dose of reality—reality TV, that is—be sure to catch *Fear Factor* **Live.** Audience members can sign up to be the stars of the show, but be prepared—the stunts, while toned down, are similarly challenging (and just as disgusting) as the ones on the TV show, so be sure you're up for the task before volunteering.

ISLANDS OF ADVENTURE

Universal's second theme park is even more impressive architecturally than its big brother, Universal Studios Florida. Roller coasters roar above pedestrian walkways, and water rides make some rather big splashes throughout the park. It is, bar none, *the* Orlando theme park for thrill-ride junkies, and also offers some of the best, and most unique, dining around—theme park or otherwise.

A few words of caution: *Nine of the park's 14 major rides have height restrictions.* Many rides may not be suitable for those who are tall enough but who are pregnant or have health problems—physical restrictions; heart, neck, or back problems; or a tendency toward motion sickness.

TICKET PRICES   See the "Ticket Prices" information for Universal Studios Florida on p. 510.

THE FLEXTICKET   See "The FlexTicket" information for Universal Studios Florida on p. 510.

PARKING   Parking is $9 for cars, light trucks, and vans. Valet parking is $16.

MAJOR ATTRACTIONS
Port of Entry
A towering lighthouse marks the entrance to this seemingly centuries-old marketplace, which serves as a gateway to IOA's five uniquely themed "islands." Guest Services can be found near the gates; the remaining area is filled with shops and restaurants.

Seuss Landing
You will feel as if you have jumped right into the pages of a Dr. Seuss classic as you enter the whimsically colorful Seuss Landing. Main attractions are aimed at youngsters, but anyone who loved the good Doctor as a child will enjoy the fun.

It's hard to miss the cat's candy-striped hat marking the entrance to **The Cat in the Hat** 🎏🎏, where guests follow the famous story from beginning to end. You'll pass through scenes taken right out of the famous tale of a day gone very much awry. This chaotic ride offers a few swirls and whirls along the way, making it bit spunkier than most, though that's part of the fun.

One Fish, Two Fish, Red Fish, Blue Fish 🎏 is a family favorite similar to the Magic Carpets of Aladdin and Dumbo rides at WDW (including the long lines). Here controls let you move your funky fish up or down as you circle a central hub. Watch out for "squirt posts," which spray unsuspecting riders.

Forget tradition and hop on **Caro-Seuss-El** 🎏🎏🎏. The not-so-normal carousel gives you a chance to ride whimsical characters from Dr. Seuss, including Cowfish, elephant birds, and Mulligatawnies.

The outdoor interactive play area, **If I Ran the Zoo** 🎏, features flying water snakes and a chance to tickle the toes of a Seussian animal. Kids can explore caves, fire water cannons, climb, slide, and otherwise burn off energy. They're also bound to get wet, so be prepared with extra clothes or even a swimsuit.

Marvel Super Hero Island
Adrenaline junkies and thrill seekers thrive on the twisting, turning, stomach-churning rides found on this island of larger-than-life comic superheroes and villains.

The original web master is the star of the exceptional special effects–laden ride **The Amazing Adventures of Spider-Man** 🎏🎏🎏. Passengers wearing 3-D glasses squeal as their 12-passenger cars twist and spin, plunge, and soar through a comic-book universe. A simulated 400-foot drop feels an awful lot like the real thing.

Look! Up in the sky! It's a bird, it's a plane . . . uh, it's you falling 150 feet, if you're courageous enough to climb aboard **Doctor Doom's Fearfall** 🎏. The screams that can be heard far from the ride's entrance add to the anticipation. You're fired to the top, with feet dangling, and dropped in intervals, leaving your stomach at several levels. The fall isn't quite up to Disney's Tower of Terror's (p. 505), but it's still frightening. *Note:* Minimum height is 52 inches.

On **The Incredible Hulk Coaster** 🎏🎏🎏, you're launched from a dark tunnel and hurtled into the lower ozone while accelerating from 0 to 40 mph in 2 seconds. You will spin upside down 128 feet from the ground, feel weightless, and careen through the center of the park. Coaster lovers will be pleased to know that this ride, which lasts 2 minutes and 15 seconds, includes seven inversions and two deep drops. *Note:* Riders must be at least 54 inches tall.

Toon Lagoon

More than 150 life-size cartoon images let you know you've entered an island dedicated to your favorites from the Sunday funnies.

Dudley Do-Right's Ripsaw Falls 𝄇𝄇, which lies under Dudley's staid red hat, has a lot more speed and drop than onlookers think. Six-passenger logs launch into a 75-foot dip at 50 mph. You *will* get wet. *Note:* Riders must be 44 inches or taller.

The three-story boat, **Me Ship, The Olive** 𝄇 is family-friendly from bow to stern. Kids can toot whistles, clang bells, or play the organ. Sweet Pea's Playpen is fun for young guests. Adults and kids 6 and up love Cargo Crane, which lets you drench riders on Popeye & Bluto's Bilge-Rat Barges (see below).

Popeye & Bluto's Bilge-Rat Barges 𝄇𝄇 are similar to the rafts at WDW's Kali River Rapids (p. 507), but faster and bouncier. You'll also be squirted by water cannons fired from Me Ship, The Olive (above). The rafts dip 14 feet at one point, as you travel a *c-c-cold,* wet white-water course. Riders must be at least 42 inches tall.

Jurassic Park

All of the basics and some of the high-tech wizardry from Steven Spielberg's wildly successful films are incorporated in this lushly landscaped tropical locale that includes a replica of the visitor center from the *Jurassic Park* movie.

The **Camp Jurassic** 𝄇𝄇𝄇 play area has everything from lava pits with dino bones to a rainforest. Watch out for the spitters that lurk in dark caves. The multilevel play area has plenty of places for kids to crawl through, explore, and spend energy on. But keep an eye on young ones: It's easy to get confused in the caverns.

Jurassic Park Discovery Center, a virtual replica of the lab from the movie set, is an amusing, somewhat educational pit stop that offers life-size dinosaur replicas and interactive games. The sequencer lets you combine your DNA with a dinosaur's. The highlight is watching a velociraptor "hatch" in the nursery.

On the **Jurassic Park River Adventure** 𝄇𝄇, after a leisurely raft tour along a faux river, things go awry (don't they always?). An immense T-Rex thinks you look like a rather tasty morsel, with spitters launching "venom" your way just to add insult to injury. The only way out: an 85-foot almost-vertical plunge in your log-style life raft. It's steep and quick enough to lift your fanny out of the seat. Expect to get wet. *Note:* Guests must be at least 42 inches tall.

The Lost Continent

This island is a blend of the mysterious and the mythical, with components of Atlantis, Merlin, and Sinbad. The entrance, marked by an enormous stone griffin clad in iron, sets an appropriately mystic mood.

The biggest thrill here is **Dueling Dragons** 𝄇𝄇𝄇, an intertwined set of two leg-dangling racing roller coasters that test your bravery as they send you soaring 125 feet, invert five times, and miss each other by a mere 12 inches. The ride is rougher on its riders, with quick and jerky banking turns, than the Hulk Coaster. There's a special (longer!) line for the front seat. *Note:* Riders must be at least 54 inches tall.

The Flying Unicorn 𝄇𝄇 is a smaller roller coaster that travels through a mythical forest with a fast, corkscrew run sure to earn squeals, but probably not at the risk of losing your lunch. Riders must be at least 36 inches tall.

Have fun at the **Mystic Fountain** ✵, a "smart" fountain that especially delights kids. It can "see," "hear," and "talk," leading to a lot of kibitzing with those who stand before it and take the time to kibitz back. But be careful: It can squirt you.

One of the park's two shows, **Poseidon's Fury** ✵, revolves around a battle between Poseidon, god of the sea, and Darkenon, an evil sorcerer. The most impressive effect occurs as you pass through a small vortex, where 17,500 gallons of water swirl around you before you enter a room to experience the battle's pyrotechnic glories.

SEAWORLD

This 200-acre marine-life park explores the mysteries of the deep by combining conservation awareness with entertainment (aka "edutainment"). Over the years, it has expanded, adding a handful of thrill rides, a shopping and dining area, additional entertainment venues, and more wildlife. While not as large as its neighbors (Universal and Disney), it won't leave you as exhausted or exasperated by crowds. The unique combination of its animal life, calmer atmosphere, beautifully landscaped grounds, shows, and sprinkling of rides makes it a must-see for anyone visiting Orlando.

TICKET PRICES   A **1-day ticket** costs $62 for ages 10 and over, $50 for children 3 to 9, plus 6.5% sales tax. If you purchase tickets online (at home only) at least 7 days in advance of your visit, you can save an additional $6 per ticket.

MULTIPARK PASSES   For information on the **FlexTicket,** see p. 510. The **Fun Card** is a 1-year pass good for unlimited visits to SeaWorld; SeaWorld and Busch Gardens; or SeaWorld, Busch Gardens, and Adventure Island. Prices range from $62 to $130 for adults, and $50 to $20 for kids ages 3 to 9. These are available only to Florida residents

Multiday and multipark **Passports** are also available. These are essentially annual passes, good for either 1 or 2 years, and cover one, two, or three parks, depending on which level you choose—gold, silver, or platinum. The passes start at $84.95 and run up to $299.95. For more information, call ✆ **407/351-3600** or check **www.seaworld.com**.

PARKING   Parking is $9 for cars, light trucks, and vans. For $12, you can park close to the entrance in a specially designated section.

MAJOR ATTRACTIONS

A lovable sea lion and otter, with a supporting cast of walruses and harbor seals as well as some quick-witted SeaWorld actors/trainers, appear in **Clyde & Seamore Take Pirate Island** ✵✵, a fish-breath comedy with a swashbuckling theme. It's corny but a lot of fun. Watch out if you enter too close to show time; the mime entertaining the crowds ahead of time may target you for the audience's amusement.

Taking a cue from Disney Imagineers, SeaWorld created a story to go with its $30-million water coaster, **Journey to Atlantis** ✵✵. But what really matters is the drop— a wild plunge from 60 feet with lugelike curves. *Note:* Riders must be at least 42 inches tall, and pregnant women as well as those with heart, neck, or back problems should not ride.

Atlantic bottlenose dolphins perform flips and high jumps, swim on their backs, and give rides to trainers at **Key West Dolphin Fest.** While the tricks are impressive, the show is still somewhat predictable, so if the lines are too long, opt for the next scheduled show instead of waiting around.

Kraken ✵✵✵, named for a mythological beast, is a floorless, open-sided coaster where 32-passenger trains place you on a pedestal high above the track, your feet

Tips **Shuttle Service**

SeaWorld and Busch Gardens (p. 395), both owned by Anheuser-Busch, offer round-trip shuttle service ($10 per person) to get you from Orlando to Tampa and back. The 1½- to 2-hour one-way shuttle runs daily and has five pickup locations in Orlando, including at Universal and on International Drive (© **800/ 221-1339**). The schedule allows for about 7 hours at Busch Gardens. The service is free if you hold a FlexTicket.

dangling. You'll climb 151 feet, only to fall 144 feet at speeds of up to 65 mph seconds later, passing underground a total of three times (spraying bystanders with water) and making seven loops before you finally touch ground again. It's actually higher and faster than any coaster at Universal, probably making it the longest 3 minutes and 39 seconds of your life. *Note:* Kraken has a 54-inch height minimum.

In **Manatee Rescue** *ᚥ*, underwater viewing stations, innovative cinema techniques, and interactive displays combine for a tribute to these gentle marine mammals. While this isn't as good as seeing them in the wild, it's as close as most folks get, and the habitat is much roomier and more natural than the tight quarters their kin have at Epcot's The Living Seas (p. 486).

You are transported by moving sidewalk through Arctic and Antarctic displays at **Penguin Encounter.** You'll get a glimpse of penguins as they preen, socialize, and swim at bullet speed in their 22°F (–5°C) habitat. You'll also see puffins and murres in a separate area. While it gives you a nice view of the penguins (and they are always a hit with the kids), the viewing area's surroundings are in need of a face-lift.

The 3-acre **Shamu's Happy Harbor** *ᚥᚥ* play area has a four-story net tower with a 35-foot-high crow's nest, water cannons, remote-controlled vehicles, slides, a submarine, a water maze, and three kid-friendly rides, including a cool little coaster. Most kids relish the freedom of running, jumping, and climbing (and, of course, getting wet) after hearing, "Don't wander too far away from us" all day long. It is easy to escape a parent's watchful eye here, so little ones are best accompanied by an adult.

Everyone comes to SeaWorld to see Shamu and his friends—the stars of the impressively choreographed show ***Believe*** (replacing The Shamu Adventure). An all-new set, spectacular special effects, and musical score add up to a great show. Be sure to heed the warnings, as those sitting in the first 14 rows are sure to get soaked with icy water more than once. Dolphins, acrobats, and exotic birds are the stars of ***Blue Horizons*** *ᚥᚥ*, a far cry from the ho-hum dolphin show it replaced.

SeaWorld has added 220 species to its **Shark Encounter** attraction. The pools out front contain small sharks and rays (feeding isn't allowed). The interior aquariums have big eels, poisonous lionfish, menacing barracudas, bug-eyed pufferfish, and even larger and more menacing sharks. The eerie music playing in the background adds to the ominous ambience.

Enveloping guests in the beauty, exhilaration, and danger of a polar expedition, **Wild Arctic** *ᚥ* combines a high-definition adventure film with flight-simulator technology to display breathtaking arctic panoramas. After a hazardous flight over the frozen north, visitors emerge into an exhibit where you can see a playful polar bear, beluga whales, and walruses. Kids and those prone to motion sickness may find the ride bumpy. There's a separate line if you want to skip the flight.

The Waterfront, SeaWorld's most recent expansion, is a wonderfully themed 5-acre Mediterranean seaport village featuring unique shops, a wide variety of desperately needed restaurants (each offering a very different atmosphere and menu), and, for entertainment, formal shows and street performances.

DINING AT SEAWORLD

The park offers entertaining dining experiences in addition to its collection of waterfront eateries. **Dine with Shamu** ($37 adults, $19 kids ages 3–9) offers visitors the experience of seeing Shamu up close (inside an area restricted to trainers during normal hours) while enjoying a buffet-style meal. The **Makahiki Luau** offers island-style entertainment and a luau-type meal. The cost is $46 adults, $30 kids ages 3 to 9 (park admission is *not* required). **Sharks Underwater Grill** is an upscale restaurant geared to adults and allows up-close viewing of sharks through a gigantic wall of glass. Entrees are a bit pricey, averaging around $18 (and reaching upward of $30), but the gourmet Floribbean fare is a few cuts above usual park cuisine.

DISCOVERY COVE: A DOLPHIN ENCOUNTER

Anheuser-Busch spent $100 million building SeaWorld's sister park, which debuted in 2000. Prices vary seasonally but range from $249 to $279 per person (plus 6.5% sales tax) for ages 6 and up if you want to swim with the dolphins, and $149 to $179 if you forego the experience. Double-check prices when you make your required reservations.

The **Dolphin Swim** ✻✻✻ stars an amazing group of 28 of these mammals. Guests can swim, touch, play with, and interact with these amazingly intelligent creatures. They can even take a brief, albeit thrilling, ride with one. The entire experience lasts 90 minutes, 35 to 40 minutes of which are spent in the lagoon with a dolphin. The rest is a classroom experience on these remarkable mammals.

Here's what you get for your money, with or without the dolphin encounter:

- A limit of *no more than 1,000 other guests a day.* (The average daily attendance at Disney's Magic Kingdom is 41,000.) This ensures that your experience will be more relaxing and private.
- A continental breakfast, lunch, all-day snacks and drinks, a towel, a locker, sunscreen, snorkeling gear (including a flotation vest), a souvenir photo, and free parking are also part of the deal.
- Other 9am-to-5:30pm activities include a chance to swim near (but on the other side of the Plexiglas) **barracudas** and **black-tip sharks.** There are no barriers between you and the gentle rays and tropical fish in the 1.3-million-gallon coral reef. The 3,300-foot-long Tropical River is a great place to swim or float in a mild current through a cave, two waterfalls, and a 30-foot-high aviary where you can take a stroll, becoming a human perch. There are also beaches for relaxing.
- Seven consecutive days of **unlimited admission** to either SeaWorld *or* Busch Gardens. For an additional $30 per person, you can upgrade this option to 14 days of unlimited admission to both SeaWorld *and* Busch Gardens.

Get more information on Discovery Cove by calling ✆ **877/434-7268,** or go to **www.discoverycove.com**. If you want to try it, make a reservation as far in advance as possible. Despite the high price, the park reaches its capacity almost every day.

12 Other Area Attractions

Several smaller Orlando-area attractions are well worth noting and deserve your attention. Many require less than a day (or a fortune), making them great choices for those times when you just can't face the major theme parks. We note how much time and money to budget. *Add 6.5% sales tax* to the prices below, unless otherwise stated.

IN KISSIMMEE

Along U.S. 192 you'll find an array of smaller attractions lining the highway, most of them within 10 to 15 minutes of Disney's entrance.

Gatorland ⚑ Founded in 1949 as one of Orlando's original attractions, Gatorland now houses thousands of alligators and crocodiles on its 70-acre spread. There are three shows. At **Gator Wrestlin',** trainers defy death by sticking their heads in the mouths of gators. **The Gator Jumparoo** is a crowd-pleaser in which some of these big reptiles lunge 4 or 5 feet out of the water to snatch meat from a trainer's hand. **Jungle Crocs** is a showcase of toothy carnivores. The Trainer for a Day program offers a number of hands-on experiences, including a chance to wrangle the gators with trainers by your side ($100; minimum age 12). Plan to spend 4 to 5 hours here. It makes for an entertaining afternoon away from the hustle and bustle of the major parks.

14501 S. Orange Blossom Trail (U.S. 441; between Osceola Pkwy. and Hunter's Creek Blvd.). ☎ **800/393-5297** or 407/855-5496. www.gatorland.com. Admission $20 adults, $13 children 3–12 (plus tax). Open daily at 9am; closing times vary. Free parking. From I-4, take the Osceola Pkwy. exit east to U.S. 17/92/441 and go left/north. Gatorland is 1½ miles on the right.

ON INTERNATIONAL DRIVE

Like Kissimmee's attractions, these are about a 10- to 15-minute drive from the Disney entrance, and about 10 minutes from Universal Orlando.

Wet 'n Wild ⚑⚑ Orlando's favorite non-Disney water park offers 25 acres of fun, including: **Fuji Flyer,** a six-story, four-passenger toboggan run through 450 feet of banked curves; **The Surge,** one of the longest and fastest multi-passenger tube rides in the Southeast; and **Black Hole,** a two-person, spaceship-style raft that makes a 500-foot twisting, turning voyage through darkness (all three require that kids 36–48 in. tall be accompanied by an adult). You also can ride **Raging Rapids,** a white-water run with a waterfall plunge; **Blue Niagara,** a 300-foot-long, six-story loop-and-dipster that includes a plunge (48-in. height minimum); **Knee Ski,** a cable-operated kneeboarding course that's open in warm-weather months only (56-in. height minimum); and **Mach 5,** a trio of twisting, turning flumes. **Disco H20,** an enclosed flume ride, sends riders flying through a '70s flashback, complete with mirrored lights and disco music. The park also has a large kids' area. Plan on a full day here.

In addition to the admission prices below, Wet 'n Wild is part of the multiday **FlexTicket package** that includes admission to Universal Orlando (which owns this attraction), SeaWorld, and Busch Gardens in Tampa. See "The FlexTicket" on p. 510 for details and prices.

6200 International Dr. (at Universal Blvd.). ☎ **800/992-9453** or 407/351-1800. www.wetnwild.com. Admission $35 adults, $29 children 3–9. Hours vary seasonally, weather permitting. You can rent tubes ($4), towels ($2), and lockers ($5), or all three for $9; all require an additional $2 deposit ($4 for the combo), refundable upon return. Parking is $7 for cars, light trucks, and vans. From I-4, take the Universal Orlando exit and follow the signs.

13 Staying Active

SPORTS ACTIVITIES

If you want some exercise other than walking the parks, Walt Disney World and the surrounding areas have plenty of recreational options. The following are open to everyone, no matter where you're staying.

BICYCLING   Bike rentals (single and multispeed bikes for adults, tandems, baby seats, and children's bikes) are available to Disney guests from the **Bike Barn** (© 407/ 824-2742), at Fort Wilderness Resort and Campground. Rates are $8 per hour, $22 per day (including tax). Fort Wilderness offers good bike trails.

BOATING   With a ton of man-made lakes and lagoons, WDW owns a navy of pleasure boats. **Capt. Jack's,** at Downtown Disney, rents Water Sprites and canopy boats ($24–$42 per half-hour). For information, call © **407/828-2204.**

The **Bike Barn,** at Fort Wilderness (© **407/824-2742**), rents canoes and paddle-boats ($6.50 per half-hour).

GOLF   Disney operates five 18-hole, par-72 golf courses and one 9-hole, par-36 walking course. The rates are $60 (twilight special) to $174 per 18-hole round. Resort guests are provided with free transportation between their resort and the course. For tee times and information, call © **407/939-4653** up to 30 days in advance (up to 90 days for guests of the Disney resort and official properties). Call © **407/934-7639** to inquire about golf packages, equipment rentals, tee times, and lessons.

Beyond Mickey's shadow, **Golfpac** (© **800/486-0948** or 407/260-2288; www.golf pacorlando.com) is an organization that packages golf with accommodations and arranges tee times at more than 40 Orlando-area courses.

HORSEBACK RIDING   **Disney's Fort Wilderness** offers 45-minute guided trail rides daily. The cost is $42 per person. Children must be at least 9. Maximum weight limit is 250 pounds. For information, call © **407/939-7529.**

The **Villas of Grand Cypresses' Equestrian Center** offers 45-minute walk-trot trail rides for $45. A 30-minute private lesson is $55; an hour-long lesson is $100. Call © **407/239-4700** and ask for the equestrian center.

TENNIS   There are 22 lighted tennis courts scattered throughout the Disney properties. They're free and open to resort guests on a first-come, first-served basis, with the exception of the Contemporary Resort's courts, which cost $8 per hour. The Racquet Club at the Contemporary Resort has six clay courts, all lighted for evening play, and offers private lessons ($75 per hour) and group clinics ($15). Call © **407/939-7529** to make reservations or for more information.

SPECTATOR SPORTS

BASEBALL   The **Atlanta Braves** play 18 spring-training games at Disney's Wide World of Sports beginning in early March. Tickets are $14 to $22. Call © **407/839-3900** or see **www.atlantabraves.com** for more information.

BASKETBALL   The **TD Waterhouse Centre,** 600 W. Amelia St., between I-4 and Parramore Avenue, is the home of the **Orlando Magic,** which plays 41 of its regular season games here from October to April. Call © **407/896-2442** or check out **www. nba.com/magic**. Single-game tickets are $25 to $175.

14 Shopping

Some of us get as much pleasure from shopping as from a good meal or show. But if you're going to ring registers in the theme parks, expect to pay top dollar. So plan a day out of the parks and be as savvy here as you are back home.

On International Drive, look for **Pointe Orlando,** 9101 International Dr. (© **407/ 248-2838;** www.pointeorlandofl.com), an open-air complex with dozens of stores, including Tommy Hilfiger and Abecrombie & Fitch.

There are several factory outlets, but their publicized discounts of 25% to 75% are often a mirage. It pays to know suggested retail prices. **Belz Factory Outlet World,** 5401 W. Oak Ridge Rd. (at the north end of International Dr.; © **407/354-0126;** www.belz.com); **Orlando Premium Outlets,** 8200 Vineland Ave. (© **407/238-7787;** www.premiumoutlets.com); and **Lake Buena Vista Factory Stores,** 155591 Apopka-Vineland Rd. (© **407/238-9301**), are the better ones, with Premium Outlets having the best variety and nicest atmosphere.

Mall at Millenia, 4200 Conroy Rd. (© **407/363-3555;** www.mallatmillenia. com), is the new upscale kid on the block (Bloomingdale's, Neiman Marcus, Tiffany), while **Florida Mall,** 8001 S. Orange Blossom Trail (© **407/851-6255;** www.shop simon.com), has Saks, Dillards, and more.

Downtown Disney—more specifically, the **Marketplace**—features a variety of unique shops, with merchandise mostly geared toward kids. The second-largest Disney store in the world, **World of Disney** (© **407/828-1451**), takes center stage. Other shops include **Lego Imagination Center** (© **407/828-0065**), as well as one of the best Disney stores around—**Once Upon a Toy** (© **407/934-7775**). Disney's Westside appeals more to teens, with stores such as the **Virgin Megastore** (© **407/ 828-0222**). Stores are generally open from 9:30am to 11pm.

15 Walt Disney World & Orlando After Dark

Central Florida has plenty for night owls to do. Parties last into the wee hours at **Pleasure Island, Downtown Disney, CityWalk,** and other hot spots.

DISNEY DINNER SHOWS

Disney's Spirit of Aloha Dinner Show *(Moments* While not nearly as in demand as the *Hoop De Doo* (see below), the Polynesian Resort's delightful 2-hour luau is worth attending. *Disney's Spirit of Aloha Dinner Show* features Tahitian, Samoan, and Hawaiian singers, drummers, and dancers who entertain you while you feast on tropical appetizers, Lanai roasted chicken, Polynesian wild rice, South Seas vegetables, dessert, wine, beer, and other beverages. The action takes place twice nightly, 5 nights a week, in an open-air theater (dress for nighttime weather).

1600 Seven Seas Dr. (at Disney's Polynesian Resort). © 407/939-3463. www.disneyworld.com. Reservations required. $51 adults, $26 kids 3–9, including tax and gratuity. Free parking. Show times 5:15 and 8pm Tues–Sat.

Hoop De Doo Musical Review *(★★★* *(Kids* AMERICAN This entertaining, high-energy dinner show is fun for the entire family. Featuring singing and dancing sprinkled with comedy, this show is justifiably the most popular of the Disney dinner shows. Dinner consists of country-fried chicken served in a bucket, along with corn on the cob, biscuits, and dessert. And though the food is pretty good, you may almost forget to eat, thanks to all the action going on around you. It can get a bit expensive if you have a large family, but the entertainment value is well worth the price.

4510 N. Fort Wilderness Trail, at Disney's Fort Wilderness Resort and Campground. (©) **407/WDW-DINE.** Reservations required. $51 adults, $26 children 3–11. AE, DC, DISC, MC, V. Shows at 5, 7:15, and 9pm nightly.

ENTERTAINMENT MECCAS
AT DISNEY

PLEASURE ISLAND   Every evening at 7pm, the 6-acre entertainment district of **Pleasure Island** ((©) **407/939-2648**) comes alive, bustling with activity as visitors come to party into the wee hours of the night. The price of admission (which includes entrance to all clubs) is $21; an annual pass costs $55. Every night is New Year's Eve here, with a lively street party continuing throughout the evening, and fireworks and confetti at midnight. Here's the club lineup:

Adventurers Club   The most unique of Pleasure Island's clubs, Adventurers occupies a multistory building chock-full of such artifacts as 1940s aviation photos, hunting trophies, shrunken heads, Buddhas, and a mounted "yakoose"—a half yak, half moose that occasionally speaks, whether you've been drinking or not. In the Mask Room, the 100 or so masks move their eyes, jeer, and make bizarre pronouncements. Improv comedy takes place throughout the evening in the salon.

BET Soundstage ⍟   This club grooves with traditional R&B and hip-hop. Boogie on an expansive dance floor, watch a video on one of the many screens, or kick back on the terrace. The club sometimes has concerts for a separate charge. Call (©) **407/ 934-7666.** You must be 21 to enter (the policy is strictly enforced).

The Comedy Warehouse   Performing two shows nightly, the "Who, What & Warehouse" improv comedians entertain audiences with their quick wit and spontaneous style.

8 Trax   This club brings back the '70s for those who just can't leave it behind. Boogie to the Bee Gees, the Village People, and Donna Summer in a setting dominated by flashing lights, lava lamps, and mirrored balls.

Mannequins Dance Palace ⍟⍟   Housed in a huge nightclub with a small-town movie-house facade, Mannequins resembles a converted theatrical warehouse (remember, you're still in Disney World). This high-energy club has a big rotating dance floor, and its popularity makes it one of the toughest nightspots to get into. Its three levels of bars and hangout space are filled with elaborately costumed mannequins and moving scenery suspended overhead. A DJ plays contemporary tunes filtered through

---

Moments **Not Your Ordinary Circus**

Cirque du Soleil, the famous no-animals circus in Downtown Disney West Side, seems to put all 64 performers onstage at once in the trampoline routine. Trapeze artists, high-wire walkers, an aerial gymnast, a strongman, and two zany clowns cement a show called **La Nouba** ⍟⍟⍟ (which means "live it up") into a five-star multiact performance.

But in a world of pricey attractions, this is one of the priciest. There are two ticket categories: $95 adults and $76 kids 3 to 9 (including tax) for center-of-the-theater seats; $61 adults and $49 kids 3 to 9 for seats to the right or left of the stage. The 90-minute shows are at 6 and 9pm; days rotate. Call (©) **407/939-7600** or check out **www.cirquedusoleil.com** for details.

---

speakers that could wake the dead, and the high-tech lighting effects complete the experience. You must be 21 to get in, and they're *very* serious about that.

Motion   Pleasure Island's newest dance club is two stories of action, from the huge video screens right down to the dance floor. The hottest chart-topping hits and some really cool, moody blue lighting make it easy to dance the night away here.

Rock 'n' Roll Beach Club   Live bands play classic rock from the 1960s through the 1990s. There are bars on all three floors. The first level has a dance floor; the others offer arcade-style games, pizza, and more. Top bands play nightly.

DOWNTOWN DISNEY WEST SIDE
House of Blues   This club/restaurant's darkened atmosphere is perfect for the oft-featured bluesy sounds that raise its rafters every night. Right next door, however, is the place to go for some of the city's best live entertainment. The huge three-tier concert hall has been known to feature some of the best bands around—local and big names both—and the dance floor is big enough to boogie without doing the bump with a stranger. © 407/934-2583. www.hob.com. Cover charges vary.

CITYWALK
Located between Islands of Adventure and Universal Studios Florida, this 30-acre club-and-restaurant district (© **407/363-8000;** www.citywalk.com) is five times larger than Pleasure Island. After dark (and even a bit before), the alcohol flows rather freely (don't get too excited—you still have to pay for the drinks!), as drinking is pretty much on tap everywhere, making this a hot spot for adults but not a place for kids.

   You can walk the entire area for free, but select clubs charge a cover. CityWalk also offers two types of **party passes.** A pass that includes access to all the clubs costs $9.95 plus tax. For $13 plus tax, you get a club pass and a movie at Universal Cineplex (© **407/354-5998**). *Note:* Daytime parking in the Universal Orlando garages costs $9, but parking is free after 6pm.

Bob Marley—A Tribute to Freedom   Clubbers can nibble on Jamaican and Caribbean food here as they're treated to live reggae music. Over a hundred portraits of the original Rastaman, Bob Marley, decorate the walls. The club is open daily from 4pm to 2am. © 407/224-3663. Cover $7 after 8pm, more on special nights. Must be 21 to enter after 9pm.

CityJazz   The cover includes the **Downbeat Jazz Hall of Fame** (which has memorabilia from Louis Armstrong and other greats) as well as the **Thelonious Monk Institute of Jazz,** a performance venue and site of jazz workshops. The two-story, 10,500-square-foot building holds more than 500 pieces of memorabilia representing Dixieland, swing, bebop, and jazz. On Thursday and Saturday nights, the theme gives way to comedy at BONKERZ Comedy Club. The club is open Sunday through Thursday from 8pm to 1am, and Friday and Saturday from 7pm to 2am. © 407/224-2189. Cover $7 (more for special events). Must be 18 to enter.

the groove   This often-crowded multilevel club features a huge dance floor, a number of bars, and a handful of lounges for just hanging out. The high-tech sound system will blow your hair back; if you need a sound check, try the upper-level patio for a brief reprieve. A DJ plays tunes most nights, featuring the latest in hip-hop, retro hits, techno, and alternative music. It's open 9pm to 2am daily. © 407/363-8000. Cover $7. Must be 21 to get in.

Hard Rock Cafe/Hard Rock Live   The cafe side is the chain's standard—a theme restaurant with memorabilia and other tributes to rock's greats. The difference is that this one has the first concert hall with the Hard Rock name on the door. Call ahead to find out what acts are featured. Tickets for big-name performers sell fast. Hard Rock Cafe is open daily from 11am to midnight. ℂ **407/351-LIVE.** www.hardrocklive.com. Concert prices depend on event.

Jimmy Buffett's Margaritaville   Music by the maestro booms loudly through the building, with live tunes occasionally performed on a small indoor stage later in the evening. There are three themed bars—Volcano, Land Shark, and 12 Volt—each with tropical touches. It's a Parrothead's paradise. If you opt for dinner, go for the true Key West experience. Early in the day, that means a cheeseburger; later, it's one of several kinds of fish. The open-air deck off to the side offers the quietest place to roost. Open daily from 11am to 2am. ℂ **407/224-2155.** Cover $5 after 10pm.

Latin Quarter   This two-level restaurant offers you a chance to absorb the salsa-and-samba culture. It's filled with the music of the merengue, the mambo, and the tango, along with a bit of Latin rock thrown in for good measure. So get ready to move your hips. The surprisingly intimate atmosphere is far from high tech; you'll feel like you're dancing in a Mayan temple. Open Saturday and Sunday from noon to 2am, and Monday through Friday from 11:30am to 10pm. ℂ **407/224-3663.**

Pat O'Brien's   Just like the French Quarter, which is home to the original Patty O's, drinking, drinking, and more drinking are the highlights here. Down the big drink of the Big Easy, a Hurricane, though there are plenty of other concoctions to choose from. Open daily from 4pm to 2am. ℂ **407/363-8000.**

Northeast Florida

When driving through the elongated state of Florida, many people make the grave mistake of gunning their engines and jetting through the Northeast without as much as a single stop beyond the Cracker Barrels, Denny's restaurants, and gas stations lining the highways. Thankfully, Juan Ponce de León made the *fortunate* mistake of playing accidental tourist and discovered just how magnificent the northeast part of the state truly is. You would do well to explore in his footsteps.

Northeast Florida traces its roots back to 1513, when the wanderlusty León, who later undertook a misguided quest for the Fountain of Youth, sighted this coast and landed somewhere between present-day Jacksonville and Cape Canaveral. (He was a bit off course—he meant to land in what is now Bimini—but who can blame a guy who didn't have GPS?) Observing the land's lush foliage, he named it *La Florida,* or "the flowery land." In 1565, the Spanish established a colony at St. Augustine, the country's oldest continuously inhabited European settlement.

Not much, if anything at all, has changed in St. Augustine (in a wonderful way). The streets of the restored Old City look much as they did in Spanish times. But not everything in Northeast Florida is antiquated.

To the south, there's the Jetsonian "Space Coast," where rockets blast off

from the Kennedy Space Center at Cape Canaveral. In nearby Cocoa Beach, you can witness surfers riding the rather sizeable waves. In Daytona Beach, brace yourself for the deafening roar of the stock cars and motorbikes that make this beach town the "World Center of Racing." And don't blink, because you wouldn't want to miss Daytona's other pop-cultural phenom, known as the MTV Spring Break bikini crowd.

Going north along the coast, you'll come to a far cry from spring breakers on a budget: the moneyed haven of Ponte Vedra Beach, where golf definitely takes precedence over manual labor. In Jacksonville, Florida's largest metropolis and a thriving port city and naval base, you can get a taste of city life before retreating back to the beach.

Up near the Georgia border, cross a bridge to Amelia Island, where you'll discover exclusive resorts that take full advantage of 13 miles of beautiful beaches. Amelia's Victorian-era town, Fernandina Beach, is another throwback to the past, helping to further render the Northeast region of Florida a fascinating juxtaposition of old, new, and somewhere in between. However you perceive it, do not make the mistake of missing the Northeast. Ponce de León didn't blow off Bimini for nothing, you know.

1 Cocoa Beach, Cape Canaveral, the Kennedy Space Center & Melbourne ⟨★

46 miles SE of Orlando, 186 miles N of Miami, 65 miles S of Daytona

The "Space Coast," the area around Cape Canaveral, was once a sleepy place where city dwellers escaped the exploding urban centers of Miami and Jacksonville. But then came the NASA space program. Today the region produces and accommodates its own crowds, particularly the hordes of tourists who come to visit the Kennedy Space Center and enjoy the area's 72 miles of beaches (this is, after all, the closest beach to Orlando's mega-attractions) as well as excellent fishing, surfing, and golfing.

Thanks to NASA, this is also a prime destination for nature lovers. The space agency originally took over much more land than it needed to launch rockets. Rather than sell off the unused portions, it turned them over to the Canaveral National Seashore and the Merritt Island National Wildlife Refuge (www.nbbd.com/godo/minwr), which have preserved these areas in their pristine natural states.

A handful of Caribbean-bound cruise ships also depart from Port Canaveral. The south side of the port is lined with seafood restaurants and marinas, which serve as home base for gambling ships and the area's deep-sea charter and group fishing boats.

ESSENTIALS

GETTING THERE   The nearest airport is **Melbourne International Airport** (✆ 321/723-6227; www.mlbair.com), 22 miles south of Cocoa Beach, which is served by **Continental** (✆ 800/525-0280; www.continental.com) and **Delta** (✆ 800/221-1212; www.delta.com). **Orlando International Airport** (p. 462), about 35 miles to the west, is a much larger hub with many more flight options and generally less expensive fares. It's an easy 45-minute drive from the Orlando Airport to the beaches via the Bee Line Expressway (Fla. 528, a toll road)—it can take almost that long from the Melbourne Airport, where **Avis, Budget, Hertz,** and **National** all have car-rental desks. The **Melbourne Airport Shuttle** (✆ 321/724-1600) will take you from the Melbourne Airport to most local destinations for about $10 to $20 per person.

VISITOR INFORMATION   For information on the area, contact the **Florida Space Coast Office of Tourism/Brevard County Tourist Development Council,** 8810 Astronaut Blvd., Suite 102, Cape Canaveral, FL 32920 (✆ 800/872-1969 or 321/868-1126; www.space-coast.com). The office is in the Sheldon Cove building, on Fla. A1A a block north of Central Boulevard, and is open Monday through Friday from 8am to 5pm. It also operates an information booth at the Kennedy Space Center Visitor Complex (p. 526).

GETTING AROUND   A car is essential in this area. If you're not coming by car, you can rent one at the airport. **Space Coast Area Transit** (✆ 321/633-1878; www.ridescat.com) operates buses ($1 adults, 50¢ seniors and students), but routes tend to be circuitous and, therefore, extremely time-consuming.

ATTRACTIONS

In addition to the two attractions below, Brevard College's **Astronaut Memorial Planetarium and Observatory,** 1519 Clearlake Rd., Cocoa Beach (✆ 321/634-3732; www.brevardcc.edu/planet), south of Florida 528, has its own International Hall of Space Explorers, but its big attractions are sound-and-light shows in the planetarium. Call or check the website for schedules and prices.

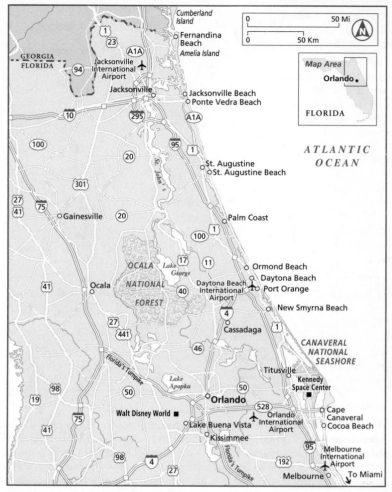

Brevard Zoo *(Kids)*   This delightful small-town zoo houses more than 500 animals, including white rhinos, red kangaroos, wallabies, crocodiles, howler monkeys, bald eagles, red wolves, and river otters. Enjoy a 10-minute train tour of the grounds ($2), a free-flight aviary, a cute and cuddly petting zoo, and alligator feedings usually 3 days a week. Check out the 10-acre Expedition Africa exhibit, where impala, gazelle, and scimitar-horned oryx chill out over the savanna. Don't miss the opportunity to kayak through the wetlands—this is the only zoo in the country that offers kayaking, and it's a bargain, at only $3 per person. For an up-close and personal view of the animals, take the behind the scenes tour with a zookeeper on Saturday and Sunday at 1pm.

8225 N. Wickham Rd., Melbourne (just east of I-95 exit 73/Wickham Rd.). ☏ **321/254-9453**. www.brevardzoo.org. Admission $9 adults, $8 seniors, $6 children 3–12, free for kids under 3. Daily 10am–5pm.

Cape Canaveral

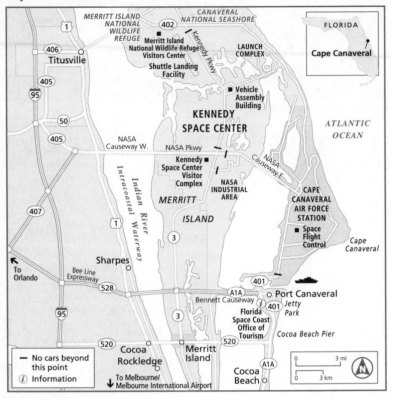

MERRITT ISLAND NATIONAL WILDLIFE REFUGE

CANAVERAL NATIONAL SEASHORE

402

Kennedy Pkwy

Merritt Island National Wildlife Refuge Visitors Center

LAUNCH COMPLEX

FLORIDA

Cape Canaveral

406

Titusville

405

95

50

405

Shuttle Landing Facility

■ Vehicle Assembly Building

KENNEDY SPACE CENTER

ATLANTIC OCEAN

NASA Causeway W.

NASA Pkwy

NASA Causeway E.

Kennedy ■ Space Center Visitor Complex

407

1

MERRITT

ISLAND

NASA INDUSTRIAL AREA

3

CAPE CANAVERAL AIR FORCE STATION

■ Space Flight Control

Cape Canaveral

Indian River Intracoastal Waterway

Sharpes

To Orlando

Bee Line Expressway

528

401

95

3

A1A

Bennett Causeway

401

Jetty Park

i

Florida Space Coast Office of Tourism

Cocoa Beach Pier

520

Cocoa

Rockledge

Merritt Island

520

Cocoa Beach

A1A

To Melbourne/ Melbourne International Airport

— No cars beyond this point

i Information

0   3 mi

0   3 km

John F. Kennedy Space Center ✪✪✪ Whether or not you're a space buff, you'll appreciate the sheer grandeur of the facilities and technological achievements displayed at NASA's primary space-launch facility. Astronauts departed Earth at this site in 1969 en route to the most famous "small step" in history—the first moon walk— and today's space shuttles still regularly lift off from here on their latest missions.

Since all roads other than Florida 405 and Florida 3 are closed to the public in the space center, you must begin your visit at the **Kennedy Space Center Visitor Complex.** A bit like a themed amusement park, this privately operated complex has received a $130-million renovation and expansion, so check beforehand to see if tours and exhibits have changed since press time. Call ahead to see what's happening on the day you intend to be here, and arrive early. You'll need at least 2 hours to see the space center's highlights on the bus tour, up to 5 hours if you linger at the stops along the way, and a full day to see and do everything here. Buy a copy of the *Official Tour Book;* it's easier to use than the rental cassette tapes, and you can take it home as a colorful souvenir (though some readers think you probably don't need the extra information, as the bus tours are narrated and the exhibits have good descriptions).

The visitor complex has real NASA rockets and the actual Mercury Mission Control Room from the 1960s. Exhibits look at early space exploration and where it's going in

---

Tips Out to Launch

If you'd like to see a shuttle launch at the **Kennedy Space Center,** first call ℂ **321/867-5000** or check NASA's official website (www.ksc.nasa.gov) for a schedule of upcoming takeoffs. You can buy launch tickets at the Kennedy Space Center Visitor Complex (ℂ **321/449-4444**) or online at www.ksctickets.com. *A word of caution:* Shuttle launches are frequently delayed due to weather, equipment malfunctions, or other factors, so you might have to make multiple visits to see one. If you don't have that flexibility, the launch window may be delayed beyond your going-home date.

If you can't get into the space center, other good viewing spots are on the causeways leading to the islands and on U.S. 1 as it skirts the waterfront in Titusville. The **Holiday Inn Riverside–Kennedy Space Center,** on Washington Avenue (U.S. 1) in Titusville (ℂ **800/465-4329** or 321/269-2121; www.holiday innksc.com), has a clear view of the launch pads across the Indian River. Area motels raise their rates and often book up at launch periods.

---

the new millennium. There are hands-on activities aimed at kids, a daily "Encounter" with a real astronaut, dining venues, and a shop selling space memorabilia. IMAX movies shown on 5½-story-high screens are both informative and entertaining.

While you could spend an entire day at the visitor complex, you must take a **KSC Tour** to see the actual space center where rockets and shuttles are prepared and launched. Take the bus tour early in your visit (the lines for these are brutal), and be sure to hit the restrooms before boarding—there's only one on the tour. Buses depart every 10 minutes or so, and you can reboard as you wish. They stop at the LC-39 Observation Gantry, with a dramatic 360-degree view over launch pads where shuttles blast off; the International Space Station Center, where scientists and engineers prepare additions to the space station now in orbit; and the Apollo/Saturn V Center, which includes artifacts, photos, films, interactive exhibits, and the 363-foot-tall Saturn V, the most powerful rocket ever launched by the United States. Unfortunately, the bus tour was the low point of my recent visit. Though the commentary on the bus was interesting, the stops were relatively dull, and waiting to board and reboard buses was more than frustrating (though touching a moon rock at the Apollo/Saturn V Center was pretty cool). If you're short on time, I suggest sticking around the visitor center.

Don't miss the Astronaut Memorial, a moving black-granite monument that bears the names of the U.S. astronauts who have died on missions or while in training. The 60-ton structure rotates on a track that follows the movement of the sun (on clear days, of course), causing the names to stand out against a brilliant reflection of the sky.

On launch days, the center is closed at least part of the day. These aren't good days to see the center, but they're great days to observe history in the making. For $37 per adult and $27 per child 3 through 11, you get a **combined ticket** that entitles you to admission to the center for the shortened operating hours, plus at least a 2-hour excursion to NASA Parkway to see the liftoff. You must pick up tickets, available 5 days before the launch, on-site.

For an out-of-this-world experience, do lunch with an astronaut, a once-in-a-lifetime opportunity available every day ($20 adults, $10 kids 3–11, in addition to space center admission). Astronauts who have participated in the past include some of the greatest, such as John Glenn, Jim Lovell, Walt Cunningham, Story Musgrave, and Jon McBride. Seating is limited; call (C) **321/449-4400** to make a reservation.

Note: Kennedy Space Center acquired many of the exhibits from the **Astronaut Hall of Fame** and added them as a separate attraction at the KSC visitor center ($17 adults, $13 kids 3–11; or $37 adults and $27 kids for a 2-day Maximum Access Admission to the Center and the Hall of Fame). The attraction includes exhibits and tributes to the heroes of the Mercury, Gemini, and Apollo space programs. There's also a collection of spacecraft, including a Mercury 7 capsule, a Gemini training capsule, and an Apollo 14 command module. In "Simulator Station," guests can experience four times the force of gravity, ride a Rover across Mars, and land a Space Shuttle.

NASA Pkwy. (Fla. 405), 6 miles east of Titusville, ½ mile west of Fla. 3. (C) 321/449-4444 for general information, or 321/449-4444 for guided bus tours and launch reservations. www.kennedyspacecenter.com. Admission $30 adults, $20 children 3–11. Annual passes $48 adults, $32 children 3–11. Audio tours $5 per person. All tours and movies free for children under 3. Daily 9am–5:30pm. Shuttle-bus tours daily 9:45am–2:15pm. Closed Christmas and some launch days.

BEACHES & WILDLIFE REFUGES

To the north of the Kennedy Space Center, **Canaveral National Seashore** 🅡🅡🅡 is a protected 13-mile stretch of barrier-island beach backed by cabbage palms, sea grapes, palmettos, marshes, and Mosquito Lagoon. This is a great area for watching herons, egrets, ibises, willets, sanderlings, turnstones, terns, and other birds. You might also glimpse dolphins and manatees in Mosquito Lagoon. Canoeists can paddle along a marked trail through the marshes of Shipyard Island, and backcountry camping is possible November through April (permits required; see below).

The main **visitor center** is at 7611 S. Atlantic Ave., New Smyrna Beach, FL 32169 ((C) **321/867-4077,** or 321/867-0677 for recorded information; www.nps.gov/cana), on Apollo Beach, at the north end of the island. The southern access gate to the island is 8 miles east of Titusville on Florida 402, just east of Florida 3. A paved road leads from the gate to undeveloped **Playalinda Beach** 🅡🅡🅡, one of Florida's most beautiful. Though illegal, nude sunbathing has long been a tradition here (at least, for those willing to walk a few miles to the more deserted areas). The beach has toilets but no running water or other amenities, so bring everything you'll need. The seashore is open daily from 6am to 8pm during daylight saving time, daily from 6am to 6pm during standard time. Entry fees are $5 per motor vehicle, $3 per pedestrian or bicyclist. National Park Service passports are accepted. Backcountry camping permits cost $10 for up to six people and must be obtained from the New Smyrna Beach visitor center. For advance information, contact the seashore headquarters at 308 Julia St., Titusville, FL 32796 ((C) **321/867-4077** or 321/267-1110; www.nps.gov/cana).

Canaveral National Seashore's neighbor to the south and west is the 140,000-acre **Merritt Island National Wildlife Refuge** 🅡🅡, home to hundreds of species of shorebirds, waterfowl, reptiles, alligators, and mammals, many of them endangered. Pick up a map and other information at the visitor center, on Florida 402 about 4 miles east of Titusville (it's on the way to Playalinda Beach). The center has a ¼-mile boardwalk along the edge of the marsh. Displays show the animals you may spot from 6-mile Black Point Wildlife Drive or from one of the nature trails through the hammocks and marshes. The visitor center is open Monday through Friday from 8am to 4:30pm, Saturday and Sunday from 9am to 5pm (closed Sun Apr–Oct). Entry is free. For more information and a schedule of programs, contact the refuge at P.O. Box 6504, Titusville, FL 32782 ((C) **321/861-0667;** www.nbbd.com/godo/minwr).

Note: Those parts of the national seashore near the Kennedy Space Center and all of the refuge close 4 days before a shuttle launch and usually reopen the day after a launch.

Another good beach area is **Lori Wilson Park,** on Atlantic Avenue at Antigua Drive in Cocoa Beach (© 321/868-1123), which preserves a stretch of sand backed by a forest of live oaks. It's home to a small but interesting nature center, and restrooms are available. The park is open daily from sunrise to sunset; the nature center, Monday through Friday from 1 to 4pm.

The beach at **Cocoa Beach Pier,** on Meade Avenue east of Florida A1A (© 321/ 783-7549), is a popular spot with surfers, who consider it the East Coast's surfing capital. The rustic pier was built in 1962 and has 842 feet of fishing, shopping, and dining overlooking a wide, sandy beach (see "Where to Dine," below). Because this is not a public park, there are no restrooms other than the ones in restaurants on the pier.

Jetty Park, 400 E. Jetty Rd., at the south entry to Port Canaveral (© 321/783-7111; www.portcanaveral.org/funport/parks.htm), has lifeguards, a fishing pier with bait shop, a playground, a volleyball court, a horseshoe pit, picnic tables, a snack bar, a grocery store, restrooms and changing facilities, and the area's only campground. From here, you can watch the big cruise ships as they enter and leave the port's narrow passage. The park is open daily from 7am to 10pm; the pier is open 24 hours for fishing. Admission is $5 per car, $7 per RV. The 150 tent and RV campsites (some of them shady, most with hookups) cost $18 to $31 a night, depending on location and time of year. No pets are allowed.

OUTDOOR ACTIVITIES & SPECTATOR SPORTS

BASEBALL   The **Washington Nationals** play spring-training games at **Space Coast Stadium,** 5800 Stadium Pkwy., Viera (© 321/633-4487), located south of Cape Canaveral and north of Melbourne. Tickets are $5 to $18. The stadium also hosts minor-league action from the Brevard County Manatees, an affiliate of the Nationals.

ECO-TOURS   **Funday Discovery Tours** (© 321/725-0796; www.fundaytours.com) offers a variety of day trips, including dinner and sunset cruises, airboat and swamp-buggy rides, dolphin-watching cruises, bird-watching expeditions, and personalized tours of the Kennedy Space Center and Merritt Island National Wildlife Refuge. Reservations are required.

FISHING   Head to Port Canaveral for catches such as snapper and grouper. **Jetty Park** (© 321/783-7111), at the south entry to the port, has a fishing pier equipped with a bait shop (see "Beaches & Wildlife Refuges," above). The south bank of the port is lined with charter boats. Try deep-sea fishing on *Miss Cape Canaveral* (© 321/ 783-5274, or 321/648-2211 in Orlando; www.misscape.com), one of the party boats based here. All-day voyages departing daily at 8am cost $50 to $65 for adults, $45 to $60 for seniors, $40 to $55 for students 11 to 17, and $30 to $45 for kids 6 to 10.

GOLF   You can read about Northeast Florida's best courses in the free *Golfer's Guide,* available at the tourist information offices and in many hotel lobbies. See p. 51 for information on ordering copies.

The municipal **Cocoa Beach Country Club,** 500 Tom Warringer Blvd. (© 321/868-3351), has 27 holes of golf and 10 lighted tennis courts set on acres of natural woodland, rivers, and lakes. Greens fees (including cart) are about $40 in winter, dropping to about $35 in summer.

On Merritt Island south of the Kennedy Space Center, the **Savannahs at Sykes Creek,** 3915 Savannahs Trail (© **321/455-1377**), has 18 holes over 6,636 yards bordered by hardwood forests, lakes, and savannahs inhabited by a host of wildlife. You'll have to hit over a lake to reach the seventh hole. Fees with cart are about $40 in winter, lower in summer.

The best nearby course is the Gary Player–designed **Baytree National Golf Club,** 8010 N. Wickham Rd., ½ mile east of I-95 in Melbourne (© **321/259-9060**), where challenging marshy holes are flanked by towering palms. This par-72 course has 7,043 yards with a unique red-shale waste area. Fees are about $90 in winter, dropping to about $50 in summer, including cart.

For course information, go to www.golf.com or www.floridagolfing.com, or call the **Florida Sports Foundation** (© **850/488-8347**) or **Florida Golfing** (© **866/833-2663**).

SURFING   Rip through some occasionally awesome waves (by Florida's standards, not California's or Hawaii's) at the **Cocoa Beach Pier** area or down south at **Sebastian Inlet.** Get outfitted at **Ron Jon Surf Shop,** 4151 N. Atlantic Ave. (© **321/799-8888;** www.ronjons.com), or learn how to hang 5 or 10 with **Cocoa Beach Surfing School** ⚡, 150 E. Columbia Lane (© **321/868-1980;** www.cocoabeachsurfing school.com). The school offers equipment and lessons for beginners and pros at area beaches. Be sure to bring along a towel, flip-flops, sunscreen, and a lot of nerve.

WHERE TO STAY

The hotels listed below are all in Cocoa Beach, the closest resort area to the Kennedy Space Center, about a 30-minute drive to the north. (For pop-culture junkies, Cocoa Beach was where the show *I Dream of Jeannie* took place.) Closest to the space center and Port Canaveral is the **Radisson Resort at the Port,** 8701 Astronaut Blvd. (Fla. A1A), in Cape Canaveral (© **800/333-3333** or 321/784-0000; www.radisson.com). It isn't on the beach, but you can relax in its landscaped courtyard, where a waterfall cascades over fake rocks into a heated pool. This well-equipped hotel caters to business travelers and passengers waiting to board cruise ships (with free transportation to the port and free parking while you cruise); it offers a great complimentary breakfast.

The newest chain motels in this area are the **Hampton Inn Cocoa Beach,** 3425 Atlantic Blvd. (© **877/492-3224** or 321/799-4099; www.hamptoninncocoabeach.com), and **Courtyard by Marriott,** 3435 Atlantic Blvd. (© **800/321-2211** or 321/784-4800; www.marriott.com). They stand side by side and access the beach via a pathway through a condominium complex.

The **Florida Space Coast Office of Tourism,** 8810 Astronaut Blvd. no. 102, Cape Canaveral, FL 32920 (© **800/93-OCEAN** or 321/868-1126; www.space-coast.com), publishes a booklet of the area's "Superior Small Lodgings."

The area has a plethora of rental condominiums and cottages. **King Rentals, Inc.,** 102 W. Central Blvd., Cape Canaveral, FL 32920 (© **888/295-0934** or 321/784-5046; www.kingrentals.com), has a wide selection in its inventory.

Given the proximity of Orlando, the generally warm weather year-round, and the business travelers visiting the space complex, there is little, if any, seasonal fluctuation in room rates here. They are highest on weekends, holidays, and during special events, such as space-shuttle launches.

Tent and RV camping are available at **Jetty Park,** in Port Canaveral (see "Beaches & Wildlife Refuges," above).

You'll pay a 4% hotel tax on top of the Florida 6% sales tax here.

DoubleTree Hotel Cocoa Beach Oceanfront ⚡ Although not as upscale as the Hilton Cocoa Beach Oceanfront (see below), this is the pick of the full-service beachside hotels. All rooms have balconies with ocean views, and 10 suites have living rooms with sleeper sofas and separate bedrooms. A charming dining room serves decent Mediterranean fare; it faces the beach and opens onto a brick patio where water cascades between two heated pools. Conference facilities draw groups.

2080 N. Atlantic Ave., Cocoa Beach, FL 32931. © 800/552-3224 or 321/783-9222. Fax 321/799-3234. www.cocoa beachdoubletree.com. 148 units. $114–$179 double; $185–$294 suite. AE, DC, DISC, MC, V. **Amenities:** Restaurant; bar; 2 heated outdoor pools; exercise room; game room; limited room service; laundry service; coin-op washers and dryers; concierge-level rooms. *In room:* A/C, TV, dataport, coffeemaker, hair dryer, iron.

Hilton Cocoa Beach Oceanfront Damaged by Hurricane Frances, the Hilton Cocoa Beach Oceanfront reopened in early 2005 after a $21-million renovation to guest rooms, pool area, restaurant, and lounge. The rooms at this seven-story Hilton lack balconies or patios; instead, they have small, sealed-shut windows, and only 16 of the rooms face the beach. These and other architectural features make this seem more like a downtown hotel transplanted to a beachside location. Nevertheless, it's one of the few upscale beachfront properties here. No doubt you'll run into a crew of name-tagged conventioneers, since it's especially popular with groups. Despite their lack of fresh air, the rooms are spacious and comfortable, especially since the renovations.

1550 N. Atlantic Ave., Cocoa Beach, FL 32931. © 800/445-8667 or 321/799-0003. Fax 321/799-0344. www.hilton. com. 296 units. $134–$294 double. AE, DC, DISC, MC, V. **Amenities:** Restaurant; 2 bars; heated outdoor pool; exercise room; watersports equipment rentals; game room; business center; limited room service; laundry service; coin-op washers and dryers; concierge-level rooms. *In room:* A/C, TV, dataport, coffeemaker, hair dryer, iron.

The Inn at Cocoa Beach ⚡⚡⚡ Despite having 50 units, this seaside inn has an intimate B&B ambience and is far and away the most romantic place in the area. Owner Karen Simpler, a skilled interior decorator, has furnished each unit with an elegant mix of pine, tropical, and French country pieces. Rooms in the three- and four-story buildings are much more spacious and have better sea views from their balconies than the "standard" units in the original two-story motel wing (all but six units here have balconies or patios). The older units open onto a courtyard with a pool tucked behind the dunes. Highest on the romance scale are the two rooms with Jacuzzi tubs and easy chairs facing gas fireplaces. Guests are treated to continental breakfast, afternoon tea, and evening wine and cheese. There's also an honor bar where you can pour your own drinks, and a library from which to feed your head.

4300 Ocean Blvd., Cocoa Beach, FL 32932. © 800/343-5307 or 321/799-3460. Fax 321/784-8632. www.theinnat cocoabeach.com. 50 units. $135–$325 double. Rates include continental breakfast and afternoon tea. AE, DISC, MC, V. No children under 12 accepted. **Amenities:** Bar (guests only); heated outdoor pool; sauna; massage; laundry service. *In room:* A/C, TV, dataport.

Riverview Hotel ⚡⚡⚡ Located right on the Intracoastal Waterway in New Smyrna Beach, the Riverview Hotel, a former fishing and hunting shack for sportsmen scoping the Indian River Lagoon, is a spectacularly restored hotel featuring a 5,000-foot spa complete with mineral pool. There's jazz on the deck every night and a fabulous restaurant, to boot (some consider Riverview Charlie's one of the state's best seafood spots). Owners Christa and Jim Kelsey used to work at the Faro Blanco Marina Resort in the Florida Keys, so they are well versed in the art of hospitality. Some rooms have private patios or porches; all are immaculate, charming, and stocked with modern amenities. If I had a choice, however, I'd go for the two-bedroom cottage or house with private pool, which are bargains at $175 to $210!

103 Flagler Ave., New Smyrna Beach 32169. ℭ **800/945-7416** or 386/428-5858. Fax 321/423-8927. www.riverview hotel.com. 18 units. $110–$125 double; $170 suite; private cottage $175, 3-bedroom house for up to 4 people $225. Rates include expanded continental breakfast. AE, DISC, MC, V. **Amenities:** Restaurant; heated pool; spa; sauna; massage. *In room:* A/C, TV.

WHERE TO DINE

On the **Cocoa Beach Pier,** at the beach end of Meade Avenue, you'll get a fine view down the coast to accompany the seafood offerings at **Atlantic Ocean Grill** (ℭ **321/ 783-7549**) and the mediocre pub fare at adjacent **Marlins Good Times Bar & Grill** (same phone). The restaurants may not justify spending an entire evening on the pier, but the outdoor, tin-roofed **Boardwalk Tiki Bar** 𝒦, where live music plays most nights, is a prime spot to have a cold one while watching the surfers or a sunset.

Bernard's Surf/Fischer's Seafood Bar & Grill 𝒦 SEAFOOD/STEAK Photos on the walls testify that many astronauts come to these adjoining establishments to celebrate their landings. It started as Bernard's Surf in 1948, serving standard steak-and-seafood fare in a nautical setting. The present Bernard's offers specials such as stone-crab claws, chargrilled red snapper, and a belly-busting platter of shrimp, scallops, grouper, crab cakes, lobster, and oysters. You can even get Russian beluga or Sevruga caviar, if you so desire. The fresh seafood also finds its way into Fischer's Seafood Bar & Grill, a *Cheers*-like lounge popular with locals. The menu here features fried combo platters and mussels with a wine sauce over pasta, as well as burgers and other pub fare. It has the same 25¢ happy-hour oysters and spicy wings as a branch of **Rusty's Seafood & Oyster Bar** (see below), also part of this complex.

2 S. Atlantic Ave. (at Minuteman Causeway Rd.), Cocoa Beach. ℭ **321/783-2401.** Reservations recommended in Bernard's, not accepted in Fischer's. Bernard's main courses $14–$55. Fischer's main courses $9–$16; sandwiches and salads $4–$9. AE, DC, DISC, MC, V. Bernard's Mon–Fri 4–10pm; Sat 4–11pm. Fischer's Mon–Fri 11am–10pm; Sat 11am–11pm. Closed Christmas.

The Mango Tree 𝒦𝒦 CONTINENTAL Gourmet seafood, pastas, and chicken are served in a plantation-home atmosphere with elegant furnishings in this stucco house, the finest dining venue around. Although the ambience borders on Tavern on the Green tourist-tacky, the restaurant is rather picturesque. Indoor goldfish ponds and an outdoor waterfall splashing into a koi pond in the gardens provide pleasing backdrops. Start with Indian River crab cakes, then go on to the chef's expert spin on roast Long Island duckling, beef tips with peppercorn-mushroom sauce, or other excellent dishes drawing their inspiration from the Continent.

118 N. Atlantic Ave. (Fla. A1A, between N. 1st and N. 2nd sts.), Cocoa Beach. ℭ **321/799-0513.** Reservations recommended. Main courses $16–$40. AE, MC, V. Tues–Sun 6–10pm.

Rusty's Seafood & Oyster Bar *Value* SEAFOOD This lively sports bar beside Port Canaveral's man-made harbor offers inexpensive chow ranging from spicy seafood gumbo to a pot of seafood that will give two people their fill of steamed oysters, clams, shrimp, crab legs, potatoes, and corn on the cob. Raw or steamed fresh oysters and clams from the raw bar are first rate and a good value, as is a weekday lunch buffet. Seating is indoors or out, but the inside tables have the best view of the fishing boats and cruise liners going in and out of the port. Daily happy hour from 3 to 6pm sees beers drafted at 60¢ a mug, and tons of raw or steamed oysters and spicy Buffalo wings go for 25¢ each. The joint is busy and sometimes noisy, especially on weekend afternoons, but the clientele tends to be older and better behaved than those at other pubs along the banks of Port Canaveral. There's another **Rusty's** in the

Bernard's Surf/Fischer's Seafood Bar & Grill restaurant complex in Cocoa Beach (see above).

628 Glen Cheek Dr. (south side of the harbor), Port Canaveral. ℂ 321/783-2033. Main courses $7–$25; sandwiches and salads $4–$7; lunch buffet $6. AE, DC, DISC, MC, V. Sun–Thurs 11am–11:30pm; Fri–Sat 11am–12:30am (lunch buffet Mon–Fri 11am–2pm).

THE SPACE COAST AFTER DARK

For a rundown of current performances and exhibits, call the **Brevard Cultural Alliance's Arts Line** (ℂ 321/690-6819). For live music, walk out on the **Cocoa Beach Pier,** on Meade Avenue at the beach, where **Oh Shuck's Seafood Bar & Grill** (ℂ 321/783-7549), **Marlins Good Times Bar & Grill** (ℂ 321/783-7549), and the alfresco **Boardwalk Tiki Bar** ⚓ (same phone as Marlins) feature bands on weekends, more often during the summer season. The Tiki Bar is a great place to hang out over a cold beer all afternoon and evening.

2 Daytona Beach ⚓⚓

54 miles NE of Orlando, 251 miles N of Miami, 78 miles S of Jacksonville

Daytona Beach is a town with many personalities. It is at once the self-proclaimed "World's Most Famous Beach" and "World Center of Racing," a mecca for tattooed motorcyclists and pierced spring-breakers, *and* the home of a surprisingly good art museum. The city and developers spent millions of dollars to turn the somewhat seedy beachfront area (complete with the requisite T-shirt and souvenir shops) around the famous Main Street Pier into Ocean Walk Village, a redevelopment area of upscale shops, entertainment, and resort facilities.

Daytona Beach has been a destination for racing enthusiasts since the early 1900s, when "horseless carriages" raced on the hard-packed sand beach. One thing is for sure: Daytonans still love their cars. Recent debate over the environmental impact of unrestricted driving on the beach caused an uproar from citizens who couldn't imagine it any other way. As it worked out, they can still drive on the sand, but not everywhere, and especially not in areas where sea turtles are nesting.

Today hundreds of thousands of race enthusiasts come to the home of the National Association for Stock Car Auto Racing (NASCAR) for the Daytona 500, the Pepsi 400, and other races throughout the year. The Speedway is also home to DAYTONA USA, a motor-sports entertainment attraction worth a visit even by nonracing fans.

Be sure to check the "Florida Calendar of Events" (p. 32) to know when the town belongs to college students during spring break, thousands of leather-clad motorcycle buffs during Bike Week (March) and Biketoberfest (Oct), or racing enthusiasts for big competitions. You won't be able to find a hotel room, drive the highways, or enjoy a peaceful vacation when they're in town.

ESSENTIALS

GETTING THERE   Continental (ℂ 800/525-0280) and **Delta** (ℂ 800/221-1212) fly into the small, pleasant, and calm **Daytona Beach International Airport** (ℂ 386/248-8030; http://flydaytonafirst.com), 4 miles inland from the beach on International Speedway Boulevard (U.S. 92), but you can usually find less expensive fares to **Orlando International Airport** (p. 462), about an hour's drive away. **Daytona-Orlando Transit Service** (**DOTS;** ℂ 800/231-1965 or 386/257-5411; www.dots-daytonabeach.com) provides van transportation to and from Orlando International Airport. One-way fares are about $28 for adults, $15 for children 11 and under. The service takes passengers to the company's terminal at 1034 N. Nova Rd., between 3rd and 4th streets, or to beach hotels for an additional fee.

If you fly into the Daytona Airport, rates for the **Daytona Shuttle** (© **386/255-2294**) run up to $12 per person, $14 per couple, and $6 per person for parties of three or more. The ride from the airport to most beach hotels via **Yellow Cab Co.** (© **386/255-5555**) is between $7 and $18.

Alamo (© 800/327-9622), **Avis** (© 800/831-2847), **Budget** (© 800/527-0700), **Dollar** (© 800/800-4000), **Enterprise** (© 800/325-8007), **Hertz** (© 800/654-3131), and **National** (© 800/227-7368) have booths at the airport. Or why not rent a Harley? This is Daytona, after all. Contact **Daytona Harley-Davidson** (© 800/307-4464 or 386/258-0638; www.daytonahd.com). Rates are $135 to $155 daily, $600 to $640 weekly. A special sunset rate of $75 is available from 4pm to 9am.

Amtrak (© **800/872-7245;** www.amtrak.com) trains stop at Deland, about 15 miles southwest of Daytona Beach, with bus service from Deland to the beach.

VISITOR INFORMATION   The **Daytona Beach Area Convention & Visitors Bureau,** 126 E. Orange Ave. (P.O. Box 910), Daytona Beach, FL 32115 (© **800/544-0415** or 386/255-0415; www.daytonabeach.com), can help you with information on attractions, accommodations, dining, and events. The office is on the mainland just west of the Memorial Bridge. The information area of the lobby is open daily from 9am to 5pm. The bureau also maintains a branch at DAYTONA USA, 1801 W. International Speedway Blvd. (daily 9am–7pm), as well as a kiosk at the airport.

GETTING AROUND   Although Daytona is primarily a driver's town, Volusia County's public transit system, **VOTRAN** (© **386/761-7700;** http://votran.org), runs a **free shuttle** in the Main Street Pier/Ocean Walk Village area and a pay **trolley** along Atlantic Avenue on the beach, Monday through Saturday from noon to midnight. Fares are $1 for adults, 50¢ for seniors and children 6 to 17, and free for kids under 6 riding with an adult. VOTRAN also runs **buses** through downtown and the beaches.

For a taxi, call **Yellow Cab** (© **386/255-5555**) or **Southern Komfort Cab** (© **386/252-2222**).

A VISIT TO THE WORLD CENTER OF RACING

Daytona International Speedway/DAYTONA USA ✸✸   You don't have to be a racing fan to enjoy a visit to the **Daytona International Speedway,** 4 miles west of the beach. Opened in 1959 with the first Daytona 500, this 480-acre complex is one of the key reasons for the city's fame. The track presents about 9 weekends of major racing events annually, featuring stock cars, sports cars, motorcycles, and go-karts, and is used for automobile and motorbike testing and other events many other days of the year. Its grandstands can accommodate more than 150,000 fans. Big events sell out months in advance—tickets to the Daytona 500 in February can be gone a year ahead of time—so buy yours and make hotel reservations as early as possible.

Start your visit at the **World Center of Racing Visitor Center,** in the NASCAR office complex at the east end of the speedway. Admission to the center is free, and you can walk out and see the track during non-race days (there's a small admission to the track during qualifying races leading up to the main events). Entertaining 30-minute guided tram tours of the facility (garage area, pit road, and so on) depart from the visitor center and are well worth taking.

The visitor center houses a large souvenir shop, a snack bar, and the phenomenally popular **DAYTONA USA,** a 60,000-square-foot, state-of-the-art interactive motor-sports

Daytona Beach

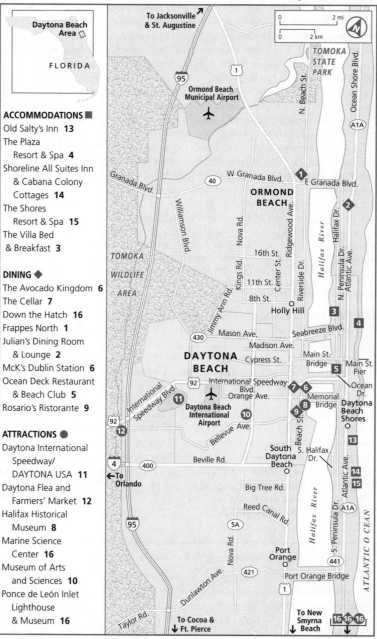

attraction. Here you can learn about the history, color, and excitement of stock car, go-kart, and motorcycle racing in Daytona. In Daytona Dream Laps, you get the feel of what it's like to zoom around the track from a 32-seat motion simulator. If that doesn't get your stomach churning, hop inside your own 80%-scale NASCAR vehicle in Acceleration Alley, buckle up, and roar up to 200 mph in a spectacular simulator for the ultimate virtual-reality–like racing experience ($5 per ride). On the milder side, you can participate in a pit stop on a NASCAR Winston Cup stock car, see an actual winning Daytona 500 car still covered in track dust, talk via video with favorite competitors, and play radio or television announcer by calling the finish of a race. An action-packed IMAX film will put you in the winner's seat of a Daytona 500 race.

To really experience what it's like, you can make (for $134) three laps around the track in a stock car from May to October with the **Richard Petty Driving Experience Ride-Along Program** (© **800/237-3889;** www.1800bepetty.com). Professional drivers (sorry, none is named Petty) are at the wheel as you see and feel what it's like to travel an average of 115 mph.

Allow at least 4 hours to see everything, and bring your video camera.

1801 W. International Speedway Blvd. (U.S. 92, at Bill France Blvd.). © **386/253-7223** for race tickets, 386/253-7223 for information, or 386/947-6404 or 386/947-6800 for DAYTONA USA. www.daytonaintlspeedway.com and www.daytonausa.com. Speedway free admission except on race days; tram rides $7.50. DAYTONA USA admission $22 adults, $19 seniors, $16 children 6–12,. free admission for children under 6. Speedway daily 9am–7pm; trams depart every 30 min. 9:30am–5pm except during races and special events. DAYTONA USA daily 9am–7pm (later during race events). Closed Christmas.

HITTING THE WORLD'S MOST FAMOUS BEACH

The beautiful and hard-packed beach here runs for 24 miles along a skinny peninsula separated from the mainland by the Halifax River. The bustling hub of activity is at the end of Main Street, where you'll find the **Main Street Pier** (also known as the Daytona Beach Pier or Ocean Pier), the longest wooden pier on the East Coast. Out here you'll find a restaurant, bar, bait shop, beach-toy concessions, chairlift running its length, and views from the 180-foot-tall Space Needle. Admission as far out as the restaurant and bar is free (at about a third of the way, this is far enough for a good view down the beach), but you'll have to pay $1 to walk beyond that point, and more than that if you fish (see "Outdoor Activities," below). Beginning at the pier, the city's famous oceanside **Boardwalk** is lined with restaurants, bars, and T-shirt shops, as are the 4 blocks of Main Street nearest the beach. The city's $400 million **Ocean Walk Village** redevelopment project begins here and runs several blocks north, featuring a movie theater, boutiques, restaurants, and even a 175-room hotel/condo, the **Ocean Walk Resort** (© **877/845-WALK**).

Tips   Driving on the Beach

You can drive and park directly on sections of the sand along 18 miles of the beach during daylight hours and at low tide (Hurricane Floyd and other recent storms have greatly reduced the beach's width), but watch for signs warning of nesting sea turtles. There's a $5-per-vehicle access fee and 10-mph speed limit. *Watch out for the tides.* If you park on an incoming tide and lose track of time, your vehicle may become an inadvertent rust bucket or artificial reef!

There's another busy beach area at the end of **Seabreeze Boulevard,** which has a multitude of restaurants, bars, and shops.

Couples seeking greater privacy usually prefer the northern or southern extremities of the beach. **Ponce Inlet,** at the very southern tip of the peninsula, is especially peaceful, since there is little commerce or traffic there to disturb the silence.

OUTDOOR ACTIVITIES

CRUISES   Take a leisurely cruise on the Halifax River aboard the 14-passenger, 25-foot *Fancy,* a replica of an 1890s-style fantail launch. It's operated by **A tiny Cruise Line River Excursions,** 425 S. Beach St., at Halifax Harbor Marina (© **386/226-2343**). Captain Jim regales passengers with river lore and points out dolphins (which are more commonly spotted in the mornings), manatees, herons, cormorants, pelicans, egrets, and osprey during his 2-hour midday cruise. In the afternoon, you can see the man-made estates along the river. Cruises range from $11 to $16 for adults, $6.50 to $9.50 for children 4 to 12. Weather permitting, the midday cruises depart year-round (with a brief hiatus during the holidays) Monday through Saturday at 11:30am. The 1-hour tour of riverfront homes is at 2pm, the tour of historic downtown at 3:30pm; there are no Monday cruises in winter months. Romantic sunset cruises are available; call for reservations. Rumor has it that Ponce de León discovered his Fountain of Youth along the St. Johns River in Volusia County. While you may not find it today, you will find a cool tour, the **Fountain of Youth Eco-History Tour,** which begins on the Spring Garden Run in the **De León Springs State Park**, 601 Ponce de León Blvd. (© **386/985-4212**). The 90-minute tour on a pontoon boat will give you great insight into the so-called healing waters of the springs in the 603-acre park. Tours cost $16 for adults, $14 for seniors. For more information, call (© **386/ 837-5537**) or go to www.foytours.com.

FISHING   The easiest and least expensive way to fish offshore for marlin, sailfish, king mackerel, grouper, red snapper, and more is with the **Critter Fleet,** 4950 S. Peninsula Dr., just past the lighthouse in Ponce Inlet (© **800/338-0850** or 386/767-7676; www.critterfleet.com), which operates two party boats. One goes on all-day trips (about $60 adults, $35 kids under 12), while the other makes morning and afternoon voyages (about $40 adults, $25 kids under 12). The fares include rod, reel, and bait. Call for schedules, prices, and reservations.

Save the cost of a boat by fishing with the locals at **Main Street Pier,** at the ocean end of Main Street (© **386/253-1212**). Admission for anglers is $5 for adults, $3.50 for kids under 12. Bait and gear are available for $13, and no license is required.

GOLF   There are more than 25 courses within 30 minutes of the beach, and most hotels can arrange starting times for you. **Golf Daytona Beach,** 126 E. Orange Ave., Daytona Beach, FL 32114 (© **800/881-7065** or 386/239-7065; fax 386/239-0064), publishes an annual brochure describing the major courses. It's available at the tourist information offices (see "Essentials," above).

For course information, go to www.golf.com or www.floridagolfing.com, or call the **Florida Sports Foundation** (© **850/488-8347**) or **Florida Golfing** (© **866/833-2663**).

Two of the nation's top-rated links for women golfers are at the **LPGA International** ✶✶, 1000 Championship Dr. (© **386/274-5742;** www.lpgainternational.com): the Champions course, designed by Rees Jones, and the Legends course, designed by Arthur Hills. Each boasts 18 outstanding holes. LPGA International is a center offering workshops and teaching programs for professional and amateur women golfers, and the pro shop carries a great selection of ladies' equipment and clothing. Greens fees with a cart are usually about $75, lower in summer. *Pssst*—they let guys play here, too!

A Lloyd Clifton–designed course, the centrally located 18-hole, par-72 **Indigo Lakes Golf Course,** 2620 W. International Speedway Blvd. (© **386/254-3607;** www.indigolakesgolf.com), has flat fairways and large bunkered Bermuda greens. Fees here are about $40 in winter (including a cart), lower in summer.

The semi-private South Course at **Pelican Bay Country Club,** 550 Sea Duck Dr. (© **386/756-0034;** www.pelicanbaygolfclub.com), is one of the area's favorites, with fast greens to test your putting skills. Fees are about $45 with cart in winter, lower in summer (no walking allowed). The North Course is for members only.

The city's prime municipal course is the **Daytona Beach Country Club,** 600 Wilder Blvd. (© **386/258-3119**), which has 36 holes. Winter fees are about $20 to walk, $30 to share a cart. They drop $3 in summer.

HELICOPTER RIDES   Take a helicopter ride around the Daytona area to see the city from a different point of view. **Air Florida** (© **386/257-6993;** www.airflorida helicopters.com) offers rides starting at $20 (two-person minimum), leaving from the Daytona Flea and Farmers' Market (see below).

HORSEBACK RIDING   **Shenandoah Stables,** 1759 Tomoka Farms Rd., off U.S. 92 (© **386/257-1444**), offers daily trail rides and lessons. Call for prices and schedules.

SPECTATOR SPORTS   The **Daytona Cubs** (© **386/872-2827;** www.daytonacubs. com), a Class A minor-league affiliate of the Chicago Cubs, play April through August at Jackie Robinson Ballpark, on City Island downtown. A game here is a treat, since the park has been restored to its classic 1914 style by the designers of Baltimore's Camden Yards and Cleveland's Jacobs Field. Tickets are $6 to $9.

WATERSPORTS   Watersports equipment, bicycles, beach buggies, and mopeds can be rented along the Boardwalk, at the ocean end of Main Street (see "Hitting the World's Most Famous Beach," above), and in front of major beachfront hotels.

MUSEUMS & ATTRACTIONS

Halifax Historical Museum ⋆   Located on Beach Street, Daytona's original river-front commercial district on the mainland side of the Halifax River (see "Shopping," below), this local museum is worth a look just for the 1912 neoclassical architecture of its home, a former bank. A mural of Old Florida wildlife graces one wall, the stained-glass ceiling reflects sunlight, and across the room is an original teller's window. The eclectic collection includes tools and household items from the Spanish and British periods, thousands of historic photographs, possessions of past residents (even a ball gown worn at Lincoln's inauguration), and, of course, model cars. A race exhibit opens annually in mid-January as a stage-setter for Race Week.

252 S. Beach St. (just north of Orange Ave.). © 386/255-6976. www.halifaxhistorical.org. Admission $4 adults, $1 children 11 and under; free Sat for children. Tues–Sat 10am–4pm.

Marine Science Center *Kids*   This marine museum has interior displays (with exhibits on mangroves, mosquitoes, shells, artificial reefs, dune habitats, and pollution solutions), a 5,000-gallon aquarium, and educational programs and activities. Though the exhibit area is rather small, there's more than enough information for a child to digest at one time. Perhaps the most interesting part of the center is the space reserved for the rehabilitation of endangered and threatened sea turtles. You can watch them in any of seven turtle tanks—look for the ones that need life jackets to stay afloat!

Crossing Over into Cassadaga

If you're in the Daytona Beach/Orlando area, suspend your disbelief for a few hours and make a pit stop in Cassadaga, the tiny century-old community composed completely of psychics and mediums who will be happy to tell you your fortune or put you in touch with the deceased—for a price, of course.

Should you find the whole concept of psychics and talking to the dead completely kooky and out of whack, consider the history of Cassadaga, which is fascinating in its own right.

At the risk of sounding like the intro to the SciFi Channel show *Crossing Over with John Edward,* the story goes that, as a young man from New York, George Colby was told during a séance that he would someday establish a spiritualist community in the South. In 1875, the prophecy came true when Colby was led through the wilderness of Central Florida by his spiritual guide to a 35-acre area that was to become the Cassadaga Spiritualist Camp.

Although it sounds like a bizarre cult, it's not. Consisting of about 57 acres and 55 no-nonsense clapboard houses, Cassadaga caters to those who have chosen to share in a community of like-minded people who happen to believe in the otherworldly. Yes, the people are eccentric, to say the least, but they're all very friendly. Designated a Historic District on the National Register of Historic Places, Cassadaga is the spiritualist version of Lourdes, to which skeptics and believers alike flock for answers, or at least kicks.

When you get to town, head straight for the information center (see below for directions), where you can find out which psychics and mediums are working that day, and make an appointment for a session, which ranges from $25 and up for a palm reading to $50 and up for a session with a medium. A general store, a restaurant, a hotel, and a few shops selling crystals and potions of sorts will keep you occupied while you wait for your appointment. Whether you're a believer or not, an hour or 2 in Cassadaga will make for interesting cocktail conversation.

From Daytona, take I-4 to exit 114. Turn right onto Highway 472 at the end of the exit ramp toward Orange City/Deland. At the traffic light, turn right onto Dr. Martin Luther King, Jr., Parkway. Turn right at the first light, which is Cassadaga Road. Continue 1½ miles to the intersection with Stevens Street. The information center is on the right. For more information, call ℭ 386/228-3171 or go to www.cassadaga.org.

---

100 Lighthouse Dr., Ponce Inlet. ℭ 386/304-5545. www.marinesciencecenter.com. Admission $3 adults, $1 children 5–12, free for children under 5. Tues–Sat 10am–4pm; Sun noon–4pm. Closed Mon. See directions for Ponce de León Inlet Lighthouse & Museum (below).

Museum of Arts and Sciences ℛℛ   An exceptional institution for a town of Daytona's size and reputation (as a culturally devoid, trashy, spring-break mecca), this museum is best known for its *Cuba: A History of Art* exhibit, with paintings acquired in 1956, when Cuban dictator Fulgencio Batista donated his private collection to the city. Among them is a portrait of Eva ("Evita") Perón, said to be the only existing painting completed while she was alive (it hangs near the lobby, not within the Cuban exhibit). The Dow Gallery displays American decorative arts, while the Bouchelle Study Center for the Decorative Arts contains American and European jewelry, furniture, mirrors, and more. Other rooms include the Schulte Gallery of Chinese Art; Africa: Life and Ritual, with the largest collection of Ashante gold ornaments in the U.S. (these are stunning); and the Center for Florida History, with the skeleton of a 13-foot-tall, 130,000-year-old giant ground sloth. Check out the unique collection of the late Chapman S. Root, a Daytona philanthropist and a founder of the Coca-Cola empire; among the memorabilia are the mold for the original Coke bottle and the Root family's two private railroad cars. The planetarium presents 30-minute shows of what the night sky will look like on the date of your visit. *Note:* Even though this is a first-class art museum, children are apt to be bored here.

1040 Museum Blvd. (off Nova Rd./Fla. 5A between International Speedway Blvd. and Bellevue Ave.). ℂ 386/255-0285. www.moas.org. Museum $8 adults, $4 children and students with ID, free for children 5 and under. Planetarium shows $3 adults, $2 children and students. Tues–Fri 9am–4pm; Sat–Sun noon–5pm. Planetarium shows Tues–Fri 2pm; Sat–Sun 1 and 3pm. Closed Thanksgiving, Christmas Eve, and Christmas Day. Take International Speedway Blvd. west, make a left on Nova Rd. (Fla. 5A), and look for a sign on your right.

Ponce de León Inlet Lighthouse & Museum 🎯🎯   This National Historic Landmark is well worth a stop even if you're not a lighthouse enthusiast. The 175-foot brick-and-granite structure is the second-tallest lighthouse in the United States. Built in the 1880s, the lighthouse and the graceful Victorian brick buildings surrounding it have been restored. There are no guided tours, but you can walk through the 12 areas, which feature different exhibits (lighthouse lenses, historical artifacts, and a film of early car racing on the nearby beach), and around the tugboat *F. D. Russell,* now sitting high and dry in the sand. Use common sense if you climb the 203 steps to the top of the lighthouse; it's a grinding ascent, but the view from up there is spectacular.

4931 S. Peninsula Dr., Ponce Inlet. ℂ 386/761-1821. www.ponceinlet.org. Admission $5 adults, $1.50 children under 12. Memorial Day to Labor Day daily 10am–9pm; rest of year daily 10am–5pm. Follow Atlantic Ave. south, make a right on Beach St., and follow the signs.

SHOPPING

On the mainland, Daytona Beach's main riverside drag, **Beach Street,** is one of the few areas in town where people actually stroll. The street is wide and inviting, with palms down its median, and decorative wrought-iron archways and fancy brickwork overlooking a branch of the Halifax River. Today Beach Street between Bay Street and Orange Avenue offers antiques and collectibles shops, galleries, clothiers, a magic shop, a historical museum (see "Museums & Attractions," above), and several good cafes. At 154 S. Beach St., you'll find the home of the **Angell & Phelps Chocolate Factory** (ℂ 386/252-6531; www.angellandphelps.com), which has been making candy for more than 75 years. Watch the goodies being made (and get a free sample!).

"Hog" riders will find several shops to your liking along Beach Street, north of International Speedway Boulevard, including the **Harley-Davidson Store,** 290 N. Beach St., at Dr. Mary McLeod Bethune Boulevard (ℂ 386/253-2453), a 20,000-square-foot retail outlet and diner serving breakfast and lunch. It's one of the nation's largest Harley dealerships. In addition to hundreds of gleaming new and used Hogs, you'll find as much fringed leather as you've ever seen in one place.

The **Daytona Flea and Farmers' Market,** on Tomoka Farms Road at the junction of I-95 and U.S. 92, a mile west of the Speedway (ℂ 386/253-3330; www.daytona fleamarket.com), is huge, with 1,000 covered outdoor booths plus 100 antiques and collectibles vendors in an air-conditioned building. Most of the booths feature new (though not necessarily first-rate) wares along the lines of socks, sunglasses, luggage, handbags, jewelry, tools, and the like. It's open year-round Friday through Sunday from 8am to 5pm. Admission and parking are free.

Ocean Walk Shoppes, at Ocean Walk Village, 250 N. Atlantic Ave. (© 386/257-5077; www.oceanwalkvillage.com), is a collection of upscale boutiques and restaurants, and a 10-screen movie theater.

WHERE TO STAY

Room rates here are among the most affordable in Florida. Some properties have several rate periods during the year, but generally they are somewhat higher from the beginning of the races in February all the way to Labor Day. They skyrocket during major events at the Speedway, during bikers' gatherings, and during spring break (see the "Florida Calendar of Events," beginning on p. 32), when hotels fill to the bursting point. Even if you can find a room then, there's often a minimum-stay requirement.

Hundreds of hotels and motels line Atlantic Avenue along the beach, many of them family owned and operated. The **Daytona Beach Area Convention & Visitors Bureau** (see "Essentials," earlier in this chapter) distributes a brochure that lists "Superior Small Lodgings" for Daytona Beach, Deland, and New Smyrna Beach. All of the small motels listed below are members.

If you're going to the races and don't care about staying on the beach, some upper-floor rooms at the **Hilton Garden Inn Daytona Beach Airport,** 189 Midway Ave. (© 877/944-4001 or 386/944-4000), overlook the international speedway track. Unlike most members of Hilton's Garden Inn chain, this one has a restaurant.

Thousands of rental condominiums line the beach. Among the most luxurious is the new 150-unit condominium hotel **Ocean Walk Resort,** 300 N. Atlantic Ave., Daytona Beach, FL 32118 (© 800/649-3566 or 386/323-4800; www.oceanwalk resort.com), which is part of the Ocean Walk Village redevelopment. Near the Main Street Pier, it's in the center of the action and has one- and two-bedroom apartments with full kitchens, washers and dryers, and all of the usual hotel amenities, plus a wondrous computer-golf simulator, a "lazy river" in the outdoor pool, an island putting green, and much more—including the gaudiest lobby I've ever seen. One of the largest rental agents is **Peck Realty,** 2340 S. Atlantic Ave., Daytona Beach Shores, FL 32118 (© 800/447-3255 or 386/257-5000; www.peckrealty.com).

In addition to the 6% state sales tax, Volusia County levies a 4% tax on hotel bills.

Old Salty's Inn *Value*   The most unusual of the many mom-and-pop beachside motels here, Old Salty's is a lush tropical enclave with a *Gilligan's Island* theme, littered with old motors, rotting boats, life preservers, and a Jeep. The TV series' main characters are depicted in murals painted on the buildings. The two-story wings flank a courtyard festooned with palms and banana trees (you can pick a banana for breakfast). Facing this vista, the bright rooms have microwaves, refrigerators, and front and back windows. The choice units have picture windows overlooking the beach. There are gas grills and rocking chairs under a gazebo by a heated beachside pool.

1921 S. Atlantic Ave. (Fla. A1A, at Flamingo Ave.), Daytona Beach Shores, FL 32118. © 800/417-1466 or 386/252-8090. Fax 386/947-9980. www.visitdaytona.com/oldsaltys. 19 units. $53–$71 double; $63–$93 efficiency; $75–$121 suite. AE, DISC, MC, V. **Amenities:** Heated outdoor pool; free use of bikes; coin-op washers and dryers. *In room:* A/C, TV, kitchen, fridge, coffeemaker, hair dryer, iron.

The Plaza Resort & Spa ★★ These elegant adjoining 7- and 13-story buildings hold some of Daytona Beach's best rooms (in a much more tasteful atmosphere than many of the neighboring hotels)—provided you don't need a large bathroom. The best units are the corner suites, each with a sitting area and two balconies overlooking the Atlantic; some even have a Jacuzzi. All units have balconies and microwaves (an on-premises store sells frozen dinners). The full-service **Ocean Waters Spa** ★★ (© **386/ 267-1660;** www.oceanwatersspa.com) has 16 treatment rooms and a soothing menu of facials, massages, and wraps.

600 N. Atlantic Ave. (at Seabreeze Ave.), Daytona Beach, FL 32118. © **800/874-7420** or 386/255-4471. Fax 386/ 238-7984. www.plazaresortandspa.com. 323 units. $139–$229 double; $189–$449 suite. AE, DC, DISC, MC, V. **Amenities:** Restaurant; bar; heated outdoor pool; exercise room; spa; Jacuzzi; watersports equipment rentals; game room; business center; limited room service; massage; babysitting; laundry service; coin-op washers and dryers; concierge-level rooms. *In room:* A/C, TV, dataport, fridge, microwave, coffeemaker, hair dryer, iron.

Shoreline All Suites Inn & Cabana Colony Cottages ★ *Value* The Shoreline All Suites Inn features one- and two-bedroom suites that occupy two buildings separated by a walkway leading to the beach. Most have small bathrooms with scant vanity space and—shall we say—intimate shower stalls. Every unit has a full kitchen, plus barbecue grills on the premises. For a change of scenery, consider the Shoreline's sister property, the **Cabana Colony Cottages** ★★. All 12 of the cottages were built in 1927 but have been upgraded. They aren't much bigger than a motel room with a kitchen, but they're light, airy, and attractively furnished. The cottages share a heated pool with the Shoreline.

2435 S. Atlantic Ave. (Fla. A1A, at Dundee Rd.), Daytona Beach Shores, FL 32118. © **800/293-0653** or 386/252-1692. Fax 386/239-7068. www.daytonashoreline.com. 30 units, including 12 cottages. $79–$350 suites and cottages. Rates include continental breakfast. Golf packages available. AE, DISC, MC, V. **Amenities:** Heated outdoor pool; coin-op washers and dryers. *In room:* A/C, TV/VCR, kitchen, coffeemaker.

The Shores Resort & Spa ★★ Far enough south to escape the madding crowds of Main Street, and set in an upscale residential area directly on the beach, this hotel is the newest and most luxurious hotel here. It welcomes guests with an elegant terra-cotta-tiled lobby with a fountain and potted palms. The large guest rooms are grouped in pairs and can be joined to form suites; only one of each pair has a balcony. Ocean-front rooms are preferable; all have sea and/or river views. Baleen restaurant (with locations in Miami and Naples, too) is one of Daytona's most beautiful, offering stellar seafood with a gourmet and regional twist; patio dining overlooking the ocean is a fine option. The SpaTerre offers an Indonesian-inspired menu of treatments.

2637 S. Atlantic Ave. (Fla. A1A, between Florida Shores Blvd. and Richard's Lane), Daytona Beach Shores, FL 32118. © **866/934-SHORES** or 386/767-7350. Fax 386/760-3651. www.shoresresort.com. 212 units. Winter $259–$489 double, $549–$1,129 suite; off season $179–$359 double, $509–$829 suite. AE, DC, DISC, MC, V. **Amenities:** Restaurant; bar; heated outdoor pool; exercise room; spa; salon; room service; babysitting; laundry service; dry cleaning. *In room:* A/C, TV, dataport, wireless Internet access, kitchen, coffeemaker, hair dryer, iron.

The Villa Bed & Breakfast ★★★ You'll think you're in Iberia upon entering this 70+-year-old Spanish mansion's great room with its fireplace, baby grand piano, and terra-cotta floors. A sunroom equipped with a TV and VCR, a formal dining room, and a breakfast nook are also located downstairs. The lush backyard surrounds a pool and a covered Jacuzzi. Upstairs, the nautically themed Christopher Columbus room has a vaulted ceiling and a small balcony overlooking the pool. The largest unit here is the King Carlos suite, once the original master bedroom, with a four-poster bed, entertainment system, fridge, rooftop deck, and bathroom equipped with four-head shower.

The Queen Isabella room has a portrait of the queen over a queen-size bed, while the Marco Polo room features Chinese black-lacquer furniture and Oriental rugs.

801 N. Peninsula Dr. (at Riverview Blvd.), Daytona Beach, FL 32118. ℭ/fax **386/248-2020.** www.thevillabb.com. 4 units. $125–$400 double. Rates include continental breakfast. AE, MC, V. No children or pets accepted. **Amenities:** Heated outdoor pool; Jacuzzi. *In room:* A/C, TV, hair dryer, no phone.

WHERE TO DINE

Daytona Beach has a few interesting dining venues, but not many are likely to leave an indelible memory. A profusion of fast-food joints lines the major thoroughfares, especially along Atlantic Avenue on the beach and International Speedway Boulevard (U.S. 92) near the racetrack. Restaurants come and go in the Beach Street district on the mainland, and along Main Street and Seabreeze Boulevard on the beach. A casual restaurant out on the Main Street Pier serves burgers, chicken wings, and lots of suds.

In addition to the local **Shells** seafood restaurant (200 S. Atlantic Ave.; (ℭ **386/258-0007;** www.shellsseafood.com; see p. 412 for details), two other outlets of chain restaurants are worth a special mention here. **Buca di Beppo,** 2514 W. International Speedway Blvd. (ℭ **386/253-6523;** www.bucadibeppo.com), a boisterous restaurant serving family-style Southern Italian specialties, is open for dinner only. Expect to take home leftovers, as the portions are huge and the food surprisingly good, especially for a "theme" restaurant. **Stonewood Tavern & Grill,** 100 S. Atlantic Ave., in Ormond Beach (ℭ **386/671-1200;** www.stonewoodgrill.com), is a casual upscale restaurant with a nice but dark mahogany interior, good American food, and excellent service. Also open only for dinner; you won't be disappointed with its menu of steaks, seafood, and the like.

AT THE BEACHES

Down the Hatch *✿ Value* SEAFOOD   Occupying a 1940s fish camp on the Halifax River, Down the Hatch serves big portions of fresh fish and seafood (note its shrimp boat docked outside). Inexpensive burgers and sandwiches are available, too. The scenic views include boats and shorebirds visible through the picture windows. At night, arrive early to catch the sunset over the river, and also to beat the crowd to this very popular place. In summer, light fare is served on a covered deck.

4894 Front St., Ponce Inlet. ℭ **386/761-4831.** Call ahead for Priority Seating. Main courses $9–$25 (most $10–$16); breakfast $2–$5; burgers and sandwiches $3–$6.50; early-bird menu (served 11am–5pm) $6–$8. AE, MC, V. Daily 8am–10pm. Closed 1st week in Dec. Take Atlantic Ave. south, make a right on Beach St., and follow the signs.

Julian's Dining Room & Lounge *✿* AMERICAN   This family-owned restaurant has catered to locals and tourists since 1967, offering a casual atmosphere and friendly service. Unlike most eateries in this area, it specializes in prime Western beef (filet mignon, strip steak, and T-bone), but the seafood is far from second fiddle here. Good choices include broiled snapper, softshell crab, and king crab au gratin.

88 S. Atlantic Ave., Ormond Beach. ℭ **386/677-6767.** www.juliansrest.com. Reservations suggested. Main courses $9–$26. AE, DC, MC, V. Daily 4–11pm. From Daytona Beach, take Atlantic Ave./Fla. A1A N. and look for the large A-frame on the left, 2 blocks before Fla. 40.

Ocean Deck Restaurant & Beach Club *Value* SEAFOOD/PUB FARE   Known by spring-breakers, bikers, and other beachgoers as Daytona's best "beach pub" since 1940, the three-story Ocean Deck is also the best restaurant in the busy area around the Main Street Pier. The downstairs reggae bar is as sweaty and packed as ever (a band plays nightly 9pm–2:30am). The upstairs dining room can be noisy, too, but come here for good food, reasonable prices, and great ocean views. You can choose from a wide range of seafood, chicken, sandwiches, and the best burgers on the beach, but don't pass up the mahimahi (look for "trophy" on the menu), a bargain at $9. There's valet parking after dark, or you can park free at the lot behind the Ocean Deck's Reggae Republic surf shop, a block away on Atlantic Avenue.

127 S. Ocean Ave. (at Kemp St.). ℂ 386/253-5224. www.oceandeck.com. Main courses $9–$18; salads and sandwiches $5–$8. AE, DISC, MC, V. Daily 11am–2am (bar to 3am).

ON THE MAINLAND
The Avocado Kingdom ✿ VEGETARIAN   A healthful place to start your day or to have lunch while touring downtown, this establishment purveys a number of vegetarian omelets, burritos, salads, pizzas, and sandwiches such as an avocado Reuben. A few chicken and turkey items are on the menu, but the only red-meat selection is a burger. You can dine outside or inside the store, which has brick walls and ceiling fans suspended from black rafters.

110 S. Beach St. (between Magnolia St. and International Speedway Blvd.). ℂ 386/947-2022. Breakfast $2.50–$5; sandwiches, salads, and pizzas $4–$8. AE, DC, DISC, MC, V. Mon–Sat 8am–4pm.

The Cellar ✿ AMERICAN   An excellent place for ladies who lunch, this tearoom occupies the basement of a 1907 Victorian built as President Warren G. Harding's winter home and now listed on the National Register of Historic Places. The tearoom couldn't be more charming, with reproduction Tiffany windows, fresh flowers, linen tablecloths, china teacups, and a baby grand piano. A lunch menu offers the house signature chicken salad, quiche du jour, vegetarian lasagna, and chicken potpie. In warm months, there's outdoor seating on a covered patio.

220 Magnolia Ave. (between Palmetto and Ridgewood aves.). ℂ 386/258-0011. Soups, salads, and sandwiches $6–$9. AE, DISC, MC, V. Mon–Fri 11am–3pm.

Frappes North ✿✿ CREATIVE AMERICAN/FUSION   It's worth the 6-mile drive north to Bobby and Meryl Frappier's sophisticated, hip establishment, where they provide this area's most entertaining cuisine. Several chic dining rooms set the stage for an ever-changing "Menu of the Moment," fusing a multitude of styles. Ingredients are always fresh, and herbs come from the restaurant's garden. Bobby and Meryl offer at least one vegetarian main course. Lunch is a steal here. The restaurant is in a storefront on the mainland stretch of Granada Boulevard, Ormond Beach's main drag.

123 W. Granada Blvd. (Fla. 40; between Ridgewood Ave. and Washington St.), Ormond Beach. ℂ 386/615-4888. www.frappesnorth.com. Reservations recommended. Main courses $15–$26; lunch $7–$11. AE, MC, V. Mon–Fri 11:30am–2:30pm; Mon–Sat 5–10pm. From the beaches, drive 4 miles north on Fla. A1A and turn left on Granada Blvd. (Fla. 40); cross Halifax River to restaurant on right.

McK's Dublin Station AMERICAN/IRISH   Worth knowing about because it serves food after midnight, this upscale Irish pub has an eclectic menu. The fare includes club sandwiches, burgers, mahimahi wraps, and a few main courses of steak, fish, and chicken. The food isn't exceptional, but it's perfectly acceptable after a few Bass ales. The service is sometimes rushed but usually pleasant.

218 S. Beach St. (between Magnolia St. and Ivy Lane). ℂ 386/238-3321. Reservations not accepted. Main courses $6–$15; salads and sandwiches $5–$8. AE, MC, V. Mon–Wed 11am–9pm; Thurs–Sat 11am–10pm (bar open later).

Rosario's Ristorante ✿ SOUTHERN ITALIAN/TUSCAN   A Victorian boardinghouse with lace curtains makes an incongruous setting for this lively restaurant. The menu delivers pastas with Bolognese and marinara sauces, but the nightly specials are more intriguing, drawing inspiration from ancient Tuscan recipes. If the mixed grill of squirrel, pheasant, rabbit, and quail in a hunter's sauce doesn't appeal to you, opt for grouper Livornese. Many nights, there's music in the cozy bar.

In Live Oak Inn, 448 S. Beach St. (at Loomis Ave.). © **386/258-6066**. Reservations recommended. Main courses $12–$24. MC, V. Tues–Sat 5–10pm.

DAYTONA BEACH AFTER DARK

Check the Friday edition of the Daytona Beach *News-Journal* (www.n-jcenter.com) for its weekly "Go-Do," and the Sunday edition for the "Master Calendar" section, which lists upcoming events. Other good sources listing nighttime entertainment are *Happenings Magazine* and *Backstage Pass Magazine,* two tabloids available at the visitor center (see "Essentials," earlier in this chapter) and in many hotel lobbies.

Ghost tours are led by certified ghost hunters who merge legend with science. You're guaranteed to have a spooky time (at least, it's more interesting than most touristy ghost tours). A portion of all proceeds goes to cemetery preservation and restoration, so at least you can feel good about the fee. Tickets are $8 per person, free for children under 6. Contact **Haunts of Daytona** (© **386-253-6034;** www.haunts ofdaytona.com) for tours and times.

THE PERFORMING ARTS   The city-operated **Peabody Auditorium,** 600 Auditorium Blvd., between Noble Street and Wild Olive Avenue (box office © **386/254-4545** or 386/671-3460), is Daytona's major venue for serious art, including concerts by the local Symphony Society (© **386/253-2901**). Professional actors perform Broadway musicals during winter and summer at the **Seaside Music Theater,** 176 N. Beach St., downtown (© **800/854-5592** or 386/252-6200; www.seasidemusictheater.org). The **Oceanfront Bandshell** (© **386/671-3400**), on the boardwalk, hosts a series of free big-name concerts every Sunday night from early June to Labor Day. It's also the scene of raucous spring-break concerts.

THE CLUB & BAR SCENE   **Main Street** and **Seabreeze Boulevard** on the beach are happening areas where dozens of bars (and a few topless shows) cater to leather-clad bikers.

The **Boot Hill Saloon,** 310 Main St. (© **386/258-9506**), is a bluesy, brew-sy honky-tonk, especially popular during race and bike weeks.

If line dancing is your thang, then scoot your boots over to the **Rockin' Ranch,** 801 S. Nova Rd. (© **386/947-0785**), an uber-fun country-western bar with live music and line-dancing lessons.

A popular beachfront bar for more than 40 years, the **Ocean Deck Restaurant & Beach Club,** 127 S. Ocean Ave. (© **386/253-5224;** see "Where to Dine," above), is packed with a mix of locals and tourists, young and old, who come for live music and cheap drinks. Reggae or ska bands play after 9:30pm. There's valet parking after dark, or leave your vehicle at Ocean Deck's Reggae Republic surf shop on Atlantic Avenue.

3 St. Augustine: America's First City ★★

105 miles NE of Orlando, 302 miles N of Miami, 39 miles S of Jacksonville

With its 17th-century fort, old city gates, horse-drawn carriages clip-clopping along narrow streets, historic buildings, and reconstructed 18th-century Spanish Quarter, St. Augustine seems more picturesque European village than modern Floridian city. This is, after all, the oldest permanent European settlement in the United States (no, it wasn't Jamestown in 1607 or the Pilgrims' settlement at Plymouth Rock in 1620). A group of French Huguenots settled in 1562 near the mouth of the St. Johns River, in present-day Jacksonville. Three years later, a Spanish force under Pedro Menéndez de Avilés arrived on the scene, wiped out the Huguenot men (de Avilés spared their women and children), and established a settlement he named St. Augustín.

The colony survived a succession of attacks by pirates, Indians, and the British over the next 2 centuries. The Treaty of Paris, ending the French and Indian War, ceded the town to Britain in 1763, but the British gave it back to Spain 20 years later. The United States took control when it acquired Florida from Spain in 1821.

Tourism is St. Augustine's main industry these days. However, despite the daily invasion (with good reason—there is a plethora of interesting attractions), it's an exceptionally charming town, with good restaurants, a small-town nightlife, and shopping bargains. Give yourself 2 days here to see the highlights, and longer to savor this historic gem: St. Augustine is one of those places that actually lives up to most of the sickly sweet and sentimental promotional literature written about it.

ESSENTIALS

GETTING THERE   The **Daytona Beach International Airport** (p. 533) is about an hour's drive south of St. Augustine, but service is more frequent—and fares usually lower—at **Jacksonville International Airport** (p. 561), about the same distance north. The nearest **Amtrak** train station is in Jacksonville (p. 561).

VISITOR INFORMATION   Before you go, contact the **St. Augustine, Ponte Vedra & The Beaches Visitors and Convention Bureau,** 88 Riberia St., Suite 400, St. Augustine, FL 32084 (© **800/653-2489** or 904/829-1711; www.visitoldcity.com). Request the *Visitor's Guide,* which details attractions, events, restaurants, accommodations, shopping, and more.

The **St. Augustine Visitor Information Center** is at 10 Castillo Dr., at San Marco Avenue, opposite the Castillo de San Marcos National Monument (© **904/825-1000**). There are numerous ways to see the city, depending on your interests and schedule; this makes a good first stop. For $1, you can watch *Struggle to Survive,* a 42-minute video about the town's difficult first 14 years. (History buffs will enjoy it; otherwise, it's a good way to kill an hour on a rainy day.) The free 22-minute orientation video is more helpful in planning a visit. Once you've looked through the extensive information and made plans, you can buy tickets for the sightseeing trains and trolleys, which include discounted admissions to the attractions (see "Getting Around," below). The center is open daily from 8:30am to 5:30pm.

GETTING AROUND   Once you've parked at the visitor center, you can walk or take one of the sightseeing trolleys, trains, or horse-drawn carriages around the his-

---

Tips Where to Park in "St. Aug"

On-street parking is nonexistent in St. Augustine's historic district, and metered parking lots are not only difficult to find, but often full. Your best bet is to park in the large lots behind the visitor center on Castillo Drive. The $3 fee is good for 2 consecutive days, so you can leave and return at will. Plus, most of the top historic attractions are within walking distance of the center, as it is virtually across the street from the Old City Gates.

toric district. The trolleys and trains follow 7-mile routes, stopping at the visitor center and at or near most attractions between 8:30am and 5pm daily. You can get off at any stop, visit the attraction, and step aboard the next vehicle that comes along about every 20 minutes. If you don't get off at any attractions, it takes about 1 hour and 10 minutes to complete the tour. The vehicles don't all go to the same sights, so speak with their agents at the visitor center in order to pick the right one for you. You can buy tickets, as well as discounted tickets to some attractions, at the visitor center or from the drivers.

St. Augustine Historical Sightseeing (© **904/826-4218** or 904/829-3800) operates the green-and-white, open-air buses (and enclosed buses when it rains, a definite advantage). You can park your car at its headquarters (the Authentic Old Jail and the Florida Heritage Museum at the Authentic Old Jail, which are also stops on the tour). The bus tour costs $15 for adults, $5 for kids 6 to 12.

St. Augustine Sightseeing Trains (© **800/226-6545** or 904/829-6545; www.red trains.com) cover all the main sights except the Authentic Old Jail and the Florida Heritage Museum at the Authentic Old Jail, but its red open-air trains are small enough to go down more of the narrow historic-district streets. Tickets are $18 for adults, $5 for kids 6 to 12, and are good for 3 consecutive days. The company also sells package tickets for your convenience.

You may want to see the sights by horse-drawn carriage. **St. Augustine Transfer Company** (© **904/829-2391;** www.staugustinetransfer.com) has been showing people around town since 1877. Its carriages line up on Avenida Menendez, south of Castillo de San Marcos National Monument. Slow-paced, entertaining, driver-narrated 45-minute to 1-hour rides past major landmarks and attractions are offered from 8am to midnight. Private tours and hotel and restaurant pickups are available. Carriage tours cost $20 for adults, $10 for kids 5 to 11. Add $3 if you want to take a ride after dark.

For more personalized excursions, call **Tour Saint Augustine** (© **800/797-3778** or 904/825-0087), which offers guided walking tours around the historic area. Rates start at $10 per person for 1 hour.

You can also search for old spirits with the nightly **Ghost Tours of St. Augustine** ★★ (© **888/461-1009** or 904/461-1009; www.ghosttoursofstaugustine.com), in which guides in period dress lead you through the historic district or to the St. Augustine Lighthouse. Tickets are $10 to $20 per person, depending on the tour you choose. Also offered are 1-hour ghost cruises on the river in a 72-foot-tall mast schooner. These cost $35 per person, including soft drinks and snacks. Call for schedule and reservations.

The **Sunshine Bus Company** (© **904/823-4816**) operates public bus routes Monday through Saturday from 6am to 7pm. The line runs between the St. Augustine Airport on U.S. 1 and the historic district via San Marco Avenue and the Greyhound bus terminal on Malaga Street. Rides cost $1 per person. Call for the schedule.

For a taxi, call **Yellow Cab** (© **904/824-6888**).

Solano Cycle, 61 San Marco Ave. at Locust Avenue, 2 blocks north of the visitor center (© **904/825-6766;** www.solanocycle.com), rents bicycles, mopeds, and scooters. Bikes cost $18 a day, scooters are $75, and mopeds are $30. Open daily from 10am to 6pm.

SEEING THE TOP HISTORIC ATTRACTIONS
St. George Street, from King Street north to the Old City Gate (at Orange St.), is the heart of the historic district. Lined with restaurants and boutiques selling everything from T-shirts to antiques, these 4 blocks get the lion's share of the town's tourists.

You'll have much less company if you poke around the narrow streets of the primarily residential neighborhood south of King Street. Most of the town's attractions do not have guided tours, but many do have docents on hand to answer questions.

Be sure to drive through the parking lot of the Howard Johnson Express Inn, at 137 San Marco Ave., to see a gorgeous and stately **live oak tree** ★★ that is at least 600 years old; then continue east to **Magnolia Avenue** ★★, a spectacularly beautiful street with a lovely canopy of old magnolia trees.

Castillo de San Marcos National Monument ★ As far as fortresses are concerned, this one's pretty cool. America's oldest and best-preserved masonry fortification took 23 years (1672–95) to build. It is stellar in design, with a double drawbridge entrance (the only way in or out) over a 40-foot dry moat. Diamond-shape bastions in each corner, which enabled cannons to set up a deadly crossfire, contained sentry towers. The indestructible Castillo was never captured in battle, and its coquina (limestone made from broken seashells and corals) walls did not crumble when pounded by enemy artillery or violent storms throughout more than 300 years. Today the old bombproof storerooms surrounding the central plaza house exhibits about the history of the fort, a national monument since 1924. You can tour the vaulted powder magazine, a dank prison cell (supposedly haunted), the chapel, and guard rooms. Climb the stairs to get a great view of Matanzas Bay. A self-guided tour map and brochure are provided at the ticket booth. If available, the 20- to 30-minute ranger talks are well worth attending. Popular torchlight tours of the fort are offered in winter.

If you like forts, you should also check out **Fort Matanzas,** built on an island in the 1740s to warn St. Augustine of enemy attacks from the south (which were out of reach of Castillo de San Marcos). For information, call ✆ **904/471-0116** or visit www.nps.gov/foma. Fort Matanzas is open daily from 8:30am to 5:30pm, and admission and the ferry ride to the island are free, though donations are accepted.

1 E. Castillo Dr. (at San Marco Ave.). ✆ **904/829-6506.** www.nps.gov/casa. Admission $6 adults for 7-day pass, free for children 15 and under. Fort daily 8:45am–4:45pm; grounds daily 5:30am–midnight.

Colonial Spanish Quarter and Spanish Quarter Museum ★★ If H. G. Wells were alive, he'd get a load of this re-created colonial Spanish village—complete with costumed folks doing things they used to do back in the 1700s—and think he was witnessing living proof of a bona-fide time-travel machine. Watch as the blacksmiths, carpenters, leatherworkers, and homemakers demonstrate their skills and show you what life was like before the Internet. All of the architecture and landscape have been re-created within this 2-square-block park which, in my opinion, is infinitely more fun than the museum itself. Do take a 20-minute guided tour of the **DeMesa-Sanchez House** (ca. 1740–60), the only authentic colonial-era structure in the compound (the others are reproductions). If you're into this re-created history, then don't miss the Old St. Augustine Village Museum (see below), which covers even more history.

33 St. George St. (between Cuna and Orange sts.). ✆ **904/825-6830.** www.historicstaugustine.com. Admission $7 adults, $6 seniors, $4 students 6–18, free for children 5 and under; $13 per family. Daily 9am–5:30pm (last entry at 4:30pm).

Lightner Museum ★★★ Now *this* is a museum. Henry Flagler's opulent Spanish Renaissance–style Alcazar Hotel, built in 1889, closed during the Depression and stayed vacant until Chicago publishing magnate Otto C. Lightner bought the building in 1948 to house his vast collection of Victoriana. The building is an attraction in itself and makes a gorgeous museum, centering on a palm-planted courtyard with an arched stone bridge spanning a fishpond. The first floor houses a Victorian village,

St. Augustine

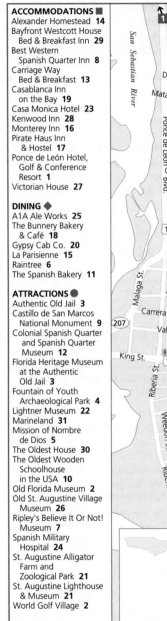

with shop fronts representing emporia selling period wares. The Victorian Science and Industry Room displays shells, rocks, and Native American artifacts in beautiful turn-of-the-20th-century cases. Other exhibits include stuffed birds, an Egyptian mummy, steam-engine models, and examples of Victorian glassblowing. (Yes, it's a strange amalgamation for a museum, but there's sure to be *something* you're interested in here.) Plan to spend about 90 minutes exploring, and be sure to be here at 11am or 2pm, when a room of automated musical instruments erupts into concerts of period music. Check out the cafe, too, housed in what used to be a stunning indoor pool.

The imposing building across King Street was Henry Flagler's rival resort, the Ponce de León Hotel. It now houses **Flagler College,** which runs don't-miss 45-minute tours daily (at 10am and 2pm) of its magnificent Tiffany stained-glass windows, ornate Spanish Renaissance architecture, and gold-leafed Maynard murals ($5 adults, $1 kids under 12). Call 𝄐 **904/823-3378** or visit www.flagler.edu/news_events/tours.html for information. Across Cordova Street stands another competitor of the day, the 1888-vintage **Casa Monica Hotel** (p. 556).

75 King St. (at Granada St.). 𝄐 **904/824-2874.** www.lightnermuseum.org. Admission $8 adults, $2 students with ID and children 12–18, free for children 11 and under. Daily 9am–5pm (last tour 4pm).

The Oldest House 𝄐𝄐
Archaeological surveys indicate that a dwelling stood on this site as early as the beginning of the 17th century. What you see today, called the Gonzáles–Alvarez House (named for two of its prominent owners), evolved from a two-room coquina dwelling built between 1702 and 1727. The rooms are furnished to evoke various historical eras. Admission also entitles you to explore the adjacent **Manucy Museum of St. Augustine History,** where artifacts, maps, and photographs document the town's history from its origins through the Flagler era a century ago. Allow about 30 minutes here.

14 St. Francis St. (at Charlotte St.). 𝄐 **904/824-2872.** www.staugustinehistoricalsociety.org/. Admission $8 adults, $7 seniors 55 and over, $4 students, free for children under 6; $16 families. Daily 9am–5pm; tours depart every half-hour (last tour at 4:30pm).

The Oldest Wooden Schoolhouse in the U.S.A. 𝄐 *Kids*
Excellent photo ops abound at this old-fashioned schoolhouse. One of three structures here dating from the Spanish colonial period, this cedar-and-cypress structure is held together by wooden pegs and handmade nails, its hand-wrought beams still intact. The last class was held in 1864. Today the old-time classroom is re-created using cheesy animated pupils and teacher, complete with a dunce and a below-stairs "dungeon" for unruly children, which will make your kids count their lucky stars that they weren't in school back then.

14 St. George St. (between Orange and Cuna sts.). 𝄐 **904/824-0192.** www.oldestschoolhouse.com. Admission $2 adults, $2.50 seniors 55 and over, $2 children 6–12, free for children 5 and under. Daily 9am–5pm (later in summer).

Old St. Augustine Village Museum 𝄐𝄐
More time travel in St. Augustine is available at this awesome museum re-creating life back in the old days. Operated by Daytona Beach's excellent Museum of Arts and Sciences (p. 539), this museum brings to life each period of the city's history, from Spanish colonial times to the early 20th century. The 10 restored homes here—built between 1790 and 1910—are on their original building sites. Since this museum is a work in progress, some houses are temporarily closed until refurbishments are complete. The reconstructed Star General Store sells preserves and other Victorian-era goods. You'll need 2 hours to see it all, including the 30-minute guided tour. Admission is good all day, so if you miss the start of a tour, you can leave and come back.

250 St. George St. (entry on Bridge St. between St. George and Cordova sts.). © **904/823-9722.** www.old-staug-village.com. Admission $7 adults, $6 seniors, $5 children under 12. Daily 9am–5pm. Guided tours on the hour 10am–3pm, except 1pm.

Spanish Military Hospital Hypochondriacs, doctors, and fans of medicine in general will love this place—but if you're squeamish in hospitals, this one isn't an exception. The clapboard building is a reconstruction of part of a hospital that stood here during the second Spanish colonial period, from 1784 to 1821. A 20-minute guided tour will show you what the apothecary, administrative offices, patients' ward, and herbarium probably looked like in 1791. The ward and a collection of actual surgical instruments of the period will enhance your appreciation of modern medicine.

3 Aviles St. (south of King St.). © **904/825-6830.** Admission $3 adults, $2.50 seniors, $2 children. Mon–Sat 10am–5pm; Sun noon–5pm.

MORE HISTORIC ATTRACTIONS

Authentic Old Jail It's no Alcatraz, but in a sinister way, this old jail is kind of quaint. The compact prison, a mile north of the visitor center, may be authentic, but it's not particularly historic. It was built in 1890 and served as the county jail until 1953. The sheriff and his wife raised their children upstairs and used the same kitchen facilities to prepare the inmates' meals and their own. Among the "regular" cells, you can also see a maximum-security cell where murderers and horse thieves were confined, a cell housing prisoners condemned to hang (they could see the gallows being constructed from their window), and a grim solitary-confinement cell—with no windows or mattress. A restaurant here serves inexpensive lunch fare.

167 San Marco Ave. (at Williams St.). © **904/829-3800.** Admission $6 adults, $4 children 6–12, free for children 5 and under. Daily 8:30am–5pm.

Florida Heritage Museum at the Authentic Old Jail Compared to the other museums in town, this one isn't so special. After you've seen the Authentic Old Jail, you can spend another 30 minutes wandering through this commercial museum documenting 400 years of Florida's past, focusing on the life of Henry Flagler, the Civil War, and the Seminole Wars. Highlights are a collection of toys and dolls, mostly from the 1870s to the 1920s, and a replica of a Spanish galleon filled with weapons, pottery, and treasures, along with display cases filled with actual gold, silver, and jewelry recovered by treasure hunters. A typical wattle-and-daub hut of a Timucuan Indian in a forest setting illustrates the lifestyle of St. Augustine's first residents.

167 San Marco Ave. (at Williams St.). © **904/829-3800.** Admission $5 adults, $4 children 6–12, free for children 5 and under. Free admission with purchase of Old Town Trolley Tour. Daily 8:30am–5pm.

Fountain of Youth Archaeological Park *Overrated* Considering that Botox and plastic surgery are the real fountains of youth, why bother? Never mind that Juan Ponce de León never found the Fountain of Youth; this 25-acre archaeological park bills itself as North America's first historic site. Smithsonian Institution archaeological digs have established that a Timucuan Indian village existed here some 1,000 years ago, but there's no evidence that Ponce de León visited the spot during his 1513 voyage. You can wander the not-so-interesting grounds yourself, but you'll learn more on a 45-minute guided tour or at a planetarium show about 16th-century celestial navigation. **Be warned:** This place could be a secondary dictionary definition for the phrase *tourist trap* (not to mention that the fountain's water smells and tastes *awful*).

Nevertheless, the grounds are lovely and the non-fountain exhibits are okay, which is good because people feel the need to visit even though it's basically a waste of time.

11 Magnolia Ave. (at Williams St.). (C) 800/356-8222 or 904/829-3168. www.fountainofyouthflorida.com. Admission $6 adults, $5 seniors, $3 children 6–12, free for children 5 and under. Daily 9am–5pm.

Mission of Nombre de Dios   This serene setting overlooking the Intracoastal Waterway is believed to be the site of the first permanent mission in the United States, founded in 1565. The mission is a popular destination of religious pilgrimages. Whatever your beliefs, it's a beautiful tree-shaded spot, ideal for quiet meditation.

27 Ocean Ave. (east of San Marco Ave.). (C) 904/824-2809. Free admission; donations appreciated. Daily 8am–5:30pm.

Old Florida Museum 𝄞𝄞 (Kids)   For those who can't resist touching things in museums, it's okay to do so here; in fact, it's encouraged! This mostly outdoors museum gives you the chance to experience historic Florida, with many hands-on activities (shelling and grinding corn, pumping water, writing with a quill pen) that kids may enjoy. Showcasing daily activities, everyday objects (games, weapons, tools, and more), and recreational pastimes, the museum demonstrates how three different eras of people in the area—the native Timucuan Indians, colonial Spaniards, and American pioneers—lived, worked, and played from the 16th to the early 20th centuries.

254-D San Marco Ave. (C) 800/813-3208 or 904/824-8874. www.oldfloridamuseum.com. Admission $6 adults, $5 kids 12 and under. Daily 10am–5pm.

St. Augustine Lighthouse & Museum 𝄞   Photo op alert! This 165-foot-tall structure, Florida's first official lighthouse, was built in 1875 to replace the old Spanish lighthouse that had stood at the inlet since 1565. The lightkeeper's cottage was destroyed by fire in 1970 but was meticulously restored to its Victorian splendor. The Victorian-style visitor center houses a museum explaining the history of the lighthouse and the area. You should be in good physical condition (children must be at least 7 years old *and* 4 ft. tall) to climb the 219 steps to the top of the lighthouse.

81 Lighthouse Ave. (off Fla. A1A east of the Bridge of Lions). (C) 904/829-0745. www.staugustinelighthouse.com. Admission to museum and tower $7.50 adults, $6.50 seniors, $5 children 7–11, free for kids under 7 and all active-duty and retired military personnel. Daily 9am–6pm. Follow Fla. A1A S. across the Bridge of Lions; take the last left before the turnoff to Anastasia State Park.

OTHER ENTERTAINING ATTRACTIONS

Dolphin Conservation Center at Marineland 𝄞   What once was a schlocky 7-acre beachfront tourist trap is now a world-class Dolphin Conservation Center. This, the world's first oceanarium (1938), is located 15 minutes south of St. Augustine and is on the National Register of Historic Places. See dolphins, sea lions, penguins, and myriad ocean life here, or snorkel or scuba in the 450,000-gallon oceanarium with some of them, if you make reservations. *Note:* Swimming with dolphins has both its critics and its supporters. You may want to visit the Whale and Dolphin Conservation Society's website at www.wdcs.org. For more information about responsible travel in general, check out www.treadlightly.org and www.ecotourism.org.

9600 Ocean Shore Blvd. (C) 904/460-1275. www.marineland.net. General admission $5. Dolphin encounter $120 (minimum height 50 in.). Scuba diving $65 (with your own equipment); snorkeling $35 (wear a bathing suit). Dolphin touch and feed (includes photo) $20. Wed–Mon 9:30am–4:30pm. South of St. Augustine on A1A.

Ripley's Believe It or Not! Museum (Kids)   A total tourist trap, this is a place to go only if it's raining outside and you have absolutely nothing to do. This is the original

Where Golf Is King

Passionate golf fans can easily spend a day at the **World Golf Hall of Fame** ⚔️ ((✆ **904/940-4123;** www.wgv.com), a state-of-the-art museum honoring professional golf, its great players, and the sport's famous supporters (including comedian Bob Hope and singer Dinah Shore). It's the centerpiece of **World Golf Village,** a complex of hotels, shops, offices, and 18-hole golf courses (see "Outdoor Activities," below). There's an IMAX screen next door.

Museum admission is $15 for adults, $13 for seniors and students, and $10 for children 5 to 12. IMAX tickets range from $7.50 to $12 for adults, $6.50 to $11 for seniors and students, and $5 to $8 for children. Combination tickets to both are $17 for adults, $15 for seniors and students, and $11 for children. A round on the putting green costs $7 for adults, $6 for seniors and students, and $5 for children. The museum is open daily from 10am to 6pm; IMAX movies run until 8pm Friday and Saturday.

You don't have to play the real courses because the village is built around a lake with a "challenge hole" sitting out in the middle, 132 feet from the shoreline. You can hit balls at it or play a round on the nearby putting course. The Walkway of Champions (whose signatures appear in pavement stones) circles the lake and passes a shopping complex where the main tenant is the two-story **Tour Stop** ((✆ **904/940-0422),** a purveyor of pricey apparel and equipment.

If you'd like to stay overnight, contact the luxurious **World Golf Village Renaissance Resort,** 500 S. Legacy Trail, St. Augustine, FL 32092 ((✆ **888/740-7020** or 904/940-8000; www.worldgolfrenaissance.com).

The village is at exit 95A off I-95. For more information, contact World Golf Village, 21 World Golf Place, St. Augustine, FL 32092 ((✆ **904/940-4000;** www.wgv.com).

Ripley's museum, housed in an architecturally interesting converted 1887 Moorish Revival residence—complete with battlements, massive chimneys, and rose windows. Like the Ripley's in a dozen other U.S. cities, the exhibits run the gamut from a Haitian voodoo doll owned by Papa Doc Duvalier to letters carved on a pencil with a chainsaw by Ray "Wild Mountain Man" Murphy.

19 San Marco Ave. (at Castillo Dr.). (✆ **904/824-1606.** www.staugustine-ripleys.com. Admission $13 adults, $8.95 seniors, $7.95 children 5–12, free for children 4 and under. June 8 to Labor Day daily 9am–9pm; rest of year 9am–7pm.

St. Augustine Alligator Farm and Zoological Park ⚔️⚔️ *Kids*   At the St. Augustine Alligator Farm and Zoological Park, gators and crocs are a dime a dozen. In fact, there are more than 2,700 of them—including some rare white ones—on display at this over-a-century-old attraction. It houses the world's only complete collection of all 22 species of crocodilians, a category that includes alligators, crocodiles, caimans, and gavials. There are also ponds and marshes filled with ducks, geese, swans, herons, egrets, ibises, and other native wading birds, as well as a petting zoo with pygmy goats, potbellied pigs, and miniature horses. Entertaining (and educational) 20-minute alligator and reptile shows take place hourly throughout the day, and you can often see narrated feedings spring through fall. Don't miss Maximo, an Australian croc that weighs 1,250 lbs.; is 15 feet, 3 inches long; and is the father to 17 baby crocs.

999 Anastasia Blvd. (Fla. A1A), east of Bridge of Lions at Old Quarry Rd. © **904/824-3337.** www.alligatorfarm.com (check for discounts). Admission $18 adults, $10 children 3–10, free for children under 3. Daily 9am–5pm; summer hours 9am–6pm.

HITTING THE BEACH

There are several places to find sand and sea: **Vilano Beach,** on the north side of St. Augustine Inlet; and **St. Augustine Beach,** on the south side (the inlet dumps the Matanzas and North rivers into the Atlantic). Be aware, however, that erosion has almost swallowed the beach from the inlet as far south as Old Beach Road in St. Augustine Beach. The U.S. Army Corps of Engineers is reclaiming the sand, but in the meantime, hotels and homes here have rock seawalls instead of sand bordering the sea.

Erosion has made a less noticeable impact on beautiful **Anastasia State Park** ★★, on Anastasia Boulevard (Fla. A1A) across the Bridge of Lions and just past the Alligator Farm, where the 4 miles of beach (on which you can drive and park) are still backed by picturesque dunes. On its riverside, the area faces a lagoon. Amenities include shaded picnic areas with grills, restrooms, windsurfing, sailing and canoeing (on a saltwater lagoon), a nature trail, and saltwater fishing (for bluefish, pompano, redfish, and flounder; a license is required for out-of-state residents). In summer, you can rent chairs, beach umbrellas, and surfboards. There's good bird-watching here, especially in spring and fall; pick up a brochure at the entrance. The 139 wooded campsites are in high demand year-round; they come with picnic tables, grills, and electricity. Admission to the park is $5 per vehicle, $1 per bicyclist or pedestrian. Campsites cost $25. For camping reservations, call © **800/326-3521** or go to www.reserveamerica.com. The day-use area is open daily from 8am to sunset. You can bring your pets. For information, contact Anastasia State Park, 1340A Fla. A1A S., St. Augustine, FL 32084 (© **904/461-2033;** www.floridastateparks.org/anastasia).

From Memorial Day to Labor Day, all St. Augustine beaches charge a fee of $3 per car at official access points; the rest of the year, you can park free, but there are no lifeguards on duty or restroom facilities on the beach.

OUTDOOR ACTIVITIES

For additional outdoor options, contact the St. Augustine, Ponte Vedra & The Beaches Visitors and Convention Bureau (p. 546) and request a copy of its *Outdoor Recreation Guide.*

CRUISES The Usina family has been running **St. Augustine Scenic Cruises** (© **904/824-1806;** www.scenic-cruise.com) on Matanzas Bay since the turn of the 20th century. They offer 75-minute narrated tours aboard the double-decker *Victory III,* departing from the Municipal Marina just south of the Bridge of Lions. You can sometimes spot dolphins, brown pelicans, cormorants, and kingfishers. Snacks, soft drinks, beer, and wine are sold onboard. Departures are usually at 11am, 1pm, 2:45pm, and 4:30pm daily except Christmas, with an additional tour at 6:15pm from April 1 to May 21 and from Labor Day to October 15. From May 22 to Labor Day there are two additional tours, at 6:45 and 8:30pm. Call ahead—schedules can change during inclement weather. Fares are $15 for adults, $9 for seniors, $8 for youths 13 to 18, and $6 for children 4 to 12. If you're driving, allow time to find parking on the street.

You can also take the free ferry to Fort Matanzas on Rattlesnake Island. There are often dolphins in the water as you make the trip, and the fort is interesting. Ferries take off from 8635 Hwy. A1A (follow A1A S. out of St. Augustine for about 15 miles). Call © **904/471-0116** or visit www.nps.gov/foma for more information.

FISHING   You can fish to your heart's content at **Anastasia State Park** (see "Hitting the Beach," above). Or you can cast your line off **St. Johns County Fishing Pier,** at the north end of St. Augustine Beach (© **904/461-0119**). The pier is open 24 hours daily and has a bait shop with rental equipment that's open from 6am to 10pm. Admission is $2 ($1 children under 12) for fishing, 50¢ for sightseeing.

For full-day, half-day, and overnight **deep-sea fishing** excursions (for snapper, grouper, porgy, amberjack, sea bass, and other species), contact the **Sea Love Marina,** 250 Vilano Rd. (Fla. A1A N.), at the eastern end of the Vilano Beach Bridge (© **904/ 824-3328;** www.sealovefishing.com). Full-day trips on the party boat *Sea Love II* cost about $50 to $65; half-day trips $35 to $45. No license is required, and rod, reel, bait, and tackle are supplied. Bring your own food and drink.

GOLF   The area's best golf resorts are in Ponte Vedra Beach—a half-hour's drive north on Florida A1A, closer to Jacksonville than St. Augustine (see p. 567 for details).

At World Golf Village, 12 miles north of St. Augustine at exit 95A off I-95 (see the box "Where Golf Is King," above), **The Slammer & The Squire** and **The King & The Bear** (© **904/940-6088;** www.wgv.com) together offer 36 holes amid a wildlife preserve. Locals say they're not as challenging as their greens fees: about $125 in summer, $165 in winter, including cart. For those not schooled in golf history, the "Slammer" is in honor of Sam Sneed, the "Squire" is for Gene Sarazen, the "King" is Arnold Palmer, and the "Bear" is Jack Nicklaus. Palmer and Nicklaus collaborated in designing their course.

Nicklaus also had a hand in the stunning course at the **Ocean Hammock Golf Club** ✾✾ (© **386/477-4600;** www.oceanhammock.com), on Florida A1A in Palm Coast, about halfway between St. Augustine and Daytona Beach. With six of its holes skirting the beach, it is the first truly oceanside course built in Florida since the 1920s.

There are only a few courses in St. Augustine, including **Ponce de León Hotel, Golf & Conference Resort,** 4000 U.S. 1 (© **904/829-5314**), with its rather flat 18; and the **St. Augustine Shores Golf Club,** 707 Shores Blvd., off U.S. 1 (© **904/794-4653**), a par-70, 18-hole course with lots of water, a lighted driving range and putting green, and a restaurant and lounge. Greens fees usually are under $30, including cart.

For more course information, go to www.golf.com or www.floridagolfing.com, or call the **Florida Sports Foundation** (© **850/488-8347**) or **Florida Golfing** (© **866/ 833-2663**).

WATERSPORTS   Jet skis and equipment for surfing and windsurfing can be rented at **Surf Station,** 1020 Anastasia Blvd. (Fla. A1A), a block south of the Alligator Farm (© **904/471-9463**); and at **Raging Water Sports,** at the Conch House Marina Resort, 57 Comares Ave. (© **904/829-5001**), off Anastasia Avenue (Fla. A1A) halfway between the Bridge of Lions and the Alligator Farm.

SHOPPING

The winding streets of the historic district are home to dozens of **antiques stores** and **galleries** stocked full of original paintings, sculptures, bric-a-brac, fine furnishings, china, and other treasures. Brick-lined **Aviles Street,** a block from the river, has an especially good mix of shops for browsing, as does **St. George Street** south of the visitor center, and the Uptown area on **San Marco Avenue** a few blocks north of the center. The **Alcazar Courtyard Shops,** at the Lightner Museum (© **904/824-2874;**

p. 548), have a good selection of antiques. Check at the visitor center for lists of art galleries and antiques shops, or contact the **Antique Dealers Association of St. Augustine,** 60 Cuna St., St. Augustine, FL 32084 (no phone).

Experience chocolate heaven at **Whetstone Chocolates,** 2 Coke Rd. (Fla. 312), between U.S. 1 and the Mickler O'Connell Bridge ((C) **904/825-1700**). Free self-guided tours of the store and factory usually take place Monday through Saturday from 10am to 5pm, but call ahead to confirm the schedule. Whetstone has a retail outlet at 42 St. George St., in the historic district.

Outlet shoppers will find plenty of good hunting 7 miles northwest of downtown on Florida 16, on the west side of I-95, in the **St. Augustine Outlet Mall** ((C) **904/825-1555;** www.staugustineoutlets.com), and at the **Belz Factory Outlet World,** on the east side of the interstate ((C) **904/826-1311;** www.belz.com). Both malls are open Monday through Saturday from 9am to 9pm, Sunday from 10am to 6pm.

WHERE TO STAY

There are plenty of moderate and inexpensive motels and hotels in St. Augustine. Most convenient to the historic district is the 40-room **Best Western Spanish Quarter Inn,** 6 Castillo Dr. ((C) **800/528-1234** or 904/824-4457; www.staugustinebest western.com), directly across from the visitor center. It's completely surrounded by an asphalt parking lot, but it does have a pool and hot tub.

If you're coming on a weekend, expect the higher end of the listed rates—almost all accommodations increase their prices on weekends, when the town is most crowded with visitors. St. Johns County charges a 9% tax on hotel bills.

HOTELS & MOTELS

Casa Monica Hotel ✹✹✹   This Moorish Revival hotel was built in 1888 as a luxury lodging by Bostonian and YMCA founder Franklin W. Smith. Unfortunately, Smith never really opened it, since the furniture he'd purchased for the hotel never made it to St. Augustine, thanks to Henry Flagler, who owned the railroad the furniture was to be shipped on as well as the neighboring hotel. In a bind and losing too much money, Smith finally sold the hotel to Flagler, for 25¢ on the dollar of what he originally spent, and the furniture mysteriously appeared almost immediately! It's easily the best hotel in town, with top-notch rooms and services. Guests here can pay $15 a day to use the pools, restaurants, and other facilities at Serenata Beach Club, an exclusive oceanfront club located 10 minutes away. Most of the guest quarters are spacious, modern hotel rooms with Iberian-style armoires, wrought-iron headboards, and tapestry drapes. "Premium" rooms have sitting areas with sofas and easy chairs. All units have big bathrooms equipped with high-end toiletries and either a large walk-in shower or a combination tub/shower. Much more interesting are the "signature suites" installed in the building's two tile-topped towers and fortresslike central turret. Each of these one- to four-bedroom units is unique. One in the turret has a half-round living room with gun-port windows overlooking the historic district, while a three-story town house in one of the towers has a huge whirlpool bathroom on its top floor.

The 95 Cordova restaurant has an excellent wine list, great service, and beautiful decor. It serves regional fare such as Calypso-spiced mahimahi and sweet-and-sour Long Island duckling. A player piano provides music in the adjoining bar.

95 Cordova St. (at King St.), St. Augustine, FL 32084. (C) **800/648-1888** or 904/827-1888. Fax 904/819-6065. www.casamonica.com. 138 units. $169–$259 double. Packages available. AE, DC, DISC, MC, V. Valet parking $13; limited free parking 2 blocks from hotel. **Amenities:** Restaurant; marketplace; bar; heated outdoor pool; access to

nearby health club; exercise room; Jacuzzi; bike rental; children's programs; concierge; business center; limited room service; babysitting; coin-op washers and dryers. *In room:* A/C, TV, dataport (high-speed Internet access), fridge, coffeemaker, hair dryer, iron, safe.

Monterey Inn *Value*   For the price, you can't find a better choice than this modest, wrought-iron-trimmed motel overlooking the Matanzas Bay and close to the attractions of the Old City. Three generations of the Six family have run this simple two-story motel, and they keep the 1960s building and grounds clean and functional. Rooms are not especially spacious, but they're good enough to sleep in after a day at the beach.

16 Avenida Menendez (between Cuna and Hypolita sts.), St. Augustine, FL 32084. ℂ **904/824-4482**. Fax 904/829-8854. www.themontereyinn.com. 59 units. $59–$159 double. AE, DC, DISC, MC, V. **Amenities:** Heated outdoor pool. *In room:* A/C, TV, dataport, hair dryer.

BED & BREAKFASTS
St. Augustine has more than two dozen bed-and-breakfasts in restored historic homes. They all provide free parking, breakfast, 24-hour refreshments, and plenty of atmosphere, but most accept neither young children nor smokers (check before booking). Those listed below are in the historic district. For more choices, contact **St. Augustine Historic Inns,** P.O. Box 5268, St. Augustine, FL 33085-5268 (no phone; www.staugustineinns.com), for descriptions of its member properties.

Alexander Homestead 👧👧   This restored 1888 Victorian beauty is spectacular, not to mention romantic, and makes a popular place for weddings and honeymoons. One room has a Jacuzzi, two have fireplaces, and all have private porches, bathrooms, and antiques. Gourmet breakfasts include baked French toast with almond syrup; at night, you can enjoy a complimentary brandy along with your complimentary chocolate. Even better, coffee is delivered directly to your door in the morning, so there's no need to stir too much before your caffeine fix.

14 Sevilla St., St. Augustine, FL 32084. ℂ **888/292-4147** or 904/826-4147. www.alexanderhomestead.com. 4 units. $159–$209 double. Rates include full breakfast. AE, DISC, MC, V. *In room:* A/C, TV.

Bayfront Westcott House Bed & Breakfast Inn 👧   Overlooking Matanzas Bay, this romantic, Key West–style wood-frame house offers rare opportunities for an uncluttered view from the porch, the second-story veranda, and a shady courtyard.

Tips **A Swashbuckling Hostel**

International travelers on the cheap congregate at the **Pirate Haus Inn & Hostel,** 32 Treasury St., at Charlotte Street (ℂ **904/808-1999;** www.pirate haus.com), smack in the middle of the historic district. Done up in a pirate theme, this Spanish-style building has a communal kitchen, living room, and rooftop terrace. The inn has five private rooms (three with their own bathrooms), each equipped with either a queen-size or double bed, plus one or two bunk beds. Two other rooms have dormitory-style bunks. Rooms cost $47 to $65 a night (higher on some weekends), while dorm beds go for $17. MasterCard and Visa are accepted. Reservations are advised, especially on weekends. Rates include the hostel's famous all-you-can-eat pancake breakfast.

The rooms—some with bay windows, two-person whirlpool tubs, and working fire-places—are immaculate and exquisitely furnished. Yours might have authentic Victorian furnishings and a brass bed made up with a white quilt and lace dust ruffle.

146 Avenida Menendez (between Bridge and Francis sts.), St. Augustine, FL 32084. ℂ **800/513-9814** or 904/824-4301. Fax 904/824-4301. www.westcotthouse.com. 9 units. $119–$229 double. Rates include full breakfast. AE, DISC, MC, V. **Amenities:** Access to nearby health club; Jacuzzi; free use of bicycles; massage. *In room:* A/C, TV, hair dryer.

Carriage Way Bed & Breakfast ✿ *Value*

Primarily occupying an 1883 Victorian wood-frame house fronted by roses and hibiscus, this B&B isn't fancy or formal, but it is comfortable and a good value. TV, books, and games are provided in a homey parlor. Guest rooms in the main house are furnished with simple reproductions, including many four-poster beds. One room retains its original fireplace. For more privacy, two more rooms are located down the street in The Cottage, a clapboard house built in 1885. The Cottage has a living room and kitchen, and both of its bedrooms have claw-foot tubs. The Miranda room also sports a two-person Jacuzzi, while the Ashton has a small back porch. Special packages provide nice little touches such as a gourmet picnic lunch, a horse-drawn carriage ride, and breakfast in bed.

70 Cuna St. (between Cordova and Spanish sts.), St. Augustine, FL 32084. ℂ **800/908-9832** or 904/829-2467. Fax 904/826-1461. www.carriageway.com. 11 units. $89–$189 double. Rates include full breakfast. AE, DISC, MC, V. **Amenities:** Free use of bikes. *In room:* A/C, dataport.

Casablanca Inn on the Bay ✿

This 1914 Mediterranean-style white-stucco house, listed on the National Register of Historic Places, faces the bay, although only a few of the rooms offer views. The most stunning are the second-floor suites with hammocks and private porches. The furnishings—a mix of turn-of-the-20th-century American oak, European, and Victorian pieces—are of a higher quality than those at many other inns. One modern convenience is a cassette player with a small selection of classical tapes. This may be appreciated, especially if you're in a ground-floor room that unfortunately suffers from the noise of the street and the next-door bar and grill. Breakfast is served alfresco on the porch or in a glass-enclosed conservatory. A porch with rocking chairs is an ideal spot to chill out, read a book, or sip a cocktail.

24 Avenida Menendez (between Hypolita and Treasury sts.), St. Augustine, FL 32084. ℂ **800/826-2626** or 904/829-0928. Fax 904/826-1892. www.casablancainn.com. 20 units. $99–$299 weeknights; $159-$399 on weekends. Rates include full breakfast. AE, DISC, MC, V. **Amenities:** Access to nearby health club; free use of bikes. *In room:* A/C, TV (18 units), no phone (6 units).

Kenwood Inn

There's lots of pink here, but what makes this inn so unusual is its relatively large outdoor space, which includes a pool, a lushly landscaped sun deck, and a secluded garden courtyard (complete with a koi pond and flower bed under a sprawling pecan tree). The Victorian wood-frame house with graceful verandas has served as a boardinghouse or inn since the late 19th century. Everything from the carpeting to the linens to the china is first class. Rooms are larger and more private than most other accommodations in converted single-family homes.

38 Marine St. (at Bridge St.), St. Augustine, FL 32084. ℂ **800/824-8151** or 904/824-2116. Fax 904/824-1689. www.thekenwoodinn.com. 14 units. $95–$175 weekdays double; $135–$185 weekends double; bridal suite $175 weeknights, $250 weekends. Rates include continental breakfast. DISC, MC, V. **Amenities:** Outdoor pool; free use of bikes. *In room:* A/C, TV (in some), fax, dataport, kitchen, minibar, fridge, coffeemaker, hair dryer, iron, no phone (in some).

Victorian House *Kids*

This 1897-vintage Victorian B&B features a wraparound porch and an adjoining old store, now dubbed the Carriage House. The latter is divided into four units, one of which has a kitchenette. What's unusual is that children can stay in the Carriage House units, all of which have TVs and private entrances. They're not welcome in the main house, however. Victorian antiques adorn all units.

11 Cadiz St. (between Aviles and Charlotte sts.), St. Augustine, FL 32084. ✆ **877/703-0432** or 904/824-5214. Fax 904/824-7990. www.victorianhouse-inn.com. 8 units. $109–$199 weekdays; $159–$209 weekends. Rates include full breakfast. AE, DISC, MC, V. **Amenities:** Free use of bikes. *In room:* A/C, TV (4 units), kitchen (1 unit), no phone.

WHERE TO DINE

In a town with as much tourist traffic as St. Augustine, there are, of course, a fair number of "tourist trap" restaurants. But on the whole, the food here, even at the popular eateries, is fairly priced and of good quality.

The historic district has a branch of Tampa's famous **Columbia,** 98 St. George St., at Hypolita Street (✆ **904/824-3341**). Like the original in Ybor City (p. 414), this one sports Spanish architecture, including intricate tilework and courtyards with fountains.

A1A Ale Works ★ SEAFOOD Anyone who has ever chugged from a beer bong or entered a beer-drinking contest, or simply loves beer must visit this brewpub. You can't miss the two-story Victorian-style building, on the waterfront opposite the Bridge of Lions. One of the city's most popular watering holes, the downstairs bar offers nightly entertainment, which sometimes filters upstairs into the restaurant. Despite the noise potential, the kitchen turns out a surprisingly good blend of New World Floribbean, Cuban, Caribbean, and Latino styles, in a nice setting with big windows and outdoor seating. Most of the seafood is very fresh, and the sauces are made to order. The spicy ahi stick appetizer (sushi-grade tuna, pickled ginger, and sesame seeds wrapped in a wonton skin, cooked rare, and topped with a wasabi and siracha aioli) is as good as it gets. Don't overlook nightly specials, either, especially the fresh fish. The house brew ranges from a very light lager to a nonalcoholic root beer.

1 King St. (at Avenida Menendez). ✆ **904/829-2977.** Call for preferred seating. Main courses $12–$28; sandwiches $7–$9. AE, DC, DISC, MC, V. Sun–Thurs 11am–10:30pm; Fri–Sat 11am–11pm. Late-night menu served downstairs.

The Bunnery Bakery & Café ★ *Value* BAKERY/DELI If you suffer from a raging sweet tooth, get thee to the Bunnery. Alluring aromas waft from this bakery and cafe in the heart of the historic district. It's a lovely spot for breakfast or for a pastry and cappuccino anytime you need a break from sightseeing. At lunch, plop yourself into one of the colorful booths and indulge in the soups, salads, burgers, or panini—or perhaps a croissant stuffed with walnut-and-pineapple chicken salad. Order at the counter; the staff will call your number when it's ready.

121 St. George St. (between Treasury and Hypolita sts.). ✆ **904/829-6166.** Breakfast $3–$7; sandwiches and salads $3.50–$8. No credit cards. Daily 8am–6pm. Closed New Year's Day, Easter, Thanksgiving, Christmas Eve, and Christmas Day.

Gypsy Cab Co. ★★ *Value* NEW AMERICAN Billing itself as a temple of "urban cuisine," Ned Pollack's high-energy establishment, with gaudy neon stripes outside and art-filled dining rooms inside, offers the town's most interesting culinary experience. Ned's creative menu changes daily, though black-bean soup is a constant winner. If it's available, try the veal with bacon-horseradish cream or the grouper in a tomato-basil sauce. As a capper, I recommend Amaretto cheesecake or Key lime pie. Also of note is the house salad dressing, which is so good they sell it by the bottle. Lunch is served (Mon–Fri 11am–4pm) in the **Gypsy Bar & Grill** (✆ **904/808-1305**) next door, which features live music Wednesday, Friday, and Saturday evenings. Taking the concept a little too far, there's a Gypsy Comedy Club right next door.

828 Anastasia Blvd. (Fla. A1A, at Ingram St., east of the Bridge of Lions). ✆ **904/824-8244**. www.gypsycab.com. Main courses $12–$25. AE, DC, DISC, MC, V. Mon–Thurs 4:30–10pm; Fri 4:30–11pm; Sat 11am–11pm; Sun 10:30am–10pm.

La Parisienne ✿✿ CONTEMPORARY FRENCH   Somewhat of an accidental tourist in these parts, La Parisienne is a welcome respite from all the nearby Americana. Despite its name, this lovely dining room evokes the French countryside, with a rough-hewn pine-beamed ceiling, lace-curtained windows, and ladder-back chairs. The seasonal menu features fresh seafood, and in fall you'll see venison and quail. If they're offered, begin with pan-seared sea scallops in a citrus sauce; then go on to steak au poivre with a Cognac-cream sauce, roast rack of lamb Provençal, or the day's treatment of fresh local fish. The weekend brunch menu features beignets, eggs Benedict, and scrambled eggs with smoked salmon.

60 Hypolita St. (between Spanish and Cordova sts.). ✆ **904/829-0055**. www.laparisienne.net. Reservations recommended. Main courses $19–$28; 5-course prix-fixe menu $60. AE, DISC, MC, V. Tues–Fri 5–9pm; Sat–Sun 11am–3pm and 5–9pm.

Raintree ✿ INTERNATIONAL   Even if you don't have a full meal at this romantic 1879 Victorian house (about ½ mile north of the historic district), the tempting variety of crepes and an exemplary crème brûlée are worth a visit. Sweetness works its way onto the main menu, as in cashew-encrusted pork tenderloin mignonettes with a champagne and ruby raspberry sauce. More traditional choices include beef Wellington and rack of New Zealand lamb. The food is all very good, though not as mod as at Gypsy Cab Co. or as expertly prepared as at La Parisienne (see above). The list of more than 300 vintages has won *Wine Spectator* awards. Keep in mind that Raintree is a destination restaurant, which means hordes of people are constantly traipsing through and marveling at the lovely old-world ambience.

102 San Marco Ave. (at Bernard St.). ✆ **904/824-7211**. www.raintreerestaurant.com. Reservations recommended. Main courses $15–$24; dessert bar $5.50. AE, DC, MC, V. Sun–Thurs 6–9:30pm; Fri–Sat 6–10pm. Courtesy car provides transportation from/to downtown hotels.

The Spanish Bakery COLONIAL   Occupying a reconstructed 17th-century building, this family-operated establishment bakes almond, lemon, and cinnamon cookies using recipes from the Spanish colonial period. These crunchy morsels make a fine snack while you're touring the historic district. Or you can have lunch here, choosing from daily specials such as spicy Spanish-style chili over rice.

Rear of 42½ St. George St. (between Cuna and Orange sts.). ✆ **904/471-3046**. Reservations not accepted. Lunch specials $5; cookies and rolls 40¢–50¢ each. No credit cards. Daily 9:30am–3pm. Closed Thanksgiving and Christmas.

ST. AUGUSTINE AFTER DARK

Especially on weekends, the Old Town is full of strollers and partiers making the rounds of dozens of bars, clubs, and restaurants. For up-to-date details on what's happening in town, check the local daily, the *St. Augustine Record* (www.staugustine.com), or the irreverent *Folio Weekly* (www.folioweekly.com). Another nighttime activity is taking one of the many ghost tours.

The best-looking and rowdiest crowd in town can be found at the **A1A Ale Works** (p. 559). Twenty-something hipsters and middle-aged partiers mingle at this New Orleans–style microbrewery and restaurant. You'll find live music Thursday through Saturday at the bar—usually light rock and R&B tunes.

Ann O'Malley's, 23 Orange St., near the Old City Gate (© 904/825-4040), is an Irish pub that's open until 1am. Besides the selection of ales, stouts, and drafts, this is one of the only spots in town where you can grab a late-night bite.

Also popular with locals, Mill Top Tavern, 19½ St. George St., at the Fort (© 904/829-2329), is a warm and rustic tavern housed in a 19th-century mill building (the water wheel is still outside). Weather permitting, it's an open-air space. There's music here every day from 1pm to 1am.

At Scarlett O'Hara's, 70 Hypolita St., at Cordova Street (© 904/824-6535; www.scarlettoharas.net), a catacomb of cozy rooms with working fireplaces in a rambling, 19th-century wood-frame house, is the setting for everything from DJs and karaoke to live music. Sporting events are aired on a large-screen TV.

Across the river, the Gypsy Bar & Grill, part of the Gypsy Cab Co. restaurant (p. 559), 828 Anastasia Blvd. (© 904/824-8244), often has live music, as well as a comedy club next door.

4 Jacksonville

36 miles S of the Georgia border, 134 miles NE of Orlando, 340 miles N of Miami

Once infamous for its smelly paper mills, the sprawling metropolis of Jacksonville—residents call it "Jax," from its airport abbreviation—is now one of the South's insurance and banking capitals. Development was rampant throughout Duval County during the 1990s, with hotels, restaurants, attractions, and clubs springing up, especially in suburban areas near the interstate highways. Aside from that, there are 20 miles of Atlantic Ocean beaches upon which to sun and swim, championship golf courses, and an abundance of beautiful and historic national and state parks to roam.

Spanning the broad, curving St. Johns River, downtown Jacksonville is a vibrant center of activity during weekdays and on weekend afternoons and evenings, when many locals head to the restaurants and bars of Jacksonville Landing and Southbank Riverwalk, two dining-and-entertainment complexes facing each other across the river that have helped revitalize downtown.

ESSENTIALS

GETTING THERE   Jacksonville International Airport, on the city's north side about 12 miles from downtown (© 904/741-2000; www.jaxairports.org), is served by Air Canada (© 888/247-2262), AirTran (© 800/247-8726), American (© 800/433-7300), Continental (© 800/525-0280), Delta (© 800/221-1212), Midway (© 800/446-4392), Northwest (© 800/225-2525), Southwest (© 800/435-9792), United (© 800/241-6522), and Metro Jet and US Airways (© 800/428-4322).

Alamo (© 800/327-9633), Avis (© 800/331-1212), Budget (© 800/527-0700), Dollar (© 800/800-4000), Enterprise (© 800/325-8007), Hertz (© 800/654-3131), and National (© 800/227-7368) have rental-car booths at the airport.

Gator City Taxi (© 904/741-0008 at the airport, or 904/355-8294 elsewhere) provides cab service. Fares for up to four persons are about $20 to downtown, $40 to $45 to beach hotels, $55 to $65 to St. Augustine, and $40 to Amelia Island. Express Shuttle (© 904/353-8880) provides van service to and from hotels and resorts throughout the area. Per-person fares are about $17 to downtown Jacksonville, $22 to $28 to the beaches, $57 to $67 to St. Augustine, and $35 to Amelia Island.

There's an Amtrak station in Jacksonville at 3570 Clifford Lane, off U.S. 1, just north of 45th Street (© 800/USA-RAIL; www.amtrak.com).

Fun Fact **Once a Cow Town**

Although Jacksonville claims to be the capital of Florida's historic "First Coast," the city dates its beginnings from an early-1800s settlement named Cowford because cattle crossed the St. Johns River here. It changed its name in 1822 to honor Gen. Andrew Jackson, who had forced Spain to cede Florida to the United States 2 years earlier.

VISITOR INFORMATION   Contact the **Jacksonville and the Beaches Convention & Visitors Bureau,** 201 E. Adams St., Jacksonville, FL 32202 (© **800/733-2668** or 904/798-9111; fax 904/789-9103; www.jaxcvb.com), for maps, brochures, calendars, and advice. The bureau is open Monday through Friday from 8am to 5pm. It operates an information booth in the upstairs food court of **Jacksonville Landing** (p. 564), open Monday through Saturday from 10am to 7pm, and Sunday from 12:30 to 5:30pm, as well as a walk-in information office in **Jacksonville Beach,** at 403 Beach Blvd., between 3rd and 4th streets (© **904/242-0024**), open Monday through Saturday from 10am to 6pm.

GETTING AROUND   In general, you're better off having a car if you want to explore this vast area. To get around downtown Jacksonville, you can take the **Skyway,** an elevated and completely automated train that runs down Hogan Street from Florida Community College's Jacksonville campus through downtown and across the river via the Acosta/Florida 13 bridge to the Southbank Riverwalk. The Skyway operates Monday through Friday from 6am to 11pm, Saturday from 10am to 11pm, and Sunday only for special events. The fare is 35¢. The **Trolley** connects with the Skyway and runs east-west through downtown, primarily along Bay Street. It's free and operates Monday through Friday from 6:30am to 7pm and Saturday from 8am to 6pm. Get maps and schedules from the visitors bureau or information booths (see above). Both the Skyway and the Trolley are operated by the **Jacksonville Transportation Authority** (© **904/630-3181;** www.jtaonthemove.com), which also provides local bus service.

You can hail a cab downtown if you spot one, though it's usually best to call **Gator City Taxi** (© **904/355-8294**) or **Yellow Cab** (© **904/260-1111**) for a pickup. Fares are $1.75 when the flag drops and 25¢ for each ⅕ mile thereafter.

Out at the beaches, the **St. Johns River Ferry** (© **904/241-9969;** www.stjohns riverferry.com) shuttles vehicles across the river between Mayport, an Old Florida fishing village on the south side, and Fort George, on the north shore. The boats run daily; times vary, so call for the current schedule. One-way fare is $3.25 per two-axle private vehicle, $1 per pedestrian or bicyclist. Even if you have to wait 30 minutes for the next ferry, the 5-minute ride greatly shortens the trip between the Jacksonville beaches and Amelia Island.

EXPLORING THE AREA

Cummer Museum of Art & Gardens *★★*   Built on the grounds of a private Tudor mansion, this modestly sized but impressive museum is worth a visit for anyone who appreciates the visual arts. The permanent collection encompasses works from 2000 B.C. to the present. It's especially rich in American Impressionist paintings, 18th-century porcelain, and 18th-century Japanese woodblock prints. Personally, I find the art here a bit boring and too focused on landscapes, but that's my taste.

Jacksonville

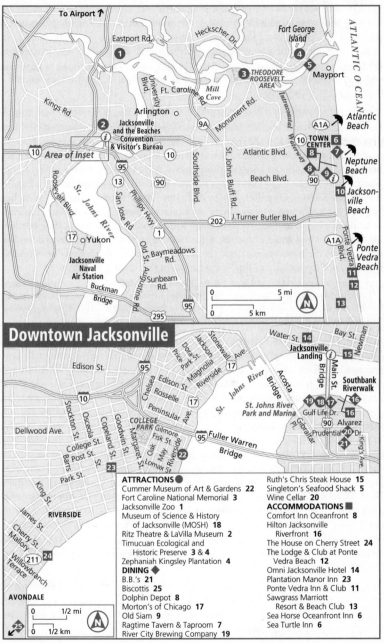

To Airport ↑

Eastport Rd. **1**

Heckscher Dr.

Fort George Island

4

5 Mayport

Kings Rd.

University Blvd.

Ft. Caroline Rd.

Mill Cove

3 THEODORE ROOSEVELT AREA

Arlington

Jacksonville and the Beaches Convention & Visitor's Bureau

2

9A

Monument Rd.

Southside Blvd.

St. Johns Bluff Rd.

Atlantic Blvd.

A1A

10 TOWN CENTER **6**

8 **7**

8 **9**

90

10 Jackson-ville Beach

Atlantic Beach

Neptune Beach

Roosevelt Blvd.

10 Area of Inset

95

San Jose Rd.

Phillips Hwy.

13

90

Beach Blvd.

St. Johns River

17 Yukon

Jacksonville Naval Air Station

Old St. Augustine Rd.

1

Baymeadows Rd.

Sunbeam Rd.

J.Turner Butler Blvd.

202

A1A

Ponte Vedra Blvd.

Ponte Vedra Beach

11

12

Buckman Bridge

95

295

0 — 5 mi
0 — 5 km

N

13

Downtown Jacksonville

Stonewall St.

Jackson St.

Dora St.

Price St.

Park St.

Magnolia St.

Riverside Ave.

17

Water St. **14**

Bay St.

Newman

Jacksonville Landing **15**

Edison St.

95

Chelsea St.

Edison St.

Rosselle St.

Peninsular Ave.

17

St. Johns River

Acosta Bridge

Main St.

Southbank Riverwalk

10

Stockton St.

Osceola St.

Copeland St.

Goodwin St.

COLLEGE PARK

Gilmore St.

Fisk St.

Margaret St.

Oak St.

May St.

Lomax St.

Riverside Ave.

95

Fuller Warren Bridge

St. Johns River Park and Marina

Gulf Life Dr.

Gibraltar Pl.

19 **18** **17**

16

16

90 Alvarez

Prudential **20** Dr.

King's Ave.

21

Dellwood Ave.

College St.

Post St.

Park St.

Barrs St.

22

23

King St.

RIVERSIDE

James St.

Cherry St.

Mallory St.

Willowbranch Terrace

24

211

AVONDALE

0 — 1/2 mi
0 — 1/2 km

N

25

ATTRACTIONS ●
Cummer Museum of Art & Gardens **22**
Fort Caroline National Memorial **3**
Jacksonville Zoo **1**
Museum of Science & History
  of Jacksonville (MOSH) **18**
Ritz Theatre & LaVilla Museum **2**
Timucuan Ecological and
  Historic Preserve **3** & **4**
Zephaniah Kingsley Plantation **4**
DINING ◆
B.B.'s **21**
Biscottis **25**
Dolphin Depot **8**
Morton's of Chicago **17**
Old Siam **9**
Ragtime Tavern & Taproom **7**
River City Brewing Company **19**

Ruth's Chris Steak House **15**
Singleton's Seafood Shack **5**
Wine Cellar **20**
ACCOMMODATIONS ■
Comfort Inn Oceanfront **8**
Hilton Jacksonville
  Riverfront **16**
The House on Cherry Street **24**
The Lodge & Club at Ponte
  Vedra Beach **12**
Omni Jacksonville Hotel **14**
Plantation Manor Inn **23**
Ponte Vedra Inn & Club **11**
Sawgrass Marriott
  Resort & Beach Club **13**
Sea Horse Oceanfront Inn **6**
Sea Turtle Inn **6**

Frankly—and art snobs may gasp at this statement—the landscaping of the museum is infinitely more spectacular. Don't miss the stunning Italian and English gardens set on the scenic St. Johns River. The museum hosts temporary and traveling exhibits, and sponsors a multitude of activities during the year, so call ahead to see what's happening.

829 Riverside Ave. (between Post and Fisk sts.). © **904/356-6857.** www.cummer.org. Admission $8 adults, $5 seniors over 65 and military, $5 students and children under 5; free Tues after 4pm. Tues and Thurs 10am–9pm; Wed and Fri–Sat 10am–5pm; Sun noon–5pm.

Jacksonville Landing   Resembling New York City's South Street Seaport, Boston's Faneuil Hall, Miami's Bayside, and Baltimore's Inner Harbor, this glass-and-steel complex on the north bank of the river serves as the focus of downtown activity. Yeah, you may see a mime or two occasionally, and there's a Hooters, a Ruby Tuesday, and a Starbucks, but there's also amazing local live music, good non-chain sushi, and Thai and Mexican restaurants. This complex is not just for tourists—it's command central for many locals looking for a lively day or night out. There are more than 65 stores here, but shopping is secondary to dining and entertainment. Choose from full-service restaurants, plus an inexpensive food court with indoor and outdoor seating overlooking the river. The Landing hosts numerous special events, from arts festivals to baseball-card shows, plus outdoor rock, blues, country, and jazz concerts on weekends. Call or check the website to find out what's going on during your stay.

2 Independent Dr. (between Main and Pearl sts.), on the St. Johns River. © **904/353-1188.** www.jacksonvillelanding. com. Free admission. Mon–Thurs 10am–8pm; Fri–Sat 10am–9pm; Sun noon–5:30pm; bars and restaurants open later. From I-95, take exit 107 downtown to Main St., go over the Blue Bridge, and turn left at Bay St. Then go 2 blocks and make a left on Laura St., which dead-ends at the Landing. Park on east side of complex.

Jacksonville Zoo and Gardens ⚜ *Kids*   Another city, another zoo. But this isn't just any zoo. Located between downtown and the airport, this environmentally sensitive zoo is well on its way to becoming one of the Southeast's best. While the zoo's Wild Florida area presents local fauna—including black bears, red wolves, Florida panthers, and alligators—the main exhibits feature an extensive and growing collection of lions, rhinos, elephants, antelopes, cheetahs, western lowland gorillas, and other African wildlife. You'll enter the 73-acre park through an authentic thatched roof built in 1995 by 24 Zulu craftsmen. Whether you go on foot or by tram, allow at least 3 hours to tour this vast zoo. Upon your arrival, ask about current animal shows and special events. Strollers and wheelchairs are available for rent. Range of the Jaguar focuses on a neotropical rainforest setting that can be found in Central or South America. Although this attraction spotlights the jaguar, you will also see other animals such as golden lion tamarins, tapirs, capybaras, giant river otters, anteaters, and a variety of bird, amphibian, fish, and reptile species, including the anaconda.

8605 Zoo Pkwy. © **904/757-4462** or 904/757-4463. www.jaxzoo.org. Admission $11 adults, $9.50 seniors, $6.50 children 3–12, free for children under 3. Daily 9am–5pm. Closed Thanksgiving and Christmas. Take I-95 N. to Hecksher Dr. (exit 124A) and follow the signs.

Ritz Theatre & LaVilla Museum   From 1921 to 1971, the Ritz Theatre was the center of cultural life in LaVilla, an African-American neighborhood so vibrant that it was known as the Harlem of the South. Many entertainers played the Ritz before moving on to the Apollo Theater in the real Harlem. Most of LaVilla's small clapboard "shotgun" houses (so called because you could fire a shotgun through the central hallway to the back room and not hit anything) have been torn down in anticipation of urban renewal, but the Ritz has been rebuilt and is once again a center of the city's cultural life. Only the northwest corner of the building, including the Ritz sign, is original, but the new 426-seat theater captures the spirit of vaudevillian times. Off the lobby, LaVilla Museum recounts local African-American history and exhibits the works of black artists.

829 N. Davis St. (between State and Union sts.). ℂ **904/632-5555.** Admission $6 adults, $3 seniors and children under 18. Tues–Fri 10am–6pm; Sat 10am–2pm; Sun 2–5pm. From downtown, take Main St. north, turn left (west) on State St. to theater and museum on Davis St.

Southbank Riverwalk *Kids*   Bordering the St. Johns River, directly opposite Jacksonville Landing (see above), this 1¼-mile wooden zigzag boardwalk is usually filled with joggers, tourists, folks sitting on benches, and lovers walking hand-in-hand, all of them watching the riverboats, the shorebirds, and downtown's skyline reflected in the water. At 200 feet in diameter, the **Friendship Fountain,** near the west end, is the nation's largest self-contained fountain; it's especially beautiful at night when illuminated by 265 colored lights. Nearby, you'll pass military memorials, a small museum dedicated to the city's history, and the **Museum of Science & History of Jacksonville (MOSH),** at Museum Circle and San Marco Boulevard (ℂ **904/396-6674;** www.themosh.org). MOSH is an interactive children's museum focusing on the science and history of Northeast Florida. One of its stars is an Allosaurus dinosaur skeleton. It also has a small planetarium, with shows included in museum admission: $8 for adults, $6.50 for seniors, and $6 for children 3 to 12. The museum is open Monday through Friday from 10am to 5pm, Saturday from 10am to 6pm, and Sunday from 1 to 6pm. The Riverwalk is the scene of special MOSH programs, seafood fests, parties, parades, and arts-and-crafts festivals.

On the south bank of St. Johns River, flanking Main St. Bridge between San Marco Blvd. and Ferry St. ℂ **904/396-4900.** Take I-95 N. to Prudential Dr. exit, make a right, and follow the signs.

AN UNUSUAL BREED OF NATIONAL PARK

Named after the American Indians who inhabited Central and North Florida some 1,000 years before European settlers arrived, the **Timucuan Ecological and Historic Preserve** offers visitors an opportunity to explore untouched wilderness, historic buildings, and informative exhibits on the area's natural history. Unusual for a national park, this 46,000-acre preserve hasn't been hacked off from the rest of the community and drawn within arbitrary boundaries. The result is a vast, intriguing system of sites joined by rural roads alongside tumbledown fish camps, trailer parks, strip malls, condominiums, and stately old homes.

Entry to all park facilities is free (though donations are accepted). The visitor centers at Fort Caroline National Memorial and Zephaniah Kingsley Plantation (see below) are open daily from 9am to 5pm, except New Year's Day, Thanksgiving, and Christmas. The Theodore Roosevelt Area is open daily from 7am to 8pm during daylight saving time and daily from 7am to 5pm during standard time, and is closed for Christmas.

SOUTH OF THE RIVER

The preserve's prime attractions are 14 miles northeast of downtown on the south bank of the St. Johns River. Your starting point is the **Fort Caroline National Memorial** ✯, 12713 Ft. Caroline Rd. (ℂ **904/641-7155;** www.nps.gov/timu), which serves as the preserve's visitor center. This was the site of the 16th-century French Huguenot settlement that was wiped out by the Spanish who landed at St. Augustine. This two-thirds-size replica shows you what the original was like. You can see archaeological artifacts and two well-produced half-hour videos highlighting the area as well.

The fort sits at the northwestern edge of the 600-acre **Theodore Roosevelt Area,** a beautiful woodland and marshland rich in history that has been undisturbed since the Civil War. On a 2-mile hike along a centuries-old park trail, you'll see a wide variety of birds, wildflowers, and maritime hammock forest. Bring binoculars, since such birds as endangered wood storks, great and snowy egrets, ospreys, hawks, and painted buntings make their homes here in spring and summer. On the ground, you might catch sight of a gray fox or raccoon. You may also want to bring a picnic basket and blanket to spread beneath the ancient oak trees that shade the banks of the wide and winding St. Johns River. After the trail crosses Hammock Creek, you're in ancient Timucuan country, where their ancestors lived as far back as 500 B.C. Farther along is the site of a wilderness cabin that belonged to the reclusive brothers Willie and Saxon Browne, who lived without the modern conveniences of indoor plumbing or electricity until the last brother's death in 1960.

If you're here on a weekend, take the fascinating 1½-hour guided tour of the fort and Theodore Roosevelt Area, offered every Saturday and Sunday (when weather and staffing permit). Call the fort for details and schedules.

The **Ribault Monument,** on St. Johns Bluff about ½ mile east of the fort, was erected in 1924 to commemorate the arrival in 1562 of French Huguenot Jean Ribault, who died defending Fort Caroline from the Spanish. It's worth a stop for the dramatic view of the area.

To get here from downtown Jacksonville, take Atlantic Boulevard (Fla. 10) east, make a left on Monument Road, and turn right on Fort Caroline Road; the Theodore Roosevelt Area is entered from Mt. Pleasant Road, about 1 mile southeast of the fort (look for the trail-head parking sign and follow the narrow dirt road to the parking lot).

NORTH OF THE RIVER

On the north side of the river, history buffs will appreciate the **Zephaniah Kingsley Plantation** (*, at 11676 Palmetto Ave. on Fort George Island (© **904/251-3537**). A winding 2½-mile dirt road runs under a canopy of dense foliage to the remains of this 19th-century plantation. The National Park Service maintains the well-preserved two-story clapboard residence, kitchen house, barn/carriage house, and remnants of 23 slave cabins built of "tabby mortar"—oyster shell and sand. Exhibits in the main house and kitchen focus on slavery as it existed in the rice-growing areas of Northern Florida, Georgia, and South Carolina. You can see it all on your own, but 40-minute ranger-guided tours are much more informative. They're usually given at 1pm Monday

Escaping Intolerance

Zephaniah Kingsley, the white man who from 1817 to 1829 owned the plantation that is now part of the Timucuan Ecological and Historic Preserve, held some seemingly contradictory views on race. Although he owned more than 200 slaves, he believed that "the coloured race were superior to us, physically and morally." He married a Senegalese woman—one of his former slaves—and in 1837 moved his mixed-race family to what is now the Dominican Republic to escape what he called the "spirit of intolerant injustice" in Florida.

through Friday, 1 and 3pm Saturday and Sunday; call to confirm. Allot time to explore the grounds. The well-stocked book-and-gift shop will keep you even longer. The plantation is open daily from 9am to 5pm, except Christmas Day.

To get here from I-95, take Heckscher Drive (Fla. 105) East and follow the signs. From Fort Caroline, take Florida 9A North over St. Johns River to Heckscher Drive East. The plantation is about 12 miles east of Florida 9A, on the left. From the beaches, take Florida A1A to the St. Johns River Ferry and ride it from Mayport to Fort George; the road to the plantation is ½ mile east of the ferry landing.

HITTING THE BEACH

You can fish, swim, snorkel, sail, sunbathe, or stroll on the sand dunes—at least from March to November, since winter can get downright chilly here. All of these activities are just a 20- to 30-minute drive east of downtown at Jacksonville's four beach communities.

Atlantic Boulevard (Fla. 10) will take you to **Atlantic Beach** and **Neptune Beach.** The boulevard divides the two towns, and where it meets the ocean, you'll come to **Town Center,** a quaint community with shops, restaurants, pubs, and a few inns.

Beach Boulevard (U.S. 90) dead-ends at **Jacksonville Beach,** where you'll find beach concessions, rental shops, and a fishing pier. This is also the most popular local surfing beach.

To the south, J. Turner Butler Boulevard (Fla. 202) leads from I-95 to the boundary between Jacksonville Beach and Ponte Vedra Beach. A right turn there will take you to **Ponte Vedra Beach** (pronounced here as Ponti *Vee-*dra). This ritzy, golf-oriented enclave is actually in St. Johns County (St. Augustine), but it's so much closer to Jacksonville that it's included in this section.

OUTDOOR ACTIVITIES & SPECTATOR SPORTS

CRUISES   Jacksonville River Cruises (© **904/396-2333;** www.rivercruise.com) operates sightseeing, dinner, and dancing cruises on the stern-wheel paddleboats the *Lady St. Johns* and the *Annabelle Lee.* They usually dock at the Radisson Riverwalk Hotel on the Southbank Riverwalk. Cost is $40; schedules vary greatly by season, so call ahead or check the website.

FISHING   The least expensive way to fish for red snapper, grouper, sea bass, small sharks, amberjack, and more, 15 to 30 miles offshore in the Atlantic Ocean, is aboard the *King Neptune,* a 65-foot, air-conditioned deep-sea party boat. The full-day trips depart at 7:30am daily from Monty's Marina, 4378 Ocean St. (Fla. A1A), ½ mile south of the Mayport Ferry landing (© **904/246-7575**); they return at 4:30pm. The price is $60 to $70 per person, including bait and tackle. You don't need a license, but reservations are required.

GOLF   The Jacksonville area offers a great variety of golf courses, some of which are ranked among the top in the country. In Ponte Vedra Beach, the Sawgrass Marriott Resort sits on the most famous course, the **TPC at Sawgrass** ☆☆☆, home of the Players Championship in March. Ranked among the nation's top courses, its island hole is one of the most photographed in the world. Nearby are the Ocean and Lagoon courses at the Ponte Vedra Inn & Club. See "Where to Stay," below, for information on the resorts.

Top courses open to the public include the **Golf Club of Jacksonville,** 10440 Tournament Lane (© **904/779-0800**), which is managed by the PGA Tour. It's a great bargain, with greens fees between $30 and $45. The semiprivate **Cimarrone,**

2690 Cimarrone Blvd. (© **904/287-2000**), is a fast and watery course with greens fees ranging from $30 to $65.

Be on the lookout for the free *Golfer's Guide* in visitor centers and hotel lobbies (see p. 51 for information on how to order a copy).

For course information, go to www.golf.com or www.floridagolfing.com, or call the **Florida Sports Foundation** (© **850/488-8347**) or **Florida Golfing** (© **866/833-2663**).

HORSEBACK RIDING   For lessons or a scenic ride along the dunes, try **Sawgrass Stables,** 23900 Marsh Landing Pkwy., off Florida A1A in Ponte Vedra Beach (© **904/ 285-3791**). Call for rates and reservations.

SPECTATOR SPORTS   The 73,000-seat **Alltel Stadium,** 1 Stadium Place, at East Duval and Haines streets (© **904/353-3309** for tickets), hosts the annual Florida– Georgia football game every October, and other college football games September through December. It's also the home field of the National Football League's **Jacksonville Jaguars** (© **877/452-4784,** or 904/633-2000 for ticket information; www.jaguars.com). One of the stadium's biggest draws is the **Toyota Gator Bowl,** usually held on New Year's Day.

The 16,000-seat **Jacksonville Veterans Memorial Arena,** 300 A. Phillip Randolph Blvd. (© **904/630-3900** for information, or 904/353-3309 for tickets), hosts National Hockey League exhibition games, college basketball games, ice-skating exhibitions, wrestling matches, and family shows.

SHOPPING & BROWSING

Jacksonville has plenty of shopping opportunities, including upscale **The Avenues Mall,** south of town at 10300 Southside Blvd., as well as a number of flea markets. At **Beach Boulevard Flea and Farmers' Market,** on Beach Boulevard/Florida 90 (© **904/645-5961**), more than 600 vendors show up Saturday and Sunday from 9am to 5pm to sell their wares in the partially covered facility. Some booths are open other days of the week as well.

San Marco Square, at San Marco and Atlantic boulevards, south of the river, is a quaint shopping district in the middle of a stunning residential area. Shops housed in meticulously refashioned Mediterranean Revival buildings sell antiques and home furnishings, in addition to clothing, books, and records.

Another worthwhile neighborhood to explore is the **Avondale/Riverside** historic district, southwest of downtown on St. Johns Avenue between Talbot Avenue and Boone Park, on the north bank of the river. More than 60 boutiques, antiques stores, art galleries, and cafes line the wide, tree-lined avenue.

Nearby, the younger set hangs out at **Five Points,** on Park Street at Avondale Avenue, where used-record stores, vintage clothiers, coffee shops, and funky galleries stay open late.

Like St. Augustine, Jacksonville is a mecca for chocoholics. If you've never tried chocolate-covered popcorn or pretzels, **Peterbrooke Chocolatier Production Center,** 1470 San Marco Blvd., on San Marco Square (© **904/398-2489;** www.peterbrooke.com), is the place if you're up for the experience. It's open Monday through Friday from 10am to 5pm. Peterbrooke also has a retail shop on St. Johns Avenue in Avondale.

WHERE TO STAY

Because Jacksonville hasn't yet made it onto the hip list, there are no boutique hotels in the city—yet. Instead, you have a choice of either a large chain hotel a la Hilton or Omni or, preferably, a much cozier, more charming bed-and-breakfast.

The accommodations listed below are arranged geographically, in and around downtown first, followed by the beach scene. The suburbs have dozens more options to choose from, especially along I-95. Many are clustered south of downtown in the **Southpoint** (exit 101, Turner Butler Blvd./Fla. 202) and **Baymeadows** (exit 101, Baymeadows Rd./Fla. 152) areas. These locales have a multitude of chain restaurants, and you can hop on the highways and zoom to the beach or downtown.

Rates in the downtown hotels are higher midweek, when rooms are in demand by business travelers. Beach accommodations are somewhat less expensive in the colder months from December to March.

Note: Hotel taxes in the area tack on an additional 12% to 14%!

IN JACKSONVILLE

Prudential Drive in the Southbank Riverwalk area is home to the **Radisson Riverwalk Hotel** (© 800/333-3333 or 904/396-5100), the **Hampton Inn Central** (© 800/426-7866 or 904/396-7770), and the all-suites **Extended Stay America Downtown** (© 800/398-7829 or 904/396-1777; www.extendedstay.com).

Hilton Jacksonville Riverfront 𝒜   Set on the Southbank Riverwalk, this 10-story tower is famous for its Elvis Presley Suite, where the King purportedly stayed half a dozen times between 1955 and 1976 when this establishment was known as the Jacksonville Hotel. Funny, but it still looks as if it's steeped in the 1970s. People don't seem to mind, though. If you can afford its $300-a-night price tag, you will see some of Elvis's million-seller gold records mounted on the walls—and then you can watch his movies on one of the suite's two VCRs. It and the other units have dark-wood furniture and smallish marble bathrooms. Riverfront rooms have balconies (those on the west end catch traffic noise from the Main St. Bridge). A branch of Ruth's Chris Steak House offers extraordinarily tender beef.

1201 Riverplace Blvd. (at Main St. on Southbank Riverwalk), Jacksonville, FL 32207. © 800/445-8667 or 904/398-8800. Fax 904/398-9170. www.jacksonvillehilton.com. 292 units. $109–$300 double. AE, DC, DISC, MC, V. Self-parking $8; valet parking $10. **Amenities:** 2 restaurants; 2 bars; heated outdoor pool; exercise room; Jacuzzi; concierge; business center; limited room service; laundry service; concierge-level rooms. *In room:* A/C, TV, dataport, coffeemaker, hair dryer, iron.

The House on Cherry Street 𝒜𝒜   This colonial-style wood-frame house, on the St. Johns River in the Riverside neighborhood, is ideal for a romantic vacation. French doors open onto a delightful screened-in porch furnished with rocking chairs; it overlooks an expanse of tree-shaded lawn (where guests play croquet) leading to the river (where they play with kayaks and canoes). You might go for the Rose Room or the Duck Room, each with canopied four-poster bed and river view. Ducks are rather a theme here, with hundreds of antique decoys on display. All units offer adjacent sitting rooms, private bathrooms, ceiling fans, and fresh flowers. No smoking is permitted inside. This place gets booked up fast, so make reservations as early as possible.

1844 Cherry St. (on St. Johns River), Jacksonville, FL 32205. © 904/384-1999. Fax 904/384-5013. www.geocities.com/houseoncherryst/. 4 units. $105–$115 double. Rates include full breakfast. AE, MC, V. No small children accepted. **Amenities:** Free use of bikes, canoes, and kayaks. *In room:* A/C, TV, hair dryer, no phone.

Omni Jacksonville Hotel 𝒜   Located directly across the street from the Times-Union Center for the Performing Arts (p. 575) and a block west of Jacksonville Landing, the Omni enjoys a more convenient location than the Hilton across the river. It caters primarily to a corporate clientele that fills the meeting facilities during the week. Most rooms are of moderate size, with the pick of the litter being the Florida suites, which have sitting areas with river or city views. The pool is on the rooftop overlooking the river. Reasonably priced Juliette's Restaurant & Bistro provides a locally famous pasta bar.

245 Water St. (between Pearl and Hogan sts.), Jacksonville, FL 32202. © **800/843-6664** or 904/355-6664. Fax 904/791-4809. www.omnihotels.com. 354 units. $139–$219 double. Weekend rates available. AE, DC, DISC, MC, V. Valet and self-parking $12. Pets accepted ($50 fee). **Amenities:** Restaurant; bar; heated outdoor pool; small exercise room; Jacuzzi; concierge; business center; limited room service; laundry service; concierge-level rooms. *In room:* A/C, TV, dataport, minibar, coffeemaker, hair dryer, iron.

Plantation Manor Inn 🏵🏵 The setting for many weddings and special events, this plantation-style B&B in the historic Riverside district is blocks from the river, 10 minutes from downtown, and a short drive to Avondale's shopping and dining. Its homey interior features a mix of thrift-store antiques, glossy pine floors, gorgeous cypress paneling, wainscoting, and carved moldings. Breakfast, which includes freshly baked muffins and breads, is served in a lovely dining room with a working fireplace. If the sun is shining, take your morning meal on the brick patio, a delightful setting with ivy-covered walls, flower beds, and garden furnishings under the shade of a massive oak tree. The patio also contains a lap pool and whirlpool spa. On the second floor, you can enjoy a big wraparound porch with seating amid potted geraniums, hibiscus, and bougainvillea. All but one of the rooms here have shower-only bathrooms.

1630 Copeland St. (between Oak and Park sts.), Jacksonville, FL 32204. © **904/384-4630.** Fax 904/387-0960. www.plantationmanorinn.com. 9 units. $150–$180 double. Rates include full breakfast. AE, DC, MC, V. **Amenities:** Outdoor pool; Jacuzzi. *In room:* A/C, TV, hair dryer, iron.

AT THE BEACHES

A dozen modest hotels line Jacksonville Beach's 1st Street, along the Atlantic. Completely renovated in 1998, the **Comfort Inn Oceanfront,** 1515 N. 1st St., 2 blocks east of Florida A1A (© **800/654-8776** or 904/241-2311; fax 904/249-3830; www.comfortinnjaxbeach.com), is one of the better values. Its rooms have balconies or screened patios, and guests can enjoy a large pool with four rock waterfalls and a palm-fringed deck, a secluded grotto whirlpool, an exercise room, a gift/sundries shop, and a multicourt sand volleyball park.

If you'd like to rent an old-fashioned cottage or a luxurious condominium in the affluent enclave of Ponte Vedra, contact **Ponte Vedra Club Realty,** 280 Ponte Vedra Blvd., Ponte Vedra Beach, FL 32082 (© **800/278-8171** or 904/285-6927; fax 904/285-5218; www.pvclubrealty.com). The company has more than 100 properties in its rental inventory, about 75% of them on the ocean. Its renters get a discount on use of facilities at the Lodge & Club at Ponte Vedra Beach, and at the Ponte Vedra Inn & Club (see below).

The Lodge & Club at Ponte Vedra Beach 🏵🏵🏵 Hello, gorgeous! One of Florida's more romantic hotels, this long two-story, Mediterranean-style building sits along the beach, affording every unit an ocean view from a private balcony or patio. All 66 rooms have been fully refurbished and are the epitome of high-end luxury, with gorgeous artwork, two-person settees recessed in front of windows looking onto the beach, and huge bathrooms with two-person tubs and separate showers. The "preferred" rooms and all of the suites also have gas fireplaces; ceiling fans hang from vaulted ceilings in the upstairs units. The suites come with sleeper sofas and kitchenettes, making them suitable for small families; some have marble-faced fireplaces and French doors as well. Down by the beach, one pool with a hot tub is reserved for couples. Guests here have access to all the facilities at Ponte Vedra Inn & Club (see below), including the spa, the tennis center, and two golf courses. Restricted to guests of the two properties, the bright Innlet Dining Room serves fine Continental cuisine with an ocean view, plus afternoon tea daily in the adjoining lounge, where a pianist performs by the fireplace at night. The poolside Oasis Bar & Grill is open daily in summer and on weekends the rest of the year. *Note:* There is a nightly gratuity charge of $12 per double room for the bellman, doorman, chambermaid, and valet-parking staff, so *don't double-tip.*

607 Ponte Vedra Blvd. (at Corona Rd.), Ponte Vedra Beach, FL 32082. © 800/243-4304 or 904/273-9500. Fax 904/273-0210. www.pvresorts.com. 66 units. Winter $220–$290 double, $340–$390 suite; summer $260–$340 double, $380–$440 suite. Packages available. AE, DC, DISC, MC, V. **Amenities:** 2 restaurants; 2 bars; 3 heated outdoor pools; health club (with lap pool); access to nearby spa; Jacuzzi; sauna; watersports equipment rentals; bike rental; concierge; business center; 24-hr. room service; babysitting; laundry service. *In room:* A/C, TV, fax, dataport, minibar, kitchen (suites only), coffeemaker, hair dryer, iron, safe.

Ponte Vedra Inn & Club ★★   This luxurious 300-acre country club and spa is a great place to pamper yourself between rounds of golf or games of tennis. The inn is ultra-elegant from the moment you drive up to its manicured front lawn, which doubles as a putting green. The gorgeous spa offers oceanview massage, herbal and seaweed wraps, facials, hydrotherapy, and much more. A new three-story building in front of the original 1937 clubhouse contains an expansive lobby downstairs and spacious, upscale guest rooms upstairs. Across the road, the condominiums are located in two-story buildings along the beach. All have furnished patios or balconies and are individually decorated; some have four-poster or sleigh beds. The larger units have full kitchens, and microwaves and small fridges are available upon request. In addition to the inn's two 18-hole golf courses, its excellent tennis center, and its fully equipped gym with six-lane Olympic pool, guests can use the three beachside pools and other facilities at the nearby Lodge & Club at Ponte Vedra Beach (see above). The Island House, a lodging favorite of guests since it was originally built in 1972, was razed in order to make way for a new and modern version: This Island House (opened in 2003) has 28 luxurious rooms and suites, all overlooking the famous Island 9th golf hole and blue lagoons. *Note:* There is a nightly gratuity charge of $12 per double room for the bellman, doorman, chambermaid, and valet-parking staff, so *don't double-tip.*

200 Ponte Vedra Blvd. (off Fla. A1A), Ponte Vedra Beach, FL 32082. © 800/234-7842 or 904/285-1111. Fax 904/285-2111. www.pvresorts.com. 221 units. Winter $180–$290 double, $340–$490 suite; summer $200–$440 double, $380–$640 suite. Packages available. AE, DC, DISC, MC, V. **Amenities:** 3 restaurants; 3 bars; indoor pool; golf courses; tennis courts; health club and spa; watersports equipment rentals; bike rental; children's programs (summer only); concierge; business center; 24-hr. room service; massage; babysitting; laundry service; coin-op washers and dryers. *In room:* A/C, TV, dataport, kitchen (some units), minibar, coffeemaker, hair dryer, iron.

Sawgrass Marriott Resort & Beach Club ★★   Swingers love this hotel. No, not *that* kind of swinger, but rather the kind that emulates Tiger Woods. One of the nation's largest golf resorts, this duffer's paradise is virtually surrounded by 99 holes, including the Pete Dye–designed **TPC at Sawgrass** ★★★, home of the annual Players Championship in March. In fact, this course has appeared on every golf critic's "best of" list since it opened in 1980. Overlooking the TPC's picturesque 13th hole, the seven-story hotel sits beside one of the lakes that make the course so challenging. The view augments the gourmet fusion cuisine served in the Augustine Grille, the hotel's signature restaurant. The guest rooms in the hotel are comfortable but of modest size. Best for families are the fully equipped one- and two-bedroom "villa suites" (condominium apartments) on or near a golf course; these offer large furnished patios or balconies. Especially luxurious are the one- to three-bedroom beachfront units, which sport huge kitchens, living rooms with fireplaces, dining rooms, and large screened decks. A complimentary shuttle takes guests to the oceanside Cabana Beach Club for snacks and meals.

1000 PGA Tour Blvd. (off Fla. A1A between U.S. 210 and J. Turner Butler Blvd.), Ponte Vedra Beach, FL 32082. ✆ 800/228-9290 or 904/285-7777. Fax 904/285-0906. www.sawgrassmarriott.com. 508 units. $109–$135 double; $175–$205 suite. Golf packages available. AE, DC, DISC, MC, V. Valet parking $12; free self-parking. **Amenities:** 6 restaurants; 4 bars; 3 outdoor pools (2 heated); 5 golf courses; 17 tennis courts; 2 health clubs; Jacuzzi; watersports equipment rentals; bike rental; children's programs; game room; concierge; activities desk; business center; limited room service; babysitting; laundry service; coin-op washers and dryers; concierge-level rooms. *In room:* A/C, TV, dataport, kitchen (condos only), minibar, coffeemaker, hair dryer, iron.

Sea Horse Oceanfront Inn *Value*   This old-school beachfront motel offers clean, spacious rooms with ocean views from its balconies and patios. Families will appreciate the six units with kitchenettes, not to mention the big beachfront lawn with pool, shuffleboard, picnic tables, and grill. Others will enjoy proximity to some of Jacksonville's top nightspots. The pool itself boasts a happening watering hole, the Lemon Bar. If you have a large family or group, consider the vast and lovely, recently remodeled third-floor penthouse—it has a big living room and dining area, full kitchen, and separate bedroom as well as sofa beds; the huge balcony is furnished with dining table and chaise longues. Town Center's restaurants and bars are across the street.

120 Atlantic Blvd. (at beach end of Atlantic Blvd.), Neptune Beach, FL 32266. ✆ 800/881-2330 or 904/246-2175. Fax 904/246-4256. www.seahorseoceanfrontinn.com. 39 units. $119–$199 double; $200–$225 penthouse suite for up to 6. AE, DC, DISC, MC, V. **Amenities:** Bar; pool. *In room:* A/C, TV, wireless Internet access, fridge, coffeemaker.

Sea Turtle Inn 🐢   Completely gutted and restored in 1999 and 2000, this elegant eight-story beachfront hotel (whose exterior facade could use some updating to match the lovely interior) is much more upscale than the Sea Horse Oceanfront Inn, which it faces across Atlantic Boulevard. (Despite their shouting-distance proximity, one technically is in Atlantic Beach, the other in Neptune Beach.) The guest units are spacious except for their somewhat cramped bathrooms. The best units, few in number, face the beach and have balconies. Plantains Restaurant is a fine spot for an alfresco beachside meal; it offers live music on weekends. There's also a lounge in the restaurant and a summertime Tiki bar beside the pool by the beach.

1 Ocean Blvd. (at beach end of Atlantic Blvd.), Atlantic Beach, FL 32233. ✆ 800/874-6000 or 904/249-7402. Fax 904/247-1517. www.seaturtle.com. 193 units. $119–$349 double. AE, DC, DISC, MC, V. **Amenities:** Restaurant; 2 bars; outdoor pool; access to nearby health club; watersports equipment rentals; limited room service; babysitting; laundry service; coin-op washers and dryers. *In room:* A/C, TV, fax, dataport, minibar, fridge, coffeemaker, hair dryer, iron.

WHERE TO DINE

The **Jacksonville and the Beaches Convention & Visitors Bureau** (p. 562) puts out an annual guide that contains a complete list of restaurants. For more choices, check listings in the "Shorelines" and "Go" sections of Friday's *Florida Times-Union* (**www.jacksonville.com**) and in *FolioWeekly* (**www.folioweekly.com**), the free local alternative paper available at restaurants, hotels, and nightspots all over town. I've concentrated here on restaurants in downtown Jacksonville and at the beaches.

IN DOWNTOWN JACKSONVILLE

Southbank Riverwalk is the city's up-and-coming mecca for eating out. In addition to B.B.'s and the River City Brewing Company, both reviewed below, the area has riverfront branches of **Ruth's Chris Steak House,** in the Hilton Jacksonville Riverfront, 1201 Riverplace Blvd. (© **904/396-6200**); **Morton's of Chicago,** 1510 Riverplace Blvd. (© **904/399-3933**); and the **Wine Cellar,** 1314 Prudential Dr. (© **904/398-8989**), which offers very good Continental fare and has a wine list to justify its name.

You'll also find a plethora of good cafes and restaurants in the San Marco Square and Avondale neighborhoods, perfect for breaking up your shopping excursions.

Don't forget that on the north side of the river, **Jacksonville Landing** (p. 564) has several full-service restaurants and an inexpensive food court with outdoor seating.

B.B.'s 🌶️🌶️ ECLECTIC   South of the Southbank Riverwalk, this bistro son of Biscottis (see below) is one of the city's hottest restaurants. You'll find local yuppies congregating at the big marble-top bar on one side of the sometimes noisy Art Deco dining room, especially during weekday "wine-downs" featuring beer and wine specials and discounted appetizers (the mozzarella bruschetta is a big hit), from 4 to 7pm. A small but inventive selection of sandwiches, salads, and pizzas is available all day. The nightly specials feature local seafood and run the gamut from roasted sea bass with citrus couscous to seared scallops with lemon grass–scented rice, sun-dried tomatoes, and lobster-flavored butter. Save room for the famous desserts. Saturday brunch sees the likes of yummy Benedict-style crab cakes and flaming bananas Foster.

1019 Hendricks Ave. (between Prudential Dr. and Home St.). © 904/306-0100. Call for priority seating. Main courses $15–$25; sandwiches and salads $5–$10; pizzas $7–$10. AE, DC, DISC, MC, V. Mon–Thurs 11am–10:30pm; Fri 11am–midnight; Sat 10am–midnight (Sat brunch 10am–2pm).

Biscottis 🌶️🌶️ *Value* ECLECTIC   This brick-walled gem in the trendy Avondale neighborhood might easily have come out of New York's East Village. Start your day here (except on Mon) with a pastry and cup of joe. At lunch and dinner, daily specials such as pan-seared tuna or pork loin are always fresh and beautifully presented. The huge and inventive salads are especially good: Try the Asian version with chicken breast, orange slices, roasted peppers, and creamy sesame dressing. Pizzas, too, are served with wonderfully exotic and delicious toppings—ever try guacamole and black beans on your slice? And by all means, don't leave without sampling the wonderful desserts. On warm days, choose a tiny sidewalk table for great people-watching. *Note:* If the wait's too long here, other choices line these 2 blocks of St. Johns Avenue, ranging from a neighborhood diner to expensive haute cuisine.

3556 St. Johns Ave. (between Talbot and Ingleside aves.), Avondale. © 904/387-2060. Main courses $9–$19; sandwiches and salads $5–$8.50; pizzas $7–$8.50. AE, DC, DISC, MC, V. Mon 11am–10pm; Tues–Thurs 7am–10pm; Fri 7am–midnight; Sat 8am–midnight; Sun 8am–3pm.

River City Brewing Company 🌶️🌶️ NEW AMERICAN/LOUISIANA   Occupying a prime location on the Southbank Riverwalk, this gorgeous restaurant and microbrewery has dramatic waterfront and skyline views. For an even better vantage point, sit outside on the enormous covered deck. The quality of the cuisine very nearly lives up to the vista, especially the coconut shrimp with a sweet mandarin-orange sauce. For a main course, try the pretzel-encrusted mahimahi with mustard-cream sauce. While you could easily drop a bundle in the main dining room, you can also devise an inexpensive, simpler meal (burgers and such) in the Brew Haus, a large sports bar that opens onto the deck and the riverbank. Bands play here on weekend evenings. Sunday brunch brings incredible buffets with decadent desserts.

835 Museum Circle (on Southbank Riverwalk). © 904/398-2299. Main courses $15–$18; sandwiches and salads $5–$11; Sun brunch buffet $22 adults, $16 seniors, $12 children 3–12. AE, DC, DISC, MC, V. Dining room Sun–Thurs

11am–3pm and 5–10pm; Fri–Sat 11am–3pm and 5–11pm; Sun 10:30am–2:30pm and 5–10pm. Pub and deck (light fare) Sun–Thurs 3–10pm (bar to midnight); Fri–Sat 3–11pm (bar to 2am). Closed Christmas. Valet parking available on weekends.

AT THE BEACHES

In addition to the Ragtime Tavern & Taproom (see below), you'll find several dining (and drinking) choices in the brick storefronts of **Town Center,** the old-time beach village at the end of Atlantic Boulevard. Among the best is the oceanfront **Plantains,** in the Sea Turtle Inn (p. 572).

Dolphin Depot ☆☆ LOW-COUNTRY CUISINE When it comes to ambience and food, this place is off the charts. Housed in a former gas station, the very rustic, antiques-filled Dolphin Depot provides a Low Country high with such dishes as shrimp and grits, she-crab soup, blackened scallops, and five fresh fish choices daily. Only adding to the restaurant's allure, the staff is Southern-style friendly, and the setting resplendent.

704 1st St. N. ✆ **904/270-1424.** Reservations recommended. Main courses $12–$26. AE, DC, DISC, MC, V. Mon–Thurs 5:30–10pm; Fri–Sat 5:30pm–midnight; Sun 5:30–9pm.

Old Siam ☆☆ THAI The best of several Thai restaurants here, this sophisticated little cafe serves fine cuisine and a good selection of wines to match the fare's spicy yet subtle flavors. The signature dish is a seafood special: shrimp, sea scallops, mussels, squid, and crab claws in a red-chile sauce accented with sweet basil. The "number three" spice level (out of six) touches the tongue but won't overwhelm the other seasonings. Standard favorites such as pad Thai are perfectly balanced with sweet and slightly sour fish sauce.

1716 N. 3rd St. (Fla. A1A, in Holiday Plaza shopping center, between 16th and 17th aves. N.), Jacksonville Beach. ✆ **904/247-7763.** Main courses $10–$23. AE, DISC, MC, V. Mon–Thurs 5–10pm; Fri–Sat 5–11pm; Sun 5–9:30pm.

Ragtime Tavern & Taproom ☆☆ SEAFOOD/CAJUN In the heart of Town Center, this lively sister of St. Augustine's A1A Ale Works (p. 559) offers six hand-crafted brews, including a refreshing pilsner known as Dolphin's Breath. You can imbibe at one of two bars on either end of the building. In between, a rabbit warren of dining rooms provides fine enough fare to keep it filled with local professionals right through the cool winter months. Try the conch fritters or the coconut shrimp as an appetizer. For a main course, choose from seared sesame-coated yellowfin tuna (the best dish here if you like rare fish) or several other treatments of fish, shrimp, chicken, and pasta. Save room for New Orleans–style beignets for dessert. Also from the Big Easy, po'boy sandwiches are served at all hours. Good local bands play here Thursday through Sunday evenings.

207 Atlantic Blvd. (at 1st Ave.), Atlantic Beach. ✆ **904/241-7877.** Call to get on waiting list. Main courses $12–$22; sandwiches and salads $6–$8. AE, DC, DISC, MC, V. Sun–Thurs 11am–10:30pm; Fri–Sat 11am–11pm (bar open later).

Singleton's Seafood Shack ☆☆ ⓥ𝘢𝘭𝘶𝘦 SEAFOOD This rustic fish camp has been serving every imaginable kind of fresh-off-the-boat seafood since 1969. And rustic it is, constructed primarily of unpainted, well-weathered plywood nailed to two-by-fours. Unlike most other fish camps that tend to overwork the deep fryer, here the fried standbys such as conch fritters, shrimp, clam strips, oysters, and squid retain their seafood taste! Singleton's also offers other preparations, such as blackened mahimahi and Cajun shrimp. Best bets at lunch are the fried shrimp or oyster po'boy sandwiches covered in crispy onion rings. At dinner, your Styrofoam plate will come stacked with a choice of sides such as black beans and rice, marvelous horseradish-y coleslaw, fries, and hush puppies. There's a selection of chicken dishes, too, but stick to the seafood.

4728 Ocean St. (Fla. A1A, at St. Johns River Ferry landing), Mayport. (© **904/246-4442**. Main courses $10–$18; sandwiches $2–$7. AE, DISC, MC, V. Sun–Thurs 10am–9pm; Fri–Sat 10am–10pm.

JACKSONVILLE AFTER DARK

In addition to the spots recommended below, check the listings in the "Shorelines" and "Go" sections of Friday's *Florida Times-Union* (**www.jacksonville.com**) and *Folio Weekly* (**www.folioweekly.com**), the free local alternative paper available all over town. Another source is **www.jaxevents.com**.

THE PERFORMING ARTS   Jacksonville has plenty of seats for concerts, touring Broadway shows, dance companies, and big-name performers at the 73,000-seat **All-tel Stadium,** at East Duval and Haines streets (© **904/630-3900**); the 16,000-seat **Jacksonville Veterans Memorial Arena,** 300 A. Phillip Randolph Blvd. (© **904/ 630-3900** for information, or 904/353-3309 for tickets); the 4,400-seat **Times-Union Center for the Performing Arts,** 300 Water St., between Hogan and Pearl streets (© **904/630-3900**); and the revitalized **Ritz Theatre** (© **904/632-5555;** p. 564). Call or check the sources above for what's playing.

THE BAR SCENE   You will find several libation options downtown at **Jacksonville Landing** (p. 564), including, if you must, a lively waterfront **Hooters** (© **904/356-5400**), plus free outdoor rock, blues, country, and jazz concerts every Friday and Saturday night except during winter. There's also live music on weekends across the river at the **River City Brewing Company** (p. 573).

Out at Town Center, at the ocean end of Atlantic Boulevard, one of several popular spots is **Ragtime Tavern & Taproom** (p. 574), where local groups play live jazz and blues Wednesday through Sunday nights. On weekends, especially, the place is really jumping and the crowd is young, but it's lively rather than rowdy. Across the street is the **Sun Dog Diner,** 207 Atlantic Blvd. (© **904/241-8221**), with nightly acoustic music and decent diner food. If these don't fit your mood, walk around Town Center until you find something you like.

The **Freebird Café,** 200 N. 1st St. (© **904/246-2473**), is a two-story homage to native Jacksonville band Lynyrd Skynyrd, run by late lead singer Ronnie Van Zant's widow and daughter, and featuring live music 6 nights a week, as well as pretty good nouveau Southern cuisine. Music fans of a different genre shouldn't miss **Stella's Piano Café,** 1521 Margaret St. (© **904/353-2900**), a restaurant housed in an old Victorian home with a second-floor piano bar.

5 Amelia Island ★★

32 miles NE of Jacksonville, 192 miles NE of Orlando, 372 miles N of Miami

Alas, paradise is found on the northernmost barrier island of Florida. With 13 beautiful miles of beach and a quaint Victorian town, Amelia Island is a charming getaway about a 45-minute drive northeast of downtown Jacksonville. Overall, this skinny barrier island, 18 miles long by 3 miles wide, has more in common with the Low Country of Georgia (across Cumberland Sound from here) and South Carolina. In fact, it's more like St. Simons Island in Georgia or Hilton Head Island in South Carolina than other beach resorts in Florida.

Amelia has five distinct personalities. First is its southern end, an exclusive real-estate development built in a forest of twisted, moss-laden live oaks. Here you'll find world-class tennis and golfing at two of Florida's most luxurious resorts. Second is modest **American Beach,** founded in the 1930s so that African Americans would have access to the ocean in this then-segregated part of the country. Today it's a modest, predominantly black community tucked away among all that south-end wealth. Third is the island's middle, a traditional beach community with a mix of affordable motels, cottages, condominiums, and a seaside inn. Fourth is the historic bayside town of **Fernandina Beach** ✦✦✦, which boasts a 50-square-block area of gorgeous Victorian, Queen Anne, and Italianate homes listed on the National Register of Historic Places. And fifth is lovely **Fort Clinch State Park,** which keeps developers from turning the island's northern end into more ritzy resorts.

The town of Fernandina Beach dates from the post–Civil War period, when Union soldiers who had occupied Fort Clinch began returning to the island. In the late 19th century, Amelia's timber, phosphate, and naval-stores industries boomed. Back then, the town was an active seaport, with 14 foreign consuls in residence. You'll see (and occasionally smell) the paper mills that still stand near the small seaport here. The island experienced another economic explosion in the 1970s and 1980s, when real-estate developers built condominiums, cottages, and two big resorts on the island's southern end. In recent years, Fernandina Beach has seen another big boom, this time in bed-and-breakfast establishments.

ESSENTIALS

GETTING THERE   The island is served by **Jacksonville International Airport** (p. 561), 12 miles north of Jacksonville's downtown and 43 miles from the island. Skirting the Atlantic in places, the scenic drive here from downtown Jacksonville is via Florida A1A and the St. Johns River Ferry. The fast, four-lane way is via I-95 North and the Buccaneer Trail (Fla. A1A) East.

VISITOR INFORMATION   For advance information, contact the **Amelia Island–Fernandina Beach–Yulee Chamber of Commerce,** 102 Centre St. (P.O. Box 472), Fernandina Beach, FL 32035 (✆ **800/226-3542** or 904/277-0717; fax 904/261-6997; www.ameliaisland.org). The chamber's visitor center, in the rustic train station at the bay end of Centre Street, is open Monday through Friday from 9am to 5pm, and Saturday from 10am to 2pm.

GETTING AROUND   There's no public transportation on this 13-mile-long island, so you'll need a vehicle. An informative and entertaining way to tour the historic district is a 30-minute ride with **Old Towne Carriage Company** (✆ **904/277-1555**), whose horse-drawn carriages leave from the waterfront on Centre Street between 6:30 and 9pm. Advance reservations are essential. Rides cost $15 for adults and $7.50 for kids under 13, with a minimum of $55 per ride. The carriage company closes from November to April, when the horses get a much-deserved rest.

Another excellent way to see the town is on a walking tour sponsored by the Amelia Island Museum of History (p. 579).

HITTING THE BEACH

Thanks to a reclamation project, the widest beaches here are at the exclusive enclave on the island's southern third. Even if you aren't staying at one of the swanky resorts here, you can enjoy this section of beach at **Peters Point Beach Front Park,** on Florida A1A, north of the Ritz-Carlton. The park has picnic shelters and restrooms.

Amelia Island

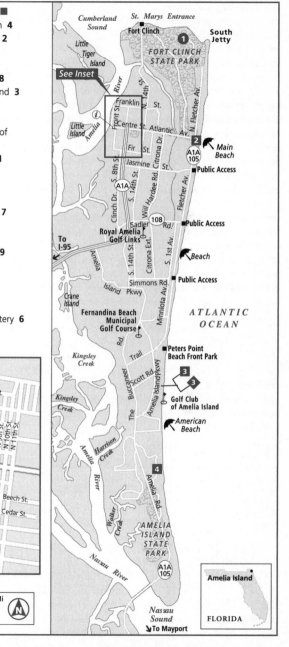

ACCOMMODATIONS ■
Amelia Island Plantation **4**
Elizabeth Pointe Lodge **2**
Fairbanks House **12**
Florida House Inn **10**
Hampton Inn & Suites **8**
Ritz-Carlton Amelia Island **3**

ATTRACTIONS ●
Amelia Island Museum of
 History **13**
Fort Clinch State Park **1**

DINING ◆
Beech Street Grill **11**
Brett's Waterway Cafe **7**
Florida House Inn **10**
The Grill **3**
Joe's 2nd Street Bistro **9**
Le Clos **9**
Marina Restaurant **7**

NIGHTLIFE ★
O'Kane's Irish Pub & Eatery **6**
Palace Saloon **5**

577

North of the resort, the beach has public-access points with free parking every ¼ mile or so. The center of activity is **Main Beach,** at the ocean end of Atlantic Avenue (Fla. A1A), with good swimming, restrooms, picnic shelters, showers, a food concession, a playground, and lots of free parking. This area is popular with families.

The beach at **Fort Clinch State Park** 🌊🌊, which wraps around the island's heavily forested northern end, is backed by rolling dunes and is filled with shells and driftwood. A jetty and pier jutting into Cumberland Sound are popular with anglers. There are showers and changing rooms at the pier. Elsewhere in the park, you might see an alligator—and certainly some of the 170 species of birds that live here—by hiking the Willow Pond nature trail. Rangers lead nature tours on the trail, usually beginning at 10:30am on Saturday. There are also 6 miles of off-road bike trails here. Construction on the remarkably well-preserved **Fort Clinch** began in 1847 on the northern tip of the island and was still underway when Union troops occupied it in 1862. The fort was abandoned shortly after the Civil War, except for a brief reactivation in 1898 during the Spanish-American War. Re-enactors gather the first full weekend of each month to re-create how the Union soldiers lived in the fort in 1864 (including wearing their wool underwear, even in summer!). Rangers are on duty at the fort year-round, and they lead candlelight tours ($3 per person) on Friday and Saturday evenings during summer, beginning about an hour after sunset. You can arrange guided tours at other times for an extra fee. The park entrance is on Atlantic Avenue near the beach. Entrance fees are $5 per vehicle with up to eight occupants, $1 per pedestrian or bicyclist. Admission to the fort costs $2, free for children under 5. The park is open daily from 8am to sunset; the fort, daily from 9am to 5pm. For a schedule of tours and events, contact the park at 2601 Atlantic Ave., Fernandina Beach, FL 32034 (© **904/277-7274;** www.floridastateparks.org/fortclinch).

The park also has 62 **campsites**—some behind the dunes at the beach (no shade out there), most in a forest along the sound side. They cost $22 per night, including tax. Pets are an extra $2 per night. You can reserve a site up to 11 months in advance (a very good idea in summer) by calling © **800/326-3521** or going to www.reserveamerica.com.

Pets on leashes are allowed on all of the island's public beaches and in Fort Clinch State Park.

OUTDOOR ACTIVITIES

BOATING, FISHING, SAILING & KAYAKING   The **Amelia Island Charter Boat Association** (© **800/229-1682** or 904/261-2870), at Tiger Point Marina on 14th Street, north of the historic district (though the boats dock at Centre St.), can help arrange deep-sea fishing charters, party-boat excursions, and dolphin-watching and sightseeing cruises. Other charter boats also dock at Fernandina Harbor Marina, downtown at the foot of Centre Street.

Windward Sailing School, based at Fernandina Harbor Marina, 3977 1st Ave. (© **904/261-9125;** www.windwardsailing.com), will teach you to skipper your boat; it also has charters and boat rentals. Call for details and reservations.

You have to be careful in the currents, but the backwaters here are great for kayaking, whether you're a beginner or a pro. However, you'll have to travel just off the island to do it. Ray and Jody Hetchka's **Kayak Amelia** 🌊🌊 (© **888/305-2925** or 904/251-0016; www.kayakamelia.com) is based near Talbot Island State Park (technically in Jacksonville) and offers beginner and advanced-level trips on back bays, creeks, and marshes. Half-day trips go for about $55 per person. Reservations are required.

GOLF If you're not staying in a resort with a golf course (see "Where to Stay," below, and note that these courses can be extremely expensive), try the new 18-hole **Royal Amelia Golf Links** (© 904/491-8500) for $110 a person, or the older and less expensive 27-hole **Fernandina Municipal Golf Course** (© 904/277-7370), where prices are $20 to $49.

For course information, go to www.golf.com or www.floridagolfing.com, or call the **Florida Sports Foundation** (© 850/488-8347) or **Florida Golfing** (© 866/833-2663).

HORSEBACK RIDING You can go riding on the beach with the **Kelly Seahorse Ranch** (© 904/491-5166; www.kellyranchinc.com), located on the southernmost tip of Amelia Island within the Amelia Island State Park. The cost is $50 per person for a 1-hour ride; the ranch is open daily from 8am to 6pm. Reservations are required. *Note:* Riders must be 13 or older, measure 4½ feet tall, and weigh less than 230 pounds. No experience is necessary.

AN OLD JAIL TURNED HISTORIC MUSEUM

Amelia Island Museum of History 🌊 Housed in the old Nassau County jail, built of brick in 1878, this award-winning local museum explains Amelia Island's fascinating history, from Timucuan Indian times through its possession by France, Spain, Great Britain, the United States, and the Confederacy. Only an upstairs photo gallery is open for casual inspection, so plan to take the 1-hour, 15-minute docent-led tour of the newly remodeled ground floor if you want to get the most out of this museum.

The museum also offers excellent **walking tours** of historic Centre Street on Thursday and Friday September through June. These depart at 3pm from the chamber of commerce (p. 576) and cost $10 for adults, $5 for students. You can't make a reservation; just show up. Longer tours of the entire 50-square-block historic district can be arranged with 24-hour notice; these cost $10 per person, with a minimum of four persons required.

233 S. 3rd St. (between Beech and Cedar sts.). © **904/261-7378**. www.ameliaislandmuseumofhistory.org. Admission by donation. Tours $5 adults, $3 students. Mon–Sat 10am–4pm. Tours Mon–Sat 11am and 2pm.

SHOPPING

Stroll down **Centre Street** in downtown Fernandina Beach, with its vintage storefronts and charming boutiques. Quality antiques shops, consignment shops, and bookstores line the wide boulevard ending at the marina. Be sure to go around the corner and poke your head into the **Island Art Association Gallery,** 18 N. 2nd St. (© 904/261-7020), a co-op exhibiting works by local artists.

On the south end of the island on Florida A1A, **Palmetto Walk,** under a canopy of live oaks; and the **Village Shops,** at the entrance to the Amelia Island Plantation (© 877/624-1854), are other good shopping bets.

WHERE TO STAY

More than two dozen of the town's charming Victorian and Queen Anne houses have been restored and turned into B&Bs. For a complete list, contact the chamber of

---

⌜Fun Fact⌝ Did You Know?

The 1988 film *The New Adventures of Pippi Longstocking* didn't take place in a Scandinavian village, but right here on Amelia Island. Pippi's house in the film, Villa Villekulla, is now a pink B&B, the Posada San Carlos.

commerce (p. 576) or the **Amelia Island Bed & Breakfast Association** (© **888/ 277-0218;** www.ameliaislandinns.com). You can tour all the B&Bs during an island-wide open house the first weekend in December.

A number of agencies can book vacation properties ranging from affordable cottages to magnificent mansions. Contact **Amelia Island Lodging Systems,** 584 S. Fletcher Ave., Fernandina Beach, FL 32034 (© **800/872-8531** or 904/261-4148; www.amelialodgings.com), which even has two lighthouse replicas for rent. *Warning:* Some properties on the website aren't as nice as they seem. Be sure to check very carefully before booking a specific property.

Your best camping option here is **Fort Clinch State Park** (p. 578).

Note: Rates are subject to a 9% hotel tax.

Amelia Island Plantation 🎇🎇   If you're comparing it to *Gone With the Wind*'s Tara, this is hardly a plantation, but rather a massive compound that could very easily host several plantations. This huge development occupies 1,350 lush beachfront acres that encompass manicured golf greens as well as a breathtaking coastal wilderness of marshes and lagoons, oceanfront property, miles and miles of lovely bike trails, and much more. The resort is so spread out that a free tram runs around the grounds every 15 minutes. Choose this rustically elegant property for its natural beauty and its outstanding sports offerings. Most notable are the four consistently top-rated championship golf courses open to resort guests; they comprise 72 holes bordering the ocean, marshes, and woodlands. The newest golf course to Amelia Island Plantation is **Royal Amelia,** open to the public and located just 3 miles from the resort's main entrance; this course is renowned as one of the best conditioned courses in the area, designed by Tom Jackson, with championship golf that all skill levels describe as "very playable." The **Long Point** 🎇🎇 course, a mind-blowingly beautiful 18-holer, has two par-3s in a row bordering the ocean. Ranked among the nation's top 50 by *Tennis* magazine, the plantation's Racquet Park, with 23 tennis courts (naturally shaded by a canopy of gorgeous trees), hosts many professional tournaments, including the annual Bausch & Lomb Championships, and is home to the renowned Gunterman Tennis School. A 13,200-square-foot spa has 25 treatment rooms and offers a rejuvenating array of massages, facials, peels, herbal wraps, and hydrotherapies; a very small island right near the spa is dedicated to Watsu massage treatments. New to the resort are guided tours using Segway Human Transporters, the latest development in personal transportation. Prices range from $40 for a 30-minute kids' excursion to $80 for a 1½-hour safari tour of the property. All tours include orientation and coaching.

Along with the adjoining convention center, the eight-story, Mediterranean-style **Amelia Inn & Beach Club** serves as the resort's focal point and holds its 249 spacious, upscale hotel rooms. Traditionally furnished, the rooms boast patios or balconies facing the ocean across a row of dunes. All of the inn's rooms are nonsmoking. (*Note:* Watch out for the minibar. My bellhop said that guests get charged for moving the contents around, even if they don't eat anything—supposedly an electronic eye monitors all minibar movement.) The other accommodations here are one- to three-bedroom privately owned condominium apartments (or "villas," in Florida speak). All but a few have balconies or patios. Each is uniquely decorated with an eclectic mix of high-end furnishings, and all offer living and dining areas (VCRs can be rented) and fully equipped kitchens. The inn's new Ocean Grill restaurant offers exceptional and expensive contemporary regional cuisine, with stunning ocean views. An adjoining lounge offers dancing and entertainment. Other restaurants and night spots are also on the property. And, really, with all you've got here, why leave?

6800 First Coast Hwy., Amelia Island, FL 32035-3000. © **888/261-6161** or 904/261-6161. Fax 904/277-5945. www. aipfl.com. 249 units, 400 1-, 2-, 3- bedroom villas. $ 156 –$ 356 double; $ 196 –$ 945 villa. Packages available. AE, DC, DISC, MC, V. Valet parking $13; free self-parking. **Amenities:** 8 restaurants; 4 bars; heated indoor pool; 23 outdoor pools; 4 golf courses; 23 tennis courts; health club and spa; Jacuzzi; sauna; bike rental; Island Hopper (golf cart–like cars to drive around the property) rental; age-specific youth programs; nature programs; game room; concierge; business center; shopping village; salon; 24-hr. room service; massage and many other spa treatments; babysitting; laundry service. *In room:* A/C, TV, dataport, kitchen (condos only), minibar (Amelia Inn only), coffeemaker, hair dryer, iron, safe.

Elizabeth Pointe Lodge 🖈🖈

You'd swear that this three-story, Nantucket-style shingled beauty sitting right on the beach is a lovingly maintained Victorian home—but you'd be wrong. Built in 1991 by David and Susan Caples, it has big-paned windows that look out from the comfy library (with stone fireplace) and dining room to an expansive front porch and the surf beyond. Antiques and reproductions, handmade quilts, and other touches lend the 20 rooms in the main building a turn-of-the-20th-century cottage ambience. All have oversize tubs. Four other rooms are located in the Harris Lodge next door, and the two-bedroom, two-bathroom Miller Cottage is also available.

98 S. Fletcher Ave. (just south of Atlantic Ave.), Fernandina Beach, FL 32034. © **800/772-3359** or 904/277-4851. Fax 904/277-6500. www.elizabethpointelodge.com. 24 units, 1 cottage. $170–$300 double; $375 cottage. Rates include full seaside buffet breakfast and morning newspaper. Packages available. AE, DISC, MC, V. **Amenities:** Restaurant; bar; access to nearby health club; Jacuzzi; watersports equipment rental; bike rental; 24-hr. room service; laundry service; free WiFi/DSL,. *In room:* A/C, TV, dataport, hair dryer, iron.

Fairbanks House 🖈🖈

Boasting all the amenities and almost as much privacy as a first-class hotel, this superbly refurbished 1885 Italianate home is a top B&B choice in the historic district. As gorgeous as it is, it used to be known as "Fairbanks' Folly," because of its pronounced decor. Many rooms and all of the cottages offer private entrances for guests who prefer not to walk through the main house. Room no. 3 is one of the finest units, with a private entrance, sitting room, plush king-size bed, period antiques, and fresh flowers. The two-bedroom Tower Suite, occupying the entire top floor, has plenty of room to spread out, plus 360-degree views and its own whirlpool tub. Five other units here have whirlpool tubs as well. Note that Fairbanks is the only B&B on the island with a pool. No smoking is permitted, indoors or out.

227 S. 7th St. (between Beech and Cedar sts.), Fernandina Beach, Amelia Island, FL 32034. © **888/891-9882** or 904/277-0500. Fax 904/277-3103. www.fairbankshouse.com. 9 units, 3 cottages. $170–$295 double; $220–$295 cottage. Rates include full breakfast and evening social hour (beverages and hors d'oeuvres). Packages available. AE, DISC, MC, V. No kids under 12. **Amenities:** Heated outdoor pool. *In room:* A/C, TV, dataport, kitchen (cottage only), minibar, fridge, coffeemaker, hair dryer, iron.

Florida House Inn 🖈 *Value*

Built near a railroad in 1857, this clapboard Victorian building is Florida's oldest operating hotel. Ulysses S. Grant stayed here, as did Cuban revolutionary José Martí; and the Rockefellers and Carnegies broke bread at the boardinghouse-style dining room that still provides family-style traditional Southern fare. You can rock away on the two gingerbread-trimmed front verandas or on a back porch overlooking a brick courtyard shaded by a huge oak tree. The 11 rooms in the original building, all mostly up to modern standards, are loaded with antiques. Most have working fireplaces; some have claw-foot tubs. Four rooms are in a wing added in 1998; one of these has log-cabin walls, the others are done in country style, and all have fireplaces and whirlpool tubs.

Fun Fact **José Martí Was Here**

Freedom fighter José Martí plotted the Cuban War for Independence (1895–1898) against Spain from his suite in Amelia's Florida House Inn, the state's oldest surviving tourist hotel. An island eavesdropper (with the makings of a modern-day tabloid reporter) heard the secret strategies, which led to the demise of the ill-fated revolution.

---

20 S. 3rd St. (between Centre and Ash sts.), Fernandina Beach, FL 32034. ✆ **800/258-3301** or 904/261-3300. Fax 904/277-3831. www.floridahouseinn.com. 15 units. $99–$299 double. Rates include full breakfast. AE, DISC, MC, V. Dogs accepted ($10 nightly fee). **Amenities:** Restaurant; bar; coin-op washers and dryers. *In room:* A/C, TV, coffeemaker, hair dryer, iron.

Hampton Inn & Suites 🏨🏨   A Hampton Inn that garners two stars, you ask? Believe it or not, it's true. When plans were announced a few years ago to build this four-story hotel in the center of the historic district, they created quite a stir among preservationists. But those fears have been put to rest—this is one of the most unusual Hampton Inns I've ever seen. Although there's only one building, the exterior looks like a row of different structures, all in the styles and sherbet hues of the Victorian storefronts lining Centre Street. Wooden floors taken from an old Jacksonville church, slatted door panels evocative of 19th-century schooners, and many other touches add to the Victorian ambience inside. About half of the guest rooms are near the top of the romance scale, with king-size beds, gas fireplaces, and two-person whirlpool tubs. The standard suites are large enough for families, and the other rooms are adequately equipped for business travelers. About a third of the units have balconies. Those higher up on the west side have fine views over the river and marshes. The only drawback: Trains slowly rumble by the west side a few times a day.

19 S. 2nd St. (between Centre and Ash sts.), Fernandina Beach, FL 32034. ✆ **800/426-7866** or 904/491-4911. Fax 904/491-4910. www.hamptoninn.com. 122 units. $109–$189 double. Rates include extensive breakfast buffet. AE, DC, DISC, MC, V. **Amenities:** Outdoor pool; exercise room; Jacuzzi; business center; babysitting; laundry service; coin-op washers and dryers. *In room:* A/C, TV, dataport, fridge, coffeemaker, hair dryer, iron.

Ritz-Carlton Amelia Island 🏨🏨🏨 *Kids*   Sprawling over 13 acres of stunning beachfront, this member of the world-renowned chain offers slightly glitzier accommodations than its neighbor, the Amelia Island Plantation, but not as much "glamour" as some of its siblings. This could be positive or negative, depending on what you want from a hotel. While some may like the fact that it's perfectly acceptable to walk through the lobby of this Ritz in shorts (it's downright relaxed in this way), others might find the service and surroundings not as polished as they might have experienced in other Ritz-Carltons. The kids' program makes well-heeled families feel just as much at home as the conventioneers who flock here to meet and make use of the extensive recreational facilities, including a beautiful 18-hole championship golf course. The spacious guest rooms—all with oceanfront or oceanview balconies or patios—have many amenities, such as scales, cosmetic mirrors, and phones in their marble bathrooms. **The Grill** leads the hotel's restaurants, with an ocean view to go along with exceptional seafood. A gourmet takeout shop sells the oft-requested Ritz dressings, condiments, and sauces, in addition to salads, sandwiches, and decadent desserts.

4750 Amelia Island Pkwy., Fernandina Beach, FL 32034. ✆ **800/241-3333** or 904/277-1100. Fax 904/277-1145. 449 units. $199–$429 double; $269–$579 suite. Golf, tennis, and other packages available. AE, DC, DISC, MC, V. Valet parking $15; no self-parking. **Amenities:** 3 restaurants; 3 bars; heated indoor and outdoor pools; golf course; 9 tennis courts; health club and spa; watersports equipment rentals; bike rental; children's programs; game room; concierge; business center; salon; 24-hr. room service; massage; babysitting; laundry service; concierge-level rooms. *In room:* A/C, TV, dataport, minibar, coffeemaker, hair dryer, iron, safe.

WHERE TO DINE

You'll find several restaurants, pubs, and snack shops along Centre Street, between the bay and 8th Street (Fla. A1A), in Fernandina Beach's old town. Two good dining options stand opposite the Hampton Inn & Suites on South 2nd Street, between Centre and Ash streets: the hip **Joe's 2nd Street Bistro** (© 904/321-2558) and the more formal but still relaxed **Le Clos** (© 904/261-8100). Joe's serves fine international fare in an old store, while Le Clos provides provincial French fare in a charming old house. Both are open for dinner only; reservations are recommended. Drop by during the day for a look at the menus posted outside each.

And don't forget **The Grill,** at the Ritz-Carlton Amelia Island (see above), where great food and impeccable service come at a high price. Lastly, the **Florida House Inn** (p. 581) serves boardinghouse-style, all-you-can-eat lunches and dinners Tuesday through Saturday from 11:30am to 2:30pm ($7 per person), and from 5:30 to 9pm ($13 per person).

Beech Street Grill ✸✸ REGIONAL NEW AMERICAN   On par with The Grill in the Ritz-Carlton, the cosmopolitan-chic Beech Street Grill pleases all palates with a rich menu of fish, chicken, and meat choices, including seasonal game dishes such as roasted venison loin in a black-currant sauce with sweet-potato-and-onion hash. Nightly fish specialties are always exceptional. The chewy steamed dumplings are great for starters, as is the huge mixed-green salad with mustard-basil vinaigrette, toasted pecans, and blue cheese. Housed in a century-old landmark home and in a newer wing to one side, the five dining rooms offer a lively atmosphere. The upstairs section features a pianist.

801 Beech St. (at 8th St./Fla. A1A), Fernandina Beach. © 904/277-3662. Reservations strongly recommended. Main courses $22–$35. AE, DC, DISC, MC, V. Daily 6–10pm.

Brett's Waterway Cafe SEAFOOD/STEAK   You'll pay for the view, but this friendly waterfront cafe at the foot of Centre Street is the only place in town to dine while watching the boats coming and going on the river—and to sip a drink (try one of the excellent martinis) while watching the sun setting over the marshes between here and the mainland. In fine weather, grab a table out by the docks. One of the best dishes is shrimp broiled with a sun-dried-tomato/cream sauce. The nightly fresh-fish specials are well prepared. Steaks and chops are also served.

1 S. Front St. (at Centre St., on the water), Fernandina Beach. © 904/261-2660. Main courses $15–$26. AE, MC, V. Mon–Sat 11:30am–2:30pm; daily 5:30–9:30pm.

Joe's 2nd Street Bistro ✸✸✸ NEW AMERICAN   In the heart of the Fernandina Beach historic district is this diminutive restored 1900s home that's filled with flavor. The island-inspired dining room features a brick fireplace, and upstairs is a private dining room, but I suggest grabbing a table out on the covered porch. A meal here is almost like eating in a chef's home, a quaint and delectable experience, to say the least. Try the loin lamb chops with a Southwestern-style rub served over three-bean ragout with roasted tomatoes and tobacco-fried onions. Yowza! For dessert, the apple bread pudding kicks that part of your body where perhaps the calories will end up. It rocks. Joe's rocks. Don't miss it. Eat at Joe's.

101 Centre St. (at Front St.), Fernandina Beach. © 904/261-5310. Reservations recommended. Main courses $14–$26. AE, DC, MC, V. Daily 6–9:30pm.

Marina Restaurant *Value* AMERICAN   Occupying a brick store built in the 1880s, this quintessential small-town restaurant has been feeding Low Country fare to locals since 1965. A lot of the seafood here is fried and broiled, but you can order grouper topped with scallops and a garlicky wine sauce. Budgeters love the $10-and-under list of Southern favorites, such as country-fried steak and breaded veal cutlet. Meatloaf with tomato-and-basil gravy, stuffed peppers with a Greek-style tomato sauce, and other lunch specials come with three fresh country-style vegetables, which are themselves worth the price of the meal. Hearty breakfasts feature eggs, omelets, French toast, and hot cakes.

101 Centre St. (at Front St.), Fernandina Beach. © 904/261-5310. Breakfast $3–$6; sandwiches $5–$9; main courses $8–$19. DC, MC, V. Daily 7–10am and 11:30am–9pm.

AMELIA ISLAND AFTER DARK

This romantic island goes to bed early. If you tire of the lounges in the island's resorts, check out the **Palace Saloon,** 117 Centre St., at 2nd Street (© **904/261-6320**). It claims to be Florida's oldest watering hole (open since 1878). Complete with a pressed-tin ceiling and a 40-foot-long mahogany bar, it once hosted the Carnegies and the du Ponts. Some nights you'll even find live local blues or rock here. It's open daily from 11am until 2am.

Another popular local watering hole, **O'Kane's Irish Pub & Eatery,** 318 Centre St., at 4th Street (© **904/261-1000**), has live music until midnight Monday through Thursday, until 1:30am Friday and Saturday.

14

Northwest Florida:
The Panhandle

The Florida Panhandle is like the Jan Brady of the state. Cindy, the cute sister, could represent Orlando and Tampa, with their amusements and attractions, while South and Southwest Florida could be Marcia, the gorgeous sister whom everyone fawns over and talks about. And then there's the misunderstood, underestimated Jan—in this case, Northwest Florida, aka the Panhandle, always getting the shaft, even though she's got some great qualities all her own, if only people took the time to discover them. For the Panhandle, this is a particular shame, since it is a dynamic, uncommonly beautiful part of Florida.

If you like beaches, you'll love the Panhandle, the land of the two-way sun, which runs east to west along the Gulf of Mexico and, therefore, offers sunrises *and* sunsets. Once and sometimes erroneously still known as the Redneck Riviera (thanks to fans in Georgia, Alabama, and Louisiana)—a refreshing change from the glitz and glamour oozing from South Florida—the Panhandle, while still rugged in a sexy, Marlboro Man kind of way, has slowly shed that rep with the emergence of upscale residential developments and boutique hotels.

Three other reasons to love this zone: water as turquoise as colored contact lenses, smaller crowds than at other Florida beaches, and ghost-white sand that's so talcumlike it squeaks when you walk on it. The sand in these parts is brilliantly white

because, over thousands of years, quartz particles were washed downstream from the eroding Appalachian Mountains and pummeled into grains as fine and soft as baby powder before finally landing at their final resting place: under the towels of the three million sunbathers who flock here every year. Speaking of walking, you can, because some 100 miles of these incomparable sands are protected in state parks and the gorgeous Gulf Islands National Seashore.

Pensacola, Destin, Fort Walton Beach, and Panama City Beach are summertime meccas for families, couples, and singles from the aforementioned adjoining states—a geographic proximity that lends this area the languid charm of the Deep South. Indeed, Southern specialties such as collard greens and cheese grits (in the South, it's a two-syllable word, pronounced *gree*-its) appear frequently on menus here.

But there's more to the northwestern Panhandle than beaches and Southern charm. Record catches of grouper, amberjack, snapper, mackerel, cobia, sailfish, wahoo, tuna, and blue marlin have made Destin one of the world's fishing capitals. In the interior near Pensacola, the Blackwater, Shoal, and Yellow rivers teem with bass, bream, catfish, and largemouth bass, and also feature some of Florida's best canoeing and kayaking adventures.

The area is steeped in history as well. Rivaling St. Augustine as Florida's oldest town, picturesque Pensacola preserves a heritage derived from Spanish, French, English, and American conquests. Famous for its oysters, Apalachicola saw the invention of the air conditioner, a moment of great historic note for Florida. And Tallahassee, seat of state government since 1824, has a host of 19th-century buildings, including the majestic Old State Capitol, not to mention a cool little town named, yes, Havana, which is one of the Southeast's largest antiques centers.

One note to those traveling the entire state: While "season" in South Florida tends to fall in the winter months, due to the Panhandle's geographic location and tendency to get chilly to downright cold during the winter, its "season" is during the summer, so hotel rates will be higher during that time while it's the opposite down south.

EXPLORING NORTHWEST FLORIDA BY CAR

Both I-10 and U.S. 98 link Tallahassee and Pensacola, some 200 miles apart. The fastest route is I-10, but all you'll see is a huge pine forest divided by two strips of concrete. Plan to take U.S. 98 instead, a scenic excursion in itself. Although it can be traffic-clogged in the beach towns during summer, U.S. 98 has some beautiful stretches out in the country, particularly as it literally skirts the bay east of Apalachicola and the Gulf west of Port St. Joe. It's also lovely along skinny Okaloosa Island and across the high-rise bridge between Fort Walton Beach and Destin. From the bridge, you'll see the brilliant hue of the Gulf and immediately understand why this is called the Emerald Coast. If you turn off U.S. 98 onto 30A, a 20-mile drive along the coastline, you will immediately be transported back in time, to the pre-Golden-Arches-lined highways of Florida. Along this scenic stretch, you'll see not only sand and surf but also, believe it or not, pine forests, saw palmettos, the Choctawhatchee Bay, and Hogtown Bayou, a magnet for fiery sunsets.

1 Pensacola ⋆ ⋆

191 miles W of Tallahassee, 354 miles W of Jacksonville

A charming blend of Old Spanish brickwork, colonial French balconies reminiscent of New Orleans, and magnificent Victorian mansions built by British and American lumber barons, Pensacola is definitely worthy of its motto, "City of Five Flags," but it's much more than just pretty buildings and a nice vibe. Thanks to the Pensacola Downtown Improvement Board, work has continued to progress on the revitalization of downtown, promoting the full occupancy of once-abandoned 125-year-old buildings and the emergence of downtown businesses, stores, historic theaters, restaurants, bars, and events such as the Florida Springfest, a 3-day music festival that lures big names like Cheap Trick, The Black Crowes, Bonnie Raitt, Trace Adkins, the Allman Brothers, and Jethro Tull, with coverage by VH-1.

West of town, the excellent National Museum of Naval Aviation at the U.S. Naval Air Station celebrates the storied past of U.S. Navy and Marine Corps pilots who trained at Pensacola. The Blue Angels, who are based here, demonstrate the high-tech present with thrilling exhibitions of precision flying in the navy's fastest fighters.

Also on the Naval Station, historic Fort Barrancas looks across the bay to Perdido Key and Santa Rosa Island, which reach out like narrow pincers to form the harbor. Out here, powdery white-sand beaches beckon sun-and-surf lovers to their spectacular Gulf shores, which include Pensacola Beach, a small family-oriented resort; and most of Florida's share of Gulf Islands National Seashore, home of historic Fort Pickens.

The Panhandle

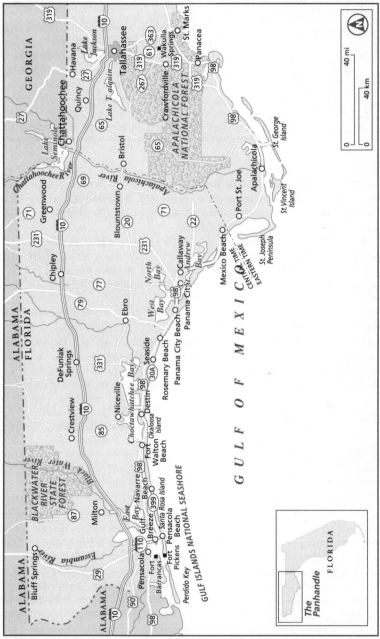

A Friendly Feud

Native Americans left pottery shards and artifacts in the coastal dunes in Pensacola centuries before Tristan de Luna arrived with a band of Spanish colonists in 1559. Although his settlement lasted only 2 years, modern Pensacolans claim de Luna made their town the oldest in North America. Pensacola actually dates its permanence from a Spanish colony established here in 1698, however, so St. Augustine wins this friendly feud, having been continuously settled since 1565. France, Great Britain, the United States, and the Confederacy subsequently captured (and, in one case, recaptured) this strategically important deepwater port.

ESSENTIALS

GETTING THERE   **Pensacola Regional Airport,** 12th Avenue at Airport Road (© 850/436-5005; www.flypensacola.com), is served by **AirTran** (© 800/247-8726), **Continental** (© 800/525-0280), **Delta** (© 800/221-1212), **Northwest** (© 800/225-2525), and **US Airways** (© 800/428-4322).

Alamo (© 800/327-9633), **Avis** (© 800/331-1212), **Budget** (© 800/527-0700), **Dollar** (© 800/800-4000), **Enterprise** (© 800/325-8007), **Hertz** (© 800/654-3131), and **National** (© 800/227-7368) have rental-car operations here.

Taxis wait outside the modern terminal. Fares are approximately $15 to downtown, $20 to Gulf Breeze, and $25 to Pensacola Beach.

The **Amtrak** (© **800/872-7245;** www.amtrak.com) transcontinental *Sunset Limited* stops in Pensacola at 980 E. Heinberg St.

VISITOR INFORMATION   The **Pensacola Visitor Information Center,** 1401 E. Gregory St., Pensacola, FL 32501 (© **800/874-1234** or 850/434-1234; fax 850/432-8211; www.visitpensacola.com), gives away helpful information about the Greater Pensacola area, including maps of self-guided tours of the historic districts, and sells a detailed street map of the area. The office is at the mainland end of the Pensacola Bay Bridge and is open daily from 8am to 5pm (until 4pm Sat–Sun Oct–Mar).

For information specific to the beach, contact the **Pensacola Beach Chamber of Commerce,** 735 Pensacola Beach Blvd. (P.O. Box 1174), Pensacola Beach, FL 32561 (© **800/635-4803** or 850/932-1500; fax 850/932-1551; www.visitpensacolabeach.com). The chamber's offices and visitor center are on the right as you drive onto Santa Rosa Island across the Bob Sikes Bridge. It's open daily from 9am to 5pm.

GETTING AROUND   To see the historic sights in town, park at the Pensacola visitor center (see above) and take the **Five Flags Trolley** (© **850/436-9383**). The one-way East Bay (Blue) Line runs Monday through Friday from 9am to 4pm between the visitor center and downtown. The Palafox (Red) Line runs Monday through Friday from 7am to 6pm north-south along Palafox Street between the waterfront and North Hill Preservation District. Both pass through Historic Pensacola Village. The 25¢ fare includes a transfer between the two lines. The visitor center has free route maps.

The free **Tiki Trolley** runs the full length of Pensacola Beach from Memorial Day weekend to Labor Day weekend, Friday and Saturday from 10am to 3am and Sunday from 10am to 10pm.

Both trolleys are operated by **Escambia County Area Transit System (ECAT;** © **850/595-3228;** www.goecat.com), which also runs public buses around town Monday through Saturday ($1 adults, 50¢ seniors)—but not to the beach. Call for schedules.

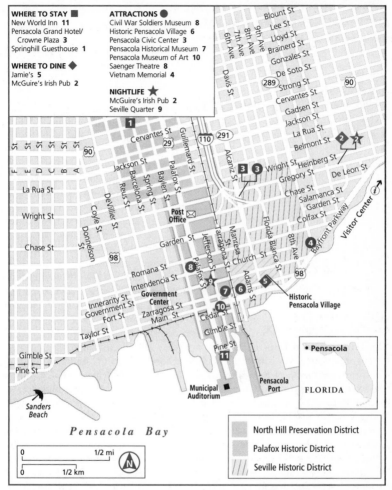

Downtown Pensacola

WHERE TO STAY ■
New World Inn **11**
Pensacola Grand Hotel/
Crowne Plaza **3**
Springhill Guesthouse **1**

WHERE TO DINE ◆
Jamie's **5**
McGuire's Irish Pub **2**

ATTRACTIONS ●
Civil War Soldiers Museum **8**
Historic Pensacola Village **6**
Pensacola Civic Center **3**
Pensacola Historical Museum **7**
Pensacola Museum of Art **10**
Saenger Theatre **8**
Vietnam Memorial **4**

NIGHTLIFE ★
McGuire's Irish Pub **2**
Seville Quarter **9**

North Hill Preservation District
Palafox Historic District
Seville Historic District

Pensacola Bay

Sanders Beach

• Pensacola

FLORIDA

If you need a cab, call **Airport Express Taxi/City Cab** (© 850/478-4477), **Orange Cab** (© 850/478-0222), or **Yellow Cab** (© 850/433-3333). Fares are $1.80 at flag fall, plus $2 a mile.

You can rent bikes from **Key Sailing,** in Pensacola Beach (© 877/932-7272 or 850/932-5520; www.keysailing.com). Rentals are $10 for 4 hours, $15 for a full day; if you call in advance, the outfitter will deliver the bikes to you. *Note:* At press time, Key Sailing was renting only pontoon boats, sailboats, and kayaks, due to the beating they took during the brutal 2005 hurricane season. Call for information.

TIME Pensacola is in the central time zone, 1 hour behind Miami, Orlando, and Tallahassee.

HITTING THE BEACH: GULF ISLANDS NATIONAL SEASHORE & MORE

Important note: As with most of Florida, the Panhandle took some hits during the brutal 2005 hurricane season. As of press time, most places were fully operational. Before planning a visit, make sure you check the status of repairs. For information, contact the Gulf Islands National Seashore, 1801 Gulf Breeze Pkwy., Gulf Breeze, FL 32561 (✆ **850/934-2600;** www.nps.gov/guis).

Stretching eastward 47 miles, from the entrance to Pensacola Bay to Fort Walton Beach, skinny Santa Rosa Island is home to the resorts, condominiums, cottages, restaurants, and shops of **Pensacola Beach,** the area's prime vacation spot. This relatively small and low-key resort began life a century ago as the site of a beach pavilion, or "casino," as such facilities were called back then; and the heart of town—at the intersection of Pensacola Beach Boulevard, Via de Luna, and Fort Pickens Road—is still known as Casino Beach. This lively area at the base of the town's water tank sports restaurants, snack bars, an arcade, a miniature golf course, public restrooms, walk-up beach bars with live bands blaring away, an indoor sports bar, and an outdoor concert pavilion with summertime entertainment. And the shops, restaurants, and bars of Quietwater Boardwalk are just across the road on the bay side of the island. If you want an active beach vacation, it's all here in one compact zone.

One reason Pensacola Beach is so small is that most of Santa Rosa Island is included in the **Gulf Islands National Seashore** ✮✮✮. Jumping from island to island from Mississippi to Florida, this magnificent preserve, possibly the best beach in the entire state, includes 150 miles of undeveloped and federally protected white-sand beach and rolling dunes covered with sea grass and sea oats. Established in 1971, the national seashore is a protected environment for more than 280 species of birds.

The most interesting part of the seashore is **Fort Pickens** (✆ **850/934-2635**), on the western end of Santa Rosa Island, about 7 miles west of Pensacola Beach. Built in the 1830s to team with Fort Barrancas in guarding Pensacola's harbor entrance, this huge brick structure saw combat during the Civil War, but it's best known as the prison home of Apache medicine man Geronimo from 1886 to 1888. The visitor center has a small museum featuring displays about Geronimo, coastal defenses, and the seashore's ecology. Plan to be here at 2pm, when rangers lead 45-minute tours of the fort (the schedule can change, so call the fort to make sure). Seven-day admission permits (that's the minimum you can get) to the Fort Pickens area are $8 per vehicle, $3 per pedestrian or bicyclist, and free for holders of National Park Service passports. The fort and museum are open March through October daily from 9:30am to 5pm, November through February daily from 8:30am to 4pm. Both are closed Christmas Day.

The Fort Pickens area has 200 **campsites** (135 with electricity) in a pine forest on the bay side of Santa Rosa Island. Nature trails lead from the camp through Blackbird Marsh and to the beach. A small store sells provisions. Sites cost $15 a night without power, $20 a night with it, and you have to pay the admission fee to the Fort Pickens area. Golden Age and Golden Access cardholders get a 50% discount. Call ✆ **800/ 365-2267** for reservations (enter code GUL) or 850/934-2621 for recorded information. You can make reservations up to 5 months in advance. *Note:* At press time, Fort Pickens was open for day use only.

The national seashore's headquarters are in the 1,378-acre **Naval Live Oaks Area,** on U.S. 98, a mile east of Gulf Breeze (✆ **850/934-2600**). This former federal tree plantation is a place of primitive beauty, with nature trails leading through the oaks and pines to picnic areas and a beach. Pick up a map at the headquarters building, which has a small museum and a gorgeous view through the pines to Santa Rosa Sound. Picnic areas and trails are open from 8am to sunset year-round, except Christmas. Admission is free. The visitor center is open daily from 8am to 5:30pm.

The national seashore maintains historic **Fort Barrancas,** on the U.S. Naval Air Station west of town. See "Pensacola's Other Fort" (p. 595) for details.

OUTDOOR ACTIVITIES

FISHING   Red snapper, grouper, mackerel, tuna, and billfish are abundant off the Panhandle. The easiest way to drop a line into the Gulf is off the new **Pensacola**

Florida's Canoe Capital

The little town of Milton, the official "Canoe Capital of Florida" (by an act of the state legislature, no less), is about 20 miles northeast of Pensacola via U.S. 90. Its title is well earned, as the nearby Blackwater River, Coldwater River, Sweetwater Creek, and Juniper Creek are perfect for canoeing, kayaking, tubing, rafting, and paddle-boating.

The Blackwater is considered one of the world's purest sand-bottom rivers. It has remained a primordial backwoods beauty, thanks chiefly to Florida's largest state forest (183,000 acres of oak, pine, and juniper) and **Blackwater River State Park** ✹✹, 7720 Deaton Bridge Rd., Holt, FL 32564 (✆ **850/983-5363;** www.floridastateparks.org/blackwaterriver), where you can closely observe plant life and wildlife along nature trails. The park has facilities for fishing, picnicking, and camping. Admission is $3 per day per vehicle, $1 per extra vehicle passenger, $1 per pedestrian or bicyclist. Campsites cost $12, plus $2 per pet with tags and vaccination papers. For camping reservations, call ✆ **800/326-3521** or go to www.reserveamerica.com.

Adventures Unlimited, Route 6, Box 283, Milton, FL 32570 (✆ **800/239-6864** or 850/623-6197; fax 850/626-3124; www.adventuresunlimited.com), is a year-round resort with day and overnight canoeing, kayaking, and rafting expeditions. Special arrangements are made for novices. Canoe trips start at $20 per person (4 miles), kayaking adventures from $25. Inner tubes start at $15. Campsites cost $15 a night, $20 with electricity. The resort also has 14 cottages on the Coldwater River ($69–$149 per night), as well as bed-and-breakfast accommodations at Wolfe Creek Old School House Inn (eight rooms, all with private bathroom; $79–$109 double). Two-night minimum stays are required (3 nights on holidays). Call for schedules and reservations for trips, accommodations, and camping.

Blackwater Canoe Rental, 10274 Pond Rd., Milton, FL 32570 (✆ **800/967-6789** or 850/623-0235; www.blackwatercanoe.com), also rents canoes, kayaks, floats, tubes, and camping equipment. It has two kinds of camping trips by canoe or kayak: a day trip, ranging from $18 to $22 per person, and an overnight excursion, ranging from $26 to $38 per person. Tents, sleeping bags, and coolers are all available for rent.

Beach Gulf Fishing Pier, on Fort Pickens Road in Pensacola Beach (© 850/934-7200; www.fishpensacolabeachpier.com). At 1,471 feet, it's the longest fishing pier on the Gulf Coast. The pier is open 24 hours a day, year-round. Fees to fish are $6.50 per day for adults, $5.50 for seniors, and $3.50 for children 6 to 12. Bait and equipment cost extra. Observers can watch for $1 per person.

Fishing-charter services are offered at Pensacola by the **Beach Marina Fishing Fleet** (© 877/650-3474 or 850/932-0304), and at Pensacola Beach by **Reel Eazy Charters** (© 877/733-5329 or 850/932-8824). Expect to pay between $400 and $900 for one to four passengers, depending on the length of your trip. You may be able to save by driving to Destin, where party boats charge less per person (see p. 605 for information). Sightseeing and evening cruises here go for $50 to $200 per person.

GOLF The Pensacola area has its share of Northwest Florida's numerous championship golf courses. Look for free copies of *South Coast Golf Guide,* an annual directory describing all of them, at the visitor center and in many hotel lobbies (see p. 51 for information on ordering copies). Reasonably priced golf packages can be arranged through many local hotels and motels.

For course information, go to www.golf.com or www.floridagolfing.com, or call the **Florida Sports Foundation** (© 850/488-8347) or **Florida Golfing** (© 866/833-2663).

Among this region's best courses is **Marcus Pointe,** on Marcus Pointe Boulevard off North W Street (© 800/362-7287 or 850/484-9770), which has hosted the Nike Tour, the American Amateur Classic, and the Pensacola Open. *Golf Digest* described this 18-hole course as a "great value," and that's not far off: Greens fees with cart are about $25 to $50, depending on the season.

The **Moors,** on Avalon Boulevard north of I-10 (© 800/727-1010 or 850/995-4653), has also greeted the Nike Tour and is home to the Emerald Coast Classic, a PGA Seniors event. Pot bunkers here make you think you're playing in Scotland. Greens fees are similarly priced. The Moors also has a lodge with eight luxury rooms.

Other courses worth considering are the **Lost Key Golf Club,** on Perdido Key (© 888/256-7853 or 850/492-1300), one of the area's more difficult courses; **Scenic Hills,** on U.S. 90 northwest of town (© 850/476-9611), whose rolling fairways are unique for this mostly flat area; the 36-hole **Tiger Point,** 1255 Country Club Rd., east of Gulf Breeze by Santa Rosa Sound (© 850/932-1330), overlooking the water (the fifth-hole green of the East Course actually sits on an island); **Hidden Creek,** 3070 PGA Blvd., in Navarre between Gulf Breeze and Fort Walton Beach (© 850/939-4604); **Creekside Golf Course,** 2355 W. Michigan Ave. (© 850/944-7969); and **Osceola Municipal Golf Course,** 300 Tonawanda, off Mobile Highway (© 850/456-2761).

In addition, the newly renovated **Sportsman Golf Resort,** 1 Doug Ford Dr. (© 866/319-2471 or 850/492-1223; www.sportsmanresort.com), on the mainland north of Perdido Key, has accommodations available for visiting golfers. It was the home of the PGA Pensacola Open from 1978 to 1987, when it was known as the Perdido Bay Golf Resort. Greens fees here range from $55 to $65.

WATERSPORTS Visibility in the waters around Pensacola can range from 30 to 50 feet deep inshore, to 100 feet deep 25 miles offshore. Although the bottom is sandy and the area is too far north for coral, the battleship USS *Massachusetts,* submerged in 30 feet of water 3 miles offshore, is one of some 35 artificial reefs where you can spot loggerhead turtles and other creatures. There are also good snorkeling sites just off the beach; get a map from the Gulf Islands National Seashore (see "Hitting the Beach: Gulf Islands National Seashore & More," above).

Scuba Shack, 711 S. Palafox St. (© **850/433-4319**), offers sales, rentals, classes, and diving and fishing charters on the *Wet Dream,* moored behind the office. **Divers Den,** 512 N. 9th Ave. (© **850/438-0650**), also provides trips, equipment rental, and PADI instruction. **MBT Divers** (© **850/455-7702;** www.mbtdivers.com) has rentals, instruction, and trips to several sites, including the habitats of sea turtles, manta rays, and nurse sharks. **Gulf Breeze Dive Pros,** 297B Gulf Breeze Pkwy. (U.S. 98), in Gulf Breeze (© **850/934-8845**), has a menu that includes rentals, all levels of instruction, and diving excursions on the 30-foot *Easy Dive.*

Key Sailing Center, 500 Quietwater Beach Rd., on the Quietwater Beach Boardwalk (© **877/932-7272** or 850/932-5520; www.keysailing.com); and **Radical Rides,** 444 Pensacola Beach Blvd., near the Bob Sikes Bridge (© **850/934-9743**), rent Hobie Cats, pontoon boats, WaveRunners, jet skis, and windsurfing boards.

EXPLORING HISTORIC PENSACOLA

Adjacent to the Historic Pensacola Village, the city's **Vietnam Memorial,** on Bayfront Parkway at 9th Avenue, is known as the "Wall South," since it is a three-quarter-size replica of the national Vietnam Veterans Memorial in Washington, D.C. Look for the "Huey" helicopter atop the wall.

Civil War Soldiers Museum ⚅   Founded by Dr. Norman Haines, Jr., a local physician who started collecting Civil War relics when he was growing up in Sharpsburg, Maryland, this 4,200-square-foot museum in the heart of the Palafox Street business district emphasizes how ordinary soldiers lived during that bloody conflict. The doctor's collection of military medical equipment and treatment methods is especially informative. A 23-minute video tells of Pensacola's role during the Civil War. The museum's bookstore carries more than 600 titles about the war.

108 S. Palafox St. (south of Romana St.). © 850/469-1900. www.cwmuseum.org. Admission $6 adults, $2.50 children 6–12. Tues–Sat 10am–4:30pm. Closed New Year's Day, Thanksgiving, Christmas Eve, and Christmas Day.

Historic Pensacola Village ⚅⚅⚅   History buffs as well as those who appreciate delightful architecture will *love* this retro-fabulous old-school village, comparable to Long Island's Old Bethpage Village Restoration or Virginia's Colonial Williamsburg. Bounded by Government, Taragona, Adams, and Alcanz streets, this original part of Pensacola resembles a shady English colonial town—albeit with Spanish street names—complete with town green and its own **Christ Church,** built in 1832 and resembling Bruton Parish in Williamsburg, Virginia. Some of Florida's oldest homes, now owned and preserved by the state, are here, and the village has charming boutiques and interesting restaurants as well. All 20 of the village's properties are on the National Register as a historic district.

In summer, costumed characters go about their daily chores and demonstrate old crafts, while University of Florida archaeologists unearth the old Spanish commanding officer's compound at Zaragosa and Tarragona streets. Among the landmarks you can visit are the **Museum of Industry,** the **Museum of Commerce,** the French Creole–style **Charles Lavalle House,** the elegant **Victorian Dorr House,** the French Colonial–Creole **Quina House,** and **St. Michael's Cemetery** (land was deeded by the king of Spain). The **Julee Cottage Black History Museum,** 204 E. Zaragosa St., is particularly fascinating: Built around 1790, this small house was owned by a freed slave who ran her business, invested in real estate, and loaned money to slaves so they could buy their freedom. Start your tour by buying tickets at **Tivoli House,** 205 E. Zaragosa St., just east of Tarragona Street, where you can get free maps and brochures. Try to take one of the 90-minute guided walking tours of the village, which will lead you through Christ Church and other buildings not otherwise open to the public.

Admission to the village includes the **T. T. Wentworth, Jr., Florida State Museum,** 330 S. Jefferson St. ((©) **850/595-5985**), at Church Street downtown, a classic yellow-brick building that houses exhibits of Western Florida's history and a special hands-on Discovery Museum for children.

205 E. Zaragosa St. (east of Tarragona St.). (©) 850/595-5985. www.historicpensacola.org. Admission $6 adults, $5 seniors, $2.50 children 4–16. Mon–Fri 10am–4pm; 90-min. guided tours 11am and 1pm. Closed New Year's Day, Thanksgiving, Christmas Eve, Christmas Day, and all other state holidays.

National Museum of Naval Aviation 🎖️🎖️   Given the present world circumstances, this museum should be required attendance for everyone. Yes, it's fascinating, but it also gives you a look into just how much blood, sweat, and tears go into defending this country. The U.S. Navy and Marine Corps have trained at the sprawling U.S. Naval Air Station since they began flying planes early in the last century. Celebrating their heroics, this remarkable museum has more than 100 aircraft dating from the 1920s to the space age, plus interesting exhibits on subjects such as POWs. There's even a torpedo bomber flown by former U.S. President George H. W. Bush during World War II. Both children and adults can sit at the controls of a jet trainer, and the mock-ups of aircraft carrier conning towers and hanger decks are realistic. You can almost feel the tug of gravity while watching the Blue Angels and other naval aviators soaring about the skies in the stunning *Magic of Flight,* one of two IMAX films shown at the museum. If the movie doesn't get your stomach churning, then a 15-minute ride in the flight-motion simulator will. Using high-tech video and real motion, it simulates a high-speed, low-level mission in the Navy's F-18 Hornet jet fighter. All guides are retired naval and Marine Corps aviators, which adds a personal touch to the hour-long museum tours. Allow at least half a day here, and save 20 minutes for a Flight Line bus tour of more than 40 aircraft parked outside the museum's restoration hangar.

Radford Blvd., U.S. Naval Air Station. (©) 850/452-3604. www.naval-air.org. Free admission. IMAX movies $7 adults; $6.50 seniors, military, and children 5–13. Add $3.50 for 2nd movie. Flight-motion simulator rides $5 per person. Daily 9am–5pm. Guided tours daily at 9:30am, 11am, 1pm, and 2:30pm. Flight Line bus tours daily every 30 min. 10am–noon and 1–4pm. IMAX movies on the hour daily 10am–4pm. Flight-motion simulator every 15 min. 9am–4:45pm. Closed New Year's Day, Thanksgiving, and Christmas. Enter naval station either at the Main Gate at the south end of Navy Blvd. (Fla. 295) or at the Back Gate on Blue Angel Pkwy. (Fla. 173) and follow the signs. No passes required.

Pensacola Historical Museum   To learn more about Pensacola's diverse, five-flag history, spend 30 to 60 minutes at this local museum in the Arbona Building, a commercial structure built around 1882. An archaeological dig of the Spanish commanding officer's compound across Zaragosa Street has a boardwalk with explanatory signposts. The museum is operated by the Pensacola Historical Society, which has a resource center and library at 117 E. Government St. ((©) **850/434-5455**).

115 E. Zaragosa St. (between Tarragona and Jefferson sts.). (©) 850/433-1559. www.pensacolahistory.org. Admission $4 adults; free for children 12 and under. Mon–Sat 10am–4:30pm.

Pensacola Museum of Art 🎖️   Housed in what was the city jail from 1906 to 1954, this museum showcases an impressive collection of decorative glass, some African tribal art, and sometimes minor works by Salvador Dalí, John Marin, Ansel

Pensacola's Other Fort

Standing on Taylor Road near the National Museum of Naval Aviation, **Fort Barrancas** *♠♠* (*©* **850/455-5167**) is definitely worth a visit while you're at the naval station. This imposing brick structure sits on a bluff overlooking the deepwater pass into Pensacola Bay. The Spanish built the water battery in 1797. Linked to it by a tunnel, the incredibly intricate brickwork of the fort's upper section was constructed by American troops between 1839 and 1844. Entry is by means of a drawbridge across a dry moat, and an interior scarp gallery goes all the way around the inside of the fort. Meticulously restored and operated by the National Park Service as part of Gulf Islands National Seashore, the fort is open March through October daily from 9:30am to 4:45pm, November through February daily from 8:30am to 3:45pm. Ranger-led, 1-hour guided tours are well worth taking. The schedule changes season-ally, so call for the latest information. Admission and tours are free.

The **Pensacola Lighthouse,** opposite the museum entrance on Radford Boulevard, has guided ships to the harbor entrance since 1825. Except for occasional guided tours (call the Pensacola visitor center, listed earlier in this chapter, for a schedule), the lighthouse is not open to the public, but you can drive right up to it. The nearby **Lighthouse Point Restaurant** (*©* **850/452-3251**) offers bountiful, all-you-can-eat luncheon buffets and magnificent bay views for about $6.50 per person Monday through Thursday and $8 per person on Friday. It's open Monday through Friday from 10:30am to 2pm, and reservations are not required.

Adams, Thomas Hart Benton, Milton Avery, Alexander Calder, and Andy Warhol, among others, all displayed in the former cell blocks. It also sponsors cool events such as Art After Dark, in which you are invited to use the walls of the museum as your personal canvas for personal, artistic expression. Call before going to see what's on.

407 S. Jefferson St. (at Main St.). *©* 850/432-6247. www.pensacolamuseumofart.org. Admission $5 adults, $2 students and active-duty military, free for children under 6; free to all Tues. Tues–Fri 10am–5pm; Sat–Sun noon–5pm.

HISTORIC DISTRICTS

In addition to Historic Pensacola Village (see above) in the Seville Historic District, the city has two other preservation areas worth a stroll. The Pensacola visitor center (p. 588) provides free walking-tour maps, if you're interested.

PALAFOX HISTORIC DISTRICT *♠♠*   Running up Palafox Street from the water to Wright Street, the Palafox Historic District is also the downtown business district. Beautiful Spanish Renaissance and Mediterranean-style buildings, including the ornate Saenger Theatre, still stand from the early days. In 1821, Gen. Andrew Jackson formally accepted Florida into the United States during a ceremony in Plaza Ferdinand VII, now a National Historic Landmark. His statue commemorates the event.

For architecture buffs, this district is a theme park, with the 1902 Theisen Building and its vivid displays of Beaux Arts details, as well as the 1925 Saenger Theatre, with its terra-cotta ornamentation and grillwork on the front facade showcasing it as an elegant gem of the Spanish baroque style.

The Palafox District is home to the **Pensacola Historical Museum;** the **Pensacola Museum of Art,** in the old city jail; and the **T. T. Wentworth, Jr., Florida State Museum** (see "Exploring Historic Pensacola," above, for all three).

For boozehounds, the **Palace Oyster Bar,** 130 E. Government St. (© **850/434-6211**), has a bar from the old Palace Hotel, where Florida's first liquor license was issued.

NORTH HILL PRESERVATION DISTRICT 🏛 Another entry in the National Register of Historic Places, the North Hill Preservation District covers the 50 square blocks north of the Palafox Historic District bounded by Wright, Blount, Palafox, and Reus streets. Descendants of Spanish nobility, timber barons, British merchants, French Creoles, buccaneers, and Civil War soldiers still live in some of the more than 500 homes. They are not open to the public, but are a bonanza for anyone interested in architecture. In 1863, Union troops erected a fort in Lee Square, at Palafox and Gadsden streets. It later was dedicated to the Confederacy, complete with a 50-foot-high obelisk and sculpture based on John Elder's painting *After Appomattox.*

A NEARBY ZOO

The Northwest Florida Zoological Park and Botanical Gardens _Kids_   Situated in a 50-acre forest 15 miles east of Pensacola, this zoo, formerly known as, well "The Zoo," has more than 700 exotic animals—including tigers, lions, rhinos, and lowland gorillas—living in landscaped habitats. Japanese gardens, a giraffe-feeding tower, and a petting farm make for a fun visit. A Safari Line train chugs through a 30-acre wildlife preserve with free-ranging herds. The 2003 birth of a Pygmy hippo and a sable antelope here garnered national attention for the zoo on the Animal Planet cable channel. Set aside 3 to 4 hours to cover the entire park. The newest addition to the zoo family is a 110-pound, 6½-foot Komodo dragon named Ivan who resides in the new Dragon World exhibit.

5701 Gulf Breeze Pkwy. (U.S. 98), Gulf Breeze. © **850/932-2229.** www.the-zoo.com. Admission $11 adults, $9.95 seniors, $7.95 children 3–11. Train rides $3 per person. Carousel rides $2 per person. Daily 9am–5pm. Closed Thanksgiving, Christmas Eve, Christmas Day, and New Year's Eve.

SHOPPING

Sightseeing and shopping can be combined in Pensacola's Palafox and Seville historic districts, where many shops are housed in renovated centuries-old buildings. The **Quayside Art Gallery,** Plaza Ferdinand, at Zaragosa and Jefferson streets (© **850/438-2363;** www.quaysidegallery.com), is the largest cooperative gallery in the Southeast. More than 100 artists display their works here. The friendly staff will direct you to other nearby galleries as well.

North T Street between West Cervantes Street and West Fairfield Drive has so many antiques dealers and small flea markets that it's known as Antique Alley. Other dealers have booths in the **Ninth Avenue Antique Mall,** 380 N. 9th Ave. between Gregory and Strong streets (© **850/438-3961**). Get a complete list of local antiques dealers from the Pensacola visitor center (p. 588).

Browsers will enjoy poking through the 400-dealer space at the **Flea Market,** on U.S. 98 opposite the Zoo, 15 miles east of Pensacola (© **850/934-1971**). It's open on Saturday and Sunday from 9am to 5pm. Admission is free.

WHERE TO STAY

The Pensacola visitor center (p. 588) publishes a complete list of rental condominiums and cottages. Among the leading rental agents are **JME Management,** 22-A Via de Luna, Pensacola Beach (© **800/554-3695;** www.jmevacations.com), and **Tristan Realty,** 1020 Fort Pickens Rd., Pensacola Beach (© **800/445-9931** or 850/932-7363; fax 850/932-8361; www.tristanrealty.com).

The **Fort Pickens Area** of Gulf Islands National Seashore is your best bet for camping (p. 590).

Escambia County adds an 11.5% tax to all hotel and campground bills.

The accommodations listed below are arranged by geographic area: downtown Pensacola and Pensacola Beach. Bear in mind that Pensacola Beach is at least a 15-minute drive from downtown.

DOWNTOWN PENSACOLA

The University Mall complex at I-10 and Davis Highway, about 5 miles north of downtown, has a host of chain motels, and there's an ample supply of inexpensive restaurants on Plantation Road and in the adjacent mall. Another good bet is the 1998-vintage **Hampton Inn Airport,** 2187 Airport Blvd. (© **800/426-7866** or 850/478-1123; fax 850/478-8519), in an area that's not as congested as that around University Mall; there's a free shuttle to nearby Cordova Mall and its adjacent chain restaurants.

Several of the town's Victorian homes have been turned into luxurious bed-and-breakfasts. Among the best is **Springhill Guesthouse,** 903 N. Spring St. (© **800/475-1956** or 850/438-6887; www.bbonline.com/fl/springhill).

New World Inn   Near the scenic bay and in the historic district, this urban version of a comfortable country inn (it looks more like a concrete fortress) is part of a meeting facility known as New World Landing. Inside, however, is an entirely different—and much more pleasing to the eye—story. From the colonial-style lobby, a grand staircase leads to high-ceilinged, spacious rooms artistically decorated with antiques. They depict aspects of Pensacola's rich history: Four of them flaunt Spanish decor, four are *très chic* French style, four portray Early Americana, and four focus on old England.

600 S. Palafox St. (at Pine St.), Pensacola, FL 32501. © **850/432-4111.** Fax 850/432-6836. www.newworldlanding.com. 15 units. $85–$95 double; $125–$145 suite. Rates include continental breakfast. AE, MC, V. **Amenities:** Access to nearby health club; laundry service. *In room:* A/C, TV, dataport.

Pensacola Grand Hotel/Crowne Plaza ⊀   Opposite the Civic Center in the Seville Historic District near the southern end of I-110, this unique hotel has turned the historic L & N Railroad Depot into a grand lobby with bar, restaurants, lounges, and cozy library. You'll see such turn-of-the-20th-century accouterments as an ornate railroad clock, oak stair rails, imported marble, mosaic-tile floors, and old-fashioned

---

⌐Tips **When Room Rates Are Lowest**

Room rates at all Panhandle beaches are highest from mid-May to mid-August, and premiums are charged at Easter, Memorial Day, July 4, and Labor Day. Hotel or motel reservations are essential during these periods. There's another high-priced peak in March, when thousands of raucous college students invade during spring break. Economical times to visit are April (except Easter) and September—the weather is warm, most establishments are open, and room rates are significantly lower than during summer. The lowest rates are available during winter, but many attractions and some restaurants may be closed then.

carved furniture. An unimpressive 15-story glass-and-steel tower behind the depot holds the rooms and suites, which are popular primarily with business travelers and groups. *Note:* As of this writing, the hotel was still closed due to damage it sustained during 2004's Hurricane Ivan.

200 E. Gregory St. (at Alcanz St.), Pensacola, FL 32501. (C) **800/348-3336** or 850/433-3336. Fax 850/432-7572. www.pensacolagrandhotel.com. 212 units. $105–$150 double; $260–$425 suite. AE, DC, DISC, MC, V. **Amenities:** Restaurant; bar; outdoor pool; exercise room; business center; limited room service; laundry service; concierge-level rooms. *In room:* A/C, TV, dataport, fridge (suites only), coffeemaker, hair dryer, iron.

PENSACOLA BEACH

Best Western Pensacola Beach Resort   It's a Best Western, yes, but this hotel has a better view than some fancier hotels could ever dream of, right on the Gulf, and it's notable for its bright, clean, and extra-spacious accommodations. Outside corridors lead to all rooms. Although none has a private balcony, the units facing the beach do have great views (and higher prices). Two pools and a playground are on the beach; restaurants are within walking distance.

16 Via de Luna Dr., Pensacola Beach, FL 32561. (C) **800/934-3301** or 850/934-3300. Fax 850/934-4366. www.best western.com. 123 units. Summer $169–$199 double; off season $89–$149 double. Rates include continental break-fast. Golf packages available. AE, DC, DISC, MC, V. **Amenities:** 2 outdoor pools; watersports equipment rental; game room. *In room:* A/C, TV, dataport, fridge, microwave, coffeemaker, hair dryer, iron.

Clarion Suites Resort & Convention Center 🏨🏨   This most unusual of Pensacola Beach's resorts resembles a village of tin-roofed, pastel-sided cottages located on the sand dunes and reminiscent of a tony rental community in New York's Hamptons. Pretty swank for Clarion Suites, I'd say. Each attractively decorated one-bedroom suite comes complete with kitchen and two TVs. The best units are those directly facing the beach; these have balconies or patios. There are no restaurants in the resort, but if you don't feel like cooking in your suite's kitchen, area eateries are within walking distance. The outdoor pool is lovely, but why use the pool when you're right on this stunning beach? As of the writing of this book, the hotel was still closed and undergoing construction due to damage sustained from Hurricane Ivan.

20 Via de Luna Dr., Pensacola Beach, FL 32561. (C) **800/874-5303** or 850/932-4300. Fax 850/934-9112. www.clarion suitesresort.com. 86 units. Summer $119–$199 up to 4 persons; off season $84–$119 up to 4 persons. Rates include continental breakfast. AE, DC, DISC, MC, V. **Amenities:** Heated outdoor pool; watersports equipment rental; coin-op washers and dryers. *In room:* A/C, TV, dataport, kitchen, coffeemaker, hair dryer, iron.

The Dunes 🏨   This eight-story beachfront tower has spacious rooms, all with balconies and Gulf or bay vistas. The penthouse suites have their own whirlpool tubs. Amenities include a restaurant, bar, jogging trail, bike path, and undeveloped dune preserve next door. A Gulf-front pool with waterfall makes a great diversion. Although this is a full-service beachfront high-rise hotel, there's something oddly impersonal about it; given the choice, I'd stay at the Clarion. As of the writing of this book, the hotel was still closed and undergoing construction due to damage sustained from Hurricane Ivan.

333 Fort Pickens Rd., Pensacola Beach, FL 32561. (C) **800/833-8637** or 850/932-3536. Fax 850/932-7088. www.the duneshotel.com. 76 units. Summer $115–$185 double, $290–$365 suite; off season $85–$115 double, $265–$305 suite. Golf and other packages available. AE, DISC, MC, V. **Amenities:** Restaurant; bar; heated outdoor pool; access to nearby health club; watersports equipment rental; limited room service; laundry service. *In room:* A/C, TV, dataport, coffeemaker, hair dryer, iron.

Five Flags Inn 🌟*Value*   Sitting between the Holiday Inn Express and the Dunes, this basic but friendly motel looks like a jail from the road, and the rooms have cinderblock walls—but if you seek location and view at a bargain-basement rate, flag this place. Big picture windows in the rooms overlook the pool (heated Mar–Oct) and the gorgeous white-sand beach, which comes right up to the property. Although the accommodations are small, trust me on this: The rates are a bargain for clean Gulf-front rooms. At the time of this writing, the hotel was closed due to damage sustained during 2005's hurricanes Katrina and Wilma.

299 Fort Pickens Rd., Pensacola Beach, FL 32561. (C) 850/932-3586. Fax 850/934-0257. 49 units. Summer $89–$109 double; off season $55–$75 double; $20 more for holidays. AE, DC, DISC, MC, V. **Amenities:** Heated outdoor pool. *In room:* A/C, TV, hair dryer, iron.

Hampton Inn Pensacola Beach ⋆ *Kids*   This pastel, four-story hotel sits on a sliver of land—600 feet, specifically—between Santa Rosa Sound and the Gulf, next to the action on Casino Beach. The bright lobby opens to a sun deck with beachside pools on either side (one is heated). Half of the oversize rooms have balconies overlooking the Gulf; these are more expensive than rooms on the bayside, which have nice views but no outside sitting areas. A Tiki bar is directly on the beach, making it a fun place to spend some time. Camp Hampton is an excellent children's program with supervised activities; it costs $20 for the first child and $10 for each additional child, and includes a meal. *Note:* At press time, this hotel was closed until mid-2006 to repair damage caused by Hurricane Ivan.

2 Via de Luna, Pensacola Beach, FL 32561. (C) 800/320-8108 or 850/932-6800. Fax 850/932-6833. www.hampton beachresort.com. 181 units. Summer $159–$199 double; off season $89–$149 double. Rates include continental breakfast. AE, DC, DISC, MC, V. **Amenities:** Bar; 2 outdoor pools; access to nearby health club; exercise room; watersports equipment rental; laundry service; coin-op washers and dryers. *In room:* A/C, TV, dataport, fridge, coffeemaker, hair dryer, iron, free local calls.

The Portofino ⋆⋆⋆ *Kids*   The one and only luxe spot in the area, the Portofino is a stunning Mediterranean-style 28-acre resort and condo at the quieter east end of Pensacola Beach. Because it's a residence-cum-resort, its richly decorated suites are spectacular and feel very much like luxury apartments, with panoramic views of the Gulf. The resort also boasts an indoor Olympic-size pool and five heated pools; whirlpool spas, saunas, and steam rooms; a spa offering many treatments; a gourmet restaurant; and shuttle service to Tiger Point, a 36-hole championship golf course.

10 Portofino Dr., Pensacola Beach, FL 32561. (C) 866/478-3400 or 850/916-5000. Fax 850/916-5010. www.theportofino. com. 150 units. Summer $693–$1,299 2- or 3-bedroom apt; off season $495–$650 2- or 3-bedroom apt. AE, DC, DISC, MC, V. **Amenities:** Restaurant; bar; 6 pools; 2 Rubico tennis courts; fitness center; watersports rental; children's program. *In room:* A/C, TV, dataport, kitchen, coffeemaker, hair dryer, iron.

WHERE TO DINE
PENSACOLA
Jamie's ⋆⋆⋆ TRADITIONAL FRENCH   Occupying a restored Victorian home in Historic Pensacola Village, the town's classiest restaurant enhances its stellar ambience with working fireplaces, fabulous antiques, romantic candlelight, and subdued background music. The excellent French provincial fare includes roast leg of lamb, tournedos of beef, and seafood specials. The wine list is also exquisite. This is as fine as Pensacola's cuisine gets.

424 E. Zaragosa St. (between Alcanz and Florida Blanca). (C) 850/434-2911. Reservations recommended for both lunch and dinner. Main courses $17–$30. AE, DISC, MC, V. Mon–Sat 11:30am–2pm and 5:30–9pm, sometimes later.

Marina Oyster Barn ⋆ *Value* SEAFOOD   Exuding the ambience of the quickly vanishing Old Florida fish camps, this plain but clean restaurant at the Johnson-Rooks

Marina is a local legend. It's been a local favorite since 1969, for both its view and its down-home seafood. Freshly shucked oysters, served raw, steamed, fried, or Rockefeller style, are the main feature; but the seafood salad is also first-rate, and the fish, shrimp, and oysters are breaded with cornmeal in true Southern fashion. The daily luncheon specials give you a light meal at a bargain price.

505 Bayou Blvd. (on Bayou Texar). 𝒞 850/433-0511. Main courses $5–$15; sandwiches $4–$7; lunch specials $4–$8. AE, DISC, MC, V. Tues–Sat 11am–9pm (lunch specials 11am–2pm). Go east on Cervantes St. (U.S. 90) across the Bayou Texar Bridge, then take 1st left on Stanley Ave., and turn left again to the end of Strong St.

McGuire's Irish Pub 𝓕 STEAKS/SEAFOOD   Every day is St. Patrick's Day at this bustling pub whose motto is "Feasting, Imbibery, and Debauchery." The menu is delectably Irish, complete with Irish stew and corned beef and cabbage. Supersize steaks are the best offerings, however, as are hickory-smoked ribs and chicken. You can also order seafood, including a hearty bouillabaisse with shrimp, red snapper, clams, mussels, and oysters. The big burgers come with a choice of more than 20 toppings, from smoked Gouda cheese to sautéed Vidalia onions. You can watch your ale being brewed in copper kettles and dine in a cellarlike room where 8,000 bottles of wine are on display. Live music is offered most nights.

600 E. Gregory St. (between 11th and 12th aves.). 𝒞 **850/433-6789**. www.mcguiresirishpub.com. Main courses $16–$25; snacks, burgers, and sandwiches $8–$12. AE, DC, DISC, MC, V. Daily 11am–midnight, later on weekends.

Skopelos on the Bay 𝓕 SEAFOOD/STEAK/GREEK   If you didn't know any better—or drank too much ouzo—you'd think you were in Santorini. Perched on a bluff overlooking the bay, this family-owned restaurant has been famous hereabouts since 1959 for its great views and creative seafood dishes, such as the scamp Cervantes (scamp is a deepwater fish with white, flaky meat) and the Mediterranean-style grouper prepared with tomato and roasted eggplant. The menu also features charcoal-grilled steaks and, befitting the owner's Greek heritage, roast lamb served with moussaka, dolmades, titopita, and spanakopita. In warm weather, opt for an outside table with a bay view.

670 Scenic Hwy. (U.S. 90 E., at E. Cervantes St.). 𝒞 **850/432-6565**. Reservations recommended. Main courses $15–$35. AE, DISC, MC, V. Tues–Thurs and Sat 5–10:30pm; Fri 11:30am–2:30pm and 5–10:30pm.

PENSACOLA BEACH

Flounder's Chowder & Ale House 𝓕𝓕 SEAFOOD   Floundering around for a place where you can get fresh fish cooked any way, accompanied by live reggae almost nightly? Then you need to be at Flounder's Chowder & Ale House, on the boardwalk overlooking the Santa Rosa Sound, where you'll find great food for breakfast, brunch, lunch, dinner, or late-night snacks. The best of the offerings include the Maine lobster and the chargrilled tuna, grouper, and mahimahi. If you're lucky, a big smoker grill outside will be producing more fish and exceptional ribs. Burgers, salads, and sandwiches are offered all day. The dining room is cool and not at all what you'd expect from a fish house; its bookshelves, confessional booth walls straight from a church, and stained-glass windows imported from a convent, of all places, contribute to a cozy, Nantucket-in-the-winter kind of feel. But when the weather's warm, you'll definitely want to be outdoors.

800 Quietwater Beach Rd. (at Via de Luna and Fort Pickens Rd.). 𝒞 **850/932-2003**. Reservations not accepted. Main courses $15–$21; burgers and sandwiches $8–$10. AE, DC, DISC, MC, V. Sun–Thurs 11am–midnight (to 11pm in winter); Fri–Sat 11am–2am (to 11pm in winter).

Fun Fact The Last Great Road House

Sitting precisely on the Florida–Alabama state line on Perdido Key, about 15 miles west of downtown Pensacola, the **Flora-Bama Lounge**, 17401 Perdido Key Dr. (© 850/492-0611; www.florabama.com), is almost a shrine to country music. Billing itself as the "Last Great American Road House," this Gulf-side pub is famous for its Saturday and Sunday jam sessions from noon until way past midnight. Flora-Bama is the prime sponsor and a key venue for the Frank Brown International Songwriters' Festival, held during the first week of November. But the wackiest shindig held here has to be the Interstate Mullet Toss and Beach Party (the last weekend in Apr), which defies more in-depth description. The raw oyster bar is popular all the time. Granted, the joint can get a bit rough from time to time, but you won't soon forget the great Gulf views while sipping a cold one at the Deck Bar. The Flora-Bama is open daily from 8:30am to 2:30am.

PENSACOLA AFTER DARK

For what's hip and happening when the sun goes down, pick up the daily *Pensacola News Journal* (www.pensacolanewsjournal.com), especially its Friday entertainment section. Another good source for nightly events is the *Pensacola Downtown Crowd* (www.burchellpublishing.com/downtown.asp), a free publication available at the visitor center (p. 588).

THE PERFORMING ARTS   Pensacola has a surprisingly sophisticated array of entertainment choices for such a relatively small city. For a schedule of events, get a copy of *Vision,* a bimonthly newsletter published by the Arts Council of Northwest Florida (© 850/432-9906; www.artsnwfl.org). Also pick up **Sneak Preview,** a calendar of events at the Pensacola Civic Center and the Saenger Theatre. Both publications are available at the visitor center (p. 588). Tickets for all major performances can be purchased from **Ticketmaster** (© 800/488-5252 or 850/433-6311; www.ticketmaster.com).

   The highlight venue here is the ornate **Saenger Theatre** ✪, 118 S. Palafox St., near Romana Street (© 850/444-7686; www.pensacolasaenger.com), a painstakingly restored masterpiece of Spanish baroque architecture. Presentations feature the local opera company and symphony orchestra, Broadway musicals, and touring performers. The 10,000-seat **Pensacola Civic Center,** 201 E. Gregory St., at Alcaniz Street (© 850/432-0800; www.pensacolaciviccenter.com), hosts a variety of concerts, exhibitions, sports events, and conventions. Call ahead for the current schedule.

THE CLUB & BAR SCENE   Pensacola's downtown nighttime entertainment center is **Seville Quarter,** 130 E. Government St., at Jefferson Street (© 850/434-6211; www.rosies.com), in the Seville Historic District. This restored antique-brick complex with New Orleans–style wrought-iron balconies is actually a collection of pubs and restaurants whose names capture the ambience: Rosie O'Grady's Goodtime Emporium, Lili Marlene's Aviator's Pub, Apple Annie's Courtyard, End o' the Alley Bar, Phineas Phogg's Balloon Works (a dance hall, not a balloon shop), and Fast Eddie's Billiard Parlor (which has electronic games, too). The pubs serve up libations, food, and live entertainment from Dixieland jazz to country and western. Get a monthly calendar at the information booth next to Rosie O'Grady's. Seville Quarter is open daily from 11am to 2am.

Every night is party time at **McGuire's Irish Pub,** the city's popular Irish pub, brewery, and eatery (p. 600). Irish bands appear nightly during summer, and on Saturday and Sunday the rest of the year.

Beach nightlife centers on **Quietwater Boardwalk,** Via de Luna at Fort Pickens Road (no phone), a shopping-and-dining complex on Santa Rosa Sound. With the lively beach-and-reggae bar at **Flounder's Chowder & Ale House** (p. 600) just a few steps away, it's easy to barhop until you find a band to your liking. Across Via de Luna at Casino Beach is **The Dock** (✆ **850/934-3314;** www.thedock.pensacola.com), which has live bands nightly in summer, and on weekends off season. Finally, **Sidelines Sports Bar & Restaurant** (✆ **850/934-3660**) has a great game lineup.

2 Destin & Fort Walton Beach ⭐⭐

40 miles E of Pensacola, 160 miles W of Tallahassee

Sitting on a round harbor off East Pass, which lets broad and beautiful Choctawhatchee Bay flow into the Gulf of Mexico, Destin, along with Fort Walton Beach and Okaloosa Island, comprises the Emerald Coast. It's justly famous for its fishing fleet, the largest in the state. It's also Northwest Florida's fastest-growing and most upscale vacation destination, with a multitude of high-rise condominiums, the huge Sandestin resort, several golf courses, and some of the Panhandle's best restaurants and lively nightspots. By and large, Destin attracts a more affluent crowd than Fort Walton Beach, its more down-to-earth neighbor.

Although Fort Walton Beach has its own strip of white sand on Okaloosa Island, it is a city whose economy is supported less by tourism than by the sprawling Eglin Air Force Base. Covering more than 700 square miles, Eglin is the world's largest air base and is home to the U.S. Air Force's Armament Museum and the 33rd Tactical Fighter Wing, the "Top Guns" of Operation Desert Storm in 1991.

To the east of Destin, development is picking up steam along the beaches of southern Walton County. Still, this picturesque area has mostly cottages nestled among rolling sand dunes covered with sea oats. Here you'll find Grayton Beach State Park, which sports one of America's finest beaches, and the quaint, albeit Stepford-esque planned village of **Seaside** ⭐⭐, which served as the set for Jim Carrey's movie *The Truman Show.* Seaside was built on a lovely stretch of beach in the 1980s—but with Victorian architecture that makes it look a century older. The village's Gulf-side honeymoon cottages make for one of Florida's most romantic retreats. It also has interesting shops and galleries; a stamp-size, Greek Revival–style post office; and a resident population of artists, writers, and other creative folks, who permit only their own cars in their relatively expensive little enclave. Don't worry; there are parking spaces for tourists on the one main road through Seaside, but you can't drive into the village itself unless you live there. Although I appreciate Seaside for what it is, the last time I was there the secret had gotten out, and Seaside was slowly falling under the weights of commercialism and tourism.

ESSENTIALS

GETTING THERE   Flights arriving at and departing from **Okaloosa Regional Airport** (✆ 850/651-7160; www.co.okaloosa.fl.us/airport.html) actually use the enormous strips at Eglin Air Force Base. The terminal is on Florida 85, north of Fort Walton Beach, and is served by **Delta** (✆ 800/221-1212), **Northwest** (✆ 800/225-2525), and **US Airways** (✆ 800/428-4322).

Avis (© 800/331-1212), **Budget** (© 800/527-0700), **Hertz** (© 800/654-3131), and **National** (© 800/CAR-RENT) have rental cars at the airport, while **Enterprise** (© 800/325-8007) is located in town.

AAA Annie's Shuttle (© 850/978-2450) provides 24-hour van transportation to and from the airport. Fares for up to three people are based on a zone system: $15 to $18 to Fort Walton Beach, $27 to Destin, and $40 to Sandestin and southern Walton County.

The **Amtrak** (© 800/872-7245; www.amtrak.com) Sunset Limited transcontinental service stops at Crestview, 26 miles north of Fort Walton Beach.

VISITOR INFORMATION For advance information on both Fort Walton Beach and Destin, contact the **Emerald Coast Convention and Visitors Bureau,** P.O. Box 609, Fort Walton Beach, FL 32549 (© 800/322-3319 or 850/651-7122; fax 850/651-7149; www.destin-fwb.com). The bureau shares quarters with the **Okaloosa County Visitors Welcome Center** in a tin-roofed, beachside building on Miracle Strip Parkway (U.S. 98), on Okaloosa Island at the eastern edge of Fort Walton Beach. Stop here for brochures, maps, and other information. This visitor center is open Monday through Friday from 8am to 5pm, Saturday and Sunday from 10am to 4pm.

The **Destin Area Chamber of Commerce,** 4484 Legendary Dr., Destin, FL 32541 (© 850/837-6241; fax 850/654-5612; www.destinchamber.com), gives away brochures and sells maps of the area. The chamber is in an office complex at the entry to Regatta Bay Golf & Country Club, on U.S. 98, ½ mile east of the Mid-Bay Bridge. It's open Monday through Friday from 9am to 5pm; closed holidays.

For information on the beaches of South Walton, contact the **South Walton Tourist Development Council,** P.O. Box 1248, Santa Rosa Beach, FL 32459 (© 800/822-6877 or 850/267-1216; fax 850/267-3943; www.beachesofsouthwalton.com). Its visitor center is at the intersection of U.S. 98 and U.S. 331, in Santa Rosa Beach (© 850/267-3511); open daily from 8:30am to 5:30pm.

GETTING AROUND The **Okaloosa County Tourist Development Authority** (© 850/651-7131) operates a free **Island Shuttle** trolley during the summer months along the entire length of Santa Rosa Boulevard on Okaloosa Island. The two trolleys run every 30 minutes Sunday through Thursday from 7am to 10pm, and Friday and Saturday from 7am to 1am. They also connect the island to the Uptown bus station, on Eglin Parkway Northeast on the Fort Walton Beach mainland.

For a cab in Fort Walton Beach, call **Black and Gold Taxi** (© 850/244-7303) or **Yellow Cab** (© 850/244-3600). In Destin, call **Destin Taxi** (© 850/654-5700). Fares are based on a zone system rather than meters, with a $5 minimum. Trips within Fort Walton Beach or Destin should range from $5 to $10.

TIME The area is in the central time zone, 1 hour behind Miami, Orlando, and Jacksonville.

HITTING THE BEACH

DESTIN Like an oasis in the middle of Destin's rapid development, the 208-acre **Henderson Beach State Park** ✺✺, east of Destin Harbor on U.S. 98, allows easy access to swimming, sunning, surf fishing, picnicking, and seabird-watching along its 1½ miles of beach. There are restrooms, outdoor showers, and surf chairs for people with disabilities. The area is open daily from 8am to sunset. Admission is $4 per vehicle with up to eight occupants, $1 per pedestrian or cyclist. Several good restaurants are just outside the park's western boundary. Pets on leashes are allowed in the park, including the beach and campground. Campers will find 60 sites in a wooded setting here; they cost $21, including electricity, and can be reserved up to 11 months in advance. For camping reservations, call © **800/326-3521** or go to www.reserveamerica. com. For more information, contact the park at 1700 Emerald Coast Pkwy., Destin, FL 32541 (© **850/837-7550;** www.floridastateparks.org/hendersonbeach).

The **James W. Lee Park,** between Destin and Sandestin on Scenic Highway 98, has a long white-sand beach overlooked by covered picnic tables, an ice-cream parlor, and a moderately priced seafood restaurant with great views.

FORT WALTON BEACH Do your loafing on the white sands of **Okaloosa Island,** joined to the mainland by the high-rise Brooks Bridge over Santa Rosa Sound. Most resort hotels and amusement parks are grouped around the Gulfarium marine park on U.S. 98, east of the bridge. Here you'll find the **Boardwalk,** a collection of tin-roofed beachside buildings that have an arcade for the kids, a saloon for adults, covered picnic areas, a summertime snack bar, and a seafood restaurant. Just to the east, you can use the restrooms, cold-water showers, and other free facilities at **Beasley Park,** home of the Okaloosa County Visitor Welcome Center.

Across U.S. 98, the Okaloosa portion of the **Gulf Islands National Seashore** has picnic areas and sailboats for rent on Choctawhatchee Bay, plus access to the Gulf. Admission to this part of the national seashore is free.

SOUTHERN WALTON COUNTY Sporting the finest stretch of white sand on the Gulf, **Grayton Beach State Park** ☆☆☆, on C.R. 30A, also has 356 acres of pine

⟨Tips⟩ How to Find a Street Address

Don't worry about getting lost, since most of what you'll want to see and do in Destin and Fort Walton Beach is either on or no more than a few blocks from U.S. 98, the area's main east-west drag. Finding a street address is another matter, however, because even many local residents don't fully comprehend the post office's bizarre naming and numbering system along U.S. 98.

In Fort Walton Beach, U.S. 98 is known as "Miracle Strip Parkway," with "southwest" and "southeast" addresses on the mainland and "east" addresses on Okaloosa Island.

In Destin, U.S. 98 is officially known as "Highway 98 East" from the Destin Bridge east to Airport Road, and street numbers get progressively higher as you head east from the bridge. East of Airport Road, however, the post office calls U.S. 98 the "Emerald Coast Parkway"—although locals still say a place is on "98 East." The highway is also known as the Emerald Coast Parkway in Walton County, but the street-numbering system changes completely once you pass the county line.

Adding to the confusion in Destin, "Old Highway 98 East" is a short spur from Airport Road to the western side of Henderson Beach State Park, and "Scenic Highway 98 East" parallels the real U.S. 98 along the beach from the eastern side of Henderson Beach to Sandestin.

In other words, call and ask for directions if you're not sure how to find an establishment here.

forests surrounding scenic Western Lake. There's a boat ramp and a campground with electric hookups on the lake. Get a leaflet at the main gate for a self-guided tour of the nature trail. Pets are not allowed anywhere in the recreation area. The park is open daily from 8am to sunset. Admission is $4 per vehicle with up to eight occupants, $1 per pedestrian or bicyclist. Campsites cost $19, including electricity. For camping reservations, call ✆ **800/326-3521** or go to www.reserveamerica.com. For general information, contact the park at 357 Main Park Rd., Santa Rosa Beach, FL 32459 (✆ **850/231-4210;** www.floridastateparks.org/graytonbeach).

Seaside has free parking along C.R. 30A and is a good spot for a day at the beach, a stroll or bike ride around the quaint village, and a tasty meal at one of its restaurants. Same goes for **Seagrove Beach**, where one of the area's most charming restaurants, **Sandor's European Cuisine**, is located (p. 617).

OUTDOOR ACTIVITIES

BOATING   Pontoon boats are highly popular for use on the back bays and Sunday-afternoon floating parties in East Pass. Several companies rent them, including **Adventure Pontoon Rentals** (✆ 850/837-3041), **B&J Boat Rentals** (✆ 850/243-4488), **East Pass Watersports** (✆ 850/654-4253), and **Destin Water Toys** (✆ 850/837-7755;** www.destinwatertoys.com), all on Destin Harbor. Expect to pay about $80 for a half-day, $125 for a full day. Destin Water Toys also has speedboats for rent ($125–$175 for 4 hr., $175–$285 for 8 hr.).

FISHING   Billing itself the "World's Luckiest Fishing Village," Destin has Florida's largest charter-boat fleet, with more than 140 vessels based at the marinas lining the north shore of Destin Harbor, on U.S. 98 east of the Destin Bridge. Arranging a trip is as easy as walking along the Destin Harbor waterfront, where you'll find the booking booths of several agents, such as **Harborwalk Charters** (✆ **800/242-2824** or 850/837-2343; www.harborwalkfishing.com), **Pelican Charters** (✆ **850/837-2343**), and **Harbor Cove Charters** (✆ **850/837-2222**). Rates for private charters range from about $440 to $1,320 per boat, depending on the length of the voyage.

For additional information on small and large group charters, check out **FishDestin. com** (✆ **850/837-9401** or 850/585-0049; www.fishdestin.com). If you're a die-hard angler, consider coming in October for the **Destin Fishing Rodeo** (✆ **850/837-6734;** www.destinfishingrodeo.org), a month-long fishing extravaganza.

You don't have to go to sea to fish from the catwalk of the 3,000-foot **Destin Bridge,** over East Pass. The marinas and bait shops at Destin Harbor can provide gear, bait, and fishing licenses. In Fort Walton Beach, you can cast a line off **Okaloosa Island Fishing Pier,** 1030 Miracle Strip Pkwy. E./U.S. 98 (✆ **850/244-1023**), open 24 hours a day. Adults pay $6.50 to fish; children 12 and under pay $3.50. Observers pay $1. Bait and equipment rentals are available.

GOLF   For advance information on area courses, contact the **Emerald Coast Golf Association,** P.O. Box 304, Destin, FL 32540. Also look for *South Coast Golf Guide,* the free annual directory published in Pensacola (see p. 51 for details). Be sure to ask whether your choice of accommodations offers golf packages, which can mean significant savings.

For course information, go to www.golf.com or www.floridagolfing.com, or call the **Florida Sports Foundation** (✆ **850/488-8347**) or **Florida Golfing** (✆ **866/833-2663**).

On the mainland, nonresidents are welcome to play at the city-owned **Fort Walton Beach Golf Club,** on Lewis Turner Boulevard (C.R. 189) north of town

(© **850/833-9530**; www.fwb.org/golf/index.htm). The club has two 18-hole courses—the **Pines** and the **Oaks** (© **850/833-9528**)—plus a pro shop. Greens fees at both courses are about $35 year-round, including cart.

In Destin, scenic **Indian Bayou Golf and Country Club,** off Airport Road (© **850/ 837-6191**), has three nine-hole courses with large greens and wide fairways. They look easy, but watch out for water hazards and strategically placed hidden bunkers! Greens fees, including cart, are about $65.

Sandestin Golf and Beach Resort (p. 610), on U.S. 98 East in southern Walton County (© **850/267-8211** for tee times), is the largest facility here. Its 72 holes are spread over three outstanding championship courses. The Baytowne and Links courses overlook Choctawhatchee Bay. Fees for 18 holes are $65 to $125 for resort guests, $85 to $145 for nonguests.

Some of the 18 championship holes at **Emerald Bay Golf Club,** 2 miles east of the Mid-Bay Bridge on U.S. 98 (© **850/837-5197**; www.emeraldbaydestin.com), run along Choctawhatchee Bay; the water adds both beauty and challenges to the otherwise wide and forgiving fairways. Greens fees are about $80 with cart, $65 in winter.

In southern Walton County, the semiprivate **Santa Rosa Golf & Beach Club,** off C.R. 30A in Dune Allen Beach (© **850/267-2229**; www.santarosaclub.com), offers a challenging 18-hole course through tall pines looking out to vistas of the Gulf. The club has a pro shop, a beachside restaurant, a lounge, and tennis courts. Fees are about $70 in summer, $50 off season.

In Niceville, a 20-minute drive north via the Mid-Bay Bridge, nonguests may play golf (4 nine-hole courses) or tennis (21 courts) at the **Bluewater Bay Resort** (© **850/ 897-3241**; www.bwbresort.com), which also has condominiums for rent.

Call ahead for reservations and current fees at all these clubs; also ask about afternoon and early-evening specials.

SAILING   Sailing South, on U.S. 98 at Destin Harbor (© **850/837-7245**; www. sailingsouth.com), has half-day cruises aboard the 72-foot schooner *Daniel Webster Clements.* The 2½-hour afternoon cruises stop for swimming and snorkeling virtually under the Destin Bridge; these cost $35 for adults and $20 for kids under 12. It also offers 2½-hour sunset cruises for the same price. The 54-foot schooner *Nathaniel Bowditch* (© **850/650-8787**; www.bowditchsailing.com) will take you on sunset and half-day shelling excursions ($35 adults, $20 kids 12 and under).

SCUBA DIVING & SNORKELING   At least a dozen dive shops are located along the beaches. Considered one of the best, **Scuba Tech Diving Charters** has two locations in Destin: at 301 U.S. 98 E. (© **850/837-2822**; www.scubatechnwfl.com) and at 10004 U.S. 98 E. (© **850/837-1933**), about ½ mile west of the Sandestin Beach Resort.

WATERSPORTS   Hobie Cats, WaveRunners, jet boats, jet skis, and parasailing are available all along the beach. The largest selection of operators is at the marinas just east of the Destin Bridge, behind the Hooters and Fat Tuesday's pubs. These include **Boogies** (© **850/654-4497**) and **Destin Watertoys** (© **888/357-2608** or 850/837-7755; www.destinwatertoys.com).

EXPLORING THE AREA

Eden Gardens State Park   Evoking images from *Gone With the Wind,* these 115 acres house the magnificent 1895 Greek Revival–style Wesley Mansion, which has been lovingly restored and richly furnished with period antiques. The second-largest collection of Louis XVI furniture in the country is here, along with a Chippendale nightstand worth about $1 million. The mansion overlooks scenic Choctawhatchee Bay and is surrounded by immense Spanish moss–draped oak trees. The house is particularly stunning during Christmastime, when it is draped in lights and decoration. The Eden Gardens are resplendent with camellias and azaleas. Your visit won't be complete without a guided tour of the house, so avoid coming here on a Tuesday or Wednesday. Picnicking is allowed on the plantation grounds.

181 Eden Gardens Rd. (off C.R. 395), Point Washington. ☏ 850/231-4214. www.floridastateparks.org/edengardens. Grounds and gardens $3 per vehicle, $1 per pedestrian or bicyclist; mansion tours $3 adults, $1 children 12 and under. Gardens and grounds daily 8am–sunset; 45-min. mansion tours on the hour. Thurs–Mon 10am–3pm. Take C.R. 395 north from Hwy. 98. Proceed for a mile; park entrance is on the left.

Florida's Gulfarium (Kids)   The country's second-oldest marine park (it opened in 1955) features ongoing 25-minute shows with dolphins, sea lions, Peruvian penguins, loggerhead turtles, sharks, stingrays, moray eels, and alligators. Fascinating exhibits include the Living Sea, with special windows for viewing undersea life. During one of the shows, a scuba diver explains the sea life while swimming among the various creatures. The Spotted Dolphin Encounter is a terrific program in which brave participants receive an up-close-and-personal hand-to-flipper encounter with two of the dolphins, Kiwi and Daphne. A trainer will guide you through the 40-minute interactive session. If you're not satisfied with just seeing a few dolphins and leaving, expect to spend about 3 hours here between all the shows and exhibits. (Be aware that swimming with dolphins has both its critics and its supporters. You may want to visit the Whale and Dolphin Conservation Society's website at www.wdcs.org. For more information about responsible travel in general, check out www.treadlightly.org and www.ecotourism.org.) *Note:* At press time, the Dolphin Encounter attraction was closed and there was no information on when it would reopen.

1010 Miracle Strip Pkwy. (U.S. 98) on Okaloosa Island. ☏ 850/244-5169. www.gulfarium.com. Admission $18 adults, $16 seniors, $11 children 4–11; Dolphin Encounter $100. Mid-May to Labor Day daily 9am–6pm (park closes 8pm); Labor Day to mid-May daily 9am–4pm (park closes 6pm).

Indian Temple Mound and Museum   This ceremonial mound, one of the largest ever discovered, dates from A.D. 1200. The museum showcases some of its 6,000 ceramic artifacts from southeastern American Indian tribes, the nation's largest such collection. Exhibits depict the lifestyles of the four tribes that lived in the Choctawhatchee Bay region for 12,000 years.

139 Miracle Strip Pkwy. SE, on the mainland. ☏ 850/833-9595. Park free; museum $2 adults, $1 children 6–17. Park daily dawn–dusk. Museum Sept–May Mon–Fri 11am–4pm, Sat 9am–4pm; June–Aug Mon–Sat 9am–4:30pm, Sun 12:30–4:30pm.

U.S. Air Force Armament Museum (⚓)   Although this fascinating museum is not on a par with Pensacola's National Museum of Naval Aviation (p. 594), you'll love it if you're into warplanes. Located on the world's largest air base, it traces military developments from World War II to Operation Desert Storm. Reconnaissance, fighter, and bomber planes, including the SR-71 Blackbird spy plane, are on display.

100 Museum Dr., off Eglin Pkwy. (Fla. 85) at Eglin Air Force Base, 5 miles north of downtown. ☏ 850/882-4062. Free admission. Daily 9:30am–4:30pm. Closed federal holidays.

SHOPPING

Silver Sands Factory Stores (★★), on U.S. 98 between Destin and Sandestin (☏ **800/510-6255** or 850/864-9771; www.silversandsfactorystores.com), has more than 120 upscale stores, such as Liz Claiborne, DKNY, J. Crew, Brooks Brothers, Coach, Bose, and so on. Shops are open Monday through Saturday from 10am to 9pm (to 7pm Jan–Feb), Sunday from 10am to 6pm (noon–6pm Jan–Feb). There are also electronic games for kids and a sports bar for adults.

Over at the Sandestin Beach Resort on U.S. 98, you can window-shop in the **Market at Sandestin,** where boutiques purvey expensive clothing, gifts, and Godiva chocolates.

WHERE TO STAY

The area has a vast supply of condominiums and cottages for rent. One good-value example is Venus by the Sea, listed below. The visitor information offices (p. 603) will provide lists of others. The largest rental agent is **Resort Quest,** 3500 Emerald Coast Pkwy., Destin (℗ **888/909-6807;** fax 850/654-2937; www.abbott-resorts.com), which publishes a magazine-size annual brochure picturing and describing its many properties throughout the area.

The **Flamingo Cottage,** on Santa Rosa Beach (℗ **832/309-5866;** www.flamingo cottage.com), is perfect for families or groups (it can sleep up to 16), with fabulous features such as stone tiles, 9-foot bead-board ceilings, crown moldings, an oak staircase, and a master suite with Jacuzzi and private covered balcony. In addition to a large den and kitchen, laundry room, and outdoor gas grill, the cottage has four bedrooms and three bathrooms. Rates are $1,475 to $3,400 per week, depending on the season.

There are several commercial campgrounds here, but the best camping is at **Henderson Beach State Park,** in Destin, and at **Grayton Beach State Park,** in south Walton County (see p. 603 and 604).

State and local governments add 9% to 11% to all hotel and campground bills.

DESTIN

The local **Motel 6,** 405 U.S. 98 E. (℗ **800/466-8356** or 850/837-0007; fax 850/837-5325; www.motel6.com), across the highway from the harbor, has rooms that are generally larger than those at other members of this cut-rate chain. There's also an outdoor pool on the premises.

Best Western SummerPlace Inn   Located just a block from the beach, this four-story, Spanish-motif Best Western is a refreshing change from its cookie-cutter siblings. It offers innlike rooms decorated with wildlife prints. A few suites have hot tubs in their living rooms. The more expensive Gulf-side units have balconies (those facing the bay do not). Doors open from an indoor pool, whirlpool, and exercise room to an outdoor pool, but you'll have to negotiate your way across busy U.S. 98 to reach the Gulf.

14047 Emerald Coast Pkwy. (U.S. 98, at Airport Rd.), Destin, FL 32541. ℗ 888/232-2499 or 850/650-8003. Fax 850/650-8004. www.bestwestern.com/summerplaceinn. 72 units. Summer $119–$179 double; off season $49–$99 double. Rates include continental breakfast. AE, DISC, MC, V. **Amenities:** Indoor and outdoor pools; exercise room; Jacuzzi; business center; coin-op washers and dryers. *In room:* A/C, TV, dataport, fridge, coffeemaker, hair dryer, free local calls.

FORT WALTON BEACH

The managers of Venus by the Sea (see below) also run the **Sea Crest Condominiums,** located next door at 895 Santa Rosa Blvd. (℗ **800/476-1885** or 850/301-9600; fax 850/301-9205; www.seacrestcondos.com). The 112 units in this seven-story building aren't as spacious as those in Venus, but they're considerably more luxurious, and those on the higher floors have great views toward the west. The complex has indoor and outdoor pools (actually one pool—you can swim under a glass partition between them), and it sits next to a county park with a boardwalk leading over the dunes to the beach.

Among the chain motels here is the **Hampton Inn Fort Walton Beach,** 1112 Santa Rosa Blvd. (© **800/426-7866** or 850/301-0906; www.hamptoninnfwb.com).

Marina Motel   This family-operated, self-described "fisherman's motel" may look like a shack from the outside, but it has clean, comfortable rooms and apartments directly across U.S. 98 from the magnificent public beach at Beasley Park. A low-slung, brick-fronted motel block holds most of the rooms. Other units are in two-story stucco structures near a marina whose 560-foot pier is home to charter-fishing boats. Two one-bedroom apartments at the end of the complex overlook the marina and bay. If traffic is too busy to cross U.S. 98 to the beach (there are no nearby over-passes or traffic lights), you can sun at the motel's little bayside beach or take a dip in its roadside pool.

1345 E. Miracle Strip Pkwy. (U.S. 98), Fort Walton Beach, FL 32548. © **800/237-7021** or 850/244-1129. Fax 850/ 243-6063. www.marinamotel.net. 38 units. Summer $69–$89 double, $115–$150 apt; off season $39–$69 double, $65–$99 apt. AE, DC, DISC, MC, V. **Amenities:** Outdoor pool; coin-op washers and dryers. *In room:* A/C, TV, kitchen (efficiencies and apts only), fridge, coffeemaker, iron.

Ramada Plaza Beach Resort ✦   This big resort boasts the prettiest outdoor areas in the region, with waterfalls cascading over lofty rocks and a romantic grotto bar, all surrounded by thick foliage. Although the resort has another pool, sun deck, and bar out by the beach, its gorgeous courtyard would have even more charm if it weren't cut off from the Gulf by a six-story block of hotel rooms. The rooms and suites in this beachfront building are the resort's best, with Gulf or courtyard views from balconies or patios. The least expensive units, in the adjacent building, overlook a parking lot. Though the decor is blasé, the hotel's views make up for that. On-site dining options include a barbecue shack out in the tropical forest. The Boardwalk beach pavilion and restaurants are next door.

1500 E. Miracle Strip Pkwy. (U.S. 98), Fort Walton Beach, FL 32548. © **800/874-8962** or 850/243-9161. Fax 850/ 243-2391. www.ramadafwb.com. 335 units. Summer $120–$185 double, $280–$350 suite; off season $70–$195 double, $160–$270 suite. AE, DC, DISC, MC, V. **Amenities:** 3 restaurants; 3 bars; 2 outdoor pools (1 heated); exercise room; Jacuzzi; watersports equipment rental; children's programs; game room; limited room service; coin-op washers and dryers. *In room:* A/C, TV, dataport, fridge, coffeemaker, hair dryer, iron, safe.

Venus by the Sea ✦ *(Value)*   Offering considerably more space than a hotel normally would at these rates, this pleasant three-story enclave on western Okaloosa Island was built in the 1970s and has been well maintained ever since, though the decor is still stuck in that era (think retirement home) and should be updated. Each of the one-, two-, and three-bedroom units has a long living/dining/kitchen area, with a rear door leading to a balcony or a patio opening onto a grassy courtyard. The beach is a short walk across the dunes, and you can stroll along the undeveloped beach at an Eglin Air Force Base auxiliary facility about 600 feet away. The same management operates the new and much more luxurious **Sea Crest Condominiums** (see above), and Venus guests can use the indoor/outdoor pool there.

885 Santa Rosa Blvd., Fort Walton Beach, FL 32548. © **800/476-1885** or 850/301-9600. Fax 850/301-9205. www. venuscondos.com. 45 units. Summer $140–$215 apt; off season $80–$110 apt. Weekly and monthly rates available. Ask about off-season specials. MC, V. **Amenities:** Outdoor pool; tennis court; coin-op washers and dryers. *In room:* A/C, TV/VCR, kitchen, coffeemaker, iron.

SOUTHERN WALTON COUNTY

If you want to stay near the Sandestin Golf and Beach Resort (see below) without paying its prices, there's a modern **Sleep Inn,** 5000 Emerald Coast Pkwy./U.S. 98 (© **800/627-5337** or 850/654-7022), just a mile west.

Hilton Sandestin Beach & Golf Resort 🏖️🏖️ (Kids)　This all-inclusive, all-suites beachside resort, housed in two adjacent towers, is the top full-service hotel here. It's nicely situated on the grounds of Sandestin Golf and Beach Resort (see the next listing) and shares its golf and tennis facilities. The elegant Elephant Walk restaurant is next door. Executive suites in one wing are equipped primarily for business travelers and conventioneers (lots of meeting space here), while the spacious junior suites in the old wing are geared toward families, with a special area for children's bunk beds. Parents can send the kids off to a supervised summertime program while pampering themselves at the full-service spa. Miniature golf, three pools, 13 tennis courts, four championship golf courses, and the stunning private beach make for a very enticing stay.

4000 Sandestin Blvd. S., Destin, FL 32541. © **800/367-1271** or 850/267-9500. Fax 850/267-3076. www.sandestin resort.hilton.com. 598 units. Summer $239–$539 suite; off season $159–$439 suite. Golf and tennis packages available. AE, DC, DISC, MC, V. **Amenities:** 2 restaurants; 2 bars; indoor and outdoor pools; golf course; tennis courts; health club; spa; Jacuzzi; watersports equipment rental; children's programs; game room; concierge; activities desk; car-rental desk; business center; shopping arcade; salon; 24-hr. room service; massage; babysitting; laundry service; coin-op washers and dryers; concierge-level rooms. *In room:* A/C, TV, dataport, minibar, coffeemaker, hair dryer, iron.

Sandestin Golf and Beach Resort 🏖️🏖️🏖️ (Kids)　Although it could be mistaken for yet another Stepfordized planned community, this luxurious real-estate development is one of Florida's biggest sports-oriented resorts and is the epitome of the great escape. It sprawls over 2,400 acres complete with a spectacular beach 5 miles west of Destin, plus a marina. It's notable for its 81 holes of championship golf and its tennis clinic (both with instruction available), plus a fully equipped sports spa and health center. An array of handsomely decorated accommodations overlooks the Gulf, Choctawhatchee Bay, the golf fairways, some lagoons, or a nature preserve. The hotel rooms and suites are in the Bayside Inn; all have kitchenettes and balconies, but you'd be wise to opt for one of the much more spacious junior suites or one-, two-, and three-bedroom condominium apartments, which are in high- and mid-rise buildings either on the Gulf or along the manicured fairways. The privately owned condominiums are individually decorated and come with full kitchen and patio or balcony; many have washers and dryers as well.

Most resort amenities are a short walk, bike ride, or free tram ride away, and a tunnel runs under U.S. 98 to connect Sandestin's Gulf and bay areas. Among the relatively limited on-site dining options is the romantic **Elephant Walk** 🏖️🏖️ (© **850/267-4800**), located on the Gulf; it serves different gourmet-quality choices for dinner every evening. On top of Elephant Walk is the **Governor's Attic,** a swanky cigar-and-cognac kind of place overlooking the Gulf. The coolest, newest addition to this resort-cum-city is the **Village of Baytowne Wharf,** a 28-acre pedestrian village overlooking the Choctawhatchee Bay, featuring a unique collection of more than two dozen specialty merchants ranging from quaint boutiques and charming eateries to lively nightclubs. It also features hotel rooms and one-, two- and three-bedroom luxury accommodations surrounding the bay, with rates ranging from $89 in the off season to $272 in the summer. Fantastic kids' and teens' offerings include Jolee Island Nature Park, a mile-long trail dotted with weather-beaten, double-wide porch swings, where you can sit and watch the waters of Horseshoe Bayou lap against the shore or catch the sunset over Choctawhatchee Bay.

⒯Tips Luxurious Cottages & Luscious Surroundings

Rosemary Beach, at the east end of C.R. 30A just 8 miles east of Seaside (© 888/855-1551; www.rosemarybeach.com), a newer, smaller, and, I think, better, seaside-style community, offers a collection of about 300 luxurious Pan-Caribbean-style cottages and carriage houses (from studios to six bedrooms), all of which are nonsmoking. This is another pedestrian-friendly community—almost everything on the 107 acres is within a 5-minute walk of the town center—and most of the homes are owned by people who live here part-time and lease to vacationers the rest of the year. The white-sand (and soft as talcum powder) beach here is ridiculously gorgeous, though guests can also choose from among four pools. Nothing on the architecturally stunning and strikingly planted property here is higher than four stories, and all the homes telescope in from the beach so everyone can have a view (or partial view) of the Gulf. Other amenities include a health club, bike rental, racquet club, 2½-mile fitness trail, spa, shops, town hall and post office, and a few very good restaurants, including the delightful Onano Neighborhood Café. Cottages are individually decorated, so check online to see pictures of the properties before deciding. Though all come with full kitchen, washer/dryer, and TV/VCR, some have added amenities such as a Jacuzzi or private pool. There is also a B&B on the premises (rooms start at $118), and the town is building a full-service hotel. The B&B's daily rates are $178 to $968 in spring and fall, $198 to $1,062 in summer, and $138 to $812 in winter.

9300 Emerald Coast Pkwy. W. (U.S. 98), Destin, FL 32541. © **800/277-0800** or 850/267-8000 in the U.S., or 800/933-7846 in Canada. Fax 850/267-8222. www.sandestin.com. 175 units, 620 condo apts. Summer $180–$210 double, $210–$560 condo apt; off season $85–$190 double, $105–$395 condo apt. Packages and weekly/monthly rates available. Rates include health club, bicycle, boogie board, canoe, and kayak use; 1 hr. tennis daily; and discounts on other amenities. AE, DC, DISC, MC, V. **Amenities:** 3 restaurants; 3 bars; 9 heated outdoor pools; 4 golf courses; 18 tennis courts; spa; Jacuzzis; watersports equipment rental; children's programs; game room; concierge; shopping arcade; salon; limited room service (hotel only); massage; babysitting; laundry service; coin-op washers and dryers. *In room:* A/C, TV, dataport, kitchen, coffeemaker, hair dryer, iron.

SEASIDE

Mayberry meets *Metropolitan Home* here in this pastel-hued community, where life is a dreamlike state of mind. If you decide to rent a home or a **romantic honeymoon cottage** 👫👫 in this quaint village, contact the **Seaside Cottage Rental Agency,** P.O. Box 4730, Seaside, FL 32459 (© **800/277-8696** or 850/231-1320; fax 850/231-2293; www.seasidefl.com). The agency has several hundred cottages in its rental inventory, from one to six bedrooms. The beachside cottages are one of Florida's best getaways for newlyweds or anyone else looking for a romantic escape, though if you want a little more privacy and less action, you might choose Rosemary Beach (see above) instead.

Josephine's French Country Inn at Seaside 👫👫👫   With its large Tuscan columns reminiscent of a Virginia mansion, Josephine's is an elegant and romantic country inn outfitted with four-poster beds, lace comforters, and marble tubs. Most

---

Tips **Picture Perfect**

Designed by renowned architect David Rockwell, the **WaterColor Inn,** 34 Goldenrod Circle (© **866/426-2656** or 850/534-500; www.watercolorinn.com), is a stunning 499-acre beachfront boutique hotel. With just 60 rooms, it feels more like a private beach house than a hotel. A ground-floor library with club chairs and a cocktail lounge opening onto the pool deck drive that feeling even further home. Guest rooms feature a pantry, a walk-in shower with views to the beach, and Adirondack chairs on the balcony. Six ground-floor bungalows sport outdoor showers enclosed by striped tents, lending a very French Riviera feel a la F. Scott Fitzgerald's *Tender Is the Night.* Rotunda guest rooms in the center tower offer stunning 180-degree views from massive balconies. Access to WaterColor community facilities, such as the Tom Fazio–designed Camp Creek Golf Club, 6 miles east, is another bonus. Five Har-Tru tennis courts are also available. A Gulf-front beach club (complete with pool deck, children's pool, and beach services including complimentary boogie boards, Hobie kayaks, surfing kayaks, beach volleyball, and snorkel equipment), as well as a lakefront boathouse (with sailboats, canoes, kids' activities, and fishing), will keep you from ever wanting to leave this fabulous piece of paradise. Rates range from $395 to $595 double, $695 suite.

---

guest rooms also have fireplaces. Conveniences such as wet bars, microwaves, and small refrigerators are neatly incorporated into the design so as not to conflict with the nostalgic charm. The suites come with fireplaces and kitchens; two have Gulf views. Sumptuous breakfasts are served in either your room or the gracious dining room. With its rich mahogany furniture and wealth of period accouterments, this intimate dining room is one of the region's finest places for a gourmet candlelit meal (by reservation only). Smoking is prohibited indoors.

C.R. 30A (P.O. Box 4767), Seaside, FL 32459. © **800/848-1840** or 850/231-1940. Fax 850/231-2446. www.josephines inn.com. 9 units, all with bathroom. Year-round $225 double; $275 suite. Rates include gourmet breakfast. Weekly rates available. AE, DISC, MC, V. **Amenities:** Restaurant; bar; free use of bikes. *In room:* A/C, TV, dataport, kitchen (in some suites), fridge, coffeemaker, hair dryer, iron.

WHERE TO DINE

Except for the strip on Okaloosa Island, a plethora of fast-food and family chain restaurants lines U.S. 98.

DESTIN

If you didn't catch a fish to be grilled at Fisherman's Wharf (see below), you can buy one to brag about at **Sexton's Seafood,** 602 Hwy. 98 E., opposite Destin Harbor (© **850/837-3040**). It's the best market here.

AJ's Seafood & Oyster Bar ★★ SEAFOOD Jimmy Buffett tunes set the tone at this fun, Tiki-topped establishment on the picturesque Destin Harbor docks, where fishing boats unload their daily catches right into the kitchen. The best items here are grilled or fried fish, but raw or steamed Apalachicola oysters also headline the menu. You can sample a bit of everything with a "run of the kitchen" seafood platter. AJ's is most famous for its topside bar, Club Bimini, open nightly and featuring live bands (you should have dinner elsewhere if you're not in a partying mood). At lunch, picnic tables on the covered dock make a fine venue with a view across the harbor. Locals love this place and you will, too.

116 Hwy. 98 E., Destin Harbor. ℂ 850/837-1913. www.ajs-destin.com. Main courses $11–$22; sandwiches and salads $6–$9. AE, DISC, MC, V. Apr–Sept Sun–Thurs 11am–10pm; Fri–Sat 11am–midnight (bar until 4am); off season daily 11am–9pm.

Back Porch ⚜ SEAFOOD   This cedar-shingled seafood shack offers glorious beach and Gulf views from its long porch. The popular casual restaurant originated charcoal-grilled amberjack, which you'll now see on menus throughout Florida. Other fish and seafood, as well as chicken and juicy hamburgers, also come from the coals. Come early, order a rum-laden Key Lime Freeze, and enjoy the sunset. The Back Porch sits with a number of other restaurants near the western boundary of the Henderson Beach State Park and is a popular hangout for Frisbee players and sunbathers.

1740 Old Hwy. 98 E. ℂ 850/837-2022. Main courses $15–$20; sandwiches, burgers, and pastas $6.50–$9. AE, DC, DISC, MC, V. Apr–Sept daily 11am–11pm; off season daily 11am–10pm. From U.S. 98, turn toward the beach at the Hampton Inn.

Callahan's Island Restaurant & Deli ⚜ _Value_ AMERICAN/DELI   The best place in the area for picnic fare, this family-operated deli offers burgers, excellent Reubens, and other made-to-order sandwiches, pastas, and nightly specials such as charcoal-grilled chicken and grilled pork chops. A long refrigerator case holds a variety of top-grade cheeses, deli meats, steaks, and chops (choose your own cut, and the chef will chargrill it to order). Tables and booths are set up garden fashion, adding an outdoorsy ambience to this pleasant storefront establishment. Locals like to do lunch here. Breakfast is served only on Saturday morning.

950 Gulf Shore Dr. (2 blocks south of U.S. 98). ℂ 850/837-6328. Main courses $10–$20; sandwiches, burgers, and salads $4–$7. DISC, MC, V. Mon–Fri 10am–9pm; Sat 8am–9pm.

Copper Grill ⚜⚜ STEAK   An upscale restaurant lit by gas torches, the Copper Grill is a delicious dichotomy of swank and kitsch—check out the zebra prints inside the dining room. Each table has its own DVD player, TV screen, and coffeemaker, and, to add to the distraction, there's an open-pit grill in the middle of the action. The Angus beef is top-notch, but order the steak fondue—it's absolutely to die for.

11225 Hwy. 98, Destin. ℂ 850/654-6900. Reservations recommended. Main courses $25–$40. AE, DISC, MC, V. Sun–Thurs 5:30–9:30pm; Fri–Sat 5:30–11pm.

Donut Hole SOUTHERN   Available around the clock, breakfasts at this popular spot feature eggs Benedict, fluffy biscuits under sausage gravy, Belgian waffles, and freshly baked doughnuts. Lunch sees deli sandwiches, half-pound burgers, and big salads. Daily specials are a bargain. The rough-hewn building has both booths and counter seating. Be prepared to wait out on the deck, especially on weekends. There's another Donut Hole in southern Walton County, on U.S. 98 E. 2½ miles east of the Sandestin Beach Resort (ℂ **850/267-3239**); it's open daily from 6am to 10pm.

635 U.S. 98 E., Destin. ℂ 850/837-8824. Breakfast $5–$9; sandwiches, salads, and burgers $5–$9; main courses $7–$10. No credit cards. Daily 24 hr. Closed 2 weeks before Christmas.

Fisherman's Wharf Seafood House ⚜⚜ SEAFOOD   Go fishing, bring your catch here, and then have the chef chargrill it at this atmospheric restaurant next to a charter-fleet marina. (The restaurant hosts most of Destin's fishing competitions.) If you struck out fishing and didn't stop by Sexton's Seafood (see above) on the way here, you can select from the restaurant's fresh-off-the-boat catch for grilling, broiling, frying, or blackening. Charcoal grilling is the house specialty—the triggerfish filet comes white and flaky but still moist. All main courses include a trip to the salad bar, rice pilaf, baked potato, or roasted vegetables. Although this building dates from 1996, it reminds me of an Old Florida fish camp, with rough-hewn wood walls and double-hung windows looking onto a large harborside deck, a venue during the warmer months for two bars, an oyster bar, live music, and great sunsets.

210D Hwy. 98 E., Destin Harbor. ✆ 850/654-4766. Main courses $11–$21; sandwiches and burgers $6–$9; cook your catch $7 lunch, $10 dinner. AE, DC, DISC, MC, V. Summer daily 11am–11pm (deck bar open later); off season daily 11am–9pm.

Fudpucker's Beachside Bar and Grill ☆ AMERICAN   A sprawling 26,000-square-foot complex, Fudpucker's is a beachside burger-and-beer joint with a twist—or, rather, many twists. For one, there's also a sushi bar. The decor is funky, with antique beer cans, mirrors, and what they call "Fud Junk." The Fudburger is the menu's most popular, but an unabridged selection of everything from fried crab to Puckeroni Pizza is available for the taking. Eight different dining rooms, a playground, and game rooms are nothing compared to Fudpucker's Gator Beach, the restaurant's very own alligator collection, located in the pond underneath the building. Live music and a new addition, Club Key West, make this place one of the area's most popular night spots. **Fudpucker's on the Island,** 108 Santa Rosa Blvd., Fort Walton Beach (✆ 850/243-3833), is the original, located on Okaloosa Island.

20001 Emerald Coast Pkwy., Destin. ✆ 850/654-4200. Reservations accepted only for hibachi tables. Main courses $12–$21. AE, DC, DISC, MC, V. Mon–Wed 11am–10pm; Thurs–Sat 11am–4am.

Harbor Docks SEAFOOD/JAPANESE   The harbor views are spectacular from indoors or out at this casual, somewhat rustic establishment. You can order your fill of fried fish, but specialties such as the daily catch sautéed with artichoke hearts are far more enjoyable. Asian influences include a sushi bar and hibachi table, which are open for dinner, and a few Thai specialties that grace the lunch menu. The bar here is popular with charter-boat skippers, and frequent live entertainment keeps the action going on the outdoor deck at night.

538 U.S. 98 E., Destin Harbor. ✆ 850/837-2506. Reservations accepted only for hibachi table. Main courses $16–$23; sushi $4.50–$8. AE, DC, DISC, MC, V. Feb–Oct daily 5:30–10:30am and 11am–11pm; Nov–Jan daily 11am–11pm. Sushi bar daily 5–10pm.

Harry T's Boat House ☆ *Kids* AMERICAN   To honor the memory of trapeze artist "Flying Harry T" Baben, his family opened this lively spot on the ground floor of Destin Harbor's tallest building. Standing guard is the stuffed Stretch, Harry's beloved giraffe. The decor includes circus memorabilia and relics from the luxury cruise ship *Thracia,* which sank off the Emerald Coast in 1927; Harry T was presented with the ship's salvaged furnishings and fixtures for personally leading the heroic rescue of its 2,000 passengers. The menu offers traditional seafood, steak, chicken, and pasta dishes. The house specialty is smokehouse ribs, juicy and full of flavor. Kids eat for 99¢ from 11am to 7pm, and Tuesday is Kids' Night, with a clown, face painting, and balloon animals. The dining room and the downstairs lounge—with live entertainment Thursday, Friday, and Saturday nights—enjoy harbor views. *Note:* As of press time they were closed and will reopen in the spring of 2007 in the lighthouse building along the harborfront, a 13,000-square-foot space overlooking the water.

320 U.S. 98 E., Destin Harbor. ☏ **850/654-4800**. www.harryts.com. Main courses $13–$24; soups and salads $3–$12. AE, DISC, MC, V. Summer Mon–Sat 11am–2am, Sun 10am–2am; off season Mon–Sat 11am–9pm, Sun 10am–9pm. Bar open later. Sun brunch year-round 10am–3pm.

Marina Cafe ✿✿✿ NEW AMERICAN   Destin's finest restaurant provides a classy atmosphere with soft candlelight, subdued music, and walls of glass overlooking the harbor. The changing menu offers nouveau preparations of seafood, such as almond-crusted mahimahi. Pizzas are topped with the likes of cayenne rock shrimp, roasted corn, and onion marmalade, while pastas might feature fusilli with roasted chicken, sun-dried tomatoes, goat cheese, broccoli, and pine nuts. Try my favorite, the chipotle-honey barbecued Gulf shrimp and roasted poblano, onion, and corn quesadilla, served with a spicy tomato-mint salsa. Weather permitting, enjoy the outdoor deck for drinks and appetizers.

404 Hwy. 98 E., Destin Harbor. ☏ **850/837-7960**. www.marinacafe.com. Reservations recommended. Main courses $15–$30; pizza and pasta $10–$17. AE, DC, DISC, MC, V. Daily 5–11pm. Closed 1st 3 weeks in Jan.

McGuire's Irish Pub & Brewery STEAK/SEAFOOD   Like Pensacola's original McGuire's (p. 600), this younger sibling sports thousands of dollar bills stuck on the ceilings and walls, plus Notre Dame football schedules, a prominent logo of the Boston Celtics, and other Irish-American memorabilia. This is Destin's most popular hangout, and local professionals congregate at the big oak bar for the live entertainment Tuesday through Sunday from 9pm. Opt for a table on either side of the bar or on a rooftop deck. Dining here is almost secondary to the see-and-be-seen scene, although the tender chargrilled steaks and giant burgers are worthy antidotes to a big appetite.

33 Hwy. 98 E., Destin Harbor (in Harborwalk Center near Destin Bridge). ☏ **850/654-0567**. Main courses $16–$25; snacks, burgers, and sandwiches $8–$12. AE, DC, DISC, MC, V. Mon–Sat 11am–midnight; later on weekends.

Rutherford's 465 ✿✿ NEW AMERICAN   An elegant restaurant overlooking Lake Regatta, Rutherford's 465 is an eclectic dining experience, thanks to chef Todd Misener's New American cuisine. Dishes like Ashley Farm's Natural Chicken (grilled breast of chicken with roasted garlic mashed potatoes, asparagus, and cider reduction sauce) and a succulent Kansas City bone-in strip loin are outstanding.

465 Regatta Bay Blvd. (inside the Regatta Bay community), Destin. ☏ **850/337-8888**. Main courses $18–$35. AE, DC, DISC, MC, V. Tues–Sat 11am–2pm and 6–10pm.

FORT WALTON BEACH

Big City Coffeehouse and Cafe COFFEE/PASTRIES/DELI   For a caffeine fix, an inexpensive breakfast or lunch, or afternoon tea, head to Tina and Jim Ivanchukov's bright cafe on the mainland near the Brooks Bridge. The owners make great salads—such as herb-roasted chicken with apples, walnuts, and tarragon dressing (sold by the pound)—and sandwiches served on homemade focaccia.

201 Miracle Strip Pkwy. SE (U.S. 98). ☏ **850/664-0664**. Sandwiches and salads $6.50–$9. MC, V. Mon–Fri 7am–7pm; Sat 8am–5pm; Sun 8am–3pm.

Café Tango ✿✿ AMERICAN   Despite the name, this restaurant has nothing to do with Argentina. Housed in a 50-year-old vine-covered red cottage, Café Tango is best known for its seafood, steaks, and pastas. With only eight tables, the restaurant is so romantic it will make you want to do some sort of after-dinner tango.

14 Vicki St., Santa Rosa Beach. ☏ **850/267-0054**. Reservations recommended. Main courses $15–$27. AE, MC, V. Summer 5–10pm; off season, call for hours.

Caffè Italia ☞☞ NORTHERN ITALIAN   Nada Eckhardt is from Croatia, but she met her American husband, Jim, while working at a restaurant named Caffè Italia in Italy. The Eckhardts duplicated that establishment in this 1925 Sears Roebuck mail-order house tucked away on the waterfront. You can dine on the patio, with a view of the sound through sprawling live oak trees (one table is set romantically under a gazebo), or sit inside, where Nada has installed floral tablecloths and photos from the Old Country. A limited but fine menu includes excellent pizzas; pasta dishes such as tortellini with tomatoes, chicken, and peas in Alfredo sauce; risotto with asparagus or smoked salmon; and meat and seafood dishes to fit the season. The cappuccino is absolutely first-rate, as are the genuine Italian desserts.

189 Brooks St., on the mainland in the block west of Brooks Bridge. ☎ 850/664-0035. Reservations recommended. Main courses $15–$18; pizza and pasta $8–$13. AE, DC, DISC, MC, V. Sun and Tues–Fri 11am–10pm; Sat 5–11pm. Closed Thanksgiving and Christmas.

Pandora's Restaurant & Lounge ☞ STEAK/PRIME RIB/SEAFOOD   The front of this unusual restaurant is a beached yacht now housing the main-deck lounge. Below is a beam-ceilinged dining room aglow with lights from copper chandeliers. Try for the private Bob Hope Booth, where you can dine below two of the great comedian's golf clubs (he used to come here to raise money for a local Air Force widow's home). Anything from the charcoal grill is excellent, including the wonderful appetizer of bacon-wrapped scallops. Several varieties of freshly caught fish are among the main-course choices, but steaks and prime rib keep the locals coming back for more. The tender beef is cut on the premises and grilled to perfection. The delicious breads and pies are homemade. There's another Pandora's in Grayton Beach, at the corner of Florida 283 and C.R. 30A (☎ **850/231-4102**).

1120B Santa Rosa Blvd. ☎ **850/244-8669.** Reservations recommended. Main courses $12–$25. AE, DISC, MC, V. Sun–Thurs 5–10pm; Fri–Sat 5–10:30pm.

Staff's Seafood Restaurant SEAFOOD/STEAK   Considered the first Emerald Coast restaurant, Staff's started as a hotel in 1913 and moved to this barnlike building in 1931. Among the memorabilia on display are an old-fashioned phonograph lamp and a 1914 cash register. Staff's tangy seafood gumbo has gained fame for this casual, historic restaurant. One of the most popular main dishes is the "seafood skillet," sizzling with broiled grouper, shrimp, scallops, and crab drenched in butter and sprinkled with cheese. Main courses are served with baskets of hot, home-baked wheat bread from a secret 70-year-old recipe, plus salad and dessert. A pianist plays at dinnertime year-round.

24 SW Miracle Strip Pkwy. (U.S. 98), on the mainland. ☎ **850/243-3526.** Main courses $12–$30. AE, DISC, MC, V. Summer daily 5–11pm; off season Mon–Thurs 5–9pm, Fri–Sat 5–10pm.

SOUTHERN WALTON COUNTY

Café Thirty-A ☞☞☞ SEAFOOD/AMERICAN   Only 1½ miles east of Seaside, along Scenic Highway 30A, this comfortable yet classy restaurant prepares exquisite seafood, steaks, and wood-oven pizzas. It's mostly a vacationing white-collar crowd here, but that shouldn't stop anyone from enjoying the remarkable offerings (including drinks from the creative martini menu and wine from the extensive, award-winning list), served up by a friendly and efficient staff. Start with skewered wood–oven roasted shrimp, sweetened and spiced with a pineapple chili sauce. Or begin more simply—an arugula salad topped with pine nuts and shaved pecorino, tossed in a lemon-garlic vinaigrette is a tasty option. For entrées, you can't miss with either the Caribbean jerked cobia or the cumin-dusted grouper. If you're feeling more surf than turf, both the filet mignon, served with shrimp bordelaise sauce and sweet pepper and corn ragout, and the New York strip, with sides of horseradish whipped potatoes and blue cheese butter, are excellent. Leave room for desserts like the luscious molten chocolate cake or the heavenly banana beignets.

3899 E. Scenic Highway 30A. Seagrove Beach. (C) **800/231-2166**. www.cafethirtya.com. Reservations highly recommended. Main courses $26–$37; wood-oven pizzas about $14. AE, DC, DISC, MC, V. Summer daily 6–10pm; off-season Mon–Fri 5:30–9pm; Sat–Sun 5:30–9:30pm.

Criolla's ✶✶✶ *Value* INTERNATIONAL   One of Florida's finest restaurants, this charming establishment features attractive decor that combines New Orleans and the Caribbean through potted palms, ceiling fans, and tropical island paintings reminiscent of another era. The menus change seasonally, but many fish dishes carry the wonderful aroma of smoke from a wood-fired grill (the bacon-wrapped swordfish, if available, is always a winner). Ask about a special four-course, fixed-price dinner, which draws inspiration from such warm spots as the Caribbean, Central America, and Tahiti. It's also worth asking in advance about special events featuring visiting chefs and spotlighting excellent vineyards. (The wine cellar here has won awards.)

170 E. Scenic Hwy. 30A, ¼ mile east of C.R. 283, Grayton Beach. (C) **850/267-1267**. Reservations recommended. Main courses $19–$32. AE, DISC, MC, V. Jan–Feb and Oct–Dec Tues–Sat 5:30–10pm; Mar–Apr and Sept Mon–Sat 5:30–10pm; May–Aug daily 5:30–10pm.

Sandor's European Cuisine ✶✶✶ INTERNATIONAL   The last thing you'd expect to see in the Panhandle of Florida of all places, is a bona fide European restaurant. But the Le Cordon Bleu–trained Hungarian immigrant Sandor Zombori fell in love with the place (as you will, too) and brought a taste of home to this seaside town. Sandor's is a tiny place—eight tables only—with brocaded linens on the tables and Mozart on the stereo. The food, European with a Panhandle flair, is to die for. The crawfish curry pastry with pickled ginger, and the ginger-and-sake-marinated sea bass with Indonesian ketchup are tough to choose between, especially when you taste the Angus filet and mushroom ragout with paprika and sour cream. And then there's the braised short ribs, which many consider to be the best they've ever eaten. Save room for deserts, all decadent, from crepes to molten chocolate cake.

2984 S. County Road., Seagrove Beach. At the corner of Hwys. 30A and 98. (C) **850/231-2858**. Reservations essential. Main courses $20–$40. AE, DISC, MC, V. May to Labor Day daily 6–10pm; off-season Mon–Sat 6–10pm.

SEASIDE
Several cafes and sandwich shops in Seaside's Gulf-side shopping complex offer inexpensive snacks to beachgoers.

Bud & Alley's *⊀⊀* SEAFOOD/STEAK/MEDITERRANEAN   In this cracked-crab-and-champagne-loving village, Bud & Alley's (named for a dog and a cat) features spectacular sunsets from the rooftop bar and a menu that changes frequently but always has savory surprises. The offerings feature an infusion of Basque, Italian, Louisiana, and Floridian dishes that might include seafood stew or sautéed head-on shrimp with garlic, shallots, and cracked pepper. You can dine indoors or out, on the screened porch or under an open-air gazebo where you'll hear waves splashing against the white sand. Jazz is usually in the spotlight on weekends. On New Year's Eve, everyone from miles around celebrates at Bud & Alley's. Call ahead to see whether a noted guest chef is cooking or a special wine-tasting dinner is scheduled. Smoking is not permitted.

C.R. 30A, in the beachside shops. ② **850/231-5900.** www.budandalleys.com. Reservations recommended. Main courses $18–$29; lunch $7.50–$23. MC, V. Apr–Sept Sun–Thurs 11:30am–3pm and 5:30–9:30pm, Fri–Sat 11:30am–3pm and 5:30–10pm; Oct–Mar Sun–Thurs 5:30–9pm, Fri–Sat 5:30–9:30pm. Closed Tues in off season.

DESTIN & FORT WALTON BEACH AFTER DARK

In summer, there's live entertainment at most resorts, including the Ramada Plaza Beach Resort, in Fort Walton Beach; and the Sandestin Hilton Beach & Golf Resort as well as Sandestin Golf and Beach Resort, in southern Walton County (see "Where to Stay," earlier in this chapter). Call ahead to find out what's scheduled, especially during the slow season between October and February.

For other ideas and listings of what's happening, pick up a copy of the weekly *Walton Sun* newspaper.

DESTIN   Several Destin restaurants offer entertainment nightly in summer, and on weekends in the off season. See "Where to Dine," earlier in this chapter, for details about restaurants. The dockside **AJ's Club Bimini,** 116 U.S. 98 E. (② **850/837-1913**), has live reggae under a big thatched-roofed deck. A somewhat older, if not more sober, crowd gathers for entertainment at the big harborside deck at **Fisherman's Wharf,** on U.S. 98 E. (② **850/654-4766**); and **The Deck,** on U.S. 98 E. at the Harbor Docks restaurant, overlooking the harbor (② **850/837-2506**). For Irish tunes nightly year-round, head for **McGuire's Irish Pub & Brewery,** in the Harborwalk Shops, U.S. 98 just east of the Destin Bridge (② **850/650-0567**). The **Grande Isle Sky Bar,** above Grazti Italian Restaurant, 1771 Old Hwy. 98 (② **850/837-7475**), draws the after-dinner crowd from the Back Porch and other adjacent restaurants.

Twenty-somethings are attracted to the dance club, rowdy saloon, Jimmy Buffett–style reggae bar, and sports TV and billiards parlor all under one roof at the acclaimed **Nightown,** 140 Palmetto St. (② **850/837-6448;** www.nightown.com), near the harbor on the inland side of U.S. 98 East. One admission covers it all. There's live music Friday and Saturday nights, and amateur boxing on Tuesday. Nearby, **Hogs Breath Destin,** 541 Hwy. 98 E. (② **850/837-5991;** www.hogsbreath.com), is another lively pub with bands playing rock, blues, and jazz.

Out toward Sandestin, **Fudpucker's Beachside Bar & Grill,** 20001 Hwy. 98 E. (② **850/654-4200**), opposite the Henderson Beach State Park, offers double the fun with two summertime stages. There's another Fudpucker's at 108 Santa Rosa Blvd., on Okaloosa Island in Fort Walton Beach (② **850/243-3833**).

FORT WALTON BEACH   Country music and dancing fans will find a home at the **Seagull,** on Miracle Strip Parkway (U.S. 98) opposite the Gulfarium (② **850/243-3413**). The generations of pilots who have hung out here call it the "Dirty Gull."

Its main rival for the country set is the **High Tide Oyster Bar,** at Okaloosa Island off the Brooks Bridge (✆ **850/244-2624**).

3 Panama City Beach

100 miles E of Pensacola, 100 miles SW of Tallahassee

Panama City Beach, a spring-break mecca once erroneously featured as a bleak, desolate wasteland of sun and strip malls in the Ashley Judd film *Ruby in Paradise,* has long been known as the "Redneck Riviera," since it's a mecca for millions of vacationers from the bordering states of Georgia, Alabama, Mississippi, and Louisiana. It still has a seemingly unending strip of bars, amusement parks, and old-fashioned motels. But this lively and crowded destination (in season) also has luxury resorts and condominiums to go along with its 20-plus miles of sandy beaches, golf courses, fishing, boating, and fresh seafood.

Panama City Beach is the most seasonal resort in Northwest Florida, since many restaurants, attractions, and some hotels close between October and March. Spring break is a big deal here; MTV sets up shop in Panama City Beach for annual beach-party broadcasts.

ESSENTIALS

GETTING THERE The commuter arms of **Delta** (✆ 800/221-1212), **Northwest** (✆ 800/225-2525), and **US Airways** (✆ 800/428-4322) fly into **Panama City/Bay County International Airport,** on Lisenby Avenue, north of St. Andrews Boulevard, in Panama City (✆ 850/763-6751; www.pcairport.com).

Alamo (✆ 800/327-9633), **Avis** (✆ 800/331-1212), **Budget** (✆ 800/527-0700), **Enterprise** (✆ 800/325-8007), **Hertz** (✆ 800/654-3131), and **National** (✆ 800/CAR-RENT) have rental-car offices here.

Taxi fares to the beach are about $25.

The **Amtrak** (✆ **800/USA-RAIL;** www.amtrak.com) transcontinental Sunset Limited service stops at Chipley, 45 miles north of Panama City.

VISITOR INFORMATION For advance information, contact the **Panama City Beach Convention & Visitors Bureau,** P.O. Box 9473, Panama City Beach, FL 32417 (✆ **800/722-3224** in the U.S., 800/553-1330 in Canada, or 850/233-6503; fax 850/233-5072; www.800pcbeach.com). It operates a visitor center in the city-hall complex, 17001 Panama City Beach Pkwy. (U.S. 98), at Florida 79. The center is open daily from 8am to 5pm; closed New Year's Day, Thanksgiving, and Christmas.

GETTING AROUND The **Bay Town Trolley** (✆ **850/769-0557**) runs along Thomas Drive and on Front Beach Road as far west as Florida 79; it operates year-round Monday through Friday five times a day. Rides cost 50¢. Call for the schedule.

For a taxi, call **Yellow Cab** (✆ **850/763-4691**). Fares at the beach are $3 to climb aboard and $1.80 per mile, or $5 to $10 for rides within Panama City Beach.

TIME The Panama City area is in the central time zone, 1 hour behind Miami, Orlando, and Tallahassee.

HITTING THE BEACH: ST. ANDREWS STATE PARK

A nearly unbroken strand of fine white sand fronts all 22 miles of Panama City Beach, but the highlight for many is **St. Andrews State Park** ★★★, at the east end. With more than 1,000 acres of dazzling white sand and dunes, this preserved wilderness demonstrates what the area looked like before motels and condominiums lined the beach. Lacy, golden sea oats sway in the refreshing Gulf breezes, and fragrant rosemary grows wild. Picnic areas (on the Gulf beach and the Grand Lagoon), restrooms, and open-air showers are available for beachgoers. Anglers will find jetties and a boat ramp. A nature trail reveals wading birds and perhaps an alligator or two. And drive carefully here because the area is home to foxes, coyotes, and a herd of deer. A historic turpentine still on display was formerly used by lumbermen to make turpentine and rosin, both important for caulking old wooden ships.

The park's 176 RV and tent **campsites** are among the state's most beautiful, especially the 40 situated in a pine forest right on the shores of Grand Lagoon. They are very popular, so reservations are highly recommended—and absolutely essential in summer. Call ℰ **800/326-3521** or go to www.reserveamerica.com. Sites cost $24 year-round.

Park admission is $5 per car with two to eight occupants, $3 per single-occupant vehicle, and $1 per pedestrian or cyclist. The area is open daily from 8am to sunset. Pets are not allowed in the park. For more information, contact the park at 4607 State Park Lane, Panama City, FL 32408 (ℰ **850/233-5140;** www.floridastateparks.org/standrews).

Pristine **Shell Island** 𝓡𝓡, a 7½-mile-long, 1-mile-wide barrier island accessible only by boat, sits a few hundred yards across an inlet from St. Andrews State Park. This uninhabited natural preserve is great for shelling and also fun for swimming, suntanning, or just relaxing. Visitors can bring chairs, beach gear, coolers, food, and beverages. The best way to get here is on the park's **Shell Island Shuttle** (ℰ **800/227-0132** or 850/234-7245; www.shellislandshuttle.com), which runs every 30 minutes— in summer, daily from 9am to 5pm; in spring and fall, Saturday and Sunday from 10am to 3pm. Fares are $12 for adults and $5.50 for children 11 and under, plus the admission fees to the state park (see above). A special snorkeling package costs $19 for adults and $13 for kids 12 and under, which includes the shuttle ride and equipment. Kayak rentals are $35 a day for a single-seat boat, $45 for a double-seater.

Several cruise boats go to Shell Island, including the glass-bottomed *Captain Anderson III,* which departs from Captain Anderson's Marina, 5500 N. Lagoon Dr., at Thomas Drive (ℰ **850/234-3435**). It charges $16 for adults, $10 for kids 12 and under (Mar–Oct).

OUTDOOR ACTIVITIES

BOATING   A variety of rental boats are available at the marinas near the Thomas Drive bridge over Grand Lagoon. These include the **Captain Davis Queen Fleet,** based at Captain Anderson's Marina, 5500 N. Lagoon Dr. (ℰ **800/874-2415** or 850/234-3435); the **Passport Marina,** 5325 N. Lagoon Dr. (ℰ **850/234-5609**); the **Port Lagoon Yacht Basin,** 5201 N. Lagoon Dr. (ℰ **850/234-0142**); the **Pirates Cove Marina,** 3901 Thomas Dr. (ℰ **850/234-3939**); and the **Treasure Island Marina,** 3605 Thomas Dr. (ℰ **850/234-6533**).

Many resorts and hotels provide beach toys for their guests' use. WaveRunners, jet boats, inflatables, and other equipment can also be rented from **Lagoon Rentals** (ℰ **850/234-7245**).

CRUISES   You'll have your choice of numerous cruises here, from sailing to visiting the dolphins aboard noisy jet skis. The visitor center (p. 619) has information about them all—and discount coupons for many.

Children get a kick out of the make-believe swashbucklers on the *Sea Dragon* (℡ 850/234-7400; www.piratecruise.net), an 80-foot-long replica of a pirate ship that goes on 2-hour cruises from its dock next to the Treasure Ship, on Thomas Drive at Grand Lagoon. The trip costs $17 for adults, $15 for seniors, and $13 for children 3 to 12. Call for seasonal schedules and reservations.

FISHING   The least expensive way to try your luck is with **Captain Anderson's Deep Sea Fishing,** at Captain Anderson's Marina, Thomas Drive at Grand Lagoon (℡ 800/874-2415 or 850/234-5940; www.captainandersonsmarina.com). The captain's party-boat trips last 5 to 6 hours, with prices ranging from $45 to $65 per person, including bait and tackle. Observers can go along for $20 less.

The more expensive charter-fishing boats depart daily from March to November from the marinas mentioned in "Boating," above.

You definitely won't get seasick casting your line from the **M. B. Miller County Pier,** 12213 Front Beach Rd. (℡ 850/233-3039), or the **Dan Russell Municipal Pier,** 16101 Front Beach Rd. (℡ 850/233-5080).

GOLF   At Marriott's Bay Point Resort Village (p. 625), the **Bay Point Yacht and Country Club,** 3900 Marriott Dr., off Jan Cooley Road (℡ 850/235-6950; www.baypointgolf.com), offers 36 holes of championship play, including the Bruce Devlin–designed course **Lagoon Legends** ✻✻, rated one of the country's most difficult. Both it and the Club Meadows course have clubhouses, putting greens, driving ranges, clinics, and private instruction. Greens fees with cart start at about $45 in summer and $95 in winter, depending on the day of the week.

The **Edgewater Beach Resort,** 11212 U.S. 98A (℡ 850/235-4044), also has a nine-hole resort course, and its guests have access to the **Hombre,** 120 Coyote Pass, 3 miles west of the Hathaway Bridge off Panama City Beach Parkway/U.S. 98 (℡ 850/234-3573), a par-72 championship course that is home to the Nike Panama City Beach Classic. Fifteen of its 18 holes have water hazards (the unforgiving seventh hole sits on an island). Greens fees are about $65 in summer, $60 in winter, including cart.

The course at the semiprivate **Holiday Golf Club,** 100 Fairway Blvd. (℡ 850/234-1800), sports lake-lined fairways and elevated greens. Greens fees with cart are about $45 in summer, $35 in winter. You can play at night on a lighted nine-hole, par-29 executive course.

The cheapest place to play here is the flat and forgiving **Signal Hill,** 9516 N. Thomas Dr. (℡ 850/234-3218), where you'll pay about $20 to walk 18 holes in summer, $15 in winter. Add about $10 per person for a cart.

For course information, go to www.golf.com or www.floridagolfing.com, or call the **Florida Sports Foundation** (℡ 850/488-8347) or **Florida Golfing** (℡ 866/833-2663).

SCUBA DIVING & SNORKELING   Although the area is too far north for extensive coral formations, more than 50 artificial reefs and shipwrecks in the Gulf waters off Panama City attract a wide variety of sea life. The largest local operator is **Hydrospace Dive Shop,** 6422 W. Hwy. 98 (℡ 850/234-3063; www.hydrospace.com). Others include **Panama City Dive Center,** 4823 Thomas Dr. (℡ 850/235-3390; www.pcdivecenter.com); **Emerald Coast Divers,** 5121 Thomas Dr. (℡ 800/945-DIVE or 850/233-3355); and **Pete's Scuba Center,** 9007 Front Beach Rd. (℡ 800/401-DIVE or 850/230-8006). These companies lead dives, teach courses, and take snorkelers to the grass flats off Shell Island.

EXPLORING THE AREA

Gulf World Marine Park *Kids*   This landscaped tropical garden and marine attraction features shows with talented dolphins, sea lions, penguins, and more. Not to be upstaged, parrots perform daily, too. Scuba demonstrations, shark feedings, and underwater shows keep the crowds entertained. The park has special interactive programs, including a trainer-for-a-day program ($225–$250 per person) and a dolphin encounter ($125–$150). Allow about 3½ hours to see it all, more if you do one of the encounters. *Note:* Swimming with dolphins has both its critics and its supporters. You may want to visit the Whale and Dolphin Conservation Society's website at www.wdcs.org. For more information about responsible travel in general, check out www.treadlightly.org and www.ecotourism.org.

15412 Front Beach Rd. (at Hill Ave.), Panama City Beach. ✆ 850/234-5271. www.gulfworldmarinepark.com. Admission $20 adults, $14 children 5–11. Summer daily 9am–4pm; off season daily 9am–2pm.

Museum of Man in the Sea   Owned by the Institute of Diving, this small museum exhibits relics from the first days of scuba diving, historic displays of the underwater world dating from 1500, and treasures recovered from sunken ships. Hands-on exhibits explain water and air pressure, light refraction, and why diving bells work. Both kids and adults can climb through a submarine and see live sea animals in a pool. Videos and aquariums explain the sea life found in St. Andrews Bay.

17314 Panama City Beach Pkwy. (at Heather Dr., west of Fla. 79), Panama City Beach. ✆ 850/235-4101. Admission $5 adults, $2.50 children 6–16. Daily 10am–4pm. Closed New Year's Day, Thanksgiving, and Christmas.

ZooWorld Zoological & Botanical Park *Kids*   Situated in a pine forest, this educational and entertaining zoo is an active participant in the Species Survival Plan, which helps protect endangered species by employing specific breeding and housing programs. Among the 350 guests here are orangutans and other primates; lions, tigers, and leopards; and alligators and other reptiles. The zoo's newest and most precious attraction is the Tilghman Infant Care Facility, a nursery facility that allows you to closely view the baby animals born at ZooWorld.

9008 Front Beach Rd. (near Moylan Dr.), Panama City Beach. ✆ 850/230-1243. Admission $13 adults, $8 children 3–11. Daily 9am–5:30pm (to 4:30pm in winter).

AMUSEMENT PARKS

For that Panama City–meets–Coney Island vibe, there are two amusement parks good for killing some time. A 105-foot-high roller coaster is just one of the 30 rides at the **Miracle Strip Amusement Park,** 12000 Front Beach Rd. at Alf Coleman Road (✆ **850/234-5810;** www.miraclestrippark.com; $27 adults, $22 kids 35–50 in. tall.). Little ones will love the traditional carousel. The 9 acres of fun include continuing live entertainment and tons of junk food. The adjoining **Shipwreck Island Water Park** (✆ **850/234-0368;** www.shipwreckisland.com; $27 for those over 50 in. tall, $22 for those 35–50 in., free for those under 35 in.) offers a variety of water amusements, including the 1,600-foot-long winding Lazy River for tubing and a daring 35-mph Speed Slide. The Tad Pole Hole is exclusively for young kids. Lounge chairs, umbrellas, and inner tubes are free, and lifeguards are on duty. Combination tickets are available. Both are open Saturday and Sunday from mid-March to Memorial Day, then daily until mid-August, and back to weekends from then to Labor Day weekend.

SHOPPING

The main branch of **Alvin's Island Tropical Department Store,** 12010 Front Beach Rd. (© **850/234-3048;** www.alvinsisland.com), opposite the James I. Lark, Sr., Visitor Information Center, is an attraction in itself. It not only sells a wide range of beach gear and apparel, but it has cages containing colorful parrots, tanks with small sharks, and an enclosure with alligators. The sharks are fed at 11am daily; the gators get theirs at 4pm in summer only. (Only in Florida—live sharks and alligators in a department store!)

WHERE TO STAY

There are scores of motels along the beach here, ranging from small mom-and-pop operations to sizable members of national chains. The annual guide distributed by the Panama City Beach Convention & Visitors Bureau (p. 619) has a complete list.

The most modern of the chain properties are the recently renovated **Howard Johnson Resort Hotel,** 9400 S. Thomas Dr. (© **800/654-2000** or 850/234-6521), and the **Four Points by Sheraton,** 9600 S. Thomas Dr. (© **888/625-5144** or 850/234-6511). Both are part of the redeveloped Boardwalk Beach Resort area, a center of beach action.

Panama City Beach also abounds with condominium complexes, such as the Edgewater Beach Resort, listed below. Among the many rental agents are **Coldwell Banker Beach Rental,** 726 Thomas Dr., Panama City Beach (© **800/621-2462** or 850/235-4075; fax 850/233-2833; www.panamabeachrentals.com); and **Condo World,** 8815A Thomas Dr. (P.O. Box 9456), Panama City Beach (© **800/232-6636** in the U.S., 800/824-5411 in Canada, or 850/234-5564; fax 850/233-6725; www.condoworld.net).

The best camping is at the lovely sites in **St. Andrews State Park** (p. 619), one of this area's major attractions.

Rates at even the most expensive properties here drop precipitously during winter, when the town rolls up the sidewalks. Bay County adds 3.5% tax to all hotel and campground bills, bringing the total add-on tax (with the county's 6% sales tax) to 9.5%.

Beachcomber by the Sea ⚓ Watercolors by local artist Paul Brent grace every unit in this eight-story, all-suites, spring-breaker-free (they're prohibited, really, I swear!) resort, built and opened in 1998 at the junction of Front Beach Road and Florida 79. All units also have balconies overlooking a Gulf-side pool and hot tub bordered by a concrete deck accented by palm trees. The well-equipped suites come in two sizes. Each of the larger ones has a living room with sleeper sofa, kitchenette, bathroom, and bedroom with either one king-size or two double beds. The suites are similar to those at the Flamingo Motel & Tower (see below), except that here they have air conditioners in both the living room and the bedroom. The smaller units are more like motel rooms but do contain microwaves; two have whirlpool tubs as well. There's no restaurant here, but several are nearby, and complimentary continental breakfast is available in the lobby each morning.

17101 Front Beach Rd., Panama City Beach, FL 32413. © **888/886-8916** or 850/233-3600. Fax 850/233-3622. www.beachcomberbythesea.com. 96 units. Summer $109–$250 double; off season $39–$109 double. Rates include continental breakfast. Packages available. AE, DISC, MC, V. **Amenities:** Heated outdoor pool; access to nearby health club; Jacuzzi; game room; coin-op washers and dryers. *In room:* A/C, TV, dataport, kitchen, fridge, coffeemaker, hair dryer, iron.

Edgewater Beach Resort ⚓⚓ *(Kids)* One of the Panhandle's largest condominium resorts, this sports-oriented, private gated facility enjoys a beautiful beachfront location and 110 landscaped acres. Units in five Gulf-side towers offer commanding views of the emerald water and gorgeous sunsets from their private balconies. A pedestrian overpass leads across Front Beach Road to low-rise apartments and town homes fringing the ponds and the fairways of the resort's nine-hole golf course. A daytime shuttle runs around the resort to pools, whirlpools, tennis center, and golf course. (Guests also get privileges at the 18-hole Hombre Golf Club, ¼ mile north.) The Shoppes at Edgewater restaurants are across the road. Last but not least, the gorgeous 11,000-square-foot, Polynesian-style pool features waterfalls, islands, and a deck with live entertainment daily from 11am to 4pm.

11212 Front Beach Rd. (P.O. Box 9850), Panama City Beach, FL 32407. © 800/874-8686 or 850/235-4044. Fax 850/235-6899. www.edgewaterbeachresort.com. 500 units. Summer $196–$578 condo; off season $90–$174 condo. Resort amenities fee $5 per unit per day. Weekly rates and maid service available. AE, DC, DISC, MC, V. **Amenities:** 2 restaurants; 2 bars; 12 outdoor pools; 9-hole golf course; 11 Plexicusion tennis courts; health club; spa services; Jacuzzi; watersports equipment rental; children's programs; concierge; limited room service. *In room:* A/C, TV, dataport, wireless Internet access, full kitchen, coffeemaker, hair dryer, iron, washer/dryer.

Flamingo Motel & Tower *Value* The Lancaster family takes great pride in the gorgeous tropical garden surrounding a heated pool and a sun deck overlooking the Gulf at their well-maintained motel. The brightly decorated guest rooms have either full kitchens or else refrigerators and microwaves. They can sleep two to six people, some in separate bedrooms. Kitchenette rooms in a two-story motel block across the road are less appealing, but will accommodate six to eight. Budget-conscious families can opt for the lower-priced rooms, accommodating two to four. Next door, the seven-story Flamingo Tower contains 49 suites, all sporting living rooms with sofa beds and dining tables, bedrooms with ceiling fans and their own TVs, kitchens, balconies overlooking the Gulf, and a beachside pool and hot tub. These suites have air-conditioning in their living rooms but not in their bedrooms (the ceiling fans will come in handy during the hot summer months). Some older units have shower-only bathrooms. The Dan Russell fishing pier is only ½ mile away. Gulf World Marine Park (p. 622) and Shuckums Oyster Pub & Seafood Grill (p. 626) are virtually across the road. College spring-breakers are not welcome.

15525 Front Beach Rd., Panama City Beach, FL 32413. © 800/828-0400 or 850/234-2232. Fax 850/234-1292. www.flamingomotel.com. 117 units. Summer $94–$159 double; off season $39–$139 double. AE, DISC, MC, V. **Amenities:** 2 heated outdoor pools; access to nearby health club; Jacuzzi; watersports equipment rental; coin-op washers and dryers. *In room:* A/C, TV, kitchen, fridge, coffeemaker.

Holiday Inn SunSpree Resort *Value* One building removed from the Edgewater Beach Resort and across the road from the Shoppes at Edgewater, this 15-story establishment is the top full-service Gulf-front hotel here. It's designed in an arch, with all rooms' balconies looking directly down on the beach, where a heated, lagoon-style pool and sun deck are separated from the sand by a row of palms and Polynesian torches. The hotel has won architectural awards for its dramatic lobby with a waterfall and the Fountain of Wishes (the coins go to charity). Each attractive, spacious guest room has a full-size refrigerator, microwave, and two spacious vanity areas. Decor is dramatically different from that found in your typical Holiday Inn—it's more reminiscent of a resort in, say, the Caribbean, with its pastel colors and tile floors.

11127 Front Beach Rd., Panama City Beach, FL 32407. © 800/633-0266 or 850/234-1111. Fax 850/235-1907. www.holidayinnsunspree.com. 340 units. Summer $185–$239 double; off season $89–$139 double. AE, DC, DISC, MC, V. **Amenities:** 2 restaurants; bar; heated outdoor pool; exercise room; Jacuzzi; watersports equipment rental; game room; concierge; limited room service; babysitting; laundry service; concierge-level rooms. *In room:* A/C, TV, dataport, fridge, coffeemaker, hair dryer, iron, safe.

Marriott's Bay Point Resort Village 🎯🎯 *Value*   Not only is this luxurious vacation miniworld ranked among the nation's top golf and tennis resorts, it's also an extraordinarily good value for Florida. Although guests pay extra for most activities, the room rates are among the top steals in the state. They would be higher if the property were beside the Gulf; instead, it's the centerpiece of a manicured real-estate development sprawling over 1,100 acres on a wildlife sanctuary bordered by St. Andrews Bay and the Grand Lagoon. Situated beside the lagoon, the vivid coral stucco hotel is surrounded by gardens, palm trees, oaks, and magnolias. From the glamorous three-story lobby, window walls look out to scenic water views and two pools (one in its own glass-enclosed building). The recently renovated guest rooms are spacious and luxurious, furnished in dark woods and all with balconies or patios. The highlights for duffers are the Lagoon Legends and the Club Meadows golf courses (p. 621). Watersports here are at Grand Lagoon Beach, reached by the hotel's long pier. There's also a free shuttle to the Gulf beaches. A fun locals' scene happens at Teddy's Back Bay Beach Club, a waterfront, open-air beach bar with a tin roof and sprawling docks, which attracts a lively crowd ashore from their WaveRunners, pontoon boats, yachts, and sailboats.

4200 Marriott Dr., Panama City Beach, FL 32408. 📞 800/874-7105 or 850/236-6000. Fax 850/236-6158. www. marriottbaypoint.com. 356 units. Summer $159–$495 double; off season $99–$159 double. Packages available. AE, DC, DISC, MC, V. From Thomas Dr., take Magnolia Beach Rd. and bear right on Dellwood Rd. to resort complex. **Amenities:** 2 restaurants; 2 bars; 3 heated outdoor pools; indoor pool; 2 golf courses; 4 tennis courts; health club; Jacuzzi; watersports equipment rental; bike rental; concierge; business center; limited room service; massage; babysitting; laundry service; coin-op washers and dryers; concierge-level rooms. *In room:* A/C, TV, dataport, fridge, coffeemaker, hair dryer, iron.

Sunset Inn   This well-maintained establishment, near the east end of the beach, is right on the Gulf but away from the crowds. The spacious beachside rooms accommodate families in one- and two-bedroom apartments, while refurbished efficiencies and a new building with tropically furnished one- and two-bedroom condominiums are across the street. The condominiums are the most expensive units here, but the units with patios or balconies right on the beach will better suit sun-and-sand lovers. Some of the older units have shower-only bathrooms. The best part about this motel is the quiet beach—it offers a sense of peace not necessarily found elsewhere along the strip.

8109 Surf Dr., Panama City Beach, FL 32408. 📞 850/234-7370. Fax 850/234-7370, ext. 303. www.sunsetinnfl.com. 62 units. Rooms and efficiencies: Spring break and summer $70–$130; spring $60–$95; fall and winter $45–$80. Condos (4–6 people): Spring break and summer $140–$165, spring $110–$125, fall and winter $80–$100. Weekly and monthly rates available. AE, DISC, MC, V. **Amenities:** Heated outdoor pool; coin-op washers and dryers. *In room:* A/C, TV, kitchen, fridge, coffeemaker.

WHERE TO DINE

Except for fast-food joints, there aren't many national-chain family restaurants in Panama City Beach (you'll find those along 15th and 23rd sts. over in Panama City). One local chain worth trying is the **Montego Bay Seafood House** (www.montego baypcb.com), which offers a wide range of fairly inexpensive sandwiches, burgers, and seafood main courses. Branches are at the "curve" at 4920 Thomas Dr. (📞 **850/234-8686**) and in the Shoppes at Edgewater, Front Beach Drive at 473 Beckrich Rd. (📞 **850/233-6033**).

Pay attention to the restaurant hours here, as some places are closed in winter. Even if they're open, many will close early when business is slow; call ahead to make sure.

Billy's Steamed Seafood Restaurant *Value* SEAFOOD   More a lively raw bar than a restaurant, Billy and Eloise Poole's casual spot has been serving the best crabs in town since 1982. These are hard-shell blue crabs prepared Maryland style: steamed with spicy Old Bay seasoning. Unlike crab houses in Baltimore, however, Billy and Eloise remove the crab's top shell, clean out the "mustard" (intestines), and cut the crabs in two for you; all you have to do is "pick" out the meat. Don't worry, they'll show you how. Other steamed morsels include shrimp, oysters, crabs, and lobster served with corn on the cob and garlic bread. Order anything from the briny deep here, but pass over other items.

3000 Thomas Dr. (between Grand Lagoon and Magnolia Beach Rd.). 𝄢 850/235-2349. Main courses $5.50–$18; sandwiches $3.50–$5.50. AE, DISC, MC, V. Daily 11am–9pm.

Boar's Head Restaurant ✺ STEAK/SEAFOOD   An institution since 1978, this shingle-roofed establishment appears from the road to be a South Seas resort. Inside, its impressive beamed ceiling, stone walls, and fireplaces create a warm, tavernlike atmosphere suited to the house specialties: tender, marbled prime rib of beef and perfectly cooked steaks. Beef eaters don't have the Boar's Head to themselves, however, as the coals are also used to give a charred flavor to salmon, grouper, and yellowfin tuna. Other temptations include scallops in a cream sauce over angel-hair pasta. And venison, quail, and other game dishes find their way here in winter. The extensive wine list has won awards. A cozy tavern to one side features live music, usually Wednesday through Saturday evenings.

17290 Front Beach Rd. (just west of Fla. 79). 𝄢 850/234-6628. www.boarsheadrestaurant.com. Main courses $17–$29. AE, DC, DISC, MC, V. Summer daily 4:30–10pm; off season Sun–Thurs 4:30–9pm, Fri–Sat 4:30–10pm.

Canopies ✺✺ SEAFOOD/STEAKS   This area's most elegant restaurant and purveyor of its finest cuisine occupies a 1910-vintage gray-clapboard house with a magnificent view of St. Andrews Bay. Dining is outside on the patio or on an enclosed veranda, and the dark, cozy bar in the old living room invites before- or after-dinner drinks. The menu changes monthly but always offers the consistently excellent she-crab soup under a flaky croissant dome. Other selections could include sushi-quality yellowfin tuna in a sherry-soy sauce; a "trio" of tuna, salmon, and grouper with a citrus-butter sauce served with mandarin-orange salsa and Vidalia-onion mashed potatoes; and sautéed grouper with lump crabmeat in a sherry-butter sauce. Forget the crab cakes. Landlubbers can partake of award-winning beef, veal, lamb, pork, and game dishes. White-chocolate mousse is among several wonderful sweet endings.

⸨Fun Fact⸩ **"We Shuck 'Em, You Suck 'Em"**

That's the motto at **Shuckums Oyster Pub & Seafood Grill,** 15614 Front Beach Rd., at Powell Adams Drive (𝄢 850/235-3214; www.shuckums.com). Comedian Martin Short made this noisy, lively, and smoky pub famous when he tried unsuccessfully to shuck oysters at its bar during the making of an MTV spring-break special. The original bar where Short tried to shuck is virtually papered over with dollar bills signed by old and young patrons who have been flocking here since 1967. The obvious specialty is fresh Apalachicola oysters, served raw, steamed, or baked with a variety of toppings. Otherwise, the menu consists of pub fare and mediocre seafood main courses. In summer, Shuckums is open daily from 11am to 2am. During the off season, it closes at 9pm Monday through Friday, at midnight Saturday and Sunday.

4423 W. Hwy. 98, Panama City (1 mile east of Hathaway Bridge on U.S. 98). © 850/872-8444. www.canopies pc.com. Reservations recommended. Main courses $18–$26; early-bird specials $11. AE, DC, DISC, MC, V. Daily 5–10pm (early-bird specials 5–6pm).

Captain Anderson's Restaurant & Waterfront Seafood Market ★ SEAFOOD
Since 1953, this famous restaurant has been attracting early diners, who come to watch the fishing fleet unload the catch of the day at the busy marina on Grand Lagoon. It's so popular, in fact, that you may have to wait 2 hours for a table during the peak summer months; the three bars help you pass the time. The Captain's menu is noted for grilled local fish (grouper, amberjack, and yellowfin tuna), crab-stuffed jumbo shrimp, and a heaped-high seafood platter. The food here isn't as interesting as at Hamilton's Seafood Restaurant & Lounge, across the road (see below), but the local atmosphere makes it worth a visit.

5551 N. Lagoon Dr. (at Thomas Dr.). © 850/234-2225. www.captanderson.com. Main courses $15–$37. AE, DC, DISC, MC, V. Summer Mon–Sat 4–10pm; off season Mon–Sat 4:30–10pm. Closed Nov–Jan.

Hamilton's Seafood Restaurant & Lounge ★ SEAFOOD
Proprietor Steve Stevens continues in the tradition of his noted Mississippi-born restaurateur father at this attractive blond-wood and knotty-pine restaurant on Grand Lagoon. The grilled grouper with shrimp, scallops, and crab is a real treat. Several other dishes are locally unique to Hamilton's, such as spicy snapper étouffée and a Greek-accented shrimp Christo. Mesquite-grilled fish and steaks are also house specialties, and vegetarians can order a coal-fired vegetable kabob served over angel-hair pasta. The Lagoon Saloon makes the wait for a table pass quickly. The extensive selection of California and French wines is well chosen. Hamilton's was nearly destroyed by Hurricane Ivan and is in the process of being rebuilt. Check their website for progress updates.

5711 N. Lagoon Dr. (at Thomas Dr.). © 850/234-1255. www.hamiltonspcbeach.com. Main courses $13–$25. AE, DISC, MC, V. Summer daily 4–10pm; off season Mon–Thurs 5–9pm, Fri–Sat 5–9:30pm. Closed 1 week in Jan.

SPECIAL DINING EXPERIENCES
You've got to see the **Treasure Ship,** at Treasure Island Marina, 3605 S. Thomas Dr. at Grand Lagoon (© **850/234-8881;** http://thetreasureship.com), to believe it. This amazing 2 acres of ship space claims to be the world's largest land-based Spanish galleon and a reputed replica of the three-masted sailing ships that carried loot back to Spain in the 16th and 17th centuries. You can get anything from an ice-cream cone to peel-it-yourself shrimp, to a sophisticated dinner in the restaurant and bar here, which are open daily from 4:30 to 10pm (and sometimes later); closed during the winter months. Call to make sure it's open when you want to go.

Dinner-dance cruises on the *Lady Anderson* are a romantic evening escape; they're available March through October. This modern, three-deck ship boards at Captain Anderson's Marina, 5550 N. Lagoon Dr. (© **800/360-0510** or 850/234-5940; www. ladyanderson.com), Monday through Saturday evenings, with the cruises lasting from 7 to 10pm. Buffet dinners are featured, followed by live music for dancing on Monday, Wednesday, Friday, and Saturday nights; gospel music on Tuesday and Thursday. Dinner-dance tickets cost $40 for adults, $38 for seniors, $23 for children 6 to 11, and $15 for children 2 to 5. Gospel-music cruises go for $35 adults, $33 seniors, $23 children 6 to 11, and $15 children 2 to 5. Tips are included. Summertime reservations should be made well in advance.

PANAMA CITY & PANAMA CITY BEACH AFTER DARK

THE CLUB & BAR SCENE   The **Breakers,** 12627 Front Beach Rd. (© **850/234-6060**), is the area's premier supper club, with unsurpassed Gulf views and music for dining and dancing. You'll swear the King has risen from the grave, as "Elvis Presley" and other impersonators at **Clutch Rock 'n' Roll Cafe** perform here. The show is worth the cover of $10 to $15 per person. The Beachfront **Harpoon Harry's Waterfront Cafe** is part of the same complex.

Romantic lounges with live entertainment can be found at the **Treasure Ship** (p. 627), at 3605 S. Thomas Dr. (© **850/234-8881**), where during summer the comedian-hypnotist Mike Harvey performs in the top-floor Captain's Quarters and at the **Boar's Head** (p. 626), at 17290 Front Beach Rd. (© **850/234-6628**).

The 20-something crowd likes to boogie all night at beach clubs such as **Schooners,** 5121 Gulf Dr. (© **850/235-3555**), where every table has a Gulf view; **Club La Vella,** also on the beach at 8813 Thomas Dr. (© **850/234-3866**), a bikini-contest kind of place and one of Florida's largest nightclubs; and **Sharkey's on the Gulf,** 15201 Front Beach Rd. (© **850/235-2420**). The clubs often stay open until 4am in summer. **Pineapple Willie's Lounge,** beachside at 9900 S. Thomas Dr. (© **850/235-0928**), is open from 11am until 2am, serving ribs basted with Jack Daniel's and spotlighting live entertainment during summer and a host of sports TVs year-round.

4 Apalachicola ⟨★⟨★

65 miles E of Panama City, 80 miles W of Tallahassee

Sometimes called Florida's Last Frontier (a claim that overlooks the Everglades), Apalachicola makes a fascinating day trip from Panama City Beach or Tallahassee, as well as a destination in its own right. The long, gorgeous beaches on St. George Island, 7 miles from town, are among America's best. Justifiably famous for Apalachicola oysters, the bays and estuaries are great for fishing and boating. And if you love nature, the area is rich in wildlife preserves.

The charming little town of Apalachicola (pop. 2,600) was a major seaport each autumn from 1827 to 1861, when plantations in Alabama and Georgia shipped tons of cotton down the Apalachicola River to the Gulf. The town had a racetrack, an opera house, and a civic center that hosted balls, socials, and gambling. The population shrank during the mosquito-infested summer months, however, when yellow fever and malaria epidemics struck. It was during one of these outbreaks that Dr. John Gorrie of Apalachicola tried to develop a method of cooling his patients' rooms. In doing so, he invented the forerunner of the air conditioner, a device that made Florida tourism possible and life a whole lot more bearable for locals.

Apalachicola has traditionally made its living primarily from the Gulf and the lagoonlike bay protected by a chain of offshore barrier islands. Today this area produces the bulk of Florida's oyster crop, and shrimping and fishing are major industries, too. The town has also been discovered by a number of urban expatriates, who have moved here, restored old homes, and opened interesting antiques and gift shops (there aren't many towns this size where you can buy Crabtree & Evelyn products).

ESSENTIALS

GETTING THERE   The nearest airport is 65 miles to the west at Panama City Beach (p. 619). From there, you'll have to rent a car or take an expensive taxi ride. The Tallahassee Regional Airport (p. 633) is about 85 miles to the northeast. **Croom's**

Transportation (✆ **888/653-8132** or 850/653-2400) has airport shuttle service between Tallahassee and Apalachicola ($105 for one passenger, $10 each additional person).

The scenic way to drive here is via the Gulf-hugging U.S. 98 from Panama City Beach, or via U.S. 319 and U.S. 98 from Tallahassee. From I-10, take exit 142 at Marianna, then follow Florida 71 south to Port St. Joe; from there, take U.S. 98 East to Apalachicola.

VISITOR INFORMATION The **Apalachicola Bay Chamber of Commerce,** 99 Market St., Apalachicola, FL 32320 (✆ **850/653-9419;** fax 850/653-8219; www.apalachicolabay.org), supplies information about the area from its office on Market Street (U.S. 98) between Avenue D and Avenue E. The chamber is open Monday through Friday from 9:30am to 5pm.

TIME The town is in the eastern time zone, like Orlando, Miami, and Tallahassee (1 hr. ahead of Panama City Beach and the rest of the Panhandle). ***Note:*** Many shops are closed on Wednesday afternoon, when Apalachicolans go fishing.

BEACHES, PARKS & WILDLIFE REFUGES

Some experts consider the 9 miles of beaches in **St. George Island State Park** ★★★ among America's best. This pristine nature preserve occupies the eastern end of St. George Island, about 15 miles east of Apalachicola. A 4-mile-long paved road leads through the dunes to picnic areas, restrooms, showers, and a boat launch. An unpaved trail leads another 5 miles to the island's eastern end, but be careful: It's easy to get stuck in the soft sand, even in a four-wheel-drive SUV. From a hiking trail leading from the campground out to a narrow peninsula on the bay side, you can see countless terns, snowy plovers, black skimmers, and other birds. Entry costs $3 per vehicle with one occupant, $5 per vehicle with two to eight occupants, and $1 per pedestrian or bicyclist. Campsites go for $19. The park is open daily from 8am to sunset. Pets are allowed. For more information, contact the park at 1900 E. Gulf Beach Dr., St. George Island, FL 32328 (✆ **850/927-2111;** www.floridastateparks.org/stgeorgeisland).

There are no facilities whatsoever at the **St. Vincent National Wildlife Refuge,** southwest of Apalachicola and accessible only by boat. The U.S. Fish & Wildlife Service has left this 12,358-acre barrier island in its natural state, but visitors are welcome to walk through its pine forests, marshlands, ponds, dunes, and beaches. In addition to native species such as bald eagles and alligators, the island is home to a small herd of sambar deer from Southeast Asia. Red wolves are bred here for re-establishment in other wildlife areas. **St. Vincents Island Shuttle Service** (✆ **850/229-1065;** www.stvincentisland.com), at Indian Pass, 21 miles west of Apalachicola via U.S. 98 and C.R.s 30A and 30B, will take you to the island in a pontoon boat. If you bring your bike, the boat will drop you at on one end of the island and pick you up later at the other. Call for prices and reservations, which are required. The refuge headquarters, at the north end of Market Street in town, has exhibits of wetland flora and fauna; it's open Monday through Friday from 8am to 4:30pm. Admission is free. For more information, contact the refuge at P.O. Box 447, Apalachicola, FL 32329 (✆ **850/653-8808**).

The huge **Apalachicola National Forest** (p. 646) begins a few miles northeast of town. It has a host of facilities, including canoeing and mountain-bike trails.

OUTDOOR ACTIVITIES

CRUISES Jeanni McMillan of **Journeys of St. George Island** ★ (✆ **850/927-3259;** www.sgislandjourneys.com) takes guests on narrated nature cruises to the barrier islands, and on canoe and kayak trips in the creeks and streams of the Apalachicola River basin. She also leads night hikes with blue-crab netting, shelling excursions, and fishing and scalloping trips, plus excursions tailored exclusively for children. Prices range from $70 to $100 per person. Reservations are required, so call her to find out what she's offering when you'll be in town. Jeanni also rents canoes, kayaks, sailboats, and sailboards. Closed January and February.

A less adventurous way to see the marshes, swamps, and shallow-water rivers is via a nature cruise with **EcoVentures, Inc.** (© 850/653-2593; www.apalachicolatours.com). It uses the *Osprey,* a 40-foot, all-weather boat that can carry up to 32 passengers. Fares are $25 for adults, $15 for children under 16. Call for schedule and reservations.

You can go afternoon or sunset sailing on the bay on Capt. Jerry Weber's 40-foot sloop **Wind Catcher** (© 850/653-3881). The 2½-hour voyages cost $40 for adults and $25 for children under 16, including snacks and soft drinks. Reservations are essential.

FISHING   You can't go oystering, but fishing is excellent in these waters, where trout, redfish, flounder, tarpon, shark, and drum abound. The chamber of commerce (p. 629) can help arrange charters on the local boats, many of which dock at the Rainbow Inn on Water Street. For guides, contact **Robinson Brothers Guide Service** (© 850/653-8896; fax 850/653-3118; www.flaredfish.com). Rates run about $350 for a half-day and $400 to $450 for a full day for up to four anglers.

EXPLORING THE TOWN

Start your visit by picking up a map and a self-guided tour brochure from the chamber of commerce (p. 629), and then stroll around Apalachicola's waterfront, business district, and Victorian-era homes.

Along Water Street, several tin warehouses date back to the town's seafaring days of the late 1800s, as does the 1840s-era **Sponge Exchange,** at Commerce Street and Avenue E. A highlight of the residential area, centered on Gorrie Square at Avenue D and 6th Street, is the Greek Revival–style **Trinity Episcopal Church,** built in New York and shipped here in 1837. **Battery Park,** at the water end of 6th Street, has a children's playground. A number of excellent art galleries and gift shops are grouped on Market Street, Avenue D, and Commerce Street.

The showpiece at the **John Gorrie Museum State Park** ✯, Avenue D at 6th Street (© 850/653-9347; www.floridastateparks.org/johngorriemuseum), is a replica of Dr. Gorrie's cooling machine, a prototype of today's air conditioner: It really works! The park is open Thursday through Monday from 9am to 5pm; closed New Year's Day, Thanksgiving, and Christmas. Admission is $1 (free for children 6 and under).

The renovated **Dixie Theater,** 21 Ave. E. (© 850/653-3200), a 1912 movie house, hosts live theater. It has maintained its original ticket booth and restored its facades to their original glory.

The **Estuarine Walk,** at the north end of Market Street on the grounds of the Apalachicola National Estuarine Research Reserve (© 850/653-8063), contains aquariums full of fish and turtles, along with displays of other estuarine life. It's open Monday through Friday from 8am to 5pm. Admission is free.

WHERE TO STAY

Built in 1997, the 42-room **Best Western Apalach Inn,** 249 Hwy. 98 W. (© 800/528-1234 or 850/653-9131; fax 850/653-9136; www.apalachicola.com/bestwestern), a mile west of downtown, is the only national chain hotel here.

Apalachicola River Inn ✿ The town's only waterfront lodging, this two-story motel's rough-hewn exterior timbers make it look like one of the neighboring warehouses. Units in the main building all have views across a marina to Apalachicola Bay. Those on the second floor are larger and have balconies, making them preferable to the smaller downstairs units, whose doors open directly onto the marina's boardwalk. All accommodations have been renovated, adding new carpeting, windows, and French doors. Most of the upstairs rooms have shower-only bathrooms; however, there are whirlpool tubs in two of the units, as well as in a two-bedroom apartment in a building next door.

The redone lobby now features the Frog Level Oyster Bar, a casual bar serving—what else?—oysters. Boss Oyster, the inn's popular riverfront restaurant, features Gulfwater oysters cooked many ways, such as the Oysters Greektown (with feta cheese, garlic, olives, and parsley). Caroline's, facing the river, serves breakfast, lunch, and seafood dinners (it's a bit pricey at dinner, but makes a fine spot for an alfresco lunch). The Roseate Spoonbill Lounge is *the* local watering hole, with a grand view and music on an outdoor deck on weekends.

123 Water St., Apalachicola, FL 32320. ⓒ 850/653-8139. Fax 850/653-2018. www.apalachicolariverinn.com. 26 units. $95–$115 double; $125–$160 Jacuzzi suite; $200–$400 2-bedroom suite. AE, DC, DISC, MC, V. Pets accepted in smoking rooms ($10 nightly fee). **Amenities:** Restaurant; bar. *In room:* A/C, TV.

Coombs House Inn ✿✿✿ The most luxurious place around, this large B&B occupies two Victorian homes. The main house was built in 1905 by a lumber baron, and it shows: Polished black-cypress paneling lines the entire central hall and parlor. Each of the 10 guest rooms here is tastefully decorated, with lots of Victorian reproductions. The Coombs Suite (with bay windows, sofa, four-poster bed, and whirlpool tub) is outstanding. The Love Bungalow has its own private entrance. Less grand but still impressive are eight rooms in another restored Victorian, known as Coombs House East, half a block away. One of these rooms has a whirlpool tub and bidet. A major truck route, U.S. 98, runs along the north side of both houses; request a south room to escape the periodic road noise. Guests are treated to complimentary wine receptions on weekends. The breakfast is hardly just Danish and coffee, but a home-cooked extravaganza. All rooms are nonsmoking.

80 6th St., Apalachicola, FL 32320. ⓒ 850/653-9199. Fax 850/653-2785. www.coombshouseinn.com. 18 units. $79–$199 double. Rates include full breakfast. DISC, MC, V. **Amenities:** Access to nearby health club; free use of mountain bikes. *In room:* A/C, TV, dataport, hair dryer.

Gibson Inn ✿✿✿ Built in 1907 as a seamen's hotel and gorgeously restored, this cupola-topped inn is such a brilliant example of Victorian architecture that it's listed on the National Register of Historic Inns. No two guest rooms are alike (some still have the original sinks in the sleeping areas), but all are richly furnished with period reproductions. Nonguests are welcome to wander upstairs and peek into unoccupied rooms (whose doors are left open). Reservations are advised during summer and on spring and fall weekends, and as much as 5 years in advance for the seafood festival in November. Grab a drink from the bar and relax in one of the high-backed rockers on the old-fashioned veranda. The dining room serves excellent seafood and is open to all comers, so don't expect this to be private like a B&B; instead, you'll find yourself in a reborn, absolutely charming turn-of-the-20th-century hotel—one, albeit, with wireless Internet access!

51 Ave. C, Apalachicola, FL 32320. ⓒ 850/653-2191. Fax 850/653-3521. www.gibsoninn.com. 31 units. $90–$119 double; $129–$175 suite. AE, MC, V. **Amenities:** Restaurant; bar; wireless Internet access. *In room:* A/C, TV.

Rancho Inn On the western edge of the historic district, this older Spanish-look motel has been spiffed up by owners Mark and Mary Lynn Rodgers, who keep it clean and well maintained. Although simple when compared to the more expensive properties here, these motel rooms are spacious and comfortable, and all have microwaves and fridges. Restaurants are within walking distance.

240 Hwy. 98 W., Apalachicola, FL 32320. ✆ 850/653-9435. Fax 850/653-9180. www.ranchoinn.com. 32 units. $85–$138 double. AE, DISC, MC, V. Pets accepted ($6 fee). **Amenities:** Outdoor pool; bike rental. *In room:* A/C, TV, dataport, fridge, coffeemaker.

WHERE TO DINE

Townsfolk still plop down on the round stools at the marble-topped counter to order Coca-Colas and milkshakes at the **Old Time Soda Fountain & Luncheonette,** 93 Market St. (✆ **850/653-2606**). This 1950s relic was once the town drugstore. It's open Monday through Saturday from 10am to 5pm.

The Boss Oyster ⭑ SEAFOOD You've heard about the aphrodisiac properties of Apalachicola oysters. Well, you can see if those properties are real at this rustic dock-side eatery, whose motto is "Shut Up and Shuck." This is one of the best places in Florida to try the bivalves raw, steamed, or under a dozen toppings, ranging from capers to crabmeat. Steamed shrimp are also on offer, as are delicious po'boy sandwiches. Most main courses come from the fryer, so consider this joint a great local experience, not fine dining. Sit at the picnic tables inside, on a screened porch, or out on the dock.

125 Water St. (between aves. C and D). ✆ 850/653-9364. Main courses $17–$22; oysters $4.50–$14; sandwiches and baskets $7–$10. AE, DC, DISC, MC, V. Apr–Sept Sun–Thurs 11:30am–10pm, Fri–Sat 11:30am–11pm; Oct–Mar Sun–Thurs 11:30am–9pm, Fri–Sat 11:30am–10pm.

Chef Eddie's Magnolia Grill ⭑⭑⭑ CONTINENTAL/CAJUN One of the top places to dine in Northwest Florida, Boston-bred chef-owner Eddie Cass's pleasant, homey restaurant offers nightly specials ranging from classic French rack of lamb and beef Wellington to fresh local seafood with New Orleans–style sauces. You will long remember Eddie's mahimahi Pontchartrain with cream and artichoke hearts. Start with a bowl of spicy seafood gumbo, a consistent hit during the Florida Seafood Festival. No smoking is permitted inside.

99 11th St. (between aves. E and F). ✆ 850/653-8000. www.chefeddiesmagnoliagrill.com. Reservations recommended. Main courses $12–$28. MC, V. Mon–Sat 6–9:30pm.

The Owl Cafe ⭑⭑ SEAFOOD Ensconced on the first floor of a two-story clap-board building in the heart of downtown, this sophisticated restaurant ranks only behind Chef Eddie's Magnolia Grill as having the best cuisine in town. Go for the nightly seafood specials or opt for the terrific grouper with garlic, capers, and arti-chokes. Now paneled in rich wood, the walls are adorned with the works of noted local photographer Richard Bickel.

15 Ave. D (at Commerce St.). ✆ 850/653-9888. Reservations recommended. Main courses $12–$25. MC, V. Mon–Sat 11:30am–3pm and 5:30–10pm.

Tamara's Cafe Floridita FLORIBBEAN/LATIN AMERICAN Tamara Saurez's storefront cafe offers a change of pace and, sadly, since she handed the restaurant over to her daughter and son-in-law, a change from what once was a fabulous experience to a somewhat disappointing one. The black-bean soup may still have zing, but the service is spotty and not nearly as attentive as it used to be. You'll also find Latino spices accentuating Floribbean fare, such as a creamy jalapeño sauce putting a little fire into pecan-encrusted grouper. The paella is still a winner, but be forewarned that it ain't what it used to be.

17 Ave. E. (at Commerce St.). ⓒ **850/653-4111**. Reservations recommended. Main courses $12–$24. MC, V. Daily 11am–10pm

APALACHICOLA AFTER DARK

Nocturnal diversions are scarce in this small town, but you can catch summer-stock performances of plays like *Same Time Next Year* in the lovingly restored, 1912-vintage **Dixie Theatre,** 21 Ave. D (ⓒ **850/653-3200**). Ticket prices range from $10 to $25, depending on the show.

Locals like to have their after-work drinks in the fine old bar at the **Gibson Inn,** and then hit the **Roseate Spoonbill Lounge,** in the Apalachicola River Inn (p. 631), where bands play on weekend evenings.

5 Tallahassee

163 miles W of Jacksonville, 191 miles E of Pensacola, 250 miles NW of Orlando

As a University of Miami alum, I was practically taught to hate Tallahassee, just because it's the home of the Miami Hurricanes' biggest rivals—Florida State University's Seminoles (or 'Noles, as locals refer to them). Because I couldn't care less about football, I just chalked up Tallahassee as the state capital and, later in life, command central for that pesky 2000 election bug known as the chad. Boy, was I wrong. It's not just about football and hanging chads. There's tons of charm and non-voting history here, too.

Tallahassee was selected as Florida's capital in 1823 because it was halfway between St. Augustine and Pensacola, then the state's major cities. That location puts it almost in Georgia—and, in fact, Tallahassee has more in common with Macon than with Miami. There's as much Old South ambience here as anywhere else you're likely to visit in Florida. You'll find lovingly restored 19th-century homes and buildings, including the 1845 Old Capitol. They all sit among so many towering pines and sprawling live oaks that you'll think you're in an enormous forest. The trees form virtual tunnels along Tallahassee's five official Canopy Roads, which are lined with historic plantations, ancient Native American settlement sites and mounds, gorgeous gardens, quiet parks with picnic areas, and beautiful lakes and streams. And the nearby Apalachicola National Forest is a virtual gold mine of outdoor pursuits.

While tradition and history are important here, you'll also encounter the modern era, beginning with the New Capitol Building towering 22 stories over downtown. Usually-sleepy Tallahassee takes on a very lively persona when the legislature is in session and when the football teams of Florida State University and Florida A&M University take to the gridiron.

If you're inclined to give your credit cards a workout, the nearby town of Havana is Florida's antiquing capital.

ESSENTIALS

GETTING THERE   **AirTran** (ⓒ 800/AIR-TRAN), **Delta** (ⓒ 800/221-1212), **Northwest** (ⓒ 800/225-2525), and **US Airways** (ⓒ 800/428-4322) serve **Tallahassee Regional Airport** (ⓒ 850/891-7802; http://talgov.com/citytlh/aviation), 10 miles southwest of downtown on Southeast Capital Circle.

Alamo (ⓒ 800/327-9633), **Avis** (ⓒ 800/331-1212), **Budget** (ⓒ 800/527-0700), **Hertz** (ⓒ 800/654-3131), and **National** (ⓒ 800/CAR-RENT) have airport sites;

Dollar (© 800/800-4000), **Enterprise** (© 800/325-8007), and **Thrifty** (© 800/367-2277) are nearby.

You can take a **taxi** downtown for about $15.

The **Amtrak** (© **800/872-7245;** www.amtrak.com) transcontinental Sunset Limited train stops in Tallahassee at 918½ Railroad Ave.

VISITOR INFORMATION   For advance information, contact the **Tallahassee Area Convention and Visitors Bureau,** 200 W. College Ave. (P.O. Box 1369), Tallahassee, FL 32302 (© **800/628-2866** or 850/413-9200; fax 850/487-4621; www.see tallahassee.com). The bureau's excellent quarterly visitors guide has descriptions (including hours and admission fees) of just about everything going on here.

Go to the **Tallahassee Area Visitor Information Center,** 106 E. Jefferson St., across from the capitol (© **850/413-9200**), for free street and public-transportation maps, brochures, and pamphlets outlining tours of the historic districts and the Canopy Roads. It's open Monday through Friday from 8am to 5pm, Saturday from 9am to noon.

For statewide information, a **Florida Welcome Center** is located in the west foyer of the New Capitol Building (see below).

GETTING AROUND   TALTRAN (© **850/891-5200;** www.state.fl.us/citytlh/taltran), the city's public-transportation agency, operates the free **Old Town Trolley,** the best way to see the sights of historic downtown Tallahassee. You can get on or off at any point between Adams Street Commons, at the corner of Jefferson and Adams streets, and the Governor's Mansion (see the exact route on the "Downtown Tallahassee" map). The trolley runs Monday through Friday, every 20 minutes between 7am and 6:30pm.

TALTRAN also provides city **bus** service from its downtown terminal, at Tennessee and Adams streets ($1.25 adults, 60¢ seniors and kids 12 and under). The ticket booths there and at the Tallahassee Area Visitor Information Center have route maps and schedules.

For taxi service, call **Yellow Cab** (© **850/580-8080**) or **City Taxi** (© **850/562-4222**). Fares are $1.85 at flag fall, plus $1.60 per mile.

TIME   Tallahassee is in the eastern time zone, like Orlando, Miami, and Apalachicola. It's 1 hour ahead of the rest of the Panhandle.

EXPLORING THE CITY
THE CAPITOL COMPLEX
Florida's capitol complex, on South Monroe Street at Apalachee Parkway, dominates the downtown area and should be your first stop after the Tallahassee Area Visitor Information Center, just across Jefferson Street.

The **New Capitol Building** (© **850/488-6167**), a $43-million skyscraper, was built in 1977 to replace the 1845-vintage Old Capitol. State legislators meet here for at least 60 days, usually beginning in March. The house and senate chambers have public viewing galleries. For a spectacular view, take the elevators to the 22nd-floor **observatory,** where, on a clear day, you can see all the way to the Gulf of Mexico. You can also view works by Florida artists while up here. The New Capitol is open Monday through Friday from 8am to 5pm.

Directly in front of the skyscraper is the strikingly white **Old Capitol** ⊛ (© **850/487-1902;** http://dhr.dos.state.fl.us/museum/m_sites.html). With its majestic dome, this "Pearl of Capitol Hill" has been restored to its original beauty. An eight-room

Downtown Tallahassee

ACCOMMODATIONS ■
Cabot Lodge North **1**
DoubleTree Hotel **9**
Governors Inn **10**

DINING ◆
Anthony's **3**
Bahn Thai **13**
Barnacle Bill's Seafood Restaurant **2**
Chez Pierre **4**
Kool Beanz Cafe **5**

ATTRACTIONS ●
Black Archives Research Center
   and Museum **14**
Florida State University
   Museum of Fine Arts **6**
Foster Tanner Art Center **15**
Knott House Museum
   ("The House That Rhymes") **8**
Mary Brogan Museum
   of Art and Science **11**
Meginnis-Monroe House **7**
Museum of Florida History **12**

exhibit portrays Florida's political history. Turn-of-the-20th-century furnishings, cotton gins, and other artifacts are also of interest. The Old Capitol is open Monday through Friday from 9am to 4:30pm, Saturday from 10am to 4:30pm, and Sunday and holidays from noon to 4:30pm. Admission to the old and the new capitols is free.

The twin granite towers of the **Vietnam Veterans Memorial,** honoring Florida's Vietnam vets, are across Monroe Street from the Old Capitol. Next to it, facing Apalachee Parkway, the **Union Bank Museum** (© **850/561-2603**) is housed in Florida's oldest surviving bank building. For a while, it was the Freedman's Savings and Trust Company, which served emancipated slaves. Now part of Florida Agricultural and Mechanical University's Black Archives Research Center, it houses a small but interesting collection of artifacts and documents reflecting black history and culture that are definitely worth a brief visit. The museum is open Monday through Friday from 9am to 4pm; admission is free.

The Old Town Trolley will take you north of the capitol to the lovely Georgian-style **Governor's Mansion,** at Adams and Brevard streets (© **850/488-4661**). Enhanced by a portico patterned after Andrew Jackson's columned antebellum home in Tennessee, the Hermitage, and surrounded by giant magnolia trees and landscaped lawns, the mansion is furnished with 18th- and 19th-century antiques and collectibles. Tours are given when the legislature is in session, usually beginning in March. Call for schedules and reservations.

Located adjacent to the Governor's Mansion, **The Grove** was home to Ellen Call Long, known as "The Tallahassee Girl," the first child born after Tallahassee was settled.

HISTORIC DISTRICTS

Although modern buildings have made inroads into the downtown area, Tallahassee has made an ongoing effort to preserve its historic homes and buildings. Many of them are concentrated in three historic districts within an easy walk north of the capitol complex. The information center in the New Capitol distributes free brochures of walking tours that cover the three areas. Taken together, the tours are about 4 miles long and should take half a day. Most interesting is the Park Avenue Historic District, 3 blocks north of the capitol complex, which you can see in about 1 hour.

ADAMS STREET COMMONS   This block-long, winding brick and landscaped area along Adams Street begins on the north side of the capitol complex (between Jefferson St. and College Ave.) and retains an old-fashioned town-square atmosphere. Restored buildings include the Governor's Club, a 1900s Masonic lodge, and Gallie's Hall, where Florida's first five African-American college students received their Florida A&M University diplomas in 1892. Restaurants, shops, and Gallie Alley are also here. Adams Street crosses Park Avenue 3 blocks north of the capitol complex. This is a good place for lunch at one of the several cafes that cater to downtown office workers.

PARK AVENUE HISTORIC DISTRICT   The 7 blocks of Park Avenue between Martin Luther King, Jr., Boulevard and North Meridian Street are a lovely promenade of beautiful trees, gardens, and outstanding old mansions. This broad avenue, with a shady median strip lined with moss-bearded live oaks, was originally named 200 Foot Street and then McCarty Street, but was later renamed Park Avenue to satisfy a snobbish Anglophile society matron who didn't want an Irish name imprinted on her son's wedding invitations.

Several Park Avenue historic homes are open to the public, including the **Knott House Museum,** at Calhoun Street (see "Museums, Galleries & Archaeological Sites," below). The **Columns,** at Duval Street, was built in the 1830s and is the city's oldest surviving building (it's now the home of the Tallahassee Chamber of Commerce). The **First Presbyterian Church,** at Adams Street, built in 1838, is the city's oldest church and has been an important African-American historic site since slaves were welcome to worship here without their masters' consent. The **Walker Library,** between Monroe and Calhoun streets, was one of Florida's first libraries, dating from 1903 (it's home to Springtime Tallahassee, which is the city's top special event). Just north of Park Avenue on Gadsden Street, the **Meginnis-Monroe House** contains the Lemoyne Art Gallery (see "Museums, Galleries & Archaeological Sites," below).

At Martin Luther King, Jr., Boulevard, the adjacent **Old City Cemetery** and **Episcopal Cemetery** contain the graves of Prince Achille Murat, Napoleon's nephew; and of Princess Catherine Murat, his wife and George Washington's grand-niece. Also buried here are two governors and numerous Confederate and Union soldiers who died at the Battle of Natural Bridge during the Civil War. The cemeteries are important to African-American history since a number of slaves and the first black Florida A&M graduates are interred here. The visitor center in the New Capitol offers a cemetery walking-tour brochure.

CALHOUN STREET HISTORIC DISTRICT   The 3 blocks of Calhoun Street between Tennessee and Georgia streets, and running east on Virginia Street to Leon High School, sport elaborate homes built by prominent citizens between 1830 and 1880. A highlight here is the **Brokaw-McDougall House,** built in 1856, located in front of Leon High School at the eastern end of Virginia Street.

MUSEUMS, GALLERIES & ARCHAEOLOGICAL SITES

Black Archives Research Center and Museum ✟   Housed in the columned library built by Andrew Carnegie in 1908, and located on the grounds of the Florida Agricultural and Mechanical University (FAMU), this fascinating research center and museum displays one of the nation's most extensive collections of African-American artifacts, as well as such treasures as a 500-piece Ethiopian cross collection. The archives contain one of the world's largest collections on African-American history. Visitors can listen to tapes of gospel music and of elderly people reminiscing about the past. FAMU was founded in 1887, primarily as a black institution. Today it's acclaimed for its business, engineering, and pharmacy schools.

Martin Luther King, Jr., Blvd. and Gamble St., on the Florida A&M University campus. © 850/599-3020. www.famu. edu. Free admission. Mon–Fri 9am–4pm. Closed major holidays. Parking lot next to building.

Florida State University Museum of Fine Arts ✟   This permanent, 4,000-piece collection features 16th-century Dutch paintings, 20th-century American paintings, Japanese prints, pre-Columbian artifacts, and much more. Touring exhibits are displayed every few weeks.

250 Fine Arts Building, Copeland and Call sts. (on the FSU campus). © 850/644-6836. www.mofa.fsu.edu. Free admission. Sept–Apr Mon–Fri 9am–4pm; Sat–Sun 1–4pm. Closed Aug.

Foster Tanner Art Center   This gallery focuses on works by local, national, and international African-American artists, with a wide variety of paintings, sculptures, and more.

Florida A&M University (between Osceola and Gamble sts., off Martin Luther King, Jr., Blvd.). © 850/599-3161. www.famu.edu. Free admission. Mon–Fri 9am–5pm.

Knott House Museum ("The House That Rhymes") ★★ Adorned by a columned portico, this stately mansion was constructed in 1843, probably by a free black builder named George Proctor. Florida's first reading of the Emancipation Proclamation took place here in 1865. In 1928, it was purchased by politician William Knott, whose wife, Louella, wrote eccentric (read: kooky) rhymes about the house and its elegant Victorian furnishings (including the nation's largest collection of 19th-century gilt-framed mirrors). She also wrote about social, economic, and political events of the era. Attached by satin ribbons to tables, chairs, and lamps, her poems are the museum's most unusual feature. The house is in the Park Avenue Historic District and is listed on the National Register of Historic Places. It's preserved as it looked in 1928, when the Knott family left it and all of its contents to the city (it's now administered by the Museum of Florida History). The gift shop carries Victorian greeting cards, paper dolls, tin toy replicas, reprints of historic newspapers, and other nostalgic items.

301 E. Park Ave. (at Calhoun St.). © 850/922-2459. http://dhr.dos.state.fl.us/museum/m_sites.html. Free admission. Wed–Fri 1–4pm; Sat 10am–4pm. 1-hr. tours depart on the hour.

Mary Brogan Museum of Art and Science *Kids* This museum's mission, "to stimulate interest in and understanding of the visual arts, sciences, mathematics, and technology through experiences that educate and inspire," pretty much says it all. Associated with the Smithsonian Institution, the Mary Brogan Museum has changing exhibitions, educational programs, and lectures, as well as permanent science-museum-y exhibits.

350 S. Duval St. (at Pensacola St.). © 850/513-0700. www.thebrogan.org. Admission $6 adults; $3.50 children 3–17, seniors 60 and over, college students, and military with ID.

Meginnis-Monroe House ★★ This restored 1852 antebellum home, listed on the National Register of Historic Places, is a lovely setting for fine art. The home's **Lemoyne Art Gallery** is named in honor of Jacques LeMoyne, a member of a French expedition to Florida in 1564. Commissioned to depict the natives' dwellings and to map the seacoast, LeMoyne was the first European artist known to have visited North America. Exhibits here include permanent displays by local artists, sculpture, pottery, and photography—everything from the traditional to the avant garde. The gardens, with an old-fashioned gazebo, are spectacular during the Christmas holiday season. Programs of classical music are combined with visual arts during the year; check in advance for the current schedule.

125 N. Gadsden St. (between Park Ave. and Call St.). © 850/222-8800. www.lemoyne.org. Admission $1 adults, free for children 12 and under; free to all Sun. Tues–Sat 10am–5pm; Sun 1–5pm. Closed holidays.

Mission San Luís de Apalachee ★ A Spanish Franciscan mission named San Luís was set up in 1656 on this hilltop, already a principal village of the Apalachee Indians. From then until 1704, it served as the capital of a chain of Spanish missions in Northwest Florida. The mission complex included a tribal council house, a Franciscan church, a Spanish fort, and residential areas. Based on extensive archaeological and historical research, the council house and the 10×50-foot thatched-roofed church have been reconstructed. They are both open to the public. Interpretive markers are located across the 60-acre site, and self-guided tour brochures are available at the visitor center. Call for a schedule of ranger-led guided tours on weekends.

2021 Mission Rd. (between W. Tennessee and Tharpe sts.). © 850/487-3711. http://dhr.dos.state.fl.us/bar/san_luis. Free admission. Tues–Sun 10am–4pm. Closed Thanksgiving and Christmas. From downtown, take Tennessee St. (U.S. 90 W.) to entrance on right past Ocala St.

<Fun Fact **High Flying**

Florida State University's **Flying High Circus** (© 800/757-2146 or 850/644-6500; www.fsu.edu/~circus) calls itself the "Greatest Collegiate Show on Earth," and that's no small boast. It's arguably the grandest college circus in the country. Look for the big top and watch rehearsals during March, then enjoy perform- ances (juggling, hand balancing, bicycle, and trapeze) on the first 2 weekends of April. Tickets are $5 to $15.

Museum of Florida History   An 11-foot-tall mastodon greets you at this state history museum, where you can look back 12,000 years to the first Native Americans to live in Florida (mastodons were very much alive back then). Ancient artifacts from Native American tribes are exhibited, along with such relics from Florida's past as a reconstructed steamboat and treasures from 16th- and 17th-century sunken Spanish galleons. Inquire about guided tours and special exhibits.

Lower level of R. A. Gray Building, 500 S. Bronough St. (at Pensacola St.). © 850/245-6400. http://dhr.dos.state.fl.us/museum. Free admission (suggested donation $3 adults, $1 children). Mon–Fri 9am–4:30pm; Sat 10am–4:30pm; Sun and holidays noon–4:30pm. Closed Thanksgiving and Christmas. Parking available in garage around the corner on St. Augustine St., between Bronough and Duvall sts.

PARKS & NATURE PRESERVES

Maclay State Gardens   In 1923, New York financier Alfred B. Maclay and his wife, Louise, began planting the floral wonderland that surrounded their winter home on Lake Hall, on Tallahassee's northeastern outskirts. After her husband's death in 1944, Louise continued his dream of an ornamental garden to delight the public. In 1953, the land was bequeathed to the state of Florida. The more than 300 acres of flowers feature at least 200 varieties; 28 acres are devoted exclusively to azaleas and camellias. The surrounding park offers nature trails, canoe rentals, boating, picnick- ing, swimming, and fishing. The high blooming season is January through April, with the peak about mid-March. Beyond the house and gardens, the state park includes Lake Overstreet, around which wind 5.5 miles of hiking, biking, and horseback-rid- ing trails, making this a major venue for those outdoor activities.

3540 Thomasville Rd. (U.S. 319, north of I-10). © 850/487-4556. www.ssnow.com/maclay. Admission to park $4 per vehi- cle with up to 8 passengers, $1 per pedestrian or cyclist. May–Dec free admission to gardens; Jan–Apr $4 adults, $2 chil- dren under 12. Park daily 8am–sunset. Gardens daily 9am–5pm. Maclay House Jan–Apr daily 9am–5pm; closed May–Dec.

TRAVELING THE CANOPY ROADS

Graced by canopies of live oaks draped with Spanish moss, the St. Augustine, Mic- cousukee, Meridian, Old Bainbridge, and Centerville roads are the five official Canopy Roads leading out of Tallahassee. Driving is slow on these winding, two-lane country roads (the locals reluctantly are turning limited sections of them into four- lane highways); some of them are canopied for as long as 20 miles. Take along a pic- nic lunch, since there are few places to buy a meal along these tranquil byways. The visitor center in the New Capitol (p. 634) provides a useful driving-guide map of the Canopy Roads and Leon County's country lanes.

If you have time for only one, take **Old Bainbridge Road,** which leads to the Lake Jackson Mounds State Archaeological Site in the northwest suburbs and then on to Havana, Florida's antiquing capital (see "Shopping," below).

SHOPPING

Antiques hounds flock to the little village of **Havana** (★★), 12 miles northwest of I-10 on U.S. 27. Havana used to make its living growing shade tobacco (the outer wrapper on cigars). When that industry fizzled in the 1960s, the town went with it. Things turned around 20 years later, however, when Havana began opening art galleries and shops featuring antiques, handicrafts, and collectibles. Today these are housed in lovingly restored, turn-of-the-20th-century brick buildings along Havana's commercial streets. Just drive into town on Main Street (U.S. 27), turn left on 7th Avenue, find a parking place, and start browsing. You'll have plenty of company on weekends.

Bradley's Country Store, about 8 miles north of I-10 on Centerville Road (© 850/893-1647; www.bradleyscountrystore.com), sells more than 80,000 pounds of homemade sausage a year, both over the counter and by mail order. You can also buy coarse-ground grits, country-milled cornmeal, hogshead cheese, liver pudding, cracklings, and specially cured hams. This friendly store, which is on the National Register of Historic Places, is also a sightseeing attraction with self-guided tours. It's open Monday through Friday from 8am to 6pm, Saturday from 8am to 5pm.

OUTDOOR ACTIVITIES & SPECTATOR SPORTS

BIKING & IN-LINE SKATING The 16-mile **Tallahassee–St. Marks Historic Railroad Trail State Park** (© 850/922-6007; www.floridastateparks.org/stmarks trail) is the city's most popular bike route. Constructed with the financial assistance of wealthy Panhandle cotton-plantation owners and merchants, this was Florida's oldest railroad, functioning from 1837 to 1984. Cotton and other products were transported from Tallahassee to St. Marks for shipment to other cities. In recent years, the tracks were removed and 16 miles of the historic trail improved for joggers, hikers, bicyclists, and horseback riders. A paved parking lot is located at the north entrance, on Woodville Highway (Fla. 363), just south of Southeast Capital Circle. See "Side Trips from Tallahassee," beginning on p. 644, for more information on what you can see in the St. Marks area.

The **Apalachicola National Forest** (p. 646) also has extensive mountain-biking trails, and there are 5.5 miles of trails at **Maclay State Gardens** (p. 639).

GOLF Play golf at outstanding Hilaman Park, 2737 Blair Stone Rd., where the **Hilaman Park Municipal Golf Course** (© 850/891-3935 for information and fees) features 18 holes (par 72), a driving range, racquetball and squash courts, and a pool. Rental equipment is available at the club, and there's a restaurant, too. Compared with most courses in Florida, greens fees are a steal: about $26 on weekdays and $35 on weekends, including cart. The park also includes the **Jake Gaither Municipal Golf Course,** at Bragg and Pasco streets (© 850/891-3942), with a 9-hole, par-35 fairway and a pro shop. Call for fees.

The leading golf course is at the **Killearn Country Club and Inn** (© 800/476-4101 or 850/893-2186; www.killearncc.com), which once hosted the Sprint Classic. Moss-draped oaks enhance the beautiful 27-hole championship course, which is for members with reciprocal privileges only. Call for fees.

For course information, go to www.golf.com or www.floridagolfing.com, or call the **Florida Sports Foundation** (© 850/488-8347) or **Teebone Golfing** (© 866/833-2663).

SPECTATOR SPORTS Tallahassee succumbs to football frenzy whenever the perennially powerful Seminoles of **Florida State University (FSU)** take to the gridiron. Call © 888/378-6653 or 850/644-1830, or go to www.seminoles.com, well in

---

⟨Fun Fact⟩ *Semi-Tough:* **The Prequel**

Burt Reynolds played defensive back for Florida State University's football team in 1957 and is still an avid 'Noles booster.

---

advance, for tickets. Even when the Seminoles play on the road, everything except Tallahassee's many sports bars comes to a stop while fans watch the games on TV.

The **Florida A&M University (FAMU)** Rattlers are cheered on by the school's high-stepping, world-famous Marching 100 Band. Call ℂ **850/599-3230** or check www.famu.edu/athletics for FAMU schedules and tickets.

Both FSU and FAMU have seasonal basketball, baseball, tennis, and track schedules. Call the numbers above for information.

WHERE TO STAY

There is no high or low season here, but every hotel and motel for miles around is completely booked during FSU and FAMU football weekends from September to November, at graduation in May and, to a far lesser degree, weekdays during the 60-day legislative session that begins in March. Reserve well in advance—or you may have to stay 60 miles or more from the city. For the game schedules, call FSU or FAMU (see "Spectator Sports," above).

Most hotels are concentrated in three areas: in downtown Tallahassee, north of downtown along North Monroe Street at exit 199 off I-10 (where you'll find most chains), and along Apalachee Parkway east of downtown.

Tax on all hotel and campground bills is 10% in Leon County.

Cabot Lodge North ⟨Value⟩   It looks like a random motel, really, but look closer: There's charm to be found here. A clapboard plantation-style house with a tin roof and a wraparound porch provides Southern country charm that distinguishes this friendly motel from its nearby competitors. Guests can relax in rockers on the porch or on comfy sofas by the fireplace in the living room. Although the guest rooms in the two-story buildings out back don't hold up their end of the atmosphere factor, they're still quite satisfactory at these rates, and they give quick access to the outdoor pool. Guests can also enjoy a complimentary continental breakfast buffet and evening cocktails.

2735 N. Monroe St., Tallahassee, FL 32303. ℂ **800/223-1964** or 850/386-8880. Fax 850/386-4254. www.cabot lodgenorthmonroe.com. 160 units. $78–$84 double. Rates include continental breakfast, evening reception. AE, DC, DISC, MC, V. **Amenities:** Outdoor pool; access to nearby health club; laundry service. *In room:* A/C, TV, dataport, hair dryer (king-size rooms only), local calls.

DoubleTree Hotel   Most of the media covering the Bush–Gore 2000 election case before the Florida Supreme Court stayed at this 16-story hotel, one of the tallest buildings in town. The best things about it are the location, just 2 blocks north of the Capitol Building at Park Avenue, and the views from the spacious rooms, especially those on the upper floors. It's usually booked solid by politicians and lobbyists during legislative sessions from March to May.

101 S. Adams St., Tallahassee, FL 32301. ℂ **800/222-8733** or 850/224-5000. Fax 850/513-9516. 243 units. $89–$169 double. AE, DC, DISC, MC, V. **Amenities:** Restaurant; bar; outdoor pool; exercise room; limited room service; laundry service; concierge-level rooms. *In room:* A/C, TV, dataport, coffeemaker, hair dryer, iron.

Governors Inn 🍴🍴 Legislators, lobbyists, groupies, and Southern gentry stay at this elegantly furnished inn, just half a block north of the Old Capitol in the Adams Street Commons historic district. It's very old-school Washington, D.C. The building was once a livery stable, and part of its original architecture has been preserved, including the impressive beams. The guest rooms are distinctive, with four-poster beds, black-oak writing desks, rock-maple armoires, and antique accouterments. Of the suites, each one named for a Florida governor, one has a whirlpool tub; another has a loft bedroom with wood-burning fireplace. Complimentary continental breakfast and afternoon cocktails are presented in the pine-paneled Florida Room, and a restaurant across the street provides limited room service. Hang out in the bar area and eavesdrop on amusing political banter. The staff here is superfriendly and helpful.

209 S. Adams St., Tallahassee, FL 32301. ℂ 800/342-7717 in Florida, or 850/681-6855. Fax 850/222-3105. www. thegovinn.com. 40 units. $159–$239 double; $219–$309 suite. Rates include continental breakfast and evening cocktails. AE, DC, DISC, MC, V. **Amenities:** Access to nearby health club; limited room service; laundry service. *In room:* A/C, TV, dataport.

Quality Inn & Suites 🍴*Value* In contrast to most Quality Inns, this property loses some of the motel-chain-gang feel in favor of a classy, marble-lined lobby and guest rooms furnished with sofas and reclining wing chairs. A complimentary continental breakfast is served in a lounge with views of the inn's pool, and guests can partake of a free wine bar Monday through Thursday evenings. A nearby restaurant will deliver food, and several fast-food and family-style eateries are within a short walk.

2020 Apalachee Pkwy., Tallahassee, FL 32301. ℂ 800/228-5151 or 850/877-4437. Fax 850/878-9964. www.quality inn.com. 100 units. $89 double; $139 suite. Rates include full breakfast and evening drinks. AE, DC, DISC, MC, V. **Amenities:** Outdoor pool; access to nearby health club; Jacuzzi; business center; limited room service; laundry service. *In room:* A/C, TV, dataport, fridge, coffeemaker, hair dryer, iron, safe, local calls.

WHERE TO DINE

Anthony's 🍴 SOUTHERN ITALIAN Locals flock to Dick Anthony's elegantly relaxed trattoria, which supplies the city's best Italian cuisine. Among his specialties is *pesce Venezia*, spinach fettuccine tossed in a cream sauce with scallops, crab, and fish. Chicken piccata and chicken San Marino are also favorites, and Dick's thick, juicy steaks are always popular with beef eaters. A wall-size wine cupboard features choices from Italy and the United States by the bottle or the glass. Espresso pie leads the dessert menu.

1950 Thomasville Rd., at Bradford Rd. in the Betton Place Shops. ℂ 850/224-1447. Reservations recommended. Main courses $12–$23. AE, DC, DISC, MC, V. Daily 5–9pm.

Bahn Thai THAI/CANTONESE Lamoi (Sue) Snyder and progeny have been serving the spicy cuisine of her native Thailand at this storefront since 1979. In deference to local Southerners, who may never have sampled anything spicier than cheese grits, much of her menu is devoted to mild Cantonese-style Chinese dishes. More adventurous diners, however, flock here to order such authentic tongue-burners as *yon voon-sen*, a combination of shrimp, chicken, bean threads, onions, lemon grass, ground peanuts, and the obligatory chile peppers. Sue's specialty is a deliciously sweet, slightly gingered version of Penang curry. You can ask her to turn down the heat in her other Thai dishes. Come at lunch and sample everything from the all-you-can-eat buffet—a real bargain.

1319 S. Monroe St. (between Oakland Ave. and Harrison St.). ℂ 850/224-4765. Main courses $6–$15. Lunch buffet $7; dinner buffet $11. DISC, MC, V. Mon–Thurs 11am–2:30pm and 5–10pm; Fri 11am–2:30pm and 5–10:30pm; Sat 5–10:30pm.

Barnacle Bill's Seafood Restaurant SEAFOOD   There's always plenty of action at this noisy, casual spot, a favorite of the downtown crowd, including journalists, bureaucrats, and politicians. Freshly shucked Apalachicola oysters are the stars at the enormous raw bar, but the menu also offers a mélange of seafood. The cooking is simple and usually done by Florida State University students working part-time jobs. Best bets are charcoal-grilled mahimahi, tuna, amberjack, and grouper. For a smoked sensation, try the mahimahi and amberjack cured on the premises. A downstairs bar serves the regular seafood items, plus sushi, deli sandwiches, and salads.

1830 N. Monroe St. (north of Tharpe St.). ✆ 850/385-8734. www.barnaclebills.com. Main courses $8–$17 (most $10–$12); sandwiches and salads $5–$9. AE, DC, DISC, MC, V. Sun–Thurs 11am–11pm; Fri–Sat 11am–midnight.

Chez Pierre ✹✹ TRADITIONAL FRENCH   You become an instant Francophile in Florida at this chic restaurant, situated in a beautifully restored 1920s brick home. French-born chef Eric Favier and his American wife and partner, Karen Cooley, offer traditional French cuisine either inside the house or out on a large deck partly shaded by live oaks draped with Spanish moss. Opening onto the deck, a bistro-style bar provides a light-fare menu between lunch and dinner. Among the winning daily specials are rack of lamb, a version of Provençal-style ratatouille, and crab cakes with a luscious mustard and thyme demi-glace. French table wines are moderately priced, and California house wines are also served. Live music regularly accompanies dining. No smoking is permitted except on the front porch, where you can enjoy stogies and brandy while lounging in wicker chairs. Book as early as possible for Bastille Day (July 14), which sees a grand fete here.

1215 Thomasville Rd. (at 6th Ave.). ✆ 850/222-0936. www.chezpierre.com. Reservations recommended. Main courses $15–$29. AE, DC, DISC, MC, V. Mon–Sat 11am–10pm; Sun 11am–2:30pm and 6–9pm.

Kool Beanz Cafe ✹✹ ECLECTIC   The coolest cafe in town, this noisy emporium of trendy cooking draws lots of patrons in their late 20s and early 30s who appreciate the exciting blends of flavors. The joint is dimly lit but painted in bright pastels from the Caribbean. You'll find many island-style items on the constantly changing menu, including Jamaican jerk grouper served with black beans, rice, and a sweet tropical-fruit relish. You may want to get here early: The more inventive items, like the seared rare tuna crusted with spice and served with a terrific roasted-peanut sauce, will sell out early, as will the curried lamb shank and the pork tenderloin marinated with orange molasses.

921 Thomasville Rd. (at Williams St.). ✆ 850/224-2466. Main courses $13–$18. AE, DISC, MC, V. Mon–Fri 11am–2:30pm and 5:30–10pm; Sat 5:30–10pm.

TALLAHASSEE AFTER DARK

Check the "Limelight" section of Friday's *Tallahassee Democrat* (www.tallahassee democrat.com) for weekend entertainment listings.

As a college town, Tallahassee has numerous pubs and clubs with live dance music, not to mention a multitude of sports bars. Pick up a copy of *Break* and other entertainment tabloids at **Barnacle Bill's Seafood Restaurant** (see above) or other venues.

West Tennessee Street is where you'll find most of the happening bars in town. One of the best bars in Tallahassee is **Bullwinkle's Saloon,** 620 W. Tennessee St. (✆ 850/224-0651), a capital institution with a laid-back vibe and even a Thirsty Moose Club, in which members never pay a cover and drink free every Wednesday and Friday. For live music, **Floyd's Music Store,** 666 W. Tennessee St. (✆ 850/222-3506), features local and national bands and, for the daring, a mosh pit that fills up quickly, so get here early.

The major performing-arts venue is the **Tallahassee–Leon County Civic Center,** 505 W. Pensacola St. (© **800/322-3602** or 850/222-0400; www.tlccc.org), which features a Broadway series, concerts, and sporting events including Florida State University (FSU) collegiate basketball games. Special concerts are presented by the **Tallahassee Symphony Orchestra** (www.tsolive.org) at FSU Ruby Diamond Auditorium, at College Avenue and Copeland Street (© **850/224-0461**). The **FSU Mainstage/School of Theatre,** at the Fine Arts Building, Call and Copeland streets (© **850/644-6500**), presents excellent productions, from classic dramas to comedies.

SIDE TRIPS FROM TALLAHASSEE

The following excursions are generally on the way to Apalachicola, so if you're headed that way, plan to make a detour or two.

WAKULLA SPRINGS 🐊🐊

The world's largest and deepest freshwater spring is 15 miles south of Tallahassee in the 2,860-acre **Edward W. Ball Wakulla Springs State Park** 🐊🐊, on Florida 267 just east of its junction with Florida 61. Ball, a financier who administered the du Pont estate, turned the springs and the moss-draped surrounding forest into a preservation area. Divers have mapped an underwater cave system extending more than 6,000 feet back from the spring's mouth. Wakulla has been known to dispense an amazing 14,325 gallons of water per second at certain times. Mastodon bones, including those of Herman, now in Tallahassee's Museum of Florida History, were found in the caves. The 1930s *Tarzan* movies, starring Johnny Weissmuller, were also filmed here.

A free 10-minute orientation movie is offered at the park's theater at the waterfront. You can hike or bike along the nature trails, and swimming is allowed in designated areas. *Note:* It's important to observe swimming rules since alligators are present here.

If the spring water is clear enough, 30-minute glass-bottomed boat sightseeing trips depart every 45 minutes daily, from 9:45am to 5pm during daylight saving time, and from 9:15am to 4:30pm the rest of the year. Even if the water is murky, you're likely to see alligators, birds, and other wildlife on 30-minute riverboat cruises, which operate during these same hours. Either boat ride costs $6 for adults, $4 for children under 13.

Entrance fees to the park are $4 per vehicle with up to eight passengers, $1 per pedestrian or bicyclist. The park is open daily from 8am to dusk. For more information, contact the park at 550 Wakulla Springs Dr., Wakulla Springs, FL 32305 (© **850/224-5950;** fax 850/561-7251; www.floridastateparks.org/wakullasprings).

Where to Stay & Dine

Wakulla Springs Lodge 🐊   On the shore of Wakulla Springs, this dated but charming lodge is distinctive for its magnificent Spanish architecture and ornate old-world furnishings, such as rare Spanish tiles, black-granite tables, marble floors, and ceiling beams painted with Florida scenes by a German artist (supposedly Kaiser Wilhelm's court painter). The guest rooms are simple by today's standards (you'll get a marble bathroom and phone, but no TV). By all means, ask for a room in the front so you'll have a lake view. You don't have to be a lodge guest to enjoy the warm, smoky ambience of the great lobby, with its huge stone fireplace and arched windows looking onto the springs, or to enjoy reasonably priced meals featuring Southern cuisine in the lovely Ball Room (reservations recommended). The fountain (a 60-ft.-long marble drugstore-style counter for old-fashioned ice-cream sodas) provides snacks and sandwiches. The only things missing here are taxidermic specimens—no boar, deer, or bear heads perched high on the walls.

550 Wakulla Park Dr., Wakulla Springs, FL 32305. (℃) 850/224-5950. Fax 850/561-7251. 27 units. $85–$105 double. AE, DISC, MC, V. **Amenities:** Restaurant. *In room:* A/C.

THE ST. MARKS AREA

Rich history lives in the area around the little village of **St. Marks,** 18 miles south of the capital at the end of both Florida 363 and the Tallahassee–St. Marks Historic Railroad Trail State Park (p. 540).

Parts of an old Spanish bastion wall and Confederate earthworks built during the Civil War are in the **San Marcos de Apalache Historic State Park,** reached by turning right at the end of Florida 363 in St. Marks and following the paved road. A museum built on the foundation of the old marine hospital contains exhibits and artifacts covering the area's history. The site is open Thursday through Monday from 9am to 5pm (closed New Year's Day, Thanksgiving, and Christmas). Entrance to the site is free; admission to the museum costs $1 (free for children 6 and under). For more information, contact the site at 1022 DeSoto Park Dr., Tallahassee, FL 32301 (℃ **850/ 922-6007;** www.floridastateparks.org/sanmarcos).

De Soto's men marked the harbor entrance in what is now the **St. Marks Lighthouse and National Wildlife Refuge** ⚓, P.O. Box 68, St. Marks, FL 32355 (℃ **850/ 925-6121**). Operated by the U.S. Fish and Wildlife Service, this 65,000-acre preserve occupies much of the coast from the Aucilla River east of St. Marks to the Ochlockonee River west of Panacea, and is home to more species of birds than anyplace else in Florida except the Everglades. The visitor center is 3½ miles south of U.S. 98 on Lighthouse Road (Fla. 59); turn south off U.S. 98 at Newport, about 2 miles east of St. Marks. Stop at the center for self-guided tour maps of the roads and extensive hiking trails, some of them built atop levees running through the marshland. Located 8 miles south of the visitor center, the 80-foot-tall **St. Marks Lighthouse** was built in 1842 of limestone blocks 4 feet thick at the base. The nearby beach is a popular crabbing spot. Admission to the refuge is $4 per vehicle, $1 per pedestrian or bicyclist (federal Duck Stamps and National Park Service passports accepted). The refuge is open daily from sunrise to sunset; the visitor center, Monday through Friday from 8am to 4pm, and Saturday and Sunday from 10am to 5pm (closed all federal holidays). Contact the refuge for information about seasonal tours and hunting.

In 1865, during the final weeks of the Civil War, federal troops landed at the lighthouse and launched a surprise attack on Tallahassee. The Confederates quickly assembled an impromptu army of wounded soldiers, old men, and boys as young as 14. This ragtag bunch fought the federal regulars for 5 days at what is now the **Natural Bridge Battlefield State Historic Site.** Surprisingly, the old men and boys won. As a result, Tallahassee remained the only Confederate state capital east of the Mississippi never to fall into Yankee hands. The historic site is on C.R. 2192, 6 miles east of Woodville on the St. Marks River, halfway between Tallahassee and St. Marks. Follow the signs from Florida 363 to the end of the pavement. It's open daily from 8am to sunset; admission is free. For more information, contact the San Marcos de Apalache Historic State Park (see above) or go to www.floridastateparks.org/naturalbridge.

Index

THE NEW TRAVELOCITY GUARANTEE

EVERYTHING YOU BOOK WILL BE RIGHT, OR WE'LL WORK WITH OUR TRAVEL PARTNERS TO MAKE IT RIGHT, RIGHT AWAY.

*To drive home the point,
we're going to use the word "right" in every single sentence.*

Let's get right to it. Right to the meat! Only Travelocity guarantees everything about your booking will be right, or we'll work with our travel partners to make it right, right away. Right on!

Here's a picture taken smack dab right in the middle of Antigua, where the guarantee also covers you.

The guarantee covers all but one of the items pictured to the right.

Now, you may be thinking, "Yeah, right, I'm so sure." That's OK; you have the right to remain skeptical. That is until we mention help is always right around the corner. Call us right off the bat, knowing that our customer service reps are there for you 24/7. Righting wrongs. Left and right.

For example, what if the ocean view you booked actually looks out at a downright ugly parking lot? You'd be right to call – we're there for you. And no one in their right mind would be pleased to learn the rental car place has closed and left them stranded. Call Travelocity and we'll help get you back on the right track.

Now if you're guessing there are some things we can't control, like the weather, well you're right. But we can help you with most things – to get all the details in righting,* visit **travelocity.com/guarantee**.

*Sorry, spelling things right is one of the few things not covered under the guarantee.

I'd give my right arm for a guarantee like this, although I'm glad I don't have to.